# A Little Literature

## Reading * Writing * Argument

**SYLVAN BARNET**
*Tufts University*

**WILLIAM BURTO**
*University of Massachusetts Lowell*

**WILLIAM E. CAIN**
*Wellesley College*

PEARSON
Longman

New York    San Francisco    Boston
London    Toronto    Sydney    Tokyo    Singapore    Madrid
Mexico City    Munich    Paris    Cape Town    Hong Kong    Montreal

Editor
Devel
Senior
Media
Execu
Produ
Project                                                                    ny, Inc.
Cover
Cover
Photo
Senior
Printer
Cover

For per                                                                    he copy-
right hc                                                                    ge.

Library

A little
    Wili
    p.
    Inc
    ISBN
    1. L                                                                   m E.,
    195.

PN6014.L635 2007
808--dc22

Visit us at www.ablongman.com

ISBN 0–321–39619–7

84-2

*I heard a Fly buzz - when I died.*
*The Stillness in the Room*
*Was like the Stillness in the Air*
*Between the Heaves of Storm -*

*The Eyes Around - had wrung them Dry -*
*And Breaths were gathering firm*
*For that last Onset - when the King*
*Be witnessed - in the Room -*

*I willed my Keepsakes - Signed away*
*What portion of me be*
*Assignable - and then it was*
*There interposed a Fly -*

*With Blue - uncertain stumbling Buzz -*
*Between the light - and me -*
*And then the Windows failed - and then*
*I could not see to see -*

Manuscript of Emily Dickinson's "I heard a Fly buzz—when I died" (see page 580).

# CONTENTS

**PART II**

# The Pleasures of Fiction   75

PART III

# The Pleasures of Poetry  383

## 11  Approaching Poetry: Responding in Writing  385

## 12  Narrative Poetry  399

## 13  Lyric Poetry  407

## 14   The Speaking Tone of Voice   422

## 15   Figurative Language: Simile, Metaphor, Personification, Apostrophe   441

Contents    xi

## 19  In Brief: Writing Arguments about Poetry    509

## 20  American Voices: Poems for a Diverse Nation    522

## PART IV

# The Pleasures of Drama   615

## 24  How to Read a Play   617

## 25  In Brief: Writing Arguments about Drama   700

## 26  American Voices: Drama for a Diverse Nation   719

## APPENDIXES

## C  Writing Essay Examinations   1146

## D  The Pleasures of Rereading   1151

"A big book," said the Greek poet and scholar Callimachus, "is a big misfortune." He might have added that a big book is heavy. Aware that many instructors have found needlessly bulky most of the textbooks designed for introductory courses in literature, the editors and publisher of *A Little Literature: Reading, Writing, Argument* have produced a book that is smaller than most books intended for such courses. We have kept in mind Dr. Johnson's maxim: "Books that you may ... hold readily in your hand are the most useful after all."

The relative brevity of this volume has been achieved partly by assuming (hopefully) that much of what is here included will please instructors and students and therefore need not be reinforced by numerous alternative selections, and partly by offering apparatus that we think is ample and is yet concise—apparatus that tells students what they need to know and yet does not overwhelm them or usurp the province of the instructor. Each of these points deserves further comment.

We offer what we believe is a judicious mixture of classic and contemporary material: Sophocles, Shakespeare, Hawthorne, Maupassant, Chekhov, Chopin, Eliot, Yeats, and Langston Hughes are here, but so too are Gish Jen, Tim O'Brien, Adrienne Rich, Amy Tan, Michele Serros, Tobias Wolff, and many other contemporary writers who have written work that we believe will endure. In short, we include abundant classical material but we do not hesitate to include contemporary writing that we value and that we believe students will value. We should add, too, that we have included several older things that ought to be much better known, for instance, the manuscript of Robert Frost's "Stopping by Woods on a Snowy Evening," several pages of manuscript from Faulkner's "A Rose for Emily" that were cut from the published version, and facsimiles of a page from the quarto and the folio versions of *Othello*. (By studying facsimiles of the two versions of Othello's last big speech—beginning "Soft you, a word or two before you go"—students can glimpse the play as Shakespeare's first readers encountered it, and they can examine a significant difference in the texts: In the quarto, Othello compares himself to the "base Indian," but in the folio he compares himself to the "base Judean.")

The editorial material is brief and yet rather complete. The paradox is easily explained: This book does not try to do what only the teacher can really do. The proper place for a detailed discussion of the multiple meanings in a word or line is, we believe, the classroom. The object of an anthology of literature is to enable students to read and to think critically, but it is doubtful if a long exegesis we might provide will do much to stimulate a student to think. On the contrary, we have found that short questions of the sort that we give after many of the selections ("Topics for Critical Thinking and Writing") do far more to help students to think about literature, to develop arguments that they set forth in engaging essays, and to enjoy literature.

# USING THE BOOK

Probably most instructors teach fiction first, then poetry, and then drama—the order followed here—but because each of our three sections is relatively independent the material can be taught in any sequence. Each of the three sections contains, for example, a discussion of symbolism, and although the three discussions have a cumulative effect, instructors can use as a first discussion of symbolism any one of the three. This flexibility runs throughout the book. We hope that instructors will not feel that the first chapter must be taught first, though we do think that the main point of the first chapter—that literature gives *pleasure*—is worth setting forth at the beginning of the course. A similar flexibility characterizes each of the three chief sections of the book: An instructor can teach a section straight through, or skip around within a section.

Although comparatively brief, *A Little Literature* contains ample material for a one-semester course. We have tried to make our apparatus sufficiently broad so that it can serve as an aid to whatever additional books are read. The introduction to tragedy is not an introduction to *Oedipus* or *Othello* but an introduction to *tragedy;* because it examines definitions of tragedy by a Jacobean dramatist, a Soviet critic, and an American dramatist, and discusses such terms as *hamartia, hybris,* and *catharsis,* it will be helpful in thinking about all tragedies, from Greek to contemporary American, for instance to *Death of a Salesman,* which is included in the book.

The features of this book, then, as we see them are:

- **Portability.**  The book is easy to carry.
- **Strong representation of classic texts.**  Instructors who are looking for works by such authors as Sophocles, Shakespeare, Hawthorne, Dickinson, Maupassant, Chopin, Chekhov, Yeats, and Eliot will find them here.

- **Strong representation of contemporary texts, especially texts by women and minority writers.** In addition to offering works by women and minority authors throughout the book, we include three chapters—one for each genre—called "American Voices," in which we give literary works that are concerned with American diversity. Diversity is broadly interpreted to include not only representations of ethnic minorities but also of gay populations.
- **Authors given in depth.** Flannery O'Connor, Langston Hughes, and Robert Frost are represented not only by literary works but by some of their critical writings.
- **Unit on translating poetry.** This chapter, with suggested writing assignments, allows students familiar with a language other than English to discuss the difficulties of translation.
- **Drama is presented with attention to the play on the stage.** Some of the Topics for Critical Thinking and Writing invite students to imagine that they are directors or spectators: How would they stage this scene?

# Writing Arguments about Literature

Instructors know that one of the best ways to become an active reader is to read with a pencil in hand—that is, to annotate a text, to make jottings in a journal, and ultimately to draft and revise essays. We think that students, too, will find themselves saying of their experiences with literature what the philosopher Arthur C. Danto said about his experience with works of art:

> I get a lot more out of art, now that I am writing about it, than I ever did before. I think what is true of me must be true of everyone, that until one tries to write about it, the work of art remains a sort of aesthetic blur.... I think in a way everyone might benefit from becoming a critic in his or her own right. After seeing the work, write about it. You cannot be satisfied for very long in simply putting down what you felt. You have to go further.
>
> —*Embodied Meanings* (1994)

In short, writing a good argumentative essay begins with *arguing with oneself,* which we take to be the essential ingredient in critical thinking. When writers begin to *examine their responses and their own assumptions,* they have taken essential steps in developing an argument that they can then set forth for readers. To this end, we have included the following:

- **Samples of annotated pages, entries in journals, and essays by students.** To prompt students to respond to the works of literature in this book and then to think and write critically about their responses, we include pages devoted to the concepts of getting ideas and revising them by means of writing, examples of annotated pages, entries in journals, and essays by students (some with the students' preliminary journal entries).

- **Explorative questions.** About half of the selections in the book are equipped with Topics for Critical Thinking and Writing, topics that offer questions intended to help draw attention to matters that deserve careful thinking.
- **Eight checklists for writers.** Checklists on topics such as "Revising Paragraphs," "Drafting an Explication," "Reviewing a Revised Draft," and "Avoiding Plagiarism" offer concise help to writers.
- **Appendices on manuscript form, research, and writing essay examinations.**

# RESOURCES FOR STUDENTS AND INSTRUCTORS

For qualified adopters:

*MyLiteratureLab.com* is a Web-based, state-of-the-art, interactive learning system designed to enhance introductory literature courses. It adds a whole new dimension to the study of literature with *Longman Lectures*—evocative, richly illustrated audio readings along with advice on how to read, interpret, and write about literary works from our own roster of Longman authors. This powerful program also features Diagnostic Tests, Interactive Readings with clickable prompts, sample student papers, Literature Timelines, Avoiding Plagiarism and Research Navigator research tools, and "Exchange," an electronic instructor/peer feedback tool. MyLiteratureLab.com can be delivered within Course Compass, Web CT, or Blackboard course management systems enabling instructors to administer their entire course online.

*Writing about Literature: Craft of Argument CD-ROM* This CD-ROM allows students to learn the skills of writing and argumentation interactively through writing activities and assignments. Paintings, photographs, and audio and film clips spark student interest in the literacy selections. All media are supported with apparatus and assignments. This CD-ROM is available free when value-packed with *An Introduction to Literature,* Fourteenth Edition. ISBN 0-321-10763-2.

*Instructor's Manual* An instructor's manual with detailed comments and suggestions for teaching each selection is available. This important resource also contains references to critical articles and books that we have found to be most useful. ISBN 0-321-36490-2.

***Video Program***    For qualified adopters, an impressive selection of videotapes is available to enrich students' experience of literature. Contact your sales representative to learn how to qualify.

***Responding to Literature: A Writer's Journal***    This journal provides students with their own personal space for writing. Helpful prompts for responding to fiction, poetry, and drama are also included. Available free when value-packed with *An Introduction to Literature*, Fourteenth Edition. ISBN 0-321-09542-1.

***Evaluating a Performance***    Perfect for the student assigned to review a local production, this supplement offers students a convenient place to record their evaluation. Useful tips and suggestions of things to consider when evaluating a production are included. Available free when value-packed with *An Introduction to Literature*, Fourteenth Edition ISBN 0-321-09541-3.

***Take Note!***    A complete information management tool for students who are working on research papers or other projects that require the use of outside sources. This cross-platform CD-ROM integrates note taking, outlining, and bibliography management into one easy-to-use package. Available at a discount when value-packed with *An Introduction to Literature*, Fourteenth Edition. ISBN 0-321-13608-X.

***Merriam-Webster's Reader's Handbook: Your Complete Guide to Literary Terms***    Includes nearly 2,000 entries, including Greek and Latin terminology, and descriptions for every major genre, style, and era of writing. Assured authority from the combined resources of Merriam-Webster and Encyclopedia Britannica. Available at a significant discount when value-packed with *An Introduction to Literature*, Fourteenth Edition. ISBN 0-321-10541-9.

***Penguin Discount Novel Program***    In cooperation with Penguin Putnam, Inc., one of our sibling companies, Longman is proud to offer a variety of Penguin paperbacks at a significant discount when packaged with any Longman title. The available titles include works by authors as diverse as Toni Morrison, Julia Alvarez, Mary Shelley, and Shakespeare. To review the complete list of titles available, visit the Longman-Penguin-Putnam Website *http://www.ablongman.com/penguin*. Discounted prices of individual Penguin novels are available on the Website.

# ACKNOWLEDGMENTS

We wish to thank the people who helped us write this book. For the preparation of this edition, we are indebted to Joe Terry, Katharine Glynn, Eric Jorgensen, John Callahan of Longman, and Katy Faria at Pre-Press Company. The book in many ways reflects their guidance. For expert assistance in obtaining permission to reprint copyrighted material, we are indebted to Virginia Creeden.

We are grateful to the reviewers of our manuscript: Glenda Bryant, South Plains College; Dr. Oralee Holder, Grossmont College; Kerry McShane-Moley, Palm Beach Community College; Kathleen McWilliams, Cuyamaca College; Deborah D. Reilly, Chesapeake College; Paul Rosenberg, Florida Community College at Jacksonville; Christopher Rossing, Asnuntuck Community College; and Diane Williams, College of Lake County.

We are also grateful for the comments and suggestions offered by the following scholars: Priscilla B. Bellair, Carroll Britch, Don Brunn, Malcolm B. Clark, Terence A. Dalrymple, Franz Douskey, Gerald Duchovnay, Peter Dumanis, Estelle Easterly, Adam Fischer, Martha Flint, Robert H. Fossum, Gerald Hasham, Richard Henze, Catherine M. Hoff, Grace S. Kehrer, Nancy E. Kensicki, Linda Kraus, Juanita Laing, Vincent J. Liesenfeld, Martha McGowan, John H. Meagher III, Stuart Millner, Edward Anthony Nagel, Peter L. Neff, Robert F. Panara, Ronald E. Pepin, Jane Pierce, Robert M. Post, Kris Rapp, Mark Reynolds, John Richardson, Donald H. Sanborn, Marlene Sebeck, Frank E. Sexton, Peggy Skaggs, David Stuchler, James E. Tamer, Carol Teaff, C. Uejio, Hugh Witemeyer, Manfred Wolf, Joseph Zaitchik.

Finally, we are also grateful for valuable suggestions made by Barbara Harman, X. J. Kennedy, Carolyn Potts, Marcia Stubbs, Helen Vendler, and Ann Chalmers Watts.

SYLVAN BARNET
WILLIAM BURTO
WILLIAM E. CAIN

We hope that you already enjoy reading literature and that *A Little Literature* will help you enjoy it even more. But as you begin your course this semester with our book, we want to say a little more about why we wrote it, how we believe it can help you, and in what ways we think it can deepen and enrich your pleasure in studying literature.

Throughout the process of writing and rewriting *A Little Literature* we saw ourselves as teachers, offering the kinds of suggestions and strategies that, over many years, we have offered to our students.

As you can tell from a glance at the Contents, *A Little Literature* includes practical advice about reading and responding to literature and writing analytical and argumentative papers, advice that comes directly from our experience not only as readers and writers but also as teachers. This experience derives from classrooms, from conferences with students, and from assignments we have given, read, responded to, and graded. We have learned from our experiences and have done our best to give you the tools that will help you make yourself a more perceptive reader and a more careful, cogent writer.

Speaking of making and remaking, we are reminded of a short poem by William Butler Yeats, who was a persistent reviser of his work. (We include two of his poems.)

> The friends that have it I do wrong
> Whenever I remake a song,
> Should know what issue is at stake:
> It is myself that I remake.

Like Yeats, you will develop throughout your life: you will find you have new things to say, and you may even come to find that the tools you acquired in college—and that suited you for a while—are not fully adequate to the new self that you have become. We can't claim to equip you for the rest of your life—though some of these works of literature surely will remain in your mind as sources of pleasure for years—but we do claim that, with your instructor, we are helping you develop skills that are important for your mental progress. We have in mind skills useful not merely in the course in which you are now enrolled, or other literature courses, or even courses in the humanities in general that you may take. We go further. We think that these skills in reading and writing are important for your development as an educated adult. Becoming an alert reader and an effective writer should be among the central goals of your education, and they are goals that *A Little Literature* is designed to help you reach.

The skills we stress in *A Little Literature* will enable you to gain confidence as a reader of literary works so that you will increase your understanding of what literature offers. You need not enjoy all authors equally. You'll have your favorites—and also some authors whom you do not like much at all. There's nothing wrong with that; reading literature is very much a personal encounter. But at the same time, the skills we highlight in *A Little Literature* can help you know and explain why one author means much to you and another does not. In this respect, reading and studying literature is more than personal; as we share our responses and try to express them effectively in writing, the analytical and argumentative work that we perform becomes cooperative and communal, a type of cultural conversation among fellow students, teachers, and friends.

As you proceed through *A Little Literature* and gain further experience as a reader and writer, you will start to see features of poems, stories, and plays that you had not noticed before, or that you had noticed but not really understood, or that you had understood but not, so to speak, fully experienced. You may even find yourself enjoying an author you thought you disliked and would never be able to understand. The study of literature calls for concentration, commitment, and discipline. It's work—sometimes hard, challenging work. But it is rewarding work, and we believe that it will lead you to find literature more engaging and more pleasurable.

We hope that *A Little Literature* will have this effect for you. Feel free to contact us with your comments and suggestions. We are eager to know what in this book has served you well, and what we might do better. You can write to us in care of Literature Editor, Longman Publishers, 1185 Avenue of the Americas, New York, NY 10036.

SYLVAN BARNET
WILLIAM BURTO
WILLIAM E. CAIN

# I

# Reading, Thinking, and Writing Critically about Literature

My task . . . is by the power of the written word to make you hear, to make you feel—it is, before all, to make you see.

—Joseph Conrad

A book must be the ax that breaks the frozen sea within us.

—Franz Kafka

A conventional good read is usally a bad read, a relaxing bath in what we know already. A true good read is surely an act of innovative creation in which we, the readers, become conspirators.

—Malcolm Bradbury

The best of all ways to make one's reading valuable is to write about it.

—Ralph Waldo Emerson

# 1

## Reading, Thinking, and Writing Critically about Literature

# 1

# Writing Arguments about Literature: A Crash Course in Critical Thinking and Writing

A bit oddly, perhaps, we want to begin our discussion of literature not by defining it, but by expressing our hope that the readings in this book will give you pleasure, and by arguing that your own writing about literature will heighten your understanding of literature and increase your pleasure in it.

## GETTING IDEAS FOR WRITING: ASKING QUESTIONS AND ANNOTATING A TEXT

We offer at the outset a song from one of Shakespeare's plays (*Much Ado about Nothing*) that we hope entertains you.

> Sigh no more, ladies, sigh no more;
>     Men were deceivers ever;
> One foot in sea and one on shore,
>     To one thing constant never;
>         Then sigh not so,
>         But let them go,
> And be you blithe and bonny;
> Converting all your sounds of woe
>     Into Hey nonny, nonny.

Sing no more ditties, sing no mo,°        *more*
Of dumps° so dull and heavy;              *mournful songs or dance*
The fraud of men was ever so,
Since summer first was leavy.°            *leafy, i.e., having trees with leaves*
    Then sigh not so,
    But let them go,
And be you blithe and bonny,°             *carefree and in good spirits*
Converting all your sounds of woe
Into Hey, nonny, nonny.  (2.3.62–79)

This song about male infidelity, by the way, is sung by a male to an onstage audience that is all male. Possibly, men—or at least certain kinds of men—enjoy hearing about their own infidelity. Possibly women—or at least certain kinds of women—enjoying hearing that while men are unfaithful, there is no use wasting time lamenting this obvious fact; rather, women may conclude that if they are to maintain their psychic equilibrium they should not take the vows of men seriously.

We are not saying that the song is true and is therefore good literature; rather, we are saying that it is *engaging,* it catches and holds our attention. It communicates a state of mind; it makes us mentally say, "Ah, yes, I myself have never thought exactly this way, but I can see that some people might—and it's an interesting angle. Certainly there are times when a woman wants to wash her hands of men. And, perhaps astoundingly, there are times when men seem quite pleased with being regarded as 'inconstant.'"

Our subject here is writing about literature. Robert Frost once said (admittedly with some overstatement), "All there is to writing is having ideas." But how do you get ideas? One of the best ways to get ideas—to educate yourself, so to speak—is to ask yourself questions and to answer them honestly.

Here are some basic questions:

**What is my first response to the work?** Am I bored, puzzled, amused, shocked, or what? And exactly *why* do I have this response?

**Who is speaking?** What voice do I hear—for instance, a happy (or an unhappy) lover, a troubled child, a puzzled parent? In "Sigh no more, ladies," we might believe the reader hears the voice of a wise counselor. This is *not* to say that in real life readers must follow the speaker's advice; it is only to say that for the moment the voice engages our full interest.

**What does the form contribute?** The work is a song, with rhymes, so even though it talks of unfaithful men and sighing women it offers pleasing patterns of sound. Further, although the two stanzas are pretty similar—in fact, the last four lines of each stanza are identical—there is, in a very quiet way, a sort of plot or narrative. If we reverse the sequence of the two stanzas, the feel of the poem is different, and in our view, less satisfactory. In the first stanza the singer tells us that men are "To one thing constant never"; in the second he or she says that "The fraud of men was ever so." Because of the word *fraud,* this assertion seems a bit stronger than the first, and that—at least while we are reading the song—justifies the advice to "let them go."

The best way to get ideas—to *discover* ideas you didn't know you had—is to annotate the text, with underlinings, marginal queries, and tentative responses of all sorts. These jottings will generate further thoughts, will *teach* you, and in time you will be able to teach the reader of your paper. One of our students, Anne Rose Washington, has kindly let us reprint her annotations of Shakespeare's song.

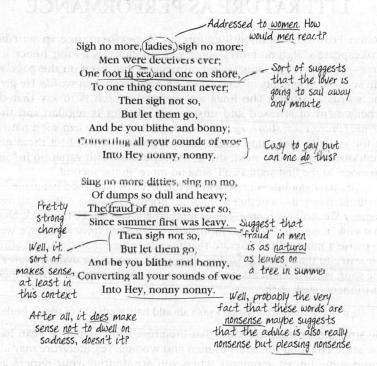

Addressed to _women_. How would _men_ react?

Sigh no more, (ladies,) sigh no more;
   Men were deceivers ever;
One foot in sea) and one on shore, — Sort of suggests that the lover is going to sail away any minute
   To one thing constant never;
      Then sigh not so,
      But let them go,
   And be you blithe and bonny;
   Converting all your sounds of woe ⎤ Easy to say but can one do this?
      Into Hey nonny, nonny. ⎦

Sing no more ditties, sing no mo,
   Of dumps so dull and heavy;
Pretty strong charge   The (fraud) of men was ever so,
   Since summer first was leavy.   Suggest that "fraud" in men is as _natural_ as leaves on a tree in summer
Well, it sort of makes sense, at least in this context   ⎧ Then sigh not so,
      ⎨ But let them go,
   And be you blithe and bonny,
   Converting all your sounds of woe
      Into Hey, nonny nonny.

After all, it _does_ make sense _not_ to dwell on sadness, doesn't it?

Well, probably the very fact that these words are _nonsense_ maybe suggests that the advice is also really nonsense but pleasing nonsense

With notes like these, a student is well on the way to furthering his or her understanding of the poem and to helping a reader see what is going on.

What counts most for you, of course, is *your* response. Here are a few questions that may help you to think about "Sigh no more, ladies."

▨ TOPICS FOR
CRITICAL THINKING AND WRITING

1. Is Shakespeare's "Sigh no more, ladies" offensive? Trivial? Engaging? All of the above? Please set forth your argument in an essay consisting of one or two paragraphs.

2. Do you think that men and women will differ in their responses to this poem? If so, will they differ a lot, or only a little?
3. How would you respond to someone who says, "Poems from long ago rarely interest me. They are too far away from the problems and issues we care about today"?

# LITERATURE AS PERFORMANCE

Robert Frost once defined literature as **"A performance in words."** Shakespeare's "Sigh no more, ladies, sigh no more," is a song, hence it is sung—performed by singers and musicians—but even on the page we can see some elements of Shakespeare's performance in words. He gives the words a pattern: The lines are metrical, which is to say that the arrangement of stressed and unstressed syllables is regular; and they rhyme (*more, ever, shore, never*, and so on). Further, we can see a pattern in the repetition of some lines ("Then sigh not so, / But let them go") from one stanza to the next, and in the repetition with variation in "Sigh no more" in the first stanza and "Sing no more" in the second.

You have doubtless experienced the force of patterned language—of rhythmic thought—whether from other poems and songs ("We shall overcome, / We shall overcome") or of football chants ("Block that kick, block that kick"). Because "Sigh no more, ladies" is a song from a play, we want to pause a moment to reiterate that literature, like music, should afford **pleasure** to the hearer. In Shakespeare's play one rather cynical hearer of the song wryly comments on the power of music produced by stringed instruments such as the lute:

Is it not strange that sheep's guts should hale souls out of men's bodies.

No stranger, we suppose, than that literature—ink on paper—can have the same effect on the souls of men and women. Yes, literature may also cause some uneasy moments when you are drafting your papers and preparing for examinations, but we are confident that these uneasy moments themselves will, in the long run, produce pleasure. Your efforts to write about the literature in this book will ultimately result in a deeper understanding of stories, poems, and plays, and this understanding will greatly heighten your pleasure in reading them. By way of analogy, consider this: The person who knows a fair amount about baseball will enjoy a given baseball game more than the person who knows little or nothing about the sport. Similarly, when we see a slow-motion rerun of the Kentucky Derby—when we have a chance to examine and study the race—we can better appreciate the race that the winning rider has run. We believe that if you do not agree with us now, by the end of the course you will be won over.

# A SECOND POEM AND TWO INTERPRETATIONS

When you write about a work, you will want to do much more than say, "I really like this story," or "This poem bored me." You may indeed jot down some such words for a start, but you will want to go further, partly because you know that your instructor wants a good deal more, but also partly because you will find that, having written these words, *you* want to say more. If the work puzzles or bores or in some other way displeases you, you probably want to find out *why* you have this response. And, to your surprise, you may find that at this stage you do not know why you feel the way you do. In the process of returning to the work in order to find out why you feel the way you do—that is, to find supporting evidence for your ideas—you may change your mind.

We do not mean to suggest that you will inevitably come to like the work, but when you better understand your own response you will arrive at a better understanding of the work. Similarly, it is possible that when you return to a work that pleases you, looking for the causes of your pleasure, you may find that it is not as interesting as you thought at first. Perhaps you will come to see it as unimaginative, cliché ridden, or sentimental. In either case, a thoughtful examination of the work will, in the long run, prove satisfying.

Let's begin with a poem that you are probably familiar with.

# ROBERT FROST (1874–1963)

## *Stopping by Woods on a Snowy Evening*

Whose woods these are I think I know.
His house is in the village, though;
He will not see me stopping here
To watch his woods fill up with snow.

My little horse must think it queer                    5
To stop without a farmhouse near
Between the woods and frozen lake
The darkest evening of the year.

He gives his harness bells a shake
To ask if there is some mistake.                       10
The only other sound's the sweep
Of easy wind and downy flake.

The woods are lovely, dark and deep,
But I have promises to keep,
And miles to go before I sleep.
And miles to go before I sleep.                                    15

---

Later in this chapter we will look at two interpretations of Frost's poem. For the moment we can define **interpretation** as a setting forth of meaning, or in this context, a setting forth of one or more of the meanings of a work of literature.

## What Characterizes a Sound Interpretation?

Almost no one believes that all interpretations are equal, or that "It's all just a matter of opinion." If all opinions about literature (or art or music) are equal, no one would take college courses in these subjects. Why spend good money listening to an "expert" when all opinions are equal?

An interpretive essay is offered against a background of ideas, shared by essayist and reader, as to what constitutes a **persuasive argument.** Thus, any essay worth reading (or writing) will be

- coherent,
- plausible, and
- rhetorically effective—that is, written so that the reader is persuaded to share, at least in some degree, the author's view.

The presentation—the rhetoric—as well as the basic idea or interpretation, is significant. This means that the writer cannot merely set down random expressions of feeling or unsupported opinions. The writer must, on the contrary, in an orderly and a convincing way **argue a thesis**—must **point to evidence** so that the reader will know not only what the writer believes, but also understand *why* he or she believes it.

There are lots of ways of making sense (and even more ways of making nonsense), but one important way of helping readers to see things from your point of view is to do your best to address all of the complexities of the work. Put it this way: Some interpretations strike a reader as better than others because they are more inclusive, that is, because they *account for more of the details of the work.* Less satisfactory interpretations leave a reader pointing to some aspects of the work—to some parts of the whole—and saying, "Yes, but your explanation doesn't take account of. . . ." This does not mean that a reader must feel that a persuasive interpretation says the last word about the work. We always realize that the work is richer than the discussion; but, again, for us to value an interpretation we must find the interpretation plausible and inclusive.

Here is the first of two interpretations that students wrote of "Stopping by Woods on a Snowy Evening."

Peter Franken

Professor Gomez

English 102

2 November 2005

The Meaning of "Stopping by Woods
on a Snowy Evening"

Although on the surface there is nothing about religion in Robert Frost's "Stopping by Woods on a Snowy Evening," I think the poem is basically about a person's realization that he or she has a religious duty to help other people.

In Stanza One the poet tells us that he knows who owns the woods. The owner is God. Of course some individual, during his lifetime, thinks that he owns the woods, but he is only the steward of the woods, a sort of caretaker. The true owner is God, whose "house is in the village," that is, who has a church in the village. At this stage in the poem, the poet is mistaken when he says that God will not see him, because God sees everything. So the poet's statement here is an example of unconscious irony.

In Stanzas Two and Three the poet tells us that God sent a message to him, through the horse. The horse shakes his harness bells, telling the speaker that he (the speaker) is making a "mistake." It may also be that in the picture of a snowy night and a domestic animal Robert Frost is trying to subtly suggest that we remember the scene of the birth of Jesus, in a manger, with domestic animals. In any case, although the scene is very peaceful and quiet (except for the harness bells and the sound of the "easy wind"), God is watching over the speaker of this poem.

In Stanza Four, in the first line ("The woods are lovely, dark and deep") Robert Frost tells us of man's love of God's creation, and in the other lines of the stanza he says that proper love of the creation leads to an awareness of our responsibilities to other human beings. Robert Frost is very effective because he uses the device of understatement. He does not tell us exactly what these responsibilities are, so he leaves it to our imagination, but we can easily think of our many duties to our family and our fellow-citizens and our country.

## Work Cited

Frost, Robert. "Stopping by Woods on a Snowy Evening." A Little Literature. Ed. Sylvan Barnet, William Burto, and William E. Cain. New York: Longman, 2007. 7-8.

To return to our basic question: What characterizes a good interpretation? The short answer is, **evidence,** and especially evidence that seems to cover all relevant issues. In an essay it is not enough merely to assert an interpretation. Your readers don't expect you to make an airtight case, but because you are trying to help readers understand a work—to see a work the way you have come to see it after carefully questioning your initial responses—you are obliged to

- offer reasonable supporting evidence, and
- take account of what might be set forth as counterevidence to your thesis.

Your essay might originate in an intuition or an emotional response, a sense that the work is about such-and-such; this intuition or emotion must then be examined, and it must stand a test of reasonableness. (It's usually a good idea to jot your first responses to a work down in a journal, and reflect on them in later entries.) It is not enough in an essay merely to set forth your response. Your readers will expect you to demonstrate that your response is something that they can to a large degree understand. They may not be convinced that the interpretation is right or true, but they must at least feel that the interpretation is plausible and in accord with the details of the work, rather than highly eccentric or irreconcilable with some details.

[▨] TOPICS FOR
CRITICAL THINKING AND WRITING

1. What is the thesis of Peter Franken's essay on Frost's poem?
2. Does Peter offer convincing evidence to support his thesis?
3. Do you consider his essay to be well written, poorly written, or something in between? On what evidence do you base your opinion?

# THINKING CRITICALLY ABOUT
# RESPONSES TO LITERATURE:
# ARGUING WITH YOURSELF

Usually you will begin with a strong response to your reading—interest, boredom, bafflement, annoyance, shock, pleasure, etc. Fine. If you are going to think critically about what you have read, you will *examine* your response by checking it against the work. Revisiting the reading in the context of your response to it can help you deepen or change your response.

How can you change an instinctive emotional response? **Critical thinking** involves seeing an issue from all sides, to as great a degree as possible. As you know, in ordinary language "to criticize" usually means to find fault, but in literary studies the term does not have a negative connotation. Rather, it means "to examine carefully." (The word "criticism" comes from a Greek verb meaning "to distinguish," "to decide," "to judge.") Nevertheless, in one sense the term "critical thinking" does approach the usual meaning of "criticism," since critical thinking requires you to take a skeptical view of your own response. You will, so to speak, argue with yourself or seek to find fault with your initial view. That is, you try to raise questions that a skeptical reader might raise, in an effort to improve your position.

Because we spent a moment talking about the word "critical," we should also spend a minute talking about the words "argue" and "argument." These words bring up images of people shouting at each other, people not really listening to the opposition but merely digging in their heels and raising their voices. But when we say that you should argue with yourself, and that your essay offers an argument, we are talking about a *reasoned* account that sets forth a view clearly. In fact, the word "argue" goes back to a Latin word meaning "to make clear." Thus, when the seventeenth-century poet John Milton sought to assist his readers by offering prefatory summaries of the plot of each of the twelve parts of his long poem, *Paradise Lost,* he called each summary an "argument," i.e., a helpful comment. When you argue with yourself—when you ask yourself if, for instance, you can point to evidence that supports an assertion you have made—you are in fact trying to make clear—*to yourself*—your own views. As André Maurois said, "The difficult part of an argument is not to defend one's opinion, but rather to know it." And when we say that your essay is an argument, we mean that the essay offers a reasoned account of a position that has become clear and reasonable to you.

Critical thinking, in short, means examining or exploring one's own responses by questioning and testing them. Critical thinking is not so much a skill (though it does involve the ability to understand a text) as it is a habit of mind, or, rather, several habits, including

- open-mindedness,
- intellectual curiosity, and
- a willingness to work.

Here is a second essay, also by a student, on "Stopping by Woods on a Snowy Evening."

Sara Fong

Professor Fish

English 102

3 December 2005

"Stopping by Woods on a Snowy Evening"

as a Short Story

Robert Frost's "Stopping by Woods on a
Snowy Evening" can be read as a poem about
a man who pauses to observe the beauty
of nature, and it can also be read as a
poem about a man with a death wish, a
man who seems to long to give himself up
completely to nature and thus escape his
responsibilities as a citizen. Much depends
on what a reader wants to emphasize. For
instance, a reader can emphasize especially
appealing lines about the beauty of nature:
"The only other sound's the sweep / Of easy
wind and downy flake," and "The woods are
lovely, dark and deep." On the other hand,
a reader can emphasize lines that show
the speaker is fully aware of the
responsibilities that most of us agree we
have. For instance, at the very start of
the poem he recognizes that the woods are
not his but are owned by someone else, and
at the end of the poem he recognizes that
he has "promises to keep" and that before
he sleeps (dies?) he must accomplish many
things (go for "miles").

Does a reader have to choose between
these two interpretations? I don't think

so; to the contrary, I think it makes sense
to read the poem as a kind of very short
story, with a character whose developing
thoughts make up a plot with four stages.
In the first stage, the central figure is
an ordinary person with rather ordinary
thoughts. His very first thought is of
the owner of the woods. He knows who the
owner is, and since the owner lives in
the village, the poet feels safe in
trespassing, or at least in watching the
woods "fill up with snow." Then, very
subtly, the poet begins to tell us that
although this seems to be an ordinary
person thinking ordinary thoughts, he is
a somewhat special person in a special
situation. First of all, the horse thinks
something is strange. He shakes his bells,
wondering why the driver doesn't keep
moving, as presumably ordinary drivers
would. Second, we are told that this is
"The darkest evening of the year." Frost
could simply have said that the evening is
dark, but he goes out of his way to make
the evening a special evening.

   We are now through with the first ten
lines, and only six lines remain, yet in
these six lines the story goes through two
additional phases. The first three of these
lines ("the only other sound's the sweep /
Of easy wind and downy flake" and "The
woods are lovely, dark and deep") are
probably the most beautiful lines, in the

Fong 3

sense that they are the ones that makes us
say, "I wish I were there," or "I'd love
to experience this." We feel that the poet
has moved from the ordinary thoughts of
the first stanza, about such businesslike
things as who owns the woods and where the
owner's house is, to less materialistic
thoughts, thoughts about the beauty of the
nonhuman world of nature. And now, with the
three final lines, we get the fourth stage
of the story, the return to the ordinary
world of people, the world of "promises."
But, just as in a short story such as
John Updike's "A&P" or William Faulkner's
"A Rose for Emily," the world that we get
at the end is not exactly the same as the
world we get at the beginning. The world
at the beginning of the poem is a world
of property (who owns the woods, and where
the house is), but the world at the end
to the poem is a world of unspecified
and rather mysterious responsibilities
("promises to keep," "miles to go before
I sleep").

It is almost as though the poet's
experience of the beauty of nature--a
beauty that for a moment made him forget
the world of property--has in fact served
to sharpen his sense that human beings have
responsibilities. He clearly sees that "The
woods are lovely, dark and deep," and then
he says (I add the italics), "But I have
promises to keep." The "but" seems, on

first thought, to be illogical. "But" would
be logical if after saying that the woods
are lovely, dark and deep, Frost has said
something like "But in the daylight they
look frightening," or "But one can freeze
to death in them." The logic of what Frost
in fact says, however, is not at all clear:
"The woods are lovely, dark and deep, / But
I have promises to keep." What is the
logical connection? We have to supply one,
something like "but, *because we are human
beings we have responsibilities*; we can
refresh ourselves by perceiving the
beauties of nature, and we can even for
a moment get so caught up that we seem to
enter an enchanted forest ('The woods are
lovely, dark and deep'), but we cannot
forget our responsibilities."

My point is not that Frost ends with an
important moral, and it is also not that we
have to choose between saying it is a poem
about nature or a poem about a man with a
death wish. Rather, my point is that the
poem takes us through several stages and
that, although the poem begins and ends
with the speaker in the woods, the speaker
has undergone mental experiences--he has,
we might say, gone through a plot with a
conflict (the appeal of the snowy woods
versus the call to return to the human
world). It's not a matter of good versus
evil and of one side winning. Frost in no

Fong 5

way suggests that it is wrong to feel the
beauty of nature--even to the momentary
exclusion of all other thoughts. But the
poem is certainly not simply a praise
of the beauty of nature. Frost shows us,
in this mini-story or mini-drama, one
character who sees the woods as property,
then sees them as a place of almost
overwhelming beauty, and then (maybe
refreshed by this experience) rejoins the
world of chores and responsibilities.

Fong 6

Work Cited

Frost, Robert. "Stopping by Woods on a Snowy
    Evening." A Little Literature. Ed. Sylvan
    Barnet, William Burto, and William E.
    Cain. New York: Longman, 2007. 7-8.

## ⁂ TOPICS FOR
## CRITICAL THINKING AND WRITING

1. What is the thesis of Sara Fong's essay?
2. Does she offer convincing evidence to support the thesis?
3. Do you consider the essay to be well written, poorly written, or something in between? On what evidence do you base your opinion?
4. What is the benefit of writing an essay about a literary work? Can you imagine other activities that would benefit your study of literature as much, or more? How do you feel, for instance, about memorizing a short poem?

# FOUR VERY SHORT STORIES

## EMILY WU

*Emily Wu has written on a variety of topics, especially East Asian art.*

## The Lesson of the Master

In fourteenth-century China a Buddhist monk named Tung-ming, who was also a painter, was fortunate in having a merchant who supported him by buying his ink-paintings. Tung-ming excelled in his art, a very difficult art because an Asian ink painting, unlike a Western oil painting, cannot be changed as the artist works on it. Once the brush touches the paper, the ink makes its mark, and it cannot be removed. The brush stroke cannot even be widened or lengthened because a knowledgeable observer will easily detect the change, the place where the first strike was widened or extended or whatever; the painting's lack of grace and spontaneity will be evident. Part of the beauty of ink painting is that the viewer understands the difficulty, and appreciates the skill that is evident in each line.

Tung-ming excelled in paintings of plum branches, but one day the merchant, who was a wholesaler of fish, asked him if he would paint a carp. The monk assured the merchant that he would paint the picture, and he then departed. A week passed. Then two weeks. Then three weeks, and still there was no painting. It was not that the merchant and the monk did not meet. No, they met every few days because the merchant often invited the monk to dinner. And in the past the monk sometimes invited the merchant to have a cup of tea at the temple and to discuss matters of Buddhism, but he had not invited the merchant since the conversation about the carp.

After the second week the merchant began to fret: "Have I offended Tung-ming?" he wondered. "Might he think that I don't sufficiently appreciate his paintings of plum blossoms?" And: "Is it possible that he thinks it is vulgar of me to ask for a picture of a fish because I am a fish merchant?" And: "Could it be that he thinks, because I am a specialist in fish, I will notice that in fact his picture of a carp is not very good, that he can't catch the essence of its fishiness?" Day after day, week after week, month after month the merchant tormented himself with such thoughts.

Now that months had gone by, the merchant summoned up the courage to ask Tung-ming if they might not, for a change, meet at the temple and have a cup of tea. Tung-ming agreed.

5      On the appointed day they met in the monk's quarters, drank tea, talked about Buddhist matters and other things, and then the merchant— having noticed that brush, ink-cake, and paper were in view—nervously

broached the subject of the picture of the carp. Tung-ming moistened the ink-case and ground some fresh ink from it, dipped the brush in the ink, stood over the paper, paused for five seconds (but the pause seemed like eternity to the merchant) and then, in another five seconds, with five strokes brushed a marvelous silvery-gray carp and handed the sheet to the merchant.

The merchant was beside himself with joy. When he recovered his composure, he hesitantly asked Tung-ming why had had not produced a picture months earlier. Tung-ming walked across the room, opened the door of a cabinet, and hundreds of sheets of paper—each with a picture of a carp—streamed to the floor.

### ▨ TOPICS FOR CRITICAL THINKING AND WRITING

1. In one sentence tell the *plot* of the story (*what happens* in it) and in a second sentence summarize the *theme* of the story (what the happenings *add up to,* what the story is *about*).

2. Although the title of a story may be the last thing the author writes, it is the first thing that the reader encounters, and it is therefore highly important. The story called "The Lesson of the Master" *might* have been called "A Very Short Story," or "Tung-ming's Fish" or "A Fishy Story" or "The Patron and the Painter" or "The Painter and the Patron" or "Easy When You Know How" or .... Consider the original title and the six alternate titles. Which do you think is the best? Why? Can you think of a title that is better than the original and the proposed alternatives? If so, state it and explain why you think it is better.

3. This story was originally written in Chinese. Was it worth translating, and worth your time as a reader? Do you think you will remember this story six months from now? Please explain.

4. Is there some literature—perhaps even a nursery rhyme or a fairy tale—that you read a long time ago but that has stayed in your mind? If so, *why* has it remained with you? The catchiness of the sounds (as in "Jack and Jill / Went up a hill")? Sharply-drawn characters? A surprising plot? The moral? Please explain.

# TOBIAS WOLFF

*Tobias Wolff was born in Alabama in 1945, but he grew up in the state of Washington. He left high school before graduating, served as an apprentice seaman and as a weight-guesser in a carnival, and then joined the army, where he served four years as a paratrooper. After his discharge from the army, he hired private tutors to enable him to pass the entrance examination to Oxford University. At Oxford he did spectacularly well, graduating with First Class Honors in English. Wolff has written stories, novels, and an autobiography* (This Boy's Life); *he now teaches in the Creative Writing Program at Stanford.*

## Powder
[1992]

Just before Christmas my father took me skiing at Mount Baker. He'd had to fight for the privilege of my company, because my mother was still angry with him for sneaking me into a nightclub during his last visit, to see Thelonius Monk.

He wouldn't give up. He promised, hand on heart, to take good care of me and have me home for dinner on Christmas Eve, and she relented. But as we were checking out of the lodge that morning it began to snow, and in this snow he observed some quality that made it necessary for us to get in one last run. We got in several last runs. He was indifferent to my fretting. Snow whirled around us in bitter, blinding squalls, hissing like sand, and still we skied. As the lift bore us to the peak yet again, my father looked at his watch and said: "Criminey. This'll have to be a fast one."

By now I couldn't see the trail. There was no point in trying. I stuck to him like white on rice and did what he did and somehow made it to the bottom without sailing off a cliff. We returned our skis and my father put chains on the Austin-Healy while I swayed from foot to foot, clapping my mittens and wishing I were home. I could see everything. The green tablecloth, the plates with the holly pattern, the red candles waiting to be lit.

We passed a diner on our way out. "You want some soup?" my father asked. I shook my head. "Buck up," he said. "I'll get you there. Right, doctor?"

5    I was supposed to say, "Right, doctor," but I didn't say anything.

A state trooper waved us down outside the resort. A pair of sawhorses were blocking the road. The trooper came up to our car and bent down to my father's window. His face was bleached by the cold. Snowflakes clung to his eyebrows and to the fur trim of his jacket and cap.

"Don't tell me," my father said.

The trooper told him. The road was closed. It might get cleared, it might not. Storm took everyone by surprise. So much, so fast. Hard to get people moving. Christmas Eve. What can you do?

My father said: "Look. We're talking about four, five inches. I've taken this car through worse than that."

10    The trooper straightened up, boots creaking. His face was out of sight but I could hear him. "The road is closed."

My father sat with both hands on the wheel, rubbing the wood with his thumbs. He looked at the barricade for a long time. He seemed to be trying to master the idea of it. Then he thanked the trooper, and with a weird, old-maidy show of caution turned the car around. "Your mother will never forgive me for this," he said.

"We should have left before," I said. "Doctor."

He didn't speak to me again until we were both in a booth at the diner, waiting for our burgers. "She won't forgive me," he said. "Do you understand? Never."

"I guess," I said, but no guesswork was required; she wouldn't forgive him.

15      "I can't let that happen." He bent toward me. "I'll tell you what I want. I want us to be all together again. Is that what you want?"

"Yes, sir."

He bumped my chin with his knuckles. "That's all I needed to hear."

When we finished eating he went to the pay phone in the back of the diner, then joined me in the booth again. I figured he'd called my mother, but he didn't give a report. He sipped at his coffee and stared out the window at the empty road. "Come on, come on," he said. A little while later he said, "Come on!" When the trooper's car went past, lights flashing, he got up and dropped some money on the check. "O.K. Vámonos."

The wind had died. The snow was falling straight down, less of it now; lighter. We drove away from the resort, right up to the barricade. "Move it," my father told me. When I looked at him he said, "What are you waiting for?" I got out and dragged one of the sawhorses aside, then put it back after he drove through. He pushed the door open for me. "Now you're an accomplice," he said. "We go down together." He put the car into gear and gave me a look. "Joke, doctor."

20      "Funny, doctor."

Down the first long stretch I watched the road behind us, to see if the trooper was on our tail. The barricade vanished. Then there was nothing but snow: snow on the road, snow kicking up from the chains, snow on the trees, snow in the sky; and our trail in the snow. I faced around and had a shock. The lie of the road behind us had been marked by our own tracks, but there were no tracks ahead of us. My father was breaking virgin snow between a line of tall trees. He was humming "Stars Fell on Alabama." I felt snow brush along the floorboards under my feet. To keep my hands from shaking, I clamped them between my knees.

My father grunted in a thoughtful way and said, "Don't ever try this yourself."

"I won't."

"That's what you say now, but someday you'll get your license and then you'll think you can do anything. Only you won't be able to do this. You need, I don't know—a certain instinct."

25        "Maybe I have it."
          "You don't. You have your strong points, but not . . . this. I only men-
tion it, because I don't want you to get the idea this is something just anybody can do. I'm a great driver. That's not a virtue, O.K.? It's just a fact, and
one you should be aware of. Of course you have to give the old heap some
credit, too—there aren't many cars I'd try this with. Listen!"
          I listened. I heard the slap of the chains, the stiff, jerky rasps of the
wipers, the purr of the engine. It really did purr. The car was almost new.
My father couldn't afford it, and kept promising to sell it, but here it was.
          I said, "Where do you think that policeman went to?"
          "Are you warm enough?" He reached over and cranked up the
blower. Then he turned off the wipers. We didn't need them. The clouds
had brightened. A few sparse, feathery flakes drifted into our slipstream
and were swept away. We left the trees and entered a broad field of snow
that ran level for a while and then tilted sharply downward. Orange stakes
had been planted at intervals in two parallel lines and my father steered a
course between them, though they were far enough apart to leave considerable doubt in my mind as to where exactly the road lay. He was humming again, doing little scat riffs around the melody.

30        "O.K. then. What are my strong points?"
          "Don't get me started," he said. "It'd take all day."
          "Oh, right. Name one."
          "Easy. You always think ahead."
          True. I always thought ahead. I was a boy who kept his clothes on
numbered hangers to insure proper rotation. I bothered my teachers for
homework assignments far ahead of their due dates so I could make up
schedules. I thought ahead, and that was why I knew that there would be
other troopers waiting for us at the end of our ride, if we got there. What I
did not know was that my father would wheedle and plead his way past
them—he didn't sing "O Tannenbaum" but just about—and get me home
for dinner, buying a little more time before my mother decided to make
the split final. I knew we'd get caught; I was resigned to it. And maybe for
this reason I stopped moping and began to enjoy myself.

35        Why not? This was one for the books. Like being in a speedboat, but
better. You can't go downhill in a boat. And it was all ours. And it kept
coming, the laden trees, the unbroken surface of snow, the sudden white
vistas. Here and there I saw hints of the road, ditches, fences, stakes, but
not so many that I could have found my way. But then I didn't have to. My
father was driving. My father in his 48th year, rumpled, kind, bankrupt of
honor, flushed with certainty. He was a great driver. All persuasion, no co-
ercion. Such subtlety at the wheel, such tactful pedalwork. I actually
trusted him. And the best was yet to come—the switchbacks and hair-
pins. Impossible to describe. Except maybe to say this: If you haven't driven fresh powder, you haven't driven.

## ▓ TOPICS FOR
## CRITICAL THINKING AND WRITING

1. In a paragraph characterize the father.
2. What is the boy's attitude toward his father? Does it change during the story? What is your attitude toward the father? Does it change during the story?


# MITSUYE YAMADA

*Mitsuye Yamada, the daughter of Japanese immigrants to the United States, was born in Japan in 1923, during her mother's return visit to her native land. She was raised in Seattle, but in 1942 she and her family were incarcerated and then relocated to an internment camp in Idaho. This was the result of Executive Order 9066, signed by President Franklin Roosevelt in February 1942. This order, in the aftermath of the Japanese attack on Pearl Harbor in December 1941, gave military authorities the right to remove any and all persons from "military areas." In 1954 Yamada became an American citizen. In addition to* Camp Notes and Other Poems *(1992, the source of the following poem),* Yamada *has written* Desert Run: Poems and Stories *(1988) and edited* Sowing TI Leaves: Writings by Multicultural Women *(1991).*

Note: *From 1942 to 1945, before leaving an internment camp for eastern sections of the United States, Japanese Americans were expected to sign a statement known as "The Loyalty Oath."*


## The Question of Loyalty                                    [1976]

I met the deadline
for alien registration
once before
was numbered fingerprinted
and ordered not to travel                                        5
without permit.

But alien still they said I must
forswear allegiance to the emperor.
for me that was easy
I didn't even know him                                          10
but my mother who did cried out
　　If I sign this
　　What will I be?
　　I am doubly loyal

to my American children                                           15
also to my own people.
How can double mean nothing?
I wish no one to lose this war.
Everyone does.

I was poor                                                       20
at math.
I signed
my only ticket out.

## ▓ TOPICS FOR CRITICAL THINKING AND WRITING

1. Who is speaking the poem?
2. What conflict does the mother experience? Do you see it as a serious conflict, or did the mother make an unnecessary fuss?
3. How would you characterize the tone of the last four lines of the poem? Do you assume that indeed the speaker is "poor at math"?

# GWENDOLYN BROOKS

*Gwendolyn Brooks (1917–2000) was born in Topeka, Kansas, but was raised in Chicago's South Side, where she spent most of her life. In 1950, when she won the Pulitzer Prize for Poetry, she became the first African-American writer to win a Pulitzer Prize.*

## *We Real Cool*                                           [1960]

*The Pool Players.*
*Seven at the Golden Shovel.*

We real cool. We
Left school. We

Lurk late. We
Strike straight. We

Sing sin. We                                                      5
Thin gin. We

Jazz June. We
Die soon.

## ▨ TOPICS FOR
## CRITICAL THINKING AND WRITING

1. Characterize the speaker of the poem. What evidence can you point to in order to support your characterization?
2. The stanzas could have been written thus:

   We real cool.
   We left school.

   We lurk late.
   We strike straight.

   And so forth. Why do you think Brooks wrote them, or printed them, the way she did?

# WHY WE WRITE ARGUMENTS
# ABOUT LITERATURE

The poems and the stories we have looked at get us to a point that we want to make about experiencing literature—about reading, thinking about, and writing about literature. We do *not* claim that it makes a reader materially richer or morally better, but we do claim that it opens a reader's eyes to points of view, to states of feeling, that he or she might not have been aware of. When we experience a work of literature we hear a report about a range of behavior, whether or not the author is trying to tell us how we should behave.

Later chapters in this book will go into detail about writing about specific forms of literature—fiction, drama, and poetry—but we want to end this chapter with a few words about why people write about literature, and then look at an overview of the writing process. We write about literature in order to clarify and to account for our responses to works that interest or excite or frustrate us. In putting words on paper, we have to take a second and a third look at what is in front of us and at what is within us. Writing is a way of learning, largely by thinking about and questioning our responses, *in effect arguing with ourselves* until we are reasonably satisfied with what our responses are, and *why* we have them. Writing, in short, is a form of critical thinking.

The last word is never said about complex thoughts and feelings—and works of literature as well as our responses to them embody complex thoughts and feelings. Still, when we write about literature we hope to make at least a little progress in the difficult but rewarding job of talking about our responses. When we write we learn; we also hope to interest our reader by communicating our responses to material that is worth talking about.

But to respond usefully—helpfully—to anything and then to communicate responses, we must have

- some understanding of the thing, and
- some skill at converting responses into words.

This book tries to help you deepen your understanding of literature—what literature does and the ways in which it does it—and also tries to help you convert your responses into words that will let your reader share your perceptions, your enthusiasms, and even your doubts. This sharing is, in effect, teaching. You may think that you are writing for the teacher, but such a view is a misconception; when you write, *you* are the teacher. An essay on literature is an attempt to help your reader to see the work as you see it.

# The Writing Process

---
**A RULE FOR WRITERS**

You are not knocking off an assignment; you are writing an essay, engaging in a process that, first, will teach you, and second, will ultimately engage the interest of your readers.

---

No one process works for all writers—indeed, most writers use different processes for different kinds of writing—but the following advice may help you get started.

1. **Consider the writing situation:**
   a. *Is the specific topic assigned, or do you choose your own?* If the choice is yours, choose a work you like—but allow plenty of time, because you may find, once you get to work, that you want to change your topic.
   b. *How long will the essay be?* Schedule an appropriate amount of time.
   c. *What kinds of sources are you expected to use?* Only your own insights, supplemented by conversations with friends, and perhaps familiarity with your textbooks? Some research? Substantial research? Again, allow the appropriate amount of time.
   d. *Who is the audience?* Classmates? The general public, for example, readers of *Time* magazine? Awareness of your audience will help you to determine the amount of detail you need to provide. Unless your instructor tells you otherwise, assume that you are writing for readers pretty much like yourself—in short, for your

classmates. They will not have to be told, for instance, that Shakespeare is an English dramatist or that Robert Frost is an American poet, but they will have to be told your reasons for the ways you respond to their works.

  e. *When is the essay due?* Allow time to type, proofread, and check any sources.

2. **Get at least a few ideas before you write a first draft.** You can immediately generate some ideas by thinking about the impact the work makes on you—why does it please or displease or even anger you? *Annotate the text in an effort to help you to grasp it:* Underline words in the text that you think are especially significant, draw lines connecting key words that, though in separate lines, seem linked to you, and jot down your tentative responses in the margin. Did some words puzzle you? Look them up, and think about why the writer may have used unusual words. You may also get some starting ideas by thinking about relevant assertions you heard in classroom discussions—for instance, ideas concerning literature and truth, symbolism, the depiction of women, or the use of dialect. (In your final essay be sure to give credit for any ideas that you borrow.) Jot down whatever comes to mind—key phrases will do—and you probably will find that these jottings engender further ideas.

3. **Rearrange your ideas into a scratch outline, i.e., a tentative plan for a draft.** A list of a few phrases indicating (a) the topics you plan to address (for instance, "conflict," "differences in gender responses," "characterization") and (b) the sequence of your ideas will help you to get going. This outline will probably indicate that the first paragraph will name the writers or the works of literature you are addressing and will specify the general approach or scope of the paper. Additional jottings, in sequence, indicate the gist of what each paragraph might be concerned with.

4. **Start writing, without worrying about correctness.** Yes, you have been putting down words, but these activities are what composition instructors call "pre-writing." Now you are in a position to really write. If you have made an outline, begin by following it, but remember, the outline is a helpful guide to get you going, not a road map that must be followed. Write freely, get your ideas down on paper or up on the screen. At this stage, you are still wrestling with ideas, trying things out, clarifying things for yourself, engaging in a search-and-discovery operation. These pages are not a first draft; rather they are what writing teachers call a zero draft, so don't worry about mechanical matters such as spelling and punctuation and stylistic elegance. Such things will be important when you revise and edit, but at the moment you are trying to find out what your ideas are, and how much sense they make. Don't be afraid to set forth your hunches. As E. M. Forster put it, "How do I know what I think until I

see what I say?"Write in a spirit of confidence, and if you are using a computer, be sure to save your material.

Later, of course, you will reread with a critical (and skeptical) mind what you have written—you will want to make sure that assertions are supported by evidence—but for now, follow your instincts.

5. **Reread and revise the material,** preferably after in interval of a few hours or even a day.

You are now prepared to write a serious draft. Your tentative or working thesis—the main point that you will support with evidence—has now evolved into a point that you have confidence in. *Do not try to revise merely by reading the computer's monitor.* You need to see the essay as your reader will see it, on paper. Only a hard copy will let you see if a paragraph is too long, or if quotations are too long and too frequent. Revise the hard copy with a pen or pencil, and then keyboard your revisions into the computer.

Revisions will be of two sorts: global (large scale, such as reorganization) and local (the substitution of a precise word for an imprecise one, or a spelling correction). Generally speaking, try to begin by making the necessary global revisions—you may, for instance, decide that introductory background material is or is not needed, or that background material should be distributed throughout the essay rather than given all at once at the start, or that additional evidence is needed to support some assertion, or that some material in our final paragraph ought to appear earlier—but of course if you spot a spelling error, or realize that a particular word is not the best word, there is no harm in pausing to make such a correction when you first see the need.

Now is the time to keep asking yourself questions like

- What will my audience—my readers—make of this word, this sentence, this paragraph?
- Do I offer adequate support for this generalization?
- Is my point clear, and is it expressed effectively?

Put yourself in your reader's shoes; ask yourself if readers will be aware of where they are going. You are inventing a skeptical reader, who in fact will be your helpful collaborator.

## A RULE FOR WRITERS

When you draft and especially when you revise an essay, keep your audience in mind. Tell them what they need to know, in an orderly way, and in language that they will understand and that will teach them.

6. **Reread and revise the draft again,** asking yourself what your reader will make out of each sentence.

Read your prose carefully, and try to hear it in the mind's ear. You might even read the draft aloud to yourself, or to a friend. Writing an essay is not the same thing as having a conversation, of course, but you'll want to write the essay in a voice that is natural to you.

---

## A RULE FOR WRITERS

The words that you put on the page will convey an image of you to the reader; make sure that image is favorable.

---

Pay special attention to your *opening and closing paragraphs.* These two are especially difficult, but after you have drafted and revised the essay you will often find you can revise the beginning and the ending effectively. (A good opening paragraph is often the last thing the writer writes. It may well be as simple as an engaging statement of the thesis that you have at last come to recognize and develop.)

---

## A RULE FOR WRITERS
(Attributed to Truman Capote)

Good writing is rewriting.

---

7. **Make certain that the mechanics are according to specifications.** Here you are acting not so much as an author but as an editor.

- An author, in the heat of drafting material, may be indifferent to mechanical details, but
- an editor must be cool, detached, and finicky.

In short, when you are in the role of editor, you must tell yourself, as the author, to come down to earth and package the essay correctly.

- Margins, spacing, and page numbering should follow the instructor's requirements.
- All sources must be documented.

### A RULE FOR WRITERS

Acknowledge your sources, including computer-generated text,

1. if you quote directly and put the quoted words in quotation marks.
2. if you summarize or paraphrase someone's material, even though you do not retain one word of your source.
3. if you borrow a distinctive idea, even though the words and the concrete application are your own.

8. **If possible, get a classmate or a friend to read your essay and make suggestions.** This representative of your audience should not rewrite the essay for you, but he or she can call your attention to paragraphs that need development, unclear organization, unconvincing arguments, awkward sentences, and even errors in punctuation and spelling.

### A RULE FOR WRITERS

Organize your essay so that your readers can easily follow the argument you use—the reasons you give—to support your thesis.

9. **Consider the reader's suggestions, and revise where you think necessary.** If your reader finds some terms obscure, or an argument unsubstantiated, you will almost surely want to revise, clarifying the terms and providing evidence for the argument. As before, in the process of revising, try to imagine yourself as your own hypothetical—and skeptical—reader.
10. **Print out a copy of the revised draft, read it, and revise again**—and again—as needed.

### A RULE FOR WRITERS

You may or may not want to sketch a rough outline before drafting your essay, but you should certainly outline what you hope is your final draft, to see (a) if it is organized, and (b) if the organization will be evident to the reader.

✔ **CHECKLIST**:  Basic Writing Strategies

❏ Is my title engaging?
❏ Does my introduction provide essential information (artist, work, topic, or approach of the essay)?
❏ Does my paper have a thesis, a point?
❏ Do I support my argument with sufficient persuasive detail?
❏ Have I kept the needs of my audience in mind—for instance, have I defined unfamiliar terms?
❏ Is the paper organized, and is the organization clear to the reader?
❏ Have I set forth my views effectively and yet not talked too much about myself?
❏ Does the essay fulfill the assignment (length, scope)?

# READING FOR PLEASURE

Through the study of literature, we acquire important analytical skills that make us better interpreters of literary meaning, and that assist us in becoming more focused, effective writers of critical essays, and that perhaps, even more, help us to live decent lives. But it is important not to lose sight of the fact that we read for pleasure as well. The experience of literature is often challenging—it tests our beliefs and values—but it is also enjoyable. To put it simply: it is something that we like to do.

When we read a good story, for example, we might find pleasure in an unexpected turn of the plot or in a surprise ending. Perhaps we feel satisfied with how things have turned out for the characters: good has been rewarded and evil punished. Or, on the other hand, since we probably all have not only a moral sense but also a tendency toward anarchy, we may feel in a story the delight that comes—at least sometimes—when strict justice has been evaded.

In the case of drama, there is pleasure in encountering a memorable character, such as Ibsen's Nora Helmer or Miller's Willy Loman, someone who seems as alive on the page and on the stage as in real life. And in poetry, there is the pleasure we take in the writer's craftsmanship—the deft handling of word, phrase, image, rhyme, meter, insight, and idea—and the sense that the writer has caught a state of mind—let's say of young love, or of loneliness, or of the pleasure of remembering youthful joy. In many poems we make the acquaintance of lines and stanzas that stay with us. We enjoy remembering them, as when Robert Frost writes:

The woods are lovely, dark and deep,
But I have promises to keep,
And miles to go before I sleep,
And miles to go before I sleep.

("Stopping by Woods on a Snowy Evening")

There are many ways for us to spend our spare time, and in our highly technological age we have access to all sorts of pleasures and distractions—on the computer, on television, in movies, on CDs. Yet reading literature still offers something unique. We read a book or see a play that catches hold of us and leads us to read more of the author's work—and to spread the word about it to other people we know. Literature is a source of both instruction and delight: it matters to us (as any child reciting a nursery rhyme knows) because it offers special pleasures that we cannot do without.

# 2

# Writing about Literature: From Idea to Essay

## MORE ABOUT WRITING ARGUMENTS ABOUT LITERATURE

If you have ever put exclamation points or questions marks or brief annotations ("this is ridiculous," or "great!") in the margins of your books, you are aware of the *pleasure* one gets from putting responses into writing. But people also write about literature—not only in margins of books but, let's say, in notebooks or journals and ultimately in essays—in order to clarify and account for their responses to works that interest or excite or frustrate them.

In putting words on paper you will have to take a second and a third look at what is in front of you and what is within you. Writing, then, is not only a way of expressing pleasure but also a way of *learning*. The last word about complex thoughts and feelings is never said, but when we write we hope to make at least a little progress in the difficult but rewarding job of talking about our responses. We learn, and then we hope to interest our readers because we are communicating to them our responses to something that for one reason or another is worth talking about.

This communication is, in effect, teaching. You may think that you are writing for the teacher, but that is a misconception; when you write, *you* are the teacher. An essay on literature is an attempt to help someone see the work as you see it. If this chapter had to be boiled down to a single sentence, that sentence would be: Because you are teaching, your essay should embody those qualities that you value in teachers—intelligence, open-mindedness, effort; a desire to offer what help one can.

# GETTING IDEAS: PRE-WRITING

We have already quoted Robert Frost: "All there is to writing is having ideas. To learn to write is to learn to have ideas." But how does one "learn to have ideas"? Among the methods are these: reading with a pen or pencil in hand, so that you can annotate the text; keeping a journal, in which you jot down reflections about your reading; talking with others (including your instructor) about the reading. In the first chapter we printed the annotations a student wrote for Shakespeare's "Sigh no more, ladies, sigh no more." Now let's look at a second example of an annotated text. We begin with a short biography of the poet, then we give the text of the poem and then we reprint the text along with the student's annotations.

## Pat Mora's "Immigrants"

*Pat Mora, after graduating from Texas Western College, earned a master's degree at the University of Texas at El Paso. She is best known for her poems, but she has also published essays on Chicano culture.*

### Immigrants

[1986]

wrap their babies in the American flag,
feed them mashed hot dogs and apple pie,
name them Bill and Daisy,
buy them blonde dolls that blink blue
eyes or a football and tiny cleats                                5
before the baby can even walk,
speak to them in thick English, hallo, babee, hallo.
whisper in Spanish or Polish
when the babies sleep, whisper
in a dark parent bed, that dark                                  10
parent fear, "Will they like
our boy, our girl, our fine american
boy, our fine american girl?"

And now the poem with the student's first thoughts.

*unusual to use title as first word?*

## Immigrants

wrap their babies in the American flag,     *so what's wrong with hot dogs and apple pie?*
feed them mashed hot dogs and apple pie,
name them Bill and Daisy,
buy them (blonde) dolls that blink (blue)
eyes or a football and tiny cleats     *Anglo types — not*  5
*Is Mora making fun of immigrants?* speak to them in thick English,    *Asian American or Latino types*
(hallo, babee, hallo,)
whisper in Spanish or Polish
*do only immigrants show a "parent fear"? Don't all parents fear for their children?* when the babies sleep, whisper
(in a dark parent bed, that dark     10
parent fear, "Will they like)     *why not a capital letter?*
our boy, our girl, our fine american
boy, our fine american girl?"

Notice that most of these annotations are questions that the student is asking herself. Asking questions is an excellent way to get yourself thinking. We will return to this method shortly.

## ▓ TOPICS FOR CRITICAL THINKING AND WRITING

1. Consider the mimicry of the immigrants talking to their children: "hallo, babee, hallo." If this mimicry came from an outsider it would be condescending and offensive, but since it is written by someone known for her concern with Mexican-American culture, it probably is not offensive. It is almost affectionate. Or is it? Your view? Your *reasons*?

2. Reread the poem—preferably aloud—and then try to decide exactly what Mora's attitude is toward the immigrants. Do you think that she fully approves of their hopes? On what do you base your answer?

3. What does it mean to say that someone—a politician, for instance— "wraps himself in the American flag"? What does Mora mean when she says that immigrants "wrap their babies in the American flag"? How would you paraphrase the line?

4. After reading the poem aloud two or three times, what elements of "verbal performance"—we might say of skillful play—do you notice? Mora does not use rhyme, but she does engage in some verbal play. What examples can you point to?

5. What is your own attitude toward the efforts of some immigrants to assimilate themselves to an Anglo-American model? How does your attitude affect your reading of the poem?

# Brainstorming for Ideas for Writing

Unlike annotating, which consists of making brief notes and small marks on the printed page, "brainstorming"—the free jotting down of ideas—asks that you jot down at length whatever comes to mind, without inhibition. But before we talk further about brainstorming, read the following short story.

## KATE CHOPIN

*Kate Chopin (1851-1904)—the name is pronounced in the French way, somewhat like "show pan"—was born in St. Louis, with the name Katherine O'Flaherty. Her father was an immigrant from Ireland, and her mother was descended from an old Creole family. (In the United States, a Creole is a person descended from the original French settlers in Lousiana or the original Spanish settlers in the Gulf States.) At the age of nineteen she married Oscar Chopin, a cotton broker in New Orleans. They had six children, and though Kate Chopin had contemplated a literary career, she did not turn seriously to writing until after her husband's death in 1883. Most of her fiction concerns the lives of the descendants of the French who had settled in Louisiana.*

## The Story of an Hour                                     [1894]

Knowing that Mrs. Mallard was afflicted with a heart trouble, great care was taken to break to her as gently as possible the news of her husband's death.

It was her sister Josephine who told her, in broken sentences, veiled hints that revealed in half concealing. Her husband's friend Richards was there, too, near her. It was he who had been in the newspaper office when intelligence of the railroad disaster was received, with Brently Mallard's name leading the list of "killed." He had only taken the time to assure himself of its truth by a second telegram, and had hastened to forestall any less careful, less tender friend in bearing the sad message.

She did not hear the story as many women have heard the same, with a paralyzed inability to accept its significance. She wept at once, with sudden, wild abandonment, in her sister's arms. When the storm of grief had spent itself she went away to her room alone. She would have no one follow her.

There stood, facing the open window, a comfortable, roomy armchair. Into this she sank, pressed down by a physical exhaustion that haunted her body and seemed to reach into her soul.

5      She could see in the open square before her house the tops of trees that were all aquiver with the new spring life. The delicious breath of rain

was in the air. In the street below a peddler was crying his wares. The notes of a distant song which some one was singing reached her faintly, and countless sparrows were twittering in the eaves.

There were patches of blue sky showing here and there through the clouds that had met and piled one above the other in the west facing her window. She sat with her head thrown back upon the cushion of the chair quite motionless, except when a sob came up into her throat and shook her, as a child who has cried itself to sleep continues to sob in its dreams.

She was young, with a fair, calm face, whose lines bespoke repression and even a certain strength. But now there was a dull stare in her eyes, whose gaze was fixed away off yonder on one of those patches of blue sky. It was not a glance of reflection, but rather indicated a suspension of intelligent thought.

There was something coming to her and she was waiting for it, fearfully. What was it? She did not know; it was too subtle and elusive to name. But she felt it, creeping out of the sky, reaching toward her through the sounds, the scents, the color that filled the air.

Now her bosom rose and fell tumultuously. She was beginning to recognize this thing that was approaching to possess her, and she was striving to beat it back with her will—as powerless as her two white slender hands would have been.

10    When she abandoned herself a little whispered word escaped her slightly parted lips. She said it over and over under her breath: "Free, free, free!" The vacant stare and the look of terror that had followed it went from her eyes. They stayed keen and bright. Her pulses beat fast, and the coursing blood warmed and relaxed every inch of her body.

She did not stop to ask if it were not a monstrous joy that held her. A clear and exalted perception enabled her to dismiss the suggestion as trivial.

She knew that she would weep again when she saw the kind, tender hands folded in death; the face that had never looked save with love upon her, fixed and gray and dead. But she saw beyond that bitter moment a long procession of years to come that would belong to her absolutely. And she opened and spread her arms out to them in welcome.

There would be no one to live for her during those coming years; she would live for herself. There would be no powerful will bending her in that blind persistence with which men and women believe they have a right to impose a private will upon a fellow creature. A kind intention or a cruel intention made the act seem no less a crime as she looked upon it in that brief moment of illumination.

And yet she had loved him—sometimes. Often she had not. What did it matter! What could love, the unsolved mystery, count for in face of this possession of self-assertion which she suddenly recognized as the strongest impulse of her being.

15    "Free! Body and soul free!" she kept whispering.

Josephine was kneeling before the closed door with her lips to the keyhole, imploring for admission. "Louise, open the door! I beg; open the door—you will make yourself ill. What are you doing, Louise? For heaven's sake open the door."

"Go away. I am not making myself ill." No; she was drinking in a very elixir of life through that open window.

Her fancy was running riot along those days ahead of her. Spring days, and summer days, and all sorts of days that would be her own. She breathed a quick prayer that life might be long. It was only yesterday she had thought with a shudder that life might be long.

She arose at length and opened the door to her sister's importunities. There was a feverish triumph in her eyes, and she carried herself unwittingly like a goddess of Victory. She clasped her sister's waist, and together they descended the stairs. Richards stood waiting for them at the bottom.

20    Some one was opening the front door with a latchkey. It was Brently Mallard who entered, a little travel-stained, composedly carrying his gripsack and umbrella. He had been far from the scene of accident, and did not even know there had been one. He stood amazed at Josephine's piercing cry; at Richards' quick motion to screen him from the view of his wife.

But Richards was too late.

When the doctors came they said she had died of heart disease—of joy that kills.

---

In brainstorming, don't worry about spelling, about writing complete sentences, or about unifying your thoughts; just let one thought lead to another. Later you can review your jottings, deleting some, connecting with arrows others that are related, expanding still others, but for now you want to get going, and so there is no reason to look back. Thus you might jot down something about the title.

```
Title speaks of an hour, and story covers an
hour, but maybe takes five minutes to read
```

And then, perhaps prompted by "an hour," you might happen to add something to this effect:

```
Doubt that a woman who got news of the death of
her husband could move from grief to joy within
an hour
```

Your next jotting might have little or nothing to do with this issue; it might simply say:

```
Enjoyed "Hour" especially because "Hour" is so
shocking
```

And then you might ask yourself:

> By shocking, do I mean "improbable," or what?
> Come to think of it, maybe it's not so improbable.
> A lot depends on what the marriage was like.

# Focused Free Writing

Focused, or directed, free writing is a method related to brainstorming that some writers use to uncover ideas they may want to write about. Concentrating on one issue—for instance, a question that strikes them as worth puzzling over (What kind of person is Mrs. Mallard?)—they write at length, nonstop, for perhaps 5 or 10 minutes.

Writers who find free writing helpful put down everything they can think of that has bearing on the one issue or question they are examining. They do not stop at this stage to evaluate the results, and they do not worry about niceties of sentence structure or of spelling. They just pour out their ideas in a steady stream of writing, drawing on whatever associations come to mind. If they pause in their writing, it is only to refer to the text, to search for more detail—perhaps a quotation—that will help them answer their question.

After the free-writing session, these writers usually go back and reread what they have written, highlighting or underlining what seems to be of value. Of course they find much that is of little or no use, but they also usually find that some strong ideas have surfaced and have received some development. At this point the writers are often able to make a scratch outline and then begin a draft.

Here is an example of one student's focused free writing, again on Chopin's "The Story of an Hour."

> What do I know about Mrs. Mallard? Let me
> put everything down here I know about her or can
> figure out from what Kate Chopin tells me. When
> she finds herself alone after the death of her
> husband, she says, "Free. Body and soul free" and
> before that she said, "Free, free, free." Three
> times. So she has suddenly perceived that she has
> not been free: she has been under the influence
> of a "powerful will." In this case it has been
> her husband, but she says no one, man nor woman,
> should impose their will on anyone else. So it's

not a feminist issue--it's a power issue. No one
should push anyone else around is what I guess
Chopin means, force someone to do what the
other person wants. I used to have a friend
that did that to me all the time; he had to run
everything. They say that fathers--before the
women's movement--used to run things, with the
father in charge of all the decisions, so maybe
this is an honest reaction to having been pushed
around by a husband. I think Mrs. Mallard is a
believable character, even if the plot is not
all that believable--all those things happening
in such quick succession.

## Listing and Clustering

In your preliminary thinking you may find it useful to make lists or to jot
down clusters of your ideas, insights, comments, questions. For "The Story
of an Hour" you might list Mrs. Mallard's traits, or you might list the stages
of her development. (Such a list is not the same as a summary of a plot. The
list helps the writer to see the sequence of psychological changes, and it
will help assist her to offer a coherent argument about what happens.)

weeps (when she gets the news)
goes to room, alone
"pressed down by a physical exhaustion"
"dull stare"
"something coming to her"
strives to beat back "this thing"
"Free, free, free!" The "vacant stare went from
    her eyes"
"A clear and exalted perception"
rejects Josephine
"she was drinking in a very elixir of life"
gets up, opens door, "a feverish triumph in
    her eyes"
sees B, and dies

Unlike brainstorming and annotating, which let you go in all directions, listing requires that you first make a decision about what you will be listing—traits of character, images, puns, or whatever. Once you make the decision, you can then construct the list, and, with a list in front of you, you will probably see patterns that you were not fully conscious of earlier.

On the other hand, don't be unduly concerned if something does not seem to fit into a list or cluster. You can return to it, and give it more thought—maybe it will come to fit later. But you might also realize that this point needs to be placed to the side. As far as you can tell, it doesn't appear to belong in one of your lists or to link well to other points you have begun to make, and in this way you may come to realize that it is not relevant to your development of possible topics for your essay.

# Developing an Awareness of the Writer's Use of Language

In the first line of the story, Chopin notes that "Mrs. Mallard was afflicted with a heart trouble." You might want to look up "afflicted" in your dictionary. Why do you think that Chopin chose this word, as opposed to other words she might have chosen? How would the effect of the opening line be different if, for example, Chopin had written "Mrs. Mallard had a heart problem" or "Mrs. Mallard's heart was weak"?

Earlier we recommended that you keep a dictionary at hand when you read. It will help you, especially if you get into the habit of asking questions about the writer's choice of language. And this brings us to our next point.

# Asking Questions

If you feel stuck, ask yourself questions. We suggest questions for fiction also on pages 164-167, for poetry on pages 509-511, and for drama on pages 701-704. If, for instance, you are thinking about a work of fiction, you might ask yourself questions about the plot and the characters—are they believable, are they interesting, and what does it all add up to? What does the story mean *to you?* One student found it helpful to jot down the following questions:

```
Plot
    Ending false? unconvincing? or prepared for?
Character?
    Mrs. M. unfeeling? Immoral?
```

```
    Mrs. M. unbelievable character?
     What might her marriage have been like? Many
        gaps. (Can we tell what her husband was
        like?) "And yet she loved him--sometimes."
        Fickle? Realistic?
     What is "this thing that was approaching to
        possess her"?
   Symbolism
     Set on spring day = symbolic of new life?
```

But, again, you don't have to be as tidy as this student was. You can begin by jotting down notes and queries about what you like or dislike and about what puzzles or amuses you. Here are the jottings of another student. They are, obviously, in no particular order—the student is brainstorming, putting down whatever occurs to her—though it is equally obvious that one note sometimes led to the next:

```
   Title nothing special. What might be better
      title?
   Could a woman who loved her husband be so
      heartless?
   Is she heartless? Did she love him?
   What are (were) Louise's feelings about her
      husband?
   Did she want too much? What did she want?
   Could this story happen today? Feminist
      interpretation?
   Sister (Josephine)--a busybody?
   Tricky ending--but maybe it could be true
   "And yet she loved him--sometimes. Often she
      had not."
   Why does one love someone "sometimes"?
   Irony: plot has reversal. Are characters ironic
      too?
```

These jottings will help the reader-writer to think about the story, to find a special point of interest and to develop a thoughtful argument about it.

# Keeping a Journal

A journal is not a diary, a record of what the writer did each day ("today I read Chopin's 'Hour'"); rather, a journal is a place to store some of the thoughts that you may have inscribed on a scrap of paper or in the margin of the text—for instance, your initial response to the title of a work or to the ending. It's also a place to jot down some further reflections. These reflections may include thoughts about what the work means to you or what was said in the classroom about writing in general or about specific works. You may, for instance, want to reflect on why your opinion is so different from that of another student, or you may want to apply a concept such as "character" or "irony" or "plausibility" to a story that later you may write an essay about.

You might even make an entry in the form of a letter to the author or in the form of a letter from one character to another. Similarly, you might write a dialogue between characters in two works or between two authors, or you might record an experience of your own that is comparable to something in the work.

A student who wrote about "The Story of an Hour" began with the following entry in his journal. In reading this entry, notice that one idea stimulates another. The student was, quite rightly, concerned with getting and exploring ideas, not with writing a unified paragraph.

Apparently a "well-made" story, but seems clever rather than moving or real. Doesn't seem plausible. Mrs. M's change comes out of the blue--maybe some women might respond like this, but probably not most.

Does literature deal with unusual people, or with usual (typical?) people? Shouldn't it deal with typical? Maybe not. (Anyway, how can I know?) Is "typical" same as "plausible"? Come to think of it, prob. not.

Anyway, whether Mrs. M. is typical or not, is her change plausible, believable?

Why did she change? Her husband dominated her life and controlled her action; he did "impose a private will upon a fellow creature." She calls this a crime. Why? Why not?

# Arriving at a Thesis to Argue

Having raised some questions, a reader goes back to the story, hoping to read it now with increased awareness. Some of the jottings will be dead ends, but some will lead to further ideas that can be arranged in lists. What the **thesis** of the essay will be—the idea that will be asserted and supported—is still in doubt, but there is no doubt about one thing: A good essay will have a thesis, a point, an argument. You ought to be able to state your point in a **thesis sentence.**

Consider these candidates as possible thesis sentences, as assertions that can be supported in an argument:

1. Mrs. Mallard dies soon after hearing that her husband had died.

True, but scarcely a point that can be argued, or even developed. About the most the essayist can do with this sentence is to amplify it by summarizing the plot of the story, a task not worth doing. An analysis may include a sentence or two of summary, to give readers their bearings, but a summary is not an essay.

2. The story is a libel on women.

In contrast to the first statement, this one can be developed into an argument. Probably the writer will try to demonstrate that Mrs. Mallard's behavior is despicable. Whether this point can be convincingly argued is another matter; the thesis may be untenable, but it is a thesis. A second problem, however, is this: Even if the writer demonstrates that Mrs. Mallard's behavior is despicable, he or she will have to go on to demonstrate that the presentation of one despicable woman constitutes a libel on women in general. That's a pretty big order.

3. The story is clever but superficial because it is based on an unreal character.

Here, too, is a thesis, a point of view that can be argued. Whether or not this thesis is true is another matter. The writer's job will be to support it by presenting evidence. Probably the writer will have no difficulty in finding evidence that the story is "clever"; the difficulty probably will be in establishing a case that the characterization of Mrs. Mallard is "unreal." The writer will have to set forth some ideas about what makes a character real and then will have to show that Mrs. Mallard is an "unreal" (unbelievable) figure.

4. The irony of the ending is believable partly because it is consistent with earlier ironies in the story.

It happens that the student who wrote the essay printed on page 00 began by drafting an essay based on the third of these thesis topics, but as she worked on a draft she found that she couldn't support her assertion that the character was unconvincing. In fact, she came to believe that although Mrs. Mallard's joy was the reverse of what a reader might expect, several early reversals in the story helped to make Mrs. Mallard's shift from grief to joy acceptable.

# WRITING A DRAFT

After jotting down notes and then adding more notes stimulated by rereading and further thinking, you'll probably be able to formulate a tentative thesis. At this point most writers find it useful to clear the air by glancing over their preliminary notes and by jotting down the thesis and a few especially promising notes—brief statements of what they think their key points may be. These notes may include some brief key quotations that the writer thinks will help to support the thesis.

Here are the notes (not the original brainstorming notes, but a later selection from them, with additions) and a draft (following) that makes use of them. The final version of the essay—the product produced by the process—is given on page 52.

```
title: Ironies in an Hour (?) An Hour of Irony (?)
    Kate Chopin's Irony (?)
thesis: irony at the end is prepared for by
    earlier ironies
chief irony: Mrs. M. dies just as she is
    beginning to enjoy life
smaller ironies: 1. "sad message" brings her joy
                 2. Richards is "too late" at end
                 3. Richards is too early at start
```

## Sample Draft of an Essay on Kate Chopin's "The Story of an Hour"

Now for the student's draft—not the first version, but a revised draft with some of the irrelevancies of the first draft omitted and some evidence added.

The digits within the parentheses refer to the page numbers from which the quotations are drawn, though with so short a work as "The

Story of an Hour," page references are hardly necessary. Unless instructed otherwise, always provide page numbers for your quotations. This will enable your readers to quickly locate the passages to which you refer. (Detailed information about how to document a paper is given on pages 1130-1145.)

---

Crowe 1

Lynn Crowe

Professor O'Brian

English 102

1 November 2005

Ironies in an Hour

After we know how the story turns out,
if we reread it we find irony at the very
start, as is true of many other stories.
Mrs. Mallard's friends assume, mistakenly,
that Mrs. Mallard was deeply in love with
her husband, Brently Mallard. They take
great care to tell her gently of his death.
The friends mean well, and in fact they do
well. They bring her an hour of life, an
hour of freedom. They think their news is
sad. Mrs. Mallard at first expresses grief
when she hears the news, but soon she finds
joy in it. So Richards's "sad message"
(36), though sad in Richards's eyes, is
in fact a happy message.

Among the ironic details is the statement
that when Mallard entered the house,
Richards tried to conceal him from Mrs.
Mallard, but "Richards was too late" (38).
This is ironic because earlier Richards
"hastened" (36) to bring his sad message;

Crowe 2

if he had at the start been "too late" (38),
Brently Mallard would have arrived at home
first, and Mrs. Mallard's life would not
have ended an hour later but would simply
have gone on as it had before. Yet another
irony at the end of the story is the
diagnosis of the doctors. The doctors say
she died of "heart disease--of joy that
kills" (38). In one sense the doctors are
right: Mrs. Mallard has experienced a great
joy. But of course the doctors totally
misunderstood the joy that kills her.

The central irony resides not in the
well-intentioned but ironic actions of
Richards, nor in the unconsciously ironic
words of the doctors, but in her own life.
In a way she has been dead. She "sometimes"
(36) loved her husband, but in a way she
has been dead. Now, his apparent death
brings her new life. This new life comes to
her at the season of the year when "the
tops of trees . . . were all aquiver with
the new spring life" (38). But, ironically,
her new life will last only an hour. She
looks forward to "summer days" (38) but she
will not see even the end of this spring
day. Her years of marriage were ironic.
They brought her a sort of living death
instead of joy. Her new life is ironic too.
It grows out of her moment of grief for her
supposedly dead husband, and her vision of
a new life is cut short.

**[New page]**

<br>

Crowe 3

Work Cited

Chopin, Kate. "The Story of an Hour."
<u>A Little Literature</u>. Ed. Sylvan Barnet,
William Burto, and William E. Cain. New
York: Longman, 2007. 36-38.

<br>

# Revising a Draft

The draft, although thoughtful and clear, is not yet a finished essay. The student went on to improve it in many small but important ways.

First, the draft needs a good introductory paragraph, a paragraph that will let readers know where the writer will be taking them. Doubtless you know from your own experience as a reader that readers can follow an argument more easily—and with more pleasure—if early in the discussion the writer alerts them to the gist of the argument. (The title, too, can strongly suggest the thesis.) Second, some of the paragraphs could be clearer.

In revising paragraphs—or, for that matter, in revising an entire draft— writers unify, organize, clarify, and polish. Let's look at the nouns implicit in these verbs.

1. **Unity** is achieved partly by eliminating irrelevancies. Notice that in the final version, printed on pages 52-54, the writer has deleted "as is true of many other stories" from the first sentence of the draft.
2. **Organization** is largely a matter of arranging material into a sequence that will assist the reader to grasp the point.
3. **Clarity** is achieved largely by providing concrete details and quotations to support generalizations and by providing helpful transitions ("for instance," "furthermore," "on the other hand," "however").
4. **Polish** is small-scale revision. For instance, one deletes unnecessary repetitions. In the second paragraph of the draft, the phrase "the doctors" appears three times, but it appears only once in the final version of the paragraph. Similarly, in polishing, a writer combines choppy sentences into longer sentences, and breaks overly long sentences into shorter sentences.

Later, after producing a draft that seems close to a finished essay, writers engage in yet another activity.

5. **Editing** concerns such things as checking the accuracy of quotations by comparing them with the original, checking a dictionary for the spelling of doubtful words, checking a handbook for doubtful punctuation—for instance, whether a comma or a semicolon is needed in a particular sentence.

---

## ✔ CHECKLIST:  Revising Paragraphs

❑ Does the paragraph *say* anything? Does it have substance?

❑ Does the paragraph have a topic sentence? If so, is it in the best place? If the paragraph doesn't have a topic sentence, might one improve the paragraph? Or does it have a clear topic idea?

❑ If the paragraph is an opening paragraph, is it interesting enough to attract and to hold a reader's attention? If it is a later paragraph, does it easily evolve out of the previous paragraph and lead into the next paragraph?

❑ Does the paragraph contain some principle of development, for instance from cause to effect, or from general to particular?

❑ Does each sentence clearly follow from the preceding sentence? Have you provided transitional words or cues to guide your reader? Would it be useful to repeat certain key words for clarity?

❑ What is the purpose of the paragraph? Do you want to summarize, to give an illustration, to concede a point, or what? Will your purpose be clear to your reader, and does the paragraph fulfill your purpose?

❑ Is the closing paragraph effective and not merely an unnecessary restatement of the obvious?

# Peer Review

Your instructor may encourage (or even require) you to discuss your draft with another student or with a small group of students. That is, you may be asked to get a review from your peers. Such a procedure is helpful in several ways. First, it gives the writer a real audience, readers who can point to what pleases or puzzles them, who make suggestions, who may often disagree (with the writer or with each other), and who frequently, though not intentionally, *misread*. Though writers don't necessarily like everything they hear (they seldom hear "This is perfect. Don't change a word!"), reading and discussing their work with others almost always gives them a fresh perspective on their work, and a fresh perspective may stimulate thoughtful revision. (Having your intentions *misread* because your writing isn't clear enough can be particularly stimulating.)

The writer whose work is being reviewed is not the sole beneficiary. When students regularly serve as readers for each other, they become better readers of their own work and consequently better revisers.

When you produce a draft of your paper for peer review, it will not be in final form; the draft is an important step toward shaping the paper and bringing it to final form. But aim to do the best job possible on your draft; let your classmates respond to the best work you can do at this stage of the process.

---

QUESTIONS FOR PEER REVIEW            ENGLISH 125A

Read each draft once, quickly. Then read it again, with the following questions in mind.

1. What is the essay's topic? Is it one of the assigned topics, or a variation from it? Does the draft show promise of fulfilling the assignment?

2. Looking at the essay as a whole, what thesis (main idea) is stated or implied? If implied, try to state it in your own words.

3. Is the thesis plausible? How might the argument be strengthened?

4. Looking at each paragraph separately:

   a. What is the basic point? (If it isn't clear to you, ask for clarification.)

   b. How does the paragraph relate to the essay's main idea or to the previous paragraph?

   c. Should some paragraphs be deleted? Be divided into two or more paragraphs? Be combined? Be put elsewhere? (If you outline the essay by jotting down the gist of each paragraph, you will get help in answering these questions.)

> d. Is each sentence clearly related to the sentence that precedes it and to the sentence that follows?
>
> e. Is each paragraph adequately developed?
>
> f. Are there sufficient details, perhaps brief supporting quotations from the text?
>
> 5. What are the paper's chief strengths?
>
> 6. Make at least two specific suggestions that you think will assist the author to improve the paper.

You will have more work to do on this paper—you know that. But you don't want your classmates to be pointing out mistakes that you know are in the draft and that you could have fixed yourself.

If peer review is a part of the writing process in your course, the instructor may distribute a sheet with some suggestions and questions. An example of such a sheet is shown here.

---

✔ CHECKLIST: Thinking Critically about a Draft

❑ Is the title of my essay at least moderately informative and interesting?

❑ Do I identify the subject of my essay (author and title) early?

❑ What is my thesis? Do I state it soon enough (perhaps even in the title) and keep it in view?

❑ Is the organization reasonable? Does each point lead into the next without irrelevancies and without anticlimaxes?

❑ Is each paragraph unified by a topic sentence or a topic idea? Are there adequate transitions from one paragraph to the next?

❑ Are generalizations supported by appropriate concrete details, especially by brief quotations from the text?

❑ Is the opening paragraph interesting and, by its end, focused on the topic? Is the final paragraph conclusive without being repetitive?

❑ Is the tone appropriate? No sarcasm, no apologies, no condescension?

❑ If there is a summary, is it as brief as possible, given its purpose?

❑ Are the quotations adequately introduced, and are they accurate? Do they provide evidence and let the reader hear the author's voice, or do they merely add words to the essay?

❑ Is the present tense used to describe the author's work and the action of the work ("Shakespeare shows," "Hamlet dies")?
❑ Have I kept in mind the needs of my audience, for instance, by defining unfamiliar terms or by briefly summarizing works or opinions with which the reader may be unfamiliar?
❑ Is documentation provided where necessary?
❑ Are the spelling and punctuation correct? Are other mechanical matters (such as margins, spacing, and citations) in correct form? Have I proofread carefully?
❑ Is the paper properly identified—author's name, instructor's name, course number, and date?

# THE FINAL VERSION

Here is the final version of the student's essay. The essay that was submitted to her instructor had been retyped, but here, so that you can easily see how the draft has been revised, we print the draft with the final changes written in by hand.

Crowe 1

Lynn Crowe
Professor O'Brian
English 102
1 November 2005

Ironies of Life in Kate Chopin's "The Story of an Hour"
~~Ironies in an Hour~~

Despite its title, Kate Chopin's "The Story of an Hour" ironically takes only a few minutes to read. In addition, the story turns out to have an ironic ending, but on rereading it one sees that the irony is not concentrated only in the outcome of the plot—Mrs. Mallard dies just when she is beginning to live—but is also present in many details.

After we know how the story turns out, if we
reread it we find irony at the very start. / ~~as is true~~
                                        Because                   and her sister
~~of many other stories~~. ∧Mrs. Mallard's friends∧ assume,
                    she
mistakenly, that ~~Mrs. Mallard~~ was deeply in love with

her husband, Brently Mallard. ~~They~~ They take great care to

tell her gently of his death. ~~The friends~~ They mean well,

and in fact they _do_ well. ~~They~~ bring[ing] her an hour of

life, an hour of [joyous] freedom. ~~but it is ironic that~~ They think their news is

[True,] sad. Mrs. Mallard at first expresses grief when she

hears the news, but soon [(unknown to her friends)] she finds joy in it. So

Richards's "sad message" (36), though sad in

Richards's eyes, is in fact a happy message.

Among the [small but significant] ironic details is the statement [near the end of the story] that

when Mallard entered the house, Richards tried to

conceal him from Mrs. Mallard, but "Richards was too

late" (38). This is ironic because [almost at the start of the story, in the second] ~~earlier~~ Richards [paragraph,]

"hastened" (36) to bring his sad message; if he had

at the start been "too late" (38), Brently Mallard

would have arrived at home first, and Mrs. Mallard's

life would not have ended an hour later but would

simply have gone on as it had before. Yet another

irony at the end of the story is the diagnosis of the

doctors. ~~The doctors~~ They say she died of "heart disease--

life would not have ended an hour later but would

simply have gone on as it had before. Yet another

irony at the end of the story is the diagnosis of the

doctors. ~~The doctors~~ They say she died of "heart disease--

of joy that kills" (38). In one sense ~~the doctors~~ they are

right: Mrs. Mallard [for the last hour] experienced a great joy. But of

course the doctors totally misunderstand the joy that

kills her. It is not joy at seeing her husband alive, but her realization that the great joy she experienced during the last hour is over.

All of these ironic details add richness to the story, but The central irony resides not in the well-

intentioned but ironic actions of Richards, nor in the

unconsciously ironic words of the doctors, but in ~~her~~ *Mrs. Mallard's*

own life. ~~In a way she has been dead.~~ She "sometimes"

(36) loved her husband, but in a way she has been

dead, *a body subjected to her husband's will* Now, his apparent death brings her new life.

This new life comes to her at the season of the year

when "the tops of trees . . . were all aquiver with

the new spring life" (38). But, ironically, her new

life will last only an hour. *She is "free, free, free"—but only until her husband walks through* She looks forward to *the doorway.*

"summer days" (38) but she will not see even the end

of this spring day. *If* Her years of marriage were

ironic, *bringing* ~~They brought~~ her a sort of living death

instead of joy. Her new life is ironic too, *not only because* It grows

out of her moment of grief for her supposedly dead

husband, *but also because her vision of "a long progression of years"* and her vision of a new life is cut short *within an hour on a spring day.*

**[New page]**

Work Cited

Chopin, Kate. "The Story of an Hour." A Little

   Literature. Ed. Sylvan Barnet, William Burto,

   and William E. Cain. New York: Longman, 2007. 36-38.

# A Brief Overview of the Final Version

Finally, as a quick review, let's look at several principles illustrated by this essay.

1. The **title of the essay** is not merely the title of the work discussed; rather, it gives the readers a clue, a small idea of the essayist's topic.
2. The **opening** or **introductory paragraph** does not begin by saying "In this story . . ." Rather, by naming the author and the title, it lets the reader know exactly what story is being discussed. It also develops the writer's thesis so readers know where they will be going.

3. The **organization** is effective. The smaller ironies are discussed in the second and third paragraphs, the central (chief) irony in the last paragraph. That is, the essay does not dwindle or become anticlimactic; rather, it builds up from the least important to the most important point.

4. Some **brief quotations** are used, both to provide evidence and to let the reader hear—even if only fleetingly—Kate Chopin's writing.

5. The essay is chiefly devoted to **analysis** (how the parts relate to each other), not to summary (a brief restatement of the happenings). The writer, properly assuming that the reader has read the work, does not tell the plot in great detail. But, aware that the reader has not memorized the story, the writer gives helpful reminders.

6. The **present tense** is used in narrating the action: "Mrs. Mallard dies"; "Mrs. Mallard's friends and her sister assume."

7. Although a **concluding paragraph** is often useful—if it does more than merely summarize what has already been clearly said—it is not essential in a short analysis. In this essay, the last sentence explains the chief irony and therefore makes an acceptable ending.

# EXPLICATION

A line-by-line commentary on what is going on in a text is an explication (literally, unfolding, or spreading out). Although your explication will for the most part move steadily from the beginning to the end of the selection, try to avoid writing along these lines (or, one might say, along this one line): "In line one. . . . In the second line. . . . In the third line. . . ." That is, don't hesitate to write such things as

The poem begins. . . . In the next line. . . . The

speaker immediately adds. . . . He then introduces.

. . . The next stanza begins by saying. . . .

And of course you can discuss the second line before the first if that seems the best way of handling the passage.

An explication is not concerned with the writer's life or times, and it is not a paraphrase (a rewording)—though it may include paraphrase if a passage in the original seems unclear, perhaps because of an unusual word or an unfamiliar expression. On the whole, however, an explication goes beyond paraphrase, seeking to make explicit what the reader perceives as implicit in the work. To this end it calls attention, as it proceeds, to the implications of words (for instance, to their tone), the function of rhymes (for instance, how they may connect ideas, as in "throne" and "alone"), the development of contrasts, and any other contributions to the meaning.

Obviously you will have ideas about the merit and the meaning of a poem, and your paper will implicitly have a *thesis*—an argument, for instance this poem is very difficult, or this poem begins effectively but quickly goes downhill, or this poem is excessively sentimental. Your essay, however, is largely devoted not to making assertions of this sort but to explaining how the details make the meaning.

A good way to stimulate responses to the poem is to ask some of the questions given on pages 509–511.

Many students find that by copying the poem (by hand, or on a computer) they gain an understanding of the uses of language in a literary work. *Don't* photocopy the poem; the act of writing or typing it will help you to get into the piece, word by word, comma by comma. Double-space, so that you have ample room for annotations.

If you use a word processing program, you can highlight key words, lines, stanzas. You can also rearrange lines and stanzas, and perhaps substitute different words for the words that the poet has selected. Some students like to make multiple printouts for contrast and comparison—the poem as the poet wrote it, the poem as the student has marked it up by using the highlighting feature of the computer program, the poem as it stands after the student has somewhat rearranged it.

A computer cannot interpret a poem or story for you. But you can employ it as a tool to deepen your own sense of how a poem is structured—why this or that word or image is crucial at this juncture, why this or that stanza or passage belongs here and could not be placed elsewhere, and so on. Your goal is to gain insight into how writers of literary texts use their artistic medium, and often a computer can be a good complement to the dictionary that you always keep nearby.

# A Sample Explication

Read this short poem (published in 1917) by the Irish poet William Butler Yeats (1865–1939). The "balloon" in the poem is a dirigible, a blimp.

# WILLIAM BUTLER YEATS

## *The Balloon of the Mind*                                   [1917]

Hands, do what you're bid:
Bring the balloon of the mind
That bellies and drags in the wind
Into its narrow shed.

A student began thinking about the poem by copying it, double-spaced. Then she jotted down her first thoughts.

*sounds abrupt*

Hands, do what you're bid:

Bring the balloon of the mind

That bellies and drags in the wind

Into its narrow shed.

—balloon imagined by the mind? Or a mind like a balloon?

no real rhymes?

line seems to drag— it's so long!

Later she wrote some notes in a journal.

I'm still puzzled about the meaning of the words, "The balloon of the mind." Does "balloon of the mind" mean a balloon that belongs to the mind, sort of like "a disease of the heart."? If so, it means a balloon that the mind has, a balloon that the mind possesses, I guess by imagining it. Or does it mean that the mind is _like_ a balloon, as when you say "he's a pig of a man," meaning he is like a pig, he is a pig? Can it mean both? What's a balloon that the mind imagines? Something like dreams of fame, wealth? Castles in Spain.

Is Yeats saying that the "hands" have to work hard to make dreams a reality? Maybe. But maybe the idea really is that the mind is _like_ a balloon—hard to keep under control, floating around. Very hard to keep the mind on the job. If the mind is like a balloon, it's hard to get it into the hangar (shed).

"Bellies." Is there such a verb? In this poem it seems to mean something like "puffs out" or "flops around in the wind." Just checked _The American Heritage Dictionary_, and it says "belly" can be a verb, "to swell out," "to bulge." Well, you learn something every day.

**A later entry:**

OK; I think the poem is about a writer trying
to keep his balloon-like mind from floating around,
trying to keep the mind under control, trying to
keep it working at the job of writing something,
maybe writing something with the "clarity, unity,
and coherence" I keep hearing about in this course.

**Here is the student's final version of the explication.**

Yeats's "Balloon of the Mind" is about writing
poetry, specifically about the difficulty of getting
one's floating thoughts down in lines on the page.
The first line, a short, stern, heavily stressed
command to the speaker's hands, perhaps implies by
its severe or impatient tone that these hands will
be disobedient or inept or careless if not watched
closely: the poor bumbling body so often fails to
achieve the goals of the mind. The bluntness of the
command in the first line is emphasized by the fact
that all the subsequent lines have more syllables.
Furthermore, the first line is a grammatically
complete sentence, whereas the thought of line 2
spills over into the next lines, implying the
difficulty of fitting ideas into confining spaces,
that is, of getting one's thoughts into order,
especially into a coherent poem.

Lines 2 and 3 amplify the metaphor already stated
in the title (the product of the mind is an airy but
unwieldy balloon), and they also contain a second
command, "Bring." Alliteration ties this command,
"Bring," to the earlier "bid"; it also ties both of
these verbs to their object, "balloon," and to the
verb that most effectively describes the balloon,
"bellies." In comparison with the abrupt first line
of the poem, lines 2 and 3 themselves seem almost
swollen, bellying and dragging, an effect aided by

using adjacent unstressed syllables ("of the,"
"[bell]ies and," "in the") and by using an eye rhyme
("mind" and "wind") rather than an exact rhyme. And
then comes the short last line: almost before we
could expect it, the cumbersome balloon--here, the
idea that is to be packed into the stanza--is
successfully lodged in its "narrow shed."

Aside from the relatively colorless "into," the
only words of more than one syllable in the poem are
"balloon," "bellies," and "narrow," and all three
emphasize the difficulty of the task. But after
"narrow"--the word itself almost looks long and
narrow, in this context like a hangar--we get the
simplicity of the monosyllable "shed." The difficult
job is done, the thought is safely packed away,
the poem is completed--but again with an off rhyme
("bid" and "shed"), for neatness can go only so far
when hands and mind and a balloon are involved.

*Note:* The reader of an explication needs to see the text, and because
the explicated text is usually short, it is advisable to quote it all. (Remember, your imagined audience probably consists of your classmates; even if
they have already read the work you are explicating, they have not memorized it, and so you helpfully remind them of the work by quoting it.) You
can quote the entire text at the outset, or you can quote the first unit (for
example, a stanza), then explicate that unit, and then quote the next unit,
and so on. And if the poem or passage of prose is longer than, say, six lines,
it is advisable to number every fifth line at the right for easy reference, or
every fourth line if the poem is written in four-line stanzas.

# Explication as Argument

An explication unfolds or interprets a work; it is partly an exposition but
it is also an *argument,* offering assertions that are supported by *reasons.*
Reread the explication of "The Balloon of the Mind," and notice that the
first sentence makes a claim—the poem is "about" such-and-such—and
notice, too, that the subsequent assertions are supported by evidence. For
instance, when the writer says that lines 2 and 3 seem to drag, she goes on
to support the claim by calling attention to "adjacent unstressed syllables."
She does not merely assert; she argues.

## ✔ CHECKLIST:  Drafting an Explication

### Overall Considerations

❑ Does the poem imply a story of some sort, for instance the speaker's report of a love affair, or of a response to nature? If so, what is its beginning, middle, and end?

❑ If you detect a story in the speaker's mind, a change of mood—for instance a shift from bitterness that a love affair has ended to hope for its renewal—is this change communicated in part by the connotations of certain words? By syntax? By metrical shifts?

❑ Do the details all cohere into a meaningful whole? If so, your explication will largely be an argument on behalf of this thesis.

### Detailed Considerations

❑ If the poem has a title other than the first line, what are the implications of the title?

❑ Are there clusters or patterns of imagery, for instance religious images, economic images, or images drawn from nature? If so, how do they contribute to the meaning of the poem?

❑ Is irony (understatement or overstatement) used? To what effect?

❑ How do the connotations of certain words (for instance, *dad* rather than *father*) help to establish the meaning?

❑ What are the implications of the syntax—for instance, of notably simple or notably complex sentences? What do such sentences tell us about the speaker?

❑ Do metrical variations occur, and if so, what is their significance?

❑ Do rhyming words have some meaningful connection, as in the clichés *moon* and *June, dove* and *love*?

❑ What are the implications of the poem's appearance on the page—for example, of an indented line, or of the stanzaic pattern? (For instance, if the poem consists of two stanzas of four lines each, does the second stanza offer a reversal of the first?)

# COMPARISON AND CONTRAST: A WAY OF ARGUING

Something should be said about an essay organized around a comparison or a contrast, say, of the settings in two short stories, of two characters in a novel, or of the symbolism in two poems. (A comparison emphasizes resemblances whereas a contrast emphasizes differences, but we can use the word "comparison" to cover both kinds of writing.) Probably the student's first thought, after making some jottings, is to discuss one-half of the comparison and then go on to the second half. Instructors and textbooks (though not this one) usually condemn such an organization, arguing that the essay breaks into two parts and that the second part involves a good deal of repetition of categories set up in the first part. Usually they recommend that students organize their thoughts differently, making point-by-point comparisons. For example, in comparing *Huckleberry Finn* with *The Catcher in the Rye,* you might organize the material like this:

1. First similarity: the narrator and his quest
   a. Huck
   b. Holden
2. Second similarity: the corrupt world surrounding the narrator
   a. society in *Huckleberry Finn*
   b. society in *Catcher*
3. First difference: degree to which the narrator fulfills his quest and escapes from society
   a. Huck's plan to "light out" to the frontier
   b. Holden's breakdown

Here is another way of organizing a comparison and contrast:

1. First point: the narrator and his quest
   a. similarities between Huck and Holden
   b. differences between Huck and Holden
2. Second point: the corrupt world
   a. similarities between the worlds in *Huck* and *Catcher*
   b. differences between the worlds in *Huck* and *Catcher*
3. Third point: degree of success
   a. similarities between Huck and Holden
   b. differences between Huck and Holden

But a comparison need not employ either of these structures. There is even the danger that an essay employing either of them may not come into focus until the essayist stands back from the seven-layer cake and announces, in the concluding paragraph, that the odd layers taste better. In your preparatory thinking, you may want to make comparisons in pairs, but you must come to some conclusions about what these add up to before writing the final version. This final version should not duplicate the thought processes; rather, it should be organized to make the point clearly and effectively. You are not making a list; you are arguing a case.

The point of the essay presumably is not to list pairs of similarities or differences, but to illuminate a work or works by making thoughtful comparisons. Although in a long essay the writer cannot postpone until page 30 a discussion of the second half of the comparison, in an essay of, say, fewer than ten pages nothing is wrong with setting forth one-half of the comparison and then, in light of it, the second half. The essay will break into two unrelated parts if the second half makes no use of the first or if it fails to modify the first half, but not if the second half looks back to the first half and calls attention to differences that the new material reveals. Learning how to write an essay with interwoven comparisons is worthwhile, but be aware that there is another, simpler and clearer way to write a comparison.

---

✔ C H E C K L I S T :   Revising a Comparison

❑ Does it make sense to compare these things? (What question will the comparison help to answer? What argument does it advance? What do you hope your reader will learn?)
❑ Is the point of the comparison—the reason for making it—clear?
❑ Does the comparison cover all significant similarities and differences?
❑ Is the comparison readable; that is, is it clear and yet not tediously mechanical?
❑ Is the organization that is used—perhaps treating one text first and then the other, or perhaps shifting back and forth between texts—the best way to make this comparison?
❑ If the essay offers a value judgment, is the judgment fair? Does the essay offer enough evidence to bring a reader into at least partial agreement?

# ADDITIONAL READINGS
# FOR PLEASURE AND FOR
# ARGUMENTATIVE WRITING

## LUKE

*Luke, the author of the third of the four Gospels in the New Testament, was a second-generation Christian. He probably was a Roman, though some early accounts refer to him as a Syrian; in any case, he wrote in Greek, probably composing the Gospel about 80–85 CE. In Chapter 15, verses 11–32, Luke reports a story that Jesus told. This story, which occurs only in Luke's Gospel, is of a type called a parable, an extremely brief narrative from which a moral may be drawn.*

### The Parable of the Prodigal Son

And he said, "A certain man had two sons: and the younger of them said to his father, 'Father, give me a portion of goods that falleth to me.' And he divided unto them his living. And not many days after, the younger son gathered all together, and took his journey into a far country, and there wasted his substance with riotous living.

"And when he had spent all, there arose a mighty famine in that land, and he began to be in want. And he went and joined himself to a citizen of that country, and he sent him into his fields to feed swine. And he would fain have filled his belly with the husks that the swine did eat: and no man gave unto him. And when he came to himself, he said, 'How many hired servants of my father's have bread enough and to spare, and I perish with hunger? I will arise and go to my father, and will say unto him, "Father, I have sinned against heaven, and before thee, and am no more worthy to be called thy son: make me as one of thy hired servants."'

"And he arose, and came to his father. But when he was yet a great way off, his father saw him, and had compassion, and ran, and fell on his neck, and kissed him. And the son said unto him, 'Father, I have sinned against heaven, and in thy sight, and am no more worthy to be called thy son.' But the father said to his servants, 'Bring forth the best robe, and put it on him, and put a ring on his hand, and shoes on his feet. And bring hither the fatted calf, and kill it, and let us eat, and be merry. For this my son was dead, and is alive again; he was lost, and is found.' And they began to be merry.

"Now his elder son was in the field, and as he came and drew nigh to the house, he heard music and dancing. And he called one of the servants, and asked what these things meant. And he said unto him 'Thy brother is come, and thy father hath killed the fatted calf, because he hath received him safe and sound.' And he was angry, and would not go in: therefore came his father out, and entreated him. And he answering said to his father 'Lo, these many years do I serve thee, neither transgressed I at any time thy commandment, and yet thou never gavest me a kid, that I might make merry with friends: but as soon as this thy son was come, which hath devoured thy living with harlots, thou hast killed for him the fatted calf.' And he said unto him, 'Son, thou art ever with me, and all that I have is thine. It was meet that we should make merry, and be glad: for this thy brother was dead, and is alive again: and was lost, and is found.'"

## ▨ TOPICS FOR CRITICAL THINKING AND WRITING

1. What parallels or contrasts (or both) do you find in the parable of the prodigal son? What *function* does the older brother serve? If he were omitted, what if anything would be lost? (Characterize him, partly by comparing him with the younger brother and with the father.)
2. Is the father foolish and sentimental? Do you approve or disapprove of his behavior at the end? Why?

3. Jesus told the story, so it must have had a meaning consistent with his other teachings. Christians customarily interpret the story as meaning that God (like the father in the parable) rejoices in the return of a sinner. What meaning, if any, can it have for readers who are not Christians? Explain.

# GRACE PALEY

*Born in 1922 in New York City, Grace Paley attended Hunter College and New York University, but left without a degree. While raising two children she wrote poetry and then, in the 1950s, turned to writing fiction.*

*Paley's chief subject is the life of little people struggling in the Big City. Of life she has said, "How daily life is lived is a mystery to me. You write about what's mysterious to you. What is it like? Why do people do this?" Of the short story she has said, "It can be just telling a little tale, or writing a complicated philosophical story. It can be a song, almost."*

## Samuel                                                             [1968]

Some boys are very tough. They're afraid of nothing. They are the ones who climb a wall and take a bow at the top. Not only are they brave on the roof, but they make a lot of noise in the darkest part of the cellar where even the super hates to go. They also jiggle and hop on the platform between the locked doors of the subway cars.

Four boys are jiggling on the swaying platform. Their names are Alfred, Calvin, Samuel, and Tom. The men and the women in the cars on either side watch them. They don't like them to jiggle or jump but don't want to interfere. Of course some of the men in the cars were once brave boys like these. One of them had ridden the tail of a speeding truck from New York to Rockaway Beach without getting off, without his sore fingers losing hold. Nothing happened to him then or later. He had made a compact with other boys who preferred to watch: Starting at Eighth Avenue and Fifteenth Street, he would get to some specified place, maybe Twenty-third and the river, by hopping the tops of the moving trucks. This was hard to do when one truck turned a corner in the wrong direction and the nearest truck was a couple of feet too high. He made three or four starts before succeeding. He had gotten his idea from a film at school called *The Romance of Logging*. He had finished high school, married a good friend, was in a responsible job and going to night school.

These two men and others looked at the four boys jumping and jig-gling on the platform and thought, It must be fun to ride that way, espe-cially now the weather is nice and we're out of the tunnel and way high over the Bronx. Then they thought, These kids do seem to be acting sort of stupid. They *are* little. Then they thought of some of the brave things they had done when they were boys and jiggling didn't seem so risky.

The ladies in the car became very angry when they looked at the four boys. Most of them brought their brows together and hoped the boys could see their extreme disapproval. One of the ladies wanted to get up and say, Be careful you dumb kids, get off that platform or I'll call a cop. But three of the boys were Negroes and the fourth was something else she couldn't tell for sure. She was afraid they'd be fresh and laugh at her and embarrass her. She wasn't afraid they'd hit her, but she was afraid of embarrassment. Another lady thought, Their mothers never know where they are. It wasn't true in this particular case. Their mothers all knew that they had gone to see the missile exhibit on Fourteenth Street.

5      Out on the platform, whenever the train accelerated, the boys would raise their hands and point them up to the sky to act like rockets going off, then they rat-tat-tatted the shatterproof glass pane like machine guns, although no machine guns had been exhibited.

For some reason known only to the motorman, the train began a sud-den slowdown. The lady who was afraid of embarrassment saw the boys jerk forward and backward and grab the swinging guard chains. She had her own boy at home. She stood up with determination and went to the door. She slid it open and said, "You boys will be hurt. You'll be killed. I'm going to call the conductor if you don't just go into the next car and sit down and be quiet."

Two of the boys said, "Yes'm," and acted as though they were about to go. Two of them blinked their eyes a couple of times and pressed their lips together. The train resumed its speed. The door slid shut, parting the lady and the boys. She leaned against the side door because she had to get off at the next stop.

The boys opened their eyes wide at each other and laughed. The lady blushed. The boys looked at her and laughed harder. They began to pound each other's back. Samuel laughed the hardest and pounded Alfred's back until Alfred coughed and the tears came. Alfred held tight to the chain hook. Samuel pounded him even harder when he saw the tears. He said, "Why you bawling? You a baby, huh?" and laughed. One of the men whose boyhood had been more watchful than brave became angry. He stood up straight and looked at the boys for a couple of seconds. Then he walked in a citizenly way to the end of the car, where he pulled the emergency cord. Almost at once, with a terrible hiss, the pressure of air abandoned the brakes and the wheels were caught and held.

People standing in the most secure places fell forward, then back-ward. Samuel had let go of his hold on the chain so he could pound Tom as well as Alfred. All the passengers in the cars whipped back and forth, but he pitched only forward and fell head first to be crushed and killed between the cars.

10        The train had stopped hard, halfway into the station, and the conductor called at once for the trainmen who knew about this kind of death and how to take the body from the wheels and brakes. There was silence except for passengers from other cars who asked, What happened! What happened! The ladies waited around wondering if he might be an only child. The men recalled other afternoons with very bad endings. The little boys stayed close to each other, leaning and touching shoulders and arms and legs.

When the policeman knocked at the door and told her about it, Samuel's mother began to scream. She screamed all day and moaned all night, though the doctors tried to quiet her with pills.

Oh, oh, she hopelessly cried. She did not know how she could ever find another boy like that one. However, she was a young woman and she became pregnant. Then for a few months she was hopeful. The child born to her was a boy. They brought him to be seen and nursed. She smiled. But immediately she saw that this baby wasn't Samuel. She and her husband together have had other children, but never again will a boy exactly like Samuel be known.

_____

You might think about the ways in which "Samuel" differs from a newspaper story of an accident in a subway. (You might even want to write a newspaper version of the happening.) In some ways, Paley's story faintly resembles an account that might appear in a newspaper. Journalists are taught to give information about Who, What, When, Where, and Why, and Paley does provide this. Thus, the *characters* (Samuel and others) are the journalist's Who; the *plot* (the boys were jiggling on the platform, and when a man pulled the emergency cord one of them was killed) is the What; the *setting* (the subway, presumably in modern times) is the When and the Where; the *motivation* (the irritation of the man who pulls the emergency cord) is the Why.

Ask yourself questions about each of these elements, and think about how they work in Paley's story. You might also think about responses to the following questions. Your responses will teach you a good deal about what literature is and about some of the ways in which it works.

## ▨ TOPICS FOR CRITICAL THINKING AND WRITING

1. Paley wrote the story, but an unspecified person *tells* it. Describe the voice of this narrator in the first paragraph. Is the voice neutral and objective, or do you hear some sort of attitude, a point of view? If you do hear an attitude, what words or phrases in the story indicate it?

2. What do you know about the setting of "Samuel"? What can you infer about the neighborhood?
3. In the fourth paragraph we are told that "three of the boys were Negroes and the fourth was something else." Is race important in this story? Is Samuel "Negro" or "something else"? Does it matter?
4. Exactly *why* did a man walk "in a citizenly way to the end of the car, where he pulled the emergency cord"? Do you think the author blames him? What evidence can you offer to support your view? Do *you* blame him? Or do you blame the boys? Or anyone? Explain.
5. The story is called "Samuel," and it is, surely, about him. But what happens after Samuel dies? (You might want to list the events.) What else is the story about? (You might want to comment on why you believe the items in your list are important.)
6. Can you generalize about what the men think of the jigglers and about what the women think? Is Paley saying something about the sexes? About the attitudes of onlookers in a big city?

# KATHERINE MANSFIELD

*Katherine Mansfield (1888-1923), née Kathleen Mansfield Beauchamp, was born in New Zealand. In 1902 she went to London for schooling; in 1906 she returned to New Zealand, but, dissatisfied with its provincialism, in 1908 she returned to London to become a writer. After a disastrous marriage and a love affair, she went to Germany, where she wrote stories; in 1910 she returned to London, published a book of stories in 1911, and in 1912 met and began living with the writer John Middleton Murry. In 1918, after her first husband at last divorced her, she married Murry. She died of tuberculosis in 1923, a few months after her thirty-fourth birthday.*

*Mansfield published about seventy stories, and left some others unpublished. An early admirer of Chekhov, she read his works in German translations before they were translated into English.*

## Miss Brill [1920]

Although it was so brilliantly fine—the blue sky powdered with gold and great spots of light like white wine splashed over the Jardins Publiques[1]— Miss Brill was glad that she had decided on her fur. The air was motionless, but when you opened your mouth there was just a faint chill, like a chill from a glass of iced water before you sip, and now and again a leaf

---

[1]**Jardins Publiques** Public Gardens (French).

came drifting—from nowhere, from the sky. Miss Brill put up her hand and touched her fur. Dear little thing! It was nice to feel it again. She had taken it out of its box that afternoon, shaken out the moth-powder, given it a good brush, and rubbed the life back into the dim little eyes. "What has been happening to me?" said the sad little eyes. Oh, how sweet it was to see them snap at her again from the red eiderdown! . . . But the nose, which was of some black composition, wasn't at all firm. It must have had a knock, somehow. Never mind—a little dab of black sealing-wax when the time came—when it was absolutely necessary. . . . Little rogue! Yes, she really felt like that about it. Little rogue biting its tail just by her left ear. She could have taken it off and laid it on her lap and stroked it. She felt a tingling in her hands and arms, but that came from walking, she supposed. And when she breathed, something light and sad—no, not sad, exactly—something gentle seemed to move in her bosom.

There were a number of people out this afternoon, far more than last Sunday. And the band sounded louder and gayer. That was because the Season had begun. For although the band played all year round on Sundays, out of season it was never the same. It was like some one playing with only the family to listen; it didn't care how it played if there weren't any strangers present. Wasn't the conductor wearing a new coat, too? She was sure it was new. He scraped with his foot and flapped his arms like a rooster about to crow, and the bandsmen sitting in the green rotunda blew out their cheeks and glared at the music. Now there came a little "flutey" bit—very pretty!—a little chain of bright drops. She was sure it would be repeated. It was; she lifted her head and smiled.

Only two people shared her "special" seat: a fine old man in a velvet coat, his hands clasped over a huge carved walking-stick, and a big old woman, sitting upright, with a roll of knitting on her embroidered apron. They did not speak. This was disappointing, for Miss Brill always looked forward to the conversation. She had become really quite expert, she thought, at listening as though she didn't listen, at sitting in other people's lives just for a minute while they talked round her.

She glanced, sideways, at the old couple. Perhaps they would go soon. Last Sunday, too, hadn't been as interesting as usual. An Englishman and his wife, he wearing a dreadful Panama hat and she button boots. And she'd gone on the whole time about how she ought to wear spectacles; she knew she needed them; but that it was no good getting any; they'd be sure to break and they'd never keep on. And he'd been so patient. He'd suggested everything—gold rims, the kind that curved round your ears, little pads inside the bridge. No, nothing would please her. "They'll always be sliding down my nose!" Miss Brill had wanted to shake her.

5    The old people sat on the bench, still as statues. Never mind, there was always the crowd to watch. To and fro, in front of the flower-beds and the band rotunda, the couples and groups paraded, stopped to talk, to greet, to buy a handful of flowers from the old beggar who had his tray

fixed to the railings. Little children ran among them, swooping and laughing; little boys with big white silk bows under their chins, little girls, little French dolls, dressed up in velvet and lace.And sometimes a tiny staggerer came suddenly rocking into the open from under the trees, stopped, stared, as suddenly sat down "flop," until its small high-stepping mother, like a young hen, rushed scolding to its rescue. Other people sat on the benches and green chairs, but they were nearly always the same, Sunday after Sunday, and—Miss Brill had often noticed—there was something funny about nearly all of them.They were odd, silent, nearly all old, and from the way they stared they looked as though they'd just come from dark little rooms or even—even cupboards!

Behind the rotunda the slender trees with yellow leaves down drooping, and through them just a line of sea, and beyond the blue sky with gold-veined clouds.

Tum-tum-tum tiddle-um! tiddle-um! tum tiddley-um tum ta! blew the band.

Two young girls in red came by and two young soldiers in blue met them, and they laughed and paired and went off arm-in-arm.Two peasant women with funny straw hats passed, gravely, leading beautiful smoke-colored donkeys. A cold, pale nun hurried by.A beautiful woman came along and dropped her bunch of violets, and a little boy ran after to hand them to her, and she took them and threw them away as if they'd been poisoned. Dear me! Miss Brill didn't know whether to admire that or not! And now an ermine toque[2] and a gentleman in grey met just in front of her. He was tall, stiff, dignified, and she was wearing the ermine toque she'd bought when her hair was yellow. Now everything, her hair, her face, even her eyes, was the same color as the shabby ermine, and her hand, in its cleaned glove, lifted to dab her lips, was a tiny yellowish paw. Oh, she was so pleased to see him—delighted! She rather thought they were going to meet that afternoon. She described where she'd been—everywhere, here, there, along by the sea.The day was so charming—didn't he agree? And wouldn't he, perhaps? . . . But he shook his head, lighted a cigarette, slowly breathed a great deep puff into her face, and, even while she was still talking and laughing, flicked the match away and walked on.The ermine toque was alone; she smiled more brightly than ever. But even the band seemed to know what she was feeling and played more softly, played tenderly, and the drum beat, "The Brute! The Brute!" over and over. What would she do? What was going to happen now? But as Miss Brill wondered, the ermine toque turned, raised her hand as though she'd seen some one else, much nicer, just over there, and pattered away. And the band changed again and played more quickly, more gaily than ever, and the old couple on Miss Brill's seat got up and marched away, and such a funny old man with long

---

[2]**toque** a brimless, close-fitting woman's hat.

whiskers hobbled along in time to the music and was nearly knocked over by four girls walking abreast.

Oh, how fascinating it was! How she enjoyed it! How she loved sitting here, watching it all! It was like a play. It was exactly like a play. Who could believe the sky at the back wasn't painted? But it wasn't till a little brown dog trotted on solemn and then slowly trotted off, like a little "theatre" dog, a little dog that had been drugged, that Miss Brill discovered what it was that made it so exciting. They were all on the stage. They weren't only the audience, not only looking on; they were acting. Even she had a part and came every Sunday. No doubt somebody would have noticed if she hadn't been there; she was part of the performance after all. How strange she'd never thought of it like that before! And yet it explained why she made such a point of starting from home at just the same time each week—so as not to be late for the performance—and it also explained why she had quite a queer, shy feeling at telling her English pupils how she spent her Sunday afternoons. No wonder! Miss Brill nearly laughed out loud. She was on the stage. She thought of the old invalid gentleman to whom she read the newspaper four afternoons a week while he slept in the garden. She had got quite used to the frail head on the cotton pillow, the hollowed eyes, the open mouth and the high pinched nose. If he'd been dead she mightn't have noticed for weeks; she wouldn't have minded. But suddenly he knew he was having the paper read to him by an actress! "An actress!" The old head lifted; two points of light quivered in the old eyes. "An actress—are ye?" And Miss Brill smoothed the newspaper as though it were the manuscript of her part and said gently: "Yes, I have been an actress for a long time."

10    The band had been having a rest. Now they started again. And what they played was warm, sunny, yet there was just a faint chill—a something, what was it?—not sadness—no, not sadness—a something that made you want to sing. The tune lifted, lifted, the light shone; and it seemed to Miss Brill that in another moment all of them, all the whole company, would begin singing. The young ones, the laughing ones who were moving together, they would begin, and the men's voices, very resolute and brave, would join them. And then she too, she too, and the others on the benches—they would come in with a kind of accompaniment—something low, that scarcely rose or fell, something so beautiful—moving. . . . And Miss Brill's eyes filled with tears and she looked smiling at all the other members of the company. Yes, we understand, we understand, she thought—though what they understood she didn't know.

Just at that moment a boy and a girl came and sat down where the old couple had been. They were beautifully dressed; they were in love. The hero and heroine, of course, just arrived from his father's yacht. And still soundlessly singing, still with that trembling smile, Miss Brill prepared to listen.

"No, not now," said the girl. "Not here, I can't."

"But why? Because of that stupid old thing at the end there?" asked the boy. "Why does she come here at all—who wants her? Why doesn't she keep her silly old mug at home?"

"It's her fu-fur which is so funny," giggled the girl. "It's exactly like a fried whiting."[3]

15      "Ah, be off with you!" said the boy in an angry whisper. Then: "Tell me, my petite chère[4]—"

"No, not here," said the girl. "Not *yet.*"

On her way home she usually bought a slice of honey-cake at the baker's. It was her Sunday treat. Sometimes there was an almond in her slice, sometimes not. It made a great difference. If there was an almond it was like carrying home a tiny present—a surprise—something that might very well not have been there. She hurried on the almond Sundays and struck the match for the kettle in quite a dashing way.

But today she passed the baker's by, climbed the stairs, went into the little dark room—her room like a cupboard—and sat down on the red eiderdown. She sat there for a long time. The box that the fur came out of was on the bed. She unclasped the necklet quickly; quickly, without looking, laid it inside. But when she put the lid on she thought she heard something crying.

---

[3]**whiting** a kind of fish.   [4]*petite chère* darling.

### ▨ TOPICS FOR CRITICAL THINKING AND WRITING

1. Why do you think Mansfield did not give Miss Brill a first name?
2. What would be lost (or gained?) if the first paragraph were omitted?
3. Suppose someone said that the story is about a woman who is justly punished for her pride. What might be your response?

## JAMES MERRILL

*James Merrill (1926-1995) published his first book of poems in 1950, three years after graduating from college. (His manuscript was chosen by W. H. Auden for the Yale Younger Poets series.) Merrill was extremely inventive in his forms, and admirably successful in combining an engaging or even a playful tone with serious topics.*

## *Christmas Tree*                                                    [1997]

To be
Brought down at last
From the cold sighing mountain
Where I and the others
Had been fed, looked after, kept still,                          5
Meant, I knew—of course I knew—
That it would be only a matter of weeks,
That there was nothing more to do.
Warmly they took me in, made much of me,
The point from the start was to keep my spirits up.         10
I could assent to that. For honestly,
It did help to be wound in jewels, to send
Their colors flashing forth from vents in the deep
Fragrant sables that cloaked me head to foot.
Over me they wove a spell of shining—                        15
Purple and silver chains, eavesdripping tinsel,
Amulets, milagros: software of silver,
A heart, a little girl, a Model T,
Two staring eyes. Then angels, trumpets, BUD and BEA
(The children's names) in clownlike capitals,               20
Somewhere a music box whose tiny song
Played and replayed I ended before long
By loving. And in shadow behind me, a primitive IV
To keep the show going. Yes, yes, what lay ahead
Was clear: the stripping, the cold street, my chemicals     25
Plowed back into the Earth for lives to come—
No doubt a blessing, a harvest, but one that doesn't bear,
Now or ever, dwelling upon. To have grown so thin.
Needles and bone. The little boy's hands meeting
About my spine. The mother's voice: *Holding up wonderfully!*  30
No dread. No bitterness. The end beginning. Today's
Dusk room aglow
For the last time
With candlelight.
Faces love-lit,                                             35
Gifts underfoot.
Still to be so poised, so
Receptive. Still to recall, to praise.

## ❋ TOPICS FOR CRITICAL THINKING AND WRITING

1. How would you characterize the tone of the first sentence (lines 1–8)? That is, what do you take to be the speaker's attitude(s)?
2. Beginning with the last line of the lowest branches ("No dread"), and continuing to the end of the poem, how would you characterize the tone(s)? Does this ending satisfy you? Why, or why not? (In your response to this question about the ending, you will of course take into consideration everything that precedes the ending.)
3. About two-thirds of the way through the poem, the tree speaks of "a primitive IV / To keep the show going." What is an IV literally, and what is it in this poem?
4. If you find some lines that strike you as especially witty, point them out. And do you find some lines especially moving? If so, which ones, and why?
5. If someone asked you what the poem is about, what would you say?
6. When did you become aware of the shape that this poem makes on the page? Does this shaping of the poem make it more or less effective? Explain your position.

# II

# The Pleasures of Fiction

Fiction reveals truths that reality obscures.

—Jessamyn West

Again and again the story-teller sees something in his own life or in the life around him that is so important he cannot bear to let it pass into oblivion. There must never come a time, the writer feels, when people do not know about this.

—Lady Murasaki

There are only two or three human stories, and they go on repeating themselves as fiercely as if they had never happened before.

—Willa Cather

We are lonesome animals. We spend all our life trying to be less lonesome. One of our ancient methods is to tell a story begging the listener to say—and to feel—"Yes, that's the way it is, or at least that's the way I feel it. You're not as alone as you thought."

– John Steinbeck

# 3

# Approaching Fiction:
# Responding in Writing

The next four chapters will look at specific elements, one by one, in fiction—plot, character, symbolism, and so on—but first let's read a brief story by Ernest Hemingway and then talk about it (and see how one student talked about it) with little or no technical language.

## ERNEST HEMINGWAY

*Ernest Hemingway (1899-1961) was born in Oak Park, Illinois. After graduating from high school in 1917 he worked on the* Kansas City Star, *but left to serve as a volunteer ambulance driver in Italy, where he was wounded in action. He returned home, married, and then served as European correspondent for the* Toronto Star, *but he soon gave up journalism for fiction. In 1922 he settled in Paris, where he moved in a circle of American expatriates that included Ezra Pound, Gertrude Stein, and F. Scott Fitzgerald. It was in Paris that he wrote stories and novels about what Gertrude Stein called a "lost generation" of rootless Americans in Europe. (For Hemingway's reminiscences of the Paris years, see his posthumously published* A Moveable Feast.) *He served as a journalist during the Spanish Civil War and during the Second World War, but he was also something of a private soldier.*

*After the Second World War his reputation sank, though he was still active as a writer (for instance, he wrote* The Old Man and the Sea *in 1952). In 1954 Hemingway was awarded the Nobel Prize in Literature, but in 1961, depressed by a sense of failing power, he took his own life.*

## *Cat in the Rain*                                           [1925]

There were only two Americans stopping at the hotel. They did not know any of the people they passed on the stairs on their way to and from their room. Their room was on the second floor facing the sea. It also faced the public garden and the war monument. There were big palms and green benches in the public garden. In the good weather there was always an artist with his easel. Artists liked the way the palms grew and the bright colors of the hotels facing the gardens and the sea. Italians came from a long way off to look up at the war monument. It was made of bronze and glistened in the rain. It was raining. The rain dripped from the palm trees. Water stood in pools on the gravel paths. The sea broke in a long line in the rain and slipped back down the beach to come up and break again in a long line in the rain. The motor cars were gone from the square by the war monument. Across the square in the doorway of the café a waiter stood looking out at the empty square.

The American wife stood at the window looking out. Outside right under their window a cat was crouched under one of the dripping green tables. The cat was trying to make herself so compact that she would not be dripped on.

"I'm going down and get that kitty," the American wife said.

"I'll do it," her husband offered from the bed.

5      "No, I'll get it. The poor kitty out trying to keep dry under a table."

The husband went on reading, lying propped up with the two pillows at the foot of the bed.

"Don't get wet," he said.

The wife went downstairs and the hotel owner stood up and bowed to her as she passed the office. His desk was at the far end of the office. He was an old man and very tall.

"Il piove,"[1] the wife said. She liked the hotel-keeper.

10      "Si, si, Signora, brutto tempo. It is very bad weather."

He stood behind his desk in the far end of the dim room. The wife liked him. She liked the deadly serious way he received any complaints. She liked his dignity. She liked the way he wanted to serve her. She liked the way he felt about being a hotel-keeper. She liked his old, heavy face and big hands.

Liking him she opened the door and looked out. It was raining harder. A man in a rubber cape was crossing the empty square to the café. The cat would be around to the right. Perhaps she could go along under the eaves. As she stood in the doorway an umbrella opened behind her. It was the maid who looked after their room.

"You must not get wet," she smiled, speaking Italian. Of course, the hotel-keeper had sent her.

---

[1] **Il piove** It's raining (Italian).

With the maid holding the umbrella over her, she walked along the gravel path until she was under their window. The table was there, washed bright green in the rain, but the cat was gone. She was suddenly disappointed. The maid looked up at her.

15    "Ha perduto qualque coas, Signora?"[2]

"There was a cat," said the American girl.

"A cat?"

"Si, il gatto."

"A cat?" the maid laughed. "A cat in the rain?"

20    "Yes," she said, "under the table." Then. "Oh, I wanted it so much. I wanted a kitty."

When she talked English the maid's face tightened.

"Come, Signora," she said. "We must get back inside. You will be wet."

"I suppose so," said the American girl.

They went back along the gravel path and passed in the door. The maid stayed outside to close the umbrella. As the American girl passed the office, the padrone bowed from his desk. Something felt very small and tight inside the girl. The padrone made her feel very small and at the same time really important. She had a momentary feeling of being of supreme importance. She went on up the stairs. She opened the door of the room. George was on the bed, reading.

25    "Did you get the cat?" he asked, putting the book down.

"It was gone."

"Wonder where it went to," he said, resting his eyes from reading.

She sat down on the bed.

"I wanted it so much," she said. "I don't know why I wanted it so much. I wanted that poor kitty. It isn't any fun to be a poor kitty out in the rain."

30    George was reading again.

She went over and sat in front of the mirror of the dressing table looking at herself with the hand glass. She studied her profile, first one side and then the other. Then she studied the back of her head and her neck.

"Don't you think it would be a good idea if I let my hair grow out?" she asked, looking at her profile again.

George looked up and saw the back of her neck, clipped close like a boy's.

"I like it the way it is."

35    "I get so tired of it," she said. "I get so tired of looking like a boy."

George shifted his position in the bed. He hadn't looked away from her since she started to speak.

"You look pretty darn nice," he said.

She laid the mirror down on the dresser and went over to the window and looked out. It was getting dark.

---

[2]**Ha . . . Signora?** Have you lost something, Madam?

"I want to pull my hair back tight and smooth and make a big knot at the back that I can feel," she said. "I want to have a kitty to sit on my lap and purr when I stroke her."

40      "Yeah?" George said from the bed.

"And I want to eat at a table with my own silver and I want candles. And I want it to be spring and I want to brush my hair out in front of a mirror and I want a kitty and I want some new clothes."

"Oh, shut up and get something to read," George said. He was reading again.

His wife was looking out of the window. It was quite dark now and still raining in the palm trees.

"Anyway, I want a cat," she said, "I want a cat. I want a cat now. If I can't have long hair or any fun, I can have a cat."

45      George was not listening. He was reading his book. His wife looked out of the window where the light had come on in the square.

Someone knocked at the door.

"Avanti,"[3] George said. He looked up from his book.

In the doorway stood the maid. She held a big tortoise-shell cat pressed tight against her and swung down against her body.

"Excuse me," she said, "the padrone asked me to bring this for the Signora."

---

[3] **Avanti** Come in.

# RESPONSES: ANNOTATIONS AND JOURNAL ENTRIES

When you read a story—or, perhaps more accurately, when you reread a story before discussing it or writing about it—you'll find it helpful to jot an occasional note (for instance, a brief response or a question) in the margins and to underline or highlight passages that strike you as especially interesting. Here is part of the story, with a student's annotations.

The cat was trying to make herself so compact that she would not be dripped on.
"I'm going down and get that kitty," the American wife said.
"I'll do it," her husband offered from the bed. *He doesn't make a move*
"No, I'll get it. The poor kitty out trying to keep dry under a table."
The husband went on reading, lying propped up with the two pillows at the foot of the bed. *still doesn't move!*

"Don't get wet," he said.

*contrast with the husband* — The wife went downstairs and the hotel owner stood up and bowed to her as she passed the office. His desk was at the far end of the office. He was an old man and very tall.

*Is he making a joke? Or maybe he just isn't even thinking about what he is saying?*

"Il piove," the wife said. She liked the hotel-keeper.

"Si, si, Signora, brutto tempo. It is very bad weather."

He stood behind his desk in the far end of the dim room. The wife liked him. She liked the deadly serious way he received any complaints. She liked his dignity. She liked the way he wanted to serve her. She liked the way he felt about being a hotel-keeper. She liked his old, heavy face and big hands.

*She respects him and she is pleased by the attention he shows*

*to emphasize the bad weather??* — Liking him she opened the door and looked out. It was raining harder. A man in a rubber cape was crossing the empty square to the café. The cat would be around to the right.

*Everything* in a story presumably is important, but having read the story once, probably something has especially interested (or puzzled) you, such as the relationship between two people, or the way the end of the story is connected to the beginning. On rereading, then, pen in hand, you'll find yourself noticing things that you missed or didn't find especially significant on your first reading. Now that you know the end of the story, you will read the beginning in a different way.

And of course if your instructor asks you to think about certain questions, you'll keep these in mind while you reread, and you will find ideas coming to you. In "Cat in the Rain," suppose you are asked (or you ask yourself) if the story might just as well be about a dog in the rain. Would anything be lost?

Here are a few questions that you can ask of almost any story. After scanning the questions, you will want to reread the story, pen in hand, and then jot down your responses on a sheet of paper. As you write, doubtless you will go back and reread the story or at least parts of it.

1. *What happens?* In two or three sentences—say 25–50 words—summarize the gist of what happens in the story.
2. *What sorts of people are the chief characters?* In "Cat in the Rain" the chief characters are George, George's wife, and the innkeeper (the padrone). Jot down the traits that each seems to possess, and next to each trait briefly give some supporting evidence.
3. *What especially pleased or displeased you in the story?* Devote at least a sentence or two to the end of the story. Do you find the end satisfying? Why or why not? What evidence can you offer to support an argument with someone whose response differs from yours?
4. *Have you any thoughts about the title?* If so, what are they? If the story did not have a title, what would you call it?

*After* you have made your own jottings, compare them with these responses by a student. No two readers will respond in exactly the same way, but all readers can examine their responses and try to account for them, at least in part. If your responses are substantially different, how do you account for the differences?

1. A summary. A young wife, stopping with her
   husband at an Italian hotel, from her room
   sees a cat in the rain. She goes to get it,
   but it is gone, and so she returns empty-
   handed. A moment later the maid knocks at the
   door, holding a tortoise-shell cat.

2. The characters: The woman.
   kind-hearted (pities cat in rain)
   appreciates innkeeper's courtesy ("liked the
      way he wanted to serve her") and admires him
      ("She liked his dignity")
   unhappy (wants a cat, wants to change her hair,
      wants to eat at a table with her own silver)
   The husband, George.
   not willing to put himself out (says he'll go
      to garden to get cat but doesn't move)
   doesn't seem very interested in wife (hardly
      talks to her--he's reading; tells her to
      "shut up")
   but he does say he finds her attractive ("You
      look pretty darn nice")
   The innkeeper.
   serious, dignified ("She liked the deadly
      serious way he received any complaints. She
      liked his dignity")
   courteous, helpful (sends maid with umbrella;
      at end sends maid with cat)

3. Dislikes and likes. "Dislikes" is too strong,
   but I was disappointed that more didn't happen
   at the end. What is the husband's reaction to
   the cat? Or his final reaction to his wife? I

mean, what did he think about his wife when the
maid brings the cat? And, for that matter,
what is the wife's reaction? Is she satisfied?
Or does she realize that the cat can't really
make her happy? Now for the likes. (1) I guess
I did like the way it turned out; it's sort of
a happy ending, I think, since she wants the
cat and gets it. (2) I also especially like the
innkeeper. Maybe I like him partly because the
wife likes him, and if she likes him he must
be nice. And he is nice -very helpful. And I
also like the way Hemingway shows the husband.
I don't mean that I like the man himself, but
I like the way Hemingway shows he is such a
bastard--not getting off the bed to get the
cat, telling his wife to shut up and read.

Another thing about him is that the one
time he says something nice about her, it's
about her hair, and she isn't keen on the way
her hair is. She says it makes her look "like
a boy," and she is "tired" of looking like
a boy. There's something wrong with this
marriage. George hardly pays attention to
his wife, but he wants her to look like a
boy. Maybe the idea is that this macho guy
wants to keep her looking like an inferior
(immature) version of himself. Anyway, he
certainly doesn't seem interested in letting
her fulfill herself as a woman.

I think my feelings add up to this: I like
the way Hemingway shows us the relation
between the husband and wife (even though
the relation is pretty bad), and I like the
innkeeper. Even if the relation with the
couple ends unhappily, the story has a sort
of happy ending, so far as it goes, since the

innkeeper does what he can to please his
guest: he sends the maid, with the cat.
There's really nothing more that he can do.
  More about the ending. The more I think
about it, the more I feel that the ending is
as happy as it can be. George is awful. When
his wife says "I want a cat and I want a cat
now," Hemingway tells us "George was not
listening." And then, a moment later, almost
like a good fairy the maid appears and grants
the wife's wish.

4. The title. I don't suppose that I would have
called it "Cat in the Rain," but I don't know
what I would have called it. Maybe "An American
Couple in Italy." Or maybe "The Innkeeper."
I really do think that the innkeeper is very
important, even though he only has a few lines.
He's very impressive--not only to the girl,
but to me (and maybe to all readers), since
at the end of the story we see how caring the
innkeeper is.

  But the more I think about Hemingway's
title, the more I think that maybe it also
refers to the girl. Like the "poor kitty"
in the rain, the wife is in a pretty bad
situation. "It isn't any fun to be a poor
kitty out in the rain." Of course the woman
is indoors, but her husband generates lots
of unpleasant weather. She may as well be
out in the rain. She says "I want to have
a kitty to sit on my lap and purr when I
stroke her." This shows that she wants to
be affectionate and that she also wants to
have someone respond to her affection. She
is like a cat in the rain.

> Oh, I just noticed that the wife at first
> calls the cat "her" rather than "it." ("The
> cat was trying to make herself compact. . . .")
> Later she says "it," but at first she thinks
> of the cat as female--because (I think) she
> identifies with the cat.

The responses of this student probably include statements that you want to take issue with. Or perhaps you feel that the student did not even mention some things that you think are important. You may want to jot down some notes and raise some questions in class.

## A SAMPLE ESSAY BY A STUDENT

The responses that we have quoted were written by Bill Yanagi, who later wrote an essay developing one of them. Here is the essay.

---

Yanagi 1

Bill Yanagi
Prof. Lange
English 10B
20 October 2005

          Hemingway's American Wife

    My title alludes not to any of the four
women to whom Hemingway was married, but
to "the American wife" who is twice called
by this term in his short story, "Cat in
the Rain." We first meet her in the first
sentence of the story ("There were only two
Americans stopping at the hotel"), and the
next time she is mentioned (apart from a
reference to the wife and her husband as
"they") it is as "the American wife," at
the beginning of the second paragraph of

Yanagi 2

the story. The term is used again at the
end of the third paragraph.

She is, then, at least in the early
part of this story, just an American or an
American wife--someone identified only by
her nationality and her marital status,
but not at all by her personality, her
individuality, her inner self. She first
becomes something of an individual when
she separates herself from her husband by
leaving the hotel room and going to look
for a cat that she has seen in the garden,
in the rain. This act of separation,
however, has not the slightest effect on
her husband, who "went on reading" (78).

When she returns, without the cat, he
puts down his book and speaks to her, but
it is obvious that he has no interest in
her, beyond as a physical object ("You look
pretty darn nice"). This comment is produced
when she says she is thinking of letting her
hair grow out, because she is "so tired of
looking like a boy" (79). Why, a reader
wonders, does her husband, who has paid
almost no attention to her up to now, assure
her that she looks "pretty darn nice"? I
think it is reasonable to conclude that he
wants her to look like someone who is not
truly a woman, in particular someone who is
immature. That she does not feel she has
much identity is evident when she continues
to talk about letting her hair grow, and she

Yanagi 3

says "I want to pull my hair back tight and smooth and make a big knot at the back that I can feel" (80). Long hair is, or at least was, the traditional sign of a woman; she wants long hair, and at the same time she wants to keep it under her control by tying it in a "big knot," a knot that she can feel, a knot whose presence reminds her, because she can feel it, of her feminine nature.

She goes on to say that she wants to brush her hair "in front of a mirror." That is, she wants to see and to feel her femininity, since her husband apparently-- so far as we can see in the story, at least--scarcely recognizes it or her. Perhaps her desire for the cat ("I want a cat") is a veiled way of saying that she wants to express her animal nature, and not be simply a neglected woman who is made by her husband to look like a boy. Hemingway tells us, however, that when she looked for the cat in the garden she could not find it, a sign, I think, of her failure to break from the man. At the end of the story the maid brings her the cat, but a woman cannot just be handed a new nature and accept it, just like that. She has to find it herself, and in herself, so I think the story ends with "the American wife" still nothing more than an American wife.

**[New page]**

---

Yanagi 4

Work Cited

Hemingway, Ernest. "Cat in the Rain."
  A Little Literature. Ed. Sylvan Barnet,
  William Burto, and William E. Cain. New
  York: Longman, 2007. 78-80.

---

A few comments and questions may be useful.

- Do you find the essay interesting? Explain your response.
- Do you find the essay well written? Explain.
- Do you find the essay convincing? Can you suggest ways of strengthening it, or do you think its argument is mistaken? Carefully reread "Cat in the Rain," taking note of passages that give further support to this student's argument, or that seem to challenge or qualify it.
- We often say that a good critical essay sends us back to the literary work with a fresh point of view. Our rereading differs from our earlier reading. Does this essay change your reading of Hemingway's story?

# ▨ TOPICS FOR CRITICAL THINKING AND WRITING

1. Can we be certain that the cat at the end of the story is the cat that the woman saw in the rain? (When we first hear about the cat in the rain we are not told anything about its color, and at end of the story we are not told that the tortoiseshell cat is wet.) Does it matter if there are two cats?
2. One student argued that the cat represents the child that the girl wants to have. Do you think there is something to this idea? How might you support or refute it?
3. Consider the following passage:

   As the American girl passed the office, the padrone bowed from his desk. Something felt very small and tight inside the girl. The padrone made her feel very small and at the same time really important. She had a momentary feeling of being of supreme importance.

Do you think there is anything sexual here? And if so, that the passage tells us something about her relations with her husband? Support your view.

4. What do you suppose Hemingway's attitude was toward each of the three chief characters? How might you support your hunch?

5. Hemingway wrote the story in Italy, when his wife Hadley was pregnant. In a letter to F. Scott Fitzgerald he said,

> Cat in the Rain wasn't about Hadley. . . . When I wrote that we were at Rapallo but Hadley was 4 months pregnant with Bumby. The Inn Keeper was the one at Cortina D'Ampezzo. . . . Hadley never made a speech in her life about wanting a baby because she had been told various things by her doctor and I'd—no use going into all that. (*Letters*, p. 180)

According to some biographers, the story shows that Hemingway knew his marriage was going on the rocks (Hemingway and Hadley divorced). Does knowing that Hemingway's marriage turned out unhappily help you to understand the story? Does it make the story more interesting? And do you think that the story tells a biographer something about Hemingway's life?

6. It is sometimes said that a good short story does two things at once: It provides a believable picture of the surface of life, and it also illuminates some moral or psychological complexity that we feel is part of the essence of human life. This dual claim may not be true, but for the moment accept it. Do you think that Hemingway's story fulfills either or both of these specifications? Support your view.

Later chapters will offer some technical vocabulary and will examine specific elements of fiction, but familiarity with technical vocabulary will not itself ensure that you will understand and enjoy fiction. There is no substitute for reading carefully, thinking about your responses, and (pen in hand) rereading the text, looking for evidence that accounts for your responses or that will lead you to different and perhaps richer responses. The essays that you will submit to your instructor are, finally, rooted in the annotations that you make in your text and the notes in which you record and explore your responses.

# 4

# Stories and Meanings: Plot, Character, Theme

In some stories we are chiefly interested in plot (the arrangement of happenings or doings), in others we are chiefly interested in character (the personalities of the doers), but on the whole the two are so intertwined that interest in one involves interest in the other. Happenings occur (people cross paths), and personalities respond, engendering further happenings. As Henry James asked rhetorically a hundred years ago (using the word "incident" for what we call "doings" or "happenings"),

> What is character but the determination of incident? What is incident but the illustration of character?

The idea that who and what we are—our character—partly determines what we do and what is done to us (the plots we are engaged in), is far older than Henry James. Two thousand five hundred years ago Heraclitus said,

> Character is destiny

and only a few decades ago a figure in Jean-Luc Godard's film, *Breathless,* astutely said,

> Informers inform, assassins assassinate, lovers love.

For this reason, then, we discuss plot and character in a single chapter. The reason we also discuss *theme* will soon be evident.

People tell stories for many reasons, including the sheer delight of talking, but probably most of the best storytelling proceeds from one of two more commendable desires: a desire to entertain or a desire to instruct. Among the most famous of the stories designed to instruct are the parables that Jesus told, including the Parable of the Prodigal Son, which we discussed in Chapter 2. (*Parable* comes from the Greek word meaning to "throw beside," that is, "to compare." We are to compare these little stories with our own behavior.) We can say that the parable is told for the sake of the point; we also can say that it is told for our sake, because we are implicitly invited to see ourselves in the story, and to live our lives in accordance with it. This simple but powerful story, with its memorable characters—though nameless and briefly sketched—makes us feel the point in our hearts.

Even older than Jesus' parables are the **fables** attributed to Aesop, some of which go back to the seventh century before Jesus. These stories also teach lessons by recounting brief incidents from which homely morals may easily be drawn, even though the stories are utterly fanciful. Among famous examples are the stories of the hare and the tortoise, the boy who cried "Wolf," the ant and the grasshopper, and a good many others that stick in the mind because of the sharply contrasted characters in sharply imagined situations. The fables just mentioned take only four or five sentences apiece, but brief as they are, Aesop told some briefer ones. Here is the briefest of all, about a female fox and a lioness.

# AESOP

*Aesop, a semi-legendary Greek storyteller, was said to have lived in the sixth century BCE, but some of the stories are found in Egypt, in texts that are hundreds of years earlier.*

## The Vixen and the Lioness

A vixen sneered at a lioness because she never bore more than one cub. "Only one," the lioness replied, "but a lion."

Just that: a situation with a **conflict** (the mere confrontation of a fox and a lion brings together the ignoble and the noble) and a resolution (*something* must come out of such a confrontation). There is no setting (we are not told that "one day in June a vixen, walking down a road, met a lioness"), but none is needed here. What there is—however briefly set forth—is characterization. The fox's baseness is effectively communicated through the verb "sneered" and through her taunt, and the lioness's nobility is even more effectively communicated through the brevity and decisiveness of her reply. This reply at first seems to agree with the fox ("Only one") and then, after a suspenseful delay provided by the words "the lioness replied," the reply is tersely and powerfully completed ("but a lion"), placing the matter firmly in a new light. Granted that the story is not much of a story, still, it is finely told, and more potent—more memorable, more lively, we might even say more real, despite its talking animals—than the mere moral: "Small-minded people confuse quantity with quality."

The fable is frankly imaginative, made-up; no one believes that foxes and lions discuss their offspring, or, for that matter, that tortoises and hares engage in races. Here is another fable, this one not about animals but still quite evidently not to be taken as history.

# W. SOMERSET MAUGHAM

*W(illiam) Somerset Maugham (1874-1965), born in Paris but of English origin, grew up in England, where he was trained as a physician, but he never practiced medicine. Rather, he preferred to make his living as a novelist, playwright, and writer of short stories. The following story is in fact a speech uttered by a character in one of Maugham's plays,* Sheppey *(1933).*

## The Appointment in Samarra          [1933]

*Death speaks:* There was a merchant in Bagdad who sent his servant to market to buy provisions and in a little while the servant came back, white and trembling, and said, Master, just now when I was in the market-place I was jostled by a woman in the crowd and when I turned I saw it was Death that jostled me. She looked at me and made a threatening gesture, now, lend me your horse, and I will ride away from the city and avoid my fate. I will go to Samarra and there Death will not find me. The merchant lent him his horse, and the servant mounted it, and he dug his spurs in its flanks and as fast as the horse could gallop he went. Then the merchant went down to the marketplace and he saw me standing in the crowd and he came to me and said, Why did you make a threatening gesture to my servant when you saw him this morning? That was not a threatening gesture, I said, it was only a start of surprise. I was astonished to see him in Bagdad, for I had an appointment with him tonight in Samarra.

---

The moral is not stated explicitly, and perhaps we might quibble a little about how we might word the moral, but the gist surely is clear: We cannot elude death; it comes to us at an appointed time. Man proposes, God disposes.

This is the sort of story that Maugham was especially fond of, the story with a decisive ending, and with relatively little interest in the personalities involved. The emphasis is on *plot* (what happens), not on *character* (what kinds of people these are). Another sort of very short story, however, the **anecdote,** is likely to emphasize character as well as plot. An anecdote is a short narrative that is supposed to be true, such as the story of George Washington and the cherry tree. The six-year-old Washington, given a hatchet, tried it out on a cherry tree on his father's farm. When the father asked if the boy had chopped down the tree, George supposedly answered. "I cannot tell a lie; you know I cannot tell a lie. I cut it with my hatchet." In fact the story is an invention of Parson Weems, who told it in his *Life of Washington* (1800). Of course one can easily moralize an anecdote ("You should be honest, just as George Washington was"), but the emphasis in an anecdote usually is on the person involved, not the moral. (Think of numerous anecdotes that essentially show how unpretentious Abraham Lincoln was, or how witty Winston Churchill was.)

Here is a nineteenth-century Japanese anecdote of anonymous authorship. It is said to be literally true, but whether it really occurred or not is scarcely of any importance. It is the story, not the history, that counts.

## Muddy Road

Two monks, Tanzan and Ekido, were once traveling together down a muddy road. A heavy rain was still falling.

Coming around a bend, they met a lovely girl in a silk kimono and sash, unable to cross the intersection.

"Come on, girl," said Tanzan at once. Lifting her in his arms, he carried her over the mud.

Ekido did not speak again until that night when they reached a lodging temple. Then he no longer could restrain himself. "We monks don't go near females," he told Tanzan, "especially not young and lovely ones. It is dangerous. Why did you do that?"

"I left the girl there," said Tanzan. "Are you still carrying her?"

---

A superb story: The opening paragraph, though simple and matter-of-fact, holds our attention as we sense that something interesting is going to happen during this journey along a muddy road on a rainy day. Perhaps we even sense, somehow, by virtue of the references to the mud and the rain, that the journey itself rather than the travelers' destination will be the heart of the story: getting there will be more than half the fun. And then, after the introduction of the two **characters** and the **setting,** we quickly get the **complication,** the encounter with the girl. Still there is apparently no **conflict,** though in "Ekido did not speak again until that night" we sense an unspoken conflict, an action (or, in this case, an inaction) that must be explained, an imbalance that must be righted before we are finished. At last Ekido, no longer able to contain his thoughts, lets his indignation burst out: "We monks don't go near females, especially not young and lovely ones. It is dangerous. Why did you do that?" His statement and his question reveal not only his moral principles, but also his insecurity and the anger that grows from it. And now, when the conflict is out in the open, comes the brief reply that reveals Tanzan's very different character as clearly as the outburst revealed Ekido's. This reply—though we could not have predicted it—strikes us as exactly right, bringing the story to a perfect end, that is to a point (like the ends of Jesus' parable and Aesop's fable) at which there is no more to be said. It provides the **dénouement** (literally, "unknotting"), or **resolution.**

Let's look now at another short piece, though this one is somewhat longer than the stories we have just read, and it is less concerned than they are with teaching a lesson.

# ANTON CHEKHOV

*Anton Chekhov (1860–1904) was born in Russia, the son of a shopkeeper. While a medical student at Moscow University, Chekhov wrote stories, sketches, and reviews to help support his family and to finance his education. In 1884 he received his medical degree, began to practice medicine, published his first book of stories, and suffered the first of a series of hemorrhages from tuberculosis. In his remaining twenty years, in addition to writing several hundred stories, he wrote plays, half a dozen of which have established themselves as classics. He died from tuberculosis at the age of forty-four.*

## Misery                                                          [1886]

*Translated by Constance Garnett*

   *"To Whom Shall I Tell My Grief?"*

The twilight of evening. Big flakes of wet snow are whirling lazily about the street lamps, which have just been lighted, and lying in a thin soft layer on roofs, horses' backs, shoulders, caps. Iona Potapov, the sledge-driver, is all white like a ghost. He sits on the box without stirring, bent as double as the living body can be bent. If a regular snowdrift fell on him it seems as though even then he would not think it necessary to shake it off. . . . His little mare is white and motionless too. Her stillness, the angularity of her lines, and the stick-like straightness of her legs make her look like a halfpenny gingerbread horse. She is probably lost in thought. Anyone who has been torn away from the plough, from the familiar gray landscapes, and cast into this slough, full of monstrous lights, of unceasing uproar and hurrying people, is bound to think.

It is a long time since Iona and his nag have budged. They came out of the yard before dinner-time and not a single fare yet. But now the shades of evening are falling on the town. The pale light of the street lamps changes to a vivid color, and the bustle of the street grows noisier.

"Sledge to Vyborgskaya!" Iona hears. "Sledge!"

Iona starts, and through his snow-plastered eyelashes sees an officer in a military overcoat with a hood over his head.

5      "To Vyborgskaya," repeats the officer. "Are you asleep? To Vyborgskaya!"

In token of assent Iona gives a tug at the reins which sends cakes of snow flying from the horse's back and shoulders. The officer gets into the sledge. The sledge-driver clicks to the horse, cranes his neck like a swan, rises in his seat, and more from habit than necessity brandishes his whip. The mare cranes her neck, too, crooks her stick-like legs, and hesitatingly sets off. . . .

"Where are you shoving, you devil?" Iona immediately hears shouts from the dark mass shifting to and fro before him. "Where the devil are you going? Keep to the r-right!"

"You don't know how to drive! Keep to the right," says the officer angrily.

A coachman driving a carriage swears at him; a pedestrian crossing the road and brushing the horse's nose with his shoulder looks at him angrily and shakes the snow off his sleeve. Iona fidgets on the box as though he were sitting on thorns, jerks his elbows, and turns his eyes about like one possessed, as though he did not know where he was or why he was there.

10     "What rascals they all are!" says the officer jocosely. "They are simply doing their best to run up against you or fall under the horse's feet. They must be doing it on purpose."

Iona looks at his fare and moves his lips. . . . Apparently he means to say something, but nothing comes out but a sniff.

"What?" inquires the officer.

Iona gives a wry smile, and straining his throat, brings out huskily: "My son . . . , er . . . my son died this week, sir."

"H'm! What did he die of?"

15     Iona turns his whole body round to his fare, and says:

"Who can tell! It must have been from fever. . . . He lay three days in the hospital and then he died. . . . God's will."

"Turn round, you devil!" comes out of the darkness. "Have you gone cracked, you old dog? Look where you are going!"

"Drive on! drive on! . . . " says the officer. "We shan't get there till tomorrow going on like this. Hurry up!"

The sledge-driver cranes his neck again, rises in his seat, and with heavy grace swings his whip. Several times he looks round at the officer, but the latter keeps his eyes shut and is apparently disinclined to listen. Putting his fare down at Vyborgskaya, Iona stops by a restaurant, and again sits huddled up on the box. . . . Again the wet snow paints him and his horse white. One hour passes, and then another. . . .

20      Three young men, two tall and thin, one short and hunchbacked, come up, railing at each other and loudly stamping on the pavement with their galoshes.

"Cabby, to the Police Bridge!" the hunchback cries in a cracked voice. "The three of us, . . . twenty kopecks!"

Iona tugs at the reins and clicks to his horse. Twenty kopecks is not a fair price, but he has no thoughts for that. Whether it is a rouble or whether it is five kopecks does not matter to him now so long as he has a fare. . . . The three young men, shoving each other and using bad language, go up to the sledge, and all three try to sit down at once. The question remains to be settled: Which are to sit down and which one is to stand? After a long altercation, ill-temper, and abuse, they come to the conclusion that the hunchback must stand because he is the shortest.

"Well, drive on," says the hunchback in his cracked voice, settling himself and breathing down Iona's neck. "Cut along! What a cap you've got, my friend! You wouldn't find a worse one in all Petersburg. . . ."

"He-he! . . . he-he! . . . " laughs Iona. "It's nothing to boast of!"

25      "Well, then, nothing to boast of, drive on! Are you going to drive like this all the way? Eh? Shall I give you one in the neck?"

"My head aches," says one of the tall ones. "At the Dukmasovs' yesterday Vaska and I drank four bottles of brandy between us."

"I can't make out why you talk such stuff," says the other tall one angrily. "You lie like a brute."

"Strike me dead, its the truth! . . . "

"It's about as true as that a louse coughs."

30      "He-he!" grins Iona. "Me-er-ry gentlemen!"

"Tfoo! the devil take you!" cries the hunchback indignantly. "Will you get on, you old plague, or won't you? Is that the way to drive? Give her one with the whip. Hang it all, give it her well."

Iona feels behind his back the jolting person and quivering voice of the hunchback. He hears abuse addressed to him, he sees people, and the feeling of loneliness begins little by little to be less heavy on his heart. The hunchback swears at him, till he chokes over some elaborately whimsical string of epithets and is overpowered by his cough. His tall companions begin talking of a certain Nadyezhda Petrovna. Iona looks round at them. Waiting till there is a brief pause, he looks round once more and says:

"This week . . . er . . . my . . . er . . . son died!"

"We shall all die, . . . " says the hunchback with a sigh, wiping his lips after coughing. "Come, drive on! drive on! My friends, I simply cannot stand crawling like this! When will he get us there?"

35      "Well, you give him a little encouragement . . . one in the neck!"

"Do you hear, you old plague? I'll make you smart. If one stands on ceremony with fellows like you one may as well walk. Do you hear, you old dragon? Or don't you care a hang what we say?"

And Iona hears rather than feels a slap on the back of his neck.

"He-he! . . . " he laughs. "Merry gentlemen . . . God give you health!"

"Cabman, are you married?" asks one of the tall ones.

40    "I? He-he! Me-er-ry gentlemen. The only wife for me now is the damp earth. . . . He-ho-ho! . . . The grave that is! . . . Here my son's dead and I am alive. . . . It's a strange thing, death has come in at the wrong door. . . . Instead of coming for me it went for my son. . . ."

And Iona turns round to tell them how his son died, but at that point the hunchback gives a faint sigh and announces that, thank God! they have arrived at last. After taking his twenty kopecks, Iona gazes for a long while after the revelers, who disappear into a dark entry. Again he is alone and again there is silence for him. . . . The misery which has been for a brief space eased comes back again and tears his heart more cruelly than ever. With a look of anxiety and suffering Iona's eyes stray restlessly among the crowds moving to and fro on both sides of the street: can he not find among those thousands someone who will listen to him? But the crowds flit by heedless of him and his misery. . . . His misery is immense, beyond all bounds. If Iona's heart were to burst and his misery to flow out, it would flood the whole world, it seems, but yet it is not seen. It has found a hiding-place in such an insignificant shell that one would not have found it with a candle by daylight. . . .

Iona sees a house-porter with a parcel and makes up his mind to address him.

"What time will it be, friend?" he asks.

"Going on for ten. . . . Why have you stopped here? Drive on!"

45    Iona drives a few paces away, bends himself double, and gives himself up to his misery. He feels it is no good to appeal to people. But before five minutes have passed he draws himself up, shakes his head as though he feels a sharp pain, and tugs at the reins. . . . He can bear it no longer.

"Back to the yard!" he thinks. "To the yard!"

And his little mare, as though she knew his thoughts, falls to trotting. An hour and a half later Iona is sitting by a big dirty stove. On the stove, on the floor, and on the benches are people snoring. The air is full of smells and stuffiness. Iona looks at the sleeping figures, scratches himself, and regrets that he has come home so early. . . .

"I have not earned enough to pay for the oats, even," he thinks "That's why I am so miserable. A man who knows how to do his work, . . . who has had enough to eat, and whose horse has had enough to eat, is always at ease. . . ."

In one of the corners a young cabman gets up, clears his throat sleepily, and makes for the waterbucket.

50    "Want a drink?" Iona asks him.

"Seems so."

"May it do you good. . . . But my son is dead, mate. . . . Do you hear? This week in the hospital. . . . It's queer business. . . ."

Iona looks to see the effect produced by his words, but he sees nothing. The young man has covered his head over and is already asleep. The old man sighs and scratches himself. . . . Just as the young man had been thirsty for water, he thirsts for speech. His son will soon have been dead a week, and he has not really talked to anybody yet. . . . He wants to talk of it properly, with deliberation. . . . He wants to tell how his son was taken ill, how he suffered, what he said before he died, how he died. . . . He wants to describe the funeral, and how he went to the hospital to get his son's clothes. He still has his daughter Anisya in the country. . . . And he wants to talk about her too. . . . Yes, he has plenty to talk about now. His listener ought to sigh and exclaim and lament. . . . It would be even better to talk to women. Though they are silly creatures, they blubber at the first word.

"Let's go out and have a look at the mare," Iona thinks. "There is always time for sleep. . . . You'll have sleep enough, no fear. . . ."

55    He puts on his coat and goes into the stables where his mare is standing. He thinks about oats, about hay, about the weather. . . . He cannot think about his son when he is alone. . . . To talk about him with someone is possible, but to think of him and picture him is insufferable anguish. . . .

"Are you munching?" Iona asks his mare, seeing her shining eyes. "There, munch away, munch away. . . . Since we have not earned enough for oats, we will eat hay. . . . Yes, . . . I have grown too old to drive. . . . My son ought to be driving, not I. . . . He was a real coachman. . . . He ought to have lived. . . ."

Iona is silent for a while, and then he goes on:

"That's how it is, old girl. . . . Kuzma Ionitch is gone. . . . He said goodby to me. . . . He went and died for no reason. . . . Now, suppose you had a little colt, and you were mother to that little colt. . . . And all at once that same little colt went and died. . . . You'd be sorry, wouldn't you? . . . "

The little mare munches, listens, and breathes on her master's hands. Iona is carried away and tells her all about it.

Let's look at Chekhov's "Misery" as a piece of craftsmanship. The happenings (here, a cabman seeks to tell his grief to several people, but is rebuffed and finally tells it to his horse) are the **plot;** the participants (cabman, officer, drunks, etc.) are the **characters;** the locale, time, and social circumstances (a snowy city in Russia, in the late nineteenth century) are the **setting;** and (though, as we will urge later, this word should be used with special caution) the meaning or point is the **theme.**

The traditional plot has this structure:

1. **Exposition** (setting forth of the initial situation)
2. **Conflict** (a complication that moves to a climax)
3. **Dénouement** (the outcome of the conflict; the resolution)

Chekhov's first paragraph, devoted to **exposition,** begins by introducing a situation that seems to be static: It briefly describes a motionless cabdriver, who "is all white like a ghost," and the cabdriver's mare, whose immobility and angularity "make her look like a halfpenny gingerbread horse." A reader probably anticipates that something will intrude into this apparently static situation; some sort of conflict will be established, and then in all probability will be (in one way or another) resolved. In fact, the inertia described at the very beginning is disturbed even before the paragraph ends, when Chekhov rather surprisingly takes us into the mind not of the cabdriver but of the horse, telling us that if we were in such a situation as the horse finds itself, we too would find it difficult not to think.

By the middle of the first paragraph, we have been given a brief but entirely adequate view of the **setting:** a Russian city in the days of horse-drawn sleighs, that is, in Chekhov's lifetime. Strictly speaking, the paragraph does not specify Russia or the period, but the author is a Russian writing in the late nineteenth century, the character has a Russian name, and there is lots of snow so one concludes that the story is set in Russia. (A reader somewhat familiar with Chekhov does not even have to read the first paragraph of this story to know the setting, since all of Chekhov's work is set in the Russia of his day.)

One might almost say that by the end of the first paragraph we have met all the chief **characters**—though we can't know this until we finish the story. In later paragraphs we will meet additional figures, but the chief characters—the characters whose fates we are concerned with—are simply the cabdriver and the horse. It's odd to call the horse a character, but as we noticed, even in the first paragraph Chekhov takes us into the mind of the horse. Notice, too, how Chekhov establishes connections between the man and the horse; for instance, when the first fare gets into the sleigh, the driver "cranes his neck" and "then the mare cranes her neck, too." By the end of the story, the horse seems almost a part of Iona. Perhaps the horse will be the best possible listener, since perhaps grief of Iona's sort can be told only to the self.

Before talking further about the characters, we should point out that the word "character" has two chief meanings:

1. A figure in a literary work (thus Iona is a character, the officer who hires the cab is another character, and the drunks are additional characters).

2. Personality, as when we say that Iona's character is described only briefly, or that Hamlet's character is complex, or that So-and-So's character is unpleasant.

Usually the context makes clear the sense in which the word is used, but in your own writing, make sure that there is no confusion.

It is sometimes said that figures in literature are either **flat characters** (one-dimensional figures, figures with simple personalities) or **round characters** (complex figures). The usual implication is that good writers give us round characters, believable figures who are more than cardboard cutouts holding up signs saying "jealous lover," "cruel landlord," "kind mother," and so forth. But a short story scarcely has space to show the complexity or roundness of several characters, and in fact, many good stories do not give even their central characters much complexity. In "Misery," for instance, Iona is shown chiefly as a grieving father aching to speak of the death of his son. We don't know what sort of food he likes, whether he ever gets drunk, what he thinks of the Czar, or whether he belongs to the church. But it is hard to imagine that knowing any of these things would be relevant and would increase our interest in him. Similarly, the other characters in the story are drawn with a few simple lines. The officer who first hires the cab is arrogant ("Sledge to Vyborgskaya! . . . Are you asleep? To Vyborgskaya!"), and though he at first makes a little joke that leads Iona to think the officer will listen to his story, the officer quickly changes the subject. We know of him only that he wants to get to Vyborg. The three noisy drunks whom Iona next picks up can be fairly characterized as just that—three noisy drunks. Again, we can hardly imagine that the story would be better if we knew much more about these drunks.

On the other hand, Iona is not quite so flat as we have perhaps implied. A careful reader notices, for instance, that Iona reveals other things about himself in addition to his need to express his grief. For instance, he treats his horse as kindly as possible. When the officer gets into the cab, Iona "more from habit than necessity brandishes his whip"—but he gets the horse moving by making a clicking sound, and he actually whips the horse only when the officer tells him to hurry. Later the hunchback will say of the mare, "Give her one with the whip. Hang it all, give it her well," but we feel that Iona uses his horse as gently as is possible.

It should be noted, however, that the drunks, though they are not much more than drunks, are not less than drunks either. They are quarrelsome and they even display touches of cruelty, but we cannot call them villains. In some degree, the fact that they are drunk excuses their "bad language," their "ill-tempers," and even their displays of cruelty. If these characters are fairly flat, they nevertheless are thoroughly believable, and we know as much about them as we need to know for the purposes of the story. Furthermore, the characters in a story help to characterize other characters, by their resemblances or their differences. How Iona might behave if he were an officer, or if he were drunk, we do not know, but he is in some degree contrasted with the other characters and thus gains some complexity, to the extent that we can at least say that he is *not* drunk, arrogant, or quarrelsome.

We need hardly ask if there is **motivation** (compelling grounds, external and also within one's personality) for Iona's final action. He has tried to express his grief to the officer, and then to the drunks. Next, his eyes search the crowds to "find someone who will listen to him." After speaking to the house-porter, Iona sees, Chekhov tells us, that "it is no good to appeal to people."When we read this line, we probably do not think, or at least do not think consciously, that he will turn from people to the mare, but when at the end of the story he does turn to the mare, the action seems entirely natural, inevitable.

We began this chapter by saying that in some stories readers are chiefly interested in plot—in what happens—and in other stories they are chiefly interested in characters—the personalities involved in the story. We also quoted Henry James's remark about the interrelationship between plot (which he calls "incident") and character:"What is character but the determination of incident? What is incident but the illustration of character?" Commonly, as a good story proceeds and we become increasingly familiar with the characters, we get intimations of what they may do in the future. We may not know precisely how they will act, but we have a fairly good idea, and when we see their subsequent actions, we usually recognize the appropriateness. Sometimes there are hints of what is to come, and because of this **foreshadowing,** we are not shocked by what happens later, but rather we experience suspense as we wait for the expected to come about. Coleridge had Shakespeare's use of foreshadowing in mind when he praised him for giving us not surprise, but expectation— the active reader participates in the work by reading it responsively—and then the fulfillment of expectation. E. M. Forster, in *Aspects of the Novel,* has a shrewd comment on the importance of both fulfilling expectation and offering a slight surprise:"Shock, followed by the feeling,'Oh, that's all right,' is a sign that all is well with plot: characters, to be real, ought to run smoothly, but a plot ought to cause surprise."

Finally, a few words about **theme.** Usually we feel that a story is about something, it has a point—a theme. (What happens is the plot; what the happenings add up to is the theme.) But a word of caution is needed here. What is the theme of "Misery"? One student formulated the theme thus:

Human beings must utter their grief, even if only to an animal.

Another student formulated it thus:

Human beings are indifferent to the sufferings of others.

Still another student offered this:

Deep suffering is incommunicable, but the sufferer must try to find an outlet.

Many other formulations are possible. Probably there is no "right" statement of the theme of "Misery" or of any other good story: a story is not simply an illustration of an abstract statement of theme. A story has a complex variety of details that modify any summary statement we may offer when we try to say what it is about. And what lives in our memory is not an abstract statement—certainly not a thesis, that is, a proposition offered and argued, such as "We should pay attention to the suffering of others."

What lives is an image that by every word in the story has convinced us that it is a representation, if not of "reality," of at least an aspect of reality.

Still, the writer is guided by a theme in the choice of details; of many possible details, Chekhov decided to present only a few. The musical sense of the word "theme" can help us to understand what a theme in literature is: "a melody constituting the basis of variation, development, or the like." The variations and the development cannot be random, but must have a basis. (We have already suggested that the episodes in "Misery"—the movement from the officer to the drunks and then to the house-porter and the other cabman—are not random, but somehow seem exactly "right," just as the remarks about the man and the horse both stretching their necks seem "right.") What is it, Robert Frost asks, that prevents the writer from jumping "from one chance suggestion to another in all directions as of a hot afternoon in the life of a grasshopper?" Frost's answer: "Theme alone can steady us down."

We can, then, talk about the theme—again, what the story adds up to—as long as we do not think a statement of the theme is equivalent to or is a substitute for the whole story. As Flannery O'Connor said, "Some people have the notion that you can read the story and then climb out of it into the meaning, but for the fiction writer himself the whole story is the meaning." A theme, she said, is not like a string tying a sack of chicken feed, to be pulled out so that the feed can be got at. "A story is a way to say something that can't be said any other way." That "something"—which can't be said in any other way—is the theme. (On theme, see also page 167.)

## ▩ TOPICS FOR CRITICAL THINKING AND WRITING

1. What do you admire or not admire about Chekhov's story? Why?
2. Try to examine in detail your response to the ending. Do you think the ending is, in a way, a happy ending? Would you prefer a different ending? For instance, should the story end when the young cabman falls asleep? Or when Iona sets out for the stable? Or can you imagine a better ending? If so, what?
3. A literary critic has said of "Misery": "For the story it tells, its length is perfect." Do you agree? Do you think that the story could be made even shorter? If so, where would you seek to cut or condense it? Could this story be made longer? If so, which features of it would you expand and develop further?
4. From working on the previous topic, what have you learned about Chekhov as a writer? What have you learned about the craft involved in the writing of a short story?
5. Which do you think is more challenging: writing a short story about a sad experience or about a happy one? Please be as specific as you

can about the nature of the challenge and how you, as the writer of such a story, would attempt to deal with it. What would you do to make the story effective?

# ALICE WALKER

*Alice Walker was born in 1944 in Eatonton, Georgia, where her parents eked out a living as sharecroppers and dairy farmers; her mother also worked as a domestic. (In a collection of essays,* In Search of Our Mothers' Gardens *[1984], Walker celebrates women who, like her mother, passed on a "respect for the possibilities [of life]—and the will to grasp them.") Walker attended Spelman College in Atlanta, and in 1965 she finished her undergraduate work at Sarah Lawrence College near New York City. She then became active in the welfare rights movement in New York and in the voter registration movement in Georgia. Later she taught writing and literature in Mississippi, at Jackson State College and Tougaloo College, and at Wellesley College, the University of Massachusetts, and Yale University.*

*Walker has written essays, poetry, and fiction. Her best-known novel,* The Color Purple *(1982), won a Pulitzer Prize and the National Book Award. She has said that her chief concern is "exploring the oppressions, the insanities, the loyalties, and the triumphs of black women."*

## Everyday Use

[1973]

*For your grandmama*

I will wait for her in the yard that Maggie and I made so clean and wavy yesterday afternoon. A yard like this is more comfortable than most people know. It is not just a yard. It is like an extended living room. When the hard clay is swept clean as a floor and the fine sand around the edges lined with tiny, irregular grooves, anyone can come and sit and look up into the elm tree and wait for the breezes that never come inside the house.

Maggie will be nervous until after her sister goes: she will stand hopelessly in corners homely and ashamed of the burn scars down her arms and legs, eyeing her sister with a mixture of envy and awe. She thinks her sister had held life always in the palm of one hand, that "no" is a word the world never learned to say to her.

You've no doubt seen those TV shows where the child who has "made it" is confronted, as a surprise, by her own mother and father, tottering in weakly from backstage. (A pleasant surprise, of course: What would they do if parent and child came on the show only to curse out and insult each other?) On TV mother and child embrace and smile into each other's faces. Sometimes the mother and father weep, the child wraps them in her arms and leans across the table to tell how she would not have made it without their help. I have seen these programs.

Sometimes I dream a dream in which Dee and I are suddenly brought together on a TV program of this sort. Out of a dark and soft-seated limousine I am ushered into a bright room filled with many people. There I meet a smiling, gray, sporty man like Johnny Carson who shakes my hand and tells me what a fine girl I have. Then we are on the stage and Dee is embracing me with tears in her eyes. She pins on my dress a large orchid, even though she has told me once that she thinks orchids are tacky flowers.

5    In real life I am a large, big-boned woman with rough, man-working hands. In the winter I wear flannel nightgowns to bed and overalls during the day. I can kill and clean a hog as mercilessly as a man. My fat keeps me hot in zero weather. I can work outside all day, breaking ice to get water for washing. I can eat pork liver cooked over the open fire minutes after it comes steaming from the hog. One winter I knocked a bull calf straight in the brain between the eyes with a sledge hammer and had the meat hung up to chill before nightfall. But of course all this does not show on television. I am the way my daughter would want me to be: a hundred pounds lighter, my skin like an uncooked barley pancake. My hair glistens in the hot bright lights. Johnny Carson has much to do to keep up with my quick and witty tongue.

But that is a mistake. I know even before I wake up. Who ever knew a Johnson with a quick tongue? Who can even imagine me looking a strange white man in the eye? It seems to me I have talked to them always with one foot raised in flight, with my head turned in whichever way is farthest from them. Dee, though. She would always look anyone in the eye. Hesitation was no part of her nature.

"How do I look, Mama?" Maggie says, showing just enough of her thin body enveloped in pink skirt and red blouse for me to know she's there, almost hidden by the door.

"Come out into the yard," I say.

Have you ever seen a lame animal, perhaps a dog run over by some careless person rich enough to own a car, sidle up to someone who is ignorant enough to be kind to him? That is the way my Maggie walks. She has been like this, chin on chest, eyes on ground, feet in shuffle, ever since the fire that burned the other house to the ground.

10    Dee is lighter than Maggie, with nicer hair and a fuller figure. She's a woman now, though sometimes I forget. How long ago was it that the other house burned? Ten, twelve years? Sometimes I can still hear the flames and feel Maggie's arms sticking to me, her hair smoking and her dress falling off her in little black papery flakes. Her eyes seemed

stretched open, blazed open by the flames reflected in them. And Dee. I see her standing off under the sweet gum tree she used to dig gum out of; a look of concentration on her face as she watched the last dingy gray board of the house fall in toward the red-hot brick chimney. Why don't you do a dance around the ashes? I'd wanted to ask her. She had hated the house that much.

I used to think she hated Maggie, too. But that was before we raised the money, the church and me, to send her to Augusta to school. She used to read to us without pity; forcing words, lies, other folks' habits, whole lives upon us two, sitting trapped and ignorant underneath her voice. She washed us in a river of make-believe, burned us with a lot of knowledge we didn't necessarily need to know. Pressed us to her with the serious way she read, to shove us away at just the moment, like dimwits, we seemed about to understand.

Dee wanted nice things. A yellow organdy dress to wear to her graduation from high school; black pumps to match a green suit she'd made from an old suit somebody gave me. She was determined to stare down any disaster in her efforts. Her eyelids would not flicker for minutes at a time. Often I fought off the temptation to shake her. At sixteen she had a style of her own: and knew what style was.

I never had an education myself. After second grade the school was closed down. Don't ask me why: in 1927 colored asked fewer questions than they do now. Sometimes Maggie reads to me. She stumbles along goodnaturedly but can't see well. She knows she is not bright. Like good looks and money, quickness passed her by. She will marry John Thomas (who has mossy teeth in an earnest face) and then I'll be free to sit here and I guess just sing church songs to myself. Although I never was a good singer. Never could carry a tune. I was always better at a man's job. I used to love to milk till I was hoofed in the side in '49. Cows are soothing and slow and don't bother you, unless you try to milk them the wrong way.

I have deliberately turned my back on the house. It is three rooms, just like the one that burned, except the roof is tin; they don't make shingle roofs any more. There are no real windows, just some holes cut in the sides, like the portholes in a ship, but not round and not square, with rawhide holding the shutters up on the outside. This house is in a pasture, too, like the other one. No doubt when Dee sees it she will want to tear it down. She wrote me once that no matter where we "choose" to live, she will manage to come see us. But she will never bring her friends. Maggie and I thought about this and Maggie asked me, "Mama, when did Dee ever *have* any friends?"

15    She had a few. Furtive boys in pink shirts hanging about on washday after school. Nervous girls who never laughed. Impressed with her they worshiped the well-turned phrase, the cute shape, the scalding humor that erupted like bubbles in lye. She read to them.

When she was courting Jimmy T she didn't have much time to pay to us, but turned all her faultfinding power on him. He *flew* to marry a cheap gal from a family of ignorant flashy people. She hardly had time to recompose herself.

When she comes I will meet—but there they are!

Maggie attempts to make a dash for the house, in her shuffling way, but I stay her with my hand. "Come back here," I say. And she stops and tries to dig a well in the sand with her toe.

It is hard to see them clearly through the strong sun. But even the first glimpse of leg out of the car tells me it is Dee. Her feet were always neat-looking, as if God himself had shaped them with a certain style. From the other side of the car comes a short, stocky man. Hair is all over his head a foot long and hanging from his chin like a kinky mule tail. I hear Maggie suck in her breath. "Uhnnnh," is what it sounds like. Like when you see the wriggling end of a snake just in front of your foot on the road. "Uhnnnh."

20        Dee next. A dress down to the ground, in this hot weather. A dress so loud it hurts my eyes. There are yellows and oranges enough to throw back the light of the sun. I feel my whole face warming from the heat waves it throws out. Earrings, too, gold and hanging down to her shoulders. Bracelets dangling and making noises when she moves her arm up to shake the folds of the dress out of her armpits. The dress is loose and flows, and as she walks closer, I like it. I hear Maggie go "Uhnnnh" again. It is her sister's hair. It stands straight up like the wool on a sheep. It is black as night and around the edges are two long pigtails that rope about like small lizards disappearing behind her ears.

"Wa-su-zo-Tean-o!" she says, coming on in that gliding way the dress makes her move. The short stocky fellow with the hair to his navel is all grinning and he follows up with "Asalamalakim, my mother and sister!" He moves to hug Maggie but she falls back, right up against the back of my chair. I feel her trembling there and when I look up I see the perspiration falling off her chin.

"Don't get up," says Dee. Since I am stout it takes something of a push. You can see me trying to move a second or two before I make it. She turns, showing white heels through her sandals, and goes back to the car. Out she peeks next with a Polaroid. She stoops down quickly and lines up picture after picture of me sitting there in front of the house with Maggie cowering behind me. She never takes a shot without making sure the house is included. When a cow comes nibbling around the edge of the yard she snaps it and me and Maggie *and* the house. Then she puts the Polaroid in the back seat of the car, and comes up and kisses me on the forehead.

Meanwhile Asalamalakim is going through the motions with Maggie's hand. Maggie's hand is as limp as a fish, and probably as cold, despite the sweat, and she keeps trying to pull it back. It looks like Asalamalakim

wants to shake hands but wants to do it fancy. Or maybe he don't know
how people shake hands. Anyhow, he soon gives up on Maggie.

"Well," I say. "Dee."

25  "No, Mama," she says. "Not 'Dee,' Wangero Leewanika Kemanjo!"

"What happened to 'Dee'?" I wanted to know.

"She's dead," Wangero said. "I couldn't bear it any longer being named
after the people who oppress me."

"You know as well as me you was named after your aunt Dicie," I said.
Dicie is my sister. She named Dee. We called her "Big Dee" after Dee was born.

"But who was *she* named after?" asked Wangero.

30  "I guess after Grandma Dee," I said.

"And who was she named after?" asked Wangero.

"Her mother," I said, and saw Wangero was getting tired. "That's about
as far back as I can trace it," I said. Though, in fact, I probably could have
carried it back beyond the Civil War through the branches.

"Well," said Asalamalakim, "there you are."

"Uhnnnh," I heard Maggie say.

35  "There I was not," I said, "before 'Dicie' cropped up in our family, so
why should I try to trace it that far back?"

He just stood there grinning, looking down on me like somebody inspecting a Model A car. Every once in a while he and Wangero sent eye signals over my head.

"How do you pronounce this name?" I asked.

"You don't have to call me by it if you don't want to," said Wangero.

"Why shouldn't I?" I asked. "If that's what you want us to call you,
we'll call you."

40  "I know it might sound awkward at first," said Wangero.

"I'll get used to it," I said. "Ream it out again."

Well, soon we got the name out of the way. Asalamalakim had a name
twice as long and three times as hard. After I tripped over it two or three
times he told me to just call him Hakim-a-barber. I wanted to ask him was
he a barber, but I didn't really think he was, so I didn't ask.

"You must belong to those beef-cattle peoples down the road," I said.
They said "Asalamalakim" when they met you, too, but they didn't shake
hands. Always too busy: feeding the cattle, fixing the fences, putting up
saltlick shelters, throwing down hay. When the white folks poisoned some
of the herd the men stayed up all night with rifles in their hands. I walked
a mile and a half just to see the sight.

Hakim-a-barber said, "I accept some of their doctrines, but farming
and raising cattle is not my style." (They didn't tell me, and I didn't ask,
whether Wangero [Dee] had really gone and married him.)

45  We sat down to eat and right away he said he didn't eat collards and
pork was unclean. Wangero, though, went on through the chitlins and
corn bread, the greens and everything else. She talked a blue streak over
the sweet potatoes. Everything delighted her. Even the fact that we still

used the benches her daddy made for the table when we couldn't afford to buy chairs.

"Oh, Mama!" she cried. Then turned to Hakim-a-barber. "I never knew how lovely these benches are. You can feel the rump prints," she said, running her hands underneath her and along the bench. Then she gave a sigh and her hand closed over Grandma Dee's butter dish. "That's it!" she said. "I knew there was something I wanted to ask you if I could have." She jumped up from the table and went over in the corner where the churn stood, the milk in it clabber by now. She looked at the churn and looked at it.

"This churn top is what I need," she said. "Didn't Uncle Buddy whittle it out of a tree you all used to have?"

"Yes," I said.

"Uh huh," she said happily. "And I want the dasher, too."

50    "Uncle Buddy whittle that, too?" asked the barber.

Dee (Wangero) looked up at me.

"Aunt Dee's first husband whittled the dash," said Maggie so low you almost couldn't hear her. "His name was Henry, but they called him Stash."

"Maggie's brain is like an elephant's," Wangero said, laughing. "I can use the churn top as a centerpiece for the alcove table," she said, sliding a plate over the churn, "and I'll think of something artistic to do with the dasher."

When she finished wrapping the dasher the handle stuck out. I took it for a moment in my hands. You didn't even have to look close to see where hands pushing the dasher up and down to make butter had left a kind of sink in the wood. In fact, there were a lot of small sinks; you could see where thumbs and fingers had sunk into the wood. It was beautiful light yellow wood, from a tree that grew in the yard where Big Dee and Stash had lived.

55    After dinner Dee (Wangero) went to the trunk at the foot of my bed and started rifling through it. Maggie hung back in the kitchen over the dishpan. Out came Wangero with two quilts. They had been pieced by Grandma Dee and then Big Dee and me had hung them on the quilt frames on the front porch and quilted them. One was in the Lone Star pattern. The other was Walk Around the Mountain. In both of them were scraps of dresses Grandma Dee had worn fifty and more years ago. Bits and pieces of Grandpa Jarrell's paisley shirts. And one teeny faded blue piece, about the piece of a penny matchbox, that was from Great Grandpa Ezra's uniform that he wore in the Civil War.

"Mama," Wangero said sweet as a bird. "Can I have these old quilts?"

I heard something fall in the kitchen, and a minute later the kitchen door slammed.

"Why don't you take one or two of the others?" I asked. "These old things was just done by me and Big Dee from some tops your grandma pieced before she died."

Quilt made by a slave in
Mississippi about 1855–1858.
(Courtesy of Michigan State
University Museum.)

The crafting of a family heirloom.

"No," said Wangero. "I don't want those. They are stitched around the borders by machine."

60      "That'll make them last better," I said.

"That's not the point," said Wangero. "These are all pieces of dresses Grandma used to wear. She did all this stitching by hand. Imagine!" She held the quilts securely in her arms, stroking them.

"Some of the pieces, like those lavender ones, come from old clothes her mother handed down to her," I said, moving up to touch the quilts. Dee (Wangero) moved back just enough so that I couldn't reach the quilts. They already belonged to her.

"Imagine!" she breathed again, clutching them closely to her bosom.

"The truth is," I said, "I promised to give them quilts to Maggie, for when she marries John Thomas."

65      She gasped like a bee had stung her.

"Maggie can't appreciate these quilts!" she said. "She'd probably be backward enough to put them to everyday use."

"I reckon she would," I said. "God knows I been saving 'em for long enough with nobody using 'em. I hope she will!" I didn't want to bring up how I had offered Dee (Wangero) a quilt when she went away to college. Then she had told me they were old-fashioned, out of style.

"But they're *priceless!*" she was saying now, furiously; for she has a temper. "Maggie would put them on the bed and in five years they'd be in rags. Less than that!"

"She can always make some more," I said. "Maggie knows how to quilt."

70      Dee (Wangero) looked at me with hatred. "You just will not understand. The point is these quilts, these quilts!"

"Well," I said, stumped. "What would *you* do with them?"

"Hang them," she said. As if that was the only thing you *could* do with quilts.

Maggie by now was standing in the door. I could almost hear the sound her feet made as they scraped over each other.

"She can have them, Mama," she said, like somebody used to never winning anything, or having anything reserved for her. "I can 'member Grandma Dee without the quilts."

75      I looked at her hard. She had filled her bottom lip with checkerberry snuff and it gave her face a kind of dopey, hangdog look. It was Grandma Dee and Big Dee who taught her how to quilt herself. She stood there with her scarred hands hidden in the folds of her skirt. She looked at her sister with something like fear but she wasn't mad at her. This was Maggie's portion. This was the way she knew God to work.

When I looked at her like that something hit me in the top of my head and ran down to the soles of my feet. Just like when I'm in church and the spirit of God touches me and I get happy and shout. I did something I never had done before: hugged Maggie to me, then dragged her on into the room, snatched the quilts out of Miss Wangero's hands and dumped them into Maggie's lap. Maggie just sat there on my bed with her mouth open.

"Take one or two of the others," I said to Dee.

But she turned without a word and went out to Hakim-a-barber.

"You just don't understand," she said, as Maggie and I came out to the car.

80    "What don't I understand?" I wanted to know.

"Your heritage," she said. And then she turned to Maggie, kissed her, and said, "You ought to try to make something of yourself, too, Maggie. It's really a new day for us. But from the way you and Mama still live you'd never know it."

She put on some sunglasses that hid everything above the tip of her nose and her chin.

Maggie smiled; maybe at the sunglasses. But a real smile, not scared. After we watched the car dust settle I asked Maggie to bring me a dip of snuff. And then the two of us sat there just enjoying, until it was time to go in the house and go to bed.

## ❄ TOPICS FOR CRITICAL THINKING AND WRITING

1. Alice Walker wrote the story, but the story is narrated by one of the characters, Mama. How would you characterize Mama?

2. At the end of the story, Dee tells Maggie, "It's really a new day for us. But from the way you and Mama still live you'd never know it." What does Dee mean? And how do Maggie and Mama respond?

3. In paragraph 76 the narrator says, speaking of Maggie, "When I looked at her like that something hit me in the top of my head and ran down to the soles of my feet." What "hit" Mama? That is, what does she understand at this moment that she had not understood before?

4. In "Everyday Use" why does the family conflict focus on who will possess the quilts? Why are the quilts important? What do they symbolize?

# 5

# Narrative Point of View

Every story is told by someone. Mark Twain wrote *Adventures of Huckleberry Finn,* but he does not tell the story; Huck tells the story, and he begins thus:

> You don't know about me without you have read a book by the name of *The Adventures of Tom Sawyer,* but that ain't no matter. That book was made by Mr. Mark Twain, and he told the truth, mainly. There was things which he stretched, but mainly he told the truth.

Similarly, Edgar Allan Poe wrote "The Cask of Amontillado," but the story is told by a man whose name, we learn later, is Montresor. Here is the opening:

> The thousand injuries of Fortunato I had borne as I best could, but when he ventured upon insult, I vowed revenge.

Each of these passages gives a reader a very strong sense of the narrator, that is, of the invented person who tells the story, and it turns out that the works are chiefly about the speakers. Compare those opening passages, however, with two others, which sound far more objective. The first comes from Chekhov's "Misery" (page 94):

> The twilight of evening. Big flakes of wet snow are whirling lazily about the street lamps, which have just been lighted, and lying in a thin soft layer on roofs, horses' backs, shoulders, caps. Iona Potapov, the sledge-driver, is all white like a ghost. He sits on the box without stirring, bent as double as the living body can be bent.

And another example, this one from Hawthorne's "Young Goodman Brown" (page 136):

> Young Goodman Brown came forth, at sunset, into the street at Salem village; but put his head back, after crossing the threshold, to exchange a parting kiss with his young wife. And Faith, as the wife was aptly named, thrust her own pretty head into the street, letting the

wind play with the pink ribbons of her cap while she called to Goodman Brown.

In each of these two passages, a reader is scarcely aware of the personality of the narrator; our interest is almost entirely in the scene that each speaker reveals, not in the speaker's response to the scene.

The narrators of *Huckleberry Finn* and of "The Cask of Amontillado" immediately impress us with their distinctive personalities. We realize that whatever happenings they report will be colored by the special ways in which such personalities see things. But what can we say about the narrators of "Misery" and of "Young Goodman Brown"? A reader hardly notices them, at least in comparison with Huck and Montresor. We look, so to speak, not *at* these narrators, but at others (the cabman and Goodman Brown and Faith).

Of course, it is true that as we read "Misery" and "Young Goodman Brown" we are looking through the eyes of the narrators, but these narrators seem (unlike Huck and Montresor) to have 20/20 vision. This is not to say, however, that these apparently colorless narrators really are colorless or invisible. The narrator of "Misery" seems, at least if we judge from the opening sentences, to want to evoke an atmosphere. He describes the setting in some detail, whereas the narrator of "Young Goodman Brown" seems chiefly concerned with reporting the actions of people whom he sees. Moreover, if we listen carefully to Hawthorne's narrator, perhaps we can say that when he mentions that Faith was "aptly" named, he makes a judgment. Still, it is clear that the narrative voices we hear in "Misery" and "Young Goodman Brown" are relatively impartial and inconspicuous; when we hear them, we feel, for the most part, that they are talking about something objective, about something "out there." These narrative voices will produce stories very different from the narrative voices used by Twain and Poe. The voice that the writer chooses, then, will in large measure shape the story; different voices, different stories.

The narrative point of view of *Huckleberry Finn* and of "The Cask of Amontillado" (and of any other story in which a character in the story tells the story) is a **participant** (or **first-person**) point of view. The point of view of "Young Goodman Brown" (and of any other story in which a nearly invisible outsider tells the story) is a **nonparticipant** (or **third-person**) point of view.

# PARTICIPANT (OR FIRST-PERSON) POINTS OF VIEW

In John Updike's "A & P" on page 117 the narrator is, like Mark Twain's Huck and Poe's Montresor, a major character. Updike has invented an adolescent boy who undergoes certain experiences and who comes to certain perceptions. Since the story is narrated by one of its characters, we can say that the author uses a first-person (or participant) point of view.

It happens that in Updike's "A & P" the narrator is the central character, the character whose actions—whose life, we might say—most interests the reader. But sometimes a first-person narrator tells a story that focuses on another character; the narrator still says "I" (thus the point of view is first person), but the reader feels that the story is not chiefly about this "I" but is about some other figure. For instance, the narrator may be a witness to a story about Jones, and our interest is in what happens to Jones, though we get the story of Jones filtered through, say, the eyes of Jones's friend, or brother, or cat.

When any of us tells a story (for instance, why we quit a job), our hearers may do well to take what we say with a grain of salt. After all, we are giving *our* side, our version of what happened. And so it is with first-person narrators of fiction. They may be reliable, in which case the reader can pretty much accept what they say, or they may be **unreliable narrators,** perhaps because they have an ax to grind, perhaps because they are not perceptive enough to grasp the full implications of what they report, or perhaps because they are mentally impaired, even insane. Poe's Montresor, in "The Cask of Amontillado," is so obsessed that we cannot be certain that Fortunato really did inflict a "thousand injuries" on him.

One special kind of unreliable first-person narrator (whether major or minor) is the **innocent eye:** the narrator is naive (usually a child, or a not-too-bright adult), telling what he or she sees and feels; the contrast between what the narrator perceives and what the reader understands produces an ironic effect. Such a story, in which the reader understands more than the teller himself does, is Ring Lardner's "Haircut," a story told by a garrulous barber who does not perceive that the "accident" he is describing is in fact a murder.

# NONPARTICIPANT (OR THIRD-PERSON) POINTS OF VIEW

In a story told from a nonparticipant (third-person) point of view, the teller of the tale is not a character in the tale. The narrator has receded from the story. If the point of view is **omniscient,** the narrator relates what he or she wishes about the thoughts as well as the deeds of the characters. The omniscient teller can at any time enter the mind of any or all of the characters; whereas the first-person narrator can only say, "I was angry," or "Jones seemed angry to me," the omniscient narrator can say, "Jones was inwardly angry but gave no sign; Smith continued chatting, but he sensed Jones's anger."

Furthermore, a distinction can be made between **neutral omniscience** (the narrator recounts deeds and thoughts, but does not judge) and **editorial omniscience** (the narrator not only recounts, but also judges). The narrator in Hawthorne's "Young Goodman Brown" knows what goes on in the mind of Brown, and he comments approvingly or disapprovingly: "With this excellent resolve for the future, Goodman Brown felt himself justified in making more haste on his present evil purpose."

Because a short story can scarcely hope to effectively develop a picture of several minds, an author may prefer to limit his or her omniscience to the minds of only a few of the characters, or even to that of one of the characters; that is, the author may use **selective omniscience** as the point of view. Selective omniscience provides a focus, especially if it is limited to a single character. When thus limited, the author hovers over the shoulder of one character, seeing him or her from outside and from inside and seeing other characters only from the outside and from the impact they make on the mind of this selected receptor. In "Young Goodman Brown" the reader sees things mostly as they make their impact on the protagonist's mind.

He could have well nigh sworn that the shape of his own dead father beckoned him to advance, looking downward from a smoke wreath, while a woman, with dim features of despair, threw out her hand to warn him back. Was it his mother? But he had no power to retreat one step, nor to resist, even in thought, when the minister and good old Deacon Gookin seized his arms and led him to the blazing rock.

When selective omniscience attempts to record mental activity ranging from consciousness to the unconscious, from clear perceptions to confused longings, it is sometimes labeled the **stream-of-consciousness** point of view. In an effort to reproduce the unending activity of the mind, some authors who use the stream-of-consciousness point of view dispense with conventional word order, punctuation, and logical transitions. The last forty-six pages in James Joyce's *Ulysses* are an unpunctuated flow of one character's thoughts.

Finally, sometimes a third-person narrator does not enter even a single mind, but records only what crosses a dispassionate eye and ear. Such a point of view is **objective** (sometimes called the **camera** or **fly-on-the-wall narrator**). The absence of editorializing and of dissection of the mind often produces the effect of a play; we see and hear the characters in action. Much of Hemingway's "Cat in the Rain" (page 78) is objective, consisting of bits of dialogue that make the story look like a play:

"I'm going down and get that kitty," the American wife said.
"I'll do it," her husband offered from the bed.
"No, I'll get it. The poor kitty out trying to keep dry under a table."
The husband went on reading, lying propped up with the two pillows at the foot of the bed.
"Don't get wet," he said.    (78)

The absence of comment on the happenings forces readers to make their own evaluations of the happenings. In the passage just quoted, when Hemingway writes "'Don't get wet,' he said," readers probably are forced to think (and to sense that Hemingway is guiding them to think) that the husband is indifferent to his wife. After all, how can she go out into the rain and not get wet? A writer can use an objective point of view, then, and still control the feelings of the reader.

# THE POINT OF A POINT OF VIEW

Generalizations about the effect of a point of view are risky, but two have already been made: that the innocent eye can achieve an ironic effect otherwise unattainable, and that an objective point of view (because we hear dialogue but get little or no comment about it) is dramatic. Three other generalizations are often made: (1) that a first-person point of view lends a sense of immediacy or reality, (2) that an omniscient point of view suggests human littleness, and (3) that the point of view must be consistent.

To take the first of these: it is true that when Poe begins a story "The thousand injuries of Fortunato I had borne as I best could, but when he ventured upon insult, I vowed revenge," we feel that the author has gripped us by the lapels; but, on the other hand, we know that we are only reading a piece of fiction, and we do not really believe in the existence of the "I" or of Fortunato; and furthermore, when we pick up a story that begins with *any* point of view, we agree (by picking up the book) to pretend to believe the fictions we are being told. That is, all fiction—whether in the first person or not—is known to be literally false but is read with the pretense that it is true (probably because we hope to get some sort of insight, or truth). The writer must hold our attention, and make us feel that the fiction is meaningful, but the use of the first-person pronoun does not of itself confer reality.

The second generalization, that an omniscient point of view can make puppets of its characters, is equally misleading; this point of view also can reveal in them a depth and complexity quite foreign to the idea of human littleness.

The third generalization, that the narrator's point of view must be consistent lest the illusion of reality be shattered, has been much preached by the followers of Henry James. But E. M. Forster has suggested, in *Aspects of the Novel*, that what is important is not consistency but "the power of the writer to bounce the reader into accepting what he says." Forster notes that in *Bleak House* Dickens uses in Chapter I an omniscient point of view, in Chapter II a selective omniscient point of view, and in Chapter III a first-person point of view. "Logically," Forster says, "*Bleak House* is all to pieces, but Dickens bounces us, so that we do not mind the shiftings of the viewpoint."

Perhaps the only sound generalizations possible are these:

1. Because point of view is one of the things that give form to a story, a good author chooses the point (or points) of view that he or she feels best for the particular story.
2. The use of any other point or points of view would turn the story into a different story.

# JOHN UPDIKE

*John Updike (b. 1932) grew up in Shillington, Pennsylvania, where his father was a teacher and his mother a writer. After receiving a B.A. degree in 1954 from Harvard, where he edited the Harvard Lampoon (for which he both wrote and drew), he studied drawing at Oxford for a year, but an offer from* The New Yorker *brought him back to the United States. He was hired as a reporter for the magazine but soon began contributing poetry, essays, and fiction. In 1957 he left* The New Yorker *in order to write independently full-time, though his stories and book reviews appear regularly in it.*

*In 1959 Updike published his first book of stories (*The Same Door*) as well as his first novel (*The Poorhouse Fair*); the next year he published* Rabbit, Run, *a highly successful novel whose protagonist, "Rabbit" Angstrom, has reappeared in three later novels,* Rabbit Redux *(1971),* Rabbit Is Rich *(1981), and* Rabbit at Rest *(1990). The first and the last* Rabbit *books each won a Pulitzer Prize.*

## A & P                                                                  [1962]

In walks these three girls in nothing but bathing suits. I'm in the third checkout slot, with my back to the door, so I don't see them until they're over by the bread. The one that caught my eye first was the one in the plaid green two-piece. She was a chunky kid, with a good tan and a sweet broad soft-looking can with those two crescents of white just under it, where the sun never seems to hit, at the top of the backs of her legs. I stood there with my hand on a box of HiHo crackers trying to remember if I rang it up or not. I ring it up again and the customer starts giving me hell. She's one of these cash-register-watchers, a witch about fifty with rouge on her cheekbones and no eyebrows, and I know it made her day to trip me up. She'd been watching cash registers for fifty years and probably never seen a mistake before.

By the time I got her feathers smoothed and her goodies into a bag—
she gives me a little snort in passing, if she'd been born at the right time
they would have burned her over in Salem—by the time I get her on her
way the girls had circled around the bread and were coming back, without a pushcart, back my way along the counters, in the aisle between the
checkouts and the Special bins. They didn't even have shoes on. There was
this chunky one, with the two-piece—it was bright green and the seams
on the bra were still sharp and her belly was still pretty pale so I guessed
she just got it (the suit)—there was this one, with one of those chubby
berry-faces, the lips all bunched together under her nose, this one, and a
tall one, with black hair that hadn't quite frizzed right, and one of these
sunburns right across under the eyes, and a chin that was too long—you
know, the kind of girl other girls think is very "striking" and "attractive" but
never quite makes it, as they very well know, which is why they like her
so much—and then the third one, that wasn't quite so tall. She was the
queen. She kind of led them, the other two peeking around and making
their shoulders round. She didn't look around, not this queen, she just
walked straight on slowly, on these long white prima-donna legs. She
came down a little hard on her heels, as if she didn't walk in her bare feet
that much, putting down her heels and then letting the weight move
along to her toes as if she was testing the floor with every step, putting a
little deliberate extra action into it. You never know for sure how girls'
minds work (do you really think it's a mind in there or just a little buzz
like a bee in a glass jar?) but you got the idea she had talked the other two
into coming in here with her, and now she was showing them how to do
it, walk slow and hold yourself straight.

   She had on a kind of dirty pink—beige maybe, I don't know—bathing
suit with a little nubble all over it and, what got me, the straps were down.
They were off her shoulders looped loose around the cool tops of her
arms, and I guess as a result the suit had slipped on her, so all around the
top of the cloth there was this shining rim. If it hadn't been there you
wouldn't have known there could have been anything whiter than those
shoulders. With the straps pushed off, there was nothing between the top
of the suit and the top of her head except just her, this clean bare plane
of the top of her chest down from the shoulder bones like a dented sheet
of metal tilted in the light. I mean, it was more than pretty.

   She had sort of oaky hair that the sun and salt had bleached, done up
in a bun that was unravelling, and a kind of prim face. Walking into the
A & P with your straps down, I suppose it's the only kind of face you *can*
have. She held her head so high her neck, coming up out of those white
shoulders, looked kind of stretched, but I didn't mind. The longer her neck
was, the more of her there was.

5       She must have felt in the corner of her eye me and over my shoulder
Stokesie in the second slot watching, but she didn't tip. Not this queen.
She kept her eyes moving across the racks, and stopped, and turned so

slow it made my stomach rub the inside of my apron, and buzzed to the other two, who kind of huddled against her for relief, and then they all three of them went up the cat and dog food-breakfast cereal-macaroni-rice-raisins-seasonings-spreads-spaghetti-soft drinks-crackers-and-cookies aisle. From the third slot I look straight up this aisle to the meat counter, and I watched them all the way. The fat one with the tan sort of fumbled with the cookies, but on second thought she put the package back. The sheep pushing their carts down the aisle—the girls were walking against the usual traffic (not that we have one-way signs or anything)—were pretty hilarious. You could see them, when Queenie's white shoulders dawned on them, kind of jerk, or hop, or hiccup, but their eyes snapped back to their own baskets and on they pushed. I bet you could set off dynamite in the A & P and the people would by and large keep reaching and checking oatmeal off their lists and muttering "Let me see, there was a third thing, began with A, asparagus, no, ah, yes, applesauce!" or whatever it is they do mutter. But there was no doubt, this jiggled them. A few house slaves in pin curlers even look around after pushing their carts past to make sure what they had seen was correct.

You know, it's one thing to have a girl in a bathing suit down on the beach, where what with the glare nobody can look at each other much anyway, and another thing in the cool of the A & P, under the fluorescent lights, against all those stacked packages, with her feet paddling along naked over our checker-board green-and-cream rubber-tile floor.

"Oh, Daddy," Stokesie said beside me. "I feel so faint."

"Darling," I said. "Hold me tight." Stokesie's married, with two babies chalked up on his fuselage already, but as far as I can tell that's the only difference. He's twenty-two, and I was nineteen this April.

"Is it done?" he asks, the responsible married man finding his voice. I forgot to say he thinks he's going to be a manager some sunny day, maybe in 1990 when it's called the Great Alexandrov and Petrooshki Tea Company or something.

10      What he meant was, our town is five miles from a beach, with a big summer colony out on the Point, but we're right in the middle of town, and the women generally put on a shirt or shorts or something before they get out of the car into the street. And anyway these are usually women with six children and varicose veins mapping their legs and nobody, including them, could care less. As I say, we're right in the middle of town, and if you stand at our front doors you can see two banks and the Congregational church and the newspaper store and three real estate offices and about twenty-seven old freeloaders tearing up Central Street because the sewer broke again. It's not as if we're on the Cape; we're north of Boston and there's people in this town haven't seen the ocean for twenty years.

The girls had reached the meat counter and were asking McMahon something. He pointed, they pointed, and they shuffled out of sight behind a pyramid of Diet Delight peaches. All that was left for us to see was old McMahon patting his mouth and looking after them sizing up their joints. Poor kids, I began to feel sorry for them, they couldn't help it.

Now here comes the sad part of the story, at least my family says it's sad, but I don't think it's so sad myself. The store's pretty empty, it being Thursday afternoon, so there was nothing much to do except lean on the register and wait for the girls to show up again. The whole store was like a pinball machine and I didn't know which tunnel they'd come out of. After a while they come around out of the far aisle, around the light bulbs, records at discount of the Caribbean Six or Tony Martin Sings or some such gunk you wonder they waste the wax on, six-packs of candy bars, and plastic toys done up in cellophane that fall apart when a kid looks at them anyway. Around they come, Queenie still leading the way, and holding a little gray jar in her hand. Slots Three through Seven are unmanned and I could see her wondering between Stokes and me, but Stokesie with his usual luck draws an old party in baggy gray pants who stumbles up with four giant cans of pineapple juice (what do these bums *do* with all that pineapple juice? I've often asked myself) so the girls come to me. Queenie puts down the jar and I take it into my fingers icy cold. Kingfish Fancy Herring Snacks in Pure Sour Cream: 49¢. Now her hands are empty, not a ring or a bracelet, bare as God made them, and I wonder where the money's coming from. Still with the prim look she lifts a folded dollar bill out of the hollow at the center of her nubbled pink top. The jar went heavy in my hand. Really, I thought that was so cute.

Then everybody's luck begins to run out. Lengel comes in from haggling with a truck full of cabbages on the lot and is about to scuttle into the door marked MANAGER behind which he hides all day when the girls touch his eye. Lengel's pretty dreary, teaches Sunday school and the rest, but he doesn't miss that much. He comes over and says, "Girls, this isn't the beach."

Queenie blushes, though maybe it's just a brush of sunburn I was noticing for the first time, now that she was so close. "My mother asked me to pick up a jar of herring snacks." Her voice kind of startled me, the way voices do when you see the people first, coming out so flat and dumb yet kind of tony, too, the way it ticked over "pick up" and "snacks." All of a sudden I slid right down her voice into her living room. Her father and the other men were standing around in ice-cream coats and bow ties and the women were in sandals picking up herring snacks on toothpicks off a big glass plate and they were all holding drinks the color of water with olives and sprigs of mint in them. When my parents have somebody over they get lemonade and if it's a real racy affair Schlitz in tall glasses with "They'll Do It Every Time" cartoons stencilled on.

15    "That's all right," Lengel said. "But this isn't the beach." His repeating this struck me as funny, as if it had just occurred to him, and he had been

thinking all these years the A & P was a great big dune and he was the head lifeguard. He didn't like my smiling—as I say he doesn't miss much—but he concentrates on giving the girls that sad Sunday-school-superintendent stare.

Queenie's blush is no sunburn now, and the plump one in plaid, that I liked better from the back—a really sweet can—pipes up, "We weren't doing any shopping. We just came in for the one thing."

"That makes no difference," Lengel tells her, and I could see from the way his eyes went that he hadn't noticed she was wearing a two-piece before. "We want you decently dressed when you come in here."

"We are decent," Queenie says suddenly, her lower lip pushing, getting sore now that she remembers her place, a place from which the crowd that runs the A & P must look pretty crummy. Fancy Herring Snacks flashed in her very blue eyes.

"Girls, I don't want to argue with you. After this come in here with your shoulders covered. It's our policy." He turns his back. That's policy for you. Policy is what the kingpins want. What the others want is juvenile delinquency.

20     All this while, the customers had been showing up with their carts but, you know, sheep, seeing a scene, they had all bunched up on Stokesie, who shook open a paper bag as gently as peeling a peach, not wanting to miss a word. I could feel in the silence everybody getting nervous, most of all Lengel, who asks me, "Sammy, have you rung up this purchase?"

I thought and said "No" but it wasn't about that I was thinking. I go through the punches, 4, 9, GROC, TOT—it's more complicated than you think and after you do it often enough, it begins to make a little song, that you hear words to, in my case "Hello (*bing*) there, you (*gung*) hap-py *pee*pul (*splat*)!"—the *splat* being the drawer flying out. I uncrease the bill, tenderly as you may imagine, it just having come from between the two smoothest scoops of vanilla I had ever known were there, and pass a half and a penny into her narrow pink palm and nestle the herrings in a bag and twist its neck and hand it over, all the time thinking.

The girls, and who'd blame them, are in a hurry to get out, so I say "I quit" to Lengel quick enough for them to hear, hoping they'll stop and watch me, their unsuspected hero. They keep right on going, into the electric eye; the door flies open and they flicker across the lot to their car, Queenie and Plaid and Big Tall Goony-Goony (not that as raw material she was so bad), leaving me with Lengel and a kink in his eyebrow.

"Did you say something, Sammy?"

"I said I quit."

25     "I thought you did."

"You didn't have to embarrass them."

"It was they who were embarrassing us."

I started to say something that came out "Fiddle-de-doo." It's a saying of my grandmother's, and I know she would have been pleased.

"I don't think you know what you're saying," Lengel said.

30      "I know you don't," I said. "But I do." I pull the bow at the back of my apron and start shrugging it off my shoulders. A couple customers that had been heading for my slot begin to knock against each other, like scared pigs in a chute.

Lengel sighs and begins to look very patient and old and gray. He's been a friend of my parents for years. "Sammy, you don't want to do this to your Mom and Dad," he tells me. It's true, I don't. But it seems to me that once you begin a gesture it's fatal not to go through with it. I fold the apron, "Sammy" stitched in red on the pocket, and put it on the counter, and drop the bow tie on top of it. The bow tie is theirs, if you've ever wondered. "You'll feel this for the rest of your life," Lengel says, and I know that's true, too, but remembering how he made that pretty girl blush makes me so scrunchy inside I punch the No Sale tab and the machine whirs "pee-pul" and the drawer splats out. One advantage to this scene taking place in summer, I can follow this up with a clean exit, there's no fumbling around getting your coat and galoshes, I just saunter into the electric eye in my white shirt that my mother ironed the night before, and the door heaves itself open, and outside the sunshine is skating around on the asphalt.

I look around for my girls, but they're gone, of course. There wasn't anybody but some young married screaming with her children about some candy they didn't get by the door of a powder-blue Falcon station wagon. Looking back in the big windows, over the bags of peat moss and aluminum lawn furniture stacked on the pavement, I could see Lengel in my place in the slot, checking the sheep through. His face was dark gray and his back stiff, as if he'd just had an injection of iron, and my stomach kind of fell as I felt how hard the world was going to be to me hereafter.

## ▨ TOPICS FOR
## CRITICAL THINKING AND WRITING

1. In what sort of community is this A & P located? To what extent does this community resemble yours?

2. Do you think Sammy is a male chauvinist pig? Why, or why not? And if you think he is, do you find the story offensive? Again, why or why not?

3. In the last line of the story Sammy says, "I felt how hard the world was going to be to me hereafter." Do you think the world is going to be hard to Sammy? Why, or why not? And if it is hard to him, is this because of a virtue or a weakness in Sammy?

4. Write Lengel's version of the story (500–1000 words) as he might narrate it to his wife during dinner. Or write the story from Queenie's point of view.

5. In speaking of contemporary fiction Updike said:

> I want stories to startle and engage me within the first few sentences, and in their middle to widen or deepen or sharpen my knowledge of human activity, and to end by giving me a sensation of completed statement.

Let's assume that you share Updike's view of what a story should do. To what extent do you think "A & P" fulfills these demands? (You may want to put your response in the form of a letter to Updike.)

6. During the course of an interview published in the *Southern Review* (Spring 2002), Updike said that the original ending of "A & P" differed from the present ending. In the original, after Sammy resigns he "goes down to the beach to try to see these three girls on whose behalf he's made this sacrifice of respectability, on whose behalf he's broken with the bourgeois norm and let his parents down and Mr. Lengel down. And he doesn't see the girls, and the story ended somewhere there." Updike's editor at *The New Yorker* persuaded him that the story "ended with the resignation." Your view?

# KATHERINE ANNE PORTER

*Katherine Anne Porter (1890–1980) had the curious habit of inventing details in her life, but it is true that she was born in a log cabin in Indian Creek, Texas, that she was originally named Callie Russell Porter, that her mother died when she was two years old, and that Callie was brought up by her maternal grandmother in Kyle, Texas. Apparently the family was conscious of former wealth and position in Louisiana and Kentucky. She was sent to convent schools, where, in her words, she received "a strangely useless and ornamental education." At sixteen she left school, married (and soon divorced), and worked as a reporter, first in Texas and later in Denver and Chicago. She moved around a good deal, both within the United States and abroad; she lived in Mexico, Belgium, Switzerland, France, and Germany.*

*Even as a child Porter was interested in writing, but she did not publish her first story until she was thirty-three. She wrote essays and one novel (Ship of Fools), but she is best known for her stories. Porter's* Collected Stories *won the Pulitzer Prize and the National Book Award in 1965.*

*The Jilting of Granny Weatherall*                                    [1929]

She flicked her wrist neatly out of Doctor Harry's pudgy careful fingers and pulled the sheet up to her chin. The brat ought to be in knee breeches. Doctoring around the country with spectacles on his nose! "Get along now, take your schoolbooks and go. There's nothing wrong with me."

Doctor Harry spread a warm paw like a cushion on her forehead where the forked green vein danced and made her eyelids twitch. "Now, now, be a good girl, and we'll have you up in no time."

"That's no way to speak to a woman nearly eighty years old just because she's down. I'd have you respect your elders, young man."

"Well, Missy, excuse me." Doctor Harry patted her cheek. "But I've got to warn you, haven't I? You're a marvel, but you must be careful or you're going to be good and sorry."

5      "Don't tell me what I'm going to be. I'm on my feet now, morally speaking. It's Cornelia. I had to go to bed to get rid of her."

Her bones felt loose, and floated around in her skin, and Doctor Harry floated like a balloon around the foot of the bed. He floated and pulled down his waistcoat and swung his glasses on a cord. "Well, stay where you are, it certainly can't hurt you."

"Get along and doctor your sick," said Granny Weatherall. "Leave a well woman alone. I'll call for you when I want you. . . . Where were you forty years ago when I pulled through milk leg and double pneumonia? You weren't even born. Don't let Cornelia lead you on," she shouted, because Doctor Harry appeared to float up to the ceiling and out. "I pay my own bills, and I don't throw my money away on nonsense!"

She meant to wave good-by, but it was too much trouble. Her eyes closed of themselves, it was like a dark curtain drawn around the bed. The pillow rose and floated under her, pleasant as a hammock in a light wind. She listened to the leaves rustling outside the window. No, somebody was swishing newspapers: no, Cornelia and Doctor Harry were whispering together. She leaped broad awake, thinking they whispered in her ear.

"She was never like this, *never* like this! "Well, what can we expect?" "Yes, eighty years old. . . ."

10     Well, and what if she was? She still had ears. It was like Cornelia to whisper around doors. She always kept things secret in such a public way. She was always being tactful and kind. Cornelia was dutiful; that was the trouble with her. Dutiful and good: "So good and dutiful," said Granny, "and I'd like to spank her." She saw herself spanking Cornelia and making a fine job of it.

"What'd you say, Mother?"

Granny felt her face tying up in hard knots.

"Can't a body think, I'd like to know?"

"I thought you might want something."

15     "I do. I want a lot of things. First off, go away and don't whisper."

She lay and drowsed, hoping in her sleep that the children would keep out and let her rest a minute. It had been a long day. Not that she was tired. It was always pleasant to snatch a minute now and then. There was always so much to be done, let me see: tomorrow.

Tomorrow was far away and there was nothing to trouble about. Things were finished somehow when the time came; thank God there was always a little margin over for peace: then a person could spread out the plan of life and tuck in the edges orderly. It was good to have everything clean and folded away, with the hair brushes and tonic bottles sitting straight on the white embroidered linen: the day started without fuss and the pantry shelves laid out with rows of jelly glasses and brown jugs and white stone-china jars with blue whirligigs and words painted on them: coffee, tea, sugar, ginger, cinnamon, allspice: and the bronze clock with the lion on top nicely dusted off. The dust that lion could collect in twenty-four hours! The box in the attic with all those letters tied up, she'd have to go through that tomorrow. All those letters—George's letters and John's letters and her letters to them both—lying around for the children to find afterwards made her uneasy. Yes, that would be tomorrow's business. No use to let them know how silly she had been once.

While she was rummaging around she found death in her mind and it felt clammy and unfamiliar. She had spent so much time preparing for death there was no need for bringing it up again. Let it take care of itself now. When she was sixty she had felt very old, finished, and went around making farewell trips to see her children and grandchildren, with a secret in her mind: This is the very last of your mother, children! Then she made her will and came down with a long fever. That was all just a notion like a lot of other things, but it was lucky too, for she had once for all got over the idea of dying for a long time. Now she couldn't be worried. She hoped she had better sense now. Her father had lived to be one hundred and two years old and had drunk a noggin of strong hot toddy on his last birthday. He told the reporters it was his daily habit, and he owed his long life to that. He had made quite a scandal and was very pleased about it. She believed she'd just plague Cornelia a little.

"Cornelia! Cornelia!" No footsteps, but a sudden hand on her cheek. "Bless you, where have you been?"

20        "Here, Mother."

"Well, Cornelia, I want a noggin of hot toddy."

"Are you cold, darling?"

"I'm chilly, Cornelia. Lying in bed stops the circulation. I must have told you that a thousand times."

Well, she could just hear Cornelia tell her husband that her Mother was getting a little childish and they'd have to humor her. The thing that most annoyed her was that Cornelia thought she was deaf, dumb, and blind. Little hasty glances and tiny gestures tossed around her and over her head saying, "Don't cross her, let her have her way, she's eighty years old," and she sitting there as if she lived in a thin glass cage. Sometimes Granny almost made up her mind to pack up and move back to her own house where nobody could remind her every minute that she was old. Wait, wait, Cornelia, till your own children whisper behind your back!

25        In her day she had kept a better house and had got more work done. She wasn't too old yet for Lydia to be driving eighty miles for advice when one of the children jumped the track, and Jimmy still dropped in and talked things over: "Now, Mammy, you've a good business head, I want to know what you think of this? . . ." Old. Cornelia couldn't change the furniture around without asking. Little things, little things! They had been so sweet when they were little. Granny wished the old days were back again with the children young and everything to be done over. It had been a hard pull, but not too much for her. When she thought of all the food she had cooked, and all the clothes she had cut and sewed, and all the gardens she had made—well, the children showed it. There they were, made out of her, and they couldn't get away from that. Sometimes she wanted to see John again and point to them and say, Well, I didn't do so badly, did I? But that would have to wait. That was for tomorrow. She used to think of him as a man, but now all the children were older than their father, and he would be a child beside her if she saw him now. It seemed strange and there was something wrong in the idea. Why he couldn't possibly recognize her. She had fenced in a hundred acres once, digging the post holes herself and clamping the wires with just a negro boy to help. That changed a woman. John would be looking for a young woman with the peaked Spanish comb in her hair and the painted fan. Digging post holes changed a woman. Riding country roads in the winter when women had their babies was another thing: sitting up nights with sick horses and sick negroes and sick children and hardly ever losing one. John, I hardly ever lost one of them! John would see that in a minute, that would be something he could understand, she wouldn't have to explain anything!

It made her feel like rolling up her sleeves and putting the whole place to rights again. No matter if Cornelia was determined to be everywhere at once, there were a great many things left undone on this place. She would start tomorrow and do them. It was good to be strong enough for everything, even if all you made melted and changed and slipped under your hands, so that by the time you finished you almost forgot what you were working for. What was it I set out to do? she asked herself intently, but she could not remember. A fog rose over the valley, she saw it marching across the creek swallowing the trees and moving up the hill like an army of ghosts. Soon it would be at the near edge of the orchard, and then it was time to go in and light the lamps. Come in, children, don't stay out in the night air.

Lighting the lamps had been beautiful. The children huddled up to her and breathed like little calves waiting at the bars in the twilight. Their eyes followed the match and watched the flame rise and settle in a blue curve, then they moved away from her. The lamp was lit, they didn't have to be scared and hang on to mother any more. Never, never, never more. God, for all my life I thank Thee. Without Thee, my God, I could never have done it. Hail, Mary, full of grace.

I want you to pick all the fruit this year and see that nothing is wasted. There's always someone who can use it. Don't let good things rot for want of using. You waste life when you waste good food. Don't let things get lost. It's bitter to lose things. Now, don't let me get to thinking, not when I am tired and taking a little nap before supper. . . .

The pillow rose about her shoulders and pressed against her heart and the memory was being squeezed out of it: oh, push down the pillow, somebody: it would smother her if she tried to hold it. Such a fresh breeze blowing and such a green day with no threats in it. But he had not come, just the same. What does a woman do when she has put on the white veil and set out the white cake for a man and he doesn't come? She tried to remember. No, I swear he never harmed me but in that. He never harmed me but in that . . . and what if he did? There was the day, the day, but a whirl of dark smoke rose and covered it, crept up and over into the bright field where everything was planted so carefully in orderly rows. That was hell, she knew hell when she saw it. For sixty years she had prayed against remembering him and against losing her soul in the deep pit of hell, and now the two things were mingled in one and the thought of him was a smoky cloud from hell that moved and crept in her head when she had just got rid of Doctor Harry and was trying to rest a minute. Wounded vanity, Ellen, said a sharp voice in the top of her mind. Don't let your wounded vanity get the upper hand of you. Plenty of girls get jilted. You were jilted, weren't you? Then stand up to it. Her eyelids wavered and let in streamers of blue-gray light like tissue paper over her eyes. She must get up and pull the shades down or she'd never sleep. She was in bed again and the shades were not down. How could that happen? Better turn over, hide from the light, sleeping in the light gave you nightmares. "Mother, how do you feel now?" and a stinging wetness on her forehead. But I don't like having my face washed in cold water!

30    Hapsy? George? Lydia? Jimmy? No, Cornelia, and her features were swollen and full of little puddles. "They're coming, darling, they'll all be here soon." Go wash your face, child, you look funny.

Instead of obeying, Cornelia knelt down and put her head on the pillow. She seemed to be talking but there was no sound. "Well, are you tongue-tied? Whose birthday is it? Are you going to give a party?"

Cornelia's mouth moved urgently in strange shapes. "Don't do that, you bother me, daughter."

"Oh, no, Mother. Oh, no. . . ."

Nonsense. It was strange about children. They disputed your every word. "No what, Cornelia?"

35    "Here's Doctor Harry."

"I won't see that boy again. He just left five minutes ago."

"That was this morning, Mother. It's night now. Here's the nurse."

"This is Doctor Harry, Mrs. Weatherall. I never saw you look so young and happy!"

"Ah, I'll never be young again—but I'd be happy if they'd let me lie in peace and get rested."

40      She thought she spoke up loudly, but no one answered. A warm weight on her forehead, a warm bracelet on her wrist, and a breeze went on whispering, trying to tell her something. A shuffle of leaves in the everlasting hand of God. He blew on them and they danced and rattled. "Mother, don't mind, we're going to give you a little hypodermic." Look here, daughter, how do ants get in this bed? I saw sugar ants yesterday. Did you send for Hapsy too?

It was Hapsy she really wanted. She had to go a long way back through a great many rooms to find Hapsy standing with a baby on her arm. She seemed to herself to be Hapsy also, and the baby on Hapsy's arm was Hapsy and himself and herself, all at once, and there was no surprise in the meeting. Then Hapsy melted from within and turned flimsy as gray gauze and the baby was a gauzy shadow, and Hapsy came up close and said, "I thought you'd never come," and looked at her very searchingly and said, "You haven't changed a bit!" They leaned forward to kiss, when Cornelia began whispering from a long way off, "Oh, is there anything you want to tell me? Is there anything I can do for you?"

Yes, she had changed her mind after sixty years and she would like to see George. I want you to find George. Find him and be sure to tell him I forgot him. I want him to know I had my husband just the same and my children and my house like any other woman. A good house too and a good husband that I loved and fine children out of him. Better than I hoped for even. Tell him I was given back everything he took away and more. Oh, no, oh, God, no, there was something else besides the house and the man and the children, Oh, surely they were not all? What was it? Something not given back. . . . Her breath crowded down under her ribs and grew into a monstrous frightening shape with cutting edges; it bored up into her head, and the agony was unbelievable: Yes, John, get the doctor now, no more talk, my time has come.

When this one was born it should be the last. The last. It should have been born first, for it was the one she had truly wanted. Everything came in good time. Nothing left out, left over. She was strong, in three days she would be as well as ever. Better. A woman needed milk in her to have her full health.

"Mother, do you hear me?"

45      "I've been telling you—"

"Mother, Father Connolly's here."

"I went to Holy Communion only once last week. Tell him I'm not so sinful as all that."

"Father just wants to speak to you."

He could speak as much as he pleased. It was like him to drop in and inquire about her soul as if it were a teething baby, and then stay on for a cup of tea and a round of cards and gossip. He always had a funny story of some sort, usually about an Irishman who made his little mistakes and confessed them, and the point lay in some absurd thing he would blurt out in the confessional showing his struggles between native piety and original sin. Granny felt easy about her soul. Cornelia, where are your manners? Give Father Connolly a chair. She had her secret comfortable understanding with a few favorite saints who cleared a straight road to God for her. All as surely signed and sealed as the papers for the new Forty Acres. Forever . . . heirs and assigns forever. Since the day the wedding cake was not cut, but thrown out and wasted. The whole bottom dropped out of the world, and there she was blind and sweating with nothing under her feet and walls falling away. His hand had caught her under the breast, she had not fallen, there was the freshly polished floor with the green rug on it, just as before. He had cursed like a sailor's parrot and said, "I'll kill him for you." Don't lay a hand on him, for my sake leave something to God. "Now, Ellen, you must believe what I tell you. . . ."

50    So there was nothing, nothing to worry about any more, except sometimes in the night one of the children screamed in a nightmare, and they both hustled out shaking and hunting for the matches and calling, "There, wait a minute, here we are!" John, get the doctor now, Hapsy's time has come. But there was Hapsy standing by the bed in a white cap. "Cornelia, tell Hapsy to take off her cap. I can't see her plain."

Her eyes opened very wide and the room stood out like a picture she had seen somewhere. Dark colors with the shadows rising towards the ceiling in long angles. The tall black dresser gleamed with nothing on it but John's picture, enlarged from a little one, with John's eyes very black when they should have been blue. You never saw him, so how do you know how he looked? But the man insisted the copy was perfect, it was very rich and handsome. For a picture, yes, but it's not my husband. The table by the bed had a linen cover and a candle and a crucifix. The light was blue from Cornelia's silk lampshade. No sort of light at all, just frippery. You had to live forty years with kerosene lamps to appreciate honest electricity. She felt very strong and saw Doctor Harry with a rosy nimbus around him.

"You look like a saint, Doctor Harry, and I vow that's as near as you'll ever come to it."

"She's saying something."

"I heard you, Cornelia. What's all this carrying on?"

55    "Father Connolly's saying—"

Cornelia's voice staggered and bumped like a cart in a bad road. It rounded corners and turned back again and arrived nowhere. Granny stepped up in the cart very lightly and reached for the reins, but a man sat beside her and she knew him by his hands, driving the cart. She did not look in his face, for she knew without seeing, but looked instead down the road where the trees leaned over and bowed to each other and a thousand birds were singing a Mass. She felt like singing too, but she put her hand in the bosom of her dress and pulled out a rosary, and Father Connolly murmured Latin in a very solemn voice and tickled her feet. My God, will you stop that nonsense? I'm a married woman. What if he did run away and leave me to face the priest by myself? I found another a whole world better. I wouldn't have exchanged my husband for anybody except St. Michael himself, and you may tell him that for me with a thank you in the bargain.

Light flashed on her closed eyelids, and a deep roaring shook her. Cornelia, is that lightning? I hear thunder. There's going to be a storm. Close all the windows. Call all the children in. . . . "Mother, here we are, all of us." "Is that you, Hapsy?" "Oh, no, I'm Lydia. We drove as fast as we could." Their faces drifted above her, drifted away. The rosary fell out of her hands and Lydia put it back. Jimmy tried to help, their hands fumbled together, and Granny closed two fingers around Jimmy's thumb. Beads wouldn't do, it must be something alive. She was so amazed her thoughts ran round and round. So, my dear Lord, this is my death and I wasn't even thinking about it. My children have come to see me die. But I can't, it's not time. Oh, I always hated surprises. I wanted to give Cornelia the amethyst set—Cornelia, you're to have the amethyst set, but Hapsy's to wear it when she wants, and, Doctor Harry, do shut up. Nobody sent for you. Oh, my dear Lord, do wait a minute. I meant to do something about the Forty Acres, Jimmy doesn't need it and Lydia will later on, with that worthless husband of hers. I meant to finish the altar cloth and send six bottles of wine to Sister Borgia for her dyspepsia. I want to send six bottles of wine to Sister Borgia, Father Connolly, now don't let me forget.

Cornelia's voice made short turns and tilted over and crashed, "Oh, Mother, oh, Mother, oh, Mother. . . ."

"I'm not going, Cornelia. I'm taken by surprise. I can't go."

60    You'll see Hapsy again. What about her? "I thought you'd never come." Granny made a long journey outward, looking for Hapsy. What if I don't find her? What then? Her heart sank down and down, there was no bottom to death, she couldn't come to the end of it. The blue light from Cornelia's lampshade drew into a tiny point in the center of her brain, it flickered and winked like an eye, quietly it fluttered and dwindled. Granny lay curled down within herself, amazed and watchful, staring at the point of light that was herself; her body was now only a deeper mass of shadow in an endless darkness and this darkness would curl around the light and swallow it up. God, give a sign!

For the second time there was no sign. Again no bridegroom and the priest in the house. She could not remember any other sorrow because this grief wiped them all away. Oh, no, there's nothing more cruel than this—I'll never forgive it. She stretched her self with a deep breath and blew out the light.

## ▓ TOPICS FOR CRITICAL THINKING AND WRITING

1. How would you describe Granny Weatherall? In what ways does her name suit her?
2. The final paragraph begins: "For the second time there was no sign." What happened the first time? What is happening now? How are the two events linked? (The paragraph alludes to Christ's parable of the bridegroom, in Matthew 25.1–13. If you are unfamiliar with the parable, read it in the Gospel according to St. Matthew.)
3. What do you think happens in the last line of the story?

# 6

# Allegory and Symbolism

In Chapter 4 we looked at some fables, short fictions that were meant to teach us: the characters clearly stood for principles of behavior, and the fictions as a whole evidently taught lessons. If you think of a fable such as "The Ant and the Grasshopper" (the ant wisely collects food during the summer in order to provide for the winter, whereas the grasshopper foolishly sings all summer and goes hungry in the winter), you can easily see that the characters may stand for something other than themselves. The ant, let's say, is the careful, foresighted person, and the grasshopper is the person who lives for the moment. Similarly, in the fable of the tortoise and the hare, the tortoise represents the person who is slow but steady, the rabbit the person who is talented but overly confident and, in the end, foolish.

A story in which each character is understood to have an equivalent is an **allegory.** Further, in an allegory, not only characters but also things (roads, forests, houses) have fairly clear equivalents. Thus, in John Bunyan's *The Pilgrim's Progress,* we meet a character named Christian, who, on the road to the Celestial City, meets Giant Despair, Mr. Worldly Wiseman, and Faithful, and passes through the City of Destruction and Vanity Fair. What all of these are equivalent to is clear from their names. It is also clear that Christian's journey stands for the trials of the soul in this world. There is, so to speak, a one-to-one relationship: A = B =, and so on. If, for example, we are asked what the road represents in *The Pilgrim's Progress,* we can confidently say that it stands for the journey of life. Thus, *The Pilgrim's Progress* tells two stories, the surface story of a man making a trip, during which he meets various figures and visits various places, and a second story, understood through the first, of the trials that afflict the soul during its quest for salvation.

Modern short stories rarely have the allegory's clear system of equivalents, but we may nevertheless feel that certain characters and certain things in the story stand for more than themselves, or hint at larger meanings. We feel, that is, that they are **symbolic**. But here we must be careful. How does one know that this or that figure or place is symbolic? In Hemingway's "Cat in the Rain" (page 78), is the cat symbolic? Is the innkeeper? Is the rain? Reasonable people may differ in their answers. Again, in Chopin's "The Story of an Hour" (page 36), is the railroad accident a symbol? Is Josephine a symbol? Is the season (springtime) a symbol? And again, reasonable people may differ in their responses.

Let's assume for the moment, however, that if writers use symbols, they want readers to perceive—at least faintly—that certain characters or places or seasons or happenings have rich implications, stand for something more than what they are on the surface. How do writers help us to perceive these things? By emphasizing them—for instance, by describing them at some length, or by introducing them at times when they might not seem strictly necessary, or by calling attention to them repeatedly.

Consider, for example, Chopin's treatment of the season in which "The Story of an Hour" takes place. The story has to take place at *some* time, but Chopin does not simply say, "On a spring day," or an autumn day, and let things go at that. Rather, she tells us about the sky, the trees, the rain, the twittering sparrows—and all of this in an extremely short story where we might think there is no time for talk about the setting. After all, none of this material is strictly necessary to a story about a woman who has heard that her husband was killed in an accident, who grieves, then recovers, and then dies when he suddenly reappears

Why, then, does Chopin give such emphasis to the season? Because, we think, she is using the season symbolically. In this story, the spring is not just a bit of detail added for realism. It is rich with suggestions of renewal, of the new life that Louise achieves for a moment. But here, a caution. We think that the spring in this story is symbolic, but this is not to say that whenever spring appears in a story, it always stands for renewal, any more than whenever winter appears it always symbolizes death. Nor does it mean that since spring recurs, Louise will be reborn. In short, in *this* story Chopin uses the season to convey specific implications.

Is the railroad accident also a symbol? Our answer is no—though we don't expect all readers to agree with us. We think that the railroad accident in "The Story of an Hour" is just a railroad accident. It's our sense that Chopin is *not* using this event to say something about (for instance) modern travel, or about industrialism. The steam-propelled railroad train could of course be used, symbolically, to say something about industrialism displacing an agrarian economy, but does Chopin give her train any such suggestion? We don't think so. Had she wished to do so, she would probably have talked about the enormous power of the train, the shriek of its whistle, the smoke pouring out of the smokestack, the intense fire burning in the engine, its indifference as it charged through the countryside, and so forth. Had she done so, the story would be a different story. Or she might have made the train a symbol of fate overriding human desires. But, again in our opinion, Chopin does not endow her train with such suggestions. She gives virtually no emphasis to the train, and so we believe it has virtually no significance for the reader.

And here, as we talk about symbolism we are getting into the theme of the story. An apparently inconsequential and even puzzling action may cast a long shadow. As Robert Frost once said,

> There is no story written that has any value at all, however straightforward it looks and free from doubleness, double entendre, that you'd value at all if it didn't have intimations of something more than itself.

The stranger, the more mysterious the story, the more likely we are to suspect some sort of significance, but even realistic stories such as Chopin's "The Storm" and "The Story of an Hour" may be rich in suggestions. This is not to say, however, that the suggestions (rather than the details of the surface) are what count. A reader does not discard the richly detailed, highly specific narrative (Mrs. Mallard learned that her husband was dead and reacted in such-and-such a way) in favor of some supposedly universal message or theme that it implies. We do not throw away the specific narrative—the memorable characters, or the interesting things that happen in the story—and move on to some "higher truth." Robert Frost went on to say, "The anecdote, the parable, the surface meaning has got to be good and got to be sufficient in itself."

Between these two extremes—on the one hand, writing that is almost all a richly detailed surface and, on the other hand, writing that has a surface so thin that we are immediately taken up with the implications or meanings—are stories in which we strongly feel both the surface happenings and their implications. In *Place in Fiction,* Eudora Welty uses an image of a china lamp to explain literature that presents an interesting surface texture filled with rich significance. When unlit, the lamp showed London; when lit, it showed the Great Fire of London. Like a painted porcelain lamp that, when illuminated, reveals an inner picture shining through the outer, the physical details in a work are illuminated from within by the author's imaginative vision. The outer painting (the literal details) presents "a continuous, shapely, pleasing, and finished surface to the eye," but this surface is not the whole. Welty happens to be talking about the novel, but her words apply equally to the short story:

> The lamp alight is the combination of internal and external, glowing at the imagination as one; and so is the good novel. . . . The good novel should be steadily alight, revealing.

Details that glow, that are themselves and are also something more than themselves, are symbols. Readers may disagree about whether in any particular story something is or is not symbolic—let's say the season in "The

Story of an Hour." And an ingenious reader may overcomplicate or overemphasize the symbolism of a work or may distort it by omitting some of the details and by unduly focusing on others. In many works the details glow, but the glow is so gentle and subtle that even to talk about the details is to overstate them and to understate other equally important aspects of the work.

Yet if it is false to overstate the significance of a detail, it is also false to understate a significant detail. The let's-have-no-nonsense literal reader who holds that "the figure of a man" whom Brown meets in the forest in Hawthorne's "Young Goodman Brown" is simply a man—rather than the Devil—impoverishes the story by neglecting the rich implications just as much as the symbol-hunter impoverishes "The Story of an Hour" by losing sight of Mrs. Mallard in an interpretation of the story as a symbolic comment on industrialism. To take only a single piece of evidence: the man whom Brown encounters holds a staff, "which bore the likeness of a great black snake, so curiously wrought that it might almost be seen to twist and wriggle itself like a living serpent." If we are familiar with the story of Adam and Eve, in which Satan took the form of a serpent, it is hard not to think that Hawthorne is here implying that Brown's new acquaintance is Satan. And, to speak more broadly, when reading the story one can hardly not set up opposing meanings (or at least suggestions) for the village (from which Brown sets out) and the forest (into which he enters). The village is associated with daylight, faith, and goodness; the forest with darkness, loss of faith, and evil. This is not to say that the story sets up neat categories. If you read the story, you will find that Hawthorne is careful to be ambiguous. Even in the passage quoted, about the serpent-staff, you'll notice that he does not say it twisted and wriggled, but that it "might almost be seen to twist and wriggle."

# A NOTE ON SETTING

The **setting** of a story—not only the physical locale but also the time of day or the year or the century—may or may not be symbolic. Sometimes the setting is lightly sketched, presented only because the story has to take place somewhere and at some time. Often, however, the setting is more important, giving us the feel of the people who move through it. But if scenery is drawn in detail, yet adds up to nothing, we share the impatience Robert Louis Stevenson expressed in a letter: "'Roland approached the house; it had green doors and window blinds; and there was a scraper on the upper step.' To hell with Roland and the scraper."

Yes, of course, but if the green doors and the scraper were to tell us something about the tenant, they could be important. As the novelist Elizabeth Bowen said, "Nothing can happen nowhere. The locale of the happening always colors the happening, and often, to a degree, shapes it." And as Henry James neatly said, in fiction "landscape is character." But don't believe it simply because Bowen and James say it. Read the stories, and test the view for yourself.


# NATHANIEL HAWTHORNE

*Nathaniel Hawthorne (1804–1864) was born in Salem, Massachusetts, the son of a sea captain. Two of his ancestors were judges; one had persecuted Quakers, and another had served at the Salem witch trials. In his stories and novels Hawthorne keeps returning to the Puritan past, studying guilt, sin, and isolation. "Young Goodman Brown" was published in 1835, the same year as "The Maypole of Merry Mount."*


## Young Goodman Brown                                    [1835]

Young Goodman[1] Brown came forth, at sunset, into the street at Salem village; but put his head back, after crossing the threshold, to exchange a parting kiss with his young wife. And Faith, as the wife was aptly named, thrust her own pretty head into the street, letting the wind play with the pink ribbons of her cap while she called to Goodman Brown.

"Dearest heart," whispered she, softly and rather sadly, when her lips were close to his ear, "prithee put off your journey until sunrise and sleep in your own bed to-night. A lone woman is troubled with such dreams and such thoughts that she's afeared of herself sometimes. Pray tarry with me this night, dear husband, of all nights in the year."

"My love and my Faith," replied young Goodman Brown, "of all nights in the year, this one night must I tarry away from thee. My journey, as thou callest it, forth and back again, must needs be done 'twixt now and sunrise. What, my sweet, pretty wife, dost thou doubt me already, and we but three months married?"

"Then God bless you!" said Faith, with the pink ribbons; "and may you find all well when you come back."

5        "Amen!" cried Goodman Brown. "Say thy prayers, dear Faith, and go to bed at dusk, and no harm will come to thee."

So they parted; and the young man pursued his way until, being about to turn the corner by the meeting-house, he looked back and saw the head of Faith still peeping after him with a melancholy air, in spite of her pink ribbons.

---

[1]**Goodman** polite term of address for a man of humble standing. (All notes are by editors.)

"Poor little Faith!" thought he, for his heart smote him. "What a wretch am I to leave her on such an errand! She talks of dreams, too. Methought as she spoke there was trouble in her face, as if a dream had warned her what work is to be done to-night. But no, no; 'twould kill her to think it. Well, she's a blessed angel on earth; and after this one night, I'll cling to her skirts and follow her to heaven."

With this excellent resolve for the future, Goodman Brown felt himself justified in making more haste on his present evil purpose. He had taken a dreary road, darkened by all the gloomiest trees of the forest, which barely stood aside to let the narrow path creep through, and closed immediately behind. It was all as lonely as could be; and there is this peculiarity in such a solitude, that the traveler knows not who may be concealed by the innumerable trunks and the thick boughs overhead; so that with lonely footsteps he may yet be passing through an unseen multitude.

"There may be a devilish Indian behind every tree," said Goodman Brown, to himself and he glanced fearfully behind him as he added, "What if the devil himself should be at my very elbow!"

His head being turned back, he passed a crook of the road, and, looking forward again, beheld the figure of a man, in grave and decent attire, seated at the foot of an old tree. He arose at Goodman Brown's approach and walked onward side by side with him.

"You are late, Goodman Brown," said he. "The clock of the Old South was striking as I came through Boston, and that is full fifteen minutes agone."

"Faith kept me back a while," replied the young man, with a tremor in his voice, caused by the sudden appearance of his companion, though not wholly unexpected.

It was now deep dusk in the forest, and deepest in that part of it where these two were journeying. As nearly as could be discerned, the second traveller was about fifty years old, apparently in the same rank of life as Goodman Brown, and bearing a considerable resemblance to him, though perhaps more in expression than features. Still they might have been taken for father and son. And yet, though the elder person was as simply clad as the younger, and as simple in manner too, he had an indescribable air of one who knew the world, and who would not have felt abashed at the governor's dinner table or in King William's court, were it possible that his affairs should call him thither. But the only thing about him that could be fixed upon as remarkable was his staff, which bore the likeness of a great black snake, so curiously wrought that it might almost be seen to twist and wriggle itself like a living serpent. This, of course, must have been an ocular deception, assisted by the uncertain light.

"Come, Goodman Brown," cried his fellow-traveller, "this is a dull pace for the beginning of a journey. Take my staff, if you are so soon weary."

15        "Friend," said the other, exchanging his slow pace for a full stop, "having kept covenant by meeting thee here, it is my purpose now to return whence I came. I have scruples touching the matter thou wot'st² of."

"Sayest thou so?" replied he of the serpent, smiling apart. "Let us walk on, nevertheless, reasoning as we go; and if I convince thee not thou shalt turn back. We are but a little way in the forest yet."

"Too far! too far!" exclaimed the goodman, unconsciously resuming his walk. "My father never went into the woods on such an errand, nor his father before him. We have been a race of honest men and good Christians since the days of the martyrs; and shall I be the first of the name of Brown that ever took this path and kept—"

"Such company, thou wouldst say," observed the elder person, interpreting his pause. "Well said, Goodman Brown! I have been as well acquainted with your family as with ever a one among the Puritans; and that's no trifle to say. I helped your grandfather, the constable, when he lashed the Quaker woman so smartly through the streets of Salem; and it was I that brought your father a pitch-pine knot, kindled at my own hearth, to set fire to an Indian village, in King Philip's war.³ They were my good friends, both; and many a pleasant walk have we had along this path, and returned merrily after midnight. I would fain be friends with you for their sake."

"If it be as thou sayest," replied Goodman Brown, "I marvel they never spoke of these matters; or, verily, I marvel not, seeing that the least rumor of the sort would have driven them from New England. We are a people of prayer, and good works to boot, and abide no such wickedness."

20        "Wickedness or not," said the traveller with the twisted staff, "I have a very general acquaintance here in New England. The deacons of many a church have drunk the communion wine with me; the selectmen of divers towns make me their chairman; and a majority of the Great and General Court are firm supporters of my interest. The governor and I, too—But these are state secrets."

"Can this be so?" cried Goodman Brown, with a stare of amazement at his undisturbed companion. "Howbeit, I have nothing to do with the governor and council; they have their own ways, and are no rule for a simple husbandman⁴ like me. But, were I to go on with thee, how should I meet the eye of that good old man, our minister, at Salem village? Oh, his voice would make me tremble both Sabbath day and lecture day."

Thus far the elder traveller had listened with due gravity; but now burst into a fit of irrepressible mirth, shaking himself so violently that his snake-like staff actually seemed to wriggle in sympathy.

---

²**wot'st** knowest.    ³**King Philip's war** war waged by the Colonists (1675–76) against the Wampanoag Indian leader Metcom, known as "King Philip."
⁴**husbandman** farmer, or, more generally, any man of humble standing.

"Ha! ha! ha!" shouted he again and again; then composing himself, "Well, go on, Goodman Brown, go on; but, prithee, don't kill me with laughing."

"Well, then, to end the matter at once," said Goodman Brown, considerably nettled, "there is my wife, Faith. It would break her dear little heart; and I'd rather break my own."

25      "Nay, if that be the case," answered the other, "e'en go thy ways, Goodman Brown. I would not for twenty old women like the one hobbling before us that Faith should come to any harm."

As he spoke he pointed his staff at a female figure on the path, in whom Goodman Brown recognized a very pious and exemplary dame, who had taught him his catechism in youth, and was still his moral and spiritual adviser, jointly with the minister and Deacon Gookin.

"A marvel, truly, that Goody⁵ Cloyse should be so far in the wilderness at nightfall," said he. "But with your leave, friend, I shall take a cut through the woods until we have left this Christian woman behind. Being a stranger to you, she might ask whom I was consorting with and whither I was going."

"Be it so," said his fellow traveller "Betake you the woods, and let me keep the path."

Accordingly the young man turned aside, but took care to watch his companion, who advanced softly along the road until he had come within a staff's length of the old dame. She, meanwhile, was making the best of her way, with singular speed for so aged a woman, and mumbling some indistinct words—a prayer, doubtless—as she went. The traveller put forth his staff and touched her withered neck with what seemed the serpent's tail.

30      "The devil!" screamed the pious old lady.

"Then Goody Cloyse knows her old friend?" observed the traveller, confronting her and leaning on his writhing stick.

"Ah, forsooth, and is it your worship indeed?" cried the good dame. "Yea, truly is it, and in the very image of my old gossip, Goodman Brown, the grandfather of the silly fellow that now is. But—would your worship believe it?—my broomstick hath strangely disappeared, stolen, as I suspect, by that unhanged witch, Goody Cory, and that, too, when I was all anointed with the juice of smallage and cinquefoil, and wolf's bane—"

"Mingled with fine wheat and the fat of a new-born babe," said the shape of old Goodman Brown.

"Ah, your worship knows the recipe," cried the old lady, cackling aloud. "So, as I was saying, being all ready for the meeting, and no horse to ride on, I made up my mind to foot it; for they tell me there is a nice young man to be taken into communion to-night. But now your good worship will lend me your arm, and we shall be there in a twinkling."

---

⁵**Goody** contraction of Goodwife, a polite term of address for a married woman of humble standing.

35     "That can hardly be," answered her friend. "I may not spare you my arm, Goody Cloyse; but here is my staff, if you will."

So saying, he threw it down at her feet, where, perhaps, it assumed life, being one of the rods which its owner had formerly lent to the Egyptian magi. Of this fact, however, Goodman Brown could not take cognizance. He had cast up his eyes in astonishment, and, looking down again, beheld neither Goody Cloyse nor the serpentine staff but his fellow-traveller alone, who waited for him as calmly as if nothing had happened.

"That old woman taught me my catechism," said the young man; and there was a world of meaning in this simple comment.

They continued to walk onward, while the elder traveller exhorted his companion to make good speed and persevere in the path, discoursing so aptly that his arguments seemed rather to spring up in the bosom of his auditor than to be suggested by himself. As they went, he plucked a branch of maple to serve for a walking stick, and began to strip it of the twigs and little boughs, which were wet with evening dew. The moment his fingers touched them they became strangely withered and dried up as with a week's sunshine. Thus the pair proceeded, at a good free pace, until suddenly, in a gloomy hollow of the road, Goodman Brown sat himself down on the stump of a tree and refused to go any farther.

"Friend," said he, stubbornly, "my mind is made up. Not another step will I budge on this errand. What if a wretched old woman do choose to go to the devil when I thought she was going to heaven: is that any reason why I should quit my dear Faith and go after her?"

40     "You will think better of this by and by," said his acquaintance, composedly. "Sit here and rest yourself a while; and when you feel like moving again, there is my staff to help you along."

Without more words, he threw his companion the maple stick, and was as speedily out of sight as if he had vanished into the deepening gloom. The young man sat a few moments by the roadside, applauding himself greatly, and thinking with how clear a conscience he should meet the minister in his morning walk, nor shrink from the eye of good old Deacon Gookin. And what calm sleep would be his that very night, which was to have been spent so wickedly, but so purely and sweetly now, in the arms of Faith! Amidst these pleasant and praiseworthy meditations, Goodman Brown heard the tramp of horses along the road, and deemed it advisable to conceal himself within the verge of the forest, conscious of the guilty purpose that had brought him thither, though now so happily turned from it.

On came the hoof-tramps and the voices of the riders, two grave old voices, conversing soberly as they drew near. These mingled sounds appeared to pass along the road, within a few yards of the young man's hiding-place; but, owing doubtless to the depth of the gloom at that particular spot, neither the travellers nor their steeds were visible. Though their figures brushed the small boughs by the wayside, it could not be seen that they intercepted, even for a moment, the faint gleam from the strip of bright sky athwart which they must have passed. Goodman Brown alternately crouched and stood on tiptoe, pulling aside the branches and thrusting forth his head as far as he durst without discerning so much as a shadow. It vexed him the more, because he could have sworn, were such a thing possible, that he recognized the voices of the minister and Deacon Gookin, jogging along quietly, as they were wont to do, when bound to some ordination or ecclesiastical council. While yet within hearing, one of the riders stopped to pluck a switch.

"Of the two, reverend sir," said the voice like the deacon's, "I had rather miss an ordination dinner than to-night's meeting. They tell me that some of our community are to be here from Falmouth and beyond, and others from Connecticut and Rhode Island, besides several of the Indian powwows, who, after their fashion, know almost as much deviltry as the best of us. Moreover, there is a goodly young woman to be taken into communion."

"Mighty well, Deacon Gookin!" replied the solemn old tones of the minister. "Spur up, or we shall be late. Nothing can be done, you know, until I get on the ground."

45    The hoofs clattered again; and the voices, talking so strangely in the empty air, passed on through the forest, where no church had ever been gathered or solitary Christian prayed. Whither, then, could these holy men be journeying so deep into the heathen wilderness? Young Goodman Brown caught hold of a tree for support, being ready to sink down on the ground, faint and overburdened with the heavy sickness of his heart. He looked up to the sky, doubting whether there really was a heaven above him. Yet there was the blue arch, and the stars brightening in it.

"With heaven above and Faith below, I will yet stand firm against the devil!" cried Goodman Brown.

While he still gazed upward into the deep arch of the firmament and had lifted his hands to pray, a cloud, though no wind was stirring, hurried across the zenith and hid the brightening stars. The blue sky was still visible, except directly overhead, where this black mass of cloud was sweeping swiftly northward. Aloft in the air, as if from the depths of the cloud, came a confused and doubtful sound of voices. Once the listener fancied that he could distinguish the accents of towns-people of his own, men and women, both pious and ungodly, many of whom he had met at the communion table, and had seen others rioting at the tavern. The next moment, so indistinct were the sounds, he doubted whether he had heard aught but the murmur of the old forest, whispering without a wind. Then came a stronger swell of those familiar tones, heard daily in the sunshine at Salem village, but never until now from a cloud of night. There was one voice, of a young woman, uttering lamentations, yet with an uncertain sorrow, and entreating for some favor, which, perhaps, it would grieve her to obtain; and all the unseen multitude, both saints and sinners, seemed to encourage her onward.

"Faith!" shouted Goodman Brown, in a voice of agony and desperation; and the echoes of the forest mocked him, crying, "Faith! Faith!" as if bewildered wretches were seeking her all through the wilderness.

The cry of grief, rage, and terror was yet piercing the night, when the unhappy husband held his breath for a response. There was a scream, drowned immediately in a louder murmur of voices, fading into far-off laughter, as the dark cloud swept away, leaving the clear and silent sky above Goodman Brown. But something fluttered lightly down through the air and caught on the branch of a tree. The young man seized it, and beheld a pink ribbon.

50    "My Faith is gone!" cried he, after one stupefied moment. "There is no good on earth; and sin is but a name. Come, devil; for to thee is this world given."

And, maddened with despair, so that he laughed loud and long, did Goodman Brown grasp his staff and set forth again, at such a rate that he seemed to fly along the forest path rather than to walk or run. The road grew wilder and drearier and more faintly traced, and vanished at length, leaving him in the heart of the dark wilderness, still rushing onward with the instinct that guides mortal man to evil. The whole forest was peopled with frightful sounds—the creaking of the trees, the howling of wild beasts, and the yell of Indians; while sometimes the wind tolled like a distant church bell, and sometimes gave a broad roar around the traveller, as if all Nature were laughing him to scorn. But he was himself the chief horror of the scene, and shrank not from its other horrors.

"Ha! ha! ha!" roared Goodman Brown when the wind laughed at him. "Let us hear which will laugh loudest. Think not to frighten me with your deviltry. Come witch, come lizard, come Indian powwow, come devil himself, and here comes Goodman Brown. You may as well fear him as he fear you!"

In truth, all through the haunted forest there could be nothing more frightful than the figure of Goodman Brown. On he flew among the black pines, brandishing his staff with frenzied gestures, now giving vent to an inspiration of horrid blasphemy, and now shouting forth such laughter as set all the echoes of the forest laughing like demons around him. The fiend in his own shape is less hideous than when he rages in the breast of man. Thus sped the demoniac on his course, until, quivering among the trees, he saw a red light before him, as when the felled trunks and branches of a clearing have been set on fire, and throw up their lurid blaze against the sky, at the hour of midnight. He paused, in a lull of the tempest that had driven him onward, and heard the swell of what seemed a hymn, rolling solemnly from a distance with the weight of many voices. He knew the tune; it was a familiar one in the choir of the village meeting-house. The verse died heavily away, and was lengthened by a chorus, not of human voices, but of all the sounds of the benighted wilderness peal-ing in awful harmony together. Goodman Brown cried out; and his cry was lost to his own ear by its unison with the cry of the desert.

In the interval of silence he stole forward until the light glared full upon his eyes. At one extremity of an open space, hemmed in by the dark wall of the forest, arose a rock, bearing some rude, natural resemblance either to an altar or a pulpit, and surrounded by four blazing pines, their tops aflame, their stems untouched, like candles at an evening meeting. The mass of foliage that had overgrown the summit of the rock was all on fire, blazing high into the night and fitfully illuminating the whole field. Each pendent twig and leafy festoon was in a blaze. As the red light arose and fell, a numerous congregation alternately shone forth, then disappeared in shadow, and again grew, as it were, out of the darkness, peopling the heart of the solitary woods at once.

55        "A grave and dark-clad company," quoth Goodman Brown.

In truth they were such. Among them, quivering to-and-fro between gloom and splendor, appeared faces that would be seen next day at the council board of the province, and others which, Sabbath after Sabbath, looked devoutly heavenward, and benignantly over the crowded pews, from the holiest pulpits in the land. Some affirm that the lady of the governor was there. At least three were high dames well known to her, and wives of honored husbands, and widows, a great multitude, and ancient maidens, all of excellent repute, and fair young girls, who trembled lest their mothers should espy them. Either the sudden gleams of light flashing over the obscure field bedazzled Goodman Brown, or he recognized a score of the church-members of Salem village famous for their especial sanctity. Good old Deacon Gookin had arrived, and waited at the skirts of that venerable saint, his revered pastor. But, irreverently consorting with these grave, reputable, and pious people, these elders of the church, these chaste dames and dewy virgins, there were men of dissolute lives and women of spotted fame, wretches given over to all mean and filthy vice, and suspected even of horrid crimes. It was strange to see that the good shrank not from the wicked, nor were the sinners abashed by the saints. Scattered also among their pale-faced enemies were the Indian priests, or powwows, who had often scared their native forest with more hideous incantations than any known to English witchcraft.

"But where is Faith?" thought Goodman Brown; and, as hope came into his heart, he trembled.

Another verse of the hymn arose, a slow and mournful strain, such as the pious love, but joined to words which expressed all that our nature can conceive of sin, and darkly hinted at far more. Unfathomable to mere mortals is the lore of fiends. Verse after verse was sung; and still the chorus of the desert swelled between, like the deepest tone of a mighty organ; and with the final peal of that dreadful anthem there came a sound, as if the roaring wind, the rushing streams, the howling beasts, and every other voice of the unconcerted wilderness were mingling and according with the voice of guilty man in homage to the prince of all. The four blazing pines threw up a loftier flame, and obscurely discovered shapes and visages of horror on the smoke wreaths above the impious assembly. At the same moment the fire on the rock shot redly forth and formed a glowing arch above its base, where now appeared a figure. With reverence be it spoken, the figure bore no slight similitude, both in garb and manner, to some grave divine of the New England churches.

"Bring forth the converts!" cried a voice that echoed through the field and rolled into the forest.

60    At the word, Goodman Brown stepped forth from the shadow of the trees and approached the congregation, with whom he felt a loathful brotherhood by the sympathy of all that was wicked in his heart. He could have wellnigh sworn that the shape of his own dead father beckoned him to advance, looking downward from a smoke wreath, while a woman, with dim features of despair, threw out her hand to warn him back. Was it his mother? But he had no power to retreat one step, nor to resist, even in thought, when the minister and good old Deacon Gookin seized his arms and led him to the blazing rock. Thither came also the slender form of a veiled female, led between Goody Cloyse, that pious teacher of the catechism, and Martha Carrier, who had received the devil's promise to be queen of hell. A rampant hag was she. And there stood the proselytes beneath the canopy of fire.

"Welcome, my children," said the dark figure, "to the communion of your race. Ye have found thus young your nature and your destiny. My children, look behind you!"

They turned; and flashing forth, as it were, in a sheet of flame, the fiend worshippers were seen; the smile of welcome gleamed darkly on every visage.

"There," resumed the sable form, "are all whom ye have reverenced from youth. Ye deemed them holier than yourselves, and shrank from your own sin, contrasting it with their lives of righteousness and prayerful aspirations heavenward. Yet here are they all in my worshipping assembly. This night it shall be granted you to know their secret deeds: how hoary-bearded elders of the church have whispered wanton words to the young maids of their households; how many a woman, eager for widows' weeds, has given her husband a drink at bedtime and let him sleep his last sleep in her bosom; how beardless youths have made haste to inherit their fathers' wealth; and how fair damsels—blush not, sweet ones—have dug little graves in the garden, and bidden me, the sole guest, to an infant's funeral. By the sympathy of your human hearts for sin ye shall scent out all the places—whether in church, bedchamber, street, field, or forest—where crime has been committed, and shall exult to behold the whole earth one stain of guilt, one mighty blood spot. Far more than this. It shall be yours to penetrate, in every bosom, the deep mystery of sin, the fountain of all wicked arts, and which inexhaustibly supplies more evil impulses than human power—than my power at its utmost—can make manifest in deeds. And now, my children, look upon each other."

They did so; and, by the blaze of the hell-kindled torches, the wretched man beheld his Faith, and the wife her husband, trembling before that unhallowed altar.

65 "Lo, there ye stand, my children," said the figure, in a deep and solemn tone, almost sad with its despairing awfulness, as if his once angelic nature could yet mourn for our miserable race. "Depending upon one another's hearts, ye had still hoped that virtue were not all a dream. Now are ye undeceived. Evil is the nature of mankind. Evil must be your only happiness. Welcome, again, my children, to the communion of your race."

"Welcome," repeated the fiend worshippers, in one cry of despair and triumph.

And there they stood, the only pair, as it seemed, who were yet hesitating on the verge of wickedness in this dark world. A basin was hollowed, naturally, in the rock. Did it contain water, reddened by the lurid light? or was it blood? or, perchance, a liquid flame? Herein did the shape of evil dip his hand and prepare to lay the mark of baptism upon their foreheads, that they might be partakers of the mystery of sin, more conscious of the secret guilt of others, both in deed and thought, than they could now be of their own. The husband cast one look at his pale wife, and Faith at him. What polluted wretches would the next glance show them to each other, shuddering alike at what they disclosed and what they saw!

"Faith! Faith!" cried the husband, "look up to heaven, and resist the wicked one."

Whether Faith obeyed he knew not. Hardly had he spoken when he found himself amid calm night and solitude, listening to a roar of the wind which died heavily away through the forest. He staggered against the rock, and felt it chill and damp; while a hanging twig, that had been all on fire, besprinkled his cheek with the coldest dew.

70 The next morning young Goodman Brown came slowly into the street of Salem village, staring around him like a bewildered man. The good old minister was taking a walk along the graveyard to get an appetite for breakfast and meditate his sermon, and bestowed a blessing, as he passed, on Goodman Brown. He shrank from the venerable saint as if to avoid an anathema. Old Deacon Gookin was at domestic worship, and the holy words of his prayer were heard through the open window. "What God doth the wizard pray to?" quoth Goodman Brown. Goody Cloyse, that excellent old Christian, stood in the early sunshine at her own lattice, catechizing a little girl who had brought her a pint of morning's milk. Goodman Brown snatched away the child as from the grasp of the fiend himself. Turning the corner by the meeting-house, he spied the head of Faith, with the pink ribbons, gazing anxiously forth, and bursting into such joy at sight of him that she skipped along the street and almost kissed her

husband before the whole village. But Goodman Brown looked sternly and sadly into her face, and passed on without a greeting.

Had Goodman Brown fallen asleep in the forest and only dreamed a wild dream of a witch-meeting?

Be it so, if you will; but alas! it was a dream of evil omen for young Goodman Brown. A stern, a sad, a darkly meditative, a distrustful, if not a desperate man did he become from the night of that fearful dream. On the Sabbath day, when the congregation were singing a holy psalm, he could not listen because an anthem of sin rushed loudly upon his ear and drowned all the blessed strain. When the minister spoke from the pulpit with power and fervid eloquence, and, with his hand on the open Bible, of the sacred truths of our religion, and of saint-like lives and triumphant deaths, and of future bliss or misery unutterable, then did Goodman Brown turn pale, dreading lest the roof should thunder down upon the gray blasphemer and his hearers. Often, awaking suddenly at midnight, he shrank from the bosom of Faith; and at morning or eventide, when the family knelt down at prayer, he scowled and muttered to himself, and gazed sternly at his wife, and turned away. And when he had lived long, and was borne to his grave a hoary corpse, followed by Faith, an aged woman, and children and grandchildren, a goodly procession, besides neighbors not a few, they carved no hopeful verse upon his tombstone, for his dying hour was gloom.

## ▓ TOPICS FOR CRITICAL THINKING AND WRITING

1. Do you take Faith to stand only for religious faith, or can she here also stand for one's faith in one's fellow human beings? Explain.

2. Hawthorne describes the second traveler as "about fifty years old, apparently in the same rank as Goodman Brown, and bearing a considerable resemblance to him." Further, "they might have been taken for father and son." What do you think Hawthorne is getting at here?

3. In the forest Brown sees (or thinks he sees) Goody Cloyse, the minister, Deacon Gookin, and others. Does he in fact meet them, or does he dream of them? Or does he encounter "figures" and "forms" (rather than real people) whom the devil conjures up in order to deceive Brown?

4. Evaluate the view that when Brown enters the dark forest he is really entering his own evil mind.

5. A Hawthorne scholar we know says that he finds this story "terrifying." Do you agree? Or would you characterize your response to it differently? Explain, making reference to passages in the text.

6. Does a person have to be a Christian in order to understand "Young Goodman Brown"? Would a Christian reader find this story reassuring

or disturbing? Can a non-Christian reader understand and appreciate the story? What might he or she learn from reading it?.

7. Having read and studied "Young Goodman Brown," do you find you want to read more of Hawthorne's stories? Are you very eager, a little eager, or not really? Please explain.

8. "Young Goodman Brown" is often included in anthologies of American literature and in collections of short stories. In your view, why is this the case? Do you agree with this decision, or does it puzzle you?

# JOHN STEINBECK

*John Steinbeck (1902–1968) was born in Salinas, California, and much of his fiction concerns this landscape and its people. As a young man he worked on ranches, farms, and road gangs, and sometimes attended Stanford University—he never graduated—but he wrote whenever he could find the time. His early efforts at writing, however, were uniformly rejected by publishers. Even when he did break into print, he did not achieve much notice for several years: a novel in 1929, a book of stories in 1932, and another novel in 1933 attracted little attention. But the publication of* Tortilla Flat *(1935), a novel about Mexican Americans, changed all that. It was followed by other successful novels—In* Dubious Battle *(1936) and* Of Mice and Men *(1937)—and by* The Long Valley *(1938), a collection of stories that included "The Chrysanthemums." His next book,* The Grapes *of* Wrath *(1939), about dispossessed sharecropper migrants from the Oklahoma dustbowl, was also immensely popular and won a Pulitzer Prize. During the Second World War Steinbeck sent reports from battlefields in Italy and Africa. In 1962 he was awarded the Nobel Prize in Literature.*

## The Chrysanthemums                                    [1937]

The high grey-flannel fog of winter closed off the Salinas Valley[1] from the sky and from all the rest of the world. On every side it sat like a lid on the mountains and made of the great valley a closed pot. On the broad, level land floor the gang plows bit deep and left the black earth shining like metal where the shares had cut. On the foothill ranches across the Salinas River, the yellow stubble fields seemed to be bathed in pale cold sunshine, but there was no sunshine in the valley now in December. The thick willow scrub along the river flamed with sharp and positive yellow leaves.

---

[1]**the Salinas Valley** a fertile area in central California.

It was a time of quiet and of waiting. The air was cold and tender. A light wind blew up from the southwest so that the farmers were mildly hopeful of a good rain before long; but fog and rain do not go together.

Across the river, on Henry Allen's foothill ranch there was little work to be done, for the hay was cut and stored and the orchards were plowed up to receive the rain deeply when it should come. The cattle on the higher slopes were becoming shaggy and rough-coated.

Elisa Allen, working in her flower garden, looked down across the yard and saw Henry, her husband, talking to two men in business suits. The three of them stood by the tractor shed, each man with one foot on the side of the little Fordson.[2] They smoked cigarettes and studied the machine as they talked.

5    Elisa watched them for a moment and then went back to her work. She was thirty-five. Her face was lean and strong and her eyes were as clear as water. Her figure looked blocked and heavy in her gardening costume, a man's black hat pulled low down over her eyes, clod-hopper shoes, a figured print dress almost completely covered by a big corduroy apron with four big pockets to hold the snips, the trowel and scratcher, the seeds and the knife she worked with. She wore heavy leather gloves to protect her hands while she worked.

She was cutting down the old year's chrysanthemum stalks with a pair of short and powerful scissors. She looked down toward the tractor shed now and then. Her face was eager and mature and handsome; even her work with the scissors was over-eager, over-powerful. The chrysanthemum stems seemed too small and easy for her energy.

She brushed a cloud of hair out of her eyes with the back of her glove, and left a smudge of earth on her cheek in doing it. Behind her stood the neat white farm house with red geraniums close-banked around it as high as the windows. It was a hard-swept looking little house with hard-polished windows, and a clean mud-mat on the front steps.

Elisa cast another glance toward the tractor shed. The strangers were getting into their Ford coupe. She took off a glove and put her strong fingers down into the forest of new green chrysanthemum sprouts that were growing around the old roots. She spread the leaves and looked down among the close-growing stems. No aphids were there, no sowbugs or snails or cutworms. Her terrier fingers destroyed such pests before they could get started.

Elisa started at the sound of her husband's voice. He had come near quietly, and he leaned over the wire fence that protected her flower garden from the cattle and dogs and chickens.

10    "At it again," he said. "You've got a strong new crop coming."

Elisa straightened her back and pulled on the gardening glove again. "Yes, they'll be strong this coming year." In her tone and on her face there was a little smugness.

---

[2]**Fordson** a two-door Ford car.

"You've got a gift with things," Henry observed. "Some of those yellow chrysanthemums you had this year were ten inches across. I wish you'd work out in the orchard and raise some apples that big."

Her eyes sharpened. "Maybe I could do it, too. I've a gift with things, all right. My mother had it. She could stick anything in the ground and make it grow. She said it was having planters' hands that knew how to do it."

"Well, it sure works with flowers," he said.

15    "Henry, who were those men you were talking to?"

"Why, sure, that's what I came to tell you. They were from the Western Meat Company. I sold those thirty head of three-year-old steers. Got nearly my own price, too."

"Good," she thought. "Good for you."

"And I thought," he continued, "I thought how it's Saturday afternoon, and we might go into Salinas for dinner at a restaurant, and then to a picture show—to celebrate, you see."

"Good," she repeated. "Oh, yes. That will be good."

20    Henry put on his joking tone. "There's fights tonight. How'd you like to go to the fights?"

"Oh, no," she said breathlessly. "No, I wouldn't like the fights."

"Just fooling, Elisa. We'll go to a movie. Let's see. It's two now. I'm going to take Scotty and bring down those steers from the hill. It'll take us maybe two hours. We'll go in town about five and have dinner at the Cominos Hotel. Like that?"

"Of course I'll like it. It's good to eat away from home."

"All right, then. I'll go get up a couple of horses."

25    She said, "I'll have plenty of time to transplant some of these sets, I guess."

She heard her husband calling Scotty down by the barn. And a little later she saw the two men ride up the pale yellow hillside in search of the steers.

There was a little square sandy bed kept for rooting the chrysanthemums. With her trowel she turned the soil over and over, and smoothed it and patted it firm. Then she dug ten parallel trenches to receive the sets. Back at the chrysanthemum bed she pulled out the little crisp shoots, trimmed off the leaves of each one with her scissors and laid it on a small orderly pile.

A squeak of wheels and plod of hoofs, came from the road. Elisa looked up. The country road ran along the dense bank of willows and cottonwoods that bordered the river, and up this road came a curious vehicle, curiously drawn. It was an old springwagon, with a round canvas top on it like the cover of a prairie schooner. It was drawn by an old bay horse and a little grey-and-white burro. A big stubble-bearded man sat between the cover flaps and drove the crawling team. Underneath the wagon, between the hind wheels, a lean and rangy mongrel dog walked sedately. Words were painted on the canvas, in clumsy, crooked letters. "Pots, pans, knives,

sisors, lawn mores, Fixed." Two rows of articles, and the triumphantly de-
finitive "Fixed" below. The black paint had run down in little sharp points
beneath each letter.

Elisa, squatting on the ground, watched to see the crazy, loose-jointed
wagon pass by. But it didn't pass. It turned into the farm road in front of
her house, crooked old wheels skirling and squeaking. The rangy dog
darted from between the wheels and ran ahead. Instantly the two ranch
shepherds flew out at him. Then all three stopped, and with stiff and quivering tails, with taut straight legs, with ambassadorial dignity, they slowly
circled, sniffing daintily. The caravan pulled up to Elisa's wire fence and
stopped. Now the newcomer dog, feeling out-numbered, lowered his tail
and retired under the wagon with raised hackles and bared teeth.

30      The man on the wagon called out, "That's a bad dog in a fight when
he gets started."

Elisa laughed. "I see he is. How soon does he generally get started?"

The man caught up her laughter and echoed it heartily. "Sometimes
not for weeks and weeks," he said. He climbed stiffly down, over the
wheel. The horse and donkey drooped like unwatered flowers.

Elisa saw that he was a very big man. Although his hair and beard
were greying, he did not look old. His worn black suit was wrinkled and
spotted with grease. The laughter had disappeared from his face and eyes
the moment his laughing voice ceased. His eyes were dark, and they were
full of the brooding that gets in the eyes of teamsters and sailors. The cal-
loused hands he rested on the wire fence were cracked, and every crack
was a black line. He took off his battered hat.

"I'm off my general road, ma'am," he said. "Does this dirt road cut over
across the river to the Los Angeles highway?"

35      Elisa stood up and shoved the thick scissors in her apron pocket.
"Well, yes, it does, but it winds around and then fords the river. I don't
think your team could pull it through the sand."

He replied with some asperity. "It might surprise you what them
beasts can pull through."

"When they get started?" She asked.

He smiled for a second. "Yes. When they get started."

"Well," said Elisa, "I think you'll save time if you go back to the Salinas
road and pick up the highway there."

40      He drew a big finger around the chicken wire and made it sing. "I
ain't in any hurry, ma'am. I go from Seattle to San Diego and back every
year. Takes all my time. About six months each way. I aim to follow nice
weather."

Elisa took off her gloves and stuffed them in the apron pocket with
the scissors. She touched under the edge of her man's hat, searching for
fugitive hairs. "That sounds like a nice kind of a way to live," she said.

He leaned confidentially over the fence. "Maybe you noticed the writing on my wagon. I mend pots and sharpen knives and scissors. You got
any of them things to do?"

"Oh, no," she said quickly. "Nothing like that." Her eyes hardened with resistance.

"Scissors is the worst thing," he explained. "Most people just ruin scissors trying to sharpen 'em, but I know how. I got a special tool. It's a little bobbit kind of thing, and patented. But it sure does the trick."

45      "No. My scissors are all sharp."

"All right, then. Take a pot," he continued earnestly, "a bent pot, or a pot with a hole. I can make it like new so you don't have to buy no new ones. That's a saving for you."

"No," she said shortly. "I tell you I have nothing like that for you to do."

His face fell to an exaggerated sadness. His voice took on a whining undertone. "I ain't had a thing to do today. Maybe I won't have no supper tonight. You see I'm off my regular road. I know folks on the highway clear from Seattle to San Diego. They save their things for me to sharpen up because they know I do it so good and save them money."

"I'm sorry," Elisa said irritably. "I haven't anything for you to do."

50      His eyes left her face and fell to searching the ground. They roamed about until they came to the chrysanthemum bed where she had been working. "What's them plants, ma'am?"

The irritation and resistance melted from Elisa's face. "Oh, those are chrysanthemums, giant whites and yellows. I raise them every year, bigger than anybody around here."

"Kind of a long-stemmed flower?" Looks like a quick puff of colored smoke?" he asked.

"That's it. What a nice way to describe them."

"They smell kind of nasty till you get used to them," he said.

55      "It's a good bitter smell," she retorted, "not nasty at all."

He changed his tone quickly. "I like the smell myself."

"I had ten-inch blooms this year," she said.

The man leaned farther over the fence. "Look. I know a lady down the road a piece, has got the nicest garden you ever seen. Got nearly every kind of flower but no chrysanthemums. Last time I was mending a copper-bottom wash-tub for her (that's a hard job but I do it good), she said to me, 'If you ever run acrost some nice chrysanthemums I wish you'd try to get me a few seeds.' That's what she told me."

Elisa's eyes grew alert and eager. "She couldn't have known much about chrysanthemums. You *can* raise them from seed, but it's much easier to root the little sprouts you see here."

60      "Oh," he said. "I s'pose I can't take none to her then."

"Why yes you can," Elisa cried. "I can put some in damp sand, and you can carry them right along with you. They'll take root in the pot if you keep them damp. And then transplant them."

"She'd sure like to have some, ma'am. You say they're nice ones?"

"Beautiful," she said. "Oh, beautiful." Her eyes shone. She tore off the battered hat and shook out her dark pretty hair. "I'll put them in a flower pot, and you can take them right with you. Come into the yard."

While the man came through the picket gate Elisa ran excitedly along the geranium-bordered path to the back of the house. And she returned carrying a big red flower pot. The gloves were forgotten now. She kneeled on the ground by the starting bed and dug up the sandy soil with her fingers and scooped it into the bright new flower pot. Then she picked up the little pile of shoots she had just prepared. With her strong fingers she pressed them into the sand and tamped around them with her knuckles. The man stood over her. "I'll tell you what to do," she said. "You remember so you can tell the lady."

65    "Yes, I'll try to remember."

"Well, look. These will take root in about a month. Then she must set them out, about a foot apart in good rich earth like this, see?" She lifted a handful of dark soil for him to look at. "They'll grow fast and tall. Now remember this: In July tell her to cut them down, about eight inches from the ground."

"Before they bloom?" he asked.

"Yes, before they bloom." Her face was tight with eagerness. "They'll grow right up again. About the last of September the buds will start."

She stopped and seemed perplexed. "It's the budding that takes the most care," she said hesitantly. "I don't know how to tell you." She looked deep into his eyes, searchingly. Her mouth opened a little, and she seemed to be listening. "I'll try to tell you," she said. "Did you ever hear of planting hands?"

70    "Can't say I have, ma'am."

"Well, I can only tell you what it feels like. It's when you're picking off the buds you don't want. Everything goes right down into your fingertips. You watch your fingers work. They do it themselves. You can feel how it is. They pick and pick the buds. They never make a mistake. They're with the plant. Do you see? Your fingers and the plant. You can feel that, right up your arm. They know. They never make a mistake. You can feel it. When you're like that you can't do anything wrong. Do you see that? Can you understand that?"

She was kneeling on the ground looking up at him. Her breast swelled passionately.

The man's eyes narrowed. He looked away self-consciously. "Maybe I know," he said. "Sometimes in the night in the wagon there—"

Elisa's voice grew husky. She broke in on him, "I've never lived as you do, but I know what you mean. When the night is dark—why, the stars are sharp-pointed, and there's quiet. Why, you rise up and up! Every pointed star gets driven into your body. It's like that. Hot and sharp and—lovely."

75    Kneeling there, her hand went out toward his legs in the greasy black trousers. Her hesitant fingers almost touched the cloth. Then her hand dropped to the ground. She crouched low like a fawning dog.

He said, "It's nice, just like you say. Only when you don't have no dinner, it ain't."

She stood up then, very straight, and her face was ashamed. She held the flower pot out to him and placed it gently in his arms. "Here. Put it in your wagon, on the seat, where you can watch it. Maybe I can find something for you to do."

At the back of the house she dug in the can pile and found two old and battered aluminum saucepans. She carried them back and gave them to him. "Here, maybe you can fix these."

His manner changed. He became professional. "Good as new I can fix them." At the back of his wagon he set a little anvil, and out of an oily tool box dug a small machine hammer. Elisa came through the gate to watch him while he pounded out the dents in the kettles. His mouth grew sure and knowing. At a difficult part of the work he sucked his under-lip,

80     "You sleep right in the wagon?" Elisa asked.

"Right in the wagon, ma'am. Rain or shine I'm dry as a cow in there."

"It must be nice," she said. "It must be very nice. I wish women could do such things."

"It ain't the right kind of life for a woman."

Her upper lip raised a little, showing her teeth. "How do you know? How can you tell?" she said.

85     "I don't know, ma'am," he protested. "Of course I don't know. Now here's your kettles done. You don't have to buy no new ones."

"How much?"

"Oh, fifty cents'll do. I keep my prices down and my work good. That's why I have all them satisfied customers up and down the highway."

Elisa brought him a fifty-cent piece from the house and dropped it in his hand. "You might be surprised to have a rival some time. I can sharpen scissors, too. And I can beat the dents out of little pots. I could show you what a woman might do."

He put his hammer back in the oily box and shoved the little anvil out of sight. "It would be a lonely life for a woman, ma'am, and a scarey life, too, with animals creeping under the wagon all night." He climbed over the singletree, steadying himself with a hand on the burro's white rump. He settled himself in the seat, picked up the lines. "Thank you kindly, ma'am," he said. "I'll do like you told me; I'll go back and catch the Salinas road."

90     "Mind," she called, "if you're long in getting there, keep the sand damp."

"Sand, ma'am? . . . Sand? Oh, sure. You mean around the chrysanthemums. Sure I will." He clucked his tongue. The beasts leaned luxuriously into their collars. The mongrel dog took his place between the back wheels. The wagon turned and crawled out the entrance road and back the way it had come, along the river.

Elisa stood in front of her wire fence watching the slow progress of the caravan. Her shoulders were straight, and her head thrown back, her eyes half-closed, so that the scene came vaguely into them. Her lips moved silently, forming the words "Good-bye—good-bye." Then she whispered,

"That's a bright direction. There's a glowing there." The sound of her whisper startled her. She shook herself free and looked about to see whether anyone had been listening. Only the dogs had heard. They lifted their heads toward her from their sleeping in the dust, and then stretched out their chins and settled asleep again. Elisa turned and ran hurriedly into the house.

In the kitchen she reached behind the stove and felt the water tank. It was full of hot water from the noonday cooking. In the bathroom she tore off her soiled clothes and flung them into the corner. And then she scrubbed herself with a little block of pumice, legs and thighs, loins and chest and arms, until her skin was scratched and red. When she had dried herself she stood in front of a mirror in her bedroom and looked at her body. She tightened her stomach and threw out her chest. She turned and looked over her shoulder at her back.

After a while she began to dress, slowly. She put on her newest underclothing and her nicest stockings and the dress which was the symbol of her prettiness. She worked carefully on her hair, penciled her eyebrows and rouged her lips.

95    Before she was finished she heard the little thunder of hoofs and the shouts of Henry and his helper as they drove the red steers into the corral. She heard the gate bang shut and set herself for Henry's arrival.

His step sounded on the porch. He entered the house calling, "Elisa, where are you?"

"In my room, dressing. I'm not ready. There's hot water for your bath. Hurry up. It's getting late."

When she heard him splashing in the tub, Elisa laid his dark suit on the bed, and shirt and socks and tie beside it. She stood his polished shoes on the floor beside the bed. Then she went to the porch and sat primly and stiffly down. She looked toward the river road where the willow-line was still yellow with frosted leaves so that under the high grey fog they seemed a thin band of sunshine. This was the only color in the grey afternoon. She sat unmoving for a long time. Her eyes blinked rarely.

Henry came banging out of the door shoving his tie inside his vest as he came. Elisa stiffened and her face grew tight. Henry stopped short and looked at her. "Why—why, Elisa. You look so nice!"

100    "Nice? You think I look nice? What do you mean by 'nice'?"

Henry blundered on. "I don't know. I mean you look different, strong and happy."

"I am strong? Yes, strong. What do you mean by 'strong'?"

He looked bewildered. "You're playing some kind of a game," he said helplessly. "It's a kind of a play. You look strong enough to break a calf over your knee, happy enough to eat it like a watermelon."

For a second she lost her rigidity. "Henry! Don't talk like that. You didn't know what you said." She grew complete again. "I'm strong," she boasted. "I never knew before how strong."

105    Henry looked down toward the tractor shed, and when he brought his eyes back to her, they were his own again. "I'll get out the car. You can put on your coat while I'm starting."

Elisa went into the house. She heard him drive to the gate and idle down his motor, and then she took a long time to put on her hat. She pulled it here and pressed it there. When Henry turned the motor off she slipped into her coat and went out.

The little roadster bounced along on the dirt road by the river, raising the birds and driving the rabbit into the brush. Two cranes flapped heavily over the willow-line and dropped into the river-bed.

Far ahead on the road Elisa saw a dark speck. She knew.

She tried not to look as they passed it, but her eyes would not obey. She whispered to herself sadly, "He might have thrown them off the road. That wouldn't have been much trouble, not very much. But he kept the pot," she explained. "He had to keep the pot. That's why he couldn't get them off the road."

110    The roadster turned a bend and she saw the caravan ahead. She swung full around toward her husband so she could not see the little covered wagon and the mismatched team as the car passed them.

In a moment it was over. The thing was done. She did not look back.

She said loudly, to be heard above the motor, "It will be good, tonight, a good dinner."

"Now you're changed again," Henry complained. He took one hand from the wheel and patted her knee. "I ought to take you in to dinner oftener. It would be good for both of us. We get so heavy out on the ranch."

"Henry," she asked, "could we have wine at dinner?"

115    "Sure we could. Say! That will be fine."

She was silent for a while; then she said, "Henry, at those prize fights, do the men hurt each other very much?"

"Sometimes a little, not often. Why?"

"Well, I've read how they break noses, and blood runs down their chests. I've read how the fighting gloves get heavy and soggy with blood."

He looked around at her. "What's the matter, Elisa? I didn't know you read things like that." He brought the car to a stop, then turned to the right over the Salinas River bridge.

120    "Do any women ever go to the fights?" she asked.

"Oh, sure, some. What's the matter, Elisa? Do you want to go? I don't think you'd like it, but I'll take you if you really want to go."

She relaxed limply in the seat. "Oh, no. No. I don't want to go. I'm sure I don't." Her face was turned away from him. "It will be enough if we can have wine. It will be plenty." She turned up her coat collar so he could not see that she was crying weakly—like an old woman.

## ✱ TOPICS FOR CRITICAL THINKING AND WRITING

1. In the first paragraph of the story, the valley, shut off by fog, is said to be "a closed pot." Is this setting significant? Would any other setting do equally well? Why, or why not?
2. What does Elisa's clothing tell us about her? By the way, do you believe that all clothing says something about the wearers? Please explain.
3. Should we make anything special out of Elisa's interest in gardening? If so, what?
4. Describe Elisa's and Henry's marriage.
5. Evaluate the view that Elisa is responsible for her troubles.

# EUDORA WELTY

*Eudora Welty (1909-2001) was born in Jackson, Mississippi. Although she earned a bachelor's degree at the University of Wisconsin, and she spent a year studying advertising in New York City at the Columbia University Graduate School of Business, she lived almost all of her life in Jackson.*

*In the preface to her* Collected Stories *she says:*

> *I have been told, both in approval and in accusation, that I seem to love all my characters. What I do in writing of any character is to try to enter into the mind, heart and skin of a human being who is not myself. Whether this happens to be a man or a woman, old or young, with skin black or white, the primary challenge lies in making the jump itself. It is the act of a writer's imagination that I set most high.*

*In addition to writing stories and novels, Welty has written a book about fiction,* The Eye of the Story *(1977), and a memoir,* One Writer's Beginnings *(1984).*

## *A Worn Path*

[1941]

It was December—a bright frozen day in the early morning. Far out in the country there was an old Negro woman with her head tied in a red rag, coming along a path through the pinewoods. Her name was Phoenix Jackson. She was very old and small and she walked slowly in the dark pine shadows, moving a little from side to side in her steps, with the balanced heaviness and lightness of a pendulum in a grandfather clock. She carried a thin, small cane made from an umbrella, and with this she kept tapping the frozen earth in front of her. This made a grave and persistent noise in the still air, that seemed meditative like the chirping of a solitary little bird.

She wore a dark striped dress reaching down to her shoe tops, and an equally long apron of bleached sugar sacks, with a full pocket: all neat and tidy, but every time she took a step she might have fallen over her shoe-laces, which dragged from her unlaced shoes. She looked straight ahead. Her eyes were blue with age. Her skin had a pattern all its own of num-berless branching wrinkles and as though a whole little tree stood in the middle of her forehead, but a golden color ran underneath, and the two knobs of her cheeks were illuminated by a yellow burning under the dark. Under the red rag her hair came down on her neck in the frailest of ringlets, still black, and with an odor like copper.

Now and then there was a quivering in the thicket. Old Phoenix said, "Out of my way, all you foxes, owls, beetles, jack rabbits, coons, and wild animals! . . . Keep out from under these feet, little bob-whites. . . . Keep the big wild hogs out of my path. Don't let none of those come running my direction. I got a long way." Under her small black-freckled hand her cane, limber as a buggy whip, would switch at the brush as if to rouse up any hiding things.

On she went. The woods were deep and still. The sun made the pine needles almost too bright to look at, up where the wind rocked. The cones dropped as light as feathers. Down in the hollow was the mourning dove—it was not too late for him.

5    The path ran up a hill. "Seem like there is chains about my feet, time I get this far," she said, in the voice of argument old people keep to use with themselves. "Something always take a hold of me on this hill—pleads I should stay."

After she got to the top she turned and gave a full, severe look behind her where she had come. "Up through pines," she said at length. "Now down through oaks."

Her eyes opened their widest, and she started down gently. But be-fore she got to the bottom of the hill a bush caught her dress.

Her fingers were busy and intent, but her skirts were full and long, so that before she could pull them free in one place they were caught in another. It was not possible to allow the dress to tear. "I in the thorny bush," she said. "Thorns, you doing your appointed work. Never want to let folks pass—no sir. Old eyes thought you was a pretty little *green* bush."

Finally, trembling all over, she stood free, and after a moment dared to stoop for her cane.

10    "Sun so high!" she cried, leaning back and looking, while the thick tears went over her eyes. "The time getting all gone here."

At the foot of this hill was a place where a log was laid across the creek.

"Now comes the trial," said Phoenix.

Putting her right foot out, she mounted the log and shut her eyes. Lift-ing her skirt, levelling her cane fiercely before her, like a festival figure in some parade, she began to march across. Then she opened her eyes and she was safe on the other side.

"I wasn't as old as I thought," she said.

15    But she sat down to rest. She spread her skirts on the bank around her and folded her hands over her knees. Up above her was a tree in a pearly cloud of mistletoe. She did not dare to close her eyes, and when a little boy brought her a little plate with a slice of marble-cake on it she spoke to him. "That would be acceptable," she said. But when she went to take it there was just her own hand in the air.

So she left that tree, and had to go through a barbed-wire fence. There she had to creep and crawl, spreading her knees and stretching her fingers like a baby trying to climb the steps. But she talked loudly to herself: she could not let her dress be torn now, so late in the day, and she could not pay for having her arm or leg sawed off if she got caught fast where she was.

At last she was safe through the fence and risen up out in the clearing. Big dead trees, like black men with one arm, were standing in the purple stalks of the withered cotton field. There sat a buzzard.

"Who you watching?"

In the furrow she made her way along.

20    "Glad this not the season for bulls," she said, looking sideways, "and the good Lord made his snakes to curl up and sleep in the winter. A pleasure I don't see no two-headed snake coming around that tree, where it come once. It took a while to get by him, back in the summer."

She passed through the old cotton and went into a field of dead corn. It whispered and shook and was taller than her head. "Through the maze now," she said, for there was no path.

Then there was something tall, black, and skinny there, moving before her.

At first she took it for a man. It could have been a man dancing in the field. But she stood still and listened, and it did not make a sound. It was as silent as a ghost.

"Ghost," she said sharply, "who be you the ghost of? For I have heard of nary death close by."

25    But there was no answer—only the ragged dancing in the wind.

She shut her eyes, reached out her hand, and touched a sleeve. She found a coat and inside that an emptiness, cold as ice.

"You scarecrow," she said. Her face lighted. "I ought to be shut up for good," she said with laughter. "My senses is gone, I too old. I the oldest people I ever know. Dance, old scarecrow," she said, "while I dancing with you."

She kicked her foot over the furrow, and with mouth drawn down, shook her head once or twice in a little strutting way. Some husks blew down and whirled in streamers about her skirts.

Then she went on, parting her way from side to side with the cane, through the whispering field. At last she came to the end, to a wagon track where the silver grass blew between the red ruts. The quail were walking around like pullets, seeming all dainty and unseen.

30    "Walk pretty," she said. "This the easy place. This the easy going."
     She followed the track, swaying through the quiet bare fields, through
the little strings of trees silver in their dead leaves, past cabins silver from
weather, with the doors and windows boarded shut, all like old women
under a spell sitting there. "I walking in their sleep," she said, nodding her
head vigorously.
     In a ravine she went where a spring was silently flowing through a
hollow log. Old Phoenix bent and drank. "Sweet-gum makes the water
sweet," she said, and drank more. "Nobody know who made this well, for
it was here when I was born."
     The track crossed a swampy part where the moss hung as white as
lace from every limb. "Sleep on, alligators, and blow your bubbles." Then
the track went into the road.
     Deep, deep the road went down between the high green-colored
banks. Overhead the live-oaks met, and it was as dark as a cave.
35    A black dog with a lolling tongue came up out of the weeds by the
ditch. She was meditating, and not ready, and when he came at her she
only hit him a little with her cane. Over she went in the ditch, like a little
puff of milk-weed.
     Down there, her senses drifted away. A dream visited her, and she
reached her hand up, but nothing reached down and gave her a pull. So
she lay there and presently went to talking. "Old woman," she said to herself, "that black dog come up out of the weeds to stall you off, and now
there he sitting on his fine tail, smiling at you."
     A white man finally came along and found her—a hunter, a young
man, with his dog on a chain.
     "Well, Granny!" he laughed. "what are you doing there?"
     "Lying on my back like a June-bug waiting to be turned over, mister,"
she said, reaching up her hand.
40    He lifted her up, gave her a swing in the air, and set her down. "Anything broken, Granny?"
     "No sir, them old dead weeds is springy enough," said Phoenix, when
she had got her breath. "I thank you for your trouble."
     "Where do you live, Granny?" he asked, while the two dogs were
growling at each other.
     "Away back yonder, sir, behind the ridge. You can't even see it from
here."
     "On your way home?"
45    "No, sir, I going to town."
     "Why, that's too far! That's as far as I walk when I come out myself,
and I get something for my trouble." He patted the stuffed bag he carried, and there hung down a little closed claw. It was one of the bob-
whites, with its beak hooked bitterly to show it was dead. "Now you go on
home, Granny!"
     "I bound to go to town, mister," said Phoenix. "The time come
around."

He gave another laugh, filling the whole landscape. "I know you old colored people! Wouldn't miss going to town to see Santa Claus!"

But something held Old Phoenix very still. The deep lines in her face went into a fierce and different radiation. Without warning, she had seen with her own eyes a flashing nickel fall out of the man's pocket onto the ground.

50      "How old are you, Granny?" he was saying.

"There is no telling, mister," she said, "no telling."

Then she gave a little cry and clapped her hands and said, "Git on away from here, dog! Look! Look at that dog!" She laughed as if in admiration. "He ain't scared of nobody. He a big black dog." She whispered, "Sic him!"

"Watch me get rid of that cur," said the man. "Sic him, Pete! Sic him!"

Phoenix heard the dogs fighting, and heard the man running and throwing sticks. She even heard a gunshot. But she was slowly bending forward by that time, further and further forward, the lids stretched down over her eyes, as if she were doing this in her sleep. Her chin was lowered almost to her knees. The yellow palm of her hand came out from the fold of her apron. Her fingers slid down and along the ground under the piece of money with the grace and care they would have in lifting an egg from under a sitting hen. Then she slowly straightened up, she stood erect, and the nickel was in her apron pocket. A bird flew by. Her lips moved. "God watching me the whole time. I come to stealing."

55      The man came back, and his own dog panted about them. "Well, I scared him off that time," he said, and then he laughed and lifted his gun and pointed it at Phoenix.

She stood straight and faced him.

"Doesn't the gun scare you?" he said, still pointing it.

"No, sir, I seen plenty go off closer by, in my day, and for less than what I done," she said, holding utterly still.

He smiled, and shouldered the gun. "Well, Granny," he said, "you must be a hundred years old, and scared of nothing. I'd give you a dime if I had any money with me. But you take my advice and stay home, and nothing will happen to you."

60      "I bound to go on my way, mister," said Phoenix. She inclined her head in the red rag. Then they went in different directions, but she could hear the gun shooting again and again over the hill.

She walked on. The shadows hung from the oak trees to the road like curtains. Then she smelled wood-smoke, and smelled the river, and she saw a steeple and the cabins on their steep steps. Dozens of little black children whirled around her. There ahead was Natchez shining. Bells were ringing. She walked on.

In the paved city it was Christmas time. There were red and green electric lights strung and crisscrossed everywhere, and all turned on in the daytime. Old Phoenix would have been lost if she had not distrusted her eyesight and depended on her feet to know where to take her.

She paused quietly on the sidewalk where people were passing by. A lady came along in the crowd, carrying an armful of red-, green-, and silver-wrapped presents; she gave off perfume like the red roses in hot summer, and Phoenix stopped her.

"Please, missy, will you lace up my shoe?" She held up her foot.

65    "What do you want, Grandma?"

"See my shoe," said Phoenix. "Do all right for out in the country, but wouldn't look right to go in a big building."

"Stand still then, Grandma," said the lady. She put her packages down on the sidewalk beside her and laced and tied both shoes tightly.

"Can't lace 'em with a cane," said Phoenix. "Thank you, missy. I doesn't mind asking a nice lady to tie up my shoe, when I gets out on the street."

Moving slowly and from side to side, she went into the big building and into a tower of steps, where she walked up and around and around until her feet knew to stop.

70    She entered a door, and there she saw nailed up on the wall the document that had been stamped with the gold seal and framed in the gold frame, which matched the dream that was hung up in her head.

"Here I be," she said. There was a fixed and ceremonial stiffness over her body.

"A charity case, I suppose," said an attendant who sat at the desk before her.

But Phoenix only looked above her head. There was sweat on her face, the wrinkles in her skin shone like a bright net.

"Speak up, Grandma," the woman said. "What's your name? We must have your history, you know. Have you been here before? What seems to be the trouble with you?"

75    Old Phoenix only gave a twitch to her face as if a fly were bothering her.

"Are you deaf?" cried the attendant.

But then the nurse came in.

"Oh, that's just old Aunt Phoenix," she said. "She doesn't come for herself—she has a little grandson. She makes these trips just as regular as clockwork. She lives away back off the old Natchez Trace." She bent down. "Well, Aunt Phoenix, why don't you just take a seat? We won't keep you standing after your long trip." She pointed.

The old woman sat down, bolt upright in the chair.

80    "Now, how is the boy?" asked the nurse.

Old Phoenix did not speak.

"I said, how is the boy?"

But Phoenix only waited and stared straight ahead, her face very solemn and withdrawn into rigidity.

"Is his throat any better?" asked the nurse. "Aunt Phoenix, don't you hear me? Is your grandson's throat any better since the last time you came for the medicine?"

85    With her hands on her knees, the old woman waited, silent, erect and
motionless, just as if she were in armor.
"You mustn't take up our time this way, Aunt Phoenix," the nurse said.
"Tell us quickly about your grandson, and get it over. He isn't dead, is he?"
At last there came a flicker and then a flame of comprehension across
her face, and she spoke.
"My grandson. It was my memory had left me. There I sat and forgot
why I made my long trip."
"Forgot?" The nurse frowned. "After you came so far?"

90    Then Phoenix was like an old woman begging a dignified forgiveness
for waking up frightened in the night. "I never did go to school, I was too
old at the Surrender," she said in a soft voice. "I'm an old woman without
an education. It was my memory fail me. My little grandson, he is just the
same, and I forgot it in the coming."
"Throat never heals, does it?" said the nurse, speaking in a loud, sure
voice to Old Phoenix. By now she had a card with something written on
it, a little list. "Yes. Swallowed lye. When was it—January—two-three years
ago—"
Phoenix spoke unasked now. "No, missy, he not dead, he just the same.
Every little while his throat begin to close up again, and he not able to swallow. He not get his breath. He not able to help himself. So the time come
around, and I go on another trip for the soothing medicine."
"All right. The doctor said as long as you came to get it, you could
have it," said the nurse. "But it's an obstinate case."
"My little grandson, he sit up there in the house all wrapped up, waiting by himself," Phoenix went on. "We is the only two left in the world. He
suffer and it don't seem to put him back at all. He got a sweet look. He going to last. He wear a little patch quilt and peep out holding his mouth
open like a little bird. I remembers so plain now. I not going to forget him
again, no, the whole enduring time. I could tell him from all the others in
creation."

95    "All right." The nurse was trying to hush her now. She brought her a
bottle of medicine. "Charity," she said, making a check mark in a book.
Old Phoenix held the bottle close to her eyes and then carefully put
it into her pocket.
"I thank you," she said.
"It's Christmas time, Grandma," said the attendant. "Could I give you a
few pennies out of my purse?"
"Five pennies is a nickel," said Phoenix stiffly.

100   "Here's a nickel," said the attendant.
Phoenix rose carefully and held out her hand. She received the nickel
and then fished the other nickel out of her pocket and laid it beside the
new one. She stared at her palm closely, with her head on one side.
Then she gave a tap with her cane on the floor.

"This is what come to me to do," she said. "I going to the store and buy my child a little windmill they sells, made out of paper. He going to find it hard to believe there such a thing in the world. I'll march myself back where he waiting, holding it straight up in his hand."

She lifted her free hand, gave a little nod, turned round, and walked out of the doctor's office. Then her slow step began on the stairs, going down.

## ▓ TOPICS FOR
## CRITICAL THINKING AND WRITING

1. If you do not know the legend of the Phoenix, look it up in a dictionary or, even better, in an encyclopedia. Then carefully reread *A Worn Path*, to learn whether the story in any way connects with the legend.

2. What do you think of the hunter?

3. What would be lost if the episode (with all of its dialogue) of Phoenix falling into the ditch and being helped out of it by the hunter were omitted?

4. Is Christmas a particularly appropriate time in which to set the story? Why or why not?

5. What do you make of the title?

6. "A Worn Path" treats race relations as one of its themes. Is this theme primary, or would you say instead that it is secondary? How would the story be different in its effect if everything stayed the same except for Phoenix's race?

7. Have you ever made a difficult trip by foot? Was there a point when you were tempted to turn back? What kept you going? Do you think that your experience could be made the basis for a short story? How would you structure such a story—its beginning, middle, and end?

# 7

# In Brief: Writing Arguments about Fiction

The following questions will help to stimulate ideas about stories. Not every question is, of course, relevant to every story, but if after reading a story and thinking about it, you then run your eye over these pages, you will find some questions that will help you to think further about the story—in short, that will help you to get ideas to develop a thesis that can effectively be supported with evidence.

It's best to do your thinking with a pen or pencil in hand. If some of the following questions seem to you to be especially relevant to the story you will be writing about, jot down—freely, without worrying about spelling—your initial responses, interrupting your writing only to glance again at the story when you feel the need to check the evidence you are offering in support of your thesis.

## PLOT

1. Does the plot grow out of the characters, or does it depend on chance or coincidence? Did something at first strike you as irrelevant that later you perceived as relevant? Do some parts continue to strike you as irrelevant?

2. Does surprise play an important role, or does foreshadowing? If surprise is very important, can the story be read a second time with any interest? If so, what gives it this further interest?

3. What conflicts does the story include? Conflicts of one character against another? Of one character against the setting, or against society? Conflicts within a single character?

4. Are certain episodes narrated out of chronological order? If so, were you puzzled? Annoyed? On reflection, does the arrangement of episodes seem effective? Why or why not? Are certain situations repeated? If so, what do you make out of the repetitions?

# CHARACTER

1. Which character chiefly engages your interest? Why?
2. What purposes do minor characters serve? Do you find some who by their similarities and differences help to define each other or help to define the major character? How else is a particular character defined—by his or her words, actions (including thoughts and emotions), dress, setting, narrative point of view? Do certain characters act differently in the same, or in a similar, situation?
3. How does the author reveal character? By explicit authorial (editorial) comment, for instance, or, on the other hand, by revelation through dialogue? Through depicted action? Through the actions of other characters? How are the author's methods especially suited to the whole of the story?
4. Is the behavior plausible—that is, are the characters well motivated?
5. If a character changes, why and how does he or she change? (You may want to jot down each event that influences a change.) Or did you change your attitude toward a character not because the character changes but because you came to know the character better?
6. Are the characters round or flat? Are they complex, or, on the other hand, highly typical (for instance, one-dimensional representatives of a social class or age)? Are you chiefly interested in a character's psychology, or does the character strike you as standing for something, such as honesty or the arrogance of power?
7. How has the author caused you to sympathize with certain characters? How does your response—your sympathy or lack of sympathy—contribute to your judgment of the conflict?

# POINT OF VIEW

1. Who tells the story? How much does the narrator know? Does the narrator strike you as reliable? What effect is gained by using this narrator?
2. How does the point of view help shape the theme? After all, the basic story of "Little Red Riding Hood"—what happens—remains unchanged whether told from the wolf's point of view or the girl's, but

if we hear the story from the wolf's point of view we may feel that the story is about terrifying yet pathetic compulsive behavior; if from the girl's point of view, about terrified innocence and male violence.

3. Does the narrator's language help you to construct a picture of the narrator's character, class, attitude, strengths, and limitations? (Jot down some evidence, such as colloquial or—on the other hand—formal expressions, ironic comments, figures of speech.) How far can you trust the narrator? Why?

# SETTING

1. Do you have a strong sense of the time and place? Is the story very much about, say, New England Puritanism, or race relations in the South in the late nineteenth century, or midwestern urban versus small-town life? If time and place are important, how and at what points in the story has the author conveyed this sense? If you do not strongly feel the setting, do you think the author should have made it more evident?

2. What is the relation of the setting to the plot and the characters? (For instance, do houses or rooms or their furnishings say something about their residents?) Would anything be lost if the descriptions of the setting were deleted from the story or if the setting were changed?

# SYMBOLISM

1. Do certain characters seem to you to stand for something in addition to themselves? Does the setting—whether a house, a farm, a landscape, a town, a period—have an extra dimension?

2. If you do believe that the story has symbolic elements, do you think they are adequately integrated within the story, or do they strike you as being too obviously stuck in?

# STYLE

**Style** may be defined as *how* the writer says what he or she says. It is the writer's manner of expression. The writer's choice of words, of sentence structure, and of sentence length are all aspects of style. Example: "Shut the door," and "Would you mind closing the door, please," differ substantially in style. Another example: Lincoln begins the Gettysburg Address by speaking of "Four score and seven years ago"—that is, by using language that has a biblical overtone. If he had said "Eighty-seven years ago," his style would have been different.

1. How would you characterize the style? Simple? Understated? Figurative?
2. How has the point of view shaped or determined the style?
3. Do you think that the style is consistent? If it isn't—for instance, if there are shifts from simple sentences to highly complex ones—what do you make of the shifts?

# THEME

1. Is the title informative? What does it mean or suggest? Did the meaning change after you read the story? Does the title help you to formulate a theme? If you had written the story, what title would you use?
2. Do certain passages—dialogue or description—seem to you to point especially toward the theme? Do you find certain repetitions of words or pairs of incidents highly suggestive and helpful in directing your thoughts toward stating a theme? Flannery O'Connor, in *Mystery and Manners,* says, "In good fiction, certain of the details will tend to accumulate meaning from the action of the story itself, and when that happens, they become symbolic in the way they work." Does this story work that way?
3. Is the meaning of the story embodied in the whole story, or does it seem stuck in, for example in certain passages of editorializing?
4. Suppose someone asked you to state the point—the theme—of the story. Could you? And if you could, would you say that the theme of a particular story reinforces values you hold, or does it to some degree challenge them? (It is sometimes said that the best writers are subversive, forcing readers to see something that they do not want to see.)

# A STORY, NOTES, AND AN ESSAY

In Chapter 2, we demonstrate the importance of annotating a text and of keeping a journal. The chapter also contains a sample draft, and the revision of the draft, for an essay on a short story, Kate Chopin's "The Story of an Hour." Chapter 3 includes annotations, journal entries, and a sample essay on Hemingway's "Cat in the Rain."

The purpose of the present chapter is both broader and narrower; it is broader in the sense that we have in the preceding pages covered a range of aspects of fiction that will provide topics for writing, but narrower in the sense that we are not here concerned with annotating a text or keeping a journal. We will give only the last stage of a student's preliminary notes and the final version of the essay that grew out of these notes. The student's topic is the personality of the narrator in Poe's story, "The Cask of Amontillado." Other topics might be chosen, such as symbolism in the story, or irony. But before looking at what the student wrote, read the story.

# EDGAR ALLAN POE

*Edgar Allan Poe (1809-1849) was the son of traveling actors. His father abandoned the family almost immediately after Poe was born, and his mother died when he was two. The child was adopted—though never legally—by a prosperous merchant and his wife in Richmond. The tensions were great, aggravated by Poe's drinking and heavy gambling, and in 1827 Poe left Richmond for Boston. He wrote, served briefly in the army, attended West Point but left within a year, and became an editor for the remaining eighteen years of his life. It was during these years, too, that he wrote the poems, essays, and fiction—especially detective stories and horror stories—that have made him famous.*

## The Cask of Amontillado                    [1846]

The thousand injuries of Fortunato I had borne as I best could, but when he ventured upon insult, I vowed revenge. You, who so well know the nature of my soul, will not suppose, however, that I gave utterance to a threat. At *length* I would be avenged; this was a point definitely settled—but the very definitiveness with which it was resolved precluded the idea of risk. I must not only punish, but punish with impunity. A wrong is unredressed when retribution overtakes its redresser. It is equally unredressed when the avenger fails to make himself felt as such to him who has done the wrong.

It must be understood that neither by word nor deed had I given Fortunato cause to doubt my good will. I continued, as was my wont, to smile in his face, and he did not perceive that my smile *now* was at the thought of his immolation.

He had a weak point—this Fortunato—although in other regards he was a man to be respected and even feared. He prided himself on his connoisseurship in wine. Few Italians have the true virtuoso spirit. For the most part their enthusiasm is adopted to suit the time and opportunity to practice imposture upon the British and Austrian *millionaires.* In painting and gemmary Fortunato, like his countrymen, was a quack, but in the matter of old wines he was sincere. In this respect I did not differ from him materially;—I was skillful in the Italian vintages myself, and bought largely whenever I could.

It was about dusk, one evening during the supreme madness of the carnival season, that I encountered my friend. He accosted me with excessive warmth, for he had been drinking much. The man wore motley. He had on a tight-fitting parti-striped dress, and his head was surmounted by the conical cap and bells. I was so pleased to see him, that I thought I should never have done wringing his hand.

5    I said to him—"My dear Fortunato, you are luckily met. How remarkably well you are looking to-day! But I have received a pipe[1] of what passes for Amontillado, and I have my doubts."

"How?" said he, "Amontillado? A pipe? Impossible! And in the middle of the carnival?"

"I have my doubts," I replied; "and I was silly enough to pay the full Amontillado price without consulting you in the matter. You were not to be found, and I was fearful of losing a bargain."

"Amontillado!"

"I have my doubts."

10    "Amontillado!"

"And I must satisfy them."

"Amontillado!"

"As you are engaged, I am on my way to Luchesi. If any one has a critical turn, it is he. He will tell me—"

"Luchesi cannot tell Amontillado from Sherry."

15    "And yet some fools will have it that his taste is a match for your own."

"Come, let us go."

"Whither?"

"To your vaults."

"My friend, no; I will not impose upon your good nature. I perceive you have an engagement. Luchesi—"

20    "I have no engagement; come."

"My friend, no. It is not the engagement, but the severe cold with which I perceive you are afflicted. The vaults are insufferably damp. They are encrusted with nitre."

"Let us go, nevertheless. The cold is merely nothing. Amontillado! You have been imposed upon; and as for Luchesi, he cannot distinguish Sherry from Amontillado."

Thus speaking, Fortunato possessed himself of my arm. Putting on a mask of black silk, and drawing a *roquelaure*[2] closely about my person, I suffered him to hurry me to my palazzo.

---

[1]**pipe** wine cask.   [2]*roquelaure* short cloak.

There were no attendants at home; they had absconded to make merry in honor of the time. I had told them that I should not return until the morning, and had given them explicit orders not to stir from the house. These orders were sufficient, I well knew, to insure their immediate disappearance, one and all, as soon as my back was turned.

25    I took from their sconces two flambeaux, and giving one to Fortunato, bowed him through several suites of rooms to the archway that led into the vaults. I passed down a long and winding staircase, requesting him to be cautious as he followed. We came at length to the foot of the descent, and stood together on the damp ground of the catacombs of the Montresors.

The gait of my friend was unsteady, and the bells upon his cap jingled as he strode.

"The pipe," said he.

"It is farther on," said I; "but observe the white web-work which gleams from these cavern walls."

He turned towards me, and looked into my eyes with two filmy orbs that distilled the rheum of intoxication.

30    "Nitre?" he asked, at length.

"Nitre," I replied. "How long have you had that cough?"

"Ugh! ugh! ugh!—ugh! ugh! ugh!—ugh! ugh! ugh!—ugh! ugh! ugh!—ugh! ugh! ugh!"

My poor friend found it impossible to reply for many minutes.

"It is nothing," he said, at last.

35    "Come," I said, with decision, "we will go back; your health is precious. You are rich, respected, admired, beloved; you are happy, as once I was. You are a man to be missed. For me it is no matter. We will go back; you will be ill, and I cannot be responsible. Besides, there is Luchesi—"

"Enough," he said; "the cough is a mere nothing: it will not kill me. I shall not die of a cough."

"True—true," I replied; "and, indeed, I had no intention of alarming you unnecessarily—but you should use all proper caution. A draught of this Medoc will defend us from the damps."

Here I knocked off the neck of a bottle which I drew from a long row of its fellows that lay upon the mould.

"Drink," I said, presenting him the wine.

40    He raised it to his lips with a leer. He paused and nodded to me familiarly, while his bells jingled.

"I drink," he said, "to the buried that repose around us."

"And I to your long life."

He again took my arm, and we proceeded.

"These vaults," he said, "are extensive."

45    "The Montresors," I replied, "were a great and numerous family."

"I forget your arms."

"A huge human foot d'or, in a field azure; the foot crushes a serpent rampant whose fangs are imbedded in the heel."

"And the motto?"

*"Nemo me impune lacessit."*[3]

50    "Good!" he said.

The wine sparkled in his eyes and the bells jingled. My own fancy grew warm with the Medoc. We had passed through walls of piled bones, with casks and puncheons intermingling, into the inmost recesses of the catacombs. I paused again, and this time I made bold to seize Fortunato by an arm above the elbow.

"The nitre!" I said; "see, it increases. It hangs like moss upon the vaults. We are below the river's bed. The drops of moisture trickle among the bones. Come, we will go back ere it is too late. Your cough—"

"It is nothing," he said; "let us go on. But first, another draught of the Medoc."

I broke and reached him a flagon of De Grâve. He emptied it at a breath. His eyes flashed with a fierce light. He laughed and threw the bottle upwards with a gesticulation I did not understand.

55    I looked at him in surprise. He repeated the movement—a grotesque one.

"You do not comprehend?" he said.

"Not I," I replied.

"Then you are not of the brotherhood."

"How?"

60    "You are not of the masons."

"Yes, yes," I said, "yes, yes."

"You? Impossible! A mason?"

"A mason," I replied.

"A sign," he said.

65    "It is this," I answered, producing a trowel from beneath the folds of my *roquelaure.*

"You jest," he exclaimed, recoiling a few paces. "But let us proceed to the Amontillado."

"Be it so," I said, replacing the tool beneath the cloak, and again offering him my arm. He leaned upon it heavily. We continued our route in search of the Amontillado. We passed through a range of low arches, descended, passed on, and descending again, arrived at a deep crypt, in which the foulness of the air caused our flambeaux rather to glow than flame.

At the most remote end of the crypt there appeared another less spacious. Its walls had been lined with human remains piled to the vault overhead, in the fashion of the great catacombs of Paris. Three sides of this interior crypt were still ornamented in this manner. From the fourth the bones had been thrown down, and lay promiscuously upon the earth, forming at one point a mound of some size. Within the wall thus exposed by the dis-

---

[3] ***Nemo me impune lacessit.*** No one dare attack me with impunity (the motto of Scotland).

placing of the bones, we perceived a still interior recess, in depth about four feet, in width three, in height six or seven. It seemed to have been constructed for no especial use within itself, but formed merely the interval between two of the colossal supports of the roof of the catacombs, and was backed by one of their circumscribing walls of solid granite.

It was in vain that Fortunato, uplifting his dull torch, endeavored to pry into the depths of the recess. Its termination the feeble light did not enable us to see.

70 "Proceed," I said; "herein is the Amontillado. As for Luchesi—"

"He is an ignoramus," interrupted my friend, as he stepped unsteadily forward, while I followed immediately at his heels. In an instant he had reached the extremity of the niche, and finding his progress arrested by the rock, stood stupidly bewildered. A moment more and I had fettered him to the granite. In its surface were two iron staples, distant from each other about two feet, horizontally. From one of these depended a short chain, from the other a padlock. Throwing the links about his waist, it was but the work of a few seconds to secure it. He was too much astounded to resist. Withdrawing the key I stepped back from the recess.

"Pass your hand," I said, "over the wall; you cannot help feeling the nitre. Indeed it is *very* damp. Once more let me *implore* you to return. No? Then I must positively leave you. But I must first render you all the little attentions in my power."

"The Amontillado!" ejaculated my friend, not yet recovered from his astonishment.

"True," I replied; "the Amontillado."

75 As I said these words I busied myself among the pile of bones of which I have before spoken. Throwing them aside, I soon uncovered a quantity of building-stone and mortar. With these materials and with the aid of my trowel, I began vigorously to wall up the entrance of the niche.

I had scarcely laid the first tier of masonry when I discovered that the intoxication of Fortunato had in a great measure worn off. The earliest indication I had of this was a low moaning cry from the depth of the recess. It was *not* the cry of a drunken man. There was then a long and obstinate silence. I laid the second tier, and the third, and the fourth; and then I heard the furious vibrations of the chain. The noise lasted for several minutes, during which, that I might hearken to it with the more satisfaction, I ceased my labors and sat down upon the bones. When at last the clanking subsided, I resumed the trowel, and finished without interruption the fifth, the sixth, and the seventh tier. The wall was now nearly upon a level with my breast. I again paused, and holding the flambeaux over the masonwork, threw a few feeble rays upon the figure within.

A succession of loud and shrill screams, bursting suddenly from the throat of the chained form, seemed to thrust me violently back. For a brief moment I hesitated—I trembled. Unsheathing my rapier, I began to grope with it about the recess; but the thought of an instant reassured me. I placed my hand upon the solid fabric of the catacombs, and felt satisfied. I reapproached the wall. I replied to the yells of him who clamored. I re-echoed—I aided—I surpassed them in volume and in strength. I did this, and the clamorer grew still.

It was now midnight, and my task was drawing to a close. I had completed the eighth, the ninth, and the tenth tier. I had finished a portion of the last and the eleventh; there remained but a single stone to be fitted and plastered in. I struggled with its weight; I placed it partially in its destined position. But now there came from out the niche a low laugh that erected the hairs upon my head. It was succeeded by a sad voice, which I had difficulty in recognizing as that of the noble Fortunato. The voice said—

"Ha! ha! ha!—he! he! he!—a very good joke indeed—an excellent jest. We will have many a rich laugh about it at the palazzo—he! he! he!—over our wine—he! he! he!"

80     "The Amontillado!" I said.

"He! he! he!—he! he! he!—yes, the Amontillado. But is it not getting late? Will not they be awaiting us at the palazzo, the Lady Fortunato and the rest? Let us be gone."

"Yes," I said, "let us be gone."

*"For the love of God, Montresor!"*

"Yes," I said, "for the love of God!"

85     But to these words I hearkened in vain for a reply. I grew impatient. I called aloud:

"Fortunato!"

No answer. I called again;

"Fortunato!"

No answer still. I thrust a torch through the remaining aperture and let it fall within. There came forth in return only a jingling of the bells. My heart grew sick—on account of the dampness of the catacombs. I hastened to make an end of my labor. I forced the last stone into its position; I plastered it up. Against the new masonry I reerected the old rampart of bones. For the half of a century no mortal has disturbed them. *In pace requiescat!*[4]

---

[4]*In pace requiescat!* May he rest in place!

# A STUDENT'S WRITTEN RESPONSE TO A STORY

# Notes

If your instructor assigns a topic in advance—such as "Irony in 'The Cask of Amontillado'" or "Is Montresor Insane?"—even on your first reading of the story you will be thinking in a specific direction, looking for relevant evidence. But if a topic is not assigned, it will be up to you to find something that you think is worth talking about to your classmates. (All writers must imagine a fairly specific audience, such as the readers of *Ms.*, or the readers of *Playboy*—these audiences are quite different—or the readers of the high school newspaper, or the readers of a highly technical professional journal, and so on. It's a good idea to imagine your classmates as your audience.)

You may want to begin by asking yourself (and responding in your journal) what you like or dislike in the story; or you may want to think about some of the questions mentioned, at the beginning of this chapter, on plot, character, point of view, setting, symbolism, style, and theme. Or you may have annotated some passage that puzzled you, and, on rereading, you may feel that *this* passage is what you want to talk about. In any case, after several readings of the story you will settle not only on a *topic* (for instance, symbolism) but also on a *thesis,* an argument, a point (for instance, the symbolism is for the most part effective but in two places is annoyingly obscure).

It happens that the student whose essay we reprint decided to write about the narrator. The following notes are not her earliest jottings but are the jottings she recorded after she had tentatively chosen her topic.

```
Two characters: narrator (Montresor) and his
    enemy, Fortunato
1st person narrator, so we know Fort. only
    through what M. tells us

Fortunato
    has wronged Montresor ("thousand injuries";
        but is M. telling the truth?)
    drinks a lot ("he had been drinking much")
    vain (Fort. insists he knows much more than
        Luchesi)
    courteous (in the vaults, drinks to M's buried
        relatives)
    foolish (?? hard to be sure about this)

Montresor
    first parag. tells us he seeks vengeance ("I
        vowed revenge") for "the thousand injuries"
        he suffered from Fort. ("I would be
        avenged")
```

of high birth
1) he comes from a family with a motto: Nemo me
   impune lacessit (no one dare attack me with
   impunity)
2) has coat of arms (human foot crushing
   serpent whose fangs are in heel). But what's
   the connection? Is the idea that he and his
   noble family are like the foot crushing a
   serpent that has bitten them, or on the
   other hand is the idea that he and family
   are like the serpent--if stepped on
   (attacked, insulted), they will fight back?
   Maybe we are supposed to think that he
   thinks he is like the human foot, but we
   see that he is like the serpent.

highly educated? At least he uses hard words
   ("unredressed," "the thought of his immolation"). (Check "immolation")   *Dictionary says it is a
                                   sacrifice, a ritual killing*
cunning: knows how to work on Fortunato
   (implies that Luchesi is more highly regarded
   than F)

rich: lives in a "palazzo," and has servants
crazy:
1) murders for vengeance
2) enjoys hearing the sound of Fort. shaking
   chains ("that I might hearken to it with the
   more satisfaction, I ceased my labors")
3) when he hears the screams of F., he screams
   ("I surpassed them in volume and in
   strength")

   Can we possibly sympathize with him? Can
he possibly be acting fairly? Do we judge him?
Do we judge (condemn) ourselves for liking
the story? Why do I find the story interesting

instead of repulsive? Because (thesis here) his
motive is good, he thinks he is upholding family
honor (in his eyes the killing is a family duty,
a sacrifice; "immolation")

# A Sample Response Essay

Here is the final version of the essay that grew out of the notes.

---

Geraghty 1

Ann Geraghty

Professor Duff

English 102

1 December 2005

Revenge, Noble and Ignoble

Because Poe's "The Cask of Amontillado"
is told by a first person narrator, a man
named Montresor, we cannot be sure that
what the narrator tells us is true. There
are some things in the story, however,
that we can scarcely believe. For instance,
we can accept the fact that there is a
character (even though we never see him)
named Luchesi, because the narrator
mentions him and the other character in the
story--Fortunato--also talks about him. But
how sure can we be that Fortunato is the
sort of man that the narrator says
Fortunato is?

In the first paragraph, Montresor says
that Fortunato has done him a "thousand

injuries" (168). He is never specific about these, and Fortunato never says anything that we can interpret as evidence that he has injured Montresor. Further, Fortunato is courteous when he meets Montresor, which seems to suggest that he is not aware that he has injured Montresor. It seems fair to conclude, then, that Fortunato has not really injured Montresor, and that Montresor has insanely imagined that Fortunato has injured him.

What evidence is there that Montresor is insane? First, we should notice the intensity with which Montresor speaks, especially in the first paragraph. He tells us that he "vowed revenge" (168) and that he "would be avenged" (168) and that he would "punish with impunity" (168). He also tells us, all in the first paragraph, that he himself must not get punished for his act of vengeance ("A wrong is unredressed when retribution overtakes its redresser"), and, second, that "It is equally unredressed when the avenger fails to make himself felt as such to him who has done the wrong." There is a common saying, "Don't get mad, get even," but Montresor is going way beyond getting even, and anyway it's not certain that he was injured in the first place. He _is_ getting "mad," not in the sense of "angry" but in the sense of "crazy."

Geraghty 3

If we agree that Montresor is insane, we
can ask ourselves two questions about this
story. First, is "The Cask of Amontillado"
just a story about a mysterious madman, a
story that begins and ends with a madman
and does not even try to explain his
madness? Second, why have people read this
story for almost a hundred and fifty years?
If we can answer the first question
negatively, we may be able to answer the
second.

I think that Montresor is insane, but
his insanity is understandable, and it is
even based on a concept of honor. He comes
from a noble family, a family with a coat
of arms (a foot is crushing a serpent that
is biting the heel) and a motto (Nemo me
impune lacessit, which means "No one dare
attack me with impunity"). Fortunato may
not have really injured him, but for some
reason Montresor thinks he has been
injured. As a nobleman who must uphold the
honor of his family, Montresor acts with a
degree of energy that is understandable for
someone in his high position. That is, he
must live up to his coat of arms, which
shows a gold foot (symbolizing a nobleman)
crushing a serpent. The motto in effect
means that Montresor must take vengeance if
he is to uphold his family honor. In fact,
the unusual word "immolation" (168) in the

Geraghty 4

second paragraph tells us a good deal about
Montresor's action. To "immolate" is to
"sacrifice," to perform a ritual killing.
Since Montresor says his vengeance will be
the "immolation" of Fortunato, we can
assume that Montresor thinks that he has a
duty, imposed by his noble family, to kill
Fortunato. He sees himself as a priest
performing a solemn sacrifice.

Interestingly, however, the reader can
interpret the motto in a different way. The
reader may see Montresor as the serpent,
viciously stinging an enemy, and Fortunato
is an almost innocent victim who has
somehow accidentally offended (stepped on)
Montresor. In reading the story we take
pleasure in hearing, and seeing, a
passionate nobleman performing what he
thinks is a duty imposed on him by his
rank. We also take pleasure in judging him
accurately, that is, in seeing that his
action is not really noble but is serpent-
like, or base. We can thus eat our cake and
have it too; we see a wicked action, a
clever murder (and we enjoy seeing it),
and, on the other hand, we can sit back and
judge it as wicked (we see Montresor as a
serpent) and therefore we can feel that we
are highly moral.

Geraghty 5

Work Cited

Poe, Edgar Allen. "The Cask of Amontillado."
A Little Literature. Ed. Sylvan Barnet,
William Burto, and William E. Cain. New
York: Longman, 2007. 168-173.

## ✸ TOPICS FOR CRITICAL THINKING AND WRITING

In reading this essay, you may wish to ask yourself the following questions (with an eye toward applying them also to your own writing):

1. Is the title appropriate and at least moderately interesting?
2. Does the essay have a thesis? If so, what is it?
3. Is the thesis (if there is one) adequately supported by evidence?
4. Is the organization satisfactory? Does one paragraph lead easily into the next, and is the argument presented in reasonable sequence?

# 8

# A Fiction Writer in Depth: Flannery O'Connor

We read stories by authors we are unfamiliar with, just as we try new foods or play new games or listen to the music of new groups, because we want to extend our experience. But we also sometimes stay with the familiar, for pretty much the same reason, oddly. We want, so to speak, to taste more fully, to experience not something utterly unfamiliar but a variation on a favorite theme. Having read, say, one story by Poe or by Alice Walker, we want to read another, and another, because we like the sort of thing that this author does, and we find that with each succeeding story we get deeper into an interesting mind talking about experiences that interest us.

## FLANNERY O'CONNOR

*Flannery O'Connor (1925-1964)—her first name was Mary but she did not use it—was born in Savannah, Georgia, but spent most of her life in Milledgeville, Georgia, where her family moved when she was twelve. She was educated in parochial schools and at the local college and then went to the School for Writers at the University of Iowa, where she earned an M.F.A. in 1946. For a few months she lived at a writers' colony in Saratoga Springs, New York, and then for a few weeks she lived in New York City, but most of her life was spent back in Milledgeville, where she tended her peacocks and wrote stories, novels, essays (posthumously published as* Mystery and Manners *[1970]), and letters (posthumously published under the title* The Habit of Being *[1979]).*

*In 1951, when she was twenty-five, Flannery O'Connor discovered that she was a victim of lupus erythematosus, an incurable autoimmune disease that had crippled and then killed her father ten years before. She died at the age of thirty-nine. O'Connor faced her illness with stoic courage, Christian fortitude—and tough humor. Here is a glimpse, from one of her letters, of how she dealt with those who pitied her:*

> *An old lady got on the elevator behind me and as soon as I turned around she fixed me with a moist gleaming eye and said in a loud voice, "Bless you, darling!" I felt exactly like the Misfit [in "A Good Man Is Hard to Find"] and I gave her a weakly lethal look, whereupon greatly encouraged she grabbed my arm and whispered (very loud) in my ear, "Remember what they said to John at the gate, darling!" It was not my floor but I got off and I suppose the old lady was astounded at how quick I could get away on crutches. I have a one-legged friend and I asked her what they said to John at the gate. She said she reckoned they said, "The lame shall enter first." This may be because the lame will be able to knock everybody else aside with their crutches.*

*A devout Catholic, O'Connor forthrightly summarized the relation between her belief and her writing:*

> *I see from the standpoint of Christian orthodoxy. This means that for me the meaning of life is centered in our Redemption by Christ and what I see in the world I see in its relation to that.*

## A Good Man Is Hard to Find                                    [1953]

The grandmother didn't want to go to Florida. She wanted to visit some of her connections in east Tennessee and she was seizing every chance to change Bailey's mind. Bailey was the son she lived with, her only boy. He was sitting on the edge of his chair at the table, bent over the orange sports section of the *Journal*. "Now look here, Bailey," she said, "see here, read this," and she stood with one hand on her thin hip and the other rattling the newspaper at his bald head. "Here this fellow that calls himself The Misfit is aloose from the Federal Pen and headed toward Florida and you read here what it says he did to these people. Just you read it. I wouldn't take my children in any direction with a criminal like that aloose in it. I couldn't answer to my conscience if I did."

Bailey didn't look up from his reading so she wheeled around then and faced the children's mother, a young woman in slacks. whose face was as broad and innocent as a cabbage and was tied around with a green headkerchief that had two points on the top like rabbit's ears. She was sitting on the sofa, feeding the baby his apricots out of a jar. "The children have been to Florida before," the old lady said. "You all ought to take them somewhere else for a change so they would see different parts of the world and be broad. They never have been to east Tennessee."

The children's mother didn't seem to hear her, but the eight-year-old boy, John Wesley, a stocky child with glasses, said. "If you don't want to go to Florida, why dontcha stay at home?" He and the little girl, June Star, were reading the funny papers on the floor.

"She wouldn't stay at home to be queen for a day," June Star said without raising her yellow head.

5      "Yes, and what would you do if this fellow, The Misfit, caught you?" the grandmother said.

"I'd smack his face," John Wesley said.

"She wouldn't stay at home for a million bucks," June Star said. "Afraid she'd miss something. She has to go everywhere we go."

"All right, Miss," the grandmother said. "Just remember that the next time you want me to curl your hair."

June Star said her hair was naturally curly.

10     The next morning the grandmother was the first one in the car, ready to go. She had her big black valise that looked like the head of a hippopotamus in one corner, and underneath it she was hiding a basket with Pitty Sing, the cat, in it. She didn't intend for the cat to be left alone in the house for three days because he would miss her too much and she was afraid he might brush against one of the gas burners and accidentally asphyxiate himself. Her son, Bailey, didn't like to arrive at a motel with a cat.

She sat in the middle of the back seat with John Wesley and June Star on either side of her. Bailey and the children's mother and the baby sat in front and they left Atlanta at eight forty-five with the mileage on the car at 55890. The grandmother wrote this down because she thought it would be interesting to say how many miles they had been when they got back. It took them twenty minutes to reach the outskirts of the city.

The old lady settled herself comfortably, removing her white cotton gloves and putting them up with her purse on the shelf in front of the back window. The children's mother still had on slacks and still had her head tied up in a green kerchief, but the grandmother had on a navy blue straw sailor hat with a bunch of white violets on the brim and a navy blue dress with a small white dot in the print. Her collars and cuffs were white organdy trimmed with lace and at her neckline she had pinned a purple spray of cloth violets containing a sachet. In case of an accident, anyone seeing her dead on the highway would know at once that she was a lady.

She said she thought it was going to be a good day for driving, neither too hot nor too cold, and she cautioned Bailey that the speed limit was fifty-five miles an hour and that the patrolmen hid themselves behind billboards and small clumps of trees and sped out after you before you had a chance to slow down. She pointed out interesting details of the scenery: Stone Mountain; the blue granite that in some places came up to both sides of the highway; the brilliant red clay banks slightly streaked with purple; and the various crops that made rows of green lace-work on the ground. The trees were full of silver-white sunlight and the meanest of them sparkled. The children were reading comic magazines and their mother had gone back to sleep.

"Let's go through Georgia fast so we won't have to look at it much," John Wesley said.

15      "If I were a little boy," said the grandmother, "I wouldn't talk about my native state that way. Tennessee has the mountains and Georgia has the hills."

"Tennessee is just a hillbilly dumping ground," John Wesley said, "and Georgia is a lousy state too."

2

*the grandmother*

~~Of course she~~ was the first one ready to load up the next morning at six o'clock. She had Baby Brother's bucking bronco ~~that~~ and ~~harnessing~~ what she called her "*git Lee*" and Pitty Sing, the cat, ~~she went~~ packed in the car before Boatwrite had a chance to ~~get anything at meeting come out of the door with the~~ *git the* rest of the luggage out of the hall. They got off at seven-thirty, Boatwrite and ~~baby~~ the children's mother in the front and Granny, John Wesley, Baby Brother, Little Sister Mary Ann, Pitty Sing, and the bucking bronco in the back.

"Why the hell did you bring that goddam rocking horse?" Boatwrite asked because as soon as ~~the car began to move~~ *they were out of the city and on the smooth highway*, Baby Brother began to squall to get on the bucking bronco. "He can't get on that thing in this car and that's final," his father who was a stern man said.

"Can we open the lunch now?" Little Sister ~~Mary Ann~~ asked. "It'll shut Baby Brother up. Mamma, can we open up the lunch?"

"No," their grandmother said. *It's only eight-thirty*

Their mother was ~~still~~ reading SCREEN MOTHERS AND THEIR CHILDREN. "Yeah, sure," she said without looking up. She was all dressed up today. She had on a purple silk dress and a hat and ~~gimcrackinged~~ a choker of pink beads and a new *for real* pocket book, and high heel pumps.

"Let's go through Georgia quick so we won't have to look at it much," John Wesley said. "~~I seen enough of it already.~~"

"You should see Tennessee," his grandmother said. "Now there is a *beautiful* state."

"I like hell," John Wesley said. "That's just a hillbilly dumping ground."

"Ha," his mother said, and nudged Boatwrite. "Didjer hear that?" *she was from Arkansas.*

They ate their lunch and got along fine ~~after that~~ for a while until Pitty Sing who had been asleep jumped into the front of the car and caused Boatwrite to swerve to the right into a ditch. Pitty Sing was a large grey-striped cat with a yellow hind leg and a ~~big~~ soiled white face. Granny thought that she was the only person in the world that he really loved but he had never ~~really~~ *the truth was* looked ~~anything but straight at her~~ *up* farther than her middle and he didn't even like other cats. He jumped snarling into the front seat and Boatwrite's shoulders

Manuscript page from Flannery O'Connor's "A Good Man Is Hard to Find."

"You said it," June Star said.

"In my time," said the grandmother, folding her thin veined fingers, "children were more respectful of their native states and their parents and everything else. People did right then. Oh look at the cute little pickaninny!" she said and pointed to a Negro child standing in the door of a shack. "Wouldn't that make a picture, now?" she asked and they all turned and looked at the little Negro out of the back window. He waved.

"He didn't have any britches on," June Star said.

20    "He probably didn't have any," the grandmother explained. "Little niggers in the country don't have things like we do. If I could paint, I'd paint that picture," she said.

The children exchanged comic books.

The grandmother offered to hold the baby and the children's mother passed him over the front seat to her. She set him on her knee and bounced him and told him about the things they were passing. She rolled her eyes and screwed up her mouth and stuck her leathery thin face into his smooth bland one. Occasionally he gave her a faraway smile. They passed a large cotton field with five or six graves fenced in the middle of it, like a small island. "Look at the graveyard!" the grandmother said, pointing it out. "That was the old family burying ground. That belonged to the plantation."

"Where's the plantation?" John Wesley asked.

"Gone With the Wind," said the grandmother. "Ha. Ha."

25    When the children finished all the comic books they had brought, they opened the lunch and ate it. The grandmother ate a peanut butter sandwich and an olive and would not let the children throw the box and the paper napkins out the window. When there was nothing else to do they played a game by choosing a cloud and making the other two guess what shape it suggested. John Wesley took one the shape of a cow and June Star guessed a cow and John Wesley said, no, an automobile, and June Star said he didn't play fair, and they began to slap each other over the grandmother.

The grandmother said she would tell them a story if they would keep quiet. When she told a story, she rolled her eyes and waved her head and was very dramatic. She said once when she was a maiden lady she had been courted by a Mr. Edgar Atkins Teagarden from Jasper, Georgia. She said he was a very good-looking man and a gentleman and that he brought her a watermelon every Saturday afternoon with his initials cut in it, E.A.T. Well, one Saturday, she said, Mr. Teagarden brought the watermelon and there was nobody at home and he left it on the front porch and returned in his buggy to Jasper, but she never got the watermelon, she said, because a nigger boy ate when he saw the initials, E.A.T.! This story tickled John Wesley's funny bone and he giggled and giggled but June Star didn't think it was any good. She said she wouldn't marry a man that just brought her a watermelon on Saturday. The grandmother said she would have done

well to marry Mr. Teagarden because he was a gentleman and had bought
Coca-Cola stock when it first came out and that he had died only a few
years ago, a very wealthy man.

They stopped at The Tower for barbecued sandwiches. The Tower was
a part-stucco and part-wood filling station and dance hall set in a clearing
outside of Timothy. A fat man named Red Sammy Butts ran it and there
were signs stuck here and there on the building and for miles up and
down the highway saying, TRY RED SAMMY'S FAMOUS BARBECUE. NONE LIKE
FAMOUS RED SAMMY'S! RED SAM! THE FAT BOY WITH THE HAPPY LAUGH. A VETERAN! RED
SAMMY'S YOUR MAN!

Red Sammy was lying on the bare ground outside The Tower with his
head under a truck while a gray monkey about a foot high, chained to a
small chinaberry tree, chattered nearby. The monkey sprang back into the
tree and got on the highest limb as soon as he saw the children jump out
of the car and run toward him.

Inside, The Tower was a long dark room with a counter at one end
and tables at the other and dancing space in the middle. They all sat down
at a broad table next to the nickelodeon and Red Sam's wife, a tall burnt-
brown woman with hair and eyes lighter than her skin, came and took
their order. The children's mother put a dime in the machine and played
"The Tennessee Waltz," and the grandmother said that tune always made
her want to dance. She asked Bailey if he would like to dance but he only
glared at her. He didn't have a naturally sunny disposition like she did and
trips made him nervous. The grandmother's brown eyes were very bright.
She swayed her head from side to side and pretended she was dancing in
her chair. June Star said play something she could tap to so the children's
mother put in another dime and played a fast number and June Star
stepped out onto the dance floor and did her tap routine.

30    "Ain't she cute?" Red Sam's wife said, leaning over the counter. "Would
you like to come be my little girl?"

"No, I certainly wouldn't," June Star said. "I wouldn't live in a broken-
down place like this for a million bucks!" and she ran back to the table.

"Ain't she cute?" the woman repeated, stretching her mouth politely.

"Aren't you ashamed?" hissed the grandmother.

Red Sam came in and told his wife to quit lounging on the counter
and hurry with these people's order. His khaki trousers reached just to his
hip bones and his stomach hung over them like a sack of meal swaying
under his shirt. He came over and sat down at a table nearby and let out a
combination sigh and yodel. "You can't win," he said, "You can't win," and
he wiped his sweating red face off with a gray handkerchief. "These days
you don't know who to trust," he said. "Ain't that the truth?"

35    "People are certainly not nice like they used to be," said the grandmother.

"Two fellers come in here last week," Red Sammy said, "driving a
Chrysler. It was an old beat-up car but it was a good one and these boys

looked all right to me. Said they worked at the mill and you know I let them fellers charge the gas they bought? Now why did I do that?"

"Because you're a good man!" the grandmother said at once.

"Yes'm, I suppose so," Red Sam said as if he were struck with this answer.

His wife brought the orders, carrying the five plates all at once without a tray, two in each hand and one balanced on her arm. "It isn't a soul in this green world of God's that you can trust," she said. "And I don't count nobody out of that, not nobody," she repeated, looking at Red Sammy.

40      "Did you read about that criminal, The Misfit, that's escaped?" asked the grandmother.

"I wouldn't be a bit surprised if he didn't attack this place right here," said the woman. "If he hears about it being here, I wouldn't be none surprised to see him. If he hears it's two cent in the cash register, I wouldn't be a tall surprised if he . . ."

"That'll do," Red Sam said. "Go bring these people their Co'Colas," and the woman went off to get the rest of the order.

"A good man is hard to find," Red Sammy said. "Everything is getting terrible. I remember the day you could go off and leave your screen door unlatched. Not no more."

He and the grandmother discussed better times. The old lady said that in her opinion Europe was entirely to blame for the way things were now. She said the way Europe acted you would think we were made of money and Red Sam said it was no use talking about it, she was exactly right. The children ran outside into the white sunlight and looked at the monkey in the lacy chinaberry tree. He was busy catching fleas on himself and biting each one carefully between his teeth as if it were a delicacy.

45      They drove off again into the hot afternoon. The grandmother took cat naps and woke up every five minutes with her own snoring. Outside of Toombsboro she woke up and recalled an old plantation that she had visited in this neighborhood once when she was a young lady. She said the house had six white columns across the front and that there was an avenue of oaks leading up to it and two little wooden trellis arbors on either side in front where you sat down with your suitor after a stroll in the garden. She recalled exactly which road to turn off to get to it. She knew that Bailey would not be willing to lose any time looking at an old house, but the more she talked about it, the more she wanted to see it once again and find out if the little twin arbors were still standing. "There was a secret panel in this house," she said craftily, not telling the truth but wishing that she were, "and the story went that all the family silver was hidden in it when Sherman came through but it was never found . . ."

"Hey!" John Wesley said. "Let's go see it! We'll find it! We'll poke all the woodwork and find it! Who lives there? Where do you turn off at? Hey, Pop, can't we turn off there?"

"We never have seen a house with a secret panel!" June Star shrieked. "Let's go to the house with the secret panel! Hey, Pop, can't we go see the house with the secret panel!"

"It's not far from here, I know," the grandmother said. "It wouldn't take over twenty minutes."

Bailey was looking straight ahead. His jaw was as rigid as a horseshoe. "No," he said.

50    The children began to yell and scream that they wanted to see the house with the secret panel. John Wesley kicked the back of the front seat and June Star hung over her mother's shoulder and whined desperately into her ear that they never had any fun even on their vacation, that they could never do what THEY wanted to do. The baby began to scream and John Wesley kicked the back of the seat so hard that his father could feel the blows in his kidney.

"All right!" he shouted and drew the car to a stop at the side of the road. "Will you all shut up? Will you all just shut up for one second? If you don't shut up, we won't go anywhere."

"It would be very educational for them," the grandmother murmured.

"All right," Bailey said, "but get this. This is the only time we're going to stop for anything like this. This is the one and only time."

"The dirt road that you have to turn down is about a mile back," the grandmother directed. "I marked it when we passed."

55    "A dirt road," Bailey groaned.

After they had turned around and were headed toward the dirt road, the grandmother recalled other points about the house, the beautiful glass over the front doorway and the candle lamp in the hall. John Wesley said that the secret panel was probably in the fireplace.

"You can't go inside this house," Bailey said. "You don't know who lives there."

"While you all talk to the people in front, I'll run around behind and get in a window," John Wesley suggested.

"We'll all stay in the car," his mother said.

60    They turned onto the dirt road and the car raced roughly along in a swirl of pink dust. The grandmother recalled the times when there were no paved roads and thirty miles was a day's journey. The dirt road was hilly and there were sudden washes in it and sharp curves on dangerous embankments. All at once they would be on a hill, looking down over the blue tops of trees for miles around, then the next minute, they would be in a red depression with the dust-coated trees looking down on them.

"This place had better turn up in a minute," Bailey said, "or I'm going to turn around."

The road looked as if no one had traveled on it in months.

"It's not much farther," the grandmother said and just as she said it, a horrible thought came to her. The thought was so embarrassing that she turned red in the face and her eyes dilated and her feet jumped up, upsetting her valise in the corner. The instant the valise moved, the newspaper top she had over the basket under it rose with a snarl and Pitty Sing, the cat, sprang onto Bailey's shoulder.

The children were thrown to the floor and their mother, clutching the baby, was thrown out the door onto the ground; the old lady was thrown into the front seat. The car turned over once and landed right-side-up in a gulch on the side of the road. Bailey remained in the driver's seat with the cat—gray-striped with a broad white face and an orange nose—clinging to his neck like a caterpillar.

65    As soon as the children saw they could move their arms and legs, they scrambled out of the car, shouting, "We've had an ACCIDENT!" The grandmother was curled up under the dashboard, hoping she was injured so that Bailey's wrath would not come down on her all at once. The horrible thought she had had before the accident was that the house she had remembered so vividly was not in Georgia but in Tennessee.

Bailey removed the cat from his neck with both hands and flung it out the window against the side of a pine tree. Then he got out of the car and started looking for the children's mother. She was sitting against the side of the red gutted ditch, holding the screaming baby, but she only had a cut down her face and a broken shoulder. "We've had an ACCIDENT!" the children screamed in a frenzy of delight.

"But nobody's killed," June Star said with disappointment as the grandmother limped out of the car, her hat still pinned to her head but the broken front brim standing up at a jaunty angle and the violet spray hanging off the side. They all sat down in the ditch, except the children, to recover from the shock. They were all shaking.

"Maybe a car will come along," said the children's mother hoarsely.

"I believe I have injured an organ," said the grandmother, pressing her side, but no one answered her. Bailey's teeth were clattering. He had on a yellow sport shirt with bright blue parrots designed in it and his face was as yellow as the shirt. The grandmother decided that she would not mention that the house was in Tennessee.

70    The road was about ten feet above and they could see only the tops of the trees on the other side of it. Behind the ditch they were sitting in there were more woods, tall and dark and deep. In a few minutes they saw a car some distance away on top of a hill, coming slowly as if the occupants were watching them. The grandmother stood up and waved both arms dramatically to attract their attention. The car continued to come on slowly, disappeared around a bend and appeared again, moving even slower on top of the hill they had gone over. It was a big black battered hearselike automobile. There were three men in it.

It came to a stop just over them and for some minutes, the driver looked down with a steady expressionless gaze to where they were sitting, and didn't speak. Then he turned his head and muttered something to the other two and they got out. One was a fat boy in black trousers and a red sweat shirt with a silver stallion embossed on the front of it. He moved around on the right side of them and stood staring, his mouth partly open in a kind of loose grin. The other had on khaki pants and a blue striped coat and a gray hat pulled down very low, hiding most of his face. He came around slowly on the left side. Neither spoke.

The driver got out of the car and stood by the side of it, looking down at them. He was an older man than the other two. His hair was just beginning to gray and he wore silver-rimmed spectacles that gave him a scholarly look. He had a long creased face and didn't have on any shirt or undershirt. He had on blue jeans that were too tight for him and was holding a black hat and a gun. The two boys also had guns.

"We've had an ACCIDENT!" the children screamed.

The grandmother had the peculiar feeling that the bespectacled man was someone she knew. His face was as familiar to her as if she had known him all her life but she could not recall who he was. He moved away from the car and began to come down the embankment, placing his feet carefully so that he wouldn't slip. He had on tan and white shoes and no socks, and his ankles were red and thin. "Good afternoon," he said. "I see you all had you a little spill."

75    "We turned over twice!" said the grandmother.

"Oncet," he corrected. "We seen it happen. Try their car and see will it run, Hiram," he said quietly to the boy with the gray hat.

"What you got that gun for?" John Wesley asked. "Whatcha gonna do with that gun?"

"Lady," the man said to the children's mother, "would you mind calling them children to sit down by you? Children make me nervous. I want all you to sit down right together there where you're at."

"What are you telling us what to do for?" June Star asked.

80    Behind them the line of woods gaped like a dark open mouth. "Come here," said their mother.

"Look here now," Bailey began suddenly, "we're in a predicament! We're in . . ."

The grandmother shrieked. She scrambled to her feet and stood staring. "You're The Misfit!" she said. "I recognized you at once!"

"Yes'm," the man said, smiling slightly as if he were pleased in spite of himself to be known, "but it would have been better for all of you, lady, if you hadn't of reckernized me."

Bailey turned his head sharply and said something to his mother that shocked even the children. The old lady began to cry and The Misfit reddened.

85    "Lady," he said, "don't get upset. Sometimes a man says things he don't mean. I don't reckon he meant to talk to you thataway."

"You wouldn't shoot a lady, would you?" the grandmother said and removed a clean handkerchief from her cuff and began to slap at her eyes with it.

The Misfit pointed the toe of his shoe into the ground and made a little hole and then covered it up again. "I would hate to have to," he said.

"Listen," the grandmother almost screamed, "I know you're a good
man. You don't look a bit like you have common blood. I know you must
come from nice people!"

"Yes ma'm," he said, "finest people in the world." When he smiled he
showed a row of strong white teeth. "God never made a finer woman than
my mother and my daddy's heart was pure gold," he said. The boy with the
red sweat shirt had come around behind them and was standing with his
gun at his hip. The Misfit squatted down on the ground. "Watch them children, Bobby Lee," he said. "You know they make me nervous." He looked
at the six of them huddled together in front of him and he seemed to be
embarrassed as if he couldn't think of anything to say. "Ain't a cloud in the
sky," he remarked, looking up at it. "Don't see no sun but don't see no
cloud neither."

90      "Yes, it's a beautiful day," said the grandmother. "Listen," she said, "you
shouldn't call yourself The Misfit because I know you're a good man at
heart. I can just look at you and tell."

"Hush!" Bailey yelled, "Hush! Everybody shut up and let me handle
this!" He was squatting in the position of a runner about to sprint forward
but he didn't move.

"I pre-chate that, lady," The Misfit said and drew a little circle in the
ground with the butt of his gun.

"It'll take a half a hour to fix this here car," Hiram called, looking over
the raised hood of it.

"Well, first you and Bobby Lee get him and that little boy to step over
yonder with you," The Misfit said, pointing to Bailey and John Wesley. "The
boys want to ask you something," he said to Bailey. "Would you mind stepping back in them woods there with them?"

95      "Listen," Bailey began, "we're in a terrible predicament! Nobody realizes what this is," and his voice cracked. His eyes were as blue and intense
as the parrots in his shirt and he remained perfectly still.

The grandmother reached up to adjust her hat brim as if she were going to the woods with him but it came off in her hand. She stood staring
at it and after a second she let it fall on the ground. Hiram pulled Bailey
up by the arm as if he were assisting an old man. John Wesley caught hold
of his father's hand and Bobby Lee followed. They went off toward the
woods and just as they reached the dark edge, Bailey turned and supporting himself against a gray naked pine trunk, he shouted, "I'll be back in a
minute, Mamma, wait on me!"

"Come back this instant!" his mother shrilled but they all disappeared
into the woods.

"Bailey Boy!" the grandmother called in a tragic voice but she found
she was looking at The Misfit squatting on the ground in front of her. "I just
know you're a good man," she said desperately. "You're not a bit common!"

"Nome, I ain't a good man," The Misfit said after a second as if he had considered her statement carefully, "but I ain't the worst in the world either. My daddy said I was a different breed of dog from my brothers and sisters. 'You know,' Daddy said, 'It's some that can live their whole life without asking about it and it's others has to know why it is, and this boy is one of the latters. He's going to be into everything!'" He put on his black hat and looked up suddenly and then away deep into the woods as if he were embarrassed again. "I'm sorry I don't have on a shirt before you ladies," he said, hunching his shoulders slightly. "We buried our clothes that we had on when we escaped and we're just making do until we can get better. We borrowed these from some folks we met," he explained.

100    "That's perfectly all right," the grandmother said. "Maybe Bailey has an extra shirt in his suitcase."

"I'll look and see terrectly," The Misfit said.

"Where are they taking him?" the children's mother screamed.

"Daddy was a card himself," The Misfit said. "You couldn't put anything over on him. He never got in trouble with the Authorities though. Just had the knack of handling them."

"You could be honest too if you'd only try," said the grandmother. "Think how wonderful it would be to settle down and live a comfortable life and not have to think about somebody chasing you all the time."

105    The Misfit kept scratching in the ground with the butt of his gun as if he were thinking about it. "Yes'm, somebody is always after you," he murmured.

The grandmother noticed how thin his shoulder blades were just behind his hat because she was standing up looking down on him. "Do you ever pray?" she asked.

He shook his head. All she saw was the black hat wiggle between his shoulder blades. "Nome," he said.

There was a pistol shot from the woods, followed closely by another. Then silence. The old lady's head jerked around. She could hear the wind move through the tree tops like a long satisfied insuck of breath. "Bailey Boy!" she called.

"I was a gospel singer for a while," The Misfit said. "I been most everything. Been in the arm service, both land and sea, at home and abroad, been twict married, been an undertaker, been with the railroads, plowed Mother Earth, been in a tornado, seen a man burnt alive oncet," and he looked up at the children's mother and the little girl who were sitting close together, their faces white and their eyes glassy; "I even seen a woman flogged," he said.

110    "Pray, pray," the grandmother began, "pray, pray. . . ."

"I never was a bad boy that I remember of," The Misfit said in an almost dreamy voice, "but somewheres along the line I done something wrong and got sent to the penitentiary. I was buried alive," and he looked up and held her attention to him by a steady stare.

"That's when you should have started to pray," she said. "What did you do to get sent up to the penitentiary that first time?"

"Turn to the right, it was a wall," The Misfit said, looking up again at the cloudless sky. "Turn to the left, it was a wall. Look up it was a ceiling, look down it was a floor. I forget what I done, lady. I set there and set there, trying to remember what it was I done and I ain't recalled it to this day. Oncet in a while, I would think it was coming to me, but it never come."

"Maybe they put you in by mistake," the old lady said vaguely.

115     "Nome," he said. "It wasn't no mistake. They had the papers on me."

"You must have stolen something," she said.

The Misfit sneered slightly. "Nobody had nothing I wanted," he said. "It was a head-doctor at the penitentiary said what I had done was kill my daddy but I known that for a lie. My daddy died in nineteen ought nineteen of the epidemic flu and I never had a thing to do with it. He was buried in the Mount Hopewell Baptist churchyard and you can go there and see for yourself."

"If you would pray," the old lady said, "Jesus would help you."

"That's right," The Misfit said.

120     "Well then, why don't you pray?" she asked trembling with delight suddenly.

"I don't want no hep," he said. "I'm doing all right by myself."

Bobby Lee and Hiram came ambling back from the woods. Bobby Lee was dragging a yellow shirt with bright blue parrots in it.

"Throw me that shirt, Bobby Lee," The Misfit said. The shirt came flying at him and landed on his shoulder and he put it on. The grandmother couldn't name what the shirt reminded her of. "No, lady," The Misfit said while he was buttoning it up, "I found out the crime don't matter. You can do one thing or you can do another, kill a man or take a tire off his car, because sooner or later you're going to forget what it was you done and just be punished for it."

The children's mother had begun to make heaving noises as if she couldn't get her breath. "Lady," he asked, "would you and that little girl like to step off yonder with Bobby Lee and Hiram and join your husband?"

125     "Yes, thank you," the mother said faintly. Her left arm dangled helplessly and she was holding the baby, who had gone to sleep, in the other. "Hep that lady up, Hiram," The Misfit said as she struggled to climb out of the ditch, "and Bobby Lee, you hold onto that little girl's hand."

"I don't want to hold hands with him," June Star said. "He reminds me of a pig."

The fat boy blushed and laughed and caught her by the arm and pulled her off into the woods after Hiram and her mother.

Alone with The Misfit, the grandmother found that she had lost her voice. There was not a cloud in the sky nor any sun. There was nothing around her but woods. She wanted to tell him that he must pray. She opened and closed her mouth several times before anything came out.

Finally she found herself saying, "Jesus, Jesus," meaning, Jesus will help you, but the way she was saying it, it sounded as if she might be cursing.

"Yes'm," The Misfit said as if he agreed. "Jesus thown everything off balance. It was the same case with Him as with me except He hadn't committed any crime and they could prove I had committed one because they had the papers on me. Of course," he said, "they never shown me my papers. That's why I sign myself now. I said long ago, you get you a signature and sign everything you do and keep a copy of it. Then you'll know what you done and you can hold up the crime to the punishment and see do they match and in the end you'll have something to prove you ain't been treated right. I call myself The Misfit," he said, "because I can't make what all I done wrong fit what all I gone through in punishment."

130    There was a piercing scream from the woods, followed closely by a pistol report. "Does it seem right to you, lady, that one is punished a heap and another ain't punished at all?"

"Jesus!" the old lady cried. "You've got good blood! I know you wouldn't shoot a lady! I know you come from nice people! Pray! Jesus, you ought not to shoot a lady. I'll give you all the money I've got!"

"Lady," The Misfit said, looking beyond her far into the woods, "there never was a body that give the undertaker a tip."

There were two more pistol reports and the grandmother raised her head like a parched old turkey hen crying for water and called, "Bailey Boy, Bailey Boy!" as if her heart would break.

"Jesus was the only One that ever raised the dead," The Misfit continued, "and He shouldn't have done it. He thown everything off balance. If He did what He said, then it's nothing for you to do but thow away everything and follow Him, and if He didn't, then it's nothing for you to do but enjoy the few minutes you got left the best way you can—by killing somebody or burning down his house or doing some other meanness to him. No pleasure but meanness," he said and his voice had become almost a snarl.

135    "Maybe He didn't raise the dead," the old lady mumbled, not knowing what she was saying and feeling so dizzy that she sank down in the ditch with her legs twisted under her.

"I wasn't there so I can't say He didn't," The Misfit said. "I wisht I had of been there," he said, hitting the ground with his fist. "It ain't right I wasn't there because if I had of been there I would of known. Listen lady," he said in a high voice, "if I had of been there I would of known and I wouldn't be like I am now." His voice seemed about to crack and the grandmother's head cleared for an instant. She saw the man's face twisted close to her own as if he were going to cry and she murmured, "Why you're one of my babies. You're one of my own children!" She reached out and touched him on the shoulder. The Misfit sprang back as if a snake had bitten him and shot her three times through the chest. Then he put his gun down on the ground and took off his glasses and began to clean them.

Hiram and Bobby Lee returned from the woods and stood over the ditch, looking down at the grandmother who half sat and half lay in a puddle of blood with her legs crossed under her like a child's and her face smiling up at the cloudless sky.

Without his glasses, The Misfit's eyes were red-rimmed and pale and defenseless-looking. "Take her off and thow her where you thown the others," he said, picking up the cat that was rubbing itself against his leg.

"She was a talker, wasn't she?" Bobby Lee said, sliding down the ditch with a yodel.

140     "She would of been a good woman," The Misfit said, "if it had been somebody there to shoot her every minute of her life."

"Some fun!" Bobby Lee said.

"Shut up, Bobby Lee," The Misfit said. "It's no real pleasure in life."

## ▓ TOPICS FOR CRITICAL THINKING AND WRITING

1. Explain the significance of the title.
2. Interpret and evaluate The Misfit's comment on the grandmother: "She would of been a good woman if it had been somebody there to shoot her every minute of her life."
3. O'Connor reported that once, when she read aloud "A Good Man Is Hard to Find," one of her hearers said that "it was a shame someone with so much talent should look upon life as a horror show." Two questions: What evidence of O'Connor's "talent" do you see in the story, and does the story suggest that O'Connor looked on life as a horror story?
4. What are the values of the members of the family?
5. Flannery O'Connor, a Roman Catholic, wrote, "I see from the standpoint of Christian orthodoxy. This means that for me the meaning of life is centered in our Redemption by Christ and what I see in the world I see in relation to that." In the light of this statement, and drawing on "A Good Man Is Hard to Find," explain what O'Connor saw in the world.

## Revelation                                                            [1964]

The doctor's waiting room, which was very small, was almost full when the Turpins entered and Mrs. Turpin, who was very large, made it look even smaller by her presence. She stood looming at the head of the magazine table set in the center of it, a living demonstration that the room was inadequate and ridiculous. Her little bright black eyes took in all the patients as she sized up the seating situation. There was one vacant chair and a place on a sofa occupied by a blond child in a dirty blue romper who should have been told to move over and make room for the lady. He was five or six, but Mrs. Turpin saw at once that no one was going to tell him to move over. He was slumped down in the seat, his arms idle at his sides and his eyes idle in his head; his nose ran unchecked.

Mrs. Turpin put a firm hand on Claud's shoulder and said in a voice that included anyone who wanted to listen, "Claud, you sit in that chair there," and gave him a push down into the vacant one. Claud was florid and bald and sturdy, somewhat shorter than Mrs. Turpin, but he sat down as if he were accustomed to doing what she told him to.

Mrs. Turpin remained standing. The only man in the room besides Claud was a lean stringy old fellow with a rusty hand spread out on each knee, whose eyes were closed as if he were asleep or dead or pretending to be so as not to get up and offer her his seat. Her gaze settled agreeably on a well-dressed grey-haired lady whose eyes met hers and whose expression said: If that child belonged to me, he would have some manners and move over—there's plenty of room there for you and him too.

Claud looked up with a sigh and made as if to rise.

5    "Sit down," Mrs. Turpin said. "You know you're not supposed to stand on that leg. He has an ulcer on his leg," she explained.

Claud lifted his foot onto the magazine table and rolled his trouser leg up to reveal a purple swelling on a plump marble-white calf.

"My!" the pleasant lady said. "How did you do that?"

"A cow kicked him," Mrs. Turpin said.

"Goodness!" said the lady.

10    Claud rolled his trouser leg down.

"Maybe the little boy would move over," the lady suggested, but the child did not stir.

"Somebody will be leaving in a minute," Mrs. Turpin said. She could not understand why a doctor—with as much money as they made charging five dollars a day to just stick their head in the hospital door and look at you—couldn't afford a decent-sized waiting room. This one was hardly bigger than a garage. The table was cluttered with limp-looking magazines and at one end of it there was a big green glass ash tray full of cigaret butts and cotton wads with little blood spots on them. If she had had anything to do with the running of the place, that would have been emptied every so often. There were no chairs against the wall at the head of the room. It had a rectangular-shaped panel in it that permitted a view of the office where the nurse came and went and the secretary listened to the radio. A plastic fern in a gold pot sat in the opening and trailed its fronds down almost to the floor. The radio was softly playing gospel music.

Just then the inner door opened and a nurse with the highest stack of yellow hair Mrs. Turpin had ever seen put her face in the crack and called for the next patient. The woman sitting beside Claud grasped the two arms of her chair and hoisted herself up; she pulled her dress free from her legs and lumbered through the door where the nurse had disappeared.

Mrs. Turpin eased into the vacant chair, which held her tight as a corset. "I wish I could reduce," she said, and rolled her eyes and gave a comic sigh.

15    "Oh, *you* aren't fat," the stylish lady said.

"Ooooo I am too," Mrs. Turpin said. "Claud he eats all he wants to and never weighs over one hundred and seventy-five pounds, but me I just look at something good to eat and I gain some weight," and her stomach and shoulders shook with laughter. "You can eat all you want to, can't you, Claud?" she asked, turning to him.

Claud only grinned.

"Well, as long as you have such a good disposition," the stylish lady said, "I don't think it makes a bit of difference what size you are. You just can't beat a good disposition."

Next to her was a fat girl of eighteen or nineteen, scowling into a thick blue book which Mrs. Turpin saw was entitled *Human Development.* The girl raised her head and directed her scowl at Mrs. Turpin as if she did not like her looks. She appeared annoyed that anyone should speak while she tried to read. The poor girl's face was blue with acne and Mrs. Turpin thought how pitiful it was to have a face like that at that age. She gave the girl a friendly smile but the girl only scowled the harder. Mrs. Turpin herself was fat but she had always had good skin, and, though she was forty-seven years old, there was not a wrinkle in her face except around her eyes from laughing too much.

20    Next to the ugly girl was the child, still in exactly the same position, and next to him was a thin leathery old woman in a cotton print dress. She and Claud had three sacks of chicken feed in their pump house that was in the same print. She had seen from the first that the child belonged with the old woman. She could tell by the way they sat—kind of vacant and white-trashy, as if they would sit there until Doomsday if nobody called and told them to get up. And at right angles but next to the well-dressed pleasant lady was a lank-faced woman who was certainly the child's mother. She had on a yellow sweat shirt and wine-colored slacks, both gritty-looking, and the rims of her lips were stained with snuff. Her dirty yellow hair was tied behind with a little piece of red paper ribbon. Worse than niggers any day, Mrs. Turpin thought.

The gospel hymn playing was, "When I looked up and He looked down," and Mrs. Turpin, who knew it, supplied the last line mentally, "And wona these days I know I'll we-era crown."

Without appearing to, Mrs. Turpin always noticed people's feet. The well-dressed lady had on red and grey suede shoes to match her dress. Mrs. Turpin had on her good black patent leather pumps. The ugly girl had on Girl Scout shoes and heavy socks. The old woman had on tennis shoes and the white-trashy mother had on what appeared to be bedroom slippers, black straw with gold braid threaded through them—exactly what you would have expected her to have on.

Sometimes at night when she couldn't go to sleep, Mrs. Turpin would occupy herself with the question of who she would have chosen to be if she couldn't have been herself. If Jesus had said to her before he made her, "There's only two places available for you. You can either be a nigger or white-trash," what would she have said? "Please, Jesus, please," she would have said, "just let me wait until there's another place available," and he would have said, "No, you have to go right now and I have only those two places so make up your mind." She would have wiggled and squirmed and begged and pleaded but it would have been no use and finally she would have said, "All right, make me a nigger then—but that don't mean a trashy one." And he would have made her a neat clean respectable Negro-woman, herself but black.

Next to the child's mother was a red-headed youngish woman, reading one of the magazines and working a piece of chewing gum, hell for leather, as Claud would say. Mrs. Turpin could not see the woman's feet. She was not white-trash, just common. Sometimes Mrs. Turpin occupied herself at night naming the classes of people. On the bottom of the heap were most colored people, not the kind she would have been if she had been one, but most of them; then next to them—not above, just away from—were the white-trash; then above them were the homeowners, and above them the home-and-land owners, to which she and Claud belonged. Above she and Claud were people with a lot of money and much bigger houses and much more land. But here the complexity of it would begin to bear in on her, for some of the people with a lot of money were common and ought to be below she and Claud and some of the people who had good blood had lost their money and had to rent and then there were colored people who owned their homes and land as well. There was a colored dentist in town who had two red Lincolns and a swimming pool and a farm with registered white-face cattle on it. Usually by the time she had fallen asleep all the classes of people were moiling and roiling around in her head, and she would dream they were all crammed in together in a box car, being ridden off to be put in a gas oven.

25    "That's a beautiful clock," she said and nodded to her right. It was a big wall clock, the face encased in a brass sunburst.

"Yes, it's very pretty," the stylish lady said agreeably. "And right on the dot too," she added, glancing at her watch.

The ugly girl beside her cast an eye upward at the clock, smirked, then looked directly at Mrs. Turpin and smirked again. Then she returned her eyes to her book. She was obviously the lady's daughter because, although they didn't look anything alike as to disposition, they both had the same shape of face and the same blue eyes. On the lady they sparkled pleasantly but in the girl's seared face they appeared alternately to smolder and to blaze.

What if Jesus had said, "All right, you can be white-trash or a nigger or ugly"!

Mrs. Turpin felt an awful pity for the girl, though she thought it was one thing to be ugly and another to act ugly.

30    The woman with the snuff-stained lips turned around in her chair and looked up at the clock. Then she turned back and appeared to look a little to the side of Mrs. Turpin. There was a cast in one of her eyes. "You want to know wher you can get one of themther clocks?" she asked in a loud voice.

"No, I already have a nice clock," Mrs. Turpin said. Once somebody like her got a leg in the conversation, she would be all over it.

"You can get you one with green stamps," the woman said. "That's most likely wher he got hisn. Save you up enough, you can get you most anything. I got me some joo'ry."

Ought to have got you a wash rag and some soap, Mrs. Turpin thought.

"I get contour sheets with mine," the pleasant lady said.

35    The daughter slammed her book shut. She looked straight in front of her, directly through Mrs. Turpin and on through the yellow curtain and the plate glass window which made the wall behind her. The girl's eyes seemed lit all of a sudden with a peculiar light, an unnatural light like night road signs give. Mrs. Turpin turned her head to see if there was anything going on outside that she should see, but she could not see anything. Figures passing cast only a pale shadow through the curtain. There was no reason the girl should single her out for her ugly looks.

"Miss Finley," the nurse said, cracking the door. The gum chewing woman got up and passed in front of her and Claud and went into the office. She had on red high-heeled shoes.

Directly across the table, the ugly girl's eyes were fixed on Mrs. Turpin as if she had some very special reason for disliking her.

"This is wonderful weather, isn't it?" the girl's mother said.

"It's good weather for cotton if you can get the niggers to pick it," Mrs. Turpin said, "but niggers don't want to pick cotton any more. You can't get the white folks to pick it and now you can't get the niggers—because they got to be right up there with the white folks."

40    "They gonna *try* anyways," the white-trash woman said, leaning forward.

"Do you have one of those cotton-picking machines?" the pleasant lady asked.

"No," Mrs. Turpin said, "they leave half the cotton in the field. We don't have much cotton anyway. If you want to make it farming now, you have to have a little of everything. We got a couple of acres of cotton and a few hogs and chickens and just enough white-face that Claud can look after them himself."

"One thang I don't want," the white-trash woman said, wiping her mouth with the back of her hand. "Hogs. Nasty stinking things, a-gruntin and a-rootin all over the place."

Mrs. Turpin gave her the merest edge of her attention. "Our hogs are not dirty and they don't stink," she said. "They're cleaner than some children I've seen. Their feet never touch the ground. We have a pig-parlor—that's where you raise them on concrete," she explained to the pleasant lady, "and Claud scoots them down with the hose every after-noon and washes off the floor." Cleaner by far than that child right there, she thought. Poor nasty little thing. He had not moved except to put the thumb of his dirty hand into his mouth.

45    The woman turned her face away from Mrs. Turpin. "I know I would-n't scoot down no hog with no hose," she said to the wall.

You wouldn't have no hog to scoot down, Mrs. Turpin said to herself.

"A-gruntin and a-rootin and a-groanin," the woman muttered.

"We got a little of everything," Mrs. Turpin said to the pleasant lady. "It's no use in having more than you can handle yourself with help like it is. We found enough niggers to pick our cotton this year but Claud he has to go after them and take them home again in the evening. They can't walk that half a mile. No they can't. I tell you," she said and laughed mer-rily, "I sure am tired of buttering up niggers, but you got to love em if you want em to work for you. When they come in the morning, I run out and I say, 'Hi yawl this morning?' and when Claud drives them off to the field I just wave to beat the band and they just wave back." And she waved her hand rapidly to illustrate.

"Like you read out of the same book," the lady said, showing she un-derstood perfectly.

50    "Child, yes," Mrs. Turpin said. "And when they come in from the field, I run out with a bucket of icewater. That's the way it's going to be from now on," she said. "You may as well face it."

"One thang I know," the white-trash woman said. "Two thangs I ain't going to do: love no niggers or scoot down no hog with no hose." And she let out a bark of contempt.

The look that Mrs. Turpin and the pleasant lady exchanged indicated they both understood that you had to *have* certain things before you could *know* certain things. But every time Mrs. Turpin exchanged a look with the lady, she was aware that the ugly girl's peculiar eyes were still on her, and she had trouble bringing her attention back to the conversation.

"When you got something," she said, "you got to look after it." And when you ain't got a thing but breath and britches, she added to herself, you can afford to come to town every morning and just sit on the Court House coping and spit.

A grotesque revolving shadow passed across the curtain behind her and was thrown palely on the opposite wall. Then a bicycle clattered down against the outside of the building. The door opened and a colored boy glided in with a tray from the drug store. It had two large red and white paper cups on it with tops on them. He was a tall, very black boy in discolored white pants and a green nylon shirt. He was chewing gum slowly. as if to music. He set the tray down in the office opening next to the fern and stuck his head through to look for the secretary. She was not in there. He rested his arms on the ledge and waited, his narrow bottom stuck out, swaying slowly to the left and right. He raised a hand over his head and scratched the base of his skull.

55 "You see that button there, boy?" Mrs. Turpin said. "You can punch that and she'll come. She's probably in the back somewhere."

"Is that right?" the boy said agreeably, as if he had never seen the button before. He leaned to the right and put his finger on it. "She sometime out," he said and twisted around to face his audience, his elbows behind him on the counter. The nurse appeared and he twisted back again. She handed him a dollar and he rooted in his pocket and made the change and counted it out to her. She gave him fifteen cents for a tip and he went out with the empty tray. The heavy door swung to slowly and closed at length with the sound of suction. For a moment no one spoke.

"They ought to send all them niggers back to Africa," the white-trash woman said. "That's wher they come from in the first place."

"Oh, I couldn't do without my good colored friends," the pleasant lady said.

"There's a heap of things worse than a nigger," Mrs. Turpin agreed. "It's all kinds of them just like it's all kinds of us."

60 "Yes, and it takes all kinds to make the world go round," the lady said in her musical voice.

As she said it, the raw-complexioned girl snapped her teeth together. Her lower lip turned downwards and inside out, revealing the pale pink inside of her mouth. After a second it rolled back up. It was the ugliest face Mrs. Turpin had ever seen anyone make and for a moment she was certain that the girl had made it at her. She was looking at her as if she had known and disliked her all her life—all of Mrs. Turpin's life, it seemed too, not just all the girl's life. Why, girl, I don't even know you, Mrs. Turpin said silently.

She forced her attention back to the discussion. "It wouldn't be practical to send them back to Africa," she said. "They wouldn't want to go. They got it too good here."

"Wouldn't be what they wanted—if I had anything to do with it," the woman said.

"It wouldn't be a way in the world you could get all the niggers back over there," Mrs. Turpin said. "They'd be hiding out and lying down and turning sick on you and wailing and hollering and raring and pitching. It wouldn't be a way in the world to get them over there."

65 "They got over here," the trashy woman said. "Get back like they got over."

"It wasn't so many of them then," Mrs. Turpin explained.

The woman looked at Mrs. Turpin as if here was an idiot indeed but Mrs. Turpin was not bothered by the look, considering where it came from.

"Nooo," she said, "they're going to stay here where they can go to New York and marry white folks and improve their color. That's what they all want to do, every one of them, improve their color."

"You know what comes of that, don't you?" Claud asked.

70 "No, Claud, what?" Mrs. Turpin said.

Claud's eyes twinkled. "White-faced niggers," he said with never a smile.

Everybody in the office laughed except the white-trash and the ugly girl. The girl gripped the book in her lap with white fingers. The trashy woman looked around her from face to face as if she thought they were all idiots. The old woman in the feed sack dress continued to gaze expressionless across the floor at the high-top shoes of the man opposite her, the one who had been pretending to be asleep when the Turpins came in. He was laughing heartily, his hands still spread out on his knees. The child had fallen to the side and was lying now almost face down in the old woman's lap.

While they recovered from their laughter, the nasal chorus on the radio kept the room from silence.

> You go to blank blank
> And I'll go to mine
> But we'll all blank along
> To-geth-ther,
> And all along the blank
> We'll hep each other out
> Smile-ling in any kind of
> Weath-ther!

Mrs. Turpin didn't catch every word but she caught enough to agree with the spirit of the song and it turned her thoughts sober. To help anybody out that needed it was her philosophy of life. She never spared herself when she found somebody in need, whether they were white or black, trash or decent. And of all she had to be thankful for, she was most thankful that this was so. If Jesus had said, "You can be high society and have all the money you want and be thin and svelte-like, but you can't be a good woman with it," she would have had to say, "Well don't make me that then. Make me a good woman and it don't matter what else, how fat or how ugly or how poor!" Her heart rose. He had not made her a nigger or white-trash or ugly! He had made her herself and given her a little of everything. Jesus, thank you! she said. Thank you thank you thank you! Whenever she counted her blessings she felt as buoyant as if she weighed one hundred and twenty-five pounds instead of one hundred and eighty.

75    "What's wrong with your little boy?" the pleasant lady asked the white-trashy woman.

"He has a ulcer," the woman said proudly. "He ain't give me a minute's peace since he was born. Him and her are just alike," she said, nodding at the old woman, who was running her leathery fingers through the child's pale hair. "Look like I can't get nothing down them two but Co'Cola and candy."

That's all you try to get down em, Mrs. Turpin said to herself. Too lazy to light the fire. There was nothing you could tell her about people like them that she didn't know already. And it was not just that they didn't have anything. Because if you gave them everything, in two weeks it would all be broken or filthy or they would have chopped it up for lightwood. She knew all this from her own experience. Help them you must, but help them you couldn't.

All at once the ugly girl turned her lips inside out again. Her eyes were fixed like two drills on Mrs. Turpin. This time there was no mistaking that there was something urgent behind them.

Girl, Mrs. Turpin exclaimed silently, I haven't done a thing to you! The girl might be confusing her with somebody else. There was no need to sit by and let herself be intimidated "You must be in college," she said boldly, looking directly at the girl. "I see you reading a book there."

80    The girl continued to stare and pointedly did not answer.

Her mother blushed at this rudeness. "The lady asked you a question, Mary Grace," she said under her breath.

"I have ears," Mary Grace said.

The poor mother blushed again. "Mary Grace goes to Wellesley College," she explained. She twisted one of the buttons on her dress. "In Massachusetts," she added with a grimace. "And in the summer she just keeps right on studying. Just reads all the time, a real book worm. She's done real well at Wellesley; she's taking English and Math and History and Psychology and Social Studies," she rattled on, "and I think it's too much. I think she ought to get out and have fun."

The girl looked as if she would like to hurl them all through the plate glass window.

85    "Way up north," Mrs. Turpin murmured and thought, well, it hasn't done much for her manners.

"I'd almost rather to have him sick," the white-trash woman said, wrenching the attention back to herself. "He's so mean when he ain't. Look like some children just take natural to meanness. It's some gets bad when they get sick but he was the opposite. Took sick and turned good. He don't give me no trouble now. It's me waitin to see the doctor," she said.

If I was going to send anybody back to Africa, Mrs. Turpin thought, it would be your kind, woman. "Yes, indeed," she said aloud, but looking up at the ceiling, "it's a heap of things worse than a nigger." And dirtier than a hog, she added to herself.

"I think people with bad dispositions are more to be pitied than anyone on earth," the pleasant lady said in a voice that was decidedly thin.

"I thank the Lord he has blessed me with a good one," Mrs. Turpin said. "The day has never dawned that I couldn't find something to laugh at."

90    "Not since she married me anyways," Claud said with a comical straight face.

Everybody laughed except the girl and the white-trash.

Mrs. Turpin's stomach shook. "He's such a caution," she said, "that I can't help but laugh at him."

The girl made a loud ugly noise through her teeth.
Her mother's mouth grew thin and tight. "I think the worst thing in
the world," she said, "is an ungrateful person. To have everything and not
appreciate it. I know a girl," she said, "who has parents who would give her
anything, a little brother who loves her dearly, who is getting a good education, who wears the best clothes, but who can never say a kind word to
anyone, who never smiles, who just criticizes and complains all day long."

95          "Is she too old to paddle?" Claud asked.
The girl's face was almost purple.
"Yes," the lady said. "I'm afraid there's nothing to do but leave her to
her folly. Some day she'll wake up and it'll be too late."
"It never hurt anyone to smile," Mrs. Turpin said. "It just makes you feel
better all over."
"Of course," the lady said sadly, "but there are just some people you
can't tell anything to. They can't take criticism."

100          "If it's one thing I am," Mrs. Turpin said with feeling, "it's grateful.
When I think who all I could have been besides myself and what all I got,
a little of everything, and a good disposition besides, I just feel like shouting, 'Thank you, Jesus, for making everything the way it is!' It could have
been different!" For one thing, somebody else could have got Claud. At the
thought of this, she was flooded with gratitude and a terrible pang of joy
ran through her. "Oh thank you, Jesus, Jesus, thank you!" she cried aloud.

The book struck her directly over her left eye. It struck almost at the
same instant that she realized the girl was about to hurl it. Before she
could utter a sound, the raw face came crashing across the table toward
her, howling. The girl's fingers sank like clamps into the soft flesh of her
neck. She heard the mother cry and Claud shout, "Whoa!" There was an instant when she was certain that she was about to be in an earthquake.

All at once her vision narrowed and she saw everything as if it were
happening in a small room far away, or as if she were looking at it through
the wrong end of a telescope. Claud's face crumpled and fell out of sight.
The nurse ran in, then out, then in again. Then the gangling figure of the
doctor rushed out of the inner door. Magazines flew this way and that as
the table turned over. The girl fell with a thud and Mrs. Turpin's vision suddenly reversed itself and she saw everything large instead of small. The
eyes of the white-trashy woman were staring hugely at the floor. There the
girl, held down on one side by the nurse and on the other by her mother,
was wrenching and turning in their grasp. The doctor was kneeling astride
her, trying to hold her arm down. He managed after a second to sink a
long needle into it.

Mrs. Turpin felt entirely hollow except for her heart which swung
from side to side as if it were agitated in a great empty drum of flesh.

"Somebody that's not busy call for the ambulance," the doctor said in
the off-hand voice young doctors adopt for terrible occasions.

105    Mrs. Turpin could not have moved a finger. The old man who had been sitting next to her skipped nimble into the office and made the call, for the secretary still seemed to be gone.

"Claud!" Mrs. Turpin called.

He was not in his chair. She knew she must jump up and find him but she felt like someone trying to catch a train in a dream, when everything moves in slow motion and the faster you try to run the slower you go.

"Here I am," a suffocated voice, very unlike Claud's, said.

He was doubled up in the corner on the floor, pale as paper, holding his leg. She wanted to get up and go to him but she could not move. Instead, her gaze was drawn slowly downward to the churning face on the floor, which she could see over the doctor's shoulder.

110    The girl's eyes stopped rolling and focused on her. They seemed a much lighter blue than before, as if a door that had been tightly closed behind them was now open to admit light and air.

Mrs. Turpin's head cleared and her power of motion returned. She leaned forward until she was looking directly into the fierce brilliant eyes. There was no doubt in her mind that the girl did know her, knew her in some intense and personal way, beyond time and condition. "What you got to say to me?" she asked hoarsely and held her breath, waiting, as for a revelation.

The girl raised her head. Her gaze locked with Mrs. Turpin's. "Go back to hell where you came from, you old wart hog," she whispered. Her voice was low but clear. Her eyes burned for a moment as if she saw with pleasure that her message had struck its target.

Mrs. Turpin sank back in her chair.

After a moment the girl's eyes closed and she turned her head wearily to the side.

115    The doctor rose and handed the nurse the empty syringe. He leaned over and put both hands for a moment on the mother's shoulders, which were shaking. She was sitting on the floor, her lips pressed together, holding Mary Grace's hand in her lap. The girl's fingers were gripped like a baby's around her thumb. "Go on to the hospital," he said. "I'll call and make the arrangements."

"Now let's see that neck," he said in a jovial voice to Mrs. Turpin. He began to inspect her neck with his first two fingers. Two little moonshaped lines like pink fish bones were indented over her windpipe. There was the beginning of an angry red swelling above her eye. His fingers passed over this also.

"Lea' me be," she said thickly and shook him off. "See about Claud. She kicked him."

"I'll see about him in a minute," he said and felt her pulse. He was a thin gray-haired man, given to pleasantries. "Go home and have yourself a vacation the rest of the day," he said and patted her on the shoulder.

Quit your pattin me, Mrs. Turpin growled to herself.

120    "And put an ice pack over that eye," he said. Then he went and squatted down beside Claud and looked at his leg. After a moment he pulled him up and Claud limped after him into the office.

Until the ambulance came, the only sounds in the room were the tremulous moans of the girl's mother, who continued to sit on the floor. The white-trash woman did not take her eyes off the girl. Mrs. Turpin looked straight ahead at nothing. Presently the ambulance drew up, a long dark shadow, behind the curtain. The attendants came in and set the stretcher down beside the girl and lifted her expertly onto it and carried her out. The nurse helped the mother gather up her things. The shadow of the ambulance moved silently away and the nurse came back in the office.

"That ther girl is going to be a lunatic, ain't she?" the white-trash woman asked the nurse, but the nurse kept on to the back and never answered her.

"Yes, she's going to be a lunatic," the white-trash woman said to the rest of them.

"Po' critter," the old woman murmured. The child's face was still in her lap. His eyes looked idly out over her knees. He had not moved during the disturbance except to draw one leg up under him.

125    "I thank Gawd," the white-trash woman said fervently, "I ain't a lunatic." Claud came limping out and the Turpins went home.

As their pick-up truck turned into their own dirt road and made the crest of the hill, Mrs. Turpin gripped the window ledge and looked out suspiciously. The land sloped gracefully down through a field dotted with lavender weeds and at the start of the rise their small yellow frame house, with its little flower beds spread out around it like a fancy apron, sat primly in its accustomed place between two giant hickory trees. She would not have been startled to see a burnt wound between two blackened chimneys.

Neither of them felt like eating so they put on their house clothes and lowered the shade in the bedroom and lay down, Claud with his leg on a pillow and herself with a damp washcloth over her eye. The instant she was flat on her back, the image of a razor-backed hog with warts on its face and horns coming out behind its ears snorted into her head. She moaned, a low quiet moan.

"I am not," she said tearfully, "a wart hog. From hell." But the denial had no force. The girl's eyes and her words, even the tone of her voice, low but clear, directed only to her, brooked no repudiation. She had been singled out for the message, though there was trash in the room to whom it might justly have been applied. The full force of this fact struck her only now. There was a woman there who was neglecting her own child but she had been overlooked. The message had been given to Ruby Turpin, a respectable, hard-working, church-going woman. The tears dried. Her eyes began to burn instead with wrath.

130    She rose on her elbow and the washcloth fell into her hand. Claud
was lying on his back, snoring. She wanted to tell him what the girl had
said. At the same time she did not wish to put the image of herself as a
wart hog from hell into his mind.

"Hey, Claud," she muttered and pushed his shoulder.

Claud opened one pale baby blue eye.

She looked into it warily. He did not think about anything. He just
went his way.

"Wha, whasit?" he said and closed his eye again.

135    "Nothing," she said. "Does your leg pain you?"

"Hurts like hell," Claud said.

"It'll quit terreckly," she said and lay back down. In a moment Claud
was snoring again. For the rest of the afternoon they lay there. Claud slept.
She scowled at the ceiling. Occasionally she raised her fist and made a
small stabbing motion over her chest as if she was defending her innocence to invisible guests who were the comforters of Job, reasonable-
seeming but wrong.

About five thirty Claud stirred. "Got to go after those niggers," he
sighed, not moving.

She was looking straight up as if there were unintelligible handwriting on the ceiling. The protuberance over her eye had turned a greenish
blue. "Listen here," she said.

140    "What?"

"Kiss me."

Claud leaned over and kissed her loudly on the mouth. He pinched
her side and their hands interlocked. Her expression of ferocious concen
tration did not change. Claud got up, groaning and growling, and limped
off. She continued to study the ceiling.

She did not get up until she heard the pick-up truck coming back with
the Negroes. Then she rose and thrust her feet in her brown oxfords,
which she did not bother to lace, and stumped out onto the back porch
and got her red plastic bucket. She emptied a tray of ice cubes into it and
filled it half full of water and went out into the back yard. Every afternoon
after Claud brought the hands in, one of the boys helped him put out hay
and the rest waited in the back of the truck until he was ready to take them
home. The truck was parked in the shade under one of the hickory trees.

"Hi yawl this evening?" Mrs. Turpin asked grimly, appearing with the
bucket and the dipper. There were three women and a boy in the truck.

145    "Us doin nicely," the oldest woman said. "Hi you doin?" and her gaze
stuck immediately on the dark lump on Mrs. Turpin's forehead. "You done
fell down, ain't you?" she asked in a solicitous voice. The old woman was
dark and almost toothless. She had on an old felt hat of Claud's set back
on her head. The other two women were younger and lighter and they
both had new bright green sun hats. One of them had hers on her head;
the other had taken hers off and the boy was grinning beneath it.

Mrs. Turpin set the bucket down on the floor of the truck. "Yawl help yourselves," she said. She looked around to make sure Claud had gone. "No, I didn't fall down," she said. "It was something worse than that."

"Ain't nothing bad happen to you!" the old woman said. She said it as if they all knew Mrs. Turpin was protected in some special way by Divine Providence. "You just had you a little fall."

"We were in town at the doctor's office for where the cow kicked Mr. Turpin," Mrs. Turpin said in a flat tone that indicated they could leave off their foolishness. "And there was this girl there. A big fat girl with her face all broke out. I could look at that girl and tell she was peculiar but I couldn't tell how. And me and her mama were just talking and going along and all of a sudden WHAM! She throws this big book she reading at me and . . ."

"Naw!" the old woman cried out.

150 "And then she jumps over the table and commences to choke me."

"Naw!" they all exclaimed, "naw!"

"Hi come she do that?" the old woman asked. "What ail her?"

Mrs. Turpin only glared in front of her.

"Somethin ail her," the old woman said.

155 "They carried her off in an ambulance," Mrs. Turpin continued, "but before she went she was rolling on the floor and they were trying to hold her down to give her a shot and she said something to me." She paused. "You know what she said to me?"

"What she say?" they asked.

"She said," Mrs. Turpin began, and stopped, her face very dark and heavy. The sun was getting whiter and whiter, blanching the sky overhead so that the leaves of the hickory tree were black in the face of it. She could not bring forth the words. "Something real ugly," she muttered.

"She sho shouldn't said nothin ugly to you," the old woman said. "You so sweet. You're the sweetest lady I know."

"She pretty too," the one with the hat on said.

160 "And stout," the other one said. "I never knowed no sweeter white lady."

"That's the truth befo' Jesus," the old woman said. "Amen! You des as sweet and pretty as you can be."

Mrs. Turpin knew just exactly how much Negro flattery was worth and it added to her rage. "She said," she began again and finished this time with a fierce rush of breath, "that I was an old wart hog from hell."

There was an astounded silence.

"Where she at?" the youngest woman cried in a piercing voice.

165 "Lemme see her. I'll kill her!"

"I'll kill her with you!" the other one cried.

"She b'long in the sylum," the old woman said emphatically. "You the sweetest white lady I know."

"She pretty too," the other two said. "Stout as she can be and sweet. Jesus satisfied with her!"

"Deed he is," the old woman declared.

170    Idiots! Mrs. Turpin growled to herself. You could never say anything intelligent to a nigger. You could talk at them but not with them. "Yawl ain't drunk your water," she said shortly. "Leave the bucket in the truck when you're finished with it. I got more to do than just stand around and pass the time of day," and she moved off and into the house.

She stood for a moment in the middle of the kitchen. The dark protuberance over her eye looked like a miniature tornado cloud which might any moment sweep across the horizon of her brow. Her lower lip protruded dangerously. She squared her massive shoulders. Then she marched into the front of the house and out the side door and started down the road to the pig parlor. She had the look of a woman going single-handed, weaponless, into battle.

The sun was a deep yellow now like a harvest moon and was riding westward very fast over the far tree line as if it meant to reach the hogs before she did. The road was rutted and she kicked several good-sized stones out of her path as she strode along. The pig parlor was on a little knoll at the end of a lane that ran off from the side of the barn. It was a square of concrete as large as a small room, with a board fence about four feet high around it. The concrete floor sloped slightly so that the hog wash could drain off into a trench where it was carried to the field for fertilizer. Claud was standing on the outside, on the edge of the concrete, hanging onto the top board, hosing down the floor inside. The hose was connected to the faucet of a water trough nearby.

Mrs. Turpin climbed up beside him and glowered down at the hogs inside. There were seven long-snouted bristly shoats in it—tan with liver-colored spots—and an old sow a few weeks off from farrowing. She was lying on her side grunting. The shoats were running about shaking themselves like idiot children, their little slit pig eyes searching the floor for anything left. She had read that pigs were the most intelligent animal. She doubted it. They were supposed to be smarter than dogs. There had even been a pig astronaut. He had performed his assignment perfectly but died of a heart attack afterwards because they left him in his electric suit, sitting upright throughout his examination when naturally a hog should be on all fours.

A-gruntin and a-rootin and a-groanin.

175    "Gimme that hose," she said, yanking it away from Claud. "Go on and carry them niggers home and then get off that leg."

"You look like you might have swallowed a mad dog," Claud observed, but he got down and limped off. He paid no attention to her humors.

Until he was out of earshot, Mrs. Turpin stood on the side of the pen, holding the hose and pointing the stream of water at the hind quarter of any shoat that looked as if it might try to lie down. When he had had time to get over the hill, she turned her head slightly and her wrathful eyes scanned the path. He was nowhere in sight. She turned back again and seemed to gather herself up. Her shoulders rose and she drew in her breath.

"What do you send me a message like that for?" she said in a low fierce voice, barely above a whisper but with the force of a shout in its concentrated fury. "How am I a hog and me both? How am I saved and from hell too?" Her free fist was knotted and with the other she gripped the hose, blindly pointing the stream of water in and out of the eye of the old sow whose outraged squeal she did not hear.

The pig parlor commanded a view of the back pasture where their twenty beef cows were gathered around the hay-bales Claud and the boy had put out. The freshly cut pasture sloped down to the highway. Across it was their cotton field and beyond that a dark green dusty wood which they owned as well. The sun was behind the wood, very red, looking over the paling of trees like a farmer inspecting his own hogs.

180     "Why me?" she rumbled. "It's no trash around here, black or white, that I haven't given to. And break my back to the bone every day working. And do for the church."

She appeared to be the right size woman to command the arena before her. "How am I a hog?" she demanded. "Exactly how am I like them?" and she jabbed the stream of water at the shoats. "There was plenty of trash there. It didn't have to be me."

"If you like trash better, go get yourself some trash then," she railed. "You could have made me trash. Or a nigger. If trash is what you wanted why didn't you make me trash?" She shook her fist with the hose in it and a watery snake appeared momentarily in the air. "I could quit working and take it easy and be filthy," she growled. "Lounge about the sidewalks all day drinking root beer. Dip snuff and spit in every puddle and have it all over my face. I could be nasty."

"Or you could have made me a nigger. It's too late for me to be a nigger," she said with deep sarcasm, "but I could act like one. Lay down in the middle of the road and stop traffic. Roll on the ground."

In the deepening light everything was taking on a mysterious hue. The pasture was growing a peculiar glassy green and the streak of highway had turned lavender. She braced herself for a final assault and this time her voice rolled out over the pasture. "Go on," she yelled, "call me a hog! Call me a hog again. From hell. Call me a wart hog from hell. Put that bottom rail on top. There'll still be a top and bottom!"

185     A garbled echo returned to her.

A final surge of fury shook her and she roared, "Who do you think you are?"

The color of everything, field and crimson sky, burned for a moment with a transparent intensity. The question carried over the pasture and across the highway and the cotton field and returned to her clearly like an answer from beyond the wood.

She opened her mouth but no sound came out of it.

A tiny truck, Claud's, appeared on the highway, heading rapidly out of sight. Its gears scraped thinly. It looked like a child's toy. At any moment a bigger truck might smash into it and scatter Claud's and the niggers' brains all over the road.

190        Mrs. Turpin stood there, her gaze fixed on the highway, all her muscles rigid, until in five or six minutes the truck reappeared, returning. She waited until it had had time to turn into their own road. Then like a monumental statue coming to life, she bent her head slowly and gazed, as if through the very heart of the mystery, down into the pig parlor at the hogs. They had settled all in one corner around the old sow who was grunting softly. A red glow suffused them. They appeared to pant with a secret life.

Until the sun slipped finally behind the tree line, Mrs. Turpin remained there with her gaze bent to them as if she were absorbing some abysmal life-giving knowledge. At last she lifted her head. There was only a purple streak in the sky, cutting through a field of crimson and leading, like an extension of the highway, into the descending dusk. She raised her hands from the side of the pen in a gesture hieratic and profound. A visionary light settled in her eyes. She saw the streak as a vast swinging bridge extending upward from the earth through a field of living fire. Upon it a vast horde of souls were rumbling toward heaven. There were whole companies of white-trash, clean for the first time in their lives, and bands of black niggers in white robes, and battalions of freaks and lunatics shouting and clapping and leaping like frogs. And bringing up the end of the procession was a tribe of people whom she recognized at once as those who, like herself and Claud, had always had a little of everything and the God-given wit to use it right. She leaned forward to observe them closer. They were marching behind the others with great dignity, accountable as they had always been for good order and common sense and respectable behavior. They alone were on key. Yet she could see by their shocked and altered faces that even their virtues were being burned away. She lowered her hands and gripped the rail of the hog pen, her eyes small but fixed unblinkingly on what lay ahead. In a moment the vision faded but she remained where she was, immobile.

At length she got down and turned off the faucet and made her slow way on the darkening path to the house. In the woods around her the invisible cricket choruses had struck up, but what she heard were the voices of the souls climbing upward into the starry field and shouting hallelujah.

▨ TOPICS FOR
CRITICAL THINKING AND WRITING

1. Why does Mary Grace attack Mrs. Turpin?
2. Characterize Mrs. Turpin before her revelation. Did your attitude toward her change at the end of the story?

3. The two chief settings are a doctor's waiting room and a "pig parlor." Can these settings reasonably be called "symbolic"? if so, symbolic of what?

4. When Mrs. Turpin goes toward the pig parlor, she has "the look of a woman going single-handed, weaponless, into battle." Once there, she dismisses Claud, uses the hose as a weapon against the pigs, and talks to herself "in a low fierce voice." What is she battling, besides the pigs?

# ON FICTION: REMARKS FROM ESSAYS AND LETTERS

## From *"The Fiction Writer and His Country"*

In the greatest fiction, the writer's moral sense coincides with his dramatic sense, and I see no way for it to do this unless his moral judgment is part of the very act of seeing, and he is free to use it. I have heard it said that belief in Christian dogma is a hindrance to the writer, but I myself have found nothing further from the truth. Actually, it frees the storyteller to observe. It is not a set of rules which fixes what he sees in the world. It affects his writing primarily by guaranteeing his respect for mystery. . . .

When I look at stories I have written I find that they are, for the most part, about people who are poor, who are afflicted in both mind and body, who have little—or at best a distorted—sense of spiritual purpose, and whose actions do not apparently give the reader a great assurance of the joy of life.

Yet how is this? For I am no disbeliever in spiritual purpose and no vague believer. I see from the standpoint of Christian orthodoxy. This means that for me the meaning of life is centered in our Redemption by Christ and what I see in the world I see in its relation to that. . . .

The novelist with Christian concerns will find in modern life distortions which are repugnant to him, and his problem will be to make these appear as distortions to an audience which is used to seeing them as natural; and he may well be forced to take ever more violent means to get his vision across to this hostile audience. When you can assume that your audience holds the same beliefs you do, you can relax a little and use more normal means of talking to it; when you have to assume that it does not, then you have to make your vision apparent by shock—to the hard of hearing you shout, and for the almost-blind you draw large and startling figures.

## From "Some Aspects of the Grotesque in Southern Fiction"

If the writer believes that our life is and will remain essentially mysterious, if he looks upon us as beings existing in a created order to whose laws we freely respond, then what he sees on the surface will be of interest to him only as he can go through it into an experience of mystery itself. His kind of fiction will always be pushing its own limits outward toward the limits of mystery, because for this kind of writer, the meaning of a story does not begin except at a depth where adequate motivation and adequate psychology and the various determinations have been exhausted. Such a writer will be interested in what we don't understand rather than in what we do. He will be interested in possibility rather than in probability. He will be interested in characters who are forced out to meet evil and grace and who act on a trust beyond themselves—whether they know very clearly what it is they act upon or not. To the modern mind, this kind of character, and his creator, are typical Don Quixotes, tilting at what is not there.

## From "The Nature and Aim of Fiction"

The novel works by a slower accumulation of detail than the short story does. The short story requires more drastic procedures than the novel because more has to be accomplished in less space. The details have to carry more immediate weight. In good fiction, certain of the details will tend to accumulate meaning from the story itself, and when this happens, they become symbolic in their action.

Now the word *symbol* scares a good many people off, just as the word *art* does. They seem to feel that a symbol is some mysterious thing put in arbitrarily by the writer to frighten the common reader—sort of a literary Masonic grip that is only for the initiated. They seem to think that it is a way of saying something that you aren't actually saying, and so if they can be got to read a reputedly symbolic work at all, they approach it as if it were a problem in algebra. Find *x*. And when they do find or think they find this abstraction, *x*, then they go off with an elaborate sense of satisfaction and the notion that they have "understood" the story. Many students confuse the *process* of understanding a thing with understanding it.

I think that for the fiction writer himself, symbols are something he uses simply as a matter of course. You might say that these are details that, while having their essential place in the literal level of the story, operate in depth as well as on the surface, increasing the story in every direction. . . .

People have a habit of saying, "What is the theme of your story?" and they expect you to give them a statement: "The theme of my story is the economic pressure of the machine on the middle class"—or some such absurdity. And when they've got a statement like that, they go off happy and feel it is no longer necessary to read the story.

Some people have the notion that you read the story and then climb out of it into the meaning, but for the fiction writer himself the whole story is the meaning, because it is an experience, not an abstraction.

## From "Writing Short Stories"

Being short does not mean being slight. A short story should be long in depth and should give us an experience of meaning. . . .

Meaning is what keeps the short story from being short. I prefer to talk about the meaning in a story rather than the theme of a story. People talk about the theme of a story as if the theme were like the string that a sack of chicken feed is tied with. They think that if you can pick out the theme, the way you pick the right thread in the chicken-feed sack, you can rip the story open and feed the chickens. But this is not the way meaning works in fiction.

When you can state the theme of a story, when you can separate it from the story itself, then you can be sure the story is not a very good one. The meaning of a story has to be embodied in it, has to be made concrete in it. A story is a way to say something that can't be said any other way, and it takes every word in the story to say what the meaning is. You tell a story because a statement would be inadequate. When anybody asks what a story is about, the only proper thing is to tell him to read the story. The meaning of fiction is not abstract meaning but experienced meaning, and the purpose of making statements about the meaning of a story is only to help you to experience that meaning more fully.

## "A Reasonable Use of the Unreasonable" [1957]

Last fall I received a letter from a student who said she would be "graciously appreciative" if I would tell her "just what enlightenment" I expected her to get from each of my stories. I suspect she had a paper to write. I wrote her back to forget about the enlightenment and just try to enjoy them. I knew that was the most unsatisfactory answer I could have given because, of course, she didn't want to enjoy them, she just wanted to figure them out.

In most English classes the short story has become a kind of literary specimen to be dissected. Every time a story of mine appears in a Freshman anthology, I have a vision of it, with its little organs laid open, like a frog in a bottle.

I realize that a certain amount of this what-is-the-significance has to go on, but I think something has gone wrong in the process when, for so many students, the story becomes simply a problem to be solved, something which you evaporate to get Instant Enlightenment.

A story really isn't any good unless it successfully resists paraphrase, unless it hangs on and expands in the mind. Properly, you analyze to enjoy, but it's equally true that to analyze with any discrimination, you have to have enjoyed already, and I think that the best reason to hear a story read is that it should stimulate that primary enjoyment.

I don't have any pretensions to being an Aeschylus or Sophocles and providing you in this story with a cathartic experience out of your mythic background, though this story I'm going to read certainly calls up a good deal of the South's mythic background, and it should elicit from you a degree of pity and terror, even though its way of being serious is a comic one. I do think, though, that like the Greeks you should know what is going to happen in this story so that any element of suspense in it will be transferred from its surface to its interior.

I would be most happy if you have already read it, happier still if you knew it well, but since experience has taught me to keep my expectations along these lines modest, I'll tell you that this is the story of a family of six which, on its way driving to Florida, gets wiped out by an escaped convict who calls himself The Misfit. The family is made up of the Grandmother and her son, Bailey, and his children, John Wesley and June Star and the baby, and there is also the cat and the children's mother. The cat is named Pitty Sing, and the Grandmother is taking him with them, hidden in a basket.

Now I think it behooves me to try to establish with you the basis on which reason operates in this story. Much of my fiction takes its character from a reasonable use of the unreasonable, though the reasonableness of my use of it may not always be apparent. The assumptions that underlie this use of it, however, are those of the central Christian mysteries. These are assumptions to which a large part of the modern audience takes exception. About this I can only say that there are perhaps other ways than my own in which this story could be read, but none other by which it could have been written. Belief, in my own case anyway, is the engine that makes perception operate.

The heroine of this story, the Grandmother, is in the most significant position life offers the Christian. She is facing death. And to all appearances she, like the rest of us, is not too well prepared for it. She would like to see the event postponed. Indefinitely.

I've talked to a number of teachers who use this story in class and who tell their students that the Grandmother is evil, that in fact, she's a witch, even down to the cat. One of these teachers told me that his students, and particularly his Southern students, resisted this interpretation with a certain bemused vigor, and he didn't understand why. I had to tell him that they resisted it because they all had grandmothers or great-aunts just like her at home, and they knew, from personal experience, that the old lady lacked comprehension, but that she had a good heart. The Southerner is usually tolerant of those weaknesses that proceed from innocence, and he knows that a taste for self-preservation can be readily combined with the missionary spirit.

This same teacher was telling his students that morally The Misfit was several cuts above the Grandmother. He had a really sentimental attachment to The Misfit. But then a prophet gone wrong is almost always more interesting than your grandmother, and you have to let people take their pleasures where they find them.

It is true that the old lady is a hypocritical old soul; her wits are no match for The Misfit's, nor is her capacity for grace equal to his; yet I think the unprejudiced reader will feel that the Grandmother has a special kind of triumph in the story which instinctively we do not allow to someone altogether bad.

I often ask myself what makes a story work, and what makes it hold up as a story, and I have decided that it is probably some action, some gesture of a character that is unlike any other in the story, one which indicates where the real heart of the story lies. This would have to be an action or a gesture which was both totally right and totally unexpected; it would have to be one that was both in character and beyond character; it would have to suggest both the world and eternity. The action or gesture I'm talking about would have to be on the anagogical level, that is, the level which has to do with the Divine life and our participation in it. It would be a gesture that transcended any neat allegory that might have been intended or any pat moral categories a reader could make. It would be a gesture which somehow made contact with mystery.

There is a point in this story where such a gesture occurs. The Grandmother is at last alone, facing The Misfit. Her head clears for an instant and she realizes, even in her limited way, that she is responsible for the man before her and joined to him by ties of kinship which have their roots deep in the mystery she has been merely prattling about so far. And at this point, she does the right thing, she makes the right gesture.

I find that students are often puzzled by what she says and does here, but I think myself that if I took out this gesture and what she says with it, I would have no story. What was left would not be worth your attention. Our age not only does not have a very sharp eye for the almost imperceptible intrusions of grace, it no longer has much feeling for the nature of the violences which precede and follow them. The devil's greatest wile, Baudelaire has said, is to convince us that he does not exist.

I suppose the reasons for the use of so much violence in modern fiction will differ with each writer who uses it, but in my own stories I have found that violence is strangely capable of returning my characters to reality and preparing them to accept their moment of grace. Their heads are so hard that almost nothing else will do the work. This idea, that reality is something to which we must be returned at considerable cost, is one which is seldom understood by the casual reader, but it is one which is implicit in the Christian view of the world.

I don't want to equate The Misfit with the devil. I prefer to think that, however unlikely this may seem, the old lady's gesture, like the mustard-seed, will grow to be a great crow-filled tree in The Misfit's heart, and will be enough of a pain to him there to turn him into the prophet he was meant to become. But that's another story.

This story has been called grotesque, but I prefer to call it literal. A good story is literal in the same sense that a child's drawing is literal. When a child draws, he doesn't intend to distort but to set down exactly what he sees, and as his gaze is direct, he sees the lines that create motion. Now the lines of motion that interest the writer are usually invisible. They are lines of spiritual motion. And in this story you should be on the lookout for such things as the action of grace in the Grandmother's soul, and not for the dead bodies.

We hear many complaints about the prevalence of violence in modern fiction, and it is always assumed that this violence is a bad thing and meant to be an end in itself. With the serious writer, violence is never an end in itself. It is the extreme situation that best reveals what we are essentially, and I believe these are times when writers are more interested in what we are essentially than in the tenor of our daily lives. Violence is a form which can be used for good or evil, and among other things taken by it is the kingdom of heaven. But regardless of what can be taken by it, the man in the violent situation reveals those qualities least dispensable in his personality, those qualities which are all he will have to take into eternity with him; and since the characters in this story are all on the verge of eternity, it is appropriate to think of what they take with them. In any case, I hope that if you consider these points in connection with the story, you will come to see it as something more than an account of a family murdered on the way to Florida.

# ON INTERPRETING "A GOOD MAN IS HARD TO FIND"

*A professor of English had sent Flannery the following letter:"I am writing as spokesman for three members of our department and some ninety university students in three classes who for a week now have been discussing your story 'A Good Man Is Hard to Find.' We have debated at length several possible interpretations, none of which fully satisfies us. In general we believe that the appearance of the Misfit is not 'real' in the same sense that the incidents of the first half of the story are real. Bailey, we believe, imagines the appearance of the Misfit, whose activities have been called to his attention on the night before the trip and again during the stopover at the roadside restaurant. Bailey, we further believe, identifies himself with the Misfit and so plays two roles in the imaginary last half of the story. But we cannot, after great effort, determine the point at which reality fades into illusion or reverie. Does the accident literally occur, or is it a part of Bailey's dream? Please believe me when I say we are not seeking an easy way out of our difficulty. We admire your story and have examined it with great care, but we are convinced that we are missing something important which you intended for us to grasp. We will all be very grateful if you comment on the interpretation which I have outlined above and if you will give us further comments about your intention in writing 'A Good Man Is Hard to Find.'"*

   *She replied:*

To a Professor of English

28 March 61

   The interpretation of your ninety students and three teachers is fantastic and about as far from my intentions as it could get to be. If it were a legitimate interpretation, the story would be little more than a trick and its interest would be simply for abnormal psychology. I am not interested in abnormal psychology.

   There is a change of tension from the first part of the story to the second where The Misfit enters, but this is no lessening of reality. This story is, of course, not meant to be realistic in the sense that it portrays the everyday doings of people in Georgia. It is stylized and its conventions are comic even though its meaning is serious.

   Bailey's only importance is as the Grandmother's boy and the driver of the car. It is the Grandmother who first recognizes The Misfit and who is most concerned with him throughout. The story is a duel of sorts between the Grandmother and her superficial beliefs and The Misfit's more profoundly felt involvement with Christ's action which set the world off balance for him.

   The meaning of a story should go on expanding for the reader the more he thinks about it, but meaning cannot be captured in an interpretation. If teachers are in the habit of approaching a story as if it were a research problem for which any answer is believable so long as it is not obvious, then I think students will never learn to enjoy fiction. Too much interpretation is certainly worse than too little and where feeling for a story is absent, theory will not supply it.

   My tone is not meant to be obnoxious. I am in a state of shock.

# 9

# American Voices: Fiction for a Diverse Nation

Almost a century ago the American writer Willa Cather, in her novel *O Pioneers* (1913), shrewdly observed:

> There are only two or three human stories, and they go on repeating themselves as if they had never happened before.

Among these is the story that essentially ends, "And they lived happily ever after." Not that *everyone* in the story need live happily ever after: Fiction often reassures us that the bad end badly, essentially showing us stories that support the Biblical assertion that "Whoso diggeth a pit shall fall therein, and he that rolleth a stone, it will return upon him" (Proverbs 26.27). There are, of course, countless variations on this theme—and we never tire of reading stories about it. Perhaps people keep writing about it, and reading about it, because it is true. Or perhaps, on the other hand, we read and write about it because life is such a mess, such a chaotic welter, that we are trying to impose order, trying to convince ourselves that indeed this pattern exists.

For all the sameness of many stories, there are countless local variations, especially variations taking account of different cultures, and especially in America—proverbially a nation of immigrants—fiction shows us distinctive kinds of behavior, behavior rooted in customs not shared by the population as a whole. In this chapter we offer stories about persons who belong to one or another of a range of minority groups: Native Americans, gays and lesbians, Asian Americans, African Americans, and Hispanic Americans. These stories remind us that diversity and difference take multiple forms, and not all of them are sexual, religious, racial, or ethnic. We believe, however, that *all* of these stories speak to *all* readers, and we call your attention to the fact that other chapters also contain stories about members of some of these groups.

Somewhat comparable chapters appear later in the book, with poems and with plays about diverse cultures.

# LESLIE MARMON SILKO

*Leslie Marmon Silko was born in 1948 in Albuquerque, New Mexico, and grew up on the Laguna Pueblo Reservation some fifty miles to the west. Of her family she says,*

> *We are mixed blood—Laguna, Mexican, white. . . . All those languages, all those ways of living are combined, and we live somewhere on the fringes of all three. But I don't apologize for this any more—not to whites, not to full bloods—our origin is unlike any other. My poetry, my storytelling rise out of this source.*

*After graduating from the University of New Mexico in 1969, Silko entered law school but soon left to become a writer. She taught for two years at Navajo Community College at Many Farms, Arizona, and then went to Alaska for two years where she studied Eskimo-Aleut culture and worked on a novel,* Ceremony. *After returning to the Southwest, she taught at the University of Arizona and then at the University of New Mexico.*

*In addition to writing stories, a novel, and poems, Silko has written the screenplay for Marlon Brando's film,* Black Elk. *In 1981 she was awarded one of the so-called genius grants from the MacArthur Foundation, which supports "exceptionally talented individuals."*

## The Man to Send Rain Clouds                                        [1969]

### One

They found him under a big cottonwood tree. His Levi jacket and pants were faded light-blue so that he had been easy to find. The big cottonwood tree stood apart from a small grove of winterbare cottonwoods which grew in the wide, sandy arroyo. He had been dead for a day or more, and the sheep had wandered and scattered up and down the arroyo. Leon and his brother-in-law, Ken, gathered the sheep and left them in the pen at the sheep camp before they returned to the cottonwood tree. Leon waited under the tree while Ken drove the truck through the deep sand to the edge of the arroyo. He squinted up at the sun and unzipped his jacket—it sure was hot for this time of year. But high and northwest the blue mountains were still deep in snow. Ken came sliding down the low, crumbling bank about fifty yards down, and he was bringing the red blanket.

Before they wrapped the old man, Leon took a piece of string out of his pocket and tied a small gray feather in the old man's long white hair. Ken gave him the paint. Across the brown wrinkled forehead he drew a streak of white and along the high cheekbones he drew a strip of blue paint. He paused and watched Ken throw pinches of corn meal and pollen into the wind that fluttered the small gray feather. Then Leon painted with yellow under the old man's broad nose, and finally, when he had painted green across the chin, he smiled.

"Send us rain clouds, Grandfather." They laid the bundle in the back of the pickup and covered it with a heavy tarp before they started back to the pueblo.

They turned off the highway onto the sandy pueblo road. Not long after they passed the store and post office they saw Father Paul's car coming toward them. When he recognized their faces he slowed his car and waved for them to stop. The young priest rolled down the car window.

5      "Did you find old Teofilo?" he asked loudly.

Leon stopped the truck. "Good morning, Father. We were just out to the sheep camp. Everything is O.K., now."

"Thank God for that. Teofilo is a very old man. You really shouldn't allow him to stay at the sheep camp alone."

"No, he won't do that any more now."

"Well, I'm glad you understand. I hope I'll be seeing you at Mass this week—we missed you last Sunday. See if you can get old Teofilo to come with you." The priest smiled and waved at them as they drove away.

## Two

10    Louise and Teresa were waiting. The table was set for lunch, and the coffee was boiling on the black iron stove. Leon looked at Louise and then at Teresa.

"We found him under a cottonwood tree in the big arroyo near sheep camp. I guess he sat down to rest in the shade and never got up again." Leon walked toward the old man's head. The red plaid shawl had been shaken and spread carefully over the bed, and a new brown flannel shirt and pair of stiff new Levis were arranged neatly beside the pillow. Louise held the screen door open while Leon and Ken carried in the red blanket. He looked small and shriveled, and after they dressed him in the new shirt and pants he seemed more shrunken.

It was noontime now because the church bells rang the Angelus.[1] They ate the beans with hot bread, and nobody said anything until after Teresa poured the coffee.

[1]**Angelus** a devotional prayer commemorating the Annunciation (the angel Gabriel's announcement of the Incarnation of God in the human form of Jesus).

Ken stood up and put on his jacket. "I'll see about the gravediggers. Only the top layer of soil is frozen. I think it can be ready before dark."

Leon nodded his head and finished his coffee. After Ken had been gone for a while, the neighbors and clanspeople came quietly to embrace Teofilo's family and to leave food on the table because the gravediggers would come to eat when they were finished.

## *Three*

15    The sky in the west was full of pale-yellow light. Louise stood outside with her hands in the pockets of Leon's green army jacket that was too big for her. The funeral was over, and the old men had taken their candles and medicine bags and were gone. She waited until the body was laid into the pickup before she said anything to Leon. She touched his arm, and he noticed that her hands were still dusty from the corn meal that she had sprinkled around the old man. When she spoke, Leon could not hear her.

"What did you say? I didn't hear you."

"I said that I had been thinking about something."

"About what?"

"About the priest sprinkling holy water for Grandpa. So he won't be thirsty."

20    Leon stared at the new moccasins that Teofilo had made for the cere-monial dances in the summer. They were nearly hidden by the red blan-ket. It was getting colder, and the wind pushed gray dust down the nar-row pueblo road. The sun was approaching the long mesa where it disappeared during the winter. Louise stood there shivering and watching his face. Then he zipped up his jacket and opened the truck door. "I'll see if he's there."

Ken stopped the pickup at the church, and Leon got out; and then Ken drove down the hill to the graveyard where people were waiting. Leon knocked at the old carved door with its symbols of the Lamb. While he waited he looked up at the twin bells from the king of Spain with the last sunlight pouring around them in their tower.

The priest opened the door and smiled when he saw who it was. "Come in! What brings you here this evening?"

The priest walked toward the kitchen, and Leon stood with his cap in his hand, playing with the earflaps and examining the living room—the brown sofa, the green armchair, and the brass lamp that hung down from the ceiling by links of chain. The priest dragged a chair out of the kitchen and offered it to Leon.

"No thank you, Father. I only came to ask you if you would bring your holy water to the graveyard."

25    The priest turned away from Leon and looked out the window at the patio full of shadows and the dining-room windows of the nuns' cloister

across the patio. The curtains were heavy, and the light from within faintly penetrated; it was impossible to see the nuns inside eating supper. "Why didn't you tell me he was dead? I could have brought the Last Rites anyway."

Leon smiled. "It wasn't necessary, Father."

The priest stared down at his scuffed brown loafers and the worn hem of his cassock. "For a Christian burial it was necessary."

His voice was distant, and Leon thought that his blue eyes looked tired.

"It's O.K., Father, we just want him to have plenty of water."

30    The priest sank down in the green chair and picked up a glossy missionary magazine. He turned the colored pages full of lepers and pagans without looking at them.

"You know I can't do that, Leon. There should have been the Last Rites and a funeral Mass at the very least."

Leon put on his green cap and pulled the flaps down over his ears. "It's getting late, Father. I've got to go."

When Leon opened the door Father Paul stood up and said, "Wait." He left the room and came back wearing a long brown overcoat. He followed Leon out the door and across the dim churchyard to the adobe steps in front of the church. They both stooped to fit through the low adobe entrance. And when they started down the hill to the graveyard only half of the sun was visible above the mesa.

The priest approached the grave slowly, wondering how they had managed to dig into the frozen ground and then he remembered that this was New Mexico, and saw the pile of cold loose sand beside the hole. The people stood close to each other with little clouds of steam puffing from their faces. The priest looked at them and saw a pile of jackets, gloves, and scarves in the yellow, dry tumbleweeds that grew in the graveyard. He looked at the red blanket, not sure that Teofilo was so small, wondering if it wasn't some perverse Indian trick—something they did in March to ensure a good harvest—wondering if maybe old Teofilo was actually at sheep camp corraling the sheep for the night. But there he was, facing into a cold dry wind and squinting at the last sunlight, ready to bury a red wool blanket while the faces of the parishioners were in shadow with the last warmth of the sun on their backs.

35    His fingers were stiff, and it took them a long time to twist the lid off the holy water. Drops of water fell on the red blanket and soaked into dark icy spots. He sprinkled the grave and the water disappeared almost before it touched the dim, cold sand; it reminded him of something—he tried to remember what it was, because he thought if he could remember he might understand this. He sprinkled more water; he shook the container until it was empty, and the water fell through the light from sundown like August rain that fell while the sun was still shining, almost evaporating before it touched the wilted squash flowers.

The wind pulled at the priest's brown Franciscan robe and swirled away the corn meal and pollen that had been sprinkled on the blanket. They lowered the bundle into the ground, and they didn't bother to untie the stiff pieces of new rope that were tied around the ends of the blanket. The sun was gone, and over on the highway the eastbound lane was full of headlights. The priest walked away slowly. Leon watched him climb the hill, and when he had disappeared within the tall, thick walls, Leon turned to look up at the high blue mountains in the deep snow that reflected a faint red light from the west. He felt good because it was finished, and he was happy about the sprinkling of the holy water, now the old man could send them big thunderclouds for sure.

## ▨ TOPICS FOR CRITICAL THINKING AND WRITING

1. How would you describe the response of Leon, Ken, Louise, and Teresa to Teofilo's death? To what degree does it resemble or differ from responses to death that you are familiar with?
2. How do the funeral rites resemble or differ from those of your community?
3. How well does Leon understand the priest? How well does the priest understand Leon?
4. At the end of the story we are told that Leon "felt good." Do you assume that the priest also felt good? Why, or why not?
5. From what point of view is the story told? Mark the passages where the narrator enters a character's mind, and then explain what, in your opinion, Silko gains (or loses) by doing so.

## JACK FORBES

*Jack Forbes was born in California in 1934 of Powhattan and Delaware background. He teaches anthropology and Native-American studies at the University of California, Davis, and is the author of fiction and nonfiction, including* Columbus and Other Cannibals *(1992) and* African and Native Americans *(1993), a study of Red-Black peoples.*

## Only Approved Indians Can Play: Made in USA    [1983]

The All-Indian Basketball Tournament was in its second day. Excitement was pretty high, because a lot of the teams were very good or at least eager and hungry to win. Quite a few people had come to watch, mostly Indians. Many were relatives or friends of the players. A lot of people were betting money and tension was pretty great.

A team from the Tucson Inter-Tribal House was set to play against a group from the Great Lakes region. The Tucson players were mostly very dark young men with long black hair. A few had little goatee beards or mustaches though, and one of the Great Lakes fans had started a rumor that they were really Chicanos. This was a big issue since the Indian Sports League had a rule that all players had to be of one-quarter or more Indian blood and that they had to have their BIA[1] roll numbers available if challenged.

And so a big argument started. One of the biggest, darkest Indians on the Tucson team had been singled out as a Chicano, and the crowd wanted him thrown out. The Great Lakes players, most of whom were pretty light, refused to start. They all had their BIA identification cards, encased in plastic. This proved that they were all real Indians, even a blonde-haired guy. He was really only about one-sixteenth but the BIA rolls had been changed for his tribe so legally he was one-fourth. There was no question about the Great Lakes team. They were all land-based, federally-recognized Indians, although living in a big midwestern city, and they had their cards to prove it.

Anyway, the big, dark Tucson Indian turned out to be a Papago. He didn't have a BIA card but he could talk Papago so they let him alone for the time being. Then they turned towards a lean, very Indian-looking guy who had a pretty big goatee. He seemed to have a Spanish accent, so they demanded to see his card.

5    Well, he didn't have one either. He said he was a full-blood Tarahumara Indian and he could also speak his language. None of the Great Lakes Indians could talk their languages so they said that was no proof of anything, that you had to have a BIA roll number.

The Tarahumara man was getting pretty angry by then. He said his father and uncle had been killed by the whites in Mexico and that he did not expect to be treated with prejudice by other Indians.

But all that did no good. Someone demanded to know if he had a reservation and if his tribe was recognized. He replied that his people lived high up in the mountains and that they were still resisting the Mexicanos, that the government was trying to steal their land.

"What state do your people live in," they wanted to know. When he said that his people lived free, outside of control of any state, they only shook their fists at him. "You're not an official Indian. All official Indians are under the whiteman's rule now. We all have a number given to us, to show that we are recognized."

Well, it all came to an end when someone shouted that "Tarahumaras don't exist. They're not listed in the BIA dictionary." Another fan yelled, "He's a Mexican. He can't play. This tournament is only for Indians."

10   The officials of the tournament had been huddling together. One blew his whistle and an announcement was made. "The Tucson team is

---

[1]**BIA** Bureau of Indian Affairs.

disqualified. One of its member is a Yaqui. One is a Tarahumara. The rest are Papagos. None of them have BIA enrollment cards. They are not Indians within the meaning of the laws of the government of the United States. The Great Lakes team is declared the winner by default."

A tremendous roar of applause swept through the stands. A white BIA official wiped the tears from his eyes and said to a companion, "God Bless America. I think we've won."

## ▨ TOPICS FOR CRITICAL THINKING AND WRITING

1. What expectations did the title, with its reference to "Approved Indians" and "Made in USA," suggest to you?
2. How would you describe the narrator's tone?

## GLORIA NAYLOR

*Gloria Naylor (b. 1950), a native of New York City, holds a bachelor's degree from Brooklyn College and a master's degree in Afro-American Studies from Yale University. "The Two" comes from* The Women of Brewster Place *(1982), a book that won the American Book Award for First Fiction. Naylor has subsequently published four novels and* Centennial *(1986), a work of nonfiction.*

## *The Two*                                                    [1982]

At first they seemed like such nice girls. No one could remember exactly when they had moved into Brewster. It was earlier in the year before Ben[1] was killed—of course, it had to be before Ben's death. But no one remembered if it was in the winter or spring of that year that the two had come. People often came and went on Brewster Place like a restless night's dream, moving in and out in the dark to avoid eviction notices or neighborhood bulletins about the dilapidated condition of their furnishings. So it wasn't until the two were clocked leaving in the mornings and returning in the evenings at regular intervals that it was quietly absorbed that they now claimed Brewster as home. And Brewster waited, cautiously prepared to claim them, because you never knew about young women, and obviously single at that. But when no wild music or drunken friends careened out of the corner building on weekends, and especially, when no

---

[1]**Ben** the custodian of Brewster Place.

slightly eager husbands were encouraged to linger around that first-floor apartment and run errands for them, a suspended sigh of relief floated around the two when they dumped their garbage, did their shopping, and headed for the morning bus.

The women of Brewster had readily accepted the lighter, skinny one. There wasn't much threat in her timid mincing walk and the slightly protruding teeth she seemed so eager to show everyone in her bell-like good mornings and evenings. Breaths were held a little longer in the direction of the short dark one—too pretty, and too much behind. And she insisted on wearing those thin Qiana dresses that the summer breeze molded against the maddening rhythm of the twenty pounds of rounded flesh that she swung steadily down the street. Through slitted eyes, the women watched their men watching her pass, knowing the bastards were praying for a wind. But since she seemed oblivious to whether these supplications went answered, their sighs settled around her shoulders too. Nice girls.

And so no one even cared to remember exactly when they had moved into Brewster Place, until the rumor started. It had first spread through the block like a sour odor that's only faintly perceptible and easily ignored until it starts growing in strength from the dozen mouths it had been lying in, among clammy gums and scum-coated teeth. And then it was everywhere—lining the mouths and whitening the lips of everyone as they wrinkled up their noses at its pervading smell, unable to pinpoint the source or time of its initial arrival. Sophie could—she had been there.

It wasn't that the rumor had actually begun with Sophie. A rumor needs no true parent. It only needs a willing carrier, and it found one in Sophie. She had been there—on one of those August evenings when the sun's absence is a mockery because the heat leaves the air so heavy it presses the naked skin down on your body, to the point that a sheet becomes unbearable and sleep impossible. So most of Brewster was outside that night when the two had come in together, probably from one of those air-conditioned movies downtown, and had greeted the ones who were loitering around their building. And they had started up the steps when the skinny one tripped over a child's ball and the darker one had grabbed her by the arm and around the waist to break her fall. "Careful, don't wanna lose you now." And the two of them had laughed into each other's eyes and went into the building.

5      The smell had begun there. It outlined the image of the stumbling woman and the one who had broken her fall. Sophie and a few other women sniffed at the spot and then, perplexed, silently looked at each other. Where had they seen that before? They had often laughed and touched each other—held each other in joy or its dark twin—but where had they seen *that* before? It came to them as the scent drifted down the steps and entered their nostrils on the way to their inner mouths. They had seen that—done that—with their men. That shared moment of invisible communion reserved for two and hidden from the rest of the world

behind laughter or tears or a touch. In the days before babies, miscar-
riages, and other broken dreams, after stolen caresses in barn stalls and
cotton houses, after intimate walks from church and secret kisses with
boys who were now long forgotten or permanently fixed in their lives—
that was where. They could almost feel the odor moving about in their
mouths, and they slowly knitted themselves together and let it out into
the air like a yellow mist that began to cling to the bricks on Brewster.

So it got around that the two in 312 were *that* way. And they had
seemed like such nice girls. Their regular exits and entrances to the block
were viewed with a jaundiced eye. The quiet that rested around their door
on the weekends hinted of all sorts of secret rituals, and their friendly indifference to the men on the street was an insult to the women as a
brazen flaunting of unnatural ways.

Since Sophie's apartment windows faced theirs from across the air
shaft, she became the official watchman for the block, and her opinions
were deferred to whenever the two came up in conversation. Sophie took
her position seriously and was constantly alert for any telltale signs that
might creep out around their drawn shades, across from which she kept a
religious vigil. An entire week of drawn shades was evidence enough to
send her flying around with reports that as soon as it got dark they pulled
their shades down and put on the lights. Heads nodded in knowing unison—a definite sign. If doubt was voiced with a "But I pull my shades
down at night too," a whispered "Yeah, but you're not *that* way" was argument enough to win them over.

Sophie watched the lighter one dumping their garbage, and she went
outside and opened the lid. Her eyes darted over the crushed tin cans, vegetable peelings, and empty chocolate chip cookie boxes. What do they do
with all them chocolate chip cookies? It was surely a sign, but it would
take some time to figure that one out. She saw Ben go into their apartment, and she waited and blocked his path as he came out, carrying his
toolbox.

"What ya see?" She grabbed his arm and whispered wetly in his face.

10      Ben stared at her squinted eyes and drooping lips and shook his head
slowly. "Uh, uh, uh, it was terrible."

"Yeah?" She moved in a little closer.

"Worst busted faucet I seen in my whole life." He shook her hand off
his arm and left her standing in the middle of the block.

"You old sop bucket," she muttered, as she went back up on her
stoop. A broken faucet, huh? Why did they need to use so much water?

Sophie had plenty to report that day. Ben had said it was terrible
in there. No, she didn't know exactly what he had seen, but you can
imagine—and they did. Confronted with the difference that had been
thrust into their predictable world, they reached into their imaginations
and, using an ancient pattern, weaved themselves a reason for its existence. Out of necessity they stitched all of their secret fears and lingering
childhood nightmares into this existence, because even though it was de-

ceptive enough to try and look as they looked, talk as they talked, and do as they did, it had to have some hidden stain to invalidate it—it was impossible for them both to be right. So they leaned back, supported by the sheer weight of their numbers and comforted by the woven barrier that kept them protected from the yellow mist that enshrouded the two as they came and went on Brewster Place.

15      Lorraine was the first to notice the change in the people on Brewster Place. She was a shy but naturally friendly woman who got up early, and had read the morning paper and done fifty sit-ups before it was time to leave for work. She came out of her apartment eager to start her day by greeting any of her neighbors who were outside. But she noticed that some of the people who had spoken to her before made a point of having something else to do with their eyes when she passed, although she could almost feel them staring at her back as she moved on. The ones who still spoke only did so after an uncomfortable pause, in which they seemed to be peering through her before they begrudged her a good morning or evening. She wondered if it was all in her mind and she thought about mentioning it to Theresa, but she didn't want to be accused of being too sensitive again. And how would Tee even notice anything like that anyway? She had a lousy attitude and hardly ever spoke to people. She stayed in that bed until the last moment and rushed out of the house fogged-up and grumpy, and she was used to being stared at—by men at least—because of her body.

Lorraine thought about these things as she came up the block from work, carrying a large paper bag. The group of women on her stoop parted silently and let her pass.

"Good evening," she said, as she climbed the steps.

Sophie was standing on the top step and tried to peek into the bag. "You been shopping, huh? What ya buy?" It was almost an accusation.

"Groceries." Lorraine shielded the top of the bag from view and squeezed past her with a confused frown. She saw Sophie throw a knowing glance to the others at the bottom of the stoop. What was wrong with this old woman? Was she crazy or something?

20      Lorraine went into her apartment. Theresa was sitting by the window, reading a copy of *Mademoiselle*. She glanced up from her magazine. "Did you get my chocolate chip cookies?"

"Why good evening to you, too, Tee. And how was my day? Just wonderful." She sat the bag down on the couch. "The little Baxter boy brought in a puppy for show-and-tell, and the damn thing pissed all over the floor and then proceeded to chew the heel off my shoe, but, yes, I managed to hobble to the store and bring you your chocolate chip cookies."

Oh, Jesus, Theresa thought, she's got a bug up her ass tonight.

"Well, you should speak to Mrs. Baxter. She ought to train her kid better than that." She didn't wait for Lorraine to stop laughing before she tried to stretch her good mood. "Here, I'll put those things away. Want me to make dinner so you can rest? I only worked half a day, and the most tragic thing that went down was a broken fingernail and that got caught in my typewriter."

Lorraine followed Theresa into the kitchen. "No, I'm not really tired, and fair's fair, you cooked last night. I didn't mean to tick off like that; it's just that . . . well, Tee, have you noticed that people aren't as nice as they used to be?"

25    Theresa stiffened. Oh, God, here she goes again. "What people, Lorraine? Nice in what way?"

"Well, the people in this building and on the street. No one hardly speaks anymore. I mean, I'll come in and say good evening—and just silence. It wasn't like that when we first moved in. I don't know, it just makes you wonder; that's all. What are they thinking?"

"I personally don't give a shit what they're thinking. And their good evenings don't put any bread on my table."

"Yeah, but you didn't see the way that woman looked at me out there. They must feel something or know something. They probably—"

"They, they, they!" Theresa exploded. "You know, I'm not starting up with this again, Lorraine. Who in the hell are they? And where in the hell are we? Living in some dump of a building in this God-forsaken part of town around a bunch of ignorant niggers with the cotton still under their fingernails because of you and your theys. They knew something in Linden Hills, so I gave up an apartment for you that I'd been in for the last four years. And then they knew in Park Heights, and you made me so miserable there we had to leave. Now these mysterious theys are on Brewster Place. Well, look out that window, kid. There's a big wall down that block, and this is the end of the line for me. I'm not moving anymore, so if that's what you're working yourself up to—save it!"

30    When Theresa became angry she was like a lump of smoldering coal, and her fierce bursts of temper always unsettled Lorraine.

"You see, that's why I didn't want to mention it." Lorraine began to pull at her fingers nervously. "You're always flying up and jumping to conclusions— no one said anything about moving. And I didn't know your life has been so miserable since you met me. I'm sorry about that," she finished tearfully.

Theresa looked at Lorraine, standing in the kitchen door like a wilted leaf, and she wanted to throw something at her. Why didn't she ever fight back? The very softness that had first attracted her to Lorraine was now a frequent cause for irritation. Smoked honey. That's what Lorraine had reminded her of, sitting in her office clutching that application. Dry autumn days in Georgia woods, thick bloated smoke under a beehive, and the first glimpse of amber honey just faintly darkened about the edges by the burning twigs. She had flowed just that heavily into Theresa's mind and had stuck there with a persistent sweetness.

But Theresa hadn't known then that this softness filled Lorraine up to the very middle and that she would bend at the slightest pressure, would be constantly seeking to surround herself with the comfort of everyone's goodwill, and would shrivel up at the least touch of disapproval. It was becoming a drain to be continually called upon for this nurturing and support that she just didn't understand. She had supplied it at first out of love for Lorraine, hoping that she would harden eventually, even as honey does when exposed to the cold. Theresa was growing tired of being clung to—of being the one who was leaned on. She didn't want a child—she wanted someone who could stand toe to toe with her and be willing to slug it out at times. If they practiced that way with each other, then they could turn back to back and beat the hell out of the world for trying to invade their territory. But she had found no such sparring partner in Lorraine, and the strain of fighting alone was beginning to show on her.

"Well, if it was that miserable, I would have been gone a long time ago," she said, watching her words refresh Lorraine like a gentle shower.

35      "I guess you think I'm some sort of sick paranoid, but I can't afford to have people calling my job or writing letters to my principal. You know I've already lost a position like that in Detroit. And teaching is my whole life, Tee."

"I know," she sighed, not really knowing at all. There was no danger of that ever happening on Brewster Place. Lorraine taught too far from this neighborhood for anyone here to recognize her in that school. No, it wasn't her job she feared losing this time, but their approval. She wanted to stand out there and chat and trade makeup secrets and cake recipes. She wanted to be secretary of their block association and be asked to mind their kids while they ran to the store. And none of that was going to happen if they couldn't even bring themselves to accept her good evenings.

Theresa silently finished unpacking the groceries. "Why did you buy cottage cheese? Who eats that stuff?"

"Well, I thought we should go on a diet."

"If *we* go on a diet, then you'll disappear. You've got nothing to lose but your hair."

40      "Oh, I don't know. I thought that we might want to try and reduce our hips or something." Lorraine shrugged playfully.

"No, thank you. We are very happy with our hips the way they are," Theresa said, as she shoved the cottage cheese to the back of the refrigerator. "And even when I lose weight, it never comes off there. My chest and arms just get smaller, and I start looking like a bottle of salad dressing."

The two women laughed, and Theresa sat down to watch Lorraine fix dinner. "You know, this behind has always been my downfall. When I was coming up in Georgia with my grandmother, the boys used to promise me penny candy if I would let them pat my behind. And I used to love those jawbreakers—you know, the kind that lasted all day and kept changing colors in your mouth. So I was glad to oblige them, because in one afternoon I could collect a whole week's worth of jawbreakers."

"Really. That's funny to you? Having some boy feeling all over you."

Theresa sucked her teeth. "We were only kids, Lorraine. You know, you remind me of my grandmother. That was one straight-laced old lady. She had a fit when my brother told her what I was doing. She called me into the smokehouse and told me in this real scary whisper that I could get pregnant from letting little boys pat my butt and that I'd end up like my cousin Willa. But Willa and I had been thick as fleas, and she had already given me a step-by-step summary of how she'd gotten into her predicament. But I sneaked around to her house that night just to double-check her story, since that old lady had seemed so earnest. 'Willa, are you sure?' I whispered through her bedroom window. 'I'm tellin' ya, Tee,' she said. 'Just keep both feet on the ground and you home free.' Much later I learned that advice wasn't too biologically sound, but it worked in Georgia because those country boys didn't have much imagination."

45     Theresa's laughter bounced off of Lorraine's silent, rigid back and died in her throat. She angrily tore open a pack of the chocolate chip cookies. "Yeah," she said, staring at Lorraine's back and biting down hard into the cookie, "it wasn't until I came up north to college that I found out there's a whole lot of things that a dude with a little imagination can do to you even with both feet on the ground. You see, Willa forgot to tell me not to bend over or squat or—"

"Must you!" Lorraine turned around from the stove with her teeth clenched tightly together.

"Must I what, Lorraine? Must I talk about things that are as much a part of life as eating or breathing or growing old? Why are you always so uptight about sex or men?"

"I'm not uptight about anything. I just think it's disgusting when you go on and on about—"

"There's nothing disgusting about it, Lorraine. You've never been with a man, but I've been with quite a few—some better than others. There were a couple who I still hope to this day will die a slow, painful death, but then there were some who were good to me—in and out of bed."

50     "If they were so great, then why are you with me?" Lorraine's lips were trembling.

"Because—" Theresa looked steadily into her eyes and then down at the cookie she was twirling on the table. "Because," she continued slowly, "you can take a chocolate chip cookie and put holes in it and attach it to your ears and call it an earring, or hang it around your neck on a silver chain and pretend it's a necklace—but it's still a cookie. See—you can toss it in the air and call it a Frisbee or even a flying saucer, if the mood hits you, and it's still just a cookie. Send it spinning on a table—like this—until it's a wonderful blur of amber and brown light that you can imagine to be a topaz or rusted gold or old crystal, but the law of gravity has got to come into play, sometime, and it's got to come to rest—sometime. Then all the spinning and pretending and hoopla is over with. And you know what you got?"

"A chocolate chip cookie," Lorraine said.

"Uh-huh." Theresa put the cookie in her mouth and winked. "A lesbian." She got up from the table. "Call me when dinner's ready, I'm going back to read." She stopped at the kitchen door. "Now, why are you putting gravy on that chicken, Lorraine? You know it's fattening."

## ▓ TOPICS FOR CRITICAL THINKING AND WRITING

1. The first sentence says, "At first they seemed like such nice girls." What do we know about the person who says it? What does it tell us (and imply) about the "nice girls"?
2. What is Sophie's role in the story?
3. In the second part of the story, who is the narrator? Does she or he know Theresa's thoughts, or Lorraine's, or both?
4. How does the story end? What do you think will happen between Lorraine and Theresa?
5. Try writing a page or less that is the *end* of a story about two people (men, women, children—but *people*) whose relationship is going to end soon, or is going to survive, because of, or despite, its difficulties.

# DIANA CHANG

*Diana Chang, author of several novels and books of poems, teaches creative writing at Barnard College. She identifies herself as an American writer whose background is mostly Chinese.*

## *The Oriental Contingent*                                    [1989]

Connie couldn't remember whose party it was, whose house. She had an impression of kerosene lamps on brown wicker tables, of shapes talking in doorways. It was summer, almost the only time Connie has run into her since, too, and someone was saying, "You must know Lisa Mallory."

"I don't think so."

"She's here. You must know her."

Later in the evening, it was someone else who introduced her to a figure perched on the balustrade of the steps leading to the lawn where more shapes milled. In stretching out a hand to shake Connie's, the figure almost fell off sideways. Connie had pushed her back upright onto her perch and, peering, took in the fact that Lisa Mallory had a Chinese face. For a long instant, she felt nonplussed, and was rendered speechless.

5    But Lisa Mallory was filling the silence. "Well, now, Connie Sung," she said, not enthusiastically but with a kind of sophisticated interest, "I'm not

in music myself, but Paul Wu's my cousin. Guilt by association!" She laughed. "No-tone music, I call his. He studied with John Cage, Varese, and so forth."

Surprised that Lisa knew she was a violinist, Connie murmured something friendly, wondering if she should simply ask outright, "I'm sure I should know, but what do you do?" but she hesitated, taking in her appearance instead, while Lisa went on with, "It's world class composing. Nothing's wrong with the level. But it's hard going for the layman, believe me."

Lisa Mallory wore a one-of-a-kind kimono dress, but it didn't make her look Japanese at all, and her hair was drawn back tightly in a braid which stood out from close to the top of her head horizontally. You could probably lift her off her feet by grasping it, like the handle of a pot.

"You should give a concert here, Connie," she said, using her first name right away, Connie noticed, like any American. "Lots of culturati around." Even when she wasn't actually speaking, she pursued her own line of thought actively and seemed to find herself mildly amusing.

"I'm new to the area," Connie said, deprecatingly. "I've just been a weekend guest, actually, till a month ago.

10      "It's easy to be part of it. Nothing to it. I should know. You'll see."

"I wish it weren't so dark," Connie found herself saying, waving her hand in front of her eyes as if the night were a veil to brush aside. She recognized in herself that intense need to see, to see into fellow Orientals, to fathom them. So far, Lisa Mallory had not given her enough clues, and the darkness itself seemed to be interfering.

Lisa dropped off her perch. "It's important to be true to oneself," she said. "Keep the modern stuff out of your repertory. Be romantic. Don't look like that! You're best at the romantics. Anyhow, take it from me. I know. And *I* like what I like."

Released by her outspokenness, Connie laughed and asked, "I'm sure I should know, but what is it that you do?" She was certain Lisa would say something like, "I'm with a public relations firm." "I'm in city services."

But she replied, "What do all Chinese excel at?" Not as if she'd asked a rhetorical question, she waited, then answered herself. "Well, aren't we all physicists, musicians, architects, or in software?"

15      At that point a voice broke in, followed by a large body which put his arms around both women, "The Oriental contingent! I've got to break this up."

Turning, Lisa kissed him roundly, and said over her shoulder to Connie, "I'll take him away before he tells us we look alike!"

They melted into the steps below, and Connie, feeling put off balance and somehow slow-witted, was left to think over her new acquaintance.

"Hello, Lisa Mallory," Connie Sung always said on the infrequent occasions when they ran into one another. She always said "Hello, Lisa Mallory," with a shyness she did not understand in herself. It was strange, but they had no mutual friends except for Paul Wu, and Connie had not seen him in ages. Connie had no one of whom to ask her questions. But sometime soon, she'd be told Lisa's maiden name. Sometime she'd simply call her Lisa. Sometime what Lisa did with her life would be answered.

Three, four years passed, with their running into one another at receptions and openings, and still Lisa Mallory remained an enigma. Mildly amused herself, Connie wondered if other people, as well, found her inscrutable. But none of her American friends (though, of course, Lisa and she were Americans, too, she had to remind herself), none of the Caucasian friends seemed curious about backgrounds. In their accepting way, they did not wonder about Lisa's background, or about Connie's or Paul Wu's. Perhaps they assumed they were all cut from the same cloth. But to Connie, the Orientals she met were unread books, books she never had the right occasion or time to fully pursue.

20    She didn't even see the humor in her situation—it was such an issue with her. The fact was she felt less, much less, sure of herself when she was with real Chinese.

As she was realizing this, the truth suddenly dawned on her. Lisa Mallory never referred to her own background because it was more Chinese than Connie's, and therefore a higher order. She was tact incarnate. All along, she had been going out of her way not to embarrass Connie. Yes, yes. Her assurance was definitely uppercrust (perhaps her father had been in the diplomatic service), and her offhand didacticness, her lack of self-doubt, was indeed characteristically Chinese Chinese. Connie was not only impressed by these traits, but also put on the defensive because of them.

Connie let out a sigh—a sigh that follows the solution to a nagging problem . . . Lisa's mysteriousness. But now Connie knew only too clearly that her own background made her decidedly inferior. Her father was a second-generation gynecologist who spoke hardly any Chinese. Yes, inferior and totally without recourse.

Of course, at one of the gatherings, Connie met Bill Mallory, too. He was simply American, maybe Catholic, possibly lapsed. She was not put off balance by him at all. But most of the time he was away on business, and Lisa cropped up at functions as single as Connie.

Then one day, Lisa had a man in tow—wiry and tall, he looked Chinese from the Shantung area, or perhaps from Beijing, and his styled hair made him appear vaguely artistic.

25    "Connie," I'd like you to meet Eric Li. He got out at the beginning of the *détente*, went to Berkeley, and is assimilating a mile-a-minute," Lisa said, with her usual irony. "Bill found him and is grooming him, though he came with his own charisma."

Eric waved her remark aside. "Lisa has missed her calling. She was born to be in PR," he said, with an accent.

"Is that what she does?" Connie put in at once, looking only at him. "Is that her profession?"

"You don't know?" he asked, with surprise.

Though she was greeting someone else, Lisa turned and answered, "I'm a fabrics tycoon, I think I can say without immodesty." She moved away and continued her conversation with the other friend.

30    Behind his hand, he said, playfully, as though letting Connie in on a secret, "Factories in Hongkong and Taipei, and now he's—Bill, that is—is exploring them on the mainland."

"With her fabulous contacts over there!" Connie exclaimed, now seeing it all. "Of course, what a wonderful business combination they must make."

Eric was about to utter something, but stopped, and said flatly, "I have all the mainland contacts, even though I was only twenty when I left, but my parents ..."

"How interesting," Connie murmured lamely. "I see," preoccupied as she was with trying to put two and two together.

Lisa was back and said without an introduction, continuing her line of thought, "You two look good together, if I have to say so myself. Why don't you ask him to one of your concerts? And you, Eric, you're in America now, so don't stand on ceremony, or you'll be out in left field." She walked away with someone for another drink.

35    Looking uncomfortable, but recovering himself with a smile, Eric said, "Lisa makes me feel more Chinese than I am becoming—it is her directness, I suspect. In China, we'd say she is too much like a man."

At which Connie found herself saying, "She makes me feel *less* Chinese."

"Less!"

"Less Chinese than she is."

"That is not possible," Eric said, with a shade of contempt—for whom? Lisa or Connie? He barely suppressed a laugh, cold as Chinese laughter could be.

40    Connie blurted out, "I'm a failed Chinese. Yes, and it's to you that I need to say it." She paused and repeated emphatically, "I am a failed Chinese." Her hear was beating quicker, but she was glad to have got that out, a confession and a definition that might begin to free her. "Do you know you make me feel that, too? You've been here only about ten years, right?"

"Right, and I'm thirty-one."

"You know what I think? I think it's harder for a Chinese to do two things."

At that moment, an American moved in closer, looking pleased somehow to be with them.

She continued, "It's harder for us to become American than, say, for a German, and it's also harder not to remain residually Chinese, even if you are third generation."

45      Eric said blandly,"Don't take yourself so seriously.You can't help being an American product.
        Trying to be comforting, the American interjected with,"The young
lady is not a product, an object. She is a human being, and there is no difference among peoples that I can see."
        "I judge myself both as a Chinese and as an American," Connie said.
        "You worry too much," Eric said, impatiently.Then he looked around
and though she wasn't in sight, he lowered his voice."She is what she is.
I know what she is. But she avoids going to Hongkong. She avoids it."
        Connie felt turned around."Avoids it?"
50      "Bill's in Beijing right now. She's here. How come?"
        "I don't know," Connie replied, as though an answer had been re-
quired of her.
        "She makes up many excuses, reasons.Ask her.Ask her yourself," he
said, pointedly.
        "Oh, I couldn't do that. By the way, I'm going on a concert tour next
year in three cities—Shanghai, Beijing and Nanking," Connie said."It'll be
my first time in China."
        "Really! You must be very talented to be touring at your age," he said,
genuinely interested for the first time. Because she was going to China, or
because she now came across as an over-achiever, even though Chinese
American?
55      "I'm just about your age," she said, realizing then that maybe Lisa Mallory had left them alone purposely.
        "You could both pass as teenagers!" the American exclaimed.

        Two months later, she ran into Lisa again. As usual, Lisa began in the
middle of her own thought."Did he call?"
        "Who? Oh. No, no."
        "Well, it's true he's been in China the last three weeks with Bill.
They'll be back this weekend."
60      Connie saw her opportunity."Are you planning to go to China yourself?"
        For the first time, Lisa seemed at a loss for words. She raised her
shoulders, then let them drop.Too airily, she said, "You know, there's always Paris. I can't bear not to go to Paris, if I'm to take a trip."
        "But you're Chinese.You *have* been to China, you came from China
originally, didn't you?"
        "I could go to Paris twice a year, I love it so," Lisa said. "And then
there's London, Florence,Venice."
        "But—but your business contacts?"
65      "*My* contacts? Bill, he's the businessman who makes the contacts.Al-
ways has. I take care of the New York office, which is a considerable job.
We have a staff of eighty-five."
        Connie said,"I told Eric I'll be giving a tour in China. I'm taking Chi-
nese lessons right now."

Lisa Mallory laughed, "Save your time. They'll still be disdainful over there. See, *they* don't care," and she waved her hand at the crowd. "Some of them have been born in Buffalo, too! It's the Chinese you can't fool. They know you're not the genuine article—you and I."

Her face was suddenly heightened in color, and she was breathing as if ready to flee from something. "Yes, you heard right. I was born in Buffalo."

"You were!" Connie exclaimed before she could control her amazement.

70      "Well, what about you?" Lisa retorted. She was actually shaking and trying to hide it by making sudden gestures.

"Westchester."

"But your parents at least were Chinese."

"Well, so were, so are, yours!"

"I was adopted by Americans. My full name is Lisa Warren Mallory."

75      Incredulous, Connie said, "I'm more Chinese than you!"

"Who isn't?" She laughed, unhappily. "Having Chinese parents makes all the difference. We're worlds apart."

"And all the time I thought . . . never mind what I thought."

"You have it over me. It's written all over you. I could tell even in the dark that night."

"Oh, Lisa," Connie said to comfort her, "none of this matters to anybody except us. Really and truly. They're too busy with their own problems."

80      "The only time I feel Chinese is when I'm embarrassed. I'm not more Chinese—which is a totally Chinese reflex I'd give anything to be rid of!"

"I know what you mean."

"And as for Eric looking down his nose at me, he's knocking himself out to be so American, *but as a secure Chinese!* What's so genuine about that article?"

Both of them struck their heads laughing, but their eyes were not merry.

"Say it again," Connie asked of her, "say it again that my being more Chinese is written all over me."

85      "Consider it said," Lisa said. "My natural mother happened to be there at the time—I can't help being born in Buffalo."

"I know, I know," Connie said with feeling. "If only you had had some say in the matter."

"It's only Orientals who haunt me!" Lisa stamped her foot. "Only them!"

"I'm so sorry," Connie Sung said, for all of them. "It's all so turned around."

"So I'm made in America, so there!" Lisa Mallory declared, making a sniffing sound, and seemed to be recovering her sangfroid.

90      Connie felt tired—as if she'd traveled—but a lot had been settled on the way.

## ▓ TOPICS FOR
## CRITICAL THINKING AND WRITING

1. In the first paragraph, a person (whose name we don't know) says, "You must know Lisa Mallory." Why does she make that assumption?
2. During their first meeting Connie thinks "she recognized in herself that intense need to see, to see into fellow Orientals, to fathom them" and she waves "her hand in front of her eyes." Does she know what she is looking for?
3. What does Eric do in the story? What is his function? And what about "the American" (paragraph 43)?
4. In paragraph 88 we read, "'I'm so sorry,' Connie Sung said, for all of them. 'It's all so turned around.'" What does the writer mean by "for all of them"? And what does Connie mean by "It's all so turned around"?

## GISH JEN

*Gish Jen, born in 1955 in Yonkers, New York, and the daughter of Chinese immigrants, was named Lillian Jen by her parents. She disliked the name Lillian, and her school friends created a new name for her, derived from the name of a famous actress of the silent screen—Lillian Gish. Jen graduated from Harvard and then, in accordance with her parents' wishes, went to Stanford Business School (M.B.A., 1980). Then, following her own wishes, Jen went to the University of Iowa, where in 1983 she earned an M.F.A. in the writing program. She has published three novels and a book of short stories, Who's Irish? We reprint the title story.*

### Who's Irish?
[1998]

In China, people say mixed children are supposed to be smart, and definitely my granddaughter Sophie is smart. But Sophie is wild, Sophie is not like my daughter Natalie, or like me. I am work hard my whole life, and fierce besides. My husband always used to say he is afraid of me, and in our restaurant, busboys and cooks all afraid of me too. Even the gang members come for protection money, they try to talk to my husband. When I am there, they stay away. If they come by mistake, they pretend they are come to eat. They hide behind the menu, they order a lot of food. They talk about their mothers. Oh, my mother have some arthritis, need to take herbal medicine, they say. Oh, my mother getting old, her hair all white now.

I say, Your mother's hair used to be white, but since she dye it, it become black again. Why don't you go home once in a while and take a look? I tell them, Confucius[1] say a filial son knows what color his mother's hair is.

My daughter is fierce too, she is vice president in the bank now. Her new house is big enough for everybody to have their own room, including me. But Sophie take after Natalie's husband's family, their name is Shea. Irish. I always thought Irish people are like Chinese people, work so hard on the railroad, but now I know why the Chinese beat the Irish. Of course, not all Irish are like the Shea family, of course not. My daughter tell me I should not say Irish this, Irish that.

How do you like it when people say the Chinese this, the Chinese that, she say.

5    You know, the British call the Irish heathen, just like they call the Chinese, she say.

You think the Opium War[2] was bad, how would you like to live right next door to the British, she say.

And that is that. My daughter have a funny habit when she win an argument, she take a sip of something and look away, so the other person is not embarrassed. So I am not embarrassed. I do not call anybody anything either. I just happen to mention about the Shea family, an interesting fact: four brothers in the family, and not one of them work. The mother, Bess, have a job before she got sick, she was executive secretary in a big company. She is handle everything for a big shot, you would be surprised how complicated her job is, not just type this, type that. Now she is a nice woman with a clean house. But her boys, every one of them is on welfare, or so-called severance pay, or so-called disability pay. Something. They say they cannot find work, this is not the economy of the fifties, but I say, Even the black people doing better these days, some of them live so fancy, you'd be surprised. Why the Shea family have so much trouble? They are white people, they speak English. When I come to this country, I have no money and do not speak English. But my husband and I own our restaurant before he die. Free and clear, no mortgage. Of course, I understand I am just lucky, come from a country where the food is popular all over the world. I understand it is not the Shea family's fault they come from a country where everything is boiled. Still, I say.

She's right, we should broaden our horizons, say one brother, Jim, at Thanksgiving. Forget about the car business. Think about egg rolls.

Pad thai, say another brother, Mike. I'm going to make my fortune in pad thai. It's going to be the new pizza.

10    I say, You people too picky about what you sell. Selling egg rolls not good enough for you, but at least my husband and I can say, We made it. What can you say? Tell me. What can you say?

---

[1]**Confucius** Chinese religious leader and philosopher (551–479 BCE). [2]**Opium War** conflicts, 1839–42 and 1856–60, between China and Great Britain involving the opium trade.

Everybody chew their tough turkey.

I especially cannot understand my daughter's husband John, who has no job but cannot take care of Sophie either. Because he is a man, he say, and that's the end of the sentence.

Plain boiled food, plain boiled thinking. Even his name is plain boiled: John. Maybe because I grew up with black bean sauce and hoisin sauce and garlic sauce, I always feel something is missing when my son-in-law talk.

But, okay: so my son-in-law can be man, I am baby-sitter. Six hours a day, same as the old sitter, crazy Amy, who quit. This is not so easy, now that I am sixty-eight, Chinese age almost seventy. Still, I try. In China, daughter take care of mother. Here it is the other way around. Mother help daughter, mother ask, Anything else I can do? Otherwise daughter complain mother is not supportive. I tell daughter, We do not have this word in Chinese, *supportive*. But my daughter too busy to listen, she has to go to meeting, she has to write memo while her husband go to the gym to be a man, My daughter say otherwise he will be depressed. Seems like all his life he has this trouble, depression.

15    No one wants to hire someone who is depressed, she say. It is important for him to keep his spirits up.

Beautiful wife, beautiful daughter, beautiful house, oven can clean itself automatically. No money left over, because only one income, but lucky enough, got the baby-sitter for free. If John lived in China, he would be very happy. But he is not happy. Even at the gym things go wrong. One day, he pull a muscle. Another day, weight room too crowded. Always something.

Until finally, hooray, he has a job. Then he feel pressure.

I need to concentrate, he say. I need to focus.

He is going to work for insurance company. Salesman job. A paycheck, he say, and at least he will wear clothes instead of gym shorts. My daughter buy him some special candy bars from the health-food store. They say THINK! on them, and are supposed to help John think.

20    John is a good-looking boy, you have to say that, especially now that he shave so you can see his face.

I am an old man in a young man's game, say John.

I will need a new suit, say John.

This time I am not going to shoot myself in the foot, say John.

Good, I say.

25    She means to be supportive, my daughter say. Don't start the send her back to China thing, because we can't.

Sophie is three years old American age, but already I see her nice Chinese side swallowed up by her wild Shea side. She looks like mostly Chinese. Beautiful black hair, beautiful black eyes. Nose perfect size, not so flat looks like something fell down, not so large looks like some big deal got stuck in wrong face. Everything just right, only her skin is a brown surprise to John's family. So brown, they say. Even John say it. She never goes in the sun, still she is that color, he say. Brown. They say, Nothing the matter with brown. They are just surprised. So brown. Nattie is not that brown, they say. They say, It seems like Sophie should be a color in between Nattie and John. Seems funny, a girl named Sophie Shea be brown. But she is brown, maybe her name should be Sophie Brown. She never go in the sun, still she is that color, they say. Nothing the matter with brown. They are just surprised.

The Shea family talk is like this sometimes, going around and around like a Christmas-tree train.

Maybe John is not her father, I say one day, to stop the train. And sure enough, train wreck. None of the brothers ever say the word *brown* to me again.

Instead, John's mother, Bess, say, I hope you are not offended.

30      She say, I did my best on those boys. But raising four boys with no father is no picnic.

You have a beautiful family, I say.

I'm getting old, she say.

You deserve a rest, I say. Too many boys make you old.

I never had a daughter, she say. You have a daughter.

35      I have a daughter, I say. Chinese people don't think a daughter is so great, but you're right. I have a daughter.

I was never against the marriage, you know, she say. I never thought John was marrying down. I always thought Nattie was just as good as white.

I was never against the marriage either, I say. I just wonder if they look at the whole problem.

Of course you pointed out the problem, you are a mother, she say. And now we both have a granddaughter. A little brown granddaughter, she is so precious to me.

I laugh. A little brown granddaughter, I say. To tell you the truth, I don't know how she came out so brown.

40      We laugh some more. These days Bess need a walker to walk. She take so many pills, she need two glasses of water to get them all down. Her favorite TV show is about bloopers, and she love her bird feeder. All day long, she can watch that bird feeder, like a cat.

I can't wait for her to grow up, Bess say. I could use some female company.

Too many boys, I say.

Boys are fine, she say. But they do surround you after a while.

You should take a break, come live with us, I say. Lots of girls at our house.

45      Be careful what you offer, say Bess with a wink. Where I come from, people mean for you to move in when they say a thing like that.

Nothing the matter with Sophie's outside, that's the truth. It is inside that she is like not any Chinese girl I ever see. We go to the park, and this is

what she does. She stand up in the stroller. She take off all her clothes and
throw them in the fountain.
    Sophie! I say. Stop!
    But she just laugh like a crazy person. Before I take over as baby-sit-
ter, Sophie has that crazy-person sitter, Amy the guitar player. My daughter
thought this Amy very creative—another word we do not talk about in
China. In China, we talk about whether we have difficulty or no difficulty.
We talk about whether life is bitter or not bitter. In America, all day long,
people talk about creative. Never mind that I cannot even look at this
Amy, with her shirt so short that her belly button showing. This Amy think
Sophie should love her body. So when Sophie take off her diaper, Amy
laugh. When Sophie run around naked, Amy say she wouldn't want to
wear a diaper either. When Sophie go *shu-shu* in her lap, Amy laugh and
say there are no germs in pee. When Sophie take off her shoes, Amy say
bare feet is best, even the pediatrician say so. That is why Sophie now
walk around with no shoes like a beggar child. Also why Sophie love to
take off her clothes.
    Turn around! say the boys in the park. Let's see that ass!
50    Of course, Sophie does not understand. Sophie clap her hands, I am
the only one to say, No! This is not a game.
    It has nothing to do with John's family, my daughter say. Amy was too
permissive, that's all.
    But I think if Sophie was not wild inside, she would not take off her
shoes and clothes to begin with.
    You never take off your clothes when you were little, I say. All my
Chinese friends had babies, I never saw one of them act wild like that.
    Look, my daughter say. I have a big presentation tomorrow.
55    John and my daughter agree Sophie is a problem, but they don't
know what to do.
    You spank her, she'll stop, I say another day.
    But they say, Oh no.
    In America, parents not supposed to spank the child.
    It gives them low self-esteem, my daughter say. And that leads to prob-
lems later, as I happen to know.
60    My daughter never have big presentation the next day when the subject of spanking come up.
    I don't want you to touch Sophie, she say. No spanking, period.
    Don't tell me what to do, I say.
    I'm not telling you what to do, say my daughter. I'm telling you how
I feel.
    I am not your servant, I say. Don't you dare talk to me like that.
65    My daughter have another funny habit when she lose an argument.
She spread out all her fingers and look at them, as if she like to make sure
they are still there.

My daughter is fierce like me, but she and John think it is better to explain to Sophie that clothes are a good idea. This is not so hard in the cold weather. In the warm weather, it is very hard.

Use your words, my daughter say. That's what we tell Sophie. How about if you set a good example.

As if good example mean anything to Sophie. I am so fierce, the gang members who used to come to the restaurant all afraid of me, but Sophie is not afraid.

I say, Sophie, if you take off your clothes, no snack.

70    I say, Sophie, if you take off your clothes, no lunch.

I say, Sophie, if you take off your clothes, no park.

Pretty soon we are stay home all day, and by the end of six hours she still did not have one thing to eat. You never saw a child stubborn like that.

I'm hungry! she cry when my daughter come home.

What's the matter, doesn't your grandmother feed you? My daughter laugh.

75    No! Sophie say. She doesn't feed me anything!

My daughter laugh again. Here you go, she say.

She say to John, Sophie must be growing.

Growing like a weed, I say.

Still Sophie take off her clothes, until one day I spank her. Not too hard, but she cry and cry, and when I tell her if she doesn't put her clothes back on I'll spank her again, she put her clothes back on. Then I tell her she is good girl, and give her some food to eat. The next day we go to the park and, like a nice Chinese girl, she does not take off her clothes.

80    She stop taking off her clothes, I report. Finally!

How did you do it? my daughter ask.

After twenty-eight years experience with you, I guess I learn something, I say.

It must have been a phase, John say, and his voice is suddenly like an expert.

His voice is like an expert about everything these days, now that he carry a leather briefcase, and wear shiny shoes, and can go shopping for a new car. On the company, he say. The company will pay for it, but he will be able to drive it whenever he want.

85    A free car, he say. How do you like that.

It's good to see you in the saddle again, my daughter say. Some of your family patterns are scary.

At least I don't drink, he say. He say, And I'm not the only one with scary family patterns.

That's for sure, say my daughter.

Everyone is happy. Even I am happy, because there is more trouble with Sophie, but now I think I can help her Chinese side fight against her wild side. I teach her to eat food with fork or spoon or chopsticks, she cannot just grab into the middle of a bowl of noodles. I teach her not to play with garbage cans. Sometimes I spank her, but not too often, and not too hard.

90 Still, there are problems. Sophie like to climb everything. If there is a railing, she is never next to it. Always she is on top of it. Also, Sophie like to hit the mommies of her friends. She learn this from her playground best friend, Sinbad, who is four. Sinbad wear army clothes every day and like to ambush his mommy. He is the one who dug a big hole under the play structure, a foxhole he call it, all by himself. Very hardworking. Now he wait in the foxhole with a shovel full of wet sand. When his mommy come, he throw it right at her.

Oh, it's all right, his mommy say. You can't get rid of war games, it's part of their imaginative play. All the boys go through it.

Also, he like to kick his mommy, and one day he tell Sophie to kick his mommy too.

I wish this story is not true.

Kick her, kick her! Sinbad say.

95 Sophie kick her. A little kick, as if she just so happened was swinging her little leg and didn't realize that big mommy leg was in the way. Still I spank Sophie and make Sophie say sorry, and what does the mommy say?

Really, it's all right, she say. It didn't hurt.

After that, Sophie learn she can attack mommies in the playground, and some will say, Stop, but others will say, Oh, she didn't mean it, especially if they realize Sophie will be punished.

This is how, one day, bigger trouble come. The bigger trouble start when Sophie hide in the foxhole with that shovel full of sand. She wait, and when I come look for her, she throw it at me. All over my nice clean clothes.

Did you ever see a Chinese girl act this way?

100 Sophie! I say. Come out of there, say you're sorry.

But she does not come out. Instead, she laugh. Naaah, naah-na, naaa-naaa, she say.

I am not exaggerate: millions of children in China, not one act like this.

Sophie! I say. Now! Come out now!

But she know she is in big trouble. She know if she come out, what will happen next. So she does not come out. I am sixty-eight, Chinese age almost seventy, how can I crawl under there to catch her? Impossible. So I yell, yell, yell, and what happen? Nothing. A Chinese mother would help, but American mothers, they look at you, they shake their head, they go home. And, of course, a Chinese child would give up, but not Sophie.

105 I hate you! she yell. I hate you, Meanie!

Meanie is my new name these days.

Long time this goes on, long long time. The foxhole is deep, you cannot see too much, you don't know where is the bottom. You cannot hear too much either. If she does not yell, you cannot even know she is still there or not. After a while, getting cold out, getting dark out. No one left in the playground, only us.

Sophie, I say. How did you become stubborn like this? I am go home without you now.

I try to use a stick, chase her out of there, and once or twice I hit her, but still she does not come out. So finally I leave. I go outside the gate.

110    Bye-bye! I say. I'm go home now.

But still she does not come out and does not come out. Now it is dinnertime, the sky is black. I think I should maybe go get help, but how can I leave a little girl by herself in the playground? A bad man could come. A rat could come. I go back in to see what is happen to Sophie. What if she have a shovel and is making a tunnel to escape?

Sophie! I say.

No answer.

Sophie!

115    I don't know if she is alive. I don't know if she is fall asleep down there. If she is crying, I cannot hear her.

So I take the stick and poke.

Sophie! I say. I promise I no hit you. If you come out, I give you a lollipop.

No answer. By now I worried. What to do, what to do, what to do? I poke some more, even harder, so that I am poking and poking when my daughter and John suddenly appear.

What are you doing? What is going on? say my daughter.

120    Put down that stick! say my daughter.

You are crazy! say my daughter.

John wiggle under the structure, into the foxhole, to rescue Sophie.

She fell asleep, say John the expert. She's okay. That is one big hole.

Now Sophie is crying and crying.

125    Sophie, my daughter say, hugging her. Are you okay, peanut? Are you okay?

She's just scared, say John.

Are you okay? I say too. I don't know what happen, I say.

She's okay, say John. He is not like my daughter, full of questions. He is full of answers until we get home and can see by the lamplight.

Will you look at her? he yell then. What the hell happened?

130    Bruises all over her brown skin, and a swollen-up eye.

You are crazy! say my daughter. Look at what you did! You are crazy!

I try very hard, I say.

How could you use a stick? I told you to use your words!

She is hard to handle, I say.

135    She's three years old! You cannot use a stick! say my daughter.

She is not like any Chinese girl I ever saw, I say.

I brush some sand off my clothes. Sophie's clothes are dirty too, but at least she has her clothes on.

Has she done this before? ask my daughter. Has she hit you before?
She hits me all the time, Sophie say, eating ice cream.
140   Your family, say John.
Believe me, say my daughter.

A daughter I have, a beautiful daughter. I took care of her when she could
not hold her head up. I took care of her before she could argue with me,
when she was a little girl with two pigtails, one of them always crooked. I
took care of her when we have to escape from China, I took care of her
when suddenly we live in a country with cars everywhere, if you are not
careful your little girl get run over. When my husband die, I promise him I
will keep the family together, even though it was just two of us, hardly a
family at all.

But now my daughter take me around to look at apartments. After all,
I can cook, I can clean, there's no reason I cannot live by myself, all I need
is a telephone. Of course, she is sorry. Sometimes she cry, I am the one to
say everything will be okay. She say she have no choice, she doesn't want
to end up divorced. I say divorce is terrible, I don't know who invented
this terrible idea. Instead of live with a telephone, though, surprise, I come
to live with Bess. Imagine that, Bess make an offer and, sure enough,
where she come from, people mean for you to move in when they say
things like that. A crazy idea, go to live with someone else's family, but she
like to have some female company, not like my daughter, who does not believe in company These days when my daughter visit, she does not bring
Sophie. Bess say we should give Nattie time, we will see Sophie again
soon. But seems like my daughter have more presentation than ever before, every time she come she have to leave.

I have a family to support, she say, and her voice is heavy, as if soaking
wet. I have a young daughter and a depressed husband and no one to
turn to.
145   When she say no one to turn to, she mean me.
These days my beautiful daughter is so tired she can just sit there in a
chair and fall asleep. John lost his job again, already, but still they rather
hire a baby-sitter than ask me to help, even they can't afford it. Of course,
the new baby-sitter is much younger, can run around. I don't know if Sophie these days is wild or not wild. She call me Meanie, but she like to kiss
me too, sometimes. I remember that every time I see a child on TV. Sophie
like to grab my hair, a fistful in each hand, and then kiss me smack on the
nose. I never see any other child kiss that way.

The satellite TV has so many channels, more channels than I can
count, including a Chinese channel from the Mainland and a Chinese
channel from Taiwan, but most of the time I watch bloopers with Bess.
Also, I watch the bird feeder—so many, many kinds of birds come. The
Shea sons hang around all the time, asking when will I go home, but Bess
tell them, Get lost.

She's a permanent resident, say Bess. She isn't going anywhere.

Then she wink at me, and switch the channel with the remote control.
150    Of course, I shouldn't say Irish this, Irish that, especially now I am become honorary Irish myself, according to Bess. Me! Who's Irish? I say, and
she laugh. All the same, if I could mention one thing about some of the
Irish, not all of them of course, I like to mention this: Their talk just stick. I
don't know how Bess Shea learn to use her words, but sometimes I hear
what she say a long time later. *Permanent resident. Not going anywhere.*
Over and over I hear it, the voice of Bess.

## ⊠ TOPICS FOR
## CRITICAL THINKING AND WRITING

1. The word "fierce" is used several times in "Who's Irish?" Please look
   up the definition of "fierce" in a good dictionary, and explain its significance for your understanding of the story.
2. Does the narrator change as a result of the experiences she describes?
3. Imagine that you have been assigned to teach "Who's Irish?" in a
   course on creative writing. What are the features of its style and structure that you would highlight for your students?
4. Now that you have read and studied "Who's Irish?," what is your response to Jen's choice of title? If the author asked you to suggest an
   alternate title, what would it be? Explain in detail why you feel that
   your title would be a good one.
5. Does this story help you to perceive something new about "diversity"? Do you think that "diversity" is an overused term? Why or
   why not?
6. How would you describe the differences between the generations as
   these are expressed in Jen's story? Do you think in general that there
   are significant differences between members of older and younger
   generations, or would you say that these are exaggerated?
7. Do you believe that sometimes these are good reasons for classifying
   people by race and ethnicity? What are these reasons? Do you find
   them convincing? How should we classify "mixed race" persons?

## TONI CADE BAMBARA

*Toni Cade Bambara (1939-1995), an African-American writer, was
born in New York City and grew up in black districts of the city. After
studying at the University of Florence and at City College in New York,
where she received a master's degree, she worked for a while as a case
investigator for the New York State Welfare Department. Later she di-*

*rected a recreation program for hospital patients. Once her literary rep-*
*utation was established, she spent most of her time writing, though she*
*also served as writer in residence at Spelman College in Atlanta.*

# The Lesson

[1972]

Back in the days when everyone was old and stupid or young and foolish
and me and Sugar were the only ones just right, this lady moved on our
block with nappy hair and proper speech and no makeup. And quite naturally we laughed at her, laughed the way we did at the junk man who went
about his business like he was some big-time president and his sorry-ass
horse his secretary. And we kinda hated her too, hated the way we did the
winos who cluttered up our parks and pissed on our handball walls and
stank up our hallways and stairs so you couldn't halfway play hide-and-
seek without a goddam gas mask. Miss Moore was her name. The only
woman on the block with no first name. And she was black as hell, cept for
her feet, which were fish-white and spooky. And she was always planning
these boring ass things for us to do, us being my cousin, mostly, who lived
on the block cause we all moved North the same time and to the same
apartment then spread out gradual to breathe. And our parents would yank
our heads into some kinda shape and crisp up our clothes so we'd be pre-
sentable for travel with Miss Moore, who always looked like she was going
to church, though she never did. Which is just one of the things the
grownups talked about when they talked behind her back like a dog. But
when she came calling with some sachet she'd sewed up or some gingerbread she'd made or some book, why then they'd all be too embarrassed
to turn her down and we'd get handed over all spruced up. She'd been to
college and said it was only right that she should take responsibility for the
young ones' education, and she not even related by marriage or blood. So
they'd go for it. Specially Aunt Gretchen. She was the main gofer in the family. You got some old dumb shit foolishness you want somebody to go for,
you send for Aunt Gretchen. She been screwed into the go-along for so
long, it's a blood-deep natural thing with her. Which is how she got saddled
with me and Sugar and Junior in the first place while our mothers were in
la-de-da apartment up the block having a good ole time.

So this one day Miss Moore rounds us all up at the mailbox and it's
puredee hot and she's knockin herself out about arithmetic. And school
suppose to let up in summer I heard, but she don't never let up. And the
starch in my pinafore scratching the shit outta me and I'm really hating
this nappy-head bitch and her goddam college degree. I'd much rather go
to the pool or to the show where it's cool. So me and Sugar leaning on the
mailbox being surly, which is a Miss Moore word. And Flyboy checking
out what everybody brought for lunch. And Fat Butt already wasting his
peanut-butter-and-jelly sandwich like the pig he is. And Junebug punchin

on Q.T.'s arm for potato chips. And Rosie Giraffe shifting from one hip to the other waiting for somebody to step on her foot or ask her if she from Georgia so she can kick ass, preferably Mercedes'. And Miss Moore asking us do we know what money is, like we a bunch of retards. I mean real money, she say, like it's only poker chips or monopoly papers we lay on the grocer. So right away I'm tired of this and say so. And would much rather snatch Sugar and go to the Sunset and terrorize the West Indian kids and take their hair ribbons and their money too. And Miss Moore files that remark away for next week's lesson on brotherhood, I can tell. And finally I say we oughta get to the subway cause it's cooler and besides we might meet some cute boys. Sugar done swiped her mama's lipstick, so we ready.

So we heading down the street and she's boring us silly about what things cost and what our parents make and how much goes for rent and how money ain't divided up right in this country. And then she gets to the part about we all poor and live in the slums, which I don't feature. And I'm ready to speak on that, but she steps out in the street and hails two cabs just like that. Then she hustles half the crew in with her and hands me a five-dollar bill and tells me to calculate 10 percent tip for the driver. And we're off. Me and Sugar and Junebug and Flyboy hangin out the window and hollering to everybody, putting lipstick on each other cause Flyboy a faggot anyway, and making farts with our sweaty armpits. But I'm mostly trying to figure how to spend this money. But they all fascinated with the meter ticking and Junebug starts laying bets as to how much it'll read when Flyboy can't hold his breath no more. Then Sugar lays bets as to how much it'll be when we get there. So I'm stuck. Don't nobody want to go for my plan, which is to jump out at the next light and run off to the first bar-b-que we can find. Then the driver tells us to get the hell out cause we there already. And the meter reads eighty-five cents. And I'm stalling to figure out the tip and Sugar say give him a dime. And I decide he don't need it bad as I do, so later for him. But then he tries to take off with Junebug foot still in the door so we talk about his mama something ferocious. Then we check out that we on Fifth Avenue and everybody dressed up in stockings. One lady in a fur coat, hot as it is. White folks crazy.

"This is the place," Miss Moore say, presenting it to us in the voice she uses at the museum. "Let's look in the windows before we go in."

5    "Can we steal?" Sugar asks very serious like she's getting the ground rules squared away before she plays. "I beg your pardon," say Miss Moore, and we fall out. So she leads us around the windows of the toy store and me and Sugar screamin, "This is mine, that's mine. I gotta have that, that was made for me. I was born for that," till Big Butt drowns us out.

"Hey, I'm going to buy that there."

"That there? You don't even know what it is, stupid."

"I do so," he say punchin on Rosie Giraffe. "It's a microscope."

"Whatcha gonna do with a microscope, fool?"

10    "Look at things."

"Like what, Ronald?" ask Miss Moore. And Big Butt ain't got the first notion. So here go Miss Moore gabbing about the thousands of bacteria in a drop of water and the somethinorother in a speck of blood and the million and one living things in the air around us is invisible to the naked eye. And what she say that for? Junebug go to town on that "naked" and we rolling. Then Miss Moore ask what it cost. So we all jam into the window smudgin it up and the price tag say $300. So then she ask how long'd take for Big Butt and Junebug to save up their allowances. "Too long," I say. "Yeh," adds Sugar, "outgrown it by that time." And Miss Moore say no, you never outgrow learning instruments. "Why, even medical students and interns and," blah, blah, blah. And we ready to choke Big Butt for bringing it up in the first damn place.

"This here cost four hundred eighty dollars," say Rosie Giraffe. So we pile up all over her to see what she pointin out. My eyes tell me it's a chunk of glass cracked with something heavy, and different-color inks dripped into the spits, then the whole thing put into a oven or something. But for $480 it don't make sense.

"That's a paperweight made of semi-precious stones fused together under tremendous pressure," she explains slowly, with her hands doing the mining and all the factory work.

"So what's a paperweight?" asks Rosie Giraffe.

15    "To weight paper with, dumbbell," say Flyboy, the wise man from the East.

"Not exactly," say Miss Moore, which is what she say when you warm or way off too. "It's to weigh paper down so it won't scatter and make your desk untidy." So right away me and Sugar curtsy to each other and then to Mercedes who is more the tidy type.

"We don't keep paper on top of the desk in my class," say Junebug, figuring Miss Moore crazy or lyin one.

"At home, then," she say. "Don't you have a calendar and a pencil case and a blotter and a letter-opener on your desk at home where you do your homework?" And she know damn well what our homes look like cause she nosys around in them every chance she gets.

"I don't even have a desk," say Junebug. "Do we?"

20    "No. And I don't get no homework neither," says Big Butt.

"And I don't even have a home," say Flyboy, like he do at school to keep the white folks off his back and sorry for him. Send this poor kid to camp posters, is his specialty.

"I do," says Mercedes. "I have a box of stationery on my desk and a picture of my cat. My godmother bought the stationery and the desk. There's a big rose on each sheet and the envelopes smell like roses."

"Who wants to know about your smelly-ass stationery," say Rosie Giraffe fore I can get my two cents in.

"It's important to have a work area all your own so that . . ."

25     "Will you look at this sailboat, please," say Flyboy, cuttin her off and pointin to the thing like it was his. So once again we tumble all over each other to gaze at this magnificent thing in the toy store which is just big enough to maybe sail two kittens across the pond if you strap them to the posts tight. We all start reciting the price tag like we in assembly. "Hand-crafted sailboat of fiberglass at one thousand one hundred ninety-five dollars."

"Unbelievable," I hear myself say and am really stunned. I read it again for myself just in case the group recitation put me in a trance. Same thing. For some reason this pisses me off. We look at Miss Moore and she lookin at us, waiting for I dunno what.

"Who'd pay all that when you can buy a sailboat set for a quarter at Pop's, a tube of glue for a dime, and a ball of string for eight cents? It must have a motor and a whole lot else besides," I say. "My sailboat cost me about fifty cents."

"But will it take water?" say Mercedes with her smart ass.

"Took mine to Alley Pond Park once," say Flyboy. "String broke. Lost it. Pity."

30     "Sailed mine in Central Park and it keeled over and sank. Had to ask my father for another dollar."

"And you got the strap," laugh Big Butt. "The jerk didn't even have a string on it. My old man wailed on his behind."

Little Q.T. was staring hard at the sailboat and you could see he wanted it bad. But he too little and somebody'd just take it from him. So what the hell. "This boat for kids, Miss Moore?"

"Parents silly to buy something like that just to get all broke up," say Rosie Giraffe.

"That much money it should last forever," I figure.

35     "My father'd buy it for me if I wanted it."

"Your father, my ass," say Rosie Giraffe getting a chance to finally push Mercedes.

"Must be rich people shop here," say Q.T.

"You are a very bright boy," say Flyboy. "What was your first clue?" And he rap him on the head with the back of his knuckles, since Q.T. the only one he could get away with. Though Q.T. liable to come up behind you years later and get his licks in when you half expect it.

"What I want to  know is," I says to Miss Moore though I never talk to her, I wouldn't give the bitch that satisfaction, "is how much a real boat costs? I figure a thousand'd get you a yacht any day."

40     "Why don't you check that out," she says, "and report back to the group?" Which really pains my ass. If you gonna mess up a perfectly good swim day least you could do is have some answers. "Let's go in," she say like she got something up her sleeve. Only she don't lead the way. So me and Sugar turn the corner to where the entrance is, but when we get

there I kinda hang back. Not that I'm scared, what's there to be afraid of, just a toy store. But I feel funny, shame. But what I got to be shamed about? Got as much right to go in as anybody. But somehow I can't seem to get hold of the door, so I step away for Sugar to lead. But she hangs back too. And I look at her and she looks at me and this is ridiculous. I mean, damn, I have never ever been shy about doing nothing or going nowhere. But then Mercedes steps up and then Rosie Giraffe and Big Butt crowd in behind and shove, and next thing we all stuffed into the doorway with only Mercedes squeezing past us, smoothing out her jumper and walking right down the aisle. Then the rest of us tumble in like a glued-together jigsaw done all wrong. And people lookin at us. And it's like the time me and Sugar crashed into the Catholic church on a dare. But once we got in there and everything so hushed and holy and the candles and the bowin and the handkerchiefs on all the drooping heads, I just couldn't go through with the plan. Which was for me to run up to the altar and do a tap dance while Sugar played the nose flute and messed around in the holy water. And Sugar kept giving me the elbow. Then later teased me so bad I tied her up in the shower and turned it on and locked her in. And she'd be there till this day if Aunt Gretchen hadn't finally figured I was lying about the boarder takin a shower.

Same thing in the store. We all walkin on tiptoe and hardly touchin the games and puzzles and things. And I watched Miss Moore who is steady watchin us like she waiting for a sign. Like Mama Drewery watches the sky and sniffs the air and takes note of just how much slant is in the bird formation. Then me and Sugar bump smack into each other, so busy gazing at the toys, 'specially the sailboat. But we don't laugh and go into our fat-lady bump-stomach routine. We just stare at that price tag. Then Sugar run a finger over the whole boat. And I'm jealous and want to hit her. Maybe not her, but I sure want to punch somebody in the mouth.

"Watcha bring us here for, Miss Moore?"

"You sound angry, Sylvia. Are you mad about something?" Givin me one of them grins like she tellin a grown-up joke that never turns out to be funny. And she's looking very closely at me like maybe she plannin to do my portrait from memory. I'm mad, but I won't give her the satisfaction. So I slouch around the store being very bored and say, "Let's go."

Me and Sugar at the back of the train watchin the tracks whizzin by large then small then gettin gobbled up in the dark. I'm thinkin about this tricky toy I saw in the store. A clown that somersaults on a bar then does chin-ups just cause you yank lightly at his leg. Cost $35. I could see me askin my mother for a $35 birthday clown. "You wanna who that costs what?" she'd say, cocking her head to the side to get a better view of the hole in my head. Thirty-five dollars could buy new bunk beds for Junior and Gretchen's boy. Thirty-five dollars and the whole household could go visit Granddaddy Nelson in the country. Thirty-five dollars would pay for the rent and the piano bill too. Who are these people that spend that much for performing clowns and $1000 for toy sailboats? What kinda work they do and how they live and how come we ain't in on it? Where we are is who we are, Miss Moore always pointin out. But it don't necessarily have to be that way, she always adds then waits for somebody to say that poor people have to wake up and demand their share of the pie and don't none of us know what kind of pie she talkin about in the first damn place. But she ain't so smart cause I still got her four dollars from the taxi and she sure ain't getting it. Messin up my day with this shit. Sugar nudges me in my pocket and winks.

45      Miss Moore lines us up in front of the mailbox where we started from, seem like years ago, and I got a headache for thinkin so hard. And we lean all over each other so we can hold up under the draggy-ass lecture she always finishes off with at the end before we thank her for borin us to tears. But she just looks at us like she readin tea leaves. Finally she say, "Well, what did you think of F.A.O. Schwarz?"

Rosie Giraffe mumbles, "White folks crazy."

"I'd like to go there again when I get my birthday money," says Mercedes, and we shove her out the pack so she has to lean on the mailbox by herself.

"I'd like a shower. Tiring day," say Flyboy.

Then Sugar surprises me by saying, "You know, Miss Moore, I don't think all of us here put together eat in a year what that sailboat costs." And Miss Moore lights up like somebody goosed her. "And?" she say, urging Sugar on. Only I'm standin on her foot so she don't continue.

50      "Imagine for a minute what kind of society it is in which some people can spend on a toy what it would cost to feed a family of six or seven. What do you think?"

"I think," say Sugar pushing me off her feet like she never done before, cause I whip her ass in a minute, "that this is not much of a democracy if you ask me. Equal chance to pursue happiness means an equal crack at the dough, don't it?" Miss Moore is beside herself and I am disgusted with Sugar's treachery. So I stand on her foot one more time to see if she'll shove me. She shuts up, and Miss Moore looks at me, sorrowfully I'm thinkin. And somethin weird is goin on, I can feel it in my chest.

"Anybody else learn anything today?" lookin dead at me. I walk away and Sugar has to run to catch up and don't even seem to notice when I shrug her arm off my shoulder.

"Well, we got four dollars anyway," she says.

"Uh hunh."

55      "We could go to Hascombs and get half a chocolate layer and then go to the Sunset and still have plenty of money for potato chips and ice cream sodas."

"Un hunh."

"Race you to Hascombs," she say.

We start down the block and she gets ahead which is O.K. by me cause I'm going to the West End and then over to the Drive to think this day through. She can run if she want to and even run faster. But ain't nobody gonna beat me at nuthin.

## ❖ TOPICS FOR CRITICAL THINKING AND WRITING

1. What is "the lesson" that Miss Moore is trying to teach the children? How much, if any, of this lesson does Sylvia learn? Point to specific passages to support your answers.
2. Since Miss Moore intends the lesson for the children's own good, why is Sylvia so resistant to it, so impatient and exasperated?
3. Toward the end of the story, Sylvia says that she is "disgusted with Sugar's treachery." Describe their relationship. What would be missing from the story if Bambara had not included Sugar among its characters?

# MICHELE SERROS

*Michele Serros, born in Oxnard, California, in 1966, published her first book of poems and stories,* Chicana Falsa *and Other Stories of Death, Identity, and Oxnard, while she was still a student at Santa Monica City College. We reprint a story from her second book,* How to Be a Chicana Role Model *(2000), which achieved national attention.*

## Senior Picture Day

Sometimes I put two different earrings in the same ear. And that's on a day I'm feeling preppy, not really new wave or anything. One time, during a track meet over at Camarillo High, I discovered way too late that I'd forgot to put on deodorant and that was the worst 'cause everyone knows how snooty those girls at Camarillo can be. Hmmm. Actually the worst thing I've ever forgotten to do was take my pill. That happened three mornings in a row and you can bet I was praying for weeks after that.

So many things to remember when you're seventeen years old and your days start at six A.M. and sometimes don't end until five in the afternoon. But today of all days there's one thing I have to remember to do and that's to squeeze my nose. I've been doing it since the seventh grade. Every morning with my thumb and forefinger I squeeze the sides of it, firmly pressing my nostrils as close as they possibly can get near the base. Sometimes while I'm waiting for the tortilla to heat up, or just when I'm brushing my teeth, I squeeze. Nobody ever notices. Nobody ever asks. With all the other shit seniors in high school go through, squeezing my nose is nothing. It's just like some regular early-morning routine, like yawning or wiping the egg from my eyes. Okay, so you might think it's just a total waste of time, but to tell you the truth, I do see the difference. Just last week I lined up all my class pictures and could definitely see the progress. My nose has actually become smaller, narrower. It looks less Indian. *I* look less Indian and you can bet that's the main goal here. Today, when I take my graduation pictures, my nose will look just like Terri's and then I'll have the best picture in the yearbook. I think about this as Mrs. Milne's Duster comes honking in the driveway to take me to school.

Terri was my best friend in seventh grade. She came from Washington to Rio Del Valle Junior high halfway through October. She was the first girl I knew who had contact lenses and *four* pairs of Chemin de Fers. Can you believe that? She told everyone that her daddy was gonna build 'em a swimming pool for the summer. She told me that I could go over to swim anytime I wanted. But until then, she told me, I could go over and we could play on her dad's CB.[1]

"You dad's really got a CB?" I asked her.

5    "Oh, yeah," she answered, jiggling her locker door. "You can come over and we can make up handles for ourselves and meet lots of guys. Cute ones."

Whaddaya mean, handles?" I asked.

"Like names, little nicknames. I never use my real name. I'm 'G.G.' when I get on. That stands for Golden Girl. Oh, and you gotta make sure you end every sentence with 'over.' You're like a total nerd if you don't finish with 'over.' I never talk to anyone who doesn't say 'over.' They're the worst."

Nobody's really into citizen band radios anymore. I now see 'em all lined up in pawnshops over on Oxnard Boulevard. But back in the seventh grade, everyone was getting them. They were way better than using a phone 'cause, first of all, there was no phone bill to bust you for talking to boys who lived past The Grade and second, you didn't have your stupid sister yelling at you for tying up the phone line. Most people had CBs in their cars, but Terri's dad had his in the den.

When I showed up at Terri's to check out the CB, her mama was in the front yard planting some purple flowers.

10    "Go on in already." She waved me in. "She's in her father's den."

I found Terri just like her mama said. She was already on the CB, looking flustered and sorta excited.

---

[1]**CB** Citizens Band (a radio frequency used by the general public to talk to one another over a short distance).

"Hey," I called out to her, and plopped my tote bag on her dad's desk. She didn't answer but rather motioned to me with her hands to hurry up. Her mouth formed an exaggerated, "Oh, *my* God!" She held out a glass bowl of Pringles and pointed to a glass of Dr Pepper on the desk.

It turned out Terri had found a boy on the CB. An older *interested* one. He was fifteen, a skateboarder, and his handle was Lightning Bolt.

15      "Lightning Bolt," he bragged to Terri. "Like, you know, powerful and fast. That's the way I skate. So," he continued, "where you guys live? Over."

"We live near Malibu." Terri answered. "Between Malibu and Santa Barbara. Over."

"Oh, excuse me, fan-ceee. Over."

"That's right." Terri giggled. "Over."

We actually lived in Oxnard. Really, in El Rio, a flat patch of houses, churches, and schools surrounded by lots of strawberry fields and some new snooty stucco homes surrounded by chainlink. But man, did Terri have this way of making things sound better. I mean, it *was* the truth, geographically, and besides it sounded way more glamorous.

20      I took some Pringles from the bowl and thought we were gonna have this wonderful afternoon of talking and flirting with Lightning Bolt until Terri's dad happened to come home early and found us gabbing in his den.

"What the . . . !" he yelled as soon as he walked in and saw us hunched over his CB, "What do you think this is? Party Central? Get off that thing!" He grabbed the receiver from Terri's hand. "This isn't a toy! It's a tool. A tool for communication, you don't use it just to meet boys!"

"Damn, Dad," Terri complained as she slid off her father's desk. "Don't have a cow." She took my hand and led me to her room. "Come on, let's pick you out a handle."

"You mean, like California?" she asked.

25      "Yeah, sorta."

"But you're Mexican."

"So?"

"So, you look like you're more from Mexico than California."

"What do you mean?"

30      "I mean, California is like, blond girls, you know."

"Yeah, but I *am* Californian. I mean, real Californian. Even my greatgrandma was born here."

"It's just that you don't look like you're from California."

"And you're not exactly golden," I snapped.

We decided to talk to Lightning Bolt the next day, Friday, right after school. Terri's dad always came home real late on Fridays, sometimes even early the next Saturday morning. It would be perfect. When I got to her house the garage door was wide open and I went in through the side door. I almost bumped into Terri's mama. She was spraying the house with Pine Scent and offered me some Hi-C.

35    "Help yourself to a Pudding Pop, too," she said before heading into the living room through a mist of aerosol. "They're in the freezer."

Man, Terri's mama made their whole life like an afternoon commercial. Hi-C, Pringles in a bowl, the whole house smelling like a pine forest. Was Terri lucky or what? I grabbed a Pudding Pop out of the freezer and was about to join her when I picked up on her laugh. She was already talking to Lightning Bolt. Dang, she didn't waste time!

"Well, maybe we don't ever want to meet you," I heard Terri flirt with Lightning Bolt. "How do you know we don't already have boyfriends? Over."

"Well, you both sound like foxes. So, uh, what *do* you look like? Over."

"I'm about five-four and have green eyes and ginger-colored hair. Over."

40    Green? Ginger? I always took Terri for having brown eyes and brown hair.

"What about your friend? Over."

"What about her? Over."

Oh, this was about me! I *had* to hear this. Terri knew how to pump up things good.

"I mean, what does she look like?" Lightning Bolt asked. "She sounds cute. Over."

45    "Well . . ." I overheard Terri hesitate. "Well, she's real skinny and, uh . . ."

"I like skinny girls!"

"You didn't let me finish!" Terri interrupted. "And you didn't say 'over.' Over."

"Sorry," Lightning Bolt said. "Go ahead and finish. Over."

I tore the wrapper off the Pudding Pop and continued to listen.

50    "Well," Terri continued. "She's also sorta flat-chested, I guess. Over."

*What?* How could Terri say that?

"Flat-chested? Oh yeah? Over." Lightning Bolt answered.

"Yeah. Over."

Terri paused uncomfortably. It was as if she knew what she was saying was wrong and bad and she should've stopped but couldn't. She was saying things about a friend, things a real friend shouldn't be saying about another friend, but now there was a boy involved and he was interested in that other friend, in me, and her side was losing momentum. She would have to continue to stay ahead.

55    "Yeah, and she also has this, this nose, a nose like . . . like an *Indian*. Over."

"An, Indian?" Lightning Bolt asked. "What do ya mean an Indian? Over."

"You know, *Indian*. Like powwow Indian."

"Really?" Lightning Bolt laughed on the other end. "Like Woo-Woo-Woo Indian?" He clapped his palm over his mouth and wailed. A sound I knew all too well.

"Yeah, just like that!" Terri laughed. "In fact, I think she's gonna pick 'Li'l Squaw' as her handle!"

60      I shut the refrigerator door quietly. I touched the ridge of my nose. I felt the bump my mother had promised me would be less noticeable once my face "filled out." The base of my nose was far from feminine and was broad, like, well, like Uncle Rudy's nose, Grandpa Rudy's nose, and yeah, a little bit of Uncle Vincente's nose, too. Men in my family who looked like Indians and here their Indian noses were lumped together on me, on my face. My nose made me look like I didn't belong, made me look less Californian than my blond counterparts. After hearing Terri and Lightning Bolt laugh, more than anything I hated the men in my family who had given me such a hideous nose.

I grabbed my tote bag and started to leave out through the garage door when Terri's mama called out from the living room. "You're leaving already?" she asked. "I know Terri would love to have you for dinner. Her daddy's working late again."

I didn't answer and I didn't turn around. I just walked out and went home.

And so that's how the squeezing began. I eventually stopped hanging out with Terri and never got a chance to use my handle on her dad's CB. I know it's been almost four years since she said all that stuff about me, about my nose, but man, it still stings.

65      During freshman year I heard that Terri's dad met some lady on the CB and left her mama for this other woman. Can you believe that? Who'd wanna leave a house that smelled like a pine forest and always had Pudding Pops in the freezer?

As Mrs. Milne honks from the driveway impatiently, I grab my books and run down the driveway, squeezing my nose just a little bit more. I do it because today is Senior Picture Day and because I do notice the difference. I might be too skinny. My chest might be too flat. But God forbid I look too Indian.

## �֍ TOPICS FOR CRITICAL THINKING AND WRITING

1. How would you characterize the narrator? Do you regard her with amusement, pity, contempt, sympathy—or all of the above, or none? Please explain.

2. Briefly recounted within this story about the narrator is another story about Terri's parents. Why do you suppose Serros included this story?

3. In your library find a book about the Maya, with illustrations of Mayan sculpture. In an essay of 250 words, describe the noses of the figures and summarize—giving credit to your source—any comments that the book makes about Mayan ideas of beauty.

# 10

# A Collection of Short Fiction

The stories of Cain and Abel, Ruth, Samson, and Joseph in the Hebrew Bible and the parables of Jesus in the New Testament are sufficient evidence that brief narratives existed in ancient times. The short tales in Boccaccio's *Decameron* and Chaucer's *Canterbury Tales* (the latter an amazing variety of narrative poems ranging from bawdy stories to legends of saints) are medieval examples of the ancient form. But, speaking generally, short narratives before the nineteenth century were either didactic pieces, with the narrative existing for the sake of a moral point, or they were "curious and striking" tales (to use Somerset Maugham's words for his favorite kind of story) recounted in order to entertain.

The contemporary short story is rather different from both of these genres, which can be called the parable and the anecdote. Like the parable, the contemporary short story has a point, a meaning; but unlike the parable, it has a richness of surface as well as depth, so that it is interesting whether or not the reader goes on to ponder "the meaning." Like the anecdote, the short story relates a happening, but whereas the happening in the anecdote is curious and is the center of interest, the happening in the contemporary story often is less interesting in itself than as a manifestation of a character's state of mind. A good short story usually has a psychological interest that an anecdote lacks.

The anecdotal story is what "story" means for most readers. It is an interesting happening or series of happenings, usually with a somewhat surprising ending. The anecdotal story, however, is quite different from most of the contemporary short stories in this book. The anecdote is good entertainment, and good entertainment should not be lightly dismissed. But it has two elements within it that prevent it (unless it is something in addition to an anecdote) from taking a high place among the world's literature. First, it cannot be reread with increasing or even continued pleasure. Even when it is well told, once we know the happening we may lose patience with the telling. Second, effective anecdotes are often highly implausible. Now, implausible anecdotes alleged to be true have a special impact by virtue of their alleged truth: they make us say to ourselves, "Truth is stranger than fiction." But the invented anecdote lacks this power; its unlikely coincidence, its unconvincing ironic situation, its surprise ending, are both untrue and unbelievable. It is entertaining but it is usually not especially meaningful.

The short story of the last hundred and fifty years is not an anecdote and is not an abbreviated novel. If it were the latter, *Reader's Digest* condensations of novels would be short stories. But they aren't; they are only eviscerated novels. Novelists usually cover a long period of time, presenting not only a few individuals but also something of a society. They often tell of the development of several many-sided figures. In contrast, short-story writers, having only a few pages, usually focus on a single figure in a single episode, revealing a character rather than recording its development.

Whereas the novel is narrative, the contemporary short story often seems less narrative than lyric or dramatic. in the short story we have a sense of a present mood or personality revealed, rather than the sense of a history reported. The revelation in a story is presented through incidents, of course, but the interest commonly resides in the character revealed through the incidents, rather than in the incidents themselves. Little "happens," in the sense that there is little rushing from place to place. What does "happen" is usually a mental reaction to an experience, and the mental reaction, rather than the external experience, is the heart of the story. In older narratives the plot usually involves a conflict that is resolved, bringing about a change in the protagonist's condition; in contemporary stories the plot usually is designed to reveal a protagonist's state of mind. This de-emphasis of overt actions results in a kinship with the lyric and the drama.

One way of looking at the matter is to distinguish between literature of *resolution* and literature of *revelation*, that is, between (1) literature that resolves a plot (literature that stimulates us to ask, "And what happened next?" and that finally leaves us with a settled state of affairs), and (2) literature that reveals a condition (literature that causes us to say, "Ah, now I understand how these people feel"). Two great writers of the later nineteenth century can be taken as representatives of the two kinds: Guy de Maupassant (1850–1893) usually put the emphasis on resolution, Anton Chekhov (1860–1904) usually on revelation. Maupassant's tightly plotted stories move to a decisive end, ordinarily marked by a great change in fortune (usually to the characters' disadvantage). Chekhov's stories, on the other hand, seem loosely plotted and may end with the characters pretty much in the condition they were in at the start, but *we* see them more clearly, even if *they* have not achieved any self-knowledge.

A slightly different way of putting the matter is this: much of the best short fiction from Chekhov onward is less concerned with *what happens* than it is with how a character (often the narrator) *feels* about the happenings. Thus the emphasis is not on external action but on inner action, feeling. Perhaps one can say that the reader is left with a mood rather than with an awareness of a decisive happening.

The distinction between a story of resolution and a story of revelation will probably be clear enough if you are familiar with stories by Maupassant and Chekhov, but of course the distinction should not be overemphasized. These are poles; most stories exist somewhere in between, closer to one pole or the other, but not utterly apart from the more remote pole. Consider again The Parable of the Prodigal Son, in Chapter 2. Insofar as the story stimulates responses such as "The son left, *and then what happened? Did he prosper?*" it is a story of resolution. Insofar as it makes increasingly evident the unchanging love of the father, it is a story of revelation.

The de-emphasis on narrative in the contemporary short story is not an invention of the twentieth-century mind. It goes back at least to three important American writers of the early nineteenth century—Washington Irving, Nathaniel Hawthorne, and Edgar Allan Poe. In 1824 Irving wrote:

> I fancy much of what I value myself upon in writing, escapes the observation of the great mass of my readers: who are intent more upon the story than the way in which it is told. For my part I consider a story merely as a frame on which to stretch my materials. It is the play of thought, and sentiments and language; the weaving in of characters, lightly yet expressively delineated; the familiar and faithful exhibition of scenes in common life; and the half-concealed vein of humor that is often playing through the whole—these are among what I aim at, and upon which I felicitate myself in proportion as I think I succeed.

Hawthorne and Poe may seem stranger than Irving as forebears of the contemporary short story: both are known for their fantastic narratives (and, in addition, Poe is known as the inventor of the detective story, a genre in which there is strong interest in curious happenings). But because Hawthorne's fantastic narratives are, as he said, highly allegorical, the reader's interest is pushed beyond the narrative to the moral significance. Poe's "arabesques," as he called his fanciful tales (in distinction from his detective tales of "ratiocination"), are aimed at revealing and arousing unusual mental states. The weird happenings and personages are symbolic representations of the mind or soul. In "The Cask of Amontillado," for instance, perhaps the chief interest is not in what happens but rather in the representation of an almost universal fear of being buried alive. But, it must be noted, in both Hawthorne and Poe we usually get what is commonly called the tale rather than the short story: We get short prose fiction dealing with the strange rather than the usual.

A paragraph from Poe's review (1842) of Hawthorne's *Twice Told Tales*, though more useful in revealing Poe's theory of fiction than Hawthorne's, illuminates something of the kinship between the contemporary short story and the best short fictions of the earlier nineteenth century. In the review Poe has been explaining that because "unity of effect or impression" is essential, a tale (Poe doubtless uses "tale" to mean short fiction in general, rather than the special type just discussed) that can be read at a single sitting has an advantage over the novel.

> A skillful artist has constructed a tale. He has not fashioned his thoughts to accommodate his incidents, but having deliberately conceived a certain single effect to be wrought, he then invents such incidents, he then combines such events, and discusses them in such tone as may best serve him in establishing this preconceived effect. If his very first sentence tends not to be outbringing of this effect, then in his very first step has he committed a blunder. In the whole composition there should be no word written of which the tendency, direct or indirect, is not to the one pre-established design. And by such means, with such care and skill a picture is at length painted which leaves in the mind of him who contemplates it with a kindred art, a sense of the fullest satisfaction. The idea of the tale, its thesis, has been presented unblemished, because undisturbed—an end absolutely demanded, yet, in the novel, altogether unattainable.

Nothing that we have said should be construed as suggesting that short fiction from the mid-nineteenth century to the present is necessarily better than older short narratives. The object of these comments has been less to evaluate than to call attention to the characteristics dominating short fiction of the last century and a half. Not that all of this fiction is of a piece; the stories in this book demonstrate something of its variety. Readers who do not like one story need not despair; they need only (in the words of an early writer of great short fiction) "turne over the leef and chese another tale."

# GUY DE MAUPASSANT

*Born and raised in Normandy, the French novelist and short-story writer Guy de Maupassant (1850–1893) studied law in Paris, then served in the Franco-Prussian War. Afterward he worked for a time as a clerk for the government until, with the support of the novelist Gustave Flaubert (a friend of Maupassant's mother) and later Émile Zola, he decided to pursue a career as a writer. Ironic and pointed, detached yet compassionate, Maupassant explores human folly and its both grim and comic consequences. His first great success came in April 1880, with the publication of the story "Boule de Suif" ("Ball of Fat"), about a prostitute traveling by coach, with a number of bourgeois companions, through Prussian-occupied France during wartime. Maupassant published six novels, including* Bel-Ami *(1885) and* Pierre et Jean *(1888), and a number of collections of stories, before his untimely death from the effects of syphilis, a month short of his forty-third birthday. Like many of his stories, "The Necklace" uses realistic observation and keenly chosen detail to tell its story of a misunderstanding and the years of hard labor that follow from it.*

# The Necklace

[1885]

*Translated by Marjorie Laurie*

She was one of those pretty and charming girls who are sometimes, as if by a mistake of destiny, born in a family of clerks. She had no dowry, no expectations, no means of being known, understood, loved, wedded by any rich and distinguished man; and she let herself be married to a little clerk at the Ministry of Public Instruction.

She dressed plainly because she could not dress well, but she was as unhappy as though she had really fallen from her proper station, since with women there is neither caste nor rank: and beauty, grace and charm act instead of family and birth. Natural fineness, instinct for what is elegant, suppleness of wit, are the sole hierarchy, and make from women of the people the equals of the very greatest ladies.

She suffered ceaselessly, feeling herself born for all the delicacies and all the luxuries. She suffered from the poverty of her dwelling, from the wretched look of the walls, from the worn-out chairs, from the ugliness of the curtains. All those things, of which another woman of her rank would never even have been conscious, tortured her and made her angry. The sight of the little Breton peasant who did her humble housework aroused in her regrets which were despairing, and distracted dreams. She thought of the silent antechambers hung with Oriental tapestry, lit by tall bronze candelabra, and of the two great footmen in knee breeches who sleep in the big armchairs, made drowsy by the heavy warmth of the hot-air stove. She thought of the long *salons*[1] fitted up with ancient silk, of the delicate furniture carrying priceless curiosities, and of the coquettish perfumed boudoirs made for talks at five o'clock with intimate friends, with men fa-

---

[1]*salons* drawing rooms.

mous and sought after, whom all women envy and whose attention they all desire.

When she sat down to dinner, before the round table covered with a table-cloth three days old, opposite her husband, who uncovered the soup tureen and declared with an enchanted air, "Ah, the good *pot-au-feu!*[2] I don't know anything better than that," she thought of dainty dinners, of shining silverware, of tapestry which peopled the walls with ancient personages and with strange birds flying in the midst of a fairy forest; and she thought of delicious dishes served on marvelous plates, and of the whispered gallantries which you listen to with a sphinxlike smile, while you are eating the pink flesh of a trout or the wings of a quail.

5      She had no dresses, no jewels, nothing. And she loved nothing but that; she felt made for that. She would so have liked to please, to be envied, to be charming, to be sought after.

She had a friend, a former schoolmate at the convent, who was rich, and whom she did not like to go and see any more, because she suffered so much when she came back.

But one evening, her husband returned home with a triumphant air, and holding a large envelope in his hand.

"There," said he. "Here is something for you."

She tore the paper sharply, and drew out a printed card which bore these words:

10     "The Minister of Public Instruction and Mme. Georges Ramponneau request the honor of M. and Mme. Loisel's company at the palace of the Ministry on Monday evening, January eighteenth."

Instead of being delighted, as her husband hoped, she threw the invitation on the table with disdain, murmuring:

"What do you want me to do with that?"

"But, my dear, I thought you would be glad. You never go out, and this is such a fine opportunity. I had awful trouble to get it. Everyone wants to go; it is very select, and they are not giving many invitations to clerks. The whole official world will be there."

She looked at him with an irritated glance, and said, impatiently:

15     "And what do you want me to put on my back?"

He had not thought of that; he stammered:

"Why, the dress you go to the theater in. It looks very well, to me."

He stopped, distracted, seeing his wife was crying. Two great tears descended slowly from the corners of her eyes toward the corners of her mouth. He stuttered:

"What's the matter? What's the matter?"

20     But, by violent effort, she had conquered her grief, and she replied, with a calm voice, while she wiped her wet cheeks:

---

[2]*pot-au-feu* stew.

"Nothing. Only I have no dress and therefore I can't go to this ball. Give your card to some colleague whose wife is better equipped than I."

He was in despair. He resumed:

"Come, let us see, Mathilde. How much would it cost, a suitable dress, which you could use on other occasions, something very simple?"

She reflected several seconds, making her calculations and wondering also what sum she could ask without drawing on herself an immediate refusal and a frightened exclamation from the economical clerk.

25     Finally, she replied, hesitatingly:

"I don't know exactly, but I think I could manage it with four hundred francs."

He had grown a little pale, because he was laying aside just that amount to buy a gun and treat himself to a little shooting next summer on the plain of Nanterre, with several friends who went to shoot larks down there, of a Sunday.

But he said:

"All right. I will give you four hundred francs. And try to have a pretty dress."

30     The day of the ball drew near, and Mme. Loisel seemed sad, uneasy, anxious. Her dress was ready, however. Her husband said to her one evening:

"What is the matter? Come, you've been so queer these last three days."

And she answered:

"It annoys me not to have a single jewel, not a single stone, nothing to put on. I shall look like distress. I should almost rather not go at all."

He resumed:

35     "You might wear natural flowers. It's very stylish at this time of the year. For ten francs you can get two or three magnificent roses."

She was not convinced.

"No; there's nothing more humiliating than to look poor among other women who are rich."

But her husband cried:

"How stupid you are! Go look up your friend Mme. Forestier, and ask her to lend you some jewels. You're quite thick enough with her to do that."

40     She uttered a cry of joy:

"It's true. I never thought of it."

The next day she went to her friend and told of her distress.

Mme. Forestier went to a wardrobe with a glass door, took out a large jewel-box, brought it back, opened it, and said to Mme. Loisel:

"Choose, my dear."

45     She saw first of all some bracelets, then a pearl necklace, then a Venetian cross, gold and precious stones of admirable workmanship. She tried on the ornaments before the glass, hesitated, could not make up her mind to part with them, to give them back. She kept asking:

"Haven't you any more?"

"Why, yes. Look. I don't know what you like."

All of a sudden she discovered, in a black satin box, a superb necklace of diamonds, and her heart began to beat with an immoderate desire. Her hands trembled as she took it. She fastened it around her throat, outside her high-necked dress, and remained lost in ecstasy at the sight of herself. Then she asked, hesitating, filled with anguish:

50     "Can you lend me that, only that?"

"Why, yes, certainly."

She sprang upon the neck of her friend, kissed her passionately, then fled with her treasure.

The day of the ball arrived. Mme. Loisel made a great success. She was prettier than them all, elegant, gracious, smiling, and crazy with joy. All the men looked at her, asked her name, endeavored to be introduced. All the attachés of the Cabinet wanted to waltz with her. She was remarked by the minister himself.

She danced with intoxication, with passion, made drunk by pleasure, forgetting all, in the triumph of her beauty, in the glory of her success, in a sort of cloud of happiness composed of all this homage, of all this admiration, of all these awakened desires, and of that sense of complete victory which is so sweet to a woman's heart.

55     She went away about four o'clock in the morning. Her husband had been sleeping since midnight, in a little deserted anteroom, with three other gentlemen whose wives were having a very good time. He threw over her shoulders the wraps which he had brought, modest wraps of common life, whose poverty contrasted with the elegance of the ball dress. She felt this, and wanted to escape so as not to be remarked by the other women, who were enveloping themselves in costly furs.

Loisel held her back.

"Wait a bit. You will catch cold outside. I will go and call a cab."

But she did not listen to him, and rapidly descended the stairs. When they were in the street they did not find a carriage; and they began to look for one, shouting after the cabmen whom they saw passing by at a distance.

They went down toward the Seine, in despair, shivering with cold. At last they found on the quay one of those ancient noctambulant coupés which, exactly as if they were ashamed to show their misery during the day, are never seen round Paris until after nightfall.

60     It took them to their door in the Rue des Martyrs, and once more, sadly, they climbed up homeward. All was ended, for her. And as to him, he reflected that he must be at the Ministry at ten o'clock.

She removed the wraps which covered her shoulders, before the glass, so as once more to see herself in all her glory. But suddenly she uttered a cry. She no longer had the necklace around her neck!

Her husband, already half undressed, demanded:

"What is the matter with you?"

She turned madly toward him:

65    "I have—I have—I've lost Mme. Forestier's necklace."

He stood up, distracted.

"What!—how?—impossible!"

And they looked in the folds of her dress, in the folds of her cloak, in her pockets, everywhere. They did not find it.

He asked:

70    "You're sure you had it on when you left the ball?"

"Yes, I felt it in the vestibule of the palace."

"But if you had lost it in the street we should have heard it fall. It must be in the cab."

"Yes. Probably. Did you take his number?"

"No. And you, didn't you notice it?"

75    "No."

They looked, thunderstruck, at one another. At last Loisel put on his clothes.

"I shall go back on foot," said he, "over the whole route which we have taken to see if I can find it."

And he went out. She sat waiting on a chair in her ball dress, without strength to go to bed, overwhelmed, without fire, without a thought.

Her husband came back about seven o'clock. He had found nothing.

80    He went to Police Headquarters, to the newspaper offices, to offer a reward: he went to the cab companies—everywhere, in fact, whither he was urged by the least suspicion of hope.

She waited all day, in the same condition of mad fear before this terrible calamity.

Loisel returned at night with a hollow, pale face; he had discovered nothing.

"You must write to your friend," said he, "that you have broken the clasp of her necklace and that you are having it mended. That will give us time to turn round."

She wrote at his dictation.

85    At the end of a week they had lost all hope.

And Loisel, who had aged five years, declared:

"We must consider how to replace that ornament."

The next day they took the box which had contained it, and they went to the jeweler whose name was found within. He consulted his books.

"It was not I, madame, who sold that necklace; I must simply have furnished the case."

90    Then they went from jeweler to jeweler, searching for a necklace like the other, consulting their memories, sick both of them with chagrin and anguish.

They found, in a shop at the Palais Royal, a string of diamonds which seemed to them exactly like the one they looked for. It was worth forty thousand francs. They could have it for thirty-six.

So they begged the jeweler not to sell it for three days yet. And they made a bargain that he should buy it back for thirty-four thousand francs, in case they found the other one before the end of February.

Loisel possessed eighteen thousand francs which his father had left him. He would borrow the rest.

He did borrow, asking a thousand francs of one, five hundred of another, five louis here, three louis[3] there. He gave notes, took up ruinous obligations, dealt with usurers and all the race of lenders. He compromised all the rest of his life, risked his signature without even knowing if he could meet it; and, frightened by the pains yet to come, by the black misery which was about to fall upon him, by the prospect of all the physical privation and of all the moral tortures which he was to suffer, he went to get the new necklace, putting down upon the merchant's counter thirty-six thousand francs.

95     When Mme. Loisel took back the necklace, Mme. Forestier said to her, with a chilly manner:

"You should have returned it sooner; I might have needed it."

She did not open the case, as her friend had so much feared. If she had detected the substitution, what would she have thought, what would she have said? Would she not have taken Mme. Loisel for a thief?

Mme. Loisel now knew the horrible existence of the needy. She took her part, moreover, all of a sudden, with heroism. That dreadful debt must be paid. She would pay it. They dismissed their servant; they changed their lodgings; they rented a garret under the roof.

She came to know what heavy housework meant and the odious cares of the kitchen. She washed the dishes, using her rosy nails on the greasy pots and pans. She washed the dirty linen, the shirts, and the dishcloths, which she dried upon a line; she carried the slops down to the street every morning, and carried up the water, stopping for breath at every landing. And, dressed like a woman of the people, she went to the fruiterer, the grocer, the butcher, her basket on her arm, bargaining, insulted, defending her miserable money sou by sou.

100    Each month they had to meet some notes, renew others, obtain more time.

Her husband worked in the evening making a fair copy of some tradesman's accounts, and late at night he often copied manuscript for five sous a page.

And this life lasted for ten years.

---

[3]**louis** a gold coin worth 20 francs.

At the end of ten years, they had paid everything, everything, with the rates of usury, and the accumulations of the compound interest.

Mme. Loisel looked old now. She had become the woman of impoverished households—strong and hard and rough. With frowsy hair, skirts askew, and red hands, she talked loud while washing the floor with great swishes of water. But sometimes, when her husband was at the office, she sat down near the window, and she thought of that gay evening of long ago, of the ball where she had been so beautiful and so fêted.

105    What would have happened if she had not lost that necklace? Who knows? Who knows? How life is strange and changeful! How little a thing is needed for us to be lost or to be saved!

But, one Sunday, having gone to take a walk in the Champs Elysées to refresh herself from the labor of the week, she suddenly perceived a woman who was leading a child. It was Mme. Forestier, still young, still beautiful, still charming.

Mme. Loisel felt moved. Was she going to speak to her? Yes, certainly. And now that she had paid, she was going to tell her all about it. Why not? She went up.

"Good day, Jeanne."

110    The other, astonished to be familiarly addressed by this plain goodwife, did not recognize her at all, and stammered:

"But—madam!—I do not know—You must be mistaken."

"No. I am Mathilde Loisel."

Her friend uttered a cry.

"Oh, my poor Mathilde! How you are changed!"

115    "Yes, I have had days hard enough, since I have seen you, days wretched enough—and that because of you!"

"Of me! How so?"

"Do you remember that diamond necklace which you lent me to wear at the ministerial ball?"

"Yes. Well?"

"Well, I lost it."

120    "What do you mean? You brought it back."

"I brought you back another just like it. And for this we have been ten years paying. You can understand that it was not easy for us, us who had nothing. At last it is ended, and I am very glad."

Mme. Forestier had stopped.

"You say that you bought a necklace of diamonds to replace mine?"

"Yes. You never noticed it, then! They were very like."

125    And she smiled with a joy which was proud and naïve at once.

Mme. Forestier, strongly moved, took her two hands.

"Oh, my poor Mathilde! Why, my necklace was paste. It was worth at most five hundred francs!"

# CHARLOTTE PERKINS GILMAN

*Charlotte Perkins Gilman (1860–1935), née Charlotte Perkins, was born in Hartford, Connecticut. Her father deserted the family soon after Charlotte's birth; she was brought up by her mother, who found it difficult to make ends meet. For a while Charlotte worked as an artist and teacher of art, and in 1884, when she was twenty-four, she married an artist. In 1885 she had a daughter, but soon after the birth of the girl Charlotte had a nervous breakdown. At her husband's urging she spent a month in the sanitarium of Dr. S. Weir Mitchell, a physician who specialized in treating women with nervous disorders. (Mitchell is specifically named in "The Yellow Wallpaper.") Because the treatment—isolation and total rest—nearly drove her to insanity, she fled Mitchell and her husband. In California she began a career as a lecturer and writer on feminist topics. (She also supported herself by teaching school and by keeping a boardinghouse.) Among her books are* Women and Economics *(1899) and* The Man-Made World *(1911), which have been revived by the feminist movement. In 1900 she married a cousin, George Gilman. From all available evidence, the marriage was successful. Certainly it did not restrict her activities as a feminist. In 1935, suffering from inoperable cancer, she took her own life.*

*"The Yellow Wallpaper," written in 1892—that is, written after she had been treated by S. Weir Mitchell for her nervous breakdown—was at first interpreted either as a ghost story or as a Poe-like study of insanity. Only in recent years has it been seen as a feminist story. (One might ask oneself if these interpretations are mutually exclusive.)*

## The Yellow Wallpaper

[1892]

It is very seldom that mere ordinary people like John and myself secure ancestral halls for the summer.

A colonial mansion, a hereditary estate. I would say a haunted house, and reach the height of romantic felicity—but that would be asking too much of fate!

Still I will proudly declare that there is something queer about it.

Else, why should it be let so cheaply? And why have stood so long untenanted?

5      John laughs at me, of course, but one expects that in marriage.

John is practical in the extreme. He has no patience with faith, an intense horror of superstition, and he scoffs openly at any talk of things not to be felt and seen and put down in figures.

John is a physician, and *perhaps*—(I would not say it to a living soul, of course, but this is dead paper and a great relief to my mind)—*perhaps* that is one reason I do not get well faster.

You see he does not believe I am sick!

And what can one do?

10     If a physician of high standing, and one's own husband, assures friends and relatives that there is really nothing the matter with one but temporary nervous depression—a slight hysterical tendency—what is one to do?

My brother is also a physician, and also of high standing, and he says the same thing.

So I take phosphates or phosphites—whichever it is, and tonics, and journeys, and air, and exercise, and am absolutely forbidden to "work" until I am well again.

Personally, I disagree with their ideas.

Personally, I believe that congenial work, with excitement and change, would do me good.

15     But what is one to do?

I did write for a while in spite of them; but it *does* exhaust me a good deal—having to be so sly about it, or else meet with heavy opposition.

I sometimes fancy that in my condition if I had less opposition and more society and stimulus—but John says the very worst thing I can do is to think about my condition, and I confess it always makes me feel bad.

So I will let it alone and talk about the house.

The most beautiful place! It is quite alone, standing well back from the road, quite three miles from the village. It makes me think of English places that you read about, for there are hedges and walls and gates that lock, and lots of separate little houses for the gardeners and people.

20     There is a *delicious* garden! I never saw such a garden—large and shady, full of box-bordered paths, and lined with long grape-covered arbors with seats under them.

There were greenhouses, too, but they are all broken now. There was some legal trouble, I believe, something about the heirs and coheirs; anyhow, the place has been empty for years.

That spoils my ghostliness. I am afraid, but I don't care—there is something strange about the house—I can feel it.

I even said so to John one moonlight evening, but he said what I felt was a *draught,* and shut the window.

I get unreasonably angry with John sometimes. I'm sure I never used to be so sensitive. I think it is due to this nervous condition.

25     But John says if I feel so, I shall neglect proper self-control; so I take pains to control myself—before him, at least, and that makes me very tired.

I don't like our room a bit. I wanted one downstairs that opened on the piazza and had roses all over the window, and such pretty old-fashioned chintz hangings! but John would not hear of it.

He said there was only one window and not room for two beds, and no near room for him if he took another.

He is very careful and loving, and hardly lets me stir without special direction.

I have a schedule prescription for each hour in the day; he takes all care from me, and so I feel basely ungrateful not to value it more.

30    He said we came here solely on my account, that I was to have perfect rest and all the air I could get. "Your exercise depends on your strength, my dear," said he, "and your food somewhat on your appetite; but air you can absorb all the time." So we took the nursery at the top of the house.

It is a big, airy room, the whole floor nearly, with windows that look all ways, and air and sunshine galore. It was nursery first and then playroom and gymnasium, I should judge; for the windows are barred for little children, and there are rings and things in the walls.

The paint and paper look as if a boys' school had used it. It is stripped off—the paper—in great patches all around the head of my bed, about as far as I can reach, and in a great place on the other side of the room low down. I never saw a worse paper in my life.

One of those sprawling flamboyant patterns committing every artistic sin.

It is dull enough to confuse the eye in following, pronounced enough to constantly irritate and provoke study, and when you follow the lame uncertain curves for a little distance they suddenly commit suicide—plunge off at outrageous angles, destroy themselves in unheard of contradictions.

35    The color is repellent, almost revolting; a smouldering unclean yellow, strangely faded by the slow-turning sunlight.

It is a dull yet lurid orange in some places, a sickly sulphur tint in others.

No wonder the children hated it! I should hate it myself if I had to live in this room long.

There comes John, and I must put this away,—he hates to have me write a word.

We have been here two weeks, and I haven't felt like writing before, since that first day.

40    I am sitting by the window now, up in this atrocious nursery, and there is nothing to hinder my writing as much as I please, save lack of strength.

John is away all day, and even some nights when his cases are serious.

I am glad my case is not serious!

But these nervous troubles are dreadfully depressing.

John does not know how much I really suffer. He knows there is no *reason* to suffer, and that satisfies him.

45    Of course it is only nervousness. It does weigh on me so not to do my duty in any way!

I meant to be such a help to John, such a real rest and comfort, and here I am a comparative burden already!

Nobody would believe what an effort it is to do what little I am able,—to dress and entertain, and order things.

It is fortunate Mary is so good with the baby. Such a dear baby!

And yet I *cannot* be with him, it makes me so nervous.

50     I suppose John never was nervous in his life. He laughs at me so about this wallpaper!

At first he meant to repaper the room, but afterwards he said that I was letting it get the better of me, and that nothing was worse for a nervous patient than to give way to such fancies.

He said that after the wallpaper was changed it would be the heavy bedstead, and then the barred windows, and then that gate at the head of the stairs, and so on.

"You know the place is doing you good," he said, "and really, dear, I don't care to renovate the house just for a three months' rental."

"Then do let us go downstairs." I said, "there are such pretty rooms there."

55     Then he took me in his arms and called me a blessed little goose, and said he would go down to the cellar, if I wished, and have it whitewashed into the bargain.

But he is right enough about the beds and windows and things.

It is an airy and comfortable room as any one need wish, and, of course, I would not be so silly as to make him uncomfortable just for a whim.

I'm really getting quite fond of the big room, all but that horrid paper.

Out of one window I can see the garden, those mysterious deep-shaded arbors, the riotous old-fashioned flowers, and bushes and gnarly trees.

60     Out of another I get a lovely view of the bay and a little private wharf belonging to the estate. There is a beautiful shaded lane that runs down there from the house. I always fancy I see people walking in these numerous paths and arbors, but John has cautioned me not to give way to fancy in the least. He says that with my imaginative power and habit of story-making, a nervous weakness like mine is sure to lead to all manner of excited fancies, and that I ought to use my will and good sense to check the tendency. So I try.

I think sometimes that if I were only well enough to write a little it would relieve the press of ideas and rest me.

But I find I get pretty tired when I try.

It is so discouraging not to have any advice and companionship about my work. When I get really well, John says we will ask Cousin Henry and Julia down for a long visit; but he says he would as soon put fireworks in my pillow-case as to let me have those stimulating people about now.

I wish I could get well faster.

65     But I must not think about that. This paper looks to me as if it *knew* what a vicious influence it had!

There is a recurrent spot where the pattern lolls like a broken neck and two bulbous eyes stare at you upside down.

I get positively angry with the impertinence of it and the everlastingness. Up and down and sideways they crawl, and those absurd, unblinking eyes are everywhere. There is one place where two breadths didn't match, and the eyes go all up and down the line, one a little higher than the other.

I never saw so much expression in an inanimate thing before, and we all know how much expression they have! I used to lie awake as a child and get more entertainment and terror out of blank walls and plain furniture than most children could find in a toystore.

I remember what a kindly wink the knobs of our big, old bureau used to have, and there was one chair that always seemed like a strong friend.

70      I used to feel that if any of the other things looked too fierce I could always hop into that chair and be safe.

The furniture in this room is no worse than inharmonious, however, for we had to bring it all from downstairs. I suppose when this was used as a playroom they had to take the nursery things out, and no wonder! I never saw such ravages as the children have made here.

The wallpaper, as I said before, is torn off in spots, and it sticketh closer than a brother—they must have had perseverance as well as hatred.

Then the floor is scratched and gouged and splintered, the plaster itself is dug out here and there, and this great heavy bed which is all we found in the room, looks as if it had been through the wars.

But I don't mind it a bit—only the paper.

75      There comes John's sister. Such a dear girl as she is, and so careful of me! I must not let her find me writing.

She is a perfect and enthusiastic housekeeper, and hopes for no better profession. I verily believe she thinks it is the writing which made me sick!

But I can write when she is out, and see her a long way off from these windows.

There is one that commands the road, a lovely shaded winding road, and one that just looks off over the country. A lovely country, too, full of great elms and velvet meadows.

This wallpaper has a kind of sub-pattern in a different shade, a particularly irritating one, for you can only see it in certain lights, and not clearly then.

80      But in the places where it isn't faded and where the sun is just so—I can see a strange, provoking, formless sort of figure, that seems to skulk about behind that silly and conspicuous front design.

There's sister on the stairs!

Well, the Fourth of July is over! The people are all gone and I am tired out. John thought it might do me good to see a little company, so we just had mother and Nellie and the children down for a week.

Of course I didn't do a thing. Jennie sees to everything now. But it tired me all the same.

John says if I don't pick up faster he shall send me to Weir Mitchell in the fall.

85      But I don't want to go there at all. I had a friend who was in his hands once, and she says he is just like John and my brother, only more so!

Besides, it is such an undertaking to go so far.

I don't feel as if it was worth while to turn my hand over for anything, and I'm getting dreadfully fretful and querulous.

I cry at nothing, and cry most of the time.

Of course I don't when John is here, or anybody else, but when I am alone.

90      And I am alone a good deal just now. John is kept in town very often by serious cases, and Jennie is good and lets me alone when I want her to.

So I walk a little in the garden or down that lovely lane, sit on the porch under the roses, and lie down up here a good deal.

I'm getting really fond of the room in spite of the wallpaper. Perhaps *because* of the wallpaper.

It dwells in my mind so!

I lie here on this great immovable bed—it is nailed down, I believe—and follow that pattern about by the hour. It is as good as gymnastics, I assure you. I start, we'll say, at the bottom, down in the corner over there where it has not been touched, and I determine for the thousandth time that I *will* follow that pointless pattern to some sort of a conclusion.

95      I know a little of the principle of design, and I know this thing was not arranged on any laws of radiation, or alternation, or repetition, or symmetry, or anything else that I ever heard of.

It is repeated, of course, by the breadths, but not otherwise.

Looked at in one way each breadth stands alone, the bloated curves and flourishes—a kind of "debased Romanesque" with *delirium tremens*—go waddling up and down in isolated columns of fatuity.

But, on the other hand, they connect diagonally, and the sprawling outlines run off in great slanting waves of optic horror, like a lot of wallowing seaweeds in full chase.

The whole thing goes horizontally, too, at least it seems so, and I exhaust myself in trying to distinguish the order of its going in that direction.

100     They have used a horizontal breadth for a frieze, and that adds wonderfully to the confusion.

There is one end of the room where it is almost intact, and there, when the crosslights fade and the low sun shines directly upon it, I can almost fancy radiation after all,—the interminable grotesques seem to form around a common center and rush off in headlong plunges of equal distraction.

It makes me tired to follow it. I will take a nap I guess.

I don't know why I should write this.

I don't want to.

105    I don't feel able.

And I know John would think it absurd. But I *must* say what I feel and think in some way—it is such a relief.

But the effort is getting to be greater than the relief!

Half the time now I am awfully lazy, and lie down ever so much.

John says I mustn't lose my strength, and has me take cod liver oil and lots of tonics and things, to say nothing of ale and wine and rare meat.

110    Dear John! He loves me very dearly, and hates to have me sick. I tried to have a real earnest reasonable talk with him the other day, and tell him how I wish he would let me go and make a visit to Cousin Henry and Julia.

But he said I wasn't able to go, nor able to stand it after I got there; and I did not make out a very good case for myself, for I was crying before I had finished.

It is getting to be a great effort for me to think straight. Just this nervous weakness I suppose.

And dear John gathered me up in his arms, and just carried me upstairs and laid me on the bed, and sat by me and read to me till it tired my head.

He said I was his darling and his comfort and all he had, and that I must take care of myself for his sake, and keep well.

115    He says no one but myself can help me out of it, that I must use my will and self-control and not let any silly fancies run away with me.

There's one comfort, the baby is well and happy, and does not have to occupy this nursery with the horrid wallpaper.

If we had not used it, that blessed child would have! What a fortunate escape! Why, I wouldn't have a child of mine, an impressionable little thing, live in such a room for worlds.

I never thought of it before, but it is lucky that John kept me here after all. I can stand it so much easier than a baby, you see.

Of course I never mention it to them any more—I am too wise,—but I keep watch of it all the same.

120    There are things in that paper that nobody knows but me, or ever will.

Behind that outside pattern the dim shapes get clearer every day.

It is always the same shape, only very numerous.

And it is like a woman stooping down and creeping about behind that pattern. I don't like it a bit. I wonder—I begin to think—I wish John would take me away from here!

It is so hard to talk to John about my case, because he is so wise, and because he loves me so.

125    But I tried last night.

It was moonlight. The moon shines in all around just as the sun does.

I hate to see it sometimes, it creeps so slowly, and always comes in by one window or another.

John was asleep and I hated to waken him, so I kept still and watched the moonlight on that undulating wallpaper till I felt creepy.

The faint figure behind seemed to shake the pattern, just as if she wanted to get out.

130    I got up softly and went to feel and see if the paper did move, and when I came back John was awake.

"What is it, little girl?" he said. "Don't go walking about like that— you'll get cold."

I thought it was a good time to talk, so I told him that I really was not gaining here, and that I wished he would take me away.

"Why darling!" said he, "our lease will be up in three weeks, and I can't see how to leave before.

"The repairs are not done at home, and I cannot possibly leave town just now. Of course if you were in any danger, I could and would, but you really are better, dear, whether you can see it or not. I am a doctor, dear, and I know. You are gaining flesh and color, your appetite is better, I feel really much easier about you."

135    "I don't weigh a bit more," said I, "nor as much; and my appetite may be better in the evening when you are here, but it is worse in the morning when you are away!"

"Bless her little heart!" said he with a big hug, "she shall be as sick as she pleases! But now let's improve the shining hours by going to sleep, and talk about it in the morning!"

"And you won't go away?" I asked gloomily.

"Why, how can I, dear? It is only three weeks more and then we will take a nice little trip of a few days while Jennie is getting the house ready. Really dear you are better!"

"Better in body perhaps—" I began, and stopped short, for he sat up straight and looked at me with such a stern, reproachful look that I could not say another word.

140    "My darling," said he, "I beg of you, for my sake and for our child's sake, as well as for your own, that you will never for one instant let that idea enter your mind! There is nothing so dangerous, so fascinating, to a temperament like yours. It is a false and foolish fancy. Can you trust me as a physician when I tell you so?"

So of course I said no more on that score, and we went to sleep before long. He thought I was asleep first, but I wasn't and lay there for hours trying to decide whether that front pattern and the back pattern really did move together or separately.

On a pattern like this, by daylight, there is a lack of sequence, a defiance of law, that is a constant irritant to a normal mind.

The color is hideous enough, and unreliable enough, and infuriating enough, but the pattern is torturing.

You think you have mastered it, but just as you get well underway in following, it turns a back-somersault and there you are. It slaps you in the face, knocks you down, and tramples upon you. It is like a bad dream.

145    The outside pattern is a florid arabesque, reminding one of a fungus. If you can imagine a toadstool in joints, an interminable string of toad-stools, budding and sprouting in endless convolutions—why, that is something like it.

That is, sometimes!

There is one marked peculiarity about this paper, a thing nobody seems to notice but myself, and that is that it changes as the light changes.

When the sun shoots in through the east window—I always watch for that first long, straight ray—it changes so quickly that I never can quite believe it.

That is why I watch it always.

150    By moonlight—the moon shines in all night when there is a moon—I wouldn't know it was the same paper.

At night in any kind of light, in twilight, candle light, lamplight, and worst of all by moonlight, it becomes bars! The outside pattern I mean, and the woman behind it as plain as can be.

I didn't realize for a long time what the thing was that showed behind, that dim sub-pattern, but now I am quite sure it is a woman.

By daylight she is subdued, quiet. I fancy it is the pattern that keeps her so still. It is so puzzling. It keeps me quiet by the hour.

I lie down ever so much now. John says it is good for me, and to sleep all I can.

155    Indeed he started the habit by making me lie down for an hour after each meal.

It is a very bad habit I am convinced, for you see I don't sleep.

And that cultivates deceit, for I don't tell them I'm awake—O no!

The fact is I am getting a little afraid of John.

He seems very queer sometimes, and even Jennie has an inexplicable look.

160    It strikes me occasionally, just as a scientific hypothesis,—that perhaps it is the paper!

I have watched John when he did not know I was looking, and come into the room suddenly on the most innocent excuses, and I've caught him several times *looking at the paper!* And Jennie too. I caught Jennie with her hand on it once.

She didn't know I was in the room, and when I asked her in a quiet, a very quiet voice, with the most restrained manner possible, what she was doing with the paper—she turned around as if she had been caught stealing, and looked quite angry—asked me why I should frighten her so!

Then she said that the paper stained everything it touched, that she had found yellow smooches on all my clothes and John's, and she wished we would be more careful!

Did not that sound innocent? But I know she was studying that pattern, and I am determined that nobody shall find it out but myself!

165    Life is very much more exciting now than it used to be. You see I have something more to expect, to look forward to, to watch. I really do eat better, and am more quiet than I was.

John is so pleased to see me improve! He laughed a little the other day, and said I seemed to be flourishing in spite of my wallpaper.

I turned it off with a laugh. I had no intention of telling him it was *because* of the wallpaper—he would make fun of me. He might even want to take me away.

I don't want to leave now until I have found it out. There is a week more, and I think that will be enough.

I'm feeling ever so much better! I don't sleep much at night, for it is so interesting to watch developments; but I sleep a good deal in the daytime.

170    In the daytime it is tiresome and perplexing.

There are always new shoots on the fungus, and new shades of yellow all over it. I cannot keep count of them, though I have tried conscientiously.

It is the strangest yellow, that wallpaper! It makes me think of all the yellow things I ever saw—not beautiful ones like buttercups, but old foul, bad yellow things.

But there is something else about that paper—the smell! I noticed it the moment we came into the room, but with so much air and sun it was not bad. Now we have had a week of fog and rain, and whether the windows are open or not, the smell is here.

It creeps all over the house.

175    I find it hovering in the dining-room, skulking in the parlor, hiding in the hall, lying in wait for me on the stairs.

It gets into my hair.

Even when I go to ride, if I turn my head suddenly and surprise it— there is that smell!

Such a peculiar odor, too! I have spent hours in trying to analyze it, to find what it smelled like.

It is not bad—at first, and very gentle, but quite the subtlest, most enduring odor I ever met.

180    In this damp weather it is awful, I wake up in the night and find it hanging over me.

It used to disturb me at first. I thought seriously of burning the house—to reach the smell.

But now I am used to it. The only thing I can think of that it is like is the *color* of the paper! A yellow smell.

There is a very funny mark on this wall, low down, near the mop-board. A streak that runs round the room. It goes behind every piece of furniture, except the bed, a long, straight, even *smooch*, as if it had been rubbed over and over.

I wonder how it was done and who did it, and what they did it for. Round and round and round—round and round and round—it makes me dizzy!

185    I really have discovered something at last.

Through watching so much at night, when it changes so, I have finally found out.

The front pattern *does* move—and no wonder! The woman behind shakes it!

Sometimes I think there are a great many women behind, and sometimes only one, and she crawls around fast, and her crawling shakes it all over.

Then in the very bright spots she keeps still, and in the very shady spots she just takes hold of the bars and shakes them hard.

190    And she is all the time trying to climb through. But nobody could climb through that pattern—it strangles so; I think that is why it has so many heads.

They get through, and then the pattern strangles them off and turns them upside down, and makes their eyes white!

If those heads were covered or taken off it would not be half so bad.

I think that woman gets out in the daytime!

And I'll tell you why—privately—I've seen her!

195    I can see her out of every one of my windows!

It is the same woman, I know, for she is always creeping, and most women do not creep by daylight.

I see her on that long road under the trees, creeping along, and when a carriage comes she hides under the blackberry vines.

I don't blame her a bit. It must be very humiliating to be caught creeping by daylight!

I always lock the door when I creep by daylight. I can't do it at night, for I know John would suspect something at once.

200    And John is so queer now, that I don't want to irritate him. I wish he would take another room! Besides, I don't want anybody to get that woman out at night but myself.

I often wonder if I could see her out of all the windows at once.

But, turn as fast as I can, I can only see out of one at one time. And though I always see her, she *may* be able to creep faster than I can turn!

I have watched her sometimes away off in the open country, creeping as fast as a cloud shadow in a high wind.

If only that top pattern could be gotten off from the under one! I mean to try it, little by little.

205    I have found out another funny thing, but I shan't tell at this time! It does not do to trust people too much.

There are only two more days to get this paper off, and I believe John is beginning to notice. I don't like the look in his eyes.

And I heard him ask Jennie a lot of professional questions about me. She had a very good report to give.

She said I slept a good deal in the daytime.

John knows I don't sleep very well at night, for all I'm so quiet!

210    He asked me all sorts of questions, too, and pretended to be very loving and kind.

As if I couldn't see through him!

Still, I don't wonder he acts so, sleeping under this paper for three months.

It only interests me, but I feel sure John and Jennie are secretly affected by it.

Hurrah! This is the last day, but it is enough. John is to stay in town over night, and won't be out until this evening.

215    Jennie wanted to sleep with me—the sly thing! But I told her I should undoubtedly rest better for a night all alone.

That was clever, for really I wasn't alone a bit! As soon as it was moonlight and that poor thing began to crawl and shake the pattern, I got up and ran to help her.

I pulled and she shook, I shook and she pulled, and before morning we had peeled off yards of that paper.

A strip about as high as my head and half round the room. And then when the sun came and that awful pattern began to laugh at me, I declared I would finish it to-day!

We go away to-morrow, and they are moving all the furniture down again to leave things as they were before.

220    Jennie looked at the wall in amazement, but I told her merrily that I did it out of pure spite at the vicious thing.

She laughed and said she wouldn't mind doing it herself, but I must not get tired.

How she betrayed herself that time!

But I am here, and no person touches this paper but me—not *alive!*

She tried to get me out of the room—it was too patent! But I said it was so quiet and empty and clean now that I believed I would lie down again and sleep all I could, and not to wake me even for dinner—I would call when I woke.

225    So now she is gone, and the servants are gone, and the things are gone, and there is nothing left but that great bedstead nailed down, with the canvas mattress we found on it.

We shall sleep downstairs to-night, and take the boat home to-morrow.

I quite enjoy the room, now it is bare again.

How those children did tear about here!

This bedstead is fairly gnawed!

230     But I must get to work.

I have locked the door and thrown the key down into the front path.

I don't want to go out, and I don't want to have anybody come in, till John comes.

I want to astonish him.

I've got a rope up here that even Jennie did not find. If that woman does get out, and tries to get away, I can tie her!

235     But I forgot I could not reach far without anything to stand on! This bed will not move!

I tried to lift and push it until I was lame, and then I got so angry I bit off a little piece at one corner—but it hurt my teeth.

Then I peeled off all the paper I could reach standing on the floor. It sticks horribly and the pattern just enjoys it! All those strangled heads and bulbous eyes and waddling fungus growths just shriek with derision!

I am getting angry enough to do something desperate. To jump out of the window would be admirable exercise, but the bars are too strong even to try.

Besides I wouldn't do it. Of course not. I know well enough that a step like that is improper and might be misconstrued.

240     I don't like to *look* out of the windows even—there are so many of those creeping women, and they creep so fast.

I wonder if they all come out of that wallpaper as I did?

But I am securely fastened now by my well-hidden rope—you don't get *me* out in the road there!

I suppose I shall have to get back behind the pattern when it comes night, and that is hard!

It is so pleasant to be out in this great room and creep around as I please!

245     I don't want to go outside. I won't, even if Jennie asks me to.

For outside you have to creep on the ground, and everything is green instead of yellow.

But here I can creep smoothly on the floor, and my shoulder just fits in that long smooch around the wall, so I cannot lose my way.

Why there's John at the door!

It is no use, young man, you can't open it!

250     How he does call and pound!

Now he's crying for an axe.

It would be a shame to break down that beautiful door!

"John dear!" said I in the gentlest voice, "the key is down by the front steps, under a plantain leaf!"

That silenced him for a few moments.
255    Then he said—very quietly indeed, "Open the door, my darling!"
"I can't," said I. "The key is down by the front door under a plantain leaf!"

And then I said it again, several times, very gently and slowly, and said it so often that he had to go and see, and he got it of course, and came in. He stopped short by the door.

"What is the matter?" he cried. "For God's sake, what are you doing!"

I kept on creeping just the same, but I looked at him over my shoulder.

260    "I've got out at last," said I, "in spite of you and Jane. And I've pulled off most of the paper, so you can't put me back!"

Now why should that man have fainted? But he did, and right across my path by the wall, so that I had to creep over him every time!


# JAMES JOYCE

*James Joyce (1882-1941) was born into a middle-class family in Dublin, Ireland. His father drank, became increasingly irresponsible and unemployable, and the family sank in the social order. Still, Joyce received a strong classical education at excellent Jesuit schools and at University College, Dublin, where he studied modern languages. In 1902, at the age of twenty, he left Ireland so that he might spend the rest of his life writing about life in Ireland. ("The shortest way to Tara," he said, "is via Holyhead," i.e., the shortest way to the heart of Ireland is to take ship away.) In Trieste, Zurich, and Paris he supported his family in a variety of ways, sometimes teaching English in a Berlitz language school. His fifteen stories, collected under the title of* Dubliners, *were written between 1904 and 1907, but he could not get them published until 1914. Next came a highly autobiographical novel,* A Portrait of the Artist as a Young Man *(1916).* Ulysses *(1922), a large novel covering eighteen hours in Dublin, was for some years banned by the United States Post Office, though few if any readers today find it offensive. Joyce spent most of his remaining years working on* Finnegans Wake *(1939).*

*Nine years before he succeeded in getting* Dubliners *published, Joyce described the manuscript in these terms:*

> *My intention was to write a chapter of the moral history of my country and I chose Dublin for the scene because that city seemed to me the centre of paralysis. . . . I have written it for the most part in a style of scrupulous meanness and with the conviction that he is a very bold man who dares to alter in the presentment, still more to deform, whatever he has seen and heard.*

# Araby

[1905]

North Richmond Street, being blind,[1] was a quiet street except at the hour when the Christian Brothers' School set the boys free. An uninhabited house of two stories stood at the blind end, detached from its neighbors in a square ground. The other houses of the street, conscious of decent lives within them, gazed at one another with brown imperturbable faces.

The former tenant of our house, a priest, had died in the back drawing-room. Air, musty from having long been enclosed, hung in all the rooms, and the waste room behind the kitchen was littered with old useless papers. Among these I found a few papercovered books, the pages of which were curled and damp: *The Abbot,* by Walter Scott, *The Devout Communicant* and *The Memoirs of Vidocq.*[2] I liked the last best because its leaves were yellow. The wild garden behind the house contained a central apple-tree and a few straggling bushes under one of which I found the late tenant's rusty bicycle-pump. He had been a very charitable priest; in his will he had left all his money to institutions and the furniture of his house to his sister.

When the short days of winter came dusk fell before we had well eaten our dinners. When we met in the street the houses had grown sombre. The space of sky above us was the colour of everchanging violet and towards it the lamps of the street lifted their feeble lanterns. The cold air stung us and we played till our bodies glowed. Our shouts echoed in the silent street. The career of our play brought us through the dark muddy lanes behind the houses where we ran the gauntlet of the rough tribes from the cottages, to the back doors of the dark dripping gardens where odours arose from the ashpits, to the dark odorous stables where a coachman smoothed and combed the horse or shook music from the buckled harness. When we returned to the street light from the kitchen windows had filled the area. If my uncle was seen turning the corner we hid in the shadow until we had seen him safely housed. Or if Mangan's sister came out on the doorstep to call her brother in to his tea we watched her from our shadow peer up and down the street. We waited to see whether she would remain or go in and, if she remained, we left our shadow and walked up to Mangan's steps resignedly. She was waiting for us, her figure defined by the light from the half-opened door. Her brother always teased her before he obeyed and I stood by the railings looking at her. Her dress swung as she moved her body and the soft rope of her hair tossed from side to side.

---

[1]**blind** a dead-end street.    [2]***The Abbot*** was one of Scott's popular historical romances; ***The Devout Communicant*** was a Catholic religious manual; ***The Memoirs of Vidocq*** were the memoirs of the chief of the French detective force.

Every morning I lay on the floor in the front parlour watching her door. The blind was pulled down to within an inch of the sash so that I could not be seen. When she came out on the doorstep my heart leaped. I ran to the hall, seized my books and followed her. I kept her brown figure always in my eye and, when we came near the point at which our ways diverged, I quickened my pace and passed her. This happened morning after morning. I had never spoken to her, except for a few casual words, and yet her name was like a summons to all my foolish blood.

5      Her image accompanied me even in places the most hostile to romance. On Saturday evenings when my aunt went marketing I had to go to carry some of the parcels. We walked through the flaring streets, jostled by drunken men and bargaining women, amid the curses of labourers, the shrill litanies of shop-boys who stood on guard by the barrels of pigs' cheeks, the nasal chanting of street-singers, who sang a *come-all-you* about O'Donovan Rossa,[3] or a ballad about the troubles in our native land. These noises converged in a single sensation of life for me: I imagined that I bore my chalice safely through a throng of foes. Her name sprang to my lips at moments in strange prayers and praises which I myself did not understand. My eyes were often full of tears (I could not tell why) and at times a flood from my heart seemed to pour itself out into my bosom. I thought little of the future. I did not know whether I would ever speak to her or not or, if I spoke to her, how I could tell her of my confused adoration. But my body was like a harp and her words and gestures were like fingers running upon the wires.

One evening I went into the back drawing-room in which the priest had died. It was a dark rainy evening and there was no sound in the house. Through one of the broken panes I heard the rain impinge upon the earth, the fine incessant needles of water playing in the sodden beds. Some distant lamp or lighted window gleamed below me. I was thankful that I could see so little. All my senses seemed to desire to veil themselves and, feeling that I was about to slip from them, I pressed the palms of my hands together until they trembled, murmuring: *O love! O love!* many times.

At last she spoke to me. When she addressed the first words to me I was so confused that I did not know what to answer. She asked me was I going to Araby.

I forget whether I answered yes or no. It would be a splendid bazaar, she said; she would love to go.

—And why can't you? I asked.

10      While she spoke she turned a silver bracelet round and round her wrist. She could not go, she said, because there would be a retreat that

---

[3]**Jeremiah O'Donovan** (1831–1915), a popular Irish leader who was jailed by the British for advocating violent rebellion. A **come-all-you** was a topical song that began "Come all you gallant Irishmen."

week in her convent. Her brother and two other boys were fighting for their caps and I was alone at the railings. She held one of the spikes, bowing her head towards me. The light from the lamp opposite our door caught the white curve of her neck, lit up her hair that rested there and, falling, lit up the hand upon the railing. It fell over one side of her dress and caught the white border of a petticoat, just visible as she stood at ease.

—It's well for you, she said.

—If I go, I said, I will bring you something.

What innumerable follies laid waste my waking and sleeping thoughts after that evening! I wished to annihilate the tedious intervening days. I chafed against the work of school. At night in my bedroom and by day in the classroom her image came between me and the page I strove to read. The syllables of the word *Araby* were called to me through the silence in which my soul luxuriated and cast an Eastern enchantment over me. I asked for leave to go to the bazaar on Saturday night. My aunt was surprised and hoped it was not some Freemason[4] affair. I answered a few questions in class. I watched my master's face pass from amiability to sternness; he hoped I was not beginning to idle. I could not call my wandering thoughts together. I had hardly any patience with the serious work of life which, now that it stood between me and my desire, seemed to me child's play, ugly monotonous child's play.

On Saturday morning I reminded my uncle that I wished to go to the bazaar in the evening. He was fussing at the hallstand, looking for the hatbrush, and answered me curtly:

15    —Yes, boy, I know.

As he was in the hall I could not go into the front parlour and lie at the window. I left the house in bad humour and walked slowly towards the school. The air was pitilessly raw and already my heart misgave me.

When I came home to dinner my uncle had not yet been home. Still it was early. I sat staring at the clock for some time and, when its ticking began to irritate me, I left the room. I mounted the staircase and gained the upper part of the house. The high cold empty gloomy rooms liberated me and I went from room to room singing. From the front window I saw my companions playing below in the street. Their cries reached me weakened and indistinct and, leaning my forehead against the cool glass, I looked over at the dark house where she lived. I may have stood there for an hour, seeing nothing but the brown-clad figure cast by my imagination, touched discreetly by the lamplight at the curved neck, at the hand upon the railings and at the border below the dress.

When I came downstairs again I found Mrs. Mercer sitting at the fire. She was an old garrulous woman, a pawnbroker's widow, who collected used stamps for some pious purpose. I had to endure the gossip of the

[4]Irish Catholics viewed the Masons as their Protestant enemies.

tea-table. The meal was prolonged beyond an hour and still my uncle did not come. Mrs. Mercer stood up to go: she was sorry she couldn't wait any longer, but it was after eight o'clock and she did not like to be out late, as the night air was bad for her. When she had gone I began to walk up and down the room, clenching my fists. My aunt said:

—I'm afraid you may put off your bazaar for this night of Our Lord.

20    At nine o'clock I heard my uncle's latchkey in the halldoor. I heard him talking to himself and heard the hallstand rocking when it had received the weight of his overcoat. I could interpret these signs. When he was midway through his dinner I asked him to give me the money to go to the bazaar. He had forgotten.

—The people are in bed and after their first sleep now, he said.

I did not smile. My aunt said to him energetically:

—Can't you give him the money and let him go? You've kept him late enough as it is.

My uncle said he was very sorry he had forgotten. He said he believed in the old saying: *All work and no play makes Jack a dull boy.* He asked me where I was going and, when I had told him a second time he asked me did I know *The Arab's Farewell to His Steed.*[5] When I left the kitchen he was about to recite the opening lines of the piece to my aunt.

25    I held a florin tightly in my hand as I strode down Buckingham Street towards the station. The sight of the streets thronged with buyers and glaring with gas recalled to me the purpose of my journey. I took my seat in a third-class carriage of a deserted train. After an intolerable delay the train moved out of the station slowly. It crept onward among ruinous houses and over the twinkling river. At Westland Row Station a crowd of people pressed to the carriage doors; but the porters moved them back, saying that it was a special train for the bazaar. I remained alone in the bare carriage. In a few minutes the train drew up beside an improvised wooden platform. I passed out on to the road and saw by the lighted dial of a clock that it was ten minutes to ten. In front of me was a large building which displayed the magical name.

I could not find any sixpenny entrance and, fearing that the bazaar would be closed, I passed in quickly through a turnstile, handing a shilling to a weary-looking man. I found myself in a big hall girdled at half its height by a gallery. Nearly all the stalls were closed and the greater part of the hall was in darkness. I recognised a silence like that which pervades a church after a service. I walked into the center of the bazaar timidly. A few people were gathered about the stalls which were still open. Before a curtain, over which the words *Café Chantant* were written in coloured lamps, two men were counting money on a salver. I listened to the fall of the coins.

---

[5]"The Arab to His Favorite Steed" was a popular sentimental poem by Caroline Norton (1808–77).

Remembering with difficulty why I had come I went over to one of the stalls and examined porcelain vases and flowered tea-sets. At the door of the stall a young lady was talking and laughing with two young gentlemen. I remarked their English accents and listened vaguely to their conversation.

—O, I never said such a thing!

—O, but you did!

30 —O, but I didn't!

—Didn't she say that?

—Yes! I heard her.

—O, there's a . . . fib!

Observing me the young lady came over and asked me did I wish to buy anything. The tone of her voice was not encouraging; she seemed to have spoken to me out of a sense of duty. I looked humbly at the great jars that stood like eastern guards at either side of the dark entrance to the stall and murmured:

35 —No, thank you.

The young lady changed the position of one of the vases and went back to the two young men. They began to talk of the same subject. Once or twice the young lady glanced at me over her shoulder.

I lingered before her stall, though I knew my stay was useless, to make my interest in her wares seem the more real. Then I turned away slowly and walked down the middle of the bazaar. I allowed the two pennies to fall against the sixpence in my pocket. I heard a voice call from one end of the gallery that the light was out. The upper part of the hall was now completely dark.

Gazing up into the darkness I saw myself as a creature driven and derided by vanity; and my eyes burned with anguish and anger.

# WILLIAM FAULKNER

*William Faulkner (1897-1962) was brought up in Oxford, Mississippi. His great-grandfather had been a Civil War hero, and his father was treasurer of the University of Mississippi in Oxford; the family was no longer rich, but it was still respected. In 1918 he enrolled in the Royal Canadian Air Force, though he never saw overseas service. After the war he returned to Mississippi and went to the university for two years. He then moved to New Orleans, where he became friendly with Sherwood Anderson, who was already an established writer. In New Orleans Faulkner worked for the* Times-Picayune; *still later, even after he had established himself as a major novelist with* The Sound and the Fury *(1929), he had to do some work in Hollywood in order to make ends meet. In 1950 he was awarded the Nobel Prize in Literature.*

*Almost all of Faulkner's writing is concerned with the people of Yoknapatawpha, an imaginary county in Mississippi."I discovered," he said, "that my own little postage stamp of native soil was worth writing about and that I would never live long enough to exhaust it." Though he lived for brief periods in Canada, New Orleans, New York, Hollywood, and Virginia (where he died), he spent most of his life in his native Mississippi.*

# A Rose for Emily

[1930]

## I

When Miss Emily Grierson died, our whole town went to her funeral: the men through a sort of respectful affection for a fallen monument, the women mostly out of curiosity to see the inside of her house, which no one save an old manservant—a combined gardener and cook—had seen in at least ten years.

It was a big, squarish frame house that had once been white, decorated with cupolas and spires and scrolled balconies in the heavily lightsome style of the seventies, set on what had once been our most select street. But garages and cotton gins had encroached and obliterated even the august names of that neighborhood; only Miss Emily's house was left, lifting its stubborn and coquettish decay above the cotton wagons and the gasoline pumps—an eyesore among eyesores. And now Miss Emily had gone to join the representatives of those august names where they lay in the cedar-bemused cemetery among the ranked and anonymous graves of Union and Confederate soldiers who fell at the battle of Jefferson.

Alive, Miss Emily had been a tradition, a duty, and a care; a sort of hereditary obligation upon the town, dating from that day in 1894 when Colonel Sartoris, the mayor—he who fathered the edict that no Negro woman should appear on the streets without an apron—remitted her taxes, the dispensation dating from the death of her father on into perpetuity. Not that Miss Emily would have accepted charity. Colonel Sartoris invented an involved tale to the effect that Miss Emily's father had loaned money to the town, which the town, as a matter of business, preferred this way of repaying. Only a man of Colonel Sartoris' generation and thought could have invented it, and only a woman could have believed it.

When the next generation, with its more modern ideas, became mayors and aldermen, this arrangement created some little dissatisfaction. On the first of the year they mailed her a tax notice. February came, and there was no reply. They wrote her a formal letter, asking her to call at the sheriff's office at her convenience. A week later the mayor wrote her himself, offering to call or to send his car for her, and received in reply a note on paper of an archaic shape, in a thin, flowing calligraphy in faded ink, to the effect that she no longer went out at all. The tax notice was also enclosed, without comment.

5    They called a special meeting of the Board of Aldermen. A deputation waited upon her, knocked at the door through which no visitor had passed since she ceased giving china-painting lessons eight or ten years earlier. They were admitted by the old Negro into a dim hall from which a staircase mounted into still more shadow. It smelled of dust and disuse—a close, dank smell. The Negro led them into the parlor. It was furnished in heavy, leather-covered furniture. When the Negro opened the blinds of one window they could see that the leather was cracked; and when they sat down, a faint dust rose sluggishly about their thighs, spinning with slow motes in the single sunray. On a tarnished gilt easel before the fireplace stood a crayon portrait of Miss Emily's father.

They rose when she entered—a small, fat woman in black, with a thin gold chain descending to her waist and vanishing into her belt, leaning on an ebony cane with a tarnished gold head. Her skeleton was small and spare; perhaps that was why what would have been merely plumpness in another was obesity in her. She looked bloated, like a body long submerged in motionless water, and of that pallid hue. Her eyes, lost in the fatty ridges of her face, looked like two small pieces of coal pressed into a lump of dough as they moved from one face to another while the visitors stated their errand.

She did not ask them to sit. She just stood in the door and listened quietly until the spokesman came to a stumbling halt. Then they could hear the invisible watch ticking at the end of the gold chain.

Her voice was dry and cold. "I have no taxes in Jefferson. Colonel Sartoris explained it to me. Perhaps one of you can gain access to the city records and satisfy yourselves."

"But we have. We are the city authorities, Miss Emily. Didn't you get a notice from the sheriff, signed by him?"

10    "I received a paper, yes," Miss Emily said. "Perhaps he considers himself the sheriff. . . . I have no taxes in Jefferson."

"But there is nothing on the books to show that, you see. We must go by the—"

"See Colonel Sartoris. I have no taxes in Jefferson."

"But, Miss Emily—"

"See Colonel Sartoris." (Colonel Sartoris had been dead almost ten years.) "I have no taxes in Jefferson. Tobe!" The Negro appeared. "Show these gentlemen out."

*II*

15    So she vanquished them, horse and foot, just as she had vanquished their fathers thirty years before about the smell. That was two years after her father's death and a short time after her sweetheart—the one we believed

would marry her—had deserted her. After her father's death she went out very little; after her sweetheart went away, people hardly saw her at all. A few of the ladies had the temerity to call, but were not received, and the only sign of life about the place was the Negro man—a young man then—going in and out with a market basket.

"Just as if a man—any man—could keep a kitchen properly," the ladies said; so they were not surprised when the smell developed. It was another link between the gross, teeming world and the high and mighty Griersons.

A neighbor, a woman, complained to the mayor, Judge Stevens, eighty years old.

"But what will you have me do about it, madam?" he said.

"Why, send her word to stop it," the woman said. "Isn't there a law?"

20    "I'm sure that won't be necessary," Judge Stevens said. "It's probably just a snake or a rat that nigger of hers killed in the yard. I'll speak to him about it."

The next day he received two more complaints, one from a man who came in diffident deprecation. "We really must do something about it, Judge, I'd be the last one in the world to bother Miss Emily, but we've got to do something." That night the Board of Aldermen met—three gray-beards and one younger man, a member of the rising generation.

"It's simple enough," he said. "Send her word to have her place cleaned up. Given her a certain time to do it in, and if she don't . . . ."

"Dammit, sir," Judge Stevens said, "will you accuse a lady to her face of smelling bad?"

So the next night, after midnight, four men crossed Miss Emily's lawn and slunk about the house like burglars, sniffing along the base of the brickwork and at the cellar openings while one of them performed a regular sowing motion with his hand out of a sack slung from his shoulder. They broke open the cellar door and sprinkled lime there, and in all the out-buildings. As they recrossed the lawn, a window that had been dark was lighted and Miss Emily sat in it, the light behind her, and her upright torso motionless as that of an idol. They crept quietly across the lawn and into the shadow of the locusts that lined the street. After a week or two the smell went away.

25    That was when people had begun to feel really sorry for her. People in our town remembering how old lady Wyatt, her great-aunt, had gone completely crazy at last, believed that the Griersons held themselves a little too high for what they really were. None of the young men were quite good enough for Miss Emily and such. We had long thought of them as a tableau; Miss Emily a slender figure in white in the background, her father a spraddled silhouette in the foreground, his back to her and clutching a horsewhip, the two of them framed by the back-flung front door. So when she got to be thirty and was still single, we were not pleased exactly, but vindicated; even with insanity in the family she wouldn't have turned down all of her chances if they had really materialized.

When her father died, it got about that the house was all that was left to her; and in a way, people were glad. At last they could pity Miss Emily. Being left alone, and a pauper, she had become humanized. Now she too would know the old thrill and the old despair of a penny more or less.

The day after his death all the ladies prepared to call at the house and offer condolence and aid, as is our custom. Miss Emily met them at the door, dressed as usual and with no trace of grief on her face. She told them that her father was not dead. She did that for three days, with the ministers calling on her, and the doctors, trying to persuade her to let them dispose of the body. Just as they were about to resort to law and force, she broke down, and they buried her father quickly.

We did not say she was crazy then. We believed she had to do that. We remembered all the young men her father had driven away, and we knew that with nothing left, she would have to cling to that which had robbed her, as people will.

## III

She was sick for a long time. When we saw her again, her hair was cut short, making her look like a girl, with a vague resemblance to those angels in colored church windows—sort of tragic and serene.

30  The town had just let the contracts for paving the sidewalks, and in the summer after her father's death they began to work. The construction company came with niggers and mules and machinery, and a foreman named Homer Barron, a Yankee—a big, dark, ready man, with a big voice and eyes lighter than his face. The little boys would follow in groups to hear him cuss the niggers, and the niggers singing in time to the rise and fall of picks. Pretty soon he knew everybody in town. Whenever you heard a lot of laughing anywhere about the square, Homer Barron would be in the center of the group. Presently we began to see him and Miss Emily on Sunday afternoons driving in the yellow-wheeled buggy and the matched team of bays from the livery stable.

At first we were glad that Miss Emily would have an interest, because the ladies all said. "Of course a Grierson would not think seriously of a Northerner, a day laborer." But there were still others, older people, who said that even grief could not cause a real lady to forget *noblesse oblige*— without calling it *noblesse oblige*. They just said, "Poor Emily. Her kinsfolk should come to her." She had some kin in Alabama; but years ago her father had fallen out with them over the estate of old lady Wyatt, the crazy woman, and there was no communication between the two families. They had not even been represented at the funeral.

And as soon as the old people said, "Poor Emily," the whispering began. "Do you suppose it's really so?" they said to one another. "Of course it is. . . ." This behind their hands; rustling of craned silk and satin behind jalousies closed upon the sun of Sunday afternoon as the thin, swift clop-clop-clop of the matched team passed: "Poor Emily."

She carried her head high enough—even when we believed that she was fallen. It was as if she demanded more than ever the recognition of her dignity as the last Grierson; as if it had wanted that touch of earthiness to reaffirm her imperviousness. Like when she bought the rat poison, the arsenic. That was over a year after they had begun to say "Poor Emily," and while the two female cousins were visiting her.

"I want some poison," she said to the druggist. She was over thirty then, still a slight woman, though thinner than usual, with cold, haughty black eyes in a face the flesh of which was strained across the temples and about the eyesockets as you imagine a lighthouse-keeper's face ought to look. "I want some poison," she said.

35          "Yes, Miss Emily. What kind? For rats and such? I'd recom—"

"I want the best you have. I don't care what kind."

The druggist named several. "They'll kill anything up to an elephant. But what you want is—"

"Arsenic." Miss Emily said. "Is that a good one?"

"Is . . . arsenic? Yes ma'am. But what you want—"

40          "I want arsenic."

The druggist looked down at her. She looked back at him, erect, her face like a strained flag. "Why, of course," the druggist said. "If that's what you want. But the law requires you to tell what you are going to use it for."

Miss Emily just stared at him, her head tilted back in order to look him eye for eye, until he looked away and went and got the arsenic and wrapped it up. The Negro delivery boy brought her the package; the druggist didn't come back. When she opened the package at home there was written on the box, under the skull and bones: "For rats."

## IV

So the next day we all said, "She will kill herself"; and we said it would be the best thing. When she had first begun to be seen with Homer Barron, we had said, "She will marry him." Then we said, "She will persuade him yet," because Homer himself had remarked—he liked men, and it was known that he drank with the younger men in the Elks' Club—that he was not a marrying man. Later we said, "Poor Emily," behind the jalousies as they passed on Sunday afternoon in the glittering buggy, Miss Emily with her head high and Homer Barron with his hat cocked and a cigar in his teeth, reins and whip in a yellow glove.

Then some of the ladies began to say that it was a disgrace to the town and a bad example to the young people. The men did not want to interfere, but at last the ladies forced the Baptist minister—Miss Emily's people were Episcopal—to call upon her. He would never divulge what happened during that interview, but he refused to go back again. The next Sunday they again drove about the streets, and the following day the minister's wife wrote to Miss Emily's relations in Alabama.

45      So she had blood-kin under her roof again and we sat back to watch developments. At first nothing happened. Then we were sure that they were to be married. We learned that Miss Emily had been to the jeweler's and ordered a man's toilet set in silver, with the letters H.B. on each piece. Two days later we learned that she had bought a complete outfit of men's clothing, including a nightshirt, and we said, "They are married." We were really glad. We were glad because the two female cousins were even more Grierson than Miss Emily had ever been.

So we were surprised when Homer Barron—the streets had been finished some time since—was gone. We were a little disappointed that there was not a public blowing-off but we believed that he had gone on to prepare for Miss Emily's coming, or to give a chance to get rid of the cousins. (By that time it was a cabal, and we were all Miss Emily's allies to help circumvent the cousins.) Sure enough, after another week they departed. And, as we had expected all along, within three days Homer Barron was back in town. A neighbor saw the Negro man admit him at the kitchen door at dusk one evening.

And that was the last we saw of Homer Barron. And of Miss Emily for some time. The Negro man went in and out with the market basket, but the front door remained closed. Now and then we would see her at a window for a moment, as the men did that night when they sprinkled the lime, but for almost six months she did not appear on the streets. Then we knew that this was to be expected too; as if that quality of her father which had thwarted her woman's life so many times had been too virulent and too furious to die.

When we next saw Miss Emily, she had grown fat and her hair was turning gray. During the next few years it grew grayer and grayer until it attained an even pepper-and-salt iron-gray, when it ceased turning. Up to the day of her death at seventy-four it was still that vigorous iron-gray, like the hair of an active man.

From that time on her front door remained closed, save for a period of six or seven years, when she was about forty, during which she gave lessons in china-painting. She fitted up a studio in one of the downstairs rooms, where the daughters and granddaughters of Colonel Sartoris' contemporaries were sent to her with the same regularity and in the same spirit that they were sent on Sundays with a twenty-five cent piece for the collection plate. Meanwhile her taxes had been remitted.

50      Then the newer generation became the backbone and the spirit of the town, and the painting pupils grew up and fell away and did not send their children to her with boxes of color and tedious brushes and pictures cut from the ladies' magazines. The front door closed upon the last one and remained closed for good. When the town got free postal delivery

Miss Emily alone refused to let them fasten the metal numbers above her door and attach a mailbox to it. She would not listen to them.

Daily, monthly, yearly we watched the Negro grow grayer and more stooped, going in and out with the market basket. Each December we sent her a tax notice, which would be returned by the post office a week later, unclaimed. Now and then we could see her in one of the downstairs windows—she had evidently shut up the top floor of the house—like the carven torso of an idol in a niche, looking or not looking at us, we could never tell which. Thus she passed from generation to generation—dear, inescapable, impervious, tranquil, and perverse.

And so she died. Fell ill in the house filled with dust and shadows, with only a doddering Negro man to wait on her. We did not even know she was sick; we had long since given up trying to get any information from the Negro. He talked to no one, probably not even to her, for his voice had grown harsh and rusty, as if from disuse.

She died in one of the downstairs rooms, in a heavy walnut bed with a curtain, her gray head propped on a pillow yellow and moldy with age and lack of sunlight.

## V

The Negro met the first of the ladies at the front door and let them in, with their hushed, sibilant voices and their quick, curious glances, and then he disappeared. He walked right through the house and out the back and was not seen again.

55        The two female cousins came at once. They held the funeral on the second day, with the town coming to look at Miss Emily beneath a mass of bought flowers, with the crayon face of her father musing profoundly above the bier and the ladies sibilant and macabre; and the very old men—some in their brushed Confederate uniforms—on the porch and the lawn, talking of Miss Emily as if she had been a contemporary of theirs, believing that they had danced with her and courted her perhaps, confusing time with its mathematical progression, as the old do, to whom all the past is not a diminishing road, but, instead, a huge meadow which no winter ever quite touches, divided from them now by the narrow bottleneck of the most recent decade of years.

Already we knew that there was one room in that region above stairs which no one had seen in forty years, and which would have to be forced. They waited until Miss Emily was decently in the ground before they opened it.

The violence of breaking down the door seemed to fill this room with pervading dust. A thin, acrid pall as of the tomb seemed to lie everywhere upon this room decked and furnished as for a bridal: upon the valance curtains of faded rose color, upon the rose-shaded lights, upon the

dust and shadows, with only a doddering negro man to wait on
her. We did not even know she was sick; we had long since given up
trying to get any information from the negro. He talked to no
one, probably not even to her, for his voice had grown ~~fussy~~
harsh and ~~and~~ rusty, as though with disuse; the sparse words
which he did speak sounded as though he had learned them that
morning by rote---just enough of them to carry him through
the day.

She died in one of the downstairs rooms, in a heavy
walnut bed with a curtain, her gray head propped on a pillow
yellow and moldy with age and lack of sunlight, her voice
gold and strong to the last.

"But not till I'm gone," she said. "Dont you let a
soul in until I'm gone, do you hear?" Standing beside the bed,
his head in the dim light nimbused by a faint halo of napped,
perfectly white hair, the negro made a brief gesture with his
hand. Miss Emily lay with her eyes open, gazing into the opposite shadows of the room. Upon the coverlet her hands lay on
her breast, gnarled, blue with age, motionless. "Hah," she said.
"Then they can. Let 'em go up there and see what's in that
room. ~~And/you/hpax/be/the/last/one/shall/fellow~~ Fools. ~~And~~ Let
'em. ~~And/you/hpax/be/the/last/one/shall~~ Satisfy their minds that
I am crazy. Do you think I am?" The negro made no reply, no
movement. He stood above the bed, ~~stoppped/unseen/like/an/angel~~
~~let/~~ motionless, musing: a secret and unfathomable soul behind
the death-mask of an ape and haloed like an angel. "Let 'em
go up there and open that door. And you wont be the last one,

13.

The printed version of Faulkner's "A Rose for Emily" omitted several passages of dialogue, shown here in the typed manuscript of pages 13 to 15, between Miss Emily and
her longtime manservant.    (*continued*)

either. Will you?"

"I wont have to," the negro said. "I know what's in
that room. I dont have to see."

"Hah," Miss Emily said. "You do, do you. How long have
you known?" Again he made that brief sign with his hand. Miss
Emily had not turned her head. She stared into the shadows where
the high ceiling was lost. "You should be glad. Now you can go
to Chicago, like you've been talking about for thirty years. And
with what you'll get for the house and furniture.... Colonel Sartoris has the will. He'll see they dont rob you."

"I dont want any house," the negro said.

"You cant help yourself. It's signed and sealed thirty-
five years ago. Wasn't that our agreement when I found I couldn't
pay you any wages? that you were to have everything that was left
if you outlived me, and I was to bury you ~~will~~ in a coffin with
your name on a gold plate if I outlived you?" He said nothing.
"Wasn't it?" Miss Emily said.

"I was young then. Wanted to be rich. But now I dont
want any house."

"Not when you have wanted to go to Chicago for thirty
years?" Their breathing was alike: each that harsh, rasping
breath of the old, the short inhalations that do not reach the
bottom of the lungs: tireless, precarious, on the verge of ces-
sation for all time, as if anything might suffice: a word, a
look. "What are you going to do, then?"

"Going to the poorhouse."

"The poorhouse? When I'm trying to fix you so you'll

14.

have neither to worry nor lift your hand as long as you live?

"I dont want nothing," the negro said. "I'm going t.
the poorhouse. I already told them."

"Well," Miss Emily said. She had not moved her head,
not moved at all. "Do you mind telling me why you want to go
to the poorhouse?"

Again he mused. The room was still save for their brea
ing: it was as though they had both quitted all living and all
dying; all the travail of mortality and of breath. "So I can
set on that hill in the sun all day and watch them trains pass.
See them at night too, with the engine puffing and lights in
all the windows.

"Oh," Miss Emily said. Motionless, her knotted hands
lying on the yellowed coverlet beneath her chin and her chin
resting upon her breast, she appeared to muse intently, as
though she were listening to dissolution setting up within her.
"Hah," she said.

Then she died, and the negro met the first of the ladies at the front door and let them in, with their hushed sibilant voices and their quick curious glances, and he went on
to the back and disappeared. He walked right through the house
and out the back and was not seen again.

The two female cousins came at once. They held the
funeral on the second day, with the town coming to look at
Miss Emily beneath a mass of bought flowers, with the crayon
face of her father musing profoundly above the bier and the la-

15.

grin cemented into what had once been a pillow by a substance like
hardened sealing-wax. One side of the covers was flung back, as
though he were preparing to rise; we lifted the covers completely
away, liberating still another sluggish cloud of infinitesimal
dust, invisible and tainted. The body had apparently once lain
in the attitude of an embrace, but now the long sleep that outlasts love, that conquers even the grimace of love, had cuckolded
him: what was left of him lay beneath what was left of the
nightshirt, become inextricable with the bed in which he lay,
and upon him and upon the pillow beside him lay that even coating of the patient and biding dust. /0/ Then we noticed that in
the second pillow was the indentation of a head; one of us
lifted something from it, and leaning forward, that faint and
invisible dust lean and acrid in the nostrils, we saw a long
strand of iron-gray hair.

The final paragraph of the typed manuscript was reworded and made into two paragraphs in the published version.

dressing table, upon the delicate array of crystal and the man's toilet things backed with tarnished silver, silver so tarnished that the monogram was obscured. Among them lay a collar and tie, as if they had just been removed, which, lifted, left upon the surface a pale crescent in the dust. Upon a chair hung the suit, carefully folded; beneath it the two mute shoes and the discarded socks.

The man himself lay in the bed.

For a long while we just stood there, looking down at the profound and fleshless grin. The body had apparently once lain in the attitude of an embrace, but now the long sleep that outlasts love, that conquers even the grimace of love, had cuckolded him. What was left of him, rotted beneath what was left of the nightshirt, had become inextricable from the bed in which he lay; and upon him and upon the pillow beside him lay that even coating of the patient and biding dust.

60      Then we noticed that in the second pillow was the indentation of a head. One of us lifted something from it, and leaning forward, that faint and invisible dust dry and acrid in the nostrils, we saw a long strand of iron-gray hair.

# LANGSTON HUGHES

*Langston Hughes (1902–1967), an African-American writer, was born in Joplin, Missouri, lived part of his youth in Mexico, spent a year at Columbia University, served as a merchant seaman, and worked in a Paris nightclub, where he showed some of his poems to Dr. Alain Locke, a strong advocate of African-American literature. Encouraged by Locke, when Hughes returned to the United States he continued to write, publishing fiction, plays, essays, and biographies; he also founded theaters, gave public readings, and was, in short, a highly visible presence.*

## One Friday Morning                                    [1941]

The thrilling news did not come directly to Nancy Lee, but it came in little indirections that finally added themselves up to one tremendous fact: she had won the prize! But being a calm and quiet young lady, she did not say anything, although the whole high school buzzed with rumors, guesses, reportedly authentic announcements on the part of students who had no right to be making announcements at all—since no student really knew yet who had won this year's art scholarship.

But Nancy Lee's drawing was so good, her lines so sure, her colors so bright and harmonious, that certainly no other student in the senior art class at George Washington High was thought to have very much of a chance. Yet you never could tell. Last year nobody had expected Joe

Williams to win the Artist Club scholarship with that funny modernistic water color he had done of the high-level bridge. In fact, it was hard to make out there was a bridge until you had looked at the picture a long time. Still, Joe Williams got the prize, was feted by the community's leading painters, club women, and society folks at a big banquet at the Park-Rose Hotel, and was now an award student at the Art School—the city's only art school.

Nancy Lee Johnson was a colored girl, a few years out of the South. But seldom did her high-school classmates think of her as colored. She was smart, pretty, and brown, and fitted in well with the life of the school. She stood high in scholarship, played a swell game of basketball, had taken part in the senior musical in a soft, velvety voice, and had never seemed to intrude or stand out, except in pleasant ways, so it was seldom even mentioned—her color.

Nancy Lee sometimes forgot she was colored herself. She liked her classmates and her school. Particularly she liked her art teacher, Miss Dietrich, the tall red-haired woman who taught her law and order in doing things; and the beauty of working step by step until a job is done; a picture finished; a design created; or a block print carved out of nothing but an idea and a smooth square of linoleum, inked, proofs made, and finally put down on paper—clean, sharp, beautiful, individual, unlike any other in the world, thus making the paper have a meaning nobody else could give it except Nancy Lee. That was the wonderful thing about true creation. You made something nobody else on earth could make—but you.

5     Miss Dietrich was the kind of teacher who brought out the best in her students—but their own best, not anybody else's copied best. For anybody else's best, great though it might be, even Michelangelo's, wasn't enough to please Miss Dietrich, dealing with the creative impulses of young men and women living in an American city in the Middle West, and being American.

Nancy Lee was proud of being American, a Negro American with blood out of Africa a long time ago, too many generations back to count. But her parents had taught her the beauties of Africa, its strength, its song, its mighty rivers, its early smelting of iron, its building of the pyramids, and its ancient and important civilizations. And Miss Dietrich had discovered for her the sharp and humorous lines of African sculpture, Benin, Congo, Makonde. Nancy Lee's father was a mail carrier, her mother a social worker in a city settlement house. Both parents had been to Negro colleges in the South. And her mother had gotten a further degree in social work from a Northern university. Her parents were, like most Americans, simple, ordinary people who had worked hard and steadily for their education. Now they were trying to make it easier for Nancy Lee to achieve learning than it had been for them. They would be very happy when they heard of the award to their daughter—yet Nancy did not tell them. To surprise them would be better. Besides, there had been a promise.

Casually, one day, Miss Dietrich asked Nancy Lee what color frame she thought would be best on her picture. That had been the first inkling.

"Blue," Nancy Lee said. Although the picture had been entered in the Artist Club contest a month ago, Nancy Lee did not hesitate in her choice of a color for the possible frame, since she could still see her picture clearly in her mind's eye—for that picture waiting for the blue frame had come out of her soul, her own life, and had bloomed into miraculous being with Miss Dietrich's help. It was, she knew, the best water color she had painted in her four years as a high-school art student, and she was glad she had made something Miss Dietrich liked well enough to permit her to enter in the contest before she graduated.

It was not a modernistic picture in the sense that you had to look at it a long time to understand what it meant. It was just a simple scene in the city park on a spring day, with the trees still leaflessly lacy against the sky, the new grass fresh and green, a flag on a tall pole in the center, children playing, and an old Negro woman sitting on a bench with her head turned. A lot for one picture, to be sure, but it was not there in heavy and final detail like a calendar. Its charm was that everything was light and airy, happy like spring, with a lot of blue sky; paper-white clouds, and air showing through. You could tell that the old Negro woman was looking at the flag, and that the flag was proud in the spring breeze, and that the breeze helped to make the children's dresses billow as they played.

10    Miss Dietrich had taught Nancy Lee how to paint spring, people, and a breeze on what was only a plain white piece of paper from the supply closet. But Miss Dietrich had not said make it like any other spring-people-breeze ever seen before. She let it remain Nancy Lee's own. That is how the old Negro woman happened to be there looking at the flag—for in her mind the flag, the spring, and the woman formed a kind of triangle holding a dream Nancy Lee wanted to express. White stars on a blue field, spring, children, ever-growing life, and an old woman. Would the judges at the Artist Club like it?

One wet, rainy April afternoon Miss O'Shay, the girls' vice-principal, sent for Nancy Lee to stop by her office as school closed. Pupils without umbrellas or raincoats were clustered in doorways, hoping to make it home between showers. Outside the skies were gray. Nancy Lee's thoughts were suddenly gray, too.

She did not think she had done anything wrong, yet that tight little knot came in her throat just the same as she approached Miss O'Shay's door. Perhaps she had banged her locker too often and too hard. Perhaps the note in French she had written to Sallie halfway across the study hall just for fun had never gotten to Sallie but into Miss O'Shay's hands instead. Or maybe she was failing in some subject and wouldn't be allowed to graduate. Chemistry! A pang went through the pit of her stomach.

She knocked on Miss O'Shay's door. That familiarly solid and competent voice said, "Come in."

Miss O'Shay had a way of making you feel welcome, even if you came to be expelled.

15    "Sit down, Nancy Lee Johnson," said Miss O'Shay. "I have something to tell you." Nancy Lee sat down. "But I must ask you to promise not to tell anyone yet."

"I won't, Miss O'Shay," Nancy Lee said, wondering what on earth the principal had to say to her.

"You are about to graduate," Miss O'Shay ˚said. "And we shall miss you. You have been an excellent student, Nancy, and you will not be without honors on the senior list, as I am sure you know."

At that point there was a light knock on the door. Miss O'Shay called out, "Come in," and Miss Dietrich entered. "May I be a part of this, too?" she asked, tall and smiling.

"Of course," Miss O'Shay said. "I was just telling Nancy Lee what we thought of her. But I hadn't gotten around to giving her the news. Perhaps, Miss Dietrich, you'd like to tell her yourself."

20    Miss Dietrich was always direct. "Nancy Lee," she said, "your picture has won the Artist Club scholarship."

The slender brown girl's eyes widened, her heart jumped, then her throat tightened again. She tried to smile, but instead tears came to her eyes.

"Dear Nancy Lee," Miss O'Shay said, "we are so happy for you." The elderly white woman took her hand and shook it warmly while Miss Dietrich beamed with pride.

Nancy Lee must have danced all the way home. She never remembered quite how she got there through the rain. She hoped she had been dignified. But certainly she hadn't stopped to tell anybody her secret on the way. Raindrops, smiles, and tears mingled on her brown cheeks. She hoped her mother hadn't yet gotten home and that the house was empty. She wanted to have time to calm down and look natural before she had to see anyone. She didn't want to be bursting with excitement—having a secret to contain.

Miss O'Shay's calling her to the office had been in the nature of a preparation and a warning. The kind, elderly vice-principal said she did not believe in catching young ladies unawares, even with honors, so she wished her to know about the coming award. In making acceptance speeches she wanted her to be calm, prepared, not nervous, overcome, and frightened. So Nancy Lee was asked to think what she would say when the scholarship was conferred upon her a few days hence, both at the Friday morning high-school assembly hour, when the announcement would be made, and at the evening banquet of the Artist Club. Nancy Lee promised the vice-principal to think calmly about what she would say.

25    Miss Dietrich had then asked for some facts about her parents, her background, and her life, since such material would probably be desired for the papers. Nancy Lee had told her how, six years before, they had

come up from the Deep South, her father having been successful in achieving a transfer from the one post office to another, a thing he had long sought in order to give Nancy Lee a chance to go to school in the North. Now they lived in a modest Negro neighborhood, went to see the best plays when they came to town, and had been saving to send Nancy Lee to art school, in case she were permitted to enter. But the scholarship would help a great deal, for they were not rich people.

"Now Mother can have a new coat next winter," Nancy Lee thought, "because my tuition will all be covered for the first year. And once in art school, there are other scholarships I can win."

Dreams began to dance through her head, plans and ambitions, beauties she would create for herself, her parents, and the Negro people—for Nancy Lee possessed a deep and reverent race pride. She could see the old woman in her picture (really her grandmother in the South) lifting her head to the bright stars on the flag in the distance. A Negro in America! Often hurt, discriminated against, sometimes lynched—but always there were the stars on the blue body of the flag. Was there any other flag in the world that had so many stars? Nancy Lee thought deeply, but she could remember none in all the encyclopedias or geographies she had ever looked into.

"Hitch your wagon to a star," Nancy Lee thought, dancing home in the rain. "Who were our flag-makers?"

Friday morning came, the morning when the world would know— her high-school world, the newspaper world, her mother and dad. Dad could not be there at the assembly to hear the announcement, nor see her prize picture displayed on the stage, nor to listen to Nancy Lee's little speech of acceptance, but Mother would be able to come, although Mother was much puzzled as to why Nancy Lee was so insistent she be at school on that particular Friday morning.

30    When something is happening, something new and fine, something that will change your very life, it is hard to go to sleep at night for thinking about it, and hard to keep your heart from pounding, or a strange little knot of joy from gathering in your throat. Nancy Lee had taken her bath, brushed her hair until it glowed, and had gone to bed thinking about the next day, the big day, when before three thousand students, she would be the one student honored, her painting the one painting to be acclaimed as the best of the year from all the art classes of the city. Her short speech of gratitude was ready. She went over it in her mind, not word for word (because she didn't want it to sound as if she had learned it by heart), but she let the thoughts flow simply and sincerely through her consciousness many times.

When the president of the Artist Club presented her with the medal and scroll of the scholarship award, she would say:

"Judges and members of the Artist Club. I want to thank you for this award that means so much to me personally and through me to my people, the colored people of this city, who, sometimes, are discouraged and bewildered, thinking that color and poverty are against them. I accept this award with gratitude and pride, not for myself alone, but for my race that believes in American opportunity and American fairness—and the bright stars in our flag. I thank Miss Dietrich and the teachers who made it possible for me to have the knowledge and training that lie behind this honor you have conferred upon my painting. When I came here from the South a few years ago, I was not sure how you would receive me. You received me well. You have given me a chance and helped me along the road I wanted to follow. I suppose the judges know that every week here at assembly the students of this school pledge allegiance to the flag. I shall try to be worthy of that pledge, and of the help and friendship and understanding of my fellow citizens of whatever race or creed, and of our American dream of 'Liberty and justice for all!'"

That would be her response before the students in the morning. How proud and happy the Negro pupils would be, perhaps almost as proud as they were of the one colored star on the football team. Her mother would probably cry with happiness. Thus Nancy Lee went to sleep dreaming of a wonderful tomorrow.

The bright sunlight of an April morning woke her. There was breakfast with her parents—their half-amused and puzzled faces across the table, wondering what could be this secret that made her eyes so bright. The swift walk to school; the clock in the tower almost nine; hundreds of pupils streaming into the long, rambling old building that was the city's largest high school; the sudden quiet of the homeroom after the bell rang; then the teacher opening her record book to call the roll. But just before she began, she looked across the room until her eyes located Nancy Lee.

35          "Nancy," she said, "Miss O'Shay would like to see you in her office, please."

Nancy Lee rose and went out while the names were being called and the word *present* added its period to each name. Perhaps, Nancy Lee thought, the reporters from the papers had already come. Maybe they wanted to take her picture before assembly, which wasn't until ten o'clock. (Last year they had had the photograph of the winner of the award in the morning papers as soon as the announcement had been made.)

Nancy Lee knocked at Miss O'Shay's door.

"Come in."

The vice-principal stood at her desk. There was no one else in the room. It was very quiet.

40          "Sit down, Nancy Lee," she said. Miss O'Shay did not smile. There was a long pause. The seconds went by slowly. "I do not know how to tell you what I have to say," the elderly woman began, her eyes on the papers on her desk. "I am indignant and ashamed for myself and for this city." Then she lifted her eyes and looked at Nancy Lee in the neat blue dress, sitting there before her. "You are not to receive the scholarship this morning."

Outside in the hall the electric bells announcing the first period rang, loud and interminably long. Miss O'Shay remained silent. To the brown girl there in the chair, the room, grew suddenly smaller, smaller, smaller, and there was no air. She could not speak.

Miss O'Shay said, "When the committee learned that you were colored, they changed their plans."

Still Nancy Lee said nothing, for there was no air to give breath to her lungs.

"Here is the letter from the committee, Nancy Lee." Miss O'Shay picked it up and read the final paragraph to her.

45      "'It seems to us wiser to arbitrarily rotate the award among the various high schools of the city from now on. And especially in this case since the student chosen happens to be colored, a circumstance which unfortunately, had we known, might have prevented this embarrassment. But there have never been any Negro students in the local art school, and the presence of one there might create difficulties for all concerned. We have high regard for the quality of Nancy Lee Johnson's talent, but we do not feel it would be fair to honor it with the Artist Club award.'" Miss O'Shay paused. She put the letter down.

"Nancy Lee, I am very sorry to have to give you this message."

"But my speech," Nancy Lee said, "was about. . . " The words stuck in her throat. ". . . about America. . . ."

Miss O'Shay had risen; she turned her back and stood looking out the window at the spring tulips in the school yard.

"I thought, since the award would be made at assembly right after our oath of allegiance," the words tumbled almost hysterically from Nancy Lee's throat now, "I would put part of the flag salute in my speech. You know, Miss O'Shay, that part about 'liberty and justice for all.'"

50      "I know," said Miss O'Shay, slowly facing the room again. "But America is only what we who believe in it make it. I am Irish. You may not know, Nancy Lee, but years ago we were called the dirty Irish, and mobs rioted against us in the big cities, and we were invited to go back where we came from. But we didn't go. And we didn't give up, because we believed in the American dream, and in our power to make that dream come true. Difficulties, yes. Mountains to climb, yes. Discouragements to face, yes. Democracy to make, yes. That is it, Nancy Lee! We still have in this world of ours democracy to *make*. You and I, Nancy Lee. But the premise and the base are here, the lines of the Declaration of Independence and the words of Lincoln are here, and the stars in our flag. Those who deny you this scholarship do not know the meaning of those stars, but it's up to us to make them know. As a teacher in the public schools of this city, I myself will go before the school board and ask them to remove from our system the offer of any prizes or awards denied to any student because of race or color."

Suddenly Miss O'Shay stopped speaking. Her clear, clear blue eyes looked like those of the girl before her. The woman's eyes were full of strength and courage. "Lift up your head, Nancy Lee, and smile at me."

Miss O'Shay stood against the open window with the green lawn and the tulips beyond, the sunlight tangled in her gray hair, her voice an electric flow of strength to the hurt spirit of Nancy Lee. The Abolitionists who believed in freedom when there was slavery must have been like that. The first white teachers who went into the Deep South to teach the freed slaves must have been like that. All those who stand against ignorance, narrowness, hate, and mud on stars must be like that.

Nancy Lee lifted her head and smiled. The bell for assembly rang. She went through the long hall filled with students, toward the auditorium.

"There will be other awards," Nancy Lee thought. "There're schools in other cities. This won't keep me down. But when I'm a woman, I'll fight to see that these things don't happen to other girls as this has happened to me. And men and women like Miss O'Shay will help me."

55      She took her seat among the seniors. The doors of the auditorium closed. As the principal came onto the platform, the students rose and turned their eyes to the flag on the stage.

One hand went to the heart, the other outstretched toward the flag. Three thousand voices spoke. Among them was the voice of a dark girl whose cheeks were suddenly wet with tears, ". . . one nation indivisible, with liberty and justice for all."

"That is the land we must make," she thought.

# RALPH ELLISON

*Ralph Ellison (1913–1994—though the year of birth is often mistakenly given as 1914) was born in Oklahoma City. His father died when Ellison was three, and his mother supported herself and her child by working as a domestic. A trumpeter since boyhood, after graduating from high school Ellison went to study music at Tuskegee Institute, a black college in Alabama founded by Booker T. Washington. In 1936 he dropped out of Tuskegee and went to Harlem to study music composition and the visual arts; there he met Langston Hughes and Richard Wright, who encouraged him to turn to fiction. Ellison published stories and essays, and in 1942 became the managing editor of* Negro Quarterly. *During the Second World War he served in the Merchant Marines. After the war he returned to writing and later taught in universities.*

*"Battle Royal" was first published in 1947 and slightly revised (a transitional paragraph was added at the end of the story) for the opening chapter of Ellison's novel,* Invisible Man *(1952), a book cited by* Book-Week *as "the most significant work of fiction written by an American" in the years between 1945 and 1965. In addition to publishing stories and one novel, Ellison published critical essays, which are brought together in* The Collected Essays of Ralph Ellison *(1995).*

# Battle Royal

[1947]

It goes a long way back, some twenty years. All my life I had been looking for something, and everywhere I turned someone tried to tell me what it was. I accepted their answers too, though they were often in contradiction and even self-contradictory. I was naïve. I was looking for myself and asking everyone except myself questions which I, and only I, could answer. It took me a long time and much painful boomeranging of my expectations to achieve a realization everyone else appears to have been born with: That I am nobody but myself. But first I had to discover that I am an invisible man!

And yet I am no freak of nature, nor of history. I was in the cards, other things having been equal (or unequal) eighty-five years ago. I am not ashamed of my grandparents for having been slaves. I am only ashamed of myself for having at one time been ashamed. About eighty-five years ago they were told that they were free, united with others of our country in everything pertaining to the common good, and, in everything social, separate like the fingers of the hand. And they believed it. They exulted in it. They stayed in their place, worked hard, and brought up my father to do the same. But my grandfather is the one. He was an odd old guy, my grandfather, and I am told I take after him. It was he who caused the trouble. On his deathbed he called my father to him and said, "Son, after I'm gone I want you to keep up the good fight. I never told you, but our life is a war and I have been a traitor all my born days, a spy in the enemy's country ever since I give up my gun back in the Reconstruction. Live with your head in the lion's mouth. I want you to overcome 'em with yeses, undermine 'em with grins, agree 'em to death and destruction, let 'em swoller you till they vomit or bust wide open." They thought the old man had gone out of his mind. He had been the meekest of men. The younger children were rushed from the room, the shades drawn and the flame of the lamp turned so low that it sputtered on the wick like the old man's breathing. "Learn it to the younguns," he whispered fiercely; then he died.

But my folks were more alarmed over his last words than over his dying. It was as though he had not died at all, his words caused so much anxiety. I was warned emphatically to forget what he had said and, indeed, this is the first time it has been mentioned outside the family circle. It had a tremendous effect upon me, however. I could never be sure of what he meant. Grandfather had been a quiet old man who never made any trouble, yet on his deathbed he had called himself a traitor and a spy, and he had spoken of his meekness as a dangerous activity. It became a constant puzzle which lay unanswered in the back of my mind. And whenever things went well for me I remembered my grandfather and felt guilty and uncomfortable. It was as though I was carrying out his advice in spite of myself. And to make it worse, everyone loved me for it. I was praised by

Gordon Parks, *Ralph Ellison.* Parks, an African-American photographer with an international reputation, has published many books of photographs, including *Camera Portraits,* where this picture appears.

the most lily-white men of the town. I was considered an example of desirable conduct—just as my grandfather had been. And what puzzled me was that the old man had defined it as *treachery.* When I was praised for my conduct I felt a guilt that in some way I was doing something that was really against the wishes of the white folks, that if they had understood they would have desired me to act just the opposite, that I should have been sulky and mean, and that that really would have been what they wanted, even though they were fooled and thought they wanted me to act as I did. It made me afraid that some day they would look upon me as a traitor and I would be lost. Still I was more afraid to act any other way because they didn't like that at all. The old man's words were like a curse. On my graduation day I delivered an oration in which I showed that humility was the secret, indeed, the very essence of progress. (Not that I believed this—how could I, remembering my grandfather?—I only believed that it worked.) It was a great success. Everyone praised me and I was invited to give the speech at a gathering of the town's leading white citizens. It was a triumph for our whole community.

It was in the main ballroom of the leading hotel. When I got there I discovered that it was on the occasion of a smoker, and I was told that since I was to be there anyway I might as well take part in the battle royal to be fought by some of my schoolmates as part of the entertainment. The battle royal came first.

5       All of the town's big shots were there in their tuxedoes, wolfing down the buffet foods, drinking beer and whiskey and smoking black cig-

ars. It was a large room with a high ceiling. Chairs were arranged in neat rows around three sides of a portable boxing ring. The fourth side was clear, revealing a gleaming space of polished floor. I had some misgivings over the battle royal, by the way. Not from a distaste for fighting, but because I didn't care too much for the other fellows who were to take part. They were tough guys who seemed to have no grandfather's curse worrying their minds. No one could mistake their toughness. And besides, I suspected that fighting a battle royal might detract from the dignity of my speech. In those pre-invisible days I visualized myself as a potential Booker T. Washington. But the other fellows didn't care too much for me either, and there were nine of them. I felt superior to them in my way, and I didn't like the manner in which we were all crowded together into the servants' elevator. Nor did they like my being there. In fact, as the warmly lighted floors flashed past the elevator we had words over the fact that I, by taking part in the fight, had knocked one of their friends out of a night's work.

We were led out of the elevator through a rococo hall into an anteroom and told to get into our fighting togs. Each of us was issued a pair of boxing gloves and ushered out into the big mirrored hall, which we entered looking cautiously about us and whispering, lest we might accidentally be heard above the noise of the room. It was foggy with cigar smoke. And already the whiskey was taking effect. I was shocked to see some of the most important men of the town quite tipsy. They were all there—bankers, lawyers, judges, doctors, fire chiefs, teachers, merchants. Even one of the more fashionable pastors. Something we could not see was going on up front. A clarinet was vibrating sensuously and the men were standing up and moving eagerly forward. We were a small tight group, clustered together, our bare upper bodies touching and shining with anticipatory sweat; while up front the big shots were becoming increasingly excited over something we still could not see. Suddenly I heard the school superintendent, who had told me to come, yell. "Bring up the shines, gentlemen! Bring up the little shines!"

We were rushed up to the front of the ballroom, where it smelled even more strongly of tobacco and whiskey. Then we were pushed into place. I almost wet my pants. A set of faces, some hostile, some amused, ringed around us, and in the center, facing us, stood a magnificent blonde—stark naked. There was dead silence. I felt a blast of cold air chill me. I tried to back away, but they were behind me and around me. Some of the boys stood with lowered heads, trembling. I felt a wave of irrational guilt and fear. My teeth chattered, my skin turned to goose flesh, my knees knocked. Yet I was strongly attracted and looked in spite of myself. Had the price of looking been blindness, I would have looked. The hair was yellow like that of a circus kewpie doll, the face heavily powdered and rouged, as though to form an abstract mask, the eyes hollow and smeared a cool blue, the color of a baboon's butt. I felt a desire to spit upon her as my eyes brushed slowly over her body. Her breasts were firm and round as the domes of East Indian temples, and I stood so close as to see the fine skin texture and beads of pearly perspiration glistening like dew around the pink and erected buds of her nipples. I wanted at one and the same time to run from the room, to sink through the floor, or go to her and cover her from my eyes and the eyes of the others with my body; to feel the soft thighs, to caress her and destroy her, to love her and murder her, to hide from her, and yet to stroke where below the small American flag tattooed upon her belly her thighs formed a capital V. I had a notion that of all in the room she saw only me with her impersonal eyes.

And then she began to dance, a slow sensuous movement; the smoke of a hundred cigars clinging to her like the thinnest of veils. She seemed like a fair bird-girl girdled in veils calling to me from the angry surface of some gray and threatening sea. I was transported. Then I became aware of the clarinet playing and the big shots yelling at us. Some threatened us if we looked and others if we did not. On my right I saw one boy faint. And now a man grabbed a silver pitcher from a table and stepped close as he dashed ice water upon him and stood him up and forced two of us to support him as his head hung and moans issued from his thick bluish lips. Another boy began to plead to go home. He was the largest of the group, wearing dark red fighting trunks much too small to conceal the erection which projected from him as though in answer to the insinuating low-registered moans of the clarinet. He tried to hide himself with his boxing gloves.

And all the while the blonde continued dancing, smiling faintly at the big shots who watched her with fascination, and faintly smiling at our fear. I noticed a certain merchant who followed her hungrily, his lips loose and drooling. He was a large man who wore diamond studs in a shirtfront which swelled with the ample paunch underneath, and each time the blonde swayed her undulating hips he ran his hand through the thin hair of his bald head and, with his arms upheld, his posture clumsy like that of an intoxicated panda, wound his belly in a slow and obscene grind. This creature was completely hypnotized. The music had quickened. As the dancer flung herself about with a detached expression on her face, the men began reaching out to touch her. I could see their beefy fingers sink into her soft flesh. Some of the others tried to stop them and she began to move around the floor in graceful circles, as they gave chase, slipping and sliding over the polished floor. It was mad. Chairs went crashing, drinks were spilt, as they ran laughing and howling after her. They caught her just as she reached a door, raised her from the floor, and tossed her as college boys are tossed at a hazing, and above her red, fixed-smiling lips I saw the terror and disgust in her eyes, almost like my own terror and that which I saw in some of the other boys. As I watched, they tossed her twice and her soft breasts seemed to flatten against the air and her legs flung wildly as she spun. Some of the more sober ones helped her to escape. And I started off the floor, heading for the anteroom with the rest of the boys.

10      Some were still crying and in hysteria. But as we tried to leave we were stopped and ordered to get into the ring. There was nothing to do but what we were told. All ten of us climbed under the ropes and allowed ourselves to be blindfolded with broad bands of white cloth. One of the men seemed to feel a bit sympathetic and tried to cheer us up as we stood with our backs against the ropes. Some of us tried to grin. "See that boy over there?" one of the men said. "I want you to run across at the bell and give it to him right in the belly. If you don't get him, I'm going to get you. I don't like his looks." Each of us was told the same. The blindfolds were put on. Yet even then I had been going over my speech. In my mind each word was as bright as flame. I felt the cloth pressed into place, and frowned so that it would be loosened when I relaxed.

But now I felt a sudden fit of blind terror. I was unused to darkness. It was as though I had suddenly found myself in a dark room filled with poisonous cottonmouths. I could hear the bleary voices yelling insistently for the battle royal to begin.

"Get going in there!"

"Let me at that big nigger!"

I strained to pick up the school superintendent's voice, as though to squeeze some security out of that slightly more familiar sound.

15      "Let me at those black sonsabitches!" someone yelled.

"No, Jackson, no!" another voice yelled. "Here, somebody, help me hold Jack."

"I want to get at that ginger-colored nigger. Tear him limb from limb," the first voice yelled.

I stood against the ropes trembling. For in those days I was what they called ginger colored, and he sounded as though he might crunch me between his teeth like a crisp ginger cookie.

Quite a struggle was going on. Chairs were being kicked about and I could hear voices grunting as with a terrific effort. I wanted to see, to see more desperately than ever before. But the blindfold was as tight as a thick skin-puckering scab and when I raised my gloved hands to push the layers of white aside a voice yelled, "Oh, no, you don't, black bastard! Leave that alone!"

20      "Ring the bell before Jackson kills him a coon!" someone boomed in the sudden silence. And I heard the bell clang and the sound of the feet scuffling forward.

A glove smacked against my head. I pivoted, striking out stiffly as someone went past, and felt the jar ripple along the length of my arm to my shoulder. Then it seemed as though all nine of the boys had turned upon me at once. Blows pounded me from all sides while I struck out as best I could. So many blows landed upon me that I wondered if I were not the only blindfolded fighter in the ring, or if the man called Jackson hadn't succeeded in getting me after all.

Blindfolded, I could no longer control my motions. I had no dignity. I stumbled about like a baby or a drunken man. The smoke had become thicker and with each new blow it seemed to sear and further restrict my lungs. My saliva became like hot bitter glue. A glove connected with my head, filling my mouth with warm blood. It was everywhere. I could not tell if the moisture I felt upon my body was sweat or blood. A blow landed hard against the nape of my neck. I felt myself going over, my head hitting the floor. Streaks of blue light filled the black world behind the blindfold. I lay prone, pretending that I was knocked out, but felt myself seized by hands and yanked to my feet. "Get going, black boy! Mix it up!" My arms were like lead, my head smarting from blows. I managed to feel my way to the ropes and held on, trying to catch my breath. A glove landed in my mid-section and I went over again, feeling as though the smoke had become a knife jabbed into my guts. Pushed this way and that by the legs milling around me, I finally pulled erect and discovered that I could see the black, sweat-washed forms weaving in the smoky-blue atmosphere like drunken dancers weaving to the rapid drum-like thuds of blows.

Everyone fought hysterically. It was complete anarchy. Everybody fought everybody else. No group fought together for long. Two, three, four, fought one, then turned to fight each other, were themselves attacked. Blows landed below the belt and in the kidney, with the gloves open as well as closed, and with my eye partly opened now there was not so much terror. I moved carefully, avoiding blows, although not too many to attract attention, fighting from group to group. The boys groped about like blind, cautious crabs crouching to protect their mid-sections, their heads pulled in short against their shoulders, their arms stretched nervously before them, with their fists testing the smoke-filled air like the knobbed feelers of hypersensitive snails. In one corner I glimpsed a boy violently punching the air and heard him scream in pain as he smashed his hand against a ring post. For a second I saw him bent over holding his hand, then going down as a blow caught his unprotected head. I played one group against the other, slipping and throwing a punch then stepping out of range while pushing the others into the melee to take the blows blindly aimed at me. The smoke was agonizing and there were no rounds, no bells at three minute intervals to relieve our exhaustion. The room spun round me, a swirl of lights, smoke, sweating bodies surrounded by tense white faces. I bled from both nose and mouth, the blood spattering upon my chest.

The men kept yelling, "Slug him, black boy! Knock his guts out!"

25      "Uppercut him! Kill him! Kill that big boy!"

Taking a fake fall, I saw a boy going down heavily beside me as though we were felled by a single blow, saw a sneaker-clad foot shoot into his groin as the two who had knocked him down stumbled upon him. I rolled out of range, feeling a twinge of nausea.

The harder we fought the more threatening the men became. And yet, I had begun to worry about my speech again. How would it go? Would they recognize my ability? What would they give me?

I was fighting automatically and suddenly I noticed that one after another of the boys was leaving the ring. I was surprised, filled with panic, as though I had been left alone with an unknown danger. Then I understood. The boys had arranged it among themselves. It was the custom for the two men left in the ring to slug it out for the winner's prize. I discovered this too late. When the bell sounded two men in tuxedoes leaped into the ring and removed the blindfold. I found myself facing Tatlock, the biggest of the gang. I felt sick at my stomach. Hardly had the bell stopped ringing in my ears than it clanged again and I saw him moving swiftly toward me. Thinking of nothing else to do I hit him smash on the nose. He kept coming, bringing the rank sharp violence of stale sweat. His face was a black bank of a face, only his eyes alive—with hate of me and aglow with a feverish terror from what had happened to us all. I became anxious. I wanted to deliver my speech and he came at me as though he meant to beat it out of me. I smashed him again and again, taking his blows as they came. Then on a sudden impulse I struck him lightly as we clinched, I whispered, "Fake like I knocked you out, you can have the prize."

"I'll break your behind," he whispered hoarsely.

30    "For *them?*"

"For *me*, sonofabitch!"

They were yelling for us to break it up and Tatlock spun me half around with a blow, and as a joggled camera sweeps in a reeling scene, I saw the howling red faces crouching tense beneath the cloud of blue-gray smoke. For a moment the world wavered, unraveled, flowed, then my head cleared and Tatlock bounced before me. That fluttering shadow before my eyes was his jabbing left hand. Then falling forward, my head against his damp shoulder, I whispered,

"I'll make it five dollars more."

"Go to hell!"

35    But his muscles relaxed a trifle beneath my pressure and I breathed, "Seven!"

"Give it to your ma," he said, ripping me beneath the heart.

And while I still held him I butted him and moved away. I felt myself bombarded with punches. I fought back with hopeless desperation. I wanted to deliver my speech more than anything else in the world, because I felt that only these men could judge truly my ability, and now this stupid clown was ruining my chances. I began fighting carefully now, moving in to punch him and out again with my greater speed. A lucky blow to his chin and I had him going too—until I heard a loud voice yell, "I got my money on the big boy."

Hearing this, I almost dropped my guard. I was confused: Should I try to win against the voice out there? Would not this go against my speech, and was not this a moment for humility, for nonresistance? A blow to my head as I danced about sent my right eye popping like a jack-in-the-box and settled my dilemma. The room went red as I fell. It was a dream fall, my body languid and fastidious as to where to land, until the floor became impatient and smashed up to meet me. A moment later I came to. An hypnotic voice said FIVE emphatically. And I lay there, hazily watching a dark red spot of my own blood shaping itself into a butterfly, glistening and soaking into the soiled gray world of the canvas.

When the voice drawled TEN I was lifted up and dragged to a chair. I sat dazed. My eye pained and swelled with each throb of my pounding heart and I wondered if now I would be allowed to speak. I was wringing wet, my mouth still bleeding. We were grouped along the wall now. The other boys ignored me as they congratulated Tatlock and speculated as to how much they would be paid. One boy whimpered over his smashed hand. Looking up front, I saw attendants in white jackets rolling the portable ring away and placing a small square rug in the vacant space surrounded by chairs. Perhaps, I thought, I will stand on the rug to deliver my speech.

40    Then the M.C. called to us, "Come on up here boys and get your money."

We ran forward to where the men laughed and talked in their chairs, waiting. Everyone seemed friendly now.

"There it is on the rug," the man said. I saw the rug covered with coins of all dimensions and a few crumpled bills. But what excited me, scattered here and there, were the gold pieces.

"Boys, it's all yours," the man said. "You get all you grab."

"That's right, Sambo," a blond man said, winking at me confidentially.

45    I trembled with excitement, forgetting my pain. I would get the gold and the bills, I thought. I would use both hands. I would throw my body against the boys nearest me to block them from the gold.

"Get down around the rug now," the man commanded, "and don't anyone touch it until I give the signal."

"This ought to be good," I heard.

As told, we got around the square rug on our knees. Slowly the man raised his freckled hand as we followed it upward with our eyes.

I heard, "These niggers look like they're about to pray!"

50    Then, "Ready," the man said. "Go!"

I lunged for a yellow coin lying on the blue design of the carpet, touching it and sending a surprised shriek to join those rising around me. I tried frantically to remove my hand but could not let go. A hot, violent force tore through my body, shaking me like a wet rat. The rug was electrified. The hair bristled up on my head as I shook myself free. My muscles jumped, my nerves jangled, writhed. But I saw that this was not stopping the other boys. Laughing in fear and embarrassment, some were holding back and scooping up the coins knocked off by the painful contortions of the others. The men roared above us as we struggled.

"Pick it up, goddamnit, pick it up!" someone called like a bass-voiced parrot. "Go on, get it!"

I crawled rapidly around the floor, picking up the coins, trying to avoid the coppers and to get greenbacks and the gold. Ignoring the shock by laughing, as I brushed the coins off quickly, I discovered that I could contain the electricity—a contradiction, but it works. Then the men began to push us onto the rug. Laughing embarrassedly, we struggled out of their hands and kept after the coins. We were all wet and slippery and hard to hold. Suddenly I saw a boy lifted into the air, glistening with sweat like a circus seal, and dropped, his wet back landing flush upon the charged rug, heard him yell and saw him literally dance upon his back, his elbows beating a frenzied tatoo upon the floor, his muscles twitching like the flesh of a horse stung by many flies. When he finally rolled off, his face was gray and no one stopped him when he ran from the floor amid booming laughter.

"Get the money," the M.C. called. "That's good hard American cash!"

55    And we snatched and grabbed, snatched and grabbed. I was careful not to come too close to the rug now, and when I felt the hot whiskey breath descend upon me like a cloud of foul air I reached out and grabbed the leg of a chair. It was occupied and I held on desperately.

"Leggo, nigger! Leggo!"

The huge face wavered down to mine as the tried to push me free. But my body was slippery and he was too drunk. It was Mr. Colcord, who owned a chain of movie houses and "entertainment palaces." Each time he grabbed me I slipped out of his hands. It became a real struggle. I feared the rug more than I did the drunk, so I held on, surprising myself for a moment by trying to topple *him* upon the rug. It was such an enormous idea that I found myself actually carrying it out. I tried not to be obvious, yet when I grabbed his leg, trying to tumble him out of the chair, he raised up roaring with laughter, and, looking at me with soberness dead in the eye, kicked me viciously in the chest. The chair leg flew out of my hand. I felt myself going and rolled. It was as though I had rolled through a bed of hot coals. It seemed a whole century would pass before I would roll free, a century in which I was seared through the deepest levels of my body to the fearful breath within me and the breath seared and heated to the point of explosion. It'll all be over in a flash, I thought as I rolled clear. It'll all be over in a flash.

But not yet, the men on the other side were waiting, red faces swollen as though from apoplexy as they bent forward in their chairs. Seeing their fingers coming toward me I rolled away as a fumbled football rolls off the receiver's fingertips, back into the coals. That time I luckily sent the rug sliding out of place and heard the coins ringing against the floor and the boys scuffling to pick them up and the M.C. calling, "All right, boys, that's all. Go get dressed and get your money."

I was limp as a dish rag. My back felt as though it had been beaten with wires.

60    When we had dressed the M.C. came in and gave us each five dollars, except Tatlock, who got ten for being the last in the ring. Then he told us to leave. I was not to get a chance to deliver my speech, I thought. I was going out into the dim alley in despair when I was stopped and told to go

back. I returned to the ballroom, where the men were pushing back their chairs and gathering in groups to talk.

The M.C. knocked on a table for quiet. "Gentlemen," he said, "we almost forgot an important part of the program. A most serious part, gentlemen. This boy was brought here to deliver a speech which he made at his graduation yesterday. . . ."

"Bravo!"

"I'm told that he is the smartest boy we've got out there in Greenwood. I'm told that he knows more big words than a pocket-sized dictionary."

Much applause and laughter.

65      "So now, gentlemen, I want you to give him your attention."

There was still laughter as I faced them, my mouth dry, my eye throbbing. I began slowly, but evidently my throat was tense, because they began shouting, "Louder! Louder!"

"We of the younger generation extol the wisdom of that great leader and educator," I shouted, "who first spoke these flaming words of wisdom: 'A ship lost at sea for many days suddenly sighted a friendly vessel. From the mast of the unfortunate vessel was seen a signal: "Water, water; we die of thirst!" The answer from the friendly vessel came back: "Cast down your bucket where you are." The captain of the distressed vessel, at last heeding the injunction, cast down his bucket, and it came up full of fresh sparkling water from the mouth of the Amazon River.' And like him I say, and in his words, 'To those of my race who depend upon bettering their condition in a foreign land, or who underestimate the importance of cultivating friendly relations with the Southern white man, who is his next-door neighbor, I would say: "Cast down your bucket where you are"—cast it down in making friends in every manly way of the people of all races by whom we are surrounded. . . .'"

I spoke automatically and with such fervor that I did not realize that the men were still talking and laughing until my dry mouth, filling up with blood from the cut, almost strangled me. I coughed, wanting to stop and go to one of the tall brass, sand-filled spittoons to relieve myself, but a few of the men, especially the superintendent, were listening and I was afraid. So I gulped it down, blood, saliva and all, and continued. (What powers of endurance I had during those days! What enthusiasm! What a belief in the rightness of things!) I spoke even louder in spite of the pain. But still they talked and still they laughed, as though deaf with cotton in dirty ears. So I spoke with greater emotional emphasis. I closed my ears and swallowed blood until I was nauseated. The speech seemed a hundred times as long as before, but I could not leave out a single word. All had to be said, each memorized nuance considered, rendered. Nor was that all. Whenever I uttered a word of three or more syllables a group of voices would yell for me to repeat it. I used the phrase "social responsibility" and they yelled:

"What's the word you say, boy?"

70      "Social responsibility," I said.

"What?"

"Social . . ."

"Louder."

". . . . responsibility."

75      "More!"

"Respon—"

"Repeat!"

"—sibility."

The room filled with the uproar of laughter until, no doubt, distracted by having to gulp down my blood, I made a mistake and yelled a phrase I had often seen denounced in newspaper editorials, heard debated in private.

80      "Social . . ."

"What?" they yelled.

". . . equality—"

The laughter hung smokelike in the sudden stillness. I opened my eyes, puzzled. Sounds of displeasure filled the room. The M.C. rushed forward. They shouted hostile phrases at me. But I did not understand.

A small dry mustached man in the front row blared out, "Say that slowly, son!"

85      "What sir?"

"What you just said!"

"Social responsibility, sir," I said.

"You weren't being smart, were you, boy?" he said, not unkindly.

"No, sir!"

90      "You sure that about 'equality' was a mistake?"

"Oh, yes, sir," I said. "I was swallowing blood."

"Well, you had better speak more slowly so we can understand. We mean to do right by you, but you've got to know your place at all times. All right now, go on with your speech."

I was afraid. I wanted to leave but I wanted also to speak and I was afraid they'd snatch me down.

"Thank you, sir," I said, beginning where I had left off, and having them ignore me as before.

95      Yet when I finished there was a thunderous applause. I was surprised to see the superintendent come forth with a package wrapped in white tissue paper, and gesturing for quiet, address the men.

"Gentlemen you see that I did not overpraise this boy. He makes a good speech and some day he'll lead his people in the proper paths. And I don't have to tell you that that is important in these days and times. This is a good, smart boy, and so to encourage him in the right direction, in the name of the Board of Education I wish to present him a prize in the form of this . . ."

He paused, removing the tissue paper and revealing a gleaming calfskin brief case.

". . . in the form of this first-class article from Shad Whitmore's shop."
"Boy," he said, addressing me, "take this prize and keep it well. Consider it a badge of office. Prize it. Keep developing as you are and some day it will be filled with important papers that will help shape the destiny of your people."

100   I was so moved that I could hardly express my thanks. A rope of bloody saliva forming a shape like an undiscovered continent drooled upon the leather and I wiped it quickly away. I felt an importance that I had never dreamed.

"Open it and see what's inside," I was told.

My fingers a-tremble I complied, smelling the fresh leather and finding an official-looking document inside. It was a scholarship to the state college for Negroes. My eyes filled with tears and I ran awkwardly off the floor.

I was overjoyed; I did not even mind when I discovered that the gold pieces I had scrambled for were brass pocket tokens advertising a certain make of automobile.

When I reached home everyone was excited. Next day the neighbors came to congratulate me. I even felt safe from grandfather, whose deathbed curse usually spoiled my triumphs. I stood beneath his photograph with my brief case in hand and smiled triumphantly into his stolid black peasant's face. It was a face that fascinated me. The eyes seemed to follow everywhere I went.

105   That night I dreamed I was at a circus with him and that he refused to laugh at the clowns no matter what they did. Then later he told me to open my brief case and read what was inside and I did, finding an official envelope stamped with the state seal; and inside the envelope I found another and another, endlessly, and I thought I would fall of weariness. "Them's years," he said. "Now open that one." And I did and in it I found an engraved document containing a short message in letters of gold. "Read it," my grandfather said. "Out loud."

"To Whom It May Concern," I intoned, "Keep This Nigger-Boy Running."

I awoke with the old man's laughter ringing in my ears.

(It was a dream I was to remember and dream again for many years after. But at the time I had no insight into its meaning. First I had to attend college.)

# JOYCE CAROL OATES

*Joyce Carol Oates was born in 1938 in Millerport, New York. She won a scholarship to Syracuse University, from which she graduated (Phi Beta Kappa and valedictorian) in 1960. She then did graduate work in English, first at the University of Wisconsin and then at Rice University, but she withdrew from Rice to devote more time to writing. Her first collec-*

*tion of stories,* By the North Gate, *was published in 1963; since then she has published at least forty books—stories, poems, essays, and (in twenty-five years) twenty-two novels. She has received many awards, has been elected to the American Academy and Institute of Arts and Letters, and now teaches creative writing at Princeton University.*

## Where Are You Going, Where Have You Been?    [1966]

*To Bob Dylan*

Her name was Connie. She was fifteen and she had a quick nervous giggling habit of craning her neck to glance into mirrors or checking other people's faces to make sure her own was all right. Her mother, who noticed everything and knew everything and who hadn't much reason any longer to look at her own face, always scolded Connie about it. "Stop gawking at yourself, who are you? You think you're so pretty?" she would say. Connie would raise her eyebrows at these familiar complaints and look right through her mother, into a shadowy vision of herself as she was right at that moment: she knew she was pretty and that was everything. Her mother had been pretty once too, if you could believe those old snapshots in the album, but now her looks were gone and that was why she was always after Connie.

"Why don't you keep your room clean like your sister? How've you got your hair fixed—what the hell stinks? Hair spray? You don't see your sister using that junk."

Her sister June was twenty-four and still lived at home. She was a secretary in the high school Connie attended, and if that wasn't bad enough—with her in the same building—she was so plain and chunky and steady that Connie had to hear her praised all the time by her mother and her mother's sisters. June did this, June did that, she saved money and helped clean the house and cooked and Connie couldn't do a thing, her mind was all filled with trashy daydreams. Their father was away at work most of the time and when he came home he wanted supper and he read the newspaper at supper and after supper he went to bed. He didn't bother talking much to them, but around his bent head Connie's mother kept picking at her until Connie wished her mother was dead and she herself was dead and it was all over. "She makes me want to throw up sometimes," she complained to her friends. She had a high, breathless, amused voice which made everything she said sound a little forced, whether it was sincere or not.

There was one good thing: June went places with girlfriends of hers, girls who were just as plain and steady as she, and so when Connie wanted to do that her mother had no objections. The father of Connie's best girlfriend drove the girls the three miles to town and left them off at a shopping plaza, so that they could walk through the stores or go to a movie, and when he came to pick them up again at eleven he never bothered to ask what they had done.

5    They must have been familiar sights, walking around that shopping plaza in their shorts and flat ballerina slippers that always scuffed the sidewalk, with charm bracelets jingling on their thin wrists; they would lean together to whisper and laugh secretly if someone passed by who amused or interested them. Connie had long dark blond hair that drew anyone's eye to it, and she wore part of it pulled up on her head and puffed out and the rest of it she let fall down her back. She wore a pull-over jersey blouse that looked one way when she was at home and another way when she was away from home. Everything about her had two sides to it, one for home and one for anywhere that was not home: her walk that could be childlike and bobbing, or languid enough to make anyone think she was hearing music in her head, her mouth which was pale and smirking most of the time, but bright and pink on these evenings out, her laugh which was cynical and drawling at home—"Ha, ha, very funny"—but high-pitched and nervous anywhere else, like the jingling of the charms on her bracelet.

Sometimes they did go shopping or to a movie, but sometimes they went across the highway, ducking fast across the busy road, to a drive-in restaurant where older kids hung out. The restaurant was shaped like a big bottle, though squatter than a real bottle, and on its cap was a revolving figure of a grinning boy who held a hamburger aloft. One night in midsummer they ran across, breathless with daring, and right away someone leaned out a car window and invited them over, but it was just a boy from high school they didn't like. It made them feel good to be able to ignore him. They went up through the maze of parked and cruising cars to the bright-lit, fly-infested restaurant, their faces pleased and expectant as if they were entering a sacred building that loomed out of the night to give them what haven and what blessing they yearned for. They sat at the counter and crossed their legs at the ankles, their thin shoulders rigid with excitement, and listened to the music that made everything so good: the music was always in the background like music at a church service, it was something to depend upon.

A boy named Eddie came in to talk with them. He sat backward on his stool, turning himself jerkily around in semicircles and then stopping and turning again, and after a while he asked Connie if she would like something to eat. She said she did and so she tapped her friend's arm on her way out—her friend pulled her face up into a brave droll look—and Connie said she would meet her at eleven, across the way. "I just hate to leave her like that," Connie said earnestly, but the boy said that she wouldn't be alone for long. So they went out to his car and on the way Connie couldn't help but let her eyes wander over the windshields and faces all around her, her face gleaming with a joy that had nothing to do with

Eddie or even this place; it might have been the music. She drew her shoulders up and sucked in her breath with the pure pleasure of being alive, and just at that moment she happened to glance at a face just a few feet from hers. It was a boy with shaggy black hair, in a convertible jalopy painted gold. He stared at her and then his lips widened into a grin. Connie slit her eyes at him and turned away, but she couldn't help glancing back and there he was still watching her. He wagged a finger and laughed and said, "Gonna get you, baby," and Connie turned away again without Eddie noticing anything.

She spent three hours with him, at the restaurant where they ate hamburgers and drank Cokes in wax cups that were always sweating, and then down an alley a mile or so away, and when he left her off at five to eleven only the movie house was still open at the plaza. Her girlfriend was there, talking with a boy. When Connie came up the two girls smiled at each other and Connie said, "How was the movie?" and the girl said, "You should know." They rode off with the girl's father, sleepy and pleased, and Connie couldn't help but look at the darkened shopping plaza with its big empty parking lot and its signs that were faded and ghostly now, and over at the drive-in restaurant where cars were still circling tirelessly. She couldn't hear the music at this distance.

Next morning June asked her how the movie was and Connie said, "So-so."

10    She and that girl and occasionally another girl went out several times a week that way, and the rest of the time Connie spent around the house—it was summer vacation—getting in her mother's way and thinking, dreaming, about the boys she met. But all the boys fell back and dissolved into a single face that was not even a face, but an idea, a feeling, mixed up with the urgent insistent pounding of the music and the humid night air of July. Connie's mother kept dragging her back to the daylight by finding things for her to do or saying, suddenly, "What's this about the Pettinger girl?"

And Connie would say nervously, "Oh, her. That dope." She always drew thick clear lines between herself and such girls, and her mother was simple and kindly enough to believe her. Her mother was so simple, Connie thought, that it was maybe cruel to fool her so much. Her mother went scuffling around the house in old bedroom slippers and complained over the telephone to one sister about the other, then the other called up and the two of them complained about the third one. If June's name was mentioned her mother's tone was approving, and if Connie's name was mentioned it was disapproving. This did not really mean she disliked Connie and actually Connie thought that her mother preferred her to June because she was prettier, but the two of them kept up a pretense of exasperation, a sense that they were tugging and struggling over something of little value to either of them. Sometimes, over coffee, they were almost friends, but something would come up—some vexation that was like a fly buzzing suddenly around their heads—and their faces went hard with contempt.

One Sunday Connie got up at eleven—none of them bothered with church—and washed her hair so that it could dry all day long, in the sun. Her parents and sister were going to a barbecue at an aunt's house and Connie said no, she wasn't interested, rolling her eyes to let her mother know just what she thought of it. "Stay home alone then," her mother said sharply. Connie sat out back in a lawn chair and watched them drive away, her father quiet and bald, hunched around so that he could back the car out, her mother with a look that was still angry and not at all softened through the windshield, and in the back seat poor old June all dressed up as if she didn't know what a barbecue was, with all the running yelling kids and the flies. Connie sat with her eyes closed in the sun, dreaming and dazed with the warmth about her as if this were a kind of love, the caresses of love, and her mind slipped over onto thoughts of the boy she had been with the night before and how nice he had been, how sweet it always was, not the way someone like June would suppose but sweet, gentle, the way it was in movies and promised in songs; and when she opened her eyes she hardly knew where she was, the back yard ran off into weeds and a fence line of trees and behind it the sky was perfectly blue and still. The asbestos "ranch house" that was now three years old startled her—it looked small. She shook her head as if to get awake.

It was too hot. She went inside the house and turned on the radio to drown out the quiet. She sat on the edge of her bed, barefoot, and listened for an hour and a half to a program called XYZ Sunday Jamboree, record after record of hard, fast, shrieking songs she sang along with, interspersed by exclamations from "Bobby King": "An' look here you girls at Napoleon's—Son and Charley want you to pay real close attention to this song coming up!"

And Connie paid close attention herself, bathed in a glow of slow-pulsed joy that seemed to rise mysteriously out of the music itself and lay languidly about the airless little room, breathed in and breathed out with each gentle rise and fall of her chest.

15    After a while she heard a car coming up the drive. She sat up at once, startled, because it couldn't be her father so soon. The gravel kept crunching all the way in from the road—the driveway was long—and Connie ran to the window. It was a car she didn't know. It was an open jalopy, painted a bright gold that caught the sunlight opaquely. Her heart began to pound and her fingers snatched at her hair, checking it, and she whispered "Christ, Christ," wondering how bad she looked. The car came to a stop at the side door and the horn sounded four short taps as if this were a signal Connie knew.

She went into the kitchen and approached the door slowly, then hung out the screen door, her bare toes curling down off the step. There were two boys in the car and now she recognized the driver: he had

shaggy, shabby black hair that looked crazy as a wig and he was grinning
at her.

"I ain't late, am I?" he said.

"Who the hell do you think you are?" Connie said.

"Toldja I'd be out, didn't I?"

20    "I don't even know who you are."

She spoke sullenly, careful to show no interest or pleasure, and he
spoke in a fast bright monotone. Connie looked past him to the other boy,
taking her time. He had fair brown hair, with a lock that fell onto his
forehead. His sideburns gave him a fierce, embarrassed look, but so far he
hadn't even bothered to glance at her. Both boys wore sunglasses. The driver's glasses were metallic and mirrored everything in miniature.

"You wanta come for a ride?" he said.

Connie smirked and let her hair fall loose over one shoulder.

"Don'tcha like my car? New paint job," he said. "Hey."

25    "What?"

"You're cute."

She pretended to fidget, chasing flies away from the door.

"Don'tcha believe me, or what?" he said

"Look, I don't even know who you are," Connie said in disgust.

30    "Hey, Ellie's got a radio, see. Mine's broke down." He lifted his friend's
arm and showed her the little transistor the boy was holding, and now
Connie began to hear the music. It was the same program that was playing inside the house.

"Bobby King?" she said.

"I listen to him all the time. I think he's great."

"He's kind of great." Connie said reluctantly.

"Listen, that guy's *great*. He knows where the action is."

35    Connie blushed a little, because the glasses made it impossible for her
to see just what this boy was looking at. She couldn't decide if she liked
him or if he was just a jerk, and so she dawdled in the doorway and
wouldn't come down or go back inside. She said, "What's all that stuff
painted on your car?"

"Can'tcha read it?" He opened the door very carefully, as if he was
afraid it might fall off. He slid out just as carefully, planting his feet firmly
on the ground, the tiny metallic world in his glasses slowing down like
gelatine hardening and in the midst of it Connie's bright green blouse.
"This here is my name, to begin with," he said. ARNOLD FRIEND was written
in tarlike black letters on the side, with a drawing of a round grinning face
that reminded Connie of a pumpkin, except it wore sunglasses. "I wanta
introduce myself, I'm Arnold Friend and that's my real name and I'm
gonna be your friend, honey, and inside the car's Ellie Oscar, he's kinda
shy." Ellie brought his transistor radio up to his shoulder and balanced it
there. "Now these numbers are a secret code, honey," Arnold Friend explained. He read off the numbers 33, 19, 17 and raised his eyebrows at her

to see what she thought of that, but she didn't think much of it. The left rear fender had been smashed and around it was written, on the gleaming gold background: DONE BY CRAZY WOMAN DRIVER. Connie had to laugh at that. Arnold Friend was pleased at her laughter and looked up at her. "Around the other side's a lot more—you wanta come and see them?"

"No."

"Why not?"

"Why should I?"

40    "Don'tcha wanta see what's on the car? Don'tcha wanta go for a ride?"

"I don't know."

"Why not?"

"I got things to do."

"Like what?"

45    "Things."

He laughed as if she had said something funny. He slapped his thighs. He was standing in a strange way, leaning back against the car as if he were balancing himself. He wasn't tall, only an inch or so taller than she would be if she came down to him. Connie liked the way he was dressed, which was the way all of them dressed: tight faded jeans stuffed into black, scuffed boots, a belt that pulled his waist in and showed how lean he was, and a white pullover shirt that was a little soiled and showed the hard small muscles of his arms and shoulders. He looked as if he probably did hard work, lifting and carrying things. Even his neck looked muscular. And his face was a familiar face, somehow: the jaw and chin and cheeks slightly darkened, because he hadn't shaved for a day or two, and the nose long and hawklike, sniffing as if she were a treat he was going to gobble up and it was all a joke.

"Connie, you ain't telling the truth. This is your day set aside for a ride with me and you know it," he said, still laughing. The way he straightened and recovered from his fit of laughing showed that it had been all fake.

"How do you know what my name is?" she said suspiciously.

"It's Connie."

50    "Maybe and maybe not."

"I know my Connie," he said, wagging his finger. Now she remembered him even better, back at the restaurant, and her cheeks warmed at the thought of how she sucked in her breath just at the moment she passed him—how she must have looked to him. And he had remembered her. "Ellie and I come out here especially for you," he said. "Ellie can sit in back. How about it?"

"Where?"

"Where what?"

"Where're we going?"

55    He looked at her. He took off the sunglasses and she saw how pale the skin around his eyes was, like holes that were not in shadow but instead in light. His eyes were like chips of broken glass that catch the light

in an amiable way. He smiled. It was as if the idea of going for a ride somewhere, to some place, was a new idea to him.

"Just for a ride, Connie sweetheart."

"I never said my name was Connie," she said.

"But I know what it is. I know your name and all about you, lots of
things," Arnold Friend said. He had not moved yet but stood still leaning
back against the side of his jalopy. "I took a special interest in you, such a
pretty girl, and found out all about you like I know your parents and sister
are gone somewheres and I know where and how long they're going to
be gone, and I know who you were with last night, and your best girlfriend's name is Betty. Right?"

He spoke in a simple lilting voice, exactly as if he were reciting the
words to a song. His smile assured her that everything was fine. In the car
Ellie turned up the volume on his radio and did not bother to look around
at them.

60      "Ellie can sit in the back seat," Arnold Friend said. He indicated his
friend with a casual jerk of his chin, as if Ellie did not count and she
should not bother with him.

"How'd you find out all that stuff?" Connie said.

"Listen: Betty Schultz and Tony Fitch and Jimmy Pettinger and Nancy
Pettinger," he said, in a chant. "Raymond Stanley and Bob Hutter—"

"Do you know all those kids?"

"I know everybody."

65      "Look, you're kidding. You're not from around here."

"Sure."

"But—how come we never saw you before?"

"Sure you saw me before," he said. He looked down at his boots, as if
he were a little offended. "You just don't remember."

"I guess I'd remember you," Connie said.

70      "Yeah?" He looked up at this, beaming. He was pleased. He began to
mark time with the music from Ellie's radio, tapping his fists lightly together. Connie looked away from his smile to the car, which was painted
so bright it almost hurt her eyes to look at it. She looked at that name,
arnold friend. And up at the front fender was an expression that was familiar—man the flying saucers. It was an expression kids had used the year
before, but didn't use this year. She looked at it for a while as if the words
meant something to her that she did not yet know.

"What're you thinking about? Huh?" Arnold Friend demanded. "Not
worried about your hair blowing around in the car, are you?"

"No."

"Think I maybe can't drive good?"

"How do I know?"

75      "You're a hard girl to handle. How come?" he said. "Don't you
know I'm your friend? Didn't you see me put my sign in the air when you
walked by?"

"What sign?"

"My sign." And he drew an X in the air, leaning out toward her. They were maybe ten feet apart. After his hand fell back to his side the X was still in the air, almost visible. Connie let the screen door close and stood perfectly still inside it, listening to the music from her radio and the boy's blend together. She stared at Arnold Friend. He stood there so stiffly relaxed, pretending to be relaxed, with one hand idly on the door handle as if he were keeping himself up that way and had no intention of ever moving again. She recognized most things about him, the tight jeans that showed his thighs and buttocks and the greasy leather boots and the tight shirt, and even that slippery friendly smile of his, that sleepy dreamy smile that all the boys used to get across ideas they didn't want to put into words. She recognized all this and also the singsong way he talked, slightly mocking, kidding, but serious and a little melancholy, and she recognized the way he tapped one fist against the other in homage to the perpetual music behind him. But all these things did not come together.

She said suddenly, "Hey, how old are you?"

His smile faded. She could see then that he wasn't a kid, he was much older—thirty, maybe more. At this knowledge her heart began to pound faster.

80    "That's a crazy thing to ask. Can'tcha see I'm your own age?"

"Like hell you are."

"Or maybe a coupla years older, I'm eighteen."

"Eighteen?" she said doubtfully.

He grinned to reassure her and lines appeared at the corners of his mouth. His teeth were big and white. He grinned so broadly his eyes became slits and she saw how thick the lashes were, thick and black as if painted with a black tarlike material. Then he seemed to become embarrassed, abruptly, and looked over his shoulder at Ellie. "Him, he's crazy," he said. "Ain't he a riot, he's a nut, a real character." Ellie was still listening to the music. His sunglasses told nothing about what he was thinking. He wore a bright orange shirt unbuttoned halfway to show his chest, which was a pale, bluish chest and not muscular like Arnold Friend's. His shirt collar was turned up all around and the very tips of the collar pointed out past his chin as if they were protecting him. He was pressing the transistor radio up against his ear and sat there in a kind of daze, right in the sun.

85    "He's kinda strange," Connie said.

"Hey, she says you're kinda strange! Kinda strange!" Arnold Friend cried. He pounded on the car to get Ellie's attention. Ellie turned for the first time and Connie saw with shock that he wasn't a kid either—he had a fair, hairless face, cheeks reddened slightly as if the veins grew too close to the surface of his skin, the face of a forty-year-old baby. Connie felt a wave of dizziness rise in her at this sight and she stared at him as if waiting for something to change the shock of the moment, make it all right again. Ellie's lips kept shaping words, mumbling along, with the words blasting in his ear.

"Maybe you two better go away," Connie said faintly.

"What? How come?" Arnold Friend cried. "We come out here to take you for a ride. It's Sunday." He had the voice of the man on the radio now. It was the same voice, Connie thought. "Don'tcha know it's Sunday all day and honey, no matter who you were with last night today you're with Arnold Friend and don't you forget it!—Maybe you better step out here," he said, and this last was in a different voice. It was a little flatter, as if the heat was finally getting to him.

"No. I got things to do."

90      "Hey."

"You two better leave."

"We ain't leaving until you come with us."

"Like hell I am—"

"Connie, don't fool around with me. I mean, I mean, don't fool *around*," he said, shaking his head. He laughed incredulously. He placed his sunglasses on top of his head, carefully, as if he were indeed wearing a wig, and brought the stems down behind his ears. Connie stared at him, another wave of dizziness and fear rising in her so that for a moment he wasn't even in focus but was just a blur, standing there against his gold car, and she had the idea that he had driven up the driveway all right but had come from nowhere before that and belonged nowhere and that everything about him and even about the music that was so familiar to her was only half real.

95      "If my father comes and sees you—"

"He ain't coming. He's at a barbecue."

"How do you know that?"

"Aunt Tillie's. Right now they're—uh—they're drinking. Sitting around," he said vaguely, squinting as if he were staring all the way to town and over to Aunt Tillie's back yard. Then the vision seemed to get clear and he nodded energetically. "Yeah. Sitting around. There's your sister in a blue dress, huh? And high heels, the poor sad bitch—nothing like you, sweetheart! And your mother's helping some fat woman with the corn, they're cleaning the corn—husking the corn—"

"What fat woman?" Connie cried.

100     "How do I know what fat woman. I don't know every goddam fat woman in the world!" Arnold Friend laughed.

"Oh, that's Mrs. Hornby. . . . Who invited her?" Connie said. She felt a little light-headed. Her breath was coming quickly.

"She's too fat. I don't like them fat. I like them the way you are, honey," he said, smiling sleepily at her. They stared at each other for a while, through the screen door. He said softly, "Now what you're going to do is this: you're going to come out that door. You're going to sit up front with me and Ellie's going to sit in the back, the hell with Ellie, right? This isn't Ellie's date. You're my date. I'm your lover, honey."

"What? You're crazy—"

"Yes, I'm your lover. You don't know what that is but you will," he said. "I know that too. I know all about you. But look: it's real nice and you couldn't ask for nobody better than me, or more polite. I always keep my word. I'll tell you how it is, I'm always nice at first, the first time. I'll hold you so tight you won't think you have to try to get away or pretend anything because you'll know you can't. And I'll come inside you where it's all secret and you'll give in to me and you'll love me—"

105    "Shut up! You're crazy!" Connie said. She backed away from the door. She put her hands against her ears as if she'd heard something terrible, something not meant for her. "People don't talk like that, you're crazy," she muttered. Her heart was almost too big now for her chest and its pumping made sweat break out all over her. She looked out to see Arnold Friend pause and then take a step toward the porch lurching. He almost fell. But, like a clever drunken man, he managed to catch his balance. He wobbled in his high boots and grabbed hold of one of the porch posts.

"Honey?" he said. "You still listening?"

"Get the hell out of here!"

"Be nice, honey. Listen."

"I'm going to call the police—"

110    He wobbled again and out of the side of his mouth came a fast spat curse, an aside not meant for her to hear. But even this "Christ!" sounded forced. Then he began to smile again. She watched this smile come, awkward as if he were smiling from inside a mask. His whole face was a mask, she thought wildly, tanned down onto his throat but then running out as if he had plastered makeup on his face but had forgotten about his throat.

"Honey—? Listen, here's how it is. I always tell the truth and I promise you this: I ain't coming in that house after you."

"You better not! I'm going to call the police if you—if you don't—"

"Honey," he said, talking right through her voice, "honey, I'm not coming in there but you are coming out here. You know why?"

She was panting. The kitchen looked like a place she had never seen before, some room she had run inside but which wasn't good enough, wasn't going to help her. The kitchen window had never had a curtain, after three years, and there were dishes in the sink for her to do—probably—and if you ran your hand across the table you'd probably feel something sticky there.

115    "You listening, honey? Hey?"

"—going to call the police—"

"Soon as you touch the phone I don't need to keep my promise and can come inside. You won't want that."

She rushed forward and tried to lock the door. Her fingers were shaking. "But why lock it," Arnold Friend said gently, talking right into her face.

"It's just a screen door. It's just nothing." One of his boots was at a strange angle, as if his foot wasn't in it. It pointed out to the left, bent at the ankle. "I mean, anybody can break through a screen door and glass and wood and iron or anything else if he needs to, anybody at all and specially Arnold Friend. If the place got lit up with a fire honey you'd come runnin' out into my arms, right into my arms an' safe at home—like you knew I was your lover and'd stopped fooling around. I don't mind a nice shy girl but I don't like no fooling around." Part of those words were spoken with a slight rhythmic lilt, and Connie somehow recognized them—the echo of a song from last year, about a girl rushing into her boyfriend's arms and coming home again—

Connie stood barefoot on the linoleum floor, staring at him. "What do you want?" she whispered.

120        "I want you," he said.

"What?"

"Seen you that night and thought, that's the one, yes sir. I never needed to look any more."

"But my father's coming back. He's coming to get me. I had to wash my hair first—" She spoke in a dry, rapid voice, hardly raising it for him to hear.

"No, your Daddy is not coming and yes, you had to wash your hair and you washed it for me. It's nice and shining and all for me, I thank you, sweetheart," he said, with a mock bow, but again he almost lost his balance. He had to bend and adjust his boots. Evidently his feet did not go all the way down; the boots must have been stuffed with something so that he would seem taller. Connie stared out at him and behind him Ellie in the car, who seemed to be looking off toward Connie's right into nothing. This Ellie said, pulling the words out of the air one after another as if he were just discovering them, "You want me to pull out the phone?"

125        "Shut your mouth and keep it shut," Arnold Friend said, his face red from bending over or maybe from embarrassment because Connie had seen his boots. "This ain't none of your business."

"What—what are you doing? What do you want?" Connie said. "If I call the police they'll get you, they'll arrest you—"

"Promise was not to come in unless you touch that phone, and I'll keep that promise," he said. He resumed his erect position and tried to force his shoulders back. He sounded like a hero in a movie, declaring something important. He spoke too loudly and it was as if he were speaking to someone behind Connie. "I ain't made plans for coming in that house where I don't belong but just for you to come out to me, the way you should. Don't you know who I am?"

"You're crazy," she whispered. She backed away from the door but did not want to go into another part of the house, as if this would give him permission to come through the door. "What do you . . . You're crazy, you . . . ."

"Huh? What're you saying, honey?"

130        Her eyes darted everywhere in the kitchen. She could not remember
what it was, this room.
       "This is how it is, honey: you come out and we'll drive away, have a
nice ride. But if you don't come out we're gonna wait till your people
come home and then they're all going to get it."
       "You want that telephone pulled out?" Ellie said. He held the radio
away from his ear and grimaced, as if without the radio the air was too
much for him.
       "I toldja shut up, Ellie," Arnold Friend said, "you're deaf, get a hearing
aid, right? Fix yourself up. This little girl's no trouble and's gonna be nice
to me, so Ellie keep to yourself, this ain't your date—right? Don't hem in
on me. Don't hog. Don't crush. Don't bird dog. Don't trail me," he said in a
rapid meaningless voice, as if he were running through all the expressions
he'd learned but was no longer sure which one of them was in style, then
rushing on to new ones, making them up with his eyes closed, "Don't
crawl under my fence, don't squeeze in my chipmunk hole, don't sniff my
glue, suck my popsicle, keep your own greasy fingers on yourself!" He
shaded his eyes and peered in at Connie, who was backed against the
kitchen table. "Don't mind him honey he's just a creep. He's a dope. Right?
I'm the boy for you and like I said you come out here nice like a lady and
give me your hand, and nobody else gets hurt, I mean, your nice old bald-
headed daddy and your mummy and your sister in her high heels. Because
listen: why bring them in this?"
       "Leave me alone," Connie whispered.
135        "Hey, you know that old woman down the road, the one with the
chickens and stuff—you know her?"
       "She's dead!"
       "Dead? What? You know her?" Arnold Friend said.
       "She's dead—"
       "Don't you like her?"
140        "She's dead—she's—she isn't here any more—"
       "But don't you like her, I mean, you got something against her? Some
grudge or something?" Then his voice dipped as if he were conscious of a
rudeness. He touched the sunglasses perched on top of his head as if to
make sure they were still there. "Now you be a good girl."
       "What are you going to do?"
       "Just two things, or maybe three," Arnold Friend said. "But I promise it
won't last long and you'll like me the way you get to like people you're
close to. You will. It's all over for you here, so come on out. You don't want
your people in any trouble, do you?"
       She turned and bumped against a chair or something, hurting her leg,
but she ran into the back room and picked up the telephone. Something
roared in her ear, a tiny roaring, and she was so sick with fear that she
could do nothing but listen to it—the telephone was clammy and very
heavy and her fingers groped down to the dial but were too weak to touch

it. She began to scream into the phone, into the roaring. She cried out, she cried for her mother, she felt her breath start jerking back and forth in her lungs as if it were something Arnold Friend were stabbing her with again and again with no tenderness. A noisy sorrowful wailing rose all about her and she was locked inside it the way she was locked inside the house.

145   After a while she could hear again. She was sitting on the floor with her wet back against the wall.

Arnold Friend was saying from the door, "That's a good girl. Put the phone back."

She kicked the phone away from her.

"No, honey. Pick it up. Put it back right."

She picked it up and put it back. The dial tone stopped.

150   "That's a good girl. Now come outside."

She was hollow with what had been fear, but what was now just an emptiness. All that screaming had blasted it out of her. She sat, one leg cramped under her, and deep inside her brain was something like a pin-point of light that kept going and would not let her relax. She thought, I'm not going to see my mother again. She thought, I'm not going to sleep in my bed again. Her bright green blouse was all wet.

Arnold Friend said, in a gentle-loud voice that was like a stage voice, "The place where you came from ain't there any more, and where you had in mind to go is canceled out. This place you are now—inside your daddy's house—is nothing but a cardboard box I can knock down any time. You know that and always did know it. You hear me?"

She thought, I have got to think. I have to know what to do.

"We'll go out to a nice field, out in the country here where it smells so nice and it's sunny," Arnold Friend said. "I'll have my arms tight around you so you won't need to try to get away and I'll show you what love is like, what it does. The hell with this house! It looks solid all right," he said. He ran a fingernail down the screen and the noise did not make Connie shiver, as it would have the day before. "Now put your hand on your heart, honey. Feel that? That feels solid too but we know better, be nice to me, be sweet like you can because what else is there for a girl like you but to be sweet and pretty and give in?—and get away before her people come back?"

155   She felt her pounding heart. Her hand seemed to enclose it. She thought for the first time in her life that it was nothing that was hers, that belonged to her, but just a pounding, living thing inside this body that wasn't really hers either.

"You don't want them to get hurt," Arnold Friend went on. "Now get up, honey. Get up all by yourself."

She stood up.

"Now turn this way. That's right. Come over here to me—Ellie, put that away, didn't I tell you? You dope. You miserable creepy dope," Arnold Friend said. His words were not angry but only part of an incantation. The incantation was kindly. "Now come out through the kitchen to me honey, and let's see a smile, try it, you're a brave sweet little girl and now they're eating corn and hot dogs cooked to bursting over an outdoor fire, and they don't know one thing about you and never did and honey you're better than them because not a one of them would have done this for you."

Connie felt the linoleum under her feet; it was cool. She brushed her hair back out of her eyes. Arnold Friend let go of the post tentatively and opened his arms for her, his elbows pointing in toward each other and his wrists limp, to show that this was an embarrassed embrace and a little mocking, he didn't want to make her self-conscious.

160    She put out her hand against the screen. She watched herself push the door slowly open as if she were safe back somewhere in the other doorway, watching this body and this head of long hair moving out into the sunlight where Arnold Friend waited.

"My sweet little blue-eyed girl," he said, in a half-sung sigh that had nothing to do with her brown eyes but was taken up just the same by the vast sunlit reaches of the land behind him and on all sides of him, so much land that Connie had never seen before and did not recognize except to know that she was going to it.

# BOBBIE ANN MASON

*Bobbie Ann Mason, born in 1940 in rural western Kentucky and a graduate of the University of Kentucky, now lives in Pennsylvania. She took a master's degree at the State University of New York at Binghamton, and a Ph.D. at the University of Connecticut, writing a dissertation on a novel by Vladimir Nabokov. Between graduate degrees she worked for various magazines, including* T.V. Star Parade. *In 1974 she published her first book—the dissertation on Nabokov—and in 1975 she published her second,* The Girl Sleuth: A Guide to the Bobbsey Twins, Nancy Drew and Their Sisters. *She is, however, most widely known for her fiction, which usually deals with blue-collar people in rural Kentucky.*

> *I write, she says, about people trapped in circumstances. . . . I identify with people who are ambivalent about their situation. And I guess in my stories, I'm in a way imagining myself as I would have felt if I had not gotten away and gotten a different perspective on things—if, for example, I had gotten pregnant in high school and had to marry a truck driver as the woman did in my story "Shiloh."*

## Shiloh                                              [1982]

Leroy Moffitt's wife, Norma Jean, is working on her pectorals. She lifts three-pound dumbbells to warm up, then progresses to a twenty-pound barbell. Standing with her legs apart, she reminds Leroy of Wonder Woman.

"I'd give anything if I could just get these muscles to where they're real hard," says Norma Jean. "Feel this arm. It's not as hard as the other one."

"That's cause you're right-handed," says Leroy, dodging as she swings the barbell in an arc.

"Do you think so?"

5    "Sure."

Leroy is a truckdriver. He injured his leg in a highway accident four months ago, and his physical therapy, which involves weights and a pulley, prompted Norma Jean to try building herself up. Now she is attending a body-building class. Leroy has been collecting temporary disability since his tractor-trailer jackknifed in Missouri, badly twisting his left leg in its socket. He has a steel pin in his hip. He will probably not be able to drive his rig again. It sits in the backyard, like a gigantic bird that has flown home to roost. Leroy has been home in Kentucky for three months, and his leg is almost healed, but the accident frightened him and he does not want to drive any more long hauls. He is not sure what to do next. In the meantime, he makes things from craft kits. He started by building a miniature log cabin from notched Popsicle sticks. He varnished it and placed it on the TV set, where it remains. It reminds him of a rustic Nativity scene. Then he tried string art (sailing ships on black velvet), a macramé owl kit, a snap-together B-17 Flying Fortress, and a lamp made out of a model truck, with a light fixture screwed in the top of the cab. At first the kits were diversions, something to kill time, but now he is thinking about building a full-scale log house from a kit. It would be considerably cheaper than building a regular house, and besides, Leroy has grown to appreciate how things are put together. He has begun to realize that in all the years he was on the road he never took time to examine anything. He was always flying past scenery.

"They won't let you build a log cabin in any of the new subdivisions," Norma Jean tells him.

"They will if I tell them it's for you," he says, teasing her. Ever since they were married, he has promised Norma Jean he would build her a new home one day. They have always rented, and the house they live in is small and nondescript. It does not even feel like a home, Leroy realizes now.

Norma Jean works at the Rexall drugstore, and she has acquired an amazing amount of information about cosmetics. When she explains to Leroy the three stages of complexion care, involving creams, toners, and moisturizers, he thinks happily of other petroleum products—axle grease, diesel fuel. This is a connection between him and Norma Jean. Since he has been home, he has felt unusually tender about his wife and guilty over his long absences. But he can't tell what she feels about him. Norma Jean has never complained about his traveling; she has never made hurt remarks, like calling his truck a "widow-maker." He is reasonably certain she has been faithful to him, but he wishes she would celebrate his permanent home-coming more happily. Norma Jean is often startled to find Leroy at home, and he thinks she seems a little disappointed about it. Perhaps he reminds her too much of the early days of their marriage, before he went on the road. They had a child who died as an infant, years ago. They never speak about their memories of Randy, which have almost faded, but now that Leroy is home all the time, they sometimes feel awkward around each other, and Leroy wonders if one of them should mention the child. He has the feeling that they are waking up out of a dream together—that they must create a new marriage, start afresh. They are lucky they are still married. Leroy has read that for most people losing a child destroys the marriage—or else he heard this on *Donahue*. He can't always remember where he learns things anymore.

10     At Christmas, Leroy bought an electric organ for Norma Jean. She used to play the piano when she was in high school. "It don't leave you," she told him once. "It's like riding a bicycle."

The new instrument had so many keys and buttons that she was bewildered by it at first. She touched the keys tentatively, pushed some buttons, then pecked out "Chopsticks." It came out in an amplified fox-trot rhythm, with marimba sounds.

"It's an orchestra!" she cried.

The organ had a pecan-look finish and eighteen preset chords, with optional flute, violin, trumpet, clarinet, and banjo accompaniments. Norma Jean mastered the organ almost immediately. At first she played Christmas songs. Then she bought *The Sixties Songbook* and learned every tune in it, adding variations to each with the rows of brightly colored buttons.

"I didn't like these old songs back then," she said. "But I have this crazy feeling I missed something."

15     "You didn't miss a thing," said Leroy.

Leroy likes to lie on the couch and smoke a joint and listen to Norma Jean play "Can't Take My Eyes Off You" and "I'll Be Back." He is back again. After fifteen years on the road, he is finally settling down with the woman he loves. She is still pretty. Her skin is flawless. Her frosted curls resemble pencil trimmings.

Now that Leroy has come home to stay, he notices how much the town has changed. Subdivisions are spreading across western Kentucky like an oil slick. The sign at the edge of town says "Pop: 11,500"—only seven hundred more than it said twenty years before. Leroy can't figure out who is living in all the new houses. The farmers who used to gather around the courthouse square on Saturday afternoons to play checkers and spit tobacco juice have gone. It has been years since Leroy has thought about the farmers, and they have disappeared without his noticing.

Leroy meets a kid named Stevie Hamilton in the parking lot at the new shopping center. While they pretend to be strangers meeting over a stalled car, Stevie tosses an ounce of marijuana under the front seat of Leroy's car. Stevie is wearing orange jogging shoes and a T-shirt that says

CHATTAHOOCHEE SUPER-RAT. His father is a prominent doctor who lives in one of the expensive subdivisions in a new white-columned brick house that looks like a funeral parlor. In the phone book under his name there is a separate number, with the listing "Teenagers."

"Where do you get this stuff?" asks Leroy. "From your pappy?"

20    "That's for me to know and you to find out," Stevie says. He is slit-eyed and skinny.

"What else you got?"

"What you interested in?"

"Nothing special. Just wondered."

Leroy used to take speed on the road. Now he has to go slowly. He needs to be mellow. He leans back against the car and says, "I'm aiming to build me a log house, soon as I get time. My wife, though, I don't think she likes the idea."

25    "Well, let me know when you want me again," Stevie says. He has a cigarette in his cupped palm, as though sheltering it from the wind. He takes a long drag, then stomps it on the asphalt and slouches away.

Stevie's father was two years ahead of Leroy in high school. Leroy is thirty-four. He married Norma Jean when they were both eighteen, and their child Randy was born a few months later, but he died at the age of four months and three days. He would be about Stevie's age now. Norma Jean and Leroy were at the drive-in, watching a double feature (*Dr. Strangelove* and *Lover Come Back*), and the baby was sleeping in the back seat. When the first movie ended, the baby was dead. It was the sudden infant death syndrome. Leroy remembers handing Randy to a nurse at the emergency room, as though he were offering her a large doll as a present. A dead baby feels like a sack of flour. "It just happens sometimes," said the doctor, in what Leroy always recalls as a nonchalant tone. Leroy can hardly remember the child anymore, but he still sees vividly a scene from *Dr. Strangelove* in which the President of the United States was talking in a folksy voice on the hot line to the Soviet premier about the bomber accidentally headed toward Russia. He was in the War Room, and the world map was lit up. Leroy remembers Norma Jean standing catatonically beside him in the hospital and himself thinking: Who is this strange girl? He had forgotten who she was. Now scientists are saying that crib death is caused by a virus. Nobody knows anything, Leroy thinks. The answers are always changing.

When Leroy gets home from the shopping center, Norma Jean's mother, Mabel Beasley, is there. Until this year, Leroy has not realized how much time she spends with Norma Jean. When she visits, she inspects the closets and then the plants, informing Norma Jean when a plant is droopy or yellow. Mabel calls the plants "flowers," although there are never any blooms. She also notices if Norma Jean's laundry is piling up. Mabel is a short, overweight woman whose tight, brown-dyed curls look more like a wig than the actual wig she sometimes wears. Today she has brought

Norma Jean an off-white dust ruffle she made for the bed; Mabel works in a custom-upholstery shop.

"This is the tenth one I made this year," Mabel says. "I got started and couldn't stop."

"It's real pretty," says Normal Jean.

30    "Now we can hide things under the bed," says Leroy, who gets along with his mother-in-law primarily by joking with her. Mabel has never really forgiven him for disgracing her by getting Norma Jean pregnant. When the baby died, she said that fate was mocking her.

"What's that thing?" Mabel says to Leroy in a loud voice, pointing to a tangle of yarn on a piece of canvas.

Leroy holds it up for Mabel to see. "It's my needlepoint," he explains. "This is a *Star Trek* pillow cover."

"That's what a woman would do," says Mabel. "Great day in the morning!"

"All the big football players on TV do it," he says.

35    "Why, Leroy, you're always trying to fool me. I don't believe you for one minute. You don't know what to do with yourself—that's the whole trouble. Sewing!"

"I'm aiming to build us a log house," says Leroy. "Soon as my plans come."

"Like *heck* you are," says Norma Jean. She takes Leroy's needlepoint and shoves it into a drawer. "You have to find a job first. Nobody can afford to build now anyway."

Mabel straightens her girdle and says. "I still think before you get tied down y'all ought to take a little run to Shiloh."

"One of these days, Mama," Norma Jean says impatiently.

40    Mabel is talking about Shiloh, Tennessee. For the past few years, she has been urging Leroy and Norma Jean to visit the Civil War battleground there. Mabel went there on her honeymoon—the only real trip she ever took. Her husband died of a perforated ulcer when Norma Jean was ten, but Mabel, who was accepted into the United Daughters of the Confederacy in 1975, is still preoccupied with going back to Shiloh.

"I've been to kingdom come and back in that truck out yonder," Leroy says to Mabel, "but we never yet set foot in that battleground. Ain't that something? How did I miss it?"

"It's not even that far," Mabel says.

After Mabel leaves, Norma Jean reads to Leroy from a list she has made. "Things you could do," she announces. "You could get a job as a guard at Union Carbide, where they'd let you set on a stool. You could get on at the lumberyard. You could do a little carpenter work, if you want to build so bad. You could—"

"I can't do something where I'd have to stand up all day."

45    "You ought to try standing up all day behind a cosmetics counter. It's amazing that I have strong feet, coming from two parents that never had

strong feet at all." At the moment Norma Jean is holding on to the kitchen counter, raising her knees one at a time as she talks. She is wearing two-pound ankle weights.

"Don't worry," says Leroy. "I'll do something."

"You could truck calves to slaughter for somebody. You wouldn't have to drive any big old truck for that."

"I'm going to build you this house," says Leroy. "I want to make you a real home."

"I don't want to live in any log cabin."

50    "It's not a cabin. It's a house."

"I don't care. It looks like a cabin."

"You and me together could lift those logs. It's just like lifting weights."

Norma Jean doesn't answer. Under her breath, she is counting. Now she is marching through the kitchen. She is doing goose steps.

Before his accident, when Leroy came home he used to stay in the house with Norma Jean, watching TV in bed and playing cards. She would cook fried chicken, picnic ham, chocolate pie—all his favorites. Now he is home alone much of the time. In the mornings, Norma Jean disappears, leaving a cooling place in the bed. She eats a cereal called Body Buddies, and she leaves the bowl on the table, with the soggy tan balls floating in a milk puddle. He sees things about Norma Jean that he never realized before. When she chops onions, she stares off into a corner, as if she can't bear to look. She puts on her house slippers almost precisely at nine o'clock every evening and nudges her jogging shoes under the couch. She saves bread heels for the birds. Leroy watches the birds at the feeder. He notices the peculiar way goldfinches fly past the window. They close their wings, then fall, then spread their wings to catch and lift themselves. He wonders if they close their eyes when they fall. Norma Jean closes her eyes when they are in bed. She wants the lights turned out. Even then, he is sure she closes her eyes.

55    He goes for long drives around town. He tends to drive a car rather carelessly. Power steering and an automatic shift make a car feel so small and inconsequential that his body is hardly involved in the driving process. His injured leg stretches out comfortably. Once or twice he has almost hit something, but even the prospect of an accident seems minor in a car. He cruises the new subdivisions, feeling like a criminal rehearsing for a robbery. Norma Jean is probably right about a log house being inappropriate here in the new subdivision. All the houses look grand and complicated. They depress him.

One day when Leroy comes home from a drive he finds Norma Jean in tears. She is in the kitchen making a potato and mushroom-soup casserole, with grated cheese topping. She is crying because her mother caught her smoking.

"I didn't hear her coming. I was standing here puffing away pretty as you please," Norma Jean says, wiping her eyes.

"I knew it would happen sooner or later," says Leroy, putting his arm around her.

"She don't know the meaning of the word 'knock,'" says Norma Jean. "It's a wonder she hadn't caught me years ago."

60      "Think of it this way," Leroy says. "What if she caught me with a joint?"

"You better not let her!" Norma Jean shrieks. "I'm warning you, Leroy Moffitt!"

"I'm just kidding. Here, play me a tune. That'll help you relax."

Norma Jean puts the casserole in the oven and sets the timer. Then she plays a ragtime tune, with horns and banjo, as Leroy lights up a joint and lies on the couch, laughing to himself about Mabel's catching him at it. He thinks of Stevie Hamilton—a doctor's son pushing grass. Everything is funny. The whole town seems crazy and small. He is reminded of Virgil Mathis, a boastful policeman Leroy used to shoot pool with. Virgil recently led a drug bust in a back room at a bowling alley, where he seized ten thousand dollars' worth of marijuana. The newspaper had a picture of him holding up the bags of grass and grinning widely. Right now, Leroy can imagine Virgil breaking down the door and arresting him with a lungful of smoke. Virgil would probably have been alerted to the scene because of all the racket Norma Jean is making. Now she sounds like a hard-rock band. Norma Jean is terrific. When she switches to a Latin-rhythm version of "Sunshine Superman," Leroy hums along. Norma Jean's foot goes up and down, up and down.

"Well, what do you think?" Leroy says, when Norma Jean pauses to search through her music.

65      "What do I think about what?"

His mind has gone blank. Then he says, "I'll sell my rig and build us a house." That wasn't what he wanted to say. He wanted to know what she thought—what she *really* thought—about them.

"Don't start in on that again," says Norma Jean. She begins playing "Who'll Be the Next in Line?"

Leroy used to tell hitchhikers his whole life story—about his travels, his hometown, the baby. He would end with a question: "Well, what do you think?" It was just a rhetorical question. In time, he had the feeling that he'd been telling the same story over and over to the same hitchhikers. He quit talking to hitchhikers when he realized how his voice sounded—whining and self-pitying, like some teenage-tragedy song. Now Leroy has the sudden impulse to tell Norma Jean about himself, as if he had just met her. They have known each other so long they have forgotten a lot about each other. They could become reacquainted. But when the oven timer goes off and she runs to the kitchen, he forgets why he wants to do this.

The next day, Mabel drops by. It is Saturday and Norma Jean is cleaning. Leroy is studying the plans of his log house, which have finally come in the mail. He has them spread out on the table—big sheets of stiff blue paper, with diagrams and numbers printed in white. While Norma Jean runs the vacuum, Mabel drinks coffee. She sets her coffee cup on a blueprint.

70 "I'm just waiting for time to pass," she says to Leroy, drumming her fingers on the table.

As soon as Norma Jean switches off the vacuum, Mabel says in a loud voice. "Did you hear about the datsun dog that killed the baby?"

Norma Jean says, "The word is 'dachshund.' "

"They put the dog on trial. It chewed the baby's legs off. The mother was in the next room all the time." She raises her voice. "They thought it was neglect."

Norma Jean is holding her ears. Leroy manages to open the refrigerator and get some Diet Pepsi to offer Mabel. Mabel still has some coffee and she waves away the Pepsi.

75 "Datsuns are like that," Mabel says. "They're jealous dogs. They'll tear a place to pieces if you don't keep an eye on them."

"You better watch out what you're saying, Mabel," says Leroy.

"Well, facts is facts."

Leroy looks out the window at his rig. It is like a huge piece of furniture gathering dust in the backyard. Pretty soon it will be an antique. He hears the vacuum cleaner. Norma Jean seems to be cleaning the living room rug again.

Later, she says to Leroy, "She just said that about the baby because she caught me smoking. She's trying to pay me back."

80 "What are you talking about?" Leroy says, nervously shuffling blueprints.

"You know good and well," Norma Jean says. She is sitting in a kitchen chair with her feet up and her arms wrapped around her knees. She looks small and helpless. She says, "The very idea, her bringing up a subject like that! Saying it was neglect."

"She didn't mean that," Leroy says.

"She might not have *thought* she meant it. She always says things like that. You don't know how she goes on."

"But she didn't really mean it. She was just talking."

85 Leroy opens a king-sized bottle of beer and pours it into two glasses dividing it carefully. He hands a glass to Norma Jean and she takes it from him mechanically. For a long time, they sit by the kitchen window watching the birds at the feeder.

Something is happening. Norma Jean is going to night school. She has graduated from her six-week body-building course and now she is taking an adult-education course in composition at Paducah Community College. She spends her evenings outlining paragraphs.

"First, you have a topic sentence," she explains to Leroy. "Then you divide it up. Your secondary topic has to be connected to your primary topic."

To Leroy, this sounds intimidating. "I never was any good in English," he says.

"It makes a lot of sense."

90    "What are you doing this for, anyhow?"

She shrugs. "It's something to do." She stands up and lifts her dumbbells a few times.

"Driving a rig, nobody cared about my English."

"I'm not criticizing your English."

Norma Jean used to say, "If I lose ten minutes' sleep, I just drag all day." Now she stays up late, writing compositions. She got a B on her first paper—a how-to theme on soup-based casseroles. Recently Norma Jean has been cooking unusual foods—tacos, lasagna, Bombay chicken. She doesn't play the organ anymore, though her second paper was called "Why Music Is Important to Me." She sits at the kitchen table, concentrating on her outlines, while Leroy plays with his log house plans, practicing with a set of Lincoln Logs. The thought of getting a truckload of notched, numbered logs scares him, and he wants to be prepared. As he and Norma Jean work together at the kitchen table, Leroy has the hopeful thought that they are sharing something, but he knows he is a fool to think this. Norma Jean is miles away. He knows he is going to lose her. Like Mabel, he is just waiting for time to pass.

95    One day, Mabel is there before Norma Jean gets home from work, and Leroy finds himself confiding in her. Mabel, he realizes, must know Norma Jean better than he does.

"I don't know what's got into that girl," Mabel says. "She used to go to bed with the chickens. Now you say she's up all hours. Plus her a-smoking. I like to died."

"I want to make her this beautiful home," Leroy says, indicating the Lincoln Logs. "I don't think she even wants it. Maybe she was happier with me gone."

"She don't know what to make of you, coming home like this."

"Is that it?"

100    Mabel takes the roof off his Lincoln Log cabin. "You couldn't get *me* in a log cabin," she says. "I was raised in one. It's no picnic, let me tell you."

"They're different now," says Leroy.

"I tell you what," Mabel says, smiling oddly at Leroy.

"What?"

"Take her on down to Shiloh. Y'all need to get out together, stir a little. Her brain's all balled up over them books."

105    Leroy can see traces of Norma Jean's features in her mother's face. Mabel's worn face has the texture of crinkled cotton, but suddenly she looks pretty. It occurs to Leroy that Mabel has been hinting all along that she wants them to take her with them to Shiloh.

"Let's all go to Shiloh," he says. "You and me and her. Come Sunday."

Mabel throws up her hand in protest. "Oh, no, not me. Young folks want to be by theirselves."

When Norma Jean comes in with groceries, Leroy says excitedly. "Your mama here's been dying to go to Shiloh for thirty-five years. It's about time we went, don't you think?"

"I'm not going to butt in on anybody's second honeymoon," Mabel says.

110       "Who's going on a honeymoon, for Christ's sake?" Norma Jean says loudly.

"I never raised no daughter of mine to talk that-a-way," Mabel says.

"You ain't seen nothing yet," says Norma Jean. She starts putting away boxes and cans, slamming cabinet doors.

"There's a log cabin at Shiloh," Mabel says. "It was there during the battle. There's bullet holes in it."

"When are you going to *shut up* about Shiloh, Mama?" asks Norma Jean.

115       "I always thought Shiloh was the prettiest place, so full of history," Mabel goes on. "I just hoped y'all could see it once before I die, so you could tell me about it." Later, she whispers to Leroy. "You do what I said. A little change is what she needs."

"Your name means 'the king.'" Norma Jean says to Leroy that evening. He is trying to get her to go to Shiloh, and she is reading a book about another century.

"Well, I reckon I ought to be right proud."

"I guess so."

"Am I still king around here?"

120       Norma Jean flexes her biceps and feels them for hardness. "I'm not fooling around with anybody, if that's what you mean," she says.

"Would you tell me if you were?"

"I don't know."

"What does *your* name mean?"

"It was Marilyn Monroe's real name."

125       "No kidding!"

"Norma comes from the Normans. They were invaders," she says. She closes her book and looks hard at Leroy. "I'll go to Shiloh with you if you'll stop staring at me."

On Sunday, Norma Jean packs a picnic and they go to Shiloh. To Leroy's relief Mabel says she does not want to come with them. Norma Jean drives, and Leroy, sitting beside her, feels like some boring hitchhiker she has picked up. He tries some conversation, but she answers him in monosyllables. At Shiloh, she drives aimlessly through the park, past bluffs and trails and steep ravines. Shiloh is an immense place, and Leroy cannot see it as a battleground. It is not what he expected. He thought it would look like a golf course. Monuments are everywhere, showing through the thick clusters of trees. Norma Jean passes the log cabin Mabel mentioned. It is surrounded by tourists looking for bullet holes.

"That's not the kind of log house I've got in mind," says Leroy apologetically.

"I know *that.*"

130    "This is a pretty place. Your mama was right."

"It's O.K.," says Norma Jean. "Well, we've seen it. I hope she's satisfied." They burst out laughing together.

At the park museum, a movie on Shiloh is shown every half hour, but they decide that they don't want to see it. They buy a souvenir Confederate flag for Mabel, and then they find a picnic spot near the cemetery. Norma Jean has brought a picnic cooler, with pimento sandwiches, soft drinks, and Yodels. Leroy eats a sandwich and then smokes a joint, hiding it behind the picnic cooler. Norma Jean has quit smoking altogether. She is picking cake crumbs from the cellophane wrapper, like a fussy bird.

Leroy says, "So the boys in gray ended up in Corinth. The Union soldiers zapped 'em finally. April 7, 1862."

135    They both know that he doesn't know any history. He is just talking about some of the historical plaques they have read. He feels awkward, like a boy on a date with an older girl. They are still just making conversation.

"Corinth is where Mama eloped to," says Norma Jean.

They sit in silence and stare at the cemetery for the Union dead and, beyond, at a tall cluster of trees. Campers are parked nearby, bumper to bumper, and small children in bright clothing are cavorting and squealing. Norma Jean wads up the cake wrapper and squeezes it tightly in her hand. Without looking at Leroy, she says, "I want to leave you."

Leroy takes a bottle of Coke out of the cooler and flips off the cap. He holds the bottle poised near his mouth but cannot remember to take a drink. Finally he says, "No, you don't."

"Yes, I do."

140    "I won't let you."

"You can't stop me."

"Don't do me that way."

Leroy knows Norma Jean will have her own way. "Didn't I promise to be home from now on?" he says.

"In some ways, a woman prefers a man who wanders," says Norma Jean. "That sounds crazy, I know."

145    "You're not crazy."

Leroy remembers to drink from his Coke. Then he says, "Yes, you *are* crazy. You and me could start all over again. Right back at the beginning."

"We *have* started all over again," says Norma Jean. "And this is how it turned out."

"What did I do wrong?"

"Nothing."

150     "Is this one of those women's lib things?" Leroy asks.

"Don't be funny."

The cemetery, a green slope dotted with white markers, looks like a subdivision site. Leroy is trying to comprehend that his marriage is breaking up, but for some reason he is wondering about white slabs in a graveyard.

"Everything was fine till Mama caught me smoking," says Norma Jean, standing up. "That set something off."

"What are you talking about?"

155     "She won't leave me alone—*you* won't leave me alone." Norma Jean seems to be crying, but she is looking away from him. "I feel eighteen again. I can't face that all over again." She starts walking away. "No, it *wasn't* fine. I don't know what I'm saying. Forget it."

Leroy takes a lungful of smoke and closes his eyes as Norma Jean's words sink in. He tries to focus on the fact that thirty-five hundred soldiers died on the grounds around him. He can only think of that war as a board game with plastic soldiers. Leroy almost smiles, as he compares the Confederates' daring attack on the Union camps and Virgil Mathis's raid on the bowling alley. General Grant, drunk and furious, shoved the Southerners back to Corinth, where Mabel and Jet Beasley were married years later, when Mabel was still thin and good-looking. The next day, Mabel and Jet visited the battleground, and then Norma Jean was born, and then she married Leroy and they had a baby, which they lost, and now Leroy and Norma Jean are here at the same battleground. Leroy knows he is leaving out a lot. He is leaving out the insides of history. History was always just names and dates to him. It occurs to him that building a house of logs is similarly empty—too simple. And the real inner workings of a marriage, like most of history, have escaped him. Now he sees that building a log house is the dumbest idea he could have had. It was clumsy of him to think Norma Jean would want a log house. It was a crazy idea. He'll have to think of something else, quickly. He will wad the blueprints into tight balls and fling them into the lake. Then he'll get moving again. He opens his eyes. Norma Jean has moved away and is walking through the cemetery, following a serpentine brick path.

Leroy gets up to follow his wife, but his good leg is asleep and his bad leg still hurts him. Norma Jean is far away, walking rapidly toward the bluff by the river, and he tries to hobble toward her. Some children run past him, screaming noisily. Norma Jean has reached the bluff, and she is looking out over the Tennessee River. Now she turns toward Leroy and waves her arms. Is she beckoning to him? She seems to be doing an exercise for her chest muscles. The sky is unusually pale—the color of the dust ruffle Mabel made for their bed.

# JAMAICA KINCAID

*Jamaica Kincaid (b. 1949) was born in St. John's, Antigua, in the West Indies. She was educated at the Princess Margaret School in Antigua, and, briefly, at Westchester Community College and Franconia College. Since 1974 she has been a contributor to The New Yorker.*

*Kincaid is the author of several books, including* At the Bottom of the River *(1983, a collection of short pieces, including "Girl"),* Annie John *(1985, a second book recording a girl's growth, including "Columbus in Chains"),* A Small Place *(1988, a passionate essay about the destructive effects of colonialism), and* Lucy *(1990, a short novel about a young black woman who comes to the United States from the West Indies).*

## Girl                                              [1978]

Wash the white clothes on Monday and put them on the stone heap; wash the color clothes in Tuesday and put them on the clotheslines to dry; don't walk barehead in the hot sun; cook pumpkin fritters in very hot sweet oil; soak your little clothes right after you take them off; when buying cotton to make yourself a nice blouse, be sure that it doesn't have gum on it, because that way it won't hold up well after a wash; soak salt fish overnight before you cook it; is it true that you sing benna[1] in Sunday School? always eat your food in such a way that it won't turn someone else's stomach; on Sundays don't sing benna in Sunday School; you musn't speak to wharf-rat boys, not even to give directions; don't eat fruits on the street—flies will follow you; *but I don't sing benna on Sundays at all and never in Sunday school;* this is how to sew on a button; this is how to make a buttonhole for the button you have just sewed on; this is how to hem a dress when you see the hem coming down and so to prevent yourself from looking like the slut I know you are so bent on becoming; this i show you iron your father's khaki shirt so that it doesn't have a crease; this is how you iron your father's khaki pants so that they don't have a crease; this is how you grow okra—far from the house, because okra tree harbors red ants; when you are growing dasheen, make sure it gets plenty of water or else it makes your throat itch when you are eating it; this is how you sweep a corner; this is how you sweep a whole house; this is how you sweep a yard; this is how you smile to someone you don't like too much; this is how you set a table for dinner with an important guest; this is how

---

[1]**benna** Calypso music.

you smile to some you don't like at all; this is how you smile to someone you like completely; this is how you set a table for tea; this is how you set a table for dinner; this is how you set a table for lunch; this is how you set a table for breakfast; this is how to behave in the presence of men who don't know you very well, and this way they won't recognize immediately the slut I have warned you against becoming; be sure to wash every day, even if it is with your own spit; don't squat down to play marbles—you are not a boy, you know; don't pick people's flowers—you might catch something; don't throw stones at blackbirds, because it might not be a blackbird at all; this is how to make a bread pudding; this is how to make duokona[2]; this is how to make a pepper pot; this is how to make a good medicine for a cold; this is how to make a good medicine to throw away a child before it even becomes a child; this is how to catch a fish; this is how to throw back a fish you don't like, and that way something bad won't fall on you; this is how to bully a man; this is how a man bullies you; this is how to love a man, and if this doesn't work there are other ways, and if they don't work don't feel too bad about giving up; this is how to spit up in the air if you feel like it, and this is how to move quick so that it doesn't fall on you; this is how to make ends meet; always squeeze bread to make sure it's fresh; *but what if the baker won't let me feel the bread?*; you mean to say that after all you are really going to be the kind of woman who the baker won't let near the bread?

---

[2]**duokona** a spicy pudding made of plantains.

# TIM O'BRIEN

*Tim O'Brien, born in 1947 in Austin, Minnesota, was drafted into the army in 1968 and served as an infantryman in Vietnam. Drawing on this experience he wrote a memoir,* If I Die in a Combat Zone *(1973), in which he explains that he did not believe in the Vietnam War, considered dodging the draft, but, lacking the courage to do so, he served, largely out of fear and embarrassment. A later book, a novel called* Going after Cacciato, *won the National Book Award in 1979.*

*"The Things They Carried," first published in 1986, was republished in 1990 as one of a series of interlocking stories in a book entitled* The Things They Carried. *In one of the stories, entitled "How to Tell a True War Story," O'Brien writes,*

> *A true war story is never moral. It does not instruct, nor encourage virtue, nor suggest models of proper human behavior.... If a story seems moral, do not believe it. If at the end of a war story you feel uplifted, or if you feel that some small bit of rectitude has been salvaged from the larger waste, then you have been made the victim of*

*a very old and terrible lie. There is no rectitude whatsoever. There is no virtue. As a first rule of thumb, therefore, you can tell a true war story by its absolute and uncompromising allegiance to obscenity and evil.*

## The Things They Carried [1986]

First Lieutenant Jimmy Cross carried letters from a girl named Martha, a junior at Mount Sebastian College in New Jersey. They were not love letters, but Lieutenant Cross was hoping, so he kept them folded in plastic at the bottom of his rucksack. In the late afternoon, after a day's march, he would dig his foxhole, wash his hands under a canteen, unwrap the letters, hold them with the tips of his fingers, and spend the last hour of light pretending. He would imagine romantic camping trips into the White Mountains in New Hampshire. He would sometimes taste the envelope flaps, knowing her tongue had been there. More than anything, he wanted Martha to love him as he loved her, but the letters were mostly chatty, elusive on the matter of love. She was a virgin, he was almost sure. She was an English major at Mount Sebastian, and she wrote beautifully about her professors and roommates and midterm exams, about her respect for Chaucer and her great affection for Virginia Woolf. She often quoted lines of poetry; she never mentioned the war, except to say, Jimmy, take care of yourself. The letters weighed ten ounces. They were signed "Love, Martha," but Lieutenant Cross understood that Love was only a way of signing and did not mean what he sometimes pretended it meant. At dusk, he would carefully return the letters to his rucksack. Slowly, a bit distracted, he would get up and move among his men, checking the perimeter, then at full dark he would return to his hole and watch the night and wonder if Martha was a virgin.

The things they carried were largely determined by necessity. Among the necessities or near-necessities were P-38 can openers, pocket knives, heat tabs, wrist watches, dog tags, mosquito repellent, chewing gum, candy, cigarettes, salt tablets, packets of Kool-Aid, lighters, matches, sewing kits, Military Payment Certificates, C rations, and two or three canteens of water. Together, these items weighed between fifteen and twenty pounds, depending upon a man's habits or rate of metabolism. Henry Dobbins, who was a big man, carried extra rations; he was especially fond of canned peaches in heavy syrup over pound cake. Dave Jensen, who practiced field hygiene, carried a toothbrush, dental floss, and several hotel-size bars of soap he'd stolen on R&R[1] in Sydney, Australia. Ted Lavender, who was scared, carried tranquilizers until he was shot in the head outside the village of Than Khe in mid-April. By necessity, and because it was SOP,[2] they

---

[1]**R&R** rest and rehabilitation leave. [2]**SOP** standard operating procedure.

all carried steel helmets that weighed five pounds including the liner and camouflage cover. They carried the standard fatigue jackets and trousers. Very few carried underwear. On their feet they carried jungle boots—2.1 pounds—and Dave Jensen carried three pairs of socks and a can of Dr. Scholl's foot powder as a precaution against trench foot. Until he was shot, Ted Lavender carried six or seven ounces of premium dope, which for him was a necessity. Mitchell Sanders, the RTO,[3] carried condoms. Norman Bowker carried a diary. Rat Kiley carried comic books. Kiowa, a devout Baptist, carried an illustrated New Testament that had been presented to him by his father, who taught Sunday school in Oklahoma City, Oklahoma. As a hedge against bad times, however, Kiowa also carried his grandmother's distrust of the white man, his grandfather's old hunting hatchet. Necessity dictated. Because the land was mined and booby-trapped, it was SOP for each man to carry a steel-centered, nylon-covered flak jacket, which weighed 6.7 pounds, but which on hot days seemed much heavier. Because you could die so quickly, each man carried at least one large compress bandage, usually in the helmet band for easy access. Because the nights were cold, and because the monsoons were wet, each carried a green plastic poncho that could be used as a raincoat or groundsheet or makeshift tent. With its quilted liner, the poncho weighed almost two pounds, but it was worth every ounce. In April, for instance, when Ted Lavender was shot, they used his poncho to wrap him up, then to carry him across the paddy, then to lift him into the chopper that took him away.

They were called legs or grunts.

To carry something was to "hump" it, as when Lieutenant Jimmy Cross humped his love for Martha up the hills and through the swamps. In its intransitive form, "to hump" meant "to walk," or "to march," but it implied burdens far beyond the intransitive.

5      Almost everyone humped photographs. In his wallet, Lieutenant Cross carried two photographs of Martha. The first was a Kodachrome snapshot signed "Love," though he knew better. She stood against a brick wall. Her eyes were gray and neutral, her lips slightly open as she stared straight-on at the camera. At night, sometimes, Lieutenant Cross wondered who had taken the picture, because he knew she had boyfriends, because he loved her so much, and because he could see the shadow of the picture taker spreading out against the brick wall. The second photograph had been clipped from the 1968 Mount Sebastian yearbook. It was an action shot—women's volleyball—and Martha was bent horizontal to the floor, reaching, the palms of her hands in sharp focus, the tongue taut, the expression frank and competitive. There was no visible sweat. She wore white gym shorts. Her legs, he thought, were almost certainly the legs of a virgin, dry

---

[3]**RTO** radio and telephone operator.

and without hair, the left knee cocked and carrying her entire weight, which was just over one hundred pounds. Lieutenant Cross remembered touching that left knee. A dark theater, he remembered, and the movie was *Bonnie and Clyde,* and Martha wore a tweed skirt, and during the final scene, when he touched her knee, she turned and looked at him in a sad, sober way that made him pull his hand back, but he would always remember the feel of the tweed skirt and the knee beneath it and the sound of the gunfire that killed Bonnie and Clyde, how embarrassing it was, how slow and oppressive. He remembered kissing her goodnight at the dorm door. Right then, he thought, he should've done something brave. He should've carried her up the stairs to her room and tied her to the bed and touched that left knee all night long. He should've risked it. Whenever he looked at the photographs, he thought of new things he should've done.

What they carried was partly a function of rank, partly of field specialty.

As a first lieutenant and platoon leader, Jimmy Cross carried a compass, maps, code books, binoculars, and a .45-caliber pistol that weighed 2.9 pounds fully loaded. He carried a strobe light and the responsibility for the lives of his men.

As an RTO, Mitchell Sanders carried the PRC-25 radio, a killer, twenty-six pounds with its battery.

As a medic, Rat Kiley carried a canvas satchel filled with morphine and plasma and malaria tablets and surgical tape and comic books and all the things a medic must carry, including M&M's[4] for especially bad wounds, for a total weight of nearly twenty pounds.

10     As a big man, therefore a machine gunner, Henry Dobbins carried the M-60, which weighed twenty-three pounds unloaded, but which was almost always loaded. In addition, Dobbins carried between ten and fifteen pounds of ammunition draped in belts across his chest and shoulders.

As PFCs or Spec 4s, most of them were common grunts and carried the standard M-16 gas-operated assault rifle. The weapon weighed 7.5 pounds unloaded, 8.2 pounds with its full twenty-round magazine. Depending on numerous factors, such as topography and psychology, the riflemen carried anywhere from twelve to twenty magazines, usually in cloth bandoliers, adding on another 8.4 pounds at minimum, fourteen pounds at maximum. When it was available, they also carried M-16 maintenance gear—rods and steel brushes and swabs and tubes of LSA oil—all of which weighed about a pound. Among the grunts, some carried the M-79 grenade launcher, 5.9 pounds unloaded, a reasonably light weapon except for the ammunition, which was heavy. A single round weighed ten ounces. The typical load was twenty-five rounds. But Ted Lavender, who was scared, carried thirty-four rounds when he was shot and killed outside

---

[4]**M&M** joking term for medical supplies.

Than Khe, and he went down under an exceptional burden, more than twenty pounds of ammunition, plus the flak jacket and helmet and rations and water and toilet paper and tranquilizers and all the rest, plus the unweighed fear. He was dead weight. There was no twitching or flopping. Kiowa, who saw it happen, said it was like watching a rock fall, or a big sandbag or something—just boom, then down—not like the movies where the dead guy rolls around and does fancy spins and goes ass over teakettle—not like that, Kiowa said, the poor bastard just flat-fuck fell. Boom. Down. Nothing else. It was a bright morning in mid-April. Lieutenant Cross felt the pain. He blamed himself. They stripped off Lavender's canteens and ammo, all the heavy things, and Rat Kiley said the obvious, the guy's dead, and Mitchell Sanders used his radio to report one U.S. KIA[5] and to request a chopper. Then they wrapped Lavender in his poncho. They carried him out to a dry paddy, established security, and sat smoking the dead man's dope until the chopper came. Lieutenant Cross kept to himself. He pictured Martha's smooth young face, thinking he loved her more than anything, more than his men, and now Ted Lavender was dead because he loved her so much and could not stop thinking about her. When the dust-off arrived, they carried Lavender aboard. Afterward they burned Than Khe. They marched until dusk, then dug their holes, and that night Kiowa kept explaining how you had to be there, how fast it was, how the poor guy just dropped like so much concrete. Boom-down, he said. Like cement.

In addition to the three standard weapons—the M-60, M-16, and M-79—they carried whatever presented itself, or whatever seemed appropriate as a means of killing or staying alive. They carried catch-as-catch-can. At various times, in various situations, they carried MD14s and CARD15s and Swedish Ks and grease guns and captured AK-47s and Chi-Coms and RPGs and Simonov carbines and black-market Uzis and .38-caliber Smith & Wesson handguns and 66 mm LAWs and shotguns and silencers and blackjacks and bayonets and C-4 plastic explosives. Lee Strunk carried a slingshot; a weapon of last resort, he called it. Mitchell Sanders carried brass knuckles. Kiowa carried his grandfather's feathered hatchet. Every third or fourth man carried a Claymore antipersonnel mine—3.5 pounds with its firing device. They all carried fragmentation grenades—fourteen ounces each. They all carried at least one M-18 colored smoke grenade—twenty-four ounces. Some carried CS or tear-gas grenades. Some carried white-phosphorus grenades. They carried all they could bear, and then some, including a silent awe for the terrible power of the things they carried.

In the first week of April, before Lavender died, Lieutenant Jimmy Cross received a good-luck charm from Martha. It was a simple pebble, an

---

[5]**KIA** killed in action.

ounce at most. Smooth to the touch, it was a milky-white color with flecks of orange and violet, oval-shaped, like a miniature egg. In the accompanying letter, Martha wrote that she had found the pebble on the Jersey shoreline, precisely where the land touched water at high tide, where things came together but also separated. It was this separate-but-together quality, she wrote, that had inspired her to pick up the pebble and to carry it in her breast pocket for several days, where it seemed weightless, and then to send it through the mail, by air, as a token of her truest feelings for him. Lieutenant Cross found this romantic. But he wondered what her truest feelings were, exactly, and what she meant by separate-but-together. He wondered how the tides and waves had come into play on that afternoon along the Jersey shoreline when Martha saw the pebble and bent down to rescue it from geology. He imagined bare feet. Martha was a poet, with the poet's sensibilities, and her feet would be brown and bare, the toenails unpainted, the eyes chilly and somber like the ocean in March, and though it was painful, he wondered who had been with her that afternoon. He imagined a pair of shadows moving along the strip of sand where things came together but also separated. It was phantom jealousy, he knew, but he couldn't help himself. He loved her so much. On the march, through the hot days of early April, he carried the pebble in his mouth, turning it with his tongue, tasting sea salts and moisture. His mind wandered. He had difficulty keeping his attention on the war. On occasion he would yell at his men to spread out the column, to keep their eyes open, but then he would slip away into daydreams, just pretending, walking barefoot along the Jersey shore, with Martha, carrying nothing. He would feel himself rising. Sun and waves and gentle winds, all love and lightness.

What they carried varied by mission.

15    When a mission took them to the mountains, they carried mosquito netting, machetes, canvas tarps, and extra bugjuice.

If a mission seemed especially hazardous, or if it involved a place they knew to be bad, they carried everything they could. In certain heavily mined AOs,[6] where the land was dense with Toe Poppers and Bouncing Betties, they took turns humping a twenty-eight-pound mine detector. With its headphones and big sensing plate, the equipment was a stress on the lower back and shoulders, awkward to handle, often useless because of the shrapnel in the earth, but they carried it anyway, partly for safety, partly for the illusion of safety.

On ambush, or other night missions, they carried peculiar little odds and ends. Kiowa always took along his New Testament and a pair of moccasins for silence. Dave Jensen carried night-sight vitamins high in carotin.

---

[6]**AOs** areas of operation.

Lee Strunk carried his slingshot; ammo, he claimed, would never be a problem. Rat Kiley carried brandy and M&M's. Until he was shot, Ted Lavender carried the starlight scope, which weighed 6.3 pounds with its aluminum carrying case. Henry Dobbins carried his girlfriend's panty hose wrapped around his neck as a comforter. They all carried ghosts. When dark came, they would move out single file across the meadows and paddies to their ambush coordinates, where they would quietly set up the Claymores and lie down and spend the night waiting.

Other missions were more complicated and required special equipment. In mid-April, it was their mission to search out and destroy the elaborate tunnel complexes in the Than Khe area south of Chu Lai. To blow the tunnels, they carried one-pound blocks of pentrite high explosives, four blocks to a man, sixty-eight pounds in all. They carried wiring, detonators, and battery-powdered clackers. Dave Jensen carried earplugs. Most often, before blowing the tunnels, they were ordered by higher command to search them, which was considered bad news, but by and large they just shrugged and carried out orders. Because he was a big man, Henry Dobbins was excused from tunnel duty. The others would draw numbers. Before Lavender died there were seventeen men in the platoon, and whoever drew the number seventeen would strip off his gear and crawl in headfirst with a flashlight and Lieutenant Cross's .45-caliber pistol. The rest of them would fan out as security. They would sit down or kneel, not facing the hole, listening to the ground beneath them, imagining cobwebs and ghosts, whatever was down there—the tunnel walls squeezing in— how the flashlight seemed impossibly heavy in the hand and how it was tunnel vision in the very strictest sense, compression in all ways, even time, and how you had to wiggle in—ass and elbows—a swallowed-up feeling—and how you found yourself worrying about odd things—will your flashlight go dead? Do rats carry rabies? If you screamed, how far would the sound carry? Would your buddies hear it? Would they have the courage to drag you out? In some respects, though not many, the waiting was worse than the tunnel itself. Imagination was a killer.

On April 16, when Lee Strunk drew the number seventeen, he laughed and muttered something and went down quickly. The morning was hot and very still. Not good, Kiowa said. He looked at the tunnel opening, then out across a dry paddy toward the village of Than Khe. Nothing moved. No clouds or birds or people. As they waited, the men smoked and drank Kool-Aid, not talking much, feeling sympathy for Lee Strunk but also feeling the luck of the draw. You win some, you lose some, said Mitchell Sanders, and sometimes you settle for a rain check. It was a tired line and no one laughed.

20      Henry Dobbins ate a tropical chocolate bar. Ted Lavender popped a tranquilizer and went off to pee.

After five minutes, Lieutenant Jimmy Cross moved to the tunnel, leaned down, and examined the darkness. Trouble, he thought—a cave-in maybe. And then suddenly, without willing it, he was thinking about Martha. The stresses and fractures, the quick collapse, the two of them buried alive under all that weight. Dense, crushing love. Kneeling, watching the hole, he tried to concentrate on Lee Strunk and the war, all the dangers, but his love was too much for him, he felt paralyzed, he wanted to sleep inside her lungs and breathe her blood and be smothered. He wanted her to be a virgin and not a virgin, all at once. He wanted to know her intimate secrets—why poetry? Why so sad? Why that grayness in her eyes? Why so alone? Not lonely, just alone—riding her bike across campus or sitting off by herself in the cafeteria. Even dancing, she danced alone—and it was the aloneness that filled him with love. He remembered telling her that one evening. How she nodded and looked away. And how, later, when he kissed her, she received the kiss without returning it, her eyes wide open, not afraid, not a virgin's eyes, just flat and uninvolved.

Lieutenant Cross gazed at the tunnel. But he was not there. He was buried with Martha under the white sand at the Jersey shore. They were pressed together, and the pebble in his mouth was her tongue. He was smiling. Vaguely, he was aware of how quiet the day was, the sullen paddies, yet he could not bring himself to worry about matters of security. He was beyond that. He was just a kid at war, in love. He was twenty-two years old. He couldn't help it.

A few moments later Lee Strunk crawled out of the tunnel. He came up grinning, filthy but alive. Lieutenant Cross nodded and closed his eyes while the others clapped Strunk on the back and made jokes about rising from the dead.

Worms, Rat Kiley said. Right out of the grave. Fuckin' zombie.

25      The men laughed. They all felt great relief.

Spook City, said Mitchell Sanders.

Lee Strunk made a funny ghost sound, a kind of moaning, yet very happy, and right then, when Strunk made that high happy moaning sound, when he went *Ahhooooo,* right then Ted Lavender was shot in the head on his way back from peeing. He lay with his mouth open. The teeth were broken. There was a swollen black bruise under his left eye. The cheekbone was gone. Oh shit, Rat Kiley said, the guy's dead. The guy's dead, he kept saying, which seemed profound—the guy's dead. I mean really.

The things they carried were determined to some extent by superstition. Lieutenant Cross carried his good-luck pebble. Dave Jensen carried a rabbit's foot. Norman Bowker, otherwise a very gentle person, carried a thumb that had been presented to him as a gift by Mitchell Sanders. The thumb was dark brown, rubbery to the touch, and weighed four ounces at most. It had been cut from a VC corpse, a boy of fifteen or sixteen. They'd found him at the bottom of an irrigation ditch, badly burned, flies in his mouth and eyes. The boy wore black shorts and sandals. At the time of his death he had been carrying a pouch of rice, a rifle, and three magazines of ammunition.

You want my opinion, Mitchell Sanders said, there's a definite moral here.

30   He put his hand on the dead boy's wrist. He was quiet for a time, as if counting a pulse, then he patted the stomach, almost affectionately, and used Kiowa's hunting hatchet to remove the thumb.

Henry Dobbins asked what the moral was.

Moral?

You know. *Moral.*

Sanders wrapped the thumb in toilet paper and handed it across to Norman Bowker. There was no blood. Smiling, he kicked the boy's head, watched the flies scatter, and said, It's like with that old TV show—Paladin. Have gun, will travel.

35   Henry Dobbins thought about it.

Yeah, well, he finally said. I don't see no moral.

There it *is,* man.

Fuck off.

They carried USO stationery and pencils and pens. They carried Sterno, safety pins, trip flares, signal flares, spools of wire, razor blades, chewing tobacco, liberated joss sticks and statuettes of the smiling Buddha, candles, grease pencils, *The Stars and Stripes,* fingernail clippers, Psy Ops leaflets, bush hats, bolos, and much more. Twice a week, when the re-supply choppers came in, they carried hot chow in green Mermite cans and large canvas bags filled with iced beer and soda pop. They carried plastic water containers, each with a two gallon capacity. Mitchell Sanders carried a set of starched tiger fatigues for special occasions. Henry Dobbins carried Black Flag insecticide. Dave Jensen carried empty sandbags that could be filled at night for added protection. Lee Strunk carried tanning lotion. Some things they carried in common. Taking turns, they carried the big PRC-77 scrambler radio, which weighed thirty pounds with its battery. They shared the weight of memory. They took up what others could no longer bear. Often, they carried each other, the wounded or weak. They carried infections. They carried chess sets, basketballs, Vietnamese-English dictionaries, insignia of rank, Bronze Stars and Purple Hearts, plastic cards imprinted with the Code of Conduct. They carried diseases, among them malaria and dysentery. They carried lice and ring-worm and leeches and paddy algae and various rots and molds. They carried the land itself—Vietnam, the place, the soil—a powdery orange-red dust that covered their boots and fatigues and faces. They carried the sky. The whole atmosphere, they carried it, the humidity, the monsoons, the stink of fungus and decay, all of it, they carried gravity. They moved like mules. By daylight they took sniper fire, at night they were mortared, but it was not battle, it was just the endless march, village to village, without purpose, nothing won or lost. They marched for the sake of the march. They plodded along slowly, dumbly, leaning forward against the heat, unthinking, all blood and bone, simple grunts, soldiering with their legs, toiling up the hills and down into the paddies and across the rivers and up again and down, just humping, one step and then the next and then another, but no volition, no will, because it was automatic, it was anatomy, and the war was entirely a matter of posture and carriage, the hump was everything, a kind of inertia, a kind of emptiness, a dullness of desire and intellect and conscience and hope and human sensibility. Their principles were in their feet. Their calculations were biological. They had no sense of strategy or mission. They searched the villages without knowing what to look for, nor caring, kicking over jars of rice, frisking children and old men, blowing tunnels, sometimes setting fires and sometimes not, then forming up and moving on to the next village, then other villages, where it would always be the same. They carried their own lives. The pressures were enormous. In the heat of early afternoon, they would remove their helmets and flak jackets, walking bare, which was dangerous but which helped ease the strain. They would often discard things along the route of march. Purely for comfort, they would throw away rations, blow their Claymores and grenades, no matter, because by nightfall the resupply choppers would arrive with more of the same, then a day or two later still more, fresh watermelons and crates of ammunition and sunglasses and woolen sweaters—the resources were stunning—sparklers for the Fourth of July, colored eggs for Easter. It was the great American war chest—the fruits of sciences, the smoke stacks, the canneries, the arsenals at Hartford, the Minnesota forests, the machine shops, the vast fields of corn and wheat—they carried like freight trains; they carried it on their backs and shoulders—and for all the ambiguities of Vietnam, all the mysteries and unknowns, there was at least the single abiding certainty that they would never be at a loss for things to carry.

40        After the chopper took Lavender away, Lieutenant Jimmy Cross led his men into the village of Than Khe. They burned everything. They shot chickens and dogs, they trashed the village well, they called in artillery and watched the wreckage, then they marched for several hours through the hot afternoon, and then at dusk, while Kiowa explained how Lavender died, Lieutenant Cross found himself trembling.

He tried not to cry. With his entrenching tool, which weighed five pounds, he began digging a hole in the earth.

He felt shame. He hated himself. He had loved Martha more than his men, and as a consequence Lavender was now dead, and this was something he would have to carry like a stone in his stomach for the rest of the war.

All he could do was dig. He used his entrenching tool like an ax, slashing, feeling both love and hate, and then later, when it was full dark, he sat at the bottom of his foxhole and wept. It went on for a long while. In part, he was grieving for Ted Lavender, but mostly it was for Martha, and for himself, because she belonged to another world, which was not quite real, and because she was a junior at Mount Sebastian College in New Jersey, a poet and a virgin and uninvolved, and because he realized she did not love him and never would.

Like cement, Kiowa whispered in the dark. I swear to God—boom-down. Not a word.

45    I've heard this, said Norman Bowker.

A pisser, you know? Still zipping himself up. Zapped while zipping.

All right, fine. That's enough.

Yeah, but you had to see it, the guy just—

I *heard*, man. Cement. So why not shut the fuck *up?*

50    Kiowa shook his head sadly and glanced over at the hole where Lieutenant Jimmy Cross sat watching the night. The air was thick and wet. A warm, dense fog had settled over the paddies and there was the stillness that precedes rain.

After a time Kiowa sighed.

One thing for sure, he said. The lieutenant's in some deep hurt. I mean that crying jag—the way he was carrying on—it wasn't fake or anything, it was real heavy-duty hurt. The man cares.

Sure, Norman Bowker said.

Say what you want, the man does care.

55    We all got problems.

Not Lavender.

No, I guess not, Bowker said. Do me a favor, though.

Shut up?

That's a smart Indian. Shut up.

60    Shrugging, Kiowa pulled off his boots. He wanted to say more, just to lighten up his sleep, but instead he opened his New Testament and arranged it beneath his head as a pillow. The fog made things seem hollow and unattached. He tried not to think about Ted Lavender, but then he was thinking how fast it was, no drama, down and dead, and how it was hard to feel anything except surprise. It seemed unchristian. He wished he could find some great sadness, or even anger, but the emotion wasn't there and he couldn't make it happen. Mostly he felt pleased to be alive. He liked the smell of the New Testament under his cheek, the leather and ink and paper and glue, whatever the chemicals were. He liked hearing the sounds of night. Even his fatigue, it felt fine, the stiff muscles and the prickly awareness of his own body, a floating feeling. He enjoyed not being dead. Lying there, Kiowa admired Lieutenant Jimmy Cross's capacity for grief. He wanted to share the man's pain, he wanted to care as Jimmy Cross cared. And yet when he closed his eyes, all he could think was Boom-down, and all he could feel was the pleasure of having his boots off and the fog curling in around him and the damp soil and the Bible smells and the plush comfort of night.

After a moment Norman Bowker sat up in the dark.

What the hell, he said. You want to talk, *talk*. Tell it to me.

Forget it.

No, man, go on. One thing I hate, it's a silent Indian.

65    For the most part they carried themselves with poise, a kind of dignity. Now and then, however, there were times of panic, when they squealed or wanted to squeal but couldn't, when they twitched and made moaning sounds and covered their heads and said Dear Jesus and flopped around on the earth and fired their weapons blindly and cringed and sobbed and begged for the noise to stop and went wild and made stupid promises to themselves and to God and to their mothers and fathers, hoping not to die. In different ways, it happened to all of them. Afterward, when the firing ended, they would blink and peek up. They would touch their bodies, feeling shame, then quickly hiding it. They would force themselves to stand. As if in slow motion, frame by frame, the world would take on the old logic—absolute silence, then the wind, then sunlight, then voices. It was the burden of being alive. Awkwardly, the men would reassemble themselves, first in private, then in groups, becoming soldiers again. They would repair the leaks in their eyes. They would check for casualties, call in dustoffs, light cigarettes, try to smile, clear their throats and spit and begin cleaning their weapons. After a time someone would shake his head and say, No lie, I almost shit my pants, and someone else would laugh, which meant it was bad, yes, but the guy had obviously not shit his pants, it wasn't that bad, and in any case nobody would ever do such a thing and then go ahead and talk about it. They would squint into the dense, oppressive sunlight. For a few moments, perhaps, they would fall silent, lighting a joint and tracking its passage from man to man, inhaling, holding in the humiliation. Scary stuff, one of them might say. But then someone else would grin or flick his eyebrows and say, Roger-dodger, almost cut me a new asshole, *almost*.

There were numerous such poses. Some carried themselves with a sort of wistful resignation, others with pride or stiff soldierly discipline or good humor or macho zeal. They were afraid of dying but they were even more afraid to show it.

They found jokes to tell.

They used a hard vocabulary to contain the terrible softness. *Greased,* they'd say. *Offed, lit up, zapped while zipping.* It wasn't cruelty, just stage presence. They were actors and the war came at them in 3-D. When someone died, it wasn't quite dying, because in a curious way it seemed scripted, and because they had their lines mostly memorized, irony mixed with tragedy, and because they called it by other names, as if to encyst and destroy the reality of death itself. They kicked corpses. They cut off thumbs. They talked grunt lingo. They told stories about Ted Lavender's supply of tranquilizers, how the poor guy didn't feel a thing, how incredibly tranquil he was.

There's a moral here, said Mitchell Sanders.

70      They were waiting for Lavender's chopper, smoking the dead man's dope.

The moral's pretty obvious, Sanders said, and winked. Stay away from drugs. No joke, they'll ruin your day every time.

Cute, said Henry Dobbins.

Mind-blower, get it? Talk about wiggy—nothing left, just blood and brains.

They made themselves laugh.

75      There it is, they'd say, over and over, as if the repetition itself were an act of poise, a balance between crazy and almost crazy, knowing without going. There it is, which meant be cool, let it ride, because oh yeah, man, you can't change what can't be changed, there it is, there it absolutely and positively and fucking well *is*.

They were tough.

They carried all the emotional baggage of men who might die. Grief, terror, love, longing—these were intangibles, but the intangibles had their own mass and specific gravity, they had tangible weight. They carried shameful memories. They carried the common secret of cowardice barely restrained, the instinct to run or freeze or hide, and in many respects this was the heaviest burden of all, for it could never be put down, it required perfect balance and perfect posture. They carried their reputations. They carried the soldier's greatest fear, which was the fear of blushing. Men killed, and died, because they were embarrassed not to. It was what had brought them to the war in the first place, nothing positive, no dreams of glory or honor, just to avoid the blush of dishonor. They died so as not to die of embarrassment. They crawled into tunnels and walked point and advanced under fire. Each morning, despite the unknowns, they made their legs move. They endured. They kept humping. They did not submit to the obvious alternative, which was simply to close the eyes and fall. So easy, really. Go limp and tumble to the ground and let the muscles unwind and not speak and not budge until your buddies picked you up and lifted you into the chopper that would roar and dip its nose and carry you off to the world. A mere matter of falling, yet no one ever fell. It was not courage, exactly; the object was not valor. Rather, they were too frightened to be cowards.

By and large they carried these things inside, maintaining the masks of composure. They sneered at sick call. They spoke bitterly about guys who had found release by shooting off their own toes or fingers. Pussies, they'd say. Candyasses. It was fierce, mocking talk, with only a trace of envy or awe, but even so, the image played itself out behind their eyes.

They imagined the muzzle against flesh. They imagined the quick, sweet pain, then the evacuation to Japan, then a hospital with warm beds and cute geisha nurses.

80      They dreamed of freedom birds.

At night, on guard, staring into the dark, they were carried away by jumbo jets. They felt the rush of takeoff. *Gone!* they yelled. And then velocity, wings and engines, a smiling stewardess—but it was more than a plane, it was a real bird, a big sleek silver bird with feathers and talons and high screeching. They were flying. The weights fell off, there was nothing to bear. They laughed and held on tight, feeling the cold slap of wind and altitude, soaring, thinking *It's over, I'm gone!*—they were naked, they were light and free—it was all lightness, bright and fast and buoyant, light as light, a helium buzz in the brain, a giddy bubbling in the lungs as they were taken up over the clouds and the war, beyond duty, beyond gravity and mortification and global entanglements—*Sin loi!*[7] they yelled, *I'm sorry, motherfuckers, but I'm out of it, I'm goofed, I'm on a space cruise, I'm gone!*—and it was a restful, disencumbered sensation, just riding the light waves, sailing that big silver freedom bird over the mountains and oceans, over America, over the farms and great sleeping cities and cemeteries and highways and the Golden Arches of McDonald's. It was flight, a kind of fleeing, a kind of falling, falling higher and higher, spinning off the edge of the earth and beyond the sun and through the vast, silent vacuum where there were no burdens and where everything weighed exactly nothing. *Gone!* they screamed, *I'm sorry but I'm gone!* And so at night, not quite dreaming, they gave themselves over to lightness, they were carried, they were purely borne.

On the morning after Ted Lavender died, First Lieutenant Jimmy Cross crouched at the bottom of his foxhole and burned Martha's letters. Then he burned the two photographs. There was a steady rain falling, which made it difficult, but he used heat tabs and Sterno to build a small fire, screening it with his body, holding the photographs over the tight blue flame with the tips of his fingers.

He realized it was only a gesture. Stupid, he thought. Sentimental, too, but mostly just stupid.

Lavender was dead. You couldn't burn the blame.

85      Besides, the letters were in his head. And even now, without photographs, Lieutenant Cross could see Martha playing volleyball in her white gym shorts and yellow T-shirt. He could see her moving in the rain.

When the fire died out, Lieutenant Cross pulled his poncho over his shoulders and ate breakfast from a can.

There was no great mystery, he decided.

In those burned letters Martha had never mentioned the war, except to say, Jimmy, take care of yourself. She wasn't involved. She signed the letters "Love," but it wasn't love, and all the fine lines and technicalities did not matter.

---

[7]*Sin loi* Sorry.

The morning came up wet and blurry. Everything seemed part of everything else, the fog and Martha and the deepening rain.

90    It was a war, after all.

Half smiling, Lieutenant Jimmy Cross took out his maps. He shook his head hard, as if to clear it, then bent forward and began planning the day's march. In ten minutes, or maybe twenty, he would rouse the men and they would pack up and head west, where the maps showed the country to be green and inviting. They would do what they had always done. The rain might add some weight, but otherwise it would be one more day layered upon all the other days.

He was realistic about it. There was that new hardness in his stomach. No more fantasies, he told himself.

Henceforth, when he thought about Martha, it would be only to think that she belonged elsewhere. He would shut down the daydreams. This was not Mount Sebastian, it was another world, where there were no pretty poems or midterm exams, a place where men died because of carelessness and gross stupidity. Kiowa was right. Boom-down, and you were dead, never partly dead.

95    Briefly, in the rain, Lieutenant Cross saw Martha's gray eyes gazing back at him.

He understood.

It was very sad, he thought. The things men carried inside. The things men did or felt they had to do.

He almost nodded at her, but didn't.

Instead he went back to his maps. He was now determined to perform his duties firmly and without negligence. It wouldn't help Lavender, he knew that, but from this point on he would comport himself as a soldier. He would dispose of his good-luck pebble. Swallow it, maybe, or use Lee Strunk's slingshot, or just drop it along the trail. On the march he would impose strict field discipline. He would be careful to send out flank security, to prevent straggling or bunching up, to keep his troops moving at the proper pace and at the proper interval. He would insist on clean weapons. He would confiscate the remainder of Lavender's dope. Later in the day, perhaps, he would call the men together and speak to them plainly. He would accept the blame for what had happened to Ted Lavender. He would be a man about it. He would look them in the eyes, keeping his chin level, and he would issue the new SOPs in a calm, impersonal tone of voice, an officer's voice, leaving no room for argument or discussion. Commencing immediately, he'd tell them, they would no longer abandon equipment along the route of march. They would police up their acts. They would get their shit together, and keep it together, and maintain it neatly and in good working order.

100    He would not tolerate laxity. He would show strength, distancing himself.

Among the men there would be grumbling, of course, and maybe worse, because their days would seem longer and their loads heavier, but Lieutenant Cross reminded himself that his obligation was not to be loved but to lead. He would dispense with love; it was not now a factor. And if anyone quarreled or complained, he would simply tighten his lips and arrange his shoulders in the correct command posture. He might give a curt little nod. Or he might not. He might just shrug and say Carry on, then they would saddle up and form into a column and move out toward the villages west of Than Khe.

# AMY TAN

*Amy Tan was born in 1952 in Oakland, California, two and a half years after her parents had emigrated from China. She entered Linfield College in Oregon but then followed a boyfriend to California State University at San Jose, where she shifted her major from premedical studies to English. After earning a master's degree in linguistics from San Jose, Tan worked as a language consultant and then, under the name of May Brown, as a freelance business writer.*

*In 1985, having decided to try her hand at fiction, she joined the Squaw Valley Community of Writers, a fiction workshop. In 1987 she visited China with her mother; on her return to the United States she learned that her agent had sold her first book,* The Joy Luck Club, *a collection of sixteen interwoven stories (including "Two Kinds") about four Chinese mothers and their four American daughters. She is also author of* The Kitchen God's Wife *(1991),* The Hundred Secret Senses *(1995), and* The Bonesetter's Daughter *(2001).*

## Two Kinds                                    [1989]

My mother believed you could be anything you wanted to be in America. You could open a restaurant. You could work for the government and get good retirement. You could buy a house with almost no money down. You could become rich. You could become instantly famous.

"Of course you can be prodigy, too," my mother told me when I was nine. "You can be best anything. What does Auntie Lindo know? Her daughter, she is only best tricky."

America was where all my mother's hopes lay. She had come to San Francisco in 1949 after losing everything in China: her mother and father, her family home, her first husband, and two daughters, twin baby girls. But she never looked back with regret. Things could get better in so many ways.

We didn't immediately pick the right kind of prodigy. At first my mother thought I could be a Chinese Shirley Temple. We'd watch Shirley's old movies on TV as though they were training films. My mother would poke my arm and say, "*Ni kan*—You watch." And I would see Shirley tapping her feet, or singing a sailor song, or pursing her lips into a very round O while saying, "Oh my goodness."

5    "*Ni kan*," said my mother as Shirley's eyes flooded with tears. "You already know how. Don't need talent for crying!"

Soon after my mother got this idea about Shirley Temple, she took me to a beauty training school in the Mission district and put me in the hands of a student who could barely hold the scissors without shaking. Instead of getting big fat curls, I emerged with an uneven mass of crinkly black fuzz. My mother dragged me off to the bathroom and tried to wet down my hair.

"You look like Negro Chinese," she lamented, as if I had done this on purpose.

The instructor of the beauty training school had to lop off these soggy clumps to make my hair even again. "Peter Pan is very popular these days," the instructor assured my mother. I now had hair the length of a boy's, with straight-across bangs that hung at a slant two inches above my eyebrows. I liked the haircut and it made me actually look forward to my future fame.

In fact, in the beginning, I was just as excited as my mother, maybe even more so. I pictured this prodigy part of me as many different images, and I tried each one on for size. I was a dainty ballerina girl standing by the curtains, waiting to hear the right music that would send me floating on my tiptoes. I was like the Christ child lifted out of the straw manger, crying with holy indignity. I was Cinderella stepping from her pumpkin carriage with sparkly cartoon music filling the air.

10    In all of my imaginings, I was filled with a sense that I would soon become perfect. My mother and father would adore me. I would be beyond reproach. I would never feel the need to sulk, or to clamor for anything.

But sometimes the prodigy in me became impatient. "If you don't hurry up and get me out of here, I'm disappearing for good," it warned. "And then you'll always be nothing."

Every night after dinner, my mother and I would sit at the Formica-topped kitchen table. She would present new tests, taking her examples from stories of amazing children she had read in *Ripley's Believe It or Not*, or *Good Housekeeping, Reader's Digest*, and any of a dozen other magazines she kept in a pile in our bathroom. My mother got these magazines from people whose houses she cleaned. And since she cleaned many houses each week, we had a great assortment. She would look through them all, searching for stories about remarkable children.

The first night she brought out a story about a three-year-old boy who knew the capitals of all the states and even most of the European countries. A teacher was quoted as saying the little boy could also pronounce the names of the foreign cities correctly. "What's the capital of Finland?" my mother asked me, looking at the magazine story.

All I knew was the capital of California, because Sacramento was the name of the street we lived on in Chinatown. "Nairobi!" I guessed, saying the most foreign word I could think of. She checked to see if that might be one way to pronounce *Helsinki* before showing me the answer.

15    The tests got harder—multiplying numbers in my head, finding the queen of hearts in a deck of cards, trying to stand on my head without using my hands, predicting the daily temperatures in Los Angeles, New York, and London. One night I had to look at a page from the Bible for three minutes and then report everything I could remember. "Now Jehoshaphat had riches and honor in abundance and . . . that's all I remember, Ma," I said.

And after seeing, once again, my mother's disappointed face, something inside of me began to die. I hated the tests, the raised hopes and failed expectations. Before going to bed that night I looked in the mirror above the bathroom sink and when I saw only my face staring back—and understood that it would always be this ordinary face—I began to cry. Such a sad, ugly girl! I made high-pitched noises like a crazed animal, trying to scratch out the face in the mirror.

And then I saw what seemed to be the prodigy side of me—a face I had never seen before. I looked at my reflection, blinking so I could see more clearly. The girl staring back at me was angry, powerful. She and I were the same. I had new thoughts, willful thoughts, or rather, thoughts filled with lots of won'ts. I won't let her change me, I promised myself. I won't be what I'm not.

So now on nights when my mother presented her tests, I performed listlessly, my head propped on one arm. I pretended to be bored. And I was. I got so bored I started counting the bellows of the foghorns out on the bay while my mother drilled me in other areas. The sound was comforting and reminded me of the cow jumping over the moon. And the next day, I played a game with myself, seeing if my mother would give up on me before eight bellows. After a while I usually counted only one, maybe two bellows at most. At last she was beginning to give up hope.

Two or three months had gone by without any mention of my being a prodigy again. And then one day my mother was watching the *Ed Sullivan Show* on TV. The TV was old and the sound kept shorting out. Every time my mother got halfway up from the sofa to adjust the set, the sound would go back on and Sullivan would be talking. As soon as she sat down, Sullivan would go silent again. She got up, the TV broke into loud piano music. She sat down—silence. Up and down, back and forth, quiet and loud. It was like a stiff embraceless dance between her and the TV set. Finally she stood by the set with her hand on the sound dial.

20    She seemed entranced by the music, a frenzied little piano piece with this mesmerizing quality, which alternated between quick, playful passages and teasing, lilting ones.

"*Ni kan*," my mother said, calling me over with hurried hand gestures, "Look here."

I could see why my mother was fascinated by the music. It was being pounded out by a little Chinese girl, about nine years old, with a Peter Pan haircut. The girl had the sauciness of a Shirley Temple. She was proudly modest, like a proper Chinese child. And she also did a fancy sweep of a curtsy, so that the fluffy skirt of her white dress cascaded slowly to the floor like the petals of a large carnation.

In spite of these warning signs, I wasn't worried. Our family had no piano and we couldn't afford to buy one, let alone reams of sheet music and piano lessons. So I could be generous in my comments when my mother bad-mouthed the little girl on TV.

"Play note right, but doesn't sound good!" complained my mother. "No singing sound."

25    "What are you picking on her for?" I said carelessly. "She's pretty good. Maybe she's not the best, but she's trying hard." I knew almost immediately I would be sorry I said that.

"Just like you," she said. "Not the best. Because you not trying." She gave a little huff as she let go of the sound dial and sat down on the sofa.

The little Chinese girl sat down also to play an encore of "Anitra's Dance" by Grieg.[1] I remember the song, because later on I had to learn how to play it.

Three days after watching the *Ed Sullivan Show*, my mother told me what my schedule would be for piano lessons and piano practice. She had talked to Mr. Chong, who lived on the first floor of our apartment building. Mr. Chong was a retired piano teacher, and my mother had traded housecleaning services for weekly lessons and a piano for me to practice on every day, two hours a day, from four until six.

When my mother told me this, I felt as though I had been sent to hell. I whined, and then kicked my foot a little when I couldn't stand it any more.

30    "Why don't you like me the way I am? I'm not a genius! I can't play the piano. And even if I could, I wouldn't go on TV if you paid me a million dollars!"

My mother slapped me. "Who ask you be genius?" she shouted. "Only ask you be your best. For you sake. You think I want you be genius? Hnnh! What for! Who ask you!"

"So ungrateful," I heard her mutter in Chinese. "If she had as much talent as she has temper, she would be famous now."

Mr. Chong, whom I secretly nicknamed Old Chong, was very strange, always tapping his fingers to the silent music of an invisible orchestra. He looked ancient in my eyes. He had lost most of the hair on top of his head and he wore thick glasses and had eyes that always looked tired. But he

---

[1]**"Anitra's Dance"** section from the incidental music that Edvard Grieg (1843–1907) wrote for *Peer Gynt*, a play by Henrik Ibsen.

must have been younger than I thought, since he lived with his mother and was not yet married.

I met Old Lady Chong once and that was enough. She had this peculiar smell like a baby that had done something in its pants and her fingers felt like a dead person's, like an old peach I once found in the back of the refrigerator; the skin just slid off the meat when I picked it up.

35      I soon found out why Old Chong had retired from teaching piano. He was deaf. "Like Beethoven!" he shouted to me. "We're both listening only in our head!" And he would start to conduct his frantic silent sonatas.

Our lessons went like this. He would open the book and point to different things, explaining their purpose: "Key! Treble! Bass! No sharps or flats! So this is C major! Listen now and play after me!"

And then he would play the C scale a few times, a simple chord, and then, as if inspired by an old, unreachable itch, he gradually added more notes and running trills and a pounding bass until the music was really something quite grand.

I would play after him, the simple scale, the simple chord, and then I just played some nonsense that sounded like a cat running up and down on top of garbage cans. Old Chong smiled and applauded and then said, "Very good! But now you must learn to keep time!"

So that's how I discovered that Old Chong's eyes were too slow to keep up with the wrong notes I was playing. He went through the motions in half-time. To help me keep rhythm, he stood behind me, pushing down on my right shoulder for every beat. He balanced pennies on top of my wrists so I would keep them still as I slowly played scales and arpeggios. He had me curve my hand around an apple and keep that shape when playing chords. He marched stiffly to show me how to make each finger dance up and down, staccato, like an obedient little soldier.

40      He taught me all these things, and that was how I also learned I could be lazy and get away with mistakes, lots of mistakes. If I hit the wrong notes because I hadn't practiced enough, I never corrected myself. I just kept playing in rhythm. And Old Chong kept conducting his own private reverie.

So maybe I never really gave myself a fair chance. I did pick up the basics pretty quickly, and I might have become a good pianist at that young age. But I was so determined not to try, not to be anybody different that I learned to play only the most ear-splitting preludes, the most discordant hymns.

Over the next year, I practiced like this, dutifully in my own way. And then one day I heard my mother and her friend Lindo Jong both talking in a loud bragging tone of voice so others could hear. It was after church, and I was leaning against the brick wall, wearing a dress with stiff white petticoats. Auntie Lindo's daughter, Waverly, who was about my age, was standing farther down the wall about five feet away. We had grown up together and shared all the closeness of two sisters squabbling over crayons and dolls. In other words, for the most part, we hated each other. I thought she was snotty. Waverly Jong had gained a certain amount of fame as "Chinatown's Littlest Chinese Chess Champion."

"She bring home too many trophy," Auntie Lindo lamented that Sunday. "All day she play chess. All day I have no time do nothing but dust off her winnings." She threw a scolding look at Waverly, who pretended not to see her.

"You lucky you don't have this problem," said Auntie Lindo with a sigh to my mother.

45    And my mother squared her shoulders and bragged: "Our problem worser than yours. If we ask Jing-mei wash dish, she hear nothing but music. It's like you can't stop this natural talent."

And right then, I was determined to put a stop to her foolish pride.

A few weeks later Old Chong and my mother conspired to have me play in a talent show that was held in the church hall. By then my parents had saved up enough to buy me a secondhand piano, a black Wurlitzer spinet with a scarred bench. It was the showpiece of our living room.

For the talent show, I was to play a piece called "Pleading Child," from Schumann's *Scenes from Childhood*.[2] It was a simple, moody piece that sounded more difficult than it was. I was supposed to memorize the whole thing. But I dawdled over it, playing a few bars and then cheating, looking up to see what notes followed. I never really listened to what I was playing. I daydreamed about being somewhere else, about being someone else.

The part I liked to practice best was the fancy curtsy: right foot out, touch the rose on the carpet with a pointed foot, sweep to the side, bend left leg, look up, and smile.

50    My parents invited all the couples from the Joy Luck Club to witness my debut. Auntie Lindo and Uncle Tin were there. Waverly and her two older brothers had also come. The first two rows were filled with children either younger or older than I was. The littlest ones got to go first. They recited simple nursery rhymes, squawked out tunes on miniature violins, twisted hula hoops, in pink ballet tutus, and when they bowed or curtsied, the audience would sigh in unison, "*Awww*," and then clap enthusiastically.

When my turn came, I was very confident. I remember my childish excitement. It was as if I knew, without a doubt, that the prodigy side of me really did exist. I had no fear whatsoever, no nervousness. I remember thinking, This is it! This is it! I looked out over the audience, at my mother's blank face, my father's yawn, Auntie Lindo's stiff-lipped smile, Waverly's sulky expression. I had on a white dress layered with sheets of lace, and a pink bow in my Peter Pan haircut. As I sat down I envisioned people

---

[2]*Scenes from Childhood* a piano work by Robert Schumann (1810–56) with twelve titled sections and an epilogue.

jumping to their feet and Ed Sullivan rushing up to introduce me to everyone on TV.

And I started to play. It was so beautiful. I was so caught up in how
lovely I looked that at first I didn't worry how I would sound. So I was surprised when I hit the first wrong note. And then I hit another. And another.
A chill started at the top of my head and began to trickle down. Yet I
couldn't stop playing, as though my hands were bewitched. I kept thinking my fingers would adjust themselves back, like a train switching to the
right track. I played this strange jumble through to the end, the sour notes
staying with me all the way.

When I stood up, I discovered my legs were shaking. Maybe I had just
been nervous, and the audience, like Old Chong, had seen me go through
the right motions and had not heard anything wrong at all. I swept my
right foot out, went down on my knee, looked up and smiled. The room
was quiet, except for Old Chong, who was beaming and shouting, "Bravo!
Bravo! Well done!" But then I saw my mother's face, her stricken face. The
audience clapped weakly, and as I walked back to my chair, with my
whole face quivering as I tried not to cry, I heard a little boy whisper
loudly to his mother, "That was awful," and the mother whispered back,
"Well, she certainly tried."

And now I realized how many people were in the audience—the
whole world, it seemed. I was aware of eyes burning into my back. I felt
the shame of my mother and father as they sat stiffly throughout the rest
of the show.

55      We could have escaped during intermission. Pride and some strange
sense of honor must have anchored my parents to their chairs. And so we
watched it all: the eighteen-year-old boy with a fake moustache who did a
magic show and juggled flaming hoops while riding a unicycle. The
breasted girl with white makeup who sang from *Madame Butterfly* and
got honorable mention. And the eleven-year-old boy who won first prize
playing a tricky violin song that sounded like a busy bee.

After the show, the Hsus, the Jongs, and the St. Clairs from the Joy
Luck Club came up to my mother and father.

"Lots of talented kids," Auntie Lindo said vaguely, smiling broadly.

"That was somethin' else," said my father, and I wondered if he was referring to me in a humorous way, or whether he even remembered what I
had done.

Waverly looked at me and shrugged her shoulders. "You aren't a genius like me," she said matter-of-factly. And if I hadn't felt so bad, I would
have pulled her braids and punched her stomach.

60      But my mother's expression was what devastated me: a quiet, blank
look that said she had lost everything. I felt the same way, and everybody
seemed now to be coming up, like gawkers at the scene of an accident, to
see what parts were actually missing.

When we got on the bus to go home, my father was humming the busy-bee tune and my mother was silent. I kept thinking she wanted to wait until we got home before shouting at me. But when my father unlocked the door to our apartment, my mother walked in and then went straight to the back, into the bedroom. No accusations. No blame. And in a way, I felt disappointed. I had been waiting for her to start shouting, so I could shout back and cry and blame her for all my misery.

I assumed my talent-show fiasco meant I would never have to play the piano again. But two days later, after school, my mother came out of the kitchen and saw me watching TV.

"Four clock," she reminded me as if it were any other day. I was stunned, as though she were asking me to go through the talent-show torture again. I wedged myself more tightly in front of the TV.

"Turn off TV," she called from the kitchen five minutes later.

65    I didn't budge. And then I decided. I didn't have to do what my mother said anymore. I wasn't her slave. This wasn't China. I had listened to her before and look what happened. She was the stupid one.

She came out from the kitchen and stood in the arched entryway of the living room. "Four clock," she said once again, louder.

"I'm not going to play anymore," I said nonchalantly. "Why should I? I'm not a genius."

She walked over and stood in front of the TV. I saw her chest was heaving up and down in an angry way.

"No!" I said, and I now felt stronger, as if my true self had finally emerged. So this was what had been inside me all along.

70    "No! I won't!" I screamed.

She snapped off the TV, yanked me by the arm and pulled me off the floor. She was frighteningly strong, half pulling, half carrying me toward the piano as I kicked the throw rugs under my feet. She lifted me up and onto the hard bench. I was sobbing by now, looking at her bitterly. Her chest was heaving even more and her mouth was open, smiling crazily as if she were pleased I was crying.

"You want me to be someone that I'm not!" I sobbed. "I'll never be the kind of daughter you want me to be!"

"Only two kinds of daughters," she shouted in Chinese. "Those who are obedient and those who follow their own mind! Only one kind of daughter can live in this house. Obedient daughter!"

"Then I wish I wasn't your daughter. I wish you weren't my mother," I shouted. As I said these things I got scared. It felt like worms and toads and slimy things crawling out of my chest, but it also felt good, that this awful side of me had surfaced, at last.

75    "Too late change this," said my mother shrilly.

And I could sense her anger rising to its breaking point. I wanted to see it spill over. And that's when I remembered the babies she had lost in

China, the ones we never talked about. "Then I wish I'd never been born!" I shouted. "I wish I were dead! Like them."

It was as if I had said the magic words. Alakazam!—and her face went blank, her mouth closed, her arms went slack, and she backed out of the room, stunned, as if she were blowing away like a small brown leaf, thin, brittle, lifeless.

It was not the only disappointment my mother felt in me. In the years that followed, I failed her so many times, each time asserting my own will, my right to fall short of expectations. I didn't get straight As. I didn't become class president. I didn't get into Stanford. I dropped out of college.

Unlike my mother, I did not believe I could be anything I wanted to be. I could only be me.

80    And for all those years, we never talked about the disaster at the recital or my terrible declarations afterward at the piano bench. Neither of us talked about it again, as if it were a betrayal that was now unspeakable. So I never found a way to ask her why she had hoped for something so large that failure was inevitable.

And even worse, I never asked her what frightened me the most: Why had she given up hope? For after our struggle at the piano, she never mentioned my playing again. The lessons stopped. The lid to the piano was closed, shutting out the dust, my misery, and her dreams.

So she surprised me. A few years ago, she offered to give me the piano, for my thirtieth birthday. I had not played in all those years. I saw the offer as a sign of forgiveness, a tremendous burden removed.

"Are you sure?" I asked shyly. "I mean, won't you and Dad miss it?"

"No, this your piano," she said firmly. "Always your piano. You only one can play."

85    "Well, I probably can't play anymore," I said. "It's been years."

"You pick up fast," said my mother, as if she knew this was certain. "You have natural talent. You could been genius if you want to."

"No I couldn't."

"You just not trying," said my mother. And she was neither angry nor sad. She said it as if to announce a fact that could never be disproved. "Take it," she said.

But I didn't at first. It was enough that she had offered it to me. And after that, every time I saw it in my parents' living room, standing in front of the bay windows, it made me feel proud, as if it were a shiny trophy I had won back.

90    Last week I sent a tuner over to my parents' apartment and had the piano reconditioned, for purely sentimental reasons. My mother had died a few months before and I had been getting things in order for my father, a little bit at a time. I put the jewelry in special silk pouches. The sweaters she had knitted in yellow, pink, bright orange—all the colors I hated—I

put those in mothproof boxes. I found some old Chinese silk dresses, the kind with little slits up the sides. I rubbed the old silk against my skin, then wrapped them in tissue and decided to take them home with me.

After I had the piano tuned, I opened the lid and touched the keys. It sounded even richer than I remembered. Really, it was a very good piano. Inside the bench were the same exercise notes with handwritten scales, the same secondhand music books with their covers held together with yellow tape.

I opened up the Schumann book to the dark little piece I had played at the recital. It was on the left-hand page, "Pleading Child." It looked more difficult than I remembered. I played a few bars, surprised at how easily the notes came back to me.

And for the first time, or so it seemed, I noticed the piece on the right-hand side. It was called "Perfectly Contented." I tried to play this one as well. It had a lighter melody but the same flowing rhythm and turned out to be quite easy. "Pleading Child" was shorter but slower; "Perfectly Contented" was longer, but faster. And after I played them both a few times, I realized they were two halves of the same song.

# ELIZABETH TALLENT

*Elizabeth Tallent was born in Washington, D.C., in 1954 and educated at Illinois State University at Normal. The author of novels and short stories, she has won many awards, including a fellowship from the National Endowment for the Arts and the O. Henry Award.*

## No One's a Mystery                                          [1985]

For my eighteenth birthday Jack gave me a five-year diary with a latch and a little key, light as a dime. I was sitting beside him scratching at the lock, which didn't seem to want to work, when he thought he saw his wife's Cadillac in the distance, coming toward us. He pushed me down onto the dirty floor of the pickup and kept one hand on my head while I inhaled the musk of his cigarettes in the dashboard ashtray and sang along with Rosanne Cash on the tape deck. We'd been drinking tequila and the bottle was between his legs, resting up against his crotch, where the seam of his Levi's was bleached linen-white, though the Levi's were nearly new. I don't know why his Levi's always bleached like that, along the seams and at the knees. In a curve of cloth his zipper glinted, gold.

"It's her," he said. "She keeps the lights on in the daytime. I can't think of a single habit in a woman that irritates me more than that." When he saw that I was going to stay still he took his hand from my head and ran it through his own dark hair.

"Why does she?" I said.

"She thinks it's safer. Why does she need to be safer? She's driving exactly fifty-five miles an hour. She believes in those signs: 'Speed Monitored by Aircraft.' It doesn't matter that you can look up and see that the sky is empty."

5       "She'll see your lips move, Jack. She'll know you're talking to someone."

"She'll think I'm singing along with the radio."

He didn't lift his head, just raised the fingers in salute while the pressure of his palm steadied the wheel, and I heard the Cadillac honk twice, musically; he was driving easily eighty miles an hour. I studied his boots. The elk heads stitched into the leather were bearded with frayed thread, the toes were scuffed, and there was a compact wedge of muddy manure between the heel and the sole—the same boots he'd been wearing for the two years I'd known him. On the tape deck Rosanne Cash sang, "Nobody's into me, no one's a mystery."

"Do you think she's getting famous because of who her daddy is or for herself?" Jack said.

"There are about a hundred pop tops on the floor, did you know that? Some little kid could cut a bare foot on one of these, Jack."

10      "No little kids get into this truck except for you."

"How come you let it get so dirty?"

"'How come,'" he mocked. "You even sound like a kid. You can get back into the seat now, if you want. She's not going to look over her shoulder and see you."

"How do you know?"

"I just know," he said. "Like I know I'm going to get meat loaf for supper. It's in the air. Like I know what you'll be writing in that diary."

15      "What will I be writing?" I knelt on my side of the seat and craned around to look at the butterfly of dust printed on my jeans. Outside the window Wyoming was dazzling in the heat. The wheat was fawn and yellow and parted smoothly by the thin dirt road. I could smell the water in the irrigation ditches hidden in the wheat.

"Tonight you'll write, 'I love Jack. This is my birthday present from him. I can't imagine anybody loving anybody more than I love Jack.'"

"I can't."

"In a year you'll write, 'I wonder what I ever really saw in Jack. I wonder why I spent so many days just riding around in his pickup. It's true he taught me something about sex. It's true there wasn't ever much else to do in Cheyenne.'"

"I won't write that."

20      "In two years you'll write, 'I wonder what that old guy's name was, the one with the curly hair and the filthy dirty pickup truck and time on his hands.'"

"I won't write that."

"No?"

"Tonight I'll write,'I love Jack.This is my birthday present from him. I can't imagine anybody loving anybody more than I love Jack.'"

"No, you can't," he said."You can't imagine it."

25      "In a year I'll write,'Jack should be home any minute now.The table's set—my grandmother's linen and her old silver and the yellow candles left over from the wedding—but I don't know if I can wait until after the trout à la Navarra to make love to him.'"

"It must have been a fast divorce."

"In two years I'll write,'Jack should be home by now. Little Jack is hungry for his supper. He said his first word today besides "Mama" and "Papa." He said "kaka."'"

Jack laughed. "He was probably trying to finger-paint with kaka on the bathroom wall when you heard him say it."

"In three years I'll write,'My nipples are a little sore from nursing Eliza Rosamund.'"

30      "Rosamund. Every little girl should have a middle name she hates."

"'Her breath smells like vanilla and her eyes are just Jack's color of blue.'"

"That's nice," Jack said.

"So, which one do you like?"

"I like yours," he said."But I believe mine."

35      "It doesn't matter. I believe mine."

"Not in your heart of hearts, you don't."

"You're wrong."

"I'm not wrong," he said."And her breath would smell like your milk, and it's kind of a bittersweet smell, if you want to know the truth."

# LOUISE ERDRICH

*Louise Erdrich, born in 1954 in Little Falls, Minnesota, grew up in North Dakota, a member of the Turtle Mountain Band of Chippewa. Her father had been born in Germany; her mother was French Ojibwe; both parents taught at the Bureau of Indian Affairs School. After graduating from Dartmouth College (with a major in anthropology) in 1976, Erdrich returned briefly to North Dakota to teach in the Poetry in the Schools Program, and went to Johns Hopkins University, where she earned a master's degree in creative writing. She now lives in Minneapolis, Minnesota.*

*Erdrich has published two books of poems and several novels, one of which,* Love Medicine *(1986), won the National Book Critics Circle Award."The Red Convertible" is a self-contained story, but it is also part of* Love Medicine, *which consists of narratives about life on a North Dakota reservation.*

# The Red Convertible [1984]

Lyman Lamartine

I was the first one to drive a convertible on my reservation. And of course it was red, a red Olds. I owned that car along with my brother Henry Junior. We owned it together until his boots filled with water on a windy night and he bought out my share. Now Henry owns the whole car, and his youngest brother Lyman (that's myself), Lyman walks everywhere he goes.

How did I earn enough money to buy my share in the first place? My own talent was I could always make money. I had a touch for it, unusual in a Chippewa. From the first I was different that way, and everyone recognized it. I was the only kid they let in the American Legion Hall to shine shoes, for example, and one Christmas I sold spiritual bouquets for the mission door to door. The nuns let me keep a percentage. Once I started, it seemed the more money I made the easier the money came. Everyone encouraged it. When I was fifteen I got a job washing dishes at the Joliet Café, and that was where my first big break happened.

It wasn't long before I was promoted to bussing tables, and then the short-order cook quit and I was hired to take her place. No sooner than you know it I was managing the Joliet. The rest is history. I went on managing. I soon became part owner, and of course there was no stopping me then. It wasn't long before the whole thing was mine.

After I'd owned the Joliet for one year, it blew over in the worst tornado ever seen around here. The whole operation was smashed to bits. A total loss. The fryalator was up in a tree, the grill torn in half like it was paper. I was only sixteen. I had it all in my mother's name, and I lost it quick, but before I lost it I had every one of my relatives, and their relatives, to dinner, and I also bought that red Olds I mentioned, along with Henry.

5      The first time we saw it! I'll tell you when we first saw it. We had gotten a ride up to Winnipeg, and both of us had money. Don't ask me why, because we never mentioned a car or anything, we just had all our money. Mine was cash, a big bankroll from the Joliet's insurance. Henry had two checks—a week's extra pay for being laid off, and his regular check from the Jewel Bearing Plant.

We were walking down Portage anyway, seeing the sights, when we saw it. There it was, parked, large as life. Really as *if* it was alive. I thought of the word *repose*, because the car wasn't simply stopped, parked, or whatever. That car reposed, calm and gleaming, a FOR SALE sign in its left front window. Then, before we had thought it over at all, the car belonged to us and our pockets were empty. We had just enough money for gas back home.

We went places in that car, me and Henry. We took off driving all one whole summer. We started off toward the Little Knife River and Mandaree in Fort Berthold and then we found ourselves down in Wakpala somehow, and then suddenly we were over in Montana on the Rocky Boys, and yet the summer was not even half over. Some people hang on to details when they travel, but we didn't let them bother us and just lived our everyday lives here to there.

I do remember this one place with willows. I remember I laid under those trees and it was comfortable. So comfortable. The branches bent down all around me like a tent or a stable. And quiet, it was quiet, even though there was a powwow close enough so I could see it going on. The air was not too still, not too windy either. When the dust rises up and hangs in the air around the dancers like that, I feel good. Henry was asleep with his arms thrown wide. Later on, he woke up and we started driving again. We were somewhere in Montana, or maybe on the Blood Reserve— it could have been anywhere. Anyway it was where we met the girl.

All her hair was in buns around her ears, that's the first thing I noticed about her. She was posed alongside the road with her arm out, so we stopped. That girl was short, so short her lumber shirt looked comical on her, like a nightgown. She had jeans on and fancy moccasins and she carried a little suitcase.

10       "Hop on in," says Henry. So she climbs in between us.
         "We'll take you home," I says. "Where do you live?"
         "Chicken," she says.
         "Where the hell's that?" I ask her.
         "Alaska."
15       "Okay," says Henry, and we drive.

We got up there and never wanted to leave. The sun doesn't truly set there in summer, and the night is more a soft dusk. You might doze off, sometimes, but before you know it you're up again, like an animal in nature. You never feel like you have to sleep hard or put away the world. And things would grow up there. One day just dirt or moss, the next day flowers and long grass. The girl's name was Susy. Her family really took to us. They fed us and put us up. We had our own tent to live in by their house, and the kids would be in and out of there all day and night. They couldn't get over me and Henry being brothers, we looked so different. We told them we knew we had the same mother, anyway.

One night Susy came in to visit us. We sat around in the tent talking of this thing and that. The season was changing. It was getting darker by that time, and the cold was even getting just a little mean. I told her it was time for us to go. She stood up on a chair.

"You never seen my hair," Susy said.

That was true. She was standing on a chair, but still, when she unclipped her buns the hair reached all the way to the ground. Our eyes opened. You couldn't tell how much hair she had when it was rolled up so neatly. Then my brother Henry did something funny. He went up to the

chair and said, "Jump on my shoulders." So she did that, and her hair
reached down past his waist, and he started twirling, this way and that, so
her hair was flung out from side to side.

20    "I always wondered what it was like to have long pretty hair," Henry
says. Well we laughed. It was a funny sight, the way he did it. The next
morning we got up and took leave of those people.

On to greener pastures, as they say. It was down through Spokane and
across Idaho then Montana and very soon we were racing the weather
right along under the Canadian border through Columbus, Des Lacs, and
then we were in Bottineau County and soon home. We'd made most of the
trip, that summer, without putting up the car hood at all. We got home just
in time, it turned out, for the army to remember Henry had signed up to
join it.

I don't wonder that the army was so glad to get my brother that they
turned him into a Marine. He was built like a brick outhouse anyway. We
liked to tease him that they really wanted him for his Indian nose. He had
a nose big and sharp as a hatchet, like the nose on Red Tomahawk, the Indian who killed Sitting Bull, whose profile is on signs all along the North
Dakota highways. Henry went off to training camp, came home once during Christmas, then the next thing you know we got an overseas letter
from him. It was 1970, and he said he was stationed up in the northern
hill country. Whereabouts I did not know. He wasn't such a hot letter
writer, and only got off two before the enemy caught him. I could never
keep it straight, which direction those good Vietnam soldiers were from.

I wrote him back several times, even though I didn't know if those
letters would get through. I kept him informed all about the car. Most of
the time I had it up on blocks in the yard or half taken apart, because that
long trip did a hard job on it under the hood.

I always had good luck with numbers, and never worried about the
draft myself. I never even had to think about what my number was. But
Henry was never lucky in the same way as me. It was at least three years
before Henry came home. By then I guess the whole war was solved in the
government's mind, but for him it would keep on going. In those years I'd
put his car into almost perfect shape. I always thought of it as his car while
he was gone, even though when he left he said, "Now it's yours," and threw
me his key.

25    "Thanks for the extra key," I'd say. "I'll put it up in your drawer just in
case I need it." He laughed.

When he came home, though, Henry was very different, and I'll say
this: the change was no good. You could hardly expect him to change for
the better, I know. But he was quiet, so quiet, and never comfortable sitting still anywhere but always up and moving around. I thought back to
times we'd sat still for whole afternoons, never moving a muscle, just
shifting our weight along the ground, talking to whoever sat with us,
watching things. He'd always had a joke, then, too, and now you couldn't
get him to laugh, or when he did it was more the sound of a man chok-

ing, a sound that stopped up the throats of other people around him.
They got to leaving him alone most of the time, and I didn't blame them.
It was a fact: Henry was jumpy and mean.

I'd bought a color TV set for my mom and the rest of us while Henry
was away. Money still came very easy. I was sorry I'd ever bought it
though, because of Henry. I was also sorry I'd bought color, because with
black-and-white the pictures seem older and farther away. But what are
you going to do? He sat in front of it, watching it, and that was the only
time he was completely still. But it was the kind of stillness that you see
in a rabbit when it freezes and before it will bolt. He was not easy. He sat
in his chair gripping the armrests with all his might, as if the chair itself
was moving at a high speed and if he let go at all he would rocket forward
and maybe crash right through the set.

Once I was in the room watching TV with Henry and I heard his
teeth click at something. I looked over, and he'd bitten through his lip.
Blood was going down his chin. I tell you right then I wanted to smash
that tube to pieces. I went over to it but Henry must have known what I
was up to. He rushed from his chair and shoved me out of the way, against
the wall. I told myself he didn't know what he was doing.

My mom came in, turned the set off real quiet, and told us she had
made something for supper. So we went and sat down. There was still
blood going down Henry's chin, but he didn't notice it and no one said
anything, even though every time he took a bit of his bread his blood fell
onto it until he was eating his own blood mixed in with the food.

30      While Henry was not around we talked about what was going to happen to him. There were no Indian doctors on the reservation, and my
mom was afraid of trusting Old Man Pillager because he courted her long
ago and was jealous of her husbands. He might take revenge through her
son. We were afraid that if we brought Henry to a regular hospital they
would keep him.

"They don't fix them in those places," Mom said; "they just give them
drugs."

"We wouldn't get him there in the first place," I agreed, "so let's just
forget about it."

Then I thought about the car.

Henry had not even looked at the car since he'd gotten home, though
like I said, it was in tip-top condition and ready to drive. I thought the car
might bring the old Henry back somehow. So I bided my time and waited
for my chance to interest him in the vehicle.

35      One night Henry was off somewhere. I took myself a hammer. I went
out to that car and I did a number on its underside. Whacked it up. Bent
the tail pipe double. Ripped the muffler loose. By the time I was done
with the car it looked worse than any typical Indian car that has been driven all its life on reservation roads, which they always say are like government promises—full of holes. It just about hurt me, I'll tell you that! I
threw dirt in the carburetor and I ripped all the electric tape off the seats.

I made it look just as beat up as I could. Then I sat back and waited for Henry to find it.

Still, it took him over a month. That was all right, because it was just getting warm enough, not melting, but warm enough to work outside.

"Lyman," he says, walking in one day, "that red car looks like shit."

"Well it's old," I says. "You got to expect that."

"No way!" says Henry. "That car's a classic! But you went and ran the piss right out of it, Lyman, and you know it don't deserve that. I kept that car in A-one shape. You don't remember. You're too young. But when I left, that car was running like a watch. Now I don't even know if I can get it to start again, let alone get it anywhere near its old condition."

40      "Well you try," I said, like I was getting mad, "but I say it's a piece of junk."

Then I walked out before he could realize I knew he'd strung together more than six words at once.

After that I thought he'd freeze himself to death working on that car. He was out there all day, and at night he rigged up a little lamp, ran a cord out the window, and had himself some light to see by while he worked. He was better than he had been before, but that's still not saying much. It was easier for him to do the things the rest of us did. He ate more slowly and didn't jump up and down during the meal to get this or that or look out the window. I put my hand in the back of the TV set, I admit, and fiddled around with it good, so that it was almost impossible now to get a clear picture. He didn't look at it very often anyway. He was always out with that car or going off to get parts for it. By the time it was really melting outside, he had it fixed.

I had been feeling down in the dumps about Henry around this time. We had always been together before. Henry and Lyman. But he was such a loner now that I didn't know how to take it. So I jumped at the chance one day when Henry seemed friendly. It's not that he smiled or anything. He just said, "Let's take that old shitbox for a spin." Just the way he said it made me think he could be coming around.

We went out to the car. It was spring. The sun was shining very bright. My only sister, Bonita, who was just eleven years old, came out and made us stand together for a picture. Henry leaned his elbow on the red car's windshield, and he took his other arm and put it over my shoulder, very carefully, as though it was heavy for him to lift and he didn't want to bring the weight down all at once.

45      "Smile," Bonita said, and he did.

That picture, I never look at it anymore. A few months ago, I don't know why, I got his picture out and tacked it on the wall. I felt good about Henry at the time, close to him. I felt good having his picture on the wall, until one night when I was looking at television. I was a little drunk and stoned. I looked up at the wall and Henry was staring at me. I don't know what it was, but his smile had changed, or maybe it was gone. All I know is I couldn't stay in the same room with that picture. I was shaking. I got up, closed the door, and went into the kitchen. A little later my friend Ray came over and we both went back into that room. We put the picture in a brown bag, folded the bag over and over tightly, then put it way back in a closet.

I still see that picture now, as if it tugs at me, whenever I pass that closet door. The picture is very clear in my mind. It was so sunny that day Henry had to squint against the glare. Or maybe the camera Bonita held flashed like a mirror, blinding him, before she snapped the picture. My face is right out in the sun, big and round. But he might have drawn back, because the shadows on his face are deep as holes. There are two shadows curved like little hooks around the ends of his smile, as if to frame it and try to keep it there—that one, first smile that looked like it might have hurt his face. He has his field jacket on and the worn-in clothes he'd come back in and kept wearing ever since. After Bonita took the picture, she went into the house and we got into the car. There was a full cooler in the trunk. We started off, east, toward Pembina and the Red River because Henry said he wanted to see the high water.

The trip over there was beautiful. When everything starts changing, drying up, clearing off, you feel like your whole life is starting. Henry felt it, too. The top was down and the car hummed like a top. He'd really put it back in shape, even the tape on the seats was very carefully put down and glued back in layers. It's not that he smiled again or even joked, but his face looked to me as if it was clear, more peaceful. It looked as though he wasn't thinking of anything in particular except the bare fields and wind breaks and houses we were passing.

The river was high and full of winter trash when we got there. The sun was still out, but it was colder by the river. There were still little clumps of dirty snow here and there on the banks. The water hadn't gone over the banks yet, but it would, you could tell. It was just at its limit, hard swollen glossy like an old gray scar. We made ourselves a fire, and we sat down and watched the current go. As I watched it I felt something squeezing inside me and tightening and trying to let go all at the same time. I knew I was not just feeling it myself; I knew I was feeling what Henry was going through at that moment. Except that I couldn't stand it, the closing and opening. I jumped to my feet. I took Henry by the shoulders and I started shaking him. "Wake up," I says, "wake up, wake up, wake up!" I didn't know what had come over me. I sat down beside him again.

50 His face was totally white and hard. Then it broke, like stones break all of a sudden when water boils up inside them.

"I know it," he says. "I know it. I can't help it. It's no use."

We start talking. He said he knew what I'd done with the car. It was obvious it had been whacked out of shape and not just neglected. He said

he wanted to give the car to me for good now, it was no use. He said he'd
fixed it just to give it back and I should take it.

"No way," I says, "I don't want it."

"That's okay," he says, "you take it."

55      "I don't want it, though," I says back to him, and then to emphasize, just
to emphasize, you understand, I touch his shoulder. He slaps my hand off.

"Take that car," he says.

"No," I say, "make me," I say, and then he grabs my jacket and rips the
arm loose. That jacket is a class act, suede with tags and zippers. I push
Henry backwards, off the log. He jumps up and bowls me over. We go
down in a clinch and come up swinging hard, for all we're worth, with our
fists. He socks my jaw so hard I feel like it swings loose. Then I'm at his
ribcage and land a good one under his chin so his head snaps back. He's
dazzled. He looks at me and I look at him and then his eyes are full of tears
and blood and at first I think he's crying. But no, he's laughing. "Ha! Ha!"
he says. "Ha! Ha! Take good care of it."

"Okay," I says, "okay, no problem. Ha! Ha!"

I can't help it, and I start laughing, too. My face feels fat and strange,
and after a while I get a beer from the cooler in the trunk, and when I
hand it to Henry he takes his shirt and wipes my germs off. "Hoof-and-
mouth disease," he says. For some reason this cracks me up, and so we're
really laughing for a while, and then we drink all the rest of the beers one
by one and throw them in the river and see how far, how fast, the current
takes them before they fill up and sink.

60      "You want to go on back?" I ask after a while. "Maybe we could snag a
couple nice Kashpaw girls."

He says nothing. But I can tell his mood is turning again.

"They're all crazy, the girls up here, every damn one of them."

"You're crazy too," I say, to jolly him up. "Crazy Lamartine boys!"

He looks as though he will take this wrong at first. His face twists,
then clears, and he jumps up on his feet. "That's right!" he says. "Crazier 'n
hell. Crazy Indians!"

65      I think it's the old Henry again. He throws off his jacket and starts
swinging his legs out from the knees like a fancy dancer. He's down doing
something between a grouse dance and a bunny hop, no kind of dance I
ever saw before, but neither has anyone else on all this green growing
earth. He's wild. He wants to pitch whoopee! He's up and at me and all
over. All this time I'm laughing so hard, so hard my belly is getting tied up
in a knot.

"Got to cool me off!" he shouts all of a sudden. Then he runs over to
the river and jumps in.

There's boards and other things in the current. It's so high. No sound
comes from the river after the splash he makes, so I run right over. I look
around. It's getting dark. I see he's halfway across the water already, and I

know he didn't swim there but the current took him. It's far. I hear his voice, though, very clearly across it.

"My boots are filling," he says.

He says this in a normal voice, like he just noticed and he doesn't know what to think of it. Then he's gone. A branch comes by. Another branch. And I go in.

70    By the time I get out of the river, off the snag I pulled myself onto, the sun is down. I walk back to the car, turn on the high beams, and drive it up the bank. I put it in first gear and then I take my foot off the clutch. I get out, close the door, and watch it plow softly into the water. The headlights reach in as they go down, searching, still lighted even after the water swirls over the back end. I wait. The wires short out. It is all finally dark. And then there is only the water, the sound of it going and running and going and running and running.

# 11

# Approaching Poetry: Responding in Writing

The title of this chapter is a bit misleading, since we have already spent a few pages discussing poems in our first two chapters, "Writing Arguments about Literature" and "Writing about Literature: From Idea to Essay." But here we will begin again, taking a different approach.

First, some brief advice.

1. Read the poem aloud; or, if you can't bring yourself to read aloud, at least sound the poem in your mind's ear. Try to catch the speaker's tone of voice.
2. Pay attention not only to the black marks on the white paper but also to the white spaces between groups of lines. If a space follows some lines, pause briefly, and take the preceding lines as a unit of thought.
3. Read the poem a second and a third time. Now that you know how it ends, you'll be able to see the connections between the beginning and what follows.

## LANGSTON HUGHES

*The following short poem is by Langston Hughes (1902-1967), an African-American writer born in Joplin, Missouri. Hughes lived part of his youth in Mexico, spent a year at Columbia University, served as a merchant seaman, and worked in a Paris nightclub. There, he showed some of his poems to Dr. Alain Locke, a strong advocate of African-American literature. Encouraged by Locke, when Hughes returned to the United States he continued to write, publishing fiction, plays, essays, and biographies; he also founded theaters, gave public readings, and was, in short, a highly visible presence. The poem that we reprint, "Harlem" (1951), provided Lorraine Hansberry with the title of her well-known play,* A Raisin in the Sun *(1958). For a generous selection of poems by Langston Hughes, see Chapter 21.*

# Harlem                                                    [1951]

What happens to a dream deferred?

Does it dry up
like a raisin in the sun?
Or fester like a sore—
And then run?                                                          5
Does it stink like rotten meat?
Or crust and sugar over—
like a syrupy sweet?

Maybe it just sags
like a heavy load.                                                     10

*Or does it explode?*

---

Read the poem at least twice, and then think about its effect on you.

1. Do you find the poem interesting? Why or why not?
2. Do some things in it interest you more than others? If so, why?
3. Does anything in it puzzle you? If so, what?

Before reading any further, you might jot down your responses to some of these questions. And, whatever your responses, can you point to features of the poem to account for them?

Of course, different readers will respond at least somewhat differently to any work. On the other hand, since writers want to communicate, they try to control their readers' responses, and they count on their readers to understand the meanings of words as the writers understand them. Thus, Hughes assumed his readers knew that Harlem was the site of a large African-American community in New York City.

Let's assume that the reader understands Hughes is talking about Harlem, New York, and, further, that the reader understands the "dream deferred" to refer to the unfulfilled hopes of African-Americans who live in a society dominated by whites. But Hughes does not say "hopes," he says "dream," and he does not say "unfulfilled," he says "deferred." You might ask yourself exactly what differences there are between these words. Next,

# III

# The Pleasures of Poetry

Poetry should surprise by a fine excess; . . . it should strike the reader as a wording of his own highest thoughts, and appear almost a remembrance.

—John Keats

Poetry is emotion put into measure. The emotion must come by nature, but the measure can be acquired by art.

—Thomas Hardy

A poet's work is to name the unnameable, to point at frauds, to take sides, state arguments, shape the world, and stop it going to sleep.

—Salman Rushdie

Poetry is the language of a state of crisis.

—Stéphane Mallarmé

He ate and drank the precious Words,
His Spirit grew robust;
He knew no more than he was poor,
Nor that his frame was dust.

—Emily Dickinson

when you have read the poem several times, you might think about which expression is better in the context, "unfulfilled hopes" or "dream deferred," and why.

# Thinking about "Harlem"

Let's turn to an analysis of the poem, an examination of how the parts fit. As you look at the poem, think about the parts, and jot down whatever notes come to mind. After you have written your own notes, consider the annotations of one student.

These annotations chiefly get at the structure of the poem, the relationship of the parts. The student notices that the poem begins with a line set off by itself and ends with a line set off by itself, and he also notices that each of these lines is a question. Further, he indicates that each of these two lines is emphasized in other ways. The first begins further to the left than any of the other lines—as though the other lines are subheadings or are in some way subordinate—and the last is italicized. In short, he comments on the structure of the poem.

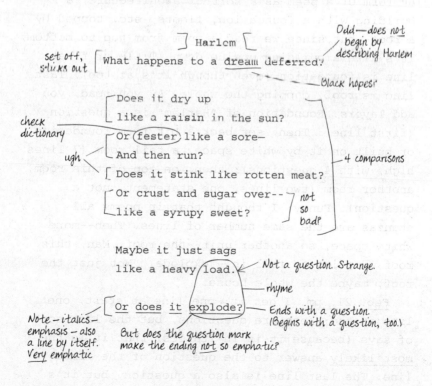

# Some Journal Entries

The student who made these annotations later wrote an entry in his journal:

Feb. 18. Since the title is "Harlem," it's obvious that the "dream" is by African-American people. Also, obvious that Hughes thinks that if the "dream" doesn't become real there may be riots ("explode"). I like "raisin in the sun" (maybe because I like the play), and I like the business about "a syrupy sweet"--much more pleasant than the festering sore and the rotten meat. But if the dream becomes "sweet," what's wrong with that? Why should something "sweet" explode?

Feb. 21. Prof. McCabe said to think of structure or form of a poem as a sort of architecture, a building with a foundation, floors, etc. topped by a roof--but since we read a poem from top to bottom, it's like a building upside down. Title or first line is foundation (even though it's at top); last line is roof, capping the whole. As you read, you add layers. Foundation of "Harlem" is a question (first line). Then, set back a bit from foundation, or built on it by white space, a tall room (7 lines high, with 4 questions); then, on top of this room, another room (two lines, one statement, not a question). Funny; I thought that in poems all stanzas are the same number of lines. Then--more white space, so another unit--the roof. Man, this roof is going to fall in--"explode." Not just the roof, maybe the whole house.

Feb. 21, pm. I get it; one line at start, one line at end; both are questions, but the last sort of says (because it is in italics) that it is the most likely answer to the question of the first line. The last line is also a question, but it's

still an answer. The big stanza (7 lines) has 4
questions: 2 lines, 2 lines, 1 line, 2 lines. Maybe
the switch to 1 line is to give some variety, so as
not to be dull? It's exactly in the middle of the
poem. I get the progress from raisin in the sun
(dried, but not so terrible), to festering sore and
to stinking meat, but I still don't see what's so
bad about "a syrupy sweet." Is Hughes saying that
after things are very bad they will get better? But
why, then, the explosion at the end?

    <u>Feb. 23</u>. "Heavy load" and "sags" in next-to-last
stanza seems to me to suggest slaves with bales of
cotton, or maybe poor cotton pickers dragging big
sacks of cotton. Or maybe people doing heavy labor
in Harlem. Anyway, very tired. Different from running sore and stinking meat earlier; not disgusting,
but pressing down, deadening. Maybe <u>worse</u> than a
sore or rotten meat--a hard, hopeless life. And
then the last line. Just one line, no fancy (and
disgusting) simile. Boom! Not just pressed down and
tired, like maybe some racist whites think (hope?)
blacks will be? Bang! Will there be survivors?

    Drawing chiefly on these notes, the student jotted down some key
ideas to guide him through a draft of an analysis of the poem. (The organization of the draft posed no problem; the student simply followed the organization of the poem.)

*11 lines; short, but powerful; explosive*
*Question (first line)*
*Answers (set off by space & also indented)*
*"raisin in the sun": shrinking*
*"sore"* ⎫
*"rotten meat"* ⎬ *disgusting*
            ⎭
*"syrupy sweet": relief from disgusting comparisons*
*final question (last line): explosion?*
  *explosive (powerful) because:*
    *short, condensed, packed*
    *in italics*
    *stands by itself--like first line*
    *no fancy comparison; very direct*

# Final Draft

Locke 1

Michael Locke

Professor Stahl

English 2B

10 December 2005

Langston Hughes's "Harlem"

"Harlem" is a poem that is only eleven
lines long, but it is charged with power.
It explodes. Hughes sets the stage, so
to speak, by telling us in the title that
he is talking about Harlem, and then he
begins by asking, "What happens to a dream
deferred?" The rest of the poem is set
off by being indented, as though it is the
answer to his question. This answer is in
three parts (three stanzas, of different
lengths).

In a way, it's wrong to speak of the
answer, since the rest of the poem consists
of questions, but I think Hughes means
that each question (for instance, does a
"deferred" hope "dry up / like a raisin in
the sun?") really is an answer, something
that really has happened and that will
happen again. The first question, "Does it
dry up / like a raisin in the sun?," is a
famous line. To compare hope to a raisin
dried in the sun is to suggest a terrible
shrinking. The next two comparisons are
to a "sore" and to "rotten meat." These
comparisons are less clever, but they are

Locke 2

very effective because they are disgusting.
Then, maybe because of the disgusting
comparisons, he gives a comparison that is
not at all disgusting. In this comparison
he says that maybe the "dream deferred"
will "crust and sugar over-- / like a
syrupy sweet."

The seven lines with four comparisons
are followed by a stanza of two lines with
just one comparison:

Maybe it just sags
like a heavy load.

So if we thought that this postponed dream
might finally turn into something "sweet,"
we were kidding ourselves. Hughes comes
down to earth, in a short stanza, with an
image of a heavy load, which probably also
calls to mind images of people bent under
heavy loads, maybe of cotton, or maybe
just any sort of heavy load carried by
African-Americans in Harlem and elsewhere.

The opening question ("What happens to
a dream deferred?") was followed by four
questions in seven lines, but now, with
"Maybe it just sags / like a heavy load,"
we get a statement, as though the poet at
last has found an answer. But at the end we
get one more question, set off by itself
and in italics: "<u>Or does it explode?</u>" This
line itself is explosive for three reasons:
it is short, it is italicized, and it is
a stanza in itself. It's also interesting

```
                                        Locke 3
that this line, unlike the earlier lines,
does not use a simile. It's almost as
though Hughes is saying, "OK, we've had
enough fancy ways of talking about this
terrible situation; here it is, straight."
```

# ▨ TOPICS FOR CRITICAL THINKING AND WRITING

1. The student's analysis suggests that the comparison with "a syrupy sweet" is a deliberately misleading happy ending that serves to make the real ending even more powerful. In class another student suggested that Hughes may be referring to African-Americans who play the Uncle Tom, people who adopt a smiling manner in order to cope with an oppressive society. Which explanation do you prefer, and why? What do you think of combining the two? Or can you offer a different explanation?
2. Do you suppose that virtually all African-Americans respond to this poem in a way that is substantially different from the way virtually all Caucasians or Asian-Americans respond? Explain your position.
3. When Hughes reprinted this poem in 1959, he retitled it "Dream Deferred." Your response?

Let's now look at another poem, and at the responses of another student. Here is a seventeenth-century poem—actually a song—that makes use of the idea that the eyes of the beloved woman can dart fire, and that she can kill (or at least severely wound) the sighing, helpless male lover. The male speaker describes the appearance of Cupid, the tyrannic god of love, who (he claims) is equipped with darts and death-dealing fire taken from the eyes of the proud, cruel woman whom the speaker loves.

# APHRA BEHN

*Aphra Behn (1640–1689) is regarded as the first English woman to have made a living by writing. Not much is known of her life, but she seems to have married a London merchant of Dutch descent, and after his death to have served as a spy in the Dutch Wars (1665–1667). After her return to England she took up playwriting, and she gained fame with* The Rover *(1677). Behn also wrote novels, the most important of which is* Oroonoko, *or* The Royal Slave *(1688), which is among the first works in English to express pity for enslaved Africans.*

## Song: Love Armed

[1676]

Love in fantastic triumph sate,
   Whilst bleeding hearts around him flowed,
For whom fresh pains he did create,
   And strange tyrannic power he showed:
From thy bright eyes he took his fire,         5
   Which round about in sport he hurled;
But 'twas from mine he took desire,
   Enough to undo the amorous world.

From me he took his sighs and tears:
   From thee, his pride and cruelty;        10
From me, his languishments and fears;
   And every killing dart from thee
Thus thou and I the god have armed
   And set him up a deity;
But my poor heart alone is harmed,        15
   Whilst thine the victor is, and free.

## ▓ TOPICS FOR CRITICAL THINKING AND WRITING

1. The speaker talks of the suffering he is undergoing. Can we neverthe-less feel that he enjoys his plight? *Why,* by the way, do we (as readers, singers, or listeners) often enjoy songs of unhappy love?
2. The woman ("thee") is said to exhibit "pride and cruelty" (line 10). Is the poem sexist? Is it therefore offensive?
3. Do you suppose that men can enjoy the poem more than women? Explain.

## Journal Entries

The subject is Aphra Behn's "Song." We begin with two entries in a journal, kept by a first-year student, Geoffrey Sullivan, and we follow these entries with Sullivan's completed essay.

   October 10. The title "Love Armed" puzzled me at first; funny, I somehow was thinking of the expression "strong-armed" and at first I didn't understand that "Love" in this poem is a human--no, not a human, but the god Cupid, who has a human form--and that he is shown as armed, with darts and so forth.

October 13. This god of "Love" is Cupid, and so he is something like what is on a valentine card-- Cupid with his bow and arrow. But valentine cards just show cute little Cupids, and in this poem Cupid is a real menace. He causes lots of pain ("bleeding hearts," "tears," "killing dart," etc.). So what is Aphra Behn telling us about the god of love, or love? That love hurts? And she is singing about it! But we do sing songs about how hard life is. But do we sing them when we are really hurting, or only when we are pretty well off and just thinking about being hurt?

When you love someone and they don't return your love, it hurts, but even when love isn't returned it still gives some intense pleasure. Strange, but I think true. I wouldn't say that love always has this two-sided nature, but I do see the idea that love can have two sides, pleasure and pain. And love takes two kinds of people, male and female. Well, for most people, anyway. Maybe there's also something to the idea that "opposites attract." Anyway, Aphra Behn seems to be talking about men vs. women, pain vs. pleasure, power vs. weakness, etc. Pairs, opposites. And in two stanzas (a pair of stanzas?).

# A Sample Essay by a Student: "The Double Nature of Love"

The final essay makes use of some, but not all, of the preliminary jottings. It includes much that Sullivan did not think of until he reread his jottings, reread the poem, and began drafting the essay.

Geoffrey Sullivan

Professor Diaz

English 2G

15 October 2005

The Double Nature of Love

Aphra Behn's "Love Armed" is in two
stanzas, and it is about two people, "me"
and "thee"--that is, you and I, the lover
and the woman he loves. I think the speaker
is a man, since according to the usual code
men are supposed to be the active lovers
and women are the (relatively) passive
people who are loved. In this poem, the
beloved--the woman, I think--has "bright
eyes" (line 5) that provide the god of Love
with fire, and she also provides the god
with "pride and cruelty" (10). This of
course is the way the man sees it if a woman
doesn't respond to him; if she doesn't love
him in return, she is (he thinks) arrogant
and cruel. What does the man give to Love?
He provides "desire" (7), "sighs and tears"
(9), "languishments and fears" (11). None of
this sounds very manly, but the joke is that
the god of love--which means love--can turn
a strong man into a crybaby when a woman
does not respond to him.

Although both stanzas are clever
descriptions of the god of love, the poem
is not just a description. Of course there
is not a plot in the way that a short story
has a plot, but there is a sort of a switch

at the end, giving the story something of
a plot. The poem is, say, ninety percent
expression of feeling and description of
love, but during the course of expressing
feelings and describing love something
happens, so there is a tiny story. The
first stanza sets the scene ("Love in
fantastic triumph sate" [1]) and tells of
some of the things that the speaker and
the woman contributed to the god of Love.
The woman's eyes provided Love with fire,
and the man's feelings provided Love with
"desire" (7). The second stanza goes on to
mention other things that Love got from the
speaker ("sighs and tears," etc. [9]), and
other things that Love got from the beloved
("pride and cruelty," etc. [10]), and in
line 13 the poet says, "Thus thou and I the
god have armed," so the two humans share
something. They have both given Love his
weapons. But--and this is the story I spoke
of--the poem ends by emphasizing their
difference: Only the man is "harmed," and
the woman is the "victor" because her heart
is not captured, as the man's heart is.
In the battle that Love presides over,
the woman is the winner; the man's heart
has fallen for the woman, but, according
to the last line, the woman's heart remains
"free."

   We have all seen the god of Love on
valentine cards, a cute little Cupid armed

with a bow and arrow. But despite the bow
and arrow that the Valentine's Day Cupid
carries, I think that until I read Aphra
Behn's "Love Armed" I had never really
thought about Cupid as <u>powerful</u> and as
capable of causing real pain. On valentine
cards, he is just cute, but when I think
about it, I realize the truth of Aphra
Behn's concept of love. Love <u>is</u> (or can be)
two-sided, whereas the valentine cards show
only the sweet side.

   I think it is interesting to notice that
although the poem is about the destructive
power of love, it is fun to read. I am not
bothered by the fact that the lover is
miserable. Why? I think I enjoy the poem,
rather than am bothered by it, because <u>he
is enjoying his misery</u>. After all, he is
singing about it, sort of singing in the
rain, telling anyone who will listen about
how miserable he is, and he is having a
very good time doing it.

**[New page]**

                    Work Cited
Behn, Aphra. "Love Armed." <u>A Little
   Literature</u>. Ed. Sylvan Barnet, William
   Burto, and William E. Cain. New York:
   Longman, 2007. 393.

# TOPICS FOR
# CRITICAL THINKING AND WRITING

1. What do you think of the essay's title? Is it sufficiently interesting and focused?
2. What are the writer's chief points? Are they clear, and are they adequately developed?
3. Do you think the writer is too concerned with himself, and that he loses sight of the poem? Or do you find it interesting that he connects the poem with life?
4. Focus on the writer's use of quotations. Does he effectively introduce and examine quoted lines and phrases?
5. What grade would you give the essay? Why?

# 12

# Narrative Poetry

Most of us are so used to reading stories—whether factual in history books or fictional in novels—that we normally associate storytelling with prose, not with poetry. But in fact some of the world's great stories have been told in poetry—for instance, the Greek epics the *Iliad* (about the Trojan War) and the *Odyssey* (about Odysseus's ten years of wandering), and medieval tales of King Arthur. Non-Western (i.e., non-European) cultures, too, have their great narrative poems, notably the Sanskrit epic *The Mahabharata* (about a war in ancient India) and African and Native-American tales of the creation of the world and of the sublime deeds of heroes. And, to descend to the ridiculous, countless narratives are still being told in the form of the limerick:

> There was a young fellow of Riga,
> Who smiled as he rode on a tiger.
>     They returned from the ride,
>     With the fellow inside,
> And the smile on the face of the tiger.

In short, although we are accustomed to thinking of a story as prose in a book, until a few hundred years ago stories were commonly poetry that was sung or recited. In nonliterate societies people got their stories from storytellers who relied on memory rather than on the written word; the memorized stories were often poems, partly because (in the words of Shakespeare's early contemporary, Sir Philip Sidney), "Verse far exceedeth prose in the knitting up of the memory." Even in literate societies, few people could read or write until the invention of the printing press in the middle of the fifteenth century. Although the printing press did not immediately destroy oral verse narratives, as the centuries passed, an increasingly large reading public developed that preferred prose narratives.

# THOMAS HARDY

*Thomas Hardy (1840-1928) was born in Dorset, England, the son of a stonemason. Despite great obstacles he studied the classics and architecture, and in 1862 he moved to London to study and practice as an architect. Ill health forced him to return to Dorset, where he continued to work as an architect and to write. Best known for his novels, Hardy ceased writing fiction after the hostile reception of* Jude the Obscure *in 1896 and turned to writing lyric poetry.*

## *The Convergence of the Twain*                    [1912]

Lines on the Loss of the Titanic

### *I*

In a solitude of the sea
Deep from human vanity,
And the Pride of Life that planned her, stilly couches she.

### *II*

Steel Chambers, late the pyres
Of her salamandrine fires,
Cold currents thrid,° and turn to rhythmic tidal lyres.          5

### *III*

Over the mirrors meant
To glass the opulent
The sea-worm crawls—grotesque, slimed, dumb, indifferent.

### *IV*

Jewels in joy designed                                          10
To ravish the sensuous mind
Lie lightless, all their sparkles bleared and black and blind.

------
**6 thrid** thread.

## V

Dim moon-eyed fishes near
Gaze at the gilded gear
And query: "What does this vaingloriousness down here?"    15

## VI

Well; while was fashioning
This creature of cleaving wing,
The Immanent Will that stirs and urges everything

## VII

Prepared a sinister mate
For her—so gaily great—    20
A Shape of Ice, for the time far and dissociate.

## VIII

And as the smart ship grew
In stature, grace, and hue,
In shadowy silent distance grew the Iceberg too.

## IX

Alien they seemed to be:    25
No mortal eye could see
The intimate welding of their later history,

## X

Or sign that they were bent
By paths coincident
On being anon twin halves of one august event,    30

## XI

Till the Spinner of the Years
Said "Now!" And each one hears,
And consummation comes, and jars two hemispheres.

# ⊠ TOPICS FOR CRITICAL THINKING AND WRITING

1. Does Hardy assign a cause to the disaster? What do you make of "The Immanent Will" (line 18) and "the Spinner of the Years" (line 31)?
2. In line 19 Hardy speaks of the "sinister mate." What other words in the poem suggest that the ship and the iceberg participate in a marriage?
3. After you have read and thought carefully about the poem, consider the title and subtitle. Why, in your view, did Hardy use the phrase "The Convergence of the Twain" as his title? Would the poem be more effective if the title and subtitle were reversed? Explain.
4. Examine the form and structure of the poem, looking closely at the ways in which Hardy has organized his lines and stanzas. Stanza I, for example, could be rewritten with the final words coming first: "She couches stilly in a solitude of the sea." What poetic effects does Hardy achieve through this change (and others like it) in normal or typical syntax and word order? And why does he use a series of three-line stanzas, each headed by a roman numeral? Why not simply present the poem as a single long stanza?

# SIEGFRIED SASSOON

*Siegfried Sassoon (1886–1967), a wealthy Englishman, served with such distinction in the First World War—in 1915 under heavy fire he helped a wounded soldier to safety—that he was awarded the Military Cross. Later, wounded by a bullet in the chest, he was sent from France back to England, where, upon reflection, he concluded that the war was not a war of defense but of aggression. Military officials shrewdly chose not to dispute him, but merely asserted that he was shell-shocked. When Sassoon recovered from the bullet wound, he was again sent into combat, and in 1919 was again wounded and hospitalized.*

*Sassoon expressed his views in* Memoirs of a Fox-Hunting Man *(1928) and* Memoirs of an Infantry Officer *(1930), as well as in several volumes of poetry.*

## The General                                          [1917]

"Good-morning, good-morning!" the General said
When we met him last week on our way to the line.
Now the soldiers he smiled at are most of 'em dead,
And we're cursing his staff for incompetent swine.
"He's a cheery old card," grunted Harry to Jack
As they slogged up to Arras with rifle and pack.

But he did for them both by his plan of attack.

# ▓ TOPICS FOR
# CRITICAL THINKING AND WRITING

1. Who is the storyteller, and what is the story he tells?
2. Why do you suppose Sassoon put an extra space between the next-to-last line and the last line? Speaking of the last line, notice that it rhymes with the two preceding lines—i.e., the last three lines end with identical sounds, whereas in the preceding four lines, no two adjacent lines rhyme. Why do you suppose Sassoon changed the rhyme scheme for the final lines?
3. How would you characterize the General? How would you characterize Harry? How would you characterize the storyteller?

# COUNTEE CULLEN

*Countee Cullen (1903-1946) was born Countee Porter in New York City, raised by his grandmother, and then adopted by the Reverend Frederick A. Cullon, a Methodist minister in Harlem. Cullen received a bachelor's degree from New York University (Phi Beta Kappa) and a master's degree from Harvard. He earned his living as a high school teacher of French, but his literary gifts were recognized in his own day. Eric Walrond (1898-1966), to whom the poem is dedicated, was an essayist and writer of short stories.*

## Incident                                                              [1925]

*(For Eric Walrond)*

Once riding in Old Baltimore,
　Heart-filled, head-filled with glee,
I saw a Baltimorean
　Keep looking straight at me.                                              4

Now I was eight and very small,
　And he was no whit bigger,
And so I smiled, but he poked out
　His tongue, and called me, "Nigger."                                      8

I saw the whole of Baltimore
　From May until December;
Of all the things that happened there
　That's all that I remember.                                               12

▧ TOPICS FOR
CRITICAL THINKING AND WRITING

1. How would you define an "incident"? A serious occurrence? A minor occurrence, or what? Think about the word, and then think about Cullen's use of it as a title for the event recorded in this poem. Test out one or two other possible titles as a way of helping yourself to see the strengths or weaknesses of Cullen's title.

2. The dedicatee, Eric Walrond (1898–1966), was an African-American essayist and writer of fiction, who in an essay, "On Being Black," had described his experiences of racial prejudice. How does the presence of the dedication bear on our response to Cullen's account of the "incident"?

3. What is the tone of the poem? Indifferent? Angry? Or what? What do you think is the speaker's attitude toward the "incident"? What is your attitude?

4. Ezra Pound, poet and critic, once defined literature as "news that *stays* news." What do you think he meant by this? Do you think that the definition fits Cullen's poem?

# EDWIN ARLINGTON ROBINSON

*Edwin Arlington Robinson (1869–1935) grew up in Gardiner, Maine, spent two years at Harvard, and then returned to Maine, where he published his first book of poetry in 1896. Though he received encouragement from neighbors, his finances were precarious, even after President Theodore Roosevelt, having been made aware of the book, secured for him an appointment as customs inspector in New York from 1905 to 1909. Additional books won fame for Robinson, and in 1922 he was awarded the first of the three Pulitzer Prizes for poetry that he would win.*

## Richard Cory                                                   [1896]

Whenever Richard Cory went down town,
We people on the pavement looked at him:
He was a gentleman from sole to crown,
Clean favored, and imperially slim.                                  4

And he was always quietly arrayed,
And he was always human when he talked;
But still he fluttered pulses when he said,
"Good-morning," and he glittered when he walked.                     8

And he was rich—yes, richer than a king—
And admirably schooled in every grace:
In fine,° we thought that he was everything
To make us wish that we were in his place.          12

So on we worked, and waited for the light,
And went without the meat, and cursed the bread;
And Richard Cory, one calm summer night,
Went home and put a bullet through his head.          16

---

[11] *In fine* in short.

## ▨ TOPICS FOR CRITICAL THINKING AND WRITING

1. Consult the entry on irony in the glossary. Then read the pages referred to in the entry. Finally, write an essay of 500 words on irony in "Richard Cory."

2. What do you think were Richard Cory's thoughts shortly before he "put a bullet through his head"? In 500 words, set forth his thoughts and actions (what he sees and does). If you wish, you can write in the first person, from Cory's point of view. Further, if you wish, your essay can be in the form of a suicide note.

3. Write a sketch (250-350 words) setting forth your early impression or understanding of someone whose later actions revealed you had not understood the person.

# EMILY DICKINSON

*Emily Dickinson (1830-1886), born into a proper New England family in Amherst, Massachusetts, was brought up as a Protestant. Much of her poetry concerns death and heaven, but it is far from being conventionally Christian.*

## *Because I could not stop for Death*

Because I could not stop for Death—
He kindly stopped for me—
The Carriage held but just Ourselves—
And Immortality.          4

We slowly drove—He knew no haste
And I had put away
My labor and my leisure too,
For His Civility—                                                  8

We passed the School, where Children strove
At Recess—in the Ring—
We passed the Fields of Gazing Grain—
We passed the Setting Sun—                                         12

Or rather—He passed Us—
The Dews drew quivering and chill—
For only Gossamer, my Gown—
My Tippet—only Tulle—                                             16

We paused before a House that seemed
A Swelling of the Ground—
The Roof was scarcely visible—
The Cornice—in the Ground—                                        20

Since then—'tis Centuries—and yet
Feels shorter than the Day
I first surmised the Horses' Heads
Were toward Eternity—                                             24

## ▩ TOPICS FOR CRITICAL THINKING AND WRITING

1. Characterize death as it appears in lines 1-8.
2. What is the significance of the details and their arrangement in the third stanza? Why "strove" rather than "played" (line 9)? What meaning does "Ring" (line 10) have? Is "Gazing Grain" better than "Golden Grain"?
3. The "House" in the fifth stanza is a sort of riddle. What is the answer? Does this stanza introduce an aspect of death not present—or present only very faintly—in the rest of the poem? Explain.
4. Evaluate this statement about the poem (from Yvor Winters's *In Defense of Reason*): "In so far as it concentrates on the life that is being left behind, it is wholly successful; in so far as it attempts to experience the death to come, it is fraudulent, however exquisitely."

# 13

# Lyric Poetry

For the ancient Greeks, a **lyric** was a song accompanied by a lyre. It was short, and it usually expressed a single emotion, such as joy or sorrow. The word is now used more broadly, referring to a poem that, neither narrative (telling a story) nor strictly dramatic (performed by actors), is an emotional or reflective soliloquy. Still, it is rarely very far from a singing voice. James Joyce saw the lyric as the "verbal vesture of an instant of emotion, a rhythmical cry such as ages ago cheered on the man who pulled at the oar." Such lyrics, too, were sung more recently than "ages ago." Here is a song that American slaves sang when rowing heavy loads.

## ANONYMOUS

### *Michael Row the Boat Ashore*

Michael row the boat ashore, Hallelujah!
Michael's boat's a freedom boat, Hallelujah!
Sister, help to trim the sail, Hallelujah!
Jordan stream is wide and deep, Hallelujah!
Freedom stands on the other side, Hallelujah!

---

We might pause for a moment to comment on why people sing at work. There are at least three reasons: (1) work done rhythmically goes more efficiently; (2) the songs relieve the boredom of the work; and (3) the songs—whether narrative or lyrical—provide something of an outlet for the workers' frustrations.

Speaking roughly, we can say that whereas a narrative (whether in prose or poetry) is set in the past, telling what happened, a lyric is set in the present, catching a speaker in a moment of expression. But a lyric can, of course, glance backward or forward, as in this folk song, usually called "Careless Love."

# ANONYMOUS

## Careless Love

Love, O love, O careless love,
You see what careless love can do.
When I wore my apron low,
Couldn't keep you from my do,°
    Fare you well, fare you well.                                    5
Now I wear my apron high,
Scarce see you passin' by,
    Fare you well, fare you well.

---

4 **do** door.

---

Notice, too, that a lyric, like a narrative, can have a plot: "Michael" moves toward the idea of freedom, and "Careless Love" implies a story of desertion—something has happened between the time that the singer could not keep the man from her door and now, when she "scarce" sees him passing by—but, again, the emphasis is on a present state of mind.

Lyrics are sometimes differentiated among themselves. For example, if a lyric is melancholy or mournfully contemplative, especially if it laments a death, it may be called an **elegy**. If a lyric is rather long, elaborate, and on a lofty theme such as immortality or a hero's victory, it may be called an **ode** or a **hymn**. Distinctions among lyrics are often vague, and one person's ode may be another's elegy. Still, when writers use one of these words in their titles, they are inviting the reader to recall the tradition in which they are working. Of the poet's link to tradition T. S. Eliot said:

> No poet, no artist of any art, has his complete meaning alone. His significance, his appreciation is the appreciation of his relation to the dead poets and artists. You cannot value him alone; you must set him, for contrast and comparison, among the dead.

Although the lyric is often ostensibly addressed to someone (the "you" in "Careless Love"), the reader usually feels that the speaker is really talking to himself or herself. In "Careless Love," the speaker need not be in the presence of her man; rather, her heart is overflowing (the reader senses) and she pretends to address him.

A comment by John Stuart Mill on poetry is especially true of the lyric:

> Eloquence is *heard*, poetry is *over*heard. Eloquence supposes an audience; the peculiarity of poetry appears to us to lie in the poet's utter unconsciousness of a listener. Poetry is feeling confessing itself to itself, in moments of solitude.

This is particularly true in work songs such as "Michael Row the Boat Ashore," where there is no audience: the singers sing for themselves, participating rather than performing. As one prisoner in Texas said: "They really be singing about the way they feel inside. Since they can't say it to nobody, they sing a song about it." The sense of "feeling confessing itself to itself, in moments of solitude" or of "singing about the way they feel inside" is strong and clear in this short cowboy song.

# ANONYMOUS

## The Colorado Trail

Eyes like the morning star,
Cheeks like a rose,
Laura was a pretty girl
God Almighty knows.                                                                    4

Weep all ye little rains,
Wail winds wail,
All along, along, along
The Colorado trail.                                                                    8

When we read a lyric poem, no matter who the speaker is, for a moment—while we recite or hear the words—we become the speaker. That is, we get into the speaker's mind, or, perhaps more accurately, the speaker takes charge of our mind, and we undergo (comfortably seated in a chair or sprawled on a bed) the mental experience that is embodied in the words.

Next, another anonymous poem, this one written in England, probably in the early sixteenth century. Aside from modern reprintings, it survives in only one manuscript, a song book, the relevant portion of which we reproduce here. But first, here is the poem in modern spelling.

*Westron wynde when wilt thou blow.* Musical setting in a tenor part-book; early sixteenth
century. (Reproduced by permission of the British Library Royal Appendix 58 f.5.)

# ANONYMOUS

## Western Wind

Westron wind, when will thou blow?
The small rain down can rain.
Christ, that my love were in my arms,
And I in my bed again.

The angular handwriting is in a style quite different from modern
writing, but when you are told that the first three words are "Westron
[i.e., western] wynde when," you can probably see some connections.
And you can probably make out the last handwritten word on the second line ("And"), and all of the third line: "I yn my bed A gayne" ("I in my
bed again"). Incidentally—we hope we are not boring you with trifles—
some controversy surrounds the transcription of one of the words—the
fifth word in the second line of writing, the word that looks like a *y* followed by an *f* (just after "Chryst" and just before "my"). The issue is this:
Is the letter a *y*, in which case the word is "if," or is it a letter we no longer
have, a letter called *thorn*, which was pronounced "th," as in either "thin"
or "this"? If indeed it is a thorn, the next letter is a *t*, not an *f*, and the
word therefore is not "if" but "that." (Incidentally, signs that say "Ye Olde
Antique Shoppe" make no sense; "Ye" was never used as a definite article.
What these signs are reproducing is a thorn, and the word really is "The,"
not "Ye.")

## ▓ TOPICS FOR
## CRITICAL THINKING AND WRITING

1. In "Western Wind," what do you think is the tone of the speaker's voice in the first two lines? Angry? Impatient? Supplicating? Be as precise as possible. What is the tone in the next two lines?
2. In England the west wind, warmed by the Gulf Stream, rises in the spring. What associations link the wind and rain of lines 1 and 2 with lines 3 and 4?
3. Should we have been told why the lovers are separated? Explain.

Love poems are by no means all the same—to take an obvious point, some are happy and some are sad—but those that are about the loss of a beloved or about the pains of love seem to be especially popular.

# JULIA WARD HOWE

*Julia Ward Howe (1819–1910) was born in New York City. A social reformer, her work for the emancipation of African-Americans and the right of women to vote is notable. She was the first woman to be elected to the American Academy of Arts and Letters.*

## *Battle Hymn of the Republic*                                    [1861]

Mine eyes have seen the glory of the coming of the Lord:
He is trampling out the vintage where the grapes of wrath are stored;
He hath loosed the fateful lightning of his terrible swift sword;
   His truth is marching on.                                    4

*Chorus*
   Glory! glory! Hallelujah!
   Glory! glory! Hallelujah!
   Glory! glory! Hallelujah!
      His truth is marching on!                                    8

I have seen him in the watch-fires of a hundred circling camps;
They have builded him an altar in the evening dews and damps;
I can read his righteous sentence by the dim and flaring lamps;
   His day is marching on.                                    12

I have read a fiery gospel, writ in burnished rows of steel:
"As ye deal with my contemners, so with you my grace shall deal;
Let the Hero, born of woman, crush the serpent with his heel,
   Since God is marching on."                                    16

He has sounded forth the trumpet that shall never call retreat;
He is sifting out the hearts of men before his judgment seat;
Oh, be swift, my soul, to answer him! be jubilant, my feet!
    Our God is marching on.                                    20

In the beauty of the lilies Christ was born across the sea,
With a glory in his bosom that transfigures you and me:
As he died to make men holy, let us die to make men free,
    While God is marching on.                                  24

## ⊞ TOPICS FOR
## CRITICAL THINKING AND WRITING

1. This poem of the Civil War, written to the tune of "John Brown's Body," draws some of its militant imagery from the Bible, especially from Isaiah 63.1–6 and Revelation 19.11–15. Do you think the lines about Christ are inappropriate here? Explain.
2. If you know the tune to which "Battle Hymn of the Republic" is sung, think about the interplay between the music and the words. Do you think people have a different response to Howe's words when they read her text as a poem, rather than experienced it as a song?

# LANGSTON HUGHES

*For a biographical note, see page 385.*

## Evenin' Air Blues

[194?]

Folks, I come up North
Cause they told me de North was fine.
I come up North
Cause they told me de North was fine.
Been up here six months                                    5
I'm about to lose my mind.

This mornin' for breakfast
I chawed de mornin' air.
This mornin' for breakfast
Chawed de mornin' air.                                    10
But this evenin' for supper,
I got evenin' air to spare.

Believe I'll do a little dancin'
Just to drive my blues away—
A little dancin'                                              15
To drive my blues away,
Cause when I'm dancin'
De blues forgets to stay.

But if you was to ask me
How de blues they come to be,                              20
Says if you was to ask me
How de blues they come to be—
You wouldn't need to ask me:
Just look at me and see!

## ▓ TOPIC FOR CRITICAL THINKING OR WRITING

In what ways (subject, language) does this poem resemble blues you may have heard? Does it differ in any ways? If so, how?

# LI-YOUNG LEE

*Li-Young Lee was born in 1957 in Jakarta, Indonesia, of Chinese parents. In 1964 his family brought him to the United States. He was educated at the University of Pittsburgh, the University of Arizona, and the State University of New York, Brockport. He now lives in Chicago.*

## *I Ask My Mother to Sing*                    [1986]

She begins, and my grandmother joins her.
Mother and daughter sing like young girls.
If my father were alive, he would play
his accordion and sway like a boat.            4

I've never been in Peking, or the Summer Palace,
nor stood on the great Stone Boat to watch
the rain begin on Kuen Ming Lake, the picnickers
running away in the grass.                      8

But I love to hear it sung;
how the waterlilies fill with rain until
they overturn, spilling water into water,
then rock back, and fill with more.            12

Both women have begun to cry.
But neither stops her song.

## ▓ TOPICS FOR CRITICAL THINKING AND WRITING

1. Why might the speaker ask the women to sing?
2. Why do the women cry? Why do they continue to sing?

# EDNA ST. VINCENT MILLAY

*Edna St. Vincent Millay (1892-1950) was born in Rockland, Maine. Even as a child she wrote poetry, and by the time she graduated from Vassar College (1917) she had achieved some notice as a poet. Millay settled for a while in Greenwich Village, a center of Bohemian activity in New York City, where she wrote, performed in plays, and engaged in feminist causes. In 1923, the year she married, she became the first woman to win the Pulitzer Prize for Poetry. Numerous other awards followed. Though she is best known as a lyric poet—especially as a writer of sonnets—she also wrote memorable political poetry and nature poetry as well as short stories, plays, and a libretto for an opera.*

## The Spring and the Fall

[1923]

In the spring of the year, in the spring of the year,
I walked the road beside my dear.
The trees were black where the bark was wet.
I see them yet, in the spring of the year.
He broke me a bough of the blossoming peach          5
That was out of the way and hard to reach.

In the fall of the year, in the fall of the year,
I walked the road beside my dear.
The rooks went up with a raucous trill.
I hear them still, in the fall of the year.            10
He laughed at all I dared to praise,
And broke my heart, in little ways.

Year be springing or year be falling,
The bark will drip and the birds be calling.
There's much that's fine to see and hear               15
In the spring of a year, in the fall of a year.
'Tis not love's going hurts my days,
But that it went in little ways.

## ▓ TOPICS FOR
## CRITICAL THINKING AND WRITING

1. The first stanza describes the generally happy beginning of a love story. Where do you find the first hint of an unhappy ending?
2. Describe the rhyme scheme of the first stanza, including internal rhymes. Do the second and third stanzas repeat the pattern, or are there some variations? What repetition of sounds other than rhyme do you note?

3. Put the last two lines into your own words. How do you react to them; that is, do you find the conclusion surprising, satisfying, recognizable from your own experience, anticlimactic, or what?

4. In two or three paragraphs, explain how the imagery of the poem (drawn from the seasons of the year) contributes to its meaning.

# WILFRED OWEN

*Wilfred Owen (1893-1918) was born in Shropshire, in England, and studied at London University. He enlisted in the army at the outbreak of World War I and fought in the Battle of the Somme until he was hospitalized with shell shock. After his recuperation in England, he returned to the front, only to be killed in action one week before the end of the war. His collected poems were published posthumously.*

## Anthem for Doomed Youth                    [1920]

What passing-bells for these who die as cattle?
Only the monstrous anger of the guns.
Only the stuttering rifles' rapid rattle
Can patter out their hasty orisons.
No mockeries for them from prayers or bells,                    5
Nor any voice of mourning save the choirs—
The shrill, demented choirs of wailing shells;
And bugles calling for them from sad shires.

What candles may be held to speed° them all?
Not in the hands of boys, but in their eyes                    10
Shall shine the holy glimmers of good-byes.
The pallor of girls' brows shall be their pall;
Their flowers the tenderness of patient minds,
And each slow dusk a drawing-down of blinds.

9 **speed** aid.

## ▒ TOPICS FOR
## CRITICAL THINKING AND WRITING

1. What is an anthem? What are some of the words or phrases in this poem that might be found in a traditional anthem? What are some of the words or phrases that you would not expect in an anthem?

2. How would you characterize the speaker's state of mind? (Your response probably will require more than one word.)

# WALT WHITMAN

*Walt Whitman (1819-1892) was born on Long Island, the son of a farmer. The young Whitman taught school and worked as a carpenter, a printer, a newspaper editor, and, during the Civil War, as a volunteer nurse on the Union side. After the war he supported himself by doing secretarial jobs. In Whitman's own day his poetry was highly controversial because of its unusual form (formlessness, many people said) and (though not in the following poem) its abundant erotic implications.*

## A Noiseless Patient Spider
[1862–63]

A noiseless patient spider,
I mark'd where on a little promontory it stood isolated,
Mark'd how to explore the vacant vast surrounding,
It launch'd forth filament, filament, filament, out of itself,
Ever unreeling them, ever tirelessly speeding them.      5

And you O my soul where you stand,
Surrounded, detached, in measureless oceans of space,
Ceaselessly musing, venturing, throwing, seeking the spheres to
    connect them,
Till the bridge you will need be form'd, till the ductile anchor hold,
Till the gossamer thread you fling catch somewhere, O my soul.      10

## ▧ TOPICS FOR CRITICAL THINKING AND WRITING

1. How are the suggestions in "launch'd" (line 4) and "unreeling" (line 5) continued in the second stanza?
2. How are the varying lengths of lines 1, 4, and 8 relevant to their ideas?
3. The second stanza is not a complete sentence. Why? The poem is unrhymed. What effect does the near-rhyme (*hold: soul*) in the last two lines have on you?

# JOHN KEATS

*John Keats (1795-1821), son of a London stable keeper, was taken out of school at age fifteen and apprenticed to a surgeon and apothecary. In 1816 he was licensed to practice as an apothecary-surgeon, but he almost immediately abandoned medicine and decided to make a career as a poet. His progress was amazing; he published books of poems—to mixed reviews—in 1817, 1818, and 1820, before dying of tuberculosis at the age of twenty-five. Today he is esteemed as one of England's greatest poets.*

## Ode on a Grecian Urn                                    [1820]

### I

Thou still unravished bride of quietness,
  Thou foster-child of silence and slow time,
Sylvan historian, who canst thus express
  A flowery tale more sweetly than our rhyme:
What leaf-fringed legend haunts about thy shape            5
  Of deities or mortals, or of both,
    In Tempe or the dales of Arcady?
  What men or gods are these? What maidens loth?
What mad pursuit? What struggle to escape?
  What pipes and timbrels? What wild ecstasy?            10

### II

Heard melodies are sweet, but those unheard
  Are sweeter; therefore, ye soft pipes, play on;
Not to the sensual° ear, but, more endeared,
  Pipe to the spirit ditties of no tone:
Fair youth, beneath the trees, thou canst not leave      15
  Thy song, nor ever can those trees be bare;
    Bold Lover, never, never canst thou kiss,
Though winning near the goal—yet, do not grieve;
  She cannot fade, though thou hast not thy bliss,
    For ever wilt thou love, and she be fair!            20

### III

Ah, happy, happy boughs! that cannot shed
  Your leaves, nor ever bid the Spring adieu;
And, happy melodist, unwearied,
  For ever piping songs for ever new;
More happy love! more happy, happy love!                 25
  For ever warm and still to be enjoyed,
    For ever panting, and for ever young;

---

**13 sensual** sensuous.

All breathing human passion far above,
  That leaves a heart high-sorrowful and cloyed,
  A burning forehead, and a parching tongue.         30

## IV

Who are these coming to the sacrifice?
  To what green altar, O mysterious priest,
Lead'st thou that heifer lowing at the skies,
  And all her silken flanks with garlands drest?
What little town by river or sea shore,              35
  Or mountain-built with peaceful citadel,
    Is emptied of this folk, this pious morn?
And, little town, thy streets for evermore
  Will silent be; and not a soul to tell
    Why thou art desolate can e'er return.           40

## V

O Attic shape! Fair attitude! with brede°
Of marble men and maidens overwrought,
With forest branches and the trodden weed;
  Thou, silent form, dost tease us out of thought
As doth eternity: Cold Pastoral!                     45
When old age shall this generation waste,
  Thou shalt remain, in midst of other woe
Than ours, a friend to man, to whom thou say'st,
"Beauty is truth, truth beauty,"—that is all
  Ye know on earth, and all ye need to know.         50

---

**41 brede** design.

## ▓ TOPICS FOR CRITICAL THINKING AND WRITING

1. If you do not know the meaning of "sylvan," check a dictionary. Why does Keats call the urn a "sylvan" historian (line 3)? As the poem continues, what evidence is there that the urn cannot "express" (line 3) a tale so sweetly as the speaker said?
2. What do you make of lines 11–14?
3. What do you think the urn may stand for in the first three stanzas? In the third stanza, is the speaker caught up in the urn's world or is he sharply aware of his own?

4. Do you take "tease us out of thought" (line 44) to mean "draw us into a realm of imaginative experience superior to that of reason" or to mean "draw us into futile and frustrating questions"? Or both? Or neither? What suggestions do you find in "Cold Pastoral" (line 45)?
5. Do lines 49-50 perhaps mean that imagination, stimulated by the urn, achieves a realm richer than the daily world? Or perhaps that art, the highest earthly wisdom, suggests there is a realm wherein earthly troubles are resolved?

# PAUL LAURENCE DUNBAR

*Paul Laurence Dunbar (1872-1906), born in Ohio to parents who had been slaves in Kentucky, achieved fame for his dialect poetry. He published early—even while in high school—and by 1896, with the publication of* Lyrics of Lowly Life, *had three books to his credit. Because he often used black speech patterns and pronunciation, Dunbar's work was sometimes thought to present demeaning racial stereotypes, but in recent years critics have seen the protest beneath the quaint surface. In the following poem, however, he works entirely within a traditional white idiom, although the subject is distinctively African-American.*

## Sympathy                                                      [1899]

I know what the caged bird feels, alas!
　　When the sun is bright on the upland slopes;
When the wind stirs soft through the spring grass,
And the river flows like a stream of glass.
　　When the first bird sings and the first bud opes,           5
And the faint perfume from its chalice steals—
I know what the caged bird feels!

I know why the caged bird beats his wing
　　Till its blood is red on the cruel bars;
For he must fly back to his perch and cling                     10
When he fain would be on the bough a-swing;
　　And a pain still throbs in the old, old scars
And they pulse again with a keener sting—
I know why he beats his wing!

I know why the caged bird sings, ah me,                         15
　　When his wing is bruised and his bosom sore,—
When he beats his bars and he would be free;
It is not a carol of joy or glee,
　　But a prayer that he sends from his heart's deep core,
But a plea, that upward to Heaven he flings—                    20
　　I know why the caged bird sings

# ▨ TOPICS FOR
# CRITICAL THINKING AND WRITING

1. Pay careful attention to Dunbar's use of language. Describe, for example, what the comparison "like a stream of glass" in the first stanza expresses about the river, and comment on the implications of the word "chalice."
2. Some readers have felt that the second stanza is the weakest in the poem, and that the poem improves if this stanza is omitted. Why do you suppose they hold this view? Do you agree with it? Explain. Should Dunbar have dropped this stanza?
3. After reading and rereading the poem, try to summarize its overall effect. Explain why the speaker sees such an intimate connection between himself and the "caged bird."

# LINDA PASTAN

*Linda Pastan was born in New York City in 1932. The author of ten books of poems, she has won numerous prizes and has received grants from the National Endowment for the Arts. In the following poem she wittily plays with repetitions and with pauses.*

## Jump Cabling                                            [1984]

| | |
|---|---|
| When our cars | touched |
| When you lifted the hood | of mine |
| To see the intimate workings | underneath, |
| When we were bound | together |
| By a pulse of pure | energy, |
| When my car like the | princess |
| In the tale woke with a | start, |

I thought why not ride the rest of the way together?

# ▨ TOPICS FOR
# CRITICAL THINKING AND WRITING

1. Suppose someone argued that this is merely prose broken up into arbitrary units. Would you agree? Explain.
2. As you read the poem aloud, think about the spacing that Pastan designed for it. What is the effect of the space between the first and second parts of the first seven lines? Why does she do something different for the final line?

# 14

# The Speaking Tone of Voice

Everything is as good as it is dramatic. . . . [A poem is] heard as sung or spoken by a person in a scene—in character, in a setting. By whom, where and when is the question. By the dreamer of a better world out in a storm in Autumn; by a lover under a window at night.

—Robert Frost, Preface, *A Way Out*

If we fall into the habit of saying, "Julia Ward Howe says that her 'eyes have seen the glory of the coming of the Lord,' " or "Robert Frost says that he thinks he knows 'Whose woods these are,' " we neglect the important truth in Frost's comment about poetry as drama: A poem is written by an author (Howe, Frost), but it is spoken by an invented speaker. The author counterfeits the speech of a person in a particular situation.

The anonymous author of "Western Wind" (page 410), for instance, invents the speech of an unhappy lover who longs for the spring ("Westron wind, when will thou blow?"); Julia Ward Howe (page 411) invents the speech of someone who has seen God working in this world; Robert Frost, in "Stopping by Woods on a Snowy Evening" (page 7), invents a speaker who, sitting in a horse-drawn sleigh, watches the woods fill up with snow.

The speaker's voice often has the ring of the author's own voice—certainly Robert Frost did a great deal to cultivate the idea that he was a farmer-poet—but even when the resemblance seems close, we should recall that in the poem we get a particular speaker in a particular situation. That is, we get, for instance, not the whole of Frost (the father, the competitive poet, the public lecturer, and so on), but only a man in a horse-drawn sleigh watching the woods fill up with snow. It is customary, then, in writing about the voice one hears in a poem, to write not about the author but about the **speaker,** or **voice,** or **mask,** or **persona** (Latin for "mask") that speaks the poem.

In reading a poem, the first and most important question to ask yourself is this: *Who is speaking?* If an audience and a setting are suggested, keep them in mind, too. Consider, for example, the following poem.

# EMILY DICKINSON

*Emily Dickinson (1830–1886) was born into a proper New England family in Amherst, Massachusetts. Because she never married, and because in her last twenty years she may never have left her house, she has sometimes been pitied. But as the critic Allen Tate said, "All pity for Miss Dickinson's 'starved life' is misdirected. Her life was one of the richest and deepest ever lived on this continent." Her brother was probably right in saying that, having seen something of the rest of the world, "she could not resist the feeling that it was painfully hollow. It was to her so thin and unsatisfying in the face of the Great Realities of Life."*

## I'm Nobody! Who are you?

[1861?]

I'm Nobody! Who are you?
Are you—Nobody—too?
Then there's a pair of us!
Don't tell! they'd banish us—you know!          4

How dreary—to be—Somebody!
How public—like a Frog—
To tell your name—the livelong June—
To an admiring Bog!          8

Let's consider the sort of person we hear in "I'm Nobody! Who are you?" (Read it aloud, to see if you agree. In fact, you should test each of our assertions by reading the poem aloud.) The voice in line 1 is rather like that of a child playing a game with a friend. In lines 2 and 3 the speaker sees the reader as a fellow spirit ("Are you—Nobody—too?") and invites the reader to join her ("Then there's a pair of us!") in forming a sort of conspiracy of silence against outsiders ("Don't tell!"). In "they'd banish us," however, we hear a word that a child would not be likely to use, and we probably feel that the speaker is a shy but (with the right companion) playful adult, who here is speaking to an intimate friend. And since we hear this voice—we are reading the poem—we are or we become the friend. Because "banish" is a word that brings to mind images of a king's court, the speaker almost comically inflates and thereby makes fun of the "they" who are opposed to "us."

In the second stanza, or we might better say in the space between the two stanzas, the speaker puts aside the childlike manner. In "How dreary," the first words of the second stanza, we hear a sophisticated voice, one might even say a world-weary voice, or a voice with perhaps more than a touch of condescension. But since by now we are paired with the speaker in a conspiracy against outsiders, we enjoy the contrast that the speaker makes between the Nobodies and the Somebodies. Who are these Somebodies, these people who would imperiously "banish" the speaker and the friend? What are the Somebodies like?

> How dreary—to be—Somebody!
> How public—like a Frog—
> To tell your name—the livelong June—
> To an admiring Bog!

The last two lines do at least two things: They amusingly explain to the speaker's new friend (the reader) in what way a Somebody is public (it proclaims its presence all day). They also indicate the absurdity of the Somebody-Frog's behavior (the audience is "an admiring Bog"). By the end of the poem we are quite convinced that it is better to be a Nobody (like Dickinson's speaker, and the reader?) than a Somebody (a loudmouth, like a croaking frog).

Often we tend to think of reading as something we do in private, and silently. But it is important to remember that writers, especially poets, care greatly about how their words *sound.* Poets pay attention not only to how the poem is arranged on the page—the length of the lines, for example—but also to how the poem sounds when actually read aloud, or, at least, when heard within the reader's mind.

One of the pleasures of reading literature, in fact, is the pleasure of listening to the sound of a voice, with its special rhythms, tones, accents, and emphases. Getting to know a poem, and becoming engaged by a poet's style, is very much a matter of getting to know a voice, acquiring a feeling for its familiar intonations, yet also being surprised, puzzled, even startled by it on occasion.

If you have done a little acting, you know from this experience how crucial it is to discover the way a character's lines in a play should sound. Directors and actors spend a great deal of time reading the lines, trying them in a variety of ways to catch their truest pace and verbal shape. And so do poets. We aren't making this up; in a letter, Robert Frost talks about "the sound of sense," a sort of abstraction in which an emotion or attitude comes through, even if the words are not clearly heard. He writes:

> The best place to get the abstract sound of sense is from voices behind a door that cuts off the words. Ask yourself how these sentences would sound without the words in which they are embodied:

> You mean to tell me you can't read?
> I said no such thing.
> Well read then.
> You're not my teacher.

In another letter, continuing the discussion of the topic, after giving some additional examples (for instance, "Unless I'm greatly mistaken," "No fool like an old fool"), Frost says, "It is so and not otherwise that we get the variety that makes it fun to write and read. *The ear does it.* The ear is the only true writer and the only true reader." (For a group of poems by Frost, see Chapter 21.)

In reading, then, your goal is to achieve a deeper sense of character—what this voice sounds like, what kind of person speaks like this. Read aloud; imagine how the writer might have meant his or her words to sound; read aloud again; and listen carefully all the while to the echoes and resonances of the words.

Consider the dramatic situation and the voices in the following poems.

# GWENDOLYN BROOKS

*Gwendolyn Brooks (1917–2000) was born in Topeka, Kansas, but was raised in Chicago's South Side, where she spent most of her life. In 1950, when she won the Pulitzer Prize for Poetry, she became the first African-American writer to win a Pulitzer Prize. We print another of Brooks's poems in Chapter 1.*

## The Mother

[1945]

Abortions will not let you forget.
You remember the children you got that you did not get,
The damp small pulps with a little or with no hair,
The singers and workers that never handled the air.
You will never neglect or beat                                      5
Them, or silence or buy with a sweet.
You will never wind up the sucking-thumb
Or scuttle off ghosts that come.
You will never leave them, controlling your luscious sigh,
Return for a snack of them, with gobbling mother-eye.          10

I have heard in the voices of the wind the voices of my
    dim killed children.
I have contracted. I have eased
My dim dears at the breasts they could never suck.
I have said, Sweets, if I sinned, if I seized
Your luck                                                          15
And your lives from your unfinished reach,
If I stole your births and your names,
Your straight baby tears and your games,
Your stilted or lovely loves, your tumults, your marriages,
    aches, and your deaths,

If I poisoned the beginnings of your breaths,                    20
Believe that even in my deliberateness I was not deliberate.
Though why should I whine,
Whine that the crime was other than mine?—
Since anyhow you are dead.
Or rather, or instead,                                           25
You were never made.
But that too, I am afraid,
Is faulty: oh, what shall I say, how is the truth to be said?
You were born, you had body, you died.
It is just that you never giggled or planned or cried.            30

Believe me, I loved you all.
Believe me, I knew you, though faintly, and I loved, I loved you
All.

## ▨ TOPICS FOR
## CRITICAL THINKING AND WRITING

1. Whom is being addressed?
2. The first ten lines sound like a chant. What gives them that quality?
   What makes them nonetheless serious?
3. In lines 20–23 the mother attempts to deny the "crime" but cannot.
   What is her reasoning here?
4. Do you find the last lines convincing? Explain.
5. The poem was first published in 1945. Do you think that the abundant debate about abortion in recent years has somehow made the
   poem seem dated, or more timely than ever? Explain.

# THE READER AS THE SPEAKER

We have been arguing that the speaker of the poem usually is not the author but a dramatized form of the author, and that we overhear this
speaker in some situation. But with poems of the sort that we have been
looking at, we can also say that *the reader* is the speaker. That is, as we
read the poem, at least to some degree *we* utter the thoughts, and *we* experience the sensations or emotions that the writer sets forth. We feel that
Dickinson has allowed us to set forth our own feelings about what it is to
be Nobody in a world where others are Somebody (and she has also
helped us to say that the Somebody is a noisy frog); with Brooks we hear
or overhear thoughts and feelings that perhaps strike us as more relevant

and more profound and more moving than most of what we hear on television or read in the newspapers about urban violence.

In the following poem you will hear at least three voices—the voice of the person who begins the poem by telling us about a dead man ("Nobody heard him, the dead man"), the voice of the dead man ("I was much further out than you thought / And not waving but drowning"), and the collective voice of the dead man's friends ("Poor chap, he always loved larking"). But see if you don't find that all of the voices together say things that you have said (or almost said).

# STEVIE SMITH

*Stevie Smith (1902-1971), christened Florence Margaret Smith, was born in England, in Hull. In addition to writing poems, she wrote stories, essays, and three novels. She is the subject of a film,* Stevie, *in which Glenda Jackson plays Smith.*

## Not Waving but Drowning

[1957]

Nobody heard him, the dead man,
But still he lay moaning:
I was much further out than you thought
And not waving but drowning.                                          4

Poor chap, he always loved larking
And now he's dead
It must have been too cold for him his heart gave way,
They said.                                                          8

Oh, no no no, it was too cold always
(Still the dead one lay moaning)
I was much too far out all my life
And not waving but drowning.                                       12

## ✻ TOPICS FOR CRITICAL THINKING AND WRITING

1. Identify the speaker of each line.
2. What sort of man did the friends of the dead man think he was? What type of man do you think he was?
3. The first line, "Nobody heard him, the dead man," is literally true. Dead men do not speak. In what other ways is it true?

# WISLAWA SZYMBORSKA

*Wislawa Szymborska (pronounced "Vislawa Zimborska"), a native of Poland, was born in 1923. In 1996 she received the Nobel Prize for poetry.*

## The Terrorist, He Watches                                   [1981]

*Translated by Robert A. Maguire and Magnus Jan Krynski*

The bomb will go off in the bar at one twenty p.m.
Now it's only one sixteen p.m.
Some will still have time to get in,
some to get out.

The terrorist has already crossed to the other side of the street.   5
The distance protects him from any danger,
and what a sight for sore eyes:

A woman in a yellow jacket, she goes in.
A man in dark glasses, he comes out.

Guys in jeans, they are talking.                                 10
One seventeen and four seconds.
That shorter guy's really got it made, and gets on a scooter,
and that taller one, he goes in.

One seventeen and forty seconds.
That girl there, she's got a green ribbon in her hair.            15
Too bad that bus just cut her off.
One eighteen p.m.
The girl's not there any more.
Was she dumb enough to go in, or wasn't she?
That we'll see when they carry them out.                         20

One nineteen p.m.
No one seems to be going in.
Instead a fat baldy's coming out.
Like he's looking for something in his pockets and
at one nineteen and fifty seconds                                25
he goes back for those lousy gloves of his.

It's one twenty p.m.
The time, how it drags.
Should be any moment now.
Not yet.                                                         30
Yes, this is it.
The bomb, it goes off.

# ▓ TOPICS FOR CRITICAL THINKING AND WRITING

1. Who speaks the poem? The terrorist? Or someone watching the terrorist? Or a sort of combination? Or what?
2. Characterize the speaker.

# JOHN UPDIKE

*John Updike (b. 1932) is best known as a writer of fiction—short stories and novels—but throughout his professional career he has also written essays and poems. (For a more complete biographical note, see page 117.)*

## Icarus

[2001]

O.K., you are sitting in an airplane and
the person in the seat next to you is a sweaty, swarthy gentleman
    of Middle Eastern origin
whose carry-on luggage consists of a bulky black brief-case he
    stashes,
in compliance with airline regulations,
underneath the seat ahead.                                          5
He keeps looking at his watch and closing his eyes in prayer,
resting his profusely dank forehead against the seatback ahead of him
just above the black briefcase,
which if you listen through the droning of the engines seems to be
    ticking, ticking
softly, softer than your heartbeat in your ears.                    10

Who wants to have all their careful packing—the travellers' checks,
    the folded underwear—
end as floating sea-wrack five miles below,
drifting in a rainbow scum of jet fuel,
and their docile hopes of a plastic-wrapped meal
dashed in a concussion whiter than the sun?                         15

I say to my companion, "Smooth flight so far."
"So far."
"That's quite a briefcase you've got there."
He shrugs and says, "It contains my life's work."
"And what is it, exactly, that you do?"                             20
"You could say I am a lobbyist."

He does not want to talk.
He wants to keep praying.
His hands, with their silky beige backs and their nails cut close like
      a technician's,
tremble and jump in handling the plastic glass of Sprite when it        25
      comes with its exploding bubbles.

Ah, but one gets swept up
in the airport throng, all those workaday faces,
faintly pampered and spoiled in the boomer style,
and those elders dressed like children for flying
in hi-tech sneakers and polychrome catsuits,                            30
and those gum-chewing attendants taking tickets
while keeping up a running flirtation with a uniformed bystander,
      a stoic blond pilot—
all so normal, who could resist
this vault into the impossible?

Your sweat has slowly dried. Your praying neighbor                      35
has fallen asleep, emitting an odor of cardamom.
His briefcase seems to have deflated.
Perhaps not this time, then.
But the possibility of impossibility will keep drawing us back
to this scrape against the numbed sky,                                  40
to this sleek sheathed tangle of color-coded wires, these million rivets,
      this wing
like a frozen lake at your elbow.

# ❋ TOPICS FOR
# CRITICAL THINKING AND WRITING

1. Take a moment to look up the Icarus myth in a classical dictionary or
   encyclopedia. Do you see connections between the myth and the
   story that Updike tells in this poem?
2. Who is the "you" in the first line?
3. What kinds of assumptions does the poem make about the "gentleman of Middle Eastern origin"? Are these assumptions challenged?
   Point to specific details in the language to explain your responses.
4. What kind of conclusion does the poem reach?
5. Does "Icarus" disturb you? If so, why?
6. Which poem do you think is more effective; Updike's "Icarus" or
   Syzmborska's "The Terrorist"? What, more generally, does it mean to
   say that one poem is more effective than another?

# THE DRAMATIC MONOLOGUE

We have said at some length that in most poems the speaker is not quite the author (say, Robert Frost) but is a dramatized version (a man sitting in a sleigh, watching the "woods fill up with snow"). We have also said that in most poems the reader can imagine himself or herself as the speaker; as we read Dickinson or even Brooks and Pastan, we say to ourselves that the poet is expressing thoughts and emotions that might be our own. But in some poems the poet creates so distinct a speaker that the character clearly is not us but is something Other. Such a poem is called a **dramatic monologue.** In it, a highly specific character speaks, in a clearly specified situation. The most famous example is Robert Browning's "My Last Duchess," where a Renaissance duke is addressing an emissary from a count.

## ROBERT BROWNING

*Born in a suburb of London into a middle-class family, Browning (1812–1889) was educated primarily at home, where he read widely. For a while he wrote for the English stage, but after marrying Elizabeth Barrett in 1846—she too was a poet—he lived with her in Italy until her death in 1861. He then returned to England and settled in London with their son. Regarded as one of the most distinguished poets of the Victorian period, he is buried in Westminster Abbey.*

### My Last Duchess [1844]

Ferrara*

That's my last Duchess painted on the wall,
Looking as if she were alive. I call
That piece a wonder, now; Frà Pandolf's° hands
Worked busily a day, and there she stands.
Will't please you sit and look at her? I said          5
"Frà Pandolf" by design, for never read
Strangers like you that pictured countenance,
The depth and passion of its earnest glance,
But to myself they turned (since none puts by

---

*Ferrara** town in Italy.   **3 Frà Pandolf** a fictitious painter.

The curtain I have drawn for you, but I)                               10
And seemed as they would ask me, if they durst,
How such a glance came there; so, not the first
Are you to turn and ask thus. Sir, 'twas not
Her husband's presence only, called that spot
Of joy into the Duchess' cheek; perhaps                                15
Frà Pandolf chanced to say "Her mantle laps
Over my Lady's wrist too much," or, "Paint
Must never hope to reproduce the faint
Half-flush that dies along her throat." Such stuff
Was courtesy, she thought, and cause enough                           20
For calling up that spot of joy. She had
A heart—how shall I say?—too soon made glad,
Too easily impressed; she liked whate'er
She looked on, and her looks went everywhere.
Sir, 'twas all one! My favor at her breast,                           25
The dropping of the daylight in the west,
The bough of cherries some officious fool
Broke in the orchard for her, the white mule
She rode with round the terrace—all and each
Would draw from her alike the approving speech,                       30
Or blush, at least. She thanked men—good! but thanked
Somehow—I know not how—as if she ranked
My gift of a nine-hundred-years-old name
With anybody's gift. Who'd stoop to blame
This sort of trifling? Even had you skill                             35
In speech—(which I have not)—to make your will
Quite clear to such an one, and say, "Just this
Or that in you disgusts me; here you miss,
Or there exceed the mark"—and if she let
Herself be lessoned so, nor plainly set                               40
Her wits to yours, forsooth, and made excuse,
—E'en then would be some stooping; and I choose
Never to stoop. Oh, Sir, she smiled, no doubt,
Whene'er I passed her; but who passed without
Much the same smile? This grew; I gave commands;                      45
Then all smiles stopped together. There she stands
As if alive. Will't please you rise? We'll meet
The company below, then. I repeat,
The Count your master's known munificence
Is ample warrant that no just pretense                                50
Of mine for dowry will be disallowed;
Though his fair daughter's self, as I avowed
At starting, is my object. Nay, we'll go

Together down, Sir. Notice Neptune, though,
Taming a sea-horse, thought a rarity,                                      55
Which Claus of Innsbruck° cast in bronze for me!

_____

**56 Claus of Innsbruck** a fictitious sculptor.

## ▨ TOPICS FOR CRITICAL THINKING AND WRITING

1. What is the occasion for the meeting?
2. What words or lines do you think especially convey the speaker's arrogance? What is your attitude toward the speaker? Loathing? Fascination? Respect? Explain.
3. The time and place are Renaissance Italy; how do they affect your attitude toward the duke? What would be the effect if the poem were set in the late twentieth century?
4. Years after writing this poem, Browning explained that the duke's "commands" (line 45) were "that she should be put to death, or he might have had her shut up in a convent." Do you think the poem should have been more explicit? Does Browning's later uncertainty indicate that the poem is badly thought out? Suppose we did not have Browning's comment on line 45. Do you think the line then could mean only that he commanded her to stop smiling and that she obeyed? Explain.

# DICTION AND TONE

From the whole of language, one consciously or unconsciously selects certain words and grammatical constructions; this selection constitutes one's **diction**. It is partly by the diction that we come to know the speaker of a poem. Stevie Smith's speaker (page 427) used words such as "chap" and "larking," which are scarcely imaginable in the mouth of Browning's Renaissance duke. But of course some words are used in both poems: "I," "you," "thought," "the," and so on. The fact remains, however, that although a large part of language is shared by all speakers, certain parts of language are used only by certain speakers.

Like some words, some grammatical constructions are used only by certain kinds of speakers. Consider these two passages:

In Adam's fall
We sinned all.

—Anonymous, *The New England Primer*

Of Man's first disobedience, and the fruit
Of that forbidden tree whose mortal taste
Brought death into the World, and all our woe,
With loss of Eden, till one greater Man
Restore us, and regain the blissful seat,
Sing, Heavenly Muse, that, on the secret top
Of Oreb, or of Sinai, didst inspire
That shepherd who first taught the chosen seed
In the beginning how the heavens and earth
Rose out of Chaos. . . .

—John Milton, *Paradise Lost*

There is an enormous difference in the diction of these two passages. Milton, speaking as an inspired poet, appropriately uses words and grammatical constructions somewhat removed from common life. Hence, while the anonymous author of the primer speaks directly of "Adam's fall," Milton speaks allusively of the fall, calling it "Man's first disobedience." Milton's sentence is nothing that any Englishman ever said in conversation; its genitive beginning ("Of Man's first disobedience"), its length (the sentence continues for six lines beyond the quoted passage), and its postponement of the main verb ("Sing") until the sixth line mark it as the utterance of a poet working in the tradition of Latin poetry. The primer's statement, by its choice of words as well as by its brevity, suggests a far less sophisticated speaker.

Speakers have attitudes toward themselves, their subjects, and their audiences, and (consciously or unconsciously) they choose their words, pitch, and modulation accordingly; all these add up to the **tone**. In written literature, tone must be detected without the aid of the ear; the reader must understand by the selection and sequence of words the way in which they are meant to be heard (that is, playfully, angrily, confidentially, sarcastically, etc.). The reader must catch what Frost calls "the speaking tone of voice somehow entangled in the words and fastened to the page of the ear of the imagination."

Finally, we should mention that although this discussion concentrates on the speaker's tone, one can also talk of the author's tone, that is, of the author's attitude toward the invented speaker. The speaker's tone might, for example, be angry, but the author's tone (as detected by the reader) might be humorous.

# ROBERT HERRICK

*Robert Herrick (1591-1674) was born in London, the son of a gold-smith. After taking an M.A. at Cambridge, he was ordained in the Church of England. Later, he was sent to the country parish of Dean*

*Prior in Devonshire, where he wrote most of his poetry. A loyal supporter of the king, in 1647 he was expelled from his parish by the Puritans, though in 1662 he was restored to Dean Prior.*

## To the Virgins, to Make Much of Time                    [1648]

Gather ye rosebuds while ye may,
   Old Time is still a-flying;
And this same flower that smiles today,
   Tomorrow will be dying.                                        4

The glorious lamp of heaven, the sun,
   The higher he's a-getting,
The sooner will his race be run,
   And nearer he's to setting.                                     8

That age is best which is the first,
   When youth and blood are warmer;
But being spent, the worse, and worst
   Times still succeed the former.                                12

Then be not coy, but use your time;
   And while ye may, go marry:
For having lost but once your prime,
   You may for ever tarry.                                         16

*Carpe diem* (Latin: "seize the day") is the theme. But if we want to get the full force of the poem, we must understand who is talking to whom. Look, for example, at "Old Time" in line 2. Time is "old" in the sense of having been around a long while, but doesn't it "old" in this context suggest also that the speaker regards Time with easy familiarity, almost affection? We visit the old school, and our friend is old George. Time is destructive, yes, and the speaker urges the young maidens to make the most of their spring. But the speaker is neither bitter nor importunate; rather, he seems to be the wise old man, the counselor, the man who has made his peace with Time and is giving advice to the young. Time moves rapidly in the poem (the rosebud of line 1 is already a flower in line 3), but the speaker is unhurried; in line 5 he has leisure to explain that the glorious lamp of heaven is the sun.

In "To the Virgins," the pauses, indicated by punctuation at the ends of the lines (except in line 11, where we tumble without stopping from "worst" to "Times"), slow the reader down. But even if there is no punctuation at the end of a line of poetry, the reader probably pauses slightly or gives the final word an additional bit of emphasis. Similarly, the space between stanzas slows a reader down, increasing the emphasis on the last word of one stanza and the first word of the next.

# THOMAS HARDY

*Thomas Hardy (1840-1928) was born in Dorset, England, the son of a stonemason. Despite great obstacles he studied the classics and architecture, and in 1862 he moved to London to study and practice as an architect. Ill health forced him to return to Dorset, where he continued to work as an architect and to write. Best known for his novels, Hardy ceased writing fiction after the hostile reception of* Jude the Obscure *in 1896 and turned to writing lyric poetry.*

## The Man He Killed
[1902]

"Had he and I but met
By some old ancient inn,
We should have sat us down to wet
Right many a nipperkin!°                                          4

"But ranged as infantry,
And staring face to face,
I shot at him as he at me,
And killed him in his place.                                      8

"I shot him dead because—
Because he was my foe,
Just so: my foe of course he was;
That's clear enough; although                                     12

"He thought he'd 'list, perhaps,
Off-hand like—just as I—
Was out of work—had sold his traps°—
No other reason why.                                              16

"Yes; quaint and curious war is!
You shoot a fellow down
You'd treat if met where any bar is,
Or help to half-a-crown."                                         20

---

**4 nipperkin** cup.    **15 traps** personal belongings.

## � TOPICS FOR
## CRITICAL THINKING AND WRITING

1. What do we learn about the speaker's life before he enlisted in the infantry? How does his diction characterize him?
2. What is the effect of the series of monosyllables in lines 7 and 8?

3. Consider the punctuation of the third and fourth stanzas. Why are the heavy, frequent pauses appropriate? What question is the speaker trying to answer?
4. In the last stanza, what attitudes toward war does the speaker express? What, from the evidence of this poem, would you infer Hardy's attitude toward war to be?

# COUNTEE CULLEN

*Countee Cullen (1903–1946) was born Countee Porter in New York City, raised by his grandmother, and then adopted by the Reverend Frederick A. Cullen, a Methodist minister in Harlem. Cullen received a bachelor's degree from New York University (Phi Beta Kappa) and a master's degree from Harvard. He earned his living as a high school teacher of French, but his literary gifts were recognized in his own day. Cullen sometimes wrote about black life, but he also wrote on other topics, insisting that African-Americans need not work only in the literary tradition exemplified by such writers as Langston Hughes.*

## For a Lady I Know                    [1925]

She even thinks that up in heaven
    Her class lies late and snores,
While poor black cherubs rise at seven
    To do celestial chores.

▧ TOPICS FOR
CRITICAL THINKING AND WRITING

1. What is the gist of what Cullen is saying?
2. How would you characterize the tone? Furious? Indifferent?

# THE VOICE OF THE SATIRIST

The writer of **satire,** in one way or another, ridicules an aspect or several aspects of human behavior, seeking to arouse in the reader some degree of amused contempt for the object. However urbane in tone, the satirist is always critical. By cleverly holding up foibles or vices for the world's derision, satire (Alexander Pope claimed) "heals with morals what it hurts with wit." The laughter of comedy is an end in itself; the laughter of satire is a weapon against the world: "The intellectual dagger," Frank O'Connor called satire, "opposing the real dagger." Jonathan Swift, of whom O'Connor is speaking, insisted that his satires were not malice but medicine:

> His satire points at no defect
> But what all mortals may correct. . . .
> He spared a hump or crooked nose,
> Whose owners set not up for beaux.

But Swift, although he claimed that satire is therapeutic, also saw its futility: "Satire is a sort of glass [i.e., mirror] wherein beholders do generally discover everybody's face but their own."

Sometimes the satirist speaks out directly as defender of public morals, abusively but wittily chopping off heads. Byron, for example, wrote:

> Prepare for rhyme—I'll publish, right or wrong:
> Fools are my theme, let Satire be my song.

But sometimes the satirist chooses to invent a speaker far removed from himself or herself, just as Browning chose to invent a Renaissance duke. The satirist may invent a callous brigadier general or a pompous judge who unconsciously annihilates himself. Consider this satirical poem by e. e. cummings (pen name of Edwin Estlin Cummings).

# e. e. cummings

*Edwin Estlin Cummings (1894-1962) grew up in Cambridge, Massachusetts, and was graduated from Harvard, where he became interested in modern literature and art, especially in the movements called cubism and futurism. His father, a conservative clergyman and a professor at Harvard, seems to have been baffled by the youth's interests, but Cummings's mother encouraged his artistic activities, including his use of unconventional punctuation as a means of expression.*

*Politically liberal in his youth, Cummings became more conservative after a visit to Russia in 1931, but early and late his work emphasizes individuality and freedom of expression.*

## next to of course god america i                                    [1926]

"next to of course god america i
love you land of the pilgrims' and so forth oh
say can you see by the dawn's early my
country 'tis of centuries come and go
and are no more what of it we should worry          5
in every language even deafanddumb

thy sons acclaim your glorious name by gorry
by jingo by gee by gosh by gum
why talk of beauty what could be more beaut-
iful than these heroic happy dead                              10
who rushed like lions to the roaring slaughter
they did not stop to think they died instead
then shall the voice of liberty be mute?"

He spoke. And drank rapidly a glass of water

---

Cummings might have written, in the voice of a solid citizen or a good
poet, a direct attack on chauvinistic windbags; instead, he chose to invent
a windbag whose rhetoric punctures itself. Yet the last line tells that we
are really hearing someone who is recounting what the windbag said; that
is, the speaker of all the lines but the last is a combination of the chauvinist *and* the satiric observer of the chauvinist. (When Cummings himself
recited these lines, there was mockery in his voice.)

Only in the final line of the poem does the author seem to speak entirely on his own, and even here he adopts a matter-of-fact pose that is
far more potent than invective (direct abuse) would be. Yet the last line
is not totally free of explicit hostility. It might, for example, have run, "He
spoke. And slowly poured a glass of water." Why does this version lack
the punch of Cummings's? And what do you think is implied by the absence of a final period in line 14?

# MARGE PIERCY

*Marge Piercy, born in Detroit in 1936, was the first member of her fam-*
*ily to attend college. After earning a bachelor's degree from the Univer-*
*sity of Michigan in 1957 and a master's degree from Northwestern Uni-*
*versity in 1958, she moved to Chicago. There she worked at odd jobs*
*while writing novels (unpublished) and engaging in action on behalf*
*of women and blacks and against the war in Vietnam. In 1970—the*
*year she moved to Wellfleet, Massachusetts, where she still lives—she*
*published her first book, a novel. Since then she has published other*
*novels, as well as short stories, poems, and essays.*

## Barbie Doll                                               [1969]

This girlchild was born as usual
and presented dolls that did pee-pee
and miniature GE stoves and irons
and wee lipsticks the color of cherry candy.

Then in the magic of puberty, a classmate said:                    5
You have a great big nose and fat legs.

She was healthy, tested intelligent,
possessed strong arms and back,
abundant sexual drive and manual dexterity.
She went to and fro apologizing.                                  10
Everyone saw a fat nose on thick legs.

She was advised to play coy,
exhorted to come on hearty,
exercise, diet, smile and wheedle.
Her good nature wore out                                          15
like a fan belt.
So she cut off her nose and her legs
and offered them up.
In the casket displayed on satin she lay
with the undertaker's cosmetics painted on,                       20
a turned-up putty nose,
dressed in a pink and white nightie.
Doesn't she look pretty? everyone said.
Consummation at last.
To every woman a happy ending.                                    25

### ▨ TOPICS FOR CRITICAL THINKING AND WRITING

1. Why is the poem called "Barbie Doll"?
2. What voice do you hear in lines 1–4? Line 6 is, we are told, the voice of "a classmate." How do these voices differ? What voice do you hear in the first three lines of the second stanza?
3. Explain in your own words what Piercy is saying about women in this poem. Does her view seem to you fair, slightly exaggerated, or greatly exaggerated?

# 15

# Figurative Language: Simile, Metaphor, Personification, Apostrophe

HIPPOLYTA.   'Tis strange, my Theseus, that these lovers speak of.
THESEUS.   More strange than true. I never may believe
These antique fables, nor these fairy toys.
Lovers and madmen have such seething brains,
Such shaping fantasies, that apprehend
More than cool reason ever comprehends.
The lunatic, the lover, and the poet,
Are of imagination all compact.
One sees more devils than vast hell can hold,
That is the madman. The lover, all as frantic,
Sees Helen's beauty in a brow of Egypt.
The poet's eye, in a fine frenzy rolling,
Doth glance from heaven to earth, from earth to heaven;
And as imagination bodies forth
The forms of things unknown, the poet's pen
Turns them to shapes, and gives to airy nothing
A local habitation and a name.
   —Shakespeare, *A Midsummer Night's Dream*, 5.1–17

Theseus was neither the first nor the last to suggest that poets, like lunatics and lovers, freely employ their imagination. Terms such as *poetic license* and *poetic justice* imply that poets are free to depict a never-never land. One has only to leaf through any anthology of poetry to encounter numerous statements that are, from a logical point of view, lunacies. Here are two quotations:

> Look like th' innocent flower,
> But be the serpent under 't.
>
> —Shakespeare

> Each outcry from the hunted hare
> A fiber from the brain does tear.
>
> —William Blake

The first of these is spoken by Lady Macbeth, when she urges her husband to murder King Duncan. How can a human being "Look like th' innocent flower," and how can a human being "be the serpent"? But Macbeth knows, and we know exactly what she means. We see and we feel her point, in a way that we would not if she had said, "Put on an innocent-looking face, but in fact kill the king."

And in the quotation from Blake, when we read that the hunted hare's plaintive cry serves to "tear" a "fiber" from our brain, we almost wince, even though we know that the statement is literally untrue.

On a literal level, then, such assertions are nonsense (so, too, is Theseus's notion that reason is cool). But of course they are not to be taken literally; rather, they employ **figures of speech**—departures from logical usage that are aimed at gaining special effects. Consider the lunacies that Robert Burns heaps up here.

# ROBERT BURNS

*Robert Burns (1759-1796) was born in Ayrshire in southwestern Scotland. Many of his best poems and songs were written in the Scots dialect, though he also wrote perfect English.*

## A Red, Red Rose                                                   [1796]

O, my luve is like a red, red rose,
  That's newly sprung in June.
O, my luve is like the melodie,
  That's sweetly played in tune.                                       4

As fair art thou, my bonnie lass,
  So deep in luve am I,
And I will luve thee still, my dear,
  Till a'° the seas gang° dry.                                         8

---

8 a' all.   gang go.

Till a' the seas gang dry, my dear,
    And the rocks melt wi' the sun!
And I will luve thee still, my dear,
    While the sands o' life shall run.                                    12

And fare thee weel, my only luve,
    And fare thee weel awhile!
And I will come again, my luve,
    Though it were ten thousand mile!                               16

---

To the charge that these lines are lunacies or untruths, at least two replies can be made. First, it might be said that the speaker is not really making assertions about a woman; he is saying he feels a certain way. His words, it can be argued, are not assertions about external reality but expressions of his state of mind, just as a tune one whistles asserts nothing about external reality but expresses the whistler's state of mind. In this view, the nonlogical language of poetry (like a groan of pain or an exclamation of joy) is an expression of emotion; its further aim, if it has one, is to induce in the hearer an emotion.

Second, and more to the point here, it can be said that nonlogical language does indeed make assertions about external reality, and even gives the reader an insight into this reality that logical language cannot. The opening comparison in Burns's poem ("my luve is like a red, red rose") brings before our eyes the lady's beauty in a way that the reasonable assertion "She is beautiful" does not. By comparing the woman to a rose, the poet invites us to see the woman through a special sort of lens: she is fragrant; her lips (and perhaps her cheeks) are like a rose in texture and color; she will not keep her beauty long. Also, "my love is like a red, red rose" says something different from "like a red, red beet," or "a red, red cabbage."

The poet, then, has not only communicated a state of mind but also discovered, through the lens of imagination, some things (both in the beloved and in the lover's own feelings) that interest us. The discovery is not world-shaking; it is less important than the discovery of America or the discovery that the meek are blessed, but it *is* a discovery and it leaves the reader with the feeling, "Yes, that's right. I hadn't quite thought of it that way, but that's right."

A poem, Robert Frost said, "assumes direction with the first line laid down, . . . runs a course of lucky events, and ends in a clarification of life—not necessarily a great clarification, such as sects and cults are founded on, but in a momentary stay against confusion." What is clarified? In another sentence Frost gives an answer: "For me the initial delight is in the surprise of remembering something I didn't know I knew." John Keats made a similar statement:"Poetry . . . should strike the Reader as a wording of his own highest thoughts, and appear almost a Remembrance."

Some figures of speech are, in effect, riddling ways of speech.To call fishermen "farmers of the sea"—a metaphor—is to give a sort of veiled description of fishermen, bringing out, when the term is properly understood, certain aspects of a fisherman's activities.And a riddle, after all, is a veiled description—though intentionally obscure or deceptive—calling attention to characteristics, especially similarities, not usually noticed. (*Riddle*, like *read*, is from Old English *redan*, "to guess,""to interpret," and thus its solution provides knowledge.) "Two sisters upstairs, often looking but never seeing each other" is (after the riddle is explained) a way of calling attention to the curious fact that the eye, the instrument of vision, never sees its mate.

# SYLVIA PLATH

*Sylvia Plath (1932-1963) was born in Boston, the daughter of German immigrants. While still an undergraduate at Smith College, she published in* Seventeen *and* Mademoiselle; *but her years at college, like her later years, were marked by manic-depressive periods.After graduating from college, she went to England to study at Cambridge University, where she met the English poet Ted Hughes, whom she married in 1956. The marriage was unsuccessful, and they separated. One day she committed suicide by turning on the kitchen gas.*

## *Metaphors*    [1960]

I'm a riddle in nine syllables,
An elephant, a ponderous house,
A melon strolling on two tendrils.
O red fruit, ivory, fine timbers!
This loaf's big with its yeasty rising.    5
Money's new-minted in this fat purse.
I'm a means, a stage, a cow in calf.
I've eaten a bag of green apples,
Boarded the train there's no getting off.

## ▓ TOPIC FOR
## CRITICAL THINKING AND WRITING

The riddling speaker says that she is, among other things, "a ponderous house" and "a cow in calf."What is she?

# SIMILE

In a **simile,** items from different classes are explicitly compared by a connective such as *like, as,* or *than* or by a verb such as *appears* or *seems.* (If the objects compared are from the same class—for example, "New York is like Chicago"—no simile is present.)

Sometimes I feel like a motherless child.

—Anonymous

It is a beauteous evening, calm and free.
The holy time is quiet as a Nun,
Breathless with adoration.

—Wordsworth

How sharper than a serpent's tooth it is
To have a thankless child.

—Shakespeare

Seems he a dove? His feathers are but borrowed.

Shakespeare

# RICHARD WILBUR

*Richard Wilbur, born in New York City in 1921, was educated at Amherst and Harvard. He served in the army during World War II and in 1947 published* The Beautiful Changes, *a book of poems that reflected some of his experience in Europe. This book and subsequent books of poetry established his literary reputation, but probably his most widely known works are the lyrics that he wrote for Leonard Bernstein's musical version of* Candide *(1956). In 1987 the Library of Congress named him U.S. Poet Laureate.*

## A Simile for Her Smile

[1950]

Your smiling, or the hope, the thought of it,
Makes in my mind such pause and abrupt ease
As when the highway bridgegates fall,
Balking the hasty traffic, which must sit
On each side massed and staring, while                    5
Deliberately the drawbridge starts to rise:

Then horns are hushed, the oilsmoke rarifies,
Above the idling motors one can tell
The packet's smooth approach, the slip,
Slip of the silken river past the sides,                    10
The ringing of clear bells, the dip
And slow cascading of the paddle wheel.

## ▦ TOPIC FOR
## CRITICAL THINKING AND WRITING

The title may lead you to think that the poet will compare the woman's smile to something. But, in fact, the comparison is not between her smile and the passing scene. What *is* being compared to the traffic?

# METAPHOR

A **metaphor** asserts the identity, without a connective such as *like* or a verb such as *appears,* of terms that are literally incompatible.

She is the rose, the glory of the day.

—Spenser

O western orb sailing the heaven.

—Whitman

Notice how in the second example only one of the terms ("orb") is stated; the other ("ship") is implied in "sailing."

# JOHN KEATS

*John Keats (1795-1821), son of a London stable keeper, was taken out of school when he was fifteen and apprenticed to a surgeon and apothecary. In 1816 he was licensed to practice as an apothecary-surgeon, but he almost immediately abandoned medicine and decided to make a career as a poet. His progress was amazing; he quickly moved from routine verse to major accomplishments, publishing books of poems—to mixed reviews—in 1817, 1818, and 1820, before dying of tuberculosis at the age of twenty-five.*

## *On First Looking into Chapman's Homer**     [1816]

Much have I traveled in the realms of gold,
And many goodly states and kingdoms seen;
Round many western islands have I been

---

*George Chapman (1559-1634?), Shakespeare's contemporary, is chiefly known for his translations (from the Greek) of Homer's *Odyssey* and *Iliad*. In lines 11-14 Keats mistakenly says that Cortés was the first European to see the Pacific, from the heights of Darien, in Panama. In fact, Balboa was the first.

Which bards in fealty to Apollo° hold.
Oft of one wide expanse have I been told                    5
That deep-browed Homer ruled as his demesne;°
Yet did I never breathe its pure serene°
Till I heard Chapman speak out loud and bold:
Then felt I like some watcher of the skies
When a new planet swims into his ken;                      10
Or like stout Cortez when with eagle eyes
He stared at the Pacific—and all his men
Looked at each other with a wild surmise—
Silent, upon a peak in Darien.

---

**4 Apollo** god of poetry.   **6 demesne** domain.
**7 serene** open space.

## ◼ TOPICS FOR CRITICAL THINKING AND WRITING

1. In line 1, what do you think "realms of gold" stands for? Chapman was an Elizabethan; how does this fact add relevance to the metaphor in the first line?
2. Does line 9 introduce a totally new idea, or can you somehow connect it to the opening metaphor?

Two types of metaphor deserve special mention. In **metonymy,** something is named that replaces something closely related to it; "City Hall," for example, sometimes is used to stand for municipal authority. In the following passage James Shirley names certain objects (scepter and crown; scythe and spade), using them to replace social classes (royalty; agricultural labor) to which they are related:

> Scepter and crown must tumble down
> And in the dust be equal made
> With the poor crooked scythe and spade.

In **synecdoche,** the whole is replaced by the part, or the part by the whole. For example, *bread* in "Give us this day our daily bread" replaces the whole class of edibles. Similarly, an automobile can be "wheels," and workers are "hands." Robert Frost was fond of calling himself "a Synecdochist" because he believed that it is the nature of poetry to "have intimations of something more than itself. It almost always comes under the head of synecdoche, a part, a hem of the garment for the whole garment."

# PERSONIFICATION

The attribution of human feelings or characteristics to abstractions or to inanimate objects is called **personification**.

> But Time did beckon to the flowers, and they
> By noon most cunningly did steal away.
>
> —Herbert

Herbert attributes a human gesture to Time and shrewdness to flowers. Of all figures, personification most surely gives to airy nothings a local habitation and a name:

> There's Wrath who has learnt every trick of guerrilla warfare,
> The shamming dead, the night-raid, the feinted retreat.
>
> —Auden

> Hope, thou bold taster of delight.
>
> —Crashaw

> The alarm clock meddling in somebody's sleep.
>
> —Brooks

> . . . neon script leering from the shuddering asphalt.
>
> —Dove

In the next poem, the speaker, addressing a former mistress ("come let us kiss and part"), seems to grant that their love is over—is dying—and he personifies this love, this passion, as a person on his deathbed ("Now at last gasp of Love's latest breath"). Further, he surrounds the dying Love with two mourners, Faith, who is kneeling by Love's bed, and Innocence, who is closing Love's eyes. But notice that the poem takes a sudden twist at the end where, it seems, Love may not have to die.

## MICHAEL DRAYTON

*Michael Drayton (1563–1631) was born in Warwickshire in England a year before Shakespeare, and like Shakespeare he wrote sonnets. Among his other works is a long poem on the geography and local lore of England.*

### Since There's No Help                                         [1619]

Since there's no help, come let us kiss and part;
Nay, I have done, you get no more of me,
And I am glad, yea glad with all my heart

That thus so cleanly I myself can free; 4
Shake hands for ever, cancel all our vows,
And when we meet at any time again,
Be it not seen in either of our brows
That we one jot of former love retain. 8
Now at the last gasp of Love's latest breath,
When, his pulse failing, Passion speechless lies,
When Faith is kneeling by his bed of death,
And Innocence is closing up his eyes, 12
    Now if thou wouldst, when all have given him over,
    From death to life you mightst him yet recover.

## ▓ TOPICS FOR CRITICAL THINKING AND WRITING

1. What do you think is the tone of lines 1–8? What words especially establish this tone? What do you think is the tone of lines 9–14?
2. Some readers find the personifications in lines 9–12 a sign that the speaker is not deeply moved, and perhaps is putting on an act. Do you agree or not? Please explain.

# APOSTROPHE

Crashaw's personification, "Hope, thou bold taster of delight," quoted a moment ago, is also an example of the figure of speech called **apostrophe,** an address to a person or thing not literally listening. Wordsworth begins a sonnet by apostrophizing John Milton:

    Milton, thou shouldst be living at this hour,

And Shelley begins an ode by apostrophizing a skylark:

    Hail to thee, blithe Spirit!

The following poem is largely built on apostrophe.

## EDMUND WALLER

*Edmund Waller (1606–1687), born into a country family of wealth in Buckinghamshire in England, attended Eton and Cambridge before spending most of his life as a member of Parliament. When the Puritans came to power, he was imprisoned and eventually banished to France, although he was soon allowed to return to England. When the monarchy was restored to the throne, he returned to Parliament.*

## Song

[1645]

Go, lovely rose,
Tell her that wastes her time and me,
    That now she knows,
When I resemble her to thee,
    How sweet and fair she seems to be.    5

Tell her that's young,
And shuns to have her graces spied,
    That hadst thou sprung
In deserts where no men abide,
    Thou must have uncommended died.    10

Small is the worth
Of beauty from the light retired:
    Bid her come forth,
Suffer her self to be desired,
    And not blush so to be admired.    15

Then die, that she
The common fate of all things rare
    May read in thee,
How small a part of time they share,
    That are so wondrous sweet and fair.    20

What conclusions, then, can we draw about **figurative language?** First, figurative language, with its literally incompatible terms, forces the reader to attend to the **connotations** (suggestions, associations) rather than to the **denotations** (dictionary definitions) of one of the terms.

Second, although figurative language is said to differ from ordinary discourse, it is found in ordinary discourse as well as in literature. "It rained cats and dogs," "War is hell," "Don't be a pig," and other tired figures are part of our daily utterances. But through repeated use, these (and most of the figures we use) have lost whatever impact they once had and are only a shade removed from expressions that, though once figurative, have become literal: the *eye* of a needle, a *branch* office, the *face* of a clock.

Third, good figurative language is usually (1) concrete, (2) condensed, and (3) interesting. The concreteness lends precision and vividness; when Keats writes that he felt "like some watcher of the skies / When a new planet swims into his ken," he more sharply characterizes his feelings than if he had said, "I felt excited." His simile isolates for us a precise kind of excitement, and the metaphoric "swims" vividly brings up the oceanic aspect of the sky. The second of these three qualities, condensation, can be seen by attempting to paraphrase some of the figures. A paraphrase or rewording will commonly use more words than the original and will have less impact—as the gradual coming of night usually has less impact on us than a sudden darkening of the sky, or as a prolonged push has less impact than a sudden blow. The third quality, interest, largely depends on the previous two: the successful figure often makes us open our eyes wider and take notice. Keats's "deep-browed Homer" arouses our interest in Homer as "thoughtful Homer" or "meditative Homer" does not. Similarly, when W. B. Yeats says (p. 583):

> An aged man is but a paltry thing,
> A tattered coat upon a stick, unless
> Soul clap its hands and sing, and louder sing
> For every tatter in its mortal dress,

the metaphoric identification of an old man with a scarecrow jolts us out of all our usual unthinking attitudes about old men as kind, happy folk content to have passed from youth to senior citizenship.

Finally, the point must be made that although figurative language is one of the poet's chief tools, a poem does not have to contain figures. Robert Frost's "The Pasture" (p. 538) contains no figures, yet surely it is a poem, and no one would say that the addition of figures would make it a better poem.

Here is a poem by William Carlos Williams. Does it contain any figures of speech?

# WILLIAM CARLOS WILLIAMS

*William Carlos Williams (1883–1963) was the son of an English traveling salesman and a Basque-Jewish woman. The couple met in Puerto Rico and settled in Rutherford, New Jersey, where Williams was born. He spent his life there, practicing as a pediatrician and writing poems in the moments between seeing patients who were visiting his office.*

## The Red Wheelbarrow [1923]

so much depends
upon

a red wheel
barrow

4

glazed with rain
water

beside the white
chickens.                                                                    8

---

The following poems rely heavily on figures of speech.

# DANA GIOIA

*Dana Gioia (pronounced "JOY uh"), born in 1950, was named chair
of the National Endowment for the Arts. in 2002. He is a poet and the
co-author of a textbook on literature, and he has also had a successful
career as a businessman.*

## Money                                                                  [1991]

*Money is a kind of poetry.*

—Wallace Stevens

Money, the long green,
cash, stash, rhino, jack
or just plain dough.

Chock it up, fork it over,
shell it out. Watch it                                                      5
burn holes through pockets.

To be made of it! To have it
to burn! Greenbacks, double eagles,
megabucks and Ginnie Maes.

It greases the palm, feathers a nest,                                       10
holds heads above water,
makes both ends meet.

Money breeds money.
Gathering interest, compounding daily.
Always in circulation                                                       15

Money. You don't know where it's been,
but you put it where your mouth is.
And it talks.

# ❖ TOPICS FOR CRITICAL THINKING AND WRITING

1. Are any of the terms in the poem unfamiliar to you? If so, check a dictionary, and if you don't find an explanation in a dictionary, turn to other resources—the Internet, and friends and classmates. Do some of the terms come from particular worlds of discourse—for instance, banking, gambling, or drug dealing?
2. Suppose the last stanza had been placed first. Would the poem be better? Or worse? Why?
3. Write a somewhat comparable poem on a topic of your choice—for instance, students, teachers, athletes, or work.

# WILLIAM SHAKESPEARE

*You will encounter Shakespeare (1564-1616) several times in this book—for instance, as the author of songs, sonnets, and a tragedy.*

*Here we give one of his sonnets (probably written in the mid-1590s), in which he playfully rejects similes and other figures of speech. His contemporaries often compared a woman's hair to fine spun gold, her lips to coral or to cherries, her cheeks to roses, her white breast to snow; when such a woman walked, she seemed to walk on air (the grass did not bend beneath her), and when she spoke, her voice was music. Shakespeare himself uses such figures in some of his poems and plays, but in this sonnet he praises his beloved by saying she does not need such figures.*

## Sonnet 130

My mistress' eyes are nothing like the sun;
Coral is far more red than her lips' red;
If snow be white, why then her breasts are dun;
If hairs be wires, black wires grow on her head.    4
I have seen roses damasked, red and white,
But no such roses see I in her cheeks;
And in some perfumes is there more delight
Than in the breath that from my mistress reeks.    8
I love to hear her speak, yet well I know
That music hath a far more pleasing sound;
I grant I never saw a goddess go;°

---

**11 go** walk.

My mistress, when she walks, treads on the ground.                    12
And yet, by heaven, I think my love as rare°
As any she belied° with false compare.

---

**13 rare** exceptional.   **14 any she belied** any woman misrepresented.

## ▦ TOPIC FOR
## CRITICAL THINKING AND WRITING

As we said a moment ago, Shakespeare here seems to ridicule figurative language, yet he uses figurative language in his sonnets and his
plays. How can this be explained?

# LORNA DEE CERVANTES

*Lorna Dee Cervantes, born in San Francisco in 1954, founded a press
and a poetry magazine,* Mango, *chiefly devoted to Chicano literature. In
1978 she received a fellowship from the National Endowment for the
Arts, and in 1981 she published her first book of poems. "Refugee Ship,"
originally written in 1974, was revised for the book. We print the revised
version.*

## *Refugee Ship*                                              [1981]

Like wet cornstarch, I slide
past my grandmother's eyes. Bible
at her side, she removes her glasses.
The pudding thickens.

Mama raised me without language.                                    5
I'm orphaned from my Spanish name.
The words are foreign, stumbling
on my tongue. I see in the mirror
my reflection: bronzed skin, black hair.

I feel I am a captive                                              10
aboard the refugee ship.
The ship that will never dock.
*El barco que nunca atraca.*°

---

**13 *El barco que nunca atraca*** The ship that never docks.

### ▨ TOPICS FOR
### CRITICAL THINKING AND WRITING

1. What do you think the speaker means by the comparison with "wet cornstarch" in line 1? And what do you take her to mean in line 6 when she says, "I'm orphaned from my Spanish name"?

2. Judging from the poem as a whole, why does the speaker feel she is "a captive / aboard the refugee ship"? How would you characterize such feelings?

3. In an earlier version of the poem, instead of "my grandmother's eyes" Cervantes wrote "*mi abuelita's* eyes"; that is, she used the Spanish words for "my grandmother." In line 5 instead of "Mama" she wrote "*mamá*" (again, the Spanish equivalent), and in line 9 she wrote "brown skin" instead of "bronzed skin." The final line of her original version was not in Spanish but in English, a repetition of the preceding line, which ran thus: "A ship that will never dock." How does each of these changes strike you?

CHAPTER

# 16

# Imagery and Symbolism

When we read the word "rose"—or, for that matter, "finger" or "thumb"—we may more or less call to mind a picture, an image. The term **imagery** is used to refer to whatever in a poem appeals to any of our sensations, including sensations of pressure and heat as well as of sight, smell, taste, touch, and sound.

Edmund Waller's rose in "Go, Lovely Rose" (page 450) is an image that happens to be compared in the first stanza to a woman ("I resemble her to thee"); later in the poem this image comes to stand for "all things rare." Yet we never forget that the rose is a rose, and that the poem is chiefly a revelation of the poet's attitude toward his beloved.

If a poet says "my rose" and is speaking about a rose, we have an image, even though we do not have a figure of speech. If a poet says "my rose" and, we gather, is speaking not really or chiefly about a rose but about something else—let's say the transience of beauty—we can say that the poet is using the rose as a symbol.

Some symbols are **natural symbols,** recognized as standing for something in particular even by people from different cultures. Rain, for instance, usually stands for fertility or the renewal of life. A forest often stands for mental darkness or chaos, a mountain for stability, a valley for a place of security, and so on. There are many exceptions, but by and large these meanings prevail.

Other symbols, however, are **conventional symbols,** which people have agreed to accept as standing for something other than themselves: A poem about the cross would probably be about Christianity. Similarly, the rose has long been a symbol for love. In Virginia Woolf's novel *Mrs. Dalloway,* the husband communicates his love by proffering this conventional symbol: "He was holding out flowers—roses, red and white roses. (But he could not bring himself to say he loved her; not in so many words.)" Objects that are not conventional symbols, however, also may give rise to rich, multiple, indefinable associations. The following poem uses the symbol of the rose, but uses it in a nontraditional way.

# WILLIAM BLAKE

*A biography of Blake, followed by three additional poems, appears on page 573.*

## The Sick Rose

[1794]

O rose, thou are sick!
The invisible worm
That flies in the night
In the howling storm                                                    4

Has found out thy bed
Of crimson joy,
And his dark secret love
Does thy life destroy.                                                  8

---

One might argue that the worm is "invisible" (line 2) merely because it is hidden within the rose, but an "invisible worm / That flies in the night" is more than a long, slender, soft-bodied creeping animal; and a rose that has, or is, a "bed / Of crimson joy" is more than a gardener's rose.

Blake's worm and rose suggest things beyond themselves—a stranger, more vibrant world than the world we are usually aware of. Many readers find themselves half-thinking, for example, that the worm is male, the rose female, and that the poem is about the violation of virginity. Or that the poem is about the destruction of beauty: woman's beauty, rooted in joy, is destroyed by a power that feeds on her. But these interpretations are not fully satisfying: the poem presents a worm and a rose, and yet it is not merely about a worm and a rose. These objects resonate, stimulating our thoughts toward something else, but the something else is elusive, whereas it is not elusive in Burns's "A Red, Red Rose" (page 442).

A **symbol**, then, is an image so loaded with significance that it is not simply literal, and it does not simply stand for something else; it is both itself *and* something else that it richly suggests, a manifestation of something too complex or too elusive to be otherwise revealed. Blake's poem is about a blighted rose and at the same time about much more. In a symbol, as Thomas Carlyle wrote, "the Infinite is made to blend with the Finite, to stand visible, and as it were, attainable there." Probably it is not fanciful to say that the American slaves who sang "Joshua fought the battle of Jericho, / And the walls came tumbling down" were singing both about an ancient occurrence *and* about a new embodiment of the ancient, the imminent collapse of slavery in the nineteenth century. Not one or the other, but both: the present partook of the past, and the past partook of the present.

# WALT WHITMAN

*Walt Whitman (1819-1892) was born in a farmhouse in rural Long Island, New York, but was brought up in Brooklyn, then an independent city in New York. He attended public school for a few years (1825-1830), apprenticed as a printer in the 1830s, and then worked as a typesetter, journalist, and newspaper editor. In 1855 he published the first edition of a collection of his poems,* Leaves of Grass, *a book that he revised and published in one edition after another throughout the remainder of his life. During the Civil War he served as a volunteer nurse for the Union army.*

*In the third edition of* Leaves of Grass *(1860), Whitman added two groups of poems, one called "Children of Adam" and the other (named for an aromatic grass that grows near ponds and swamps) called "Calamus." "Children of Adam" celebrates heterosexual relations, whereas "Calamus" celebrates what Whitman called "manly love." Although many of the "Calamus" poems seem clearly homosexual, perhaps the very fact that Whitman published them made them seem relatively innocent; in any case, those nineteenth-century critics who condemned Whitman for the sexuality of his writing concentrated on the poems in "Children of Adam."*

*"I Saw in Louisiana" is from the "Calamus" section. It was originally published in the third edition of* Leaves of Grass *and was revised into its final form in the 1867 edition. We give it in the 1867 version. We also give the manuscript, showing it in its earliest extant version.*

## I Saw in Louisiana a Live-Oak Growing                [1867]

I saw in Louisiana a live-oak growing,
All alone stood it and the moss hung down from the branches,
Without any companion it grew there uttering joyous leaves
    of dark green,
And its look, rude, unbending, lusty, made me think of myself,
But I wonder'd how it could utter joyous leaves standing alone there
    without its friend near, for I knew I could not,          5
And I broke off a twig with a certain number of leaves upon it,
    and twined around it a little moss,
And brought it away, and I have placed it in sight in my room,
It is not needed to remind me as of my own dear friends,
(For I believe lately I think of little else than of them,)
Yet it remains to me a curious token, it makes me think of manly love;   10
For all that, and though the live-oak glistens there in Louisiana
    solitary in a wide flat space,
Uttering joyous leaves all its life without a friend a lover near,
I know very well I could not.

Walt Whitman, "I Saw in Louisiana a Live-Oak Growing," manuscript of 1860. On the first leaf, in line 3 Whitman deleted "with." On the second leaf (see page 460), in the third line (line 8 of the printed text) he added, with a caret, "lately." In the sixth line on this leaf he deleted "I write these pieces, and name them after it," replacing the deletion with "it makes me think of manly love." In the next line he deleted "tree" and inserted "live oak." When he reprinted the poem in the 1867 version of *Leaves of Grass*, he made further changes, as you will see if you compare the printed text with this manuscript version.

It is not needed to remind
me as of my friends, (for I
believe lately think of little
else than of them,)
Yet it remains to me a
curious token — it makes
~~me think of man love,~~
~~these pieces and name~~
~~them after it~~ ;
For all that, and though the
~~live oak tree~~ glistens there in Louis:
iana, solitary in a wide
flat space, uttering joyous
leaves all its life, without
a friend, a lover, near — I
know very well I could
not.

ठ

## TOPIC FOR
## CRITICAL THINKING AND WRITING

Compare the final version (1867) of the poem with the manuscript
version of 1860. Which version do you prefer? Why?

# SAMUEL TAYLOR COLERIDGE

*Samuel Taylor Coleridge (1772-1834) was born in Devonshire in England, the son of a clergyman. He attended Christ's Hospital school in London and Cambridge University, which he left without receiving a degree. With his friend William Wordsworth in 1798 he published, anonymously, a volume of poetry,* Lyrical Ballads, *which became the manifesto of the Romantic movement.*

## Kubla Khan

[1798]

Or, A Vision in a Dream. A Fragment.

In Xanadu did Kubla Khan
A stately pleasure-dome decree:
Where Alph, the sacred river, ran
Through caverns measureless to man
    Down to a sunless sea.                                    5
So twice five miles of fertile ground
With walls and towers were girdled round:
And here were gardens bright with sinuous rills,
Where blossomed many an incense-bearing tree;
And here were forests ancient as the hills,                       10
Enfolding sunny spots of greenery.

But oh! that deep romantic chasm which slanted
Down the green hill athwart a cedarn cover!
A savage place! as holy and enchanted
As e'er beneath a waning moon was haunted                        15
By woman wailing for her demon-lover!
And from this chasm, with ceaseless turmoil seething,
As if this earth in fast thick pants were breathing
A mighty fountain momently was forced;
Amid whose swift half-intermitted burst                          20
Huge fragments vaulted like rebounding hail,
Or chaffy grain beneath the thresher's flail:
And 'mid these dancing rocks at once and ever
It flung up momently the sacred river.
Five miles meandering with a mazy motion                         25
Through wood and dale the sacred river ran,
Then reached the caverns measureless to man,
And sank in tumult to a lifeless ocean:
And 'mid this tumult Kubla heard from far
Ancestral voices prophesying war!                                30

The shadow of the dome of pleasure
Floated midway on the waves;
Where was heard the mingled measure
From the fountain and the caves.
It was a miracle of rare device,                                    35
A sunny pleasure-dome with caves of ice!
    A damsel with a dulcimer
    In a vision once I saw:
    It was an Abyssinian maid,
    And on her dulcimer she played,                                40
    Singing of Mount Abora.
    Could I revive within me
    Her symphony and song,
    To such a deep delight 'twould win me,
That with music loud and long,                                     45
I would build that dome in air,
That sunny dome! those caves of ice!
And all who heard should see them there,
And all should cry, Beware! Beware!
His flashing eyes, his floating hair!                              50
Weave a circle round him thrice,
And close your eyes with holy dread,
For he on honey-dew hath fed,
And drunk the milk of Paradise.

---

When Coleridge published "Kubla Khan" in 1816, he prefaced it with this
explanatory note:

> The following fragment is here published at the request of a poet of
> great and deserved celebrity, and, as far as the author's own opinions
> are concerned, rather as a psychological curiosity, than on the ground
> of any supposed *poetic* merits.
>
>     In the summer of the year 1797, the author, then in ill health, had
> retired to a lonely farmhouse between Porlock and Linton, on the Ex-
> moor confines of Somerset and Devonshire. In consequence of a
> slight indisposition, an anodyne had been prescribed, from the effects
> of which he fell asleep in his chair at the moment that he was reading
> the following sentence, or words of the same substance, in *Purchas'
> Pilgrimage:* "Here the Khan Kubla commanded a palace to be built,
> and a stately garden thereunto. And thus ten miles of fertile ground
> were inclosed with a wall." The author continued for about three
> hours in a profound sleep, at least of the external senses, during
> which time he has the most vivid confidence that he could not have
> composed less than from two to three hundred lines; if that indeed

can be called composition in which all the images rose up before him as *things,* with a parallel production of the correspondent expressions, without any sensation or consciousness of effort. On awaking he appeared to himself to have a distinct recollection of the whole, and taking his pen, ink, and paper, instantly and eagerly wrote down the lines that are here preserved. At this moment he was unfortunately called out by a person on business from Porlock, and detained by him above an hour, and on his return to his room, found, to his no small surprise and mortification, that though he still retained some vague and dim recollection of the general purport of the vision, yet, with the exception of some eight or ten scattered lines and images, all the rest had passed away like the images on the surface of a stream into which a stone has been cast, but, alas! without the after restoration of the latter!

Then all the charm
Is broken— all that phantom world so fair
Vanishes, and a thousand circlets spread,
And each misshape[s] the other. Stay awhile,
Poor youth! who scarcely dar'st lift up thine eyes—
The stream will soon renew its smoothness, soon
The visions will return! And lo, he stays,
And soon the fragments dim of lovely forms
Come trembling back, unite, and now once more
The pool becomes a mirror.
                —Coleridge, *The Picture; or, the Lover's Resolution,*
                                        lines 91–100

Yet from the still surviving recollections in his mind, the author has frequently purposed to finish for himself what had been originally, as it were, given to him. Σαμερου αδιου ασω [today I shall sing more sweetly]:"But the tomorrow is yet to come."

## ❖ TOPICS FOR CRITICAL THINKING AND WRITING

1. Coleridge changed the "palace" of his source into a "dome" (line 2). What do you think are the relevant associations of "dome"?
2. What pairs of contrasts (e.g., underground river, fountain) do you find? What do you think they contribute to the poem?
3. If Coleridge had not said that the poem is a fragment, might you take it as a complete poem, the first thirty-six lines describing the creative imagination, and the remainder lamenting the loss of poetic power?

# CLAUDE McKAY

*Claude McKay (1889–1948), born in Jamaica, briefly served as a police officer in Jamaica, published two books of dialect poems in 1912, and in the same year left Jamaica forever—although, as the poem we reprint shows, it remained a source of inspiration. In the United States he studied briefly at Tuskegee Institute, then for two years at Kansas State University, and then went to New York, writing poems and working on a radical journal, The Liberator. In 1922 he visited Russia, and from 1923 to 1934 he lived abroad, chiefly in France and North Africa, writing fiction and journalism as well as poetry. He returned to the United States, recanted his Communist beliefs, and in 1945 converted to Catholicism. He then wrote a good deal of prose and poetry that did not get published in his lifetime.*

*Although the earliest poems were in dialect, McKay quickly repudiated such diction; his later work uses traditional diction and traditional British poetic forms (here, three quatrains, with alternating rhymes), in contrast to the vernacular language used by his contemporary, Langston Hughes.*

## The Tropics in New York                                    [1922]

Bananas ripe and green, and ginger-root,
    Cocoa in pods and alligator pears,
And tangerines and mangoes and grape fruit,
    Fit for the highest prize at parish fairs,                    4

Set in the window, bringing memories
    Of fruit-trees laden by low-singing rills,
And dewy dawns, and mystical blue skies
    In benediction over nun-like hills.                           8

My eyes grew dim, and I could no more gaze;
    A wave of longing through my body swept,
And, hungry for the old, familiar ways,
    I turned aside and bowed my head and wept.                   12

## ▓ TOPICS FOR
## CRITICAL THINKING AND WRITING

1. Describe as fully as possible the effect of the details given in the first three lines. What kind of basis or foundation do these details establish for the rest of the poem?

2. What is the purpose of the religious terms and images that the poet uses?
3. Is the poem sentimental? If it is sentimental, is that a bad thing? Why, or why not?

# ADRIENNE RICH

*Adrienne Rich's most recent books of poetry are* The School Among the Ruins: Poems 2000–2004, *and* Fox: Poems 1998–2000 *(Norton). A selection of her essays,* Arts of the Possible: Essays and Conversations, *was published in 2001. A new edition of* What Is Found There: Notebooks on Poetry and Policitics, *appeared in 2003. She is a recipient of the Lannan Foundation Lifetime Achievement Award, the Lambda Book Award, the Lenore Marshall/Nation Prize, the Wallace Stevens Award, and the Bollingen Prize in Poetry, among other honors. She lives in California.*

## Diving into the Wreck                          [1973]

First having read the book of myths,
and loaded the camera,
and checked the edge of the knife-blade,
I put on
the body-armor of black rubber                                5
the absurd flippers
the grave and awkward mask.
I am having to do this
not like Cousteau° with his
assiduous team                                               10
aboard the sun-flooded schooner
but here alone.

There is a ladder.
The ladder is always there
hanging innocently                                           15
close to the side of the schooner.
We know what it is for,
we who have used it.
Otherwise
it's a piece of maritime floss                               20
some sundry equipment.

---

**9 Jacques Cousteau** (1910–97) French underwater explorer.

I go down.
Rung after rung and still
the oxygen immerses me
the blue light                                              25
the clear atoms
of our human air.
I go down.
My flippers cripple me,
I crawl like an insect down the ladder               30
and there is no one
to tell me when the ocean
will begin.

First the air is blue and then
it is bluer and then green and then               35
black I am blacking out and yet
my mask is powerful
it pumps my blood with power
the sea is another story
the sea is not a question of power               40
I have to learn alone
to turn my body without force
in the deep element.

And now: it is easy to forget
what I came for                                              45
among so many who have always
lived here
swaying their crenellated fans
between the reefs
and besides                                                    50
you breathe differently down here.

I came to explore the wreck.
The words are purposes.
The words are maps.
I came to see the damage that was done       55
and the treasures that prevail.
I stroke the beam of my lamp
slowly along the flank
of something more permanent
than fish or weed                                           60

the thing I came for:
the wreck and not the story of the wreck
the thing itself and not the myth

the drowned face always staring
toward the sun                                                        65
the evidence of damage
worn by salt and sway into this threadbare beauty
the ribs of the disaster
curving their assertion
among the tentative haunters.                              70

This is the place.
And I am here, the mermaid whose dark hair
streams black, the merman in his armored body
We circle silently
about the wreck                                                    75
we dive into the hold.
I am she: I am he

whose drowned face sleeps with open eyes
whose breasts still bear the stress
whose silver, copper, vermeil cargo lies      80
obscurely inside barrels
half-wedged and left to rot
we are the half-destroyed instruments
that once held to a course
the water-eaten log                                             85
the fouled compass

We are, I am, you are
by cowardice or courage
the one who find our way
back to this scene                                               90
carrying a knife, a camera
a book of myths
in which
our names do not appear.

# CHRISTINA ROSSETTI

*Christina Rossetti (1830–1894) was the daughter of an exiled Italian
patriot who lived in London and the sister of the poet and painter
Dante Gabriel Rossetti. After her father became an invalid, she led an
extremely ascetic life, devoting most of her life to doing charitable work.
Her first and best-known volume of poetry,* Goblin Market and Other
Poems, *was published in 1862.*

## Uphill    [1858]

Does the road wind uphill all the way?
　Yes, to the very end.
Will the day's journey take the whole long day?
　From morn to night, my friend.    4

But is there for the night a resting-place?
　A roof for when the slow dark hours begin.
May not the darkness hide it from my face?
　You cannot miss that inn.    8

Shall I meet other wayfarers at night?
　Those who have gone before.
Then must I knock, or call when just in sight?
　They will not keep you standing at that door.    12

Shall I find comfort, travel-sore and weak?
　Of labor you shall find the sum.
Will there be beds for me and all who seek?
　Yea, beds for all who come.    16

## ▓ TOPICS FOR
## CRITICAL THINKING AND WRITING

1. Suppose that someone told you this poem is about a person preparing to go on a hike. The person is supposedly making inquiries about
   the road and the possible hotel arrangements. What would you reply?
2. Who is the questioner? A woman? A man? All human beings collectively? "Uphill" does not use quotation marks to distinguish between
   two speakers. Can one say that in "Uphill" the questioner and the an-
   swerer are the same person?
3. Are the answers unambiguously comforting? Or can it, for instance,
   be argued that the "roof" is (perhaps among other things) the lid of a
   coffin—hence the questioner will certainly not be kept "standing at
   that door"? If the poem can be read along these lines, is it chilling
   rather than comforting?

# 17

# Irony

There is a kind of discourse which, though nonliteral, need not use similes, metaphors, apostrophes, personification, or symbols. Without using these figures, speakers may say things that are not to be taken literally. They may, in short, employ **irony.**

In Greek comedy, the *eiron* was the sly underdog who, by dissembling inferiority, outwitted his opponent. As Aristotle puts it, irony (employed by the *eiron*) is a "pretense tending toward the underside" of truth. Later, Cicero somewhat altered the meaning of the word: He defined it as saying one thing and meaning another, and he held that Socrates, who feigned ignorance and let his opponents entrap themselves in their own arguments, was the perfect example of an ironist.

In **verbal irony,** as the term is now used, what is *stated* is in some degree negated by what is *suggested*. A classic example is Lady Macbeth's order to get ready for King Duncan's visit: "He that's coming / Must be provided for." The words seem to say that she and Macbeth must busy themselves with household preparations so that the king may be received in appropriate style, but this suggestion of hospitality is undercut by an opposite meaning: preparations must be made for the murder of the king. Two other examples of verbal irony are Melville's comment

> What like a bullet can undeceive!

and the lover's assertion (in Marvell's "To His Coy Mistress") that

> The grave's a fine and private place,
> But none, I think, do there embrace.

Under Marvell's cautious words ("I think") we detect a wryness; the **understatement** masks yet reveals a deep-felt awareness of mortality and the barrenness of the grave. The self-mockery in this understatement proclaims modesty, but suggests assurance. The speaker here, like most ironists, is both playful and serious at once. Irony packs a great deal into a few words.* What we call irony here, it should be mentioned, is often called **sarcasm,** but a distinction can be made: sarcasm is notably contemptuous and crude or heavy-handed ("You're a great guy, a real friend," said to a friend who won't lend you ten dollars). Sarcasm is only one kind of irony, and a kind almost never found in literature.

**Overstatement (hyperbole),** like understatement, is ironic when it contains a contradictory suggestion:

> For Brutus is an honorable man;
> So are they all, all honorable men.

The sense of contradiction that is inherent in verbal irony is also inherent in a paradox. **Paradox** has several meanings for philosophers, but we need only be concerned with its meaning of an apparent contradiction. Some paradoxes are

> The child is father of the man;
>
> —Wordsworth

and (on the soldiers who died to preserve the British Empire)

> The saviors come not home tonight;
> Themselves they could not save;
>
> —Housman

and

> One short sleep past, we wake eternally,
> And Death shall be no more; Death, thou shalt die.
>
> —Donne

Donne's lines are a reminder that paradox is not only an instrument of the poet. Christianity embodies several paradoxes: God became a human being; through the death on the cross, human beings can obtain eternal life; human beings do not live fully until they die.

Some critics have put a high premium on ironic and paradoxical poetry. Briefly, their argument runs that great poetry recognizes the complexity of experience, and that irony and paradox are ways of doing justice to this complexity. I. A. Richards uses "irony" to denote "The bringing in of the opposite, the complementary impulses," and suggests (in *The Principles of Literary Criticism*) that irony in this sense is a characteristic of poetry of "the highest order." It is dubious that all poets must always bring in the opposite, but it is certain that much poetry is ironic and paradoxical.

---

*A word of caution: We have been talking about verbal irony, not **irony of situation.** Like ironic words, ironic situations have in them an element of contrast. A clown whose heart is breaking must make his audience laugh; an author's worst book is her only financial success; a fool solves a problem that vexes the wise.

# PERCY BYSSHE SHELLEY

*Percy Bysshe Shelley (1792-1822) was born in Sussex in England, the son of a prosperous country squire. Educated at Eton, he went on to Oxford but was expelled for having written a pamphlet supporting a belief in atheism. Like John Keats he was a member of the second generation of English romantic poets. (The first generation included Wordsworth and Coleridge.) And like Keats, Shelley died young; he was drowned during a violent storm off the coast of Italy while sailing with a friend.*

## Ozymandias                                                      [1817]

I met a traveler from an antique land
Who said: Two vast and trunkless legs of stone
Stand in the desert . . . Near them, on the sand,
Half sunk, a shattered visage lies, whose frown,
And wrinkled lip, and sneer of cold command,                      5
Tell that its sculptor well those passions read
Which yet survive, stamped on these lifeless things,
The hand that mocked them, and the heart that fed:
And on the pedestal these words appear:
"My name is Ozymandias, king of kings:                            10
Look on my works, ye Mighty, and despair!"
Nothing beside remains. Round the decay
Of that colossal wreck, boundless and bare
The lone and level sands stretch far away.

Lines 4-8 are somewhat obscure, but the gist is that the passions—still evident in the "shattered visage"—survive the sculptor's hand that "mocked"—that is, (1) imitated or copied, (2) derided—them, and the passions also survive the king's heart that had nourished them.

[※] TOPIC FOR CRITICAL THINKING AND WRITING

> There is an irony of plot here: Ozymandias believed that he created enduring works, but his intentions came to nothing. However, another irony is also present: How are his words, in a way he did not intend, true?

# ANDREW MARVELL

*Born in 1621 near Hull in England, Marvell attended Trinity College, Cambridge, and graduated in 1638. During the English Civil War he was tutor to the daughter of Sir Thomas Fairfax in Yorkshire at Nun Appleton House, where most of his best-known poems were written. In 1657 he was appointed assistant to John Milton, the Latin Secretary for the Commonwealth. After the Restoration of the monarchy in 1659, Marvell represented Hull as a member of Parliament until his death. Most of his poems were not published until after his death in 1678.*

## To His Coy Mistress [1681]

Had we but world enough, and time,
This coyness, lady, were no crime.
We would sit down, and think which way
To walk, and pass our long love's day.
Thou by the Indian Ganges' side                      5
Should'st rubies find: I by the tide
Of Humber would complain.° I would
Love you ten years before the Flood,
And you should, if you please, refuse
Till the conversion of the Jews.                     10
My vegetable° love should grow
Vaster than empires, and more slow.
An hundred years should go to praise
Thine eyes, and on thy forehead gaze:
Two hundred to adore each breast:                    15
But thirty thousand to the rest.
An age at least to every part,
And the last age should show your heart.
For, lady, you deserve this state,
Nor would I love at lower rate.                       20
    But at my back I always hear
Time's winged chariot hurrying near;
And yonder all before us lie
Deserts of vast eternity.
Thy beauty shall no more be found,                   25
Nor in thy marble vault shall sound
My echoing song; then worms shall try
That long preserved virginity,
And your quaint honor turn to dust,
And into ashes all my lust.                          30
The grave's a fine and private place,
But none, I think, do there embrace.
    Now therefore, while the youthful hue
Sits on thy skin like morning dew,

---

**7 complain** write love poems.    **11 vegetable** i.e., unconsciously growing.

And while thy willing soul transpires                          35
At every pore with instant fires,
Now let us sport us while we may;
And now, like am'rous birds of prey,
Rather at once our time devour,
Than languish in his slow-chapt° power,                        40
Let us roll all our strength, and all
Our sweetness, up into one ball;
And tear our pleasures with rough strife
Thorough° the iron gates of life.
Thus, though we cannot make our sun                            45
Stand still, yet we will make him run.

---

**40 slow-chapt** slowly devouring.    **44 Thorough** through.

## ▨ TOPICS FOR CRITICAL THINKING AND WRITING

1. Do you find the assertions in lines 1–20 so inflated that you detect behind them a playfully ironic tone? Explain. Why does the speaker say,
   in line 8, that he would love "ten years before the Flood," rather than
   merely "since the Flood"?
2. Explain lines 21–24. Why is time behind the speaker, and eternity in
   front of him? Is this "eternity" the same as the period discussed in
   lines 1–20? What do you make of the change in the speaker's tone after line 20?
3. Do you agree with the comment on page 469 about the understatement in lines 31–32? What more can you say about these lines, in
   context?
4. Why "am'rous birds of prey" (line 38) rather than the conventional
   doves? Is the idea of preying continued in the poem?
5. Try to explain the last two lines, and characterize the speaker's tone.
   Do you find these lines anticlimactic?
6. The poem is organized in the form of an argument. Trace the steps.

## JOHN DONNE

*John Donne (1572–1631) was born into a Roman Catholic family in
England, but in the 1590s he abandoned that faith. In 1615 he became
an Anglican priest and soon was known as a great preacher. Of his ser-
mons 160 survive, including one with the famous line, "No man is an
island, entire of itself; every man is a piece of the continent, a part of*

*the main; if a clod be washed away by the sea, Europe is the less . . . ;*
*and therefore never send to know for whom the bell tolls; it tolls for*
*thee." From 1621 until his death, Donne was dean of St. Paul's Cathe-*
*dral in London. His love poems (often bawdy and cynical) are said to*
*be his early work, and his "Holy Sonnets" (among the greatest religious*
*poems written in English) his later work.*

## Holy Sonnet XIV                                                [1633]

Batter my heart, three-personed God; for you
As yet but knock, breathe, shine, and seek to mend;
That I may rise and stand, o'erthrow me, and bend
Your force, to break, blow, burn, and make me new.
I, like an usurped town, to another due,                              5
Labor to admit you, but oh, to no end,
Reason, your viceroy in me, me should defend,
But is captived, and proves weak or untrue.
Yet dearly I love you, and would be loved fain,
But am betrothed unto your enemy:                                    10
Divorce me, untie, or break that knot again,
Take me to you, imprison me, for I
Except you enthrall me, never shall be free,
Nor ever chaste, except you ravish me.

## ▨ TOPICS FOR
## CRITICAL THINKING AND WRITING

1. Explain the paradoxes in lines 1, 3, 13, and 14. Explain the double
   meanings of "enthrall" (line 13) and "ravish" (line 14).
2. In lines 1-4, what is God implicitly compared to (considering especially lines 2 and 4)? How does this comparison lead into the comparison that dominates lines 5-8? What words in lines 9-12 are especially
   related to the earlier lines?
3. What do you think is gained by piling up verbs in lines 2-4?
4. Do you find sexual references irreverent in a religious poem? (As
   already mentioned, Donne was an Anglican priest.)

## MARTÍN ESPADA

*Martín Espada was born in Brooklyn in 1957. He received a bachelor's*
*degree from the University of Wisconsin and a law degree from North-*
*eastern University. He is now an associate professor of English at the*
*University of Massachusetts (Amherst).*

# Tony Went to the Bodega*
# but He Didn't Buy Anything

[1987]

*para Angel Guadalupe*

Tony's father left the family
and the Long Island city projects,
leaving a mongrel-skinny puertorriqueño boy
nine years old
who had to find work.                                              5

Makengo the Cuban
let him work at the bodega.
In grocery aisles
he learned the steps of the dry-mop mambo,
banging the cash register                                          10
like piano percussion
in the spotlight of Machito's orchestra,
polite with the abuelas° who bought on credit,
practicing the grin on customers
he'd seen Makengo grin                                             15
with his bad yellow teeth.

Tony left the projects too,
with a scholarship for law school.
But he cursed the cold primavera°
in Boston;                                                         20
the cooking of his neighbors
left no smell in the hallway
and no one spoke Spanish
(not even the radio).

So Tony walked without a map                                       25
through the city,
a landscape of hostile condominiums
and the darkness of white faces,
sidewalk-searcher lost
till he discovered the projects.                                   30

Tony went to the bodega
but he didn't buy anything:

---

*Bodega grocery and liquor store; in the dedication, after the title, *para* means "for."

13 abuelas grandmothers.    19 primavera spring season.

he sat by the doorway satisfied
to watch la gente° (people
island-brown as him)                                          35
crowd in and out,
hablando español,°
thought: this is beautiful,
and grinned
his bodega grin.                                             40

This is a rice and beans
success story:
today Tony lives on Tremont Street,
above the bodega.

_____

**34 la gente** the people.    **37 hablando español** speaking Spanish.

## ▦ TOPICS FOR CRITICAL THINKING AND WRITING

1. Why do you suppose Espada included the information about Tony's father? The information about young Tony "practicing" a grin?
2. Why does Tony leave?
3. How would you characterize Tony?

## EDNA ST. VINCENT MILLAY

*For other poems by the American poet Edna St. Vincent Millay (1892–1950) as well as a brief biography, see pages 415 and 584.*

### Love Is Not All: It Is Not Meat nor Drink                [1931]

Love is not all: it is not meat nor drink
Nor slumber nor a roof against the rain;
Nor yet a floating spar to men that sink
And rise and sink and rise and sink again;
Love can not fill the thickened lung with breath,         5
Nor clean the blood, nor set the fractured bone;
Yet many a man is making friends with death
Even as I speak, for lack of love alone.
It well may be that in a difficult hour,
Pinned down by pain and moaning for release,              10

Or nagged by want past resolution's power,
I might be driven to sell your love for peace,
Or trade the memory of this night for food.
It well may be. I do not think I would.

## ▒ TOPICS FOR
## CRITICAL THINKING AND WRITING

1. "Love Is Not All" is a sonnet. Using your own words, briefly summarize the argument of the octet (the first 8 lines). Next, paraphrase the sestet (the six lines from line 9 through line 14), line by line. On the whole, does the sestet repeat the idea of the octet, or does it add a new idea? Whom did you imagine to be speaking the octet? What does the sestet add to your knowledge of the speaker and the occasion? (And how did you paraphrase line 11?)
2. The first and last lines of the poem consist of words of one syllable, and both lines have a distinct pause in the middle. Do you imagine the lines to be spoken in the same tone of voice? If not, can you describe the difference and account for it?
3. Lines 7 and 8 appear to mean that the absence of love can be a cause of death. To what degree do you believe that to be true?
4. Would you call "Love Is Not All" a love poem? Why or why not? Describe the kind of person who might include the poem in a love letter or valentine, or who would be happy to receive it. (One of our friends recited it at her wedding. What do you think of that idea?)

## HENRY REED

*Born in Birmingham, England, Henry Reed (1914–1986) served in the British army during the Second World War. Later, in civilian life he had a distinguished career as a journalist, a translator of French and Italian literature, a writer of radio plays, and a poet.*

*"Naming of Parts" draws on his experience as a military recruit.*

## Naming of Parts                                                    [1946]

Today we have naming of parts. Yesterday,
We had daily cleaning. And tomorrow morning,
We shall have what to do after firing. But today,
Today we have naming of parts. Japonica
Glistens like coral in all of the neighboring gardens,          5
       And today we have naming of parts.

This is the lower sling swivel. And this
Is the upper sling swivel, whose use you will see,
When you are given your slings. And this is the piling swivel,
Which in your case you have not got. The branches                    10
Hold in the gardens their silent, eloquent gestures,
       Which in our case we have not got.

This is the safety-catch, which is always released
With an easy flick of the thumb. And please do not let me
See anyone using his finger. You can do it quite easy               15
If you have any strength in your thumb. The blossoms
Are fragile and motionless, never letting anyone see
       Any of them using their finger.

And this you can see is the bolt. The purpose of this
Is to open the breech, as you see. We can slide it                  20
Rapidly backwards and forwards: we call this
Easing the spring. And rapidly backwards and forwards
The early bees are assaulting and fumbling the flowers:
       They call it easing the Spring.

They call it easing the Spring: it is perfectly easy                25
If you have any strength in your thumb: like the bolt,
And the breech, and the cocking-piece, and the point of balance,
Which in our case we have not got; and the almond-blossom
Silent in all of the gardens and the bees going backwards and forwards,
       For today we have naming of parts.                          30

## ▨ TOPICS FOR
## CRITICAL THINKING AND WRITING

1. How many speakers do you hear in the poem? How would you characterize each of them?
2. Why do we include this poem in a chapter on "irony"?

# 18

# Rhythm and Versification

Up and down the City Road,
In and out the Eagle;
That's the way the money goes,
Pop goes the weasel.

Probably very few of the countless children—and adults—who sometimes
find themselves singing this ditty have the faintest idea of what it is about.
It endures because it is catchy—a strong, easily remembered rhythm. Even
if you just read it aloud without singing it, we think you will agree.

If you try to specify exactly what the rhythm is—for instance, by
putting an accent mark on each syllable that you stress heavily—you may
run into difficulties. You may become unsure of whether you stress *up*
and *down* equally; maybe you will decide that *up* is hardly stressed more
than *and*, at least compared with the heavy stress that you put on *down*.
Different readers (really, singers) will recite it differently. Does this mean
that anything goes? Of course not. No one will emphasize *and* or *the*, just
as no one will emphasize the second syllable in *city* or the second syllable in *money*. There may be some variations from reader to reader, but
there will also be a good deal that all readers will agree on. And surely all
readers agree that it is memorable.

Does this song have a meaning? Well, historians say that the Eagle was
a tavern and music hall in the City Road, in Victorian London. People went
there to eat, drink, and sing, with the result that they sometimes spent too
much money and then had to pawn (or "pop") the "weasel"—though no
one is sure what the weasel is. It doesn't really matter; the song lives by its
rhythm.

Now consider this poem by Ezra Pound (1885–1972). Pound's early
work is highly rhythmical; later he became sympathetic to Fascism and he
grew increasingly anti-Semitic, with the result that for many readers his
later work is much less interesting—just a lot of nasty ideas, rather than

memorable expressions. Pound ought to have remembered his own definition of literature: "Literature is news that *stays* news." One way of staying
is to use unforgettable rhythms.

## EZRA POUND

### *An Immorality*                                                    [1919]

Sing we for love and idleness,
Naught else is worth the having.

Though I have been in many a land,
There is naught else in living.

And I would rather have my sweet,                                          5
Though rose-leaves die of grieving,

Than do high deeds in Hungary
To pass all men's believing.

A good poem. To begin with, it sings; as Pound said, "Poetry withers and
dries out when it leaves music, or at least imagined music, too far behind
it. Poets who are not interested in music are, or become, bad poets."
Hymns and ballads, it must be remembered, are songs, and other poetry,
too, is sung, especially by children. Children reciting a counting-out
rhyme, or singing on their way home from school, are enjoying poetry:

> Pease-porridge hot,
>   Pease-porridge cold,
> Pease-porridge in the pot
>   Nine days old.

Nothing very important is being said, but for generations children have
enjoyed the music of these lines, and adults, too, have recalled them with
pleasure—though few people know what pease-porridge is.

The "music"—the catchiness of certain sounds—should not be un-
derestimated. Here are lines chanted by the witches in *Macbeth:*

> Double, double, toil and trouble;
> Fire burn and cauldron bubble.

This is rather far from words that mean approximately the same thing:
"Twice, twice, work and care; / Fire ignite, and pot boil." The difference is
more in the sounds than in the instructions. What is lost in the paraphrase

is the magic, the incantation, which resides in elaborate repetitions of sounds and stresses.

**Rhythm** (most simply, in English poetry, stresses at regular intervals) has a power of its own. A good march, said John Philip Sousa (the composer of "Stars and Stripes Forever"), "should make even someone with a wooden leg step out." A highly pronounced rhythm is common in such forms of poetry as charms, college yells, and lullabies; all of them (like the witches' speech) are aimed at inducing a special effect magically. It is not surprising that *carmen,* the Latin word for "poem" or "song," is also the Latin word for *charm,* and the word from which "charm" is derived.

> Rain, rain, go away;
> Come again another day.

> Block that kick! Block that kick! Block that kick!

> Rock-a-bye baby, on the tree top,
> When the wind blows, the cradle will rock.

In much poetry, rhythm is only half-heard, but its omnipresence is suggested by the fact that when poetry is printed it is customary to begin each line with a capital letter. Prose (from Latin *prorsus,* "forward," "straight on") keeps running across the paper until the right-hand margin is reached, and then, merely because the paper has given out, the writer or printer starts again at the left, with a small letter. But verse (Latin *versus,* "a turning") often ends well short of the right-hand margin, and the next line begins at the left—usually with a capital—not because paper has run out but because the rhythmic pattern begins again. Lines of poetry are continually reminding us that they have a pattern.

Before turning to some other highly rhythmical pieces, a word of caution: a mechanical, unvarying rhythm may be good to put the baby to sleep, but it can be deadly to readers who wish to keep awake. Poets vary their rhythm according to their purpose; a poet ought not to be so regular that he or she is (in W. H. Auden's words) an "accentual pest." In competent hands, rhythm contributes to meaning; it says something. The rhythm in the lines from *Macbeth,* for example, helps suggest the strong binding power of magic. Again Ezra Pound has a relevant comment: "Rhythm *must* have meaning. It can't be merely a careless dash off, with no grip and no real hold to the words and sense, a tumty tum tumty tum tum ta." Some examples will be useful.

Consider this description of Hell from John Milton's *Paradise Lost* (the heavier stresses are marked by ´):

> Rócks, caves, lakes, fens, bogs, dens, and shades of death.

Such a succession of stresses is highly unusual. Elsewhere in the poem Milton chiefly uses iambic feet—alternating unstressed and stressed syllables—but here he immediately follows one heavy stress with another, thereby helping to communicate the "meaning"—the impressive monotony of Hell. As a second example, consider the function of the rhythm in two lines by Alexander Pope:

> Whĕn Ájăx strĭves sŏme rŏck's văst weĭght tŏ thrŏw,
> Thĕ lĭne toŏ lábŏrs, ănd thĕ wŏrds móve slŏw.

The heavier stresses (again, marked by ´) do not merely alternate with the lighter ones (marked ˘); rather, the great weight of the rock is suggested by three consecutive stressed words, "rock's vast weight," and the great effort involved in moving it is suggested by another three consecutive stresses, "line too labors," and by yet another three, "words move slow." Note, also, the abundant pauses within the lines. In the first line, unless one's speech is slovenly, one must pause at least slightly after "Ajax," "strives," "rock's," "vast," "weight," and "throw." The grating sounds in "Ajax" and "rock's" do their work, too, and so do the explosive *t*'s. When Pope wishes to suggest lightness, he reverses his procedure and he groups *un*stressed syllables:

> Not so, when swift Camilla scours the plain,
> Fliés o'ĕr th'uńbéndĭng córn, ănd skíms ălŏng thĕ máin.

This last line has twelve syllables and is thus longer than the line about Ajax, but the addition of "along" helps to communicate lightness and swiftness because in this line (it can be argued) neither syllable of "along" is strongly stressed. If "along" is omitted, the line still makes grammatical sense and becomes more "regular," but it also becomes less imitative of lightness.

The very regularity of a line may be meaningful too. Shakespeare begins a sonnet thus:

> Whĕn Í dŏ coúnt thĕ clŏck thăt télls thĕ tíme.

This line about a mechanism runs with appropriate regularity. (It is worth noting, too, that "count the clock" and "tells the time" emphasize the regularity by the repetition of sounds and syntax.) But notice what Shakespeare does in the middle of the next line:

> Ănd sée thĕ bráve dáy suńk iń hídeŏus níght.

What has he done? And what is the effect?

Following are some poems in which the strongly felt pulsations are highly important.

# WILLIAM CARLOS WILLIAMS

*A poem by William Carlos Williams (1883-1963), along with a brief biography, appears on page 451. The Breughel (also spelled Brueghel) painting described in "The Dance" is shown on the next page.*

Pieter Breughel the Elder, *Peasant Dance,* c. 1568, oil on wood, 114 × 164 cm.
(Kunsthistorisches Museum, Vienna.)

## The Dance

[1944]

In Breughel's great picture, The Kermess,°
the dancers go round, they go round and
around, the squeal and the blare and the
tweedle of bagpipes, a bugle and fiddles
tipping their bellies (round as the thick-                    5
sided glasses whose wash they impound)
their hips and their bellies off balance
to turn them. Kicking and rolling about
the Fair Grounds, swinging their butts, those
shanks must be sound to bear up under such          10
rollicking measures, prance as they dance
in Breughel's great picture, The Kermess.

1 **Kermess** Carnival.

## ▓ TOPICS FOR
## CRITICAL THINKING AND WRITING

1. Read Williams's poem aloud several times, and decide where the
   heavy stresses fall. Mark the heavily stressed syllables ´, the lightly
   stressed ones ^, and the unstressed ones ˘. Are all the lines identical?

What effect is thus gained, especially when read aloud? What does the parenthetical statement (lines 5-6) do to the rhythm? Does a final syllable often receive a heavy stress here? Are there noticeable pauses at the ends of the lines? What is the consequence? Are the dancers waltzing?

2. What syllables rhyme or are repeated (e.g., "round" in lines 2 and 5, and "-pound" in line 6; "-ing" in lines 5, 8, 9, and 11)? What effect do they have?

3. What do you think the absence at the beginning of each line of the customary capital contributes to the meaning? Why is the last line the same as the first?

# ROBERT FRANCIS

*Robert Francis (1901-1987) was born in Upland, Pennsylvania, and educated at Harvard. He taught only briefly, a term here or there and an occasional summer, devoting himself for the most part to reading and writing.*

## The Pitcher

[1960]

His art is eccentricity, his aim
How not to hit the mark he seems to aim at,

His passion how to avoid the obvious,
His technique how to vary the avoidance.

The others throw to be comprehended. He          5
Throws to be a moment misunderstood.

Yet not too much. Not errant, arrant, wild,
But every seeming aberration willed.

Not to, yet still, still to communicate
Making the batter understand too late.          10

If you read this poem aloud, pausing appropriately where the punctuation tells you to, you will hear the poet trying to represent something of the pitcher's "eccentricity." ("Eccentric," you may know, literally means "off center.") A pitcher tries to deceive a batter, perhaps by throwing a ball that will unexpectedly curve over the plate; the poet playfully deceives the reader, for instance, with unexpected pauses. In line 5, for example, he puts a heavy pause (indicated by a period) not at the end of the line, but just before the end.

# ▨ TOPICS FOR CRITICAL THINKING AND WRITING

1. Notice that some lines contain no pauses, but the next-to-last line contains two within it (indicated by commas) and none at the end. What do you suppose Francis is getting at?
2. What significance can be attached to the fact that only the last two lines really rhyme (communicate/late), whereas other lines do not quite rhyme?

# VERSIFICATION: A GLOSSARY FOR REFERENCE

The technical vocabulary of **prosody** (the study of the principles of verse structure, including meter, rhyme, and other sound effects, and stanzaic patterns) is large. An understanding of these terms will not turn anyone into a poet, but it will enable one to discuss some aspects of poetry more efficiently. A knowledge of them, like a knowledge of most other technical terms (e.g., "misplaced modifier," "woofer," "automatic transmission"), allows for quick and accurate communication. The following are the chief terms of prosody.

## Meter

Most English poetry has a pattern of **stressed (accented)** sounds, and this pattern is the **meter** (from the Greek word for "measure"). Although in Old English poetry (poetry written in England before the Norman-French Conquest in 1066) a line may have any number of unstressed syllables in addition to four stressed syllables, most poetry written in England since the Conquest not only has a fixed number of stresses in a line but also has a fixed number of unstressed syllables before or after each stressed one. (One really ought not to talk of "unstressed" or "unaccented" syllables, since to utter a syllable—however lightly—is to give it some stress. It is really a matter of *relative* stress, but the fact is that "unstressed" or "unaccented" are parts of the established terminology of versification.)

In a line of poetry, the **foot** is the basic unit of measurement. On rare occasions it is a single stressed syllable, but generally a foot consists of two or three syllables, one of which is stressed. (Stress is indicated by ´, lack of stress by ˘.) The repetition of feet, then, produces a pattern of stresses throughout the poem.

Two cautions:

1. A poem will seldom contain only one kind of foot throughout; significant variations usually occur, but one kind of foot is dominant.
2. In reading a poem one pays attention to the sense as well as to the metrical pattern. By paying attention to the sense, one often finds that the stress falls on a word that according to the metrical pattern would be unstressed. Or a word that according to the pattern would be stressed may be seen to be unstressed. Furthermore, by reading for sense, one finds that not all stresses are equally heavy; some are almost as light as unstressed syllables, and sometimes there is a **hovering stress**; that is, the stress is equally distributed over two adjacent syllables. To repeat: *read for sense,* allowing the meaning to help indicate the stresses.

## Metrical Feet

The most common feet in English poetry are the following six.

**Iamb** (adjective: **iambic**): one unstressed syllable followed by one stressed syllable. The iamb, said to be the most common pattern in English speech, is surely the most common in English poetry. The following example has four iambic feet:

Mў héart ĭs líke ă sínğinğ bírd.

—Christina Rossetti

**Trochee (trochaic):** one stressed syllable followed by one unstressed.

Wé weře véřy tírĕd, wé wĕre véřy mérřy

—Edna St. Vincent Millay

**Anapest (anapestic):** two unstressed syllables followed by one stressed.

Thĕre aře mánў whŏ sáy thăt ă dóg hăs hĭs dáy.

—Dylan Thomas

**Dactyl (dactylic):** one stressed syllable followed by two unstressed. This trisyllabic foot, like the anapest, is common in light verse or verse suggesting joy, but its use is not limited to such material, as Longfellow's *Evangeline* shows. Thomas Hood's sentimental "The Bridge of Sighs" begins:

Táke hĕr ŭp ténderlў.

**Spondee (spondaic):** two stressed syllables; most often used as a substitute for an iamb or trochee.

Smárt lád, tŏ slíp bĕtímes ăwáy.

—A. E. Housman

**Pyrrhic:** two unstressed syllables; it is often not considered a legitimate foot in English.

## Metrical Lines

A metrical line consists of one or more feet and is named for the number of feet in it. The following names are used:

**monometer:** one foot          **pentameter:** five feet
**dimeter:** two feet            **hexameter:** six feet
**trimeter:** three feet         **heptameter:** seven feet
**tetrameter:** four feet        **octameter:** eight feet

A line is scanned for the kind and number of feet in it, and the **scansion** tells you if it is, say, anapestic trimeter (three anapests):

Ăs Ĭ cáme tŏ thĕ édge ŏf thĕ wóods.

—Robert Frost

Or, in another example, iambic pentameter:

Thĕ súmmĕr thúndĕr, líke ă wóodĕn béll

Louise Bogan

A line ending with a stress has a **masculine ending;** a line ending with an extra unstressed syllable has a **feminine ending.** The **caesura** (usually indicated by the symbol //) is a slight pause within the line. It need not be indicated by punctuation (notice the fourth and fifth lines in the following quotation), and it does not affect the metrical count:

Awake, my St. John! // leave all meaner things
To low ambition, // and the pride of kings.
Let us // (since life can little more supply
Than just to look about us // and to die)
Expatiate free // o'er all this scene of Man;
A mighty maze! // but not without a plan;
A wild, // where weeds and flowers promiscuous shoot;
Or garden, // tempting with forbidden fruit.

—Alexander Pope

The varying position of the caesura helps to give Pope's lines an informality that plays against the formality of the pairs of rhyming lines.

An **end-stopped line** concludes with a distinct syntactical pause, but a **run-on line** has its sense carried over into the next line without syntactical pause. (The running on of a line is called **enjambment.**) In the following passage, only the first is a run-on line:

Yet if we look more closely we shall find
Most have the seeds of judgment in their mind:

Nature affords at least a glimmering light;
The lines, though touched but faintly, are drawn right.

—Alexander Pope

Meter produces **rhythm,** recurrences at equal intervals; but rhythm (from a Greek word meaning "flow") is usually applied to larger units than feet. Often it depends most obviously on pauses. Thus, a poem with run-on lines will have a different rhythm from a poem with end-stopped lines, even though both are in the same meter. And prose, though it is unmetrical, can have rhythm, too.

In addition to being affected by syntactical pause, rhythm is affected by pauses attributable to consonant clusters and to the length of words. Words of several syllables establish a different rhythm from words of one syllable, even in metrically identical lines. One can say, then, that rhythm is altered by shifts in meter, syntax, and the length and ease of pronunciation. But even with no such shift, even if a line is repeated word for word, a reader may sense a change in rhythm. The rhythm of the final line of a poem, for example, may well differ from that of the line before, even though in all other respects the lines are identical, as in Frost's "Stopping by Woods on a Snowy Evening" (page 7), which concludes by repeating "And miles to go before I sleep." One may simply sense that the final line ought to be spoken, say, more slowly and with more stress on "miles."

## Patterns of Sound

Though rhythm is basic to poetry, **rhyme**—the repetition of the identical or similar stressed sound or sounds—is not. Rhyme is, presumably, pleasant in itself; it suggests order; and it may also be related to meaning, for it brings two words sharply together, often implying a relationship, as in the now trite *dove* and *love,* or in the more imaginative *throne* and *alone.*

**Perfect,** or **exact, rhyme:** Differing consonant sounds are followed by identical stressed vowel sounds, and the following sounds, if any, are identical *(foe—toe; meet—fleet; buffer—rougher).* Notice that perfect rhyme involves identity of sound, not of spelling. *Fix* and *sticks,* like *buffer* and *rougher,* are perfect rhymes.

**Half-rhyme** (or **off-rhyme**): Only the final consonant sounds of the words are identical; the stressed vowel sounds as well as the initial consonant sounds, if any, differ *(soul—oil; mirth—forth; trolley—bully).*

**Eye-rhyme:** The sounds do not in fact rhyme, but the words look as though they would rhyme *(cough—bough).*

**Masculine rhyme:** The final syllables are stressed and, after their differing initial consonant sounds, are identical in sound *(stark—mark; support—retort).*

**Feminine rhyme** (or **double rhyme**): Stressed rhyming syllables are followed by identical unstressed syllables *(revival—arrival; flatter—batter)*.

**Triple rhyme** is a kind of feminine rhyme in which identical stressed vowel sounds are followed by two identical unstressed syllables *(machinery—scenery; tenderly—slenderly)*.

**End rhyme** (or **terminal rhyme**): The rhyming words occur at the ends of the lines.

**Internal rhyme:** At least one of the rhyming words occurs within the line (Oscar Wilde's "Each narrow *cell* in which we *dwell*").

**Alliteration:** Sometimes defined as the repetition of initial sounds *("All* the *a*wful *a*uguries," or "*B*ring me my *b*ow of *b*urning gold"), and sometimes as the prominent repetition of a consonant ("*af*ter life's *f*it*f*ul *f*ever").

**Assonance:** The repetition, in words of proximity, of identical vowel sounds preceded and followed by differing consonant sounds. Whereas *tide* and *hide* are rhymes, *tide* and *mine* are assonantal.

**Consonance:** The repetition of identical consonant sounds and differing vowel sounds in words in proximity *(fail—feel; rough—roof; pitter—patter)*. Sometimes consonance is more loosely defined merely as the repetition of a consonant *(fail —peel)*.

**Onomatopoeia:** The use of words that imitate sounds, such as *hiss* and *buzz*. There is a mistaken tendency to see onomatopoeia everywhere—for example in *thunder* and *horror*. Many words sometimes thought to be onomatopoeic are not clearly imitative of the thing they refer to; they merely contain some sounds that, when we know what the word means, seem to have some resemblance to the thing they denote. Tennyson's lines from "Come down, O maid" are usually cited as an example of onomatopoeia:

> The moan of doves in immemorial elms
> And murmuring of innumerable bees.

If you have read the preceding—and, admittedly, not entirely engaging—paragraphs, you may have found yourself mentally repeating some catchy sounds, let's say our example of internal rhyme ("Each narrow cell in which we dwell") or our example of alliteration ("Bring me my bow of burning gold"). As the creators of advertising slogans know, all of us—not just poets—can be hooked by the sounds of words, but probably poets are especially fond of savoring words.

# A Note about Poetic Forms

"Art is nothing without form," the French author Gustave Flaubert maintained, and it's true that works of art have a carefully designed shape. Most obviously, for instance, a good story has an ending that satisfies the reader or hearer. In real life, things keep going, but when a good story ends, the audience feels that there is nothing more to say, at least nothing more of interest to say.

With poems that rhyme, the rhyme-scheme provides a pattern, a shape, a structure that seems inseparable from the content. If you recite a limerick, you will immediately see how the shape is inseparable from the content:

> There was a young fellow from Lynn
> Who was so exceedingly thin
>     That when he essayed
>     To drink lemonade
> He slipped through the straw and fell in.

If you put the words in a different order, and you ignore meter and rhyme—that is, if you destroy the form and turn the passage into something like "A young man, so thin that he fell through a straw into a glass of lemonade, lived in Lynn"—you can instantly see the importance of form.

Let's briefly look at a more serious example. A. E. Housman's "Eight O'Clock," a poem whose title corresponds to the hour at which executions in England used to take place.

> He stood, and heard the steeple
>     Sprinkle the quarters on the morning town.
> One, two, to market-place and people
>     It tossed them down.
>
> Strapped, noosed, nighing his hour,
>     He stood and counted them and cursed his luck;
> And then the clock collected in the tower
>     Its strength, and struck.

The rhyme of "struck" with "luck" (in this instance, bad luck) is conclusive. We don't ask if the body was removed from the gallows and buried, or if the condemned man's wife (if he had one) grieved, or if his children (if he had any) turned out well or badly. None of these things is of any relevance. There is nothing more to say. The form and the content perfectly go together. In this example, the lines, each of which rhymes with another line—we might say that each line is tied to another line—seem especially appropriate for a man who is "strapped" and "noosed."

But why do poets use forms established by rhyme? In an essay called "The Constant Symbol," Robert Frost says that a poet regards rhymes as "stepping stones. . . . The way will be zigzag, but it will be a straight crookedness like the walking stick he cuts in the bushes for an emblem." Housman's stepping-stones in the second stanza took Houseman (and take the reader) from *hour* to *luck,* then to *tower* and then with great finality to the end of the walk, *struck.* We think this stanza is inspired, and we imagine that Housman's inspiration was mightily helped by his need for rhymes—his need to get "stepping stones" that would allow him to continue the "straight crookedness" of his walk with this condemned man. His walk-with-words, or rather his walk with words-that-set-forth-ideas, produced "luck" and "struck," and enabled him to give to his readers the memorable image of the clock as a machine that executes the man.

When you read Housman's or Frost's actual lines—or better, when you read them aloud and hear and feel the effect of these rhymes—you can understand why Frost more than once said he would as soon write unrhymed poetry as he would "play tennis with the net down." The rules governing the game of tennis or the game of writing do not interfere with the game; rather, the rules allow the players to play a game. The rules allow poets to write poems; the rules—the restraints—provide the structure that allows poets to accomplish something. Poets are somewhat like Houdini, who accepted shackles so that he could triumph over them. Without the handcuffs and other restraints, he could accomplish nothing. Or consider the string on a kite; far from impeding the kite's flight, the string allows the kite to fly. Speaking in less high-flying terms, we can quote from a talk that Frost gave to college students in 1937, "The Poet's Next of Kin in College." He told them—and he was speaking not only to young poets but to all students—that in their endeavors, of whatever sort, they "must have form   performance. The thing itself is indescribable, but it is felt like athletic form. To have form, feel form in sports—and by analogy feel form in verse."

Poets have testified that they use rhyme partly because, far from impeding them, it helps them to say interesting things in a memorable way. True, some rhymes have been used so often that although they were once rich in meaning—for instance—"love" and "dove" or "moon" and "June"—they have become clichés, their use indicating not an imaginative leap but a reliance on what has been said too often. But other rhymes—let's say "earth" and "birth" or "law" and "flaw"—can lead poets to say interesting things that they might otherwise not have thought of.

In his "Letter of Advice to a Young Poet," Jonathan Swift (whom you may know as the author of *Gulliver's Travels*, 1726), said: "Verse without rhyme is a body without a soul." A striking, and indeed surprising, comment: Swift dares to propose that the soul of a poem depends not on the content but, rather, on a crucial element of its form, the presence of rhyme. In part he is reminding us here of the importance of craft in the writing of a poem, of the sheer skill and deliberation that makes the literary work feel exactly right, as though it *had* to be this way.

# Stanzaic Patterns

Lines of poetry are commonly arranged in a rhythmical unit called a stanza (from an Italian word meaning "room" or "stopping-place"). Usually all the stanzas in a poem have the same rhyme pattern. A stanza is sometimes called a **verse,** though *verse* may also mean a single line of poetry. (In discussing stanzas, rhymes are indicated by identical letters. Thus, *abab* indicates that the first and third lines rhyme with each other, while the second and fourth lines are linked by a different rhyme. An unrhymed line is denoted by *x.*) Common stanzaic forms in English poetry are the following:

**Couplet:** a stanza of two lines, usually but not necessarily with end-rhymes. *Couplet* is also used for a pair of rhyming lines. The **octosyllabic couplet** is iambic or trochaic tetrameter:

Had we but world enough and time,
This coyness, lady, were no crime.

—Andrew Marvell

**Heroic couplet:** a rhyming couplet of iambic pentameter, often "closed," that is, containing a complete thought, with a fairly heavy pause at the end of the first line and a still heavier one at the end of the second. Commonly, there is a parallel or an *antithesis* (contrast) within a line or between the two lines. It is called heroic because in England, especially in the eighteenth century, it was much used for heroic (epic) poems.

Some foreign writers, some our own despise;
The ancients only, or the moderns, prize.

—Alexander Pope

**Triplet** (or **tercet**): a three-line stanza, usually with one rhyme.

Whenas in silks my Julia goes
Then, then (methinks) how sweetly flows
That liquefaction of her clothes.

—Robert Herrick

**Quatrain:** a four-line stanza, rhymed or unrhymed. The **heroic** (or **elegiac) quatrain** is iambic pentameter, rhyming *abab.* That is, the first and third lines rhyme (so they are designated *a*), and the second and fourth lines rhyme (so they are designated *b*).

# THREE COMPLEX FORMS: THE SONNET, THE VILLANELLE, AND THE SESTINA

## The Sonnet

A sonnet is a fourteen-line poem, predominantly in iambic pentameter. The rhyme is usually according to one of two schemes. The **Italian** or **Petrarchan sonnet,** named for the Italian poet Francesco Petrarch

(1304–1374), has two divisions: The first eight lines (rhyming *abba abba*) are the octave, and the last six (rhyming *cd cd cd*, or a variant) are the sestet. Gerard Manley Hopkins's "God's Grandeur" (page 605) is an Italian sonnet. The second kind of sonnet, the **English** or **Shakespearean sonnet**, is usually arranged into three quatrains and a couplet, rhyming *abab cdcd efef gg*. (For examples see the next two poems.) In many sonnets there is a marked correspondence between the rhyme scheme and the development of the thought. Thus an Italian sonnet may state a generalization in the octave and a specific example in the sestet. Or an English sonnet may give three examples—one in each quatrain—and draw a conclusion in the couplet.

Why poets choose to imprison themselves in fourteen tightly rhymed lines is something of a mystery. Tradition has a great deal to do with it: the form, having been handled successfully by major poets, stands as a challenge. In writing a sonnet a poet gains a little of the authority of Petrarch, Shakespeare, Milton, Wordsworth, and other masters who showed that the sonnet is not merely a trick. A second reason perhaps resides in the very tightness of the rhymes, which can help as well as hinder. Many poets have felt, along with Richard Wilbur (in *Mid-Century American Poets,* ed. John Ciardi), that the need for a rhyme has suggested

. . . arbitrary connections of which the mind may take advantage if it likes. For example, if one has to rhyme with *tide*, a great number of rhyme-words at once come to mind (ride, bide, shied, confide, Akenside, etc.). Most of these, in combination with *tide*, will probably suggest nothing apropos, but one of them may reveal precisely what one wanted to say. If none of them does, *tide* must be dispensed with. Rhyme, austerely used, may be a stimulus to discovery and a stretcher of the attention.

# WILLIAM SHAKESPEARE

*William Shakespeare (1564–1616), born in Stratford-upon-Avon in England, is chiefly known as a dramatic poet, but he also wrote non-dramatic poetry. In 1609 a volume of 154 of his sonnets was published, apparently without his permission. Probably he chose to keep his sonnets unpublished not because he thought that they were of little value, but because it was more prestigious to be an amateur (unpublished) poet than a professional (published) poet. Although the sonnets were published in 1609, they were probably written in the mid-1590s, when there was a vogue for sonneteering. A contemporary writer in 1598 said that Shakespeare's "sugred Sonnets [circulate] among his private friends."*

## Sonnet 73

That time of year thou mayst in me behold
When yellow leaves, or none, or few, do hang
Upon those boughs which shake against the cold,
Bare ruined choirs° where late the sweet birds sang.          4
In me thou see'st the twilight of such day
As after sunset fadeth in the west,
Which by-and-by black night doth take away,
Death's second self that seals up all in rest,               8
In me thou see'st the glowing of such fire
That on the ashes of his youth doth lie,
As the deathbed whereon it must expire,
Consumed with that which it was nourished by.               12
   This thou perceiv'st, which makes thy love more strong,
   To love that well which thou must leave ere long.

---

4 **choir** the part of the church where services were sung.

## ▓ TOPICS FOR CRITICAL THINKING AND WRITING

1. In the first quatrain (the first four lines) to what "time of year" does Shakespeare compare himself? In the second quatrain (lines 5–8) to what does he compare himself? In the third? If the sequence of the three quatrains were reversed, what would be gained or lost?

2. In line 8, what is "Death's second self"? What implications do you perceive in "seals up all in rest," as opposed, for instance, to "brings most welcome rest"?

3. In line 13, exactly what is "This"?

4. In line 14, suppose in place of "To love that well which thou must leave ere long," Shakespeare had written "To love me well whom thou must leave ere long." What if anything would have been gained or lost?

5. What is your personal response to this sonnet? Do you feel that its lessons apply to you? Please explain.

6. Did you find this sonnet hard to understand when you read it for the first time? After you reread and studied it, did it become more difficult, or less so? Do you like to read difficult poems?

# JOHN CROWE RANSOM

*A graduate of Vanderbilt University and a Rhodes scholar at Oxford, John Crowe Ransom returned to teach at Vanderbilt, where he and others founded an important poetry journal,* The Fugitive. *In 1937 he moved to Kenyon College, where he founded and edited the* Kenyon Review. *Distinguished as a poet and a teacher, he also wrote significant literary criticism. One of his books,* The New Criticism *(1941), gave its name to a critical movement.*

## Piazza Piece
[1927]

—I am a gentleman in a dustcoat trying
To make you hear. Your ears are soft and small
And listen to an old man not at all,
They want the young men's whispering and sighing.
But see the roses on your trellis dying                          5
And hear the spectral singing of the moon;
For I must have my lovely lady soon,
I am a gentleman in a dustcoat trying.

—I am a lady young in beauty waiting
Until my truelove comes, and then we kiss.                       10
But what gray man among the vines is this
Whose words are dry and faint as in a dream?
Back from my trellis, Sir, before I scream!
I am a lady young in beauty waiting.

## ▨ TOPICS FOR
## CRITICAL THINKING AND WRITING

1. Who speaks the octave? What words especially characterize him? Characterize the speaker of the sestet.
2. In lines 9–10, the young lady is waiting for her "truelove." Comment on the suggestions in this word. In line 14 she is still "waiting." For whom does she think she is waiting? For whom does the reader know she is waiting? How do you know?
3. The first and last lines of the octave are identical, and so are the first and last lines of the sestet. What does this indicate about the degree to which the speakers communicate to each other?
4. What is the point of Ransom's poem? Is this an appropriate question to ask about a poem—whether it does or does not make a point? Please explain.

# BILLY COLLINS

*Born in New York City in 1941, Collins is a professor of English at Lehman College of the City University of New York. He is the author of six books of poetry and the recipient of numerous awards, including one from the National Endowment for the Arts. Collins's* Sailing Alone Around the Room: New and Selected Poems *was published in 2001; in the same year, he was appointed Poet Laureate of the United States.*

*The following sonnet uses the Petrarchan form of an octave and a sestet. (See page 492.) Petrarch is additionally present in the poem by the allusion in line 3 to "a little ship on love's storm-tossed seas," because Petrarch compared the hapless lover, denied the favor of his mistress, to a ship in a storm: The lover cannot guide his ship because the North Star is hidden (Petrarch's beloved Laura averts her eyes), and the sails of the ship are agitated by the lover's pitiful sighs. As you will see, Petrarch and Laura explicitly enter the poem in the last three lines.*

*In line 8 Collins refers to the stations of the cross. In Roman Catholicism, one of the devotions consists of prayers and meditations before each of fourteen crosses or images set up along a path that commemorates the fourteen places at which Jesus halted when, just before the Crucifixion, he was making his way in Jerusalem to Golgotha.*

## Sonnet                                                      [1999]

All we need is fourteen lines, well, thirteen now,
and after this next one just a dozen
to launch a little ship on love's storm-tossed seas,
then only ten more left like rows of beans.                          4
How easily it goes unless you get Elizabethan
and insist the iambic bongos must be played
and rhymes positioned at the ends of lines,
one for every station of the cross.                                  8
But hang on here while we make the turn
into the final six where all will be resolved,
where longing and heartache will find an end,
where Laura will tell Petrarch to put down his pen,                  12
take off those crazy medieval tights,
blow out the lights, and come at last to bed.

## ▨ TOPICS FOR
## CRITICAL THINKING AND WRITING

1. The headnote explains the stations of the cross (line 8), but what is the point of introducing this image into a sonnet?

2. Normally the "turn" (*volta*) in an Italian sonnet occurs at the beginning of the ninth line; the first eight lines (the octave) establish some sort of problem, and the final six lines (the sestet) respond, for instance by answering a question, or by introducing a contrasting emotion. In your view, how satisfactorily does Collins handle this form?

3. Does this sonnet interest you? Do you find it clever? Is that a good thing or a bad thing?

4. Do you think that you could have written this sonnet? Could you have written Shakespeare's sonnets 73 and 116 (pages 494 and 569)? What do your responses to these questions suggest to you about the writing of poetry?

# The Villanelle

The name comes from an Italian words, *villanella,* meaning "country song" or "peasant song," and originally, in the sixteenth century, the subject was the supposedly simple life of the shepherd, but in France in the seventeenth century elaborate rules were developed. Variations occur, but usually a villanelle has the following characteristics:

- Five stanzas with three lines each (tercets), rhyming *aba,* and a final stanza with four lines (a quatrain).
- The first line of the first stanza is repeated as the last line of the second stanza and the last line of the fourth stanza.
- The third line of the first stanza is repeated as the last line of the third stanza and the last line of the fifth stanza.
- The quatrain that concludes the villanelle rhymes *abaa,* using the first and third lines of the first stanza as the next-to-last and last lines of the final stanza—i.e., the poem ends with a couplet.

Because the villanelle repeats one sound thirteen times (in the first and last line of each tercet, and in the first, third, and fourth lines of the quatrain), it strongly conveys a sense of return, a sense of not going forward, even a sense of dwelling on the past. We give four examples of the form.

If you are going to write a villanelle, here are two tips:

- Begin by writing a couplet (a pair of rhyming lines); in fact, write several couplets on different topics, and then decide which couplet you think is most promising. Next, insert between these two lines a line that makes sense in the context but that does *not* rhyme with them.
- Each line need not end with a pause, and in fact some run-on lines probably will help to prevent the poem from becoming too singsongy.

# DYLAN THOMAS

*Dylan Thomas (1914-1953) was born and grew up in Swansea, in Wales. His first volume of poetry, published in 1934, immediately made him famous. Endowed with a highly melodious voice, on three tours of the United States he was immensely successful as a reader both of his own and of other poets' work. He died in New York City.*

## Do Not Go Gentle into That Good Night                    [1952]

Do not go gentle into that good night,
Old age should burn and rave at close of day;
Rage, rage against the dying of the light.

Though wise men at their end know dark is right,
Because their words had forked no lightning they          5
Do not go gentle into that good night.

Good men, the last wave by, crying how bright
Their frail deeds might have danced in a green bay,
Rage, rage against the dying of the light.

Wild men who caught and sang the sun in flight,          10
And learn, too late, they grieved it on its way,
Do not go gentle into that good night.

Grave men, near death, who see with blinding sight
Blind eyes could blaze like meteors and be gay,
Rage, rage against the dying of the light.               15

And you, my father, there on the sad height,
Curse, bless, me now with your fierce tears, I pray.
Do not go gentle into that good night.
Rage, rage against the dying of the light.

## ❋ TOPICS FOR CRITICAL THINKING AND WRITING

1. The intricate form of the villanelle might seem too fussy for a serious poem about dying. Do you find it too fussy? Or does the form here somehow succeed?
2. How would you describe the speaker's tone? Is it accurate or misleading to say that "Do Not Go Gentle into That Good Night" is an angry poem?
3. What is the speaker's attitude toward death? Do you share this attitude or not? Please explain.
4. This is a famous poem. Why do you think that is the case?

# WENDY COPE

*Wendy Cope was born in 1945 in Kent, in the south of England, and educated at St. Hilda's College at Oxford University, where she took a degree in history, and then at the Westminster College of Education. After working for a number of years as a music teacher in London, she became a television critic, a columnist, a freelance writer, and, above all, a poet. Her books of verse include* Making Cocoa for Kingsley Amis *(1986) and* Serious Concerns *(1991), both of which were best-sellers in England, and* If I Don't Know *(2001).*

## Reading Scheme
[1986]

Here is Peter. Here is Jane. They like fun.
Jane has a big doll. Peter has a ball.
Look, Jane, look! Look at the dog! See him run!    3

Here is Mummy. She has baked a bun.
Here is the milkman. He has come to call.
Here is Peter. Here is Jane. They like fun.    6

Go Peter! Go Jane! Come, milkman, come!
The milkman likes Mummy. She likes them all.
Look, Jane, look! Look at the dog! See him run!    9

Here are the curtains. They shut out the sun.
Let us peep! On tiptoe Jane! You are small!
Here is Peter. Here is Jane. They like fun.    12

I hear a car, Jane. The milkman looks glum.
Here is Daddy in his car. Daddy is tall.
Look, Jane, look! Look at the dog! See him run!    15

Daddy looks very cross. Has he a gun?
Up milkman! Up milkman! Over the wall!
Here is Peter. Here is Jane. They like fun.    18
Look, Jane, look! Look at the dog! See him run!

## ▨ TOPICS FOR CRITICAL THINKING AND WRITING

1. What was your first response to this poem? After you read it through several times, did your response change? Please explain.
2. What does the word "scheme" mean? What makes this word in the title a good choice for the poem that follows?
3. Do you think that Cope intends her poem to be comic in its effect on the reader? Or would you characterize the effect in different terms?

4. How does the form of this poem contribute to its meaning? Could you imagine the poem affecting you in the same way if Cope had written it in a different form—for example, without the pattern of rhymes?

5. Has this poem given you a new insight into the relationship between form and meaning? If so, please describe this insight and explain how it will affect your reading of other poems.

# The Sestina

This fiendishly elaborate form developed in twelfth-century Europe, especially in southern France, among the troubadours, court poets who sang for nobles. (The name comes from the Italian *sesto,* "sixth," because there are six stanzas of six lines each—but then, to complicate matters, there is a seventh stanza, a three-line "envoy" or "envoi," a summing up that uses key words of the first six stanzas.)

More precisely—this is mind-boggling—the six words that end the six lines of the first stanza are used at the ends of all the following lines but in a different though fixed order in each stanza. (Rhyme is *not* used in this form.) This fixed order has been characterized as a sort of bottoms-up pattern, a term that will become clear as we describe the stanzas. In the second stanza the *first* line ends with the *last* word of the *last* line (the bottom) of the first stanza; the second line of the second stanza ends with the first line of the first; the third line ends with the last word of the fifth line of the first stanza—i.e., with the next-to-bottom line of the first stanza. The fourth line of the second stanza ends with the second line of the first, the fifth with the fourth line of the first, and the sixth with the third line of the first.

Thus, if we designate the final words of the first stanza, line by line, as 1, 2, 3, 4, 5, 6,

the final words of the second stanza are 6, 1, 5, 2, 4, 3;
the third stanza: 3, 6, 4, 1, 2, 5
the fourth stanza: 5, 3, 2, 6, 1, 4
the fifth stanza: 4, 5, 1, 3, 6, 2
the sixth stanza: 2, 4, 6, 5, 3, 1

The envoy of three lines must use these six words, but there are various possible patterns—for instance, 5, 3, 1 at the ends of the three lines, and 2, 4, 6 in the middle of the lines.

If you are going to write a sestina, two tips:

- Once you have settled on your topic—let's say "loss" or "a restless spirit of adventure"—jot down six words that you think are relevant, and get going.

- You need not end each line with a pause, and in fact most good sestinas use considerable enjambment—i.e., the sense of the line runs over into the next line.

# ELIZABETH BISHOP

*Elizabeth Bishop (1911-1979) was born in Worcester, Massachusetts. Because her father died when she was eight months old and her mother was confined to a sanitarium four years later, Bishop was raised by relatives in New England and Nova Scotia. After graduation from Vassar College in 1934, where she was co-editor of the student literary magazine, she lived (on a small private income) for a while in Key West, France, and Mexico, and then for much of her adult life in Brazil, before returning to the United States to teach at Harvard.*

## Sestina

[1965]

September rain falls on the house.
In the failing light, the old grandmother
sits in the kitchen with the child
beside the Little Marvel Stove,
reading the jokes from the almanac,
laughing and talking to hide her tears.                          6

She thinks that her equinoctial tears
and the rain that beats on the roof of the house
were both foretold by the almanac,
but only known to a grandmother.
The iron kettle sings on the stove.
She cuts some bread and says to the child,                       12

*It's time for tea now;* but the child
is watching the teakettle's small hard tears
dance like mad on the hot black stove,
the way the rain must dance on the house.
Tidying up, the old grandmother
hangs up the clever almanac                                      18

on its string. Birdlike, the almanac
hovers half open above the child,
hovers above the old grandmother
and her teacup full of dark brown tears.
She shivers and says she thinks the house
feels chilly, and puts more wood in the stove.                   24

*It was to be,* says the Marvel Stove.
*I know what I know,* says the almanac.
With crayons the child draws a rigid house
and a winding pathway.Then the child
puts in a man with buttons like tears
and shows it proudly to the grandmother.                          30

But secretly, while the grandmother
busies herself about the stove,
the little moons fall down like tears
from between the pages of the almanac
into the flower bed the child
has carefully placed in the front of the house.                  36

*Time to plant tears,* says the almanac.
The grandmother sings to the marvelous stove
and the child draws another inscrutable house.


## ▓ TOPICS FOR
## CRITICAL THINKING AND WRITING

1. Does Bishop's choice of title seem strange to you? Why would she use
   the name of the poetic form for her title? Do you think that a different title might be more effective? Please give examples, and explain
   why they would or would not be better.
2. As carefully as you can, describe the effect of line 1.
3. In the first stanza, why is the grandmother crying? How are her tears
   in lines 6 and 7 related to the "small hard tears" of the teakettle in
   line 14? Note, too, the later references to tears. Please comment on
   these as well.
4. Several of the lines in this poem are italicized. Do the italics make the
   lines more forceful? Should Bishop have made the force of the lines
   clear without changing the "look" of the lines on the page?
5. What is an almanac? Have you ever seen one? Why would someone
   want an almanac? What is the significance of the almanac in this poem?
6. What is your response to the fact that this poem is a sestina? Do you
   think you could write a poem in this form? What would be the benefit to you of such an assignment?


# SHAPED POETRY OR PATTERN POETRY

We have been talking about shapes or patterns determined by rhymes, but
some poems—admittedly few—take their shape from the length of the
lines, which form a simple image, such as a sphere, an egg, a vase, or a wing.

We have already printed one poem of this sort in our first chapter, James Merrill's "Christmas Tree," which is shaped like—well, you can guess.

Here is a famous example of shaped poetry, a pair of wings. We print it sideways, as it was printed in the earliest edition, in 1633, though in that edition the first stanza was printed on the left-hand page, the second on the right-hand page.

# GEORGE HERBERT

*George Herbert (1593-1633), born into a distinguished Welsh family, studied at the University of Cambridge (England) and became a clergyman. By all accounts he lived an admirable life and was deservedly known in his community as "Holy Mr. Herbert."*

Note: *In line 1,* store *means "abundance," "plenty." In line 10, the fall refers to the loss of innocence that resulted when Adam ate the forbidden fruit in the garden of Eden. In the next-to-last line,* imp, *a term from falconry, means "to graft, to insert feathers into a wing."*

## Easter-Wings

Lord, who createdst man in wealth and store,
    Though foolishly he lost the same,
        Decaying more and more,
            Till he became
                Most poor:
                With thee
            O let me rise
        As larks, harmoniously,
    And sing this day thy victories:
Then shall the fall further the flight in me.                    10

My tender age in sorrow did begin:
    And still with sicknesses and shame
        Thou didst so punish sin,
            That I became
                Most thin.
                With thee
            Let me combine,
        And feel this day thy victory:
    For, if I imp my wing on thine,
Affliction shall advance the flight in me.                    20

## ▨ TOPICS FOR CRITICAL THINKING AND WRITING

1. Why are wings especially relevant to a poem about Easter?
2. We don't think one can argue that the length of every line is exactly suited to the meaning of the line, but we do think that some of the lengths are parallel or reinforce some of the ideas within those lines. For instance, the first line, speaking of a man's original "wealth and store," is a long line. Why is this length more appropriate to the meaning than it would be to, say, "Lord, who created a man who soon would fall"? And note especially the fifth and sixth lines of each stanza: Would you agree that their length suits their meaning?
3. Do you think this poem is a mere novelty, or do you think it deserves close attention and indeed is memorable? Please explain.

# LILLIAN MORRISON

*Lillian Morrison, born in Jersey City, New Jersey, is an anthologist and folklorist and a writer of children's books as well as a poet in her own right. The first books she published were collections of folk rhymes that she assembled and edited while working as a librarian at the New York Public Library. In 1987 Morrison received the Grolier Award for "outstanding contributions to the stimulation of reading by young people." She lives in New York City.*

## The Sidewalk Racer

[1978]

Or *On the Skateboard*

Skimming
an asphalt sea
I swerve, I curve, I
sway; I speed to whirring
sound an inch above the                                    5
ground; I'm the sailor
and the sail, I'm the
driver and the wheel
I'm the one and only
single engine                                              10
human auto
mobile.

# ☒ TOPICS FOR CRITICAL THINKING AND WRITING

1. Is the poem really about a skateboard? If not, what *is* it about?
2. The first line is "Skimming." Would the poem be improved or weakened if it began "I skim"? Please explain.
3. The second line rhymes with the fifth and seventh ("sea," "the") and with the ninth ("only"). What other rhymes do you find? What is the effect of using rhymes that are *not* at the ends of the lines?
4. From a grammatical point of view, a period could be put at the end of line 8. Why do you suppose Morrison did not put a period there?

# BLANK VERSE AND FREE VERSE

A good deal of English poetry is unrhymed, much of it in **blank verse**—that is, unrhymed iambic pentameter. Introduced into English poetry by Henry Howard, the Earl of Surrey, in the middle of the sixteenth century, late in the century it became the standard medium (especially in the hands of Marlowe and Shakespeare) of English drama. In the seventeenth century, Milton used it for *Paradise Lost,* and it has continued to be used in both dramatic and nondramatic literature. For an example see the first scene of *Othello* (page 1002). A passage of blank verse that has a rhetorical unity is sometimes called a **verse paragraph.**

The second kind of unrhymed poetry fairly common in English, especially in the twentieth century, is **free verse** (or **vers libre**): rhythmical lines varying in length, adhering to no fixed metrical pattern and usually unrhymed. Such poetry may seem formless; Robert Frost, who strongly preferred regular meter and rhyme, said that he would not consider writing free verse any more than he would consider playing tennis without a net. But free verse does have a form or pattern, often largely based on repetition and parallel grammatical structure. Whitman's "A Noiseless Patient Spider" (page 417) is an example; Arnold's "Dover Beach" (page 578) is another example, though less typical because it uses rhyme. Thoroughly typical is Whitman's "When I Heard the Learn'd Astronomer."

# WALT WHITMAN

*For a biography of the American poet Walt Whitman (1819-1892), see the note prefacing "A Noiseless Patient Spider" (page 417).*

## *When I Heard the Learn'd Astronomer* [1865]

When I heard the learn'd astronomer,
When the proofs, the figures, were ranged in columns before me,
When I was shown the charts and diagrams, to add, divide, and
        measure them,
When I sitting heard the astronomer where he lectured with much
        applause in the lecture-room,
How soon unaccountable I became tired and sick,                    5
Till rising and gliding out I wander'd off by myself,
In the mystical moist night-air, and from time to time,
Look'd up in perfect silence at the stars.

-------

What can be said about the rhythmic structure of this poem? Rhymes are
absent, and the lines vary greatly in the number of syllables, ranging from
9 (the first line) to 23 (the fourth line), but when we read the poem we
sense a rhythmic structure. The first four lines obviously hang together,
each beginning with "When"; indeed, three of these four lines begin
"When I." We may notice, too, that each of these four lines has more syllables than its predecessor (the numbers are 9, 14, 18, and 23); this increase in length, like the initial repetition, is a kind of pattern. But then,
with the fifth line, which speaks of fatigue and surfeit, there is a shrink-
age to 14 syllables, offering an enormous relief from the previous
swollen line with its 23 syllables. The second half of the poem—the pattern established by "When" in the first four lines is dropped, and in effect
we get a new stanza, also of four lines—does not relentlessly diminish
the number of syllables in each succeeding line, but it *almost* does so:
14, 14, 13, 10.

    The second half of the poem thus has a pattern too, and this pattern
is more or less the reverse of the first half of the poem. We may notice too
that the last line (in which the poet, now released from the oppressive
lecture hall, is in communion with nature) is very close to an iambic pentameter line; that is, the poem concludes with a metrical form said to be
the most natural in English. The effect of naturalness or ease in this final
line, moreover, is increased by the absence of repetitions (e.g., not only of
"When I," but even of such syntactic repetitions as "charts and diagrams,"
"tired and sick," "rising and gliding") that characterize most of the previous lines. This final effect of naturalness is part of a carefully constructed
pattern in which rhythmic structure is part of meaning. Though at first
glance free verse may appear unrestrained, as T. S. Eliot (a practitioner)
said, "No *vers* is *libre* for the man who wants to do a good job"—or for the
woman who wants to do a good job.

# THE PROSE POEM

The term *prose poem* is sometimes applied to a short work that looks like prose but that is highly rhythmical or rich in images, or both. Here is a modern example.

## CAROLYN FORCHÉ

*Carolyn Forché was born in Detroit in 1950. After earning a bachelor's degree from Michigan State University and a master's degree from Bowling Green State University, she traveled widely in the Southwest, living among Pueblo Indians. Between 1978 and 1986 she made several visits to El Salvador, documenting human rights violations for Amnesty International. Her first book of poems,* Gathering the Tribes, *won the Yale Younger Poets award in 1975. Her second book of poems,* The Country Between Us *(1981), includes "The Colonel," which has been called a prose poem.*

## *The Colonel*                                                    [1978, publ. 1981]

What you have heard is true. I was in his house. His wife carried a tray of coffee and sugar. His daughter filed her nails, his son went out for the night. There were daily papers, pet dogs, a pistol on the cushion beside him. The moon swung bare on its black cord over the house. On the television was a cop show. It was in English. Broken bottles were embedded in the walls around the house to scoop the kneecaps from a man's legs or cut his hands to lace. On the windows there were gratings like those in liquor stores. We had dinner, rack of lamb, good wine, a gold bell was on the table for calling the maid. The maid brought green mangoes, salt, a type of bread. I was asked how I enjoyed the country. There was a brief commercial in Spanish. His wife took everything away. There was some talk then of how difficult it had become to govern. The parrot said hello on the terrace. The colonel told it to shutup, and pushed himself from the table. My friend said to me with his eyes: say nothing. The colonel returned with a sack used to bring groceries home. He spilled many human ears on the table. They were like dried peach halves. There is no other way to say this. He took one of them in his hands, shook it in our faces, dropped it into a water glass. It came alive there. I am tired of fooling around he said. As for the rights of anyone, tell your people they can go fuck themselves. He swept the ears to the floor with his arm and held the last of his wine in the air. Something for your poetry, no? he said. Some of the ears on the floor caught this scrap of his voice. Some of the ears on the floor were pressed to the ground.

🔣 TOPICS FOR
CRITICAL THINKING AND WRITING

1. How would you characterize the colonel in a few sentences?
2. We are told that the colonel spoke of "how difficult it had become to govern." What do you suppose the colonel assumes is the purpose of government? What do you assume its purpose is?
3. How much do we know about the narrator? Can we guess the narrator's purpose in visiting the colonel? How would you characterize the narrator's tone? Do you believe the narrator?
4. What is your response to the last sentence?
5. What, if anything, is gained by calling this work a "prose poem" rather than a short story?

# 19

# In Brief: Writing
# Arguments about Poetry

If you are going to write about a fairly short poem (say, under 30 lines), it's not a bad idea to copy out the poem, writing or typing it double-spaced. By writing it out you will be forced to notice details, down to the punctuation. After you have copied the poem, proofread it carefully against the original. Catching an error—even the addition or omission of a comma—may help you to notice a detail in the original that you might otherwise have overlooked. And now that you have the poem with ample space between the lines, you have a worksheet with room for jottings.

A good essay is based on a genuine response to a poem; a response may be stimulated in part by first reading the poem aloud and then considering the following questions.

Remember, even an explication—an unfolding of the implications of the poem—is an argument. In the example on page 390, the student begins by asserting a thesis, a claim: "'Harlem' is only eleven lines long, but it is charged with power." The thesis, the arguable claim, of course is not that "the poem is . . . only eleven lines long," but that "it is charged with power," and the rest of the explication is devoted to supporting this claim, to pointing out almost word by word, the sources of the power.

## FIRST RESPONSE

What was your response to the poem on first reading? Did some parts especially please or displease you, or puzzle you? After some study—perhaps checking the meanings of some of the words in a dictionary and reading the poem several times—did you modify your initial response to the parts and to the whole?

# SPEAKER AND TONE

1. Who is the speaker? (Consider age, gender, personality, frame of mind, and tone of voice.) Is the speaker defined fairly precisely (for instance, an older woman speaking to a child), or is the speaker simply a voice meditating? (Jot down your first impressions, then reread the poem and make further jottings, if necessary.)
2. Do you think the speaker is fully aware of what he or she is saying, or does the speaker unconsciously reveal his or her personality and values? What is your attitude toward this speaker?
3. Is the speaker narrating or reflecting on an earlier experience or attitude? If so, does he or she convey a sense of new awareness, such as regret for innocence lost?

# AUDIENCE

To whom is the speaker speaking? What is the situation (including time and place)? (In some poems a listener is strongly implied, but in others, especially those in which the speaker is meditating, there may be no audience other than the reader, who "overhears" the speaker.)

# STRUCTURE AND FORM

1. Does the poem proceed in a straightforward way, or at some point or points does the speaker reverse course, altering his or her tone or perception? If there is a shift, what do you make of it?
2. Is the poem organized into sections? If so, what are these sections—stanzas, for instance—and how does each section (characterized, perhaps, by a certain tone of voice, or a group of rhymes) grow out of what precedes it?
3. What is the effect on you of the form—say, quatrains (stanzas of four lines) or blank verse (unrhymed lines of ten syllables of iambic pentameter)? If the sense overflows the form, running without pause from (for example) one quatrain into the next, what effect is created?

# CENTER OF INTEREST AND THEME

1. What is the poem about? Is the interest chiefly in a distinctive character, or in meditation? That is, is the poem chiefly psychological or chiefly philosophical?

2. Is the theme stated explicitly (directly) or implicitly? How might you state the theme in a sentence? What is lost by reducing the poem to a statement of a theme?

# DICTION

1. How would you characterize the language? Colloquial, or elevated, or what?
2. Do certain words have rich and relevant associations that relate to other words and help to define the speaker or the theme or both?
3. What is the role of figurative language, if any? Does it help to define the speaker or the theme?
4. What do you think is to be taken figuratively or symbolically, and what literally?

# SOUND EFFECTS

1. What is the role of sound effects, including repetitions of sound (for instance, alliteration) and of entire words, and shifts in versification?
2. If there are off-rhymes (for instance, *dizzy* and *easy*, or *home* and *come*), what effect do they have on you? Do they, for instance, add a note of tentativeness or uncertainty?
3. If there are unexpected stresses or pauses, what do they communicate about the speaker's experience? How do they affect you?

# A NOTE ON EXPLICATION

On page 55 we discuss the form known as *explication,* a line-by-line commentary seeking to make explicit or to explain the meaning that is implicit or hidden within the words. (*Explication* comes from the Latin *explicare,* meaning "to unfold," from *ex* = out + *plicare* = to fold.) The implication of such an activity is that writers "fold" a meaning into their words, and the reader perceives or unfolds the message. (*Implication,* also from the Latin word for "fold," means something entangled or involved in something else.)

An example will clarify these remarks. If we say to someone, "Shut the door," obviously we are conveying a message through these words. Also obviously, the message in "Shut the door" is *not* exactly the same as the message in "Would you mind shutting the door, please?" An explication would point out that the first sentence contains an authoritative tone that is not found in the second. In effect, the first sentence "says" (in addition to the point about the door) that the speaker may give orders to the hearer; or, to put it the other way around, folded into the second sentence (but not the first) is the speaker's awareness that the person receiving the words is the speaker's social equal. A slightly more complicated and much more interesting example is Julius Caesar's "I came, I saw, I conquered" (Latin: *veni, vidi, vici*). An explication would point out that in addition to the explicit meaning there are implicit meanings, for example that a man like Caesar does not waste words, that he is highly disciplined (the pattern of words suggests that he is a master of language), and that he is the sort of person who, on seeing something, immediately gets it under control by taking the appropriate action.

Because explication is chiefly concerned with making explicit what is implicit in a text, it is not concerned with such matters as the poet's place in history or the poet's biography, nor is it concerned with the reader's response to the poem—except to the degree that the reader's explication really may *not* be an objective decoding of the poem but may depend in large part on the reader's private associations. (Some literary critics would argue that the underlying premise of explication—that a writer puts a specific meaning into a work and that a reader can objectively recover that meaning—is based on the mistaken belief that readers can be objective.) If you look at the sample explication on pages 56–59, you can decide for yourself whether the student unfolded implicit meanings that the author (William Butler Yeats) had tucked into the words of his poem or whether the explication really is a personal response to the poem.

# A STUDENT'S WRITTEN RESPONSE TO A POEM

What we give in this chapter is not an explication but a more personal response to a poem by Louise Glück. Like an explication, it is concerned with the author's meaning; but unlike an explication, it does not hesitate to go beyond the poem and into "the real world" that the writer of the paper lives in. The essay is not so personal that the poem disappears (as it might in an essay that says something like "This poem reminds me of the time that I . . ."), but it does not claim merely to unfold meanings that Glück has embodied or entangled in her words.

First read the following biographical note and the poem.

# LOUISE GLÜCK

*One of the leading contemporary poets, Louise Glück was born in New York City in 1943, grew up on Long Island, and attended Sarah Lawrence College and Columbia University. She has taught at a number of colleges and universities, including the University of Iowa and*

*Williams College.* Firstborn, *her first book of poems, was published in 1968. Her later books include* The House on Marshland *(1975), from which the following poem is taken;* The Triumph of Achilles *(1985);* The Wild Iris *(1992); and* Vita Nova *(1999). Glück's poetry has been widely anthologized and translated.* Proofs and Theories: Essays on Poetry *(1995) is a collection of her literary criticism on Stanley Kunitz, T. S. Eliot, and other authors.*

## Gretel in Darkness

[1975]

This is the world we wanted,
All who would have seen us dead
are dead. I hear the witch's cry
break in the moonlight through a sheet
of sugar: God rewards.                                              5
Her tongue shrivels into gas. . . .

    Now, far from women's arms
and memory of women, in our father's hut
we sleep, are never hungry.
Why do I not forget?                                               10
My father bars the door, bars harm
from this house, and it is years.

No one remembers. Even you, my brother,
summer afternoons you look at me as though
you meant to leave,                                                15
as though it never happened.
But I killed for you. I see armed firs,
the spires of that gleaming kiln—

Nights I turn to you to hold me
but you are not there.                                             20
Am I alone? Spies
hiss in the stillness, Hansel,
we are there still and it is real, real,
that black forest and the fire in earnest.

----

A student named Jennifer Anderson was assigned to write about this poem in an Introduction to Literature course. Jennifer started her work by copying the poem on a sheet of paper and annotating it.

To follow up on these annotations and develop them, Jennifer turned next to her writing journal. She jotted down responses and ideas, and her questions about aspects of the poem and details of the language that intrigued and puzzled her.

Speaker ———— (Gretel) in Darkness    *Gretel and her brother*

This is the world (we) wanted.
All who would have <u>seen us</u> (dead)
are (dead). I hear the witch's cry
break in the moonlight through a sheet
of sugar: <u>God</u> rewards.    *Christian theme?*
Her tongue shrivels into gas. . . .

*why this space?*    Now, far from women's arms ———    *Women (mother) vs. Father*
and memory of women, in our <u>father's</u> hut
we sleep, are never hungry.
Why do I not forget? ——— *the Key Question*
My father (bars) the door, (bars) harm

*The speaker does*    from this house, and it is years.
<u>No one remembers</u>. Even you, my brother,
summer afternoons <u>you look at me as though
you meant to leave</u>,

*intense, direct word choice*    as though it never happened.    *oven, furnace*
But I <u>killed</u> for you. I see armed firs,
the spires of that gleaming (kiln)

Nights I turn to you to hold me    *Hansel's separation / distance from Gretel*
but <u>you are not there</u>.

*"S" sounds*    Am I alone? Spies    *compare with opening lines—everything's not dead*
hiss in the stillness, Hansel,
(we are there) still and it is (real,) (real,)    *serious + intense*
that black forest and the fire in <u>earnest</u>.

**Here are the pages from her journal:**

Great poem! Haunting, eerie. My favorite so far
in the course.

Story of Hansel and Gretel--Look this up. Should
I summarize the story in the paper?

Speaker--Gretel. Why her, and not Hansel? Not
both of them as speakers?

"in darkness"--really in darkness, or is
darkness a metaphor?

Repetition in the poem: dead/dead, bar/bar, real/real.

The tone of the opening stanza--scary, ominous. Darkness, dead.

The reference to the witch. "Shrivels into gas"--creepy detail.

But the witch has been defeated. Through the power of God? Why is God mentioned in this line?--not mentioned elsewhere.

Women (not mothers) seem the enemy in stanza two. (Odd that the second stanza is indented.) The father provides safety. But safety is not enough. Gretel cannot forget the past: the real enemy is not the witch or the mothers, but her memory.

She has to talk about her memory, her experiences. "No one remembers," but she does.

I think that this is a poem about Memory. "Why do I not forget?"

Gretel doesn't want her brother to forget. She reminds him.

"Killed"- such a strong word, very direct. Gretel is angry with her brother; she feels him pulling away from her.

Something disturbed, unnatural about the poem?-- the detail about Gretel looking for her brother to hold her. But he is absent. Where is he?

Who are the "Spies"? Lots of "s" sounds in these lines--spies, hiss, stillness, Hansel, still.

She addresses him by name.

She cannot escape, maybe she doesn't want to escape. Note that Gretel is describing her memories of what happened--not a poem that tells the story of Hansel and Gretel. Glück is interested in how Gretel remembers, how she feels about remembering.

Jennifer knew the main features of the Hansel and Gretel story—the brother and sister, their abandonment, their capture by a witch, and their escape. But she wanted to remind herself about the details, as her note to herself in her journal indicates.

As an experiment, Jennifer used one of the Internet search engines that her instructor had described during class. She went to:

Metacrawler
http://www.metacrawler.com

And she searched for "hansel and gretel." A number of the results looked promising, and she linked to this one:

Grimm's Fairy Tales—Hansel and Gretel
http://www.mordent.com/folktales/grimms/hng/hng.html

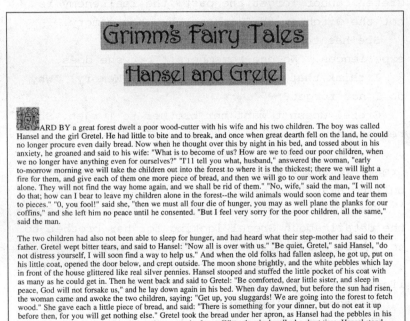

**Grimm's Fairy Tales**

**Hansel and Gretel**

ARD BY a great forest dwelt a poor wood-cutter with his wife and his two children. The boy was called Hansel and the girl Gretel. He had little to bite and to break, and once when great dearth fell on the land, he could no longer procure even daily bread. Now when he thought over this by night in his bed, and tossed about in his anxiety, he groaned and said to his wife: "What is to become of us? How are we to feed our poor children, when we no longer have anything even for ourselves?" "I'll tell you what, husband," answered the woman, "early to-morrow morning we will take the children out into the forest to where it is the thickest; there we will light a fire for them, and give each of them one more piece of bread, and then we will go to our work and leave them alone. They will not find the way home again, and we shall be rid of them." "No, wife," said the man, "I will not do that; how can I bear to leave my children alone in the forest--the wild animals would soon come and tear them to pieces." "0, you fool!" said she, "then we must all four die of hunger, you may as well plane the planks for our coffins," and she left him no peace until he consented. "But I feel very sorry for the poor children, all the same," said the man.

The two children had also not been able to sleep for hunger, and had heard what their step-mother had said to their father. Gretel wept bitter tears, and said to Hansel: "Now all is over with us." "Be quiet, Gretel," said Hansel, "do not distress yourself, I will soon find a way to help us." And when the old folks had fallen asleep, he got up, put on his little coat, opened the door below, and crept outside. The moon shone brightly, and the white pebbles which lay in front of the house glittered like real silver pennies. Hansel stooped and stuffed the little pocket of his coat with as many as he could get in. Then he went back and said to Gretel: "Be comforted, dear little sister, and sleep in peace, God will not forsake us," and he lay down again in his bed. When day dawned, but before the sun had risen, the woman came and awoke the two children, saying: "Get up, you sluggards! We are going into the forest to fetch wood." She gave each a little piece of bread, and said: "There is something for your dinner, but do not eat it up before then, for you will get nothing else." Gretel took the bread under her apron, as Hansel had the pebbles in his pocket. Then they all set out together on the way to the forest. When they had walked a short time, Hansel stood still and peeped back at the house, and did so again and again. His father said: "Hansel, what are you looking at there and staying behind for? Pay attention, and do not forget how to use your legs." "Ah, father," said Hansel, "I am looking at my little white cat, which is sitting up on the roof, and wants to say good-bye to me." The wife said: "Fool, that is not your little cat, that is the morning sun which is shining on the chimneys." Hansel, however, had not been looking back at the cat, but had been constantly throwing one of the white pebble-stones out of his pocket on the road.

"Hansel and Gretel" on the Internet (full text available; portion of first page reproduced here).

Jennifer had not reread "Hansel and Gretel" since she was a child. Rereading it now was very helpful, for it clarified a number of important details in Glück's poem. It explained, for example, "the witch's cry" in the first stanza, which alludes to the witch's "horrible howl" when Gretel pushes her into the oven. It also fills out the reference to the "women" in the second stanza, who in the story include the children's cruel step-mother as well as the evil witch. Jennifer could have prepared and written her paper without taking the time to check on the story, but it was better that she did.

# STUDENT ESSAY

Here is the essay that Jennifer wrote.

---

Anderson 1

Jennifer Anderson
Professor Washington
English 102
12 October 2005

A Memory Poem:
Louise Glück's "Gretel in Darkness"
Everyone knows the story of Hansel and
Gretel, one of the best-known of Grimm's
Fairy Tales. In her poem "Gretel in
Darkness" (513), Louise Glück takes
for granted that we know the story--the
brother and sister who are mistreated by
their father and, especially, by their
stepmother; their abandonment in a forest;
their capture by a witch who lives in a
house made of cakes and candy; the witch's
plan to fatten them up (Hansel first) and
then eat them; Gretel's killing of the
witch by pushing her into an oven; and,
finally, the children's discovery of the

Anderson 2

witch's jewels that makes them and their
father (the stepmother has died) rich
and happy at last. Glück's subject is not
the story itself, but, instead, Gretel's
memories. "Gretel in Darkness" is a
haunting poem about horrors that Gretel,
Glück's speaker, cannot forget.

The poem takes place after the witch
has been killed and Hansel and Gretel have
returned to the safety of their father's
cottage. Everything now should be fine,
Gretel says: "This is the world we wanted."
"God rewards": God has heard their prayers
and saved them. But as if it were still
present, Gretel hears "the witch's cry,"
the witch whom Gretel killed. And the image
about the witch's death that she uses is
graphic and disturbing: "Her tongue
shrivels into gas. . . ." The witch was
horrible, but this image is horrifying; it
sticks in Gretel's mind, and the reader's
too, like a shocking detail from a
nightmare.

In a way the entire poem reports on a
nightmare that Gretel is doomed to live in
forever. "Why do I not forget?"--the key
line in the poem, I think--really means
that she knows she will always remember
what happened to her and her brother. For
Gretel this fairy tale does not have a
happy ending.

Yet it does for her brother, or so it
seems to Gretel. She resents Hansel's
failure to remember as she does, and, with
a vivid, direct choice of verb, she reminds
him: "I killed for you." The nightmarish
quality of Gretel's thoughts and feelings
is shown again in the next lines, which
once more make clear how much her past
dominates the present:

> I see armed firs,
>    the spires of that gleaming kiln--

Gretel is safe but threatened, sheltered
at home but still in danger. She is caught
by a terrifying and terrible past she
cannot break free from. The repetitions--
dead/dead, bars/bar, real/real--imply that
she is trapped, not able to re-enter the
present and look forward to the future.
She turns to her brother for help, yet
without finding the support she seeks:

> Nights I turn to you to hold me
> but you are not there.

Hansel (who is only named once) is not
there for Gretel, and at first I felt her
hurt. But Glück is not meaning to criticize
Hansel for his distance, his separation
from his sister. Or if Glück is, she is
balancing that against Gretel's absorption
in the terror of her experiences. She feels
that she and her brother are still in the
middle of them.

Anderson 4

As I thought further about this poem, I
wondered: Strange as it sounds, maybe Gretel
prefers the past to the present, because the
past was so real. Life is all too safe and
comfortable now, while <u>then</u> everything, like
the fire in the oven, was so earnest, that is,
so serious and intense. It was not the world
she wanted--who would want to be in that house
of horrors! Even now her life is menaced,
as those snaky "s" sounds in the middle of
the final stanza suggest. But perhaps the
frightful feelings, in their intensity,
were (and still are) keener and deeper than
anything that Gretel knew before, or knows
now, in the secure world she lives in with her
father and brother. She and her brother then
were so absolutely close, as they are not now.
Gretel cannot let go of her past, and she does
not want to.

**[New page]**

Anderson 5

Work Cited

Glück, Louise. "Gretel in Darkness." <u>A</u>
<u>Little Literature</u>. Ed. Sylvan Barnet,
William Burto, and William E. Cain. New
York: Longman, 2007. 513.

# ▒ TOPICS FOR CRITICAL THINKING AND WRITING

1. Jennifer's instructor told the class that the essay should be "about 500 words." Jennifer's paper is more than that—about 650 words. Do you think that she uses her space well? Could she have shortened the essay, to bring it closer to the assigned length? If you had to suggest cuts, where would you propose to make them?

2. Does Jennifer omit important details in the poem that you think she should have included in the paper? Explain why these should be part of her response.

3. Give Jennifer's paper a grade, and in a paragraph written to her, highlight the strengths and limitations of this paper. Provide her, too, with one or two specific suggestions for improving her writing in the next paper.

# 20

# American Voices: Poems for a Diverse Nation

## AURORA LEVINS MORALES

*Aurora Levins Morales, born in Puerto Rico in 1954, came to the United States with her family in 1967. She has lived in Chicago and New Hampshire and now lives in the San Francisco Bay area. Levins Morales has published stories, essays, prose poems, and poems.*

## Child of the Americas                                    [1986]

I am a child of the Americas,
a light-skinned mestiza of the Caribbean,
a child of many diaspora,° born into this continent at a crossroads.

I am a U.S. Puerto Rican Jew,
a product of the ghettos of New York I have never known.                    5
An immigrant and the daughter and granddaughter of immigrants.
I speak English with passion: it's the tongue of my consciousness,
a flashing knife blade of crystal, my tool, my craft.

I am Caribeña,° island grown. Spanish is in my flesh,
ripples from my tongue, lodges in my hips:                                   10
the language of garlic and mangoes,
the singing in my poetry, the flying gestures of my hands.

---

**3 diaspora** literally, "scattering"; the term is used especially to refer to the dispersion of the Jews outside of Israel from the sixth century BCE, when they were exiled to Babylonia, to the present time.   **9 Caribeña** Caribbean woman.

I am of Latinoamerica, rooted in the history of my continent:
I speak from that body.

I am not african. Africa is in me, but I cannot return.                    15
I am not taína.° Taíno is in me, but there is no way back.
I am not european. Europe lives in me, but I have no home there.

I am new. History made me. My first language was spanglish.°
I was born at the crossroads
and I am whole.                                                            20

---

**16 taína** the Taínos were the Indian tribe native to Puerto Rico.    **18 spanglish** a mixture of Spanish and English.

# MITSUYE YAMADA

*Mitsuye Yamada, the daughter of Japanese immigrants to the United States, was born in Japan in 1923, during her mother's return visit to her native land. Yamada was raised in Seattle; but in 1942 she and her family were incarcerated and then relocated to a camp in Idaho, when Executive Order 9066 gave military authorities the right to remove any and all persons from "military areas." In 1954 she became an American citizen. She has taught in the Asian American Studies Program at the University of California at Irvine, and she is the author of poems and stories.*

## To the Lady                                                          [1976]

The one in San Francisco who asked:
Why did the Japanese Americans let
the government put them in
those camps without protest?
Come to think of it I                                                      5
   should've run off to Canada
   should've hijacked a plane to Algeria
   should've pulled myself up from my
   bra straps
   and kicked'm in the groin                                              10
   should've bombed a bank
   should've tried self-immolation
   should've holed myself up in a
   woodframe house
   and let you watch me                                                   15

burn up on the six o'clock news
should've run howling down the street
naked and assaulted you at breakfast
by AP wirephoto
should've screamed bloody murder                              20
like Kitty Genovese°

Then
YOU would've
    come to my aid in shining armor
    laid yourself across the railroad track                  25
    marched on Washington
    tatooed a Star of David on your arm
    written six million enraged
    letters to Congress.

---

**21 Kitty Genovese** In 1964 Kitty Genovese of Kew Gardens, New York, was
stabbed to death when she left her car and walked toward her home. Thirty-eight
persons heard her screams, but no one came to her assistance.

Dorothea Lange, "Grandfather and Grandchildren Awaiting Evacuation Bus."

But we didn't draw the line                                    30
anywhere
law and order Executive Order 9066°
social order moral order internal order

YOU let'm
I let'm                                                        35
All are punished.

---

32 **Executive Order 9066** an authorization, signed in 1941 by President
Franklin D. Roosevelt, allowing military authorities to relocate Japanese and
Japanese-Americans who resided on the Pacific Coast of the United States.

# YUSEF KOMUNYAKAA

*Yusef Komunyakaa was born in 1947 in Bogalusa, Louisiana. After
graduating from high school he entered the army and served in Vietnam, where he was awarded the Bronze Star. On his return to the
United States he earned a bachelor's degree at the University of Colorado, and then earned an M.A. at Colorado State University and an
M.F.A. in creative writing at the University of California, Irvine. The author of several books of poetry, he has been teaching at Indiana University in Bloomington since 1985. "Facing It" is the last poem in a book
of poems about Vietnam, Dien Cai Dau (1988). The title of the book is a
slang word for crazy.*

## Facing It                                                  [1988]

My black face fades,
hiding inside the black granite.
I said I wouldn't,
dammit: No tears.
I'm stone. I'm flesh.                                          5
My clouded reflection eyes me
like a bird of prey, the profile of night
slanted against morning. I turn
this way—the stone lets me go.
I turn that way—I'm inside                                    10
the Vietnam Veterans Memorial
again, depending on the light
to make a difference.
I go down the 58,022 names,

half-expecting to find 15
my own in letters like smoke.
I touch the name Andrew Johnson;
I see the booby trap's white flash.
Names shimmer on a woman's blouse
but when she walks away 20
the names stay on the wall.
Brushstrokes flash, a red bird's
wings cutting across my stare.
The sky. A plane in the sky.
A white vet's image floats 25
closer to me, then his pale eyes
look through mine. I'm a window.
He's lost his right arm
inside the stone. In the black mirror
a woman's trying to erase names: 30
No, she's brushing a boy's hair.

Vietnam Veterans Memorial.

# CLAUDE McKAY

*Claude McKay (1890-1948), born in Jamaica, came to the United States when he was twenty-three. McKay is known chiefly for his militant left-wing writings—novels and essays as well as poems—but he wrote a wide range of lyric poetry, and despite his radicalism he favored (like his friend Countee Cullen) traditional poetic forms such as the sonnet.*

## America

[1921]

Although she feeds me bread of bitterness,
And sinks into my throat her tiger's tooth,
Stealing my breath of life, I will confess
I love this cultured hell that tests my youth!
Her vigor flows like tides into my blood,                    5
Giving me strength against her hate.
Her bigness sweeps my being like a flood
Yet as a rebel fronts a king in state,
I stand within her walls with not a shred
Of terror, malice, not a word of jeer.                      10
Darkly I gaze into the days ahead,
And see her might and granite wonders there,
Beneath the touch of Time's unerring hand,
Like priceless treasures sinking in the sand.

# DUDLEY RANDALL

*Born in Washington, D.C., in 1914, Randall graduated from Wayne State University and the University of Michigan, and worked as a reference librarian and as poet in residence at the University of Detroit. In 1965 he founded the Broadside Press, widely recognized as influential far beyond its size. Broadside Press issues excellent small books and single sheets with poems by African-Americans.*

## The Melting Pot

[1968]

There is a magic melting pot
where any girl or man
can step in Czech or Greek or Scot,
step out American                                            4

*Johann* and *Jan* and *Jean* and *Juan,*
*Giovanni* and *Ivan*
step in and then step out again
all freshly christened *John.*                                           8

Sam, watching, said, "Why, I was here
even before they came,"
and stepped in too, but was tossed out
before he passed the brim.                                              12

And every time Sam tried that pot
they threw him out again.

"Keep out. This is our private pot
We don't want your black stain."                                        16

At last, thrown out a thousand times,
Sam said, "I don't give a damn.
Shove your old pot. You can like it or not,
but I'll be just what I am."                                            20

# MARTÍN ESPADA

*Martín Espada was born in Brooklyn in 1957. He received a bachelor's
degree from the University of Wisconsin and a law degree from North-
eastern University. A poet who publishes regularly, Espada is also Out-
reach Coordinator and Supervisor of Lawyers of the Arts at the Artists'
Foundation in Boston.*

## *Bully*                                                          [1990]

*Boston, Massachusetts, 1987*

In the school auditorium,
the Theodore Roosevelt statue
is nostalgic
for the Spanish-American War,
each fist lonely for a saber                                            5
or the reins of anguish-eyed horses,
or a podium to clatter with speeches
glorying in the malaria of conquest.

But now the Roosevelt school
is pronounced *Hernández.*                                             10
Puerto Rico has invaded Roosevelt

with its army of Spanish-singing children
in the hallways,
brown children devouring
the stockpiles of the cafeteria,                                    15
children painting *Taíno* ancestors
that leap naked across murals.

Roosevelt is surrounded
by all the faces
he ever shoved in eugenic spite                                    20
and cursed as mongrels, skin of one race,
hair and cheekbones of another.

Once Marines tramped
from the newsreel of his imagination;
now children plot to spray graffiti                                25
in parrot-brilliant colors across the Victorian mustache
and monocle.

# JIMMY SANTIAGO BACA

*Jimmy Santiago Baca, of Chicano and Apache descent, was born in
1952. When he was two his parents divorced, and a grandparent
brought him up until he was five, when he was placed in an orphan-
age in New Mexico. He ran away when he was eleven, lived on the
streets, took drugs, and at the age of twenty was convicted of drug possession. In prison he taught himself to read and write, and he began to
compose poetry. A fellow inmate urged him to send some poems to
Mother Jones magazine, and the work was accepted. In 1979 Louisiana
State University Press published a book of his poems,* Immigrants in Our
Own Land. *He has since published several other books.*

## So Mexicans Are Taking Jobs from Americans          [1979]

O Yes? Do they come on horses
with rifles, and say,
         Ese gringo,° gimmee your job?
And do you, gringo, take off your ring,
drop your wallet into a blanket                                    5
spread over the ground, and walk away?

---

**3 Ese gringo** Hey, whitey.

I hear Mexicans are taking your jobs away.
Do they sneak into town at night,
and as you're walking home with a whore,
do they mug you, a knife at your throat,                              10
saying, I want your job?

Even on TV, an asthmatic leader
crawls turtle heavy, leaning on an assistant,
and from a nest of wrinkles on his face,
a tongue paddles through flashing waves                              15
of lightbulbs, of cameramen, rasping
"They're taking our jobs away."

Well, I've gone about trying to find them,
asking just where the hell are these fighters.

The rifles I hear sound in the night                                 20
are white farmers shooting blacks and browns
whose ribs I see jutting out
and starving children,
I see the poor marching for a little work,
I see small white farmers selling out                                25
to clean-suited farmers living in New York,
who've never been on a farm,
don't know the look of a hoof or the smell
of a woman's body bending all day long in fields.

I see this, and I hear only a few people                             30
got all the money in this world, the rest
count their pennies to buy bread and butter.

Below that cool green sea of money,
millions and millions of people fight to live,
search for pearls in the darkest depths                              35
of their dreams, hold their breath for years
trying to cross poverty to just having something.

The children are dead already. We are killing them,
that is what America should be saying;
on TV, in the streets, in offices, should be saying,                 40
    "We aren't giving the children a chance to live."
Mexicans are taking our jobs, they say instead.
What they really say is, let them die,
and the children too.

# SHERMAN ALEXIE

*Sherman Alexie, born in 1966 in Spokane, Washington, holds a B.A. from Washington State University. Author of novels, stories, and poems, Alexie has been awarded a grant from the National Endowment for the Arts. Of his life and his work he says, "I am a Spokane Coeur d'Alene Indian. . . . I live on the Spokane Indian Reservation. Everything I do now, writing and otherwise, has its origin in that."*

## On the Amtrak from Boston to New York City    [1993]

The white woman across the aisle from me says, "Look,
look at all the history, that house
on the hill there is over two hundred years old,"
as she points out the window past me                                4

into what she has been taught. I have learned
little more about American history during my few days
back East than what I expected and far less
of what we should all know of the tribal stories            8

whose architecture is 15,000 years older
than the corners of the house that sits
museumed on the hill. "Walden Pond,"°
the woman on the train asks, "Did you see Walden Pond?"      12

and I don't have a cruel enough heart to break
her own by telling her there are five Walden Ponds
on my little reservation out West
and at least a hundred more surrounding Spokane,            16

the city I pretend to call my home. "Listen,"
I could have told her. "I don't give a shit
about Walden. I know the Indians were living stories
around that pond before Walden's grandparents were born     20

and before his grandparents' grandparents were born.
I'm tired of hearing about Don-fucking-Henley° saving it, too,
because that's redundant. If Don Henley's brothers and sisters
and mothers and fathers hadn't come here in the first place   24

---

11 **Walden Pond** site in Massachusetts where Henry David Thoreau (1817–62) lived from 4 July 1845 to 6 September 1847, and about which he wrote in his most famous book, *Walden* (1854).    22 **Don Henley** rock singer who was active in preserving Walden Pond.

then nothing would need to be saved."
But I didn't say a word to the woman about Walden
Pond because she smiled so much and seemed delighted
that I thought to bring her an orange juice                    28

back from the food car. I respect elders
of every color. All I really did was eat
my tasteless sandwich, drink my Diet Pepsi
and nod my head whenever the woman pointed out              32

another little piece of her country's history
while I, as all Indians have done
since this war began, made plans
for what I would do and say the next time                    36

somebody from the enemy thought I was one of their own.


# LAUREEN MAR

*Laureen Mar, a Chinese-American born in Seattle in 1953, studied creative writing at Columbia University. She has published poems in several national magazines.*


## *My Mother, Who Came from China,*
## *Where She Never Saw Snow*                        [1977]

In the huge, rectangular room, the ceiling
a machinery of pipes and fluorescent lights,
ten rows of women hunch over machines,
their knees pressing against pedals
and hands pushing the shiny fabric thick as tongues          5
through metal and thread.
My mother bends her head to one of these machines.
Her hair is coarse and wiry, black as burnt scrub.
She wears glasses to shield her intense eyes.
A cone of orange thread spins. Around her,                   10
talk flutters harshly in Toisan wah.°
Chemical stings. She pushes cloth
through a pounding needle, under, around, and out,
breaks thread with a snap against fingerbone, tooth.
Sleeve after sleeve, sleeve.                                 15
It is easy. The same piece.
For eight or nine hours, sixteen bundles maybe,
250 sleeves to ski coats, all the same.

---

**11 Toisan wah** a Chinese dialect.

It is easy, only once she's run the needle
through her hand. She earns money                                    20
by each piece, on a good day,
thirty dollars. Twenty-four years.
It is frightening how fast she works.
She and the women who were taught sewing
terms in English as Second Language.                                 25
Dull thunder passes through their fingers.

# ROBERT FROST

*For a biographical note on Robert Frost (1874–1963), see page 537.*

## The Vanishing Red                                         [1916]

He is said to have been the last Red Man
In Acton.° And the Miller is said to have laughed—
If you like to call such a sound a laugh.
But he gave no one else a laugher's license.
For he turned suddenly grave as if to say,                           5
"Whose business,—if I take it on myself,
Whose business—but why talk round the barn?—
When it's just that I hold with getting a thing done with."
You can't get back and see it as he saw it.
It's too long a story to go into now.                                10
You'd have to have been there and lived it.
Then you wouldn't have looked on it as just a matter
of who began it between the two races.

Some guttural exclamation of surprise
The Red Man gave in poking about the mill                           15
Over the great big thumping shuffling mill-stone
Disgusted the Miller physically as coming
From one who had no right to be heard from.
"Come, John," he said, 'you want to see the wheel pit?"°

He took him down below a cramping rafter,                           20
And showed him, through a manhole in the floor,
The water in desperate straits like frantic fish,
Salmon and sturgeon, lashing with their tails.
Then he shut down the trap door with a ring in it

---

2 **Acton** a town in Massachusetts, not far from where Frost spent part of his
childhood.    19 **wheel pit** the pit containing the wheel that, agitated by the water,
drives the mill.

That jangled even above the general noise,                    25
And came up stairs alone—and gave that laugh,
And said something to a man with a meal-sack
That the man with the meal-sack didn't catch—then.
Oh, yes, he showed John the wheel pit all right.

# NILA NORTHSUN

*Nila northSun was born in 1951 in Schurz, Nevada, of Shoshone-Chippewa stock. She studied at the California State University campuses at Hayward and Humboldt and the University of Montana at Missoula, beginning as a psychology major but switching to art history, specializing in Native American art. She is the author of three books of poetry and is director of an emergency youth shelter in Fallon, Nevada.*

## Moving Camp Too Far                                  [1977]

i can't speak of
    many moons
    moving camp on travois°
i can't tell of
    the last great battle                             5
    counting coup° or
    taking scalp
i don't know what it
    was to hunt buffalo
    or do the ghost dance                             10
but

i can see an eagle
    almost extinct
    on slurpee plastic cups
i can travel to powwows                                15
    in campers & winnebagos
i can eat buffalo meat
    at the tourist burger stand
i can dance to indian music
    rock-n-roll hey-a-hey-o                           20
i can
    & unfortunately
    i do

---

**3 travois** a frame slung between trailing poles that are pulled by a horse. Plains
Indians used the device to transport their goods.    **6 counting coup** recounting
one's exploits in battle.

# 21

# Two Poets in Depth:
# Robert Frost and
# Langston Hughes

## ON READING AUTHORS
## REPRESENTED IN DEPTH

If you have read several works by an author, whether tragedies by Shakespeare or detective stories about Sherlock Holmes by Arthur Conan Doyle, you know that authors return again and again to certain themes (tragedy for Shakespeare, crime for Conan Doyle), yet each treatment is different. *Hamlet, Macbeth,* and *Romeo and Juliet* are all tragedies, and they all share certain qualities that we think of as Shakespearean, yet each is highly distinctive.

When we read several works by an author, we find ourselves thinking about resemblances and differences. We enjoy seeing the author return to some theme (for instance, God, or nature, or love) or to some literary form (for instance, the sonnet, or blank verse, or pairs of rhyming lines); and we may find, to our delight, that the author has handled things differently and that we are getting a sense of the writer's variety and perhaps even of the writer's development. Indeed, we sometimes speak of the *shape* or *design* of the author's career, meaning that our careful study of the writings has led us to an understanding of the story—with its beginning, middle, and end—that the writings tell across a period of time. Often, once we read one poem by an author and find it intriguing or compelling, we want to read more: Are there other poems like this one? What kinds of poems were written before or after this one? Our enjoyment and understanding of one poem helps us to enjoy and understand others, and makes us curious about the place that each one occupies in a larger structure, the shape of the author's career.

We can go further and say that the reading of a second author can help us—perhaps by way of contrast—to understand the first. In the preface to one of his volumes of poetry, Robert Frost put it this way:

> A poem is best read in the light of all the other poems ever written. We read A the better to read B (we have to start somewhere; we may get very little out of A). We read B the better to read C, C the better to read D, D the better to go back and get something more out of A. Progress is not the aim, but circulation. The thing is to get among the poems where they hold each other apart in their places as the stars do.

In an Introduction to Literature course, although you'll often be asked to write analytical papers about a single poem, story, or play, sometimes you'll be assigned a paper that requires a comparison and contrast of, for example, two poems by different authors. Less frequent perhaps, but equally important, is the paper that examines a central theme or idea as it is expressed and explored in three or more works.

At first this might seem a daunting task, but there are helpful ways of getting in control of the assignment. One of the best is to begin with a single work and then to move outward from it, making connections to works that show interesting similarities to, or differences from, it.

One of our students, Mark Bradley, was assigned to write on a theme (which he had to define himself) in a selection of poems by Langston Hughes. Mark started by closely studying a poem by Hughes that had caught his attention when he made his way through the group of poems for the first time. In one of his journal entries, Mark wrote:

```
The poem "The South" surprised me. It wasn't
what I expected. I thought Hughes would attack
the South for being so racist--he wrote the poem
in the 1920s, when segregation was everywhere
in the South. He says some tough stuff about the
South, that's for sure: "Beast strong, / Idiot-
brained." But he also says that the South is
attractive in some ways, and I'm not convinced
that when he brings in the North at the end,
he really believes that the North is superior.
```

Intrigued by this poem, Mark made it his point of departure for the thematic paper he was assigned. He judged that if he worked intensively on this poem and came to know it well, he could review other Hughes poems and see how they were both like and unlike the poem with which he began.

When you write an essay on several works, keep two points especially in mind: the length of the assignment, and the choice of examples. You want to treat the right number of examples for the space you are given, and, furthermore, to provide sufficient detail in your analysis of each of them. You might call this the principle of proportion.

Preparing an outline can be valuable. It will lead you to think carefully about which examples you have selected for your argument and the main idea about each one that you will present. You might begin by examining one poem in depth, and then proceed to relate it to key passages in other poems. Or maybe you'll find one passage in a poem so significant that it—rather than the poem in its entirety—can serve as a good beginning. Whichever strategy you choose, when you review the rough draft, use a pen to mark off the amount of space that you have devoted to each example. Ask yourself:

* Is this example clearly connected to my argument in the paper as a whole?
* Have I not only referred to the example but also provided adequate quotation from it?
* Have I made certain to comment on the passage? (Remember that passages do not interpret themselves. You have to explicate and explain them.)
* Has each example received its due?

There is no easy rule of thumb for knowing how much space each example should be given. Some passages are more complicated than others; some demand more intensive scrutiny. But you'll be well on the way toward handling this aspect of the paper effectively if you are self-aware about your choices, alert to the principle of proportion.

# ROBERT FROST

 *Robert Frost (1874-1963) was born in California. After his father's death in 1885, Frost's mother brought the family to New England, where she taught in high schools in Massachusetts and New Hampshire. Frost studied for part of one term at Dartmouth College in New Hampshire, then did odd jobs (including teaching), and from 1897 to 1899 was enrolled as a special student at Harvard. He then farmed in New Hampshire, published a few poems in local newspapers, left the farm and*

*taught again, and in 1912 left for England, where he hoped to achieve more popular success as a writer. By 1915 he had won a considerable reputation, and he returned to the United States, settling on a farm in New Hampshire and cultivating the image of the country-wise farmer-poet. In fact he was well read in the classics, the Bible, and English and American literature.*

*Among Frost's many comments about literature, here are three: "Writing is unboring to the extent that it is dramatic"; "Every poem is . . . a figure of the will braving alien entanglements"; and, finally, a poem "begins in delight and ends in wisdom. . . . It runs a course of lucky events, and ends in a clarification of life—not necessarily a great clarification, such as sects and cults are founded on, but in a momentary stay against confusion."*

*And for good measure, here is Frost, in a letter, writing about his own work.*

> *You get more credit for thinking if you restate formulae or cite cases that fall in easily under formulae, but all the fun is outside[,] saying things that suggest formulae that won't formulate—that almost but don't quite formulate. I should like to be so subtle at this game as to seem to the casual person altogether obvious. The casual person would assume I meant nothing or else I came near enough meaning something he was familiar with to mean it for all practical purposes. Well, well, well.*

*We give ten of Frost's poems, arranged in chronological order, and we follow these poems with some of Frost's comments about poetry. The first poem, "The Pasture," is one that Frost customarily put at the beginning of his collected poems. The last words of each stanza, "You come too," are an invitation to the reader to join him.*

*Note: "Stopping by Woods on a Snowy Evening" is printed on page 7, and "The Vanishing Red" on page 533.*

## The Pasture                                          [1913]

I'm going out to clean the pasture spring;
I'll only stop to rake the leaves away
(And wait to watch the water clear, I may):
I shan't be gone long.—You come too.                            4

I'm going out to fetch the little calf
That's standing by the mother. It's so young,
It totters when she licks it with her tongue.
I shan't be gone long.—You come too.                            8

# Mending Wall

[1914]

Something there is that doesn't love a wall,
That sends the frozen-ground-swell under it,
And spills the upper boulder in the sun;
And makes gaps even two can pass abreast.
The work of hunters is another thing:                                    5
I have come after them and made repair
Where they have left not one stone on a stone,
But they would have the rabbit out of hiding,
To please the yelping dogs. The gaps I mean,
No one has seen them made or heard them made,               10
But at spring mending-time we find them there.
I let my neighbor know beyond the hill;
And on a day we meet to walk the line
And set the wall between us once again.
We keep the wall between us as we go.                                    15
To each the boulders that have fallen to each.
And some are loaves and some so nearly balls
We have to use a spell to make them balance:
"Stay where you are until our backs are turned!"
We wear our fingers rough with handling them.                   20
Oh, just another kind of outdoor game,
One on a side. It comes to little more:
There where it is we do not need the wall:
He is all pine and I am apple orchard.
My apple trees will never get across                                       25
And eat the cones under his pines, I tell him.
He only says, "Good fences make good neighbours."
Spring is the mischief in me, and I wonder
If I could put a notion in his head:
"Why do they make good neighbours? Isn't it                       30
Where there are cows? But here there are no cows.
Before I built a wall I'd ask to know
What I was walling in or walling out,
And to whom I was like to give offence.
Something there is that doesn't love a wall,                         35
That wants it down." I could say "Elves" to him,
But it's not elves exactly, and I'd rather
He said it for himself. I see him there
Bringing a stone grasped firmly by the top
In each hand, like an old-stone savage armed.                      40
He moves in darkness as it seems to me,

Not of woods only and the shade of trees.
He will not go behind his father's saying,
And he likes having thought of it so well
He says again, "Good fences make good neighbours."          45

## The Road Not Taken                                      [1916]

Two roads diverged in a yellow wood,
And sorry I could not travel both
And be one traveler, long I stood
And looked down one as far as I could
To where it bent in the undergrowth;                       5

Then took the other, as just as fair,
And having perhaps the better claim,
Because it was grassy and wanted wear;
Though as for that the passing there
Had worn them really about the same,                       10

And both that morning equally lay
In leaves no step had trodden black.
Oh, I kept the first for another day!
Yet knowing how way leads on to way,
I doubted if I should ever come back.                      15

I shall be telling this with a sigh
Somewhere ages and ages hence:
Two roads diverged in a wood, and I—
I took the one less traveled by,
And that has made all the difference.                      20

## The Aim Was Song                                        [1923]

Before man came to blow it right
    The wind once blew itself untaught,
And did its loudest day and night
    In any rough place where it caught.                    4

Man came to tell it what was wrong:
    It hadn't found the place to blow;
It blew too hard—the aim was song.
    And listen—how it ought to go!                         8

He took a little in his mouth,
    And held it long enough for north

To be converted into south,
And then by measure blew it forth.                        12

By measure. It was word and note,
The wind the wind had meant to be—
A little through the lips and throat.
The aim was song—the wind could see.                     16


## The Need of Being Versed in Country Things        [1923]

The house had gone to bring again
To the midnight sky a sunset glow.
Now the chimney was all of the house that stood,
Like a pistil after the petals go.                       4

The barn opposed across the way,
That would have joined the house in flame
Had it been the will of the wind, was left
To bear forsaken the place's name.                       8

No more it opened with all one end
For teams that came by the stony road
To drum on the floor with scurrying hoofs
And brush the mow with the summer load.                  12

The birds that came to it through the air
At broken windows flew out and in,
Their murmur more like the sigh we sigh
From too much dwelling on what has been.                 16

Yet for them the lilac renewed its leaf,
And the aged elm, though touched with fire;
And the dry pump flung up an awkward arm;
And the fence post carried a strand of wire.             20

For them there was really nothing sad.
But though they rejoiced in the nest they kept,
One had to be versed in country things
Not to believe the phoebes wept.                         24


## Acquainted with the Night        [1928]

I have been one acquainted with the night.
I have walked out in rain—and back in rain.
I have outwalked the furthest city light.

I have looked down the saddest city lane.
I have passed by the watchman on his beat    5
And dropped my eyes, unwilling to explain.

I have stood still and stopped the sound of feet
When far away an interrupted cry
Came over houses from another street,

But not to call me back or say good-bye;    10
And further still at an unearthly height,
One luminary clock against the sky

Proclaimed the time was neither wrong nor right.
I have been one acquainted with the night.


# Design
[1936]

I found a dimpled spider, fat and white,
On a white heal-all, holding up a moth
Like a white piece of rigid satin cloth—
Assorted characters of death and blight    4
Mixed ready to begin the morning right,
Like the ingredients of a witches' broth—
A snow-drop spider, a flower like froth,
And dead wings carried like a paper kite.    8

What had that flower to do with being white,
The wayside blue and innocent heal-all?
What brought the kindred spider to that height,
Then steered the white moth thither in the night?    12
What but design of darkness to appall?—
If design govern in a thing so small.


# The Silken Tent
[1942]

She is as in a field a silken tent
At midday when a sunny summer breeze
Has dried the dew and all its ropes relent,
So that in guys it gently sways at ease,    4
And its supporting central cedar pole,
That is its pinnacle to heavenward
And signifies the sureness of the soul,
Seems to owe naught to any single cord,    8
But strictly held by none, is loosely bound

By countless silken ties of love and thought
To everything on earth the compass round,
And only by one's going slightly taut                    12
In the capriciousness of summer air
Is of the slightest bondage made aware.

Page from Frost's notebooks, showing "The Silken Tent."

## Come In

[1942]

As I came to the edge of the woods.
Thrush music—hark!
Now if it was dusk outside,
Inside it was dark.                                        4

Too dark in the woods for a bird
By sleight of wing
To better its perch for the night,
Though it still could sing.                                                8

The last of the light of the sun
That had died in the west
Still lived for one song more
In a thrush's breast.                                                    12

Far in the pillared dark
Thrush music went—
Almost like a call to come in
To the dark and lament.                                                  16

But no, I was out for stars:
I would not come in.
I meant not even if asked,
And I hadn't been.                                                       20


## The Most of It                                          [1942]

He thought he kept the universe alone;
For all the voice in answer he could wake
Was but the mocking echo of his own
From some tree-hidden cliff across the lake.
Some morning from the boulder-broken beach                    5
He would cry out on life, that what it wants
Is not its own love back in copy speech,
But counter-love, original response.
And nothing ever came of what he cried
Unless it was the embodiment that crashed                    10
In the cliff's talus on the other side,
And then in the far distant water splashed,
But after a time allowed for it to swim,
Instead of proving human when it neared
And someone else additional to him,                          15
As a great buck it powerfully appeared,
Pushing the crumpled water up ahead,
And landed pouring like a waterfall,
And stumbled through the rocks with horny tread,
And forced the underbrush—and that was all.                  20

# ROBERT FROST ON POETRY

## *The Figure a Poem Makes*

Abstraction is an old story with the philosophers, but it has been like a new toy in the hands of the artists of our day. Why can't we have any one quality of poetry we choose by itself? We can have in thought. Then it will go hard if we can't in practice. Our lives for it.

Granted no one but a humanist much cares how sound a poem is if it is only *a* sound. The sound is the gold in the ore. Then we will have the sound out alone and dispense with the inessential. We do till we make the discovery that the object in writing poetry is to make all poems sound as different as possible from each other, and the resources for that of vowels, consonants, punctuation, syntax, words, sentences, meter are not enough. We need the help of context—meaning—subject matter. That is the greatest help towards variety. All that can be done with words is soon told. So also with meters—particularly in our language where there are virtually but two, strict iambic and loose iambic. The ancients with many were still poor if they depended on meters for all tune. It is painful to watch our sprung-rhythmists straining at the point of omitting one short from a foot for relief from monotony. The possibilities for tune from the dramatic tones of meaning struck across the rigidity of a limited meter are endless. And we are back in poetry as merely one more art of having something to say, sound or unsound. Probably better if sound, because deeper and from wider experience.

Then there is this wildness whereof it is spoken. Granted again that it has an equal claim with sound to being a poem's better half. If it is a wild tune, it is a poem. Our problem then is, as modern abstractionists, to have the wildness pure: to be wild with nothing to be wild about. We bring up as aberrationists, giving way to undirected associations and kicking ourselves from one chance suggestion to another in all directions as of a hot afternoon in the life of a grasshopper. Theme alone can steady us down. Just as the first mystery was how a poem could have a tune in such a straightness as meter, so the second mystery is how a poem can have wildness and at the same time a subject that shall be fulfilled.

It should be of the pleasure of a poem itself to tell how it can. The figure a poem makes. It begins in delight and ends in wisdom. The figure is the same as for love. No one can really hold that the ecstasy should be static and stand still in one place. It begins in delight, it inclines to the impulse, it assumes direction with the first line laid down, it runs a course of lucky events, and ends in a clarification of life—not necessarily a great clarification, such as sects and cults are founded on, but in a momentary stay against confusion. It has denouement. It has an outcome that though unforeseen was predestined from the first image of the original mood—and indeed from the very mood. It is but a trick poem and no poem at all if the best of it was thought of first and saved for the last. It finds its own name as it goes and discovers the best waiting for it in some final phrase at once wise and sad—the happy-sad blend of the drinking song.

No tears in the writer, no tears in the reader. No surprise for the writer, no surprise for the reader. For me the initial delight is in the surprise of remembering something I didn't know I knew. I am in a place, in a situation, as if I had materialized from cloud or risen out of the ground. There is a glad recognition of the long lost and the rest follows. Step by step the wonder of unexpected supply keeps growing. The impressions most useful to my purpose seem always those I was unaware of and so made no note of at the time when taken, and the conclusion is come to that like giants we are always hurling experience ahead of us to pave the future with against the day when we may want to strike a line of purpose across it for somewhere. The line will have the more charm for not being mechanically straight. We enjoy the straight crookedness of a good walking stick. Modern instruments of precision are being used to make things crooked as if by eye and hand in the old days.

I tell how there may be a better wildness of logic than of inconsequence. But the logic is backward, in retrospect, after the act. It must be more felt than seen ahead like prophecy. It must be a revelation, or a series of revelations, as much for the poet as for the reader. For it to be that there must have been the greatest freedom of the material to move about in it and to establish relations in it regardless of time and space, previous relation, and everything but affinity. We prate of freedom. We call our schools free because we are not free to stay away from them till we are sixteen years of age. I have given up my democratic prejudices and now willingly set the lower classes free to be completely taken care of by the upper classes. Political freedom is nothing to me. I bestow it right and left. All I would keep for myself is the freedom of my material—the condition of body and mind now and then to summons aptly from the vast chaos of all I have lived through.

Scholars and artists thrown together are often annoyed at the puzzle of where they differ. Both work from knowledge; but I suspect they differ most importantly in the way their knowledge is come by. Scholars get theirs with conscientious thoroughness along projected lines of logic; poets theirs cavalierly and as it happens in and out of books. They stick to nothing deliberately, but let what will stick to them like burrs where they walk in the fields. No acquirement is on assignment, or even self-assignment. Knowledge of the second kind is much more available in the wild free ways of wit and art. A school boy may be defined as one who can tell you what he knows in the order in which he learned it. The artist must value himself as he snatches a thing from some previous order in time and space into a new order with not so much as a ligature clinging to it of the old place where it was organic.

More than once I should have lost my soul to radicalism if it had been the originality it was mistaken for by young converts. Originality and initiative are what I ask for my country. For myself the originality need be no more than the freshness of a poem run in the way I have described: from delight to wisdom. The figure is the same as for love. Like a piece of ice on a hot stove the poem must ride on its own melting. A poem may be worked over once it is in being, but may not be worried into being. Its most precious quality will remain its having run itself and carried away the poet with it. Read it a hundred times: it will forever keep its freshness as a metal keeps its fragrance. It can never lose its sense of a meaning that once unfolded by surprise as it went.

## From "The Constant Symbol"

There are many other things I have found myself saying about poetry, but the chieftest of these is that it is metaphor, saying one thing and meaning another, saying one thing in terms of another, the pleasure of ulteriority. Poetry is simply made of metaphor. So also is philosophy and science, too, for that matter, if it will take the soft impeachment from a friend. Every poem is a new metaphor inside or it is nothing. And there is a sense in which all poems are the same old metaphor always.

Every single poem written regular is a symbol small or great of the way the will has to pitch into commitments deeper and deeper to a rounded conclusion and then be judged for whether any original intention it had has been strongly spent or weakly lost; be it in art, politics, school, church, business, love, or marriage—in a piece of work or in a career. Strongly spent is synonymous with kept.

# LANGSTON HUGHES

*Langston Hughes (1902-1967) was an accomplished poet, short-story writer, dramatist, essayist, and editor. He was born in Joplin, Missouri; he grew up in Lawrence, Kansas, and Cleveland, Ohio; and he spent a year living in Mexico before entering Columbia University in 1921. He left Columbia the following year and traveled extensively in Europe, returning to the United States in the mid-1920s. During these years, Hughes pursued his academic studies at Lincoln University in Pennsylvania (graduating in 1929) and published his first two books of verse,* The Weary Blues *(1926) and* Fine Clothes to the Jew *(1927). His many achievements in literature, drawing upon spirituals, blues, jazz, and folk expression, and his rich, productive career have led*

*his biographer, Arnold Rampersad, to describe him as "perhaps the most representative black American writer."*

*Here we provide a selection of Hughes's poetry that shows the range of his themes and the variety of his speaking voices. We begin with one of his best-known works, "The Negro Speaks of Rivers," a poem first published in the June 1921 issue of* The Crisis, *the official magazine of the NAACP. We give seven of Hughes's poems here (and we have already given some of his poems in earlier chapters), and two selections from his prose. Other poems by Hughes appear on pages 386 and 413.*

## The Negro Speaks of Rivers [1921]

I've known rivers:
I've known rivers ancient as the world and older than the flow of
human blood in human veins.

My soul has grown deep like the rivers.

I bathed in the Euphrates when dawns were young.
I built my hut near the Congo and it lulled me to sleep.                    5
I looked upon the Nile and raised the pyramids above it.
I heard the singing of the Mississippi when Abe Lincoln went
down to New Orleans, and I've seen its muddy bosom turn all golden
in the sunset.

I've known rivers:
Ancient, dusky rivers.

My soul has grown deep like the rivers.                                     10

## Mother to Son [1922]

Well, son, I'll tell you:
Life for me ain't been no crystal stair.
It's had tacks in it,
And splinters,
And boards torn up,                                                        5
And places with no carpet on the floor—
Bare.
But all the time
I'se been a-climbin' on,
And reachin' landin's,                                                     10
And turnin' corners,

And sometimes goin' in the dark
Where there ain't been no light.
So boy, don't you turn back.
Don't you set down on the steps                                    15
'Cause you finds it's kinder hard.
Don't you fall now—
For I'se still goin', honey,
I'se still climbin',
And life for me ain't been no crystal stair.                      20

## The Weary Blues

[1925]

Droning a drowsy syncopated tune,
Rocking back and forth to a mellow croon,
    I heard a Negro play.
Down on Lenox Avenue the other night
By the pale dull pallor of an old gas light                        5
    He did a lazy sway. . . .
    He did a lazy sway. . . .
To the tune o' those Weary Blues.
With his ebony hands on each ivory key
He made that poor piano moan with melody.                          10
    O Blues!
Swaying to and fro on his rickety stool
He played that sad raggy tune like a musical fool.
    Sweet Blues!
Coming from a black man's soul.                                    15
    O Blues!
In a deep song voice with a melancholy tone
I heard that Negro sing, that old piano moan—
    "Ain't got nobody in all this world,
        Ain't got nobody but ma self.                              20
        I's gwine to quit ma frownin'
        And put ma troubles on the shelf."

Thump, thump, thump, went his foot on the floor.
He played a few chords then he sang some more—
    "I got the Weary Blues                                         25
        And I can't be satisfied.
        Got the Weary Blues
        And can't be satisfied—
        I ain't happy no mo'
        And I wish that I had died."                               30
And far into the night he crooned that tune.

The stars went out and so did the moon.
The singer stopped playing and went to bed
While the Weary Blues echoed through his head.
He slept like a rock or a man that's dead.                    35


## The South                                                    [1922]

The lazy, laughing South
With blood on its mouth.
The sunny-faced South,
    Beast-strong,
    Idiot-brained.                                              5
The child-minded South
Scratching in the dead fire's ashes
For a Negro's bones.
    Cotton and the moon,
    Warmth, earth, warmth,                                      10
    The sky, the sun, the stars,
    The magnolia-scented South.
Beautiful, like a woman,
Seductive as a dark-eyed whore,
    Passionate, cruel,                                          15
    Honey-lipped, syphilitic—
    That is the South.
And I, who am black, would love her
But she spits in my face.
And I, who am black,                                            20
Would give her many rare gifts
But she turns her back upon me.
    So now I seek the North—
    The cold-faced North,
    For she, they say,                                          25
    Is a kinder mistress,
And in her house my children
May escape the spell of the South.


## Too Blue                                                      [1943]

I got those sad old weary blues.
I don't know where to turn.
I don't know where to go.

Nobody cares about you
When you sink so low.

What shall I do?
What shall I say?
Shall I take a gun
And put myself away?

I wonder if
*One* bullet would do?
As hard as my head is,
It would probably take two.

But I ain't got
Neither bullet nor gun—
And I'm too blue
To look for one.

## Harlem [1]                                    [1949]

Here on the edge of hell
Stands Harlem—
Remembering the old lies,
The old kicks in the back,
The old "Be patient"
They told us before.
Sure, we remember.
Now when the man at the corner store
Says sugar's gone up another two cents,
And bread one,
And there's a new tax on cigarettes—
We remember the job we never had,
Never could get,
And can't have now
Because we're colored.

So we stand here
On the edge of hell
In Harlem
And look out on the world
And wonder
What we're gonna do
In the face of what
We remember.

## *Theme for English B*                                          [1949]

The instructor said,

> *Go home and write*
> *a page tonight.*
> *And let that page come out of you—*
> *Then, it will be true.*                                          5

I wonder if it's that simple?
I am twenty-two, colored, born in Winston-Salem.
I went to school there, then Durham, then here
to this college on the hill above Harlem.
I am the only colored student in my class.                         10
The steps from the hill lead down into Harlem,
through a park, then I cross St. Nicholas,
Eighth Avenue, Seventh, and I come to the Y,
the Harlem Branch Y, where I take the elevator
up to my room, sit down, and write this page:                      15

It's not easy to know what is true for you or me
at twenty-two, my age. But I guess I'm what
I feel and see and hear, Harlem, I hear you:
hear you, hear me—we two—you, me, talk on this page.
(I hear New York, too.) Me—who?                                    20
Well, I like to eat, sleep, drink, and be in love.
I like to work, read, learn, and understand life.
I like a pipe for a Christmas present,
or records—Bessie, bop, or Bach.
I guess being colored doesn't make me *not* like                   25
the same things other folks like who are other races.

So will my page be colored that I write?
Being me, it will not be white.
But it will be
a part of you, instructor.                                         30
You are white—
yet a part of me, as I am a part of you.
That's American.
Sometimes perhaps you don't want to be a part of me.
Nor do I often want to be a part of you.                           35
But we are, that's true!
As I learn from you,
I guess you learn from me—
although you're older—and white—
and somewhat more free.                                            40

*This is my page for English B.*

# LANGSTON HUGHES ON POETRY

## The Negro and the Racial Mountain [1926]

*Hughes often examined the challenges he faced in writing as both an American and an African-American, as in this provocative essay published in 1926.*

One of the most promising of the young Negro poets said to me once, "I want to be a poet—not a Negro poet," meaning, I believe, "I want to write like a white poet"; meaning subconsciously, "I would like to be a white poet"; meaning behind that, "I would like to be white." And I was sorry the young man said that, for no great poet has ever been afraid of being himself. And I doubted then that, with his desire to run away spiritually from his race, this boy would ever be a great poet. But this is the mountain standing in the way of any true Negro art in America—this urge within the race toward whiteness, the desire to pour racial individuality into the mold of American standardization, and to be as little Negro and as much American as possible.

But let us look at the immediate background of this young poet. His family is of what I suppose one would call the Negro middle class: people who are by no means rich yet never uncomfortable nor hungry—smug, contented, respectable folk, members of the Baptist church. The father goes to work every morning. He is a chief steward at a large white club. The mother sometimes does fancy sewing or supervises parties for the rich families of the town. The children go to a mixed school. In the home they read white papers and magazines. And the mother often says "Don't be like niggers" when the children are bad. A frequent phrase from the father is, "Look how well a white man does things." And so the word white comes to be unconsciously a symbol of all the virtues. It holds for the children beauty, morality, and money. The whisper of "I want to be white" runs silently through their minds. This young poet's home is, I believe, a fairly typical home of the colored middle class. One sees immediately how difficult it would be for an artist born in such a home to interest himself in interpreting the beauty of his own people. He is never taught to see that beauty. He is taught rather not to see it, or if he does, to be ashamed of it when it is not according to Caucasian patterns.

For racial culture the home of a self-styled "high-class" Negro has nothing better to offer. Instead there will perhaps be more aping of things white than in a less cultured or less wealthy home. The father is perhaps a doctor, lawyer, landowner, or politician. The mother may be a social worker, or a teacher, or she may do nothing and have a maid. Father is often dark but he has usually married the lightest woman he could find. The family attend a fashionable church where few really colored faces are to be found. And they themselves draw a color line. In the North they go to white theaters and white movies. And in the South they have at least two cars and a house "like white folks." Nordic manners, Nordic faces, Nordic hair, Nordic art (if any), and an Episcopal heaven. A very high mountain indeed for the would-be racial artist to climb in order to discover himself and his people.

But then there are the low-down folks, the so-called common element, and they are the majority—may the Lord be praised! The people who have their nip of gin on Saturday nights and are not too important to themselves or the community, or too well fed, or too learned to watch the lazy world go round. They live on Seventh Street in Washington or State Street in Chicago and they do not particularly care whether they are like white folks or anybody else. Their joy runs, bang! into ecstasy. Their religion soars to a shout. Work maybe a little today, rest a little tomorrow. Play awhile. Sing awhile. O, let's dance! These common people are not afraid of spirituals, as for a long time their more intellectual brethren were, and jazz is their child. They furnish a wealth of colorful, distinctive material for any artist because they still hold their own individuality in the face of American standardizations. And perhaps these common people will give to the world its truly great Negro artist, the one who is not afraid to be himself. Whereas the better-class Negro would tell the artist what to do, the people at least let him alone when he does appear. And they are not ashamed of him—if they know he exists at all. And they accept what beauty is their own without question.

5     Certainly there is, for the American Negro artist who can escape the restrictions the more advanced among his own group would put upon him, a great field of unused material ready for his art. Without going outside his race and even among the better classes with their "white" culture and conscious American manners, but still Negro enough to be different, there is sufficient matter to furnish a black artist with a lifetime of creative work. And when he chooses to touch on the relations between Negroes and whites in this country with their innumerable overtones and undertones, surely, and especially for literature and the drama, there is an inexhaustible supply of themes at hand. To these the Negro artist can give his racial individuality, his heritage of rhythm and warmth, and his incongruous humor that so often, as in the Blues, becomes ironic laughter mixed with tears. But let us look again at the mountain.

A prominent Negro clubwoman in Philadelphia paid eleven dollars to hear Raquel Meller sing Andalusian popular songs. But she told me a few weeks before she would not think of going to hear "that woman," Clara Smith, a great black artist, sing Negro folksongs. And many an upper-class Negro church, even now, would not dream of employing a spiritual in its services. The drab melodies in white folks' hymnbooks are much to be preferred. "We want to worship the Lord correctly and quietly. We don't believe in 'shouting.' Let's be dull like the Nordics," they say, in effect.

The road for the serious black artist, then, who would produce a racial art is most certainly rocky and the mountain is high. Until recently he received almost no encouragement for his work from either white or colored people. The fine novels of Chestnutt[1] go out of print with neither race noticing their passing. The quaint charm and humor of Dunbar's[2] dialect verse brought to him, in his day, largely the same kind of encouragement one would give a sideshow freak (A colored man writing poetry! How odd!) or a clown (How amusing!).

The present vogue in things Negro, although it may do as much harm as good for the budding colored artist, has at least done this: it has brought him forcibly to the attention of his own people among whom for so long, unless the other race had noticed him beforehand, he was a prophet with little honor. I understand that Charles Gilpin acted for years in Negro theaters without any special acclaim from his own, but when Broadway gave him eight curtain calls, Negroes, too, began to beat a tin pan in his honor. I know a young colored writer, a manual worker by day, who had been writing well for the colored magazines for some years, but it was not until he recently broke into the white publications and his first book was accepted by a prominent New York publisher that the "best" Negroes in his city took the trouble to discover that he lived there. Then almost immediately they decided to give a grand dinner for him. But the society ladies were careful to whisper to his mother that perhaps she'd better not come. They were not sure she would have an evening gown.

The Negro artist works against an undertow of sharp criticism and misunderstanding from his own group and unintentional bribes from the whites. "O, be respectable, write about nice people, show how good we are," say the Negroes. "Be stereotyped, don't go too far, don't shatter our illusions about you, don't amuse us too seriously. We will pay you," say the whites. Both would have told Jean Toomer not to write "Cane." The colored people did not praise it. The white people did not buy it. Most of the colored people who did read "Cane" hate it. They are afraid of it. Although the critics gave it good reviews the public remained indifferent. Yet (excepting the work of DuBois[3]) "Cane" contains the finest prose written by a Negro in America. And like the singing of Robeson,[4] it is truly racial.

10    But in spite of the Nordicized Negro intelligentsia and the desires of some white editors we have an honest American Negro literature already with us. Now I await the rise of the Negro theater. Our folk music, having achieved world-wide fame, offers itself to the genius of the great individual American Negro composer who is to come. And within the next decade I

---

[1]**Chestnutt** Charles Chestnutt (1858–1932), African-American novelist.
[2]**Dunbar** Paul Laurence Dunbar (1872–1906), African-American poet (for an example of his work, see page 420).    [3]**DuBois** William Edward Burghardt DuBois (1868–1963), African-American historian, sociologist, writer.    [4]**Robeson** Paul Robeson (1898–1976), African-American singer and actor.

expect to see the work of a growing school of colored artists who paint and model the beauty of dark faces and create with new technique the expres- sions of their own soul-world.And the Negro dancers who will dance like flame and the singers who will continue to carry our songs to all who listen—they will be with us in even greater numbers tomorrow.

Most of my own poems are racial in theme and treatment, derived from the life I know. In many of them I try to grasp and hold some of the meanings and rhythms of jazz. I am sincere as I know how to be in these poems and yet after every reading I answer questions like these from my own people: Do you think Negroes should always write about Negroes? I wish you wouldn't read some of your poems to white folks. How do you find anything interesting in a place like a cabaret? Why do you write about black people? You aren't black.What makes you do so many jazz poems?

But jazz to me is one of the inherent expressions of Negro life in America: the eternal tom-tom beating in the Negro soul—the tom-tom of revolt against weariness in a white world, a world of subway trains, and work, work, work; the tom-tom of joy and laughter, and pain swallowed in a smile.Yet the Philadelphia clubwoman is ashamed to say that her race created it and she does not like me to write about it.The old subconscious "white is best" runs through her mind.Years of study under white teachers, a lifetime of white books, pictures, and papers, and white manners, morals, and Puritan standards made her dislike the spirituals.And now she turns up her nose at jazz and all its manifestations—likewise almost everything else distinctly racial. She doesn't care for the Winold Reiss portraits of Negroes because they are "too Negro." She does not want a true picture of herself from anybody. She wants the artist to flatter her, to make the white world believe that all Negroes are as smug and as near white in soul as she wants to be. But, to my mind, it is the duty of the younger Negro artist, if he accepts any duties at all from outsiders, to change through the force of his art that old whispering "I want to be white," hidden in the aspirations of his people, to "Why should I want to be white? I am a Negro—and beautiful!"

So I am ashamed for the black poet who says, "I want to be a poet, not a Negro poet," as though his own racial world were not as interesting as any other world. I am ashamed, too, for the colored artist who runs from the painting of Negro faces to the painting of sunsets after the manner of the academicians because he fears the strange un-whiteness of his own features.An artist must be free to choose what he does, certainly, but he must also never be afraid to do what he might choose.

Let the blare of Negro jazz bands and the bellowing voice of Bessie Smith singing Blues penetrate the closed ears of the colored near-intellectuals "until they listen and perhaps understand. Let Paul Robeson singing Water Boy, and Rudolph Fisher writing about the streets of Harlem, and Jean Toomer holding the heart of Georgia in his hands, and Aaron Douglas drawing strange black fantasies cause the smug Negro middle class to turn from their white, respectable, ordinary books and papers to catch a glimmer of their own beauty. We younger Negro artists who create now intend to express our individual dark-skinned selves without fear or shame. If white people are pleased we are glad. If they are not, it doesn't matter. We know we are beautiful. And ugly too. The tom-tom cries and the tom-tom laughs. If colored people are pleased we are glad. If they are not, their displeasure doesn't matter either. We build our temples for tomorrow, strong as we know how, and we stand on top of the mountain, free within ourselves.

## On the Cultural Achievements of African-Americans
[1960]

Without them, on my part, there would have been no poems; without their hopes and fears and dreams, no stories; without their struggles, no dramas; without their music, no songs.

Had I not heard as a child in the little churches of Kansas and Missouri, "Deep river, my home is over Jordan," or "My Lord, what a morning when the stars begin to fall," I might not have come to realize the lyric beauty of *living* poetry. . . .

There is so much richness in Negro humor, so much beauty in black dreams, so much dignity in our struggle, and so much universality in our problems, in *us*—in each living human being of color—that I do not understand the tendency today that some American Negro artists have of seeking to run away from themselves, of running away from *us*, of being afraid to sing our own songs, paint our pictures, write about ourselves—when it is our music that has given America its greatest music, our humor that has enriched its entertainment media for the past 100 years, our rhythm that has guided its dancing feet from plantation days to the Charleston. . . . Yet there are some of us who say, "Why write about Negroes? Why not be *just a writer?*" And why not—if one wants to be "just a writer?" Negroes in a free world should be whatever each wants to be—even if it means being "just a writer. . . . "

There is nothing to be ashamed of in the strength and dignity and laughter of the Negro people. And there is nothing to be afraid of in the use of their material.

Could you be possibly afraid that the rest of the world will not accept it? Our spirituals are sung and loved in the great concert halls of the whole world. Our blues are played from Topeka to Tokyo. Harlem's jive talk delights Hong Kong and Paris. Those of our writers who have *most* concerned themselves with our very special problems are translated and read around the world. The local, the regional can—and does—become universal. Sean O'Casey's Irishmen are an example. So I would say to young Negro writers, do not be afraid of yourself. *You* are the world. . . .

# 22

# Poetry and Translation

During the course of reading this section you will be invited to translate a poem. If you are competent in a language other than English, you will be asked to translate a poem of your choice from that language, and also to write about the particular difficulties you experienced while translating. Or you can construct a verse translation of one of the French, Spanish, and Japanese poems that we print in this chapter; you don't have to know any of these languages, since we provide literal English translations.

## A POEM TRANSLATED FROM SPANISH, IN AN ESSAY BY A STUDENT

We begin with a student's discussion of his translation of Federico García Lorca's short poem, "Despedida."

```
                                              Guzman 1
    George Guzman
    Professor Tredo
    English 101
    20 September 2005
              García Lorca's "Despedida"
         My father sometimes quotes, half-jokingly
    although it is a serious poem, Federico
    García Lorca's "Despedida," which he learned
```

Guzman 2

when he was a schoolboy in Cuba. Because it
is short and because he quotes it so often,
I know it by heart. In Spanish it goes like
this:

Despedida

Si muero,
dejad el balcón abierto.

El niño come naranjas.
(Desde mi balcón lo veo.)

El segador siega el trigo.
(Desde mi balcón lo siento.)

¡Si muero,
dejad el balcón abierto!

When I translated the poem for this
assignment, I didn't find any serious
difficulties--probably because the poem
does not rhyme. The only word in the
poem that I think is especially hard
to translate is the title, "Despedida."
It comes from a verb, "despedir," which
Spanish-English dictionaries define as
"to take one's leave." In English, however,
no one "takes one's leave"; we just say
"Goodbye," and go. But "Goodbye" is too
informal for "Despedida," so I settled on
"Farewell." No one speaking English ever
says "Farewell," but I think it catches the
slight formality of the Spanish, and it has
the right tone for this poem about a man
who is talking about leaving the world.
Still another possibility that seems good
to me is "parting."

Aside from the title, I at first found the poem easy to translate, but on further thinking about my translation, I found a few things that I wish I could do better. Here, for a start, is my literal translation.

### Farewell

If I die,
leave the balcony open.

The boy eats oranges.
(From my balcony I see him.)

The reaper reaps the wheat.
(From my balcony I hear him.)

If I die,
leave the balcony open!

There are subtle things in this poem, but most of them can be translated easily. For instance, in the first and the last stanzas the poet speaks of "el balcón" (the balcony), but in the middle two stanzas he speaks of "mi balcón" (my balcony). That is, in the first and last stanzas, where he imagines himself dead, he realizes the balcony is not his anymore, but is simply "the balcony." There is no difficulty in translating this idea from Spanish into English.

Because I knew the poem by heart, I translated it without first looking at the original on the page. But when I wrote it out in Spanish, too, I became aware of a small difficulty. In Spanish if a sentence

Guzman 4

ends with an exclamation point (or a
question mark) it also begins with one,
so the reader knows at the beginning of a
sentence what sort of sentence it will be.
We don't do this in English, and I think
something is lost in English. The two
exclamation marks in García Lorca's last
sentence, one at the beginning and one at
the end, seem to me to call more attention
to the sentence, and make it more sad. And
since the first and last sentences are
identical except for the exclamation marks
around the last sentence, the punctuation
makes the last sentence different from the
first. Superficially the poem begins and
ends with the same sentence, but the last
sentence is much more final.

A second difficulty is this: On
rereading my translation, I wondered if
it should try to catch the o sounds that
in the original are at the end of every line
except the third. It's hard to explain, but
I think this repeated o sound has several
effects. Certainly the repetition of the
sound gives unity to the poem. But it also
is part of the meaning, in two ways. First
of all, the sound of o is like a lament or
a cry. Second, because the sound is repeated
again and again, in line after line, it
is as if the poet wants the present to
continue, doesn't want to stop, wants to
keep living. Obviously he is not looking

forward to dying. He doesn't say anything
about hoping to go to heaven. All he thinks
of is what he sees now, and he suggests that
he would like to keep seeing it from his
balcony.

Balcón in Spanish means, as I have
translated it, "balcony," but to say "leave
the balcony open"--which is perfectly all
right in Spanish--sounds a little funny in
English, maybe especially because we don't
have many balconies here, unlike (I am
told) Spain. The idea of course is to leave
open the door, or if it is glass it is also
a window, that leads to the balcony. Maybe,
then, it makes better sense to be a little
free in the translation, and to say, "Leave
the window open," or even "Do not draw the
curtain," or some such thing. In fact, if
we can put "window" at the end of the line,
we get the o sound of the original.

     If I die,

    Leave open the window.

But in the original the first line ("Si
muero," literally "If I die") has this o
sound also, and I can't think of any way of
getting this into the translation. For a
moment I thought of beginning,

     If I go,

    Leave open the window,

but "If I go" just isn't a moving way of
saying "If I die," which is what "Si muero"
means. Still, we might translate line 4 as

Guzman 6

"I see him from my window," and line 6 as "I hear him from my window." In the end, I decided <u>not</u> to begin by saying "If I go," but (even though I lose the <u>o</u> sound in the first line) to substitute "window" for the "balcony" in lines 2, 4, and 6, in order to get the repetition and the sad <u>o</u> sound. My final version goes like this:

                    Farewell

     If I die,
leave open the window.
     The boy eats oranges.
(I see him from my window.)
     The reaper reaps the wheat.
(I hear him from my window.)
     If I die,
leave open the window!

## ▨ TOPICS FOR CRITICAL THINKING AND WRITING

Here are our responses. If yours differ, consider putting them into writing.

1. This seems like an excellent translation to us. Do you agree?
2. When the student shared his essay with others in the class, it was praised for being "thoughtful." What gives the essay this quality?

# A Note on Using the First-Person Singular Pronoun in Essays

Some handbooks on writing tell students never to use *I* in an essay. But this rule is too rigid; in the case of the essay you have just read, the personal touches make it all the more interesting and engaging. Often the problem is not really with the use of *I*, but, rather, with the absence of explanation and evidence that make clear what prompted the "I" to respond as he or she does. This student does a good job of focusing on the poem, commenting on details of language, and keeping the nature of the assignment in mind. His use of *I* occurs as part of a careful analysis and argument.

# TRANSLATING A POEM OF YOUR CHOICE, AND COMMENTING ON THE TRANSLATION

If you are at ease in a language other than English, translate a short poem from that language into English. It may be a poem that you learned in school or at home or on the street.

We suggest that you begin by jotting down a line-for-line prose translation, and then work on a poetic version. Your prose version of course will not be a word-for-word translation. After all, a word-for-word translation of the Spanish "Me llamo Juan" is "Me [or "Myself"] I call John," but no one speaking English says this. The English version of these words is "My name is John"—even though the Spanish word for *name (nombre)* does not appear in the original sentence. Similarly, a native speaker of French, when asked whether he or she is going to class this morning , may reply "Mais oui," which in a word-for-word translation would be "But yes." In English, however, we would simply say "Yes" or "Certainly," and therefore the "But" ought to be omitted in a translation. Or consider the phrase "les hommes d'équipage" in the first line of Baudelaire's "L'Albatros." A word-for-word translation would be "men of the crew," but does one say this? Perhaps "members of the crew" is better? Or perhaps simply "the crew"? Or "crewmen"? Or, perhaps best of all, "sailors"? In any case, the French *equipage* certainly cannot be translated as "equipment." (Translators call words that look alike but have different meanings "false friends." Examples: French *advertissement* means "warning"; German *also* means "therefore"; Spanish *constipado* means "having a head cold.")

The prose translation *ought to sound like English,* and this means going beyond a word-for-word translation, at least to a phrase-by-phrase translation. If English is not your native language, you may want to check your prose version with a native-born speaker of English. In any case, once you have a prose version that is in idiomatic English, try to put it into a poetic form.

This does not mean that (assuming your original uses rhyme) you must preserve the exact rhyme scheme. If the original rhymes *abab,* you may find it satisfactory to produce a version in which only the second and fourth lines rhyme. Similarly, even if the original line has 11 or 12 syllables, you may prefer to reduce the line to 10 syllables because the pentameter line (10 syllables) is so widely used in English that it seems natural. Admittedly, your task is easier if you choose an unrhymed poem, and much of the world's poetry—to cite only two instances, Native American poetry and Japanese poetry—does not use rhyme.

When you have done your best, relax for a while, and then jot down (in preparation for drafting an essay that will accompany your translation) some notes about the particular problems involved in translating the work. Is there a pun in the original that is impossible to translate? Are there historical or mythological allusions that are clear to people who belong to the culture that produced the poem but that are obscure to outsiders? Are there qualities in the original language (specialists call it "the source language") that simply cannot be reproduced in the "host" (or "target") language? For instance, Japanese has several verbs meaning "to give"; the word used in "I gave you a book" differs from the word in "You gave me a book." It is rather as if one had to say, "You bestowed a book on me"—but of course no one *does* say this in English. What, then, is a translator to do?

In the end, you will produce a translation, and an essay of some 500 words, explaining the particular difficulties you encountered, and perhaps explaining the hardest decisions that you ultimately made.

# LAST-MINUTE HELP:
# THREE SPANISH POEMS

If you don't know a poem in a language other than English, consider translating into poetry one or both of these Spanish folk songs, or, finally, the poem we print by the Chilean poet Gabriela Mistral.

| | |
|---|---|
| Ya se van los pastores, alla Estremadura | The shepherds are already leaving on their way to Estremadura |
| Ya se queda la Sierra triste y obscura. | And the mountain ridge is already sad and gloomy. |
| Ya se van los pastores ya se van marchando | The shepherds are already going, they are already departing |
| Ya las pobres niñas se queden llorando. | And the poor girls remain there, crying. |

Here is the second song:

| | |
|---|---|
| Una gallina con pollos cinco duro me costó | I bought a hen and chicks for five duros |
| Corrocloclo corrocloclo | Corrocloclo corrocloclo |
| La compré por la mañana, y a la tarde se perdió | I bought her in the morning and in the afternoon it lost its way |
| Corrocloclo corrocloclo | Corrocloclo corrocloclo |
| Yo no siento la gallina ni el dinero que costó | I'm not sorry about the hen or the money it cost |

| | |
|---|---|
| Corrocloclo corrocloclo | Corrocloclo corrocloclo |
| Solo siento los pollitos que sin | I'm only sorry for the chicks who |
| madre los quedó | are left without a mother |
| Corrocloclo corrocloclo. | Corrocloclo corrocloclo. |

# GABRIELA MISTRAL

*Lucila Godoy Alacayaga (1889-1957) adopted the pseudonym Gabriela Mistral. A teacher and a director of schools in Chile, she achieved fame there in 1914, when she won first prize in a national poetry contest; she received international fame in 1945, when she was awarded the Nobel Prize for Literature, the first Latin-American writer to win the award. She was also distinguished in two other careers, as an educator—she is esteemed for her revision of the Mexican school system and she was a beloved professor at Barnard College in New York—and as a figure in the world of international politics, representing Chile in the League of Nations and the United Nations.*

*The following poem originates in a response to a statue, Rodin's* The Thinker. *If you do work on a translation of Mistral's poem, you might keep in mind a comment by an earlier translator of her work, the poet Langston Hughes, who in his Introduction to* Selected Poems of Gabriela Mistral *(1957) wrote: "I have no theories of translation. I simply try to transfer into English as much as I can of the literal content, emotion, and style of each poem." Unfortunately Hughes did not include a translation of the following poem.*

## El Pensador de Rodin

Con el mentón caído sobre la mano ruda,
el Pensador se acuerda que es carne de la huesa,
carne fatal, delante del destino denuda,
carne que odia la muerte, y tembló de belleza.          4

Y tembló de amor, toda su primavera ardiente,
y ahora, al otoño, anégase de verdad y tristeza.
El "de morir tenemos" pasa sobre su frente,
en todo agudo bronce, cuando la noche empieza.          8

Y en la angustia, sus músculos se hienden, sufridores.
Los surcos de su carne se llenan de terrores.
Se hiende, como la hoja de otoño, al Señor fuerte

que la llama en los bronces ...Y no hay árbol torcido          12
de sol en la llanura, ni león de flanco herido,
crispados como este hombre que medita en la muerte.

Auguste Rodin, *The Thinker*. (1910. Bronze, height 27½".
The Metropolitan Museum of Art. Gift of Thomas F. Ryan.)

Here is a translation:

## Rodin's Thinker

*Translated by Gustavo Alfaro* [x]

With his chin fallen on his rough hand,
the Thinker, remembering that his flesh is of the grave,
mortal flesh, naked before its fate,
flesh that hates death, trembled for beauty.                    4

---

*Translator's note:* Mistral's *bronce* in line 8 and *bronces* in line 12 I translate
as *trumpet sound* and *trumpet calls*. Given the context, this reading seems to me
to be more plausible than a reading that takes *bronce* and *bronces* to refer to the
bronze sculpture itself.

And he trembled for love, his whole ardent spring,
and now in autumn, he is overcome with truth and sadness.
"We must die" passes across his brow,
in every piercing trumpet sound, when night begins to fall.     8

And in his anguish, his long suffering muscles split.
The furrows of his flesh are filled with terrors.
It splits, like the autumn leaf before the mighty Lord

who calls it with trumpet calls ... And there is no tree twisted     12
by the sun in the plain, nor lion wounded on its side,
as tense as this man who meditates on death.

# 23

# A Collection of Poems

## WILLIAM SHAKESPEARE

*William Shakespeare (1564–1616), born in Stratford-upon-Avon in England, is chiefly known as a dramatic poet, but he also wrote non-dramatic poetry. In 1609 a volume of 154 of his sonnets was published, apparently without his permission. Probably he chose to keep his sonnets unpublished not because he thought that they were of little value, but because it was more prestigious to be an amateur (unpublished) poet than a professional (published) poet. Although the sonnets were published in 1609, they were probably written in the mid 1590s, when there was a vogue for sonneteering. A contemporary writer in 1598 said that Shakespeare's "sugred Sonnets [circulate] among his private friends."*

## Sonnet 116

Let me not to the marriage of true minds
Admit impediments; love is not love
Which alters when it alteration finds,
Or bends with the remover to remove.
O, no, it is an ever-fixèd mark°                                                5
That looks on tempests and is never shaken;
It is the star° to every wand'ring bark,
Whose worth's unknown, although his height be taken.
Love's not Time's fool,° though rosy lips and cheeks

---

**5 mark** guide to mariners.    **7 star** the North Star.    **9 fool** plaything.

Within his bending sickle's compass° come;                                    10
Love alters not with his° brief hours and weeks
But bears° it out even to the edge of doom.°
    If this be error and upon me proved,
    I never writ, nor no man ever loved.

_____

**10 compass** range.    **11 his** Time's.    **12 bears** endures.    **doom** Judgment Day.

# JOHN DONNE

*John Donne (1572-1631) was born into a Roman Catholic family in
England, but in the 1590s he abandoned that faith. In 1615 he became
an Anglican priest and soon was known as a great preacher. Of his ser-
mons 160 survive, including one with the famous line, "No man is an
island, entire of itself; every man is a piece of the continent, a part of
the main; if a clod be washed away by the sea, Europe is the less . . . ;
and therefore never send to know for whom the bell tolls; it tolls for
thee." From 1621 until his death he was dean of St. Paul's Cathedral in
London. Most of his love poems (often bawdy and cynical) are said to
be his early work, and his "Holy Sonnets" (among the greatest religious
poems written in English) his later work.*

## *A Valediction: Forbidding Mourning*                        [1633]

As virtuous men pass mildly away;
    And whisper to their souls, to go,
Whilst some of their sad friends do say,
    "The breath goes now," and some say, "No":                          4

So let us melt, and make no noise.
    No tear-floods, nor sigh-tempests move.
'Twere profanation of our joys
    To tell the laity our love.                                          8

Moving of the earth° brings harms and fears,
    Men reckon what it did and meant;
But trepidation of the spheres,
    Though greater far, is innocent.°                                   12

_____

**9 Moving of the earth** an earthquake.    **12 But . . . innocent** But the movement
of the heavenly spheres (in Ptolemaic astronomy), though far greater, is harmless.

Dull sublunary° lovers' love
   (Whose soul is sense) cannot admit
Absence, because it doth remove
   Those things which elemented it.      16

But we, by a love so much refined
   That our selves know not what it is,
Inter-assuréd of the mind,
   Care less, eyes, lips, and hands to miss.      20

Our two souls therefore, which are one,
   Though I must go, endure not yet
A breach, but an expansion,
   Like gold to airy thinness beat.      24

If they be two, they are two so
   As stiff twin compasses° are two:
Thy soul, the fixed foot, makes no show
   To move, but doth, if the other do.      28

And though it in the center sit,
   Yet when the other far doth roam,
It leans, and hearkens after it,
   And grows erect, as that comes home.      32

Such wilt thou be to me, who must
   Like the other foot, obliquely run:
Thy firmness makes my circle just,
   And makes me end where I begun.      36

---

13 **sublunary** under the moon (i.e., earthly).   26 **twin compasses** a carpenter's
compass, used for making circles.

## The Flea

                      [1633]

Mark but this flea, and mark in this
How little that which thou deny'st me is;
It sucked me first, and now sucks thee,
And in this flea our two bloods mingled be;
Thou know'st that this cannot be said
A sin, nor shame, nor loss of maidenhead;      5
   Yet this enjoys before it woo,
     And pampered swells with one blood made of two,
   And this, alas, is more than we would do.

Oh stay, three lives in one flea spare,      10
Where we almost, yea, more than married are.

This flea is you and I, and this
Our marriage bed and marriage temple is;
Though parents grudge, and you, we are met
And cloistered in these living walls of jet.          15
  Though use° make you apt to kill me,
  Let not to that, self-murder added be,
  And sacrilege, three sins in killing three.

Cruel and sudden, has thou since
Purpled thy nail in blood of innocence?          20
Wherein could this flea guilty be,
Except in that drop which it sucked from thee?
Yet thou triumph'st and say'st that thou
Find'st not thyself, nor me the weaker now.
  'Tis true. Then learn how false fears be:          25
  Just so much honor, when thou yield'st to me,
  Will waste, as this flea's death took life from thee.

_____

16 use  custom.


# BEN JONSON

_Ben Jonson (1572–1637), born in London, was Shakespeare's contemporary. Like Shakespeare, he wrote for the theater, and in fact Shakespeare acted in Jonson's first important play,_ Every Man in His Humour _(1598). But unlike Shakespeare, Jonson produced a fairly large body of nondramatic poetry._

  _The following song is from a play,_ Epicoene, _or the Silent Woman._


## Still to Be Neat                                    [1609]
_____

Still° to be neat, still to be dressed
As° you were going to a feast;
Still to be powdered, still perfumed—
Lady, it is to be presumed,
Though art's hid causes are not found,
All is not sweet, all is not sound.          6

Give me a look, give me a face,
That makes simplicity a grace;

_____

1 Still  always.    2 As  As if.

Robes loosely flowing, hair as free:
Such sweet neglect more taketh me
Than all the adulteries° of art;
They strike mine eyes, but not my heart.          12

_____

**11 adulteries** adulterations.

# ROBERT HERRICK

*Robert Herrick (1591–1674) was born in London, the son of a gold-
smith. After taking an M.A. at Cambridge, he was ordained in the Church
of England. Later, he was sent to the country parish of Dean Prior in
Devonshire, where he wrote most of his poetry. A loyal supporter of the
king, in 1647 he was expelled from his parish by the Puritans, though
in 1662 he was restored to Dean Prior.*

## Delight in Disorder                                                  [1648]

A sweet disorder in the dress
Kindles in clothes a wantonness.
A lawn° about the shoulders thrown
Into a fine distraction;                                                 4
An erring lace, which here and there
Enthralls the crimson stomacher,°
A cuff neglectful, and thereby
Ribbons to flow confusedly;                                             8
A winning wave, deserving note,
In the tempestuous petticoat;
A careless shoestring, in whose tie
I see a wild civility;                                                   12
Do more bewitch me than when art
Is too precise in every part.

_____

**3 lawn** scarf.    **6 stomacher** ornamental cloth.

# WILLIAM BLAKE

*William Blake (1757–1827) was born in London and at age fourteen
was apprenticed for seven years to an engraver. A Christian visionary
poet, he made his living by giving drawing lessons and by illustrating
books, including his own* Songs of Innocence *(1789) and* Songs of

Experience *(1794). These two books represent, he said, "two contrary states of the human soul." ("The Lamb" comes from* Songs of Innocence; *"The Tyger" and "London" are from* Songs of Experience.*) In 1809 Blake exhibited his art, but the show was a failure. Not until he was in his sixties, when he stopped writing poetry, did he achieve any public recognition—and then it was as a painter.*

## The Lamb

[1789]

Little Lamb, who made thee?
Dost thou know who made thee?
Gave thee life, and bid thee feed
By the stream and o'er the mead;
Gave thee clothing of delight,                    5
Softest clothing, wooly, bright;
Gave thee such a tender voice,
Making all the vales rejoice?
    Little Lamb, who made thee?
    Dost thou know who made thee?              10

    Little Lamb, I'll tell thee,
    Little Lamb, I'll tell thee:
He is callèd by thy name,
For he calls himself a Lamb.
He is meek, and he is mild;                        15
He became a little child.
I a child, and thou a lamb,
We are callèd by his name.
    Little Lamb, God bless thee!
    Little Lamb, God bless thee!               20

## The Tyger

[1793]

Tyger! Tyger! burning bright
In the forests of the night,
What immortal hand or eye
Could frame thy fearful symmetry?                  4

In what distant deeps or skies
Burnt the fire of thine eyes?
On what wings dare he aspire?
What the hand dare seize the fire?                 8

And what shoulder, and what art,
Could twist the sinews of thy heart?

And, when thy heart began to beat,
What dread hand? and what dread feet?    12

What the hammer? what the chain?
In what furnace was thy brain?
What the anvil? what dread grasp
Dare its deadly terrors clasp?    16

When the stars threw down their spears,
And watered heaven with their tears,
Did he smile his work to see?
Did he who made the lamb make thee?    20

Tyger! Tyger! burning bright
In the forests of the night,
What immortal hand or eye,
Dare frame thy fearful symmetry?    24

## London    [1794]

I wander thro' each charter'd street,
Near where the charter'd Thames does flow,
And mark in every face I meet
Marks of weakness, marks of woe.    4

In every cry of every Man,
In every Infant's cry of fear,
In every voice, in every ban,
The mind-forg'd manacles I hear.    8

How the Chimney-sweeper's cry
Every black'ning Church appalls;
And the hapless Soldier's sigh
Runs in blood down Palace walls.    12

But most thro' midnight streets I hear
How the youthful Harlot's curse
Blasts the new-born Infant's tear,
And blights with plagues the Marriage hearse.    16

# WILLIAM WORDSWORTH

*William Wordsworth (1770–1850), the son of an attorney, grew up in the Lake District of England. After graduating from Cambridge University in 1791, he spent a year in France, falling in love with a French girl, with whom he had a daughter. His enthusiasm for the French*

*Revolution waned, and he returned alone to England, where, with the help of a legacy, he devoted his life to poetry. With his friend Samuel Taylor Coleridge, in 1798 he published anonymously a volume of poetry, Lyrical Ballads, which changed the course of English poetry. In 1799 he and his sister Dorothy settled in Grasmere in the Lake District, where he married and was given the office of distributor of stamps. In 1843 he was appointed poet laureate.*

## *I Wandered Lonely as a Cloud*                    [1807]

I wandered lonely as a cloud
That floats on high o'er vales and hills,
When all at once I saw a crowd,
A host, of golden daffodils,
Beside the lake, beneath the trees,                          5
Fluttering and dancing in the breeze.

Continuous as the stars that shine
And twinkle on the milky way,
They stretched in never-ending line
Along the margin of a bay;                                  10
Ten thousand saw I at a glance,
Tossing their heads in sprightly dance.

The waves beside them danced, but they
Outdid the sparkling waves in glee;
A poet could not but be gay,                                15
In such a jocund company;
I gazed—and gazed—but little thought
What wealth the show to me had brought:

For oft, when on my couch I lie
In vacant or in pensive mood,                               20
They flash upon that inward eye
Which is the bliss of solitude;
And then my heart with pleasure fills,
And dances with the daffodils.

# PHILLIS WHEATLEY

*Kidnapped in Africa when she was a child of about age seven, and brought to Boston on the schooner* Phillis, *Phillis Wheatley (1753–1784) owed her first name to the ship and her second to the family name of the merchant who bought her to attend to his wife. She was educated in English, Latin, history, and geography, and especially in the Bible, and*

*within a few years she was writing poetry in the approved manner—
that is, the manner of eighteenth-century England. In 1773, the year she
was granted freedom, she published a book of her poems in England.*

*Despite her education and the style of writing that she adopted,
Wheatley of course did not move freely in the white world. But neither
did she move freely in the black world, since her educators kept her
away from other persons of African origin. Perhaps the best single sentence ever written about Phillis Wheatley is Richard Wright's:"Before the
webs of slavery had so tightened as to snare nearly all Negroes in our
land, one was freed by accident to give in clear, bell-like limpid cadence
the hope of freedom in the New World." One other sentence about Wheatley, by another African-American writer, should also be quoted here.
Alice Walker, commenting on Wheatley's much criticized assumption of
white values, says, in an address to Wheatley, "It is not so much what
you sang, as that you kept alive, in so many of our ancestors, the notion of song."*

*"On Being Brought from Africa to America" alludes to the story of
Cain and Abel, in Genesis 4, which reports that Cain killed Abel, and
that "the Lord set a mark upon Cain" (4.15). The biblical text explicitly
says that the mark was to protect Cain from someone who might take
vengeance on him, but it does not say what the mark was. Nevertheless,
some Christians developed the idea that the color of Africans was the
mark of Cain.*

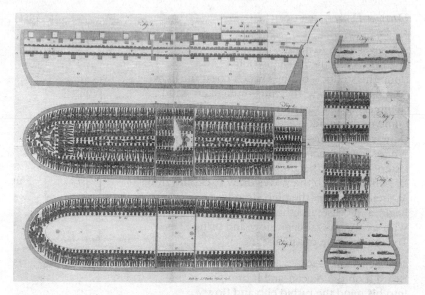

Wheatley probably was brought to America on a slave ship such as this one. Thomas
Clarkson distributed this drawing with his *Essay on the Slavery and Commerce of the
Human Species* (1804).

## On Being Brought from Africa to America [1772]

'Twas mercy brought me from my pagan land,
Taught my beknighted soul to understand
That there's a God, that there's a Savior too:
Once I redemption neither sought nor knew.
Some view our sable race with scornful eye,                5
"Their color is a diabolic dye."
Remember, Christians; Negroes, black as Cain,
May be refined, and join the angelic train.

# MATTHEW ARNOLD

*Matthew Arnold (1822–1888) was the son of a famous educator, Dr.
Thomas Arnold, the headmaster of Rugby School. After graduating
from Oxford, Matthew Arnold became an inspector of schools, a post he
held until two years before his death. Besides writing poetry, Arnold
wrote literary criticism and was appointed professor of poetry at Oxford from 1857 to 1867. He traveled widely on the Continent and lectured in the United States.*

## Dover Beach [c. 1851]

The sea is calm to-night.
The tide is full, the moon lies fair
Upon the straits;—on the French coast the light
Gleams and is gone; the cliffs of England stand,
Glimmering and vast, out in the tranquil bay.              5
Come to the window, sweet is the night-air!
Only, from the long line of spray
Where the sea meets the moon-blanch'd land,
Listen! you hear the grating roar
Of pebbles which the waves draw back, and fling,           10
At their return, up the high strand,
Begin, and cease, and then again begin,
With tremulous cadence slow, and bring
The eternal note of sadness in.

Sophocles long ago                                         15
Heard it on the Ægean, and it brought
Into his mind the turbid ebb and flow
Of human misery; we

Find also in the sound a thought,
Hearing it by this distant northern sea.                          20

The Sea of Faith
Was once, too, at the full, and round earth's shore
Lay like the folds of a bright girdle furl'd.
But now I only hear
Its melancholy, long, withdrawing roar,                           25
Retreating, to the breath
Of the night-wind, down the vast edges drear
And naked shingles° of the world.

Ah, love, let us be true
To one another! for the world, which seems                        30
To lie before us like a land of dreams,
So various, so beautiful, so new,
Hath really neither joy, nor love, nor light,
Nor certitude, nor peace, nor help for pain;
And we are here as on a darkling plain                            35
Swept with confused alarms of struggle and flight,
Where ignorant armies clash by night.

---

28 **shingles** pebbled beaches.


# EMILY DICKINSON

*Emily Dickinson (1830–1886) was born into a proper New England family in Amherst, Massachusetts. Because she never married, and because in her last twenty years she may never have left her house, she has sometimes been pitied. But as the critic Allen Tate said, "All pity for Miss Dickinson's 'starved life' is misdirected. Her life was one of the richest and deepest ever lived on this continent." Her brother was probably right in saying that, having seen something of the rest of the world, "she could not resist the feeling that it was painfully hollow. It was to her so thin and unsatisfying in the face of the Great Realities of Life."*


## Papa above!
[c. 1859]

Papa above!
Regard a Mouse
O'erpowered by the Cat!
Reserve within thy kingdom
A "Mansion" for the Rat!                                          5

Snug in seraphic Cupboards
To nibble all the day,
While unsuspecting Cycles°
Wheel solemnly away!

_____

8 **Cycles** long periods, eons.

## Wild Nights—Wild Nights! [1861]

Wild Nights—Wild Nights!
Were I with thee
Wild Nights should be
Our luxury!                                                          4

Futile—the Winds—
To a Heart in port—
Done with the Compass—
Done with the Chart!                                                 8

Rowing in Eden—
Ah, the Sea!
Might I but moor—Tonight—
In Thee!                                                            12


## I heard a Fly buzz—when I died [1862]

I heard a Fly buzz—when I died—
The Stillness in the Room
Was like the Stillness in the Air—
Between the Heaves of Storm—                                         4

The Eyes around—had wrung them dry—
And Breaths were gathering firm
For the last Onset—when the King
Be witnessed—in the Room—                                           8

I willed my Keepsakes—Signed away
What portion of me be
Assignable—and then it was
There interposed a Fly—                                             12

With Blue—uncertain stumbling Buzz—
Between the light—and me—
And then the Windows failed—and then
I could not see to see—                                             16

# GERARD MANLEY HOPKINS

*Gerard Manley Hopkins (1844–1889) was born near London and was educated at Oxford, where he studied the classics. A convert from Anglicanism to Roman Catholicism, he was ordained a Jesuit priest in 1877. After serving as a parish priest and teacher, he was appointed Professor of Greek at the Catholic University in Dublin.*

*Hopkins published only a few poems during his lifetime, partly because he believed that the pursuit of literary fame was incompatible with his vocation as a priest, and partly because he was aware that his highly individual style might puzzle readers.*

## God's Grandeur

[1877]

The world is charged with the grandeur of God.
　It will flame out, like shining from shook foil;
　It gathers to a greatness, like the ooze of oil
Crushed. Why do men then now not reck his rod?
Generations have trod, have trod, have trod;　　　　　　　　5
　And all is seared with trade; bleared, smeared with toil;
　And wears man's smudge and shares man's smell: the soil
Is bare now, nor can foot feel, being shod.

And for all this, nature is never spent;
　There lives the dearest freshness deep down things;　　　　10
And though the last lights off the black West went
　Oh, morning, at the brown brink eastward, springs—
Because the Holy Ghost over the bent
　World broods with warm breast and with ah! bright wings.

## Pied* Beauty

[1877]

Glory be to God for dappled things—
　For skies of couple-colour as a brinded° cow;
　　For rose-moles all in stipple upon trout that swim;
Fresh-firecoal chestnut-falls; finches' wings;
　Landscape plotted and pieced—fold, fallow, and plough;°　　5
　　And áll trádes, their gear and tackle and trim.°

---

*Pied Variegated, particolored.    2 brinded streaked.    5 fold, fallow, and plough fields used for pasture (sheep-fold), left fallow, or ploughed.    6 trim equipment.

All things counter, original, spare, strange;
  Whatever is fickle, freckled (who knows how?)
    With swift, slow; sweet, sour; adazzle, dim;
He fathers-forth whose beauty is past change:                    10
              Praise him.


# WILLIAM BUTLER YEATS

*William Butler Yeats (1865–1939), born in Dublin, Ireland, was awarded
the Nobel Prize for Literature in 1923.*

*In the seventh century BCE the ancient Greeks founded the city of
Byzantium in Thrace, where Istanbul, Turkey, now stands. (Constan-
tine, the first Christian ruler of the Roman empire, built a new city
there in 330 CE. Named Constantinople, the city served as the capital of
the Roman empire until 1453, when the Turks captured it. In 1930 the
name was officially changed to Istanbul.) The capital of the Roman
Empire and the "holy city" of the Greek Orthodox Church, Byzantium
had two golden ages. The first, in its early centuries, continued the traditions of the antique Greco-Roman world. The second, which is what
Yeats had in mind, extended from the mid-ninth to the mid-thirteenth
century and was a distinctive blend of classical, Christian, Slavic, and
even Islamic culture. This period is noted for mysticism, for the preser-
vation of ancient learning, and for exquisitely refined symbolic art.
In short, Byzantium (as Yeats saw it) was wise and passionless. In
A Vision, his prose treatment of his complex mystical system, Yeats says:*

> *I think that in early Byzantium, maybe never before or since in
> recorded history, religious, aesthetic and practical life were one, that
> architect and artificers—though not, it may be, poets, for language
> has been the instrument of controversy and must have grown
> abstract—spoke to the multitude and the few alike. The painter, the
> mosaic worker, the worker in gold and silver, the illuminator of sa-
> cred books, were almost impersonal, almost perhaps without the
> consciousness of individual design, absorbed in their subject mat-
> ter and that the vision of the whole people. They could copy out of
> old Gospel books those pictures that seemed as sacred as the text,
> and yet weave all into a vast design, the work of many that seemed
> the work of one, that made building, picture, pattern, metal-work of
> rail and lamp, seem but a single image.*


## Sailing to Byzantium                                    [1926]

### *I*

That is no country for old men. The young
In one another's arms, birds in the trees

—Those dying generations—at their song,
The salmon-falls, the mackerel-crowded seas,
Fish, flesh, or fowl, commend all summer long    5
Whatever is begotten, born, and dies.
Caught in that sensual music all neglect
Monuments of unaging intellect.

## II

An aged man is but a paltry thing,
A tattered coat upon a stick, unless    10
Soul clap its hands and sing, and louder sing
For every tatter in its mortal dress.
Nor is there singing school but studying
Monuments of its own magnificence;
And therefore I have sailed the seas and come    15
To the holy city of Byzantium.

## III

O sages standing in God's holy fire
As in the gold mosaic of a wall,
Come from the holy fire, perne° in a gyre,
And be the singing-masters of my soul.    20
Consume my heart away; sick with desire
And fastened to a dying animal
It knows not what it is; and gather me
Into the artifice of eternity.

## IV

Once out of nature I shall never take    25
My bodily form from any natural thing,
But such a form as Grecian goldsmiths make
Of hammered gold and gold enameling
To keep a drowsy Emperor awake;
Or set upon a golden bough to sing    30
To lords and ladies of Byzantium
Of what is past, or passing, or to come.

---

19 perne whirl down.

# JAMES WELDON JOHNSON

*Born in Jacksonville, Florida, James Weldon Johnson (1871-1938) received a bachelor's and a master's degree from Atlanta University. Johnson taught school, served as a high school principal, and founded the Daily American (1895, the first black daily in America). Later he became active in the NAACP, served as consul to Venezuela and to Nicaragua, and taught creative writing at Fisk University. On the day of his death, in an automobile accident, he was appointed to teach African-American literature at New York University.*

*Johnson wrote dialect poems as well as poems in standard English.*

## To America                                                      [1917]

How would you have us, as we are?
Or sinking 'neath the load we bear?
Our eyes fixed forward on a star?
Or gazing empty at despair?                                           4

Rising or falling? Men or things?
With dragging pace or footsteps fleet?
Strong, willing sinews in your wings?
Or tightening chains about your feet?                                 8

# EDNA ST. VINCENT MILLAY

*Edna St. Vincent Millay (1892-1950) was born in Rockland, Maine. Even as a child she wrote poetry, and by the time she graduated from Vassar College (1917) she had achieved some notice as a poet. Millay settled for a while in Greenwich Village, a center of Bohemian activity in New York City, where she wrote, performed in plays, and engaged in feminist causes. In 1923, the year she married, she became the first woman to win the Pulitzer Prize for Poetry. Numerous other awards followed. Though she is best known as a lyric poet—especially as a writer of sonnets—she also wrote memorable political poetry and nature poetry as well as short stories, plays, and a libretto for an opera.*

## Sonnet xli                                                       [1923]

I, being born a woman and distressed
By all the needs and notions of my kind,
Am urged by your propinquity to find
Your person fair, and feel a certain zest                              4
To bear your body's weight upon my breast:

So subtly is the fume of life designed,
To clarify the pulse and cloud the mind,
And leave me once again undone, possessed.    8
Think not for this, however, the poor treason
Of my stout blood against my staggering brain,
I shall remember you with love, or season
My scorn with pity,—let me make it plain:    12
I find this frenzy insufficient reason
For conversation when we meet again.

# E. E. CUMMINGS

*e. e. cummings was the pen name of Edwin Estlin Cummings (1894-1962), who grew up in Cambridge, Massachusetts, and was graduated from Harvard, where he became interested in modern literature and art, especially in the movements called cubism and futurism. His father, a conservative clergyman and a professor at Harvard, seems to have been baffled by the youth's interests, but Cummings's mother encouraged his artistic activities, including his use of unconventional punctuation and capitalization.*

*Politically liberal in his youth, Cummings became more conservative after a visit to Russia in 1931, but early and late his work emphasizes individuality and freedom of expression.*

## anyone lived in a pretty how town    [1940]

anyone lived in a pretty how town
(with up so floating many bells down)
spring summer autumn winter
he sang his didn't he danced his did.    4

Women and men(both little and small)
cared for anyone not at all
they sowed their isn't they reaped their same
sun moon stars rain    8

children guessed(but only a few
and down they forgot as up they grew
autumn winter spring summer)
that noone loved him more by more    12

when by now and tree by leaf
she laughed his joy she cried his grief
bird by snow and stir by still
anyone's any was all to her    16

someones married their everyones
laughed their cryings and did their dance
(sleep wake hope and then)they
said their nevers they slept their dream                    20

stars rain sun moon
(and only the snow can begin to explain
how children are apt to forget to remember
with up so floating many bells down)                       24

one day anyone died i guess
(and noone stooped to kiss his face)
busy folk buried them side by side
little by little and was by was                            28

all by all and deep by deep
and more by more they dream their sleep
noone and anyone earth by april
wish by spirit and if by yes.                              32

Women and men(both dong and ding)
summer autumn winter spring
reaped their sowing and went their came
sun moon stars rain                                        36

# T. S. ELIOT

*Thomas Stearns Eliot (1888-1965) was born into a New England family that had moved to St. Louis. He attended a preparatory school in Massachusetts, then graduated from Harvard and did further study in literature and philosophy in France, Germany, and England. In 1914 he began working for Lloyd's Bank in London, and three years later he published his first book of poems (it included "Prufrock"). In 1925 he joined a publishing firm, and in 1927 he became a British citizen and a member of the Church of England. Much of his later poetry, unlike "The Love Song of J.Alfred Prufrock," is highly religious. In 1948 Eliot received the Nobel Prize for Literature.*

## The Love Song of J. Alfred Prufrock                     [1917]

> *S'io credesse che mia risposta fosse*
> *A persona che mai tornasse al mondo,*
> *Questa fiamma staria senza più scosse.*
> *Ma perciocchè giammai di questo fondo*

*Non torno vivo alcun, s' i' odo il vero,*
*Senza tema d'infamia ti rispondo.**

Let us go then, you and I,
When the evening is spread out against the sky
Like a patient etherised upon a table;
Let us go, through certain half-deserted streets,
The muttering retreats                                                    5
Of restless nights in one-night cheap hotels
And sawdust restaurants with oyster-shells;
Streets that follow like a tedious argument
Of insidious intent
To lead you to an overwhelming question . . .                            10

Oh, do not ask, "What is it?"
Let us go and make our visit.

In the room the women come and go
Talking of Michelangelo.

The yellow fog that rubs its back upon the window panes,                 15
The yellow smoke that rubs its muzzle on the window panes
Licked its tongue into the corners of the evening,
Lingered upon the pools that stand in drains,
Let fall upon its back the soot that falls from chimneys,
Slipped by the terrace, made a sudden leap,                              20
And seeing that it was a soft October night,
Curled once about the house, and fell asleep.

And indeed there will be time
For the yellow smoke that slides along the street,
Rubbing its back upon the window-panes;                                  25
There will be time, there will be time
To prepare a face to meet the faces that you meet;

---

*In Dante's *Inferno* XXVII: 61–66, a damned soul who had sought absolution before committing a crime addresses Dante, thinking that his words will never reach the earth:"If I believed that my answer were to a person who could ever return to the world, this flame would no longer quiver. But because no one ever returned from this depth, if what I hear is true, without fear of infamy, I answer you."

Explanations of allusions in the poem may be helpful."Works and days" (line 29) is the title of a poem on farm life by Hesiod (eighth century BCE);"dying fall" (line 52) echoes *Twelfth Night* I.i.4; lines 81–83 allude to John the Baptist (see Matthew 14.1–11); line 92 echoes lines 41–42 of Marvell's "To His Coy Mistress" (see page 472); for "Lazarus" (line 94) see Luke 16 and John 11; lines 112–117 allude to Polonius and perhaps to other figures in *Hamlet;* "full of high sentence" (line 117) comes from Chaucer's description of the Clerk of Oxford in the *Canterbury Tales.*

There will be time to murder and create,
And time for all the works and days of hands
That lift and drop a question on your plate;                          30
Time for you and time for me,
And time yet for a hundred indecisions,
And for a hundred visions and revisions,
Before the taking of a toast and tea.

In the room the women come and go                                    35
Talking of Michelangelo.

And indeed there will be time
To wonder, "Do I dare?" and, "Do I dare?"—
Time to turn back and descend the stair,
With a bald spot in the middle of my hair—                           40
(They will say: "How his hair is growing thin!")
My morning coat, my collar mounting firmly to the chin,
My necktie rich and modest, but asserted by a simple pin—
(They will say: "But how his arms and legs are thin!")
Do I dare                                                            45
Disturb the universe?
In a minute there is time
For decisions and revisions which a minute will reverse.

For I have known them all already, known them all:—
Have known the evenings, mornings, afternoons,                       50
I have measured out my life with coffee spoons;
I know the voices dying with a dying fall
Beneath the music from a farther room.
     So how should I presume?

And I have known the eyes already, known them all—                   55
The eyes that fix you in a formulated phrase.
And when I am formulated, sprawling on a pin,
When I am pinned and wriggling on the wall,
Then how should I begin
To spit out all the butt-ends of my days and ways?                   60
     And how should I presume?

And I have known the arms already, known them all—
Arms that are braceleted and white and bare
(But in the lamplight, downed with light brown hair!)
Is it perfume from a dress                                           65
That makes me so digress?
Arms that lie along a table, or wrap about a shawl.
     And should I then presume?
     And how should I begin?

Shall I say, I have gone at dusk through narrow streets                70
And watched the smoke that rises from the pipes
Of lonely men in shirt-sleeves, leaning out of windows? . . .

I should have been a pair of ragged claws
Scuttling across the floors of silent seas.
And the afternoon, the evening, sleeps so peacefully!                 75
Smoothed by long fingers,
Asleep . . . tired . . . or it malingers,
Stretched on the floor, here beside you and me.
Should I, after tea and cakes and ices,
Have the strength to force the moment to its crisis?                  80
But though I have wept and fasted, wept and prayed,
Though I have seen my head (grown slightly bald)
     brought in upon a platter,
I am no prophet—and here's no great matter;
I have seen the moment of my greatness flicker,
And I have seen the eternal Footman hold my coat, and snicker,        85
And in short, I was afraid.

And would it have been worth it, after all,
After the cups, the marmalade, the tea,
Among the porcelain, among some talk of you and me,
Would it have been worth while,                                       90
To have bitten off the matter with a smile,
To have squeezed the universe into a ball
To roll it toward some overwhelming question,
To say:"I am Lazarus, come from the dead,
Come back to tell you all, I shall tell you all"—                    95
If one, settling a pillow by her head,
     Should say:"That is not what I meant at all;
     That is not it, at all."

And would it have been worth it, after all,
Would it have been worth while,                                      100
After the sunsets and the dooryards and the sprinkled streets,
After the novels, after the teacups, after the skirts that trail
     along the floor—
And this, and so much more?—
It is impossible to say just what I mean!
But as if a magic lantern threw the nerves in patterns on a screen:  105

Would it have been worth while
If one, settling a pillow or throwing off a shawl,
And turning toward the window, should say:
     "That is not it at all,
     That is not what I meant, at all."                              110

No! I am not Prince Hamlet, nor was meant to be;
Am an attendant lord, one that will do
To swell a progress, start a scene or two,
Advise the prince; no doubt, an easy tool,
Deferential, glad to be of use,                                  115
Politic, cautious, and meticulous;
Full of high sentence, but a bit obtuse;
At times, indeed, almost ridiculous—
Almost, at times, the Fool.

I grow old . . . I grow old . . .                                120
I shall wear the bottoms of my trousers rolled.

Shall I part my hair behind? Do I dare to eat a peach?
I shall wear white flannel trousers, and walk upon the beach.
I have heard the mermaids singing, each to each.

I do not think that they will sing to me.                        125

I have seen them riding seaward on the waves
Combing the white hair of the waves blown back
When the wind blows the water white and black.

We have lingered in the chambers of the sea
By sea-girls wreathed with seaweed red and brown,               130
Till human voices wake us, and we drown.

# ARCHIBALD MACLEISH

*Archibald MacLeish (1892-1982) was educated at Harvard and at Yale Law School. His early poetry (say, to about 1930), including "Ars Poetica," often is condensed and allusive, though his later poems and his plays are readily accessible. Under Franklin Delano Roosevelt, MacLeish served as Librarian of Congress (1939-1944) and as assistant secretary of state (1944-45). He then taught at Harvard and at Amherst until he retired in 1967.*

## Ars Poetica                                                   [1926]

A poem should be palpable and mute
As a globed fruit,

Dumb
As old medallions to the thumb,

Silent as the sleeve-worn stone                                 5
Of casement ledges where the moss has grown—

A poem should be wordless
As the flight of birds.

A poem should be motionless in time
As the moon climbs,                                    10

Leaving, as the moon releases
Twig by twig the night-entangled trees,

Leaving, as the moon behind the winter leaves,
Memory by memory the mind—

A poem should be motionless in time                    15
As the moon climbs.

A poem should be equal to:
Not true.

For all the history of grief
An empty doorway and a maple leaf.                     20

For love
The leaning grasses and two lights above the sea—

A poem should not mean
But be.

# W. H. AUDEN

*Wystan Hugh Auden (1907–1973) was born in York, England, and edu-*
*cated at Oxford. In the 1930s his left-wing poetry earned him wide ac-*
*claim as the leading poet of his generation. He went to Spain during the*
*Spanish Civil War, intending to serve as an ambulance driver for the*
*Republicans in their struggle against fascism, but he was so distressed*
*by the violence of the Republicans that he almost immediately returned*
*to England. In 1939 he came to America, and in 1946 he became a citi-*
*zen of the United States, though he returned to England for his last*
*years. Much of his poetry is characterized by a combination of collo-*
*quial diction and technical dexterity.*

## The Unknown Citizen                                 [1940]

*(To JS/07/M378*
*This Marble Monument*
*Is Erected by the State)*

He was found by the Bureau of Statistics to be
One against whom there was no official complaint,

And all the reports on his conduct agree
That, in the modern sense of an old-fashioned word, he was a saint,
For in everything he did he served the Greater Community.          5
Except for the War till the day he retired
He worked in a factory and never got fired,
But satisfied his employers, Fudge Motors Inc.
Yet he wasn't a scab or odd in his views,
For his Union reports that he paid his dues,                        10
(Our report on his Union shows it was sound)
And our Social Psychology workers found
That he was popular with his mates and liked a drink.
The Press are convinced that he bought a paper every day
And that his reactions to advertisements were normal in every way.  15
Policies taken out in his name prove that he was fully insured,
And his Health-card shows he was once in hospital but left it cured.
Both Producers Research and High-Grade Living declare
He was fully sensible to the advantages of the Installment Plan
And had everything necessary to the Modern Man,                     20
A phonograph, radio, a car and a frigidaire.
Our researchers into Public Opinion are content
That he held the proper opinions for the time of year;
When there was peace, he was for peace; when there was war,
    he went.
He was married and added five children to the population,           25
Which our Eugenist says was the right number for a parent of his
    generation,
And our teachers report that he never interfered with their education.
Was he free? Was he happy? The question is absurd:
Had anything been wrong, we should certainly have heard.

# ROBERT HAYDEN

*Robert Hayden (1913–1980) was born in Detroit, Michigan. His parents divorced when he was a child, and he was brought up by a neighboring family, whose name he adopted. In 1942, at the age of twenty-nine, he graduated from Detroit City College (now Wayne State University), and he received a master's degree from the University of Michigan. He taught at Fisk University from 1946 to 1969 and after that, for the remainder of his life, at the University of Michigan. In 1979 he was appointed Consultant in Poetry to the Library of Congress, the first African-American to hold the post.*

# Those Winter Sundays

[1962]

Sundays too my father got up early
and put his clothes on in the blueblack cold,
then with cracked hands that ached
from labor in the weekday weather made
banked fires blaze. No one ever thanked him.                    5

I'd wake and hear the cold splintering, breaking.
When the rooms were warm, he'd call,
and slowly I would rise and dress,
fearing the chronic angers of that house.

Speaking indifferently to him,                                  10
who had driven out the cold
and polished my good shoes as well.
What did I know, what did I know
of love's austere and lonely offices?

# GWENDOLYN BROOKS

*Gwendolyn Brooks (1917–2000) was born in Topeka, Kansas, but was
raised in Chicago's South Side, where she spent most of her life. Brooks
taught in several colleges and universities and wrote a novel (Maud
Martha, 1953) and a memoir (Report from Part One, 1972), but she is
best known as a poet. In 1950, when she won the Pulitzer Prize for Poetry, she became the first African-American writer to win a Pulitzer
Prize. In 1985 Brooks became Consultant in Poetry to the Library of
Congress.*

*The subject of the second poem here, the civil rights leader Martin
Luther King Jr. (1929–1968), was assassinated at the height of his
career.*

# The Bean Eaters

[1960]

They eat beans mostly, this old yellow pair.
Dinner is a casual affair.
Plain chipware on a plain and creaking wood,
Tin flatware.                                                   4

Two who are Mostly Good.
Two who have lived their day,
But keep on putting on their clothes
And putting things away.                                        8

And remembering . . .
Remembering, with twinklings and twinges,
As they lean over the beans in their rented back room that is full
    of beads and receipts and dolls and clothes, tobacco crumbs,
    vases and fringes.

## Martin Luther King Jr.                                     [1970]

A man went forth with gifts.
He was a prose poem.
He was a tragic grace.
He was a warm music.

He tried to heal the vivid volcanoes.                          5
His ashes are
    reading the world.

Funeral march for Martin Luther King Jr., held in Atlanta, Georgia.

His Dream still wishes to anoint
  the barricades of faith and of control.

His word still burns the center of the sun,    10
  above the thousands and the
  hundred thousands.

The word was Justice. It was spoken.

So it shall be spoken.
So it shall be done.    15


# ANTHONY HECHT

*Anthony Hecht (1923-2004), born in New York City, was educated at
Bard College and Columbia University. He taught at several institutions
(notably at Georgetown University), and he served as poetry consultant to the Library of Congress.*

  *Like "The Dover Bitch," which assumes a reader's familiarity with
Matthew Arnold's "Dover Beach" (page 602), much of Hecht's work
glances at earlier literature. The poem is dedicated to a critic and editor.*


## The Dover Bitch    [1967]

A Criticism of Life

*For Andrews Wanning*

So there stood Matthew Arnold and this girl
With the cliffs of England crumbling away behind them,
And he said to her, "Try to be true to me,
And I'll do the same for you, for things are bad
All over, etc., etc."    5
Well now, I knew this girl. It's true she had read
Sophocles in a fairly good translation
And caught that bitter allusion to the sea,
But all the time he was talking she had in mind
The notion of what his whiskers would feel like    10
On the back of her neck. She told me later on
That after a while she got to looking out
At the lights across the channel, and really felt sad,
Thinking of all the wine and enormous beds
And blandishments in French and the perfumes.    15
And then she got really angry. To have been brought
All the way down from London, and then be addressed

As sort of a mournful cosmic last resort
Is really tough on a girl, and she was pretty,
Anyway, she watched him pace the room                          20
And finger his watch-chain and seem to sweat a bit,
And then she said one or two unprintable things.
But you mustn't judge her by that. What I mean to say is,
She's really all right. I still see her once in a while
And she always treats me right.                                25
We have a drink
And I give her a good time, and perhaps it's a year
Before I see her again, but there she is.
Running to fat, but dependable as they come.
And sometimes I bring her a bottle of *Nuit d'Amour.*          30

# ROBERT BLY

*Robert Bly, born in 1926 in Madison, Minnesota, is one of the few poets who has been able to support himself by writing and by giving readings, rather than by teaching. In 1990 his* Iron John, *a book about male identity, became a bestseller.*

## Driving to Town Late to Mail a Letter                   [1962]

It is a cold and snowy night. The main street is deserted.
The only things moving are swirls of snow.
As I lift the mailbox door, I feel its cold iron.
There is a privacy I love in this snowy night.
Driving around, I will waste more time.

# ALLEN GINSBERG

*Allen Ginsberg (1926–1997) was born in Newark, New Jersey, and graduated from Columbia University in 1948. After eight months in Columbia Psychiatric Institute—Ginsberg had pleaded insanity to avoid prosecution when the police discovered that a friend stored stolen goods in Ginsberg's apartment—he worked at odd jobs and finally left the nine-to-five world for a freer life in San Francisco. In the 1950s he established a reputation as an uninhibited declamatory poet whose chief theme was a celebration of those who were alienated from a repressive America.*

# A Supermarket in California

[1956]

What thoughts I have of you tonight, Walt Whitman, for I walked
down the sidestreets under the trees with a headache self-conscious
looking at the full moon.

In my hungry fatigue, and shopping for images, I went into the
neon fruit supermarket, dreaming of your enumerations!

What peaches and what penumbras! Whole families shopping at
night! Aisles full of husbands! Wives in the avocados, babies in the
tomatoes!—and you, García Lorca,° what were you doing down by
the watermelons?

I saw you, Walt Whitman, childless, lonely old grubber, poking
among the meats in the refrigerator and cyeing the grocery boys.

I heard you asking questions of each: Who killed the pork chops?
What price bananas? Are you my Angel?                                        5

I wandered in and out of the brilliant stacks of cans following
you, and followed in my imagination by the store detective.

We strode down the open corridors together in our solitary
fancy tasting artichokes, possessing every frozen delicacy, and never
passing the cashier.

Where are we going, Walt Whitman? The doors close in an hour.
Which way does your beard point tonight?

(I touch your book and dream of our odyssey in the supermarket and feel absurd.)

Will we walk all night through solitary streets? The trees add
shade to shade, lights out in the houses, we'll both be lonely.          10

Will we stroll dreaming of the lost America of love past blue
automobiles in driveways, home to our silent cottage?

Ah, dear father, graybeard, lonely old courage-teacher, what America did you have when Charon quit poling his ferry and you got out
on a smoking bank and stood watching the boat disappear on the
black water of Lethe?°

---

3 **García Lorca** Federico García Lorca (1899–1936), Spanish poet (and, like
Whitman and Ginsberg, a homosexual).    **12 Lethe** In classical mythology, Charon
ferried the souls of the dead across the river Styx, to Hades, where, after drinking
from the river Lethe, they forgot the life they had lived.

# JAMES WRIGHT

*James Wright (1927-1980) was born in Martins Ferry, Ohio, which provided him with the locale for many of his poems. He is often thought of as a poet of the Midwest, but (as in the example that we give) his poems move beyond the scenery. Wright was educated at Kenyon College in Ohio and at the University of Washington. He wrote several books of poetry and published many translations of European and Latin-American poetry.*

## *Lying in a Hammock at William Duffy's Farm in Pine Island, Minnesota*                    [1963]

Over my head, I see the bronze butterfly,
Asleep on the black trunk,
Blowing like a leaf in green shadow.
Down the ravine behind the empty house,
The cowbells follow one another                                5
Into the distances of the afternoon.
To my right,
In a field of sunlight between two pines,
The droppings of last year's horses
Blaze up into golden stones.                                  10
I lean back, as the evening darkens and comes on.
A chicken hawk floats over, looking for home.
I have wasted my life.

# ANNE SEXTON

*Anne Sexton (1928-1974) was born in Newton, Massachusetts. She was a member of a well-educated New England family but did not attend college. After the birth of her second child she suffered a mental break-down, and for much of the rest of her life she was under psychiatric care. Indeed, a psychiatrist encouraged her to write poetry, and she was soon able to publish in national journals such as* The New Yorker. *Despite her success, she continued to suffer mentally, and in 1974 she took her life.*

# Her Kind

[1960]

I have gone out, a possessed witch,
haunting the black air, braver at night;
dreaming evil, I have done my hitch
over the plain houses, light by light;
lonely thing, twelve-fingered, out of mind.                      5
A woman like that is not a woman, quite.
I have been her kind.

I have found the warm caves in the woods,
filled them with skillets, carvings, shelves,
closets, silks, innumerable goods;                               10
fixed the suppers for the worms and the elves:
whining, rearranging the disaligned.
A woman like that is misunderstood.
I have been her kind.

I have ridden in your cart, driver,                              15
waved my nude arms at villages going by,
learning the last bright routes, survivor
where your flames still bite my thigh
and my ribs crack where your wheels wind.
A woman like that is not ashamed to die.                         20
I have been her kind.

# ADRIENNE RICH

Adrienne Rich's most recent books of poetry are The School Among the Ruins: Poems 2000–2004, and Fox: Poems 1998–2000 (Norton). A selection of her essays, Arts of the Possible: Essays and Conversations, was published in 2001. A new edition of What is Found There: Notebooks on Poetry and Politics, appeared in 2003. She is a recipient of the Lannan Foundation Lifetime Achievement Award, the Lambda Book Award, the Lenore Marshall/Nation Prize, the Wallace Stevens Award, and the Bollingen Prize in Poetry, among other honors. She lives in California.
In line 9 of the first poem, James and Whitehead are William James (1842–1910) and Alfred North Whitehead (1861–1947), both of whom taught philosophy at Harvard.

## For the Felling of an Elm in the Harvard Yard     [1951]

They say the ground precisely swept
No longer feeds with rich decay
The roots enormous in their age
That long and deep beneath have slept.                    4

So the great spire is overthrown,
And sharp saws have gone hurtling through
The rings that three slow centuries wore;
The second oldest elm is down.                            8

The shade where James and Whitehead strolled
Becomes a litter on the green.
The young men pause along the paths
To see the axes glinting bold.                            12

Watching the hewn trunk dragged away,
Some turn the symbol to their own,
And some admire the clean dispatch
With which the aged elm came down.                        16

# SYLVIA PLATH

*Sylvia Plath (1932–1963) was born in Boston, the daughter of German immigrants. While still an undergraduate at Smith College, she published in* Seventeen *and* Mademoiselle, *but her years at college, like her later years, were marked by manic-depressive periods. After graduating from college she went to England to study at Cambridge University, where she met the English poet Ted Hughes, whom she married in 1956. The marriage was unsuccessful, and they separated. One day she committed suicide by turning on the kitchen gas.*

## Daddy     [1965]

You do not do, you do not do
Any more, black shoe
In which I have lived like a foot
For thirty years, poor and white,
Barely daring to breathe or Achoo.                        5

Daddy, I have had to kill you.
You died before I had time—

Marble-heavy, a bag full of God,
Ghastly statue with one gray toe
Big as a Frisco seal                                        10

And a head in the freakish Atlantic
Where it pours bean green over blue
In the waters off beautiful Nauset.
I used to pray to recover you.
Ach, du.°                                                    15

In the German tongue, in the Polish town
Scraped flat by the roller
Of wars, wars, wars.
But the name of the town is common.
My Polack friend                                            20

Says there are a dozen or two.
So I never could tell where you
Put your foot, your root,
I never could talk to you
The tongue stuck in my jaw.                                 25

It stuck in a barb wire snare.
Ich, ich, ich, ich,°
I could hardly speak.
I thought every German was you.
And the language obscene                                    30

An engine, an engine
Chuffing me off like a Jew.
A Jew to Dachau, Auschwitz, Belsen.°
I began to talk like a Jew.
I think I may well be a Jew.                                35

The snows of the Tyrol, the clear beer of Vienna
Are not very pure or true.
With my gypsy ancestress and my weird luck
And my Taroc pack and my Taroc pack
I may be a bit of a Jew.                                    40

I have always been scared of *you,*
With your Luftwaffe,° your gobbledygoo.
And your neat moustache

---

**15 Ach, du** O, you (German).    **27 Ich, ich, ich, ich** I, I, I, I.    **33 Dachau . . .**
**Belsen** concentration camps.    **42 Luftwaffe** German air force.

And your Aryan eye, bright blue,
Panzer-man,° panzer-man, O You—                    45

Not God but a swastika
So black no sky could squeak through.
Every woman adores a Fascist,
The boot in the face, the brute
Brute heart of a brute like you.                    50

You stand at the blackboard, daddy,
In the picture I have of you,
A cleft in your chin instead of your foot
But no less a devil for that, no not
Any less the black man who                          55

Bit my pretty red heart in two.
I was ten when they buried you.
At twenty I tried to die
And get back, back, back to you.
I thought even the bones would do.                  60

But they pulled me out of the sack,
And they stuck me together with glue,
And then I knew what to do.
I made a model of you,
A man in black with a Meinkampf° look              65

And a love of the rack and the screw.
And I said I do, I do.
So daddy, I'm finally through.
The black telephone's off at the root,
The voices just can't worm through.                70

If I've killed one man, I've killed two—
The vampire who said he was you
And drank my blood for a year,
Seven years, if you want to know.
Daddy, you can lie back now.                        75

There's a stake in your fat black heart
And the villagers never liked you.
They are dancing and stamping on you.
They always *knew* it was you.
Daddy, daddy, you bastard, I'm through.             80

---

**45 Panzer-man** member of a tank crew.   **65 Meinkampf** My Struggle (*Mein Kampf* is the title of Hitler's autobiography).

# JOHN UPDIKE

*John Updike (b. 1932) is best known as a writer of fiction—short stories and novels—but throughout his professional career he has also written essays and poems. (For a more complete biography, see page 117.)*

## Ex-Basketball Player

[1958]

Pearl Avenue runs past the high-school lot,
Bends with the trolley tracks, and stops, cut off
Before it has a chance to go two blocks,
At Colonel McComsky Plaza. Berth's Garage
Is on the corner facing west, and there,
Most days, you'll find Flick Webb, who helps Berth out.    6

Flick stands tall among the idiot pumps—
Five on a side, the old bubble-head style,
Their rubber elbows hanging loose and low
One's nostrils are two S's, and his eyes
An E and O. And one is squat, without
A head at all—more of a football type.    12

Once Flick played for the high-school team, the Wizards.
He was good: in fact, the best. In '46
He bucketed three hundred ninety points,
A county record still. The ball loved Flick.
I saw him rack up thirty-eight or forty
In one home game. His hands were like wild birds.    18

He never learned a trade, he just sells gas,
Checks oil, and changes flats. Once in a while,
As a gag, he dribbles an inner tube,
But most of us remember anyway.
His hands are fine and nervous on the lug wrench.
It makes no difference to the lug wrench, though.    24

Off work, he hangs around Mae's Luncheonette.
Grease-gray and kind of coiled, he plays pinball,
Smokes those thin cigars, nurses lemon phosphates.
Flick seldom says a word to Mae, just nods
Beyond her face toward bright applauding tiers
Of Necco Wafers, Nibs, and Juju Beads.    30

# PAT MORA

*Pat Mora, after graduating from Texas Western College, earned a master's degree at the University of Texas at El Paso. She is best known for her poems, but she has also published essays on Chicano culture.*

## Illegal Alien                                                    [1984]

Socorro, you free me
to sit in my yellow kitchen
waiting for a poem
while you scrub and iron.

Today you stand before me                                            5
holding cleanser and sponge
and say you can't sleep at night.
"My husband's fury is a fire.
His fist can burn.
We don't fight with words                                            10
on that side of the Rio Grande."

Your eyes fill. I want
to comfort you, but my arms
feel heavy, unaccustomed
to healing grown-up bodies.                                          15

I offer foolish questions
when I should hug you hard,
when I should dry your eyes, my sister,
sister because we are both women,
both married, both warmed                                            20
by Mexican blood.

It is not cool words you need
but soothing hands.
My plastic band-aid doesn't fit
your hurt.                                                           25
I am the alien here.

## Legal Alien                                                      [1984]

Bi-lingual. Bi-cultural,
able to slip from "How's life?"
to *"Me'stan volviendo loca,"*°

---

3 *Me'stan volviendo loca*  They are driving me crazy.

able to sit in a paneled office
drafting memos in smooth English,                         5
able to order in fluent Spanish
at a Mexican restaurant,
American but hyphenated,
viewed by Anglos as perhaps exotic,
perhaps inferior, definitely different,                    10
viewed by Mexicans as alien.
(their eyes say, "You may speak
Spanish but you're not like me")
an American to Mexicans
a Mexican to Americans                                     15
a handy token
sliding back and forth
between the fringes of both worlds
by smiling
by masking the discomfort                                  20
of being pre-judged
Bi laterally.

# SHARON OLDS

*Sharon Olds was born in San Francisco in 1942. She was educated at
Stanford University and Columbia University, has published several volumes of poetry, and has received major awards.*

## Rites of Passage                                [1983]

As the guests arrive at my son's party
They gather in the living room—
short men, men in first grade
with smooth jaws and chins.
Hands in pockets, they stand around               5
jostling, jockeying for place, small fights
breaking out and calming. One says to another
*How old are you? Six. I'm seven. So?*
They eye each other, seeing themselves
tiny in the other's pupils. They clear their      10
throats a lot, a room of small bankers,
they fold their arms and frown. *I could beat you
up,* a seven says to a six,
the dark cake, round and heavy as a
turret, behind them on the table. My son,        15

freckles like specks of nutmeg on his cheeks,
chest narrow as the balsa keel of a
model boat, long hands
cool and thin as the day they guided him
out of me, speaks up as a host                                20
for the sake of the group.
*We could easily kill a two-year-old,*
he says in his clear voice. The other
men agree, they clear their throats
like Generals, they relax and get down to        25
playing war, celebrating my son's life.


# NIKKI GIOVANNI

*Nikki Giovanni was born in Knoxville, Tennessee, in 1943 and edu-*
*cated at Fisk University, the University of Pennsylvania School of Social*
*Work, and Columbia University. She has taught at Queens College, Rut-*
*gers University, and Ohio State University, and she now teaches cre-*
*ative writing at Mt. St. Joseph on the Ohio. Giovanni has published*
*many books of poems, an autobiography* (Gemini: An Extended Autobiographical Statement on My First Twenty-Five Years of Being a Black Poet),
*a book of essays, and a book consisting of a conversation with James*
*Baldwin.*

## Master Charge Blues                                      [1970]

its wednesday night baby
and i'm all alone
wednesday night baby
and i'm all alone
sitting with myself                                         5
waiting for the telephone

wanted you baby
but you said you had to go
wanted you yeah
but you said you had to go                                  10
called your best friend
but he can't come 'cross no more

did you ever go to bed
at the end of a busy day
look over and see the smooth                                15
where you hump usta lay

feminine odor and no reason why
i said feminine odor and no reason why
asked the lord to help me
he shook his head "not i"                                    20

but i'm a modern woman baby
ain't gonna let this get me down
i'm a modern woman
ain't gonna let this get me down
gonna take my master charge                                  25
and get everything in town

# LOUISE GLÜCK

*Louise Glück (b. 1943) was born in New York City
and attended Sarah Lawrence College and Columbia University. She has taught at Goddard College
in Vermont and at Warren Wilson College in North
Carolina. Her volume of poems,* The Triumph of
Achilles *(1985), won the National Book Critics Circle Award for poetry.*

## The School Children                          [1975]

The children go forward with their little satchels.
And all morning the mothers have labored
to gather the late apples, red and gold,
like words of another language.

And on the other shore                                       5
are those who wait behind great desks
to receive these offerings.

How orderly they are—the nails
on which the children hang
their overcoats of blue or yellow wool.                      10

And the teachers shall instruct them in silence
and the mothers shall scour the orchards for a way out,
drawing to themselves the gray limbs of the fruit trees
bearing so little ammunition.

# CAROL MUSKE

*Carol Muske was born in 1945 in St. Paul, Minnesota, and educated at Creighton University and San Francisco State University. She has taught creative writing at several universities and was the founder and director of Free Space (a creative writing program) at the Women's House of Detention, Riker's Island, New York. She has written several books of poetry (and a novel, Dear Digby [1989], published under her married name, Carol Muske-Dukes) and has been awarded distinguished fellowships, including a grant from the National Endowment for the Arts.*

## Chivalry
[1997]

In Benares°
the holiest city on earth
I saw an old man
toiling up the stone steps
to the ghat°                                                    5
his dead wife in his arms
shrunken to the size
of a child—
lashed to a stretcher.

The sky filled with crows.                                     10
He held her up for a moment
then placed her
in the flames.

In my time on earth
I have seen few acts of true chivalry,                         15
man's reverence
for woman.

But the memory of him
with her
in the cradle of his arms                                      20
placing her just so in the fire

---

**1 Benares** one of India's most ancient cities; located on the Ganges River, it is the holy city of the Hindus and the site of pilgrimages.   **5 ghat** a broad flight of steps on an Indian riverbank that provides access to the water.

so she would burn faster
so the kindling of the stretcher
would catch—
is enough for me now,                                                      25
will suffice
for what remains on this earth
a gesture of bereavement
in the familiar carnage of love.


# WENDY ROSE

*Wendy Rose, of Hopi and Miwok ancestry, was born in 1948 in Oakland, California. A graduate of the University of California, Berkeley, she has been editor of* American Indian Quarterly. *She teaches American Indian Studies at Fresno City College and is active as a poet, artist, and anthologist.*


## *Three Thousand Dollar Death Song*                        [1980]

*Nineteen American Indian Skeletons from Nevada . . . valued
at $3000 . . .*

                                        —Museum invoice, 1975

Is it in cold hard cash? the kind
that dusts the insides of men's pockets
lying silver-polished surface along the cloth.
Or in bills? papering the wallets of they
who thread the night with dark words. Or               5
checks? paper promises weighing the same
as words spoken once on the other side
of the grown grass and damned rivers
of history. However it goes, it goes
Through my body it goes assessing each nerve, running its edges    10
along my arteries, planning ahead
for whose hands will rip me
into pieces of dusty red paper,
whose hands will smooth or smatter me
into traces of rubble. Invoiced now,                   15
it's official how our bones are valued
that stretch out pointing to sunrise
or are flexed into one last foetal bend,
that are removed and tossed about,
catalogued, numbered with black ink                    20

on newly-white foreheads.
As we were formed to the white soldier's voice,
so we explode under white students' hands.
Death is a long trail of days
in our fleshless prison.                                              25

From this distant point we watch our bones
auctioned with our careful beadwork,
our quilled medicine bundles, even the bridles
of our shot-down horses. You: who have
priced us, you who have removed us: at what cost?                     30
What price the pits where our bones share
a single bit of memory, how one century
turns our dead into specimens, our history
into dust, our survivors into clowns.
Our memory might be catching, you know;                               35
picture the mortars, the arrowheads, the labrets°
shaking off their labels like bears
suddenly awake to find the seasons have ended
while they slept. Watch them touch each other,
measure reality, march out the museum door!                          40
Watch as they lift their faces
and smell about for us; watch our bones rise
to meet them and mount the horses once again!
The cost, then, will be paid
for our sweetgrass-smelling having-been                              45
in clam shell beads and steatite,°
dentalia° and woodpecker scalp, turquoise
and copper, blood and oil, coal
and uranium, children, a universe
of stolen things.                                                    50

---

36 **labrets** wood or bone ornaments inserted into a perforation in the lip.
46 **steatite** soapstone.  47 **dentalia** plural of *dentalium*, a kind of shellfish.

# JUDITH ORTIZ COFER

*Born in Puerto Rico in 1952 of a Puerto Rican mother and a United
States mainland father who served in the Navy, Judith Ortiz Cofer was
educated both in Puerto Rico and on the mainland. After earning a*

*bachelor's and a master's degree in English, she did further graduate work at Oxford and then taught English in Florida. The author of poems, essays, and a novel, she is now the Director of the Creative Writing Program at the University of Georgia.*

# My Father in the Navy

[1987]

A Childhood Memory

Stiff and immaculate
in the white cloth of his uniform
and a round cap on his head like a halo,
he was an apparition on leave from a shadow-world
and only flesh and blood when he rose from below    5
the waterline where he kept watch over the engines
and dials making sure the ship parted the waters
on a straight course.
Mother, brother and I kept vigil
on the nights and dawns of his arrivals,    10
watching the corner beyond the neon sign of a quasar
for the flash of white our father like an angel
heralding a new day.
His homecomings were the verses
we composed over the years making up    15
the siren's song that kept him coming back
from the bellies of iron whales
and into our nights
like the evening prayer.

# RITA DOVE

*Rita Dove was born in 1952 in Akron, Ohio. After graduating summa cum laude from Miami University (Ohio) she earned an M.F.A. at the Iowa Writers' Workshop. She has been awarded fellowships from the Guggenheim Foundation and the National Endowment for the Arts, and she now teaches at the University of Virginia. In 1993 she was appointed poet laureate for 1993-1994. Dove is currently writing a book about the experiences of an African-American volunteer regiment in France during World War I.*

# Daystar

[1986]

She wanted a little room for thinking:
but she saw diapers steaming on the line,
a doll slumped behind the door.
So she lugged a chair behind the garage
to sit out the children's naps.                                    5

Sometimes there were things to watch—
the pinched armor of a vanished cricket,
a floating maple leaf. Other days
she stared until she was assured
when she closed her eyes                                           10
she'd see only her own vivid blood.

She had an hour, at best, before Liza appeared
pouting from the top of the stairs.
And just *what* was mother doing
out back with the field mice? Why,                                15

building a palace. Later
that night when Thomas rolled over and
lurched into her, she would open her eyes
and think of the place that was hers
for an hour—where                                                 20
she was nothing,
pure nothing, in the middle of the day.

# KITTY TSUI

*Born in Hong Kong in 1953, Kitty Tsui lived there and in England until 1969, when she came to the United States. She is an actor, an artist, and a professional bodybuilder as well as a writer. Her publications include* Breathless: Erotica *(1996).*

# A Chinese Banquet

[1983]

*for the one who was not invited*

it was not a very formal affair but
all the women over twelve
wore long gowns and a corsage,
except for me.                                                    4

it was not a very formal affair, just
the family getting together,
*poa poa,*° *kuw fu*° without *kuw mow*°
(her excuse this year is a headache).                    8

aunts and uncles and cousins,
the grandson who is a dentist,
the one who drives a mercedes benz,
sitting down for shark's fin soup.                      12

they talk about buying a house and
taking a two week vacation in beijing.
i suck on shrimp and squab,
dreaming of the cloudscape in your eyes.                16

my mother, her voice beaded with sarcasm;
you're twenty six and not getting younger.
it's about time you got a decent job.
she no longer asks when i'm getting married.           20

you're twenty six and not getting younger.
what are you doing with your life?
you've got to make a living.
why don't you study computer programming?              24

she no longer asks when i'm getting married.
one day, wanting desperately to
bridge the boundaries that separate us,
wanting desperately to touch her,                       28

tell her: mother, i'm gay,
mother i'm gay and so happy with her.
but she will not listen,
she shakes her head.                                    32

she sits across from me,
emotions invading her face.
her eyes are wet but
she will not let tears fall.                            36

mother, i say,
you love a man.
i love a woman.
it is not what she wants to hear.                       40

_____

7 *poa poa* maternal grandmother. *kuw fu* uncle. *kuw mow* aunt.

aunts and uncles and cousins,
very much a family affair.
but you are not invited,
being neither my husband nor my wife.                                    44

aunts and uncles and cousins
eating longevity noodles
fragrant with ham inquire:
sold that old car of yours yet?                                          48

i want to tell them: my back is healing,
i dream of dragons and water.
my home is in her arms,
our bedroom ceiling the wide open sky.                                   52

# IV

# The Pleasures of Drama

Drama is life with the dull bits cut out.

—Alfred Hitchcock

The structure of a play is always the story of how the birds come home to roost.

—Arthur Miller

The theater is supremely fitted to say: "Behold! These things are." Yet most dramatists employ it to say: "This moral truth can be learned from beholding this action."

—Thornton Wilder

# 24

# How to Read a Play

## THINKING ABOUT
## THE LANGUAGE OF DRAMA

The earlier parts of this book have dealt with fiction and poetry. A third chief literary type is drama, texts written to be performed.

A play is written to be seen and to be heard. We go to *see* a play in a theater (*theater* is derived from a Greek word meaning "to watch"), but in the theater we also *hear* it because we become an audience (*audience* is derived from a Latin word meaning "to hear"). Hamlet was speaking the ordinary language of his day when he said, "We'll hear a play tomorrow." When we read a play rather than see and hear it in a theater, we lose a good deal. We must see it in the mind's eye and hear it in the mind's ear.

In reading a play it's not enough mentally to hear the lines. We must try to see the characters, costumed and moving within a specified setting, and we must try to hear not only their words but their tone, their joy or hypocrisy or tentativeness or aggression. Our job is much easier when we are in the theater and we have only to pay attention to the performers; as readers on our own, however, we must do what we can to perform the play in the theater of our minds.

If as a reader you develop the following principles into habits, you will get far more out of a play than if you read it as though it were a novel consisting only of dialogue.

1. *Pay attention to the **list of characters** and carefully read whatever **descriptions** the playwright has provided.* Early dramatists, such as Shakespeare, did not provide much in the way of description ("Othello, the Moor" or "Ariel, an airy spirit" is about as much as we find in Elizabethan texts), but later playwrights often are very forthcoming. Here, for instance, is Tennessee Williams introducing us to

Amanda Wingfield in *The Glass Menagerie.* (We give only the beginning of his longish description.)

> *Amanda Wingfield,* the mother. A little woman of great but confused vitality clinging frantically to another time and place.

And here is Susan Glaspell introducing us to all the characters in her one-act play, *Trifles:*

> . . . the Sheriff comes in, followed by the County Attorney and Hale. The Sheriff and Hale are men in middle life, the County Attorney is a young man; all are much bundled up and go at once to the stove. They are followed by the two women—the Sheriff's Wife, [Mrs. Peters] first; she is a slight wiry woman, a thin nervous face. Mrs. Hale is larger and would ordinarily be called more comfortable looking, but she is disturbed now and looks fearfully about as she enters. The women have come in slowly and stand close together near the door.

Glaspell's description of her characters is not nearly so explicit as Tennessee Williams's, but Glaspell does reveal much to a reader. What do we know about the men? They differ in age, they are bundled up, and they "go at once to the stove." What do we know about the women? Mrs. Peters is slight, and she has a "nervous face"; Mrs. Hale is "larger" but she too is "disturbed." The women enter "slowly," and they "stand close together near the door." In short, the men, who take over the warmest part of the room, are more confident than the women, who nervously huddle together near the door. It's a man's world.

2. *Pay attention to **gestures** and **costumes** that are specified in stage directions or are implied by the dialogue.* We have just seen how Glaspell distinguishes between the men and the women by what they do—the men take over the warm part of the room, the women stand insecurely near the door. Most dramatists from the late nineteenth century to the present have been fairly generous with their stage directions, but when we read the works of earlier dramatists we often have to deduce the gestures from the speeches. For instance, in the second scene of *Othello,* Iago—who hates Othello but who pretends to be his loyal friend—claims that he was almost tempted to stab ("yerk") Roderigo, a fool who is courting the woman whom Othello loves. Iago says:

> Nine or ten times
> I had thought t'have yerked him here under the ribs.

"Here under the ribs" pretty much suggests that Iago points to ribs—but whose? His own, or Othello's? Our view is that Iago should jab a finger into Othello's ribs, thus doing by way of illustration with his finger what in fact he would like to do with a knife. Or to move from the early part of the play to the very end, consider the concluding lines of the speech in which Othello stabs himself. Othello describes himself as "one that loved not wisely but too well," and he compares himself to someone who "threw a pearl away / richer than all his tribe." Then, speaking of his military service to Venice, he says,

> Set you down this;
> And say besides that in Aleppo once,
> Where a malignant and a turbaned Turk
> Beat a Venetian and traduced the state,
> I took by th'throat the circumcisèd dog
> And smote him thus.          [*He stabs himself.*]

Clearly when he says "thus," he stabs himself, showing *how* he killed the "turbaned Turk." Can't one also conjecture that Othello, with the hand unencumbered by the dagger, grasps *his own* throat, thus emphasizing his view that he is at least exerting just punishment on an enemy to society?

Admittedly our interpretation is conjectural; we are on safer ground when we say that the action of *kneeling* is eloquent in the play—Cassio kneels to Desdemona when we first see her, and his language suggests more than mere courtesy; it suggests that she is a spiritual force;

> Hail to thee, lady! And the grace of heaven
> Before, behind thee, and on every hand
> Enwheel thee round!

Later, when Othello vows to expel her from his heart, he kneels, thereby emphasizing the solemnity of his vow, and the monstrously hypocritical Iago joins him in this posture. Or take Othello's final gestures. After stabbing himself fatally, he kisses Desdemona—

> I kissed thee ere I killed thee. No way but this,
> Killing myself, to die upon a kiss—

and he dies on the bed with her.

In addition to thinking about gestures, don't forget the costumes the characters wear. Costumes identify characters as soldiers or housewives or kings. Shakespeare tells us nothing specific about the costumes worn in *Othello*, though in some plays he does give us clues. For instance, we know that Hamlet is dressed in black (in mourning for his father) because his mother speaks of Hamlet's "nighted color," and Hamlet himself speaks of his "inky cloak." A change of costume can be immensely significant. Consider Nora Helmer's changes in Ibsen's *A Doll's House*. In the first act she wears ordinary clothing appropriate to a bourgeois housewife, but in the middle of the second act, when she frantically rehearses her tarantella, a wild dance, she wears "a long gaily coloured shawl." The shawl is appropriate to the Italian dance, but its multitude of colors also helps express Nora's conflicting emotions. Her extreme agitation is expressed, too, in the fact that "Her hair comes undone and falls about her shoulders; she pays no attention and goes on dancing." The shawl and the disheveled hair, then, *speak* to us as clearly as the dialogue does. In the middle of the third act, after the party and just before the showdown, Nora appears in her "Italian costume," and her husband, Torvald, wears "evening dress" under an open black cloak. She is dressed for a masquerade (her whole life ahs been a masquerade, as it turns out), and Torvald's formal suit and black cloak help express the stiffness and the blight that have forced her to present a false front throughout their marriage. A little later Nora appears "in an everyday dress." The pretense is over. When she finally leaves the stage—leaves the house—she "wraps her shawl around her." This is not the "gaily coloured shawl" she used in rehearsing the dance, but the "big black shawl" she wears when she returns from the dance. The blackness of this shawl helps express the death of her old way of life.

3. *Keep in mind the* **kind of theater** *for which the play was written.* The plays in this book were written for various kinds of theaters. Sophocles, author of *Antigone* and *King Oedipus,* wrote for the ancient Greek theater, essentially a space where performers acted in front of an audience seated on a hillside. (See the photo on page 948.) This theater was open to the heavens, with a structure representing a palace or temple behind the actors, in itself a kind of image of a society governed by the laws of the state and the laws of the gods. Moreover, the chorus entered the playing space by marching down the side aisles, close to the audience, thus helping to unite the world of the audience and of the players. On the other hand, the audience in most modern theaters sits in a darkened area and looks through a proscenium arch at performers who move in a boxlike setting. The box set of the late nineteenth century and the twentieth century is, it often seems, an appropriate image of the confined lives of the unheroic characters of the play.

4. *If the playwright describes a set, try to* **envision the set** *clearly.* Glaspell, for instance, tells us a good deal about the set. We quote only the first part.

> The kitchen in the now abandoned farmhouse of John Wright, a gloomy kitchen, and left without having been put in order. . . .

These details about a gloomy and disordered kitchen may seem to be mere realism—after all, the play has to take place *somewhere*—but it turns out that the disorder and, for that matter, the gloominess are extremely important. You'll have to read the play to find out why.

Another example of a setting that provides important information is Arthur Miller's in *Death of a Salesman*. Again we quote only the beginning of the description.

> Before us is the Salesman's house. We are aware of towering, angular shapes behind it, surrounding it on all sides. Only the blue light of the sky falls upon the house and forestage; the surrounding area shows an angry glow of orange.

5. *Pay attention to whatever **sound effects** are specified in the play.* In *Death of a Salesman,* before the curtain goes up, "A melody is heard, played upon a flute. It is small and fine, telling of grass and trees and the horizon." Then the curtain rises, revealing the Salesman's house, with "towering, angular shapes behind it, surrounding it on all sides." Obviously the sound of the flute is meant to tell us of the world that the Salesman is shut off from.

A sound effect, however, need not be so evidently symbolic to be important in a play. In Glaspell's *Trifles,* almost at the very end of the play we hear the "sound of a knob turning in the other room." The sound has an electrifying effect on the audience, as it does on the two women on the stage, and it precedes a decisive action.

6. *Pay attention to what the characters say, and keep in mind that (like real people) dramatic characters are not always to be trusted.* An obvious case is Shakespeare's Iago, an utterly unscrupulous villain who knows that he is a liar. But a character may be self-deceived, or, to put it a bit differently, characters may say what they honestly think but may not know what they are talking about.

# PLOT AND CHARACTER

Although **plot** is sometimes equated with the gist of the narrative—the story—it is sometimes reserved to denote the writer's *arrangement* of the happenings in the story. Thus, all plays about the assassination of Julius Caesar have pretty much the same story, but by beginning with a scene of workmen enjoying a holiday (and thereby introducing the motif of the ficklcness of the mob), Shakespeare's play has a plot different from a play that omits such a scene.

Handbooks on drama often suggest that a plot (arrangement of happenings) should have a **rising action,** a **climax,** and a **falling action.** This sort of plot can be diagrammed as a pyramid, the tension rising through complications, or **crises,** to a climax, at which point the fate of the **protagonist** (chief character) is firmly established; the climax is the apex, and the tension allegedly slackens as we witness the **dénouement** (unknotting). Shakespeare sometimes used a pyramidal structure, placing his climax neatly in the middle of what seems to us to be the third of five acts.* Roughly the first half of Julius Caesar shows Brutus rising, reaching his height in 3.1 with the death of Caesar; but later in this scene he gives Marc Antony permission to speak at Caesar's funeral and thus he sets in motion his own fall, which occupies the second half of the play. In *Macbeth* (3.4.137–39), the protagonist attains his height in 3.1 ("Thou hast it now: King"), but he soon perceives that he is going downhill:

> I am in blood
> Stepped in so far, that, should I wade no more,
> Returning were as tedious as go o'er.

Of course, no law demands such a structure, and a hunt for the pyramid usually causes the hunter to overlook all the crises but the middle one. William Butler Yeats once suggestively diagrammed a good plot not as a pyramid but as a line moving diagonally upward, punctuated by several crises. Perhaps it is sufficient to say that a good plot has its moments of tension, but the location of these will vary with the play. They are the product of **conflict,** but not all conflict produces tension; there is conflict but little tension in a ball game when the score is 10–0 in the ninth inning with two out and no one on base.

Regardless of how a plot is diagrammed, the **exposition** is that part that tells the audience what it has to know about the past, the **antecedent action.** When two gossiping servants tell each other that after a year away in Paris the young master is coming home tomorrow with a new wife, they are giving the audience the exposition by introducing characters and establishing relationships. The Elizabethans and the Greeks sometimes tossed out all pretense at dialogue and began with a **prologue,** like the one spoken by the Chorus at the outset of *Romeo and Juliet:*

> Two households, both alike in dignity
> In fair Verona, where we lay our scene,

---

*An **act** is a main division in a drama or opera. Act divisions probably stem from Roman theory and derive ultimately from the Greek practice of separating episodes in a play by choral interludes; but Greek (and probably Roman) plays were performed without interruption, for the choral interludes were part of the plays themselves. Elizabethan plays, too, may have been performed without breaks; the division of Elizabethan plays into five acts is usually the work of editors rather than of authors. Frequently an act division today (commonly indicated by lowering the curtain and turning up the houselights) denotes change in locale and lapse of time. A **scene** is a smaller unit, either (1) a division with no change of locale or abrupt shift of time, or (2) a division consisting of an actor or group of actors on the stage; according to the second definition, the departure or entrance of an actor changes the composition of the group and thus introduces a new scene. (In an entirely different sense, the scene is the locale where a work is set.)

From ancient grudge break to new mutiny,
    Where civil blood makes civil hands unclean.
From forth the fatal loins of these two foes
    A pair of star-crossed lovers take their life. . . .

And in Tennessee Williams's *The Glass Menagerie,* Tom's first speech is a sort of prologue. However, the exposition also may extend far into the play so that the audience keeps getting bits of information that both clarify the present and build suspense about the future. Occasionally the **soliloquy** (speech of a character alone on the stage, revealing his or her thoughts) or the **aside** (speech in the presence of others but unheard by them) is used to do the job of putting the audience in possession of the essential facts. The soliloquy and the aside are not limited to exposition; they are used to reveal the private thoughts of characters who, like people in real life, do not always tell others what their inner thoughts are. The soliloquy is especially used for meditation, where we might say the character is interacting not with another character but with himself or herself.

Because a play is not simply words but words spoken with accompanying gestures by performers who are usually costumed and in a particular setting, it may be argued that to read a play (rather than to see and hear it) is to falsify it. Drama is not literature, some people hold, but theater. However, there are replies: a play can be literature as well as theater, and readers of a play can perhaps enact in the theater of their mind a more effective play than the one put on by imperfect actors.

# A NOTE ON TRAGEDY

The Greek philosopher Aristotle defined "tragedy" as a dramatization of a serious happening—not necessarily one ending with the death of the protagonist—and his definition remains among the best. But many plays have been written since Aristotle defined tragedy. When we think of Shakespeare's tragedies, we cannot resist narrowing Aristotle's definition by adding something like "showing a struggle that rends the protagonist's whole being": and when we think of the "problem plays" of the last hundred years—the serious treatments of such sociological problems as alcoholism and race prejudice—we might be inclined to exclude some of them by adding to the definition something about the need for universal appeal.

In the next few pages we will examine two comments on tragedy, neither of which is entirely acceptable, but each of which seems to have some degree of truth. The first comment is by Cyril Tourneur, a tragic dramatist of the early seventeenth century:

When the bad bleed, then is the tragedy good.

We think of Macbeth ("usurper," "butcher"). Macbeth is much more than a usurper and butcher, but it is undeniable that he is an offender against the moral order. Whatever the merits of Tourneur's statement, however, if we think of *Romeo and Juliet* (to consider only one play), we realize its inadequacy. Tourneur so stresses the guilt of the protagonist that his or her suffering becomes mere retributive justice. But we cannot plausibly say, for example, that Romeo and Juliet deserved to die because they married without their parents' consent; it is much too simple to call them "bad." Romeo and Juliet are young, in love, nobler in spirit than their parents.

Tourneur's view is probably derived ultimately from an influential passage in Aristotle's *Poetics* in which Aristotle speaks of **hamartia,** sometimes literally translated as "missing the target," sometimes as "vice" or "flaw" or "weakness," but perhaps best translated as "mistake." Aristotle seems to imply that the hero is undone because of some mistake he or she commits, but this mistake need not be the result of a moral fault; it may be simply a miscalculation—for example, failure to foresee the consequences of a deed. Brutus makes a strategic mistake when he lets Marc Antony speak at Caesar's funeral, but we can hardly call it a vice.

Because Aristotle's *hamartia* includes mistakes of this sort, the common translation "tragic flaw" is erroneous. In many Greek tragedies the hero's hamartia is **hubris** (or **hybris**), usually translated as "overweening pride." The hero forgets that he or she is fallible, acts as though he or she has the power and wisdom of the gods, and is later humbled for this arrogance. But one can argue that this self-assertiveness is not a vice but a virtue, not a weakness but a strength; if the hero is destroyed for self-assertion, he or she is nevertheless greater than the surrounding people, just as the person who tries to stem a lynch mob is greater than the mob, although that person also may be lynched for his or her virtue. Or a hero may be undone by a high-mindedness that makes him or her vulnerable. Hamlet is vulnerable because he is, as his enemy says, "most generous and free from all contriving"; because Hamlet is high-minded, he will not suspect that the proposed fencing match is a murderous plot. Othello can be tricked into murdering Desdemona not simply because he is jealous but because he is (in the words of the villainous Iago) "of a free and open nature / That thinks men honest but seem so." Iago knows, too, that out of Desdemona's "goodness" he can "make the net / That shall enmesh them all."

Next, here is a statement by Arthur Miller:

> If it is true to say that in essence the tragic hero is intent upon claiming his whole due as a personality, and if this struggle must be total and without reservation, then it automatically demonstrates the indestructible will of man to achieve his humanity. . . . It is curious, although edifying, that the plays we revere, century after century, are the tragedies. In them, and in them alone, lies the belief—optimistic, if you will—in the perfectibility of man.

There is much in Miller's suggestions that the tragic hero makes a large and total claim and that the audience often senses triumph rather than despair in tragedies. We often feel that we have witnessed human greatness—that the hero, despite profound suffering, has lived according to his or her ideals. We may feel that we have achieved new insight into human greatness. But the perfectibility of man? Do we feel that *Julius Caesar* or *Macbeth* or *Hamlet* have to do with human perfectibility? Don't these plays suggest rather that people, whatever their nobility, have within them the seeds of their own destruction? Without overemphasizing the guilt of the protagonists, don't we feel that in part the plays dramatize the *im*perfectibility of human beings? In much tragedy, after all, the destruction comes from within, not from without:

> In tragic life, God wot,
> No villain need be! Passions spin the plot:
> We are betrayed by what is false within.
>
> —George Meredith

What we are talking about is **tragic irony,** the contrast between what is believed to be so and what is so, or between expectations and accomplishments.* Several examples from *Macbeth* illustrate something of the range of tragic irony within a single play. In the first act, King Duncan bestows on Macbeth the title of Thane of Cawdor. By his kindness Duncan seals his own doom, for Macbeth, having achieved this rank, will next want to achieve a higher one. In the third act, Macbeth, knowing that Banquo will soon be murdered, hypocritically urges Banquo to "fail not our feast." But Macbeth's hollow request is ironically fulfilled: the ghost of Banquo terrorizes Macbeth during the feast. The most pervasive irony of all, of course, is that Macbeth aims at happiness when he kills Duncan and takes the throne, but he wins only sorrow.

Aristotle's discussion of **peripeteia (reversal)** and **anagnorisis (recognition)** may be a way of getting at this sort of irony. He may simply have meant a reversal of fortune (for example, good luck ceases) and a recognition of who is who (for example, the pauper is really the prince), but more likely he meant profounder things. One can say that the reversal in *Macbeth* lies in the sorrow that Macbeth's increased power brings. The recognition comes when he realizes the consequences of his deeds:

> I have lived long enough: my way of life
> Is fall'n into the sere, the yellow leaf;
> And what which should accompany old age,

---

*Tragic irony is sometimes **dramatic irony** or **Sophoclean irony.** The terms are often applied to speeches or actions that the audience understands in a sense fuller than or different from the sense in which the dramatic characters understand them.

As honor, love, obedience, troops of friends,
I must not look to have; but, in their stead,
Curses, not loud but deep, mouth-honor, breath
Which the poor heart would fain deny, and dare not.

That our deeds often undo us, that we can aim at our good and produce our ruin, was not, of course, a discovery of the tragic dramatists. The archetype is the story of Adam and Eve: these two aimed at becoming like God, and as a consequence, they brought upon themselves corruption, death, the loss of their earthly paradise. The Bible is filled with stories of tragic irony. A brief quotation from Ecclesiastes (10.8–9) can stand as an epitome of these stories:

> He that diggeth a pit shall fall into it; and whoso breaketh an hedge, a serpent shall bite him.
>
> Whoso removeth stones shall be hurt therewith; and he that cleaveth wood shall be endangered thereby.

"He that cleaveth wood shall be endangered thereby." Activity involves danger. To be inactive is, often, to be ignoble, but to be active is necessarily to imperil oneself. Perhaps we can attempt a summary of tragic figures: they act, and they suffer, usually as a consequence of their action. The question is not of the action's being particularly bad or particularly good; the action is often both good and bad, a sign of courage and also of arrogance, a sign of greatness and also of limitations.

Finally, a brief consideration of the pleasure of tragedy: Why do we enjoy plays about suffering? Aristotle has some obscure comments on **catharsis (purgation)** that are often interpreted as saying that tragedy arouses in us both pity and fear and then purges us of these emotions. The idea, perhaps, is that just as we can (it is said) harmlessly discharge our aggressive impulses by witnessing a prizefight or by shouting at an umpire, so we can harmlessly discharge our impulses to pity and to fear by witnessing the dramatization of a person's destruction. The theater in this view is an outlet for emotions that elsewhere would be harmful. But, it must be repeated, Aristotle's comments on catharsis are obscure; perhaps, too, they are wrong.

Most later theories on the pleasure of tragedy are footnotes to Aristotle's words on catharsis. Some say that our pleasure is sadistic (we enjoy the sight of suffering); some, that our pleasure is masochistic (we enjoy lacerating ourselves); some, that it lies in sympathy (we enjoy extending pity and benevolence to the wretched); some, that it lies in self-congratulation (we are reminded, when we see suffering, of our own good fortune); some, that we take pleasure in tragedy because the tragic hero acts out our secret desires, and we rejoice in his or her aggression, expiating our guilt in his or her suffering; and so on.

But this is uncertain psychology, and it mostly neglects the distinction between real suffering and dramatized suffering. In the latter, surely, part of the pleasure is in the contemplation of an aesthetic object, an object that is unified and complete. The chaos of real life seems, for a few moments in drama, to be ordered: the protagonist's action, his or her subsequent suffering, and the total cosmos seem somehow related. Tragedy has no use for the passerby who is killed by a falling brick. The events (the person's walk, the brick's fall) have no meaningful relation. But suppose a person chooses to climb a mountain, and in making the ascent sets in motion an avalanche that destroys that person. Here we find (however simple the illustration) something closer to tragedy. We do not say that people should avoid mountains, or that mountain climbers deserve to die by avalanches. But we feel that the event is unified, as the accidental conjunction of brick and passerby is not.

Tragedy thus presents some sort of ordered action; tragic drama itself is orderly. As we see or read it, we feel it cannot be otherwise; word begets word, deed begets deed, and every moment is exquisitely appropriate. Whatever the relevance on sadism, masochism, sympathy, and the rest, the pleasure of tragedy surely comes in part from the artistic shaping of the material.

# A NOTE ON COMEDY

Though etymology is not always helpful (after all, is it really illuminating to say that *tragedy* may come from a Greek word meaning "goat song"?), the etymology of *comedy* helps to reveal comedy's fundamental nature. **Comedy** (Greek: *komoidia*) is a revel song; ancient Greek comedies are descended from fertility rituals that dramatized the joy of renewal, the joy of triumphing over obstacles, the joy of being (in a sense) reborn. Whereas the movement of tragedy, speaking roughly, is from prosperity to disaster, the movement of comedy is from some sort of minor disaster to prosperity.

To say, however, that comedy dramatizes the triumph over obstacles is to describe it as though it were melodrama, a play in which, after hairbreadth adventures, good prevails over evil, often in the form of the hero's unlikely last-minute rescue of the fair Belinda from the clutches of the villain. What distinguishes comedy from melodrama is the pervasive high spirits of comedy. The joyous ending in comedy—usually a marriage—is in the spirit of what has gone before; the entire play, not only the end, is a celebration of fecundity.

The threats in the world of comedy are not taken very seriously; the parental tyranny that makes *Romeo and Juliet* and *Antigone* tragedies is, in comedy, laughable throughout. Parents may fret, fume, and lock doors, but in doing so they make themselves ridiculous, for love will find a way. Villains may threaten, but the audience never takes the threats seriously.

The marriage and renewal of society, so usual at the end of comedy, may be most improbable, but they do not therefore weaken the comedy. The stuff of comedy is, in part, improbability. In *A Midsummer Night's Dream,* Puck speaks for the spectator when he says:

> And those things do best please me
> That befall preposterously.

In tragedy, probability is important; in comedy, *im*probability is often desirable, for at least three reasons. First, comedy seeks to include as much as possible, to reveal the rich abundance of life. The motto of comedy (and the implication in the weddings with which it usually concludes) is, "The more the merrier." Second, the improbable is the surprising; surprise often evokes laughter, and laughter surely has a central place in comedy. Third, by getting the characters into improbable situations, the dramatist can show off the absurdity of their behavior. This point needs amplification.

Comedy often shows the absurdity of ideals. The miser, the puritan, the health faddist, and so on, are people of ideals, but their ideals are suffocating. The miser, for example, treats everything in terms of money; the miser's ideal causes him or her to renounce much of the abundance and joy of life. He or she is in love, but is unwilling to support a spouse; or he or she has a headache, but will not be so extravagant as to take an aspirin tablet. If a thief accosts the miser with "Your money or your life," the miser will prefer to give up life—and that is what in fact the miser has been doing all the while. Now, by putting this miser in a series of improbable situations, the dramatist can continue to demonstrate entertainingly the miser's absurdity.*

The comic protagonist's tenacious hold on his or her ideals is not very far from that of the tragic protagonist. In general, however, tragedy suggests the nobility of ideals; the tragic hero's ideals undo him or her, and they may be ideals about which we have serious reservations, but still we admire the nobility of these ideals. Romeo and Juliet will not put off their love for each other; Oedipus will not cease in his quest for the killer of Laius. But the comic protagonist who is always trying to keep his or her

---

*A character who is dominated by a single trait—avarice, jealousy, timidity, and so forth—is sometimes called a **humor character.** Medieval and Renaissance psychology held that an individual's personality depended on the mixture of four liquids (humors): blood (Latin: *sanguis*), choler, phlegm, and bile. An overabundance of one fluid produced a dominant trait, and even today "sanguine," "choleric," "phlegmatic," and "bilious" describe personalities.

Not all comedy, of course, depends on humor characters placed in situations that exhibit their absurdity. **High comedy** is largely verbal, depending on witty language; **farce,** at the other extreme, is dependent on inherently ludicrous situations—for example, a hobo is mistaken for a millionaire. Situation comedy, then, may use humor characters, but it need not do so.

hands clean is funny; we laugh at this refusal to touch dirt with the rest of us, this refusal to enjoy the abundance life has to offer. The comic protagonist who is always talking about his or her beloved is funny; we laugh at the failure to see that the world is filled with people more attractive than the one with whom he or she is obsessed.

In short, the ideals for which the tragic protagonist loses the world seem important to us and gain, in large measure, our sympathy, but the ideals for which the comic protagonist loses the world seem trivial compared with the rich variety that life has to offer, and we laugh at their absurdity. The tragic figure makes a claim on our sympathy. The absurd comic figure continually sets up obstacles to our sympathetic interest; we feel detached from, superior to, and amused by comic figures. Something along these lines is behind William Butler Yeats's insistence that *character* is always present in comedy but not in tragedy. Though Yeats is eccentric in his notion that individual character is obliterated in tragedy, he interestingly gets at one of the important elements in comedy:

> When the tragic reverie is at its height . . . [we do not say,] "How well that man is realized I should know him were I to meet him in the street," for it is always ourselves that we see upon the [tragic] stage. . . . Tragedy must always be a drowning and breaking of the dikes that separate man from man, and . . . it is upon these dikes comedy keeps house.

Most comic plays can roughly be sorted into one of two types: romantic comedy and satiric comedy. **Romantic comedy** presents an ideal world, a golden world, a world more delightful than our own; if there are difficulties in it, they are not briers but (to quote from Shakespeare's *As You Like It*) "burrs . . . thrown . . . in holiday foolery." It is the world of most of Shakespeare's comedies, a world of Illyria, of the Forest of Arden, of Belmont, of the moonlit Athens in *A Midsummer Night's Dream*. The chief figures are lovers; the course of their love is not smooth, but the outcome is never in doubt and the course is the more fun for being bumpy. Occasionally in this golden world there is a villain, but if so, the villain is a great bungler who never really does any harm; the world seems to be guided by a benevolent providence who prevents villains from seriously harming even themselves. In these plays, the world belongs to golden lads and lasses. When we laugh, we laugh not so much *at* them as *with* them.

If romantic comedy shows us a world with people more attractive than we find in our own, **satiric comedy** shows us a world with people less attractive. The satiric world seems dominated by morally inferior people—the decrepit wooer, the jealous spouse, the demanding parent. These unengaging figures go through their paces, revealing again and again their absurdity. The audience laughs *at* (rather than *with*) such figures, and writers justify this kind of comedy by claiming to reform society: antisocial members of the audience will see their grotesque images on the stage and will reform themselves when they leave the theater. But it is hard to believe that this theory is rooted in fact. Jonathan Swift was probably right when he said, "Satire is a sort of glass wherein beholders do generally discover everybody's face but their own."

Near the conclusion of a satiric comedy, the obstructing characters are dismissed, often perfunctorily, allowing for a happy ending—commonly the marriage of figures less colorful than the obstructionist(s). And so all-encompassing are the festivities at the end that even obstructionists are invited to join in the wedding feast. If they refuse to join, we may find them—yet again—laughable rather than sympathetic, though admittedly one may also feel lingering regret that this somewhat shabby world of ours cannot live up to the exalted (even if rigid and rather crazy) standards of the outsider who refuses to go along with the way of the world.

# SUSAN GLASPELL

*Susan Glaspell (1882-1948) was born in Davenport, Iowa, and educated at Drake University in Des Moines. In 1903 she married George Cram Cook and, with Cook and other writers, actors, and artists, in 1915 founded the Provincetown Players, a group that remained vital until 1929. Glaspell wrote* Trifles *(1916) for the Provincetown Players, but she also wrote stories, novels, and a biography of her husband. In 1931 she won a Pulitzer Prize for* Alison's House, *a play about the family of a deceased poet who in some ways resembles Emily Dickinson.*

## *Trifles*                                                    [1916]

SCENE: *The kitchen in the now abandoned farmhouse of John Wright, a gloomy kitchen, and left without having been put in order—unwashed pans under the sink, a loaf of bread outside the breadbox, a dish towel on the table—other signs of incompleted work. At the rear the outer door opens, and the Sheriff comes in, followed by the County Attorney and Hale. The Sheriff and Hale are men in middle life, the County Attorney is a young man; all are much bundled up and go at once to the stove. They are followed by the two women—the Sheriff's Wife first; she is a slight wiry woman, a thin nervous face. Mrs. Hale is larger and would ordinarily be called more comfortable looking, but she is disturbed now and looks fearfully about as she enters. The women have come in slowly and stand close together near the door.*

COUNTY ATTORNEY *(rubbing his hands).*  This feels good. Come up to the fire, ladies.

MRS. PETERS *(after taking a step forward).*  I'm not—cold.

Marjorie Vonnegut, Elinor M. Cox, John King, Arthur F. Hole, and T. W. Gibson in
*Trifles*, as published in *Theatre Magazine*, January 1917.

SHERIFF *(unbuttoning his overcoat and stepping away from the stove as
if to the beginning of official business).* Now, Mr. Hale, before we
move things about, you explain to Mr. Henderson just what you saw
when you came here yesterday morning.

COUNTY ATTORNEY. By the way, has anything been moved? Are things just as
you left them yesterday?

SHERIFF *(looking about).* It's just the same. When it dropped below zero
last night, I thought I'd better send Frank out this morning to make a
fire for us—no use getting pneumonia with a big case on; but I told
him not to touch anything except the stove—and you know Frank.

COUNTY ATTORNEY. Somebody should have been left here yesterday.

SHERIFF. Oh—yesterday. When I had to send Frank to Morris Center for that
man who went crazy—I want you to know I had my hands full yesterday. I knew you could get back from Omaha by today, and as long
as I went over everything here myself—

COUNTY ATTORNEY. Well, Mr. Hale, tell just what happened when you came
here yesterday morning.

HALE. Harry and I had started to town with a load of potatoes. We came
along the road from my place; and as I got here, I said, "I'm going to
see if I can't get John Wright to go in with me on a party telephone." I
spoke to Wright about it once before, and he put me off, saying folks
talked too much anyway, and all he asked was peace and quiet—I

guess you know about how much he talked himself; but I thought maybe if I went to the house and talked about it before his wife, though I said to Harry that I didn't know as what his wife wanted made much difference to John—

COUNTY ATTORNEY. Let's talk about that later, Mr. Hale. I do want to talk about that, but tell now just what happened when you got to the house.

HALE. I didn't hear or see anything; I knocked at the door, and still it was all quiet inside. I knew they must be up, it was past eight o'clock. So I knocked again, and I thought I heard somebody say, "Come in." I wasn't sure, I'm not sure yet, but I opened the door—this door *(indicating the door by which the two women are still standing)*, and there in that rocker—*(pointing to it)* sat Mrs. Wright. *(They all look at the rocker.)*

COUNTY ATTORNEY. What—was she doing?

HALE. She was rockin' back and forth. She had her apron in her hand and was kind of—pleating it.

COUNTY ATTORNEY. And how did she—look?

HALE. Well, she looked queer.

COUNTY ATTORNEY. How do you mean—queer?

HALE. Well, as if she didn't know what she was going to do next. And kind of done up.

COUNTY ATTORNEY. How did she seem to feel about your coming?

HALE. Why, I don't think she minded—one way or other. She didn't pay much attention. I said, "How do, Mrs. Wright, it's cold, ain't it?" And she said, "Is it?"—and went on kind of pleating at her apron. Well, I was surprised; she didn't ask me to come up to the stove, or to set down, but just sat there, not even looking at me, so I said, "I want to see John." And then she—laughed. I guess you would call it a laugh. I thought of Harry and the team outside, so I said a little sharp: "Can't I see John?" "No," she says, kind o' dull like. "Ain't he home?" says I. "Yes," says she, "he's home." "Then why can't I see him?" I asked her, out of patience. "'Cause he's dead," says she. *"Dead?"* says I. She just nodded her head, not getting a bit excited, but rockin' back and forth. "Why—where is he?" says I, not knowing what to say. She just pointed upstairs—like that *(himself pointing to the room above)*. I got up, with the idea of going up there. I walked from there to here—then I says, "Why, what did he die of?" "He died of a rope around his neck," says she, and just went on pleatin' at her apron. Well, I went out and called Harry. I thought I might—need help. We went upstairs, and there he was lyin'—

COUNTY ATTORNEY. I think I'd rather have you go into that upstairs, where you can point it all out. Just go on now with the rest of the story.

HALE. Well, my first thought was to get that rope off. I looked . . . *(Stops, his face twitches.)* . . . but Harry, he went up to him, and he said,

"No, he's dead all right, and we'd better not touch anything." So we went back downstairs. She was still sitting that same way. "Has anybody been notified?" I asked. "No," says she, unconcerned. "Who did this, Mrs. Wright?" said Harry. He said it business-like—and she stopped pleatin' of her apron. "I don't know," she says. "You don't *know?*" says Harry. "No," says she. "Weren't you sleepin' in the bed with him?" says Harry. "Yes," says she, "but I was on the inside." "Somebody slipped a rope round his neck and strangled him, and you didn't wake up?" says Harry. "I didn't wake up," she said after him. We must 'a looked as if we didn't see how that could be, for after a minute she said, "I sleep sound." Harry was going to ask her more questions, but I said maybe we ought to let her tell her story first to the coroner, or the sheriff, so Harry went fast as he could to Rivers' place, where there's a telephone.

COUNTY ATTORNEY.   And what did Mrs. Wright do when she knew that you had gone for the coroner?

HALE.   She moved from that chair to this over here . . . *(Pointing to a small chair in the corner.)* . . . and just sat there with her hands held together and looking down. I got a feeling that I ought to make some conversation, so I said I had come in to see if John wanted to put in a telephone, and at that she started to laugh, and then she stopped and looked at me—scared. *(The County Attorney, who has had his notebook out, makes a note.)* I dunno, maybe it wasn't scared. I wouldn't like to say it was. Soon Harry got back, and then Dr. Lloyd came, and you, Mr. Peters, and so I guess that's all I know that you don't.

COUNTY ATTORNEY *(looking around)*.   I guess we'll go upstairs first—and then out to the barn and around there. *(To the Sheriff.)* You're convinced that there was nothing important here—nothing that would point to any motive?

SHERIFF.   Nothing here but kitchen things.

*(The County Attorney, after again looking around the kitchen, opens the door of a cupboard closet. He gets up on a chair and looks on a shelf. Pulls his hand away, sticky.)*

COUNTY ATTORNEY.   Here's a nice mess.

*(The women draw nearer.)*

MRS. PETERS *(to the other woman)*.   Oh, her fruit; it did freeze. *(To the Lawyer.)* She worried about that when it turned so cold. She said the fire'd go out and her jars would break.

SHERIFF.   Well, can you beat the women! Held for murder and worryin' about her preserves.

COUNTY ATTORNEY.   I guess before we're through she may have something more serious than preserves to worry about.

HALE.   Well, women are used to worrying over trifles.

*(The two women move a little closer together.)*

COUNTY ATTORNEY *(with the gallantry of a young politician).* And yet, for all their worries, what would we do without the ladies? *(The women do not unbend. He goes to the sink, takes a dipperful of water from the pail and, pouring it into a basin, washes his hands. Starts to wipe them on the roller towel, turns it for a cleaner place.)* Dirty towels! *(Kicks his foot against the pans under the sink.)* Not much of a housekeeper, would you say, ladies?

MRS. HALE *(stiffly).* There's a great deal of work to be done on a farm.

COUNTY ATTORNEY. To be sure. And yet . . . *(With a little bow to her.)* . . . I know there are some Dickson county farmhouses which do not have such roller towels. *(He gives it a pull to expose its full length again.)*

MRS. HALE. Those towels get dirty awful quick. Men's hands aren't always as clean as they might be.

COUNTY ATTORNEY. Ah, loyal to your sex, I see. But you and Mrs. Wright were neighbors. I suppose you were friends, too.

MRS. HALE *(shaking her head).* I've not seen much of her of late years. I've not been in this house—it's more than a year.

COUNTY ATTORNEY. And why was that? You didn't like her?

MRS. HALE. I liked her all well enough. Farmers' wives have their hands full, Mr. Henderson. And then—

COUNTY ATTORNEY. Yes—?

MRS. HALE *(looking about).* It never seemed a very cheerful place.

COUNTY ATTORNEY. No—it's not cheerful. I shouldn't say she had the home-making instinct.

MRS. HALE. Well, I don't know as Wright had, either.

COUNTY ATTORNEY. You mean that they didn't get on very well?

MRS. HALE. No, I don't mean anything. But I don't think a place'd be any cheerfuler for John Wright's being in it.

COUNTY ATTORNEY. I'd like to talk more of that a little later. I want to get the lay of things upstairs now. *(He goes to the left, where three steps lead to a stair door.)*

SHERIFF. I suppose anything Mrs. Peters does'll be all right. She was to take in some clothes for her, you know, and a few little things. We left in such a hurry yesterday.

COUNTY ATTORNEY. Yes, but I would like to see what you take, Mrs. Peters, and keep an eye out for anything that might be of use to us.

MRS. PETERS. Yes, Mr. Henderson.

*(The women listen to the men's steps on the stairs, then look about the kitchen.)*

MRS. HALE. I'd hate to have men coming into my kitchen, snooping around and criticizing. *(She arranges the pans under sink which the Lawyer had shoved out of place.)*

MRS. PETERS.  Of course it's no more than their duty.

MRS. HALE.  Duty's all right, but I guess that deputy sheriff that came out to make the fire might have got a little of this on. *(Gives the roller towel a pull.)* Wish I'd thought of that sooner. Seems mean to talk about her for not having things slicked up when she had to come away in such a hurry.

MRS. PETERS *(who has gone to a small table in the left rear corner of the room, and lifted one end of a towel that covers a pan).*  She had bread set. *(Stands still.)*

MRS. HALE *(eyes fixed on a loaf of bread beside the breadbox, which is on a low shelf at the other side of the room. Moves slowly toward it).* She was going to put this in there. *(Picks up loaf, then abruptly drops it. In a manner of returning to familiar things.)* It's a shame about her fruit. I wonder if it's all gone. *(Gets up on the chair and looks.)*  I think there's some here that's all right, Mrs. Peters. Yes— here; *(Holding it toward the window.)*  this is cherries, too. *(Looking again.)* I declare I believe that's the only one. *(Gets down, bottle in her hand. Goes to the sink and wipes it off on the outside.)* She'll feel awful bad after all her hard work in the hot weather. I remember the afternoon I put up my cherries last summer. *(She puts the bottle on the big kitchen table, center of the room, front table. With a sigh, is about to sit down in the rocking chair. Before she is seated realizes what chair it is; with a slow look at it, steps back. The chair, which she has touched, rocks back and forth.)*

MRS. PETERS.  Well, I must get those things from the front room closet. *(She goes to the door at the right, but after looking into the other room steps back.)* You coming with me, Mrs. Hale? You could help me carry them. *(They go into the other room; reappear, Mrs. Peters carrying a dress and skirt, Mrs. Hale following with a pair of shoes.)*

MRS. PETERS.  My, it's cold in there. *(She puts the cloth on the big table, and hurries to the stove.)*

MRS. HALE *(examining the skirt).*  Wright was close. I think maybe that's why she kept so much to herself. She didn't even belong to the Ladies' Aid. I suppose she felt she couldn't do her part, and then you don't enjoy things when you feel shabby. She used to wear pretty clothes and be lively, when she was Minnie Foster, one of the town girls singing in the choir. But that—oh, that was thirty years ago. This all you was to take in?

MRS. PETERS.  She said she wanted an apron. Funny thing to want, for there isn't much to get you dirty in jail, goodness knows. But I suppose just to make her feel more natural. She said they was in the top drawer in this cupboard. Yes, here. And then her little shawl that always hung behind the door. *(Opens stair door and looks.)* Yes, here it is. *(Quickly shuts door leading upstairs.)*

MRS. HALE *(abruptly moving toward her).*  Mrs. Peters?

MRS. PETERS.  Yes, Mrs. Hale?

MRS. HALE.  Do you think she did it?

MRS. PETERS *(in a frightened voice).* Oh, I don't know.

MRS. HALE.  Well, I don't think she did. Asking for an apron and her little shawl. Worrying about her fruit.

MRS. PETERS *(starts to speak, glances up, where footsteps are heard in the room above. In a low voice).* Mr. Peters says it looks bad for her. Mr. Henderson is awful sarcastic in speech, and he'll make fun of her sayin' she didn't wake up.

MRS. HALE.  Well, I guess John Wright didn't wake when they was slipping that rope under his neck.

MRS. PETERS.  No, it's strange. It must have been done awful crafty and still. They say it was such a—funny way to kill a man, rigging it all up like that.

MRS. HALE.  That's just what Mr. Hale said. There was a gun in the house. He says that's what he can't understand.

MRS. PETERS.  Mr. Henderson said coming out that what was needed for the case was a motive; something to show anger, or—sudden feeling.

MRS. HALE *(who is standing by the table).* Well, I don't see any signs of anger around here. *(She puts her hand on the dish towel which lies on the table, stands looking down at the table, one half of which is clean, the other half messy).* It's wiped here. *(Makes a move as if to finish work, then turns and looks at loaf of bread outside the breadbox. Drops towel. In that voice of coming back to familiar things.)* Wonder how they are finding things upstairs? I hope she had it a little more red-up there. You know, it seems kind of *sneaking.* Locking her up in town and then coming out here and trying to get her own house to turn against her!

MRS. PETERS.  But, Mrs. Hale, the law is the law.

MRS. HALE.  I s'pose 'tis. *(Unbuttoning her coat.)* Better loosen up your things, Mrs. Peters. You won't feel them when you go out.

*(Mrs. Peters takes off her fur tippet, goes to hang it on hook at the back of room, stands looking at the under part of the small corner table.)*

MRS. PETERS.  She was piecing a quilt. *(She brings the large sewing basket, and they look at the bright pieces.)*

MRS. HALE.  It's log cabin pattern. Pretty, isn't it? I wonder if she was goin' to quilt or just knot it?

*(Footsteps have been heard coming down the stairs. The Sheriff enters, followed by Hale and the County Attorney.)*

SHERIFF.  They wonder if she was going to quilt it or just knot it. *(The men laugh, the women look abashed.)*

COUNTY ATTORNEY (*rubbing his hands over the stove*). Frank's fire didn't do much up there, did it? Well, let's go out to the barn and get that cleared up.

(*The men go outside.*)

MRS. HALE (*resentfully*). I don't know as there's anything so strange, our takin' up our time with little things while we're waiting for them to get the evidence. (*She sits down at the big table, smoothing out a block with decision.*) I don't see as it's anything to laugh about.

MRS. PETERS (*apologetically*). Of course they've got awful important things on their minds. (*Pulls up a chair and joins Mrs. Hale at the table.*)

MRS. HALE (*examining another block*). Mrs. Peters, look at this one. Here, this is the one she was working on, and look at the sewing! All the rest of it has been so nice and even. And look at this! It's all over the place! Why, it looks as if she didn't know what she was about! (*After she has said this, they look at each other, then start to glance back at the door. After an instant Mrs. Hale has pulled at a knot and ripped the sewing.*)

MRS. PETERS. Oh, what are you doing, Mrs. Hale?

MRS. HALE (*mildly*). Just pulling out a stitch or two that's not sewed very good. (*Threading a needle.*) Bad sewing always made me fidgety.

MRS. PETERS (*nervously*). I don't think we ought to touch things.

MRS. HALE. I'll just finish up this end. (*Suddenly stopping and leaning forward.*) Mrs. Peters?

MRS. PETERS. Yes, Mrs. Hale?

MRS. HALE. What do you suppose she was so nervous about?

MRS. PETERS. Oh—I don't know. I don't know as she was nervous. I sometimes sew awful queer when I'm just tired. (*Mrs. Hale starts to say something, looks at Mrs. Peters, then goes on sewing.*) Well, I must get these things wrapped up. They may be through sooner than we think. (*Putting apron and other things together.*) I wonder where I can find a piece of paper, and string.

MRS. HALE. In that cupboard, maybe.

MRS. PETERS (*looking in cupboard*). Why, here's a birdcage. (*Holds it up*). Did she have a bird, Mrs. Hale?

MRS. HALE. Why, I don't know whether she did or not—I've not been here for so long. There was a man around last year selling canaries cheap, but I don't know as she took one; maybe she did. She used to sing real pretty herself.

MRS. PETERS (*glancing around*). Seems funny to think of a bird here. But she must have had one, or why should she have a cage? I wonder what happened to it?

MRS. HALE. I s'pose maybe the cat got it.

MRS. PETERS.  No, she didn't have a cat. She's got that feeling some people have about cats—being afraid of them. My cat got in her room, and she was real upset and asked me to take it out.

MRS. HALE.  My sister Bessie was like that. Queer, ain't it?

MRS. PETERS *(examining the cage).* Why, look at this door. It's broke. One hinge is pulled apart.

MRS. HALE *(looking, too).* Looks as if someone must have been rough with it.

MRS. PETERS.  Why, yes. *(She brings the cage forward and puts it on the table.)*

MRS. HALE.  I wish if they're going to find any evidence they'd be about it. I don't like this place.

MRS. PETERS.  But I'm awful glad you came with me, Mrs. Hale. It would be lonesome for me sitting here alone.

MRS. HALE.  It would, wouldn't it? *(Dropping her sewing.)* But I tell you what I do wish, Mrs. Peters. I wish I had come over sometimes when *she* was here. I—*(Looking around the room.)*—wish I had.

MRS. PETERS.  But of course you were awful busy, Mrs. Hale—your house and your children.

MRS. HALE.  I could've come. I stayed away because it weren't cheerful—and that's why I ought to have come. I—I've never liked this place. Maybe because it's down in a hollow, and you don't see the road. I dunno what it is, but it's a lonesome place and always was. I wish I had come over to see Minnie Foster sometimes. I can see now—*(Shakes her head.)*

MRS. PETERS.  Well, you mustn't reproach yourself, Mrs. Hale. Somehow we just don't see how it is with other folks until—something comes up.

MRS. HALE.  Not having children makes less work—but it makes a quiet house, and Wright out to work all day, and no company when he did come in. Did you know John Wright, Mrs. Peters?

MRS. PETERS.  Not to know him; I've seen him in town. They say he was a good man.

MRS. HALE.  Yes—good; he didn't drink, and kept his word as well as most, I guess, and paid his debts. But he was a hard man, Mrs. Peters. Just to pass the time of day with him. *(Shivers.)* Like a raw wind that gets to the bone. *(Pauses, her eye falling on the cage.)* I should think she would 'a wanted a bird. But what do you suppose went with it?

MRS. PETERS.  I don't know, unless it got sick and died. *(She reaches over and swings the broken door, swings it again; both women watch it.)*

MRS. HALE.  You weren't raised round here, were you? *(Mrs. Peters shakes her head.)* You didn't know—her?

MRS. PETERS.  Not till they brought her yesterday.

MRS. HALE.  She—come to think of it, she was kind of like a bird herself—real sweet and pretty, but kind of timid and—fluttery. How—she—did—change. *(Silence; then as if struck by a happy thought and relieved to get back to everyday things.)* Tell you what, Mrs. Peters, why don't you take the quilt in with you? It might take up her mind.

MRS. PETERS.  Why, I think that's a real nice idea, Mrs. Hale. There couldn't possibly be any objection to it, could there? Now, just what would I take? I wonder if her patches are in here—and her things. *(They look in the sewing basket.)*

MRS. HALE.  Here's some red. I expect this has got sewing things in it. *(Brings out a fancy box.)* What a pretty box. Looks like something somebody would give you. Maybe her scissors are in here. *(Opens box. Suddenly puts her hand to her nose.)* Why—*(Mrs. Peters bends nearer, then turns her face away.)* There's something wrapped up in this piece of silk.

MRS. PETERS.  Why, this isn't her scissors.

MRS. HALE *(lifting the silk)*.  Oh, Mrs. Peters—it's—*(Mrs. Peters bends closer.)*

MRS. PETERS.  It's the bird.

MRS. HALE *(jumping up)*.  But, Mrs. Peters—look at it. Its neck! Look at its neck! It's all—other side *to*.

MRS. PETERS.  Somebody—wrung—its neck.

*(Their eyes meet. A look of growing comprehension of horror. Steps are heard outside. Mrs. Hale slips box under quilt pieces, and sinks into her chair. Enter Sheriff and County Attorney. Mrs. Peters rises.)*

COUNTY ATTORNEY *(as one turning from serious things to little pleasantries)*.  Well, ladies, have you decided whether she was going to quilt it or knot it?

MRS. PETERS.  We think she was going to—knot it.

COUNTY ATTORNEY.  Well, that's interesting, I'm sure. *(Seeing the birdcage.)* Has the bird flown?

MRS. HALE *(putting more quilt pieces over the box)*.  We think the—cat got it.

COUNTY ATTORNEY *(preoccupied)*.  Is there a cat?

*(Mrs. Hale glances in a quick covert way at Mrs. Peters.)*

MRS. PETERS.  Well, not now. They're superstitious, you know. They leave.

COUNTY ATTORNEY *(to Sheriff Peters, continuing an interrupted conversation)*.  No sign at all of anyone having come from the outside. Their own rope. Now let's go up again and go over it piece by piece. *(They start upstairs.)* It would have to have been someone who knew just the—

*(Mrs. Peters sits down. The two women sit there not looking at one another, but as if peering into something and at the same time holding back. When they talk now, it is the manner of feeling their*

*way over strange ground, as if afraid of what they are saying, but as if they cannot help saying it.)*

MRS. HALE.  She liked the bird. She was going to bury it in that pretty box.

MRS. PETERS *(in a whisper)*.  When I was a girl—my kitten—there was a boy took a hatchet, and before my eyes—and before I could get there—*(Covers her face an instant.)* If they hadn't held me back, I would have—*(Catches herself, looks upstairs where steps are heard, falters weakly.)*—hurt him.

MRS. HALE *(with a slow look around her)*.  I wonder how it would seem never to have had any children around. *(Pause.)*  No, Wright wouldn't like the bird—a thing that sang. She used to sing. He killed that, too.

MRS. PETERS *(moving uneasily)*.  We don't know who killed the bird.

MRS. HALE.  I knew John Wright.

MRS. PETERS.  It was an awful thing was done in this house that night, Mrs. Hale. Killing a man while he slept, slipping a rope around his neck that choked the life out of him.

MRS. HALE.  His neck. Choked the life out of him.

*(Her hand goes out and rests on the birdcage.)*

MRS. PETERS *(with a rising voice)*.  We don't know who killed him. We don't *know*.

MRS. HALE *(her own feeling not interrupted)*.  If there'd been years and years of nothing, then a bird to sing to you, it would be awful—still, after the bird was still.

MRS. PETERS *(something within her speaking)*.  I know what stillness is. When we homesteaded in Dakota, and my first baby died—after he was two years old, and me with no other then—

MRS. HALE *(moving)*.  How soon do you suppose they'll be through, looking for evidence?

MRS. PETERS.  I know what stillness is. *(Pulling herself back.)* The law has got to punish crime, Mrs. Hale.

MRS. HALE *(not as if answering that)*.  I wish you'd seen Minnie Foster when she wore a white dress with blue ribbons and stood up there in the choir and sang. *(A look around the room.)*  Oh, I *wish* I'd come over here once in a while! That was a crime! That was a crime! Who's going to punish that?

MRS. PETERS *(looking upstairs)*.  We mustn't—take on.

MRS. HALE.  I might have known she needed help! I know how things can be—for women. I tell you, it's queer, Mrs. Peters. We live close together and we live far apart. We all go through the same things—it's all just a different kind of the same thing. *(Brushes her eyes, noticing the bottle of fruit, reaches out for it.)* If I was you, I wouldn't tell her her fruit was gone. Tell her it *ain't*. Tell her it's all right. Take this in to prove it to her. She—she may never know whether it was broke or not.

MRS. PETERS *(takes the bottle, looks about for something to wrap it in; takes petticoat from the clothes brought from the other room, very nervously begins winding this around the bottle. In a false voice).* My, it's a good thing the men couldn't hear us. Wouldn't they just laugh! Getting all stirred up over a little thing like a—dead canary. As if that could have anything to do with—with—wouldn't they *laugh!*

*(The men are heard coming downstairs.)*

MRS. HALE *(under her breath).* Maybe they would—maybe they wouldn't.

COUNTY ATTORNEY. No, Peters, it's all perfectly clear except a reason for doing it. But you know juries when it comes to women. If there was some definite thing. Something to show—something to make a story about—a thing that would connect up with this strange way of doing it.

*(The women's eyes meet for an instant. Enter Hale from outer door.)*

HALE. Well, I've got the team around. Pretty cold out there.

COUNTY ATTORNEY. I'm going to stay here awhile by myself. *(To the Sheriff.)* You can send Frank out for me, can't you? I want to go over everything. I'm not satisfied that we can't do better.

SHERIFF. Do you want to see what Mrs. Peters is going to take in?

*(The Lawyer goes to the table, picks up the apron, laughs.)*

COUNTY ATTORNEY. Oh I guess they're not very dangerous things the ladies have picked up. *(Moves a few things about, disturbing the quilt pieces which cover the box. Steps back.)* No, Mrs. Peters doesn't need supervising. For that matter, a sheriff's wife is married to the law. Ever think of it that way, Mrs. Peters?

MRS. PETERS. Not—just that way.

SHERIFF *(chuckling).* Married to the law. *(Moves toward the other room.)* I just want you to come in here a minute, George. We ought to take a look at these windows.

COUNTY ATTORNEY *(scoffingly).* Oh, windows!

SHERIFF. We'll be right out, Mr. Hale.

*(Hale goes outside. The Sheriff follows the County Attorney into the other room. Then Mrs. Hale rises, hands tight together, looking intensely at Mrs. Peters, whose eyes take a slow turn, finally meeting Mrs. Hale's. A moment Mrs. Hale holds her, then her own eyes point the way to where the box is concealed. Suddenly Mrs. Peters throws back quilt pieces and tries to put the box in the bag she is wearing. It is too big. She opens box, starts to take the bird out, cannot touch it, goes to pieces, stands there helpless. Sound of a knob turning in the other room. Mrs. Hale snatches the box and puts it in the pocket of her big coat. Enter County Attorney and Sheriff.)*

COUNTY ATTORNEY *(facetiously)*. Well, Henry, at least we found out that she was not going to quilt it. She was going to—what is it you call it, ladies?

MRS. HALE *(her hand against her pocket)*. We call it—knot it, Mr. Henderson.

CURTAIN

# ❊ TOPICS FOR
# CRITICAL THINKING AND WRITING

## *The Play on the Page*

1. How would you characterize Mr. Henderson, the county attorney?
2. In what way or ways are Mrs. Peters and Mrs. Hale different from each other?
3. On page 640, when Mrs. Peters tells of the boy who killed her cat, she says, "If they hadn't held me back, I would have—*(catches herself, looks upstairs where steps are heard, falters weakly.)*—hurt him." What do you think she was about to say before she faltered? Why do you suppose Glaspell included this speech about Mrs. Peters's girlhood?
4. We never see Mrs. Wright on stage. Nevertheless, by the end of *Trifles* we know a great deal  about her. Explain both what we know about her—physical characteristics, habits, interests, personality, life before her marriage and after—and *how* we know these things.
5. The title of the play is ironic—the "trifles" are important. What other ironies do you find in the play. (On *irony,* see the Glossary.)
6. Do you think the play is immoral? Explain.
7. Assume that the canary has been found, thereby revealing a possible motive, and that Minnie is indicted for murder. You are the defense attorney. In 500 words set forth your defense. (Take any position you wish. For instance, you may want to argue that she committed justifiable homicide or that—on the basis of her behavior as reported by Mr. Hale—she is innocent by reason of insanity.)
8. Assume that the canary had been found and Minnie Wright convicted. Compose the speech you think she might have delivered before the sentence was given.

## *The Play on the Stage*

9. Briefly describe the setting, indicating what it "says" and what atmosphere it evokes.
10. Several times the men "laugh" or "chuckle." In their contexts, what do these expressions of amusement convey?

11. On page 641, *"the women's eyes meet for an instant."* What do you think this bit of action "says"? What do you understand by the exchange of glances?

# TENNESSEE WILLIAMS

*Tennessee Williams (1914–1983) was born Thomas Lanier Williams in Columbus, Mississippi. During his childhood his family moved to St. Louis, where his father had accepted a job as manager of a shoe company. Williams has written that neither he nor his sister Rose could adjust to the change from the South to the Midwest, but the children had already been deeply troubled. Nevertheless, at the age of sixteen he achieved some distinction as a writer when his prize-winning essay in a nationwide contest was published. After high school he attended the University of Missouri but flunked ROTC and was therefore withdrawn from school by his father. He worked in a shoe factory for a while, then attended Washington University, where he wrote several plays. He finally graduated from the University of Iowa with a major in playwrighting.*

Left to right: Anthony Ross (Jim), Laurette Taylor (Amanda), Eddie Dowling (Tom), and Julie Hayden (Laura) in the 1945 original production of *The Glass Menagerie*, The Playhouse, New York.

*After graduation he continued to write, supporting himself with odd jobs such as waiting on tables and running elevators. His first commercial success was* The Glass Menagerie *(produced in Chicago in 1944, and in New York in 1945); among his other plays are* A Streetcar Named Desire *(1947),* Cat on a Hot Tin Roof *(1955), and* Suddenly Last Summer *(1958).*

## The Glass Menagerie                                         [1944]

*nobody, not even the rain, has such small hands.*

—e. e. cummings

**LIST OF CHARACTERS**

AMANDA WINGFIELD, *the mother. A little woman of great but confused vitality clinging frantically to another time and place. Her characterization must be carefully created, not copied from type. She is not paranoiac, but her life is paranoia. There is much to admire in Amanda, and as much to love and pity as there is to laugh at. Certainly she has endurance and a kind of heroism, and though her foolishness makes her unwittingly cruel at times, there is tenderness in her slight person.*

LAURA WINGFIELD, *her daughter. Amanda, having failed to establish contact with reality, continues to live vitally in her illusions, but Laura's situation is even graver. A childhood illness has left her crippled, one leg slightly shorter than the other, and held in a brace. This defect need not be more than suggested on the stage. Stemming from this, Laura's separation increases till she is like a piece of her own glass collection, too exquisitely fragile to move from the shelf.*

TOM WINGFIELD, *her son. And the narrator of the play. A poet with a job in a warehouse. His nature is not remorseless, but to escape from a trap he has to act without pity.*

JIM O'CONNOR, *the gentleman caller. A nice, ordinary, young man.*

**SCENE.** *An alley in St. Louis.*

**PART I.** *Preparation for a Gentleman Caller.*

**PART II.** *The Gentleman Calls.*

**TIME.** *Now and the Past.*

*Scene I*

*The Wingfield apartment is in the rear of the building, one of those vast hive-like conglomerations of cellular living-units that flower as warty growths in overcrowded urban centers of lower middle-class popu-*

*lation and are symptomatic of the impulse of this largest and fundamentally enslaved section of American society to avoid fluidity and differentiation and to exist and function as one interfused mass of automatism.*

*The apartment faces an alley and is entered by a fire-escape, a structure whose name is a touch of accidental poetic truth, for all of these huge buildings are always burning with the slow and implacable fires of human desperation. The fire-escape is included in the set—that is, the landing of it and steps descending from it.*

*The scene is memory and is therefore nonrealistic. Memory takes a lot of poetic license. It omits some details; others are exaggerated, according to the emotional value of the articles it touches, for memory is seated predominantly in the heart. The interior is therefore rather dim and poetic.*

*At the rise of the curtain, the audience is faced with the dark, grim rear wall of the Wingfield tenement. This building, which runs parallel to the footlights, is flanked on both sides by dark, narrow alleys which run into murky canyons of tangled clotheslines, garbage cans and the sinister latticework of neighboring fire-escapes. It is up and down these side alleys that exterior entrances and exits are made, during the play. At the end of* TOM's *opening commentary, the dark tenement wall slowly reveals (by means of a transparency) the interior of the ground floor Wingfield apartment.*

*Downstage is the living room, which also serves as a sleeping room for* LAURA, *the sofa unfolding to make her bed. Upstage, center, and divided by a wide arch or second proscenium with transparent faded portieres (or second curtain), is the dining room. In an old-fashioned what-not in the living room are seen scores of transparent glass animals. A blown-up photograph of the father hangs on the wall of the living room, facing the audience, to the left of the archway. It is the face of a very handsome young man in a doughboy's First World War cap. He is gallantly smiling, ineluctably smiling, as if to say, "I will be smiling forever."*

*The audience hears and sees the opening scene in the dining room through both the transparent fourth wall of the building and the transparent gauze portieres of the dining-room arch. It is during this revealing scene that the fourth wall slowly ascends, out of sight.*

*This transparent exterior wall is not brought down again until the very end of the play, during* TOM's *final speech.*

*The narrator is an undisguised convention of the play. He takes whatever license with dramatic convention as is convenient to his purposes.*

TOM *enters dressed as a merchant sailor from alley, stage left, and strolls across the front of the stage to the fire-escape. There he stops and lights a cigarette. He addresses the audience.*

TOM.  Yes, I have tricks in my pocket, I have things up my sleeve. But I am the opposite of a stage magician. He gives you illusion that has the appearance of truth. I give you truth in the pleasant disguise of illusion. To begin with, I turn back time. I reverse it to that quaint period, the thirties, when the huge middle class of America was matriculating in a school for the blind. Their eyes had failed them, or they had failed their eyes, and so they were having their fingers pressed forcibly down on the fiery Braille alphabet of a dissolving economy. In Spain there was revolution. Here there was only shouting and confusion. In Spain there was Guernica. Here there were disturbances of labor, sometimes pretty violent, in otherwise peaceful cities such as Chicago, Cleveland, Saint Louis. . . . This is the social background of the play.

(*Music.*)

The play is memory. Being a memory play, it is dimly lighted, it is sentimental, it is not realistic. In memory everything seems to happen to music. That explains the fiddle in the wings. I am the narrator of the play, and also a character in it. The other characters are my mother, Amanda, my sister, Laura, and a gentleman caller who appears in the final scenes. He is the most realistic character in the play, being an emissary from a world of reality that we were somehow set apart from. But since I have a poet's weakness for symbols, I am using this character also as a symbol; he is the long delayed but always expected something that we live for. There is a fifth character in the play who doesn't appear except in this larger-than-life photograph over the mantel. This is our father who left us a long time ago. He was a telephone man who fell in love with long distances; he gave up his job with the telephone company and skipped the light fantastic out of town. . . . The last we heard of him was a picture post-card from Mazatlan, on the Pacific coast of Mexico, containing a message of two words—"Hello—Goodbye!" and no address. I think the rest of the play will explain itself. . . .

AMANDA'S *voice becomes audible through the portieres.*
    (*Legend on Screen:"Où Sont les Neiges?"*)
    *He divides the portieres and enters the upstage area.*
    AMANDA *and* LAURA *are seated at a drop-leaf table. Eating is indicated by gestures without food or utensils.* AMANDA *faces the audience.* TOM *and* LAURA *are seated in profile.*
    *The interior has lit up softly and through the scrim we see* AMANDA *and* LAURA *seated at the table in the upstage area.*

AMANDA (*calling*).  Tom?
TOM.  Yes, Mother.
AMANDA.  We can't say grace until you come to the table!

TOM. Coming, Mother. (*He bows slightly and withdraws, reappearing a few moments later in his place at the table.*)

AMANDA (*to her son*). Honey, don't *push* with your *fingers*. If you have to push with something, the thing to push with is a crust of bread. And chew—chew! Animals have sections in their stomachs which enable them to digest food without mastication, but human beings are supposed to chew their food before they swallow it down. Eat food leisurely, son, and really enjoy it. A well-cooked meal has lots of delicate flavors that have to be held in the mouth for appreciation. So chew your food and give your salivary glands a chance to function!

TOM *deliberately lays his imaginary fork down and pushes his chair back from the table.*

TOM. I haven't enjoyed one bite of this dinner because of your constant directions on how to eat it. It's you that makes me rush through meals with your hawk-like attention to every bite I take. Sickening— spoils my appetite—all this discussion of animals' secretion—salivary glands—mastication!

AMANDA (*lightly*). Temperament like a Metropolitan star! (*He rises and crosses downstage.*) You're not excused from the table.

TOM. I am getting a cigarette.

AMANDA. You smoke too much.

*LAURA rises.*

LAURA. I'll bring in the blanc mange.

*He remains standing with his cigarette by the portieres during the following.*

AMANDA (*rising.*) No, sister, no, sister—you be the lady this time and I'll be the darky.

LAURA. I'm already up.

AMANDA. Resume your seat, little sister—I want you to stay fresh and pretty—for gentlemen callers!

LAURA. I'm not expecting any gentlemen callers.

AMANDA (*crossing out to kitchenette. Airily*). Sometimes they come when they are least expected! Why, I remember one Sunday afternoon in Blue Mountain—(*Enters kitchenette.*)

TOM. I know what's coming!

LAURA. Yes. But let her tell it.

TOM. Again?

LAURA. She loves to tell it.

AMANDA *returns with bowl of dessert.*

AMANDA. One Sunday afternoon in Blue Mountain—your mother received— seventeen!—gentlemen callers! Why, sometimes there weren't chairs enough to accommodate them all. We had to send the nigger over to bring in folding chairs from the parish house.

TOM (*remaining at portieres*). How did you entertain those gentlemen callers?

AMANDA. I understood the art of conversation!

TOM. I bet you could talk.

AMANDA. Girls in those days *knew* how to talk, I can tell you.

TOM. Yes?

(*Image:* AMANDA *as a Girl on a Porch Greeting Callers.*)

AMANDA. They knew how to entertain their gentlemen callers. It wasn't enough for a girl to be possessed of a pretty face and a graceful figure—although I wasn't slighted in either respect. She also needed to have a nimble wit and a tongue to meet all occasions.

TOM. What did you talk about?

AMANDA. Things of importance going on in the world! Never anything coarse or common or vulgar. (*She addresses* TOM *as though he were seated in the vacant chair at the table though he remains by portieres. He plays this scene as though he held the book.*) My callers were gentlemen—all! Among my callers were some of the most prominent young planters of the Mississippi Delta—planters and sons of planters!

TOM *motions for music and a spot of light on* AMANDA.
        *Her eyes lift, her face glows, her voice becomes rich and elegiac.*
        (*Screen Legend:"Où Sont les Neiges?"*)

There was young Champ Laughlin who later became vice-president of the Delta Planters Bank. Hadley Stevenson who was drowned in Moon Lake and left his widow one hundred and fifty thousand in Government bonds. There were the Cutrere brothers, Wesley and Bates. Bates was one of my bright particular beaux! He got in a quarrel with that wild Wainright boy. They shot it out on the floor of Moon Lake Casino. Bates was shot through the stomach. Died in the ambulance on his way to Memphis. His widow was also well-provided for, came into eight or ten thousand acres, that's all. She married him on the rebound—never loved her—carried my picture on him the night he died! And there was that boy that every girl in Delta had set her cap for! That beautiful, brilliant young Fitzhugh boy from Green County!

TOM. What did he leave his widow?

AMANDA. He never married! Gracious, you talk as though all of my old admirers had turned up their toes to the daisies!

TOM. Isn't this the first you mentioned that still survives?

AMANDA. That Fitzhugh boy went North and made a fortune—came to be known as the Wolf of Wall Street! He had the Midas touch, whatever he touched turned to gold! And I could have been Mrs. Duncan J. Fitzhugh, mind you! But—I picked your *father!*

LAURA (*rising*). Mother, let me clear the table.

AMANDA. No dear, you go in front and study your typewriter chart. Or practice your shorthand a little. Stay fresh and pretty!—It's almost time for our gentlemen callers to start arriving. (*She flounces girlishly toward the kitchenette.*) How many do you suppose we're going to entertain this afternoon?

TOM *throws down the paper and jumps up with a groan.*

LAURA (*alone in the dining room*). I don't believe we're going to receive any, Mother.

AMANDA (*reappearing, airily*). What? No one—not one? You must be joking! (*LAURA nervously echoes her laugh. She slips in a fugitive manner through the half-open portieres and draws them gently behind her. A shaft of very clear light is thrown on her face against the faded tapestry of the curtains.*) (*Music:"The Glass Menagerie" Under Faintly.*) (*Lightly.*) Not one gentleman caller? It can't be true! There must be a flood, there must have been a tornado!

LAURA. It isn't a flood, it's not a tornado, Mother. I'm just not popular like you were in Blue Mountain. . . . (*TOM utters another groan. LAURA glances at him with a faint, apologetic smile. Her voice catching a little.*) Mother's afraid I'm going to be an old maid.

(*The Scene Dims Out with "Glass Menagerie" Music.*)

## Scene II

### *"Laura, Haven't You Ever Liked Some Boy?"*

On the dark stage the screen is lighted with the image of blue roses. Gradually LAURA'S *figure becomes apparent and the screen goes out. The music subsides.*

LAURA *is seated in the delicate ivory chair at the small clawfoot table.*

She wears a dress of soft violet material for a kimono—her hair tied back from her forehead with a ribbon.

She is washing and polishing her collection of glass.

AMANDA *appears on the fire-escape steps. At the sound of her ascent,* LAURA *catches her breath, thrusts the bowl of ornaments away and seats herself stiffly before the diagram of the typewriter keyboard as though it held her spellbound. Something has happened to* AMANDA. *It is written in her face as she climbs to the landing: a look that is grim and hopeless and a little absurd.*

She has on one of those cheap or imitation velvety-looking cloth coats with imitation fur collar. Her hat is five or six years old, one of those dreadful cloche hats that were worn in the late twenties, and she is *clasping an enormous black patent-leather pocketbook with nickel clasp and initials. This is her full-dress outfit, the one she usually wears to the D.A.R.*

*Before entering she looks through the door.*

*She purses her lips, opens her eyes wide, rolls them upward and shakes her head.*

*Then she slowly lets herself in the door. Seeing her mother's expression* LAURA *touches her lips with a nervous gesture.*

LAURA.  Hello, Mother, I was—(*She makes a nervous gesture toward the chart on the wall.* AMANDA *leans against the shut door and stares at* LAURA *with a martyred look.*)

AMANDA.  Deception? Deception? (*She slowly removes her hat and gloves, continuing the swift suffering stare. She lets the hat and gloves fall on the floor—a bit of acting.*)

LAURA (*shakily.*)  How was the D.A.R. meeting? (AMANDA *slowly opens her purse and removes a dainty white handkerchief which she shakes out delicately and delicately touches to her lips and nostrils.*) Didn't you go to the D.A.R. meeting, Mother?

AMANDA (*faintly, almost inaudibly*).  —No.—No. (*Then more forcibly.*) I did not have the strength—to go to the D.A.R. In fact, I did not have the courage! I wanted to find a hole in the ground and hide myself in it forever! (*She crosses slowly to the wall and removes the diagram of the typewriter keyboard. She holds it in front of her for a second, staring at it sweetly and sorrowfully—then bites her lips and tears it in two pieces.*)

LAURA (*faintly*).  Why did you do that, Mother? (AMANDA *repeats the same procedure with the chart of the Gregg Alphabet.*) Why are you—

AMANDA.  Why? Why? How old are you, Laura?

LAURA.  Mother, you know my age.

AMANDA.  I thought that you were an adult; it seems that I was mistaken. (*She crosses slowly to the sofa and sinks down and stares at* LAURA.)

LAURA.  Please don't stare at me, Mother.

AMANDA *closes her eyes and lowers her head. Count ten.*

AMANDA.  What are we going to do, what is going to become of us, what is the future?

*Count ten.*

LAURA.  Has something happened, Mother? (AMANDA *draws a long breath and takes out the handkerchief again. Dabbing process.*) Mother, has—something happened?

AMANDA.  I'll be all right in a minute. I'm just bewildered—(*count five*)—by life. . . .

LAURA.  Mother, I wish that you would tell me what's happened.

AMANDA. As you know, I was supposed to be inducted into my office at the D.A.R. this afternoon. (*Image: A Swarm of Typewriters.*) But I stopped off at Rubicam's Business College to speak to your teachers about your having a cold and ask them what progress they thought you were making down there.

LAURA. Oh. . . .

AMANDA. I went to the typing instructor and introduced myself as your mother. She didn't know who you were. Wingfield, she said. We don't have any such student enrolled at the school! I assured her she did, that you had been going to classes since early in January. "I wonder," she said, "if you could be talking about that terribly shy little girl who dropped out of school after only a few days' attendance?" "No," I said, "Laura, my daughter, has been going to school every day for the past six weeks!" "Excuse me," she said. She took the attendance book out and there was your name, unmistakably printed, and all the dates you were absent until they decided that you had dropped out of school. I still said, "No, there must have been some mistake! There must have been some mix-up in the records!" And she said, "No I remember her perfectly now. Her hand shook so that she couldn't hit the right keys! The first time we gave a speed-test, she broke down completely—was sick at the stomach and almost had to be carried into the wash-room! After that morning she never showed up any more. We phoned the house but never got any answer"—while I was working at Famous and Barr, I suppose, demonstrating those—Oh! I felt so weak I could barely keep on my feet. I had to sit down while they got me a glass of water! Fifty dollars' tuition, all of our plans—my hopes and ambitions for you—just gone up the spout, just gone up the spout like that. (LAURA *draws a long breath and gets awkwardly to her feet. She crosses to the victrola and winds it up.*) What are you doing?

LAURA. Oh! (*She releases the handle and returns to her seat.*)

AMANDA. Laura, where have you been going when you've gone out pretending that you were going to business college?

LAURA. I've just been going out walking.

AMANDA. That's not true.

LAURA. It is. I just went walking.

AMANDA. Walking? Walking? In winter? Deliberately courting pneumonia in that light coat? Where did you walk to, Laura?

LAURA. It was the lesser of two evils, Mother. (*Image: Winter Scene in Park.*) I couldn't go back up. I—threw up—on the floor!

AMANDA. From half past seven till after five every day you mean to tell me you walked around in the park, because you wanted to make me think that you were still going to Rubicam's Business College?

LAURA. It wasn't as bad as it sounds. I went inside places to get warmed up.

AMANDA. Inside where?

LAURA. I went in the art museum and the bird-houses at the Zoo. I visited the penguins every day! Sometimes I did without lunch and went to the movies. Lately I've been spending most of my afternoons in the Jewel-box, that big glass house where they raise the tropical flowers.

AMANDA. You did all this to deceive me, just for the deception? (LAURA *looks down.*) Why?

LAURA. Mother, when you're disappointed, you get that awful suffering look on your face, like the picture of Jesus' mother in the museum!

AMANDA. Hush!

LAURA. I couldn't face it.

> *Pause. A whisper of strings.*
> (*Legend:"The Crust of Humility."*)

AMANDA (*hopelessly fingering the huge pocketbook*). So what are we going to do the rest of our lives? Stay home and watch the parades go by? Amuse ourselves with the glass menagerie, darling? Eternally play those worn-out phonograph records your father left as a painful reminder of him? We won't have a business career—we've given that up because it gave us nervous indigestion! (*Laughs wearily.*) What is there left but dependency all our lives? I know so well what becomes of unmarried women who aren't prepared to occupy a position. I've seen such pitiful cases in the South—barely tolerated spinsters living upon the grudging patronage of sister's husband or brother's wife!— stuck away in some little mousetrap of a room—encouraged by one in-law to visit another—little birdlike women without any nest—eating the crust of humility all their life! Is that the future that we've mapped out for ourselves? I swear it's the only alternative I can think of! It isn't a very pleasant alternative, is it? Of course—some girls *do marry.* (LAURA *twists her hands nervously.*) Haven't you ever liked some boy?

LAURA. Yes. I liked one once. (*Rises.*) I came across his picture a while ago.

AMANDA (*with some interest*). He gave you his picture?

LAURA. No, it's in the year-book.

AMANDA (*disappointed*). Oh—a high-school boy.

> (*Screen Image:* JIM *as a High-School Hero Bearing a Silver Cup.*)

LAURA. Yes. His name was Jim. (LAURA *lifts the heavy annual from the clawfoot table.*) Here he is in *The Pirates of Penzance.*

AMANDA (*absently*). The what?

LAURA. The operetta the senior class put on. He had a wonderful voice and we sat across the aisle from each other Mondays, Wednesdays and Fridays in the Aud. Here he is with the silver cup for debating! See his grin?

AMANDA (*absently*).  He must have had a jolly disposition.
LAURA.  He used to call me—Blue Roses.

(*Image: Blue Roses.*)

AMANDA.  Why did he call you such a name as that?
LAURA.  When I had that attack of pleurosis—he asked me what was the matter when I came back. I said pleurosis—he thought that I said Blue Roses! So that's what he always called me after that. Whenever he saw me, he'd holler, "Hello, Blue Roses!" I didn't care for the girl that he went out with. Emily Meisenbach. Emily was the best-dressed girl at Soldan. She never struck me, though, as being sincere. . . . It says in the Personal Section—they're engaged. That's—six years ago! They must be married by now.
AMANDA.  Girls that aren't cut out for business careers usually wind up married to some nice man. (*Gets up with a spark of revival.*) Sister, that's what you'll do!

LAURA *utters a startled, doubtful laugh. She reaches quickly for a piece of glass.*

LAURA.  But, Mother—
AMANDA.  Yes? (*Crossing to photograph.*)
LAURA (*in a tone of frightened apology*).  I'm—crippled!

(*Image: Screen.*)

AMANDA.  Nonsense! Laura, I've told you never, never to use that word. Why, you're not crippled, you just have a little defect—hardly noticeable, even! When people have some slight disadvantage like that, they cultivate other things to make up for it—develop charm—and vivacity—and—*charm!* That's all you have to do! (*She turns again to the photograph.*) One thing your father had *plenty of*—was *charm!*

TOM *motions to the fiddle in the wings.*
(*The Scene Fades Out with Music.*)

## Scene III

(*Legend on the Screen:"After the Fiasco—"*)
TOM *speaks from the fire-escape landing.*

TOM.  After the fiasco at Rubicam's Business College, the idea of getting a gentleman caller for Laura began to play a more important part in Mother's calculations. It became an obsession. Like some archetype of the universal unconscious, the image of the gentleman caller haunted our small apartment. . . . (*Image: Young Man at Door with Flowers.*) An evening at home rarely passed without some allusion to this image, this specter, this hope. . . . . Even when he wasn't mentioned, his presence hung in Mother's preoccupied look and in my sister's frightened, apologetic manner—hung like a sentence passed upon the Wingfields! Mother was a woman of action as well as words. She began to take logical steps in the planned direction. Late that winter and in the early spring—realizing that extra money would be needed to properly feather the nest and plume the bird—she conducted a vigorous campaign on the telephone, roping in subscribers to one of those magazines for matrons called *The Home-maker's Companion,* the type of journal that features the serialized sublimations of ladies of letters who think in terms of delicate cuplike breasts, slim, tapering waists, rich, creamy thighs, eyes like woodsmoke in autumn, fingers that soothe and caress like strains of music, bodies as powerful as Etruscan sculpture.

*(Screen Image: Glamor Magazine Cover.)*
    AMANDA *enters with phone on long extension cord. She is spotted in the dim stage.*

AMANDA.  Ida Scott? This is Amanda Wingfield! We *missed* you at the D.A.R. last Monday! I said to myself: She's probably suffering with that sinus condition! How is that sinus condition? Horrors! Heaven have mercy!—You're a Christian martyr, yes, that's what you are, a Christian martyr! Well, I just now happened to notice that your subscription to the *Companion's* about to expire! Yes, it expires with the next issue, honey!—just when that wonderful new serial by Bessie Mae Hopper is getting off to such an exciting start. Oh, honey, it's something that you can't miss! You remember how *Gone With the Wind* took everybody by storm? You simply couldn't go out if you hadn't read it. All everybody *talked* was Scarlett O'Hara. Well, this is a book that critics already compare to *Gone With the Wind.* It's the *Gone With the Wind* of the post-World War generation!—What?—Burning?—Oh, honey, don't let them burn, go take a look in the oven and I'll hold the wire! Heavens—I think she's hung up!

*(Dim Out.)*
    *(Legend on Screen: "You Think I'm in Love with Continental Shoemakers?")*
    *Before the stage is lighted, the violent voices of* TOM *and* AMANDA *are heard. They are quarreling behind the portieres. In front of them stands* LAURA *with clenched hands and panicky expression.*
    *A clear pool of light on her figure throughout this scene.*

TOM.  What in Christ's name am I—
AMANDA *(shrilly).*  Don't you use that—
TOM.  Supposed to do!

AMANDA. Expression! Not in my—

TOM. Ohhh!

AMANDA. Presence! Have you gone out of your senses?

TOM. I have, that's true, *driven* out!

AMANDA. What is the matter with you, you—big—big—IDIOT!

TOM. Look—I've got *no thing*, no single thing—

AMANDA. Lower your voice!

TOM. In my life here that I can call my OWN! Everything is—

AMANDA. Stop that shouting!

TOM. Yesterday you confiscated my books! You had the nerve to—

AMANDA. I took that horrible novel back to the library—yes! That hideous
book by that insane Mr. Lawrence. (TOM *laughs wildly.*) I cannot control the output of diseased minds or people who cater to them—(TOM
*laughs still more wildly.*) BUT I WON'T ALLOW SUCH FILTH BROUGHT INTO
MY HOUSE! No, no, no, no, no!

TOM. House, house! Who pays rent on it, who makes a slave of himself
to—

AMANDA (*fairly screeching*). Don't you DARE to—

TOM. No, no, *I* musn't say things! *I've* got to just—

AMANDA. Let me tell you—

TOM. I don't want to hear any more! (*He tears the portieres open. The upstage area is lit with a turgid smoky red glow.*)

AMANDA'S *hair is in metal curlers and she wears a very old bathrobe,
much too large for her slight figure, a relic of the faithless* MR.
WINGFIELD.

*An upright typewriter and a wild disarray of manuscripts are
on the dropleaf table. The quarrel was probably precipitated by*
AMANDA'S *interruption of his creative labor. A chair lying overthrown
on the floor.*

*Their gesticulating shadows are cast on the ceiling by the fiery
glow.*

AMANDA. You *will* hear more, you—

TOM. No, I won't hear more, I'm going out!

AMANDA. You come right back in—

TOM. Out, out, out! Because I'm—

AMANDA. Come back here, Tom Wingfield! I'm not through talking to you!

TOM. Oh, go—

LAURA (*desperately*). Tom!

AMANDA. You're going to listen, and no more insolence from you! I'm at
the end of my patience! (*He comes back toward her.*)

TOM. What do you think I'm at? Aren't I supposed to have any patience to
reach the end of, Mother? I know, I know. It seems unimportant to
you, what I'm *doing*—what I *want* to do—having a little *difference*
between them! You don't think that—

AMANDA.  I think you've been doing things that you're ashamed of. That's why you act like this. I don't believe that you go every night to the movies. Nobody goes to the movies night after night. Nobody in their right minds goes to the movies as often as you pretend to. People don't go to the movies at nearly midnight, and movies don't let out at two A.M. Come in stumbling. Muttering to yourself like a maniac! You get three hours' sleep and then go to work. Oh, I can picture the way you're doing down there. Moping, doping, because you're in no condition.

TOM (*wildly*).  No, I'm in no condition!

AMANDA.  What right have you got to jeopardize your job? Jeopardize the security of us all? How do you think we'd manage if you were—

TOM.  Listen! You think I'm crazy *about the warehouse?* (*He bends fiercely toward her slight figure.*) You think I'm in love with the Continental Shoemakers? You think I want to spend fifty-five *years* down there in that—*celotex interior!* with—*fluorescent—tubes!* Look! I'd rather somebody picked up a crowbar and battered out my brains— than go back mornings! I go! Every time you come in yelling that God damn *"Rise and Shine!" "Rise and Shine!"* I say to myself "How *lucky dead* people are!" But I get up. I *go!* For sixty-five dollars a month I give up all that I dream of doing and being *ever!* And you say self— *self's* all I ever think of. Why, listen, if self is what I thought of, Mother, I'd be where he is—GONE! (*Pointing to father's picture.*) As far as the system of transportation reaches! (*He starts past her. She grabs his arm.*) Don't grab at me, Mother!

AMANDA.  Where are you going?

TOM.  I'm going to the *movies!*

AMANDA.  I don't believe that lie!

TOM (*crouching toward her, overtowering her tiny figure. She backs away, gasping*).  I'm going to opium dens! Yes, opium dens, dens of vice and criminals' hang-outs, Mother. I've joined the Hogan gang, I'm a hired assassin, I carry a tommy-gun in a violin case! I run a string of cat-houses in the Valley! They call me Killer, Killer Wingfield, I'm leading a double-life, a simple, honest warehouse worker by day, by night a dynamic *czar* of the *underworld, Mother.* I go to gambling casinos, I spin away fortunes on the roulette table! I wear a patch over one eye and a false mustache, sometimes I put on green whiskers. On those occasions they call me—*El Diablo!* Oh, I could tell you things to make you sleepless! My enemies plan to dynamite this place. They're going to blow us all sky-high some night! I'll be glad, very happy, and so will you! You'll go up, up on a broomstick, over Blue Mountain with seventeen gentlemen callers! You ugly—babbling old—*witch.* . . . (*He goes through a series of violent, clumsy movements, seizing his overcoat, lunging to the door, pulling it fiercely open. The women watch him, aghast. His arm catches in the sleeve of the coat as he struggles to pull it on. For a moment he is pinioned by the bulky garment. With an outraged groan he tears the coat off again, splitting the shoulders of it, and hurls it across the room. It strikes against the shelf of Laura's glass collection, there is a tinkle of shattering glass.* LAURA *cries out as if wounded.*)

(*Music Legend: "The Glass Menagerie."*)

LAURA (*shrilly*). My glass!—menagerie. . . . (*She covers her face and turns away.*)

*But* AMANDA *is still stunned and stupefied by the "ugly witch" so that she barely notices this occurrence. Now she recovers her speech.*

AMANDA (*in an awful voice*). I won't speak to you—until you apologize! (*She crosses through portieres and draws them together behind her.* TOM *is left with* LAURA. LAURA *clings weakly to the mantel with her face averted.* TOM *stares at her stupidly for a moment. Then he crosses to shelf. Drops awkwardly to his knees to collect the fallen glass, glancing at* LAURA *as if he would speak but couldn't.*)

*"The Glass Menagerie" steals in as*
(*The Scene Dims Out.*)

Scene IV

*The interior is dark. Faint light in the alley.*

*A deep-voiced bell in a church is tolling the hour of five as the scene commences.*

TOM *appears at the top of the alley. After each solemn boom of the bell in the tower, he shakes a little noise-maker or rattle as if to express the tiny spasm of man in contrast to the sustained power and dignity of the Almighty. This and the unsteadiness of his advance make it evident that he has been drinking.*

*As he climbs the few steps to the fire-escape landing light steals up inside.* LAURA *appears in night-dress, observing* TOM'S *empty bed in the front room.*

TOM *fishes in his pockets for the door-key, removing a motley assortment of articles in the search, including a perfect shower of movie-ticket stubs and an empty bottle. At last he finds the key, but just as he is about to insert it, it slips from his fingers. He strikes a match and crouches below the door.*

TOM (*bitterly*). One crack—and it falls through!

LAURA *opens the door.*

LAURA. Tom! Tom, what are you doing?
TOM. Looking for a door-key.

LAURA.  Where have you been all this time?

TOM.  I have been to the movies.

LAURA.  All this time at the movies?

TOM.  There was a very long program. There was a Garbo picture and a
Mickey Mouse and a travelogue and a newsreel and a preview of
coming attractions. And there was an organ solo and a collection for
the milk-fund—simultaneously—which ended up in a terrible fight
between a fat lady and an usher!

LAURA (*innocently*).  Did you have to stay through everything?

TOM.  Of course! And, oh, I forgot! There was a big stage show! The head-
liner on this stage show was Malvolio the Magician. He performed
wonderful tricks, many of them, such as pouring water back and forth
between pitchers. First it turned to wine and then it turned to beer
and then it turned to whiskey. I know it was whiskey it finally turned
into because he needed somebody to come up out of the audience to
help him, and I came up—both shows! It was Kentucky Straight Bourbon. A very generous fellow, he gave souvenirs. (*He pulls from his
back pocket a shimmering rainbow-colored scarf.*) He gave me this.
This is his magic scarf. You can have it, Laura. You wave it over a canary cage and you get a bowl of gold-fish. You wave it over the gold-
fish bowl and they fly away canaries. . . . But the wonderfullest trick
of all was the coffin trick. We nailed him into a coffin and he got out
of the coffin without removing one nail. (*He has come inside.*) There
is a trick that would come in handy for me—get me out of this 2 by 4
situation! (*Flops onto bed and starts removing shoes.*)

LAURA.  Tom—Shhh!

TOM.  What you shushing me for?

LAURA.  You'll wake up Mother.

TOM.  Goody, goody! Pay 'er back for all those "Rise an' Shines." (*Lies down,
groaning.*) You know it don't take much intelligence to get yourself
into a nailed-up coffin, Laura. But who in hell ever got himself out of
one without removing one nail?

*As if in answer, the father's grinning photograph lights up.*
     (*Scene Dims Out.*)
     *Immediately following: The church bell is heard striking six. At
the sixth stroke the alarm clock goes off in* AMANDA'S *room, and after a few moments we hear her calling: "Rise and Shine! Rise and
Shine!* LAURA, *go tell your brother to rise and shine!"*

TOM (*sitting up slowly*).  I'll rise—but I won't shine.

*The light increases.*

AMANDA.  Laura, tell your brother his coffee is ready.

LAURA *slips into front room.*

LAURA.  Tom! It's nearly seven. Don't make Mother nervous. (*He stares at her stupidly. Beseechingly.*) Tom, speak to Mother this morning. Make up with her, apologize, speak to her!

TOM.  She won't to me. It's her that started not speaking.

LAURA.  If you just say you're sorry she'll start speaking.

TOM.  Her not speaking—is that such a tragedy?

LAURA.  Please—please!

AMANDA (*calling from kitchenette*). Laura, are you going to do what I asked you to do, or do I have to get dressed and go out myself?

LAURA.  Going, going—soon as I get on my coat! (*She pulls on a shapeless felt hat with nervous, jerky movement, pleadingly glancing at* TOM. *Rushes awkwardly for coat. The coat is one of* AMANDA's, *inaccurately made-over, the sleeves too short for* LAURA.) Butter and what else?

AMANDA (*entering upstage*). Just butter. Tell them to charge it.

LAURA.  Mother, they make such faces when I do that.

AMANDA.  Sticks and stones may break my bones, but the expression on Mr. Garfinkel's face won't harm us! Tell your brother his coffee is getting cold.

LAURA (*at door*). Do what I asked you, will you, will you, Tom?

*He looks sullenly away.*

AMANDA.  Laura, go now or just don't go at all!

LAURA (*rushing out*). Going—going! (*A second later she cries out.* TOM *springs up and crosses to the door.* AMANDA *rushes anxiously in.* TOM *opens the door.*)

TOM.  Laura?

LAURA.  I'm all right. I slipped, but I'm all right.

AMANDA (*peering anxiously after her*). If anyone breaks a leg on those fire-escape steps, the landlord ought to be sued for every cent he possesses! (*She shuts door. Remembers she isn't speaking and returns to other room.*)

*As* TOM *enters listlessly for his coffee, she turns her back to him and stands rigidly facing the window on the gloomy gray vault of the areaway. Its light on her face with its aged but childish features is cruelly sharp, satirical as a Daumier print.*
    (*Music Under: "Ave Maria."*)
    TOM *glances sheepishly but sullenly at her averted figure and slumps at the table. The coffee is scalding hot; he sips it and gasps and spits it back in the cup. At his gasp,* AMANDA *catches her breath and half turns. Then catches herself and turns back to window.*

TOM *blows on his coffee, glancing sidewise at his mother. She clears her throat.* TOM *clears his. He starts to rise. Sinks back down again, scratches his head, clears his throat again.* AMANDA *coughs.* TOM *raises his cup in both hands to blow on it, his eyes staring over the rim of it at his mother for several moments. Then he slowly sets the cup down and awkwardly and hesitantly rises from the chair.*

TOM (*hoarsely*). Mother. I—I apologize. Mother. (AMANDA *draws a quick, shuddering breath. Her face works grotesquely. She breaks into childlike tears.*) I'm sorry for what I said, for everything that I said, I didn't mean it.

AMANDA (*sobbingly*). My devotion has made me a witch and so I make myself hateful to my children!

TOM. No you *don't.*

AMANDA. I worry so much, don't sleep, it makes me nervous!

TOM (*gently*). I understand that.

AMANDA. I've had to put up a solitary battle all these years. But you're my right-hand bower! Don't fall down, don't fail!

TOM (*gently*). I try, Mother.

AMANDA (*with great enthusiasm*). Try and you will SUCCEED! (*The notion makes her breathless.*) Why, you—you're just *full* of natural endowments! Both of my children—they're *unusual* children! Don't you think I know it? I'm so—*proud!* Happy and—feel I've—so much to be thankful for but—Promise me one thing, son!

TOM. What, Mother?

AMANDA. Promise, son, you'll—never be a drunkard!

TOM (*turns to her grinning*). I will never be a drunkard, Mother.

AMANDA. That's what frightened me so, that you'd be drinking! Eat a bowl of Purina!

TOM. Just coffee, Mother.

AMANDA. Shredded wheat biscuit?

TOM. No. No, Mother, just coffee.

AMANDA. You can't put in a day's work on an empty stomach. You've got ten minutes—don't gulp! Drinking too-hot liquids makes cancer of the stomach. . . . Put cream in.

TOM. No, thank you.

AMANDA. To cool it.

TOM. No! No, thank you, I want it black.

AMANDA. I know, but it's not good for you. We have to do all that we can to build ourselves up. In these trying times we live in, all that we have to cling to is—each other. . . . That's why it's so important to—Tom, I— I sent out your sister so I could discuss something with you. If you hadn't spoken I would have spoken to you. (*Sits down.*)

TOM (*gently*). What is it, Mother, that you want to discuss?

AMANDA. Laura!

TOM *puts his cup down slowly.*
(*Legend on Screen:* "LAURA.")
(*Music:* "*The Glass Menagerie.*")

TOM. —Oh.—Laura . . .

AMANDA (*touching his sleeve*). You know how Laura is. So quiet but—still water runs deep! She notices things and I think she—broods about them. (TOM *looks up.*) A few days ago I came in and she was crying.

TOM. What about?

AMANDA. You.

TOM. Me?

AMANDA. She has an idea that you're not happy here.

TOM. What gave her that idea?

AMANDA. What gives her any idea? However, you do act strangely. I—I'm not criticizing, understand *that!* I know your ambitions do not lie in the warehouse, that like everybody in the whole wide world—you've had to—make sacrifices, but—Tom—Tom—life's not easy, it calls for—Spartan endurance! There's so many things in my heart that I cannot describe to you! I've never told you but I—*loved* your father. . . .

TOM (*gently*). I know that, Mother.

AMANDA. And you—when I see you taking after his ways! Staying out late—and—well, you *had* been drinking the night you were in that—terrifying condition! Laura says that you hate the apartment and that you go out nights to get away from it! Is that true, Tom?

TOM. No. You say there's so much in your heart that you can't describe to me. That's true of me, too. There's so much in my heart that I can't describe to *you!* So let's respect each other's—

AMANDA. But, why—*why,* Tom—are you always so *restless?* Where do you go to, nights?

TOM. I—go to the movies.

AMANDA. Why do you go to the movies so much, Tom?

TOM. I go to the movies because—I like adventure. Adventure is something I don't have much of at work, so I go to the movies.

AMANDA. But, Tom, you go to the movies *entirely too much!*

TOM. I like a lot of adventure.

AMANDA *looks baffled, then hurt. As the familiar inquisition resumes he becomes hard and impatient again.* AMANDA *slips back into her querulous attitude toward him.*
(*Image on Screen: Sailing Vessel with Jolly Roger.*)

AMANDA. Most young men find adventure in their careers.

TOM. Then most young men are not employed in a warehouse.

AMANDA. The world is full of young men employed in warehouses and offices and factories.

TOM. Do all of them find adventure in their careers?

AMANDA. They do or they do without it! Not everybody has a craze for adventure.

TOM. Man is by instinct a lover, a hunter, a fighter, and none of those instincts are given much play at the warehouse!

AMANDA. Man is by instinct! Don't quote instinct to me! Instinct is something that people have got away from! It belongs to animals! Christian adults don't want it!

TOM. What do Christian adults want, then, Mother?

AMANDA. Superior things! Things of the mind and the spirit! Only animals have to satisfy instincts! Surely your aims are somewhat higher than theirs! Than monkeys—pigs—

TOM. I reckon they're not.

AMANDA. You're joking. However, that isn't what I wanted to discuss.

TOM (*rising*). I haven't much time.

AMANDA (*pushing his shoulders*). Sit down.

TOM. You want me to punch in red at the warehouse, Mother?

AMANDA. You have five minutes. I want to talk about Laura.

(*Legend:"Plans and Provisions."*)

TOM. All right! What about Laura?

AMANDA. We have to be making plans and provisions for her. She's older than you, two years, and nothing has happened. She just drifts along doing nothing. It frightens me terribly how she just drifts along.

TOM. I guess she's the type that people call home girls.

AMANDA. There's no such type, and if there is, it's a pity! That is unless the home is hers, with a husband!

TOM. What?

AMANDA. Oh, I can see the handwriting on the wall as plain as I see the nose in the front of my face! It's terrifying! More and more you remind me of your father! He was out all hours without explanation— Then *left! Goodbye!* And me with the bag to hold. I saw that letter you got from the Merchant Marine. I know what you're dreaming of. I'm not standing here blindfolded. Very well, then. Then *do* it! But not till there's somebody to take your place.

TOM. What do you mean?

AMANDA. I mean that as soon as Laura has got somebody to take care of her, married, a home of her own, independent—why, then you'll be free to go wherever you please, on land, on sea, whichever way the wind blows! But until that time you've got to look out for your sister. I don't say me because I'm old and don't matter! I say for your sister because she's young and dependent. I put her in business college—a dismal failure! Frightened her so it made her sick to her stomach. I took her over to the Young People's League at the church. Another fiasco. She spoke to nobody, nobody spoke to her. Now all she does is fool with those pieces of glass and play those worn-out records. What kind of a life is that for a girl to lead!

TOM. What can I do about it?

AMANDA. Overcome selfishness! Self, self, self is all that you ever think of! (TOM *springs up and crosses to get his coat. It is ugly and bulky. He pulls on a cap with earmuffs.*) Where is your muffler? Put your wool muffler on! (*He snatches it angrily from the closet and tosses it around his neck and pulls both ends tight.*) Tom! I haven't said what I had in mind to ask you.

TOM. I'm too late to—

AMANDA (*catching his arms—very importunately. Then shyly*). Down at the warehouse, aren't there some—nice young men?

TOM. No!

AMANDA. There *must* be—*some.*

TOM. Mother—

*Gesture.*

AMANDA. Find out one that's clean-living—doesn't drink and—ask him out for sister!

TOM. What?

AMANDA. For *sister! To meet! Get acquainted!*

TOM (*stamping to door*). Oh, my go osh!

AMANDA. Will you? (*He opens door. Imploringly.*) Will you? (*He starts down.*) Will you? *Will* you dear?

TOM (*calling back*). YES!

> AMANDA *closes the door hesitantly and with a troubled but faintly hopeful expression.*
>     (*Screen Image: Glamor Magazine Cover.*)
>     *Spot* AMANDA *at phone.*

AMANDA. Ella Cartwright? This is Amanda Wingfield! How are you honey? How is that kidney condition? (*Count five.*) Horrors! (*Count five.*) You're a Christian martyr, yes, honey, that's what you are, a Christian martyr! Well, I just happened to notice in my little red book that your subscription to the *Companion* has just run out! I knew that you wouldn't want to miss out on the wonderful serial starting in this new issue. It's by Bessie Mae Hopper, the first thing she's written since *Honeymoon for Three.* Wasn't that a strange and interesting story? Well, this one is even lovelier, I believe. It has a sophisticated society background. It's all about the horsey set on Long Island!

(*Fade Out.*)

### Scene V

(*Legend on Screen: "Annunciation."*) *Fade with music.*

   *It is early dusk of a spring evening. Supper has just been finished at the Wingfield apartment.* AMANDA *and* LAURA *in light-colored dresses*

*are removing dishes from the table, in the upstage area, which is shad-*
*owy, their movements formalized almost as a dance or ritual, their*
*moving forms as pale and silent as moths.*

TOM, *in white shirt and trousers, rises from the table and crosses to-*
*ward the fire-escape.*

AMANDA (*as he passes her*).  Son, will you do me a favor?

TOM.  What?

AMANDA.  Comb your hair! You look so pretty when your hair is combed!
(TOM *slouches on sofa with evening paper. Enormous caption*
*"Franco Triumphs."*) There is only one respect in which I would like
you to emulate your father.

TOM.  What respect is that?

AMANDA.  The care he always took of his appearance. He never allowed
himself to look untidy. (*He throws down the paper and crosses to*
*fire-escape.*) Where are you going?

TOM.  I'm going out to smoke.

AMANDA.  You smoke too much. A pack a day at fifteen cents a pack. How
much would that amount to in a month? Thirty times fifteen is how
much, Tom? Figure it out and you will be astounded at what you
could save. Enough to give you a night-school course in accounting
at Washington U! Just think what a wonderful thing that would be for
you, son!

TOM *is unmoved by the thought.*

TOM.  I'd rather smoke. (*He steps out on landing, letting the screen door*
*slam.*)

AMANDA (*sharply*).  I know! That's the tragedy of it. . . . (*Alone, she turns*
*to look at her husband's picture.*)

(*Dance Music:"All the World Is Waiting for the Sunrise!"*)

TOM (*to the audience*).  Across the alley from us was the Paradise Dance
Hall. On evenings in spring the windows and doors were open and
the music came outdoors. Sometimes the lights were turned out except for a large glass sphere that hung from the ceiling. It would turn
slowly about and filter the dusk with delicate rainbow colors. Then
the orchestra played a waltz or a tango, something that had a slow and
sensuous rhythm. Couples would come outside, to the relative privacy of the alley. You could see them kissing behind ashpits and telephone poles. This was the compensation for lives that passed like
mine, without any change or adventure. Adventure and change were
imminent in this year. They were waiting around the corner for all
these kids. Suspended in the mist over Berchtesgaden, caught in the
folds of Chamberlain's umbrella—In Spain there was Guernica! But
here there was only hot swing music and liquor, dance halls, bars, and

movies, and sex that hung in the gloom like a chandelier and flooded the world with brief, deceptive rainbows. . . . All the world was waiting for bombardments!

AMANDA *turns from the picture and comes outside.*

AMANDA (*sighing*). A fire-escape landing's a poor excuse for a porch. (*She spreads a newspaper on a step and sits down, gracefully and demurely as if she were settling into a swing on a Mississippi veranda.*) What are you looking at?

TOM. The moon.

AMANDA. Is there a moon this evening?

TOM. It's rising over Garfinkel's Delicatessen.

AMANDA. So it is! A little silver slipper of a moon. Have you made a wish on it yet?

TOM. Um-hum.

AMANDA. What did you wish for?

TOM. That's a secret.

AMANDA. A secret, huh? Well, I won't tell mine either. I will be just as mysterious as you.

TOM. I bet I can guess what yours is.

AMANDA. Is my head so transparent?

TOM. You're not a sphinx.

AMANDA. No, I don't have secrets. I'll tell you what I wished for on the moon. Success and happiness for my precious children! I wish for that whenever there's a moon, and when there isn't a moon, I wish for it, too.

TOM. I thought perhaps you wished for a gentleman caller.

AMANDA. Why do you say that?

TOM. Don't you remember asking me to fetch one?

AMANDA. I remember suggesting that it would be nice for your sister if you brought some nice young man from the warehouse. I think I've made that suggestion more than once.

TOM. Yes, you have made it repeatedly.

AMANDA. Well?

TOM. We are going to have one.

AMANDA. *What?*

TOM. A gentleman caller!

(*The Annunciation Is Celebrated with Music.*)
    AMANDA *rises.*
    (*Image on Screen: Caller with Bouquet.*)

AMANDA. You mean you have asked some nice young man to come over?

TOM. Yep. I've asked him to dinner.

AMANDA. You really did?

TOM. I did!

AMANDA. You did, and did he—*accept?*

TOM. He did!

AMANDA. Well, well—well, well! That's—lovely!

TOM. I thought that you would be pleased.

AMANDA. It's definite, then?

TOM. Very definite.

AMANDA. Soon?

TOM. Very soon.

AMANDA. For heaven's sake, stop putting on and tell me some things, will you?

TOM. What things do you want me to tell you?

AMANDA. Naturally I would like to know when he's *coming!*

TOM. He's coming tomorrow.

AMANDA. *Tomorrow?*

TOM. Yep. Tomorrow.

AMANDA. But, Tom!

TOM. Yes, Mother?

AMANDA. Tomorrow gives me no time!

TOM. Time for what?

AMANDA. Preparations! Why didn't you phone me at once, as soon as you asked him, the minute that he accepted? Then, don't you see, I could have been getting ready!

TOM. You don't have to make any fuss.

AMANDA. Oh, Tom, Tom, Tom, of course I have to make a fuss! I want things nice, not sloppy! Not thrown together. I'll certainly have to do some fast thinking, won't I?

TOM. I don't see why you have to think at all.

AMANDA. You just don't know. We can't have a gentleman caller in a pigsty! All my wedding silver has to be polished, the monogrammed table linen ought to be laundered! The windows have to be washed and fresh curtains put up. And how about clothes? We have to *wear* something, don't we?

TOM. Mother, this boy is no one to make a fuss over!

AMANDA. Do you realize he's the first young man we've introduced to your sister? It's terrible, dreadful, disgraceful that poor little sister has never received a single gentleman caller! Tom, come inside! (*She opens the screen door.*)

TOM. What for?

AMANDA. I want to ask you some things.

TOM. If you're going to make such a fuss, I'll call it off, I'll tell him not to come.

AMANDA. You certainly won't do anything of the kind. Nothing offends people worse than broken engagements. It simply means I'll have to work like a Turk! We won't be brilliant, but we'll pass inspection. Come on inside. (TOM *follows, groaning.*) Sit down.

TOM.  Any particular place you would like me to sit?

AMANDA.  Thank heavens I've got that new sofa! I'm also making payments on a floor lamp I'll have sent out! And put the chintz covers on, they'll brighten things up! Of course I'd hoped to have these walls repapered. . . .What is the young man's name?

TOM.  His name is O'Connor.

AMANDA.  That, of course, means fish—tomorrow is Friday! I'll have that salmon loaf—with Durkee's dressing! What does he do? He works at the warehouse?

TOM.  Of course! How else would I—

AMANDA.  Tom, he—doesn't drink?

TOM.  Why do you ask me that?

AMANDA.  Your father *did!*

TOM.  Don't get started on that!

AMANDA.  He *does* drink, then?

TOM.  Not that I know of!

AMANDA.  Make sure, be certain! The last thing I want for my daughter's a boy who drinks!

TOM.  Aren't you being a little premature? Mr. O'Connor has not yet appeared on the scene!

AMANDA.  But will tomorrow. To meet your sister, and what do I know about his character? Nothing! Old maids are better off than wives of drunkards!

TOM.  Oh, my God!

AMANDA.  Be still!

TOM  (*leaning forward to whisper*).  Lots of fellows meet girls whom they don't marry!

AMANDA.  Oh, talk sensibly, Tom—and don't be sarcastic! (*She has gotten a hairbrush.*)

TOM.  What are you doing?

AMANDA.  I'm brushing that cow-lick down! What is this young man's position at the warehouse?

TOM  (*submitting grimly to the brush and the interrogation*).  This young man's position is that of a shipping clerk, Mother.

AMANDA.  Sounds to me like a fairly responsible job, the sort of a job *you* would be in if you just had more *get-up*. What is his salary? Have you got any idea?

TOM.  I would judge it to be approximately eighty-five dollars a month.

AMANDA.  Well—not princely, but—

TOM.  Twenty more than I make.

AMANDA.  Yes, how well I know! But for a family man, eighty-five dollars a month is not much more than you can just get by on. . . .

TOM.  Yes, but Mr. O'Connor is not a family man.

AMANDA.  He might be, mightn't he? Some time in the future?

TOM.  I see. Plans and provisions.

AMANDA.  You are the only man that I know of who ignores the fact that the future becomes the present, the present the past, and the past turns into everlasting regret if you don't plan for it!

TOM.  I will think that over and see what I can make of it.

AMANDA.  Don't be supercilious with your mother! Tell me some more about this—what do you call him?

TOM.  James D. O'Connor. The D. is for Delaney.

AMANDA.  Irish on *both* sides! *Gracious!* And doesn't drink?

TOM.  Shall I call him up and ask him right this minute?

AMANDA.  The only way to find out about those things is to make discreet inquiries at the proper moment. When I was a girl in Blue Mountain and it was suspected that a young man drank, the girl whose attentions he had been receiving, if any girl *was,* would sometimes speak to the minister of his church, or rather her father would if her father was living, and sort of feel him out on the young man's character. That is the way such things are discreetly handled to keep a young woman from making a tragic mistake!

TOM.  Then how did you happen to make a tragic mistake?

AMANDA.  That innocent look of your father's had everyone fooled! He *smiled*—the world was *enchanted!* No girl can do worse than put herself at the mercy of a handsome appearance! I hope that Mr. O'Connor is not too good-looking.

TOM.  No, he's not too good-looking. He's covered with freckles and hasn't too much of a nose.

AMANDA.  He's not right-down homely, though?

TOM.  Not right-down homely. Just medium homely, I'd say.

AMANDA.  Character's what to look for in a man.

TOM.  That's what I've always said, Mother.

AMANDA.  You've never said anything of the kind and I suspect you would never give it a thought.

TOM.  Don't be suspicious of me.

AMANDA.  At least I hope he's the type that's up and coming.

TOM.  I think he really goes in for self-improvement.

AMANDA.  What reason have you to think so?

TOM.  He goes to night school.

AMANDA (*beaming*).  Splendid! What does he do, I mean study?

TOM.  Radio engineering and public speaking!

AMANDA.  Then he has visions of being advanced in the world! Any young man who studies public speaking is aiming to have an executive job some day! And radio engineering? A thing for the future! Both of these facts are very illuminating. Those are the sort of things that a mother should know concerning any young man who comes to call on her daughter. Seriously or—not.

TOM. One little warning. He doesn't know about Laura. I didn't let on that we had dark ulterior motives. I just said, why don't you come have dinner with us? He said okay and that was the whole conversation.

AMANDA. I bet it was! You're eloquent as an oyster. However, he'll know about Laura when he gets here. When he sees how lovely and sweet and pretty she is, he'll thank his lucky stars he was asked to dinner.

TOM. Mother, you mustn't expect too much of Laura.

AMANDA. What do you mean?

TOM. Laura seems all those things to you and me because she's ours and we love her. We don't even notice she's crippled any more.

AMANDA. Don't say crippled! You know that I never allow that word to be used!

TOM. But face facts, Mother. She is and—that's not all—

AMANDA. What do you mean "not all"?

TOM. Laura is very different from other girls.

AMANDA. I think the difference is all to her advantage.

TOM. Not quite all—in the eyes of others—strangers—she's terribly shy and lives in a world of her own and those things make her seem a little peculiar to people outside the house.

AMANDA. Don't say peculiar.

TOM. Face the facts. She is.

(*The Dance-Hall Music Changes to a Tango that Has a Minor and Somewhat Ominous Tone.*)

AMANDA. In what way is she peculiar—may I ask?

TOM (*gently*). She lives in a world of her own—a world of—little glass ornaments, Mother. . . . (*Gets up.* AMANDA *remains holding brush, looking at him, troubled.*) She plays old phonograph records and—that's about all—(*He glances at himself in the mirror and crosses to door.*)

AMANDA (*sharply*). Where are you going?

TOM. I'm going to the movies. (*Out screen door.*)

AMANDA. Not to the movies, every night to the movies! (*Follows quickly to screen door.*) I don't believe you always go to the movies! (*He is gone.* AMANDA *looks worriedly after him for a moment. Then vitality and optimism return and she turns from the door. Crossing to portieres.*) Laura! Laura! (LAURA *answers from kitchenette.*)

LAURA. Yes, Mother.

AMANDA. Let those dishes go and come in front! (LAURA *appears with dish towel. Gaily.*) Laura, come here and make a wish on the moon!

LAURA (*entering*). Moon—moon?

AMANDA. A little silver slipper of a moon. Look over your left shoulder, Laura, and make a wish! (LAURA *looks faintly puzzled as if called out of sleep.* AMANDA *seizes her shoulders and turns her at an angle by the door.*) Now! Now, darling, *wish!*

LAURA. What shall I wish for, Mother?

AMANDA (*her voice trembling and her eyes suddenly filling with tears*). Happiness! Good Fortune!

*The violin rises and the stage dims out.*

### Scene VI

*(Image: High School Hero.)*

TOM.    And so the following evening I brought Jim home to dinner. I had known Jim slightly in high school. In high school Jim was a hero. He had tremendous Irish good nature and vitality with the scrubbed and polished look of white chinaware. He seemed to move in a continual spotlight. He was a star in basketball, captain of the debating club, president of the senior class and the glee club and he sang the male lead in the annual light operas. He was always running or bounding, never just walking. He seemed always at the point of defeating the law of gravity. He was shooting with such velocity through his adolescence that you would logically expect him to arrive at nothing short of the White House by the time he was thirty. But Jim apparently ran into more interference after his graduation from Soldan. His speed had definitely slowed. Six years after he left high school he was holding a job that wasn't much better than mine.

*(Image: Clerk.)*

He was the only one at the warehouse with whom I was on friendly terms. I was valuable to him as someone who could remember his former glory, who had seen him win basketball games and the silver cup in debating. He knew of my secret practice of retiring to a cabinet of the washroom to work on poems when business was slack in the warehouse. He called me Shakespeare. And while the other boys in the warehouse regarded me with suspicious hostility, Jim took a humorous attitude toward me. Gradually his attitude affected the others, their hostility wore off and they also began to smile at me as people smile at an oddly fashioned dog who trots across their path at some distance.

I knew that Jim and Laura had known each other at Soldan, and I had heard Laura speak admiringly of his voice. I didn't know if Jim remembered her or not. In high school Laura had been as unobtrusive as Jim had been astonishing. If he did remember Laura, it was not as my sister, for when I asked him to dinner, he grinned and said, "You know, Shakespeare, I never thought of you as having folks!"

He was about to discover that I did. . . .

*(Light up Stage.)*
*(Legend on Screen: "The Accent of a Coming Foot.")*

*Friday evening. It is about five o'clock of a late spring evening which comes "scattering poems in the sky." A delicate lemony light is in the Wingfield apartment.* AMANDA *has worked like a Turk in preparation for the gentleman caller. The results are astonishing. The new floor lamp with its rose-silk shade is in place, a colored paper lantern conceals the broken light fixture in the ceiling, new billowing white curtains are at the windows, chintz covers are on chairs and sofa, a pair of new sofa pillows make their initial appearance.*

*Open boxes and tissue paper are scattered on the floor.*

LAURA *stands in the middle with lifted arms while* AMANDA *crouches before her, adjusting the hem of the new dress, devout and ritualistic. The dress is colored and designed by memory. The arrangement of* LAURA's *hair is changed, it is softer and more becoming. A fragile, unearthly prettiness has come out in* LAURA: *she is like a piece of translucent glass touched by light, given a momentary radiance, not actual, not lasting.*

AMANDA (*impatiently*). Why are you trembling?

LAURA. Mother, you've made me so nervous!

AMANDA. How have I made you nervous?

LAURA. By all this fuss! You make it seem so important!

AMANDA. I don't understand you, Laura. You couldn't be satisfied with just sitting home, and yet whenever I try to arrange something for you, you seem to resist it. (*She gets up.*) Now take a look at yourself. No, wait! Wait just a moment—I have an idea!

LAURA. What is it now?

AMANDA *produces two powder puffs which she wraps in handkerchiefs and stuffs in* LAURA'S *bosom.*

LAURA. Mother, what are you doing?

AMANDA. They call them "Gay Deceivers"!

LAURA. I won't wear them!

AMANDA. You will!

LAURA. Why should I?

AMANDA. Because, to be painfully honest, your chest is flat.

LAURA. You make it seem like we were setting a trap.

AMANDA. All pretty girls are a trap, a pretty trap, and men expect them to be. (*Legend: "A Pretty Trap."*) Now look at yourself, young lady. This is the prettiest you will ever be! I've got to fix myself now! You're going to be surprised by your mother's appearance! (*She crosses through portieres, humming gaily.*)

*Laura moves slowly to the long mirror and stares solemnly at herself.*

*A wind blows the white curtains inward in a slow, graceful motion and with a faint, sorrowful sighing.*

AMANDA (*off stage*). It isn't dark enough yet. (*She turns slowly before the mirror with a troubled look.*)

(*Legend on Screen:"This Is My Sister: Celebrate Her with Strings!" Music.*)

AMANDA (*laughing, off*). I'm going to show you something. I'm going to make a spectacular appearance!

LAURA. What is it, Mother?

AMANDA. Possess your soul in patience—you will see! Something I've resurrected from that old trunk! Styles haven't changed so terribly much after all. . . . (*She parts the portieres.*) Now just look at your mother! (*She wears a girlish frock of yellowed voile with a blue silk sash. She carries a bunch of jonquils—the legend of her youth is nearly revived. Feverishly.*) This is the dress in which I led the cotillion. Won the cakewalk twice at Sunset Hill, wore one spring to the Governor's ball in Jackson! See how I sashayed around the ballroom, Laura? (*She raises her skirt and does a mincing step around the room.*) I wore it on Sundays for my gentlemen callers! I had it on the day I met your father—I had malaria fever all that spring. The change of climate from East Tennessee to the Delta—weakened resistance— I had a little temperature all the time—not enough to be serious— just enough to make me restless and giddy! Invitations poured in— parties all over the Delta!—"stay in bed," said Mother, "you have fever!"—but I just wouldn't.—I took quinine but kept on going, going!—Evenings, dances!—Afternoons, long, long rides! Picnics— lovely!—So lovely, that country in May.—All lacy with dogwood, literally flooded with jonquils!—That was the spring I had the craze for jonquils. Jonquils became an absolute obsession. Mother said, "Honey, there's no more room for jonquils." And still I kept bringing in more jonquils. Whenever, wherever I saw them, I'd say, "Stop! Stop! I see jonquils!" I made the young men help me gather the jonquils! It was a joke, Amanda and her jonquils! Finally there were no more vases to hold them, every available space was filled with jonquils. No vases to hold them? All right, I'll hold them myself! And then I—(*She stops in front of the picture.*) (*Music.*) met your father! Malaria fever and jonquils and then—this—boy. . . . (*She switches on the rose-colored lamp.*) I hope they get here before it starts to rain. (*She crosses upstage and places the jonquils in bowl on table.*) I gave your brother a little extra change so he and Mr. O'Connor could take the service car home.

LAURA (*with altered look*). What did you say his name was?

AMANDA. O'Connor.

LAURA. What is his first name?
AMANDA. I don't remember. Oh, yes, I do. It was—Jim!

LAURA *sways slightly and catches hold of a chair.*
(*Legend on Screen:"Not Jim!"*)

LAURA (*faintly*). Not—Jim!
AMANDA. Yes, that was it, it was Jim! I've never known a Jim that wasn't nice!

(*Music: Ominous.*)

LAURA. Are you sure his name is Jim O'Connor?
AMANDA. Yes. Why?
LAURA. Is he the one that Tom used to know in high school?
AMANDA. He didn't say so. I think he just got to know him at the warehouse.
LAURA. There was a Jim O'Connor we both knew in high school—(*Then, with effort.*) If that is the one that Tom is bringing to dinner—you'll have to excuse me, I won't come to the table.
AMANDA. What sort of nonsense is this?
LAURA. You asked me once if I'd ever liked a boy. Don't you remember I showed you this boy's picture?
AMANDA. You mean the boy you showed me in the year-book?
LAURA. Yes, that boy.
AMANDA. Laura, Laura, were you in love with that boy?
LAURA. I don't know, Mother. All I know is I couldn't sit at the table if it was him!
AMANDA. It won't be him! It isn't the least bit likely. But whether it is or not, you will come to the table. You will not be excused.
LAURA. I'll have to be, Mother.
AMANDA. I don't intend to humor your silliness, Laura. I've had too much from you and your brother, both! So just sit down and compose yourself till they come. Tom has forgotten his key so you'll have to let them in, when they arrive.
LAURA (*panicky*). Oh, Mother—*you* answer the door!
AMANDA (*lightly*). I'll be in the kitchen—busy!
LAURA. Oh, Mother, please answer the door, don't make me do it!
AMANDA (*crossing into kitchenette*). I've got to fix the dressing for the salmon. Fuss, fuss—silliness!—over a gentleman caller!

> *Door swings shut.* LAURA *is left alone.*
> (*Legend:"Terror!"*)
> *She utters a low moan and turns off the lamp—sits stiffly on the edge of the sofa, knotting her fingers together.*
> (*Legend on Screen:"The Opening of a Door!"*)

TOM *and* JIM *appear on the fire-escape steps and climb to landing. Hearing their approach,* LAURA *rises with a panicky gesture. She retreats to the portieres.*
*The doorbell.* LAURA *catches her breath and touches her throat. Low drums.*

AMANDA (*calling*). Laura, sweetheart! The door!

LAURA *stares at it without moving.*

JIM. I think we just beat the rain.
TOM. Uh-huh. (*He rings again, nervously.* JIM *whistles and fishes for a cigarette.*)
AMANDA (*very, very gaily*). Laura, that is your brother and Mr. O'Connor! Will you let them in, darling?

LAURA *crosses toward kitchenette door.*

LAURA (*breathlessly*). Mother—you go to the door!

AMANDA *steps out of kitchenette and stares furiously at* LAURA. *She points imperiously at the door.*

LAURA. Please, please!
AMANDA (*in a fierce whisper*). What is the matter with you, you silly thing?
LAURA (*desperately*). Please, you answer it, *please!*
AMANDA. I told you I wasn't going to humor you, Laura. Why have you chosen this moment to lose your mind?
LAURA. Please, please, please, you go!
AMANDA. You'll have to go to the door because I can't!
LAURA (*despairingly*). I can't either!
AMANDA. Why?
LAURA. I'm sick!
AMANDA. I'm sick, too—of your nonsense! Why can't you and your brother be normal people? Fantastic whims and behavior! (TOM *gives a long ring.*) Preposterous goings on! Can you give me one reason—(*Calls out lyrically.*) COMING! JUST ONE SECOND!—why should you be afraid to open a door? Now you answer it, Laura!
LAURA. Oh, oh, oh . . . (*She returns through the portieres. Darts to the victrola and winds it frantically and turns it on.*)
AMANDA. Laura Wingfield, you march right to that door!
LAURA. Yes—yes, Mother!

*A faraway, scratchy rendition of "dardanella" softens the air and gives her strength to move through it. She slips to the door and draws it cautiously open.*
TOM *enters with caller,* JIM O'CONNOR.

TOM. Laura, this is Jim. Jim, this is my sister, Laura.
JIM (*stepping inside*). I didn't know that Shakespeare had a sister!

LAURA (*retreating stiff and trembling from the door*).  How—how do you do?

JIM (*heartily extending his hand*).  Okay!

LAURA *touches it hesitantly with hers.*

JIM.  Your hand's *cold*, Laura!

LAURA.  Yes, well—I've been playing the victrola. . . .

JIM.  Must have been playing classical music on it! You ought to play a little hot swing music to warm you up!

LAURA.  Excuse me—I haven't finished playing the victrola. . . .

*She turns awkwardly and hurries into the front room. She pauses a second by the victrola. Then catches her breath and darts through the portieres like a frightened deer.*

JIM (*grinning*).  What was the matter?

TOM.  Oh—with Laura? Laura is—terribly shy.

JIM.  Shy, huh? It's unusual to meet a shy girl nowadays. I don't believe you ever mentioned you had a sister.

TOM.  Well, now you know. I have one. Here is the *Post Dispatch*. You want a piece of it?

JIM.  Uh-huh.

TOM.  What piece? The comics?

JIM.  Sports! (*Glances at it.*) Ole Dizzy Dean is on his bad behavior.

TOM (*disinterest*).  Yeah? (*Lights cigarette and crosses back to fire-escape door.*)

JIM.  Where are *you* going?

TOM.  I'm going out on the terrace.

JIM (*goes after him*).  You know, Shakespeare—I'm going to sell you a bill of goods!

TOM.  What goods?

JIM.  A course I'm taking.

TOM.  Huh?

JIM.  In public speaking! You and me, we're not the warehouse type.

TOM.  Thanks—that's good news. But what has public speaking got to do with it?

JIM.  It fits you for—executive positions!

TOM.  Awww.

JIM.  I tell you it's done a helluva lot for me.

(*Image: Executive at Desk.*)

TOM.  In what respect?

JIM.  In every! Ask yourself what is the difference between you an' me and men in the office down front? Brains?—No!—Ability?—No! Then what? Just one little thing—

TOM.  What is that one little thing?

JIM.  Primarily it amounts to—social poise! Being able to square up to people and hold your own on any social level!

AMANDA (*off stage*).  Tom?

TOM.  Yes, Mother?

AMANDA.  Is that you and Mr. O'Connor?

TOM.  Yes, Mother.

AMANDA.  Well, you just make yourselves comfortable in there.

TOM.  Yes, Mother.

AMANDA.  Ask Mr. O'Connor if he would like to wash his hands.

JIM.  Aw—no—no—thank you—I took care of that at the warehouse.
Tom—

TOM.  Yes?

JIM.  Mr. Mendoza was speaking to me about you.

TOM.  Favorably?

JIM.  What do you think?

TOM.  Well—

JIM.  You're going to be out of a job if you don't wake up.

TOM.  I am waking up—

JIM.  You show no signs.

TOM.  The signs are interior.

(*Image on Screen: The Sailing Vessel with Jolly Roger Again.*)

TOM.  I'm planning to change. (*He leans over the rail speaking with quiet
exhilaration. The incandescent marquees and signs of the first-run
movie houses light his face from across the alley. He looks like a
voyager.*) I'm right at the point of committing myself to a future that
doesn't include the warehouse and Mr. Mendoza or even a night-
school course in public speaking.

JIM.  What are you gassing about?

TOM.  I'm tired of the movies.

JIM.  Movies!

TOM.  Yes, movies! Look at them—(*a wave toward the marvels of Grand
Avenue.*) All of those glamorous people—having adventures—hog-
ging it all, gobbling the whole thing up! You know what happens?
People go to the *movies* instead of *moving!* Hollywood characters
are supposed to have all the adventures for everybody in America,
while everybody in America sits in a dark room and watches them
have them! Yes, until there's a war. That's when adventure becomes
available to the masses! *Everyone's* dish, not only Gable's! Then the
people in the dark room come out of the dark room to have some adventures themselves—Goody, goody—It's our turn now, to go to the
South Sea Island—to make a safari—to be exotic, far-off—But I'm not
patient. I don't want to wait till then. I'm tired of the *movies* and I am
*about to move!*

JIM (*incredulously*).  Move?

TOM.  Yes.

JIM.  When?

TOM.  Soon!

JIM.  Where? Where?

*(Theme Three: Music Seems to Answer the Question, while* TOM *Thinks it Over. He Searches among his Pockets.)*

TOM.  I'm starting to boil inside. I know I seem dreamy, but inside—well, I'm boiling! Whenever I pick up a shoe, I shudder a little thinking how short life is and what I am doing!—Whatever that means. I know it doesn't mean shoes—except as something to wear on a traveler's feet! *(Finds paper.)* Look—

JIM.  What?

TOM.  I'm a member.

JIM *(reading)*.  The Union of Merchant Seamen.

TOM.  I paid my dues this month, instead of the light bill.

JIM.  You will regret it when they turn the lights off.

TOM.  I won't be here.

JIM.  How about your mother?

TOM.  I'm like my father. The bastard son of a bastard! See how he grins? And he's been absent going on sixteen years!

JIM.  You're just talking, you drip. How does your mother feel about it?

TOM.  Shhh—Here comes Mother! Mother is not acquainted with my plans!

AMANDA *(enters portieres)*.  Where are you all?

TOM.  On the terrace, Mother.

*They start inside. She advances to them.* TOM *is distinctly shocked at her appearance. Even* JIM *blinks a little. He is making his first contact with girlish Southern vivacity and in spite of the night-school course in public speaking is somewhat thrown off the beam by the unexpected outlay of social charm.*

*Certain responses are attempted by* JIM *but are swept aside by* AMANDA's *gay laughter and chatter.* TOM *is embarrassed but after the first shock* JIM *reacts very warmly. Grins and chuckles, is altogether won over.*

*(Image:* AMANDA *as a Girl.)*

AMANDA *(coyly smiling, shaking her girlish ringlets)*.  Well, well, well, so this is Mr. O'Connor. Introductions entirely unnecessary. I've heard so much about you from my boy. I finally said to him, Tom—good gracious!—why don't you bring this paragon to supper? I'd like to meet this nice young man at the warehouse!—Instead of just hearing him sing your praises so much! I don't know why my son is so standoffish—that's not Southern behavior! Let's sit down and—I think we could stand a little more air in here! Tom, leave the door open. I felt a nice fresh breeze a moment ago. Where has it gone? Mmm, so warm already! And not quite summer, even. We're going to burn up when summer really gets started. However, we're having—we're having a very light supper. I think light things are better fo' this time of year. The same as light clothes are. Light clothes an' light food are what warm weather calls fo'. You know our blood gets so thick during th' winter—it takes a while fo' us to *adjust* ou'selves!—when the season changes. . . . It's come so quick this year. I wasn't prepared. All of a sudden—heavens! Already summer!—I ran to the trunk an' pulled out this light dress—Terribly old! Historical almost! But feels so good—so good an' co-ol, y'know. . . . .

TOM. Mother—

AMANDA. Yes, honey?

TOM. How about—supper?

AMANDA. Honey, you go ask Sister if supper is ready! You know that Sister is in full charge of supper! Tell her you hungry boys are waiting for it. (*To* JIM.) Have you met Laura?

JIM. She—

AMANDA. Let you in? Oh, good, you've met already! It's rare for a girl as sweet an' pretty as Laura to be domestic! But Laura is, thank heavens, not only pretty but also very domestic. I'm not at all. I never was a bit. I never could make a thing but angel-food cake. Well, in the South we had so many servants. Gone, gone, gone. All vestiges of gracious living! Gone completely! I wasn't prepared for what the future brought me. All of my gentlemen callers were sons of planters and so of course I assumed that I would be married to one and raise my family on a large piece of land with plenty of servants. But man proposes—and woman accepts the proposal!—To vary that old, old saying a little bit—I married no planter! I married a man who worked for the telephone company!—that gallantly smiling gentleman over there! [*Points to the picture.*] A telephone man who—fell in love with long distance!—Now he travels and I don't even know where!—But what am I going on for about my—tribulations! Tell me yours—I hope you don't have any! Tom?

TOM (*returning*). Yes, Mother?

AMANDA. Is supper nearly ready?

TOM. It looks to me like supper is on the table.

AMANDA. Let me look—(*She rises prettily and looks through portieres.*) Oh, lovely—But where is Sister?

TOM. Laura is not feeling well and she says that she thinks she'd better not come to the table.

AMANDA. What?—Nonsense!—Laura? Oh, Laura!

LAURA (*off stage, faintly*). Yes, Mother.

AMANDA. You really must come to the table. We won't be seated until you come to the table! Come in, Mr. O'Connor. You sit over there and I'll—

Laura? Laura Wingfield! You're keeping us waiting, honey! We can't say grace until you come to the table!

*The back door is pushed weakly open and* LAURA *comes in. She is obviously quite faint, her lips trembling, her eyes wide and staring. She moves unsteadily toward the table.*

*(Legend:"Terror!")*

*Outside a summer storm is coming abruptly. The white curtains billow inward at the windows and there is a sorrowful murmur and deep blue dusk.*

LAURA *suddenly stumbles—She catches a chair with a faint moan.*

TOM.  Laura!

AMANDA.  Laura! *(There is a clap of thunder.)* *(Legend: "Ah!")* *(Despairingly.)* Why, Laura, you *are* sick, darling! Tom, help your sister into the living room, dear! Sit in the living room, Laura—rest on the sofa. Well! *(To the gentleman caller.)* Standing over the hot stove made her ill!—I told her that it was just too warm this evening, but— *(*TOM *comes back in.* LAURA *is on the sofa.)* Is Laura all right now?

TOM.  Yes.

AMANDA.  What *is* that? Rain? A nice cool rain has come up! *(She gives the gentleman caller a frightened look.)* I think we may—have grace—now . . . *(*TOM *looks at her stupidly.)* Tom, honey—you say grace!

TOM.  Oh . . . "For these and all thy mercies—" *(They bow their heads,* AMANDA *stealing a nervous glance at* JIM. *In the living room* LAURA, *stretched on the sofa, clenches her hand to her lips, to hold back a shuddering sob.)* God's Holy Name be praised—

*(The Scene Dims Out.)*


### Scene VII

### A Souvenir

*Half an hour later. Dinner is just being finished in the upstage area which is concealed by the drawn portieres.*

*As the curtain rises* LAURA *is still huddled upon the sofa, her feet drawn under her, her head resting on a pale blue pillow, her eyes wide and mysteriously watchful. The new floor lamp with its shade of rose-colored silk gives a soft, becoming light to her face, bringing out the fragile, unearthly prettiness which usually escapes attention. There is a steady murmur of rain, but it is slackening and stops soon after the scene begins; the air outside becomes pale and luminous as the moon breaks out.*

*A moment after the curtain rises, the lights in both rooms flicker and go out.*

JIM.  Hey, there, Mr. Light Bulb!

AMANDA *laughs nervously.*
(*Legend:"Suspension of a Public Service."*)

AMANDA.  Where was Moses when the lights went out? Ha-ha. Do you know the answer to that one, Mr. O'Connor?

JIM.  No, Ma'am, what's the answer?

AMANDA.  In the dark! (JIM *laughs appreciatively.*) Everybody sit still. I'll light the candles. Isn't it lucky we have them on the table? Where's a match? Which of you gentlemen can provide a match?

JIM.  Here.

AMANDA.  Thank you, sir.

JIM.  Not at all, Ma'am!

AMANDA.  I guess the fuse has burnt out. Mr. O'Connor, can you tell a burnt-out fuse? I know I can't and Tom is a total loss when it comes to mechanics. (*Sound: Getting Up: Voices Recede a Little to Kitchenette.*) Oh, be careful you don't bump into something. We don't want our gentleman caller to break his neck. Now wouldn't that be a fine howdy-do?

JIM.  Ha-ha! Where is the fuse-box?

AMANDA.  Right here next to the stove. Can you see anything?

JIM.  Just a minute.

AMANDA.  Isn't electricity a mysterious thing? Wasn't it Benjamin Franklin who tied a key to a kite? We live in such a mysterious universe, don't we? Some people say that science clears up all the mysteries for us. In my opinion it only creates more! Have you found it yet?

JIM.  No, Ma'am. All these fuses look okay to me.

AMANDA.  Tom!

TOM.  Yes, Mother?

AMANDA.  That light bill I gave you several days ago. The one I told you we got the notices about?

TOM.  Oh.—Yeah.

(*Legend:"Ha!"*)

AMANDA.  You didn't neglect to pay it by any chance?

TOM.  Why, I—

AMANDA.  Didn't! I might have known it!

JIM.  Shakespeare probably wrote a poem on that light bill, Mrs. Wingfield.

AMANDA.  I might have known better than to trust him with it! There's such a high price for negligence in this world!

JIM.  Maybe the poem will win a ten-dollar prize.

AMANDA.  We'll just have to spend the remainder of the evening in the nineteenth century, before Mr. Edison made the Mazda lamp!

JIM.  Candlelight is my favorite kind of light.

AMANDA. That shows you're romantic! But that's no excuse for Tom. Well, we got through dinner. Very considerate of them to let us get through dinner before they plunged us into everlasting darkness, wasn't it, Mr. O'Connor?

JIM. Ha-ha!

AMANDA. Tom, as a penalty for your carelessness you can help me with the dishes.

JIM. Let me give you a hand.

AMANDA. Indeed you will not!

JIM. I ought to be good for something.

AMANDA. Good for something? (*Her tone is rhapsodic.*) *You?* Why, Mr. O'Connor, nobody, *nobody's* given me this much entertainment in years—as you have!

JIM. Aw, now, Mrs. Wingfield!

AMANDA. I'm not exaggerating, not one bit! But Sister is all by her lonesome. You go keep her company in the parlor! I'll give you this lovely old candelabrum that used to be on the altar at the church of the Heavenly Rest. It was melted a little out of shape when the church burnt down. Lightning struck it one spring. Gypsy Jones was holding a revival at the time and he intimated that the church was destroyed because the Episcopalians gave card parties.

JIM. Ha-ha.

AMANDA. And how about coaxing Sister to drink a little wine? I think it would be good for her! Can you carry both at once?

JIM. Sure. I'm Superman!

AMANDA. Now, Thomas, get into this apron!

*The door of kitchenette swings closed on* AMANDA'S *gay laughter; the flickering light approaches the portieres.*

LAURA *sits up nervously as he enters. Her speech at first is low and breathless from the almost intolerable strain of being alone with a stranger.*

(Legend: "I Don't Suppose You Remember Me at All!")

*In her first speeches in this scene, before* JIM'S *warmth overcomes her paralyzing shyness,* LAURA'S *voice is thin and breathless as though she has run up a steep flight of stairs.*

JIM'S *attitude is gently humorous. In playing this scene it should be stressed that while the incident is apparently unimportant, it is to* LAURA *the climax of her secret life.*

JIM. Hello, there, Laura.

LAURA (*faintly*). Hello. (*She clears her throat.*)

JIM. How are you feeling now? Better?

LAURA. Yes. Yes, thank you.

JIM. This is for you. A little dandelion wine. (*He extends it toward her with extravagant gallantry.*)

LAURA. Thank you.

JIM. Drink it—but don't get drunk! (*He laughs heartily.* LAURA *takes the glass uncertainly; laughs shyly.*) Where shall I set the candles?

LAURA. Oh—oh, anywhere . . .

JIM. How about here on the floor? Any objections?

LAURA. No.

JIM. I'll spread a newspaper under to catch the drippings. I like to sit on the floor. Mind if I do?

LAURA. Oh, no.

JIM. Give me a pillow?

LAURA. What?

JIM. A pillow!

LAURA. Oh . . . (*Hands him one quickly.*)

JIM. How about you? Don't you like to sit on the floor?

LAURA. Oh—yes.

JIM. Why don't you, then?

LAURA. I—will.

JIM. Take a pillow! (LAURA *does. Sits on the other side of the candelabrum.* JIM *crosses his legs and smiles engagingly at her.*) I can't hardly see you sitting way over there.

LAURA. I can—see you.

JIM. I know, but that's not fair, I'm in the limelight. (LAURA *moves her pillow closer.*) Good! Now I can see you! Comfortable?

LAURA. Yes.

JIM. So am I. Comfortable as a cow. Will you have some gum?

LAURA. No, thank you.

JIM. I think that I will indulge, with your permission. (*Musingly unwraps it and holds it up.*) Think of the fortune made by the guy that invented the first piece of chewing gum. Amazing, huh? The Wrigley Building is one of the sights of Chicago.—I saw it summer before last when I went up to the Century of Progress. Did you take in the Century of Progress?

LAURA. No, I didn't.

JIM. Well, it was quite a wonderful exposition. What impressed me most was the Hall of Science. Gives you an idea of what the future will be in America, even more wonderful than the present time is! (*Pause. Smiling at her.*) Your brother tells me you're shy. Is that right, Laura?

LAURA. I—don't know.

JIM. I judge you to be an old-fashioned type of girl. Well, I think that's a pretty good type to be. Hope you don't think I'm being too personal—do you?

LAURA (*hastily, out of embarrassment*). I believe I *will* take a piece of gum, if you—don't mind. (*Clearing her throat.*) Mr. O'Connor, have you—kept up with your singing?

JIM. Singing? Me?

LAURA.  Yes. I remember what a beautiful voice you had.

JIM.  When did you hear me sing?

(*Voice Offstage in the Pause.*)

VOICE  (*offstage*).

> O blow, ye winds, heigh-ho.
> A-roving I will go!
> I'm off to my love
> With a boxing glove—
> Ten thousand miles away!

JIM.  You say you've heard me sing?

LAURA.  Oh, yes! Yes, very often . . . . I—don't suppose you remember me—at all?

JIM (*smiling doubtfully*).  You know I have an idea I've seen you before. I had that idea soon as you opened the door. It seemed almost like I was about to remember your name. But the name that I started to call you—wasn't a name! And so I stopped myself before I said it.

LAURA.  Wasn't it—Blue Roses?

JIM (*springs up, grinning*).  Blue Roses! My gosh, yes—Blue Roses! That's what I had on my tongue when you opened the door! Isn't it funny what tricks your memory plays? I didn't connect you with the high school somehow or other. But that's where it was; it was high school. I didn't even know you were Shakespeare's sister! Gosh, I'm sorry.

LAURA.  I didn't expect you to. You  barely knew me!

JIM.  But we did have a speaking acquaintance, huh?

LAURA.  Yes, we  spoke to each other.

JIM.  When did you recognize me?

LAURA.  Oh, right away!

JIM.  Soon as I came in the door?

LAURA.  When I heard your name I thought it was probably you. I knew that Tom used to know you a little in high school. So when you came in the door—Well, then I was—sure.

JIM.  Why didn't you *say* something, then?

LAURA (*breathlessly*).  I didn't know what to say, I was—too surprised!

JIM.  For goodness' sakes! You know, this sure is funny!

LAURA.  Yes! Yes, isn't it, though. . . .

JIM.  Didn't we have a class in something together?

LAURA.  Yes, we did.

JIM.  What class was that?

LAURA.  It was—singing—Chorus!

JIM.  Aw!

LAURA.  I sat across the aisle from you in the Aud.

JIM.  Aw.

LAURA.  Mondays, Wednesdays and Fridays.

JIM. Now I remember—you always came in late.

LAURA. Yes, it was so hard for me, getting upstairs. I had a brace on my leg—it clumped so loud!

JIM. I never heard any clumping.

LAURA (*wincing at the recollection*). To me it sounded like—thunder!

JIM. Well, well, well. I never even noticed.

LAURA. And everybody was seated before I came in. I had to walk in front of all those people. My seat was in the back row. I had to go clumping all the way up the aisle with everyone watching!

JIM. You shouldn't have been self-conscious.

LAURA. I know, but I was. It was always such a relief when the singing started.

JIM. Aw, yes, I've placed you now! I used to call you Blue Roses. How was it that I got started calling you that?

LAURA. I was out of school a little while with pleurosis. When I came back you asked me what was the matter. I said I had pleurosis—you thought I said Blue Roses. That's what you always called me after that!

JIM. I hope you didn't mind.

LAURA. Oh, no—I liked it. You see, I wasn't acquainted with many—people. . . .

JIM. As I remember you sort of stuck by yourself.

LAURA. I—I—never had much luck at—making friends.

JIM. I don't see why you wouldn't.

LAURA. Well, I—started out badly.

JIM. You mean being—

LAURA. Yes, it sort of—stood between me—

JIM. You shouldn't have let it!

LAURA. I know, but it did, and—

JIM. You were shy with people!

LAURA. I tried not to be but never could—

JIM. Overcome it?

LAURA. No, I—I never could!

JIM. I guess being shy is something you have to work out of kind of gradually.

LAURA (*sorrowfully*). Yes—I guess it—

JIM. Takes time!

LAURA. Yes—

JIM. People are not so dreadful when you know them. That's what you have to remember! And everybody has problems, not just you, but practically everybody has got some problems. You think of yourself as having the only problems, as being the only one who is disappointed. But just look around you and you will see lots of people as disappointed as you are. For instance, I hoped when I was going to high school that I would be further along at this time, six years after, than I am now—You remember that wonderful write-up I had in *The Torch?*

LAURA. Yes! (*She rises and crosses to table.*)

JIM. It said I was bound to succeed in anything I went into! (*Laura returns with the annual.*) Holy Jeez! *The Torch!* (*He accepts it reverently. They smile across it with mutual wonder.* LAURA *crouches beside him and they begin to turn through it.* LAURA'S *shyness is dissolving in his warmth.*)

LAURA. Here you are in *Pirates of Penzance!*

JIM (*wistfully*). I sang the baritone lead in that operetta.

LAURA (*rapidly*). So—*beautifully!*

JIM (*protesting*). Aw—

LAURA. Yes, yes—beautifully—beautifully!

JIM. You heard me?

LAURA. All three times!

JIM. No!

LAURA. Yes!

JIM. All three performances?

LAURA (*looking down*). Yes.

JIM. Why?

LAURA. I—wanted to ask you to—autograph my program.

JIM. Why didn't you ask me to?

LAURA. You were always surrounded by your own friends so much that I never had a chance to.

JIM. You should have just—

LAURA. Well, I—thought you might think I was—

JIM. Thought I might think you was —what?

LAURA. Oh—

JIM (*with reflective relish*). I was beleaguered by females in those days.

LAURA. You were terribly popular!

JIM. Yeah—

LAURA. You had such a—friendly way—

JIM. I was spoiled in high school.

LAURA. Everybody—liked you!

JIM. Including you?

LAURA. I—yes, I—I did, too—(*She gently closes the book in her lap.*)

JIM. Well, well, well!—Give me that program, Laura. (*She hands it to him. He signs it with a flourish.*) There you are—better late than never!

LAURA. Oh, I—what a—surprise!

JIM. My signature isn't worth very much right now. But some day— maybe—it will increase in value! Being disappointed is one thing and being discouraged is something else. I am disappointed but I'm not discouraged. I'm twenty-three years old. How old are you?

LAURA. I'll be twenty-four in June.

JIM. That's not old age!

LAURA. No, but—

JIM. You finished high school?

LAURA (*with difficulty*). I didn't go back.

JIM. You mean you dropped out?

LAURA. I made bad grades in my final examinations. (*She rises and re-places the book and the program. Her voice strained.*) How is— Emily Meisenbach getting along?

JIM. Oh, that kraut-head!

LAURA. Why do you call her that?

JIM. That's what she was.

LAURA. You're not still—going with her?

JIM. I never see her.

LAURA. It said in the Personal Section that you were—engaged!

JIM. I know, but I wasn't impressed by that—propaganda!

LAURA. It wasn't—the truth?

JIM. Only in Emily's optimistic opinion!

LAURA. Oh—

> (*Legend:"What Have You Done since High School?"*)
>
> JIM *lights a cigarette and leans indolently back on his elbows smiling at* LAURA *with a warmth and charm which light her inwardly with altar candles. She remains by the table and turns in her hands a piece of glass to cover her tumult.*

JIM (*after several reflective puffs on a cigarette*). What have you done since high school? (*She seems not to hear him.*) Huh? (LAURA *looks up.*) I said what have you done since high school, Laura?

LAURA. Nothing much.

JIM. You must have been doing something these six long years.

LAURA. Yes.

JIM. Well, then, such as what?

LAURA. I took a business course at business college—

JIM. How did that work out?

LAURA. Well, not very—well—I had to drop out, it gave me—indigestion—

> JIM *laughs gently.*

JIM. What are you doing now?

LAURA. I don't do anything—much. Oh, please don't think I sit around doing nothing! My glass collection takes up a good deal of my time. Glass is something you have to take good care of.

JIM. What did you say—about glass?

LAURA. Collection I said—I have one—(*She clears her throat and turns away again, acutely shy.*)

JIM (*abruptly*). You know what I judge to be the trouble with you? Inferiority complex! Know what that is? That's what they call it when someone low-rates himself! I understand it because I had it, too. Although my case was not so aggravated as yours seems to be. I had it until I took up public speaking, developed my voice, and learned that I had an aptitude for science. Before that time I never thought of myself as being outstanding in any way whatsoever! Now I've never made a regular study of it, but I have a friend who says I can analyze people better than doctors that make a profession of it. I don't claim that to be necessarily true, but I can sure guess a person's psychology, Laura! (*Takes out his gum.*) Excuse me, Laura. I always take it out when the flavor is gone. I'll use this scrap of paper to wrap it in. I know how it is to get it stuck on a shoe. Yep—that's what I judge to be your principal trouble. A lack of confidence in yourself as a person. You don't have the proper amount of faith in yourself. I'm basing that fact on a number of your remarks and also on certain observations I've made. For instance that clumping you thought was so awful in high school. You say that you even dreaded to walk into class. You see what you did? You dropped out of school, you gave up an education because of a clump, which as far as I know was practically nonexistent! A little physical defect is what you have. Hardly noticeable even! Magnified thousands of times by imagination! You know what my strong advice to you is? Think of yourself as *superior* in some way!

LAURA. In what way would I think?

JIM. Why, man alive, Laura! Just look about you a little. What do you see? A world full of common people! All of 'em born and all of 'em going to die! Which of them has one-tenth of your good points! Or mine! Or anyone else's, as far as that goes—Gosh! Everybody excels in some one thing. Some in many! (*Unconsciously glances at himself in the mirror.*) All you've got to do is discover in *what!* Take me, for instance. (*He adjusts his tie at the mirror.*) My interest happens to lie in electrodynamics. I'm taking a course in radio engineering at night school, Laura, on top of a fairly responsible job at the warehouse. I'm taking that course and studying public speaking.

LAURA. Ohhhh.

JIM. Because I believe in the future of television! (*Turning back to her.*) I wish to be ready to go up right along with it. Therefore I'm planning to get in on the ground floor. In fact, I've already made the right connections and all that remains is for the industry itself to get under way! Full steam—(*His eyes are starry.*) Knowledge—Zzzzzp! Money—Zzzzzzp!—Power! That's the cycle democracy is built on! (*His attitude is convincingly dynamic.* LAURA *stares at him, even her shyness eclipsed in her absolute wonder. He suddenly grins.*) I guess you think I think a lot of myself!

LAURA. No—o-o-o, I—

JIM. Now how about you? Isn't there something you take more interest in than anything else?

LAURA. Well, I do—as I said—have my—glass collection—

*A peal of girlish laughter from the kitchen.*

JIM.  I'm not right sure I know what you're talking about. What kind of glass is it?

LAURA.  Little articles of it, they're ornaments mostly! Most of them are little animals made out of glass, the tiniest little animals in the world. Mother calls them a glass menagerie! Here's an example of one, if you'd like to see it! This one is one of the oldest. It's nearly thirteen. (*He stretches out his hand.*) (*Music:"The Glass Menagerie."*) Oh, be careful—if you breathe, it breaks!

JIM.  I'd better not take it. I'm pretty clumsy with things.

LAURA.  Go on, I trust you with him! (*Places it in his palm.*) There now— you're holding him gently! Hold him over the light, he loves the light! You see how the light shines through him?

JIM.  It sure does shine!

LAURA.  I shouldn't be partial, but he is my favorite one.

JIM.  What kind of a thing is this one supposed to be?

LAURA.  Haven't you noticed the single horn on his forehead?

JIM.  A unicorn, huh?

LAURA.  Mmm-hmmm!

JIM.  Unicorns, aren't they extinct in the modern world?

LAURA.  I know!

JIM.  Poor little fellow, he must feel sort of lonesome.

LAURA (*smiling*).  Well, if he does he doesn't complain about it. He stays on a shelf with some horses that don't have horns and all of them seem to get along nicely together.

JIM.  How do you know?

LAURA (*lightly*).  I haven't heard any arguments among them!

JIM (*grinning*).  No arguments, huh? Well, that's a pretty good sign! Where shall I set him?

LAURA.  Put him on the table. They all like a change of scenery once in a while!

JIM (*stretching*).  Well, well, well, well—Look how big my shadow is when I stretch!

LAURA.  Oh, oh, yes—it stretches across the ceiling!

JIM (*crossing to door*).  I think it's stopped raining. (*Opens fire-escape door.*) Where does the music come from?

LAURA.  From the Paradise Dance Hall across the alley.

JIM.  How about cutting the rug a little, Miss Wingfield?

LAURA.  Oh, I—

JIM.  Or is your program filled up? Let me have a look at it. (*Grasps imaginary card.*) Why, every dance is taken! I'll just have to scratch some out. (*Waltz Music:"La Golondrina."*) Ahhh, a waltz! (*He executes some sweeping turns by himself then holds his arms toward* LAURA.)

LAURA (*breathlessly*). I—can't dance!

JIM. There you go, that inferiority stuff!

LAURA. I've never danced in my life!

JIM. Come on, try!

LAURA. Oh, but I'd step on you!

JIM. I'm not made out of glass.

LAURA. How—how—how do we start?

JIM. Just leave it to me. You hold your arms out a little.

LAURA. Like this?

JIM. A little bit higher. Right. Now don't tighten up, that's the main thing about it—relax.

LAURA (*laughing breathlessly*). It's hard not to.

JIM. Okay.

LAURA. I'm afraid you can't budge me.

JIM. What do you bet I can't? (*He swings her into motion.*)

LAURA. Goodness, yes, you can!

JIM. Let yourself go, now, Laura, just let yourself go.

LAURA. I'm—

JIM. Come on!

LAURA. Trying!

JIM. Not so stiff—Easy does it!

LAURA. I know but I'm—

JIM. Loosen th' backbone! There now, that's a lot better.

LAURA. Am I?

JIM. Lots, lots better! (*He moves her about the room in a clumsy waltz.*)

LAURA. Oh, my!

JIM. Ha-ha!

LAURA. Oh, my goodness!

JIM. Ha-ha-ha! (*They suddenly bump into the table. JIM stops.*) What did we hit on?

LAURA. Table.

JIM. Did something fall off it? I think—

LAURA. Yes.

JIM. I hope that it wasn't the little glass horse with the horn!

LAURA. Yes.

JIM. Aw, aw, aw. Is it broken?

LAURA. Now it is just like all the other horses.

JIM. It's lost its—

LAURA. Horn! It doesn't matter. Maybe it's a blessing in disguise.

JIM. You'll never forgive me. I bet that that was your favorite piece of glass.

LAURA. I don't have favorites much. It's no tragedy, Freckles. Glass breaks so easily. No matter how careful you are. The traffic jars the shelves and things fall off them.

JIM.  Still I'm awfully sorry that I was the cause.

LAURA  (*smiling*).  I'll just imagine he had an operation. The horn was removed to make him feel less—freakish! (*They both laugh.*) Now he will feel more at home with the other horses, the ones that don't have horns . . .

JIM.  Ha-ha, that's very funny! (*Suddenly serious.*) I'm glad to see that you have a sense of humor. You know—you're—well—very different! Surprisingly different from anyone else I know! (*His voice becomes soft and hesitant with a genuine feeling.*) Do you mind me telling you that? (LAURA *is abashed beyond speech.*) You make me feel sort of—I don't know how to put it! I'm usually pretty good at expressing things, but—This is something that I don't know how to say! (LAURA *touches her throat and clears it—turns the broken unicorn in her hands.*) (*Even softer.*) Has anyone ever told you that you were pretty? (*Pause: Music.*) (LAURA *looks up slowly, with wonder, and shakes her head.*) Well, you are! In a very different way from anyone else. And all the nicer because of the difference, too. (*His voice becomes low and husky.* LAURA *turns away, nearly faint with the novelty of her emotions.*) I wish that you were my sister. I'd teach you to have some confidence in yourself. The different people are not like other people, but being different is nothing to be ashamed of. Because other people are not such wonderful people. They're one hundred times one thousand. You're one times one! They walk all over the earth. You just stay here. They're common as—weeds, but—you—well, you're *Blue Roses!*

(*Image on Screen: Blue Roses.*)
(*Music Changes.*)

LAURA.  But blue is wrong for—roses . . .

JIM.  It's right for you—You're—pretty!

LAURA.  In what respect am I pretty?

JIM.  In all respects—believe me! Your eyes—your hair—are pretty! Your hands are pretty! (*He catches hold of her hand.*) You think I'm making this up because I'm invited to dinner and have to be nice. Oh, I could do that! I could put on an act for you, Laura, and say lots of things without being very sincere. But this time I am. I'm talking to you sincerely. I happened to notice you had this inferiority complex that keeps you from feeling comfortable with people. Somebody needs to build your confidence up and make you proud instead of shy and turning away and—blushing—Somebody ought to—ought to—*kiss* you. Laura! (*His hand slips slowly up her arm to her shoulder.*) (*Music Swells Tumultuously.*) (*He suddenly turns her about and kisses her on the lips. When he releases her* LAURA *sinks on the sofa with a bright, dazed look.* JIM *backs away and fishes in his pocket for a cigarette.*) (*Legend on Screen: "Souvenir."*) Stumble-john! (*He lights the cigarette, avoiding her look. There is a peal of girlish laughter from* AMANDA *in the kitchen.* LAURA *slowly raises and opens her hand. It still contains the little broken glass animal. She looks at it with a tender, bewildered expression.*) Stumble-john! I shouldn't have done that—That was way off the beam. You don't smoke, do you? (*She looks up, smiling, not hearing the question. He sits beside her a little gingerly. She looks at him speechlessly—waiting. He coughs decorously and moves a little farther aside as he considers the situation and senses her feelings, dimly, with perturbation. Gently.*) Would you—care for a—mint? (*She doesn't seem to hear him but her look grows brighter even.*) Peppermint—Life Saver? My pocket's a regular drug store—wherever I go . . . (*He pops a mint in his mouth. Then gulps and decides to make a clean breast of it. He speaks slowly and gingerly.*) Laura, you know, if I had a sister like you, I'd do the same thing as Tom. I'd bring out fellows—introduce her to them. The right type of boys—of a type to—appreciate her. Only—well—he made a mistake about me. Maybe I've got no call to be saying this. That may not have been the idea in having me over. But what if it was? There's nothing wrong about that. The only trouble is that in my case—I'm not in a situation to—do the right thing. I can't take down your number and say I'll phone. I can't call up next week and—ask for a date. I thought I had better explain the situation in case you misunderstood it and—hurt your feelings. . . . (*Pause. Slowly, very slowly,* LAURA'S *look changes, her eyes returning slowly from his to the ornament in her palm.*)

AMANDA *utters another gay laugh in the kitchen.*

LAURA (*faintly*). You—won't—call again?

JIM. No, Laura, I can't. (*He rises from the sofa.*) As I was just explaining, I've—got strings on me, Laura, I've—been going steady! I go out all the time with a girl named Betty. She's a home-girl like you, and Catholic, and Irish, and in a great many ways we—get along fine. I met her last summer on a moonlight boat trip up the river to Alton, on the *Majestic.* Well—right away from the start it was—love! (*Legend: Love!*) (LAURA *sways slightly forward and grips the arm of the sofa. He fails to notice, now enrapt in his own comfortable being.*) Being in love has made a new man of me! (*Leaning stiffly forward, clutching the arm of the sofa,* LAURA *struggles visibly with her storm. But* JIM *is oblivious, she is a long way off.*) The power of love is really pretty tremendous! Love is something that—changes the whole world, Laura! (*The storm abates a little and* LAURA *leans back. He notices her again.*) It happened that Betty's aunt took sick, she got a wire and had to go to Centralia. So Tom—when he asked me to dinner—I naturally just accepted the invitation, not knowing that you—that he—that I—(*He stops awkwardly.*) Huh—I'm a stumble-john! (*He flops back on the sofa. The holy candles in the altar of*

LAURA's *face have been snuffed out! There is a look of almost infinite desolation.* JIM *glances at her uneasily.*) I wish that you would—say something. (*She bites her lip which was trembling and then bravely smiles. She opens her hand again on the broken glass ornament. Then she gently takes his hand and raises it level with her own. She carefully places the unicorn in the palm of his hand, then pushes his fingers closed upon it.*) What are you—doing that for? You want me to have him?—Laura? (*She nods.*) What for?

LAURA.  A—souvenir . . .

*She rises unsteadily and crouches beside the victrola to wind it up.*
    (*Legend on Screen: "Things Have a Way of Turning Out So Badly."*)
    (*Or Image: "Gentleman Caller Waving Good-Bye!—Gaily."*)
    *At this moment* AMANDA *rushes brightly back in the front room. She bears a pitcher of fruit punch in an old-fashioned cut-glass pitcher and a plate of macaroons. The plate has a gold border and poppies painted on it.*

AMANDA.  Well, well, well! Isn't the air delightful after the shower? I've made you children a little liquid refreshment. (*Turns gaily to the gentleman caller.*) Jim, do you know that song about lemonade?

    "Lemonade, lemonade
    Made in the shade and stirred with a spade—
    Good enough for any old maid!"

JIM (*uneasily*).  Ha-ha! No—I never heard it.
AMANDA.  Why, Laura! You look so serious!
JIM.  We were having a serious conversation.
AMANDA.  Good! Now you're better acquainted!
JIM (*uncertainly*).  Ha-ha! Yes.
AMANDA.  You modern young people are much more serious-minded than my generation. I was so gay as a girl!
JIM.  You haven't changed, Mrs. Wingfield.
AMANDA.  Tonight I'm rejuvenated! The gaiety of the occasion, Mr. O'Connor! (*She tosses her head with a peal of laughter. Spills lemonade.*) Oooo! I'm baptizing myself!
JIM.  Here—let me—
AMANDA (*setting the pitcher down*).  There now. I discovered we had some maraschino cherries. I dumped them in, juice and all!
JIM.  You shouldn't have gone to that trouble, Mrs. Wingfield.
AMANDA.  Trouble, trouble? Why it was loads of fun! Didn't you hear me cutting up in the kitchen? I bet your ears were burning! I told Tom how outdone with him I was for keeping you to himself so long a time! He should have brought you over much, much sooner! Well, now that you've found your way, I want you to be a very frequent

caller! Not just occasional but all the time. Oh, we're going to have a lot of gay times together! I see them coming! Mmm, just breathe that air! So fresh, and the moon's so pretty! I'll skip back out—I know where my place is when young folks are having a—serious conversation!

JIM.   Oh, don't go out, Mrs. Wingfield. The fact of the matter is I've got to be going.

AMANDA.   Going, now? You're joking! Why, it's only the shank of the evening, Mr. O'Connor!

JIM.   Well, you know how it is.

AMANDA.   You mean you're a young workingman and have to keep workingmen's hours. We'll let you off early tonight. But only on the condition that next time you stay later. What's the best night for you? Isn't Saturday night the best night for you workingmen?

JIM.   I have a couple of time-clocks to punch, Mrs. Wingfield. One at morning, another one at night!

AMANDA.   My, but you *are* ambitious! You work at night, too?

JIM.   No, Ma'am, not work but—Betty! (*He crosses deliberately to pick up his hat. The band at the Paradise Dance Hall goes into a tender waltz.*)

AMANDA.   Betty? Betty? Who's—Betty! (*There is an ominous cracking sound in the sky.*)

JIM.   Oh, just a girl. The girl I go steady with! (*He smiles charmingly. The sky falls.*)

(*Legend: "The Sky Falls."*)

AMANDA (*a long-drawn exhalation*).   Ohhhh . . . Is it a serious romance, Mr. O'Connor?

JIM.   We're going to be married the second Sunday in June.

AMANDA.   Ohhhh—how nice! Tom didn't mention that you were engaged to be married.

JIM.   The cat's not out of the bag at the warehouse yet. You know how they are. They call you Romeo and stuff like that. (*He stops at the oval mirror to put on his hat. He carefully shapes the brim and the crown to give a discreetly dashing effect.*) It's been a wonderful evening, Mrs. Wingfield. I guess this is what they mean by Southern hospitality.

AMANDA.   It really wasn't anything at all.

JIM.   I hope it don't seem like I'm rushing off. But I promised Betty I'd pick her up at the Wabash depot, an' by the time I get my jalopy down there her train'll be in. Some women are pretty upset if you keep 'em waiting.

AMANDA.   Yes, I know—The tyranny of women! (*Extends her hand.*) Goodbye, Mr. O'Connor. I wish you luck—and happiness—and success! All three of them, and so does Laura!—Don't you, Laura?

LAURA.   Yes!

JIM (*taking her hand*). Goodbye, Laura. I'm certainly going to treasure that souvenir. And don't you forget the good advice I gave you. (*Raises his voice to a cheery shout.*) So long, Shakespeare! Thanks again, ladies—good night!

*He grins and ducks jauntily out.*

*Still bravely grimacing,* AMANDA *closes the door on the gentleman caller. Then she turns back to the room with a puzzled expression. She and* LAURA *don't dare to face each other.* LAURA *crouches beside the victrola to wind it.*

AMANDA (*faintly*). Things have a way of turning out so badly. I don't believe that I would play the victrola. Well, well—well—Our gentleman caller was engaged to be married! Tom!

TOM (*from back*). Yes, Mother?

AMANDA. Come in here a minute. I want to tell you something awfully funny.

TOM (*enters with macaroon and a glass of the lemonade*). Has the gentleman caller gotten away already?

AMANDA. The gentleman caller has made an early departure. What a wonderful joke you played on us!

TOM. How do you mean?

AMANDA. You didn't mention that he was engaged to be married.

TOM. Jim? Engaged?

AMANDA. That's what he just informed us.

TOM. I'll be jiggered! I didn't know about that.

AMANDA. That seems very peculiar.

TOM. What's peculiar about it?

AMANDA. Didn't you call him your best friend down at the warehouse?

TOM. He is, but how did I know?

AMANDA. It seems extremely peculiar that you wouldn't know your best friend was going to be married!

TOM. The warehouse is where I work, not where I know things about people!

AMANDA. You don't know things anywhere! You live in a dream; you manufacture illusions! (*He crosses to door.*) Where are you going?

TOM. I'm going to the movies.

AMANDA. That's right, now that you've had us make such fools of ourselves. The effort, the preparations, all the expense! The new floor lamp, the rug, the clothes for Laura! All for what? To entertain some other girl's fiancé! Go to the movies, go! Don't think about us, a mother deserted, an unmarried sister who's crippled and has no job! Don't let anything interfere with your selfish pleasure! Just go, go, go—to the movies!

TOM. All right, I will! The more you shout about my selfishness to me the quicker I'll go, and I won't go to the movies!

AMANDA.  Go, then! Then go to the moon—you selfish dreamer!

> TOM *smashes his glass on the floor. He plunges out on the fire-escape, slamming the door.* LAURA *screams—cut by door.*
> *Dance-hall music up.* TOM *goes to the rail and grips it desperately, lifting his face in the chill white moonlight penetrating the narrow abyss of the alley.*
> (*Legend on Screen:"And So Good-Bye . . ."*)
> TOM'S *closing speech is timed with the interior pantomime. The interior scene is played as though viewed through sound-proof glass.* AMANDA *appears to be making a comforting speech to* LAURA *who is huddled upon the sofa. Now that we cannot hear the mother's speech, her silliness is gone and she has dignity and tragic beauty.* LAURA'S *dark hair hides her face until at the end of the speech she lifts it to smile at her mother.* AMANDA'S *gestures are slow and graceful, almost dancelike, as she comforts the daughter. At the end of her speech she glances a moment at the father's picture— then withdraws through the portieres. At close of* TOM'S *speech,* LAURA *blows out the candles, ending the play.*

TOM.  I didn't go to the moon, I went much further—for time is the longest distance between two places—Not long after that I was fired for writing a poem on the lid of a shoe-box. I left Saint Louis. I descended the steps of this fire-escape for a last time and followed, from then on, in my father's footsteps, attempting to find in motion what was lost in space—I traveled around a great deal. The cities swept about me like dead leaves, leaves that were brightly colored but torn away from the branches. I would have stopped, but I was pursued by something. It al ways came upon me unawares, taking me altogether by surprise. Perhaps it was a familiar bit of music. Perhaps it was only a piece of transparent glass—Perhaps I am walking along a street at night, in some strange city, before I have found companions. I pass the lighted window of a shop where perfume is sold. The window is filled with pieces of colored glass, tiny transparent bottles in delicate colors, like bits of a shattered rainbow. Then all at once my sister touches my shoulder. I turn around and look into her eyes . . . Oh, Laura, Laura, I tried to leave you behind me, but I am more faithful than I intended to be! I reach for a cigarette, I cross the street, I run into the movies or a bar, I buy a drink, I speak to the nearest stranger—anything that can blow your candles out! (LAURA *bends over the candles.*)—for nowadays the world is lit by lightning! Blow out your candles, Laura—and so goodbye . . .

She blows the candles out.

(*The Scene Dissolves.*)

# A CONTEXT FOR
# *THE GLASS MENAGERIE*

## TENNESSEE WILLIAMS

### *Production Notes*

[1944]

Being a "memory play," *The Glass Menagerie* can be presented with unusual freedom of convention. Because of its considerably delicate or tenuous material, atmospheric touches and subtleties of direction play a particularly important part. Expressionism and all other unconventional techniques in drama have only one valid aim, and that is a closer approach to truth. When a play employs unconventional techniques, it is not, or certainly shouldn't be, trying to escape its responsibility of dealing with reality, or interpreting experience, but is actually or should be attempting to find a closer approach, a more penetrating and vivid expression of things as they are. The straight realistic play with its genuine frigidaire and authentic ice cubes, its characters that speak exactly as its audience speaks, corresponds to the academic landscape and has the same virtue of a photographic likeness. Everyone should know nowadays the unimportance of the photographic in art: that truth, life, or reality is an organic thing which the poetic imagination can represent or suggest, in essence, only through transformation, through changing into other forms than those which were merely present in appearance.

These remarks are not meant as comments only on this particular play. They have to do with a conception of a new, plastic theater which must take the place of the exhausted theater of realistic conventions if the theater is to resume vitality as a part of our culture.

### *The Screen Device*

There is *only one important difference between the original and acting version of the play* and that is the *omission* in the latter of the device which I tentatively included in my *original* script. This device was the use of a screen on which were projected magic-lantern slides bearing images or titles. I do not regret the omission of this device from the . . . Broadway production. The extraordinary power of Miss Taylor's performance made it suitable to have the utmost simplicity in the physical production. But I think it may be interesting to some readers to see how this device was conceived. So I am putting it into the published manuscript. These images and legends, projected from behind, were cast on a section of wall between the front-room and dining-room areas, which should be indistinguishable from the rest when not in use.

The purpose of this will probably be apparent. It is to give accent to certain values in each scene. Each scene contains a particular point (or several) which is structurally the most important. In an episodic play, such as this, the basic structure or narrative line may be obscured from the audience; the effect may seem fragmentary rather than architectural. This may not be the fault of the play so much as a lack of attention in the audience. The legend or image upon the screen will strengthen the effect of what is merely allusion in the writing and allow the primary point to be made more simply and lightly than if the entire responsibility were on the spoken lines. Aside from this structural value, I think the screen will have a definite emotional appeal, less definable but just as important. An imaginative producer or director may invent many other uses for this device than those indicated in the present script. In fact the possibilities of the device seem much larger to me than the instance of this play can possibly utilize.

## The Music

Another extra-literary accent in this play is provided by the use of music. A single recurring tune, "The Glass Menagerie," is used to give emotional emphasis to suitable passages. This tune is like circus music, not when you are on the grounds or in the immediate vicinity of the parade, but when you are at some distance and very likely thinking of something else. It seems under those circumstances to continue almost interminably and it weaves in and out of your preoccupied consciousness; then it is the lightest, most delicate music in the world and perhaps the saddest. It expresses the surface vivacity of life with the underlying strain of immutable and inexpressible sorrow. When you look at a piece of delicately spun glass you think of two things: how beautiful it is and how easily it can be broken. Both of those ideas should be woven into the recurring tune, which dips in and out of the play as if it were carried on a wind that changes. It serves as a thread of connection and allusion between the narrator with his separate point in time and space and the subject of his story. Between each episode it returns as reference to the emotion, nostalgia, which is the first condition of the play. It is primarily Laura's music and therefore comes out most clearly when the play focuses upon her and the lovely fragility of glass which is her image.

## The Lighting

The lighting in the play is not realistic. In keeping with the atmosphere of memory, the stage is dim. Shafts of light are focused on selected areas or actors, sometimes in contradistinction to what is the apparent center. For instance, in the quarrel scene between Tom and Amanda, in which Laura has no active part, the clearest pool of light is on her figure. This is also true of the supper scene. The light upon Laura should be distinct from the others, having a peculiar pristine clarity such as light used in early religious portraits of female saints or madonnas. A certain correspondence to light in religious paintings, such as El Greco's, where the figures are radiant in atmosphere that is relatively dusky, could be effectively used throughout the play. (It will also permit a more effective use of the screen.) A free, imaginative use of light can be of enormous value in giving a mobile, plastic quality to plays of a more or less static nature.

## ▓ TOPICS FOR
## CRITICAL THINKING AND WRITING
### *The Play on the Page*

1. What does the victrola offer to Laura? Why is the typewriter a better symbol (for the purposes of the play) than, for example, a piano? After all, Laura could have been taking piano lessons.

2. What do you understand of Laura's glass menagerie? Why is it especially significant that the unicorn is Laura's favorite? How do you interpret the loss of the unicorn's horn? What is Laura saying to Jim in the gesture of giving him the unicorn?

3. Laura escapes to her glass menagerie. To what do Tom and Amanda escape? How complete do you think Tom's escape is at the end of the play?

4. Jim is described as "a nice, ordinary young man." To what extent can it be said that he, like the Wingfields, lives in a dream world? Tom says (speaking of the time of the play, 1939) that "The huge middle class was matriculating in a school for the blind." Does the play suggest that Jim, apparently a spokesperson for the American dream, is one of the pupils in this school?

5. There is an implication that had Jim not been going steady he might have rescued Laura, but Jim also seems to represent (for example, in his lines about money and power) the corrupt outside world that no longer values humanity. Is this a slip on Williams's part, or is it an interesting complexity?

6. How do you interpret the episode at the end when Laura blows out the candles? Is she blowing out illusions? her own life? both? Explain.

7. Some readers have seen great importance in the religious references in the play. To cite only a few examples: Scene 5 is called (on the screen) "Annunciation"; Amanda is associated with the music "Ave Maria"; Laura's candelabrum, from the altar of the Church of Heavenly Rest, was melted out of shape when the church burned down. Do you think these references add up to anything? If so, to what?

8. On page 695, Williams says, in a stage direction, *"Now that we cannot hear the mother's speech, her silliness is gone and she has dignity*

*and tragic beauty."* Is Williams simply dragging in the word "tragic" because of its prestige, or is it legitimate? *Tragedy* is often distinguished from *pathos*: in tragedy, suffering is experienced by persons who act and are in some measure responsible for their suffering; in pathos, suffering is experienced by the passive and the innocent. For example, in discussion *The Suppliants,* a play by the ancient Greek dramatist Aeschylus, H. D. F. Kitto (in *Greek Tragedy*) says, "The Suppliants are not only pathetic, as the victims of outrage, but also tragic, as the victims of their own misconceptions." Given this distinction, to what extent are Amanda and Laura tragic? pathetic? You might take into account the following quote from an interview with Williams, reprinted in *Conversations with Tennessee Williams* (ed. Albert J. Devlin): "The mother's valor is the core of *The Glass Menagerie....* She's confused, pathetic, even stupid, but everything has *got* to be all right. She fights to make it that way in the only way she knows how."

9. Before writing *The Glass Menagerie,* Williams wrote a short story with the same plot, "Portrait of a Girl in Glass" (later published in his *Collected Stories*). You may want to compare the two works, noticing especially the ways in which Williams has turned a story into a play.

## The Play on the Stage

10. In what ways is the setting relevant to the issues raised in the play?
11. In his Production Notes (page 696) Williams called for the use of a "screen device." Over the years, some productions have incorporated it and some have not. If you were involved in producing *The Glass Menagerie,* would you use this device? Explain your reasons
12. As director, would you want the actress playing Laura to limp? Give reasons for your decision, and provide additional comments on the ways in which you would ask an actress to portray the role.
13. List the various emotions that you find for Amanda in Scenes 2 and 3. If you were advising an actress playing this role, how would you suggest she convey these different feelings? Following are some questions to consider: In what ways does she reveal her own sadnesses? Should her speeches to Tom be delivered differently from her speeches to Laura? When she looks at Laura's yearbook, should there be any physical contact between the two women? What effect would you wish to achieve at the close of Scene 3?
14. At the end of Scene 5, after an exasperated exchange between Tom and Amanda, Laura and her mother make a wish on the new moon. Three students can memorize this brief section and present it to the group. Then examine each speech, and discuss its emotion. Offer suggestions to the three actors—for instance, changes in emphasis, a slight difference in tone, a certain stance for the mother and daughter—and repeat the scene.

# 25

# In Brief:
# Writing Arguments
# about Drama

Perhaps more evidently than stories or poems, plays themselves are writings that offer arguments. Characters, pitted against other characters, are likely to try to justify their behavior. At the end of *Othello,* for instance, the protagonist offers an account of his behavior—an account that some readers and spectators find convincing and emotionally satisfying, but that others find self-deluded and emotionally unsatisfying. Essays about plays often set forth highly controversial positions, for instance, "The women in Glaspell's *Trifles* are justified in concealing evidence of the murder," or, to take a more nuanced position, "Although viewers can scarcely approve of withholding evidence of murder, in Glaspell's *Trifles* viewers probably approve for three reasons: First,...., second,..., and third...."

Assertions of a thesis will interest readers only if they are supported by evidence. In all probability you can find a thesis by examining your basic responses, or by scanning the questions we give below, but almost certainly you will modify this thesis during the course of your reexamination of the play. Thinking skeptically about *your own* assertions is the heart of critical thinking, and critical thinking is at the heart of writing an effective argument. It is not, however, the *whole* of writing an argument. Once you have drafted your argument, and you are satisfied with the position that you have taken, you still need to make sure that you set forth this position effectively, in words that will engage your readers.

The following questions may help you to formulate ideas for an essay on a play.

# PLOT AND CONFLICT

1. Does the exposition introduce elements that will be ironically fulfilled? During the exposition do you perceive things differently from the way the characters perceive them?
2. Are certain happenings or situations recurrent? If so, what significance do you attach to them?
3. If there is more than one plot, do the plots seem to you to be related? Is one plot clearly the main plot and another plot a subplot, a minor variation on the theme?
4. Do any scenes strike you as irrelevant?
5. Are certain scenes so strongly foreshadowed that you anticipated them? If so, did the happenings in these scenes merely fulfill your expectations, or did they also in some way surprise you?
6. What kinds of conflict are there? One character against another, one group against another, one part of a personality against another part in the same person?
7. How is the conflict resolved? By an unambiguous triumph of one side or by a triumph that is also in some degree a loss for the triumphant side? Do you find the resolution satisfying, or unsettling, or what? Why?

# CHARACTER

1. A dramatic character is not likely to be thoroughly realistic, a copy of someone we might know. Still, we can ask if the character is consistent and coherent. We can also ask if the character is complex or is, on the other hand, a simple representative of some human type.
2. How is the character defined? Consider what the character says and does and what others say about him or her and do to him or her. Also consider other characters who more or less resemble the character in question, because the similarities—and the differences—may be significant.
3. How trustworthy are the characters when they characterize themselves? When they characterize others?
4. Do characters change as the play goes on, or do we simply know them better at the end?
5. What do you make of the minor characters? Are they merely necessary to the plot, or are they foils to other characters? Or do they serve some other functions?

6. If a character is tragic, does the tragedy seem to you to proceed from a moral flaw, from an intellectual error, from the malice of others, from sheer chance, or from some combination of these?
7. What are the character's goals? To what degree do you sympathize with them? If a character is comic, do you laugh *with* or *at* the character?
8. Do you think the characters are adequately motivated?
9. Is a given character so meditative that you feel he or she is engaged less in a dialogue with others than in a dialogue with the self? If so, do you feel that this character is in large degree a spokesperson for the author, commenting not only on the world of the play but also on the outside world?

# TRAGEDY

1. What causes the tragedy? A flaw in the central character? A mistake (*not* the same thing as a flaw) made by this character? An outside force, such as another character, or fate?
2. Is the tragic character defined partly by other characters, for instance, by characters who help us to sense what the character *might* have done, or who in some other way reveal the strengths or weaknesses of the protagonist?
3. Does a viewer know more than the tragic figure knows? More than most or all of the characters know?
4. Does the tragic character achieve any sort of wisdom at the end of the play?
5. To what degree do you sympathize with the tragic character?
6. Is the play depressing? If not, why not?

# COMEDY

1. Do the comic complications arise chiefly out of the personalities of the characters (for instance, pretentiousness or amorousness), or out of the situations (for instance, mistaken identity)?
2. What are the chief goals of the figures? Do we sympathize with these goals, or do we laugh at persons who pursue them? If we laugh, *why* do we laugh?
3. What are the personalities of those who oppose the central characters? Do we laugh at them, or do we sympathize with them?
4. What is funny about the play? Is the comedy high (including verbal comedy) or chiefly situational and physical?

5. Is the play predominantly genial, or is there a strong satiric tone?
6. Does the comedy have any potentially tragic elements in it? Might the plot be slightly rewritten so that it would become a tragedy?
7. What, if anything, do the characters learn by the end of the play?

# NONVERBAL LANGUAGE

1. If the playwright does not provide full stage directions, try to imagine for at least one scene what gestures and tones might accompany each speech. (The first scene is usually a good one to try your hand at.)
2. What do you make of the setting? Does it help to reveal character? Do changes of scene strike you as symbolic? If so, symbolic of what?
3. Do certain costumes (dark suits, flowery shawls, stiff collars, etc.) or certain properties (books, pictures, toys, candlesticks, etc.) strike you as symbolic? If so, symbolic of what?

# THE PLAY IN PERFORMANCE

Often we can gain a special pleasure from, or insight into, a dramatic work when we actually see it produced onstage or made into a film. This gives us an opportunity to think about the choices that the director has made, and, even more, it may prompt us to imagine and ponder how we would direct the play for the theater or make a film version of it ourselves.

1. If you have seen the play in the theater or in a film version, what has been added? What has been omitted? Why?
2. In the case of a film, has the film medium been used to advantage—for example, in focusing attention through close-ups or reaction shots (shots showing not the speaker but a person reacting to the speaker)?
3. Do certain plays seem to be especially suited—maybe *only* suited—to the stage? Would they not work effectively as films? Is the reverse true: Are some plays best presented, and best understood, when they are done as films?
4. Critics have sometimes said about this or that play that it cannot really be staged successfully or presented well on film—that the best way to appreciate and understand it is as something to be *read,* like a poem or novel. Are there plays you have studied for which this observation appears to hold true? Which features of the work—its characters, settings, dialogue, central themes—might make it difficult to transfer the play from the page to the stage or to the movie screen?

5. Imagine that you are directing the play. What would be the important decisions you would have to make about character, setting, and pacing of the action? Would you be inclined to omit certain scenes? To add new scenes that are not in the work itself? What kinds of advice would you give to the performers about their roles?

# A SAMPLE STUDENT ESSAY, USING SOURCES

In Appendix A we discuss manuscript form (page 1112) and in Appendix B the use of sources (page 1118) and documentation (page 1130). Here we give a student's documented paper on Arthur Miller's *Death of a Salesman*. (The play appears in this book on page 725.) The student of course had taken notes on index cards, both from the play and from secondary sources, and had arranged and rearranged the notes as her topic and thesis became clearer to her. We preface the final version of her essay with the rough outline that she prepared before she wrote her first draft.

```
Linda
    realistic
    encourages Willy
    foolish? loving?        Both? Not so foolish; Knows how to calm
    prevented him from succeeding?              him down
    doesn't understand W's needs? or nothing else to
      do?
    quote some critics knocking Linda

    other women
5   the Woman
4   the two women in restaurant  (Forsythe first, then Letta)
3   Jenny
2   W's mother (compare with father?)
      check to see exactly what the play says about her
1   Howard's wife (and daughter?)  (discuss this first)
6   discuss Linda last
    titles?
      Linda Loman
      Women in Miller's Salesman
      Gender in . . .           Male and Female in Death . . .
    Men and Women: Arthur M's View
      Willy Loman's Women
```

Here is the final version of the essay.

Ruth Katz
Professor Ling
English 102
10 December 2005

The Women in Death of a Salesman
    Death of a Salesman is of course about a
salesman, but it is also about the American
dream of success. Somewhere in between the
narrowest topic, the death of a salesman,
and the largest topic, the examination of
American values, is Miller's picture of the
American family. This paper will chiefly
study one member of the family, Willy's
wife, Linda Loman, but before examining
Miller's depiction of her, it will look
at Miller's depiction of other women in
the play in order to make clear Linda's
distinctive traits. We will see that
although her role in society is extremely
limited, she is an admirable figure,
fulfilling the roles of wife and mother
with remarkable intelligence.
    Linda is the only woman who is on stage
much of the time, but there are several
other women in the play: "the Woman" (the
unnamed woman in Willy's hotel room), Miss
Forsythe and her friend Letta (the two women
who join the brothers in the restaurant),
Jenny (Charley's secretary), the various
women that the brothers talk about, and the

Katz 2

voices of Howard's daughter and wife. We
also hear a little about Willy's mother.

   We will look first at the least
important (but not utterly unimportant) of
these, the voices of Howard's daughter and
wife on the wire recorder. Of Howard's
seven-year-old daughter we know only that
she can whistle "Roll Out the Barrel" and
that according to Howard she "is crazy
about me." The other woman in Howard's life
is equally under his thumb. Here is the
dialogue that tells us about her--and her
relation to her husband.

       HOWARD'S VOICE. "Go on, say
            something." (Pause.) "Well, you
            gonna talk?"
       HIS WIFE. "I can't think of anything."
       HOWARD'S VOICE. "Well, talk--it's
            turning."
       HIS WIFE. (shyly, beaten). "Hello."
            (Silence.) "Oh, Howard, I can't
            talk into this . . . "
       HOWARD. (snapping the machine off).
            That was my wife. (764-65)

There is, in fact, a third woman in Howard's
life, the maid. Howard says that if he can't
be at home when the Jack Benny program comes
on, he uses the wire recorder. He tells "the
maid to turn the radio on when Jack Benny
comes on, and this automatically goes on
with the radio. . . ." (765). In short, the

women in Howard's world exist to serve (and
to worship) him.

Another woman who seems to have existed
only to serve men is Willy Loman's mother.
On one occasion, in speaking with Ben,
Willy remembers being on her lap, and Ben,
on learning that his mother is dead, utters
a platitudinous description of her, "Fine
specimen of a lady, Mother" (747), but
that's as much as we learn of her. Willy
is chiefly interested in learning about
his father, who left the family and went
to Alaska. Ben characterizes the father as
"a very great and a very wild-hearted man"
(748), but the fact that the father left
his family and apparently had no further
communication with his wife and children
seems to mean nothing to Ben. Presumably
the mother struggled alone to bring up
the boys, but her efforts are unmentioned.
Curiously, some writers defend the father's
desertion of his family. Lois Gordon says,
"The first generation (Willy's father) has
been forced, in order to make a living, to
break up the family" (278), but nothing in
the play supports this assertion that the
father was "forced" to break up the family.

Willy, like Ben, assumes that men are
heroic and women are nothing except
servants and sex machines. For instance,
Willy says to Ben, "Please tell about Dad.

Katz 4

I want my boys to hear. I want them to know
the kind of stock they spring from" (748).
As Kay Stanton, a feminist critic says,
Willy's words imply "an Edenic birth myth,"
a world "with all the Loman men springing
directly from their father's side, with no
commingling with a female" (69).

Another woman who, like Howard's maid
and Willy's mother, apparently exists only
to serve is Jenny, Charley's secretary. She
is courteous, and she is treated courteously
by Charley and by Charley's son, Bernard,
but she has no identity other than that of
a secretary. And, as a secretary--that is,
as a nonentity in the eyes of at least some
men--she can be addressed insensitively.
Willy Loman makes off-color remarks to her:

> WILLY. . . . . Jenny, Jenny, good to see
>     you. How're ya? Workin'? Or still
>     honest?
> JENNY. Fine. How've you been feeling?
> WILLY. Not much any more, Jenny.
>     Ha, ha! (772)

The first of these comments seems to
suggest that a working woman is not honest
--that is, is a prostitute or is engaged in
some other sort of hanky-panky, as is the
Woman who in exchange for silk stockings
and sex sends Willy directly into the
buyer's office. The second of Willy's
jokes, with its remark about not feeling
much, also refers to sex. In short, though

readers or viewers of the play see Jenny as
a thoroughly respectable woman, they see
her not so much as an individual but as a
person engaged in routine work and as a
person to whom Willy can speak crudely.

It is a little harder to be certain
about the characters of Miss Forsythe
and Letta, the two women in the scene in
Stanley's restaurant. For Happy, Miss
Forsythe is "strudel," an object for a man
to consume, and for Stanley she and her
friend Letta are "chippies," that is,
prostitutes. But is it clear that they are
prostitutes? When Happy tells Miss Forsythe
that he is in the business of selling, he
makes a dirty joke, saying, "You don't
happen to sell, do you?" (778). She
replies, "No, I don't sell," and if we
take this seriously and if we believe her,
we can say that she is respectable and
is rightly putting Happy in his place.
Further, her friend Letta says, "I gotta
get up very early tomorrow. I got jury
duty" (785), which implies that she is a
responsible citizen. Still, the girls do
not seem especially thoughtful. When Biff
introduces Willy to the girls, Letta says,
"Isn't he cute? Sit down with us, Pop"
(785), and when Willy breaks down in the
restaurant, Miss Forsythe says, "Say,
I don't like that temper of his" (786).
Perhaps we can say this: It is going too

far--on the basis of what we see--to agree
with Stanley that the women are "chippies,"
or with Happy, who assumes that every woman
is available for sex, but Miss Forsythe
and Letta do not seem to be especially
responsible or even interesting people.
That is, as Miller presents them, they
are of little substance, simply figures
introduced into the play in order to show
how badly Happy and Biff behave.

The most important woman in the play,
other than Linda, is "the Woman," who for
money or stockings and perhaps for pleasure
has sex with Willy, and who will use her
influence as a receptionist or secretary
in the office to send Willy directly on to
the buyer, without his having to wait at
the desk. But even though the Woman gets
something out of the relationship, she
knows that she is being used. When Biff
appears in the hotel room, she asks him,
"Are you football or baseball?" Biff
replies, "Football," and the Woman, "angry,
humiliated," says, "That's me too" (789).
We can admire her vigorous response, but,
again, like the other women whom we have
discussed, she is not really an impressive
figure. We can say that, at best, in a
society that assumes women are to be
exploited by men, she holds her own.

So far, then--though we have not yet
talked about Linda--the world of Death of a

<u>Salesman</u> is not notable for its pictures of impressive women. True, most of the males in the play--Willy, Biff, Happy, Ben, and such lesser characters as Stanley and Howard--are themselves pretty sorry specimens, but Bernard and Charley are exceptionally decent and successful people, people who can well serve as role models. Can any female character in the play serve as a role model?

Linda has evoked strongly contrasting reactions from the critics. Some of them judge her very severely. For instance, Lois Gordon says that Linda "encourages Willy's dream, yet she will not let him leave her for the New Continent, the only realm where the dream can be fulfilled" (280). True, Linda urges Willy not to follow Ben's advice of going to Alaska, but surely the spectator of the play cannot believe that Willy is the sort of man who can follow in Ben's footsteps and violently make a fortune. And, in fact, Ben is so vile a person (as when he trips Biff, threatens Biff's eye with the point of his umbrella, and says, "Never fight fair with a stranger, boy" [749]), that we would not want Willy to take Ben's advice.

A second example of a harsh view of Linda is Brian Parker's comment on "the essential stupidity of Linda's behavior. Surely it is both stupid and immoral to encourage the man you love in self-deceit and lies" (54). Parker also says that Linda's speech at the end, when she says she cannot understand why Willy killed himself, "is not only pathetic, it is also an explanation of the loneliness of Willy Loman which threw him into other women's arms" (54). Nothing in the play suggests that Linda was anything other than a highly supportive wife. If Willy turned to other women, surely it was not because Linda did not understand him. Finally, one last example of the Linda-bashing school of commentary: Guerin Bliquez speaks of "Linda's facility for prodding Willy to his doom" (383).

Very briefly, the arguments against Linda are that (1) she selfishly prevented Willy from going to Alaska, (2) she stupidly encourages him in his self-deceptions, and (3) she is materialistic, so that even at the end, in the Requiem, when she says she has made the last payment on the house, she is talking about money. But if we study the play we will see that all three of these charges are false. First, although Linda does indeed discourage Willy from taking Ben's advice and going to Alaska, she points out that there is no need for "everybody [to] conquer the world" and that Willy has "a beautiful job here" (769), a job with excellent prospects. She may be mistaken in thinking that Willy has

a good job--he may have misled her--but,
given what seems to be the situation, her
comment is entirely reasonable. So far as
the second charge goes, that she encourages
him in self-deception, there are two
answers. First, on some matters she does
not know that Willy has lied to her, and so
her encouragement is reasonable and right.
Second, on other matters she does know
that Willy is not telling the truth, but
she rightly thinks it is best not to let
him know that she knows, since such a
revelation would crush what little self-
respect remains in him. Consider, for
example, this portion of dialogue, early in
the play, when Willy, deeply agitated about
his failure to drive and about Biff, has
returned from what started out as a trip to
Boston. Linda, trying to take his mind off
his problems, urges him to go downstairs to
the kitchen to try a new kind of cheese:

> LINDA. Go down, try it. And be quiet.
> WILLY. (<u>turning to Linda, guiltily</u>).
> You're not worried about me, are you,
>    sweetheart?
>
>                 . . .
>
> LINDA. You've got too much on the
>    ball to worry about.
> WILLY. You're my foundation and my
>    support, Linda.
> LINDA. Just try to relax, dear. You
>    make mountains out of molehills.

Katz 10

WILLY. I won't fight with him any
    more. If he wants to go back to
    Texas, let him go.

LINDA. He'll find his way. (730)

Of course she does not really think he has
a great deal on the ball, and she probably
is not confident that Biff will "find his
way," but surely she is doing the best
thing possible--calming Willy, partly by
using soothing words and partly by doing
what she can to get Biff out of the house,
since she knows that Biff and Willy can't
live under the same roof.

    The third charge, that she is
materialistic, is ridiculous. She has to
count the pennies because someone has to
see that the bills are paid, and Willy is
obviously unable to do so. Here is an
example of her supposed preoccupation with
money:

    LINDA. Well, there's nine-sixty for
        the washing machine. And for the
        vacuum cleaner there's three and
        a half due on the fifteenth. Then
        the roof, you got twenty-one
        dollars remaining.

    WILLY. It don't leak, does it?

    LINDA. No, they did a wonderful job.
        Then you owe Frank for the
        carburetor.

    WILLY. I'm not going to pay that man!
        That goddam Chevrolet, they ought

to prohibit the manufacture of that
car!

LINDA. Well, you owe him three and a
half. And odds and ends, comes to
around a hundred and twenty
dollars by the fifteenth. (741)

It might be nice if Linda spent her time
taking courses at an adult education center
and thinking high thoughts, but it's
obvious that <u>someone</u> in the Loman family
(as in all families) has to keep track of
the bills.

The worst that can be said of Linda
is that she subscribes to three American
ideas of the time--that the man is the
breadwinner, that the relationship between
a father and his sons is far more important
than the relationship between a mother and
her sons, and that a woman's sole job is to
care for the house and to produce sons for
her husband. She is the maidservant to her
husband and to her sons, but in this she
is like the vast majority of women of her
time, and she should not be criticized for
not being an innovator. Compared to her
husband and her sons, Linda (though of
course not perfect) is a tower of common
sense, virtue, and strength. In fact, far
from causing Willy's failure, she does what
she can to give him strength to face the
facts, for instance when she encourages
him to talk to Howard about a job in New

Katz 12

York: "Why don't you go down to the place
tomorrow and tell Howard you've simply
got to work in New York? You're too
accommodating, dear" (728). Notice, too,
her speech in which she agrees with Biff's
decision that it is best for Biff to leave
for good: she goes to Willy and says, "I
think that's the best way, dear. 'Cause
there's no use drawing it out, you'll just
never get along" (795). Linda is not
the most forceful person alive, or the
brightest, but she is decent and she sees
more clearly than do any of the other
Lomans.

There is nothing in the play to suggest
that Arthur Miller was a feminist or was
ahead of his time in his view of the role
of women. On the contrary, the play seems
to give a pre-feminist view, with women
playing subordinate roles to men. The
images of success of the best sort--not
of Ben's ruthless sort--are Charley and
Bernard, two males. Probably Miller, writing
in the 1940s, could hardly conceive of a
successful woman other than as a wife or
mother. Notice, by the way, that Bernard--
probably the most admirable male in the
play--is not only an important lawyer but
the father of two sons, apparently a sign
of his complete success as a man. Still,
Miller's picture of Linda is by no means
condescending. Linda may not be a genius,

but she is the brightest and the most
realistic of the Lomans. Things turn out
badly, but not because of Linda. The viewer
leaves the theater with profound respect for
her patience, her strength, her sense of
decency, and, yes, her intelligence and her
competence in dealing with incompetent men.

[New page]

Katz 14

Works Cited

Bliquez, Guerin. "Linda's Role in Death of
    a Salesman." Modern Drama 10 (1968):
    383-86.

Gordon, Lois. "Death of a Salesman: An
    Appreciation." The Forties: Fiction,
    Poetry, Drama. Ed. Warren French. Deland,
    Florida: Everett/Edwards, 1969. 273-83.

Koon, Helene Wickham, ed. Twentieth Century
    Interpretations of Death of a Salesman.
    Englewood Cliffs, New Jersey: Prentice,
    1983.

Miller, Arthur. Death of a Salesman. A
    Little Literature. Ed. Sylvan Barnet
    et al. 14th ed. New York: Longman, 2007.
    725-801.

Parker, Brian. "Point of View in Arthur
    Miller's Death of a Salesman." University
    of Toronto Quarterly 35 (1966): 144-47.
    Rpt. in Koon. 41-55.

Stanton, Kay. "Women and the American Dream
    of Death of a Salesman." Feminist
    Readings of American Drama. Ed. Judith
    Schlueter. Rutherford, New Jersey:
    Fairleigh Dickinson UP, 1989. 67-102.

# 26

# American Voices: Drama for a Diverse Nation

In the first act of Arthur Miller's play *Death of a Salesman* (1947), Willy Loman (the leading character) tells his sons:

> The man who makes an appearance in the business world, the man who creates personal interest, is the man who gets ahead. Be liked and you will never want.

Against Willy's earnest remark we can juxtapose a cynical remark made more than half a century earlier by Mark Twain:

> All you need in this life is ignorance and confidence, then success is sure.

The dream of success, the American Dream—in one form or another—has motivated millions, and it has generated countless pithy remarks. Here are a few observations about America that you may want to recall as you read and reflect on the plays in this chapter.

> America means opportunity, freedom, power.
> —Ralph Waldo Emerson (1803–1882), 1864

> America has been another name for opportunity.
> —Frederick Jackson Turner (1861–1932), historian, 1893

What I do object to about America is the herd thinking. There is no room for individuals in your country—and yet you are dedicated to saving the world for individualism.

—Bertrand Russell (1872–1970),
British philosopher, 1964

The genius of America is that out of the many, we become one.

—Jesse Jackson (b. 1941), speech at the
Democratic National Convention,
Atlanta, Georgia, July 1988

If you work hard and play by the rules in this great country, you can get ahead.

—Richard A. Gephardt (b. 1941),
Missouri congressman, 1995

America must be described in romantic terms. . . . America is a romance in which we all partake.

—Newt Gingrich (b. 1943), Georgia congressman,
in *To Renew America,* 1995

People in America, of course, live in all sorts of fashions, because they are foreigners, or unlucky, or depraved, or without ambition; people live like that, but *Americans* live in white detached houses with green shutters. Rigidly, blindly, the dream takes precedence.

—Margaret Mead (1901–1978),
anthropologist, 1949

In poetry, prose, and drama, American writers have explored the meanings of the American Dream, even as they have also described the challenges that members of certain social classes and groups and racial and ethnic minorities have faced in gaining access to the Dream. In a sense, there is perhaps only one American Dream, and it involves self-reliance, success, and independence. But in life and literature, there are many different American dreamers, who from their own backgrounds and experiences have expressed their hopes and fears about the possibilities for fulfillment that America offers, as the plays in this chapter attest.

# JANE MARTIN

*Jane Martin has never given an interview and has never been photographed. The name presumably is the pseudonym of a writer who works with the Actors Theatre of Louisville, Kentucky. Rodeo is one of a collection of monologues,* Talking With . . . , *first presented at the Actors Theatre during the 1981 Humana Festival of New American Plays. Jane Martin has also written full-length plays.*

Margo Martinale, in Jane Martin's *Rodeo*, at the 6th Humana Festival of New American Plays (1982). Photographer: Sam Garst.

# Rodeo

[1981]

*A young woman in her late twenties sits working an a piece of tack ** *Beside her is a Lone Star beer in the can. As the lights come up we hear* *the last verse of a Tanya Tucker song or some other female country-* *western vocalist. She is wearing old worn jeans and boots plus a long-* *sleeved workshirt with the sleeves rolled up. She works until the song is* *over and then speaks.*

BIG EIGHT.  Shoot—Rodeo's just goin' to hell in a handbasket. Rodeo used to be somethin'. I loved it. I did. Once Daddy an' a bunch of 'em was foolin' around with some old bronc over to our place and this ol' red nose named Cinch got bucked off and my Daddy hooted and said he had him a nine-year-old girl, namely me, wouldn't have no damn trouble cowboyin' that horse. Well, he put me on up there, stuck that ridin' rein in my hand, gimme a kiss, and said, "Now there's only one thing t' remember Honey Love, if ya fall off you jest don't come home." Well I stayed up. You gotta stay on a bronc eight seconds. Otherwise the ride don't count. So from that day on my daddy called me Big Eight. Heck! That's all the name I got anymore . . . Big Eight.

---

*tack harness for a horse, including the bridle and saddle.

Used to be fer cowboys, the rodeo did. Do it in some open field, folks would pull their cars and pick-ups round it, sit on the hoods, some ranch hand'd bulldog him some rank steer and everybody'd wave their hats and call him by name. Ride us some buckin' stock, rope a few calves, git throwed off a bull, and then we'd jest git us to a bar and tell each other lies about how good we were.

Used to be a family thing. Wooly Billy Tilson and Tammy Lee had them five kids on the circuit. Three boys, two girls and Wooly and Tammy. Wasn't no two-beer rodeo in Oklahoma didn't have a Tilson entered. Used to call the oldest girl Tits. Tits Tilson. Never seen a girl that top-heavy could ride so well. Said she only fell off when the gravity got her. Cowboys used to say if she landed face down you could plant two young trees in the holes she'd leave. Ha! Tits Tilson.

Used to be people came to a rodeo had a horse of their own back home. Farm people, ranch people—lord, they *knew* what they were lookin' at. Knew a good ride from a bad ride, knew hard from easy. You broke some bones er spent the day eatin' dirt, at least ya got appreciated.

Now they bought the rodeo. Them. Coca-Cola, Pepsi Cola, Marlboro damn cigarettes. You know the ones I mean. Them. Hire some New York faggot t' sit on some ol' stuffed horse in front of a sagebrush photo n' smoke that junk. Hell, tobacco wasn't made to smoke, honey, it was made to chew. Lord wanted ya filled up with smoke he would've set ya on fire. Damn it gets me!

There's some guy in a banker's suit runs the rodeo now. Got him a pinky ring and a digital watch, honey. Told us we oughta have a watchamacallit, choriographus or somethin', some ol' ballbuster used to be with the Ice damn Capades. Wants us to ride around dressed up like Mickey Mouse, Pluto, crap like that. Told me I had to haul my butt through the barrel race done up like Minnie damn Mouse in a tu-tu. Huh uh, honey! Them people is so screwed-up they probably eat what they run over in the road.

Listen, they got the clowns wearin' Astronaut suits! I ain't lyin'. You know what a rodeo clown does! You go down, fall off whatever—the clown runs in front of the bull so's ya don't git stomped. Pin-stripes, he got 'em in space suits tellin' jokes on a microphone. First horse see 'em, done up like the Star Wars went crazy. Best buckin' horse on the circuit, name of Piss 'N' Vinegar, took one look at them clowns, had him a heart attack and died. Cowboy was ridin' him got hisself squashed. Twelve hundred pounds of coronary arrest jes fell right through 'em. Blam! Vio con dios. Crowd thought that was funnier than the astronauts. I swear it won't be long before they're strappin' ice-skates on the ponies. Big crowds now. Ain't hardly no ranch people, no farm people, nobody I know. Buncha disco babies and dee-vorce lawyers—designer jeans and day-glo Stetsons. Hell, the whole bunch of 'em wears French perfume. Oh it smells like money now! Got it on the cable T and V—hey, you know what, when ya rodeo yer just bound to kick yerself up some dust—well now, seems like that fogs up the ol'TV camera, so they told us a while back that from now on we was gonna ride on some new stuff called Astro-dirt. Dust free. Artificial damn dirt, honey. Lord have mercy.

Banker Suit called me in the other day said "Lurlene . . ." "Hold it," I said. "Who's this Lurlene? Round here they call me Big Eight." "Well, Big Eight," he said, "my name's Wallace." "Well that's a read surprise t' me," I said, "cause aroun' here everybody jes calls you Dumb-ass." My, he laughed real big, slapped his big ol' desk, an' then he said I wasn't suitable for the rodeo no more. Said they was lookin' fer another type, somethin' a little more in the showgirl line, like the Dallas Cowgirls maybe. Said the ridin' and ropin' wasn't the thing no more. Talked on about floats, costumes, dancin' choreog-aphy. If I was a man I woulda pissed on his shoe. Said he'd give me a lifetime pass though. Said I could come to his rodeo any time I wanted.

Rodeo used to be people ridin' horses for the pleasure of people who rode horses—made you feel good about what you could do. Rodeo wasn't worth no money to nobody. Money didn't have nothing to do with it! Used to be seven Tilsons riding in the rodeo. Wouldn't none of 'em dress up like Donald damn Duck so they quit. That there's the law of gravity!

There's a bunch of assholes in this country sneak around until they see ya havin' fun and then they buy the fun and start in sellin' it. See, they figure if ya love it, they can sell it. Well you look out, honey! They want to make them a dollar out of what you love. Dress *you* up like Minnie Mouse. Sell your rodeo. Turn *yer* pleasure into Ice damn Capades. You hear what I'm sayin'? You're jus' merchandise to them, sweetie. You're jus' merchandise to them.

BLACKOUT.

## ❈ TOPICS FOR CRITICAL THINKING AND WRITING

### *The Play on the Page*

1. Try to recall your response to the title and the first paragraph or two of the play. Did Big Eight fit your view (perhaps a stereotypical view) of what a cowgirl might sound like?
2. Reread *Rodeo,* this time paying attention not only to what Big Eight says but also to your responses to her. By the end of the play has she

become a somewhat more complicated figure than she seems to be after the first paragraph, or does she pretty much seem the same? Do you find that you become increasingly sympathetic? Increasingly unsympathetic? Or does your opinion not change?

3. If you have ever seen a rodeo, do you think Big Eight's characterization is on the mark? Or is she simply bitter because she has been fired?

4. If a local theater group were staging *Rodeo*, presumably with some other short plays, would you go to see it? Why, or why not?

### *The Play on the Stage*

5. If you were directing a production of *Rodeo*, would you keep the actor seated, or would you have her get up, move around the stage, perhaps hang up one piece of tack and take down another? Why?

6. If you were directing *Rodeo*, would you tell Big Eight that her speech is essentially an interior monologue—a soliloquy—or would you tell her that she is speaking directly to the audience—i.e., that the audience is, collectively, a character in the play?

7. The play ends with a stage direction, "Blackout"; that is, the stage suddenly darkens. One director of a recent production, however, chose to end with a "fade out"; the illumination decreased slowly by means of dimmers (mechanical devices that regulate the intensity of a lighting unit). If you were directing a production, what sort of lighting would you use at the end? Why?

# ARTHUR MILLER

*Arthur Miller (1915–2005) was born in New York. In 1938 he graduated from the University of Michigan, where he won several prizes for drama. Six years later he had his first Broadway production,* The Man Who Had All the Luck, *but the play was unlucky and closed after four days. By the time of his first commercial success,* All My Sons *(1947), he had already written several plays. In 1949 he won a Pulitzer Prize with* Death of a Salesman *and achieved an international reputation. Among his other works are an adaptation (1950) of Ibsen's* Enemy of the People *and a play about the Salem witch trials,* The Crucible *(1953), both containing political implications, and* The Misfits *(1961, a screenplay),* After the Fall *(1964), and* Incident at Vichy *(1965).*

Lee J. Cobb as Willy Loman in the 1949 original Broadway production of *Death of a Salesman*

# Death of a Salesman [1947]

Certain Private Conversations in Two Acts and a Requiem

## LIST OF CHARACTERS

WILLY LOMAN

LINDA

BIFF

HAPPY

BERNARD

THE WOMAN

CHARLEY

UNCLE BEN

HOWARD WAGNER

JENNY

STANLEY

MISS FORSYTHE

LETTA

**SCENE:** *The action takes place in* WILLY LOMAN'*s house and yard and in various places he visits in the New York and Boston of today.*

Dustin Hoffman as Willy Loman, and John Malkovich as Biff, in the 1984 production.

## Act 1

**SCENE:** *A melody is heard, played upon a flute. It is small and fine, telling of grass and trees and the horizon. The curtain rises.*

*Before us is the Salesman's house. We are aware of towering, angular shapes behind it, surrounding it on all sides. Only the blue light of the sky falls upon the house and forestage; the surrounding area shows an angry glow of orange. As more light appears, we see a solid vault of apartment houses around the small, fragile-seeming home. An air of the dream clings to the place, a dream rising out of reality. The kitchen at center seems actual enough, for there is a kitchen table with three chairs, and a refrigerator. But no other fixtures are seen. At the back of the kitchen there is a draped entrance, which leads to the living room. To the right of the kitchen, on a level raised two feet, is a bedroom furnished only with a brass bedstead and a straight chair. On a shelf over the bed a silver athletic trophy stands. A window opens onto the apartment house at the side.*

*Behind the kitchen, on a level raised six and a half feet, is the boys' bedroom, at present barely visible. Two beds are dimly seen, and at the back of the room a dormer window. (This bedroom is above the unseen living room.) At the left a stairway curves up to it from the kitchen.*

*The entire setting is wholly or, in some places, partially transparent. The roof-line of the house is one-dimensional; under and over it we see the apartment buildings. Before the house lies an apron, curving beyond the forestage into the orchestra. This forward area serves as the back yard as well as the locale of all* WILLY'*s imaginings and of his city scenes. Whenever the action is in the present the actors observe the imaginary wall-lines, entering the house only through its door at the left. But in the scenes of the past these boundaries are broken, and characters enter or leave a room by stepping "through" a wall onto the forestage.*

*From the right,* WILLY LOMAN, *the Salesman, enters, carrying two large sample cases. The flute plays on. He hears but is not aware of it. He is past sixty years of age, dressed quietly. Even as he crosses the stage to the doorway of the house, his exhaustion is apparent. He unlocks the door, comes into the kitchen, and thankfully lets his burden down, feeling the soreness of his palms. A word-sigh escapes his lips—it might be "Oh, boy, oh, boy." He closes the door, then carries his cases out into the living room, through the draped kitchen doorway.*

LINDA, *his wife, has stirred in her bed at the right. She gets out and puts on a robe, listening. Most often jovial, she has developed an iron repression of her exceptions to* WILLY'*s behavior—she more than loves him, she admires him, as though his mercurial nature, his temper, his massive dreams and little cruelties, served her only as sharp reminders of the turbulent longings within him, longings which she shares but lacks the temperament to utter and follow to their end.*

LINDA (*hearing* WILLY *outside the bedroom, calls with some trepidation*). Willy!

WILLY.   It's all right. I came back.

LINDA.   Why? What happened? (*Slight pause.*) Did something happen, Willy?

WILLY.   No, nothing happened.

LINDA.   You didn't smash the car, did you?

WILLY (*with casual irritation*).   I said nothing happened. Didn't you hear me?

LINDA.   Don't you feel well?

WILLY.   I'm tired to the death. (*The flute has faded away. He sits on the bed beside her, a little numb.*) I couldn't make it. I just couldn't make it, Linda.

LINDA (*very carefully, delicately*).   Where were you all day? You look terrible.

WILLY.   I got as far as a little above Yonkers. I stopped for a cup of coffee. Maybe it was the coffee.

LINDA.   What?

WILLY (*after a pause*).   I suddenly couldn't drive any more. The car kept going off onto the shoulder, y'know?

LINDA (*helpfully*).   Oh. Maybe it was the steering again. I don't think Angelo knows the Studebaker.

WILLY.   No, it's me, it's me. Suddenly I realize I'm goin' sixty miles an hour and I don't remember the last five minutes. I'm—I can't seem to—keep my mind to it.

LINDA.  Maybe it's your glasses. You never went for your new glasses.

WILLY.  No, I see everything. I came back ten miles an hour. It took me nearly four hours from Yonkers.

LINDA (*resigned*).  Well, you'll just have to take a rest, Willy, you can't continue this way.

WILLY.  I just got back from Florida.

LINDA.  But you didn't rest your mind. Your mind is overactive, and the mind is what counts, dear.

WILLY.  I'll start out in the morning. Maybe I'll feel better in the morning. (*She is taking off his shoes.*) These goddam arch supports are killing me.

LINDA.  Take an aspirin. Should I get you an aspirin? It'll soothe you.

WILLY (*with wonder*).  I was driving along, you understand? And I was fine. I was even observing the scenery. You can imagine, me looking at scenery, on the road every week of my life. But it's so beautiful up there, Linda, the trees are so thick, and the sun is warm. I opened the windshield and just let the warm air bathe over me. And then all of a sudden I'm goin' off the road! I'm tellin' ya, I absolutely forgot I was driving. If I'd've gone the other way over the white line I might've killed somebody. So I went on again—and five minutes later I'm dreamin' again, and I nearly . . . (*He presses two fingers against his eyes.*) I have such thoughts, I have such strange thoughts.

LINDA.  Willy, dear. Talk to them again. There's no reason why you can't work in New York.

WILLY.  They don't need me in New York. I'm the New England man. I'm vital in New England.

LINDA.  But you're sixty years old. They can't expect you to keep traveling every week.

WILLY.  I'll have to send a wire to Portland. I'm supposed to see Brown and Morrison tomorrow morning at ten o'clock to show the line. Goddammit, I could sell them! (*He starts putting on his jacket.*)

LINDA (*taking the jacket from him*).  Why don't you go down to the place tomorrow and tell Howard you've simply got to work in New York? You're too accommodating, dear.

WILLY.  If old man Wagner was alive I'd a been in charge of New York now! That man was a prince, he was a masterful man. But that boy of his, that Howard, he don't appreciate. When I went north the first time, the Wagner Company didn't know where New England was!

LINDA.  Why don't you tell those things to Howard, dear?

WILLY (*encouraged*).  I will, I definitely will. Is there any cheese?

LINDA.  I'll make you a sandwich.

WILLY.  No, go to sleep. I'll take some milk. I'll be up right away. The boys in?

LINDA.  They're sleeping. Happy took Biff on a date tonight.

WILLY (*interested*).  That so?

LINDA. It was so nice to see them shaving together, one behind the other, in the bathroom. And going out together. You notice? The whole house smells of shaving lotion.

WILLY. Figure it out. Work a lifetime to pay off a house. You finally own it, and there's nobody to live in it.

LINDA. Well, dear, life is a casting off. It's always that way.

WILLY. No, no, some people—some people accomplish something. Did Biff say anything after I went this morning?

LINDA. You shouldn't have criticized him, Willy, especially after he just got off the train. You mustn't lose your temper with him.

WILLY. When the hell did I lose my temper? I simply asked him if he was making any money. Is that a criticism?

LINDA. But, dear, how could he make any money?

WILLY (*worried and angered*). There's such an undercurrent in him. He became a moody man. Did he apologize when I left this morning?

LINDA. He was crestfallen, Willy. You know how he admires you. I think if he finds himself, then you'll both be happier and not fight any more.

WILLY. How can he find himself on a farm? Is that a life? A farm hand? In the beginning, when he was young, I thought, well, a young man, it's good for him to tramp around, take a lot of different jobs. But it's more than ten years now and he has yet to make thirty-five dollars a week!

LINDA. He's finding himself, Willy.

WILLY. Not finding yourself at the age of thirty-four is a disgrace!

LINDA. Shh!

WILLY. The trouble is he's lazy, goddammit!

LINDA. Willy, please!

WILLY. Biff is a lazy bum!

LINDA. They're sleeping. Get something to eat. Go on down.

WILLY. Why did he come home? I would like to know what brought him home.

LINDA. I don't know. I think he's still lost, Willy. I think he's very lost.

WILLY. Biff Loman is lost. In the greatest country in the world a young man with such—personal attractiveness, gets lost. And such a hard worker. There's one thing about Biff—he's not lazy.

LINDA. Never.

WILLY (*with pity and resolve*). I'll see him in the morning; I'll have a nice talk with him. I'll get him a job selling. He could be big in no time. My God! Remember how they used to follow him around in high school? When he smiled at one of them their faces lit up. When he walked down the street . . . (*He loses himself in reminiscences.*)

LINDA (*trying to bring him out of it*). Willy, dear, I got a new kind of American-type cheese today. It's whipped.

WILLY. Why do you get American when I like Swiss?

LINDA. I just thought you'd like a change . . .

WILLY.  I don't want a change! I want Swiss cheese. Why am I always being contradicted?

LINDA (*with a covering laugh*).  I thought it would be a surprise.

WILLY.  Why don't you open a window in here, for God's sake?

LINDA (*with infinite patience*).  They're all open, dear.

WILLY.  The way they boxed us in here. Bricks and windows, windows and bricks.

LINDA.  We should've bought the land next door.

WILLY.  The street is lined with cars. There's not a breath of fresh air in the neighborhood. The grass don't grow any more, you can't raise a carrot in the back yard. They should've had a law against apartment houses. Remember those two beautiful elm trees out there? When I and Biff hung the swing between them?

LINDA.  Yeah, like being a million miles from the city.

WILLY.  They should've arrested the builder for cutting those down. They massacred the neighborhood. (*Lost.*) More and more I think of those days, Linda. This time of year it was lilac and wisteria. And then the peonies would come out, and the daffodils. What fragrance in this room!

LINDA.  Well, after all, people had to move somewhere.

WILLY.  No, there's more people now.

LINDA.  I don't think there's more people. I think . . .

WILLY.  There's more people! That's what's ruining this country! Population is getting out of control. The competition is maddening! Smell the stink from that apartment house! And another one on the other side . . . How can they whip cheese?

*On* WILLY's *last line,* BIFF *and* HAPPY *raise themselves up in their beds, listening.*

LINDA.  Go down, try it. And be quiet.

WILLY (*turning to* LINDA, *guiltily*).  You're not worried about me, are you, sweetheart?

BIFF.  What's the matter?

HAPPY.  Listen!

LINDA.  You've got too much on the ball to worry about.

WILLY.  You're my foundation and my support, Linda.

LINDA.  Just try to relax, dear. You make mountains out of molehills.

WILLY.  I won't fight with him any more. If he wants to go back to Texas, let him go.

LINDA.  He'll find his way.

WILLY.  Sure. Certain men just don't get started till later in life. Like Thomas Edison, I think. Or B. F. Goodrich. One of them was deaf. (*He starts for the bedroom doorway.*) I'll put my money on Biff.

LINDA.  And Willy—if it's warm Sunday we'll drive in the country. And we'll open the windshield, and take lunch.

WILLY.  No, the windshields don't open on the new cars.

LINDA. But you opened it today.

WILLY. Me? I didn't. (*He stops.*) Now isn't that peculiar! Isn't that a remarkable ... (*He breaks off in amazement and fright as the flute is heard
distantly.*)

LINDA. What, darling?

WILLY. That is the most remarkable thing.

LINDA. What, dear?

WILLY. I was thinking of the Chevvy. (*Slight pause.*) Nineteen twenty-
eight ... when I had that red Chevvy ... (*Breaks off.*) That funny? I
coulda sworn I was driving that Chevvy today.

LINDA. Well, that's nothing. Something must've reminded you.

WILLY. Remarkable. Ts. Remember those days? The way Biff used to simo-
nize that car? The dealer refused to believe there was eighty thousand
miles on it. (*He shakes his head.*) Heh! (*To Linda.*) Close your eyes,
I'll be right up. (*He walks out of the bedroom.*)

HAPPY (*to* BIFF). Jesus, maybe he smashed up the car again!

LINDA (*calling after* WILLY). Be careful on the stairs, dear! The cheese is on
the middle shelf. (*She turns, goes over to the bed, takes his jacket,
and goes out of the bedroom.*)

*Light has risen on the boys' room. Unseen,* WILLY *is heard talking to
himself, "Eighty thousand miles," and a little laugh.* BIFF *gets out of
bed, comes downstage a bit, and stands attentively.* BIFF *is two years
older than his brother* HAPPY, *well built, but in these days bears a
worn air and seems less self-assured. He has succeeded less, and his
dreams are stronger and less acceptable than* HAPPY'S. HAPPY *is tall,
powerfully made. Sexuality is like a visible color on him, or a scent
that many women have discovered. He, like his brother, is lost, but
in a different way, for he has never allowed himself to turn his face
toward defeat and is thus more confused and hard-skinned, although seemingly more content.*

HAPPY (*getting out of bed*). He's going to get his license taken away if he
keeps that up. I'm getting nervous about him, y'know, Biff?

BIFF. His eyes are going.

HAPPY. No, I've driven with him. He sees all right. He just doesn't keep his
mind on it. I drove into the city with him last week. He stops at a
green light and then it turns red and he goes. (*He laughs.*)

BIFF. Maybe he's color-blind.

HAPPY. Pop? Why he's got the finest eye for color in the business. You
know that.

BIFF (*sitting down on his bed*). I'm going to sleep.

HAPPY. You're not still sour on Dad, are you, Biff?

BIFF. He's all right, I guess.

WILLY (*underneath them, in the living room*). Yes, sir, eighty thousand
miles—eighty-two thousand!

BIFF. You smoking?

HAPPY (*holding out a pack of cigarettes*). Want one?

BIFF (*taking a cigarette*). I can never sleep when I smell it.

WILLY. What a simonizing job, heh!

HAPPY (*with deep sentiment*). Funny, Biff, y'know? Us sleeping in here again? The old beds. (*He pats his bed affectionately.*) All the talk that went across those beds, huh? Our whole lives.

BIFF. Yeah. Lotta dreams and plans.

HAPPY (*with a deep and masculine laugh*). About five hundred women would like to know what was said in this room. (*They share a soft laugh.*)

BIFF. Remember that big Betsy something—what the hell was her name— over on Bushwick Avenue?

HAPPY (*combing his hair*). With the collie dog!

BIFF. That's the one. I got you in there, remember?

HAPPY. Yeah, that was my first time—I think. Boy, there was a pig. (*They laugh, almost crudely.*) You taught me everything I know about women. Don't forget that.

BIFF. I bet you forgot how bashful you used to be. Especially with girls.

HAPPY. Oh, I still am, Biff.

BIFF. Oh, go on.

HAPPY. I just control it, that's all. I think I got less bashful and you got more so. What happened, Biff? Where's the old humor, the old confidence? (*He shakes* BIFF'*s knee.* BIFF *gets up and moves restlessly about the room.*) What's the matter?

BIFF. Why does Dad mock me all the time?

HAPPY. He's not mocking you, he . . .

BIFF. Everything I say there's a twist of mockery on his face. I can't get near him.

HAPPY. He just wants you to make good, that's all. I wanted to talk to you about Dad for a long time, Biff. Something's—happening to him. He— talks to himself.

BIFF. I noticed that this morning. But he always mumbled.

HAPPY. But not so noticeable. It got so embarrassing I sent him to Florida. And you know something? Most of the time he's talking to you.

BIFF. What's he say about me?

HAPPY. I can't make it out.

BIFF. What's he say about me?

HAPPY. I think the fact that you're not settled, that you're still kind of up in the air . . .

BIFF. There's one or two other things depressing him, Happy.

HAPPY. What do you mean?

BIFF. Never mind. Just don't lay it all to me.

HAPPY. But I think if you just got started—I mean—is there any future for you out there?

BIFF. I tell ya, Hap, I don't know what the future is. I don't know—what I'm supposed to want.

HAPPY. What do you mean?

BIFF. Well, I spent six or seven years after high school trying to work myself up. Shipping clerk, salesman, business of one kind or another. And it's a measly manner of existence. To get on that subway on the hot mornings in summer. To devote your whole life to keeping stock, or making phone calls, or selling or buying. To suffer fifty weeks of the year for the sake of a two-week vacation, when all you really desire is to be outdoors, with your shirt off. And always to have to get ahead of the next fella. And still—that's how you build a future.

HAPPY. Well, you really enjoy it on a farm? Are you content out there?

BIFF (*with rising agitation*). Hap, I've had twenty or thirty different kinds of jobs since I left home before the war, and it always turns out the same. I just realized it lately. In Nebraska when I herded cattle, and the Dakotas, and Arizona, and now in Texas. It's why I came home now, I guess, because I realized it. This farm I work on, it's spring there now, see? And they've got about fifteen new colts. There's nothing more inspiring or—beautiful than the sight of a mare and a new colt. And it's cool there now, see? Texas is cool now, and it's spring. And whenever spring comes to where I am, I suddenly get the feeling, my God, I'm not gettin' anywhere! What the hell am I doing, playing around with horses, twenty-eight dollars a week! I'm thirty-four years old, I oughta be makin' my future. That's when I come running home. And now, I get here, and I don't know what to do with myself. (*After a pause.*) I've always made a point of not wasting my life, and everytime I come back here I know that all I've done is to waste my life.

HAPPY. You're a poet, you know that, Biff? You're a—you're an idealist!

BIFF. No, I'm mixed up very bad. Maybe I oughta get married. Maybe I oughta get stuck into something. Maybe that's my trouble. I'm like a boy. I'm not married, I'm not in business, I just—I'm like a boy. Are you content, Hap? You're a success, aren't you? Are you content?

HAPPY. Hell, no!

BIFF. Why? You're making money, aren't you?

HAPPY (*moving about with energy, expressiveness*). All I can do now is wait for the merchandise manager to die. And suppose I get to be merchandise manager? He's a good friend of mine, and he just built a terrific estate on Long Island. And he lived there about two months and sold it, and now he's building another one. He can't enjoy it once it's finished. And I know that's just what I would do. I don't know what the hell I'm workin' for. Sometimes I sit in my apartment—all alone. And I think of the rent I'm paying. And it's crazy. But then, it's what I always wanted. My own apartment, a car, and plenty of women. And still, goddammit, I'm lonely.

BIFF (*with enthusiasm*). Listen, why don't you come out West with me?

HAPPY. You and I, heh?

BIFF. Sure, maybe we could buy a ranch. Raise cattle, use our muscles. Men built like we are should be working out in the open.

HAPPY (*avidly*).  The Loman Brothers, heh?

BIFF (*with vast affection*).  Sure, we'd be known all over the counties!

HAPPY (*enthralled*).  That's what I dream about, Biff. Sometimes I want to just rip my clothes off in the middle of the store and outbox that goddam merchandise manager. I mean I can outbox, outrun, and outlift anybody in that store, and I have to take orders from those common, petty sons-of-bitches till I can't stand it any more.

BIFF.  I'm tellin' you, kid, if you were with me I'd be happy out there.

HAPPY (*enthused*).  See, Biff, everybody around me is so false that I'm constantly lowering my ideals ...

BIFF.  Baby, together we'd stand up for one another, we'd have someone to trust.

HAPPY.  If I were around you ...

BIFF.  Hap, the trouble is we weren't brought up to grub for money. I don't know how to do it.

HAPPY.  Neither can I!

BIFF.  Then let's go!

HAPPY.  The only thing is—what can you make out there?

BIFF.  But look at your friend. Builds an estate and then hasn't the peace of mind to live in it.

HAPPY.  Yeah, but when he walks into the store the waves part in front of him. That's fifty-two thousand dollars a year coming through the revolving door, and I got more in my pinky finger than he's got in his head.

BIFF.  Yeah, but you just said ...

HAPPY.  I gotta show some of those pompous, self-important executives over there that Hap Loman can make the grade. I want to walk into the store the way he walks in. Then I'll go with you, Biff. We'll be together yet, I swear. But take those two we had tonight. Now weren't they gorgeous creatures?

BIFF.  Yeah, yeah, most gorgeous I've had in years.

HAPPY.  I get that any time I want, Biff. Whenever I feel disgusted. The only trouble is, it gets like bowling or something. I just keep knockin' them over and it doesn't mean anything. You still run around a lot?

BIFF.  Naa. I'd like to find a girl—steady, somebody with substance.

HAPPY.  That's what I long for.

BIFF.  Go on! You'd never come home.

HAPPY.  I would! Somebody with character, with resistance! Like Mom, y'know? You're gonna call me a bastard when I tell you this. That girl Charlotte I was with tonight is engaged to be married in five weeks. (*He tries on his new hat.*)

BIFF.  No kiddin'!

HAPPY.  Sure, the guy's in line for the vice-presidency of the store. I don't know what gets into me, maybe I just have an over-developed sense of competition or something, but I went and ruined her, and furthermore I can't get rid of her. And he's the third executive I've done that to. Isn't that a crummy characteristic? And to top it all, I go to their weddings! (*Indignantly, but laughing.*) Like I'm not supposed to take bribes. Manufacturers offer me a hundred-dollar bill now and then to throw an order their way. You know how honest I am, but it's like this girl, see. I hate myself for it. Because I don't want the girl, and, still, I take it and—I love it!

BIFF. Let's go to sleep.

HAPPY. I guess we didn't settle anything, heh?

BIFF. I just got one idea that I think I'm going to try.

HAPPY. What's that?

BIFF. Remember Bill Oliver?

HAPPY. Sure, Oliver is very big now. You want to work for him again?

BIFF. No, but when I quit he said something to me. He put his arm on my shoulder, and he said, "Biff, if you ever need anything, come to me."

HAPPY. I remember that. That sounds good.

BIFF. I think I'll go to see him. If I could get ten thousand or even seven or eight thousand dollars I could buy a beautiful ranch.

HAPPY. I bet he'd back you. 'Cause he thought highly of you, Biff. I mean, they all do. You're well liked, Biff. That's why I say to come back here, and we both have the apartment. And I'm tellin' you, Biff, any babe you want . . .

BIFF. No, with a ranch I could do the work I like and still be something. I just wonder though. I wonder if Oliver still thinks I stole that carton of basketballs.

HAPPY. Oh, he probably forgot that long ago. It's almost ten years. You're too sensitive. Anyway, he didn't really fire you.

BIFF. Well, I think he was going to. I think that's why I quit. I was never sure whether he knew or not. I know he thought the world of me, though. I was the only one he'd let lock up the place.

WILLY (*below*). You gonna wash the engine, Biff?

HAPPY. Shh!

BIFF *looks at* HAPPY, *who is gazing down, listening.* WILLY *is mumbling in the parlor.*

HAPPY. You hear that?

*They listen.* WILLY *laughs warmly.*

BIFF (*growing angry*). Doesn't he know Mom can hear that?

WILLY. Don't get your sweater dirty, Biff!

*A look of pain crosses* BIFF'S *face.*

HAPPY. Isn't that terrible? Don't leave again, will you? You'll find a job here. You gotta stick around. I don't know what to do about him, it's getting embarrassing.

WILLY.  What a simonizing job!
BIFF.  Mom's hearing that!
WILLY.  No kiddin', Biff, you got a date? Wonderful!
HAPPY.  Go on to sleep. But talk to him in the morning, will you?
BIFF *(reluctantly getting into bed).* With her in the house. Brother!
HAPPY *(getting into bed).* I wish you'd have a good talk with him.

*The light on their room begins to fade.*

BIFF *(to himself in bed ).* That selfish, stupid . . .
HAPPY.  Sh . . . Sleep, Biff.

*Their light is out. Well before they have finished speaking,* WILLY*'s form is dimly seen below in the darkened kitchen. He opens the refrigerator, searches in there, and takes out a bottle of milk. The apartment houses are fading out, and the entire house and surroundings become covered with leaves. Music insinuates itself as the leaves appear.*

WILLY.  Just wanna be careful with those girls, Biff, that's all. Don't make any promises. No promises of any kind. Because a girl, y'know, they always believe what you tell 'em, and you're very young, Biff, you're too young to be talking seriously to girls.

*Light rises on the kitchen.* WILLY, *talking, shuts the refrigerator door and comes downstage to the kitchen table. He pours milk into a glass. He is totally immersed in himself, smiling faintly.*

WILLY.  Too young entirely, Biff. You want to watch your schooling first. Then when you're all set, there'll be plenty of girls for a boy like you. *(He smiles broadly at a kitchen chair.)* That so? The girls pay for you? *(He laughs.)* Boy, you must really be makin' a hit.

WILLY *is gradually addressing—physically—a point offstage, speaking through the wall of the kitchen, and his voice has been rising in volume to that of a normal conversation.*

WILLY.  I been wondering why you polish the car so careful. Ha! Don't leave the hubcaps, boys. Get the chamois to the hubcaps. Happy, use newspaper on the windows, it's the easiest thing. Show him how to do it, Biff! You see, Happy? Pad it up, use it like a pad. That's it, that's it, good work. You're doin' all right, Hap. *(He pauses, then nods in approbation for a few seconds, then looks upward.)* Biff, first thing we gotta do when we get time is clip that big branch over the house. Afraid it's gonna fall in a storm and hit the roof. Tell you what. We get a rope and sling her around, and then we climb up there with a couple of saws and take her down. Soon as you finish the car, boys, I wanna see ya. I got a surprise for you, boys.
BIFF *(offstage).* Whatta ya got, Dad?

WILLY.  No, you finish first. Never leave a job till you're finished—remember that. (*Looking toward the "big trees."*) Biff, up in Albany I saw a beautiful hammock. I think I'll buy it next trip, and we'll hang it right between those two elms. Wouldn't that be something? Just swingin' there under those branches. Boy, that would be ...

*Young* BIFF *and Young* HAPPY *appear from the direction* WILLY *was addressing.* HAPPY *carries rags and a pail of water.* BIFF, *wearing a sweater with a block "S," carries a football.*

BIFF (*pointing in the direction of the car offstage*). How's that, Pop, professional?

WILLY.  Terrific. Terrific job, boys. Good work, Biff.

HAPPY.  Where's the surprise, Pop?

WILLY.  In the back seat of the car.

HAPPY.  Boy! (*He runs off.*)

BIFF.  What is it, Dad? Tell me, what'd you buy?

WILLY (*laughing, cuffs him*). Never mind, something I want you to have.

BIFF (*turns and starts off*). What is it, Hap?

HAPPY (*offstage*). It's a punching bag!

BIFF.  Oh, Pop!

WILLY.  It's got Gene Tunney's signature on it!

HAPPY *runs onstage with a punching bag.*

BIFF.  Gee, how'd you know we wanted a punching bag?

WILLY.  Well, it's the finest thing for the timing.

HAPPY (*lies down on his back and pedals with his feet*). I'm losing weight, you notice, Pop?

WILLY (*to* HAPPY). Jumping rope is good too.

BIFF.  Did you see the new football I got?

WILLY (*examining the ball*). Where'd you get a new ball?

BIFF.  The coach told me to practice my passing.

WILLY.  That so? And he gave you the ball, heh?

BIFF.  Well, I borrowed it from the locker room. (*He laughs confidentially.*)

WILLY (*laughing with him at the theft*). I want you to return that.

HAPPY.  I told you he wouldn't like it!

BIFF (*angrily*). Well, I'm bringing it back!

WILLY (*stopping the incipient argument, to* HAPPY). Sure, he's gotta practice with a regulation ball, doesn't he? (*To* BIFF.) Coach'll probably congratulate you on your initiative!

BIFF.  Oh, he keeps congratulating my initiative all the time, Pop.

WILLY.  That's because he likes you. If somebody else took that ball there'd be an uproar. So what's the report, boys, what's the report?

BIFF.  Where'd you go this time, Dad? Gee we were lonesome for you.

WILLY (*pleased, puts an arm around each boy and they come down to the apron*). Lonesome, heh?

BIFF.  Missed you every minute.

WILLY.  Don't say? Tell you a secret, boys. Don't breathe it to a soul. Someday I'll have my own business, and I'll never have to leave home any more.

HAPPY.  Like Uncle Charley, heh?

WILLY.  Bigger than Uncle Charley! Because Charley is not—liked. He's liked, but he's not—well liked.

BIFF.  Where'd you go this time, Dad?

WILLY.  Well, I got on the road, and I went north to Providence. Met the Mayor.

BIFF.  The Mayor of Providence!

WILLY.  He was sitting in the hotel lobby.

BIFF.  What'd he say?

WILLY.  He said, "Morning!" And I said, "Morning!" And I said, "You got a fine city here, Mayor." And then he had coffee with me. And then I went to Waterbury. Waterbury is a fine city. Big clock city, the famous Waterbury clock. Sold a nice bill there. And then Boston—Boston is the cradle of the Revolution. A fine city. And a couple of other towns in Mass., and on to Portland and Bangor and straight home!

BIFF.  Gee, I'd love to go with you sometime, Dad.

WILLY.  Soon as summer comes.

HAPPY.  Promise?

WILLY.  You and Hap and I, and I'll show you all the towns. America is full of beautiful towns and fine, upstanding people. And they know me, boys, they know me up and down New England. The finest people. And when I bring you fellas up, there'll be open sesame for all of us, 'cause one thing, boys: I have friends. I can park my car in any street in New En-gland, and the cops protect it like their own. This summer, heh?

BIFF AND HAPPY (*together*).  Yeah! You bet!

WILLY.  We'll take our bathing suits.

HAPPY.  We'll carry your bags, Pop!

WILLY.  Oh, won't that be something! Me comin' into the Boston stores with you boys carryin' my bags. What a sensation!

    BIFF *is prancing around, practicing passing the ball.*

WILLY.  You nervous, Biff, about the game?

BIFF.  Not if you're gonna be there.

WILLY.  What do they say about you in school, now that they made you captain?

HAPPY.  There's a crowd of girls behind him everytime the classes change.

BIFF (*taking* WILLY'*s hand*).  This Saturday, Pop, this Saturday—just for you, I'm going to break through for a touchdown.

HAPPY.  You're supposed to pass.

BIFF.  I'm takin' one play for Pop. You watch me, Pop, and when I take off my helmet, that means I'm breakin' out. Then you watch me crash through that line!

WILLY (*kisses* BIFF). Oh, wait'll I tell this in Boston!

BERNARD *enters in knickers. He is younger than* BIFF, *earnest and loyal, a worried boy.*

BERNARD. Biff, where are you? You're supposed to study with me today.

WILLY. Hey, looka Bernard. What're you lookin' so anemic about, Bernard?

BERNARD. He's gotta study, Uncle Willy. He's got Regents next week.

HAPPY (*tauntingly, spinning* BERNARD *around*). Let's box, Bernard!

BERNARD. Biff! (*He gets away from* HAPPY.) Listen, Biff, I heard Mr. Birnbaum say that if you don't start studyin' math he's gonna flunk you, and you won't graduate. I heard him!

WILLY. You better study with him, Biff. Go ahead now.

BERNARD. I heard him!

BIFF. Oh, Pop, you didn't see my sneakers! (*He holds up a foot for* WILLY *to look at.*)

WILLY. Hey, that's a beautiful job of printing!

BERNARD (*wiping his glasses*). Just because he printed University of Virginia on his sneakers doesn't mean they've got to graduate him, Uncle Willy!

WILLY (*angrily*). What're you talking about? With scholarships to three universities they're gonna flunk him?

BERNARD. But I heard Mr. Birnbaum say ...

WILLY. Don't be a pest, Bernard! (*To his boys.*) What an anemic!

BERNARD. Okay, I'm waiting for you in my house, Biff.

BERNARD *goes off. The* LOMANS *laugh.*

WILLY. Bernard is not well liked, is he?

BIFF. He's liked, but he's not well liked.

HAPPY. That's right, Pop.

WILLY. That's just what I mean. Bernard can get the best marks in school, y'understand, but when he gets out in the business world, y'understand, you are going to be five times ahead of him. That's why I thank Almighty God you're both built like Adonises. Because the man who makes an appearance in the business world, the man who creates personal interest, is the man who gets ahead. Be liked and you will never want. You take me, for instance. I never have to wait in line to see a buyer. "Willy Loman is here!" That's all they have to know, and I go right through.

BIFF. Did you knock them dead, Pop?

WILLY. Knocked 'em cold in Providence, slaughtered 'em in Boston.

HAPPY (*on his back, pedaling again*). I'm losing weight, you notice, Pop?

LINDA *enters as of old, a ribbon in her hair, carrying a basket of washing.*

LINDA (*with youthful energy*). Hello, dear!

WILLY. Sweetheart!

LINDA.  How'd the Chevvy run?

WILLY.  Chevrolet, Linda, is the greatest car ever built. (*To the boys.*) Since when do you let your mother carry wash up the stairs?

BIFF.  Grab hold there, boy!

HAPPY.  Where to, Mom?

LINDA.  Hang them up on the line. And you better go down to your friends, Biff. The cellar is full of boys. They don't know what to do with themselves.

BIFF.  Ah, when Pop comes home they can wait!

WILLY (*laughs appreciatively*).  You better go down and tell them what to do, Biff.

BIFF.  I think I'll have them sweep out the furnace room.

WILLY.  Good work, Biff.

BIFF (*goes through wall-line of kitchen to doorway at back and calls down*).  Fellas! Everybody sweep out the furnace room! I'll be right down!

VOICES.  All right! Okay, Biff.

BIFF.  George and Sam and Frank, come out back! We're hangin' up the wash! Come on, Hap, on the double! (*He and* HAPPY *carry out the basket.*)

LINDA.  The way they obey him!

WILLY.  Well, that's training, the training. I'm tellin' you, I was sellin' thousands and thousands, but I had to come home.

LINDA.  Oh, the whole block'll be at that game. Did you sell anything?

WILLY.  I did five hundred gross in Providence and seven hundred gross in Boston.

LINDA.  No! Wait a minute. I've got a pencil. (*She pulls pencil and paper out of her apron pocket.*) That makes your commission . . . Two hundred—my God! Two hundred and twelve dollars!

WILLY.  Well, I didn't figure it yet, but . . .

LINDA.  How much did you do?

WILLY.  Well, I—I did—about a hundred and eighty gross in Providence. Well, no—it came to—roughly two hundred gross on the whole trip.

LINDA (*without hesitation*).  Two hundred gross. That's . . . (*She figures.*)

WILLY.  The trouble was that three of the stores were half-closed for inventory in Boston. Otherwise I woulda broke records.

LINDA.  Well, it makes seventy dollars and some pennies. That's very good.

WILLY.  What do we owe?

LINDA.  Well, on the first there's sixteen dollars on the refrigerator . . .

WILLY.  Why sixteen?

LINDA.  Well, the fan belt broke, so it was a dollar eighty.

WILLY.  But it's brand new.

LINDA.  Well, the man said that's the way it is. Till they work themselves in, y'know.

*They move through the wall-line into the kitchen.*

WILLY. I hope we didn't get stuck on that machine.

LINDA. They got the biggest ads of any of them!

WILLY. I know, it's a fine machine. What else?

LINDA. Well, there's nine-sixty for the washing machine. And for the vacuum cleaner there's three and a half due on the fifteenth. Then the
roof, you got twenty-one dollars remaining.

WILLY. It don't leak, does it?

LINDA. No, they did a wonderful job. Then you owe Frank for the carburetor.

WILLY. I'm not going to pay that man! That goddam Chevrolet, they ought
to prohibit the manufacture of that car!

LINDA. Well, you owe him three and a half. And odds and ends, comes to
around a hundred and twenty dollars by the fifteenth.

WILLY. A hundred and twenty dollars! My God, if business don't pick up I
don't know what I'm gonna do!

LINDA. Well, next week you'll do better.

WILLY. Oh, I'll knock 'em dead next week. I'll go to Hartford. I'm very well
liked in Hartford. You know, the trouble is, Linda, people don't seem
to take to me.

*They move onto the forestage.*

LINDA. Oh, don't be foolish.

WILLY. I know it when I walk in. They seem to laugh at me.

LINDA. Why? Why would they laugh at you? Don't talk that way, Willy.

*WILLY moves to the edge of the stage. LINDA goes into the kitchen and
starts to darn stockings.*

WILLY. I don't know the reason for it, but they just pass me by. I'm not
noticed.

LINDA. But you're doing wonderful, dear. You're making seventy to a hundred dollars a week.

WILLY. But I gotta be at it ten, twelve hours a day. Other men—I don't
know— they do it easier. I don't know why—I can't stop myself—I
talk too much. A man oughta come in with a few words. One thing
about Charley. He's a man of few words, and they respect him.

LINDA. You don't talk too much, you're just lively.

WILLY (*smiling*). Well, I figure, what the hell, life is short, a couple of jokes.
(*To himself:*) I joke too much! (*The smile goes.*)

LINDA. Why? You're . . .

WILLY. I'm fat. I'm very—foolish to look at, Linda. I didn't tell you, but
Christmas time I happened to be calling on F. H. Stewarts, and a
salesman I know, as I was going in to see the buyer I heard him say
something about—walrus. And I—I cracked him right across the

face. I won't take that. I simply will not take that. But they do laugh
at me. I know that.

LINDA. Darling ...

WILLY. I gotta overcome it. I know I gotta overcome it. I'm not dressing to
advantage, maybe.

LINDA. Willy, darling, you're the handsomest man in the world ...

WILLY. Oh, no, Linda.

LINDA. To me you are. (*Slight pause.*) The handsomest.

*From the darkness is heard the laughter of a woman.* WILLY *doesn't
turn to it, but it continues through* LINDA's *lines.*

LINDA. And the boys, Willy. Few men are idolized by their children the way
you are.

*Music is heard as behind a scrim, to the left of the house;* THE WOMAN,
*dimly seen, is dressing.*

WILLY (*with great feeling*). You're the best there is. Linda, you're a pal, you
know that? On the road—on the road I want to grab you sometimes
and just kiss the life outa you.

*The laughter is loud now, and he moves into a brightening area at
the left, where* THE WOMAN *has come from behind the scrim and is
standing, putting on her hat, looking into a "mirror" and laughing.*

WILLY. 'Cause I get so lonely—especially when business is bad and there's
nobody to talk to. I get the feeling that I'll never sell anything again,
that I won't make a living for you, or a business, a business for the
boys. (*He talks through* THE WOMAN's *subsiding laughter;* THE WOMAN
*primps at the "mirror."*) There's so much I want to make for ...

THE WOMAN. Me? You didn't make me, Willy. I picked you.

WILLY (*pleased*). You picked me?

THE WOMAN (*who is quite proper-looking,* WILLY's *age*). I did. I've been sitting at that desk watching all the salesmen go by, day in, day out. But
you've got such a sense of humor, and we do have such a good time
together, don't we?

WILLY. Sure, sure. (*He takes her in his arms.*) Why do you have to go now?

THE WOMAN. It's two o'clock ...

WILLY. No, come on in! (*He pulls her.*)

THE WOMAN. ... my sisters'll be scandalized. When'll you be back?

WILLY. Oh, two weeks about. Will you come up again?

THE WOMAN. Sure thing. You do make me laugh. It's good for me. (*She
squeezes his arm, kisses him.*) And I think you're a wonderful man.

WILLY. You picked me, heh?

THE WOMAN. Sure. Because you're so sweet. And such a kidder.

WILLY. Well, I'll see you next time I'm in Boston.

THE WOMAN. I'll put you right through to the buyers.

WILLY (*slapping her bottom*).  Right. Well, bottoms up!
THE WOMAN (*slaps him gently and laughs*).  You just kill me, Willy. (*He suddenly grabs her and kisses her roughly.*) You kill me. And thanks for the stockings. I love a lot of stockings. Well, good night.
WILLY.  Good night. And keep your pores open!
THE WOMAN.  Oh, Willy!

THE WOMAN *bursts out laughing, and* LINDA*'s laughter blends in.* THE WOMAN *disappears into the dark. Now the area at the kitchen table brightens.* LINDA *is sitting where she was at the kitchen table, but now is mending a pair of her silk stockings.*

LINDA.  You are, Willy. The handsomest man. You've got no reason to feel that . . .
WILLY (*coming out of* THE WOMAN*'s dimming area and going over to* LINDA).  I'll make it all up to you, Linda, I'll . . .
LINDA.  There's nothing to make up, dear. You're doing fine, better than . . .
WILLY (*noticing her mending*).  What's that?
LINDA.  Just mending my stockings. They're so expensive . . .
WILLY (*angrily, taking them from her*).  I won't have you mending stockings in this house! Now throw them out!

LINDA *puts the stockings in her pocket.*

BERNARD (*entering on the run*).  Where is he? If he doesn't study!
WILLY (*moving to the forestage, with great agitation*).  You'll give him the answers!
BERNARD.  I do, but I can't on a Regents! That's a state exam! They're liable to arrest me!
WILLY.  Where is he? I'll whip him, I'll whip him!
LINDA.  And he'd better give back that football, Willy, it's not nice.
WILLY.  Biff! Where is he? Why is he taking everything?
LINDA.  He's too rough with the girls, Willy. All the mothers are afraid of him!
WILLY.  I'll whip him!
BERNARD.  He's driving the car without a license!

THE WOMAN*'s laugh is heard.*

WILLY.  Shut up!
LINDA.  All the mothers . . .
WILLY.  Shut up!
BERNARD (*backing quietly away and out*).  Mr. Birnbaum says he's stuck up.
WILLY.  Get outa here!
BERNARD.  If he doesn't buckle down he'll flunk math! (*He goes off.*)
LINDA.  He's right, Willy, you've gotta . . .
WILLY (*exploding at her*).  There's nothing the matter with him! You want him to be a worm like Bernard? He's got spirit, personality . . .

*As he speaks,* LINDA, *almost in tears, exits into the living room.* WILLY *is alone in the kitchen, wilting and staring. The leaves are gone. It is night again, and the apartment houses look down from behind.*

WILLY.  Loaded with it. Loaded! What is he stealing? He's giving it back, isn't he? Why is he stealing? What did I tell him? I never in my life told him anything but decent things.

HAPPY *in pajamas has come down the stairs;* WILLY *suddenly becomes aware of* HAPPY's *presence.*

HAPPY.  Let's go now, come on.

WILLY *(sitting down at the kitchen table).*  Huh! Why did she have to wax the floors herself? Everytime she waxes the floors she keels over. She knows that!

HAPPY.  Shh! Take it easy. What brought you back tonight?

WILLY.  I got an awful scare. Nearly hit a kid in Yonkers. God! Why didn't I go to Alaska with my brother Ben that time! Ben! That man was a genius, that man was success incarnate! What a mistake! He begged me to go.

HAPPY.  Well, there's no use in . . .

WILLY.  You guys! There was a man started with the clothes on his back and ended up with diamond mines!

HAPPY.  Boy, someday I'd like to know how he did it.

WILLY.  What's the mystery? The man knew what he wanted and went out and got it! Walked into a jungle, and comes out, the age of twenty-one, and he's rich! The world is an oyster, but you don't crack it open on a mattress!

HAPPY.  Pop, I told you I'm gonna retire you for life.

WILLY.  You'll retire me for life on seventy goddam dollars a week? And your women and your car and your apartment, and you'll retire me for life! Christ's sake, I couldn't get past Yonkers today! Where are you guys, where are you? The woods are burning! I can't drive a car!

CHARLEY *has appeared in the doorway. He is a large man, slow of speech, laconic, immovable. In all he says, despite what he says, there is pity, and, now, trepidation. He has a robe over pajamas, slippers on his feet. He enters the kitchen.*

CHARLEY.  Everything all right?

HAPPY.  Yeah, Charley, everything's . . .

WILLY.  What's the matter?

CHARLEY.  I heard some noise. I thought something happened. Can't we do something about the walls? You sneeze in here, and in my house hats blow off.

HAPPY.  Let's go to bed, Dad. Come on.

CHARLEY *signals to* HAPPY *to go.*

WILLY. You go ahead, I'm not tired at the moment.

HAPPY (*to* WILLY). Take it easy, huh? (*He exits.*)

WILLY. What're you doin' up?

CHARLEY (*sitting down at the kitchen table opposite* WILLY). Couldn't sleep good. I had a heartburn.

WILLY. Well, you don't know how to eat.

CHARLEY. I eat with my mouth.

WILLY. No, you're ignorant. You gotta know about vitamins and things like that.

CHARLEY. Come on, let's shoot. Tire you out a little.

WILLY (*hesitantly*). All right. You got cards?

CHARLEY (*taking a deck from his pocket*). Yeah, I got them. Someplace. What is it with those vitamins?

WILLY (*dealing*). They build up your bones. Chemistry.

CHARLEY. Yeah, but there's no bones in a heartburn.

WILLY. What are you talkin' about? Do you know the first thing about it?

CHARLEY. Don't get insulted.

WILLY. Don't talk about something you don't know anything about.

*They are playing. Pause.*

CHARLEY. What're you doin' home?

WILLY. A little trouble with the car.

CHARLEY. Oh. (*Pause.*) I'd like to take a trip to California.

WILLY. Don't say.

CHARLEY. You want a job?

WILLY. I got a job, I told you that. (*After a slight pause.*) What the hell are you offering me a job for?

CHARLEY. Don't get insulted.

WILLY. Don't insult me.

CHARLEY. I don't see no sense in it. You don't have to go on this way.

WILLY. I got a good job. (*Slight pause.*) What do you keep comin' in here for?

CHARLEY. You want me to go?

WILLY (*after a pause, withering*). I can't understand it. He's going back to Texas again. What the hell is that?

CHARLEY. Let him go.

WILLY. I got nothin' to give him, Charley, I'm clean, I'm clean.

CHARLEY. He won't starve. None a them starve. Forget about him.

WILLY. Then what have I got to remember?

CHARLEY. You take it too hard. To hell with it. When a deposit bottle is broken you don't get your nickel back.

WILLY. That's easy enough for you to say.

CHARLEY. That ain't easy for me to say.

WILLY. Did you see the ceiling I put up in the living room?

CHARLEY. Yeah, that's a piece of work. To put up a ceiling is a mystery to me. How do you do it?

WILLY. What's the difference?

CHARLEY. Well, talk about it.

WILLY. You gonna put up a ceiling?

CHARLEY. How could I put up a ceiling?

WILLY. Then what the hell are you bothering me for?

CHARLEY. You're insulted again.

WILLY. A man who can't handle tools is not a man. You're disgusting.

CHARLEY. Don't call me disgusting, Willy.

> UNCLE BEN, *carrying a valise and an umbrella, enters the forestage from around the right corner of the house. He is a stolid man, in his sixties, with a mustache and an authoritative air. He is utterly certain of his destiny, and there is an aura of far places about him. He enters exactly as* WILLY *speaks.*

WILLY. I'm getting awfully tired, Ben.

> BEN's *music is heard.* BEN *looks around at everything.*

CHARLEY. Good, keep playing; you'll sleep better. Did you call me Ben?

> BEN *looks at his watch.*

WILLY. That's funny. For a second there you reminded me of my brother Ben.

BEN. I only have a few minutes. (*He strolls, inspecting the place.* WILLY *and* CHARLEY *continue playing.*)

CHARLEY. You never heard from him again, heh? Since that time?

WILLY. Didn't Linda tell you? Couple of weeks ago we got a letter from his wife in Africa. He died.

CHARLEY. That so.

BEN. (*chuckling*). So this is Brooklyn, eh?

CHARLEY. Maybe you're in for some of his money.

WILLY. Naa, he had seven sons. There's just one opportunity I had with that man ...

BEN. I must make a train, William. There are several properties I'm looking at in Alaska.

WILLY. Sure, sure! If I'd gone with him to Alaska that time, everything would've been totally different.

CHARLEY. Go on, you'd froze to death up there.

WILLY. What're you talking about?

BEN. Opportunity is tremendous in Alaska, William. Surprised you're not up there.

WILLY. Sure, tremendous.

CHARLEY. Heh?

WILLY. There was the only man I ever met who knew the answers.
CHARLEY. Who?
BEN. How are you all?
WILLY (*taking a pot, smiling*). Fine, fine.
CHARLEY. Pretty sharp tonight.
BEN. Is Mother living with you?
WILLY. No, she died a long time ago.
CHARLEY. Who?
BEN. That's too bad. Fine specimen of a lady, Mother.
WILLY (*to* CHARLEY). Heh?
BEN. I'd hoped to see the old girl.
CHARLEY. Who died?
BEN. Heard anything from Father, have you?
WILLY (*unnerved*). What do you mean, who died?
CHARLEY (*taking a pot*). What're you talkin' about?
BEN (*looking at his watch*). William, it's half-past eight!
WILLY (*as though to dispel his confusion he angrily stops* CHARLEY's
    *hand*). That's my build!
CHARLEY. I put the ace ...
WILLY. If you don't know how to play the game I'm not gonna throw my
    money away on you!
CHARLEY (*rising*). It was my ace, for God's sake!
WILLY. I'm through, I'm through!
BEN. When did Mother die?
WILLY. Long ago. Since the beginning you never knew how to play cards.
CHARLEY (*picks up the cards and goes to the door*). All right! Next time
    I'll bring a deck with five aces.
WILLY. I don't play that kind of game!
CHARLEY (*turning to him*). You ought to be ashamed of yourself!
WILLY. Yeah?
CHARLEY. Yeah! (*He goes out.*)
WILLY (*slamming the door after him*). Ignoramus!
BEN (*as* WILLY *comes toward him through the wall-line of the kitchen*).
    So you're William.
WILLY (*shaking* BEN's *hand*). Ben! I've been waiting for you so long!
    What's the answer? How did you do it?
BEN. Oh, there's a story in that.

   LINDA *enters the forestage, as of old, carrying the wash basket.*

LINDA. Is this Ben?
BEN (*gallantly*). How do you do, my dear.
LINDA. Where've you been all these years? Willy's always wondered why
    you ...
WILLY (*pulling* BEN *away from her impatiently*). Where is Dad? Didn't
    you follow him? How did you get started?

BEN. Well, I don't know how much you remember.

WILLY. Well, I was just a baby, of course, only three or four years old ...

BEN. Three years and eleven months.

WILLY. What a memory, Ben!

BEN. I have many enterprises, William, and I have never kept books.

WILLY. I remember I was sitting under the wagon in—was it Nebraska?

BEN. It was South Dakota, and I gave you a bunch of wild flowers.

WILLY. I remember you walking away down some open road.

BEN (*laughing*). I was going to find Father in Alaska.

WILLY. Where is he?

BEN. At that age I had a very faulty view of geography, William. I discovered
    after a few days that I was heading due south, so instead of Alaska, I
    ended up in Africa.

LINDA. Africa!

WILLY. The Gold Coast!

BEN. Principally diamond mines.

LINDA. Diamond mines!

BEN. Yes, my dear. But I've only a few minutes ...

WILLY. No! Boys! Boys! (*Young* BIFF *and* HAPPY *appear.*) Listen to this. This
    is your Uncle Ben, a great man! Tell my boys, Ben!

BEN. Why, boys, when I was seventeen I walked into the jungle, and when
    I was twenty-one I walked out. (*He laughs.*) And by God I was rich.

WILLY (*to the boys*). You see what I been talking about? The greatest things
    can happen!

BEN (*glancing at his watch*). I have an appointment in Ketchikan Tuesday
    week.

WILLY. No, Ben! Please tell about Dad. I want my boys to hear. I want them
    to know the kind of stock they spring from. All I remember is a man
    with a big beard, and I was in Mamma's lap, sitting around a fire, and
    some kind of high music.

BEN. His flute. He played the flute.

WILLY. Sure, the flute, that's right!

*New music is heard, a high, rollicking tune.*

BEN. Father was a very great and a very wild-hearted man. We would start
    in Boston, and he'd toss the whole family into the wagon, and then
    he'd drive the team right across the country; through Ohio, and Indi-
    ana, Michigan, Illinois, and all the Western states. And we'd stop in the
    towns and sell the flutes that he'd made on the way. Great inventor, Fa-
    ther. With one gadget he made more in a week than a man like you
    could make in a lifetime.

WILLY. That's just the way I'm bringing them up, Ben—rugged, well liked,
    all-around.

BEN. Yeah? (*To* BIFF.) Hit that, boy—hard as you can. (*He pounds his
    stomach.*)

BIFF.  Oh, no, sir!

BEN (*taking boxing stance*). Come on, get to me! (*He laughs.*)

WILLY.  Go to it. Biff! Go ahead, show him!

BIFF.  Okay! (*He cocks his fists and starts in.*)

LINDA (*to* WILLY). Why must he fight, dear?

BEN (*sparring with* BIFF). Good boy! Good boy!

WILLY.  How's that, Ben, heh?

HAPPY.  Give him the left, Biff!

LINDA.  Why are you fighting?

BEN.  Good boy! (*Suddenly comes in, trips* BIFF, *and stands over him, the point of his umbrella poised over* BIFF'*s eye.*)

LINDA.  Look out, Biff!

BIFF.  Gee!

BEN (*patting* BIFF'*s knee*).  Never fight fair with a stranger, boy. You'll never get out of the jungle that way. (*Taking* LINDA'*s hand and bowing.*) It was an honor and a pleasure to meet you, Linda.

LINDA (*withdrawing her hand coldly, frightened*). Have a nice—trip.

BEN (*to* WILLY).  And good luck with your—what do you do?

WILLY.  Selling.

BEN.  Yes. Well . . . (*He raises his hand in farewell to all.*)

WILLY.  No, Ben, I don't want you to think . . . (*He takes* BEN'*s arm to show him.*) It's Brooklyn, I know, but we hunt too.

BEN.  Really, now.

WILLY.  Oh, sure, there's snakes and rabbits and—that's why I moved out here. Why, Biff can fell any one of these trees in no time! Boys! Go right over to where they're building the apartment house and get some sand. We're gonna rebuild the entire front stoop right now! Watch this, Ben!

BIFF.  Yes, sir! On the double, Hap!

HAPPY (*as he and* BIFF *run off*).  I lost weight, Pop, you notice?

CHARLEY *enters in knickers, even before the boys are gone.*

CHARLEY.  Listen, if they steal any more from that building the watchman'll put the cops on them!

LINDA   (*to* WILLY). Don't let Biff . . .

BEN *laughs lustily.*

WILLY.  You shoulda seen the lumber they brought home last week. At least a dozen six-by-tens worth all kinds a money.

CHARLEY.  Listen, if that watchman . . .

WILLY.  I gave them hell, understand. But I got a couple of fearless characters there.

CHARLEY.  Willy, the jails are full of fearless characters.

BEN (*clapping* WILLY *on the back, with a laugh at* CHARLEY).  And the stock exchange, friend!

WILLY (*joining in* BEN's *laughter*). Where are the rest of your pants?

CHARLEY. My wife bought them.

WILLY. Now all you need is a golf club and you can go upstairs and go to sleep. (*To* BEN.) Great athlete! Between him and his son Bernard they can't hammer a nail!

BERNARD (*rushing in*). The watchman's chasing Biff!

WILLY (*angrily*). Shut up! He's not stealing anything!

LINDA (*alarmed, hurrying off left*). Where is he? Biff, dear! (*She exits.*)

WILLY (*moving toward the left, away from* BEN). There's nothing wrong. What's the matter with you?

BEN. Nervy boy. Good!

WILLY (*laughing*). Oh, nerves of iron, that Biff!

CHARLEY. Don't know what it is. My New England man comes back and he's bleedin', they murdered him up there.

WILLY. It's contacts, Charley, I got important contacts!

CHARLEY (*sarcastically*). Glad to hear it, Willy. Come in later, we'll shoot a little casino. I'll take some of your Portland money. (*He laughs at* WILLY *and exits.*)

WILLY (*turning to* BEN). Business is bad, it's murderous. But not for me, of course.

BEN. I'll stop by on my way back to Africa.

WILLY (*longingly*). Can't you stay a few days? You're just what I need, Ben, because I—I have a fine position here, but I—well, Dad left when I was such a baby and I never had a chance to talk to him and I still feel—kind of temporary about myself.

BEN. I'll be late for my train.

*They are at opposite ends of the stage.*

WILLY. Ben, my boys—can't we talk? They'd go into the jaws of hell for me, see, but I . . .

BEN. William, you're being first-rate with your boys. Outstanding, manly chaps!

WILLY (*hanging on to his words*). Oh, Ben, that's good to hear! Because sometimes I'm afraid that I'm not teaching them the right kind of— Ben, how should I teach them?

BEN (*giving great weight to each word, and with a certain vicious audacity*). William, when I walked into the jungle, I was seventeen. When I walked out I was twenty-one. And, by God, I was rich! (*He goes off into darkness around the right corner of the house.*)

WILLY. . . . was rich! That's just the spirit I want to imbue them with! To walk into a jungle! I was right! I was right! I was right!

BEN *is gone, but* WILLY *is still speaking to him as* LINDA, *in nightgown and robe, enters the kitchen, glances around for* WILLY, *then goes to the door of the house, looks out and sees him. Comes down to his left. He looks at her.*

LINDA. Willy, dear? Willy?

WILLY. I was right!

LINDA. Did you have some cheese? (*He can't answer.*) It's very late, darling. Come to bed, heh?

WILLY (*looking straight up*). Gotta break your neck to see a star in this yard.

LINDA. You coming in?

WILLY. Whatever happened to that diamond watch fob? Remember? When Ben came from Africa that time? Didn't he give me a watch fob with a diamond in it?

LINDA. You pawned it, dear. Twelve, thirteen years ago. For Biff's radio correspondence course.

WILLY. Gee, that was a beautiful thing. I'll take a walk.

LINDA. But you're in your slippers.

WILLY (*starting to go around the house at the left*). I was right! I was! (*Half to* LINDA, *as he goes, shaking his head.*) What a man! There was a man worth talking to. I was right!

LINDA (*calling after* WILLY). But in your slippers, Willy!

WILLY *is almost gone when* BIFF, *in his pajamas, comes down the stairs and enters the kitchen.*

BIFF. What is he doing out there?

LINDA. Sh!

BIFF. God Almighty, Mom, how long has he been doing this?

LINDA. Don't, he'll hear you.

BIFF. What the hell is the matter with him?

LINDA. It'll pass by morning.

BIFF. Shouldn't we do anything?

LINDA. Oh, my dear, you should do a lot of things, but there's nothing to do, so go to sleep.

HAPPY *comes down the stairs and sits on the steps.*

HAPPY. I never heard him so loud, Mom.

LINDA. Well, come around more often; you'll hear him. (*She sits down at the table and mends the lining of* WILLY's *jacket.*)

BIFF. Why didn't you ever write me about this, Mom?

LINDA. How would I write to you? For over three months you had no address.

BIFF. I was on the move. But you know I thought of you all the time. You know that, don't you, pal?

LINDA. I know, dear, I know. But he likes to have a letter. Just to know that there's still a possibility for better things.

BIFF. He's not like this all the time, is he?

LINDA. It's when you come home he's always the worst.

BIFF. When I come home?

LINDA. When you write you're coming, he's all smiles, and talks about the future, and—he's just wonderful. And then the closer you seem to come, the more shaky he gets, and then, by the time you get here, he's arguing, and he seems angry at you. I think it's just that maybe he can't bring himself to—to open up to you. Why are you so hateful to each other? Why is that?

BIFF (*evasively*). I'm not hateful, Mom.

LINDA. But you no sooner come in the door than you're fighting!

BIFF. I don't know why. I mean to change. I'm tryin', Mom, you understand?

LINDA. Are you home to stay now?

BIFF. I don't know. I want to look around, see what's doin'.

LINDA. Biff, you can't look around all your life, can you?

BIFF. I just can't take hold, Mom. I can't take hold of some kind of a life.

LINDA. Biff, a man is not a bird, to come and go with the spring time.

BIFF. Your hair . . . (*He touches her hair.*) Your hair got so gray.

LINDA. Oh, it's been gray since you were in high school. I just stopped dyeing it, that's all.

BIFF. Dye it again, will ya? I don't want my pal looking old. (*He smiles.*)

LINDA. You're such a boy! You think you can go away for a year and . . . You've got to get it into your head now that one day you'll knock on this door and there'll be strange people here . . .

BIFF. What are you talking about? You're not even sixty, Mom.

LINDA. But what about your father?

BIFF (*lamely*). Well, I meant him too.

HAPPY. He admires Pop.

LINDA. Biff, dear, if you don't have any feeling for him, then you can't have any feeling for me.

BIFF. Sure I can, Mom.

LINDA. No. You can't just come to see me, because I love him. (*With a threat, but only a threat, of tears.*) He's the dearest man in the world to me, and I won't have anyone making him feel unwanted and low and blue. You've got to make up your mind now, darling, there's no leeway any more. Either he's your father and you pay him that respect, or else you're not to come here. I know he's not easy to get along with—nobody knows that better than me—but . . .

WILLY (*from the left, with a laugh*). Hey, hey, Biffo!

BIFF (*starting to go out after* WILLY). What the hell is the matter with him? (HAPPY *stops him.*)

LINDA. Don't—don't go near him!

BIFF. Stop making excuses for him! He always, always wiped the floor with you. Never had an ounce of respect for you.

HAPPY. He's always had respect for . . .

BIFF. What the hell do you know about it?

HAPPY (*surlily*). Just don't call him crazy!

BIFF. He's got no character—Charley wouldn't do this. Not in his own house—spewing out that vomit from his mind.

HAPPY.  Charley never had to cope with what he's got to.

BIFF.  People are worse off than Willy Loman. Believe me, I've seen them!

LINDA.  Then make Charley your father, Biff. You can't do that, can you? I
don't say he's a great man. Willy Loman never made a lot of money.
His name was never in the paper. He's not the finest character that
ever lived. But he's a human being, and a terrible thing is happening
to him. So attention must be paid. He's not to be allowed to fall into
his grave like an old dog. Attention, attention must be finally paid to
such a person. You called him crazy . . .

BIFF.  I didn't mean . . .

LINDA.  No, a lot of people think he's lost his—balance. But you don't have
to be very smart to know what his trouble is. The man is exhausted.

HAPPY.  Sure!

LINDA.  A small man can be just as exhausted as a great man. He works for a
company thirty-six years this March, opens up unheard-of territories
to their trademark, and now in his old age they take his salary away.

HAPPY (*indignantly*).  I didn't know that, Mom.

LINDA.  You never asked, my dear! Now that you get your spending money
someplace else you don't trouble your mind with him.

HAPPY.  But I gave you money last . . .

LINDA.  Christmas time, fifty dollars! To fix the hot water it cost ninety-
seven fifty! For five weeks he's been on straight commission, like a be-
ginner, an unknown!

BIFF.  Those ungrateful bastards!

LINDA.  Are they any worse than his sons? When he brought them business,
when he was young, they were glad to see him. But now his old
friends, the old buyers that loved him so and always found some order to hand him in a pinch—they're all dead, retired. He used to be
able to make six, seven calls a day in Boston. Now he takes his valises
out of the car and puts them back and takes them out again and he's
exhausted. Instead of walking he talks now. He drives seven hundred
miles, and when he gets there no one knows him any more, no one
welcomes him. And what goes through a man's mind, driving seven
hundred miles home without having earned a cent? Why shouldn't he
talk to himself? Why? When he has to go to Charley and borrow fifty
dollars a week and pretend to me that it's his pay? How long can that
go on? How long? You see what I'm sitting here and waiting for? And
you tell me he has no character? The man who never worked a day
but for your benefit? When does he get the medal for that? Is this his
reward—to turn around at the age of sixty-three and find his sons,
who he loved better than his life, one a philandering bum . . .

HAPPY.  Mom!

LINDA.  That's all you are, my baby! (*To* BIFF.) And you! What happened to the
love you had for him? You were such pals! How you used to talk to him
on the phone every night! How lonely he was till he could come home
to you!

BIFF. All right, Mom. I'll live here in my room, and I'll get a job. I'll keep away from him, that's all.

LINDA. No, Biff. You can't stay here and fight all the time.

BIFF. He threw me out of this house, remember that.

LINDA. Why did he do that? I never knew why.

BIFF. Because I know he's a fake and he doesn't like anybody around who knows!

LINDA. Why a fake? In what way? What do you mean?

BIFF. Just don't lay it all at my feet. It's between me and him—that's all I have to say. I'll chip in from now on. He'll settle for half my paycheck. He'll be all right. I'm going to bed. (*He starts for the stairs.*)

LINDA. He won't be all right.

BIFF (*turning on the stairs, furiously*). I hate this city and I'll stay here. Now what do you want?

LINDA. He's dying, Biff.

HAPPY *turns quickly to her, shocked.*

BIFF (*after a pause*). Why is he dying?

LINDA. He's been trying to kill himself.

BIFF (*with great horror*). How?

LINDA. I live from day to day.

BIFF. What're you talking about?

LINDA. Remember I wrote you that he smashed up the car again? In February?

BIFF. Well?

LINDA. The insurance inspector came. He said that they have evidence. That all these accidents in the last year—weren't—weren't—accidents.

HAPPY. How can they tell that? That's a lie.

LINDA. It seems there's a woman . . . (*She takes a breath as:*)

BIFF (*sharply but contained*). What woman?

LINDA (*simultaneously*). . . . and this woman . . .

LINDA. What?

BIFF. Nothing. Go ahead.

LINDA. What did you say?

BIFF. Nothing. I just said what woman?

HAPPY. What about her?

LINDA. Well, it seems she was walking down the road and saw his car. She says that he wasn't driving fast at all, and that he didn't skid. She says he came to that little bridge, and then deliberately smashed into the railing, and it was only the shallowness of the water that saved him.

BIFF. Oh, no, he probably just fell asleep again.

LINDA. I don't think he fell asleep.

BIFF. Why not?

LINDA. Last month . . . (*With great difficulty.*) Oh, boys, it's so hard to say a thing like this! He's just a big stupid man to you, but I tell you there's more good in him than in many other people. (*She chokes, wipes her eyes.*) I was looking for a fuse. The lights blew out, and I went down the cellar. And behind the fuse box—it happened to fall out—was a length of rubber pipe—just short.

HAPPY. No kidding!

LINDA. There's a little attachment on the end of it. I knew right away. And sure enough, on the bottom of the water heater there's a new little nipple on the gas pipe.

HAPPY (*angrily*). That—jerk.

BIFF. Did you have it taken off?

LINDA. I'm—I'm ashamed to. How can I mention it to him? Every day I go down and take away that little rubber pipe. But, when he comes home, I put it back where it was. How can I insult him that way? I don't know what to do. I live from day to day, boys. I tell you, I know every thought in his mind. It sounds so old-fashioned and silly, but I tell you he put his whole life into you and you've turned your backs on him. (*She is bent over in the chair, weeping, her face in her hands.*) Biff, I swear to God! Biff, his life is in your hands!

HAPPY (*to BIFF*). How do you like that damned fool!

BIFF (*kissing her*). All right, pal, all right. It's all settled now. I've been remiss. I know that, Mom. But now I'll stay, and I swear to you, I'll apply myself. (*Kneeling in front of her, in a fever of self-reproach.*) It's just—you see, Mom, I don't fit in business. Not that I won't try. I'll try, and I'll make good.

HAPPY. Sure you will. The trouble with you in business was you never tried to please people.

BIFF. I know, I ...

HAPPY. Like when you worked for Harrison's. Bob Harrison said you were tops, and then you go and do some damn fool thing like whistling whole songs in the elevator like a comedian.

BIFF (*against HAPPY*). So what? I like to whistle sometimes.

HAPPY. You don't raise a guy to a responsible job who whistles in the elevator!

LINDA. Well, don't argue about it now.

HAPPY. Like when you'd go off and swim in the middle of the day instead of taking the line around.

BIFF (*his resentment rising*). Well, don't you run off? You take off sometimes, don't you? On a nice summer day?

HAPPY. Yeah, but I cover myself!

LINDA. Boys!

HAPPY. If I'm going to take a fade the boss can call any number where I'm supposed to be and they'll swear to him that I just left. I'll tell you something that I hate to say, Biff, but in the business world some of them think you're crazy.

BIFF (*angered*). Screw the business world!

HAPPY.   All right, screw it! Great, but cover yourself!

LINDA.   Hap, Hap!

BIFF.   I don't care what they think! They've laughed at Dad for years, and you know why? Because we don't belong in this nuthouse of a city! We should be mixing cement on some open plain or—or carpenters. A carpenter is allowed to whistle!

WILLY *walks in from the entrance of the house, at left.*

WILLY.   Even your grandfather was better than a carpenter. (*Pause. They watch him.*) You never grew up. Bernard does not whistle in the elevator, I assure you.

BIFF (*as though to laugh* WILLY *out of it*). Yeah, but you do, Pop.

WILLY.   I never in my life whistled in an elevator! And who in the business world thinks I'm crazy?

BIFF.   I didn't mean it like that, Pop. Now don't make a whole thing out of it, will ya?

WILLY.   Go back to the West! Be a carpenter, a cowboy, enjoy yourself!

LINDA.   Willy, he was just saying . . .

WILLY.   I heard what he said!

HAPPY (*trying to quiet* WILLY). Hey, Pop, come on now . . .

WILLY (*continuing over* HAPPY'*s line*). They laugh at me, heh? Go to Filene's, go to the Hub, go to Slattery's, Boston. Call out the name Willy Loman and see what happens! Big shot!

BIFF.   All right, Pop.

WILLY.   Big!

BIFF.   All right!

WILLY.   Why do you always insult me?

BIFF.   I didn't say a word. (*To* LINDA.) Did I say a word?

LINDA.   He didn't say anything, Willy.

WILLY (*going to the doorway of the living room*). All right, good night, good night.

LINDA.   Willy, dear, he just decided . . .

WILLY (*to* BIFF). If you get tired hanging around tomorrow, paint the ceiling I put up in the living room.

BIFF.   I'm leaving early tomorrow.

HAPPY.   He's going to see Bill Oliver, Pop.

WILLY (*interestedly*). Oliver? For what?

BIFF (*with reserve, but trying; trying*). He always said he'd stake me. I'd like to go into business, so maybe I can take him up on it.

LINDA.   Isn't that wonderful?

WILLY.   Don't interrupt. What's wonderful about it? There's fifty men in the City of New York who'd stake him. (*To* BIFF.) Sporting goods?

BIFF.   I guess so. I know something about it and . . .

WILLY.   He knows something about it! You know sporting goods better than Spalding, for God's sake! How much is he giving you?

BIFF.   I don't know, I didn't even see him yet, but . . .

WILLY. Then what're you talkin' about?

BIFF (*getting angry*). Well, all I said was I'm gonna see him, that's all!

WILLY (*turning away*). Ah, you're counting your chickens again.

BIFF (*starting left for the stairs*). Oh, Jesus, I'm going to sleep!

WILLY (*calling after him*). Don't curse in this house!

BIFF (*turning*). Since when did you get so clean?

HAPPY (*trying to stop them*). Wait a ...

WILLY. Don't use that language to me! I won't have it!

HAPPY (*grabbing* BIFF, *shouts*). Wait a minute! I got an idea. I got a feasible idea. Come here, Biff, let's talk this over now, let's talk some sense here. When I was down in Florida last time, I thought of a great idea to sell sporting goods. It just came back to me. You and I, Biff—we have a line, the Loman Line. We train a couple of weeks, and put on a couple of exhibitions, see?

WILLY. That's an idea!

HAPPY. Wait! We form two basketball teams, see? Two water-polo teams. We play each other. It's a million dollars' worth of publicity. Two brothers, see? The Loman Brothers. Displays in the Royal Palms—all the hotels. And banners over the ring and the basketball court. "Loman Brothers." Baby, we could sell sporting goods!

WILLY. That is a one-million-dollar idea!

LINDA. Marvelous!

BIFF. I'm in great shape as far as that's concerned.

HAPPY. And the beauty of it is, Biff, it wouldn't be like a business. We'd be out playin' ball again.

BIFF (*enthused*). Yeah, that's ...

WILLY. Million-dollar ...

HAPPY. And you wouldn't get fed up with it, Biff. It'd be the family again. There'd be the old honor, and comradeship, and if you wanted to go off for a swim or somethin'—well, you'd do it! Without some smart cooky gettin' up ahead of you!

WILLY. Lick the world! You guys together could absolutely lick the civilized world.

BIFF. I'll see Oliver tomorrow. Hap, if we could work that out ...

LINDA. Maybe things are beginning to ...

WILLY (*wildly enthused, to* LINDA). Stop interrupting! (*To* BIFF.) But don't wear sport jacket and slacks when you see Oliver.

BIFF. No, I'll ...

WILLY. A business suit, and talk as little as possible, and don't crack any jokes.

BIFF. He did like me. Always liked me.

LINDA. He loved you!

WILLY (*to* LINDA). Will you stop! (*To* BIFF.) Walk in very serious. You are not applying for a boy's job. Money is to pass. Be quiet, fine, and serious. Everybody likes a kidder, but nobody lends him money.

HAPPY. I'll try to get some myself, Biff. I'm sure I can.

WILLY.  I see great things for you kids, I think your troubles are over. But remember, start big and you'll end big. Ask for fifteen. How much you gonna ask for?

BIFF.  Gee, I don't know …

WILLY.  And don't say "Gee." "Gee" is a boy's word. A man walking in for fifteen thousand dollars does not say "Gee!"

BIFF.  Ten, I think, would be top though.

WILLY.  Don't be so modest. You always started too low. Walk in with a big laugh. Don't look worried. Start off with a couple of your good stories to lighten things up. It's not what you say, it's how you say it—because personality always wins the day.

LINDA.  Oliver always thought the highest of him …

WILLY.  Will you let me talk?

BIFF.  Don't yell at her, Pop, will ya?

WILLY (*angrily*).  I was talking, wasn't I?

BIFF.  I don't like you yelling at her all the time, and I'm tellin' you, that's all.

WILLY.  What're you, takin' over this house?

LINDA.  Willy …

WILLY (*turning to her*).  Don't take his side all the time, goddammit!

BIFF (*furiously*).  Stop yelling at her!

WILLY (*suddenly pulling on his cheek, beaten down, guilt ridden*).  Give my best to Bill Oliver—he may remember me. (*He exits through the living room doorway.*)

LINDA (*her voice subdued*).  What'd you have to start that for? (BIFF *turns away.*) You see how sweet he was as soon as you talked hopefully? (*She goes over to* BIFF.) Come up and say good night to him. Don't let him go to bed that way.

HAPPY.  Come on, Biff, let's buck him up.

LINDA.  Please, dear. Just say good night. It takes so little to make him happy. Come. (*She goes through the living room doorway, calling upstairs from within the living room.*) Your pajamas are hanging in the bathroom, Willy!

HAPPY (*looking toward where* LINDA *went out*).  What a woman! They broke the mold when they made her. You know that, Biff.

BIFF.  He's off salary. My God, working on commission!

HAPPY.  Well, let's face it: he's no hot-shot selling man. Except that sometimes, you have to admit, he's a sweet personality.

BIFF (*deciding*).  Lend me ten bucks, will ya? I want to buy some new ties.

HAPPY.  I'll take you to a place I know. Beautiful stuff. Wear one of my striped shirts tomorrow.

BIFF.  She got gray. Mom got awful old. Gee, I'm gonna go in to Oliver tomorrow and knock him for a …

HAPPY.  Come on up. Tell that to Dad. Let's give him a whirl. Come on.

BIFF (*steamed up*).  You know, with ten thousand bucks, boy!

HAPPY (*as they go into the living room*). That's the talk, Biff, that's the first
time I've heard the old confidence out of you! (*From within the living room, fading off*) You're gonna live with me, kid, and any babe
you want just say the word ...(*The last lines are hardly heard. They
are mounting the stairs to their parents' bedroom.*)

LINDA (*entering her bedroom and addressing* WILLY, *who is in the bathroom. She is straightening the bed for him*). Can you do anything
about the shower? It drips.

WILLY  (*from the bathroom*). All of a sudden everything falls to pieces.
Goddam plumbing, oughta be sued, those people. I hardly finished
putting it in and the thing ...(*His words rumble off.*)

LINDA. I'm just wondering if Oliver will remember him. You think he
might?

WILLY (*coming out of the bathroom in his pajamas*). Remember him?
What's the matter with you, you crazy? If he'd've stayed with Oliver
he'd be on top by now! Wait'll Oliver gets a look at him. You don't
know the average caliber any more. The average young man today—
(*he is getting into bed*)—is got a caliber of zero. Greatest thing in the
world for him was to bum around.

BIFF *and* HAPPY *enter the bedroom. Slight pause.*

WILLY (*stops short, looking at* BIFF). Glad to hear it, boy.
HAPPY.  He wanted to say good night to you, sport.
WILLY (*to* BIFF). Yeah. Knock him dead, boy. What'd you want to tell me?
BIFF.  Just take it easy, Pop. Good night. (*He turns to go.*)
WILLY (*unable to resist*). And if anything falls off the desk while you're
talking to him—like a package or something—don't you pick it up.
They have office boys for that.
LINDA.  I'll make a big breakfast ...
WILLY.  Will you let me finish? (*To* BIFF.) Tell him you were in the business
in the West. Not farm work.
BIFF.  All right, Dad.
LINDA.  I think everything ...
WILLY (*going right through her speech*). And don't undersell yourself. No
less than fifteen thousand dollars.
BIFF (*unable to bear him*). Okay. Good night, Mom. (*He starts moving.*)
WILLY.  Because you got a greatness in you, Biff, remember that. You got all
kinds of greatness ...(*He lies back, exhausted.* BIFF *walks out.*)
LINDA (*calling after* BIFF). Sleep well, darling!
HAPPY.  I'm gonna get married, Mom. I wanted to tell you.
LINDA.  Go to sleep, dear.
HAPPY (*going*). I just wanted to tell you.
WILLY.  Keep up the good work. (HAPPY *exits.*) God ... remember that
Ebbets Field game? The championship of the city?

LINDA.  Just rest. Should I sing to you?
WILLY.  Yeah. Sing to me. (LINDA *hums a soft lullaby.*) When that team came
out—he was the tallest, remember?
LINDA.  Oh, yes. And in gold.

BIFF *enters the darkened kitchen, takes a cigarette, and leaves the
house. He comes downstage into a golden pool of light. He smokes,
staring at the night.*

WILLY.  Like a young god. Hercules—something like that. And the sun, the
sun all around him. Remember how he waved to me? Right up from
the field, with the representatives of three colleges standing by? And
the buyers I brought, and the cheers when he came out—Loman, Loman, Loman! God Almighty, he'll be great yet. A star like that, magnificent, can never really fade away!

*The light on* WILLY *is fading. The gas heater begins to glow through
the kitchen wall, near the stairs, a blue flame beneath red coils.*

LINDA (*timidly*). Willy dear, what has he got against you?
WILLY.  I'm so tired. Don't talk any more.

BIFF *slowly returns to the kitchen. He stops, stares toward the heater.*

LINDA.  Will you ask Howard to let you work in New York?
WILLY.  First thing in the morning. Everything'll be all right.

BIFF *reaches behind the heater and draws out a length of rubber
tubing. He is horrified and turns his head toward* WILLY's *room, still
dimly lit, from which the strains of* LINDA's *desperate but monotonous humming rise.*

WILLY (*staring through the window into the moonlight*). Gee, look at the
moon moving between the buildings!

BIFF *wraps the tubing around his hand and quickly goes up the
stairs.*

## Act 2

**SCENE:** *Music is heard, gay and bright. The curtain rises as the music
fades away.* WILLY, *in shirt sleeves, is sitting at the kitchen table, sipping
coffee, his hat in his lap.* LINDA *is filling his cup when she can.*

WILLY.  Wonderful coffee. Meal in itself.
LINDA.  Can I make you some eggs?
WILLY.  No. Take a breath.
LINDA.  You look so rested, dear.
WILLY.  I slept like a dead one. First time in months. Imagine, sleeping till
ten on a Tuesday morning. Boys left nice and early, heh?

LINDA.  They were out of here by eight o'clock.
WILLY.  Good work!
LINDA.  It was so thrilling to see them leaving together. I can't get over the
shaving lotion in this house!
WILLY (*smiling*). Mmm ...
LINDA.  Biff was very changed this morning. His whole attitude seemed to
be hopeful. He couldn't wait to get downtown to see Oliver.
WILLY.  He's heading for a change.There's no question, there simply are cer-
tain men that take longer to get—solidified. How did he dress?
LINDA.  His blue suit. He's so handsome in that suit. He could be a—any-
thing in that suit!

> WILLY *gets up from the table.* LINDA *holds his jacket for him.*

WILLY.  There's no question, no question at all. Gee, on the way home
tonight I'd like to buy some seeds.
LINDA (*laughing*). That'd be wonderful. But not enough sun gets back
there. Nothing'll grow any more.
WILLY.  You wait, kid, before it's all over we're gonna get a little place out in
the country, and I'll raise some vegetables, a couple of chickens ...
LINDA.  You'll do it yet, dear.

> WILLY *walks out of his jacket.* LINDA *follows him.*

WILLY.  And they'll get married, and come for a weekend. I'd build a little
guest house. 'Cause I got so many fine tools, all I'd need would be a
little lumber and some peace of mind.
LINDA (*joyfully*). I sewed the lining ...
WILLY.  I could build two guest houses, so they'd both come. Did he decide
how much he's going to ask Oliver for?
LINDA (*getting him into the jacket*). He didn't mention it, but I imagine
ten or fifteen thousand.You going to talk to Howard today?
WILLY.  Yeah. I'll put it to him straight and simple. He'll just have to take me
off the road.
LINDA.  And Willy, don't forget to ask for a little advance, because we've got
the insurance premium. It's the grace period now.
WILLY.  That's a hundred ...?
LINDA.  A hundred and eight, sixty-eight. Because we're a little short again.
WILLY.  Why are we short?
LINDA.  Well, you had the motor job on the car ...
WILLY.  That goddam Studebaker!
LINDA.  And you got one more payment on the refrigerator ...
WILLY.  But it just broke again!
LINDA.  Well, it's old, dear.
WILLY.  I told you we should've bought a well-advertised machine. Charley
bought a General Electric and it's twenty years old and it's still good,
that son-of-a-bitch.

LINDA. But, Willy . . .

WILLY. Whoever heard of a Hastings refrigerator? Once in my life I would like to own something outright before it's broken! I'm always in a race with the junkyard! I just finished paying for the car and it's on its last legs. The refrigerator consumes belts like a goddam maniac. They time those things. They time them so when you finally paid for them, they're used up.

LINDA (*buttoning up his jacket as he unbuttons it*). All told, about two hundred dollars would carry us, dear. But that includes the last payment on the mortgage. After this payment, Willy, the house belongs to us.

WILLY. It's twenty-five years!

LINDA. Biff was nine years old when we bought it.

WILLY. Well, that's a great thing. To weather a twenty-five year mortgage is . . .

LINDA. It's an accomplishment.

WILLY. All the cement, the lumber, the reconstruction I put in this house! There ain't a crack to be found in it any more.

LINDA. Well, it served its purpose.

WILLY. What purpose? Some stranger'll come along, move in, and that's that. If only Biff would take this house, and raise a family . . . (*He starts to go.*) Good-by, I'm late.

LINDA (*suddenly remembering*). Oh, I forgot! You're supposed to meet them for dinner.

WILLY. Me?

LINDA. At Frank's Chop House on Forty-eighth near Sixth Avenue.

WILLY. Is that so! How about you?

LINDA. No, just the three of you. They're gonna blow you to a big meal!

WILLY. Don't say! Who thought of that?

LINDA. Biff came to me this morning, Willy, and he said, "Tell Dad, we want to blow him to a big meal." Be there six o'clock. You and your two boys are going to have dinner.

WILLY. Gee whiz! That's really somethin'. I'm gonna knock Howard for a loop, kid. I'll get an advance, and I'll come home with a New York job. Goddammit, now I'm gonna do it!

LINDA. Oh, that's the spirit, Willy!

WILLY. I will never get behind a wheel the rest of my life!

LINDA. It's changing, Willy, I can feel it changing!

WILLY. Beyond a question. G'by, I'm late. (*He starts to go again.*)

LINDA (*calling after him as she runs to the kitchen table for a handkerchief*). You got your glasses?

WILLY (*feels for them, then comes back in*). Yeah, yeah, got my glasses.

LINDA (*giving him the handkerchief*). And a handkerchief.

WILLY. Yeah, handkerchief.

LINDA. And your saccharine?

WILLY.  Yeah, my saccharine.
LINDA.  Be careful on the subway stairs.

*She kisses him, and a silk stocking is seen hanging from her hand.*
WILLY *notices it.*

WILLY.  Will you stop mending stockings? At least while I'm in the house. It
gets me nervous. I can't tell you. Please.

LINDA *hides the stocking in her hand as she follows* WILLY *across the*
*forestage in front of the house.*

LINDA.  Remember, Frank's Chop House.
WILLY *(passing the apron).* Maybe beets would grow out there.
LINDA *(laughing).* But you tried so many times.
WILLY.  Yeah. Well, don't work hard today. *(He disappears around the right*
*corner of the house.)*
LINDA.  Be careful!

*As* WILLY *vanishes,* LINDA *waves to him. Suddenly the phone rings. She*
*runs across the stage and into the kitchen and lifts it.*

LINDA.  Hello? Oh, Biff! I'm so glad you called, I just …Yes, sure, I just told
him. Yes, he'll be there for dinner at six o'clock, I didn't forget. Listen, I
was just dying to tell you. You know that little rubber pipe I told you
about? That he connected to the gas heater? I finally decided to go
down the cellar this morning and take it away and destroy it. But it's
gone! Imagine? He took it away himself, it isn't there! *(She listens.)*
When? Oh, then you took it. Oh—nothing, it's just that I'd hoped he'd
taken it away himself. Oh, I'm not worried, darling, because this morning he left in such high spirits, it was like the old days! I'm not afraid
any more. Did Mr. Oliver see you? . . . Well, you wait there then. And
make a nice impression on him, darling. Just don't perspire too much
before you see him. And have a nice time with Dad. He may have big
news too! . . . That's right, a New York job. And be sweet to him tonight,
dear. Be loving to him. Because he's only a little boat looking for a harbor. *(She is trembling with sorrow and joy.)* Oh, that's wonderful, Biff,
you'll save his life. Thanks, darling. Just put your arm around him when
he comes into the restaurant. Give him a smile. That's the boy …Good-
by, dear. . . . You got your comb? . . . That's fine. Good-by, Biff dear.

*In the middle of her speech,* HOWARD WAGNER, *thirty-six, wheels in a*
*small typewriter table on which is a wire-recording machine and*
*proceeds to plug it in. This is on the left forestage. Light slowly fades*
*on* LINDA *as it rises on* HOWARD. HOWARD *is intent on threading the ma-*
*chine and only glances over his shoulder as* WILLY *appears.*

WILLY.  Pst! Pst!
HOWARD.  Hello, Willy, come in.

WILLY.  Like to have a little talk with you, Howard.

HOWARD.  Sorry to keep you waiting. I'll be with you in a minute.

WILLY.  What's that, Howard?

HOWARD.  Didn't you ever see one of these? Wire recorder.

WILLY.  Oh. Can we talk a minute?

HOWARD.  Records things. Just got delivery yesterday. Been driving me crazy, the most terrific machine I ever saw in my life. I was up all night with it.

WILLY.  What do you do with it?

HOWARD.  I bought it for dictation, but you can do anything with it. Listen to this. I had it home last night. Listen to what I picked up. The first one is my daughter. Get this. (*He flicks the switch and "Roll out the Barrel" is heard being whistled.*) Listen to that kid whistle.

WILLY.  That is lifelike, isn't it?

HOWARD.  Seven years old. Get that tone.

WILLY.  Ts, ts. Like to ask a little favor if you . . .

*The whistling breaks off, and the voice of* HOWARD's *daughter is heard.*

HIS DAUGHTER.  "Now you, Daddy."

HOWARD.  She's crazy for me! (*Again the same song is whistled.*) That's me! Ha! (*He winks.*)

WILLY.  You're very good!

*The whistling breaks off again. The machine runs silent for a moment.*

HOWARD.  Sh! Get this now, this is my son.

HIS SON.  "The capital of Alabama is Montgomery; the capital of Arizona is Phoenix; the capital of Arkansas is Little Rock; the capital of California is Sacramento . . . " (*and on, and on.*)

HOWARD (*holding up five fingers*). Five years old, Willy!

WILLY.  He'll make an announcer some day!

HIS SON (*continuing*). "the capital . . . "

HOWARD.  Get that—alphabetical order! (*The machine breaks off suddenly.*) Wait a minute. The maid kicked the plug out.

WILLY.  It certainly is a . . .

HOWARD.  Sh, for God's sake!

HIS SON.  "It's nine o'clock, Bulova watch time. So I have to go to sleep."

WILLY.  That really is . . .

HOWARD.  Wait a minute! The next is my wife.

*They wait.*

HOWARD'S VOICE.  "Go on, say something." (*Pause.*) "Well, you gonna talk?"

HIS WIFE.  "I can't think of anything."

HOWARD'S VOICE. "Well, talk—it's turning."

HIS WIFE (*shyly, beaten*). "Hello." (*Silence.*) "Oh, Howard, I can't talk into this … "

HOWARD (*snapping the machine off*). That was my wife.

WILLY. That is a wonderful machine. Can we …

HOWARD. I tell you, Willy, I'm gonna take my camera, and my bandsaw, and all my hobbies, and out they go. This is the most fascinating relaxation I ever found.

WILLY. I think I'll get one myself.

HOWARD. Sure, they're only a hundred and a half. You can't do without it. Supposing you wanna hear Jack Benny, see? But you can't be at home at that hour. So you tell the maid to turn the radio on when Jack Benny comes on, and this automatically goes on with the radio …

WILLY. And when you come home you …

HOWARD. You can come home twelve o'clock, one o'clock, any time you like, and you get yourself a Coke and sit yourself down, throw the switch, and there's Jack Benny's program in the middle of the night!

WILLY. I'm definitely going to get one. Because lots of times I'm on the road, and I think to myself, what I must be missing on the radio!

HOWARD. Don't you have a radio in the car?

WILLY. Well, yeah, but who ever thinks of turning it on?

HOWARD. Say, aren't you supposed to be in Boston?

WILLY. That's what I want to talk to you about, Howard. You got a minute? (*He draws a chair in from the wing.*)

HOWARD. What happened? What're you doing here?

WILLY. Well …

HOWARD. You didn't crack up again, did you?

WILLY. Oh, no. No.

HOWARD. Geez, you had me worried there for a minute. What's the trouble?

WILLY. Well, tell you the truth, Howard. I've come to the decision that I'd rather not travel any more.

HOWARD. Not travel! Well, what'll you do?

WILLY. Remember, Christmas time, when you had the party here? You said you'd try to think of some spot for me here in town.

HOWARD. With us?

WILLY. Well, sure.

HOWARD. Oh, yeah, yeah. I remember. Well, I couldn't think of anything for you, Willy.

WILLY. I tell ya, Howard. The kids are all grown up, y'know. I don't need much any more. If I could take home—well, sixty-five dollars a week, I could swing it.

HOWARD. Yeah, but Willy, see I …

WILLY. I tell ya why, Howard. Speaking frankly and between the two of us, y'know—I'm just a little tired.

HOWARD.  Oh, I could understand that, Willy. But you're a road man, Willy, and we do a road business. We've only got a half-dozen salesmen on the floor here.

WILLY.  God knows, Howard. I never asked a favor of any man. But I was with the firm when your father used to carry you in here in his arms.

HOWARD.  I know that, Willy, but ...

WILLY.  Your father came to me the day you were born and asked me what I thought of the name Howard, may he rest in peace.

HOWARD.  I appreciate that, Willy, but there just is no spot here for you. If I had a spot I'd slam you right in, but I just don't have a single solitary spot.

*He looks for his lighter.* WILLY *has picked it up and gives it to him. Pause.*

WILLY (*with increasing anger*).  Howard, all I need to set my table is fifty dollars a week.

HOWARD.  But where am I going to put you, kid?

WILLY.  Look, it isn't a question of whether I can sell merchandise, is it?

HOWARD.  No, but it's business, kid, and everybody's gotta pull his own weight.

WILLY (*desperately*).  Just let me tell you a story, Howard ...

HOWARD.  'Cause you gotta admit, business is business.

WILLY (*angrily*).  Business is definitely business, but just listen for a minute. You don't understand this. When I was a boy—eighteen, nineteen—I was already on the road. And there was a question in my mind as to whether selling had a future for me. Because in those days I had a yearning to go to Alaska. See, there were three gold strikes in one month in Alaska, and I felt like going out. Just for the ride, you might say.

HOWARD (*barely interested*).  Don't say.

WILLY.  Oh, yeah, my father lived many years in Alaska. He was an adventurous man. We've got quite a little streak of self-reliance in our family. I thought I'd go out with my older brother and try to locate him, and maybe settle in the North with the old man. And I was almost decided to go, when I met a salesman in the Parker House. His name was Dave Singleman. And he was eighty-four years old, and he'd drummed merchandise in thirty-one states. And old Dave, he'd go up to his room, y'understand, put on his green velvet slippers—I'll never forget—and pick up his phone and call the buyers, and without ever leaving his room, at the age of eighty-four, he made his living. And when I saw that, I realized that selling was the greatest career a man could want. 'Cause what could be more satisfying than to be able to go, at the age of eighty-four, into twenty or thirty different cities, and pick up a phone, and be remembered and loved and helped by so many different people? Do you know? when he died—and by the way he died the death of a salesman, in his green velvet slippers in the smoker of the New York, New Haven and Hartford, going into Boston—when he died, hundreds of salesmen and buyers were at his funeral. Things were sad on a lotta trains for months after that. (*He stands up,* HOWARD *has not looked at him.*) In those days there was personality in it, Howard. There was respect, and comradeship, and gratitude in it. Today, it's all cut and dried, and there's no chance for bringing friendship to bear—or personality. You see what I mean? They don't know me any more.

HOWARD (*moving away, to the right*). That's just the thing, Willy.

WILLY. If I had forty dollars a week—that's all I'd need. Forty dollars, Howard.

HOWARD. Kid, I can't take blood from a stone, I . . .

WILLY (*desperation is on him now*). Howard, the year Al Smith was nominated, your father came to me and . . .

HOWARD (*starting to go off*). I've got to see some people, kid.

WILLY (*stopping him*). I'm talking about your father! There were promises made across this desk! You mustn't tell me you've got people to see— I put thirty-four years into this firm, Howard, and now I can't pay my insurance! You can't eat the orange and throw the peel away—a man is not a piece of fruit! (*After a pause.*) Now pay attention. Your father—in 1928 I had a big year. I averaged a hundred and seventy dollars a week in commissions.

HOWARD (*impatiently*). Now, Willy, you never averaged . . .

WILLY (*banging his hand on the desk*). I averaged a hundred and seventy dollars a week in the year of 1928! And your father came to me—or rather, I was in the office here—it was right over this desk—and he put his hand on my shoulder . . .

HOWARD (*getting up*). You'll have to excuse me, Willy, I gotta see some people. Pull yourself together. (*Going out.*) I'll be back in a little while.

*On* HOWARD'*s exit, the light on his chair grows very bright and strange.*

WILLY.  Pull myself together! What the hell did I say to him? My God, I was yelling at him! How could I? (WILLY *breaks off, staring at the light, which occupies the chair, animating it. He approaches this chair, standing across the desk from it.*) Frank, Frank, don't you remember what you told me that time? How you put your hand on my shoulder, and Frank . . . (*He leans on the desk and as he speaks the dead man's name he accidentally switches on the recorder, and instantly*)

HOWARD'S SON.  " . . . New York is Albany. The capital of Ohio is Cincinnati, the capital of Rhode Island is . . . " (*The recitation continues.*)

WILLY (*leaping away with fright, shouting*).  Ha! Howard! Howard! Howard!

HOWARD (*rushing in*).  What happened?

WILLY (*pointing at the machine, which continues nasally, childishly, with the capital cities*).  Shut it off! Shut it off!

HOWARD (*pulling the plug out*). Look, Willy ...
WILLY (*pressing his hands to his eyes*). I gotta get myself some coffee. I'll
get some coffee ...

WILLY *starts to walk out.* HOWARD *stops him.*

HOWARD (*rolling up the cord*). Willy, look ...
WILLY. I'll go to Boston.
HOWARD. Willy, you can't go to Boston for us.
WILLY. Why can't I go?
HOWARD. I don't want you to represent us. I've been meaning to tell you
for a long time now.
WILLY. Howard, are you firing me?
HOWARD. I think you need a good long rest, Willy.
WILLY. Howard ...
HOWARD. And when you feel better, come back, and we'll see if we can
work something out.
WILLY. But I gotta earn money, Howard. I'm in no position to ...
HOWARD. Where are your sons? Why don't your sons give you a hand?
WILLY. They're working on a very big deal.
HOWARD. This is no time for false pride, Willy. You go to your sons and you
tell them that you're tired. You've got two great boys, haven't you?
WILLY. Oh, no question, no question, but in the meantime ...
HOWARD. Then that's that, heh?
WILLY. All right, I'll go to Boston tomorrow.
HOWARD. No, no.
WILLY. I can't throw myself on my sons. I'm not a cripple!
HOWARD. Look, kid, I'm busy this morning.
WILLY (*grasping* HOWARD's *arm*). Howard, you've got to let me go to Boston!
HOWARD (*hard, keeping himself under control*). I've got a line of people
to see this morning. Sit down, take five minutes, and pull yourself to-
gether, and then go home, will ya? I need the office, Willy. (*He starts
to go, turns, remembering the recorder, starts to push off the table
holding the recorder.*) Oh, yeah. Whenever you can this week, stop by
and drop off the samples. You'll feel better, Willy, and then come back
and we'll talk. Pull yourself together, kid, there's people outside.

HOWARD *exits, pushing the table off left.* WILLY *stares into space, exhausted. Now the music is heard—*BEN's *music—first distantly, then
closer, closer. As* WILLY *speaks,* BEN *enters from the right. He carries
valise and umbrella.*

WILLY. Oh, Ben, how did you do it? What is the answer? Did you wind up
the Alaska deal already?
BEN. Doesn't take much time if you know what you're doing. Just a short
business trip. Boarding ship in an hour. Wanted to say good-by.
WILLY. Ben, I've got to talk to you.

BEN (*glancing at his watch*). Haven't the time, William.

WILLY (*crossing the apron to* BEN). Ben, nothing's working out. I don't know what to do.

BEN. Now, look here, William. I've bought timberland in Alaska and I need a man to look after things for me.

WILLY. God, timberland! Me and my boys in those grand outdoors!

BEN. You've a new continent at your doorstep, William. Get out of these cities, they're full of talk and time payments and courts of law. Screw on your fists and you can fight for a fortune up there.

WILLY. Yes, yes! Linda, Linda!

LINDA *enters as of old, with the wash.*

LINDA. Oh, you're back?

BEN. I haven't much time.

WILLY. No, wait! Linda, he's got a proposition for me in Alaska.

LINDA. But you've got ... (*To* BEN.) He's got a beautiful job here.

WILLY. But in Alaska, kid, I could ...

LINDA. You're doing well enough, Willy!

BEN (*To* LINDA). Enough for what, my dear?

LINDA (*frightened of* BEN *and angry at him*). Don't say those things to him! Enough to be happy right here, right now. (*To* WILLY, *while* BEN *laughs.*) Why must everybody conquer the world? You're well liked, and the boys love you, and someday— (*To* BEN)—why, old man Wagner told him just the other day that if he keeps it up he'll be a member of the firm, didn't he, Willy?

WILLY. Sure, sure. I am building something with this firm, Ben, and if a man is building something he must be on the right track, mustn't he?

BEN. What are you building? Lay your hand on it. Where is it?

WILLY (*hesitantly*). That's true, Linda, there's nothing.

LINDA. Why? (*To* BEN.) There's a man eighty-four years old ...

WILLY. That's right, Ben, that's right. When I look at that man I say, what is there to worry about?

BEN. Bah!

WILLY. It's true, Ben. All he has to do is go into any city, pick up the phone, and he's making his living and you know why?

BEN (*picking up his valise*). I've got to go.

WILLY (*holding* BEN *back*). Look at this boy!

BIFF, *in his high school sweater, enters carrying suitcase.* HAPPY *carries* BIFF's *shoulder guards, gold helmet, and football pants.*

WILLY. Without a penny to his name, three great universities are begging for him, and from there the sky's the limit, because it's not what you do, Ben. It's who you know and the smile on your face! It's contacts, Ben, contacts! The whole wealth of Alaska passes over the lunch table at the Commodore Hotel, and that's the wonder, the wonder of this country, that a man can end with diamonds here on the basis of being liked! (*He turns to* BIFF.) And that's why when you get out on that field today it's important. Because thousands of people will be rooting for you and loving you. (*To* BEN, *who has again begun to leave.*) And Ben! when he walks into a business office his name will sound out like a bell and all the doors will open to him! I've seen it, Ben, I've seen it a thousand times! You can't feel it with your hand like timber, but it's there!

BEN.  Good-by, William.

WILLY.  Ben, am I right? Don't you think I'm right? I value your advice.

BEN.  There's a new continent at your doorstep, William. You could walk out rich. Rich! (*He is gone.*)

WILLY.  We'll do it here, Ben! You hear me? We're gonna do it here!

*Young* BERNARD *rushes in. The gay music of the Boys is heard.*

BERNARD.  Oh, gee, I was afraid you left already!

WILLY.  Why? What time is it?

BERNARD.  It's half-past one!

WILLY.  Well, come on, everybody! Ebbets Field next stop! Where's the pennants? (*He rushes through the wall-line of the kitchen and out into the living room.*)

LINDA (*to* BIFF).  Did you pack fresh underwear?

BIFF (*who has been limbering up*).  I want to go!

BERNARD.  Biff, I'm carrying your helmet, ain't I?

HAPPY.  No, I'm carrying the helmet.

BERNARD.  Oh, Biff, you promised me.

HAPPY.  I'm carrying the helmet.

BERNARD.  How am I going to get in the locker room?

LINDA.  Let him carry the shoulder guards. (*She puts her coat and hat on in the kitchen.*)

BERNARD.  Can I, Biff? 'Cause I told everybody I'm going to be in the locker room.

HAPPY.  In Ebbets Field it's the clubhouse.

BERNARD.  I meant the clubhouse. Biff!

HAPPY.  Biff!

BIFF (*grandly, after a slight pause*).  Let him carry the shoulder guards.

HAPPY (*as he gives* BERNARD *the shoulder guards*).  Stay close to us now.

WILLY *rushes in with the pennants.*

WILLY (*handing them out*).  Everybody wave when Biff comes out on the field. (HAPPY *and* BERNARD *run off.*) You set now, boy?

*The music has died away.*

BIFF.  Ready to go, Pop. Every muscle is ready.

WILLY (*at the edge of the apron*).  You realize what this means?

BIFF. That's right, Pop.

WILLY (*feeling* BIFF's *muscles*). You're comin' home this afternoon captain of the All-Scholastic Championship Team of the City of New York.

BIFF. I got it, Pop. And remember, pal, when I take off my helmet, that touchdown is for you.

WILLY. Let's go! (*He is starting out, with his arm around* BIFF, *when* CHARLEY *enters, as of old, in knickers.*) I got no room for you, Charley.

CHARLEY. Room? For what?

WILLY. In the car.

CHARLEY. You goin' for a ride? I wanted to shoot some casino.

WILLY (*furiously*). Casino! (*Incredulously.*) Don't you realize what today is?

LINDA. Oh, he knows, Willy. He's just kidding you.

WILLY. That's nothing to kid about!

CHARLEY. No, Linda, what's goin' on?

LINDA. He's playing in Ebbets Field.

CHARLEY. Baseball in this weather?

WILLY. Don't talk to him. Come on, come on! (*He is pushing them out.*)

CHARLEY. Wait a minute, didn't you hear the news?

WILLY. What?

CHARLEY. Don't you listen to the radio? Ebbets Field just blew up.

WILLY. You go to hell! (CHARLEY *laughs. Pushing them out.*) Come on, come on! We're late.

CHARLEY (*as they go*). Knock a homer, Biff, knock a homer!

WILLY (*the last to leave, turning to* CHARLEY). I don't think that was funny, Charley. This is the greatest day of his life.

CHARLEY. Willy, when are you going to grow up?

WILLY. Yeah, heh? When this game is over, Charley, you'll be laughing out of the other side of your face. They'll be calling him another Red Grange. Twenty-five thousand a year.

CHARLEY (*kidding*). Is that so?

WILLY. Yeah, that's so.

CHARLEY. Well, then, I'm sorry, Willy. But tell me something.

WILLY. What?

CHARLEY. Who is Red Grange?

WILLY. Put up your hands. Goddam you, put up your hands!

CHARLEY, *chuckling, shakes his head and walks away, around the left corner of the stage.* WILLY *follows him. The music rises to a mocking frenzy.*

WILLY. Who the hell do you think you are, better than everybody else? You don't know everything, you big, ignorant, stupid . . . Put up your hands!

*Light rises, on the right side of the forestage, on a small table in the reception room of* CHARLEY's *office. Traffic sounds heard.* BERNARD, *now mature, sits whistling to himself. A pair of tennis rackets and an old overnight bag are on the floor beside him.*

WILLY (*offstage*). What are you walking away for? Don't walk away! If you're going to say something say it to my face! I know you laugh at me behind my back. You'll laugh out of the other side of your goddam face after this game. Touchdown! Touchdown! Eighty thousand people! Touchdown! Right between the goal posts.

(BERNARD *is a quiet, earnest, but self-assured young man.* WILLY's *voice is coming from right upstage now.* BERNARD *lowers his feet off the table and listens.* JENNY, *his father's secretary, enters.*)

JENNY (*distressed*). Say, Bernard, will you go out in the hall?

BERNARD. What is that noise? Who is it?

JENNY. Mr. Loman. He just got off the elevator.

BERNARD (*getting up*). Who's he arguing with?

JENNY. Nobody. There's nobody with him. I can't deal with him any more, and your father gets all upset every time he comes. I've got a lot of typing to do, and your father's waiting to sign it. Will you see him?

WILLY (*entering*). Touchdown! Touch—(*He sees* JENNY.) Jenny, Jenny, good to see you. How're ya? Workin'? Or still honest?

JENNY. Fine. How've you been feeling?

WILLY. Not much any more, Jenny. Ha, ha! (*He is surprised to see the rackets.*)

BERNARD. Hello, Uncle Willy.

WILLY (*almost shocked*). Bernard! Well, look who's here! (*He comes quickly, guiltily, to* BERNARD *and warmly shakes his hand.*)

BERNARD. How are you? Good to see you.

WILLY. What are you doing here?

BERNARD. Oh, just stopped by to see Pop. Get off my feet till my train leaves. I'm going to Washington in a few minutes.

WILLY. Is he in?

BERNARD. Yes, he's in his office with the accountant. Sit down.

WILLY (*sitting down*). What're you going to do in Washington?

BERNARD. Oh, just a case I've got there, Willy.

WILLY. That so? (*Indicating the rackets.*) You going to play tennis there?

BERNARD. I'm staying with a friend who's got a court.

WILLY. Don't say. His own tennis court. Must be fine people, I bet.

BERNARD. They are, very nice. Dad tells me Biff's in town.

WILLY (*with a big smile*). Yeah, Biff's in. Working on a very big deal, Bernard.

BERNARD. What's Biff doing?

WILLY. Well, he's been doing very big things in the West. But he decided to establish himself here. Very big. We're having dinner. Did I hear your wife had a boy?

BERNARD. That's right. Our second.

WILLY. Two boys! What do you know!

BERNARD. What kind of a deal has Biff got?

WILLY. Well, Bill Oliver—very big sporting-goods man—he wants Biff very badly. Called him in from the West. Long distance, carte blanche, special deliveries. Your friends have their own private tennis court?

BERNARD. You still with the old firm, Willy?

WILLY (*after a pause*). I'm—I'm overjoyed to see how you made the grade, Bernard, overjoyed. It's an encouraging thing to see a young man really—really . . . Looks very good for Biff—very . . . (*He breaks off, then.*) Bernard . . . (*He is so full of emotion, he breaks off again.*)

BERNARD. What is it, Willy?

WILLY (*small and alone*). What—what's the secret?

BERNARD. What secret?

WILLY. How—how did you? Why didn't he ever catch on?

BERNARD. I wouldn't know that, Willy.

WILLY (*confidentially, desperately*). You were his friend, his boyhood friend. There's something I don't understand about it. His life ended after that Ebbets Field game. From the age of seventeen nothing good ever happened to him.

BERNARD. He never trained himself for anything.

WILLY. But he did, he did. After high school he took so many correspondence courses. Radio mechanics; television; God knows what, and never made the slightest mark.

BERNARD (*taking off his glasses*). Willy, do you want to talk candidly?

WILLY (*rising, faces* BERNARD). I regard you as a very brilliant man, Bernard. I value your advice.

BERNARD. Oh, the hell with the advice, Willy. I couldn't advise you. There's just one thing I've always wanted to ask you. When he was supposed to graduate, and the math teacher flunked him . . .

WILLY. Oh, that son-of-a-bitch ruined his life.

BERNARD. Yeah, but, Willy, all he had to do was go to summer school and make up that subject.

WILLY. That's right, that's right.

BERNARD. Did you tell him not to go to summer school?

WILLY. Me? I begged him to go. I ordered him to go!

BERNARD. Then why wouldn't he go?

WILLY. Why? Why! Bernard, that question has been trailing me like a ghost for the last fifteen years. He flunked the subject, and laid down and died like a hammer hit him!

BERNARD. Take it easy, kid.

WILLY. Let me talk to you—I got nobody to talk to. Bernard, Bernard, was it my fault? Y'see? It keeps going around in my mind, maybe I did something to him. I got nothing to give him.

BERNARD. Don't take it so hard.

WILLY. Why did he lay down? What is the story there? You were his friend!

BERNARD.  Willy, I remember, it was June, and our grades came out. And he'd flunked math.

WILLY.  That son-of-a-bitch!

BERNARD.  No, it wasn't right then. Biff just got very angry, I remember, and he was ready to enroll in summer school.

WILLY (*surprised*).  He was?

BERNARD.  He wasn't beaten by it at all. But then, Willy, he disappeared from the block for almost a month. And I got the idea that he'd gone up to New England to see you. Did he have a talk with you then?

WILLY *stares in silence.*

BERNARD.  Willy?

WILLY (*with a strong edge of resentment in his voice*).  Yeah, he came to Boston. What about it?

BERNARD.  Well, just that when he came back—I'll never forget this, it always mystifies me. Because I'd thought so well of Biff, even though he'd always taken advantage of me. I loved him, Willy, y'know? And he came back after that month and took his sneakers—remember those sneakers with "University of Virginia" printed on them? He was so proud of those, wore them every day. And he took them down in the cellar, and burned them up in the furnace. We had a fist fight. It lasted at least half an hour. Just the two of us, punching each other down the cellar, and crying right through it. I've often thought of how strange it was that I knew he'd given up his life. What happened in Boston, Willy?

WILLY *looks at him as at an intruder.*

BERNARD.  I just bring it up because you asked me.

WILLY (*angrily*).  Nothing. What do you mean, "What happened?" What's that got to do with anything?

BERNARD.  Well, don't get sore.

WILLY.  What are you trying to do, blame it on me? If a boy lays down is that my fault?

BERNARD.  Now, Willy, don't get ...

WILLY.  Well, don't—don't talk to me that way! What does that mean, "What happened?"

CHARLEY *enters. He is in his vest, and he carries a bottle of bourbon.*

CHARLEY.  Hey, you're going to miss that train. (*He waves the bottle.*)

BERNARD.  Yeah, I'm going. (*He takes the bottle.*) Thanks, Pop. (*He picks up his rackets and bag.*) Good-by, Willy, and don't worry about it. You know, "If at first you don't succeed ... "

WILLY.  Yes, I believe in that.

BERNARD.  But sometimes, Willy, it's better for a man just to walk away.

WILLY.  Walk away?

BERNARD. That's right.

WILLY. But if you can't walk away?

BERNARD (*after a slight pause*). I guess that's when it's tough. (*Extending his hand.*) Good-by, Willy.

WILLY (*shaking* BERNARD's *hand*). Good-by, boy.

CHARLEY (*an arm on* BERNARD's *shoulder*). How do you like this kid? Gonna argue a case in front of the Supreme Court.

BERNARD (*protesting*). Pop!

WILLY (*genuinely shocked, pained, and happy*). No! The Supreme Court!

BERNARD. I gotta run. 'By, Dad!

CHARLEY. Knock 'em dead, Bernard!

BERNARD *goes off.*

WILLY (*as* CHARLEY *takes out his wallet*). The Supreme Court! And he didn't even mention it!

CHARLEY (*counting out money on the desk*). He don't have to—he's gonna do it.

WILLY. And you never told him what to do, did you? You never took any interest in him.

CHARLEY. My salvation is that I never took any interest in anything. There's some money—fifty dollars. I got an accountant inside.

WILLY. Charley, look . . . (*with difficulty.*) I got my insurance to pay. If you can manage it—I need a hundred and ten dollars.

CHARLEY *doesn't reply for a moment; merely stops moving.*

WILLY. I'd draw it from my bank but Linda would know, and I . . .

CHARLEY. Sit down, Willy.

WILLY (*moving toward the chair*). I'm keeping an account of everything, remember. I'll pay every penny back. (*He sits.*)

CHARLEY. Now listen to me, Willy.

WILLY. I want you to know I appreciate . . .

CHARLEY (*sitting down on the table*). Willy, what're you doin'? What the hell is going on in your head?

WILLY. Why? I'm simply . . .

CHARLEY. I offered you a job. You make fifty dollars a week. And I won't send you on the road.

WILLY. I've got a job.

CHARLEY. Without pay? What kind of a job is a job without pay? (*He rises.*) Now, look, kid, enough is enough. I'm no genius but I know when I'm being insulted.

WILLY. Insulted!

CHARLEY. Why don't you want to work for me?

WILLY. What's the matter with you? I've got a job.

CHARLEY. Then what're you walkin' in here every week for?

WILLY (*getting up*). Well, if you don't want me to walk in here . . .

CHARLEY. I'm offering you a job.

WILLY. I don't want your goddam job!

CHARLEY. When the hell are you going to grow up?

WILLY (*furiously*). You big ignoramus, if you say that to me again I'll rap you one! I don't care how big you are! (*He's ready to fight.*)

*Pause.*

CHARLEY (*kindly, going to him*). How much do you need, Willy?

WILLY. Charley, I'm strapped. I'm strapped. I don't know what to do. I was just fired.

CHARLEY. Howard fired you?

WILLY. That snotnose. Imagine that? I named him. I named him Howard.

CHARLEY. Willy, when're you gonna realize that them things don't mean anything? You named him Howard, but you can't sell that. The only thing you got in this world is what you can sell. And the funny thing is that you're a salesman, and you don't know that.

WILLY. I've always tried to think otherwise, I guess. I always felt that if a man was impressive, and well liked, that nothing . . .

CHARLEY. Why must everybody like you? Who liked J. P. Morgan? Was he impressive? In a Turkish bath he'd look like a butcher. But with his pockets on he was very well liked. Now listen, Willy, I know you don't like me, and nobody can say I'm in love with you, but I'll give you a job because—just for the hell of it, put it that way. Now what do you say?

WILLY. I—I just can't work for you, Charley.

CHARLEY. What're you, jealous of me?

WILLY. I can't work for you, that's all, don't ask me why.

CHARLEY (*angered, takes out more bills*). You been jealous of me all your life, you damned fool! Here, pay your insurance. (*He puts the money in* WILLY's *hand.*)

WILLY. I'm keeping strict accounts.

CHARLEY. I've got some work to do. Take care of yourself. And pay your insurance.

WILLY (*moving to the right*). Funny, y'know? After all the highways, and the trains, and the appointments, and the years, you end up worth more dead than alive.

CHARLEY. Willy, nobody's worth nothin' dead. (*After a slight pause.*) Did you hear what I said?

WILLY *stands still, dreaming.*

CHARLEY. Willy!

WILLY. Apologize to Bernard for me when you see him. I didn't mean to argue with him. He's a fine boy. They're all fine boys, and they'll end up big—all of them. Someday they'll all play tennis together. Wish me luck, Charley. He saw Bill Oliver today.

CHARLEY. Good luck.

WILLY (*on the verge of tears*). Charley, you're the only friend I got. Isn't that a remarkable thing? (*He goes out.*)
CHARLEY. Jesus!

CHARLEY *stares after him a moment and follows. All light blacks out. Suddenly raucous music is heard, and a red glow rises behind the screen at right.* STANLEY, *a young waiter, appears, carrying a table, followed by* HAPPY, *who is carrying two chairs.*

STANLEY (*putting the table down*). That's all right, Mr. Loman, I can handle it myself. (*He turns and takes the chairs from* HAPPY *and places them at the table.*)
HAPPY (*glancing around*). Oh, this is better.
STANLEY. Sure, in the front there you're in the middle of all kinds of noise. Whenever you got a party, Mr. Loman, you just tell me and I'll put you back here. Y'know, there's a lotta people they don't like it private, because when they go out they like to see a lotta action around them because they're sick and tired to stay in the house by theirself. But I know you, you ain't from Hackensack. You know what I mean?
HAPPY (*sitting down*). So how's it coming, Stanley?
STANLEY. Ah, it's a dog life. I only wish during the war they'd a took me in the Army. I coulda been dead by now.
HAPPY. My brother's back, Stanley.
STANLEY. Oh, he come back, heh? From the Far West.
HAPPY. Yeah, big cattle man, my brother, so treat him right. And my father's coming too.
STANLEY. Oh, your father too!
HAPPY. You got a couple of nice lobsters?
STANLEY. Hundred percent, big.
HAPPY. I want them with the claws.
STANLEY. Don't worry, I don't give you no mice. (HAPPY *laughs.*) How about some wine? It'll put a head on the meal.
HAPPY. No. You remember, Stanley, that recipe I brought you from overseas? With the champagne in it?
STANLEY. Oh, yeah, sure. I still got it tacked up yet in the kitchen. But that'll have to cost a buck apiece anyways.
HAPPY. That's all right.
STANLEY. What'd you, hit a number or somethin'?
HAPPY. No, it's a little celebration. My brother is—I think he pulled off a big deal today. I think we're going into business together.
STANLEY. Great! That's the best for you. Because a family business, you know what I mean?—that's the best.
HAPPY. That's what I think.
STANLEY. 'Cause what's the difference? Somebody steals? It's in the family. Know what I mean? (*Sotto voce.*) Like this bartender here. The boss is goin' crazy what kinda leak he's got in the cash register. You put it in but it don't come out.

HAPPY *(raising his head)*. Sh!

STANLEY. What?

HAPPY. You notice I wasn't lookin' right or left, was I?

STANLEY. No.

HAPPY. And my eyes are closed.

STANLEY. So what's the . . . ?

HAPPY. Strudel's comin'.

STANLEY *(catching on, looks around)*. Ah, no, there's no . . .

> He breaks off as a furred, lavishly dressed GIRL enters and sits at the next table. Both follow her with their eyes.

STANLEY. Geez, how'd ya know?

HAPPY. I got radar or something. *(Staring directly at her profile.)* Oooooooo . . . Stanley.

STANLEY. I think that's for you, Mr. Loman.

HAPPY. Look at that mouth. Oh, God. And the binoculars.

STANLEY. Geez, you got a life, Mr. Loman.

HAPPY. Wait on her.

STANLEY *(going to the GIRL's table)*. Would you like a menu, ma'am?

GIRL. I'm expecting someone, but I'd like a . . .

HAPPY. Why don't you bring her—excuse me, miss, do you mind? I sell champagne, and I'd like you to try my brand. Bring her a champagne, Stanley.

GIRL. That's awfully nice of you.

HAPPY. Don't mention it. It's all company money. *(He laughs.)*

GIRL. That's a charming product to be selling, isn't it?

HAPPY. Oh, gets to be like everything else. Selling is selling, y'know.

GIRL. I suppose.

HAPPY. You don't happen to sell, do you?

GIRL. No, I don't sell.

HAPPY. Would you object to a compliment from a stranger? You ought to be on a magazine cover.

GIRL *(looking at him a little archly)*. I have been.

> STANLEY comes in with a glass of champagne.

HAPPY. What'd I say before, Stanley? You see? She's a cover girl.

STANLEY. Oh, I could see, I could see.

HAPPY *(to the GIRL)*. What magazine?

GIRL. Oh, a lot of them. *(She takes the drink.)* Thank you.

HAPPY. You know what they say in France, don't you? "Champagne is the drink of the complexion"—Hya, Biff!

> BIFF *has entered and sits with* HAPPY.

BIFF. Hello, kid. Sorry I'm late.

HAPPY.  I just got here. Uh, Miss ... ?

GIRL.  Forsythe.

HAPPY.  Miss Forsythe, this is my brother.

BIFF.  Is Dad here?

HAPPY.  His name is Biff. You might've heard of him. Great football player.

GIRL.  Really? What team?

HAPPY.  Are you familiar with football?

GIRL.  No, I'm afraid I'm not.

HAPPY.  Biff is quarterback with the New York Giants.

GIRL.  Well, that is nice, isn't it? (*She drinks.*)

HAPPY.  Good health.

GIRL.  I'm happy to meet you.

HAPPY.  That's my name. Hap. It's really Harold, but at West Point they called me Happy.

GIRL (*now really impressed*).  Oh, I see. How do you do? (*She turns her profile.*)

BIFF.  Isn't Dad coming?

HAPPY.  You want her?

BIFF.  Oh, I could never make that.

HAPPY.  I remember the time that idea would never come into your head. Where's the old confidence, Biff?

BIFF.  I just saw Oliver ...

HAPPY.  Wait a minute. I've got to see that old confidence again. Do you want her? She's on call.

BIFF.  Oh, no. (*He turns to look at the* GIRL.)

HAPPY.  I'm telling you. Watch this (*Turning to the* GIRL.) Honey? (*She turns to him.*) Are you busy?

GIRL.  Well, I am ... but I could make a phone call.

HAPPY.  Do that, will you, honey? And see if you can get a friend. We'll be here for a while. Biff is one of the greatest football players in the country.

GIRL (*standing up*).  Well, I'm certainly happy to meet you.

HAPPY.  Come back soon.

GIRL.  I'll try.

HAPPY.  Don't try, honey, try hard.

*The* GIRL *exits.* STANLEY *follows, shaking his head in bewildered admiration.*

HAPPY.  Isn't that a shame now? A beautiful girl like that? That's why I can't get married. There's not a good woman in a thousand. New York is loaded with them, kid!

BIFF.  Hap, look ...

HAPPY.  I told you she was on call!

BIFF (*strangely unnerved*).  Cut it out, will ya? I want to say something to you.

HAPPY.  Did you see Oliver?

BIFF.  I saw him all right. Now look, I want to tell Dad a couple of things and I want you to help me.

HAPPY.  What? Is he going to back you?

BIFF.  Are you crazy? You're out of your goddam head, you know that?

HAPPY.  Why? What happened?

BIFF (*breathlessly*).  I did a terrible thing today, Hap. It's been the strangest day I ever went through. I'm all numb, I swear.

HAPPY.  You mean he wouldn't see you?

BIFF.  Well, I waited six hours for him, see? All day. Kept sending my name in. Even tried to date his secretary so she'd get me to him, but no soap.

HAPPY.  Because you're not showin' the old confidence, Biff. He remembered you, didn't he?

BIFF (*stopping* HAPPY *with a gesture*).  Finally, about five o'clock, he comes out. Didn't remember who I was or anything. I felt like such an idiot, Hap.

HAPPY.  Did you tell him my Florida idea?

BIFF.  He walked away. I saw him for one minute. I got so mad I could've torn the walls down! How the hell did I ever get the idea I was a salesman there? I even believed myself that I'd been a salesman for him! And then he gave me one look and—I realized what a ridiculous lie my whole life has been! We've been talking in a dream for fifteen years. I was a shipping clerk.

HAPPY.  What'd you do?

BIFF (*with great tension and wonder*).  Well, he left, see. And the secretary went out. I was all alone in the waiting room. I don't know what came over me, Hap. The next thing I know I'm in his office—paneled walls, everything. I can't explain it. I—Hap. I took his fountain pen.

HAPPY.  Geez, did he catch you?

BIFF.  I ran out. I ran down all eleven flights. I ran and ran and ran.

HAPPY.  That was an awful dumb—what'd you do that for?

BIFF (*agonized*).  I don't know, I just—wanted to take something, I don't know. You gotta help me, Hap. I'm gonna tell Pop.

HAPPY.  You crazy? What for?

BIFF.  Hap, he's got to understand that I'm not the man somebody lends that kind of money to. He thinks I've been spiting him all these years and it's eating him up.

HAPPY.  That's just it. You tell him something nice.

BIFF.  I can't.

HAPPY.  Say you got a lunch date with Oliver tomorrow.

BIFF.  So what do I do tomorrow?

HAPPY.  You leave the house tomorrow and come back at night and say Oliver is thinking it over. And he thinks it over for a couple of weeks, and gradually it fades away and nobody's the worse.

BIFF.  But it'll go on forever!

HAPPY. Dad is never so happy as when he's looking forward to something!

WILLY *enters.*

HAPPY. Hello, scout!

WILLY. Gee, I haven't been here in years!

STANLEY *has followed* WILLY *in and sets a chair for him.* STANLEY *starts off but* HAPPY *stops him.*

HAPPY. Stanley!

STANLEY *stands by, waiting for an order.*

BIFF (*going to* WILLY *with guilt, as to an invalid*). Sit down, Pop. You want a drink?

WILLY. Sure, I don't mind.

BIFF. Let's get a load on.

WILLY. You look worried.

BIFF. N-no. (*To* STANLEY.) Scotch all around. Make it doubles.

STANLEY. Doubles, right. (*He goes.*)

WILLY. You had a couple already, didn't you?

BIFF. Just a couple, yeah.

WILLY. Well, what happened, boy? (*Nodding affirmatively, with a smile.*) Everything go all right?

BIFF (*takes a breath, then reaches out and grasps* WILLY's *hand*). Pal . . . (*He is smiling bravely, and* WILLY *is smiling too.*) I had an experience today.

HAPPY. Terrific, Pop.

WILLY. That so? What happened?

BIFF (*high, slightly alcoholic, above the earth*). I'm going to tell you everything from first to last. It's been a strange day. (*Silence. He looks around, composes himself as best he can, but his breath keeps breaking the rhythm of his voice.*) I had to wait quite a while for him, and . . .

WILLY. Oliver?

BIFF. Yeah, Oliver. All day, as a matter of cold fact. And a lot of—instances— facts, Pop, facts about my life came back to me. Who was it, Pop? Who ever said I was a salesman with Oliver?

WILLY. Well, you were.

BIFF. No, Dad, I was a shipping clerk.

WILLY. But you were practically . . .

BIFF (*with determination*). Dad, I don't know who said it first, but I was never a salesman for Bill Oliver.

WILLY. What're you talking about?

BIFF. Let's hold on to the facts tonight, Pop. We're not going to get anywhere bullin' around. I was a shipping clerk.

WILLY (*angrily*). All right, now listen to me . . .

BIFF. Why don't you let me finish?

WILLY. I'm not interested in stories about the past or any crap of that kind because the woods are burning, boys, you understand? There's a big blaze going on all around. I was fired today.

BIFF (*shocked*). How could you be?

WILLY. I was fired, and I'm looking for a little good news to tell your mother, because the woman has waited and the woman has suffered. The gist of it is that I haven't got a story left in my head, Biff. So don't give me a lecture about facts and aspects. I am not interested. Now what've you got to say to me?

STANLEY *enters with three drinks. They wait until he leaves.*

WILLY. Did you see Oliver?

BIFF. Jesus, Dad!

WILLY. You mean you didn't go up there?

HAPPY. Sure he went up there.

BIFF. I did. I—saw him. How could they fire you?

WILLY (*on the edge of his chair*). What kind of a welcome did he give you?

BIFF. He won't even let you work on commission?

WILLY. I'm out! (*Driving.*) So tell me, he gave you a warm welcome?

HAPPY. Sure, Pop, sure!

BIFF (*driven*). Well, it was kind of ...

WILLY. I was wondering if he'd remember you. (*To* HAPPY.) Imagine, man doesn't see him for ten, twelve years and gives him that kind of a welcome!

HAPPY. Damn right!

BIFF (*trying to return to the offensive*). Pop, look ...

WILLY. You know why he remembered you, don't you? Because you impressed him in those days.

BIFF. Let's talk quietly and get this down to the facts, huh?

WILLY (*as though* BIFF *had been interrupting*). Well, what happened? It's great news, Biff. Did he take you into his office or'd you talk in the waiting room?

BIFF. Well, he came in, see, and ...

WILLY (*with a big smile*). What'd he say? Betcha he threw his arm around you.

BIFF. Well, he kinda ...

WILLY. He's a fine man. (*To* HAPPY.) Very hard man to see, y'know.

HAPPY (*agreeing*). Oh, I know.

WILLY (*to* BIFF). Is that where you had the drinks?

BIFF. Yeah, he gave me a couple of—no, no!

HAPPY (*cutting in*). He told him my Florida idea.

WILLY. Don't interrupt. (*To* BIFF.) How'd he react to the Florida idea?

BIFF. Dad, will you give me a minute to explain?

WILLY. I've been waiting for you to explain since I sat down here! What happened? He took you into his office and what?

BIFF. Well—I talked. And—and he listened, see.

WILLY. Famous for the way he listens, y'know. What was his answer?

BIFF. His answer was—(*He breaks off, suddenly angry.*) Dad, you're not letting me tell you what I want to tell you!

WILLY (*accusing, angered*). You didn't see him, did you?

BIFF. I did see him!

WILLY. What'd you insult him or something? You insulted him, didn't you?

BIFF. Listen, will you let me out of it, will you just let me out of it!

HAPPY. What the hell!

WILLY. Tell me what happened!

BIFF (*to* HAPPY). I can't talk to him!

*A single trumpet note jars the ear. The light of green leaves stains the house, which holds the air of night and a dream.* YOUNG BERNARD *enters and knocks on the door of the house.*

YOUNG BERNARD (*frantically*). Mrs. Loman, Mrs. Loman!

HAPPY. Tell him what happened!

BIFF (*to* HAPPY.) Shut up and leave me alone!

WILLY. No, no! You had to go and flunk math!

BIFF. What math? What're you talking about?

YOUNG BERNARD. Mrs. Loman, Mrs. Loman!

LINDA *appears in the house, as of old.*

WILLY (*wildly*). Math, math, math!

BIFF. Take it easy, Pop!

YOUNG BERNARD. Mrs. Loman!

WILLY (*furiously*). If you hadn't flunked you'd've been set by now!

BIFF. Now, look, I'm gonna tell you what happened, and you're going to listen to me.

YOUNG BERNARD. Mrs. Loman!

BIFF. I waited six hours . . .

HAPPY. What the hell are you saying?

BIFF. I kept sending in my name but he wouldn't see me. So finally he . . . (*He continues unheard as light fades low on the restaurant.*)

YOUNG BERNARD. Biff flunked math!

LINDA. No!

YOUNG BERNARD. Birnbaum flunked him! They won't graduate him!

LINDA. But they have to. He's gotta go to the university. Where is he? Biff! Biff!

YOUNG BERNARD. No, he left. He went to Grand Central.

LINDA. Grand—You mean he went to Boston!

YOUNG BERNARD. Is Uncle Willy in Boston?

LINDA.   Oh, maybe Willy can talk to the teacher. Oh, the poor, poor boy!

*Light on house area snaps out.*

BIFF (*at the table, now audible, holding up a gold fountain pen*). . . . so
     I'm washed up with Oliver, you understand? Are you listening to me?
WILLY (*at a loss*). Yeah, sure. If you hadn't flunked . . .
BIFF. Flunked what? What're you talking about?
WILLY.   Don't blame everything on me! I didn't flunk math—you did! What
     pen?
HAPPY.   That was awful dumb, Biff, a pen like that is worth—
WILLY (*seeing the pen for the first time*). You took Oliver's pen?
BIFF (*weakening*). Dad, I just explained it to you.
WILLY.   You stole Bill Oliver's fountain pen!
BIFF.   I didn't exactly steal it! That's just what I've been explaining to you!
HAPPY.   He had it in his hand and just then Oliver walked in, so he got ner-
     vous and stuck it in his pocket!
WILLY.   My God, Biff!
BIFF.   I never intended to do it, Dad!
OPERATOR'S VOICE.   Standish Arms, good evening!
WILLY (*shouting*). I'm not in my room!
BIFF (*frightened*). Dad, what's the matter? (*He and* HAPPY *stand up.*)
OPERATOR.   Ringing Mr. Loman for you!
WILLY.   I'm not there, stop it!
BIFF (*horrified, gets down on one knee before* WILLY). Dad, I'll make good,
     I'll make good. (WILLY *tries to get to his feet.* BIFF *holds him down.*) Sit
     down now.
WILLY.   No, you're no good, you're no good for anything.
BIFF.   I am, Dad, I'll find something else, you understand? Now don't worry
     about anything. (*He holds up* WILLY's *face.*) Talk to me, Dad.
OPERATOR.   Mr. Loman does not answer. Shall I page him?
WILLY (*attempting to stand, as though to rush and silence the* OPERATOR).
     No, no, no!
HAPPY.   He'll strike something, Pop.
WILLY.   No, no . . .
BIFF (*desperately, standing over* WILLY). Pop, listen! Listen to me! I'm
     telling you something good. Oliver talked to his partner about the
     Florida idea. You listening? He—he talked to his partner, and he came
     to me . . . I'm going to be all right, you hear? Dad, listen to me, he said
     it was just a question of the amount!
WILLY.   Then you . . . got it?
HAPPY.   He's gonna be terrific, Pop!
WILLY (*trying to stand*). Then you got it, haven't you? You got it! You
     got it!
BIFF (*agonized, holds* WILLY *down*). No, no. Look, Pop. I'm supposed to
     have lunch with them tomorrow. I'm just telling you this so you'll

know that I can still make an impression, Pop. And I'll make good
somewhere, but I can't go tomorrow, see.

WILLY. Why not? You simply ...

BIFF. But the pen, Pop!

WILLY. You give it to him and tell him it was an oversight!

HAPPY. Sure, have lunch tomorrow!

BIFF. I can't say that ...

WILLY. You were doing a crossword puzzle and accidentally used his pen!

BIFF. Listen, kid, I took those balls years ago, now I walk in with his fountain pen? That clinches it, don't you see? I can't face him like that! I'll
try elsewhere.

PAGE'S VOICE. Paging Mr. Loman!

WILLY. Don't you want to be anything?

BIFF. Pop, how can I go back?

WILLY. You don't want to be anything, is that what's behind it?

BIFF (*now angry at* WILLY *for not crediting his sympathy*). Don't take it
that way! You think it was easy walking into that office after what I'd
done to him? A team of horses couldn't have dragged me back to Bill
Oliver!

WILLY. Then why'd you go?

BIFF. Why did I go? Why did I go! Look at you! Look at what's become
of you!

*Off left,* THE WOMAN *laughs.*

WILLY. Biff, you're going to go to that lunch tomorrow, or ...

BIFF. I can't go. I've got no appointment!

HAPPY. Biff, for ... !

WILLY. Are you spiting me?

BIFF. Don't take it that way! Goddammit!

WILLY (*strikes* BIFF *and falters away from the table*). You rotten little
louse! Are you spiting me?

THE WOMAN. Someone's at the door, Willy!

BIFF. I'm no good, can't you see what I am?

HAPPY (*separating them*). Hey, you're in a restaurant! Now cut it out, both
of you! (*The girls enter.*) Hello, girls, sit down.

THE WOMAN *laughs, off left.*

MISS FORSYTHE. I guess we might as well. This is Letta.

THE WOMAN. Willy, are you going to wake up?

BIFF (*ignoring* WILLY). How're ya, miss, sit down. What do you drink?

MISS FORSYTHE. Letta might not be able to stay long.

LETTA. I gotta get up very early tomorrow. I got jury duty. I'm so excited!
Were you fellows ever on a jury?

BIFF. No, but I been in front of them! (*The girls laugh.*) This is my father.

LETTA. Isn't he cute? Sit down with us, Pop.

HAPPY.  Sit him down, Biff!

BIFF (*going to him*).  Come on, slugger, drink us under the table. To hell with it! Come on, sit down, pal.

*On* BIFF*'s last insistence,* WILLY *is about to sit.*

THE WOMAN (*now urgently*).  Willy, are you going to answer the door!

THE WOMAN*'s call pulls* WILLY *back. He starts right, befuddled.*

BIFF.  Hey, where are you going?

WILLY.  Open the door.

BIFF.  The door?

WILLY.  The washroom . . . the door . . . where's the door?

BIFF (*leading* WILLY *to the left*).  Just go straight down.

WILLY *moves left.*

THE WOMAN.  Willy, Willy, are you going to get up, get up, get up, get up?

WILLY *exits left.*

LETTA.  I think it's sweet you bring your daddy along.

MISS FORSYTHE.  Oh, he isn't really your father!

BIFF (*at left, turning to her resentfully*).  Miss Forsythe, you've just seen a prince walk by. A fine, troubled prince. A hardworking, unappreciated prince. A pal, you understand? A good companion. Always for his boys.

LETTA.  That's so sweet.

HAPPY.  Well, girls, what's the program? We're wasting time. Come on, Biff. Gather round. Where would you like to go?

BIFF.  Why don't you do something for him?

HAPPY.  Me!

BIFF.  Don't you give a damn for him, Hap?

HAPPY.  What're you talking about? I'm the one who . . .

BIFF.  I sense it, you don't give a good goddam about him. (*He takes the rolled-up hose from his pocket and puts it on the table in front of* HAPPY.) Look what I found in the cellar, for Christ's sake. How can you bear to let it go on?

HAPPY.  Me? Who goes away? Who runs off and . . .

BIFF.  Yeah, but he doesn't mean anything to you. You could help him—I can't! Don't you understand what I'm talking about? He's going to kill himself, don't you know that?

HAPPY.  Don't I know it! Me!

BIFF.  Hap, help him! Jesus . . . help him . . . Help me, help me, I can't bear to look at his face! (*Ready to weep, he hurries out, up right.*)

HAPPY (*starting after him*).  Where are you going?

MISS FORSYTHE.  What's he so mad about?

HAPPY.  Come on, girls, we'll catch up with him.

MISS FORSYTHE (*as* HAPPY *pushes her out*).  Say, I don't like that temper of his!

HAPPY.  He's just a little overstrung, he'll be all right!
WILLY (*off left, as* THE WOMAN *laughs*).  Don't answer! Don't answer!
LETTA.  Don't you want to tell your father ...
HAPPY.  No, that's not my father. He's just a guy. Come on, we'll catch Biff, and, honey, we're going to paint this town! Stanley, where's the check! Hey, Stanley!

*They exit.* STANLEY *looks toward left.*

STANLEY (*calling to* HAPPY *indignantly*).  Mr. Loman! Mr. Loman!

STANLEY *picks up a chair and follows them off. Knocking is heard off left.* THE WOMAN *enters, laughing.* WILLY *follows her. She is in a black slip; he is buttoning his shirt. Raw, sensuous music accompanies their speech:*

WILLY.  Will you stop laughing? Will you stop?
THE WOMAN.  Aren't you going to answer the door? He'll wake the whole hotel.
WILLY.  I'm not expecting anybody.
THE WOMAN.  Whyn't you have another drink, honey, and stop being so damn self-centered?
WILLY.  I'm so lonely.
THE WOMAN.  You know you ruined me, Willy? From now on, whenever you come to the office, I'll see that you go right through to the buyers. No waiting at my desk anymore, Willy. You ruined me.
WILLY.  That's nice of you to say that.
THE WOMAN.  Gee, you are self-centered! Why so sad? You are the saddest, self-centeredest soul I ever did see-saw. (*She laughs. He kisses her.*) Come on inside, drummer boy. It's silly to be dressing in the middle of the night. (*As knocking is heard.*) Aren't you going to answer the door?
WILLY.  They're knocking on the wrong door.
THE WOMAN.  But I felt the knocking. And he heard us talking in here. Maybe the hotel's on fire!
WILLY (*his terror rising*).  It's a mistake.
THE WOMAN.  Then tell him to go away!
WILLY.  There's nobody there.
THE WOMAN.  It's getting on my nerves, Willy. There's somebody standing out there and it's getting on my nerves!
WILLY (*pushing her away from him*).  All right, stay in the bathroom here, and don't come out. I think there's a law in Massachusetts about it, so don't come out. It may be that new room clerk. He looked very mean. So don't come out. It's a mistake, there's no fire.

*The knocking is heard again. He takes a few steps away from her, and she vanishes into the wing. The light follows him, and now he is facing* YOUNG BIFF, *who carries a suitcase.* BIFF *steps toward him. The music is gone.*

BIFF.  Why didn't you answer?

WILLY.  Biff! What are you doing in Boston?

BIFF.  Why didn't you answer? I've been knocking for five minutes, I called you on the phone . . .

WILLY.  I just heard you. I was in the bathroom and had the door shut. Did anything happen home?

BIFF.  Dad—I let you down.

WILLY.  What do you mean?

BIFF.  Dad . . .

WILLY.  Biffo, what's this about? (*Putting his arm around* BIFF.) Come on, let's go downstairs and get you a malted.

BIFF.  Dad, I flunked math.

WILLY.  Not for the term?

BIFF.  The term. I haven't got enough credits to graduate.

WILLY.  You mean to say Bernard wouldn't give you the answers?

BIFF.  He did, he tried, but I only got a sixty-one.

WILLY.  And they wouldn't give you four points?

BIFF.  Birnbaum refused absolutely. I begged him, Pop, but he won't give me those points. You gotta talk to him before they close the school. Because if he saw the kind of man you are, and you just talked to him in your way, I'm sure he'd come through for me. The class came right before practice, see, and I didn't go enough. Would you talk to him? He'd like you, Pop. You know the way you could talk.

WILLY.  You're on. We'll drive right back.

BIFF.  Oh, Dad, good work! I'm sure he'll change it for you!

WILLY.  Go downstairs and tell the clerk I'm checkin' out. Go right down.

BIFF.  Yes, sir! See, the reason he hates me, Pop—one day he was late for class so I got up at the blackboard and imitated him. I crossed my eyes and talked with a lithp.

WILLY (*laughing*).  You did? The kids like it?

BIFF.  They nearly died laughing!

WILLY.  Yeah? What'd you do?

BIFF.  The thquare root of thixthy twee is . . . (WILLY *bursts out laughing;* BIFF *joins.*) And in the middle of it he walked in!

WILLY *laughs and* THE WOMAN *joins in offstage.*

WILLY (*without hesitation*).  Hurry downstairs and . . .

BIFF.  Somebody in there?

WILLY.  No, that was next door.

THE WOMAN *laughs offstage.*

BIFF.  Somebody got in your bathroom!

WILLY.  No, it's the next room, there's a party . . .

THE WOMAN (*enters, laughing; she lisps this*).  Can I come in? There's something in the bathtub, Willy, and it's moving!

WILLY *looks at* BIFF, *who is staring open-mouthed and horrified at* THE WOMAN.

WILLY. Ah—you better go back to your room. They must be finished paint-ing by now. They're painting her room so I let her take a shower here. Go back, go back ... (*He pushes her.*)

THE WOMAN (*resisting*). But I've got to get dressed, Willy, I can't ...

WILLY. Get out of here! Go back, go back ... (*Suddenly striving for the ordinary.*) This is Miss Francis, Biff, she's a buyer. They're painting her room. Go back, Miss Francis, go back ...

THE WOMAN. But my clothes, I can't go out naked in the hall!

WILLY (*pushing her offstage*). Get outa here! Go back, go back!

(BIFF *slowly sits down on his suitcase as the argument continues offstage.*)

THE WOMAN. Where's my stockings? You promised me stockings, Willy!

WILLY. I have no stockings here!

THE WOMAN. You had two boxes of size nine sheers for me, and I want them!

WILLY. Here, for God's sake, will you get outa here!

THE WOMAN (*enters holding a box of stockings*). I just hope there's nobody in the hall. That's all I hope. (*To* BIFF.) Are you football or baseball?

BIFF. Football.

THE WOMAN (*angry, humiliated*). That's me too. G'night. (*She snatches her clothes from* WILLY, *and walks out.*)

WILLY (*after a pause*). Well, better get going. I want to get to the school first thing in the morning. Get my suits out of the closet. I'll get my valise. (BIFF *doesn't move.*) What's the matter! (BIFF *remains motion-less, tears falling.*) She's a buyer. Buys for J. H. Simmons. She lives down the hall—they're painting. You don't imagine—(*He breaks off. After a pause.*) Now listen, pal, she's just a buyer. She sees merchan-dise in her room and they have to keep it looking just so ... (*Pause. Assuming command.*) All right, get my suits. (BIFF *doesn't move.*) Now stop crying and do as I say. I gave you an order. Biff, I gave you an order! Is that what you do when I give you an order? How dare you cry! (*Putting his arm around* BIFF.) Now look, Biff, when you grow up you'll understand about these things. You mustn't—you mustn't overemphasize a thing like this. I'll see Birnbaum first thing in the morning.

BIFF. Never mind.

WILLY (*getting down beside* BIFF). Never mind! He's going to give you those points. I'll see to it.

BIFF. He wouldn't listen to you.

WILLY. He certainly will listen to me. You need those points for the U. of Virginia.

BIFF. I'm not going there.

WILLY. Heh? If I can't get him to change that mark you'll make it up in summer school. You've got all summer to . . .

BIFF (*his weeping breaking from him*). Dad . . .

WILLY (*infected by it*). Oh, my boy . . .

BIFF. Dad . . .

WILLY. She's nothing to me, Biff. I was lonely, I was terribly lonely.

BIFF. You—you gave her Mama's stockings! (*His tears break through and he rises to go.*)

WILLY (*grabbing for* BIFF). I gave you an order!

BIFF. Don't touch me, you—liar!

WILLY. Apologize for that!

BIFF. You fake! You phony little fake! You fake! (*Overcome, he turns quickly and weeping fully goes out with his suitcase.* WILLY *is left on the floor on his knees.*)

WILLY. I gave you an order! Biff, come back here or I'll beat you! Come back here! I'll whip you!

STANLEY *comes quickly in from the right and stands in front of* WILLY.

WILLY (*shouts at* STANLEY). I gave you an order . . .

STANLEY. Hey, let's pick it up, pick it up, Mr. Loman. (*He helps* WILLY *to his feet.*) Your boys left with the chippies. They said they'll see you home.

*A second waiter watches some distance away.*

WILLY. But we were supposed to have dinner together.

*Music is heard,* WILLY'*s theme.*

STANLEY. Can you make it?

WILLY. I'll—sure, I can make it. (*Suddenly concerned about his clothes.*) Do I—I look all right?

STANLEY. Sure, you look all right. (*He flicks a speck off* WILLY'*s lapel.*)

WILLY. Here—here's a dollar.

STANLEY. Oh, your son paid me. It's all right.

WILLY (*putting it in* STANLEY'*s hand*). No, take it. You're a good boy.

STANLEY. Oh, no, you don't have to . . .

WILLY. Here—here's some more, I don't need it any more. (*After a slight pause.*) Tell me—is there a seed store in the neighborhood?

STANLEY. Seeds? You mean like to plant?

*As* WILLY *turns,* STANLEY *slips the money back into his jacket pocket.*

WILLY. Yes. Carrots, peas . . .

STANLEY. Well, there's hardware stores on Sixth Avenue, but it may be too late now.

WILLY (*anxiously*). Oh, I'd better hurry. I've got to get some seeds. (*He starts off to the right.*) I've got to get some seeds, right away. Nothing's planted. I don't have a thing in the ground.

WILLY *hurries out as the light goes down.* STANLEY *moves over to the right after him, watches him off. The other waiter has been staring at* WILLY.

STANLEY (*to the waiter*). Well, whatta you looking at?

*The waiter picks up the chairs and moves off right.* STANLEY *takes the table and follows him. The light fades on this area. There is a long pause, the sound of the flute coming over. The light gradually rises on the kitchen, which is empty.* HAPPY *appears at the door of the house, followed by* BIFF. HAPPY *is carrying a large bunch of long-stemmed roses. He enters the kitchen, looks around for* LINDA. *Not seeing her, he turns to* BIFF, *who is just outside the house door, and makes a gesture with his hands, indicating "Not here, I guess." He looks into the living room and freezes. Inside,* LINDA, *unseen, is seated,* WILLY'*s coat on her lap. She rises ominously and quietly and moves toward* HAPPY, *who backs up into the kitchen, afraid.*

HAPPY. Hey, what're you doing up? (LINDA *says nothing but moves toward him implacably.*) Where's Pop? (*He keeps backing up to the right, and now* LINDA *is in full view in the doorway to the living room.*) Is he sleeping?

LINDA. Where were you?

HAPPY (*trying to laugh it off*). We met two girls, Mom, very fine types. Here, we brought you some flowers. (*Offering them to her.*) Put them in your room, Ma.

*She knocks them to the floor at* BIFF'*s feet. He has now come inside and closed the door behind him. She stares at* BIFF, *silent.*

HAPPY. Now what'd you do that for? Mom, I want you to have some flowers . . .

LINDA (*cutting* HAPPY *off, violently to* BIFF). Don't you care whether he lives or dies?

HAPPY (*going to the stairs*). Come upstairs, Biff.

BIFF (*with a flare of disgust, to* HAPPY). Go away from me! (*To* LINDA.) What do you mean, lives or dies? Nobody's dying around here, pal.

LINDA. Get out of my sight! Get out of here!

BIFF. I wanna see the boss.

LINDA. You're not going near him!

BIFF. Where is he? (*He moves into the living room and* LINDA *follows.*)

LINDA (*shouting after* BIFF). You invite him for dinner. He looks forward to it all day—(BIFF *appears in his parents' bedroom, looks around, and exits*)—and then you desert him there. There's no stranger you'd do that to!

HAPPY. Why? He had a swell time with us. Listen, when I—(LINDA *comes back into the kitchen*)—desert him I hope I don't outlive the day!

LINDA.  Get out of here!

HAPPY.  Now look, Mom . . .

LINDA.  Did you have to go to women tonight? You and your lousy rotten whores!

BIFF *re-enters the kitchen.*

HAPPY.  Mom, all we did was follow Biff around trying to cheer him up! (*To* BIFF.) Boy, what a night you gave me!

LINDA.  Get out of here, both of you, and don't come back! I don't want you tormenting him any more. Go on now, get your things together! (*To* BIFF.) You can sleep in his apartment. (*She starts to pick up the flowers and stops herself.*) Pick up this stuff, I'm not your maid any more. Pick it up, you bum, you!

HAPPY *turns his back to her in refusal.* BIFF *slowly moves over and gets down on his knees, picking up the flowers.*

LINDA.  You're a pair of animals! Not one, not another living soul would have had the cruelty to walk out on that man in a restaurant!

BIFF (*not looking at her*).  Is that what he said?

LINDA.  He didn't have to say anything. He was so humiliated he nearly limped when he came in.

HAPPY.  But, Mom, he had a great time with us . . .

BIFF (*cutting him off violently*).  Shut up!

*Without another word,* HAPPY *goes upstairs.*

LINDA.  You! You didn't even go in to see if he was all right!

BIFF (*still on the floor in front of* LINDA, *the flowers in his hand; with self-loathing*).  No. Didn't. Didn't do a damned thing. How do you like that, heh? Left him babbling in a toilet.

LINDA.  You louse. You . . .

BIFF.  Now you hit it on the nose! (*He gets up, throws the flowers in the wastebasket.*) The scum of the earth, and you're looking at him!

LINDA.  Get out of here!

BIFF.  I gotta talk to the boss, Mom. Where is he?

LINDA.  You're not going near him. Get out of this house!

BIFF (*with absolute assurance, determination*).  No. We're gonna have an abrupt conversation, him and me.

LINDA.  You're not talking to him.

*Hammering is heard from outside the house, off right.* BIFF *turns toward the noise.*

LINDA (*suddenly pleading*).  Will you please leave him alone?

BIFF.  What's he doing out there?

LINDA.  He's planting the garden!

BIFF (*quietly*).  Now? Oh, my God!

BIFF *moves outside,* LINDA *following. The light dies down on them and comes up on the center of the apron as* WILLY *walks into it. He is carrying a flashlight, a hoe, and a handful of seed packets. He raps the top of the hoe sharply to fix it firmly, and then moves to the left, measuring off the distance with his foot. He holds the flashlight to look at the seed packets, reading off the instructions. He is in the blue of night.*

WILLY.  Carrots . . . quarter-inch apart. Rows . . . one-foot rows. (*He measures it off.*) One foot. (*He puts down a package and measures off.*)  Beets. (*He puts down another package and measures again.*) Lettuce. (*He reads the package, puts it down.*) One foot—(*He breaks off as* BEN *appears at the right and moves slowly down to him.*) What a proposition, ts, ts. Terrific, terrific. 'Cause she's suffered, Ben, the woman has suffered. You understand me? A man can't go out the way he came in, Ben, a man has got to add up to something. You can't, you can't—(BEN *moves toward him as though to interrupt.*) You gotta consider now. Don't answer so quick. Remember, it's a guaranteed twenty-thousand-dollar proposition. Now look, Ben, I want you to go through the ins and outs of this thing with me. I've got nobody to talk to, Ben, and the woman has suffered, you hear me?

BEN (*standing still, considering*).  What's the proposition?

WILLY.  It's twenty thousand dollars on the barrelhead. Guaranteed, gilt-edged, you understand?

BEN.  You don't want to make a fool of yourself. They might not honor the policy.

WILLY.  How can they dare refuse? Didn't I work like a coolie to meet every premium on the nose? And now they don't pay off? Impossible!

BEN.  It's called a cowardly thing, William.

WILLY.  Why? Does it take more guts to stand here the rest of my life ringing up a zero?

BEN (*yielding*).  That's a point, William. (*He moves, thinking, turns.*) And twenty thousand—that is something one can feel with the hand, it is there.

WILLY (*now assured, with rising power*).  Oh, Ben, that's the whole beauty of it! I see it like a diamond, shining in the dark, hard and rough, that I can pick up and touch in my hand. Not like—like an appointment! This would not be another damned-fool appointment, Ben, and it changes all the aspects. Because he thinks I'm nothing, see, and so he spites me. But the funeral . . . (*Straightening up.*) Ben, that funeral will be massive! They'll come from Maine, Massachusetts, Vermont, New Hampshire! All the old-timers with the strange license plates—that boy will be thunderstruck, Ben, because he never realized—I am known! Rhode Island, New York, New Jersey—I am known, Ben, and he'll see it with his eyes once and for all. He'll see what I am, Ben! He's in for a shock, that boy!

BEN (*coming down to the edge of the garden*). He'll call you a coward.
WILLY (*suddenly fearful*). No, that would be terrible.
BEN. Yes. And a damned fool.
WILLY. No, no, he mustn't, I won't have that! (*He is broken and desperate.*)
BEN. He'll hate you, William.

    *The gay music of the Boys is heard.*

WILLY. Oh, Ben, how do we get back to all the great times? Used to be so
    full of light, and comradeship, the sleigh-riding in winter, and the rud-
    diness on his cheeks. And always some kind of good news coming up,
    always something nice coming up ahead. And never even let me carry
    the valises in the house, and simonizing, simonizing that little red car!
    Why, why can't I give him something and not have him hate me?
BEN. Let me think about it. (*He glances at his watch.*) I still have a little
    time. Remarkable proposition, but you've got to be sure you're not
    making a fool of yourself.

    BEN *drifts off upstage and goes out of sight.* BIFF *comes down from*
    *the left.*

WILLY (*suddenly conscious of* BIFF, *turns and looks up at him, then be-*
    *gins picking up the packages of seeds in confusion*). Where the hell
    is that seed? (*Indignantly.*) You can't see nothing out here! They
    boxed in the whole goddam neighborhood!
BIFF. There are people all around here. Don't you realize that?
WILLY. I'm busy. Don't bother me.
BIFF (*taking the hoe from* WILLY). I'm saying good-by to you, Pop. (WILLY
    *looks at him, silent, unable to move.*) I'm not coming back any more.
WILLY. You're not going to see Oliver tomorrow?
BIFF. I've got no appointment, Dad.
WILLY. He put his arm around you, and you've got no appointment?
BIFF. Pop, get this now, will you? Everytime I've left it's been a—fight that
    sent me out of here. Today I realized something about myself and I
    tried to explain it to you and I—I think I'm just not smart enough to
    make any sense out of it for you. To hell with whose fault it is or any-
    thing like that. (*He takes* WILLY's *arm.*) Let's just wrap it up, heh?
    Come on in, we'll tell Mom. (*He gently tries to pull* WILLY *to left.*)
WILLY (*frozen, immobile, with guilt in his voice*). No, I don't want to
    see her.
BIFF. Come on! (*He pulls again, and* WILLY *tries to pull away.*)
WILLY (*highly nervous*). No, no, I don't want to see her.
BIFF (*tries to look into* WILLY's *face, as if to find the answer there*). Why
    don't you want to see her?
WILLY (*more harshly now*). Don't bother me, will you?
BIFF. What do you mean, you don't want to see her? You don't want them
    calling you yellow, do you? This isn't your fault; it's me, I'm a bum.

Now come inside! (WILLY *strains to get away.*) Did you hear what I said to you?

WILLY *pulls away and quickly goes by himself into the house.* BIFF *follows.*

LINDA (*to* WILLY). Did you plant, dear?

BIFF (*at the door, to* LINDA). All right, we had it out. I'm going and I'm not writing any more.

LINDA (*going to* WILLY *in the kitchen*). I think that's the best way, dear. 'Cause there's no use drawing it out, you'll just never get along.

WILLY *doesn't respond.*

BIFF. People ask where I am and what I'm doing, you don't know, and you don't care. That way it'll be off your mind and you can start brightening up again. All right? That clears it, doesn't it? (WILLY *is silent, and* BIFF *goes to him.*) You gonna wish me luck, scout? (*He extends his hand.*) What do you say?

LINDA. Shake his hand, Willy.

WILLY (*turning to her, seething with hurt*). There's no necessity—to mention the pen at all, y'know.

BIFF (*gently*). I've got no appointment, Dad.

WILLY (*erupting fiercely*). He put his arm around . . . ?

BIFF. Dad, you're never going to see what I am, so what's the use of arguing? If I strike oil I'll send you a check. Meantime forget I'm alive.

WILLY (*to* LINDA). Spite, see?

BIFF. Shake hands, Dad.

WILLY. Not my hand.

BIFF. I was hoping not to go this way.

WILLY. Well, this is the way you're going. Good-by.

BIFF *looks at him a moment, then turns sharply and goes to the stairs.*

WILLY (*stops him with*). May you rot in hell if you leave this house!

BIFF (*turning*). Exactly what is it that you want from me?

WILLY. I want you to know, on the train, in the mountains, in the valleys, wherever you go, that you cut down your life for spite!

BIFF. No, no.

WILLY. Spite, spite, is the word of your undoing! And when you're down and out, remember what did it. When you're rotting somewhere beside the railroad tracks, remember, and don't you dare blame it on me!

BIFF. I'm not blaming it on you!

WILLY. I won't take the rap for this, you hear?

HAPPY *comes down the stairs and stands on the bottom step, watching.*

BIFF. That's just what I'm telling you!

WILLY (*sinking into a chair at a table, with full accusation*). You're trying to put a knife in me—don't think I don't know what you're doing!

BIFF. All right, phony! Then let's lay it on the line. (*He whips the rubber tube out of his pocket and puts it on the table.*)

HAPPY. You crazy . . .

LINDA. Biff! (*She moves to grab the hose, but* BIFF *holds it down with his hand.*)

BIFF. Leave it there! Don't move it!

WILLY (*not looking at it*). What is that?

BIFF. You know goddam well what that is.

WILLY (*caged, wanting to escape*). I never saw that.

BIFF. You saw it. The mice didn't bring it into the cellar! What is this supposed to do, make a hero out of you? This supposed to make me sorry for you?

WILLY. Never heard of it.

BIFF. There'll be no pity for you, you hear it? No pity!

WILLY (*to* LINDA). You hear the spite!

BIFF. No, you're going to hear the truth—what you are and what I am!

LINDA. Stop it!

WILLY. Spite!

HAPPY (*coming down toward* BIFF). You cut it now!

BIFF (*to* HAPPY). The man don't know who we are! The man is gonna know! (*To* WILLY.) We never told the truth for ten minutes in this house!

HAPPY. We always told the truth!

BIFF (*turning on him*). You big blow, are you the assistant buyer? You're one of the two assistants to the assistant, aren't you?

HAPPY. Well, I'm practically . . .

BIFF. You're practically full of it! We all are! and I'm through with it. (*To* WILLY.) Now hear this, Willy, this is me.

WILLY. I know you!

BIFF. You know why I had no address for three months? I stole a suit in Kansas City and I was in jail. (*To* LINDA, *who is sobbing.*) Stop crying. I'm through with it.

LINDA *turns away from them, her hands covering her face.*

WILLY. I suppose that's my fault!

BIFF. I stole myself out of every good job since high school!

WILLY. And whose fault is that?

BIFF. And I never got anywhere because you blew me so full of hot air I could never stand taking orders from anybody! That's whose fault it is!

WILLY. I hear that!

LINDA. Don't, Biff!

BIFF. It's goddam time you heard that! I had to be boss big shot in two weeks, and I'm through with it!

WILLY.  Then hang yourself! For spite, hang yourself!
BIFF.  No! Nobody's hanging himself, Willy! I ran down eleven flights with
a pen in my hand today. And suddenly I stopped, you hear me? And in
the middle of that office building, do you hear this? I stopped in the
middle of that building and I saw—the sky. I saw the things that I love
in this world. The work and the food and time to sit and smoke. And I
looked at the pen and said to myself, what the hell am I grabbing this
for? Why am I trying to become what I don't want to be? What am I
doing in an office, making a contemptuous, begging fool of myself,
when all I want is out there, waiting for me the minute I say I know
who I am! Why can't I say that, Willy? (*He tries to make* WILLY *face
him, but* WILLY *pulls away and moves to the left.*)
WILLY (*with hatred, threateningly*). The door of your life is wide open!
BIFF.  Pop! I'm a dime a dozen, and so are you!
WILLY (*turning on him now in an uncontrolled outburst*). I am not a
dime a dozen! I am Willy Loman, and you are Biff Loman!

BIFF *starts for* WILLY, *but is blocked by* HAPPY. *In his fury,* BIFF *seems on
the verge of attacking his father.*

BIFF.  I am not a leader of men, Willy, and neither are you. You were never
anything but a hard-working drummer who landed in the ash can like
all the rest of them! I'm one dollar an hour, Willy! I tried seven states
and couldn't raise it. A buck an hour! Do you gather my meaning? I'm
not bringing home any prizes any more, and you're going to stop
waiting for me to bring them home!
WILLY (*directly to* BIFF). You vengeful, spiteful mutt!

BIFF *breaks from* HAPPY. WILLY, *in fright, starts up the stairs.* BIFF *grabs
him.*

BIFF (*at the peak of his fury*). Pop! I'm nothing! I'm nothing, Pop. Can't
you understand that? There's no spite in it any more. I'm just what I
am, that's all.

BIFF'*s fury has spent itself and he breaks down, sobbing, holding on
to* WILLY, *who dumbly fumbles for* BIFF'*s face.*

WILLY (*astonished*).  What're you doing? What're you doing? (*To* LINDA.)
Why is he crying?
BIFF (*crying, broken*).  Will you let me go, for Christ's sake? Will you take
that phony dream and burn it before something happens? (*Struggling
to contain himself he pulls away and moves to the stairs.*) I'll go in
the morning. Put him—put him to bed. (*Exhausted,* BIFF *moves up the
stairs to his room.*)
WILLY (*after a long pause, astonished, elevated*).  Isn't that—isn't that remarkable? Biff—he likes me!
LINDA.  He loves you, Willy!

HAPPY (*deeply moved*). Always did, Pop.

WILLY. Oh, Biff! (*Staring wildly.*) He cried! Cried to me. (*He is choking with his love, and now cries out his promise.*) That boy—that boy is going to be magnificent!

BEN *appears in the light just outside the kitchen.*

BEN. Yes, outstanding, with twenty thousand behind him.

LINDA (*sensing the racing of his mind, fearfully, carefully.*) Now come to bed, Willy. It's all settled now.

WILLY (*finding it difficult not to rush out of the house*). Yes, we'll sleep. Come on. Go to sleep, Hap.

BEN. And it does take a great kind of a man to crack the jungle.

   *In accents of dread,* BEN's *idyllic music starts up.*

HAPPY (*his arm around* LINDA). I'm getting married, Pop, don't forget it. I'm changing everything. I'm gonna run that department before the year is up. You'll see, Mom. (*He kisses her.*)

BEN. The jungle is dark but full of diamonds, Willy.

   WILLY *turns, moves, listening to* BEN.

LINDA. Be good. You're both good boys, just act that way, that's all.

HAPPY. 'Night, Pop. (*He goes upstairs.*)

LINDA (*to* WILLY). Come, dear.

BEN (*with greater force*). One must go in to fetch a diamond out.

WILLY (*to* LINDA, *as he moves slowly along the edge of the kitchen, toward the door*). I just want to get settled down, Linda. Let me sit alone for a little.

LINDA (*almost uttering her fear*). I want you upstairs.

WILLY (*taking her in his arms*). In a few minutes, Linda. I couldn't sleep right now. Go on, you look awful tired. (*He kisses her.*)

BEN. Not like an appointment at all. A diamond is rough and hard to the touch.

WILLY. Go on now. I'll be right up.

LINDA. I think this is the only way, Willy.

WILLY. Sure, it's the best thing.

BEN. Best thing!

WILLY. The only way. Everything is gonna be—go on, kid, get to bed. You look so tired.

LINDA. Come right up.

WILLY. Two minutes.

   LINDA *goes into the living room, then reappears in her bedroom.* WILLY *moves just outside the kitchen door.*

WILLY. Loves me. (*Wonderingly.*) Always loved me. Isn't that a remarkable thing? Ben, he'll worship me for it!

BEN (*with promise*). It's dark there, but full of diamonds.

WILLY. Can you imagine that magnificence with twenty thousand dollars in his pocket?

LINDA (*calling from her room*). Willy! Come up!

WILLY (*calling into the kitchen*). Yes! Yes. Coming! It's very smart, you realize that, don't you, sweetheart? Even Ben sees it. I gotta go, baby. 'By! 'By! (*Going over to* BEN, *almost dancing.*) Imagine? When the mail comes he'll be ahead of Bernard again!

BEN. A perfect proposition all around.

WILLY. Did you see how he cried to me? Oh, if I could kiss him, Ben!

BEN. Time, William, time!

WILLY. Oh, Ben, I always knew one way or another we were gonna make it, Biff and I.

BEN (*looking at his watch*). The boat. We'll be late. (*He moves slowly off into the darkness.*)

WILLY (*elegiacally, turning to the house*). Now when you kick off, boy, I want a seventy-yard boot, and get right down the field under the ball, and when you hit, hit low and hit hard, because it's important, boy (*He swings around and faces the audience.*) There's all kinds of important people in the stands, and the first thing you know . . . (*Suddenly realizing he is alone.*) Ben! Ben, where do I . . . ? (*He makes a sudden movement of search.*) Ben, how do I . . . ?

LINDA (*calling*). Willy, you coming up?

WILLY (*uttering a gasp of fear, whirling about as if to quiet her*). Sh! (*He turns around as if to find his way; sounds, faces, voices, seem to be swarming in upon him and he flicks at them, crying*) Sh! Sh! (*Suddenly music, faint and high, stops him. It rises in intensity, almost to an unbearable scream. He goes up and down on his toes, and rushes off around the house.*) Shhh!

LINDA. Willy?

*There is no answer.* LINDA *waits.* BIFF *gets up off his bed. He is still in his clothes.* HAPPY *sits up.* BIFF *stands listening.*

LINDA (*with real fear*). Willy, answer me! Willy!

*There is the sound of a car starting and moving away at full speed.*

LINDA. No!

BIFF (*rushing down the stairs*). Pop!

*As the car speeds off the music crashes down in a frenzy of sound, which becomes the soft pulsation of a single cello string.* BIFF *slowly returns to his bedroom. He and* HAPPY *gravely don their jackets.* LINDA *slowly walks out of her room. The music has developed into a dead march. The leaves of day are appearing over everything.* CHARLEY *and* BERNARD, *somberly dressed, appear and knock on the kitchen door.* BIFF *and* HAPPY *slowly descend the stairs to the kitchen as* CHARLEY *and* BERNARD *enter. All stop a moment when* LINDA, *in clothes of mourning, bearing a little bunch of roses, comes through the draped doorway into the kitchen. She goes to* CHARLEY *and takes his arm. Now all move toward the audience, through the wall-line of the kitchen. At the limit of the apron,* LINDA *lays down the flowers, kneels, and sits back on her heels. All stare down at the grave.*

### *Requiem*

CHARLEY.  It's getting dark, Linda.

LINDA *doesn't react. She stares at the grave.*

BIFF.  How about it, Mom? Better get some rest, heh? They'll be closing the gate soon.

LINDA *makes no move. Pause.*

HAPPY (*deeply angered*).  He had no right to do that. There was no necessity for it. We would've helped him.

CHARLEY (*grunting*).  Hmmm.

BIFF.  Come along, Mom.

LINDA.  Why didn't anybody come?

CHARLEY.  It was a very nice funeral.

LINDA.  But where are all the people he knew? Maybe they blame him.

CHARLEY.  Naa. It's a rough world, Linda. They wouldn't blame him.

LINDA.  I can't understand it. At this time especially. First time in thirty-five years we were just about free and clear. He only needed a little salary. He was even finished with the dentist.

CHARLEY.  No man only needs a little salary.

LINDA.  I can't understand it.

BIFF.  There were a lot of nice days. When he'd come home from a trip; or on Sundays, making the stoop; finishing the cellar; putting on the new porch; when he built the extra bathroom; and put up the garage. You know something, Charley, there's more of him in that front stoop than in all the sales he ever made.

CHARLEY.  Yeah. He was a happy man with a batch of cement.

LINDA.  He was so wonderful with his hands.

BIFF.  He had the wrong dreams. All, all, wrong.

HAPPY (*almost ready to fight* BIFF).  Don't say that!

BIFF.  He never knew who he was.

CHARLEY (*stopping* HAPPY'*s movement and reply; to* BIFF).  Nobody dast blame this man. You don't understand: Willy was a salesman. And for a salesman, there is no rock bottom to the life. He don't put a bolt to a nut, he don't tell you the law or give you medicine. He's a man way out there in the blue, riding on a smile and a shoeshine. And when they start not smiling back—that's an earthquake. And then you get yourself a couple of spots on your hat, and you're finished. Nobody dast

blame this man. A salesman is got to dream, boy. It comes with the
territory.

BIFF. Charley, the man didn't know who he was.

HAPPY (*infuriated*). Don't say that!

BIFF. Why don't you come with me, Happy?

HAPPY. I'm not licked that easily. I'm staying right in this city, and I'm
gonna beat this racket! (*He looks at* BIFF, *his chin set.*) The Loman
Brothers!

BIFF. I know who I am, kid.

HAPPY. All right, boy. I'm gonna show you and everybody else that Willy Loman did not die in vain. He had a good dream. It's the only dream you
can have—to come out number-one man. He fought it out here, and
this is where I'm gonna win it for him.

BIFF (*with a hopeless glance at* HAPPY, *bends toward his mother*). Let's
go, Mom.

LINDA. I'll be with you in a minute. Go on, Charley. (*He hesitates.*) I want
to, just for a minute. I never had a chance to say good-by.

CHARLEY *moves away, followed by* HAPPY. BIFF *remains a slight distance up and left of* LINDA. *She sits there, summoning herself. The
flute begins, not far away, playing behind her speech.*

LINDA. Forgive me, dear. I can't cry. I don't know what it is, but I can't cry. I
don't understand it. Why did you ever do that? Help me, Willy, I can't cry.
It seems to me that you're just on another trip. I keep expecting you.
Willy, dear, I can't cry. Why did you do it? I search and search and I search,
and I can't understand it, Willy. I made the last payment on the house today. Today, dear. And there'll be nobody home. (*A sob rises in her throat.*)
We're free and clear. (*Sobbing mournfully, released.*) We're free. (BIFF
*comes slowly toward her.*) We're free . . . We're free . . .

BIFF *lifts her to her feet and moves out up right with her in his arms.*
LINDA *sobs quietly.* BERNARD *and* CHARLEY *come together and follow
them, followed by* HAPPY. *Only the music of the flute is left on the
darkening stage as over the house the hard towers of the apartment buildings rise into sharp focus and the curtain falls.*

# ▨ TOPICS FOR
# CRITICAL THINKING AND WRITING

## *The Play on the Page*

1. Miller said in the *New York Times* (February 27, 1949, Sec. II, p. 1) that
   tragedy shows man's struggle to secure "his sense of personal dignity" and that "his destruction in the attempt posits a wrong or an evil
   in his environment." Does this make sense when applied to some

earlier tragedy (for example, *Oedipus Rex* or *Hamlet*), and does it apply convincingly to *Death of a Salesman*? Is this the tragedy of an individual's own making? Or is society at fault for corrupting and exploiting Willy? Or both?

2. Is Willy pathetic rather than tragic? If pathetic, does this imply that the play is less worthy than if he is tragic?

3. Do you feel that Miller is straining too hard to turn a play about a little man into a big, impressive play? For example, do the musical themes, the unrealistic setting, the appearances of Ben, and the speech at the grave seem out of keeping in a play about the death of a salesman?

4. We don't know what Willy sells, and we don't know whether or not the insurance will be paid after his death. Do you consider these uncertainties to be faults in the play?

5. Is Howard a villain?

6. Characterize Linda.

## The Play on the Stage

7. It is sometimes said that in this realistic play that includes symbolic and expressionistic elements, Biff and Happy can be seen as two aspects of Willy. In this view, Biff more or less represents Willy's spiritual needs, and Happy represents his materialism and his sexuality. If you were directing the play, would you adopt this point of view? Whatever your interpretation, how would you costume the brothers?

8. Although Miller envisioned Willy as a small man (literally small), the role was first performed by Lee J. Cobb, a large man. If you were casting the play, what actor would you select? Why? Whom would you choose for Linda, Biff, Happy, Bernard, and Charley?

9. Select roughly thirty lines of dialogue, and discuss the movements (gestures and blocking) that as a director you would suggest to the performers.

# DAVID HENRY HWANG

*David Henry Hwang, born in 1951 in the Los Angeles suburb of San Gabriel, is the son of parents born in China. His mother's background was unusual for a Chinese-American: Her grandparents had converted to Protestant fundamentalism, and the couple—who met at the University of Southern California in the early 1950s—could not marry until David's father converted to Christianity. David's father became a banker, his mother a pianist and a teacher; the family pursued the American dream, and David especially considered himself an assimi-*

*lated American.As a senior at Stanford in 1979, he directed a production of his first play,* FOB *(i.e., "Fresh Off the Boat," an ironic reference to recent immigrants), in the lobby of a college dormitory.Within a year the play appeared on the professional stage in New York. Hwang has gone on to write other acclaimed plays, most notably* M. Butterfly *(1988).* Trying to Find Chinatown *was first produced in 1996.*

# Trying to Find Chinatown*

1996

## CHARACTERS

BENJAMIN, *Caucasian male, early twenties.*
RONNIE, *Asian-American male, mid-twenties.*

## TIME AND PLACE

*A street corner on the Lower East Side, New York City.The present.*

## NOTE ON MUSIC

*Obviously, it would be foolish to require that the actor portraying Ronnie perform the specified violin music live. The score of this play can be played on tape over the house speakers, and the actor can feign playing the violin using a bow treated with soap. However, in order to effect a convincing illusion, it is desirable that the actor possess some familiarity with the violin or another stringed instrument.*

*Darkness. Over the house speakers, sound fades in: Hendrix-like virtuoso rock 'n' roll riffs—heavy feedback, distortion, phase shifting, wah-wah—amplified over a tiny Fender pug-nose.*

*Lights fade up to reveal that the music's being played over a solid-body electric violin by Ronnie, a Chinese-American male in his mid-twenties; he is dressed in retro-'60s clothing and has a few requisite '90s body mutilations. He's playing on a sidewalk for money, his violin case open before him; change and a few stray bills have been left by previous passersby.*

*Benjamin enters; he's in his early twenties, blond, blue-eyed, a Midwestern tourist in the big city. He holds a scrap of paper in his hands, scanning street signs for an address. He pauses before Ronnie, listens for a while.With a truly bravura run, Ronnie concludes the number and falls to his knees, gasping. Benjamin applauds.*

---

BENJAMIN:  Good. That was really great. *(Pause)* I didn't . . . I mean, a fiddle . . . I mean, I'd heard them at square dances, on country stations and all, but I never . . . wow, this must really be New York City!

*(Benjamin applauds, starts to walk on. Still on his knees, Ronnie clears his throat loudly.)*

Oh, I . . . you're not just doing this for your health, right?

*(Benjamin reaches in his picket, pulls out a couple of coins. Ronnie clears his throat again.)*

Look, I'm not a millionaire, I'm just . . .

*(Benjamin pulls out his wallet, removes a dollar bill. Ronnie nods his head and gestures toward the violin case as he takes out a pack of cigarettes, lights one.)*

RONNIE:  And don't call it a "fiddle," OK?
BENJAMIN:  Oh. Well, I didn't mean to—
RONNIE:  You sound like a wuss. A hick. A dipshit.
BENJAMIN:  It just slipped out. I didn't really—
RONNIE:  If this was a fiddle, I'd be sitting here with a cob pipe, stomping my cowboy boots and kicking up hay. Then I'd go home and fuck my cousin.
BENJAMIN:  Oh! Well, I don't really think—
RONNIE:  Do you see a cob pipe? Am I fucking my cousin?
BENJAMIN:  Well, no, not at the moment, but—
RONNIE:  All right. Then this is a violin, now you give me your money, and I ignore the insult. Herein endeth the lesson.

*(Pause.)*

BENJAMIN:  Look, a dollar's more than I've ever given to a . . . to someone asking for money.
RONNIE:  Yeah, well, this is New York. Welcome to the cost of living.
BENJAMIN:  What I mean is, maybe in exchange, you could help me—?
RONNIE:  Jesus Christ! Do you see a sign around my neck reading "Big Apple Fucking Tourist Bureau"?
BENJAMIN:  I'm just looking for an address, I don't think it's far from here, maybe you could . . . ?

*(Benjamin holds out his scrap of paper, Ronnie snatches it away.)*

RONNIE:  You're lucky I'm such a goddamn softy. *(He looks at the paper.)* Oh, fuck you. Just suck my dick, you and the cousin you rode in on.
BENJAMIN:  I don't get it! What are you—?
RONNIE:  Eat me. You know exactly what I—
BENJAMIN:  I'm just asking for a little—

RONNIE: "13 Doyers Street"? Like you don't know where that is?

BENJAMIN: Of course I don't know! That's why I'm asking—

RONNIE: C'mon, you trailer-park refugee. You don't know that's Chinatown?

BENJAMIN: Sure I know that's Chinatown.

RONNIE: I know you know that's Chinatown.

BENJAMIN: So? That doesn't mean I know where Chinatown—

RONNIE: So why is it that you picked *me,* of all the street musicians in the city—to point you in the direction of Chinatown? Lemme guess—is it the earring? No, I don't think so. The Hendrix riffs? Guess again, you fucking moron.

BENJAMIN: Now, wait a minute. I see what you're—

RONNIE: What are you gonna ask me next? Where you can find the best dim sum in the city? Whether I can direct you to a genuine opium den? Or do I happen to know how you can meet Miss Saigon for a night of nookie-nookie followed by a good old-fashioned ritual suicide? Now, get your white ass off my sidewalk. One dollar doesn't even begin to make up for all this aggravation. Why don't you go back home and race bullfrogs, or whatever it is you do for—?

BENJAMIN: Brother, I can absolutely relate to your anger. Righteous rage, I suppose, would be a more appropriate term. To be marginalized, as we are, by a white racist patriarchy, to the point where the accomplishments of our people are obliterated from the history books, this is cultural genocide of the first order, leading to the fact that you must do battle with all of Euro-America's emasculating and brutal stereotypes of Asians—the opium den, the sexual objectification of the Asian female, the exoticized image of a tourist's Chinatown which ignores the exploitation of workers, the failure to unionize, the high rate of mental illness and tuberculosis—against these, each day, you rage, no, not as a victim, but as a survivor, yes, brother, a glorious warrior survivor!

*(Silence)*

RONNIE: Say what?

BENJAMIN: So, I hope you can see that my request is not—

RONNIE: Wait, wait.

BENJAMIN: —motivated by the sorts of racist assumptions—

RONNIE: But, but where . . . how did you learn all that?

BENJAMIN: All what?

RONNIE: All that—you know—oppression stuff—tuberculosis . . .

BENJAMIN: It's statistically irrefutable. TB occurs in the community at a rate—

RONNIE: Where did *you* learn it?

BENJAMIN: I took Asian-American studies. In college.

RONNIE: Where did you go to college?

BENJAMIN:   University of Wisconsin. Madison.

RONNIE:   Madison, Wisconsin?

BENJAMIN:   That's not where the bridges are, by the way.

RONNIE:   Huh? Oh, right . . .

BENJAMIN:   You wouldn't believe the number of people who—

RONNIE:   They have Asian-American studies in Madison, Wisconsin? Since when?

BENJAMIN:   Since the last Third World Unity hunger strike. *(Pause.)* Why do you look so surprised? We're down.

RONNIE:   I dunno. It just never occurred to me, the idea of Asian students in the Midwest going on a hunger strike.

BENJAMIN:   Well, a lot of them had midterms that week, so they fasted in shifts. *(Pause.)* The administration never figured it out. The Asian students put that "They all look alike" stereotype to good use.

RONNIE:   OK, so they got Asian-American studies. That still doesn't explain—

BENJAMIN:   What?

RONNIE:   Well . . . what *you* were doing taking it?

BENJAMIN:   Just like everyone else. I wanted to explore my roots. And, you know, the history of oppression which is my legacy. After a lifetime of assimilation, I wanted to find out who I really am.

*(Pause.)*

RONNIE:   And did you?

BENJAMIN:   Sure. I learned to take pride in my ancestors who built the railroads, my Popo who would make me a hot bowl of jok with thousand-day-old eggs when the white kids chased me home yelling, "Gook! Chink! Slant-eyes!"

RONNIE:   OK, OK, that's enough!

BENJAMIN:   Painful to listen to, isn't it?

RONNIE:   I don't know what kind of bullshit ethnic studies program they're running over in Wuss-consin, but did they bother to teach you that in order to find your Asian "roots," it's a good idea to first be Asian?

*(Pause.)*

BENJAMIN:   Are you speaking metaphorically?

RONNIE:   No! Literally! Look at your skin!

BENJAMIN:   You know, it's very stereotypical to think that all Asian skin tones conform to a single hue.

RONNIE:   You're white! Is this some kind of redneck joke or something? Am I the first person in the world to tell you this?

BENJAMIN:   Oh! Oh! Oh!

RONNIE:   I know real Asians are scarce in the Midwest, but . . . Jesus!

BENJAMIN:   No, of course, I . . . I see where your misunderstanding arises.

RONNIE:  Yeah. It's called, "You white."

BENJAMIN:  It's just that—in my hometown of Tribune, Kansas, and then at school—see, everyone knows me—so this sort of thing never comes up. *(He offers his hand.)*  Benjamin Wong. I forget that a society wedded to racial constructs constantly forces me to explain my very existence.

RONNIE:  Ronnie Chang. Otherwise known as "The Bow Man."

BENJAMIN:  You see, I was adopted by Chinese-American parents at birth. So, clearly, I'm an Asian-American—

RONNIE:  Even though you're blond and blue-eyed.

BENJAMIN:  Well, you can't judge my race by my genetic heritage alone.

RONNIE:  If genes don't determine race, what does?

BENJAMIN:  Perhaps you'd prefer that I continue in denial, masquerading as a white man?

RONNIE:  You can't just wake up and say, "Gee, I *feel* black today."

BENJAMIN:  Brother, I'm just trying to find what you've already got.

RONNIE:  What do I got?

BENJAMIN:  A home. With your people. Picketing with the laundry workers. Taking refuge from the daily slights against your masculinity in the noble image of Gwan Gung.

RONNIE:  Gwan who?

BENJAMIN:  C'mon—the Chinese god of warriors and—what do you take me for? There're altars to him up all over the community.

RONNIE:  I dunno what community you're talking about, but it's sure as hell not mine.

*(Pause.)*

BENJAMIN:  What do you mean?

RONNIE:  I mean, if you wanna call Chinatown *your* community, OK, knock yourself out, learn to use chopsticks, big deal. Go ahead, try and find your "roots" in some dim sum parlor with headless ducks hanging in the window. Those places don't tell you a thing about who *I* am.

BENJAMIN:  Oh, I get it.

RONNIE:  You get what?

BENJAMIN:  You're one of those self-hating, *assimilated* Chinese-Americans, aren't you?

RONNIE:  Oh, Jesus.

BENJAMIN:  You probably call yourself "Oriental," huh? Look, maybe I can help you. I have some books I can—

RONNIE:  Hey, I read all those Asian identity books when you were still slathering on industrial-strength sunblock. *(Pause.)*  Sure, I'm Chinese. But folks like you act like that means something. Like, all of a sudden, you know who I am. You think identity's that simple? That you can wrap it all up in a neat package and say, "I have ethnicity,

therefore I am"? All you fucking ethnic fundamentalists. Always settling for easy answers. You say you're looking for identity, but you
can't begin to face the real mysteries of the search. So instead, you go
skin-deep, and call it a day. *(Pause. He turns away from Benjamin
and starts to play his violin—slow and bluesy.)*

BENJAMIN: So what are you? "Just a human being"? That's like saying you
*have* no identity. If you asked me to describe my dog, I'd say more
than, "He's just a dog."

RONNIE: What—you think if I deny the importance of my race, I'm nobody? There're worlds out there, worlds you haven't even begun to
understand. Open your eyes. Hear with your ears.

*(Ronnie holds his violin at chest level, but does not attempt to play
during the following monologue. As he speaks, rock and jazz violin
tracks fade in and out over the house speakers, bringing to life the
styles of music he describes.)*

I concede—it was called a fiddle long ago—but that was even before
the birth of jazz. When the hollering in the fields, the rank injustice of
human bondage, the struggle of God's children against the plagues of
the devil's white man, when all these boiled up into that bittersweet
brew, called by later generations, the blues. That's when fiddlers like
Son Sims held their chin rests at their chests, and sawed away like the
hillbillies still do today. And with the coming of ragtime appeared the
pioneer Stuff Smith, who sang as he stroked the catgut, with his raspy,
Louis Armstrong–voice—gruff and sweet like the timber of horsehair
riding south below the fingerboard—and who finally sailed for Europe to find ears that would hear. Europe—where Stephane Grappelli
initiated a magical French violin, to be passed from generation to generation—first he, to Jean-Luc Ponty, then Ponty to Didier Lockwood.
Listening to Grappelli play "A Nightingale Sang in Berkeley Square" is
to understand not only the song of birds, but also how they learn to
fly, fall in love on the wing, and finally falter one day, to wait for darkness beneath a London street lamp. And Ponty—he showed how the
modern violin man can accompany the shadow of this own lead
lines, which cascade, one over another, into some nether world beyond the range of human hearing. Joe Venuti. Noel Pointer. Sven As-
mussen. Even the Kronos Quartet, with their arrangement of "Purple
Haze." Now, tell me, could any legacy be more rich, more crowded
with mythology and heroes to inspire pride? What can I say if the
banging of a gong or the clinking of a pickax on the Transcontinental
Railroad fails to move me even as much as one note, played through a
violin MIDI controller by Michael Urbaniak? *(He puts his violin to
his chin, begins to play a jazz composition of his own invention.)*
Does it have a sound like Chinese opera before people like you decide I know who I am?

*(Benjamin stands for a long moment, listening to Ronnie play. Then, he drops his dollar into the case, turns and exits right. Ronnie continues to play a long moment. Then Benjamin enters downstage left, illuminated in his own spotlight. He sits on the floor of the stage, his feet dangling off the lip. As he speaks, Ronnie continues playing his tune, which becomes underscoring for Benjamin's monologue. As the music continues, does it slowly begin to reflect the influence of Chinese music?)*

BENJAMIN: When I finally found Doyers Street, I scanned the buildings for Number 13. Walking down an alley where the scent of freshly steamed char siu bao lingered in the air, I felt immediately that I had entered a world where all things were finally familiar. *(Pause)* An old woman bumped me with her shopping bag—screaming to her friend in Cantonese, though they walked no more than a few inches apart. Another man—shouting to a vendor in Sze-Yup. A youth, in white undershirt, perhaps a recent newcomer, bargaining with a grocer in Hokkien. I walked through this ocean of dialects, breathing in the richness with deep gulps, exhilarated by the energy this symphony brought to my step. And when I finally saw the number 13, I nearly wept at my good fortune. An old tenement, paint peeling, inside walls no doubt thick with a century of grease and broken dreams—and yet, to me, a temple—the house where my father was born. I suddenly saw it all: Gung Gung, coming home from his sixteen-hour days pressing shirts he could never afford to own, bringing with him candies for my father, each sweet wrapped in the hope of a better life. When my father left the ghetto, he swore he would never return. But he had, this day, in the thoughts and memories of his son, just six months after his death. And as I sat on the stoop, I pulled a hua-moi from my picket, sucked on it, and felt his spirit returning. To this place where his ghost, and the dutiful hearts of all his descendants, would always call home. *(He listens for a long moment.)* And I felt an ache in my heart for all those lost souls, denied this most important of revelations: to know who they truly are.

*(Benjamin sucks his salted plum and listens to the sounds around him. Ronnie continues to play. The two remain oblivious of one another. Lights fade slowly to black.)*

END OF PLAY

# ▓ TOPICS FOR
# CRITICAL THINKING AND WRITING

## *The Play on the Page*

1. Benjamin sees his identity in the culture of the people who adopted him. In what does Ronnie see his identity? (Hwang calls him "an Asian-American male," and Ronnie at one point says, "Sure, I'm Chinese.") In their discussion of identity, is one character "right" and one "wrong," or both "right" or both "wrong," or what?

2. Benjamin, the adopted son of Chinese parents in America says, "I learned to take pride in my ancestors who built the railroads." How important is it to you to "take pride in [your] ancestors"? Perhaps it is useful to think about the issue from a different angle: Suppose all of your grandparents were engaged in disreputable activities, perhaps crimes of various sorts. You probably would be a bit embarrassed, but should you be ashamed of actions over which you had no control? If not, why should you be proud of the good actions of your ancestors? Please explain.

3. The African-American writer James Baldwin said, "An identity would seem to be arrived at by the way in which the person faces and uses his experience." What do you think Ronnie would say to this view? And what would Benjamin say?

## *The Play on the Stage*

4. Just before Benjamin speaks the monologue that concludes the play, Hwang gives us a stage direction:

   > Ronnie continues playing his tune, which becomes underscoring for Benjamin's monologue. As the music continues, does it slowly begin to reflect the influence of Chinese music?

   If you were directing the play, would you or would you not at this point use music that "reflect[s] the influence of Chinese music"? Please explain your choice.

5. The play includes language that many people would find offensive in real life. Why do you suppose Hwang uses such language when he could have chosen not to? Would the impact and meaning of the play change if this language were omitted or altered? If you wanted to direct a production but believed that many members of the audience would be deeply uncomfortable, would you ask the playwright for permission to delete the obscenities?

6. The play deals with a serious issue, but can one say that it also has comic passages? If you think the play is in some places amusing, point to two or three such places and explain what is amusing about them. How would you ensure that the comedy came across in the theater?

Scene from a production of "*Los Vendidos*" at Iowa State University Theatre

# LUIS VALDEZ

*Luis Valdez was born into a family of migrant farm workers in Delano, California, in 1940. After completing high school he entered San Jose State College on a scholarship. He wrote his first plays while still an undergraduate, and after receiving his degree (in English and drama) from San Jose in 1964 he joined the San Francisco Mime Troupe, a left-wing group that performed in parks and streets. Revolutionary in technique as well as in political content, the Mime Troupe rejected the traditional forms of drama and instead drew on the traditions of the circus and the carnival.*

*In 1965 Valdez returned to Delano, California, where Cesar Chavez had organized a strike of farm workers and a boycott against grape growers. It was here, under the wing of the United Farm Workers, that he established El Teatro Campesino (the Farm Workers' Theater), which at first specialized in doing short, improvised, satirical skits called actos. When the teatro moved to Del Rey, California, it expanded its repertoire beyond farm issues, and it became part of a cultural center that gave workshops (in English and Spanish) in such subjects as history, drama, and politics.*

*The* actos, *performed by amateurs on college campuses and on flatbed trucks and at the edges of vineyards, were highly political. Making use of stereotypes (the boss, the scab), the* actos *sought not to present the individual thoughts of a gifted playwright but to present the social vision of ordinary people—the* pueblo—*though it was acknowledged that in an oppressive society the playwright might have to help guide the people to see their own best interests.*

*Valdez moved from* actos *to* mitos *(myths)—plays that drew on Aztec mythology, Mexican folklore, and Christianity—and then to* Zoot Suit, *a play that ran for many months in California and that became the first Mexican-American play to be produced on Broadway. More recently he wrote and directed a hit movie,* La Bamba, *and in 1991 received an award from the A.T.&T. Foundation for his musical,* Bandido, *presented by El Teatro Campesino.*

Los Vendidos *was written in 1967, when Ronald Reagan was governor of California.*

# Los Vendidos*                                                    [1967]

## LIST OF CHARACTERS

HONEST SANCHO
SECRETARY
FARM WORKER
JOHNNY
REVOLUCIONARIO
MEXICAN-AMERICAN

**SCENE:** HONEST SANCHO's *Used Mexican Lot and Mexican Curio Shop. Three models are on display in* HONEST SANCHO's *shop: to the right, there is a* REVOLUCIONARIO, *complete with sombrero, carrilleras¹ and carabina 30-30. At center, on the floor, there is the* FARM WORKER, *under a broad straw sombrero. At stage left is the* PACHUCO,² *filero³ in hand.*

(HONEST SANCHO *is moving among his models, dusting them off and preparing for another day of business.*)

SANCHO.  Bueno, bueno, mis monos, vamos a ver a quien vendemos ahora, ¿no?⁴ (*To audience.*) ¡Quihubo! I'm Honest Sancho and this is my shop. Antes fui contratista pero ahora logré tener mi negocito.⁵ All I need now is a customer. (*A bell rings offstage.*) Ay, a customer!

---

*****Los Vendidos** the sellouts.    ¹**carrilleras** cartridge belts.    ²**Pachuco** an urban tough guy.    ³**filero** blade.    ⁴**Bueno . . . no?** Well, well, darlings, let's see who we can sell now, O.K.?    ⁵**Antes . . . negocito** I used to be a contractor, but now I've succeeded in having my little business.

SECRETARY (*Entering*). Good morning, I'm Miss Jiménez from—
SANCHO. ¡Ah, una chicana! Welcome, welcome Señorita Jiménez.
SECRETARY (*Anglo pronunciation*). JIM-enez.
SANCHO. ¿Qué?
SECRETARY. My name is Miss JIM-enez. Don't you speak English? What's wrong with you?
SANCHO. Oh, nothing, Señorita JIM-enez. I'm here to help you.
SECRETARY. That's better. As I was starting to say, I'm a secretary from Governor Reagan's office, and we're looking for a Mexican type for the administration.
SANCHO. Well, you come to the right place, lady. This is Honest Sancho's Used Mexican lot, and we got all types here. Any particular type you want?
SECRETARY. Yes, we were looking for somebody suave—
SANCHO. Suave.
SECRETARY. Debonair.
SANCHO. De buen aire.
SECRETARY. Dark.
SANCHO. Prieto.
SECRETARY. But of course not too dark.
SANCHO. No muy prieto.
SECRETARY. Perhaps, beige.
SANCHO. Beige, just the tone. Así como cafecito con leche.[6] ¿no?
SECRETARY. One more thing. He must be hard-working.
SANCHO. That could only be one model. Step right over here to the center of the shop, lady. (*They cross to the* FARM WORKER.) This is our standard farm worker model. As you can see, in the words of our beloved Senator George Murphy, he is "built close to the ground." Also take special notice of his four-ply Goodyear huaraches, made from the rain tire. This wide-brimmed sombrero is an extra added feature—keeps off the sun, rain, and dust.
SECRETARY. Yes, it does look durable.
SANCHO. And our farm worker model is friendly. Muy amable.[7] Watch. (*Snaps his fingers.*)
FARM WORKER (*Lifts up head*). Buenos días, señorita. (*His head drops.*)
SECRETARY. My, he's friendly.
SANCHO. Didn't I tell you? Loves his patrones! But his most attractive feature is that he's hard working. Let me show you. (*Snaps fingers.* FARM WORKER *stands.*)
FARM WORKER. ¡El jale![8] (*He begins to work.*)
SANCHO. As you can see, he is cutting grapes.
SECRETARY. Oh, I wouldn't know.

---

[6]**Así . . . leche** like coffee with milk.    [7]**Muy amable** very friendly.    [8]**El jale** the job.

SANCHO.  He also picks cotton. (*Snap.* FARM WORKER *begins to pick cotton.*)

SECRETARY.  Versatile isn't he?

SANCHO.  He also picks melons. (*Snap.* FARM WORKER *picks melons.*) That's his slow speed for late in the season. Here's his fast speed. (*Snap.* FARM WORKER *picks faster.*)

SECRETARY.  ¡Chihuahua! . . . I mean, goodness, he sure is a hard worker.

SANCHO (*Pulls the* FARM WORKER *to his feet*).  And that isn't the half of it. Do you see these little holes on his arms that appear to be pores? During those hot sluggish days in the field, when the vines or the branches get so entangled, it's almost impossible to move; these holes emit a certain grease that allow our model to slip and slide right through the crop with no trouble at all.

SECRETARY.  Wonderful. But is he economical?

SANCHO.  Economical? Señorita, you are looking at the Volkswagen of Mexicans. Pennies a day is all it takes. One plate of beans and tortillas will keep him going all day. That, and chile. Plenty of chile. Chile jalapeños, chile verde, chile colorado. But, of course, if you do give him chile (*Snap.* FARM WORKER *turns left face. Snap.* FARM WORKER *bends over.*) then you have to change his oil filter once a week.

SECRETARY.  What about storage?

SANCHO.  No problem. You know these new farm labor camps our Honorable Governor Reagan has built out by Parlier or Raisin City? They were designed with our model in mind. Five, six, seven, even ten in one of those shacks will give you no trouble at all. You can also put him in old barns, old cars, river banks. You can even leave him out in the field overnight with no worry!

SECRETARY.  Remarkable.

SANCHO.  And here's an added feature: Every year at the end of the season, this model goes back to Mexico and doesn't return, automatically, until next Spring.

SECRETARY.  How about that. But tell me: does he speak English?

SANCHO.  Another outstanding feature is that last year this model was programmed to go out on STRIKE! (*Snap.*)

FARM WORKER.  ¡HUELGA! ¡HUELGA! Hermanos, sálganse de esos files.[9] (*Snap. He stops.*)

SECRETARY.  No! Oh no, we can't strike in the State Capitol.

SANCHO.  Well, he also scabs. (*Snap.*)

FARM WORKER.  Me vendo barato, ¿y qué?[10] (*Snap.*)

SECRETARY.  That's much better, but you didn't answer my question. Does he speak English?

SANCHO.  Bueno . . . no, pero[11] he has other—

SECRETARY.  No.

---

[9]**Huelga . . . files** Strike! Strike! Brothers, leave those rows.   [10]**Me . . . qué?** I come cheap. So what?   [11]**Bueno . . . no, pero** Well, no, but.

SANCHO.  Other features.

SECRETARY.  NO! He just won't do!

SANCHO.  Okay, okay pues. We have other models.

SECRETARY.  I hope so. What we need is something a little more sophisticated.

SANCHO.  Sophisti—¿qué?

SECRETARY.  An urban model.

SANCHO.  Ah, from the city! Step right back. Over here in this corner of the shop is exactly what you're looking for. Introducing our new 1969 JOHNNY PACHUCO model! This is our fast-back model. Streamlined. Built for speed, low-riding, city life. Take a look at some of these features. Mag shoes, dual exhausts, green chartreuse paint-job, dark-tint windshield, a little poof on top. Let me just turn him on. (*Snap.* JOHNNY *walks to stage center with a pachuco bounce.*)

SECRETARY.  What was that?

SANCHO.  That, señorita, was the Chicano shuffle.

SECRETARY.  Okay, what does he do?

SANCHO.  Anything and everything necessary for city life. For instance, survival: He knife fights. (*Snap.* JOHNNY *pulls out switchblade and swings at* SECRETARY.)

(SECRETARY *screams.*)

SANCHO.  He dances. (*Snap.*)

JOHNNY (*Singing*).  "Angel Baby, my Angel Baby ..." (*Snap.*)

SANCHO.  And here's a feature no city model can be without. He gets arrested, but not without resisting, of course. (*Snap.*)

JOHNNY.  ¡En la madre, la placa![12] I didn't do it! I didn't do it! (JOHNNY *turns and stands up against an imaginary wall, legs spread out, arms behind his back.*)

SECRETARY.  Oh no, we can't have arrests! We must maintain law and order.

SANCHO.  But he's bilingual!

SECRETARY.  Bilingual?

SANCHO.  Simón que yes.[13] He speaks English! Johnny, give us some English. (*Snap.*)

JOHNNY (*Comes downstage*).  Fuck-you!

SECRETARY (*Gasps*).  Oh! I've never been so insulted in my whole life!

SANCHO.  Well, he learned it in your school.

SECRETARY.  I don't care where he learned it.

SANCHO.  But he's economical!

SECRETARY.  Economical?

SANCHO.  Nickels and dimes. You can keep Johnny running on hamburgers, Taco Bell tacos, Lucky Lager beer, Thunderbird wine, yesca—

SECRETARY.  Yesca?

---

[12]¡**En . . . la placa!** Wow, the cops!   [13]**Simón que yes** Yea, sure.

SANCHO. Mota.

SECRETARY. Mota?

SANCHO. Leños[14] . . . Marijuana. (*Snap;* JOHNNY *inhales on an imaginary joint.*)

SECRETARY. That's against the law!

JOHNNY (*Big smile, holding his breath*). Yeah.

SANCHO. He also sniffs glue. (*Snap.* JOHNNY *inhales glue, big smile.*)

JOHNNY. That's too much man, ése.[15]

SECRETARY. No, Mr. Sancho, I don't think this—

SANCHO. Wait a minute, he has other qualities I know you'll love. For example, an inferiority complex. (*Snap.*)

JOHNNY (*To* SANCHO). You think you're better than me, huh ése? (*Swings switchblade.*)

SANCHO. He can also be beaten and he bruises, cut him and he bleeds; kick him and he—(*He beats, bruises and kicks* PACHUCO.) would you like to try it?

SECRETARY. Oh, I couldn't.

SANCHO. Be my guest. He's a great scapegoat.

SECRETARY. No, really.

SANCHO. Please.

SECRETARY. Well, all right. Just once. (*She kicks* PACHUCO.) Oh, he's so soft.

SANCHO. Wasn't that good? Try again.

SECRETARY (*Kicks* PACHUCO). Oh, he's so wonderful! (*She kicks him again.*)

SANCHO. Okay, that's enough, lady. You ruin the merchandise. Yes, our Johnny Pachuco model can give you many hours of pleasure. Why, the L.A.P.D. just bought twenty of these to train their rookie cops on. And talk about maintenance. Señorita, you are looking at an entirely self-supporting machine. You're never going to find our Johnny Pachuco model on the relief rolls. No, sir, this model knows how to liberate.

SECRETARY. Liberate?

SANCHO. He steals. (*Snap.* JOHNNY *rushes the* SECRETARY *and steals her purse.*)

JOHNNY. ¡Dame esa bolsa, vieja![16] (*He grabs the purse and runs. Snap by* SANCHO. *He stops.*)

(SECRETARY *runs after* JOHNNY *and grabs purse away from him, kicking him as she goes.*)

SECRETARY. No, no, no! We can't have any *more* thieves in the State Administration. Put him back.

SANCHO. Okay, we still got other models. Come on, Johnny, we'll sell you to some old lady. (SANCHO *takes* JOHNNY *back to his place.*)

---

[14]**Leños** joints (marijuana).    [15]**ése** fellow.    [16]**¡Dame . . . vieja!** Give me that bag, old lady!

SECRETARY.  Mr. Sancho, I don't think you quite understand what we need. What we need is something that will attract the women voters. Something more traditional, more romantic.

SANCHO.  Ah, a lover. (*He smiles meaningfully.*) Step right over here, señorita. Introducing our standard Revolucionario and/or Early California Bandit type. As you can see he is well-built, sturdy, durable. This is the International Harvester of Mexicans.

SECRETARY.  What does he do?

SANCHO.  You name it, he does it. He rides horses, stays in the mountains, crosses deserts, plains, rivers, leads revolutions, follows revolutions, kills, can be killed, serves as a martyr, hero, movie star—did I say movie star? Did you ever see *Viva Zapata? Viva Villa? Villa Rides? Pancho Villa Returns? Pancho Villa Goes Back? Pancho Villa Meets Abbott and Costello*—

SECRETARY.  I've never seen any of those.

SANCHO.  Well, he was in all of them. Listen to this. (*Snap.*)

REVOLUCIONARIO (*Scream*).  ¡VIVA VILLAAAAA!

SECRETARY.  That's awfully loud.

SANCHO.  He has a volume control. (*He adjusts volume. Snap.*)

REVOLUCIONARIO (*Mousey voice*).  ¡Viva Villa!

SECRETARY.  That's better.

SANCHO.  And even if you didn't see him in the movies, perhaps you saw him on TV. He makes commercials. (*Snap.*)

REVOLUCIONARIO.  Is there a Frito Bandito in your house?

SECRETARY.  Oh yes, I've seen that one!

SANCHO.  Another feature about this one is that he is economical. He runs on raw horsemeat and tequila!

SECRETARY.  Isn't that rather savage?

SANCHO.  Al contrario,[17] it makes him a lover. (*Snap.*)

REVOLUCIONARIO (*To* SECRETARY).  ¡Ay, mamasota, cochota, ven pa'ca![18] (*He grabs* SECRETARY *and folds her back—Latin-Lover style.*)

SANCHO (*Snap.* REVOLUCIONARIO *goes back upright*).  Now wasn't that nice?

SECRETARY.  Well, it was rather nice.

SANCHO.  And finally, there is one outstanding feature about this model I KNOW the ladies are going to love: He's a GENUINE antique! He was made in Mexico in 1910!

SECRETARY.  Made in Mexico?

SANCHO.  That's right. Once in Tijuana, twice in Guadalajara, three times in Cuernavaca.

SECRETARY.  Mr. Sancho, I thought he was an American product.

SANCHO.  No, but—

---

[17]**Al contrario** on the contrary.   [18]**¡Ay . . . pa'ca!** get over here!

SECRETARY.  No, I'm sorry. We can't buy anything but American-made products. He just won't do.

SANCHO.  But he's an antique!

SECRETARY.  I don't care. You still don't understand what we need. It's true we need Mexican models such as these, but it's more important that he be *American*.

SANCHO.  American?

SECRETARY.  That's right, and judging from what you've shown me, I don't think you have what we want. Well, my lunch hour's almost over: I better—

SANCHO.  Wait a minute! Mexican but American?

SECRETARY.  That's correct.

SANCHO.  Mexican but ... (*A sudden flash.*) AMERICAN! Yeah, I think we've got exactly what you want. He just came in today! Give me a minute. (*He exits. Talks from backstage.*) Here he is in the shop. Let me just get some papers off. There. Introducing our new 1970 Mexican-American! Ta-ra-ra-ra-ra-ra-RA-RAAA!

(SANCHO *brings out the* MEXICAN-AMERICAN *model, a clean-shaven middle-class type in a business suit, with glasses.*)

SECRETARY (*Impressed*).  Where have you been hiding this one?

SANCHO.  He just came in this morning. Ain't he a beauty? Feast your eyes on him! Sturdy US STEEL frame, streamlined, modern. As a matter of fact, he is built exactly like our Anglo models except that he comes in a variety of darker shades: naugahyde, leather, or leatherette.

SECRETARY.  Naugahyde.

SANCHO.  Well, we'll just write that down. Yes, señorita, this model represents the apex of American engineering! He is bilingual, college educated, ambitious! Say the word "acculturate" and he accelerates. He is intelligent, well-mannered, clean—did I say clean? (*Snap.* MEXICAN-AMERICAN *raises his arm.*) Smell.

SECRETARY (*Smells*).  Old Sobaco, my favorite.

SANCHO (*Snap.* MEXICAN-AMERICAN *turns toward* SANCHO).  Eric! (*To* SECRETARY.) We call him Eric García. (*To* ERIC.) I want you to meet Miss JIM-enez, Eric.

MEXICAN-AMERICAN.  Miss JIM-enez, I am delighted to make your acquaintance. (*He kisses her hand.*)

SECRETARY.  Oh, my, how charming!

SANCHO.  Did you feel the suction? He has seven especially engineered suction cups right behind his lips. He's a charmer all right!

SECRETARY.  How about boards? Does he function on boards?

SANCHO.  You name them, he is on them. Parole boards, draft boards, school boards, taco quality control boards, surf boards, two-by-fours.

SECRETARY.  Does he function in politics?

SANCHO.  Señorita, you are looking at a political MACHINE. Have you ever heard of the OEO, EOC, COD, WAR ON POVERTY? That's our model! Not only that, he makes political speeches.

SECRETARY.  May I hear one?

SANCHO.  With pleasure. (*Snap.*) Eric, give us a speech.

MEXICAN-AMERICAN.  Mr. Congressman, Mr. Chairman, members of the board, honored guests, ladies and gentlemen. (SANCHO *and* SECRETARY *applaud.*) Please, please. I come before you as a Mexican-American to tell you about the problems of the Mexican. The problems of the Mexican stem from one thing and one thing alone: He's stupid. He's uneducated. He needs to stay in school. He needs to be ambitious, forward-looking, harder-working. He needs to think American, American, American, AMERICAN, AMERICAN, AMERICAN. GOD BLESS AMERICA! GOD BLESS AMERICA! GOD BLESS AMERICA!! (*He goes out of control.*)

(SANCHO *snaps frantically and the* MEXICAN-AMERICAN *finally slumps forward, bending at the waist.*)

SECRETARY.  Oh my, he's patriotic too!

SANCHO.  Sí, señorita, he loves his country. Let me just make a little adjustment here. (*Stands* MEXICAN-AMERICAN *up.*)

SECRETARY.  What about upkeep? Is he economical?

SANCHO.  Well, no, I won't lie to you. The Mexican-American costs a little bit more, but you get what you pay for. He's worth every extra cent. You can keep him running on dry Martinis, Langendorf bread.

SECRETARY.  Apple pie?

SANCHO.  Only Mom's. Of course, he's also programmed to eat Mexican food on ceremonial functions, but I must warn you: an overdose of beans will plug up his exhaust.

SECRETARY.  Fine! There's just one more question: HOW MUCH DO YOU WANT FOR HIM?

SANCHO.  Well, I tell you what I'm gonna do. Today and today only, because you've been so sweet, I'm gonna let you steal this model from me! I'm gonna let you drive him off the lot for the simple price of—let's see taxes and license included—$15,000.

SECRETARY.  Fifteen thousand DOLLARS? For a MEXICAN!

SANCHO.  Mexican? What are you talking, lady? This is a Mexican-AMERICAN! We had to melt down two pachucos, a farm worker and three gabachos[19] to make this model! You want quality, but you gotta pay for it! This is no cheap run-about. He's got class!

---

[19] **gabachos** whites.

SECRETARY.  Okay, I'll take him.
SANCHO.  You will?
SECRETARY.  Here's your money.
SANCHO.  You mind if I count it?
SECRETARY.  Go right ahead.
SANCHO.  Well, you'll get your pink slip in the mail. Oh, do you want me to wrap him up for you? We have a box in the back.
SECRETARY.  No, thank you. The Governor is having a luncheon this afternoon, and we need a brown face in the crowd. How do I drive him?
SANCHO.  Just snap your fingers. He'll do anything you want.

(SECRETARY *snaps*. MEXICAN-AMERICAN *steps forward.*)

MEXICAN-AMERICAN.  RAZA QUERIDA, ¡VAMOS LEVANTANDO ARMAS PARA LIBERARNOS DE ESTOS DESGRACIADOS GABACHOS QUE NOS EXPLOTAN! VAMOS.[20]
SECRETARY.  What did he say?
SANCHO.  Something about lifting arms, killing white people, etc.
SECRETARY.  But he's not supposed to say that!
SANCHO.  Look, lady, don't blame me for bugs from the factory. He's your Mexican-American; you bought him, now drive him off the lot!
SECRETARY.  But he's broken!
SANCHO.  Try snapping another finger.

(SECRETARY *snaps*. MEXICAN-AMERICAN *comes to life again.*)

MEXICAN-AMERICAN.  ¡ESTA GRAN HUMANIDAD HA DICHO BASTA! Y SE HA PUESTO EN MARCHA! ¡BASTA! ¡BASTA! ¡VIVA LA RAZA! ¡VIVA LA CAUSA! ¡VIVA LA HUELGA! ¡VIVAN LOS BROWN BERETS! ¡VIVAN LOS ESTUDIANTES![21] ¡CHICANO POWER!

(*The* MEXICAN-AMERICAN *turns toward the* SECRETARY, *who gasps and backs up. He keeps turning toward the* PACHUCO, FARM WORKER, *and* REVOLUCIONARIO, *snapping his fingers and turning each of them on, one by one.*)

PACHUCO (*Snap. To* SECRETARY). I'm going to get you, baby! ¡Viva La Raza!
FARM WORKER (*Snap. To* SECRETARY). ¡Viva la huelga! ¡Viva la Huelga! ¡VIVA LA HUELGA!

---

[20]**Raza . . . Vamos** Beloved Raza [persons of Mexican descent], let's take up arms to liberate ourselves from those damned whites who exploit us. Let's get going.
[21]**¡Esta . . . Estudiantes!** This great mass of humanity has said enough! And it has begun to march. Enough! Enough! Long live La Raza! Long live the Cause! Long live the strike! Long live the Brown Berets! Long live the students!

REVOLUCIONARIO (*Snap. To* SECRETARY).   ¡Viva la revolución! ¡VIVA LA REV-
OLUCIÓN!

(*The three models join together and advance toward the* SECRETARY
*who backs up and runs out of the shop screaming.* SANCHO *is at the
other end of the shop holding his money in his hand. All freeze.
After a few seconds of silence, the* PACHUCO *moves and stretches,
shaking his arms and loosening up. The* FARM WORKER *and* REVOLU-
CIONARIO *do the same.* SANCHO *stays where he is, frozen to his spot.*)

JOHNNY.   Man, that was a long one, ése.[22] (*Others agree with him.*)

FARM WORKER.   How did we do?

JOHNNY.   Perty good, look at all that lana,[23] man! (*He goes over to* SANCHO
*and removes the money from his hand.* SANCHO *stays where he is.*)

REVOLUCIONARIO.   En la madre, look at all the money.

JOHNNY.   We keep this up, we're going to be rich.

FARM WORKER.   They think we're machines.

REVOLUCIONARIO.   Burros.

JOHNNY.   Puppets.

MEXICAN-AMERICAN.   The only thing I don't like is—how come I always got
to play the godamn Mexican-American?

JOHNNY.   That's what you get for finishing high school.

FARM WORKER.   How about our wages, ése?

JOHNNY.   Here it comes right now. $3,000 for you, $3,000 for you, $3,000
for you, and $3,000 for me. The rest we put back into the business.

MEXICAN-AMERICAN.   Too much, man. Heh, where you vatos[24] going tonight?

FARM WORKER.   I'm going over to Concha's. There's a party.

JOHNNY.   Wait a minute, vatos. What about our salesman? I think he needs
an oil job.

REVOLUCIONARIO.   Leave him to me.

(*The* PACHUCO, FARM WORKER, *and* MEXICAN-AMERICAN *exit, talking loudly
about their plans for the night. The* REVOLUCIONARIO *goes over to* SAN-
CHO, *removes his derby hat and cigar, lifts him up and throws him
over his shoulder.* SANCHO *hangs loose, lifeless.*)

REVOLUCIONARIO (*To audience*).   He's the best model we got! ¡Ajua![25]

(*Exit.*)

THE END

---

[22]**ése** man.   [23]**lana** money.   [24]**vatos** guys.   [25]**¡Ajua!** Wow!

# ❋ TOPICS FOR CRITICAL THINKING AND WRITING

## *The Play on the Page*

1. If you are an Anglo (shorthand for a Caucasian with traditional Northern European values), do you find the play deeply offensive? Why, or why not? If you are a Mexican-American, do you find the play entertaining or do you find parts of it offensive? What might Anglos enjoy in the play, and what might Mexican-Americans find offensive?

2. What stereotypes of Mexican-Americans are presented here? At the end of the play, what image of the Mexican-American is presented? How does it compare with the stereotypes?

3. Putting aside the politics of the play (and your own politics), what do you think are the strengths of *Los Vendidos*? What do you think are the weaknesses?

4. The play was written in 1967. Putting aside a few specific references for instance, to Governor Reagan—do you find it dated? If not, why not?

5. In his short essay "The Actos," Valdez says that *actos* achieve the following: "Inspire the audience to social action. Illuminate specific points about social problems. Satirize the opposition. Show or hint at a solution. Express what people are feeling." How much of this do you think *Los Vendidos* does?

6. Many people assume that politics gets in the way of serious art. That is, they assume that artists ought to be concerned with issues that transcend politics. Does this point make any sense to you? Why or why not?

## *The Play on the Stage*

7. In 1971 when *Los Vendidos* was produced by El Teatro de la Esperanza, the group altered the ending by having the men decide to use the money to build a community center. Evaluate this ending.

8. Jorge Huerta, who directed the 1971 El Teatro de la Esperanza production of *Los Vendidos,* suggests that it was a mistake for Jane Fonda to be cast as Miss Jiménez, and she introduces herself as that, in the videotape of the play. "Something is lost," he says, "in the realization that this woman is not pretending to be white...." Do you agree? Explain.

9. When the play was videotaped by KNBC in Los Angeles for broadcast in 1973, Valdez changed the ending. In the revised version we discover that a scientist (played by Valdez) masterminds the operation, placing Mexican-American models wherever there are persons of Mexican descent. These models soon will become Chicanos (as opposed to persons with Anglo values) and will aid rather than work against their fellows. Evaluate this ending.

# AUGUST WILSON

*August Wilson (1945-2005) was born in Pittsburgh, the son of a black
woman and a white man. After dropping out of school at the age of fifteen, Wilson took various odd jobs, such as stock clerk and short-order
cook, in his spare time educating himself in the public library, chiefly
by reading works by such black writers as Richard Wright, Ralph Ellison, Langston Hughes, and Amiri Baraka (LeRoi Jones). In 1978 the director of a black theater in St. Paul, Minnesota, who had known Wilson
in Pittsburgh, invited him to write a play for the theater. Six months
later Wilson moved permanently to St. Paul.*

*The winner of the Pulitzer Prize for drama in 1987, Wilson's*
Fences *was first presented as a staged reading in 1983 and was later
performed in Chicago, Seattle, Rochester (New York), and New Haven
(Connecticut) before reaching New York City in 1987. An earlier play,*
Ma Rainey's Black Bottom, *was voted Best Play of the Year 1984-1985
by the New York Drama Critics' Circle. In 1981 when* Ma Rainey *was
first read at the O'Neill Center in Waterford, Connecticut, Wilson met
Lloyd Richards, an African-American director with whom he worked
closely for many years.* The Piano Lesson, *directed by Richards, won Wilson a second Pulitzer Prize in 1990.*

## Fences

[1987]

*for Lloyd Richards,
who adds to whatever he touches*

> *When the sins of our fathers visit us
> We do not have to play host.
> We can banish them with forgiveness
> As God, in His Largeness and Laws.*

—August Wilson

## LIST OF CHARACTERS

TROY MAXSON
JIM BONO, *Troy's friend*
ROSE, *Troy's wife*
LYONS, *Troy's oldest son by previous marriage*
GABRIEL, *Troy's brother*
CORY, *Troy and Rose's son*
RAYNELL, *Troy's daughter*

**SETTING:** *The setting is the yard which fronts the only entrance to the
Maxson household, an ancient two-story brick house set back off a
small alley in a big-city neighborhood. The entrance to the house is*

*gained by two or three steps leading to a wooden porch badly in need of paint.*

*A relatively recent addition to the house and running its full width, the porch lacks congruence. It is a sturdy porch with a flat roof. One or two chairs of dubious value sit at one end where the kitchen window opens onto the porch. An old-fashioned icebox stands silent guard at the opposite end.*

*The yard is a small dirt yard, partially fenced, except for the last scene, with a wooden saw horse, a pile of lumber, and other fence-building equipment set off to the side. Opposite is a tree from which*

Left to right: Frances Foster as Rose, Keith Amos as Cory, William Jay as Gabriel, and Gilbert Lewis as Troy, in the Seattle Repertory Theater production of *Fences.*

*hangs a ball made of rags. A baseball bat leans against the tree. Two oil drums serve as garbage receptacles and sit near the house at right to complete the setting.*

**THE PLAY:** *Near the turn of the century, the destitute of Europe sprang on the city with tenacious claws and an honest and solid dream. The city devoured them. They swelled its belly until it burst into a thousand furnaces and sewing machines, a thousand butcher shops and bakers' ovens, a thousand churches and hospitals and funeral parlors and money-lenders. The city grew. It nourished itself and offered each man a partnership limited only by his talent, his guile, and his willingness and capacity for hard work. For the immigrants of Europe, a dream dared and won true.*

*The descendants of African slaves were offered no such welcome or participation. They came from places called the Carolinas and the Virginias, Georgia, Alabama, Mississippi, and Tennessee. They came strong, eager, searching. The city rejected them and they fled and settled along the riverbanks and under bridges in shallow, ramshackle houses made of sticks and tarpaper. They collected rags and wood. They sold the use of their muscles and their bodies. They cleaned houses and washed clothes, they shined shoes, and in quiet desperation and vengeful pride, they stole, and lived in pursuit of their own dream. That they could breathe free, finally, and stand to meet life with the force of dignity and whatever eloquence the heart could call upon.*

*By 1957, the hard-won victories of the European immigrants had solidified the industrial might of America. War had been confronted and won with new energies that used loyalty and patriotism as its fuel. Life was rich, full, and flourishing. The Milwaukee Braves won the World Series, and the hot winds of change that would make the sixties a turbulent, racing, dangerous, and provocative decade had not yet begun to blow full.*

*Act 1*

*Scene 1*

*It is 1957.* TROY *and* BONO *enter the yard, engaged in conversation.* TROY *is fifty-three years old, a large man with thick, heavy hands; it is this largeness that he strives to fill out and make an accommodation with. Together with his blackness, his largeness informs his sensibilities and the choices he has made in his life.*

*Of the two men,* BONO *is obviously the follower. His commitment to their friendship of thirty-odd years is rooted in his admiration of* TROY's *honesty, capacity for hard work, and his strength, which* BONO *seeks to emulate.*

*It is Friday night, payday, and the one night of the week the two men engage in a ritual of talk and drink.* TROY *is usually the*

*most talkative and at times he can be crude and almost vulgar,*
*though he is capable of rising to profound heights of expression. The*
*men carry lunch buckets and wear or carry burlap aprons and are*
*dressed in clothes suitable to their jobs as garbage collectors.*

BONO.  Troy, you ought to stop that lying!

TROY.  I ain't lying! The nigger had a watermelon this big. (*He indicates*
*with his hands.*) Talking about . . . "What watermelon, Mr. Rand?" I
liked to fell out! "What watermelon, Mr. Rand?" . . . And it sitting there
big as life.

BONO.  What did Mr. Rand say?

TROY.  Ain't said nothing. Figure if the nigger too dumb to know he carrying a watermelon, he wasn't gonna get much sense out of him. Trying
to hide that great big old watermelon under his coat. Afraid to let the
white man see him carry it home.

BONO.  I'm like you . . . I ain't got no time for them kind of people.

TROY.  Now what he look like getting mad 'cause he see the man from the
union talking to Mr. Rand?

BONO.  He come to me talking about . . . "Maxson gonna get us fired." I told
him to get away from me with that. He walked away from me calling
you a troublemaker. What Mr. Rand say?

TROY.  Ain't said nothing. He told me to go down the Commissioner's office next Friday. They called me down there to see them.

BONO.  Well, as long as you got your complaint filed, they can't fire you.
That's what one of them white fellows tell me.

TROY.  I ain't worried about them firing me. They gonna fire me 'cause I
asked a question? That's all I did. I went to Mr. Rand and asked him,
"Why? Why you got the white mens driving and the colored lifting?"
Told him, "what's the matter, don't I count? You think only white fellows got sense enough to drive a truck. That ain't no paper job! Hell,
anybody can drive a truck. How come you got all whites driving and
the colored lifting?" He told me "take it to the union." Well, hell, that's
what I done! Now they wanna come up with this pack of lies.

BONO.  I told Brownie if the man come and ask him any questions . . . just
tell the truth! It ain't nothing but something they done trumped up
on you cause you filed a complaint on them.

TROY.  Brownie don't understand nothing. All I want them to do is change
the job description. Give everybody a chance to drive the truck.
Brownie can't see that. He ain't got that much sense.

BONO.  How you figure he be making out with that gal be up at Taylor's all
the time . . . that Alberta gal?

TROY.  Same as you and me. Getting just as much as we is. Which is to say
nothing.

BONO.  It is, huh? I figure you doing a little better than me . . . and I ain't saying what I'm doing.

TROY.  Aw, nigger, look here . . . I know you. If you had got anywhere near
    that gal, twenty minutes later you be looking to tell somebody.
    And the first one you gonna tell . . . that you gonna want to brag to . . .
    is me.

BONO.  I ain't saying that. I see where you be eyeing her.

TROY.  I eye all the women. I don't miss nothing. Don't never let nobody
    tell you Troy Maxson don't eye the women.

BONO.  You been doing more than eyeing her. You done bought her a drink
    or two.

TROY.  Hell yeah, I bought her a drink! What that mean? I bought you one,
    too. What that mean cause I buy her a drink? I'm just being polite.

BONO.  It's all right to buy her one drink. That's what you call being polite.
    But when you wanna be buying two or three . . . that's what you call
    eyeing her.

TROY.  Look here, as long as you known me . . . you ever known me to
    chase after women?

BONO.  Hell yeah! Long as I done known you. You forgetting I knew you
    when.

TROY.  Naw, I'm talking about since I been married to Rose?

BONO.  Oh, not since you been married to Rose. Now, that's the truth,
    there. I can say that.

TROY.  All right then! Case closed.

BONO.  I see you be walking up around Alberta's house. You supposed to
    be at Taylors' and you be walking up around there.

TROY.  What you watching where I'm walking for? I ain't watching after
    you.

BONO.  I seen you walking around there more than once.

TROY.  Hell, you liable to see me walking anywhere! That don't mean noth-
    ing cause you see me walking around there.

BONO.  Where she come from anyway? She just kinda showed up one day.

TROY.  Tallahassee. You can look at her and tell she one of them Florida
    gals. They got some big healthy women down there. Grow them right
    up out the ground. Got a little bit of Indian in her. Most of them nig-
    gers down in Florida got some Indian in them.

BONO.  I don't know about that Indian part. But she damn sure big and
    healthy. Woman wear some big stockings. Got them great big old legs
    and hips as wide as the Mississippi River.

TROY.  Legs don't mean nothing. You don't do nothing but push them out
    of the way. But them hips cushion the ride!

BONO.  Troy, you ain't got no sense.

TROY.  It's the truth! Like you riding on Goodyears!

    ROSE *enters from the house. She is ten years younger than* TROY, *her*
    *devotion to him stems from her recognition of the possibilities*
    *of her life without him: a succession of abusive men and their*

*babies, a life of partying and running the streets, the Church, or aloneness with its attendant pain and frustration. She recognizes* TROY's *spirit as a fine and illuminating one and she either ignores or forgives his faults, only some of which she recognizes. Though she doesn't drink, her presence is an integral part of the Friday night rituals. She alternates between the porch and the kitchen, where supper preparations are under way.*

ROSE. What you all out here getting into?

TROY. What you worried about what we getting into for? This is men talk, woman.

ROSE. What I care what you all talking about? Bono, you gonna stay for supper?

BONO. No, I thank you, Rose. But Lucille say she cooking up a pot of pigfeet.

TROY. Pigfeet! Hell, I'm going home with you! Might even stay the night if you got some pigfeet. You got something in there to top them pigfeet, Rose?

ROSE. I'm cooking up some chicken. I got some chicken and collard greens.

TROY. Well, go on back in the house and let me and Bono finish what we was talking about. This is men talk. I got some talk for you later. You know what kind of talk I mean. You go on and powder it up.

ROSE. Troy Maxson, don't you start that now!

TROY (*puts his arm around her*). Aw, woman ... come here. Look here, Bono ... when I met this woman ... I got out that place, say, "Hitch up my pony, saddle up my mare ... there's a woman out there for me somewhere. I looked here. Looked there. Saw Rose and latched on to her." I latched on to her and told her—I'm gonna tell you the truth—I told her, "Baby, I don't wanna marry, I just wanna be your man." Rose told me ... tell him what you told me, Rose.

ROSE. I told him if he wasn't the marrying kind, then move out the way so the marrying kind could find me.

TROY. That's what she told me. "Nigger, you in my way. You blocking the view! Move out the way so I can find me a husband." I thought it over two or three days. Come back—

ROSE. Ain't no two or three days nothing. You was back the same night.

TROY. Come back, told her ... "Okay, baby ... but I'm gonna buy me a banty rooster and put him out there in the backyard ... and when he see a stranger come, he'll flap his wings and crow ... " Look here, Bono, I could watch the front door by myself ... it was that back door I was worried about.

ROSE. Troy, you ought not talk like that. Troy ain't doing nothing but telling a lie.

TROY. Only thing is ... when we first got married ... forget the rooster ... we ain't had no yard!

BONO.  I hear you tell it. Me and Lucille was staying down there on Logan
Street. Had two rooms with the outhouse in the back. I ain't mind the
outhouse none. But when that goddamn wind blow through there in
the winter . . . that's what I'm talking about! To this day I wonder why
in the hell I ever stayed down there for six long years. But see, I did-
n't know I could do no better. I thought only white folks had inside
toilets and things.

ROSE.  There's a lot of people don't know they can do no better than they
doing now. That's just something you got to learn. A lot of folks still
shop at Bella's.

TROY.  Ain't nothing wrong with shopping at Bella's. She got fresh food.

ROSE.  I ain't said nothing about if she got fresh food. I'm talking about
what she charge. She charge ten cents more than the A&P.

TROY.  The A&P ain't never done nothing for me. I spends my money
where I'm treated right. I go down to Bella, say, "I need a loaf of bread,
I'll pay you Friday." She give it to me. What sense that make when I got
money to go and spend it somewhere else and ignore the person
who done right by me? That ain't in the Bible.

ROSE.  We ain't talking about what's in the Bible. What sense it make to
shop there when she overcharge?

TROY.  You shop where you want to. I'll do my shopping where the people
been good to me.

ROSE.  Well, I don't think it's right for her to overcharge. That's all I was
saying.

BONO.  Look here . . . I got to get on. Lucille going be raising all kind of hell.

TROY.  Where you going, nigger? We ain't finished this pint. Come here,
finish this pint.

BONO.  Well, hell, I am . . . if you ever turn the bottle loose.

TROY (*hands him the bottle*).  The only thing I say about the A&P is I'm
glad Cory got that job down there. Help him take care of his school
clothes and things. Gabe done moved out and things getting tight
around here. He got that job . . . He can start to look out for himself.

ROSE.  Cory done went and got recruited by a college football team.

TROY.  I told that boy about that football stuff. The white man ain't gonna
let him get nowhere with that football. I told him when he first come
to me with it. Now you come telling me he done went and got more
tied up in it. He ought to go and get recruited in how to fix cars or
something where he can make a living.

ROSE.  He ain't talking about making no living playing football. It's just
something the boys in school do. They gonna send a recruiter by to
talk to you. He'll tell you he ain't talking about making no living playing football. It's a honor to be recruited.

TROY.  It ain't gonna get him nowhere. Bono'll tell you that.

BONO.  If he be like you in the sports . . . he's gonna be all right. Ain't but
two men ever played baseball as good as you. That's Babe Ruth and

Josh Gibson.[1] Them's the only two men ever hit more home runs than you.

TROY. What it ever get me? Ain't got a pot to piss in or a window to throw it out of.

ROSE. Times have changed since you was playing baseball, Troy. That was before the war. Times have changed a lot since then.

TROY. How in hell they done changed?

ROSE. They got lots of colored boys playing ball now. Baseball and football.

BONO. You right about that, Rose. Times have changed, Troy. You just come along too early.

TROY. There ought not never have been no time called too early! Now you take that fellow . . . what's that fellow they had playing right field for the Yankees back then? You know who I'm talking about, Bono. Used to play right field for the Yankees.

ROSE. Selkirk?

TROY. Selkirk! That's it! Man batting .269, understand? .269. What kind of sense that make? I was hitting .432 with thirty-seven home runs! Man batting .269 and playing right field for the Yankees! I saw Josh Gibson's daughter yesterday. She walking around with raggedy shoes on her feet. Now I bet you Selkirk's daughter ain't walking around with raggedy shoes on her feet! I bet you that!

ROSE. They got a lot of colored baseball players now. Jackie Robinson[2] was the first. Folks had to wait for Jackie Robinson.

TROY. I done seen a hundred niggers play baseball better than Jackie Robinson. Hell, I know some teams Jackie Robinson couldn't even make! What you talking about Jackie Robinson. Jackie Robinson wasn't nobody. I'm talking about if you could play ball then they ought to have let you play. Don't care what color you were. Come telling me I come along too early. If you could play . . . then they ought to have let you play.

TROY *takes a long drink from the bottle.*

ROSE. You gonna drink yourself to death. You don't need to be drinking like that.

TROY. Death ain't nothing. I done seen him. Done wrassled with him. You can't tell me nothing about death. Death ain't nothing but a fastball on the outside corner. And you know what I'll do to that! Lookee here, Bono . . . am I lying? You get one of them fastballs, about waist high, over the outside corner of the plate where you can get the meat of the bat on it . . . and good god! You can kiss it goodbye. Now, am I lying?

---

[1]**Josh Gibson** African-American ballplayer (1911–47), known as the Babe Ruth of the Negro Leagues.     [2]**Jackie Robinson** In 1947 Robinson (1919–72) became the first African-American to play baseball in the major leagues.

BONO.  Naw, you telling the truth there. I seen you do it.

TROY.  If I'm lying . . . that 450 feet worth of lying! (*Pause.*) That's all death
is to me. A fastball on the outside corner.

ROSE.  I don't know why you want to get on talking about death.

TROY.  Ain't nothing wrong with talking about death. That's part of life.
Everybody gonna die. You gonna die, I'm gonna die. Bono's gonna die.
Hell, we all gonna die.

ROSE.  But you ain't got to talk about it. I don't like to talk about it.

TROY.  You the one brought it up. Me and Bono was talking about baseball
. . . you tell me I'm gonna drink myself to death. Ain't that right, Bono?
You know I don't drink this but one night out of the week. That's Friday night. I'm gonna drink just enough to where I can handle it. Then
I cuts it loose. I leave it alone. So don't you worry about me drinking
myself to death. 'Cause I ain't worried about Death. I done seen him.
I done wrestled with him.

　　　Look here, Bono . . . I looked up one day and Death was marching
straight at me. Like Soldiers on Parade! The Army of Death was
marching straight at me. The middle of July, 1941. It got real cold just
like it be winter. It seem like Death himself reached out and touched
me on the shoulder. He touch me just like I touch you. I got cold as
ice and Death standing there grinning at me.

ROSE.  Troy, why don't you hush that talk.

TROY.  I say . . . what you want, Mr. Death? You be wanting me? You done
brought your army to be getting me? I looked him dead in the eye. I
wasn't fearing nothing. I was ready to tangle. Just like I'm ready to tangle now. The Bible say be ever vigilant. That's why I don't get but so
drunk. I got to keep watch.

ROSE.  Troy was right down there in Mercy Hospital. You remember he had
pneumonia? Laying there with a fever talking plumb out of his head.

TROY.  Death standing there staring at me . . . carrying that sickle in his
hand. Finally he say, "You want bound over for another year?" See, just
like that . . . "You want bound over for another year?" I told him,
"Bound over hell! Let's settle this now!"

　　　It seem like he kinda fell back when I said that, and all the cold
went out of me. I reached down and grabbed that sickle and threw it
just as far as I could throw it . . . and me and him commenced to
wrestling.

　　　We wrestled for three days and three nights. I can't say where I
found the strength from. Everytime it seemed like he was gonna get
the best of me, I'd reach way down deep inside myself and find the
strength to do him one better.

ROSE.  Everytime Troy tell that story he find different ways to tell it. Different things to make up about it.

TROY.  I ain't making up nothing. I'm telling you the facts of what happened. I wrestled with Death for three days and three nights and I'm

standing here to tell you about it. (*Pause.*) All right. At the end of the third night we done weakened each other to where we can't hardly move. Death stood up, throwed on his robe . . . had him a white robe with a hood on it. He throwed on that robe and went off to look for his sickle. Say, "I'll be back." Just like that. "I'll be back." I told him, say, "Yeah, but . . . you gonna have to find me!" I wasn't no fool. I wasn't going looking for him. Death ain't nothing to play with. And I know he's gonna get me. I know I got to join his army . . . his camp followers. But as long as I keep my strength and see him coming . . . as long as I keep up my vigilance . . . he's gonna have to fight to get me. I ain't going easy.

BONO.  Well, look here, since you got to keep up your vigilance . . . let me have the bottle.

TROY.  Aw hell, I shouldn't have told you that part. I should have left out that part.

ROSE.  Troy be talking that stuff and half the time don't even know what he be talking about.

TROY.  Bono know me better than that.

BONO.  That's right. I know you. I know you got some Uncle Remus[3] in your blood. You got more stories than the devil got sinners.

TROY.  Aw hell, I done seen him too! Done talked with the devil.

ROSE.  Troy, don't nobody wanna be hearing all that stuff.

LYONS *enters the yard from the street. Thirty-four years old,* TROY*'s son by a previous marriage, he sports a neatly trimmed goatee, sport coat, white shirt, tieless and buttoned at the collar. Though he fancies himself a musician, he is more caught up in the rituals and "idea" of being a musician than in the actual practice of the music. He has come to borrow money from* TROY, *and while he knows he will be successful, he is uncertain as to what extent his lifestyle will be held up to scrutiny and ridicule.*

LYONS.  Hey, Pop.

TROY.  What you come "Hey, Popping" me for?

LYONS.  How you doing, Rose? (*He kisses her.*) Mr. Bono. How you doing?

BONO.  Hey, Lyons . . . how you been?

TROY.  He must have been doing all right. I ain't seen him around here last week.

ROSE.  Troy, leave your boy alone. He come by to see you and you wanna start all that nonsense.

TROY.  I ain't bothering Lyons. (*Offers him the bottle.*) Here . . . get you a drink. We got an understanding. I know why he come by to see me and he know I know.

---

[3]**Uncle Remus** narrator of traditional black tales in a book by Joel Chandler Harris.

LYONS.  Come on, Pop . . . I just stopped by to say hi . . . see how you was doing.

TROY.  You ain't stopped by yesterday.

ROSE.  You gonna stay for supper, Lyons? I got some chicken cooking in the oven.

LYONS.  No, Rose . . . thanks. I was just in the neighborhood and thought I'd stop by for a minute.

TROY.  You was in the neighborhood all right, nigger. You telling the truth there. You was in the neighborhood cause it's my payday.

LYONS.  Well, hell, since you mentioned it . . . let me have ten dollars.

TROY.  I'll be damned! I'll die and go to hell and play blackjack with the devil before I give you ten dollars.

BONO.  That's what I wanna know about . . . that devil you done seen.

LYONS.  What . . . Pop done seen the devil? You too much, Pops.

TROY.  Yeah, I done seen him. Talked to him too!

ROSE.  You ain't seen no devil. I done told you that man ain't had nothing to do with the devil. Anything you can't understand, you want to call it the devil.

TROY.  Look here, Bono . . . I went down to see Hertzberger about some furniture. Got three rooms for two-ninety-eight. That what it say on the radio. "Three rooms . . . two-ninety-eight." Even made up a little song about it. Go down there . . . man tell me I can't get no credit. I'm working every day and can't get no credit. What to do? I got an empty house with some raggedy furniture in it. Cory ain't got no bed. He's sleeping on a pile of rags on the floor. Working every day and can't get no credit. Come back here—Rose'll tell you—madder than hell. Sit down . . . try to figure what I'm gonna do. Come a knock on the door. Ain't been living here but three days. Who know I'm here? Open the door . . . devil standing there bigger than life. White fellow . . . white fellow . . . got on good clothes and everything. Standing there with a clipboard in his hand. I ain't had to say nothing. First words come out of his mouth was . . . "I understand you need some furniture and can't get no credit." I liked to fell over. He say, "I'll give you all the credit you want, but you got to pay the interest on it." I told him, "Give me three rooms worth and charge whatever you want." Next day a truck pulled up here and two men unloaded them three rooms. Man what drove the truck give me a book. Say send ten dollars, first of every month to the address in the book and every thing will be all right. Say if I miss a payment the devil was coming back and it'll be hell to pay. That was fifteen years ago. To this day . . . the first of the month I send my ten dollars, Rose'll tell you.

ROSE.  Troy lying.

TROY.  I ain't never seen that man since. Now you tell me who else that could have been but the devil? I ain't sold my soul or nothing like that, you understand. Naw, I wouldn't have truck with the devil about nothing like that. I got my furniture and pays my ten dollars the first of the month just like clockwork.

BONO.    How long you say you been paying this ten dollars a month?

TROY.    Fifteen years!

BONO.    Hell, ain't you finished paying for it yet? How much the man done charged you?

TROY.    Ah hell, I done paid for it. I done paid for it ten times over! The fact is I'm scared to stop paying it.

ROSE.    Troy lying. We got that furniture from Mr. Glickman. He ain't paying no ten dollars a month to nobody.

TROY.    Aw hell, woman. Bono know I ain't that big a fool.

LYONS.    I was just getting ready to say . . . I know where there's a bridge for sale.

TROY.    Look here, I'll tell you this . . . it don't matter to me if he was the devil. It don't matter if the devil give credit. Somebody has got to give it.

ROSE.    It ought to matter. You going around talking about having truck with the devil . . . God's the one you gonna have to answer to. He's the one gonna be at the Judgment.

LYONS.    Yeah, well, look here, Pop . . . Let me have that ten dollars. I'll give it back to you. Bonnie got a job working at the hospital.

TROY.    What I tell you, Bono? The only time I see this nigger is when he wants something. That's the only time I see him.

LYONS.    Come on, Pop, Mr. Bono don't want to hear all that. Let me have the ten dollars. I told you Bonnie working.

TROY.    What that mean to me? "Bonnie working." I don't care if she working. Go ask her for the ten dollars if she working. Talking about "Bonnie working." Why ain't you working?

LYONS.    Aw, Pop, you know I can't find no decent job. Where am I gonna get a job at? You know I can't get no job.

TROY.    I told you I know some people down there. I can get you on the rubbish if you want to work. I told you that the last time you came by here asking me for something.

LYONS.    Naw, Pop . . . thanks. That ain't for me. I don't wanna be carrying nobody's rubbish. I don't wanna be punching nobody's time clock.

TROY.    What's the matter, you too good to carry people's rubbish? Where you think that ten dollars you talking about come from? I'm just supposed to haul people's rubbish and give my money to you cause you too lazy to work. You too lazy to work and wanna know why you ain't got what I got.

ROSE.    What hospital Bonnie working at? Mercy?

LYONS.    She's down at Passavant working in the laundry.

TROY.    I ain't got nothing as it is. I give you that ten dollars and I got to eat beans the rest of the week. Naw . . . you ain't getting no ten dollars here.

LYONS.    You ain't got to be eating no beans. I don't know why you wanna say that.

TROY. I ain't got no extra money. Gabe done moved over to Miss Pearl's
paying her the rent and things done got tight around here. I can't afford to be giving you every payday.

LYONS. I ain't asked you to give me nothing. I asked you to loan me ten
dollars. I know you got ten dollars.

TROY. Yeah, I got it. You know why I got it? 'Cause I don't throw my money
away out there in the streets. You living the fast life . . . wanna be a musician . . . running around in them clubs and things . . . then, you learn
to take care of yourself. You ain't gonna find me going and asking nobody for nothing. I done spent too many years without.

LYONS. You and me is two different people, Pop.

TROY. I done learned my mistake and learned to do what's right by it. You
still trying to get something for nothing. Life don't owe you nothing.
You owe it to yourself. Ask Bono. He'll tell you I'm right.

LYONS. You got your way of dealing with the world . . . I got mine. The only
thing that matters to me is the music.

TROY. Yeah, I can see that! It don't matter how you gonna eat . . . where
your next dollar is coming from. You telling the truth there.

LYONS. I know I got to eat. But I got to live too. I need something that
gonna help me to get out of the bed in the morning. Make me feel
like I belong in the world. I don't bother nobody. I just stay with the
music cause that's the only way I can find to live in the world. Otherwise there ain't no telling what I might do. Now I don't come criticizing you and how you live. I just come by to ask you for ten dollars. I
don't wanna hear all that about how I live.

TROY. Boy, your mamma did a hell of a job raising you.

LYONS. You can't change me, Pop. I'm thirty-four years old. If you wanted
to change me, you should have been there when I was growing up. I
come by to see you . . . ask for ten dollars and you want to talk about
how I was raised. You don't know nothing about how I was raised.

ROSE. Let the boy have ten dollars, Troy.

TROY (*to* LYONS). What the hell you looking at me for? I ain't got no ten dollars. You know what I do with my money. (*To* ROSE.) Give him ten dollars if you want him to have it.

ROSE. I will. Just as soon as you turn it loose.

TROY (*handing* ROSE *the money*). There it is. Seventy-six dollars and forty-
two cents. You see this, Bono? Now, I ain't gonna get but six of that back.

ROSE. You ought to stop telling that lie. Here, Lyons. (*She hands him the
money.*)

LYONS. Thanks, Rose. Look . . . I got to run . . . I'll see you later.

TROY. Wait a minute. You gonna say, "thanks, Rose" and ain't gonna look to
see where she got that ten dollars from? See how they do me, Bono?

LYONS. I know she got it from you, Pop. Thanks. I'll give it back to you.

TROY. There he go telling another lie. Time I see that ten dollars . . . he'll be
owing me thirty more.

LYONS. See you, Mr. Bono.

BONO.  Take care, Lyons!

LYONS.  Thanks, Pop. I'll see you again.

LYONS *exits the yard.*

TROY.  I don't know why he don't go and get him a decent job and take care of that woman he got.

BONO.  He'll be all right, Troy. The boy is still young.

TROY.  The *boy* is thirty-four years old.

ROSE.  Let's not get off into all that.

BONO.  Look here . . . I got to be going. I got to be getting on. Lucille gonna be waiting.

TROY (*puts his arm around* ROSE).  See this woman, Bono? I love this woman. I love this woman so much it hurts. I love her so much . . . I done run out of ways of loving her. So I got to go back to basics. Don't you come by my house Monday morning talking about time to go to work . . . 'cause I'm still gonna be stroking!

ROSE.  Troy! Stop it now!

BONO.  I ain't paying him no mind, Rose. That ain't nothing but gin-talk. Go on, Troy. I'll see you Monday.

TROY.  Don't you come by my house, nigger! I done told you what I'm gonna be doing.

*The lights go down to black.*

## Scene 2

*The lights come up on* ROSE *hanging up clothes. She hums and sings softly to herself. It is the following morning.*

ROSE (*sings*).

Jesus, be a fence all around me every day
Jesus, I want you to protect me as I travel on my way.
Jesus, be a fence all around me every day.

TROY *enters from the house.*

Jesus, I want you to protect me
As I travel on my way.

(*To* TROY.) 'Morning. You ready for breakfast? I can fix it soon as I finish hanging up these clothes.

TROY.  I got the coffee on. That'll be all right. I'll just drink some of that this morning.

ROSE.  That 651 hit yesterday. That's the second time this month. Miss Pearl hit for a dollar . . . seem like those that need the least always get lucky. Poor folks can't get nothing.

TROY.  Them numbers don't know nobody. I don't know why you fool with them. You and Lyons both.

ROSE. It's something to do.

TROY. You ain't doing nothing but throwing your money away.

ROSE. Troy, you know I don't play foolishly. I just play a nickel here and a nickel there.

TROY. That's two nickels you done thrown away.

ROSE. Now I hit sometimes . . . that makes up for it. It always comes in handy when I do hit. I don't hear you complaining then.

TROY. I ain't complaining now. I just say it's foolish. Trying to guess out of six hundred ways which way the number gonna come. If I had all the money niggers, these Negroes, throw away on numbers for one week—just one week—I'd be a rich man.

ROSE. Well, you wishing and calling it foolish ain't gonna stop folks from playing numbers. That's one thing for sure. Besides . . . some good things come from playing numbers. Look where Pope done bought him that restaurant off of numbers.

TROY. I can't stand niggers like that. Man ain't had two dimes to rub to- gether. He walking around with his shoes all run over bumming money for cigarettes. All right. Got lucky there and hit the numbers . . .

ROSE. Troy, I know all about it.

TROY. Had good sense, I'll say that for him. He ain't throwed his money away. I seen niggers hit the numbers and go through two thousand dollars in four days. Man bought him that restaurant down there . . . fixed it up real nice . . . and then didn't want nobody to come in it! A Negro go in there and can't get no kind of service. I seen a white fel- low come in there and order a bowl of stew. Pope picked all the meat out of the pot for him. Man ain't had nothing but a bowl of meat! Ne gro come behind him and ain't got nothing but the potatoes and car- rots. Talking about what numbers do for people, you picked a wrong example. Ain't done nothing but make a worser fool out of him than he was before.

ROSE. Troy, you ought to stop worrying about what happened at work yesterday.

TROY. I ain't worried. Just told me to be down there at the Commissioner's office on Friday. Everybody think they gonna fire me. I ain't worried about them firing me. You ain't got to worry about that. (*Pause.*) Where's Cory? Cory in the house? (*Calls.*) Cory?

ROSE. He gone out.

TROY. Out, huh? He gone out 'cause he know I want him to help me with this fence. I know how he is. That boy scared of work.

     GABRIEL *enters. He comes halfway down the alley and, hearing* TROY*'s voice, stops.*

TROY (*continues*). He ain't done a lick of work in his life.

ROSE. He had to go to football practice. Coach wanted them to get in a lit- tle extra practice before the season start.

TROY.  I got his practice ... running out of here before he get his chores done.

ROSE.  Troy, what is wrong with you this morning? Don't nothing set right with you. Go on back in there and go to bed ...get up on the other side.

TROY.  Why something got to be wrong with me? I ain't said nothing wrong with me.

ROSE.  You got something to say about everything. First it's the numbers ... then it's the way the man runs his restaurant ... then you done got on Cory. What's it gonna be next? Take a look up there and see if the weather suits you ... or is it gonna be how you gonna put up the fence with the clothes hanging in the yard?

TROY.  You hit the nail on the head then.

ROSE.  I know you like I know the back of my hand. Go on in there and get you some coffee ... see if that straighten you up. 'Cause you ain't right this morning.

TROY *starts into the house and sees* GABRIEL. GABRIEL *starts singing.* TROY*'s brother, he is seven years younger than* TROY. *Injured in World War II, he has a metal plate in his head. He carries an old trumpet tied around his waist and believes with every fiber of his being that he is the Archangel Gabriel. He carries a chipped basket with an assortment of discarded fruits and vegetables he has picked up in the strip district and which he attempts to sell.*

GABRIEL (*singing*).
    Yes, ma'am I got plums
    You ask me how I sell them
    Oh ten cents apiece
    Three for a quarter
    Come and buy now
    'Cause I'm here today
    And tomorrow I'll be gone

    GABRIEL *enters.*

    Hey, Rose!

ROSE.  How you doing, Gabe?

GABRIEL.  There's Troy ... Hey, Troy!

TROY.  Hey, Gabe.

    *Exit into kitchen.*

ROSE (*to* GABRIEL). What you got there?

GABRIEL.  You know what I got, Rose. I got fruits and vegetables.

ROSE (*looking in basket*).  Where's all these plums you talking about?

GABRIEL.  I ain't got no plums today, Rose. I was just singing that. Have some tomorrow. Put me in a big order for plums. Have enough plums tomorrow for St. Peter and everybody.

TROY *reenters from kitchen, crosses to steps.*

(*To* ROSE.) Troy's mad at me.

TROY. I ain't mad at you. What I got to be mad at you about? You ain't done nothing to me.

GABRIEL. I just moved over to Miss Pearl's to keep out from in your way. I ain't mean no harm by it.

TROY. Who said anything about that? I ain't said anything about that.

GABRIEL. You ain't mad at me, is you?

TROY. Naw . . . I ain't mad at you, Gabe. If I was mad at you I'd tell you about it.

GABRIEL. Got me two rooms. In the basement. Got my own door too. Wanna see my key? (*He holds up a key.*) That's my own key! My two rooms!

TROY. Well, that's good, Gabe. You got your own key . . . that's good.

ROSE. You hungry, Gabe? I was just fixing to cook Troy his breakfast.

GABRIEL. I'll take some biscuits. You got some biscuits? Did you know when I was in heaven . . . every morning me and St. Peter would sit down by the gate and eat some big fat biscuits? Oh, yeah! We had us a good time. We'd sit there and eat us them biscuits and then St. Peter would go off to sleep and tell me to wake him up when it's time to open the gates for the Judgment.

ROSE. Well, come on . . . I'll make up a batch of biscuits.

ROSE *exits into the house.*

GABRIEL. Troy . . . St. Peter got your name in the book. I seen it. It say . . . Troy Maxson. I say . . . I know him! He got the same name like what I got. That's my brother!

TROY. How many times you gonna tell me that, Gabe?

GABRIEL. Ain't got my name in the book. Don't have to have my name. I done died and went to heaven. He got your name though. One morning St. Peter was looking at his book . . . marking it up for the judgment . . . and he let me see your name. Got it in there under M. Got Rose's name . . . I ain't seen it like I seen yours . . . but I know it's in there. He got a great big book. Got everybody's name what was ever been born. That's what he told me. But I seen your name. Seen it with my own eyes.

TROY. Go on in the house there. Rose going to fix you something to eat.

GABRIEL. Oh, I ain't hungry. I done had breakfast with Aunt Jemimah. She come by and cooked me up a whole mess of flapjacks. Remember how we used to eat them flapjacks?

TROY. Go on in the house and get you something to eat now.

GABRIEL. I got to sell my plums. I done sold some tomatoes. Got me two quarters. Wanna see? (*He shows* TROY *his quarters.*) I'm gonna save them and buy me a new horn so St. Peter can hear me when it's time to open the gates. (GABRIEL *stops suddenly. Listens.*) Hear that? That's the hellhounds. I got to chase them out of here. Go on get out of here! Get out!

GABRIEL *exits singing.*

> Better get ready for the judgment
> Better get ready for the judgment
> My Lord is coming down

ROSE *enters from the house.*

TROY.  He's gone off somewhere.

GABRIEL (*offstage*).

> Better get ready for the judgment
> Better get ready for the judgment morning
> Better get ready for the judgment
> My God is coming down

ROSE.  He ain't eating right. Miss Pearl say she can't get him to eat nothing.

TROY.  What you want me to do about it, Rose? I done did everything I can for the man. I can't make him get well. Man got half his head blown away . . . what you expect?

ROSE.  Seem like something ought to be done to help him.

TROY.  Man don't bother nobody. He just mixed up from that metal plate he got in his head. Ain't no sense for him to go back into the hospital.

ROSE.  Least he be eating right. They can help him take care of himself.

TROY.  Don't nobody wanna be locked up, Rose. What you wanna lock him up for? Man go over there and fight the war . . . messin' around with them Japs, get half his head blown off . . . and they give him a lousy three thousand dollars. And I had to swoop down on that.

ROSE.  Is you fixing to go into that again?

TROY.  That's the only way I got a roof over my head . . . 'cause of that metal plate.

ROSE.  Ain't no sense you blaming yourself for nothing. Gabe wasn't in no condition to manage that money. You done what was right by him. Can't nobody say you ain't done what was right by him. Look how long you took care of him . . . till he wanted to have his own place and moved over there with Miss Pearl.

TROY.  That ain't what I'm saying, woman! I'm just stating the facts. If my brother didn't have that metal plate in his head . . . I wouldn't have a pot to piss in or a window to throw it out of. And I'm fifty-three years old. Now see if you can understand that!

TROY *gets up from the porch and starts to exit the yard.*

ROSE.  Where you going off to? You been running out of here every Saturday for weeks. I thought you was gonna work on this fence?

TROY.  I'm gonna walk down to Taylors'. Listen to the ball game. I'll be back in a bit. I'll work on it when I get back.

*He exits the yard. The lights go to black.*

## Scene 3

*The lights come up on the yard. It is four hours later.* ROSE *is taking down the clothes from the line.* CORY *enters carrying his football equipment.*

ROSE. Your daddy like to had a fit with you running out of here this morning without doing your chores.

CORY. I told you I had to go to practice.

ROSE. He say you were supposed to help him with this fence.

CORY. He been saying that the last four or five Saturdays, and then he don't never do nothing, but go down to Taylors'. Did you tell him about the recruiter?

ROSE. Yeah, I told him.

CORY. What he say?

ROSE. He ain't said nothing too much. You get in there and get started on your chores before he gets back. Go on and scrub down them steps before he gets back here hollering and carrying on.

CORY. I'm hungry. What you got to eat, Mama?

ROSE. Go on and get started on your chores. I got some meat loaf in there. Go on and make you a sandwich . . . and don't leave no mess in there.

CORY *exits into the house.* ROSE *continues to take down the clothes.* TROY *enters the yard and sneaks up and grabs her from behind.*

Troy! Go on, now. You liked to scared me to death. What was the score of the game? Lucille had me on the phone and I couldn't keep up with it.

TROY. What I care about the game? Come here, woman. (*He tries to kiss her.*)

ROSE. I thought you went down Taylors' to listen to the game. Go on, Troy! You supposed to be putting up this fence.

TROY (*attempting to kiss her again*). I'll put it up when I finish with what is at hand.

ROSE. Go on, Troy. I ain't studying you.

TROY (*chasing after her*). I'm studying you . . . fixing to do my homework!

ROSE. Troy, you better leave me alone.

TROY. Where's Cory? That boy brought his butt home yet?

ROSE. He's in the house doing his chores.

TROY (*calling*). Cory! Get your butt out here, boy!

ROSE *exits into the house with the laundry.* TROY *goes over to the pile of wood, picks up a board, and starts sawing.* CORY *enters from the house.*

TROY. You just now coming in here from leaving this morning?

CORY.  Yeah, I had to go to football practice.

TROY.  Yeah, what?

CORY.  Yessir.

TROY.  I ain't but two seconds off you noway. The garbage sitting in there overflowing . . . you ain't done none of your chores . . . and you come in here talking about "Yeah."

CORY.  I was just getting ready to do my chores now, Pop . . .

TROY.  Your first chore is to help me with this fence on Saturday. Everything else come after that. Now get that saw and cut them boards.

> CORY *takes the saw and begins cutting the boards.* TROY *continues working. There is a long pause.*

CORY.  Hey, Pop . . . why don't you buy a TV?

TROY.  What I want with a TV? What I want one of them for?

CORY.  Everybody got one. Earl, Ba Bra . . . Jesse!

TROY.  I ain't asked you who had one. I say what I want with one?

CORY.  So you can watch it. They got lots of things on TV. Baseball games and everything. We could watch the World Series.

TROY.  Yeah . . . and how much this TV cost?

CORY.  I don't know. They got them on sale for around two hundred dollars.

TROY.  Two hundred dollars, huh?

CORY.  That ain't that much, Pop.

TROY.  Naw, it's just two hundred dollars. See that roof you got over your head at night? Let me tell you something about that roof. It's been over ten years since that roof was last tarred. See now . . . the snow come this winter and sit up there on that roof like it is . . . and it's gonna seep inside. It's just gonna be a little bit . . . ain't gonna hardly notice it. Then the next thing you know, it's gonna be leaking all over the house. Then the wood rot from all that water and you gonna need a whole new roof. Now, how much you think it cost to get that roof tarred?

CORY.  I don't know.

TROY.  Two hundred and sixty-four dollars . . . cash money. While you thinking about a TV, I got to be thinking about the roof . . . and whatever else go wrong here. Now if you had two hundred dollars, what would you do . . . fix the roof or buy a TV?

CORY.  I'd buy a TV. Then when the roof started to leak . . . when it needed fixing . . . I'd fix it.

TROY.  Where you gonna get the money from? You done spent it for a TV. You gonna sit up and watch the water run all over your brand new TV.

CORY.  Aw, Pop. You got money. I know you do.

TROY.  Where I got it at, huh?

CORY.  You got it in the bank.

TROY.  You wanna see my bankbook? You wanna see that seventy-three dollars and twenty-two cents I got sitting up in there?

CORY.  You ain't got to pay for it all at one time. You can put a down payment on it and carry it on home with you.

TROY.  Not me. I ain't gonna owe nobody nothing if I can help it. Miss a payment and they come and snatch it right out of your house. Then what you got? Now, soon as I get two hundred dollars clear, then I'll buy a TV. Right now, as soon as I get two hundred and sixty-four dollars, I'm gonna have this roof tarred.

CORY.  Aw . . . Pop!

TROY.  You go on and get you two hundred dollars and buy one if ya want it. I got better things to do with my money.

CORY.  I can't get no two hundred dollars. I ain't never seen two hundred dollars.

TROY.  I'll tell you what . . . you get you a hundred dollars and I'll put the other hundred with it.

CORY.  All right, I'm gonna show you.

TROY.  You gonna show me how you can cut them boards right now.

CORY *begins to cut the boards. There is a long pause.*

CORY.  The Pirates won today. That makes five in a row.

TROY.  I ain't thinking about the Pirates. Got an all-white team. Got that boy . . . that Puerto Rican boy . . . Clemente. Don't even half-play him. That boy could be something if they give him a chance. Play him one day and sit him on the bench the next.

CORY.  He gets a lot of chances to play.

TROY.  I'm talking about playing regular. Playing every day so you can get your timing. That's what I'm talking about.

CORY.  They got some white guys on the team that don't play every day. You can't play everybody at the same time.

TROY.  If they got a white fellow sitting on the bench . . . you can bet your last dollar he can't play! The colored guy got to be twice as good before he get on the team. That's why I don't want you to get all tied up in them sports. Man on the team and what it get him? They got colored on the team and don't use them. Same as not having them. All them teams the same.

CORY.  The Braves got Hank Aaron and Wes Covington. Hank Aaron hit two home runs today. That makes forty-three.

TROY.  Hank Aaron ain't nobody. That what you supposed to do. That's how you supposed to play the game. Ain't nothing to it. It's just a matter of timing . . . getting the right follow-through. Hell, I can hit forty-three home runs right now!

CORY.  Not off no major-league pitching, you couldn't.

TROY.   We had better pitching in the Negro leagues. I hit seven home runs off of Satchel Paige.[4] You can't get no better than that!

CORY.   Sandy Koufax. He's leading the league in strikeouts.

TROY.   I ain't thinking of no Sandy Koufax.

CORY.   You got Warren Spahn and Lew Burdette. I bet you couldn't hit no home runs off of Warren Spahn.

TROY.   I'm through with it now. You go on and cut them boards. (*Pause.*) Your mama tell me you done got recruited by a college football team? Is that right?

CORY.   Yeah. Coach Zellman say the recruiter gonna be coming by to talk to you. Get you to sign the permission papers.

TROY.   I thought you supposed to be working down there at the A&P. Ain't you suppose to be working down there after school?

CORY.   Mr. Stawicki say he gonna hold my job for me until after the football season. Say starting next week I can work weekends.

TROY.   I thought we had an understanding about this football stuff? You suppose to keep up with your chores and hold that job down at the A&P. Ain't been around here all day on a Saturday. Ain't none of your chores done . . . and now you telling me you done quit your job.

CORY.   I'm going to be working weekends.

TROY.   You damn right you are! And ain't no need for nobody coming around here to talk to me about signing nothing.

CORY.   Hey, Pop . . . you can't do that. He's coming all the way from North Carolina.

TROY.   I don't care where he coming from. The white man ain't gonna let you get nowhere with that football noway. You go on and get your book-learning so you can work yourself up in that A&P or learn how to fix cars or build houses or something, get you a trade. That way you have something can't nobody take away from you. You go on and learn how to put your hands to some good use. Besides hauling people's garbage.

CORY.   I get good grades, Pop. That's why the recruiter wants to talk with you. You got to keep up your grades to get recruited. This way I'll be going to college. I'll get a chance . . .

TROY.   First you gonna get your butt down there to the A&P and get your job back.

CORY.   Mr. Stawicki done already hired somebody else 'cause I told him I was playing football.

TROY.   You a bigger fool than I thought . . . to let somebody take away your job so you can play some football. Where you gonna get your money to take out your girlfriend and whatnot? What kind of foolishness is that to let somebody take away your job?

---

[4]**Satchel Paige** (1906–82) pitcher in the Negro leagues.

CORY. I'm still gonna be working weekends.

TROY. Naw . . . naw. You getting your butt out of here and finding you another job.

CORY. Come on, Pop! I got to practice. I can't work after school and play football too. The team needs me. That's what Coach Zellman say . . .

TROY. I don't care what nobody else say. I'm the boss . . . you understand? I'm the boss around here. I do the only saying what counts.

CORY. Come on, Pop!

TROY. I asked you . . . did you understand?

CORY. Yeah . . .

TROY. What?!

CORY. Yessir.

TROY. You go on down there to that A&P and see if you can get your job back. If you can't do both . . . then you quit the football team. You've got to take the crookeds with the straights.

CORY. Yessir. (*Pause.*) Can I ask you a question?

TROY. What the hell you wanna ask me? Mr. Stawicki the one you got the questions for.

CORY. How come you ain't never liked me?

TROY. Liked you? Who the hell say I got to like you? What law is there say I got to like you? Wanna stand up in my face and ask a damn foolass question like that. Talking about liking somebody. Come here, boy, when I talk to you.

CORY *comes over to where* TROY *is working. He stands slouched over and* TROY *shoves him on his shoulder.*

Straighten up, goddammit! I asked you a question . . . what law is there say I got to like you?

CORY. None.

TROY. Well, all right then! Don't you eat every day? (*Pause.*) Answer me when I talk to you! Don't you eat every day?

CORY. Yeah.

TROY. Nigger, as long as you in my house, you put that sir on the end of it when you talk to me.

CORY. Yes . . . sir.

TROY. You eat every day.

CORY. Yessir!

TROY. Got a roof over your head.

CORY. Yessir!

TROY. Got clothes on your back.

CORY. Yessir.

TROY. Why you think that is?

CORY. 'Cause of you.

TROY. Ah, hell I know it's 'cause of me . . . but why do you think that is?

CORY (*hesitant*). 'Cause you like me.

TROY.  Like you? I go out of here every morning . . . bust my butt . . . putting up with them crackers every day . . . cause I like you? You are the biggest fool I ever saw. (*Pause.*) It's my job. It's my responsibility! You understand that? A man got to take care of his family. You live in my house . . . sleep you behind on my bedclothes . . . fill you belly up with my food . . . 'cause you my son. You my flesh and blood. Not 'cause I like you! 'Cause it's my duty to take care of you. I owe a responsibility to you! Let's get this straight right here . . . before it go along any further . . . I ain't got to like you. Mr. Rand don't give me my money come payday 'cause he likes me. He give me 'cause he owe me. I done give you everything I had to give you. I gave you your life! Me and your mama worked that out between us. And liking your black ass wasn't part of the bargain. Don't you try and go through life worrying about if somebody like you or not. You best be making sure they doing right by you. You understand what I'm saying, boy?

CORY.  Yessir.

TROY.  Then get the hell out of my face, and get on down to that A&P.

ROSE *has been standing behind the screen door for much of the scene. She enters as* CORY *exits.*

ROSE.  Why don't you let the boy go ahead and play football, Troy? Ain't no harm in that. He's just trying to be like you with the sports.

TROY.  I don't want him to be like me! I want him to move as far away from my life as he can get. You the only decent thing that ever happened to me. I wish him that. But I don't wish him a thing else from my life. I decided seventeen years ago that boy wasn't getting involved in no sports. Not after what they did to me in the sports.

ROSE.  Troy, why don't you admit you was too old to play in the major leagues? For once . . . why don't you admit that?

TROY.  What do you mean too old? Don't come telling me I was too old. I just wasn't the right color. Hell, I'm fifty-three years old and can do better than Selkirk's .269 right now!

ROSE.  How's was you gonna play ball when you were over forty? Sometimes I can't get no sense out of you.

TROY.  I got good sense, woman. I got sense enough not to let my boy get hurt over playing no sports. You been mothering that boy too much. Worried about if people like him.

ROSE.  Everything that boy do . . . he do for you. He wants you to say "Good job, son." That's all.

TROY.  Rose, I ain't got time for that. He's alive. He's healthy. He's got to make his own way. I made mine. Ain't nobody gonna hold his hand when he get out there in that world.

ROSE.  Times have changed from when you was young, Troy. People change. The world's changing around you and you can't even see it.

TROY (*slow, methodical*). Woman . . . I do the best I can do. I come in here every Friday. I carry a sack of potatoes and a bucket of lard. You all line up at the door with your hands out. I give you the lint from my pockets. I give you my sweat and my blood. I ain't got no tears. I done spent them. We go upstairs in that room at night . . . and I fall down on you and try to blast a hole into forever. I get up Monday morning . . . find my lunch on the table. I go out. Make my way. Find my strength to carry me through to the next Friday. (*Pause.*) That's all I got, Rose. That's all I got to give. I can't give nothing else.

TROY *exits into the house. The lights go down to black.*

## Scene 4

*It is Friday. Two weeks later.* CORY *starts out of the house with his football equipment. The phone rings.*

CORY (*calling*). I got it! (*He answers the phone and stands in the screen door talking.*) Hello? Hey, Jesse. Naw . . . I was just getting ready to leave now.

ROSE (*calling*). Cory!

CORY. I told you, man, them spikes is all tore up. You can use them if you want, but they ain't no good. Earl got some spikes.

ROSE (*calling*). Cory!

CORY (*calling to* ROSE). Mam? I'm talking to Jesse. (*Into phone.*) When she say that? (*Pause.*) Aw, you lying, man. I'm gonna tell her you said that.

ROSE (*calling*). Cory, don't you go nowhere!

CORY. I got to go to the game, Ma! (*Into the phone.*) Yeah, hey, look, I'll talk to you later. Yeah, I'll meet you over Earl's house. Later. Bye, Ma.

CORY *exits the house and starts out the yard.*

ROSE. Cory, where you going off to? You got that stuff all pulled out and thrown all over your room.

CORY (*in the yard*). I was looking for my spikes. Jesse wanted to borrow my spikes.

ROSE. Get up there and get that cleaned up before your daddy get back in here.

CORY. I got to go to the game! I'll clean it up *when I get back.*

CORY *exits.*

ROSE. That's all he need to do is see that room all messed up.

ROSE *exits into the house.* TROY *and* BONO *enter the yard.* TROY *is dressed in clothes other than his work clothes.*

BONO. He told him the same thing he told you. Take it to the union.

TROY.  Brownie ain't got that much sense. Man wasn't thinking about nothing. He wait until I confront them on it . . . then he wanna come crying seniority. (*Calls.*) Hey, Rose!

BONO.  I wish I could have seen Mr. Rand's face when he told you.

TROY.  He couldn't get it out of his mouth! Liked to bit his tongue! When
they called me down there to the Commissioner's office . . . he
thought they was gonna fire me. Like everybody else.

BONO.  I didn't think they was gonna fire you. I thought they was gonna
put you on the warning paper.

TROY.  Hey, Rose! (*To* BONO.) Yeah, Mr. Rand like to bit his tongue.

TROY *breaks the seal on the bottle, takes a drink, and hands it to*
BONO.

BONO.  I see you run right down to Taylors' and told that Alberta gal.

TROY (*calling*). Hey, Rose! (*To* BONO.) I told everybody. Hey, Rose! I went
down there to cash my check.

ROSE (*entering from the house*). Hush all that hollering, man! I know you
out here. What they say down there at the Commissioner's office?

TROY.  You supposed to come when I call you, woman. Bono'll tell you
that. (*To* BONO.) Don't Lucille come when you call her?

ROSE.  Man, hush your mouth. I ain't no dog . . . talk about "come when you
call me."

TROY (*puts his arm around* ROSE). You hear this, Bono? I had me an old
dog used to get uppity like that. You say, "C'mere, Blue!" . . . and he just
lay there and look at you. End up getting a stick and chasing him away
trying to make him come.

ROSE.  I ain't studying you and your dog. I remember you used to sing that
old song.

TROY (*he sings*).
　　　　Hear it ring! Hear it ring! I had a dog his name was Blue.

ROSE.  Don't nobody wanna hear you sing that old song.

TROY (*sings*).
　　　　You know Blue was mighty true.

ROSE.  Used to have Cory running around here singing that song.

BONO.  Hell, I remember that song myself.

TROY (*sings*).
　　　　You know Blue was a good old dog.
　　　　Blue treed a possum in a hollow log.
　　　That was my daddy's song. My daddy made up that song.

ROSE.  I don't care who made it up. Don't nobody wanna hear you sing it.

TROY (*makes a song like calling a dog*). Come here, woman.

ROSE.  You come in here carrying on, I reckon they ain't fired you. What
they say down there at the Commissioner's office?

TROY.  Look here, Rose . . . Mr. Rand called me into his office today when I
got back from talking to them people down there . . . it come from up
top . . . he called me in and told me they was making me a driver.

ROSE.  Troy, you kidding!

TROY.  No I ain't. Ask Bono.

ROSE.  Well, that's great, Troy. Now you don't have to hassle them people no more.

LYONS *enters from the street.*

TROY.  Aw hell, I wasn't looking to see you today. I thought you was in jail. Got it all over the front page of the *Courier* about them raiding Sefus's place . . . where you be hanging out with all them thugs.

LYONS.  Hey, Pop . . . that ain't got nothing to do with me. I don't go down there gambling. I go down there to sit in with the band. I ain't got nothing to do with the gambling part. They got some good music down there.

TROY.  They got some rogues . . . is what they got.

LYONS.  How you been, Mr. Bono? Hi, Rose.

BONO.  I see where you playing down at the Crawford Grill tonight.

ROSE.  How come you ain't brought Bonnie like I told you? You should have brought Bonnie with you, she ain't been over in a month of Sundays.

LYONS.  I was just in the neighborhood . . . thought I'd stop by.

TROY.  Here he come . . .

BONO.  Your daddy got a promotion on the rubbish. He's gonna be the first colored driver. Ain't got to do nothing but sit up there and read the paper like them white fellows.

LYONS.  Hey, Pop . . . if you knew how to read you'd be all right.

BONO.  Naw . . . naw . . . you mean if the nigger knew how to drive he'd be all right. Been fighting with them people about driving and ain't even got a license. Mr. Rand know you ain't got no driver's license?

TROY.  Driving ain't nothing. All you do is point the truck where you want it to go. Driving ain't nothing.

BONO.  Do Mr. Rand know you ain't got no driver's license? That's what I'm talking about. I ain't asked if driving was easy. I asked if Mr. Rand know you ain't got no driver's license.

TROY.  He ain't got to know. The man ain't got to know my business. Time he find out, I have two or three driver's licenses.

LYONS *(going into his pocket).* Say, look here, Pop . . .

TROY.  I knew it was coming. Didn't I tell you, Bono? I know what kind of "Look here, Pop" that was. The nigger fixing to ask me for some money. It's Friday night. It's my payday. All them rogues down there on the avenue . . . the ones that ain't in jail . . . and Lyons is hopping in his shoes to get down there with them.

LYONS.  See, Pop . . . if you give somebody else a chance to talk sometimes, you'd see that I was fixing to pay you back your ten dollars like I told you. Here . . . I told you I'd pay you when Bonnie got paid.

TROY.  Naw . . . you go ahead and keep that ten dollars. Put it in the bank. The next time you feel like you wanna come by here and ask me for something . . . you go on down there and get that.

LYONS.  Here's your ten dollars, Pop. I told you I don't want you to give me nothing. I just wanted to borrow ten dollars.

TROY.  Naw . . . you go on and keep that for the next time you want to ask me.

LYONS.  Come on, Pop . . . here go your ten dollars.

ROSE.  Why don't you go on and let the boy pay you back, Troy?

LYONS.  Here you go, Rose. If you don't take it I'm gonna have to hear about it for the next six months. (*He hands her the money.*)

ROSE.  You can hand yours over here too, Troy.

TROY.  You see this, Bono. You see how they do me.

BONO.  Yeah, Lucille do me the same way.

GABRIEL *is heard singing off stage. He enters.*

GABRIEL.  Better get ready for the Judgment! Better get ready for . . . Hey! . . . Hey! . . . There's Troy's boy!

LYONS.  How are you doing, Uncle Gabe?

GABRIEL.  Lyons . . . The King of the Jungle! Rose . . . hey, Rose. Got a flower for you. (*He takes a rose from his pocket.*) Picked it myself. That's the same rose like you is!

ROSE.  That's right nice of you, Gabe.

LYONS.  What you been doing, Uncle Gabe?

GABRIEL.  Oh, I been chasing hellhounds and waiting on the time to tell St. Peter to open the gates.

LYONS.  You been chasing hellhounds, huh? Well . . . you doing the right thing, Uncle Gabe. Somebody got to chase them.

GABRIEL.  Oh, yeah . . . I know it. The devil's strong. The devil ain't no pushover. Hellhounds snipping at everybody's heels. But I got my trumpet waiting on the Judgment time.

LYONS.  Waiting on the Battle of Armageddon, huh?

GABRIEL.  Ain't gonna be too much of a battle when God get to waving that Judgment sword. But the people's gonna have a hell of a time trying to get into heaven if them gates ain't open.

LYONS (*putting his arm around* GABRIEL).  You hear this, Pop. Uncle Gabe, you all right!

GABRIEL (*laughing with* LYONS).  Lyons! King of the Jungle.

ROSE.  You gonna stay for supper, Gabe? Want me to fix you a plate?

GABRIEL.  I'll take a sandwich, Rose. Don't want no plate. Just wanna eat with my hands. I'll take a sandwich.

ROSE.  How about you, Lyons? You staying? Got some short ribs cooking.

LYONS.  Naw, I won't eat nothing till after we finished playing. (*Pause.*) You ought to come down and listen to me play, Pop.

TROY.  I don't like that Chinese music. All that noise.

ROSE.  Go on in the house and wash up, Gabe . . . I'll fix you a sandwich.

GABRIEL (*to* LYONS, *as he exits*).  Troy's mad at me.

LYONS. What you mad at Uncle Gabe for, Pop?
ROSE. He thinks Troy's mad at him 'cause he moved over to Miss Pearl's.
TROY. I ain't mad at the man. He can live where he want to live at.
LYONS. What he move over there for? Miss Pearl don't like nobody.
ROSE. She don't mind him none. She treats him real nice. She just don't al-
low all that singing.
TROY. She don't mind that rent he be paying ... that's what she don't mind.
ROSE. Troy, I ain't going through that with you no more. He's over there
'cause he want to have his own place. He can come and go as he
please.
TROY. Hell, he could come and go as he please here. I wasn't stopping
him. I ain't put no rules on him.
ROSE. It ain't the same thing, Troy. And you know it.

GABRIEL *comes to the door.*

Now, that's the last I wanna hear about that. I don't wanna hear noth-
ing else about Gabe and Miss Pearl. And next week ...
GABRIEL. I'm ready for my sandwich, Rose.
ROSE. And next week ... when that recruiter come from that school ... I
want you to sign that paper and go on and let Cory play football. Then
that'll be the last I have to hear about that.
TROY (*to* ROSE *as she exits into the house*). I ain't thinking about Cory
nothing.
LYONS. What ... Cory got recruited? What school he going to?
TROY. That boy walking around here smelling his piss ... thinking he's
grown. Thinking he's gonna do what he want, irrespective of what I
say. Look here, Bono ... I left the Commissioner's office and went
down to the A&P ... that boy ain't working down there. He lying to
me. Telling me he got his job back ... telling me he working weekends
... telling me he working after school ... Mr. Stawicki tell me he ain't
working down there at all!
LYONS. Cory just growing up. He's just busting at the seams trying to fill
out your shoes.
TROY. I don't care what he's doing. When he get to the point where he
wanna disobey me ... then it's time for him to move on. Bono'll tell
you that. I bet he ain't never disobeyed his daddy without paying the
consequences.
BONO. I ain't never had a chance. My daddy came on through ... but I ain't
never knew him to see him ... or what he had on his mind or where
he went. Just moving on through. Searching out the New Land. That's
what the old folks used to call it. See a fellow moving around from
place to place ... woman to woman ... called it searching out the
New Land. I can't say if he ever found it. I come along, didn't want no
kids. Didn't know if I was gonna be in one place long enough to fix

on them right as their daddy. I figured I was going searching too. As it turned out I been hooked up with Lucille near about as long as your daddy been with Rose. Going on sixteen years.

TROY. Sometimes I wish I hadn't known my daddy. He ain't cared nothing about no kids. A kid to him wasn't nothing. All he wanted was for you to learn how to walk so he could start you to working. When it come time for eating . . . he ate first. If there was anything left over, that's what you got. Man would sit down and eat two chickens and give you the wing.

LYONS. You ought to stop that, Pop. Everybody feed their kids. No matter how hard times is . . . everybody care about their kids. Make sure they have something to eat.

TROY. The only thing my daddy cared about was getting them bales of cotton in to Mr. Lubin. That's the only thing that mattered to him. Sometimes I used to wonder why he was living. Wonder why the devil hadn't come and got him. "Get them bales of cotton in to Mr. Lubin" and find out he owe him money . . .

LYONS. He should have just went on and left when he saw he couldn't get nowhere. That's what I would have done.

TROY. How he gonna leave with eleven kids? And where he gonna go? He ain't knew how to do nothing but farm. No, he was trapped and I think he knew it. But I'll say this for him . . . he felt a responsibility toward us. Maybe he ain't treated us the way I felt he should have . . . but without that responsibility he could have walked off and left us . . . made his own way.

BONO. A lot of them did. Back in those days what you talking about . . . they walk out their front door and just take on down one road or another and keep on walking.

LYONS. There you go! That's what I'm talking about.

BONO. Just keep on walking till you come to something else. Ain't you never heard of nobody having the walking blues? Well, that's what you call it when you just take off like that.

TROY. My daddy ain't had them walking blues! What you talking about? He stayed right there with his family. But he was just as evil as he could be. My mama couldn't stand him. Couldn't stand that evilness. She run off when I was about eight. She sneaked off one night after he had gone to sleep. Told me she was coming back for me. I ain't never seen her no more. All his women run off and left him. He wasn't good for nobody.

When my turn come to head out, I was fourteen and got to sniffing around Joe Canewell's daughter. Had us an old mule we called Greyboy. My daddy sent me out to do some plowing and I tied up Greyboy and went to fooling around with Joe Canewell's daughter. We done found us a nice little spot, got real cozy with each other. She about thirteen and we done figured we was grown anyway . . . so we down there enjoying ourselves . . . ain't thinking about nothing. We didn't know Greyboy had got loose and wandered back to the house and my daddy was looking for me. We down there by the creek enjoying ourselves when my daddy come up on us. Surprised us. He had them leather straps off the mule and commenced to whupping me like there was no tomorrow. I jumped up, mad and embarrassed. I was scared of my daddy. When he commenced to whupping on me . . . quite naturally I run to get out of the way. (*Pause.*) Now I thought he was mad 'cause I ain't done my work. But I see where he was chasing me off so he could have the gal for himself. When I see what the matter of it was, I lost all fear of my daddy. Right there is where I become a man . . . at fourteen years of age. (*Pause.*) Now it was my turn to run him off. I picked up them same reins that he had used on me. I picked up them reins and commenced to whupping on him. The gal jumped up and run off . . . and when my daddy turned to face me, I could see why the devil had never come to get him . . . 'cause he was the devil himself. I don't know what happened. When I woke up, I was laying right there by the creek, and Blue . . . this old dog we had . . . was licking my face. I thought I was blind. I couldn't see nothing. Both my eyes were swollen shut. I laid there and cried. I didn't know what I was gonna do. The only thing I knew was the time had come for me to leave my daddy's house. And right there the world suddenly got big. And it was a long time before I could cut it down to where I could handle it.

Part of that cutting down was when I got to the place where I could feel him kicking in my blood and knew that the only thing that separated us was the matter of a few years.

GABRIEL *enters from the house with a sandwich.*

LYONS.  What you got there, Uncle Gabe?

GABRIEL.  Got me a ham sandwich. Rose gave me a ham sandwich.

TROY.  I don't know what happened to him. I done lost touch with everybody except Gabriel. But I hope he's dead. I hope he found some peace.

LYONS.  That's a heavy story, Pop. I didn't know you left home when you was fourteen.

TROY.  And didn't know nothing. The only part of the world I knew was the forty-two acres of Mr. Lubin's land. That's all I knew about life.

LYONS.  Fourteen's kinda young to be out on your own. (*Phone rings.*) I don't even think I was ready to be out on my own at fourteen. I don't know what I would have done.

TROY.  I got up from the creek and walked on down to Mobile. I was through with farming. Figured I could do better in the city. So I walked the two hundred miles to Mobile.

LYONS.  Wait a minute . . . you ain't walked no two hundred miles, Pop. Ain't nobody gonna walk no two hundred miles. You talking about some walking there.

BONO.  That's the only way you got anywhere back in them days.

LYONS.  Shhh. Damn if I wouldn't have hitched a ride with somebody!

TROY.  Who you gonna hitch it with? They ain't had no cars and things like they got now. We talking about 1918.

ROSE (*entering*).  What you all out here getting into?

TROY (*to* ROSE).  I'm telling Lyons how good he got it. He don't know nothing about this I'm talking.

ROSE.  Lyons, that was Bonnie on the phone. She say you supposed to pick her up.

LYONS.  Yeah, okay, Rose.

TROY.  I walked on down to Mobile and hitched up with some of them fellows that was heading this way. Got up here and found out . . . not only couldn't you get a job . . . you couldn't find no place to live. I thought I was in freedom. Shhh. Colored folks living down there on the riverbanks in whatever kind of shelter they could find for themselves. Right down there under the Brady Street Bridge. Living in shacks made of sticks and tarpaper. Messed around there and went from bad to worse. Started stealing. First it was food. Then I figured, hell, if I steal money I can buy me some food. Buy me some shoes too! One thing led to another. Met your mama. I was young and anxious to be a man. Met your mama and had you. What I do that for? Now I got to worry about feeding you and her. Got to steal three times as much. Went out one day looking for somebody to rob . . . that's what I was, a robber. I'll tell you the truth. I'm ashamed of it today. But it's the truth. Went to rob this fellow . . . pulled out my knife . . . and he pulled out a gun. Shot me in the chest. I felt just like somebody had taken a hot branding iron and laid it on me. When he shot me I jumped at him with my knife. They told me I killed him and they put me in the penitentiary and locked me up for fifteen years. That's where I met Bono. That's where I learned how to play baseball. Got out that place and your mama had taken you and went on to make life without me. Fifteen years was a long time for her to wait. But that fifteen years cured me of that robbing stuff. Rose'll tell you. She asked me when I met her if I had gotten all that foolishness out of my system. And I told her, "Baby, it's you and baseball all what count with me." You hear me, Bono? I meant it too. She say, "Which one comes first?" I told her, "Baby, ain't no doubt it's baseball . . . but you stick and get old with me and we'll both outlive this baseball." Am I right, Rose? And it's true.

ROSE.  Man, hush your mouth. You ain't said no such thing. Talking about, "Baby you know you'll always be number one with me." That's what you was talking.

TROY.  You hear that, Bono. That's why I love her.

BONO.  Rose'll keep you straight. You get off the track, she'll straighten you up.

ROSE.  Lyons, you better get on up and get Bonnie. She waiting on you.

LYONS (*gets up to go*). Hey, Pop, why don't you come on down to the Grill and hear me play?

TROY. I ain't going down there. I'm too old to be sitting around in them clubs.

BONO. You got to be good to play down at the Grill.

LYONS. Come on, Pop . . .

TROY. I got to get up in the morning.

LYONS. You ain't got to stay long.

TROY. Naw, I'm gonna get my supper and go on to bed.

LYONS. Well, I got to go. I'll see you again.

TROY. Don't you come around my house on my payday.

ROSE. Pick up the phone and let somebody know you coming. And bring Bonnie with you. You know I'm always glad to see her.

LYONS. Yeah, I'll do that, Rose. You take care now. See you, Pop. See you, Mr. Bono. See you, Uncle Gabe.

GABRIEL. Lyons! King of the Jungle!

LYONS *exits.*

TROY. Is supper ready, woman? Me and you got some business to take care of. I'm gonna tear it up too.

ROSE. Troy, I done told you now!

TROY (*puts his arm around* BONO). Aw hell, woman . . . this is Bono. Bono like family. I done known this nigger since . . . how long I done know you?

BONO. It's been a long time.

TROY. I done know this nigger since Skippy was a pup. Me and him done been through some times.

BONO. You sure right about that.

TROY. Hell, I done know him longer than I known you. And we still standing shoulder to shoulder. Hey, look here, Bono . . . a man can't ask for no more than that. (*Drinks to him.*) I love you, nigger.

BONO. Hell, I love you too . . . I got to get home see my woman. You got yours in hand. I got to get mine.

BONO *starts to exit as* CORY *enters the yard, dressed in his football uniform. He gives* TROY *a hard, uncompromising look.*

CORY. What you do that for, Pop?

*He throws his helmet down in the direction of* TROY.

ROSE. What's the matter? Cory . . . what's the matter?

CORY. Papa done went up to the school and told Coach Zellman I can't play football no more. Wouldn't even let me play the game. Told him to tell the recruiter not to come.

ROSE. Troy . . .

TROY. What you Troying me for. Yeah, I did it. And the boy know why I did it.

CORY.  Why you wanna do that to me? That was the one chance I had.

ROSE.  Ain't nothing wrong with Cory playing football, Troy.

TROY.  The boy lied to me. I told the nigger if he wanna play football . . . to keep up his chores and hold down that job at the A&P. That was the conditions. Stopped down there to see Mr. Stawicki . . .

CORY.  I can't work after school during the football season, Pop! I tried to tell you that Mr. Stawicki's holding my job for me. You don't never want to listen to nobody. And then you wanna go and do this to me!

TROY.  I ain't done nothing to you. You done it to yourself.

CORY.  Just cause you didn't have a chance! You just scared I'm gonna be better than you, that's all.

TROY.  Come here.

ROSE.  Troy . . .

*CORY reluctantly crosses over to TROY.*

TROY.  All right! See. You done made a mistake.

CORY.  I didn't even do nothing!

TROY.  I'm gonna tell you what your mistake was. See . . . you swung at the ball and didn't hit it. That's strike one. See, you in the batter's box now. You swung and you missed. That's strike one. Don't you strike out!

*Lights fade to black.*

## Act 2

### Scene 1

*The following morning. CORY is at the tree hitting the ball with the bat. He tries to mimic TROY, but his swing is awkward, less sure. ROSE enters from the house.*

ROSE.  Cory, I want you to help me with this cupboard.

CORY.  I ain't quitting the team. I don't care what Poppa say.

ROSE.  I'll talk to him when he gets back. He had to go see about your Uncle Gabe. The police done arrested him. Say he was disturbing the peace. He'll be back directly. Come on in here and help me clean out the top of this cupboard.

*CORY exits into the house. ROSE sees TROY and BONO coming down the alley.*

Troy . . . what they say down there?

TROY.  Ain't said nothing. I give them fifty dollars and they let him go. I'll talk to you about it. Where's Cory?

ROSE.  He's in there helping me clean out these cupboards.

TROY.  Tell him to get his butt out here.

TROY *and* BONO *go over to the pile of wood.* BONO *picks up the saw and begins sawing.*

TROY (*to* BONO). All they want is the money. That makes six or seven times I done went down there and got him. See me coming they stick out their hands.

BONO. Yeah. I know what you mean. That's all they care about . . . that money. They don't care about what's right. (*Pause.*) Nigger, why you got to go and get some hard wood? You ain't doing nothing but building a little old fence. Get you some soft pine wood. That's all you need.

TROY. I know what I'm doing. This is outside wood. You put pine wood inside the house. Pine wood is inside wood. This here is outside wood. Now you tell me where the fence is gonna be?

BONO. You don't need this wood. You can put it up with pine wood and it'll stand as long as you gonna be here looking at it.

TROY. How you know how long I'm gonna be here, nigger? Hell, I might just live forever. Live longer than old man Horsely.

BONO. That's what Magee used to say.

TROY. Magee's a damn fool. Now you tell me who you ever heard of gonna pull their own teeth with a pair of rusty pliers.

BONO. The old folks . . . my granddaddy used to pull his teeth with pliers. They ain't had no dentists for the colored folks back then.

TROY. Get clean pliers! You understand? Clean pliers! Sterilize them! Besides we ain't living back then. All Magee had to do was walk over to Doc Goldblum's.

BONO. I see where you and that Tallahassee gal . . . that Alberta . . . I see where you all done got tight.

TROY. What you mean "got tight"?

BONO. I see where you be laughing and joking with her all the time.

TROY. I laughs and jokes with all of them, Bono. You know me.

BONO. That ain't the kind of laughing and joking I'm talking about.

CORY *enters from the house.*

CORY. How you doing, Mr. Bono?

TROY. Cory? Get that saw from Bono and cut some wood. He talking about the wood's too hard to cut. Stand back there, Jim, and let that young boy show you how it's done.

BONO. He's sure welcome to it.

CORY *takes the saw and begins to cut the wood.*

Whew-e-e! Look at that. Big old strong boy. Look like Joe Louis. Hell, must be getting old the way I'm watching that boy whip through that wood.

CORY. I don't see why Mama want a fence around the yard noways.

TROY. Damn if I know either. What the hell she keeping out with it? She ain't got nothing nobody want.

BONO.  Some people build fences to keep people out ... and other people build fences to keep people in. Rose wants to hold on to you all. She loves you.

TROY.  Hell, nigger, I don't need nobody to tell me my wife loves me. Cory ... go on in the house and see if you can find that other saw.

CORY.  Where's it at?

TROY.  I said find it! Look for it till you find it!

CORY *exits into the house.*

What's that supposed to mean? Wanna keep us in?

BONO.  Troy ... I done known you seem like damn near my whole life. You and Rose both. I done know both of you all for a long time. I remember when you met Rose. When you was hitting them baseball out the park. A lot of them old gals was after you then. You had the pick of the litter. When you picked Rose, I was happy for you. That was the first time I knew you had any sense. I said ... My man Troy knows what he's doing ... I'm gonna follow this nigger ... he might take me somewhere. I been following you too. I done learned a whole heap of things about life watching you. I done learned how to tell where the shit lies. How to tell it from the alfalfa. You done learned me a lot of things. You showed me how to not make the same mistakes ... to take life as it comes along and keep putting one foot in front of the other. (*Pause.*) Rose a good woman, Troy.

TROY.  Hell, nigger, I know she a good woman. I been married to her for eighteen years. What you got on your mind, Bono?

BONO.  I just say she a good woman. Just like I say anything. I ain't got to have nothing on my mind.

TROY.  You just gonna say she a good woman and leave it hanging out there like that? Why you telling me she a good woman?

BONO.  She loves you, Troy. Rose loves you.

TROY.  You saying I don't measure up. That's what you trying to say. I don't measure up cause I'm seeing this other gal. I know what you trying to say.

BONO.  I know what Rose means to you, Troy. I'm just trying to say I don't want to see you mess up.

TROY.  Yeah, I appreciate that, Bono. If you was messing around on Lucille I'd be telling you the same thing.

BONO.  Well, that's all I got to say. I just say that because I love you both.

TROY.  Hell, you know me ... I wasn't out there looking for nothing. You can't find a better woman than Rose. I know that. But seems like this woman just stuck onto me where I can't shake her loose. I done wrestled with it, tried to throw her off me ... but she just stuck on tighter. Now she's stuck on for good.

BONO.  You's in control ... that's what you tell me all the time. You responsible for what you do.

TROY.  I ain't ducking the responsibility of it. As long as it sets right in my
heart . . . then I'm okay. Cause that's all I listen to. It'll tell me right from
wrong every time. And I ain't talking about doing Rose no bad turn. I
love Rose. She done carried me a long ways and I love and respect her
for that.

BONO.  I know you do. That's why I don't want to see you hurt her. But what
you gonna do when she find out? What you got then? If you try and
jugle both of them . . . sooner or later you gonna drop one of them.
That's common sense.

TROY.  Yeah, I hear what you saying, Bono. I been trying to figure a way to
work it out.

BONO.  Work it out right, Troy. I don't want to be getting all up between you
and Rose's business . . . but work it so it come out right.

TROY.  Ah hell, I get all up between you and Lucille's business. When you
gonna get that woman that refrigerator she been wanting? Don't tell
me you ain't got no money now. I know who your banker is. Mellon
don't need that money bad as Lucille want that refrigerator. I'll tell
you that.

BONO.  Tell you what I'll do . . . when you finish building this fence for
Rose . . . I'll buy Lucille that refrigerator.

TROY.  You done stuck your foot in your mouth now!

TROY *grabs up a board and begins to saw.* BONO *starts to walk out the
yard.*

Hey, nigger . . . where you going?

BONO.  I'm going home. I know you don't expect me to help you now.
I'm protecting my money. I wanna see you put that fence up by yourself. That's what I want to see. You'll be here another six months without me.

TROY.  Nigger, you ain't right.

BONO.  When it comes to my money . . . I'm right as fireworks on the Fourth
of July.

TROY.  All right, we gonna see now. You better get out your bankbook.

BONO *exits, and* TROY *continues to work.* ROSE *enters from the house.*

ROSE.  What they say down there? What's happening with Gabe?

TROY.  I went down there and got him out. Cost me fifty dollars. Say he was
disturbing the peace. Judge set up a hearing for him in three weeks.
Say to show cause why he shouldn't be recommitted.

ROSE.  What was he doing that cause them to arrest him?

TROY.  Some kids was teasing him and he run them off home. Say he was
howling and carrying on. Some folks seen him and called the police.
That's all it was.

ROSE.  Well, what's you say? What'd you tell the judge?

TROY.  Told him I'd look after him. It didn't make no sense to recommit the man. He stuck out his big greasy palm and told me to give him fifty dollars and take him on home.

ROSE.  Where's he at now? Where'd he go off to?

TROY.  He's gone about his business. He don't need nobody to hold his hand.

ROSE.  Well, I don't know. Seem like that would be the best place for him if they did put him into the hospital. I know what you're gonna say. But that's what I think would be best.

TROY.  The man done had his life ruined fighting for what? And they wanna take and lock him up. Let him be free. He don't bother nobody.

ROSE.  Well, everybody got their own way of looking at it I guess. Come on and get your lunch. I got a bowl of lima beans and some cornbread in the oven. Come and get something to eat. Ain't no sense you fretting over Gabe.

ROSE *turns to go into the house.*

TROY.  Rose . . . got something to tell you.

ROSE.  Well, come on . . . wait till I get this food on the table.

TROY.  Rose!

*She stops and turns around.*

I don't know how to say this. (*Pause.*) I can't explain it none. It just sort of grows on you till it gets out of hand. It starts out like a little bush . . . and the next thing you know it's a whole forest.

ROSE.  Troy . . . what is you talking about?

TROY.  I'm talking, woman, let me talk. I'm trying to find a way to tell you . . . I'm gonna be a daddy. I'm gonna be somebody's daddy.

ROSE.  Troy . . . you're not telling me this? You're gonna be . . . what?

TROY.  Rose . . . now . . . see . . .

ROSE.  You telling me you gonna be somebody's daddy? You telling your *wife* this?

GABRIEL *enters from the street. He carries a rose in his hand.*

GABRIEL.  Hey, Troy! Hey, Rose!

ROSE.  I have to wait eighteen years to hear something like this.

GABRIEL.  Hey, Rose . . . I got a flower for you. (*He hands it to her.*) That's a rose. Same rose like you is.

ROSE.  Thanks, Gabe.

GABRIEL.  Troy, you ain't mad at me is you? Them bad mens come and put me away. You ain't mad at me is you?

TROY.  Naw, Gabe, I ain't mad at you.

ROSE.  Eighteen years and you wanna come with this.

GABRIEL (*takes a quarter out of his pocket*). See what I got? Got a brand new quarter.

TROY.  Rose … it's just …

ROSE.  Ain't nothing you can say, Troy. Ain't no way of explaining that.

GABRIEL.  Fellow that give me this quarter had a whole mess of them. I'm gonna keep this quarter till it stop shining.

ROSE.  Gabe, go on in the house there. I got some watermelon in the Frigidaire. Go on and get you a piece.

GABRIEL.  Say, Rose … you know I was chasing hellhounds and them bad mens come and get me and take me away. Troy helped me. He come down there and told them they better let me go before he beat them up. Yeah, he did!

ROSE.  You go on and get you a piece of watermelon, Gabe. Them bad mens is gone now.

GABRIEL.  Okay, Rose … gonna get me some watermelon. The kind with the stripes on it.

GABRIEL *exits into the house.*

ROSE.  Why, Troy? Why? After all these years to come dragging this in to me now. It don't make no sense at your age. I could have expected this ten or fifteen years ago, but not now.

TROY.  Age ain't got nothing to do with it, Rose.

ROSE.  I done tried to be everything a wife should be. Everything a wife could be. Been married eighteen years and I got to live to see the day you tell me you been seeing another woman and done fathered a child by her. And you know I ain't never wanted no half nothing in my family. My whole family is half. Everybody got different fathers and mothers … my two sisters and my brother. Can't hardly tell who's who. Can't never sit down and talk about Papa and Mama. It's your papa and your mama and my papa and my mama …

TROY.  Rose … stop it now.

ROSE.  I ain't never wanted that for none of my children. And now you wanna drag your behind in here and tell me something like this.

TROY.  You ought to know. It's time for you to know.

ROSE.  Well, I don't want to know, goddamn it!

TROY.  I can't just make it go away. It's done now. I can't wish the circumstance of the thing away.

ROSE.  And you don't want to either. Maybe you want to wish me and my boy away. Maybe that's what you want? Well, you can't wish us away. I've got eighteen years of my life invested in you. You ought to have stayed upstairs in my bed where you belong.

TROY.  Rose … now listen to me … we can get a handle on this thing. We can talk this out … come to an understanding.

ROSE.  All of a sudden it's "we." Where was "we" at when you was down there rolling around with some godforsaken woman? "We" should have come to an understanding before you started making a damn fool of yourself. You're a day late and a dollar short when it comes to an understanding with me.

TROY.  It's just . . . She gives me a different idea . . . a different understanding about myself. I can step out of this house and get away from the pressures and problems . . . be a different man. I ain't got to wonder how I'm gonna pay the bills or get the roof fixed. I can just be a part of myself that I ain't never been.

ROSE.  What I want to know . . . is do you plan to continue seeing her. That's all you can say to me.

TROY.  I can sit up in her house and laugh. Do you understand what I'm saying. I can laugh out loud . . . and it feels good. It reaches all the way down to the bottom of my shoes. (*Pause.*) Rose, I can't give that up.

ROSE.  Maybe you ought to go on and stay down there with her . . . if she's a better woman than me.

TROY.  It ain't about nobody being a better woman or nothing. Rose, you ain't the blame. A man couldn't ask for no woman to be a better wife than you've been. I'm responsible for it. I done locked myself into a pattern trying to take care of you all that I forgot about myself.

ROSE.  What the hell was I there for? That was my job, not somebody else's.

TROY.  Rose, I done tried all my life to live decent . . . to live a clean . . . hard . . . useful life. I tried to be a good husband to you. In every way I knew how. Maybe I come into the world backwards, I don't know. But . . . you born with two strikes on you before you come to the plate. You got to guard it closely . . . always looking for the curve ball on the inside corner. You can't afford to let none get past you. You can't afford a call strike. If you going down . . . you going down swinging. Everything lined up against you. What you gonna do. I fooled them, Rose. I bunted. When I found you and Cory and a halfway decent job . . . I was safe. Couldn't nothing touch me. I wasn't gonna strike out no more. I wasn't going back to the penitentiary. I wasn't gonna lay in the streets with a bottle of wine. I was safe. I had me a family. A job. I wasn't gonna get that last strike. I was on first looking for one of them boys to knock me in. To get me home.

ROSE.  You should have stayed in my bed, Troy.

TROY.  Then when I saw that gal . . . she firmed up my backbone. And I got to thinking that if I tried . . . I just might be able to steal second. Do you understand after eighteen years I wanted to steal second.

ROSE.  You should have held me tight. You should have grabbed me and held on.

TROY.  I stood on first base for eighteen years and I thought . . . well, goddamn it . . . go on for it!

ROSE.  We're not talking about baseball! We're talking about you going off to lay in bed with another woman . . . and then bring it home to me. That's what we're talking about. We ain't talking about no baseball.

TROY.  Rose, you're not listening to me. I'm trying the best I can to explain it to you. It's not easy for me to admit that I been standing in the same place for eighteen years.

ROSE.  I been standing with you! I been right here with you, Troy. I got a
life too. I gave eighteen years of my life to stand in the same spot
with you. Don't you think I ever wanted other things? Don't you
think I had dreams and hopes? What about my life? What about me.
Don't you think it ever crossed my mind to want to know other
men? That I wanted to lay up somewhere and forget about my responsibilities? That I wanted someone to make me laugh so I could
feel good? You not the only one who's got wants and needs. But I
held on to you, Troy. I took all my feelings, my wants and needs, my
dreams . . . and I buried them inside you. I planted a seed and
watched and prayed over it. I planted myself inside you and waited
to bloom. And it didn't take me no eighteen years to find out the soil
was hard and rocky and it wasn't never gonna bloom.

    But I held on to you, Troy. I held you tighter. You was my husband.
I owed you everything I had. Every part of me I could find to
give you. And upstairs in that room . . . with the darkness falling in on
me . . . I gave everything I had to try and erase the doubt that you
wasn't the finest man in the world. And wherever you was going . . . I
wanted to be there with you. 'Cause you was my husband. 'Cause
that's the only way I was gonna survive as your wife. You always talking about what you give . . . and what you don't have to give. But you
take too. You take . . . and don't even know nobody's giving!

    ROSE *turns to exit into the house;* TROY *grabs her arm.*

TROY.  You say I take and don't give!

ROSE.  Troy! You're hurting me!

TROY.  You say I take and don't give!

ROSE.  Troy . . . you're hurting my arm! Let go!

TROY.  I done give you everything I got. Don't you tell that lie on me.

ROSE.  Troy!

TROY.  Don't you tell that lie on me!

    CORY *enters from the house.*

CORY.  Mama!

ROSE.  Troy. You're hurting me.

TROY.  Don't you tell me about no taking and giving.

    CORY *comes up behind* TROY *and grabs him.* TROY, *surprised, is*
    *thrown off balance just as* CORY *throws a glancing blow that*
    *catches him on the chest and knocks him down.* TROY *is stunned, as*
    *is* CORY.

ROSE.  Troy. Troy. No!

    TROY *gets to his feet and starts at* CORY.

    Troy . . . no. Please! Troy!

ROSE *pulls on* TROY *to hold him back.* TROY *stops himself.*

TROY (*to* CORY). All right. That's strike two. You stay away from around me, boy. Don't you strike out. You living with a full count. Don't you strike out.

TROY *exits out the yard as the lights go down.*

### Scene 2

*It is six months later, early afternoon.* TROY *enters from the house and starts to exit the yard.* ROSE *enters from the house.*

ROSE. Troy, I want to talk to you.

TROY. All of a sudden, after all this time, you want to talk to me, huh? You ain't wanted to talk to me for months. You ain't wanted to talk to me last night. You ain't wanted no part of me then. What you wanna talk to me about now?

ROSE. Tomorrow's Friday.

TROY. I know what day tomorrow is. You think I don't know tomorrow's Friday? My whole life I ain't done nothing but look to see Friday coming and you got to tell me it's Friday.

ROSE. I want to know if you're coming home.

TROY. I always come home, Rose. You know that. There ain't never been a night I ain't come home.

ROSE. That ain't what I mean . . . and you know it. I want to know if you're coming straight home after work.

TROY. I figure I'd cash my check . . . hang out at Taylors' with the boys . . . maybe play a game of checkers . . .

ROSE. Troy, I can't live like this. I won't live like this. You livin' on borrowed time with me. It's been going on six months now you ain't been coming home.

TROY. I be here every night. Every night of the year. That's 365 days.

ROSE. I want you to come home tomorrow after work.

TROY. Rose . . . I don't mess up my pay. You know that now. I take my pay and I give it to you. I don't have no money but what you give me back. I just want to have a little time to myself . . . a little time to enjoy life.

ROSE. What about me? When's my time to enjoy life?

TROY. I don't know what to tell you, Rose. I'm doing the best I can.

ROSE. You ain't been home from work but time enough to change your clothes and run out . . . and you wanna call that the best you can do?

TROY. I'm going over to the hospital to see Alberta. She went into the hospital this afternoon. Look like she might have the baby early. I won't be gone long.

ROSE. Well, you ought to know. They went over to Miss Pearl's and got Gabe today. She said you told them to go ahead and lock him up.

TROY. I ain't said no such thing. Whoever told you that is telling a lie. Pearl ain't doing nothing but telling a big fat lie.

ROSE.  She ain't had to tell me. I read it on the papers.
TROY.  I ain't told them nothing of the kind.
ROSE.  I saw it right there on the papers.
TROY.  What it say, huh?
ROSE.  It said you told them to take him.
TROY.  Then they screwed that up, just the way they screw up everything. I ain't worried about what they got on the paper.
ROSE.  Say the government send part of his check to the hospital and the other part to you.
TROY.  I ain't got nothing to do with that if that's the way it works. I ain't made up the rules about how it work.
ROSE.  You did Gabe just like you did Cory. You wouldn't sign the paper for Cory . . . but you signed for Gabe. You signed that paper.

*The telephone is heard ringing inside the house.*

TROY.  I told you I ain't signed nothing, woman! The only thing I signed was the release form. Hell, I can't read, I don't know what they had on that paper! I ain't signed nothing about sending Gabe away.
ROSE.  I said send him to the hospital . . . you said let him be free . . . now you done went down there and signed him to the hospital for half his money. You went back on yourself, Troy. You gonna have to answer for that.
TROY.  See now . . . you been over there talking to Miss Pearl. She done got mad 'cause she ain't getting Gabe's rent money. That's all it is. She's liable to say anything.
ROSE.  Troy, I seen where you signed the paper.
TROY.  You ain't seen nothing I signed. What she doing got papers on my brother anyway? Miss Pearl telling a big fat lie. And I'm gonna tell her about it too! You ain't seen nothing I signed. Say . . . you ain't seen nothing I signed.

ROSE *exits into the house to answer the telephone. Presently she returns.*

ROSE.  Troy . . . that was the hospital. Alberta had the baby.
TROY.  What she have? What is it?
ROSE.  It's a girl.
TROY.  I better get on down to the hospital to see her.
ROSE.  Troy . . .
TROY.  Rose . . . I got to go see her now. That's only right . . . what's the matter . . . the baby's all right, ain't it?
ROSE.  Alberta died having the baby.
TROY.  Died . . . you say she's dead? Alberta's dead?
ROSE.  They said they done all they could. They couldn't do nothing for her.
TROY.  The baby? How's the baby?

ROSE.   They say it's healthy. I wonder who's gonna bury her.

TROY.   She had family, Rose. She wasn't living in the world by herself.

ROSE.   I know she wasn't living in the world by herself.

TROY.   Next thing you gonna want to know if she had any insurance.

ROSE.   Troy, you ain't got to talk like that.

TROY.   That's the first thing that jumped out your mouth. "Who's gonna bury her?" Like I'm fixing to take on that task for myself.

ROSE.   I am your wife. Don't push me away.

TROY.   I ain't pushing nobody away. Just give me some space. That's all. Just give me some room to breathe.

> ROSE *exits into the house.* TROY *walks about the yard.*

TROY   (*with a quiet rage that threatens to consume him*). All right . . . Mr. Death. See now . . . I'm gonna tell you what I'm gonna do. I'm gonna take and build me a fence around this yard. See? I'm gonna build me a fence around what belongs to me. And then I want you to stay on the other side. See? You stay over there until you're ready for me. Then you come on. Bring your army. Bring your sickle. Bring your wrestling clothes. I ain't gonna fall down on my vigilance this time. You ain't gonna sneak up on me no more. When you ready for me . . . when the top of your list say Troy Maxson . . . that's when you come around here. You come up and knock on the front door. Ain't nobody else got nothing to do with this. This is between you and me. Man to man. You stay on the other side of that fence until you ready for me. Then you come up and knock on the front door. Anytime you want. I'll be ready for you.

> *The lights go down to black.*

*Scene 3*

*The lights come up on the porch. It is late evening three days later.* ROSE *sits listening to the ball game waiting for* TROY. *The final out of the game is made and* ROSE *switches off the radio.* TROY *enters the yard carrying an infant wrapped in blankets. He stands back from the house and calls.*

> ROSE *enters and stands on the porch. There is a long, awkward silence, the weight of which grows heavier with each passing second.*

TROY.   Rose . . . I'm standing here with my daughter in my arms. She ain't but a wee bittie little old thing. She don't know nothing about grownups' business. She innocent . . . and she ain't got no mama.

ROSE.   What you telling me for, Troy?

> *She turns and exits into the house.*

TROY.   Well . . . I guess we'll just sit out here on the porch.

*He sits down on the porch. There is an awkward indelicateness about the way he handles the baby. His largeness engulfs and seems to swallow it. He speaks loud enough for* ROSE *to hear.*

A man's got to do what's right for him. I ain't sorry for nothing I done. It felt right in my heart. (*To the baby.*) What you smiling at? Your daddy's a big man. Got these great big old hands. But sometimes he's scared. And right now your daddy's scared cause we sitting out here and ain't got no home. Oh, I been homeless before. I ain't had no little baby with me. But I been homeless. You just be out on the road by your lonesome and you see one of them trains coming and you just kinda go like this . . .

*He sings as a lullaby.*

> Please, Mr. Engineer let a man ride the line
> Please, Mr. Engineer let a man ride the line
> I ain't got no ticket please let me ride the blinds

ROSE *enters from the house.* TROY, *hearing her steps behind him, stands and faces her.*

She's my daughter, Rose. My own flesh and blood. I can't deny her no more than I can deny them boys. (*Pause.*) You and them boys is my family. You and them and this child is all I got in the world. So I guess what I'm saying is . . . I'd appreciate it if you'd help me take care of her.

ROSE. Okay, Troy . . . you're right. I'll take care of your baby for you . . . 'cause . . . like you say . . . she's innocent . . . and you can't visit the sins of the father upon the child. A motherless child has got a hard time. (*She takes the baby from him.*) From right now . . . this child got a mother. But you a womanless man.

ROSE *turns and exits into the house with the baby. Lights go down to black.*

## Scene 4

*It is two months later.* LYONS *enters the street. He knocks on the door and calls.*

LYONS. Hey, Rose! (*Pause.*) Rose!

ROSE (*from inside the house*). Stop that yelling. You gonna wake up Raynell. I just got her to sleep.

LYONS. I just stopped by to pay Papa this twenty dollars I owe him. Where's Papa at?

ROSE. He should be here in a minute. I'm getting ready to go down to the church. Sit down and wait on him.

LYONS. I got to go pick up Bonnie over her mother's house.

ROSE. Well, sit it down there on the table. He'll get it.

LYONS (*enters the house and sets the money on the table*). Tell Papa I said thanks. I'll see you again.

ROSE. All right, Lyons. We'll see you.

LYONS *starts to exit as* CORY *enters.*

CORY. Hey, Lyons.

LYONS. What's happening, Cory? Say man, I'm sorry I missed your graduation. You know I had a gig and couldn't get away. Otherwise, I would have been there, man. So what you doing?

CORY. I'm trying to find a job.

LYONS. Yeah I know how that go, man. It's rough out here. Jobs are scarce.

CORY. Yeah, I know.

LYONS. Look here, I got to run. Talk to Papa . . . he know some people. He'll be able to help get you a job. Talk to him . . . see what he say.

CORY. Yeah . . . all right, Lyons.

LYONS. You take care. I'll talk to you soon. We'll find some time to talk.

LYONS *exits the yard.* CORY *wanders over to the tree, picks up the bat, and assumes a batting stance. He studies an imaginary pitcher and swings. Dissatisfied with the result, he tries again.* TROY *enters. They eye each other for a beat.* CORY *puts the bat down and exits the yard.* TROY *starts into the house as* ROSE *exits with* RAYNELL. *She is carrying a cake.*

TROY. I'm coming in and everybody's going out.

ROSE. I'm taking this cake down to the church for the bake sale. Lyons was by to see you. He stopped by to pay you your twenty dollars. It's laying in there on the table.

TROY (*going into his pocket*). Well . . . here go this money.

ROSE. Put it in there on the table, Troy. I'll get it.

TROY. What time you coming back?

ROSE. Ain't no use in you studying me. It don't matter what time I come back.

TROY. I just asked you a question, woman. What's the matter . . . can't I ask you a question?

ROSE. Troy, I don't want to go into it. Your dinner's in there on the stove. All you got to do is heat it up. And don't you be eating the rest of them cakes in there. I'm coming back for them. We having a bake sale at the church tomorrow.

ROSE *exits the yard.* TROY *sits down on the steps, takes a pint bottle from his pocket, opens it, and drinks. He begins to sing.*

TROY.
Hear it ring! Hear it ring!
Had an old dog his name was Blue

You know Blue was mighty true
You know Blue as a good old dog
Blue trees a possum in a hollow log
You know from that he was a good old dog

BONO *enters the yard.*

BONO. Hey, Troy.

TROY. Hey, what's happening, Bono?

BONO. I just thought I'd stop by to see you.

TROY. What you stop by and see me for? You ain't stopped by in a month of Sundays. Hell, I must owe you money or something.

BONO. Since you got your promotion I can't keep up with you. Used to see you every day. Now I don't even know what route you working.

TROY. They keep switching me around. Got me out in Greentree now . . . hauling white folks' garbage.

BONO. Greentree, huh? You lucky, at least you ain't got to be lifting them barrels. Damn if they ain't getting heavier. I'm gonna put in my two years and call it quits.

TROY. I'm thinking about retiring myself.

BONO. You got it easy. You can drive for another five years.

TROY. It ain't the same, Bono. It ain't like working the back of the truck. Ain't got nobody to talk to . . . feel like you working by yourself. Naw, I'm thinking about retiring. How's Lucille?

BONO. She all right. Her arthritis get to acting up on her sometime. Saw Rose on my way in. She going down to the church, huh?

TROY. Yeah, she took up going down there. All them preachers looking for somebody to fatten their pockets. (*Pause.*) Got some gin here.

BONO. Naw, thanks. I just stopped by to say hello.

TROY. Hell, nigger . . . you can take a drink. I ain't never known you to say no to a drink. You ain't got to work tomorrow.

BONO. I just stopped by. I'm fixing to go over to Skinner's. We got us a domino game going over his house every Friday.

TROY. Nigger, you can't play no dominoes. I used to whup you four games out of five.

BONO. Well, that learned me. I'm getting better.

TROY. Yeah? Well, that's all right.

BONO. Look here . . . I got to be getting on. Stop by sometime, huh?

TROY. Yeah, I'll do that, Bono. Lucille told Rose you bought her a new refrigerator.

BONO. Yeah, Rose told Lucille you had finally built your fence . . . so I figured we'd call it even.

TROY. I knew you would.

BONO. Yeah . . . okay. I'll be talking to you.

TROY. Yeah, take care, Bono. Good to see you. I'm gonna stop over.

BONO. Yeah. Okay, Troy.

BONO *exits.* TROY *drinks from the bottle.*

TROY.

> Old Blue died and I dug his grave
> Let him down with a golden chain
> Every night when I hear old Blue bark
> I know Blue treed a possum in Noah's Ark.
> Hear it ring! Hear it ring!

CORY *enters the yard. They eye each other for a beat.* TROY *is sitting in the middle of the steps.* CORY *walks over.*

CORY. I got to get by.

TROY. Say what? What's you say?

CORY. You in my way. I got to get by.

TROY. You got to get by where? This is my house. Bought and paid for. In full. Took me fifteen years. And if you wanna go in my house and I'm sitting on the steps ... you say excuse me. Like your mama taught you.

CORY. Come on, Pop ... I got to get by.

CORY *starts to maneuver his way past* TROY. TROY *grabs his leg and shoves him back.*

TROY. You just gonna walk over top of me?

CORY. I live here too!

TROY *(advancing toward him).* You just gonna walk over top of me in my own house?

CORY. I ain't scared of you.

TROY. I ain't asked if you was scared of me. I asked you if you was fixing to walk over top of me in my own house? That's the question. You ain't gonna say excuse me? You just gonna walk over top of me?

CORY. If you wanna put it like that.

TROY. How else am I gonna put it?

CORY. I was walking by you to go into the house cause you sitting on the steps drunk, singing to yourself. You can put it like that.

TROY. Without saying excuse me???

CORY *doesn't respond.*

I asked you a question. Without saying excuse me???

CORY. I ain't got to say excuse me to you. You don't count around here no more.

TROY. Oh, I see ... I don't count around here no more. You ain't got to say excuse me to your daddy. All of a sudden you done got so grown that your daddy don't count around here no more ... Around here in his own house and yard that he done paid for with the sweat of his brow. You done got so grown to where you gonna take over. You gonna take

over my house. Is that right? You gonna wear my pants. You gonna go
in there and stretch out on my bed. You ain't got to say excuse me
cause I don't count around here no more. Is that right?

CORY.  That's right. You always talking this dumb stuff. Now, why don't you
just get out my way?

TROY.  I guess you got someplace to sleep and something to put in your belly.
You got that, huh? You got that? That's what you need. You got that, huh?

CORY.  You don't know what I got. You ain't got to worry about what I got.

TROY.  You right! You one hundred percent right! I done spent the last seventeen years worrying about what you got. Now it's your turn, see? I'll
tell you what to do. You grown . . . we done established that. You a man.
Now, let's see you act like one. Turn your behind around and walk out
this yard. And when you get out there in the alley . . . you can forget
about this house. See? 'Cause this is my house. You go on and be a man
and get your own house. You can forget about this. 'Cause this is mine.
You go on and get yours 'cause I'm through with doing for you.

CORY.  You talking about what you did for me . . . what'd you ever give me?

TROY.  Them feet and bones! That pumping heart, nigger! I give you more
than anybody else is ever gonna give you.

CORY.  You ain't never gave me nothing! You ain't never done nothing but
hold me back. Afraid I was gonna be better than you. All you ever did
was try and make me scared of you. I used to tremble every time you
called my name. Every time I heard your footsteps in the house. Won
dering all the time . . . what's Papa gonna say if I do this? . . . What's he
gonna say if I do that? . . . What's Papa gonna say if I turn on the radio?
And Mama, too . . . she tries . . . but she's scared of you.

TROY.  You leave your mama out of this. She ain't got nothing to do with
this.

CORY.  I don't know how she stand you . . . after what you did to her.

TROY.  I told you to leave your mama out of this!

*He advances toward* CORY.

CORY.  What you gonna do . . . give me a whupping? You can't whup me no
more. You're too old. You just an old man.

TROY (*shoves him on his shoulder*).  Nigger! That's what you are. You just
another nigger on the street to me!

CORY.  You crazy! You know that?

TROY.  Go on now! You got the devil in you. Get on away from me!

CORY.  You just a crazy old man . . . talking about I got the devil in me.

TROY.  Yeah, I'm crazy! If you don't get on the other side of that yard . . . I'm
gonna show you how crazy I am! Go on . . . get the hell out of my yard.

CORY.  It ain't your yard. You took Uncle Gabe's money he got from the
army to buy this house and then you put him out.

TROY (*advances on* CORY).  Get your black ass out of my yard!

TROY's *advance backs* CORY *up against the tree.* CORY *grabs up the bat.*

CORY.  I ain't going nowhere! Come on . . . put me out! I ain't scared of you.
TROY.  That's my bat!
CORY.  Come on!
TROY.  Put my bat down!
CORY.  Come on, put me out.

CORY *swings at* TROY, *who backs across the yard.*

What's the matter? You so bad . . . put me out!

TROY *advances toward* CORY.

CORY (*backing up*).  Come on! Come on!
TROY.  You're gonna have to use it! You wanna draw that bat back on me . . .
you're gonna have to use it.
CORY.  Come on! . . . Come on!

CORY *swings the bat at* TROY *a second time. He misses.* TROY *continues to advance toward him.*

TROY.  You're gonna have to kill me! You wanna draw that bat back on me.
You're gonna have to kill me.

CORY, *backed up against the tree, can go no farther.* TROY *taunts him.
He sticks out his head and offers him a target.*

Come on! Come on!

CORY *is unable to swing the bat.* TROY *grabs it.*

TROY.  Then I'll show you.

CORY *and* TROY *struggle over the bat. The struggle is fierce and fully
engaged.* TROY *ultimately is the stronger and takes the bat from* CORY
*and stands over him ready to swing. He stops himself.*

Go on and get away from around my house.

CORY, *stung by his defeat, picks himself up, walks slowly out of the
yard and up the alley.*

CORY.  Tell Mama I'll be back for my things.
TROY.  They'll be on the other side of that fence.

CORY *exits.*

TROY.  I can't taste nothing. Helluljah! I can't taste nothing no more. (TROY *assumes a batting posture and begins to taunt Death, the fastball on
the outside corner.*) Come on! It's between you and me now! Come
on! Anytime you want! Come on! I be ready for you . . . but I ain't gonna
be easy.

*The lights go down on the scene.*

## Scene 5

*The time is 1965. The lights come up in the yard. It is the morning of* TROY'S *funeral. A funeral plaque with a light hangs beside the door. There is a small garden plot off to the side. There is noise and activity in the house as* ROSE, LYONS, *and* BONO *have gathered. The door opens and* RAYNELL, *seven years old, enters dressed in a flannel nightgown. She crosses to the garden and pokes around with a stick.* ROSE *calls from the house.*

ROSE. Raynell!

RAYNELL. Mam?

ROSE. What you doing out there?

RAYNELL. Nothing.

*ROSE comes to the door.*

ROSE. Girl, get in here and get dressed. What you doing?

RAYNELL. Seeing if my garden growed.

ROSE. I told you it ain't gonna grow overnight. You got to wait.

RAYNELL. It don't look like it never gonna grow. Dag!

ROSE. I told you a watched pot never boils. Get in here and get dressed.

RAYNELL. This ain't even no pot, Mama.

ROSE. You just have to give it a chance. It'll grow. Now you come on and do what I told you. We got to be getting ready. This ain't no morning to be playing around. You hear me?

RAYNELL. Yes, mam.

*ROSE exits into the house. RAYNELL continues to poke at her garden with a stick.* CORY *enters. He is dressed in a Marine corporal's uniform, and carries a duffelbag. His posture is that of a military man, and his speech has a clipped sternness.*

CORY (*to* RAYNELL). Hi. (*Pause.*) I bet your name is Raynell.

RAYNELL. Uh huh.

CORY. Is your mama home?

*RAYNELL runs up on the porch and calls through the screen door.*

RAYNELL. Mama ... there's some man out here. Mama?

*ROSE comes to the door.*

ROSE. Cory? Lord have mercy! Look here, you all!

*ROSE and CORY embrace in a tearful reunion as BONO and LYONS enter from the house dressed in funeral clothes.*

BONO. Aw, looka here ...

ROSE. Done got all grown up!

CORY. Don't cry, Mama. What you crying about?

ROSE. I'm just so glad you made it.

CORY. Hey Lyons. How you doing, Mr. Bono.

LYONS *goes to embrace* CORY.

LYONS. Look at you, man. Look at you. Don't he look good, Rose. Got them Corporal stripes.

ROSE. What took you so long?

CORY. You know how the Marines are, Mama. They got to get all their paperwork straight before they let you do anything.

ROSE. Well, I'm sure glad you made it. They let Lyons come. Your Uncle Gabe's still in the hospital. They don't know if they gonna let him out or not. I just talked to them a little while ago.

LYONS. A Corporal in the United States Marines.

BONO. Your daddy knew you had it in you. He used to tell me all the time.

LYONS. Don't he look good, Mr. Bono?

BONO. Yeah, he remind me of Troy when I first met him. (*Pause.*) Say, Rose, Lucille's down at the church with the choir. I'm gonna go down and get the pallbearers lined up. I'll be back to get you all.

ROSE. Thanks, Jim.

CORY. See you, Mr. Bono.

LYONS (*with his arm around* RAYNELL). Cory . . . look at Raynell. Ain't she precious? She gonna break a whole lot of hearts.

ROSE. Raynell, come and say hello to your brother. This is your brother, Cory. You remember Cory.

RAYNELL. No, Mam.

CORY. She don't remember me, Mama.

ROSE. Well, we talk about you. She heard us talk about you. (*To* RAYNELL.) This is your brother, Cory. Come on and say hello.

RAYNELL. Hi.

CORY. Hi. So you're Raynell. Mama told me a lot about you.

ROSE. You all come on into the house and let me fix you some breakfast. Keep up your strength.

CORY. I ain't hungry, Mama.

LYONS. You can fix me something, Rose. I'll be in there in a minute.

ROSE. Cory, you sure you don't want nothing? I know they ain't feeding you right.

CORY. No, Mama . . . thanks. I don't feel like eating. I'll get something later.

ROSE. Raynell . . . get on upstairs and get that dress on like I told you.

ROSE *and* RAYNELL *exit into the house.*

LYONS. So . . . I hear you thinking about getting married.

CORY. Yeah, I done found the right one, Lyons. It's about time.

LYONS. Me and Bonnie been split up about four years now. About the time Papa retired. I guess she just got tired of all them changes I was

putting her through. (*Pause.*) I always knew you was gonna make
something out yourself. Your head was always in the right direction.
So . . . you gonna stay in . . . make it a career . . . put in your twenty
years?

CORY. I don't know. I got six already, I think that's enough.

LYONS. Stick with Uncle Sam and retire early. Ain't nothing out here. I guess
Rose told you what happened with me. They got me down the work-
house. I thought I was being slick cashing other people's checks.

CORY. How much time you doing?

LYONS. They give me three years. I got that beat now. I ain't got but nine
more months. It ain't so bad. You learn to deal with it like anything
else. You got to take the crookeds with the straights. That's what Papa
used to say. He used to say that when he struck out. I seen him strike
out three times in a row . . . and the next time up he hit the ball over
the grandstand. Right out there in Homestead Field. He wasn't satisfied hitting in the seats . . . he want to hit it over everything! After the
game he had two hundred people standing around waiting to shake
his hand. You got to take the crookeds with the straights. Yeah, Papa
was something else.

CORY. You still playing?

LYONS. Cory . . . you know I'm gonna do that. There's some fellows down
there we got us a band . . . we gonna try and stay together when we
get out . . . but yeah, I'm still playing. It still helps me to get out of bed
in the morning. As long as it do that I'm gonna be right there playing
and trying to make some sense out of it.

ROSE (*calling*). Lyons, I got these eggs in the pan.

LYONS. Let me go on and get these eggs, man. Get ready to go bury Papa.
(*Pause.*) How you doing? You doing all right?

CORY *nods.* LYONS *touches him on the shoulder and they share a moment of silent grief.* LYONS *exits into the house.* CORY *wanders about
the yard.* RAYNELL *enters.*

RAYNELL. Hi.

CORY. Hi.

RAYNELL. Did you used to sleep in my room?

CORY. Yeah . . . that used to be my room.

RAYNELL. That's what Papa call it. "Cory's room." It got your football in the
closet.

ROSE *comes to the door.*

ROSE. Raynell, get in there and get them good shoes on.

RAYNELL. Mama, can't I wear these? Them other one hurt my feet.

ROSE. Well, they just gonna have to hurt your feet for a while. You ain't said
they hurt your feet when you went down to the store and got them.

RAYNELL.  They didn't hurt then. My feet done got bigger.

ROSE.  Don't you give me no backtalk now. You get in there and get them shoes on.

RAYNELL *exits into the house.*

Ain't too much changed. He still got that piece of rag tied to that tree. He was out here swinging that bat. I was just ready to go back in the house. He swung that bat and then he just fell over. Seem like he swung it and stood there with this grin on his face . . . and then he just fell over. They carried him on down to the hospital, but I knew there wasn't no need . . . why don't you come on in the house?

CORY.  Mama . . . I got something to tell you. I don't know how to tell you this . . . but I've got to tell you . . . I'm not going to Papa's funeral.

ROSE.  Boy, hush your mouth. That's your daddy you talking about. I don't want hear that kind of talk this morning. I done raised you to come to this? You standing there all healthy and grown talking about you ain't going to your daddy's funeral?

CORY.  Mama . . . listen . . .

ROSE.  I don't want to hear it, Cory. You just get that thought out of your head.

CORY.  I can't drag Papa with me everywhere I go. I've got to say no to him. One time in my life I've got to say no.

ROSE.  Don't nobody have to listen to nothing like that. I know you and your daddy ain't seen eye to eye, but I ain't got to listen to that kind of talk this morning. Whatever was between you and your daddy . . . the time has come to put it aside. Just take it and set it over there on the shelf and forget about it. Disrespecting your daddy ain't gonna make you a man, Cory. You got to find a way to come to that on your own. Not going to your daddy's funeral ain't gonna make you a man.

CORY.  The whole time I was growing up . . . living in his house . . . Papa was like a shadow that followed you everywhere. It weighed on you and sunk into your flesh. It would wrap around you and lay there until you couldn't tell which one was you anymore. That shadow digging in your flesh. Trying to crawl in. Trying to live through you. Everywhere I looked, Troy Maxson was staring back at me . . . hiding under the bed . . . in the closet. I'm just saying I've got to find a way to get rid of that shadow, Mama.

ROSE.  You just like him. You got him in you good.

CORY.  Don't tell me that, Mama.

ROSE.  You Troy Maxson all over again.

CORY.  I don't want to be Troy Maxson. I want to be me.

ROSE.  You can't be nobody but who you are, Cory. That shadow wasn't nothing but you growing into yourself. You either got to grow into it or cut it down to fit you. But that's all you got to make life with. That's all you got to measure yourself against that world out there. Your

daddy wanted you to be everything he wasn't . . . and at the same time
he tried to make you into everything he was. I don't know if he was
right or wrong . . . but I do know he meant to do more good than
he meant to do harm. He wasn't always right. Sometimes when he
touched he bruised. And sometimes when he took me in his arms
he cut.

When I first met your daddy I thought . . . Here is a man I can lay
down with and make a baby. That's the first thing I thought when I
seen him. I was thirty years old and had done seen my share of men.
But when he walked up to me and said, "I can dance a waltz that'll
make you dizzy," I thought, Rose Lee, here is a man that you can open
yourself up to and be filled to bursting. Here is a man that can fill all
them empty spaces you been tipping around the edges of. One of
them empty spaces was being somebody's mother.

I married your daddy and settled down to cooking his supper
and keeping clean sheets on the bed. When your daddy walked
through the house he was so big he filled it up. That was my first
mistake. Not to make him leave some room for me. For my part in
the matter. But at that time I wanted that. I wanted a house that I
could sing in. And that's what your daddy gave me. I didn't know to
keep up his strength I had to give up little pieces of mine. I did that.
I took on his life as mine and mixed up the pieces so that you could-
n't hardly tell which was which anymore. It was my choice. It was
my life and I didn't have to live it like that. But that's what life offered me in the way of being a woman and I took it. I grabbed hold
of it with both hands.

By the time Raynell came into the house, me and your daddy had
done lost touch with one another. I didn't want to make my blessing
off of nobody's misfortune . . . but I took on to Raynell like she was all
them babies I had wanted and never had.

*The phone rings.*

Like I'd been blessed to relive a part of my life. And if the Lord see fit
to keep up my strength . . . I'm gonna do her just like your daddy did
you . . . I'm gonna give her the best of what's in me.

RAYNELL (*entering, still with her old shoes*).  Mama . . . Reverend Tollivier
on the phone.

ROSE *exits into the house.*

RAYNELL.  Hi.

CORY.  Hi.

RAYNELL.  You in the Army or the Marines?

CORY.  Marines.

RAYNELL.  Papa said it was the Army. Did you know Blue?

CORY.  Blue? Who's Blue?

RAYNELL.  Papa's dog what he sing about all the time.

CORY (*singing*).

> Hear it ring! Hear it ring!
> I had a dog his name was Blue
> You know Blue was mighty true
> You know Blue was a good old dog
> Blue treed a possum in a hollow log
> You know from that he was a good old dog.
> Hear it ring! Hear it ring!

RAYNELL *joins in singing.*

CORY AND RAYNELL.

> Blue treed a possum out on a limb
> Blue looked at me and I looked at him
> Grabbed that possum and put him in a sack
> Blue stayed there till I came back
> Old Blue's feets was big and round
> Never allowed a possum to touch the ground.
> Old Blue died and I dug his grave
> I dug his grave with a silver spade
> Let him down with a golden chain
> And every night I call his name
> Go on Blue, you good dog you
> Go on Blue, you good dog you.

RAYNELL.

> Blue laid down and died like a man
> Blue laid down and died . . .

BOTH.

> Blue laid down and died like a man
> Now he's treeing possums in the Promised Land
> I'm gonna tell you this to let you know
> Blue's gone where the good dogs go
> When I hear old Blue bark
> When I hear old Blue bark
> Blue treed a possum in Noah's Ark
> Blue treed a possum in Noah's Ark.

ROSE *comes to the screen door.*

ROSE.  Cory, we gonna be ready to go in a minute.

CORY (*to* RAYNELL).  You go on in the house and change them shoes like Mama told you so we can go to Papa's funeral.

RAYNELL.  Okay, I'll be back.

RAYNELL *exits into the house.* CORY *gets up and crosses over to the tree.* ROSE *stands in the screen door watching him.* GABRIEL *enters from the alley.*

GABRIEL (*calling*). Hey, Rose!

ROSE. Gabe?

GABRIEL. I'm here, Rose. Hey, Rose, I'm here!

ROSE *enters from the house.*

ROSE. Lord ... Look here, Lyons!

LYONS. See, I told you, Rose ... I told you they'd let him come.

CORY. How you doing, Uncle Gabe?

LYONS. How you doing, Uncle Gabe?

GABRIEL. Hey, Rose. It's time. It's time to tell St. Peter to open the gates. Troy, you ready? You ready, Troy. I'm gonna tell St. Peter to open the gates. You get ready now.

GABRIEL, *with great fanfare, braces himself to blow. The trumpet is without a mouthpiece. He puts the end of it into his mouth and blows with great force, like a man who has been waiting some twenty-odd years for this single moment. No sound comes out of the trumpet. He braces himself and blows again with the same result. A third time he blows. There is a weight of impossible description that falls away and leaves him bare and exposed to a frightful realization. It is a trauma that a sane and normal mind would be unable to withstand. He begins to dance. A slow, strange dance, eerie and life-giving. A dance of atavistic signature and ritual.* LYONS *attempts to embrace him.* GABRIEL *pushes* LYONS *away. He begins to howl in what is an attempt at song, or perhaps a song turning back into itself in an attempt at speech. He finishes his dance and the gates of heaven stand open as wide as God's closet.*

That's the way that go!

BLACKOUT

## ✳ TOPICS FOR CRITICAL THINKING AND WRITING

### *The Play on the Page*

1. What do you think that Bono means when he says, early in Act 2, "Some people build fences to keep people out ... and some people build fences to keep people in"? Why is the play called *Fences*? What has fenced Troy in? What is Troy fencing in? (Take account of Troy's last speech in Act 2, Scene 2, but do not limit your discussion to this speech.)

2. What do you think Troy's reasons are—conscious and unconscious—for not wanting Cory to play football at college?
3. Compare and contrast Cory and Lyons. Consider, too, in what ways they resemble Troy and in what ways they differ from him.
4. In what ways is Troy like his father, and in what ways unlike him?
5. What do you make out of the prominence given to the song about Blue?
6. There is a good deal of anger in the play, but there is also humor. Which passages do you find humorous, and why?
7. Characterize Rose Maxson.

### The Play on the Stage

8. In what ways is the role of Gabriel a challenge for an actor? What advice might you give to the other actors on stage during Gabriel's appearances?
9. Some scenes begin by specifying that "the lights come up." Others do not, presumably beginning with an illuminated stage. All scenes except the last one end with the lights going down to blackness. Explain Wilson's use of lighting.

# TERRENCE MCNALLY

*Terrence McNally, born in 1939 in St. Petersburg, Florida, grew up in Corpus Christi, Texas, and did his undergraduate work at Columbia University. "I'm a gay man who writes plays," he has said, and most of his work concerns gay people—or the responses of straight people to gay people.*

*We give the original script of* Andre's Mother *(1988); McNally later amplified it for a 1990 television broadcast (running time is 58 minutes) that was awarded an Emmy.*

## Andre's Mother                                     [1988]

### CHARACTERS
CAL, *a young man*
ARTHUR, *his father*
PENNY, *his sister*
ANDRE'S MOTHER

TIME: *Now*
PLACE: *New York City, Central Park*

*Four people—Cal, Arthur, Penny, and Andre's Mother—enter: They are nicely dressed and each carries a white helium-filled balloon on a string.*

CAL:  You know what's really terrible? I can't think of anything terrific to say. Good-bye. I love you. I'll miss you. And I'm supposed to be so great with words!

PENNY:  What's that over there?

ARTHUR:  Ask your brother.

CAL:  It's a theatre. An outdoor theatre. They do plays there in the summer. Shakespeare's plays. *(To Andre's Mother.)* God, how much he wanted to play Hamlet again. He would have gone to Timbucktu to have another go at that part. The summer he did it in Boston, he was so happy!

PENNY:  Cal, I don't think she . . . ! It's not the time. Later.

ARTHUR:  Your son was a . . . the Jews have a word for it . . .

PENNY *(quietly appalled):*  Oh my God!

ARTHUR:  Mensch, I believe it is, and I think I'm using it right. It means warm, solid, the real thing. Correct me if I'm wrong.

PENNY:  Fine, Dad, fine. Just quit while you're ahead.

ARTHUR:  I won't say he was like a son to me. Even my son isn't always like a son to me. I mean . . . ! In my clumsy way, I'm trying to say how much I liked Andre. And how much he helped me to know my own boy. Cal was always two handsful but Andre and I could talk about anything under the sun. My wife was very fond of him, too.

PENNY:  Cal, I don't understand about the balloons.

CAL:  They represent the soul. When you let go, it means you're letting his soul ascend to Heaven. That you're willing to let go. Breaking the last earthly ties.

PENNY:  Does the Pope know about this?

ARTHUR:  Penny!

PENNY:  Andre loved my sense of humor. Listen, you can hear him laughing. *(She lets go of her white balloon.)* So long, you glorious, wonderful, I-know-what-Cal-means-about-words . . . *man*! God forgive me for wishing you were straight every time I laid eyes on you. But if any man was going to have you, I'm glad it was my brother! Look how fast it went up. I bet that means something. Something terrific.

ARTHUR *(Lets his balloon go.):*  Good-bye. God speed.

PENNY:  Cal?

CAL:  I'm not ready yet.

PENNY:  Okay. We'll be over there. Come on, Pop, you can buy your little girl a Good Humor.

ARTHUR:  They still make Good Humor?

PENNY:  Only now they're called Dove Bars and they cost twelve dollars.

*(Penny takes Arthur off. Cal and Andre's Mother stand with their balloons.)*

CAL:  I wish I knew what you were thinking. I think it would help me. You know almost nothing about me and I only know what Andre told me about you. I'd always had it in my mind that one day we would be friends, you and me. But if you didn't know about Andre and me . . . If this hadn't happened, I wonder if he would have ever told you. When he was sick, if I asked him once I asked him a thousand times, tell her. She's your mother. She won't mind. But he was so afraid of hurting you and of your disapproval. I don't know which was worse. *(No response. He sighs.)* God, how many of us live in this city because we don't want to hurt our mothers and live in mortal terror of their disapproval. We lose ourselves here. Our lives aren't furtive, just our feelings toward people like you are! A city of fugitives from our parents' scorn or heartbreak. Sometimes he'd seem a little down and I'd say, "What's the matter, babe?" and this funny sweet, sad smile would cross his face and he'd say, "Just a little homesick, Cal, just a little bit." I always accused him of being a country boy just playing at being a hotshot, sophisticated New Yorker. *(He sighs.)*

It's bullshit. It's all bullshit. *(Still no response.)*

Do you remember the comic strip *Little Lulu?* Her mother had no name, she was so remote, so formidable to all the children. She was just Lulu's mother. "Hello, Lulu's Mother," Lulu's friends would say. She was almost anonymous in her remoteness. You remind me of her. Andre's Mother. Let me answer the questions you can't ask and then I'll leave you alone and you won't ever have to see me again. Andre died of AIDS. I don't know how he got it. I tested negative. He died bravely. You would have been proud of him. The only thing that frightened him was you. I'll have everything that was his sent to you. I'll pay for it. There isn't much. You should have come up the summer he played Hamlet. He was magnificent. Yes, I'm bitter. I'm bitter I've lost him. I'm, bitter what's happening. I'm bitter even now, after all this, I can't reach you. I'm beginning to feel your disapproval and it's making me ill. *(He looks at his balloon.)* Sorry, old friend. I blew it. *(He lets go of the balloon.)*

Good night, sweet prince, and flights of angels sing thee to they rest![1] *(Beat.)*

Goodbye, Andre's Mother.

*(He goes. Andre's Mother stands alone holding her white balloon. Her lips tremble. She looks on the verge of breaking down. She is about to let go of the balloon when she pulls it down to her. She*

---

[1]**Good night . . . rest!** Cal is quoting lines that Hamlet's friend Horatio speaks (5.2.336–37) at the moment of Hamlet's death.

*looks at it awhile before she gently kisses it. She lets go of the bal-
loon. She follows it with her eyes as it rises and rises. The lights are
beginning to fade. Andre's Mother's eyes are still on the balloon. The
lights fade.)*

## ▨ TOPICS FOR
## CRITICAL THINKING AND WRITING

### *The Play on the Page*

1. Andre's Mother doesn't speak in the play, but we learn something
   about her through Cal's words, and something more through the
   description in the final stage direction. In a paragraph characterize
   Andre's Mother.
2. Cal tells Penny that the balloons "represent the soul. When you let go,
   it means you're letting his soul ascend to Heaven." Is that exactly the
   way you see the balloons, or would see them if you attended a funeral
   where white balloons were distributed? Explain.

### *The Play on the Stage*

3. McNally tells us in a stage direction that Andre's Mother "follows [the
   balloon] with her eyes," and that when the lights fade, at the very end,
   "Andre's mother's eyes are still on the balloon." If you were directing
   the play, would you suggest to the actor who is performing the role
   of the mother that she should somehow convey that she has—or has
   not—"let go" of her memory of her son?
4. Let's assume that you drafted this play, and now, on rereading it you
   decide that you want to give Andre's Mother one speech, and one
   speech only. Write the speech—it can go anywhere in the play that
   you think best—and then in a brief essay explain why you think the
   speech is effective.

# 27

# A Play about Marriage

Probably most of us think of marriage chiefly in romantic terms—

> Love and marriage, love and marriage
> Go together like a horse and carriage—

but history tells us that in most Western societies marriage has been a way for males to transfer their property and their power to their offspring. Men could sow their wild oats, but women were expected to be faithful. Speaking generally, the husband provided food and shelter, and the wife—sometimes regarded as not much more than a property of her husband—bore and reared his children, and the male offspring would inherit the estate.

Amazingly, in popular culture as evinced by cartoons and jokes, women set out to entrap men, and the man is the long-suffering member of the team. A recent cartoon, for instance, showed a husband looking up from his newspaper and saying to his stern-faced wife, "Gay marriage! Haven't they already suffered enough?" Mother-in-law jokes (it is always the wife's mother who is damaging the marriage) are another sign of the widespread view that in marriage the husband is the disadvantaged party.

In this chapter we present a play that explores the nature of marriage in the late nineteenth century. Read the play and then ask yourself if it is dated. You might also consider this topic: Can the play be called a tragedy, or comedy, or both, or neither? Please explain.

## HENRIK IBSEN

*Henrik Ibsen (1828–1906) was born in Skien, Norway, of wealthy parents who soon after his birth lost their money. Ibsen worked as a pharmacist's apprentice, but at the age of twenty-two he had written his first play, a promising melodrama entitled* Cataline. *He engaged in theater work first in Norway and then in Denmark and Germany. By 1865 his*

*plays had won him a state pension that enabled him to settle in Rome.
After writing romantic, historic, and poetic plays, he turned to realistic
drama with* The League of Youth *(1869). Among his major realistic
"problem plays" are* A Doll's House *(1879),* Ghosts *(1881), and* An Enemy of the People *(1882). In* The Wild Duck *(1884) he moved toward a
more symbolic tragic comedy, and his last plays, written in the nineties,
are highly symbolic.* Hedda Gabler *(1890) looks backward to the plays
of the eighties rather than forward to the plays of the nineties.*

# A Doll's House                                                            [1879]

*Translated by James McFarlane*

## CHARACTERS

TORVALD HELMER, *a lawyer*
NORA, *his wife*
DR. RANK
MRS. KRISTINE LINDE
NILS KROGSTAD
ANNE MARIE, *the nursemaid*
KELENE, *the maid*
THE HELMERS' THREE CHILDREN
A PORTER

*The action takes place in the Helmers' flat.*

### Act I

*A pleasant room, tastefully but not expensively furnished. On the back
wall, one door on the right leads to the entrance hall, a second door on
the left leads to* HELMER's *study. Between these two doors, a piano. In the
middle of the left wall, a door; and downstage from it, a window. Near
the window a round table with armchairs and a small sofa. In the right
wall, upstage, a door; and on the same wall downstage, a porcelain
stove with a couple of armchairs and a rocking chair. Between the stove
and the door a small table. Etchings on the walls. A whatnot with china
and other small objects d'art; a small bookcase with books in handsome
bindings. Carpet on the floor; a fire burns in the stove. A winter's day.*

*The front doorbell rings in the hall; a moment later, there is the
sound of the front door being opened.* NORA *comes into the room, happily humming to herself. She is dressed in her outdoor things, and is
carrying lots of parcels which she then puts down on the table, right.
She leaves the door into the hall standing open; a* PORTER *can be seen
outside holding a Christmas tree and a basket; he hands them to the*
MAID *who has opened the door for them.*

*A Doll's House.* In Act 3, Nora lights Dr. Rank's cigar while Torvald impatiently waits for him to leave.

NORA.  Hide the Christmas tree away carefully, Helene. The children must-n't see it till this evening when it's decorated. [*To the* PORTER, *taking out her purse.*] How much?
PORTER.  Fifty öre.
NORA.  There's a crown. Keep the change.

[*The* PORTER *thanks her and goes.* NORA *shuts the door. She continues to laugh quietly and happily to herself as she takes off her things. She takes a bag of macaroons out of her pocket and eats one or two; then she walks stealthily across and listens at her husband's door.*]

NORA.  Yes, he's in.

[*She begins humming again as she walks over to the table, right.*]

HELMER [*in his study*].  Is that my little skylark chirruping out there?
NORA [*busy opening some of the parcels*].  Yes, it is.
HELMER.  Is that my little squirrel frisking about?
NORA.  Yes!
HELMER.  When did my little squirrel get home?
NORA.  Just this minute. [*She stuffs the bag of macaroons in her pocket and wipes her mouth.*] Come on out, Torvald, and see what I've bought.

HELMER. I don't want to be disturbed! [*A moment later, he opens the door and looks out, his pen in his hand.*] "Bought," did you say? All that? Has my little spendthrift been out squandering money again?

NORA. But, Torvald, surely this year we can spread ourselves just a little. This is the first Christmas we haven't had to go carefully.

HELMER. Ah, but that doesn't mean we can afford to be extravagant, you know.

NORA. Oh yes, Torvald, surely we can afford to be just a little bit extravagant now, can't we? Just a teeny-weeny bit. You are getting quite a good salary now, and you are going to earn lots and lots of money.

HELMER. Yes, after the New Year. But it's going to be three whole months before the first pay cheque comes in.

NORA. Pooh! We can always borrow in the meantime.

HELMER. Nora! [*Crosses to her and takes her playfully by the ear.*] Here we go again, you and your frivolous ideas! Suppose I went and borrowed a thousand crowns today, and you went and spent it all over Christmas, then on New Year's Eve a slate fell and hit me on the head and there I was. . . .

NORA [*putting her hand over his mouth*]. Sh! Don't say such horrid things.

HELMER. Yes, but supposing something like that did happen . . . what then?

NORA. If anything as awful as that did happen, I wouldn't care if I owed anybody anything or not.

HELMER. Yes, but what about the people I'd borrowed from?

NORA. Them? Who cares about them! They are only strangers!

HELMER. Nora, Nora! Just like a woman! Seriously though, Nora, you know what I think about these things. No debts! Never borrow! There's always something inhibited, something unpleasant, about a home built on credit and borrowed money. We two have managed to stick it out so far, and that's the way we'll go on for the little time that remains.

NORA [*walks over to the stove*]. Very well, just as you say, Torvald.

HELMER [*following her*]. There, there! My little singing bird mustn't go drooping her wings, eh? Has it got the sulks, that little squirrel of mine? [*Takes out his wallet.*] Nora, what do you think I've got here?

NORA [*quickly turning round*]. Money!

HELMER. There! [*He hands her some notes*]. Good heavens, I know only too well how Christmas runs away with the housekeeping.

NORA [*counts*]. Ten, twenty, thirty, forty. Oh, thank you, thank you, Torvald! This will see me quite a long way.

HELMER. Yes, it'll have to.

NORA. Yes, yes, I'll see that it does. But come over here, I want to show you all the things I've bought. And so cheap! Look, some new clothes for Ivar . . . and a little sword. There's a horse and a trumpet for Bob. And a doll and a doll's cot for Emmy. They are not very grand but she'll

have them all broken before long anyway. And I've got some dress
material and some handkerchiefs for the maids. Though, really, dear
old Anne Marie should have had something better.

HELMER. And what's in this parcel here?

NORA [*shrieking*]. No, Torvald! You mustn't see that till tonight!

HELMER. All right. But tell me now, what did my little spendthrift fancy for
herself?

NORA. For me? Puh, I don't really want anything.

HELMER. Of course you do. Anything reasonable that you think you might
like, just tell me.

NORA. Well, I don't really know. As a matter of fact, though, Torvald . . .

HELMER. Well?

NORA [*toying with his coat buttons, and without looking at him*]. If you
did want to give me something, you could . . . you could always . . .

HELMER. Well, well, out with it!

NORA [*quickly*]. You could always give me money, Torvald. Only what you
think you could spare. And then I could buy myself something with it
later on.

HELMER. But Nora. . . .

NORA. Oh, please, Torvald dear! Please! I beg you. Then I'd wrap the money
up in some pretty gilt paper and hang it on the Christmas tree.
Wouldn't that be fun?

HELMER. What do we call my pretty little pet when it runs away with all
the money?

NORA. I know, I know, we call it a spendthrift. But please let's do what I
said, Torvald. Then I'll have a bit of time to think about what I need
most. Isn't that awfully sensible, now, eh?

HELMER [*smiling*]. Yes, it is indeed—that is, if only you really could hold on
to the money I gave you, and really did buy something for yourself
with it. But it just gets mixed up with the housekeeping and frittered
away on all sorts of useless things, and then I have to dig into my
pocket all over again.

NORA. Oh but, Torvald. . . .

HELMER. You can't deny it, Nora dear. [*Puts his arm round her waist.*] My
pretty little pet is very sweet, but it runs away with an awful lot of
money. It's incredible how expensive it is for a man to keep such
a pet.

NORA. For shame! How can you say such a thing? As a matter of fact I save
everything I can.

HELMER [*laughs*]. Yes, you are right there. Everything you *can*. But you simply can't.

NORA [*hums and smiles quietly and happily*]. Ah, if you only knew how
many expenses the likes of us skylarks and squirrels have, Torvald!

HELMER. What a funny little one you are! Just like your father. Always on
the lookout for money, wherever you can lay your hands on it; but as

soon as you've got it, it just seems to slip through your fingers. You
never seem to know what you've done with it. Well, one must accept
you as you are. It's in the blood. Oh yes, it is, Nora. That sort of thing is
hereditary.

NORA. Oh, I only wish I'd inherited a few more of Daddy's qualities.

HELMER. And I wouldn't want my pretty little songbird to be the least bit
different from what she is now. But come to think of it, you look
rather . . . rather . . . how shall I put it? . . . rather guilty today. . . .

NORA. Do I?

HELMER. Yes, you do indeed. Look me straight in the eye.

NORA [looks at him]. Well?

HELMER [wagging his finger at her]. My little sweet-tooth surely didn't forget herself in town today?

NORA. No, whatever makes you think that?

HELMER. She didn't just pop into the confectioner's for a moment?

NORA. No, I assure you, Torvald . . . !

HELMER. Didn't try sampling the preserves?

NORA. No, really I didn't.

HELMER. Didn't go nibbling a macaroon or two?

NORA. No, Torvald, honestly, you must believe me . . . !

HELMER. All right then! It's really just my little joke. . . .

NORA [crosses to the table]. I would never dream of doing anything you
didn't want me to.

HELMER. Of course not, I know that. And then you've given me your
word. . . . [Crosses to her.] Well then, Nora dearest, you shall keep
your little Christmas secrets. They'll all come out tonight, I dare say,
when we light the tree.

NORA. Did you remember to invite Dr. Rank?

HELMER. No. But there's really no need. Of course he'll come and have dinner with us. Anyway, I can ask him when he looks in this morning. I've
ordered some good wine. Nora, you can't imagine how I am looking
forward to this evening.

NORA. So am I. And won't the children enjoy it, Torvald!

HELMER. Oh, what a glorious feeling it is, knowing you've got a nice, safe
job, and a good fat income. Don't you agree? Isn't it wonderful, just
thinking about it?

NORA. Oh, it's marvelous!

HELMER. Do you remember last Christmas? Three whole weeks beforehand
you shut yourself up every evening till after midnight making flowers
for the Christmas tree and all the other splendid things you wanted
to surprise us with. Ugh, I never felt so bored in all my life.

NORA. I wasn't the least bit bored.

HELMER [smiling]. But it turned out a bit of an anticlimax, Nora.

NORA. Oh, you are not going to tease me about that again! How was I to
know the cat would get in and pull everything to bits?

HELMER.  No, of course you weren't. Poor little Nora! All you wanted was for
us to have a nice time—and it's the thought behind it that counts, after
all. All the same, it's a good thing we've seen the back of those lean
times.

NORA.  Yes, really it's marvelous.

HELMER.  Now there's no need for me to sit here all on my own, bored to
tears. And you don't have to strain your dear little eyes, and work
those dainty little fingers to the bone. . . .

NORA [clapping her hands].  No, Torvald, I don't, do I? Not any more. Oh,
how marvelous it is to hear that! [Takes his arm.] Now I want to tell
you how I've been thinking we might arrange things, Torvald. As soon
as Christmas is over. . . . [The door-bell rings in the hall.] Oh, there's
the bell. [Tidies one or two things in the room.] It's probably a visitor. What a nuisance!

HELMER.  Remember I'm not at home to callers.

MAID [in the doorway].  There's a lady to see you, ma'am.

NORA.  Show her in, please.

MAID [to HELMER].  And the doctor's just arrived, too, sir.

HELMER.  Did he go straight into my room?

MAID.  Yes, he did, sir.

[HELMER goes into his study. The MAID shows in MRS. LINDE, who is in
traveling clothes, and closes the door after her.]

MRS. LINDE [subdued and rather hesitantly].  How do you do, Nora?

NORA [uncertainly].  How do you do?

MRS. LINDE.  I'm afraid you don't recognize me.

NORA.  No, I don't think I . . . And yet I seem to. . . . [Bursts out suddenly.]
Why! Kristine! Is it really you?

MRS. LINDE.  Yes, it's me.

NORA.  Kristine! Fancy not recognizing you again! But how was I to,
when . . . [Gently.] How you've changed, Kristine!

MRS. LINDE.  I dare say I have. In nine . . . ten years . . . .

NORA.  Is it so long since we last saw each other? Yes, it must be. Oh, believe me these last eight years have been such a happy time. And now
you've come up to town, too? All that long journey in wintertime.
That took courage.

MRS. LINDE.  I just arrived this morning on the steamer.

NORA.  To enjoy yourself over Christmas, of course. How lovely! Oh, we'll
have such fun, you'll see. Do take off your things. You are not cold, are
you? [Helps her.] There now! Now let's sit down here in comfort beside the stove. No, here, you take the armchair, I'll sit here on the rocking chair. [Takes her hands.] Ah, now you look a bit more like your
old self again. It was just that when I first saw you. . . . But you are a
little paler, Kristine . . . and perhaps even a bit thinner!

MRS. LINDE.  And much, much older, Nora.

NORA. Yes, perhaps a little older . . . very, very little, not really very much.
[*Stops suddenly and looks serious.*] Oh, what a thoughtless creature
I am, sitting here chattering on like this! Dear, sweet Kristine, can you
forgive me?

MRS. LINDE. What do you mean, Nora?

NORA [*gently*]. Poor Kristine, of course you're a widow now.

MRS. LINDE. Yes, my husband died three years ago.

NORA. Oh, I remember now. I read about it in the papers. Oh, Kristine, believe me I often thought at the time of writing to you. But I kept
putting it off, something always seemed to crop up.

MRS. LINDE. My dear Nora, I understand so well.

NORA. No, it wasn't very nice of me, Kristine. Oh, you poor thing, what you
must have gone through. And didn't he leave you anything?

MRS. LINDE. No.

NORA. And no children?

MRS. LINDE. No.

NORA. Absolutely nothing?

MRS. LINDE. Nothing at all . . . not even a broken heart to grieve over.

NORA [*looks at her incredulously*]. But, Kristine, is that possible?

MRS. LINDE [*smiles sadly and strokes* NORA*'s hair*]. Oh, it sometimes happens, Nora.

NORA. So utterly alone. How terribly sad that must be for you. I have three
lovely children. You can't see them for the moment, because they're
out with their nanny. But now you must tell me all about yourself. . . .

MRS. LINDE. No, no, I want to hear about you.

NORA. No, you start. I won't be selfish today. I must think only about
your affairs today. But there's just one thing I really must tell you.
Have you heard about the great stroke of luck we've had in the last
few days?

MRS. LINDE. No. What is it?

NORA. What do you think? My husband has just been made Bank Manager!

MRS. LINDE. Your husband? How splendid!

NORA. Isn't it tremendous! It's not a very steady way of making a living,
you know, being a lawyer, especially if he refuses to take on anything
that's the least bit shady—which of course is what Torvald does, and I
think he's quite right. You can imagine how pleased we are! He starts
at the Bank straight after New Year, and he's getting a big salary and
lots of commission. From now on we'll be able to live quite differently . . . we'll do just what we want. Oh, Kristine, I'm so happy and
relieved. I must say it's lovely to have plenty of money and not have
to worry. Isn't it?

MRS. LINDE. Yes. It must be nice to have enough, at any rate.

NORA. No, not just enough, but pots and pots of money.

MRS. LINDE [*smiles*]. Nora, Nora, haven't you learned any sense yet? At
school you used to be an awful spendthrift.

NORA.  Yes, Torvald still says I am. [*Wags her finger.*] But little Nora isn't as
stupid as everybody thinks. Oh, we haven't really been in a position
where I could afford to spend a lot of money. We've both had to work.

MRS. LINDE.  You too?

NORA.  Yes, odd jobs—sewing, crochetwork, embroidery and things like
that. [*Casually.*] And one or two other things, besides. I suppose you
know that Torvald left the Ministry when we got married. There
weren't any prospects of promotion in his department, and of course
he needed to earn more money than he had before. But the first year
he wore himself out completely. He had to take on all kinds of extra
jobs, you know, and he found himself working all hours of the day
and night. But he couldn't go on like that; and he became seriously ill.
The doctors said it was essential for him to go South.

MRS. LINDE.  Yes, I believe you spent a whole year in Italy, didn't you?

NORA.  That's right. It wasn't easy to get away, I can tell you. It was just after I'd had Ivar. But of course we had to go. Oh, it was an absolutely
marvelous trip. And it saved Torvald's life. But it cost an awful lot of
money, Kristine.

MRS. LINDE.  That I can well imagine.

NORA.  Twelve hundred dollars. Four thousand eight hundred crowns.
That's a lot of money, Kristine.

MRS. LINDE.  Yes, but in such circumstances, one is very lucky if one has it.

NORA.  Well, we got it from Daddy, you see.

MRS. LINDE.  Ah, that was it. It was just about then your father died, I believe,
wasn't it?

NORA.  Yes, Kristine, just about then. And do you know, I couldn't even go
and look after him. Here was I expecting Ivar any day. And I also had
poor Torvald, gravely ill, on my hands. Dear, kind Daddy! I never saw
him again, Kristine. Oh, that's the saddest thing that has happened to
me in all my married life.

MRS. LINDE.  I know you were very fond of him. But after that you left for
Italy?

NORA.  Yes, we had the money then, and the doctors said it was urgent. We
left a month later.

MRS. LINDE.  And your husband came back completely cured?

NORA.  Fit as a fiddle!

MRS. LINDE.  But . . . what about the doctor?

NORA.  How do you mean?

MRS. LINDE.  I thought the maid said something about the gentleman who
came at the same time as me being a doctor.

NORA.  Yes, that was Dr. Rank. But this isn't a professional visit. He's our
best friend and he always looks in at least once a day. No, Torvald has
never had a day's illness since. And the children are fit and healthy,
and so am I. [*Jumps up and claps her hands.*] Oh God, oh God, isn't
it marvelous to be alive, and to be happy, Kristine! . . . Oh, but I ought

to be ashamed of myself . . . Here I go on talking about nothing but myself. [*She sits on a low stool near* MRS. LINDE *and lays her arms on her lap.*] Oh, please, you mustn't be angry with me! Tell me, is it really true that you didn't love your husband? What made you marry him, then?

MRS. LINDE. My mother was still alive; she was bedridden and helpless. And then I had my two young brothers to look after as well. I didn't think I would be justified in refusing him.

NORA. No, I dare say you are right. I suppose he was fairly wealthy then?

MRS. LINDE. He was quite well off, I believe. But the business was shaky. When he died, it went all to pieces, and there just wasn't anything left.

NORA. What then?

MRS. LINDE. Well, I had to fend for myself, opening a little shop, running a little school, anything I could turn my hand to. These last three years have been one long relentless drudge. But now it's finished, Nora. My poor dear mother doesn't need me any more, she's passed away. Nor the boys either, they're at work now, they can look after themselves.

NORA. What a relief you must find it. . . .

MRS. LINDE. No, Nora! Just unutterably empty. Nobody to live for any more. [*Stands up restless.*] That's why I couldn't stand it any longer being cut off up there. Surely it must be a bit easier here to find something to occupy your mind. If only I could manage to find a steady job of some kind, in an office perhaps. . . .

NORA. But, Kristine, that's terribly exhausting; and you look so worn out even before you start. The best thing for you would be a little holiday at some quiet little resort.

MRS. LINDE [*crosses to the window*]. I haven't any father I can fall back on for the money, Nora.

NORA [*rises*]. Oh, please, you mustn't be angry with me!

MRS. LINDE [*goes to her*]. My dear Nora, you mustn't be angry with me either. That's the worst thing about people in my position, they become so bitter. One has nobody to work for, yet one has to be on the look-out all the time. Life has to go on, and one starts thinking only of oneself. Believe it or not, when you told me the good news about your step up, I was pleased not so much for your sake as for mine.

NORA. How do you mean? Ah, I see. You think Torvald might be able to do something for you.

MRS. LINDE. Yes, that's exactly what I thought.

NORA. And so he shall, Kristine. Just leave things to me. I'll bring it up so cleverly . . . I'll think up something to put him in a good mood. Oh, I do so much want to help you.

MRS. LINDE. It is awfully kind of you, Nora, offering to do all this for me, particularly in your case, where you haven't known much trouble or hardship in your own life.

NORA. When I . . . ? I haven't known much . . . ?

MRS. LINDE [*smiling*].  Well, good heavens, a little bit of sewing to do and a few things like that. What a child you are, Nora!

NORA [*tosses her head and walks across the room*].  I wouldn't be too sure of that, if I were you.

MRS. LINDE.  Oh?

NORA.  You're just like the rest of them. You all think I'm useless when it comes to anything really serious. . . .

MRS. LINDE.  Come, come. . . .

NORA.  You think I've never had anything much to contend with in this hard world.

MRS. LINDE.  Nora dear, you've only just been telling me all the things you've had to put up with.

NORA.  Pooh! They were just trivialities! [*Softly.*] I haven't told you about the really big thing.

MRS. LINDE.  What big thing? What do you mean?

NORA.  I know you rather tend to look down on me, Kristine. But you shouldn't, you know. You are proud of having worked so hard and so long for your mother.

MRS. LINDE.  I'm sure I don't look down on anybody. But it's true what you say: I am both proud and happy when I think of how I was able to make Mother's life a little easier towards the end.

NORA.  And you are proud when you think of what you have done for your brothers, too.

MRS. LINDE.  I think I have every right to be.

NORA.  I think so too. But now I'm going to tell you something, Kristine. I too have something to be proud and happy about.

MRS. LINDE.  I don't doubt that. But what is it you mean?

NORA.  Not so loud. Imagine if Torvald were to hear! He must never on any account . . . nobody must know about it, Kristine, nobody but you.

MRS. LINDE.  But what is it?

NORA.  Come over here. [*She pulls her down on the sofa beside her.*] Yes, Kristine, I too have something to be proud and happy about. I was the one who saved Torvald's life.

MRS. LINDE.  Saved . . . ? How . . . ?

NORA.  I told you about our trip to Italy. Torvald would never have recovered but for that. . . .

MRS. LINDE.  Well? Your father gave you what money was necessary. . . .

NORA [*smiles*].  That's what Torvald thinks, and everybody else. But . . .

MRS. LINDE.  But . . . ?

NORA.  Daddy never gave us a penny. I was the one who raised the money.

MRS. LINDE.  You? All that money?

NORA.  Twelve hundred dollars. Four thousand eight hundred crowns. What do you say to that!

MRS. LINDE.  But, Nora, how was it possible? Had you won a sweepstake or something?

NORA [*contemptuously*]. A sweepstake? Pooh! There would have been
   nothing to it then.
MRS. LINDE. Where did you get it from, then?
NORA [*hums and smiles secretively*]. H'm, tra-la-la!
MRS. LINDE. Because what you couldn't do was borrow it.
NORA. Oh? Why not?
MRS. LINDE. Well, a wife can't borrow without her husband's consent.
NORA [*tossing her head*]. Ah, but when it happens to be a wife with a bit
   of a sense for business . . . a wife who knows her way about things,
   then. . . .
MRS. LINDE. But, Nora, I just don't understand. . . .
NORA. You don't have to. I haven't said I did borrow the money. I might
   have got it some other way. [*Throws herself back on the sofa.*]
   I might even have got it from some admirer. Anyone as reasonably
   attractive as I am. . . .
MRS. LINDE. Don't be so silly!
NORA. Now you must be dying of curiosity, Kristine.
MRS. LINDE. Listen to me now, Nora dear—you haven't done anything rash,
   have you?
NORA [*sitting up again*]. Is it rash to save your husband's life?
MRS. LINDE. I think it was rash to do anything without telling him. . . .
NORA. But the whole point was that he mustn't know anything. Good
   heavens, can't you see! He wasn't even supposed to know how desperately ill he was. It was me the doctors came and told his life was
   in danger, that the only way to save him was to go South for a while.
   Do you think I didn't try talking him into it first? I began dropping
   hints about how nice it would be if I could be taken on a little trip
   abroad, like other young wives. I wept, I pleaded. I told him he ought
   to show some consideration for my condition, and let me have a bit
   of my own way. And then I suggested he might take out a loan. But at
   that he nearly lost his temper, Kristine. He said I was being frivolous,
   that it was his duty as a husband not to give in to all these whims
   and fancies of mine—as I do believe he called them. All right, I
   thought, somehow you've got to be saved. And it was then I found
   a way. . . .
MRS. LINDE. Did your husband never find out from your father that the
   money hadn't come from him?
NORA. No, never. It was just about the time Daddy died. I'd intended letting him into the secret and asking him not to give me away. But
   when he was so ill . . . I'm sorry to say it never became necessary.
MRS. LINDE. And you never confided in your husband?
NORA. Good heavens, how could you ever imagine such a thing! When
   he's so strict about such matters! Besides, Torvald is a man with a
   good deal of pride—it would be terribly embarrassing and humiliating for him if he thought he owed anything to me. It would spoil

everything between us; this happy home of ours would never be the same again.

MRS. LINDE. Are you never going to tell him?

NORA [*reflectively, half smiling*]. Oh yes, some day perhaps . . . in many years time, when I'm no longer as pretty as I am now. You mustn't laugh! What I mean of course is when Torvald isn't quite so much in love with me as he is now, when he's lost interest in watching me dance, or get dressed up, or recite. Then it might be a good thing to have something in reserve. . . . [*Breaks off.*] What nonsense! That day will never come. Well, what have you got to say to my big secret, Kristine? Still think I'm not much good for anything? One thing, though, it's meant a lot of worry for me, I can tell you. It hasn't always been easy to meet my obligations when the time came. You know in business there is something called quarterly interest, and other things called instalments, and these are always terribly difficult things to cope with. So what I've had to do is save a little here and there, you see, wherever I could. I couldn't really save anything out of the house-keeping, because Torvald has to live in decent style. I couldn't let the children go about badly dressed either—I felt any money I got for them had to go on them alone. Such sweet little things!

MRS. LINDE. Poor Nora! So it had to come out of your own allowance?

NORA. Of course. After all, I was the one it concerned most. Whenever Torvald gave me money for new clothes and such-like, I never spent more than half. And always I bought the simplest and cheapest things. It's a blessing most things look well on me, so Torvald never noticed anything. But sometimes I did feel it was a bit hard, Kristine, because it is nice to be well dressed, isn't it?

MRS. LINDE. Yes, I suppose it is.

NORA. I have had some other sources of income, of course. Last winter I was lucky enough to get quite a bit of copying to do. So I shut myself up every night and sat and wrote through to the small hours of the morning. Oh, sometimes I was so tired, so tired. But it was tremendous fun all the same, sitting there working and earning money like that. It was almost like being a man.

MRS. LINDE. And how much have you been able to pay off like this?

NORA. Well, I can't tell exactly. It's not easy to know where you are with transactions of this kind, you understand. All I know is I've paid off just as much as I could scrape together. Many's the time I was at my wit's end. [*Smiles.*] Then I used to sit here and pretend that some rich old gentleman had fallen in love with me. . . .

MRS. LINDE. What! What gentleman?

NORA. Oh, rubbish! . . . and that now he had died, and when they opened his will, there in big letters were the words: "My entire fortune is to be paid over, immediately and in cash, to charming Mrs. Nora Helmer."

MRS. LINDE. But my dear Nora—who is this man?

NORA.  Good heavens, don't you understand? There never was any old gentleman; it was just something I used to sit here pretending, time and
time again, when I didn't know where to turn next for money. But it
doesn't make very much difference; as far as I'm concerned, the old
boy can do what he likes, I'm tired of him; I can't be bothered any
more with him or his will. Because now all my worries are over.
[*Jumping up.*] Oh God, what a glorious thought, Kristine! No more
worries! Just think of being without a care in the world . . . being
able to romp with the children, and making the house nice and attractive, and having things just as Torvald likes to have them! And
then spring will soon be here, and blue skies. And maybe we can go
away somewhere. I might even see something of the sea again. Oh,
yes! When you're happy, life is a wonderful thing!

[*The doorbell is heard in the hall.*]

MRS. LINDE [*gets up*].  There's the bell. Perhaps I'd better go.
NORA.  No, do stay, please. I don't suppose it's for me; it's probably some-
body for Torvald . . .
MAID [*in the doorway*].  Excuse me, ma'am, but there's a gentleman here
wants to see Mr. Helmer, and I didn't quite know . . . because the doc-
tor is in there. . . .
NORA.  Who is the gentleman?
KROGSTAD [*in the doorway*].  It's me, Mrs. Helmer.

[MRS. LINDE *starts, then turns away to the window.*]

NORA [*tense, takes a step towards him and speaks in a low voice*].  You?
What is it? What do you want to talk to my husband about?
KROGSTAD.  Bank matters . . . in a manner of speaking. I work at the bank,
and I hear your husband is to be the new manager. . . .
NORA.  So it's . . .
KROGSTAD.  Just routine business matters, Mrs. Helmer. Absolutely nothing
else.
NORA.  Well then, please go into his study.

[*She nods impassively and shuts the hall door behind him; then she
walks across and sees to the stove.*]

MRS. LINDE.  Nora . . . who was that man?
NORA.  His name is Krogstad.
MRS. LINDE.  So it really was him.
NORA.  Do you know the man?
MRS. LINDE.  I used to know him . . a good many years ago. He was a solici-
tor's clerk in our district for a while.
NORA.  Yes, so he was.
MRS. LINDE.  How he's changed!
NORA.  His marriage wasn't a very happy one, I believe.

MRS. LINDE.  He's a widower now, isn't he?

NORA.  With a lot of children. There, it'll burn better now.

[*She closes the stove door and moves the rocking chair a little to one side.*]

MRS. LINDE.  He does a certain amount of business on the side, they say?

NORA.  Oh? Yes, it's always possible. I just don't know. . . . But let's not think about business . . . it's all so dull.

[DR. RANK *comes in from* HELMER's *study.*]

DR. RANK [*still in the doorway*].  No, no, Torvald, I won't intrude. I'll just look in on your wife for a moment. [*Shuts the door and notices* MRS. LINDE.] Oh, I beg your pardon. I'm afraid I'm intruding here as well.

NORA.  No, not at all! [*Introduces them.*] Dr. Rank . . . Mrs. Linde.

RANK.  Ah! A name I've often heard mentioned in this house. I believe I came past you on the stairs as I came in.

MRS. LINDE.  I have to take things slowly going upstairs. I find it rather a trial.

RANK.  Ah, some little disability somewhere, eh?

MRS. LINDE.  Just a bit run down, I think, actually.

RANK.  Is that all? Then I suppose you've come to town for a good rest— doing the rounds of the parties?

MRS. LINDE.  I have come to look for work.

RANK.  Is that supposed to be some kind of sovereign remedy for being run down?

MRS. LINDE.  One must live, Doctor.

RANK.  Yes, it's generally thought to be necessary.

NORA.  Come, come, Dr. Rank. You are quite as keen to live as anybody.

RANK.  Quite keen, yes. Miserable as I am, I'm quite ready to let things drag on as long as possible. All my patients are the same. Even those with a moral affliction are no different. As a matter of fact, there's a bad case of that kind in talking with Helmer at this very moment . . .

MRS. LINDE [*softly*].  Ah!

NORA.  Whom do you mean?

RANK.  A person called Krogstad—nobody you would know. He's rotten to the core. But even he began talking about having to *live,* as though it were something terribly important.

NORA.  Oh? And what did he want to talk to Torvald about?

RANK.  I honestly don't know. All I heard was something about the Bank.

NORA.  I didn't know that Krog . . . that this Mr. Krogstad had anything to do with the Bank.

RANK.  Oh yes, he's got some kind of job down there. [*To* MRS. LINDE.] I wonder if you've got people in your part of the country too who go rushing round sniffing out cases of moral corruption, and then installing

the individuals concerned in nice, well-paid jobs where they can
keep them under observation. Sound, decent people have to be content to stay out in the cold.

MRS. LINDE. Yet surely it's the sick who most need to be brought in.

RANK [*shrugs his shoulders*]. Well, there we have it. It's that attitude that's
turning society into a clinic.

[NORA, *lost in her own thoughts, breaks into smothered laughter
and claps her hands.*]

RANK. Why are you laughing at that? Do you know in fact what society is?

NORA. What do I care about your silly old society? I was laughing about
something quite different . . . something frightfully funny. Tell me,
Dr. Rank, are all the people who work at the Bank dependent on
Torvald now?

RANK. Is that what you find so frightfully funny?

NORA [*smiles and hums*]. Never you mind! Never you mind! [*Walks
about the room.*] Yes, it really is terribly amusing to think that we . . .
that Torvald now has power over so many people. [*She takes the bag
out of her pocket.*] Dr. Rank, what about a little macaroon?

RANK. Look at this, eh? Macaroons. I thought they were forbidden here.

NORA. Yes, but these are some Kristine gave me.

MRS. LINDE. What? I . . . ?

NORA. Now, now, you needn't be alarmed. You weren't to know that Torvald had forbidden them. He's worried in case they ruin my teeth, you
know. Still . . . what's it matter once in a while! Don't you think so,
Dr. Rank? Here! [*She pops a macaroon into his mouth.*] And you too,
Kristine. And I shall have one as well; just a little one . . . or two at the
most. [*She walks about the room again.*] Really I am so happy.
There's just one little thing I'd love to do now.

RANK. What's that?

NORA. Something I'd love to say in front of Torvald.

RANK. Then why can't you?

NORA. No, I daren't. It's not very nice.

MRS. LINDE. Not very nice?

RANK. Well, in that case it might not be wise. But to us, I don't see why. . . .
What is this you would love to say in front of Helmer?

NORA. I would simply love to say: "Damn."

RANK. Are you mad!

MRS. LINDE. Good gracious, Nora . . . !

RANK. Say it! Here he is!

NORA [*hiding the bag of macaroons*]. Sh! Sh!

[HELMER *comes out of his room, his overcoat over his arm and his
hat in his hand.*]

NORA [*going over to him*]. Well, Torvald dear, did you get rid of him?

HELMER.  Yes, he's just gone.

NORA.  Let me introduce you. This is Kristine, who has just arrived in town. . . .

HELMER.  Kristine . . . ? You must forgive me, but I don't think I know . . .

NORA.  Mrs. Linde, Torvald dear. Kristine Linde.

HELMER.  Ah, indeed. A school friend of my wife's, presumably.

MRS. LINDE.  Yes, we were girls together.

NORA.  Fancy, Torvald, she's come all this long way just to have a word with you.

HELMER.  How is that?

MRS. LINDE.  Well, it wasn't really . . .

NORA.  The thing is, Kristine is terribly clever at office work, and she's frightfully keen on finding a job with some efficient man, so that she can learn even more. . . .

HELMER.  Very sensible, Mrs. Linde.

NORA.  And then when she heard you'd been made Bank Manager—there was a bit in the paper about it—she set off at once. Torvald please! You *will* try and do something for Kristine, won't you? For my sake?

HELMER.  Well, that's not altogether impossible. You are a widow, I presume?

MRS. LINDE.  Yes.

HELMER.  And you've had some experience in business?

MRS. LINDE.  A fair amount.

HELMER.  Well, it's quite probable I can find you a job, I think. . . .

NORA [*clapping her hands*].  There, you see!

HELMER.  You have come at a fortunate moment, Mrs. Linde . . .

MRS. LINDE.  Oh, how can I ever thank you . . . ?

HELMER.  Not a bit. [*He puts on his overcoat.*] But for the present I must ask you to excuse me. . . .

RANK.  Wait. I'm coming with you.

[*He fetches his fur coat from the hall and warms it at the stove.*]

NORA.  Don't be long, Torvald dear.

HELMER.  Not more than an hour, that's all.

NORA.  Are you leaving too, Kristine?

MRS. LINDE [*putting on her things*].  Yes, I must go and see if I can't find myself a room.

HELMER.  Perhaps we can all walk down the road together.

NORA [*helping her*].  What a nuisance we are so limited for space here. I'm afraid it just isn't possible. . . .

MRS. LINDE.  Oh, you mustn't dream of it! Goodbye, Nora dear, and thanks for everything.

NORA.  Goodbye for the present. But . . . you'll be coming back this evening, of course. And you too, Dr. Rank? What's that? If you are up to it? Of course you'll be up to it. Just wrap yourself up well.

[*They go out, talking, into the hall; children's voices can be heard on the stairs.*]

NORA. Here they are! Here they are! [*She runs to the front door and opens it.* ANNE MARIE, *the nursemaid, enters with the children.*] Come in! Come in! [*She bends down and kisses them.*] Ah! my sweet little darlings. . . . You see them, Kristine? Aren't they lovely!

RANK. Don't stand here chattering in this draught!

HELMER. Come along, Mrs. Linde. The place now becomes unbearable for anybody except mothers.

[DR. RANK, HELMER *and* MRS. LINDE *go down the stairs: the* NURSEMAID *comes into the room with the children, then Nora, shutting the door behind her.*]

NORA. How fresh and bright you look! My, what red cheeks you've got! Like apples and roses. [*During the following, the children keep chattering away to her.*] Have you had a nice time? That's splendid. And you gave Emmy and Bob a ride on your sledge? Did you now! Both together! Fancy that! There's a clever boy, Ivar. Oh, let me take her a little while, Anne Marie. There's my sweet little babydoll! [*She takes the youngest of the children from the* NURSEMAID *and dances with her.*] All right, Mummy will dance with Bobby too. What? You've been throwing snowballs? Oh, I wish I'd been there. No, don't bother, Anne Marie, I'll help them off with their things. No, please, let me— I like doing it. You go on in, you look frozen. You'll find some hot coffee on the stove. [*The* NURSEMAID *goes into the room, left.* NORA *takes off the children's coats and hats and throws them down anywhere, while the children all talk at once.*] Really! A great big dog came running after you? But he didn't bite. No, the doggies wouldn't bite my pretty little dollies. You mustn't touch the parcels, Ivar! What are they? Wouldn't you like to know! No, no, that's nasty. Now? Shall we play something? What shall we play? Hide and seek? Yes, let's play hide and seek. Bob can hide first. Me first? All right, let me hide first.

[*She and the children play, laughing and shrieking, in this room and in the adjacent room on the right. Finally* NORA *hides under the table; the children come rushing in to look for her but cannot find her; they hear her stifled laughter, rush to the table, lift up the tablecloth and find her. Tremendous shouts of delight. She creeps out and pretends to frighten them. More shouts. Meanwhile there has been a knock at the front door, which nobody has heard. The door half opens, and* KROGSTAD *can be seen. He waits a little; the game continues.*]

KROGSTAD. I beg your pardon, Mrs. Helmer. . . .

NORA [*turns with a stifled cry and half jumps up*].  Ah! What do you want?

KROGSTAD.  Excuse me. The front door was standing open. Somebody must have forgotten to shut it. . . .

NORA [*standing up*].  My husband isn't at home, Mr. Krogstad.

KROGSTAD.  I know.

NORA.  Well . . . what are you doing here?

KROGSTAD.  I want a word with you.

NORA.  With . . . ? [*Quietly, to the children.*] Go to Anne Marie. What? No, the strange man won't do anything to Mummy. When he's gone we'll have another game. [*She leads the children into the room, left, and shuts the door after them; tense and uneasy.*] You want to speak to me?

KROGSTAD.  Yes, I do.

NORA.  Today? But it isn't the first of the month yet. . . .

KROGSTAD.  No, it's Christmas Eve. It depends entirely on you what sort of Christmas you have.

NORA.  What do you want? Today I can't possibly . . .

KROGSTAD.  Let's not talk about that for the moment. It's something else. You've got a moment to spare?

NORA.  Yes, I suppose so, though . . .

KROGSTAD.  Good. I was sitting in Olsen's café, and I saw your husband go down the road . . .

NORA.  Did you?

KROGSTAD.  . . . with a lady.

NORA.  Well?

KROGSTAD.  May I be so bold as to ask whether that lady was a Mrs. Linde?

NORA.  Yes.

KROGSTAD.  Just arrived in town?

NORA.  Yes, today.

KROGSTAD.  And she's a good friend of yours?

NORA.  Yes, she is. But I can't see . . .

KROGSTAD.  I also knew her once.

NORA.  I know.

KROGSTAD.  Oh? So you know all about it. I thought as much. Well, I want to ask you straight: is Mrs. Linde getting a job in the Bank?

NORA.  How dare you cross-examine me like this, Mr. Krogstad? You, one of my husband's subordinates? But since you've asked me, I'll tell you. Yes, Mrs. Linde has got a job. And I'm the one who got it for her, Mr. Krogstad. Now you know.

KROGSTAD.  So my guess was right.

NORA [*walking up and down*].  Oh, I think I can say that some of us have a little influence now and again. Just because one happens to be a woman, that doesn't mean. . . . People in subordinate positions, ought to take care they don't offend anybody . . who . . . him . . .

KROGSTAD.  . . . has influence?

NORA.  Exactly.

KROGSTAD [*changing his tone*].  Mrs. Helmer, will you have the goodness to use your influence on my behalf?

NORA.  What? What do you mean?

KROGSTAD.  Will you be so good as to see that I keep my modest little job at the Bank?

NORA.  What do you mean? Who wants to take it away from you?

KROGSTAD.  Oh, you needn't try and pretend to me you don't know. I can quite see that this friend of yours isn't particularly anxious to bump up against me. And I can also see now whom I can thank for being given the sack.

NORA.  But I assure you. . . .

KROGSTAD.  All right, all right. But to come to the point: there's still time. And I advise you to use your influence to stop it.

NORA.  But, Mr. Krogstad, I *have* no influence.

KROGSTAD.  Haven't you? I thought just now you said yourself . . .

NORA.  I didn't mean it that way, of course. Me? What makes you think I've got any influence of that kind over my husband?

KROGSTAD.  I know your husband from our student days. I don't suppose he is any more steadfast than other married men.

NORA.  You speak disrespectfully of my husband like that and I'll show you the door.

KROGSTAD.  So the lady's got courage.

NORA.  I'm not frightened of you any more. After New Year's I'll soon be finished with the whole business.

KROGSTAD [*controlling himself*].  Listen to me, Mrs. Helmer. If necessary I shall fight for my little job in the Bank as if I were fighting for my life.

NORA.  So it seems.

KROGSTAD.  It's not just for the money, that's the last thing I care about. There's something else . . . well, I might as well out with it. You see it's like this. You know as well as anybody that some years ago I got myself mixed up in a bit of trouble.

NORA.  I believe I've heard something of the sort.

KROGSTAD.  It never got as far as the courts; but immediately it was as if all paths were barred to me. So I started going in for the sort of business you know about. I had to do something, and I think I can say I haven't been one of the worst. But now I have to get out of it. My sons are growing up; for their sake I must try and win back what respectability I can. That job in the Bank was like the first step on the ladder for me. And now your husband wants to kick me off the ladder again, back into the mud.

NORA.  But in God's name, Mr. Krogstad, it's quite beyond my power to help you.

KROGSTAD.  That's because you haven't the will to help me. But I have ways of making you.

NORA. You wouldn't go and tell my husband I owe you money?
KROGSTAD. Suppose I did tell him?
NORA. It would be a rotten shame. [*Half choking with tears.*] That secret is all my pride and joy—why should he have to hear about it in this nasty, horrid way . . . hear about it from *you*. You would make things horribly unpleasant for me. . . .
KROGSTAD. Merely unpleasant?
NORA [*vehemently*]. Go on, do it then! It'll be all the worse for you. Because then my husband will see for himself what a bad man you are, and then you certainly won't be able to keep your job.
KROGSTAD. I asked whether it was only a bit of domestic unpleasantness you were afraid of?
NORA. If my husband gets to know about it, he'll pay off what's owing at once. And then we'd have nothing more to do with you.
KROGSTAD [*taking a pace towards her*]. Listen, Mrs. Helmer, either you haven't a very good memory, or else you don't understand much about business. I'd better make the position a little bit clearer for you.
NORA. How do you mean?
KROGSTAD. When your husband was ill, you came to me for the loan of twelve hundred dollars.
NORA. I didn't know of anybody else.
KROGSTAD. I promised to find you the money. . . .
NORA. And you did find it.
KROGSTAD. I promised to find you the money on certain conditions. At the time you were so concerned about your husband's illness, and so anxious to get the money for going away with, that I don't think you paid very much attention to all the incidentals. So there is perhaps some point in reminding you of them. Well, I promised to find you the money against an IOU which I drew up for you.
NORA. Yes, and which I signed.
KROGSTAD. Very good. But below that I added a few lines, by which your father was to stand security. This your father was to sign.
NORA. Was to . . . ? He did sign it.
KROGSTAD. I had left the date blank. The idea was that your father was to add the date himself when he signed it. Remember?
NORA. Yes, I think. . . .
KROGSTAD. I then gave you the IOU to post to your father. Wasn't that so?
NORA. Yes.
KROGSTAD. Which of course you did at once. Because only about five or six days later you brought it back to me with your father's signature. I then paid out the money.
NORA. Well? Haven't I paid the installments regularly?
KROGSTAD. Yes, fairly. But . . . coming back to what we were talking about . . . that was a pretty bad period you were going through then, Mrs. Helmer.

NORA. Yes, it was.

KROGSTAD. Your father was seriously ill, I believe.

NORA. He was very near the end.

KROGSTAD. And died shortly afterwards?

NORA. Yes.

KROGSTAD. Tell me, Mrs. Helmer, do you happen to remember which day your father died? The exact date, I mean.

NORA. Daddy died on 29 September.

KROGSTAD. Quite correct. I made some inquiries. Which brings up a rather curious point [*takes out a paper*] which I simply cannot explain.

NORA. Curious . . . ? I don't know . . .

KROGSTAD. The curious thing is, Mrs. Helmer, that your father signed this document three days after his death.

NORA. What? I don't understand. . . .

KROGSTAD. Your father died on 29 September. But look here. Your father has dated his signature 2 October. Isn't that rather curious, Mrs. Helmer? [NORA *remains silent.*] It's also remarkable that the words '2 October' and the year are not in your father's handwriting, but in a handwriting I rather think I recognize. Well, perhaps that could be explained. Your father might have forgotten to date his signature, and then somebody else might have made a guess at the date later, before the fact of your father's death was known. There is nothing wrong in that. What really matters is the signature. And *that* is of course genuine, Mrs. Helmer? It really was your father who wrote his name here?

NORA [*after a moment's silence, throws her head back and looks at him defiantly*]. No, it wasn't. It was me who signed father's name.

KROGSTAD. Listen to me. I suppose you realize that that is a very dangerous confession?

NORA. Why? You'll soon have all your money back.

KROGSTAD. Let me ask you a question: why didn't you send that document to your father?

NORA. It was impossible. Daddy was ill. If I'd asked him for his signature, I'd have to tell him what the money was for. Don't you see, when he was as ill as that I couldn't go and tell him that my husband's life was in danger. It was simply impossible.

KROGSTAD. It would have been better for you if you had abandoned the whole trip.

NORA. No, that was impossible. This was the thing that was to save my husband's life. I couldn't give it up.

KROGSTAD. But did it never strike you that this was fraudulent . . . ?

NORA. That wouldn't have meant anything to me. Why should I worry about you? I couldn't stand you, not when you insisted on going through with all those cold-blooded formalities, knowing all the time what a critical state my husband was in.

KROGSTAD.  Mrs. Helmer, it's quite clear you still haven't the faintest idea what it is you've committed. But let me tell you, my own offence was no more and no worse than that, and it ruined my entire reputation.

NORA.  You? Are you trying to tell me that you once risked everything to save your wife's life?

KROGSTAD.  The law takes no account of motives.

NORA.  Then they must be very bad laws.

KROGSTAD.  Bad or not, if I produce this document in court, you'll be condemned according to them.

NORA.  I don't believe it. Isn't a daughter entitled to try and save her father from worry and anxiety on his deathbed? Isn't a wife entitled to save her husband's life? I might not know very much about the law, but I feel sure of one thing: it must say somewhere that things like this are allowed. You mean to say you don't know that—you, when it's your job? You must be a rotten lawyer, Mr. Krogstad.

KROGSTAD.  That may be. But when it comes to business transactions—like the sort between us two—perhaps you'll admit I know something about them? Good. Now you must please yourself. But I tell you this: if I'm pitched out a second time, you are going to keep me company.

[*He bows and goes out through the hall.*]

NORA [*stands thoughtfully for a moment, then tosses her head*].  Rubbish! He's just trying to scare me. I'm not such a fool as all that. [*Begins gathering up the children's clothes; after a moment she stops.*] Yet . . . ? No, it's impossible! I did it for love, didn't I?

THE CHILDREN [*in the doorway, left*].  Mummy, the gentleman's just gone out of the gate.

NORA.  Yes, I know. But you mustn't say anything to anybody about that gentleman. You hear? Not even to Daddy!

THE CHILDREN.  All right, Mummy. Are you going to play again?

NORA.  No, not just now.

THE CHILDREN.  But Mummy, you promised!

NORA.  Yes, but I can't just now. Off you go now, I have a lot to do. Off you go, my darlings. [*She herds them carefully into the other room and shuts the door behind them. She sits down on the sofa, picks up her embroidery and works a few stitches, but soon stops.*] No! [*She flings her work down, stands up, goes to the hall door and calls out.*] Helene! Fetch the tree in for me, please. [*She walks across to the table, left, and opens the drawer; again pauses.*] No, really, it's quite impossible!

MAID [*with the Christmas tree*].  Where shall I put it, ma'am?

NORA.  On the floor there, in the middle.

MAID.  Anything else you want me to bring?

NORA.  No, thank you. I've got what I want.

[*The* MAID *has put the tree down and goes out.*]

NORA [*busy decorating the tree*]. Candles here . . . and flowers here—
Revolting man! It's all nonsense! There's nothing to worry about. We'll
have a lovely Christmas tree. And I'll do anything you want me to, Torvald; I'll sing for you, dance for you. . . .

[HELMER, *with a bundle of documents under his arm, comes in by
the hall door.*]

NORA. Ah, back again already?
HELMER. Yes. Anybody been?
NORA. Here? No.
HELMER. That's funny. I just saw Krogstad leave the house.
NORA. Oh? O yes, that's right. Krogstad was here a minute.
HELMER. Nora, I can tell by your face he's been asking you to put a good
word in for him.
NORA. Yes.
HELMER. And you were to pretend it was your own idea? You were to keep
quiet about his having been here. He asked you to do that as well,
didn't he?
NORA. Yes, Torvald. But . . .
HELMER. Nora, Nora, what possessed you to do a thing like that? Talking to
a person like him, making him promises? And then on top of every-
thing, to tell me a lie!
NORA. A lie . . . ?
HELMER. Didn't you say that nobody had been here? [*Wagging his finger
at her.*] Never again must my little song-bird do a thing like that!
Little song-birds must keep their pretty little beaks out of mischief;
no chirruping out of tune! [*Puts his arm round her waist.*] Isn't
that the way we want things to be? Yes, of course it is. [*Lets her go.*]
So let's say no more about it. [*Sits down by the stove.*] Ah, nice and
cozy here!

[*He glances through his papers.*]

NORA [*busy with the Christmas tree, after a short pause*]. Torvald!
HELMER. Yes.
NORA. I'm so looking forward to the fancy dress ball at the Stenborgs on
Boxing Day.
HELMER. And I'm terribly curious to see what sort of surprise you've got
for me.
NORA. Oh, it's too silly.
HELMER. Oh?
NORA. I just can't think of anything suitable. Everything seems so absurd,
so pointless.
HELMER. Has my little Nora come to that conclusion?

NORA [*behind his chair, her arms on the chair-back*]. Are you very busy, Torvald?

HELMER. Oh. . . .

NORA. What are all those papers?

HELMER. Bank matters.

NORA. Already?

HELMER. I have persuaded the retiring manager to give me authority to make any changes in organization or personnel I think necessary. I have to work on it over the Christmas week. I want everything straight by the New Year.

NORA. So that was why that poor Krogstad. . . .

HELMER. Hm!

NORA [*still leaning against the back of the chair, running her fingers through his hair*]. If you hadn't been so busy, Torvald, I'd have asked you to do me an awfully big favor.

HELMER. Let me hear it. What's it to be?

NORA. Nobody's got such good taste as you. And the thing is I do so want to look my best at the fancy dress ball. Torvald, couldn't you give me some advice and tell me what you think I ought to go as, and how I should arrange my costume?

HELMER. Aha! So my impulsive little woman is asking for somebody to come to her rescue, eh?

NORA. Please, Torvald, I never get anywhere without your help.

HELMER. Very well, I'll think about it. We'll find something.

NORA. That's sweet of you. [*She goes across to the tree again; pause.*] How pretty these red flowers look.—Tell me, was it really something terribly wrong this man Krogstad did?

HELMER. Forgery. Have you any idea what that means?

NORA. Perhaps circumstances left him no choice?

HELMER. Maybe. Or perhaps, like so many others, he just didn't think. I am not so heartless that I would necessarily want to condemn a man for a single mistake like that.

NORA. Oh no, Torvald, of course not!

HELMER. Many a man might be able to redeem himself, if he honestly confessed his guilt and took his punishment.

NORA. Punishment?

HELMER. But that wasn't the way Krogstad chose. He dodged what was due to him by a cunning trick. And that's what has been the cause of his corruption.

NORA. Do you think it would . . . ?

HELMER. Just think how a man with a thing like that on his conscience will always be having to lie and cheat and dissemble; he can never drop the mask, not even with his own wife and children. And the children—that's the most terrible part of it, Nora.

NORA. Why?

HELMER.  A fog of lies like that in a household, and it spreads disease and infection to every part of it. Every breath the children take in that kind
of house is reeking with evil germs.

NORA [*closer behind him*].  Are you sure of that?

HELMER.  My dear Nora, as a lawyer I know what I'm talking about. Practically all juvenile delinquents come from homes where the mother is
dishonest.

NORA.  Why mothers particularly?

HELMER.  It's generally traceable to the mothers, but of course fathers can
have the same influence. Every lawyer knows that only too well. And
yet there's Krogstad been poisoning his own children for years with
lies and deceit. That's the reason I call him morally depraved. [*Holds
out his hands to her.*] That's why my sweet little Nora must promise
me not to try putting in any more good words for him. Shake hands
on it. Well? What's this? Give me your hand. There now! That's settled.
I assure you I would have found it impossible to work with him. I
quite literally feel physically sick in the presence of such people.

NORA [*draws her hand away and walks over to the other side of the
Christmas tree*].  How hot it is in here! And I still have such a lot to do.

HELMER [*stands up and collects his papers together*].  Yes, I'd better think
of getting some of this read before dinner. I must also think about
your costume. And I might even be able to lay my hands on something to wrap in gold paper and hang on the Christmas tree. [*He lays
his hand on her head.*] My precious little singing bird.

[*He goes into his study and shuts the door behind him.*]

NORA [*quietly, after a pause*].  Nonsense! It can't be. It's impossible. It
*must* be impossible.

MAID [*in the doorway, left*].  The children keep asking so nicely if they can
come in and see Mummy.

NORA.  No, no, don't let them in! You stay with them, Anne Marie.

MAID.  Very well, ma'am.

[*She shuts the door.*]

NORA [*pale with terror*].  Corrupt my children . . . ! Poison my home?
[*Short pause; she throws back her head.*] It's not true! It could never,
never be true!

## Act II

*The same room. In the corner beside the piano stands the Christmas
tree, stripped, bedraggled and with its candles burnt out.* NORA'S *outdoor
things lie on the sofa.* NORA, *alone there, walks about restlessly; at last
she stops by the sofa and picks up her coat.*

NORA [*putting her coat down again*]. Somebody's coming! [*Crosses to the door, listens.*] No, it's nobody. Nobody will come today, of course, Christmas Day—nor tomorrow, either. But perhaps. . . . [*She opens the door and looks out.*] No, nothing in the letter box; quite empty. [*Comes forward.*] Oh, nonsense! He didn't mean it seriously. Things like that can't happen. It's impossible. Why, I have three small children.

[*The* NURSEMAID *comes from the room, left, carrying a big cardboard box.*]

NURSEMAID.  I finally found it, the box with the fancy dress costumes.

NORA.  Thank you. Put it on the table, please.

NURSEMAID [*does this*].  But I'm afraid they are in an awful mess.

NORA.  Oh, if only I could rip them up into a thousand pieces!

NURSEMAID.  Good heavens, they can be mended all right, with a bit of patience.

NORA.  Yes, I'll go over and get Mrs. Linde to help me.

NURSEMAID.  Out again? In this terrible weather? You'll catch your death of cold, Ma'am.

NORA.  Oh, worse things might happen.—How are the children?

NURSEMAID.  Playing with their Christmas presents, poor little things, but . . .

NORA.  Do they keep asking for me?

NURSEMAID.  They are so used to being with their Mummy.

NORA.  Yes, Anne Marie, from now on I can't be with them as often as I was before.

NURSEMAID.  Ah well, children get used to anything in time.

NORA.  Do you think so? Do you think they would forget their Mummy if she went away for good?

NURSEMAID.  Good gracious—for good?

NORA.  Tell me, Anne Marie—I've often wondered—how on earth could you bear to hand your child over to strangers?

NURSEMAID.  Well, there was nothing else for it when I had to come and nurse my little Nora.

NORA.  Yes but . . . how could you *bring* yourself to do it?

NURSEMAID.  When I had the chance of such a good place? When a poor girl's been in trouble she must make the best of things. Because *he* didn't help, the rotter.

NORA.  But your daughter will have forgotten you.

NURSEMAID.  Oh no, she hasn't. She wrote to me when she got confirmed, and again when she got married.

NORA [*putting her arms round her neck*].  Dear old Anne Marie, you were a good mother to me when I was little.

NURSEMAID.  My poor little Nora never had any other mother but me.

NORA.  And if my little ones only had you, I know you would. . . . Oh, what am I talking about! [*She opens the box.*] Go in to them. I must . . . Tomorrow I'll let you see how pretty I am going to look.

NURSEMAID. Ah, there'll be nobody at the ball as pretty as my Nora.

[*She goes into the room, left.*]

NORA [*begins unpacking the box, but soon throws it down*]. Oh, if only I dare go out. If only I could be sure nobody would come. And that nothing would happen in the meantime here at home. Rubbish—nobody's going to come. I mustn't think about it. Brush this muff. Pretty gloves, pretty gloves! I'll put it right out of my mind. One, two, three, four, five, six. . . . [*Screams.*] Ah, they are coming. . . . [*She starts towards the door, but stops irresolute.* MRS. LINDE *comes from the hall, where she has taken off her things.*] Oh, it's you, Kristine. There's nobody else out there, is there? I'm so glad you've come.

MRS. LINDE. I heard you'd been over looking for me.

NORA. Yes, I was just passing. There's something you must help me with. Come and sit beside me on the sofa here. You see, the Stenborgs are having a fancy dress party upstairs tomorrow evening, and now Torvald wants me to go as a Neapolitan fisher lass and dance the tarantella. I learned it in Capri, you know.

MRS. LINDE. Well, well! So you are going to do a party piece?

NORA. Torvald says I should. Look, here's the costume, Torvald had it made for me down there. But it's got all torn and I simply don't know. . . .

MRS. LINDE. We'll soon have that put right. It's only the trimming come away here and there. Got a needle and thread? Ah, here's what we are after.

NORA. It's awfully kind of you.

MRS. LINDE. So you are going to be all dressed up tomorrow, Nora? Tell you what—I'll pop over for a minute to see you in all your finery. But I'm quite forgetting to thank you for the pleasant time we had last night.

NORA [*gets up and walks across the room*]. Somehow I didn't think yesterday was as nice as things generally are.—You should have come to town a little earlier, Kristine.—Yes, Torvald certainly knows how to make things pleasant about the place.

MRS. LINDE. You too, I should say. You are not your father's daughter for nothing. But tell me, is Dr. Rank always as depressed as he was last night?

NORA. No, last night it was rather obvious. He's got something seriously wrong with him, you know. Tuberculosis of the spine, poor fellow. His father was a horrible man, who used to have mistresses and things like that. That's why the son was always ailing, right from being a child.

MRS. LINDE [*lowering her sewing*]. But my dear Nora, how do you come to know about things like that?

NORA [*walking about the room*]. Huh! When you've got three children, you get these visits from . . . women who have had a certain amount of medical training. And you hear all sorts of things from them.

MRS. LINDE [*begins sewing again; short silence*]. Does Dr. Rank call in every day?

NORA.  Every single day. He was Torvald's best friend as a boy, and he's a good friend of mine, too. Dr. Rank is almost like one of the family.

MRS. LINDE.  But tell me—is he really genuine? What I mean is: doesn't he sometimes rather turn on the charm?

NORA.  No, on the contrary. What makes you think that?

MRS. LINDE.  When you introduced me yesterday, he claimed he'd often heard my name in this house. But afterwards I noticed your husband hadn't the faintest idea who I was. Then how is it that Dr. Rank should. . . .

NORA.  Oh yes, it was quite right what he said, Kristine. You see Torvald is so terribly in love with me that he says he wants me all to himself. When we were first married, it even used to make him sort of jealous if I only as much as mentioned any of my old friends from back home. So of course I stopped doing it. But I often talk to Dr. Rank about such things. He likes hearing about them.

MRS. LINDE.  Listen, Nora! In lots of ways you are still a child. Now, I'm a good deal older than you, and a bit more experienced. I'll tell you something: I think you ought to give up all this business with Dr. Rank.

NORA.  Give up what business?

MRS. LINDE.  The whole thing, I should say. Weren't you saying yesterday something about a rich admirer who was to provide you with money. . . .

NORA.  One who's never existed, I regret to say. But what of it?

MRS. LINDE.  Has Dr. Rank money?

NORA.  Yes, he has.

MRS. LINDE.  And no dependents?

NORA.  No, nobody. But. . . ?

MRS. LINDE.  And he comes to the house every day?

NORA.  Yes, I told you.

MRS. LINDE.  But how can a man of his position want to pester you like this?

NORA.  I simply don't understand.

MRS. LINDE.  Don't pretend, Nora. Do you think I don't see now who you borrowed the twelve hundred from?

NORA.  Are you out of your mind? Do you really think that? A friend of ours who comes here every day? The whole situation would have been absolutely intolerable.

MRS. LINDE.  It *really* isn't him?

NORA.  No, I give you my word. It would never have occurred to me for one moment. . . . Anyway, he didn't have the money to lend then. He didn't inherit it till later.

MRS. LINDE.  Just as well for you, I'd say, my dear Nora.

NORA.  No, it would never have occurred to me to ask Dr. Rank. . . . All the same I'm pretty certain if I were to ask him . . .

MRS. LINDE.  But of course you won't.

NORA.  No, of course not. I can't ever imagine it being necessary. But I'm quite certain if ever I were to mention it to Dr. Rank. . . .

MRS. LINDE.  Behind your husband's back?

NORA.  I have to get myself out of that other business. That's also behind his back. I must get myself out of that.

MRS. LINDE.  Yes, that's what I said yesterday. But . . .

NORA [*walking up and down*].  A man's better at coping with these things than a woman. . . .

MRS. LINDE.  Your own husband, yes.

NORA.  Nonsense! [*Stops.*] When you've paid everything you owe, you do get your IOU back again, don't you?

MRS. LINDE.  Of course.

NORA.  And you can tear it up into a thousand pieces and burn it—the nasty, filthy thing!

MRS. LINDE [*looking fixedly at her, puts down her sewing and slowly rises*].  Nora, you are hiding something from me.

NORA.  Is it so obvious?

MRS. LINDE.  Something has happened to you since yesterday morning. Nora, what is it?

NORA [*going towards her*].  Kristine! [*Listens.*] Hush! There's Torvald back. Look, you go and sit in there beside the children for the time being. Torvald can't stand the sight of mending lying about. Get Anne Marie to help you.

MRS. LINDE [*gathering a lot of the things together*].  All right, but I'm not leaving until we have thrashed this thing out.

[*She goes into the room, left; at the same time* HELMER *comes in from the hall.*]

NORA [*goes to meet him*].  I've been longing for you to be back, Torvald, dear.

HELMER.  Was that the dressmaker . . . ?

NORA.  No, it was Kristine; she's helping me with my costume. I think it's going to look very nice . . .

HELMER.  Wasn't that a good idea of mine, now?

NORA.  Wonderful! But wasn't it also nice of me to let you have your way?

HELMER [*taking her under the chin*].  Nice of you—because you let your husband have his way? All right, you little rogue, I know you didn't mean it that way. But I don't want to disturb you. You'll be wanting to try the costume on, I suppose.

NORA.  And I dare say you've got work to do?

HELMER.  Yes. [*Shows her a bundle of papers.*] Look at this. I've been down at the Bank. . . .

[*He turns to go into his study.*]

NORA.  Torvald!

HELMER [*stopping*].  Yes.

NORA. If a little squirrel were to ask ever so nicely . . . ?

HELMER. Well?

NORA. Would you do something for it?

HELMER. Naturally I would first have to know what it is.

NORA. Please, if only you would let it have its way, and do what it wants, it'd scamper about and do all sorts of marvelous tricks.

HELMER. What is it?

NORA. And the pretty little skylark would sing all day long. . . .

HELMER. Huh! It does that anyway.

NORA. I'd pretend I was an elfin child and dance a moonlight dance for you, Torvald.

HELMER. Nora—I hope it's not that business you started on this morning?

NORA [*coming closer*]. Yes, it is, Torvald. I implore you!

HELMER. You have the nerve to bring that up again?

NORA. Yes, yes, you *must* listen to me. You must let Krogstad keep his job at the Bank.

HELMER. My dear Nora, I'm giving his job to Mrs. Linde.

NORA. Yes, it's awfully sweet of you. But couldn't you get rid of somebody else in the office instead of Krogstad?

HELMER. This really is the most incredible obstinacy! Just because you go and make some thoughtless promise to put in a good word for him, you expect me . . .

NORA. It's not that, Torvald. It's for your own sake. That man writes in all the nastiest papers, you told me that yourself. He can do you no end of harm. He terrifies me to death. . . .

HELMER. Aha, now I see. It's your memories of what happened before that are frightening you.

NORA. What do you mean?

HELMER. It's your father you are thinking of.

NORA. Yes . . . yes, that's right. You remember all the nasty insinuations those wicked people put in the papers about Daddy? I honestly think they would have had him dismissed if the Ministry hadn't sent you down to investigate, and you hadn't been so kind and helpful.

HELMER. My dear little Nora, there is a considerable difference between your father and me. Your father's professional conduct was not entirely above suspicion. Mine is. And I hope it's going to stay that way as long as I hold this position.

NORA. But nobody knows what some of these evil people are capable of. Things could be so nice and pleasant for us here, in the peace and quiet of our home—you and me and the children, Torvald! That's why I implore you. . . .

HELMER. The more you plead for him, the more impossible you make it for me to keep him on. It's already known down at the Bank that I am going to give Krogstad his notice. If it ever got around that the new manager had been talked over by his wife. . . .

NORA. What of it?

HELMER. Oh, nothing! As long as the little woman gets her own stubborn way . . . ! Do you want me to make myself a laughing stock in the office? . . . Give people the idea that I am susceptible to any kind of outside pressure? You can imagine how soon I'd feel the consequences of that! Anyway, there's one other consideration that makes it impossible to have Krogstad in the Bank as long as I am manager.

NORA. What's that?

HELMER. At a pinch I might have overlooked his past lapses. . . .

NORA. Of course you could, Torvald!

HELMER. And I'm told he's not bad at his job, either. But we knew each other rather well when we were younger. It was one of those rather rash friendships that prove embarrassing in later life. There's no reason why you shouldn't know we were once on terms of some familiarity. And he, in his tactless way, makes no attempt to hide the fact, particularly when other people are present. On the contrary, he thinks he has every right to treat me as an equal, with his "Torvald this" and "Torvald that" every time he opens his mouth. I find it extremely irritating, I can tell you. He would make my position at the Bank absolutely intolerable.

NORA. Torvald, surely you aren't serious?

HELMER. Oh? Why not?

NORA. Well, it's all so petty.

HELMER. What's that you say? Petty? Do you think I'm petty?

NORA. No, not at all, Torvald dear! And that's why . . .

HELMER. Doesn't make any difference! . . . You call my motives petty; so I must be petty too. Petty! Indeed! Well, we'll put a stop to that, once and for all. [He opens the hall door and calls.] Helene!

NORA. What are you going to do?

HELMER [searching among his papers]. Settle things. [The maid comes in.] See this letter? I want you to take it down at once. Get hold of a messenger and get him to deliver it. Quickly. The address is on the outside. There's the money.

MAID. Very good, sir.

[She goes with the letter.]

HELMER [putting his papers together]. There now, my stubborn little miss.

NORA [breathless]. Torvald . . . what was that letter?

HELMER. Krogstad's notice.

NORA. Get it back, Torvald! There's still time! Oh, Torvald, get it back! Please for my sake, for your sake, for the sake of the children! Listen, Torvald, please! You don't realize what it can do to us.

HELMER. Too late.

NORA. Yes, too late.

HELMER.  My dear Nora, I forgive you this anxiety of yours, although it is
actually a bit of an insult. Oh, but it is, I tell you! It's hardly flattering
to suppose that anything this miserable pen-pusher wrote could
frighten *me!* But I forgive you all the same, because it is rather a
sweet way of showing how much you love me. [*He takes her in his
arms.*] This is how things must be, my own darling Nora. When it
comes to the point, I've enough strength and enough courage, believe me, for whatever happens. You'll find I'm man enough to take
everything on myself.

NORA [*terrified*].  What do you mean?

HELMER.  Everything, I said. . . .

NORA [*in command of herself*].  That is something you shall never,
never do.

HELMER.  All right, then we'll share it, Nora—as man and wife. That's what
we'll do. [*Caressing her.*] Does that make you happy now? There,
there, don't look at me with those eyes, like a little frightened dove.
The whole thing is sheer imagination.—Why don't you run through
the tarantella and try out the tambourine? I'll go into my study and
shut both the doors, then I won't hear anything. You can make all the
noise you want. [*Turns in the doorway.*] And when Rank comes, tell
him where he can find me.

[*He nods to her, goes with his papers into his room, and shuts the
door behind him.*]

NORA [*wild-eyed with terror, stands as though transfixed*].  He's quite capable of doing it! He would do it! No matter what, he'd do it.—No,
never in this world! Anything but that! Help? Some way out . . . ? [*The
doorbell rings in the hall.*] Dr. Rank . . . ! Anything but that, anything!
[*She brushes her hands over her face, pulls herself together and
opens the door into the hall.* DR. RANK *is standing outside hanging
up his fur coat. During what follows it begins to grow dark.*] Hello,
Dr. Rank. I recognized your ring. Do you mind not going in to Torvald
just yet, I think he's busy.

RANK.  And you?

[DR. RANK *comes into the room and she closes the door behind him.*]

NORA.  Oh, you know very well I've always got time for you.

RANK.  Thank you. A privilege I shall take advantage of as long as I am able.

NORA.  What do you mean—as long as you are able?

RANK.  Does that frighten you?

NORA.  Well, it's just that it sounds so strange. Is anything likely to happen?

RANK.  Only what I have long expected. But I didn't think it would come
quite so soon.

NORA [*catching at his arm*].  What have you found out? Dr. Rank, you must
tell me!

RANK. I'm slowly sinking. There's nothing to be done about it.

NORA [*with a sigh of relief*]. Oh, it's *you* you're . . . ?

RANK. Who else? No point in deceiving oneself. I am the most wretched of all my patients, Mrs. Helmer. These last few days I've made a careful analysis of my internal economy. Bankrupt! Within a month I shall probably be lying rotting up there in the churchyard.

NORA. Come now, what a ghastly thing to say!

RANK. The whole damned thing is ghastly. But the worst thing is all the ghastliness that has to be gone through first. I only have one more test to make; and when that's done I'll know pretty well when the final disintegration will start. There's something I want to ask you. Helmer is a sensitive soul; he loathes anything that's ugly. I don't want him visiting me. . . .

NORA. But Dr. Rank. . . .

RANK. On no account must he. I won't have it. I'll lock the door on him.— As soon as I'm absolutely certain of the worst, I'll send you my visiting card with a black cross on it. You'll know then the final horrible disintegration has begun.

NORA. Really, you are being quite absurd today. And here was I hoping you would be in a thoroughly good mood.

RANK. With death staring me in the face? Why should I suffer for another man's sins? What justice is there in that? Somewhere, somehow, every single family must be suffering some such cruel retribution. . . .

NORA [*stopping up her ears*]. Rubbish! Do cheer up!

RANK. Yes, really the whole thing's nothing but a huge joke. My poor innocent spine must do penance for my father's gay subaltern life.

NORA [*by the table, left*]. Wasn't he rather partial to asparagus and *pâté de foie gras*?

RANK. Yes, he was. And truffles.

NORA. Truffles, yes. And oysters, too, I believe?

RANK. Yes, oysters, oysters, of course.

NORA. And all the port and champagne that goes with them. It does seem a pity all these delicious things should attack the spine.

RANK. Especially when they attack a poor spine that never had any fun out of them.

NORA. Yes, that is an awful pity.

RANK [*looks at her sharply*]. Hm. . . .

NORA [*after a pause*]. Why did you smile?

RANK. No, it was you who laughed.

NORA. No, it was you who smiled, Dr. Rank!

RANK [*getting up*]. You are a bigger rascal than I thought you were.

NORA. I feel full of mischief today.

RANK. So it seems.

NORA [*putting her hands on his shoulders*]. Dear, dear Dr. Rank, you mustn't go and die on Torvald and me.

RANK.  You wouldn't miss me for long. When you are gone, you are soon forgotten.

NORA [*looking at him anxiously*].  Do you think so?

RANK.  People make new contacts, then . . .

NORA.  Who make new contacts?

RANK.  Both you and Helmer will, when I'm gone. You yourself are already well on the way, it seems to me. What was this Mrs. Linde doing here last night?

NORA.  Surely you aren't jealous of poor Kristine?

RANK.  Yes, I am. She'll be my successor in this house. When I'm done for, I can see this woman. . . .

NORA.  Hush! Don't talk so loud, she's in there.

RANK.  Today as well? There you are, you see!

NORA.  Just to do some sewing on my dress. Good Lord, how absurd you are! [*She sits down on the sofa.*] Now Dr. Rank, cheer up. You'll see tomorrow how nicely I can dance. And you can pretend I'm doing it just for you—and for Torvald as well, of course. [*She takes various things out of the box.*] Come here, Dr. Rank. I want to show you something.

RANK [*sits*].  What is it?

NORA.  Look!

RANK.  Silk stockings.

NORA.  Flesh-coloured! Aren't they lovely! Of course, it's dark here now, but tomorrow. . . . No, no, no, you can only look at the feet. Oh well, you might as well see a bit higher up, too.

RANK.  Hm. . . .

NORA.  Why are you looking so critical? Don't you think they'll fit?

RANK.  I couldn't possibly offer any informed opinion about that.

NORA [*looks at him for a moment*].  Shame on you. [*Hits him lightly across the ear with the stockings.*] Take that! [*Folds them up again.*]

RANK.  And what other delights am I to be allowed to see?

NORA.  Not another thing. You are too naughty. [*She hums a little and searches among her things.*]

RANK [*after a short pause*].  Sitting here so intimately like this with you, I can't imagine . . . I simply cannot conceive what would have become of me if I had never come to this house.

NORA [*smiles*].  Yes, I rather think you do enjoy coming here.

RANK [*in a low voice, looking fixedly ahead*].  And the thought of having to leave it all . . .

NORA.  Nonsense. You aren't leaving.

RANK [*in the same tone*].  . . . without being able to leave behind even the slightest token of gratitude, hardly a fleeting regret even . . . nothing but an empty place to be filled by the first person that comes along.

NORA.  Supposing I were to ask you to . . . ? No . . .

RANK.  What?

NORA.  . . . to show me the extent of your friendship . . .

RANK.  Yes?

NORA.  I mean . . . to do me a tremendous favor. . . .

RANK.  Would you really, for once, give me that pleasure?

NORA.  You have no idea what it is.

RANK.  All right, tell me.

NORA.  No, really I can't, Dr. Rank. It's altogether too much to ask . . . because I need your advice and help as well. . . .

RANK.  The more the better. I cannot imagine what you have in mind. But tell me anyway. You do trust me, don't you?

NORA.  Yes, I trust you more than anybody I know. You are my best and my most faithful friend. I know that. So I will tell you. Well then, Dr. Rank, there is something you must help me to prevent. You know how deeply, how passionately Torvald is in love with me. He would never hesitate for a moment to sacrifice his life for my sake.

RANK. [bending towards her]. Nora . . . do you think he's the only one who . . . ?

NORA [stiffening slightly]. Who . . . ?

RANK. Who wouldn't gladly give his life for your sake.

NORA [sadly]. Oh!

RANK.  I swore to myself you would know before I went. I'll never have a better opportunity. Well, Nora! Now you know. And now you know too that you can confide in me as in nobody else.

NORA [rises and speaks evenly and calmly]. Let me past.

RANK [makes way for her, but remains seated]. Nora. . . .

NORA [in the hall doorway]. Helene, bring the lamp in, please. [Walks over to the stove.] Oh, my dear Dr. Rank, that really was rather horrid of you.

RANK [getting up]. That I have loved you every bit as much as anybody? Is that horrid?

NORA.  No, but that you had to go and tell me. When it was all so unnecessary. . . .

RANK.  What do you mean? Did you know . . . ?

[The MAID comes in with the lamp, puts it on the table, and goes out again.]

RANK.  Nora . . . Mrs. Helmer . . . I'm asking you if you knew?

NORA.  How can I tell whether I did or didn't. I simply can't tell you. . . . Oh, how could you be so clumsy, Dr. Rank! When everything was so nice.

RANK.  Anyway, you know now that I'm at your service, body and soul. So you can speak out.

NORA [looking at him]. After this?

RANK.  I beg you to tell me what it is.

NORA.  I can tell you nothing now.

RANK.   You must. You can't torment me like this. Give me a chance—I'll do anything that's humanly possible.

NORA.   You can do nothing for me now. Actually, I don't really need any help. It's all just my imagination, really it is. Of course! [*She sits down in the rocking chair, looks at him and smiles.*] I must say, you are a nice one, Dr. Rank! Don't you feel ashamed of yourself, now the lamp's been brought in?

RANK.   No, not exactly. But perhaps I ought to go—for good?

NORA.   No, you mustn't do that. You must keep coming just as you've always done. You know very well Torvald would miss you terribly.

RANK.   And *you?*

NORA.   I always think it's tremendous fun having you.

RANK.   That's exactly what gave me wrong ideas. I just can't puzzle you out. I often used to feel you'd just as soon be with me as with Helmer.

NORA.   Well, you see, there are those people you love and those people you'd almost rather *be* with.

RANK.   Yes, there's something in that.

NORA.   When I was a girl at home, I loved Daddy best, of course. But I also thought it great fun if I could slip into the maids' room. For one thing they never preached at me. And they always talked about such exciting things.

RANK.   Aha! So it's their role I've taken over!

NORA   [*jumps up and crosses to him*].   Oh, my dear, kind Dr. Rank, I didn't mean that at all. But you can see how it's a bit with Torvald as it was with Daddy. . . .

[*The* MAID *comes in from the hall.*]

MAID.   Please, ma'am . . . !

[*She whispers and hands her a card.*]

NORA   [*glances at the card*]. Ah!

[*She puts it in her pocket.*]

RANK.   Anything wrong?

NORA.   No, no, not at all. It's just . . . it's my new costume. . . .

RANK.   How is that? There's your costume in there.

NORA.   That one, yes. But this is another one. I've ordered it. Torvald mustn't hear about it. . . .

RANK.   Ah, so that's the big secret, is it!

NORA.   Yes, that's right. Just go in and see him, will you? He's in the study. Keep him occupied for the time being. . . .

RANK.   Don't worry. He shan't escape me.

[*He goes into* HELMER's *study.*]

NORA   [*to the* MAID].   Is he waiting in the kitchen?

MAID.  Yes, he came up the back stairs. . . .
NORA.  But didn't you tell him somebody was here?
MAID.  Yes, but it was no good.
NORA.  Won't he go?
MAID.  No, he won't till he's seen you.
NORA.  Let him in, then. But quietly. Helene, you mustn't tell anybody about
this. It's a surprise for my husband.
MAID.  I understand, ma'am. . . .

[*She goes out.*]

NORA.  Here it comes! What I've been dreading! No, no, it can't happen, it
*can't* happen.

[*She walks over and bolts* HELMER'*s door. The* MAID *opens the hall
door for* KROGSTAD *and shuts it again behind him. He is wearing a
fur coat, overshoes, and a fur cap.*]

NORA [*goes towards him*].  Keep your voice down, my husband is at home.
KROGSTAD.  What if he is?
NORA.  What do you want with me?
KROGSTAD.  To find out something.
NORA.  Hurry, then. What is it?
KROGSTAD.  You know I've been given notice.
NORA.  I couldn't prevent it, Mr. Krogstad, I did my utmost for you, but it
was no use.
KROGSTAD.  Has your husband so little affection for you? He knows what I
can do to you, yet he dares. . . .
NORA.  You don't imagine he knows about it!
KROGSTAD.  No, I didn't imagine he did. It didn't seem a bit like my good
friend Torvald Helmer to show that much courage. . . .
NORA.  Mr. Krogstad, I must ask you to show some respect for my husband.
KROGSTAD.  Oh, sure! All due respect! But since you are so anxious to keep
this business quiet, Mrs. Helmer, I take it you now have a rather
clearer idea of just what it is you've done, than you had yesterday.
NORA.  Clearer than *you* could ever have given me.
KROGSTAD.  Yes, being as I am such a rotten lawyer. . . .
NORA.  What do *you* want with me?
KROGSTAD.  I just wanted to see how things stood, Mrs. Helmer. I've been
thinking about you all day. Even a mere money-lender, a hack jour-
nalist, a—well, even somebody like me has a bit of what you might
call feeling.
NORA.  Show it then. Think of my little children.
KROGSTAD.  Did you or your husband think of mine? But what does it matter
now? There was just one thing I wanted to say: you needn't take this
business too seriously. I shan't start any proceedings, for the present.
NORA.  Ah, I knew you wouldn't.

KROGSTAD. The whole thing can be arranged quite amicably. Nobody need know. Just the three of us.

NORA. My husband must never know.

KROGSTAD. How can you prevent it? Can you pay off the balance?

NORA. No, not immediately.

KROGSTAD. Perhaps you've some way of getting hold of the money in the next few days.

NORA. None I want to make use of.

KROGSTAD. Well, it wouldn't have been very much help to you if you had. Even if you stood there with the cash in your hand and to spare, you still wouldn't get your IOU back from me now.

NORA. What are you going to do with it?

KROGSTAD. Just keep it—have it in my possession. Nobody who isn't implicated need know about it. So if you are thinking of trying any desperate remedies . . .

NORA. Which I am. . . .

KROGSTAD. . . . if you happen to be thinking of running away . . .

NORA. Which I am!

KROGSTAD. . . . or anything worse . . .

NORA. How did you know?

KROGSTAD. . . . forget it!

NORA. How did you know I was thinking of *that?*

KROGSTAD. Most of us think of *that,* to begin with. I did, too; but I didn't have the courage. . . .

NORA [*tonelessly*]. I haven't either.

KROGSTAD [*relieved*]. So you haven't the courage either, eh?

NORA. No, I haven't! I haven't!

KROGSTAD. It would also be very stupid. There'd only be the first domestic storm to get over. . . . I've got a letter to your husband in my pocket here. . . .

NORA. And it's all in there?

KROGSTAD. In as tactful a way as possible.

NORA [*quickly*]. He must never read that letter. Tear it up. I'll find the money somehow.

KROGSTAD. Excuse me, Mrs. Helmer, but I've just told you. . . .

NORA. I'm not talking about the money I owe you. I want to know how much you are demanding from my husband, and I'll get the money.

KROGSTAD. I want no money from your husband.

NORA. What do you want?

KROGSTAD. I'll tell you. I want to get on my feet again, Mrs. Helmer; I want to get to the top. And your husband is going to help me. For the last eighteen months I've gone straight; all that time it's been hard going; I was content to work my way up, step by step. Now I'm being kicked out, and I won't stand for being taken back again as an act of charity. I'm going to get to the top, I tell you. I'm going back into that Bank—

with a better job. Your husband is going to create a new vacancy, just
for me. . . .

NORA. He'll never do that!

KROGSTAD. He will do it. I know him. He'll do it without so much as a
whimper. And once I'm in there with him, you'll see what's what. In
less than a year I'll be his right-hand man. It'll be Nils Krogstad, not
Torvald Helmer, who'll be running that Bank.

NORA. You'll never live to see that day!

KROGSTAD. You mean you . . . ?

NORA. Now I have the courage.

KROGSTAD. You can't frighten me! A precious pampered little thing like
you. . . .

NORA. I'll show you! I'll show you!

KROGSTAD. Under the ice, maybe? Down in the cold, black water? Then
being washed up in the spring, bloated, hairless, unrecognizable. . . .

NORA. You can't frighten me.

KROGSTAD. You can't frighten me, either. People don't do that sort of thing,
Mrs. Helmer. There wouldn't be any point to it, anyway, I'd still have
him right in my pocket.

NORA. Afterwards? When I'm no longer . . .

KROGSTAD. Aren't you forgetting that your reputation would then be entirely in my hands? [NORA *stands looking at him, speechless.*] Well,
I've warned you. Don't do anything silly. When Helmer gets my letter,
I expect to hear from him. And don't forget: it's him who is forcing me
off the straight and narrow again, your own husband! That's something I'll never forgive him for. Goodbye, Mrs. Helmer.

[*He goes out through the hall.* NORA *crosses to the door, opens it
slightly, and listens.*]

NORA. He's going. He hasn't left the letter. No, no, that would be impossible! [*Opens the door further and further.*] What's he doing? He's
stopped outside. He's not going down the stairs. Has he changed his
mind? Is he . . . ? [*A letter falls into the letter box. Then* KROGSTAD'S
*footsteps are heard receding as he walks downstairs.* NORA *gives a
stifled cry, runs across the room to the sofa table; pause.*] In the letter box! [*She creeps stealthily across to the hall door.*] There it is! Torvald, Torvald! It's hopeless now!

MRS. LINDE. [*comes into the room, left, carrying the costume*]. There,
I think that's everything. Shall we try it on?

NORA [*in a low, hoarse voice*]. Kristine, come here.

MRS. LINDE [*throws the dress down on the sofa*]. What's wrong with you?
You look upset.

NORA. Come here. Do you see that letter? There, look! Through the glass in
the letter box.

MRS. LINDE. Yes, yes, I can see it.

NORA.  It's a letter from Krogstad.

MRS. LINDE.  Nora! It was Krogstad who lent you the money!

NORA.  Yes. And now Torvald will get to know everything.

MRS. LINDE.  Believe me, Nora, it's best for you both.

NORA.  But there's more to it than that. I forged a signature. . . .

MRS. LINDE.  Heavens above!

NORA.  Listen, I want to tell you something, Kristine, so you can be my witness.

MRS. LINDE.  What do you mean, "witness"? What do you want me to . . . ?

NORA.  If I should go mad . . . which might easily happen . . .

MRS. LINDE.  Nora!

NORA.  Or if anything happened to me . . . which meant I couldn't be here. . . .

MRS. LINDE.  Nora, Nora! Are you out of your mind?

NORA.  And if somebody else wanted to take it all upon himself, the whole blame, you understand. . . .

MRS. LINDE.  Yes, yes. But what makes you think . . . ?

NORA.  Then you must testify that it isn't true, Kristine. I'm not out of my mind; I'm quite sane now. And I tell you this: nobody else knew anything, I alone was responsible for the whole thing. Remember that!

MRS. LINDE.  I will. But I don't understand a word of it.

NORA.  Why should you? You see something miraculous is going to happen.

MRS. LINDE.  Something miraculous?

NORA.  Yes, a miracle. But something so terrible as well, Kristine—oh, it must never happen, not for anything.

MRS. LINDE.  I'm going straight over to talk to Krogstad.

NORA.  Don't go. He'll only do you harm.

MRS. LINDE.  There was a time when he would have done anything for me.

NORA.  Him!

MRS. LINDE.  Where does he live?

NORA.  How do I know . . . ? Wait a minute. [*She feels in her pocket.*] Here's his card. But the letter, the letter . . . !

HELMER [*from his study, knocking on the door*].  Nora!

NORA [*cries out in terror*].  What's that? What do you want?

HELMER.  Don't be frightened. We're not coming in. You've locked the door. Are you trying on?

NORA.  Yes, yes, I'm trying on. It looks so nice on me, Torvald.

MRS. LINDE [*who has read the card*].  He lives just round the corner.

NORA.  It's no use. It's hopeless. The letter is there in the box.

MRS. LINDE.  Your husband keeps the key?

NORA.  Always.

MRS. LINDE.  Krogstad must ask for his letter back unread, he must find some sort of excuse. . . .

NORA.  But this is just the time that Torvald generally . . .

MRS. LINDE. Put him off! Go in and keep him busy. I'll be back as soon as I can.

[*She goes out hastily by the hall door.* NORA *walks over to* HELMER'S *door, opens it and peeps in.*]

NORA. Torvald!

HELMER [*in the study*]. Well, can a man get into his own living room again now? Come along, Rank, now we'll see . . . [*In the doorway.*] But what's this?

NORA. What, Torvald dear?

HELMER. Rank led me to expect some kind of marvelous transformation.

RANK [*in the doorway*]. That's what I thought too, but I must have been mistaken.

NORA. I'm not showing myself off to anybody before tomorrow.

HELMER. Nora dear, you look tired. You haven't been practising too hard?

NORA. No, I haven't practised at all yet.

HELMER. You'll have to, though.

NORA. Yes, I certainly must, Torvald. But I just can't get anywhere without your help: I've completely forgotten it.

HELMER. We'll soon polish it up.

NORA. Yes, do help me, Torvald. Promise? I'm so nervous. All those people. . . . You must devote yourself exclusively to me this evening. Pens away! Forget all about the office! Promise me, Torvald dear!

HELMER. I promise. This evening I am wholly and entirely at your service . . . helpless little thing that you are. Oh, but while I remember, I'll just look first . . .

[*He goes towards the hall door.*]

NORA. What do you want out there?

HELMER. Just want to see if there are any letters.

NORA. No, don't, Torvald!

HELMER. Why not?

NORA. Torvald, *please!* There aren't any.

HELMER. Just let me see.

[*He starts to go.* NORA, *at the piano, plays the opening bars of the tarantella.*]

HELMER [*at the door, stops*]. Aha!

NORA. I shan't be able to dance tomorrow if I don't rehearse it with you.

HELMER [*walks to her*]. Are you really so nervous, Nora dear?

NORA. Terribly nervous. Let me run through it now. There's still time before supper. Come and sit here and play for me, Torvald dear. Tell me what to do, keep me right—as you always do.

HELMER. Certainly, with pleasure, if that's what you want.

[*He sits at the piano.* NORA *snatches the tambourine out of the box, and also a long gaily coloured shawl which she drapes round herself, then with a bound she leaps forward.*]

NORA [*shouts*].  Now play for me! Now I'll dance!

[HELMER *plays and* NORA *dances;* DR. RANK *stands at the piano behind* HELMER *and looks on.*]

HELMER [*playing*].  Not so fast! Not so fast!

NORA.  I can't help it.

HELMER.  Not so wild, Nora!

NORA.  This is how it has to be.

HELMER [*stops*].  No, no, that won't do at all.

NORA [*laughs and swings the tambourine*].  Didn't I tell you?

RANK.  Let me play for her.

HELMER [*gets up*].  Yes, do. Then I'll be better able to tell her what to do.

[RANK *sits down at the piano and plays.* NORA *dances more and more wildly.* HELMER *stands by the stove giving her repeated directions as she dances; she does not seem to hear them. Her hair comes undone and falls about her shoulders; she pays no attention and goes on dancing.* MRS. LINDE *enters.*]

MRS. LINDE [*standing as though spellbound in the doorway*].  Ah . . . !

NORA [*dancing*].  See what fun we are having, Kristine.

HELMER.  But my dear darling Nora, you are dancing as though your life depended on it.

NORA.  It does.

HELMER.  Stop, Rank! This is sheer madness. Stop, I say.

[RANK *stops playing and* NORA *comes to a sudden halt.*]

HELMER [*crosses to her*].  I would never have believed it. You have forgotten everything I ever taught you.

NORA [*throwing away the tambourine*].  There you are, you see.

HELMER.  Well, some more instruction is certainly needed there.

NORA.  Yes, you see how necessary it is. You must go on coaching me right up to the last minute. Promise me, Torvald?

HELMER.  You can rely on me.

NORA.  You mustn't think about anything else but me until after tomorrow . . . mustn't open any letters . . . mustn't touch the letter box.

HELMER.  Ah, you are still frightened of what that man might . . .

NORA.  Yes, yes, I am.

HELMER.  I can see from your face there's already a letter there from him.

NORA.  I don't know. I think so. But you mustn't read anything like that now. We don't want anything horrid coming between us until all this is over.

RANK [*softly to* HELMER]. I shouldn't cross her.

HELMER [*puts his arm round her*]. The child must have her way. But tomorrow night, when your dance is done. . . .

NORA. Then you are free.

MAID [*in the doorway, right*]. Dinner is served, madam.

NORA. We'll have champagne, Helene.

MAID. Very good, madam.

    [*She goes.*]

HELMER. Aha! It's to be quite a banquet, eh?

NORA. With champagne flowing until dawn. [*Shouts.*] And some macaroons, Helene . . . lots of them, for once in a while.

HELMER [*seizing her hands*]. Now, now, not so wild and excitable! Let me see you being my own little singing bird again.

NORA. Oh yes, I will. And if you'll just go in . . . you, too, Dr. Rank. Kristine, you must help me to do my hair.

RANK [*softly, as they leave*]. There isn't anything . . . anything as it were, impending, is there?

HELMER. No, not at all, my dear fellow. It's nothing but these childish tears I was telling you about.

    [*They go out to the right.*]

NORA. Well?

MRS. LINDE. He's left town.

NORA. I saw it in your face.

MRS. LINDE. He's coming back tomorrow evening. I left a note for him.

NORA. You shouldn't have done that. You must let things take their course.
    Because really it's a case for rejoicing, waiting like this for the miracle.

MRS. LINDE. What is it you are waiting for?

NORA. Oh, you wouldn't understand. Go and join the other two. I'll be there in a minute.

    [MRS. LINDE *goes into the dining-room.* NORA *stands for a moment as though to collect herself, then looks at her watch.*]

NORA. Five. Seven hours to midnight. Then twenty-four hours till the next midnight. Then the tarantella will be over. Twenty-four and seven? Thirty-one hours to live.

HELMER [*in the doorway, right*]. What's happened to our little sky-lark?

NORA [*running towards him with open arms*]. Here she is!

## Act III

*The same room. The round table has been moved to the center of the room, and the chairs placed round it. A lamp is burning on the table. The door to the hall stands open. Dance music can be heard coming from the floor above.* MRS. LINDE *is sitting by the table, idly turning over the pages of a book; she tries to read, but does not seem able to concentrate. Once or twice she listens, tensely, for a sound at the front door.*

MRS. LINDE [*looking at her watch*].  Still not here. There isn't much time left. I only hope he hasn't . . . [*She listens again.*] Ah, there he is. [*She goes out into the hall, and cautiously opens the front door. Soft footsteps can be heard on the stairs. She whispers.*] Come in. There's nobody here.

KROGSTAD [*in the doorway*].  I found a note from you at home. What does it all mean?

MRS. LINDE.  I *had* to talk to you.

KROGSTAD.  Oh? And did it have to be here, in this house?

MRS. LINDE.  It wasn't possible over at my place, it hasn't a separate entrance. Come in. We are quite alone. The maid's asleep and the Helmers are at a party upstairs.

KROGSTAD [*comes into the room*].  Well, well! So the Helmers are out dancing tonight! Really?

MRS. LINDE.  Yes, why not?

KROGSTAD.  Why not indeed!

MRS. LINDE.  Well then, Nils. Let's talk.

KROGSTAD.  Have we two anything more to talk about?

MRS. LINDE.  We have a great deal to talk about.

KROGSTAD.  I shouldn't have thought so.

MRS. LINDE.  That's because you never really understood me.

KROGSTAD.  What else was there to understand, apart from the old, old story? A heartless woman throws a man over the moment something more profitable offers itself.

MRS. LINDE.  Do you really think I'm so heartless? Do you think I found it easy to break it off?

KROGSTAD.  Didn't you?

MRS. LINDE.  You didn't really believe that?

KROGSTAD.  If that wasn't the case, why did you write to me as you did?

MRS. LINDE.  There was nothing else I could do. If I had to make the break, I felt in duty bound to destroy any feeling that you had for me.

KROGSTAD [*clenching his hands*].  So that's how it was. And all that . . . was for money!

MRS. LINDE.  You mustn't forget I had a helpless mother and two young brothers. We couldn't wait for you, Nils. At that time you hadn't much immediate prospect of anything.

KROGSTAD.  That may be. But you had no right to throw me over for somebody else.

MRS. LINDE.  Well, I don't know. Many's the time I've asked myself whether I was justified.

KROGSTAD [*more quietly*]. When I lost you, it was just as if the ground had slipped away from under my feet. Look at me now: a broken man clinging to the wreck of his life.

MRS. LINDE. Help might be near.

KROGSTAD. It was near. Then you came along and got in the way.

MRS. LINDE. Quite without knowing, Nils. I only heard today it's you I'm supposed to be replacing at the Bank.

KROGSTAD. If you say so, I believe you. But now you do know, aren't you going to withdraw?

MRS. LINDE. No, that wouldn't benefit you in the slightest.

KROGSTAD. Benefit, benefit . . . ! I would do it just the same.

MRS. LINDE. I have learned to go carefully. Life and hard, bitter necessity have taught me that.

KROGSTAD. And life has taught me not to believe in pretty speeches.

MRS. LINDE. Then life has taught you a very sensible thing. But deeds are something you surely must believe in?

KROGSTAD. How do you mean?

MRS. LINDE. You said you were like a broken man clinging to the wreck of his life.

KROGSTAD. And I said it with good reason.

MRS. LINDE. And I am like a broken woman clinging to the wreck of her life. Nobody to care about, and nobody to care for.

KROGSTAD. It was your own choice.

MRS. LINDE. At the time there was no other choice.

KROGSTAD. Well, what of it?

MRS. LINDE. Nils, what about us two castaways joining forces?

KROGSTAD. What's that you say?

MRS. LINDE. Two of us on one wreck surely stand a better chance than each on his own.

KROGSTAD. Kristine!

MRS. LINDE. Why do you suppose I came to town?

KROGSTAD. You mean, you thought of me?

MRS. LINDE. Without work I couldn't live. All my life I have worked, for as long as I can remember; that has always been my one great joy. But now I'm completely alone in the world, and feeling horribly empty and forlorn. There's no pleasure in working only for yourself. Nils, give me somebody and something to work for.

KROGSTAD. I don't believe all this. It's only a woman's hysteria, wanting to be all magnanimous and self-sacrificing.

MRS. LINDE. Have you ever known me hysterical before?

KROGSTAD. Would you really do this? Tell me—do you know all about my past?

MRS. LINDE. Yes.

KROGSTAD. And you know what people think about me?

MRS. LINDE. Just now you hinted you thought you might have been a different person with me.

KROGSTAD. I'm convinced I would.

MRS. LINDE. Couldn't it still happen?

KROGSTAD. Kristine! You know what you are saying, don't you? Yes, you do. I can see you do. Have you really the courage . . . ?

MRS. LINDE. I need someone to mother, and your children need a mother. We two need each other. Nils, I have faith in what, deep down, you are. With you I can face anything.

KROGSTAD [*seizing her hands*]. Thank you, thank you, Kristine. And I'll soon have everybody looking up to me, or I'll know the reason why. Ah, but I was forgetting. . . .

MRS. LINDE. Hush! The tarantella! You must go!

KROGSTAD. Why? What is it?

MRS. LINDE. You hear that dance upstairs? When it's finished they'll be coming.

KROGSTAD. Yes, I'll go. It's too late to do anything. Of course, you know nothing about what steps I've taken against the Helmers.

MRS. LINDE. Yes, Nils, I do know.

KROGSTAD. Yet you still want to go on. . . .

MRS. LINDE. I know how far a man like you can be driven by despair.

KROGSTAD. Oh, if only I could undo what I've done!

MRS. LINDE. You still can. Your letter is still there in the box.

KROGSTAD. Are you sure?

MRS. LINDE. Quite sure. But . . .

KROGSTAD [*regards her searchingly*]. Is that how things are? You want to save your friend at any price? Tell me straight. Is that it?

MRS. LINDE. When you've sold yourself *once* for other people's sake, you don't do it again.

KROGSTAD. I shall demand my letter back.

MRS. LINDE. No, no.

KROGSTAD. Of course I will, I'll wait here till Helmer comes. I'll tell him he has to give me my letter back . . . that it's only about my notice . . . that he mustn't read it. . . .

MRS. LINDE. No, Nils, don't ask for it back.

KROGSTAD. But wasn't that the very reason you got me here?

MRS. LINDE. Yes, that was my first terrified reaction. But that was yesterday, and it's quite incredible the things I've witnessed in this house in the last twenty-four hours. Helmer must know everything. This unhappy secret must come out. Those two must have the whole thing out between them. All this secrecy and deception, it just can't go on.

KROGSTAD. Well, if you want to risk it . . . . But one thing I can do, and I'll do it at once. . . .

MRS. LINDE [*listening*]. Hurry! Go, go! The dance has stopped. We aren't safe a moment longer.

KROGSTAD. I'll wait for you downstairs.

MRS. LINDE. Yes, do. You must see me home.

KROGSTAD. I've never been so incredibly happy before.

[*He goes out by the front door. The door out into the hall remains standing open.*]

MRS. LINDE [*tidies the room a little and gets her hat and coat ready*]. How things change! How things change! Somebody to work for . . . to live for. A home to bring happiness into. Just let me get down to it. . . . I wish they'd come. . . . [*Listens.*] Ah, there they are. . . . Get my things.

[*She takes her coat and hat. The voices of* HELMER *and* NORA *are heard outside. A key is turned and* HELMER *pushes* NORA *almost forcibly into the hall. She is dressed in the Italian costume, with a big black shawl over it. He is in evening dress, and over it a black cloak, open.*]

NORA [*still in the doorway, reluctantly*]. No, no, not in here! I want to go back up again. I don't want to leave so early.

HELMER. But my dearest Nora . . .

NORA. Oh, please, Torvald, I beg you. . . . *Please,* just for another hour.

HELMER. Not another minute, Nora my sweet. You remember what we agreed. There now, come along in. You'll catch cold standing there.

[*He leads her, in spite of her resistance, gently but firmly into the room.*]

MRS. LINDE. Good evening.

NORA. Kristine!

HELMER. Why, Mrs. Linde. You here so late?

MRS. LINDE. Yes. You must forgive me but I did so want to see Nora all dressed up.

NORA. Have you been sitting here waiting for me?

MRS. LINDE. Yes, I'm afraid I wasn't in time to catch you before you went upstairs. And I felt I couldn't leave again without seeing you.

HELMER [*removing* NORA'S *shawl*]. Well take a good look at her. I think I can say she's worth looking at. Isn't she lovely, Mrs. Linde?

MRS. LINDE. Yes, I must say. . . .

HELMER. Isn't she quite extraordinarily lovely? That's what everybody at the party thought, too. But she's dreadfully stubborn . . . the sweet little thing! And what shall we do about that? Would you believe it, I nearly had to use force to get her away.

NORA. Oh Torvald, you'll be sorry you didn't let me stay, even for half an hour.

HELMER. You hear that, Mrs. Linde? She dances her tarantella, there's wild applause—which was well deserved, although the performance was

perhaps rather realistic . . . I mean, rather more so than was strictly
necessary from the artistic point of view. But anyway! The main thing
is she was a success, a tremendous success. Was I supposed to let her
stay after that? Spoil the effect? No thank you! I took my lovely little
Capri girl—my capricious little Capri girl, I might say—by the arm,
whisked her once round the room, a curtsey all round, and then—as
they say in novels—the beautiful vision vanished. An exit should
always be effective, Mrs. Linde. But I just can't get Nora to see that.
Phew! It's warm in here. [*He throws his cloak over a chair and
opens the door to his study.*] What? It's dark. Oh yes, of course. Excuse me. . . .

[*He goes in and lights a few candles.*]

NORA [*quickly, in a breathless whisper*]. Well?

MRS. LINDE [*softly*]. I've spoken to him.

NORA. And . . . ?

MRS. LINDE. Nora . . . you must tell your husband everything.

NORA [*tonelessly*]. I knew it.

MRS. LINDE. You've got nothing to fear from Krogstad. But you must speak.

NORA. I won't.

MRS. LINDE. Then the letter will.

NORA. Thank you, Kristine. Now I know what's to be done. Hush . . . !

HELMER [*comes in again*]. Well, Mrs. Linde, have you finished admiring
her?

MRS. LINDE. Yes. And now I must say good night.

HELMER. Oh, already? Is this yours, this knitting?

MRS. LINDE [*takes it*]. Yes, thank you. I nearly forgot it.

HELMER. So you knit, eh?

MRS. LINDE. Yes.

HELMER. You should embroider instead, you know.

MRS. LINDE. Oh? Why?

HELMER. So much prettier. Watch! You hold the embroidery like this in the
left hand, and then you take the needle in the right hand, like this, and
you describe a long, graceful curve. Isn't that right?

MRS. LINDE. Yes, I suppose so. . . .

HELMER. Whereas knitting on the other hand just can't help being ugly.
Look! Arms pressed into the sides, the knitting needles going up and
down—there's something Chinese about it. . . . Ah, that was marvelous champagne they served tonight.

MRS. LINDE. Well, good night, Nora! And stop being so stubborn.

HELMER. Well said, Mrs. Linde!

MRS. LINDE. Good night, Mr. Helmer.

HELMER [*accompanying her to the door*]. Good night, good night! You'll
get home all right, I hope? I'd be only too pleased to. . . . But you
haven't far to walk. Good night, good night! [*She goes; he shuts the

*door behind her and comes in again.*] There we are, got rid of her at
last. She's a frightful bore, that woman.

NORA. Aren't you very tired, Torvald?

HELMER. Not in the least.

NORA. Not sleepy?

HELMER. Not at all. On the contrary, I feel extremely lively. What about you?
Yes, you look quite tired and sleepy.

NORA. Yes, I'm very tired. I just want to fall straight off to sleep.

HELMER. There you are, you see! Wasn't I right in thinking we shouldn't
stay any longer.

NORA. Oh, everything you do is right.

HELMER [*kissing her forehead*]. There's my little sky-lark talking common
sense. Did you notice how gay Rank was this evening?

NORA. Oh, was he? I didn't get a chance to talk to him.

HELMER. I hardly did either. But it's a long time since I saw him in such a
good mood. [*Looks at* NORA *for a moment or two, then comes nearer
her.*] Ah, it's wonderful to be back in our own home again, and quite
alone with you. How irresistibly lovely you are, Nora!

NORA. Don't look at me like that, Torvald!

HELMER. Can't I look at my most treasured possession? At all this loveliness
that's mine and mine alone, completely and utterly mine.

NORA [*walks round to the other side of the table*]. You mustn't talk to me
like that tonight.

HELMER [*following her*]. You still have the tarantella in your blood, I see.
And that makes you even more desirable. Listen! The guests are beginning to leave now. [*Softly.*] Nora . . . soon the whole house will be
silent.

NORA. I should hope so.

HELMER. Of course you do, don't you, Nora my darling? You know, whenever I'm out at a party with you . . . do you know why I never talk to
you very much, why I always stand away from you and only steal a
quick glance at you now and then . . . do you know why I do that? It's
because I'm pretending we are secretly in love, secretly engaged and
nobody suspects there is anything between us.

NORA. Yes, yes. I know your thoughts are always with me, of course.

HELMER. And when it's time to go, and I lay your shawl round those
shapely, young shoulders, round the exquisite curve of your neck . . .
I pretend that you are my young bride, that we are just leaving our
wedding, that I am taking you to our new home for the first time . . .
to be alone with you for the first time . . . quite alone with your
young and trembling loveliness! All evening I've been longing for you,
and nothing else. And as I watched you darting and swaying in the
tarantella, my blood was on fire . . . I couldn't bear it any longer . . .
and that's why I brought you down here with me so early. . . .

NORA. Go away, Torvald! Please leave me alone. I won't have it.

HELMER. What's this? It's just your little game isn't it, my little Nora. Won't!
  Won't! Am I not your husband . . . ?

[*There is a knock on the front door.*]

NORA [*startled*]. Listen . . . !

HELMER [*going towards the hall*]. Who's there?

RANK [*outside*]. It's me. Can I come in for a minute?

HELMER [*in a low voice, annoyed*]. Oh, what does he want now? [*Aloud*]
  Wait a moment. [*He walks across and opens the door.*] How nice of
  you to look in on your way out.

RANK. I fancied I heard your voice and I thought I would just look in. [*He
  takes a quick glance round.*] Ah yes, this dear, familiar old place!
  How cozy and comfortable you've got things here, you two.

HELMER. You seemed to be having a pretty good time upstairs yourself.

RANK. Capital! Why shouldn't I? Why not make the most of things in this
  world? At least as much as one can, and for as long as one can. The
  wine was excellent. . . .

HELMER. Especially the champagne.

RANK. You noticed that too, did you? It's incredible the amount I was able
  to put away.

NORA. Torvald also drank a lot of champagne this evening.

RANK. Oh?

NORA. Yes, and that always makes him quite merry.

RANK. Well, why shouldn't a man allow himself a jolly evening after a day
  well spent?

HELMER. Well spent? I'm afraid I can't exactly claim that.

RANK [*clapping him on the shoulder*]. But I can, you see!

NORA. Dr. Rank, am I right in thinking you carried out a certain laboratory
  test today?

RANK. Exactly.

HELMER. Look at our little Nora talking about laboratory tests!

NORA. And may I congratulate you on the result?

RANK. You may indeed.

NORA. So it was good?

RANK. The best possible, for both doctor and patient—certainty!

NORA [*quickly and searchingly*]. Certainty?

RANK. Absolute certainty. So why shouldn't I allow myself a jolly evening
  after that?

NORA. Quite right, Dr. Rank.

HELMER. I quite agree. As long as you don't suffer for it in the morning.

RANK. Well, you never get anything for nothing in this life.

NORA. Dr. Rank . . . you are very fond of masquerades, aren't you?

RANK. Yes, when there are plenty of amusing disguises. . . .

NORA. Tell me, what shall we two go as next time?

HELMER.  There's frivolity for you . . . thinking about the next time already!

RANK.  We two? I'll tell you. You must go as Lady Luck . . . .

HELMER.  Yes, but how do you find a costume to suggest *that?*

RANK.  Your wife could simply go in her everyday clothes. . . .

HELMER.  That was nicely said. But don't you know what you would be?

RANK.  Yes, my dear friend, I know exactly what I shall be.

HELMER.  Well?

RANK.  At the next masquerade, I shall be invisible.

HELMER.  That's a funny idea!

RANK.  There's a big black cloak . . . haven't you heard of the cloak of
   invisibility? That comes right down over you, and then nobody can
   see you.

HELMER [*suppressing a smile*].  Of course, that's right.

RANK.  But I'm clean forgetting what I came for. Helmer, give me a cigar,
   one of the dark Havanas.

HELMER.  With the greatest of pleasure.

   [*He offers his case.*]

RANK [*takes one and cuts the end off* ].  Thanks.

NORA [*strikes a match*].  Let me give you a light.

RANK.  Thank you. [*She holds out the match and he lights his cigar.*]  And
   now, goodbye!

HELMER.  Goodbye, goodbye, my dear fellow!

NORA.  Sleep well, Dr. Rank.

RANK.  Thank you for that wish.

NORA.  Wish me the same.

RANK.  You? All right, if you want me to. . . .  Sleep well. And thanks for the
   light.

   [*He nods to them both, and goes.*]

HELMER [*subdued*].  He's had a lot to drink.

NORA [*absently*].  Very likely.

   [HELMER *takes a bunch of keys out of his pocket and goes into
   the hall.*]

NORA.  Torvald . . . what do you want there?

HELMER.  I must empty the letter box, it's quite full. There'll be no room for
   the papers in the morning. . . .

NORA.  Are you going to work tonight?

HELMER.  You know very well I'm not. Hello, what's this? Somebody's been
   at the lock.

NORA.  At the lock?

HELMER.  Yes, I'm sure of it. Why should that be? I'd hardly have thought the
   maids . . . ? Here's a broken hairpin. Nora, it's one of yours. . . .

NORA [*quickly*].  It must have been the children. . . .

HELMER.  Then you'd better tell them not to. Ah . . . there . . . I've managed to get it open. [*He takes the things out and shouts into the kitchen.*] Helene! . . . Helene, put the light out in the hall. [*He comes into the room again with the letters in his hand and shuts the hall door.*] Look how it all mounts up. [*Runs through them.*] What's this?

NORA.  The letter! Oh no, Torvald, no!

HELMER.  Two visiting cards . . . from Dr. Rank.

NORA.  From Dr. Rank?

HELMER [*looking at them*].  Dr. Rank, Medical Practitioner. They were on top. He must have put them in as he left.

NORA.  Is there anything on them?

HELMER.  There's a black cross above his name. Look. What an uncanny idea. It's just as if he were announcing his own death.

NORA.  He is.

HELMER.  What? What do you know about it? Has he said anything to you?

NORA.  Yes. He said when these cards came, he would have taken his last leave of us. He was going to shut himself up and die.

HELMER.  Poor fellow! Of course I knew we couldn't keep him with us very long. But so soon. . . . And hiding himself away like a wounded animal.

NORA.  When it has to happen, it's best that it should happen without words. Don't you think so, Torvald?

HELMER [*walking up and down*].  He had grown so close to us. I don't think I can imagine him gone. His suffering and his loneliness seemed almost to provide a background of dark cloud to the sunshine of our lives. Well, perhaps it's all for the best. For him at any rate. [*Pauses.*] And maybe for us as well, Nora. Now there's just the two of us. [*Puts his arms round her.*] Oh, my darling wife, I can't hold you close enough. You know, Nora . . . many's the time I wish you were threatened by some terrible danger so I could risk everything, body and soul, for your sake.

NORA [*tears herself free and says firmly and decisively*].  Now you must read your letters, Torvald.

HELMER.  No, no, not tonight. I want to be with you, my darling wife.

NORA.  Knowing all the time your friend is dying . . . ?

HELMER.  You are right. It's been a shock to both of us. This ugly thing has come between us . . . thoughts of death and decay. We must try to free ourselves from it. Until then . . . we shall go our separate ways.

NORA [*her arms round his neck*].  Torvald . . . good night! Good night!

HELMER [*kisses her forehead*].  Goodnight, my little singing bird. Sleep well, Nora, I'll just read through my letters.

[*He takes the letters into his room and shuts the door behind him.*]

NORA [*gropes around her, wild-eyed, seizes* HELMER'S *cloak, wraps it round herself, and whispers quickly, hoarsely, spasmodically*].  Never see

him again. Never, never, never. [*Throws her shawl over her head.*]
And never see the children again either. Never, never. Oh, that black
icy water. Oh, that bottomless . . . ! If only it were all over! He's got it
now. Now he's reading it. Oh no, no! Not yet! Torvald, goodbye . . .
and my children. . . .

[*She rushes out in the direction of the hall; at the same moment*
HELMER *flings open his door and stands there with an open letter in
his hand.*]

HELMER.  Nora!
NORA [*shrieks*].  Ah!
HELMER.  What is this? Do you know what is in this letter?
NORA.  Yes, I know. Let me go! Let me out!
HELMER [*holds her back*].  Where are you going?
NORA [*trying to tear herself free*].  You mustn't try to save me, Torvald!
HELMER [*reels back*].  True! Is it true what he writes? How dreadful! No, no,
it can't possibly be true.
NORA.  It *is* true. I loved you more than anything else in the world.
HELMER.  Don't come to me with a lot of paltry excuses!
NORA [*taking a step towards him*].  Torvald . . . !
HELMER.  Miserable woman . . . what is this you have done?
NORA.  Let me go. I won't have you taking the blame for me. You mustn't
take it on yourself.
HELMER.  Stop play-acting! [*Locks the front door.*] You are staying here to
give an account of yourself. Do you understand what you have done?
Answer me! Do you understand?
NORA [*looking fixedly at him, her face hardening*].  Yes, now I'm really
beginning to understand.
HELMER [*walking up and down*].  Oh, what a terrible awakening this is.
All these eight years . . . this woman who was my pride and joy . . .
a hypocrite, a liar, worse than that, a criminal! Oh, how utterly squalid it
all is! Ugh! Ugh! [NORA *remains silent and looks fixedly at him.*]
I should have realized something like this would happen. I should
have seen it coming. All your father's irresponsible ways. . . . Quiet! All
your father's irresponsible ways are coming out in you. No religion, no
morals, no sense of duty. . . . Oh, this is my punishment for turning a
blind eye to him. It was for your sake I did it, and this is what I get for it.
NORA.  Yes, this.
HELMER.  Now you have ruined my entire happiness, jeopardized my whole
future. It's terrible to think of. Here I am, at the mercy of a thoroughly
unscrupulous person; he can do whatever he likes with me, demand
anything he wants, order me about just as he chooses . . . and I
daren't even whimper. I'm done for, a miserable failure, and it's all the
fault of a feather-brained woman!
NORA.  When I've left this world behind, you will be free.

HELMER.  Oh, stop pretending! Your father was just the same, always ready
with fine phrases. What good would it do me if you left this world behind, as you put it? Not the slightest bit of good. He can still let it all
come out, if he likes; and if he does, people might even suspect me of
being an accomplice in these criminal acts of yours. They might even
think I was the one behind it all, that it was I who pushed you into it!
And it's you I have to thank for this . . . and when I've taken such good
care of you, all our married life. Now do you understand what you have
done to me?

NORA [*coldly and calmly*].  Yes.

HELMER.  I just can't understand it, it's so incredible. But we must see about
putting things right. Take that shawl off. Take it off, I tell you! I must
see if I can't find some way or other of appeasing him. The thing must
be hushed up at all costs. And as far as you and I are concerned, things
must appear to go on exactly as before. But only in the eyes of the
world, of course. In other words you'll go on living here; that's understood. But you will not be allowed to bring up the children, I can't
trust you with them. . . . Oh, that I should have to say this to the
woman I loved so dearly, the woman I still. . . . Well, that must be
all over and done with. From now on, there can be no question of
happiness. All we can do is save the bits and pieces from the wreck,
preserve appearances. . . . [*The front door-bell rings.* HELMER *gives
a start.*] What's that? So late? How terrible, supposing. . . . If he
should . . . ? Hide, Nora! Say you are not well.

[NORA *stands motionless.* HELMER *walks across and opens the door
into the hall.*]

MAID [*half dressed, in the hall*].  It's a note for Mrs. Helmer.

HELMER.  Give it to me. [*He snatches the note and shuts the door.*] Yes, it's
from him. You can't have it. I want to read it myself.

NORA.  You read it then.

HELMER [*by the lamp*].  I hardly dare. Perhaps this is the end, for both of us.
Well, I must know. [*He opens the note hurriedly, reads a few lines,
looks at another enclosed sheet, and gives a cry of joy.*] Nora! [NORA
*looks at him inquiringly.*] Nora! I must read it again. Yes, yes, it's
true! I am saved! Nora, I am saved!

NORA.  And me?

HELMER.  You too, of course, we are both saved, you as well as me. Look,
he's sent your IOU back. He sends his regrets and apologies for what
he has done. . . . His luck has changed. . . . Oh, what does it matter
what he says. We are saved, Nora! Nobody can do anything to you
now. Oh, Nora, Nora . . . but let's get rid of this disgusting thing first.
Let me see. . . . [*He glances at the IOU.*] No, I don't want to see it. I
don't want it to be anything but a dream. [*He tears up the IOU and
both letters, throws all the pieces into the stove and watches them*

*burn.*] Well, that's the end of that. He said in his note you'd known
since Christmas Eve. . . . You must have had three terrible days of
it, Nora.

NORA. These three days haven't been easy.

HELMER.  The agonies you must have gone through! When the only way out
seemed to be. . . . No, let's forget the whole ghastly thing. We can rejoice and say: It's all over! It's all over! Listen to me, Nora! You don't
seem to understand: it's all over! Why this grim look on your face? Oh,
poor little Nora, of course I understand. You can't bring yourself to
believe I've forgiven you. But I have, Nora, I swear it. I forgive you
everything. I know you did what you did because you loved me.

NORA. That's true.

HELMER.  You loved me as a wife should love her husband. It was simply
that you didn't have the experience to judge what was the best way
of going about things. But do you think I love you any the less for
that; just because you don't know how to act on your own responsibility? No, no, you just lean on me, I shall give you all the advice and
guidance you need. I wouldn't be a proper man if I didn't find a
woman doubly attractive for being so obviously helpless. You mustn't
dwell on the harsh things I said in that first moment of horror, when
I thought everything was going to come crashing down about my
ears. I have forgiven you, Nora, I swear it! I have forgiven you!

NORA.  Thank you for your forgiveness.

[*She goes out through the door, right.*]

HELMER.  No, don't go! [*He looks through the doorway.*] What are you doing in the spare room?

NORA.  Taking off this fancy dress.

HELMER [*standing at the open door*].  Yes, do. You try and get some rest,
and set your mind at peace again, my frightened little songbird. Have
a good long sleep; you know you are safe and sound under my wing.
[*Walks up and down near the door.*] What a nice, cozy little home
we have here, Nora! Here you can find refuge. Here I shall hold you
like a hunted dove I have rescued unscathed from the cruel talons of
the hawk, and calm your poor beating heart. And that will come, gradually, Nora, believe me. Tomorrow you'll see everything quite differently. Soon everything will be just as it was before. You won't need
me to keep on telling you I've forgiven you; you'll feel convinced of it
in your own heart. You don't really imagine me ever thinking of turning you out, or even of reproaching you? Oh, a real man isn't made
that way, you know, Nora. For a man, there's something indescribably
moving and very satisfying in knowing that he has forgiven his wife—
forgiven her, completely and genuinely, from the depths of his heart.
It's as though it made her his property in a double sense: he has, as it
were, given her a new life, and she becomes in a way both his wife

and at the same time his child. That is how you will seem to me after today, helpless, perplexed little thing that you are. Don't you worry your pretty little head about anything, Nora. Just you be frank with me, and I'll take all the decisions for you. . . . What's this? Not in bed? You've changed your things?

NORA [*in her everyday dress*].  Yes, Torvald, I've changed.

HELMER.  What for? It's late.

NORA.  I shan't sleep tonight.

HELMER.  But my dear Nora. . . .

NORA [*looks at her watch*].  It's not so terribly late. Sit down, Torvald. We two have a lot to talk about.

[*She sits down at one side of the table.*]

HELMER.  Nora, what is all this? Why so grim?

NORA.  Sit down. It'll take some time. I have a lot to say to you.

HELMER [*sits down at the table opposite her*].  You frighten me, Nora. I don't understand you.

NORA.  Exactly. You don't understand me. And I have never understood you, either—until tonight. No, don't interrupt. I just want you to listen to what I have to say. We are going to have things out, Torvald.

HELMER.  What do you mean?

NORA.  Isn't there anything that strikes you about the way we two are sitting here?

HELMER.  What's that?

NORA.  We have now been married eight years. Hasn't it struck you this is the first time you and I, man and wife, have had a serious talk together?

HELMER.  Depends what you mean by "serious."

NORA.  Eight whole years—no, more, ever since we first knew each other—and never have we exchanged one serious word about serious things.

HELMER.  What did you want me to do? Get you involved in worries that you couldn't possibly help me to bear?

NORA.  I'm not talking about worries. I say we've never once sat down together and seriously tried to get to the bottom of anything.

HELMER.  But, my dear Nora, would that have been a thing for you?

NORA.  That's just it. You have never understood me . . . I've been greatly wronged, Torvald. First by my father, and then by you.

HELMER.  What! Us two! The two people who loved you more than anybody?

NORA [*shakes her head*].  You two never loved me. You only thought how nice it was to be in love with me.

HELMER.  But, Nora, what's this you are saying?

NORA.  It's right, you know, Torvald. At home, Daddy used to tell me what he thought, then I thought the same. And if I thought differently, I

kept quiet about it, because he wouldn't have liked it. He used to call
me his baby doll, and he played with me as I used to play with my
dolls.Then I came to live in your house. . . .

HELMER.  What way is that to talk about our marriage?

NORA [*imperturbably*].  What I mean is: I passed out of Daddy's hands into
yours.You arranged everything to your tastes, and I acquired the same
tastes. Or I pretended to . . . I don't really know . . . I think it was a
bit of both, sometimes one thing and sometimes the other.When I
look back, it seems to me I have been living here like a beggar, from
hand to mouth. I lived by doing tricks for you,Torvald. But that's the
way you wanted it.You and Daddy did me a great wrong. It's your
fault that I've never made anything of my life.

HELMER.  Nora, how unreasonable . . . how ungrateful you are! Haven't you
been happy here?

NORA.  No, never. I thought I was, but I wasn't really.

HELMER.  Not . . . not happy!

NORA.  No, just gay.And you've always been so kind to me. But our house
has never been anything but a playroom. I have been your doll wife,
just as at home I was Daddy's doll child.And the children in turn have
been my dolls. I thought it was fun when you came and played with
me, just as they thought it was fun when I went and played with
them.That's been our marriage,Torvald.

HELMER.  There is some truth in what you say, exaggerated and hysterical
though it is. But from now on it will be different. Playtime is over;
now comes the time for lessons.

NORA.  Whose lessons? Mine or the children's?

HELMER.  Both yours and the children's, my dear Nora.

NORA.  Ah,Torvald, you are not the man to teach me to be a good wife
for you.

HELMER.  How can you say that?

NORA.  And what sort of qualifications have I to teach the children?

HELMER.  Nora!

NORA.  Didn't you say yourself, a minute or two ago, that you couldn't trust
me with that job?

HELMER.  In the heat of the moment! You shouldn't pay any attention
to that.

NORA.  On the contrary, you were quite right. I'm not up to it.There's another problem needs solving first. I must take steps to educate myself. You are not the man to help me there.That's something I must
do on my own.That's why I'm leaving you.

HELMER [*jumps up*].  What did you say?

NORA.  If I'm ever to reach any understanding of myself and the things
around me, I must learn to stand alone.That's why I can't stay here
with you any longer.

HELMER.  Nora! Nora!

NORA. I'm leaving here at once. I dare say Kristine will put me up for
tonight. . . .

HELMER. You are out of your mind! I won't let you! I forbid you!

NORA. It's no use forbidding me anything now. I'm taking with me my
own personal belongings. I don't want anything of yours, either now
or later.

HELMER. This is madness!

NORA. Tomorrow I'm going home—to what used to be my home, I mean.
It will be easier for me to find something to do there.

HELMER. Oh, you blind, inexperienced . . .

NORA. I must set about *getting* experience, Torvald.

HELMER. And leave your home, your husband and your children? Don't you
care what people will say?

NORA. That's no concern of mine. All I know is that this is necessary
for me.

HELMER. This is outrageous! You are betraying your most sacred duty.

NORA. And what do you consider to be my most sacred duty?

HELMER. Does it take me to tell you that? Isn't it your duty to your husband
and your children?

NORA. I have another duty equally sacred.

HELMER. You have not. What duty might *that* be?

NORA. My duty to myself.

HELMER. First and foremost, you are a wife and mother.

NORA. That I don't believe any more. I believe that first and foremost I am
an individual, just as much as you are—or at least I'm going to try to
be. I know most people agree with you, Torvald, and that's also what
it says in books. But I'm not content any more with what most people say, or with what it says in books. I have to think things out for
myself, and get things clear.

HELMER. Surely you are clear about your position in your own home?
Haven't you an infallible guide in questions like these? Haven't you
your religion?

NORA. Oh, Torvald, I don't really know what religion is.

HELMER. What do you say!

NORA. All I know is what Pastor Hansen said when I was confirmed. He
said religion was this, that and the other. When I'm away from all
this and on my own, I'll go into that, too. I want to find out whether
what Pastor Hansen told me was right—or at least whether it's right
for *me*.

HELMER. This is incredible talk from a young woman! But if religion cannot keep you on the right path, let me at least stir your conscience.
I suppose you do have some moral sense? Or tell me—perhaps
you don't?

NORA. Well, Torvald, that's not easy to say. I simply don't know. I'm really
very confused about such things. All I know is my ideas about such

things are very different from yours. I've also learnt that the law is different from what I thought; but I simply can't get it into my head that that particular law is right. Apparently a woman has no right to spare her old father on his deathbed, or to save her husband's life, even. I just don't believe it.

HELMER. You are talking like a child. You understand nothing about the society you live in.

NORA. No, I don't. But I shall go into that too. I must try to discover who is right, society or me.

HELMER. You are ill, Nora. You are delirious. I'm half inclined to think you are out of your mind.

NORA. Never have I felt so calm and collected as I do tonight.

HELMER. Calm and collected enough to leave your husband and children?

NORA. Yes.

HELMER. Then only one explanation is possible.

NORA. And that is?

HELMER. You don't love me any more.

NORA. Exactly.

HELMER. Nora! Can you say that!

NORA. I'm desperately sorry, Torvald. Because you have always been so kind to me. But I can't help it. I don't love you any more.

HELMER [struggling to keep his composure]. Is that also a "calm and collected" decision you've made?

NORA. Yes, absolutely calm and collected. That's why I don't want to stay here.

HELMER. And can you also account for how I forfeited your love?

NORA. Yes, very easily. It was tonight, when the miracle didn't happen. It was then I realized you weren't the man I thought you were.

HELMER. Explain yourself more clearly. I don't understand.

NORA. For eight years I have been patiently waiting. Because, heavens, I knew miracles didn't happen every day. Then this devastating business started, and I became absolutely convinced the miracle *would* happen. All the time Krogstad's letter lay there, it never so much as crossed my mind that you would ever submit to that man's conditions. I was absolutely convinced you would say to him: Tell the whole wide world if you like. And when that was done . . .

HELMER. Yes, then what? After I had exposed my own wife to dishonor and shame . . . !

NORA. When that was done, I was absolutely convinced you would come forward and take everything on yourself, and say: I am the guilty one.

HELMER. Nora!

NORA. You mean I'd never let you make such a sacrifice for my sake? Of course not. But what would my story have counted for against yours?—That was the miracle I went in hope and dread of. It was to prevent it that I was ready to end my life.

HELMER.  I would gladly toil day and night for you, Nora, enduring all manner of sorrow and distress. But nobody sacrifices his *honor* for the
one he loves.

NORA.  Hundreds and thousands of women have.

HELMER.  Oh, you think and talk like a stupid child.

NORA.  All right. But you neither think nor talk like the man I would want
to share my life with. When you had got over your fright—and you
weren't concerned about me but only about what might happen to
you—and when all danger was past, you acted as though nothing had
happened. I was your little skylark again, your little doll, exactly as before; except you would have to protect it twice as carefully as before,
now that it had shown itself to be so weak and fragile. [*Rises.*] Torvald, that was the moment I realized that for eight years I'd been living with a stranger, and had borne him three children. . . . Oh, I can't
bear to think about it! I could tear myself to shreds.

HELMER [*sadly*].  I see. I see. There is a tremendous gulf dividing us. But,
Nora, is there no way we might bridge it?

NORA.  As I am now, I am no wife for you.

HELMER.  I still have it in me to change.

NORA.  Perhaps . . . if you have your doll taken away.

HELMER.  And be separated from you! No, no, Nora, the very thought of it is
inconceivable.

NORA [*goes into the room, right*].  All the more reason why it must be
done.

[*She comes back with her outdoor things and a small traveling
bag, which she puts on the chair beside the table.*]

HELMER.  Nora, Nora, not now! Wait till the morning.

NORA [*putting on her coat*].  I can't spend the night in a strange man's
room.

HELMER.  Couldn't we go on living here like brother and sister . . . ?

NORA [*tying on her hat*].  You know very well that wouldn't last. [*She
draws the shawl round her.*] Goodbye, Torvald. I don't want to see
the children. I know they are in better hands than mine. As I am now,
I can never be anything to them.

HELMER.  But some day, Nora, some day . . . ?

NORA.  How should I know? I've no idea what I might turn out to be.

HELMER.  But you are my wife, whatever you are.

NORA.  Listen, Torvald, from what I've heard, when a wife leaves her
husband's house as I am doing now, he is absolved by law of all responsibility for her. I can at any rate free you from all responsibility.
You must not feel in any way bound, any more than I shall. There
must be full freedom on both sides. Look, here's your ring back. Give
me mine.

HELMER.  That too?

NORA. That too.

HELMER. There it is.

NORA. Well, that's the end of that. I'll put the keys down here. The maids know where everything is in the house—better than I do, in fact. Kristine will come in the morning after I've left to pack up the few things I brought with me from home. I want them sent on.

HELMER. The end! Nora, will you never think of me?

NORA. I dare say I'll often think about you and the children and this house.

HELMER. May I write to you, Nora?

NORA. No, never. I won't let you.

HELMER. But surely I can send you . . .

NORA. Nothing, nothing.

HELMER. Can't I help you if ever you need it?

NORA. I said no. I don't accept things from strangers.

HELMER. Nora, can I never be anything more to you than a stranger?

NORA [takes her bag]. Ah, Torvald, only by a miracle of miracles . . .

HELMER. Name it, this miracle of miracles!

NORA. Both you and I would have to change to the point where. . . . Oh, Torvald, I don't believe in miracles any more.

HELMER. But I will believe. Name it! Change to the point where . . .?

NORA. Where we could make a real marriage of our lives together. Goodbye!

[She goes out through the hall door.]

HELMER [sinks down on a chair near the door, and covers his face with his hands]. Nora! Nora! [He rises and looks round.] Empty! She's gone! [With sudden hope.] The miracle of miracles . . . ?

[The heavy sound of a door being slammed is heard from below.]

### TOPICS FOR CRITICAL THINKING AND WRITING

1. Near the beginning of the play, how does Mrs. Linde's presence help to define Nora's character? How does Nora's response to Krogstad's entrance tell us something about Nora?

2. What does Dr. Rank contribute to the play? If he were eliminated, what would be lost?

3. Can it be argued that although at the end Nora goes out to achieve self-realization, her abandonment of her children—especially to Torvald's loathsome conventional morality—is a crime? (By the way, exactly why does Nora leave the children? She seems to imply, in some passages, that because she forged a signature she is unfit to bring them up. But do you agree with her?)

4. Michael Meyer, in his splendid biography *Henrik Ibsen,* says that the play is not so much about women's rights as about "the need of every individual to find out the kind of person he or she really is, and to strive to become that person." What evidence can you offer to support or refute this interpretation?

5. In *The Quintessence of Ibsenism* Bernard Shaw says that Ibsen, reacting against a common theatrical preference for strange situations, "saw that . . . the more familiar the situation, the more interesting the play. Shakespear[e] had put ourselves on the stage but not our situations. Our uncles seldom murder our fathers and . . . marry our mothers. . . . Ibsen . . . gives us not only ourselves, but ourselves in our own situations. The things that happen to his stage figures are things that happen to us. One consequence is that his plays are much more important to us than Shakespear[e]'s. Another is that they are capable both of hurting us cruelly and of filling us with excited hopes of escape from idealistic tyrannies, and with visions of intenser life in the future." How much of this do you believe? Focus on details in the play to explain your response.

# 28

# Two Classic Tragedies

## A NOTE ON THE GREEK THEATER

Little or nothing is known for certain of the origin of Greek tragedy. The most common hypothesis holds that it developed from improvised speeches during choral dances honoring Dionysus, a Greek nature god associated with spring, fertility, and wine. Thespis (who perhaps never existed) is said to have introduced an actor into these choral performances in the sixth century BCE Aeschylus (525–456 BCE), Greece's first great writer of tragedies, added the second actor, and Sophocles (495?–406 BCE) added the third actor and fixed the size of the chorus at fifteen. (Because the chorus leader often functioned as an additional actor, and because the actors sometimes doubled in their parts, a Greek tragedy could have more characters than might at first be thought.)

All the extant great Greek tragedy is of the fifth century BCE It was performed at religious festivals in the winter and early spring, in large outdoor amphitheaters built on hillsides. Some of these theaters were enormous; the one at Epidaurus held about fifteen thousand people. The audience sat in tiers, looking down on the **orchestra** (a dancing place), with the acting area behind it and the **skene** (the scene building) yet farther back. The scene building served as dressing room, background (suggesting a palace or temple), and place for occasional entrances and exits. Furthermore, this building helped to provide good acoustics, for speech travels well if there is a solid barrier behind the speakers and a hard, smooth surface in front of them, and if the audience sits in tiers. The wall of the scene building provided the barrier; the orchestra provided the surface in front of the actors; and the seats on the hillside fulfilled the third requirement. Moreover, the acoustics were somewhat improved by slightly elevating

Greek theater of Epidaurus on the Peloponnesus east of Nauplia.

the actors above the orchestra, but it is not known exactly when this platform was first constructed in front of the scene building.

A tragedy commonly begins with a **prologos (prologue)**, during which the exposition is given. Next comes the **párodos,** the chorus's ode of entrance, sung while the chorus marches into the theater through the side aisles and onto the orchestra. The **epeisodion (episode)** is the ensuing scene; it is followed by a **stasimon** (choral song, ode). Usually there are four or five *epeisodia,* alternating with *stasima.* Each of these choral odes has a **strophe** (lines presumably sung while the chorus dances in one direction) and an antistrophe (lines presumably sung while the chorus retraces its steps). Sometimes a third part, an **epode,** concludes an ode. (In addition to odes that are *stasima,* there can be odes within episodes; the fourth episode of *Antigonê* contains an ode complete with *epode.*) After the last part of the last ode comes the **exodos,** the epilogue or final scene.

The actors (all male) wore masks, and they seem to have chanted much of the play. Perhaps the total result of combining speech with music and dancing was a sort of music-drama roughly akin to opera with some spoken dialogue, such as Mozart's *The Magic Flute* (1791).

# SOPHOCLES

*One of the three great writers of tragedies in ancient Greece, Sophocles (496?–406 BCE) was born in Colonus, near Athens, into a well-to-do family. Well educated, he first won public acclaim as a tragic poet at the age of twenty seven, in 468 BCE when he defeated Aeschylus in a competition for writing a tragic play. He is said to have written some 120 plays, but only seven tragedies are extant: among them are* Oedipus Rex *(or* Oedipus the King, *as in Robert Fagles's translation below),* Antigone, *and* Oedipus at Colonus. *He died, much honored, in his ninetieth year, in Athens, where he had lived his entire life.*

## Oedipus the King

*Translated by Robert Fagles*

**CHARACTERS**

OEDIPUS, *king of Thebes*
A PRIEST OF ZEUS
CREON, *brother of Jocasta*
A CHORUS *of Theban citizens and their leader*
TIRESIAS, *a blind prophet*
JOCASTA, *the queen, wife of Oedipus*
A MESSENGER *from Corinth*
A SHEPHERD
A MESSENGER *from inside the palace*
ANTIGONE, ISMENE, *daughters of Oedipus and Jocasta*
GUARDS *and attendants*
PRIESTS *of Thebes*

Laurence Olivier in *Oedipus Rex.*

[**TIME AND SCENE:** *The royal house of Thebes. Double doors dominate the façade; a stone altar stands at the center of the stage.*

*Many years have passed since* OEDIPUS *solved the riddle of the Sphinx and ascended the throne of Thebes, and now a plague has struck the city. A procession of priests enters; suppliants, broken and despondent, they carry branches wound in wool and lay them on the altar.*

*The doors open.* GUARDS *assemble.* OEDIPUS *comes forward, majestic but for a telltale limp, and slowly views the condition of his people.*]

OEDIPUS.  Oh my children, the new blood of ancient Thebes,
   why are you here? Huddling at my altar,
   praying before me, your branches wound in wool.°
   Our city reeks with the smoke of burning incense,
   rings with cries for the Healer° and wailing for the dead.     5
   I thought it wrong, my children, to hear the truth
   from others, messengers. Here I am myself—
   you all know me, the world knows my fame:
   I am Oedipus.

---

3 **branches wound in wool** Suppliants laid such offerings on the altar of Apollo, god of healing, until their request was granted. Notice that in line 161 Oedipus tells the suppliants to remove the branches, thus suggesting that he will heal them.
5 **the Healer** Apollo.

[*Helping a* PRIEST *to his feet.*]
         Speak up, old man.Your years,
your dignity—you should speak for the others.        10
Why here and kneeling, what preys upon you so?
Some sudden fear? some strong desire?
You can trust me. I am ready to help,
I'll do anything. I would be blind to misery
not to pity my people kneeling at my feet.        15
PRIEST.  Oh Oedipus, king of the land, our greatest power!
You see us before you now, men of all ages
clinging to your altars. Here are boys,
still too weak to fly from the nest,
and here the old, bowed down with the years,        20
the holy ones—a priest of Zeus° myself—and here
the picked, unmarried men, the young hope of Thebes.
And all the rest, your great family gathers now,
branches wreathed, massing in the squares,
kneeling before the two temples of queen Athena°        25
or the river-shrine where the embers glow and die
and Apollo sees the future in the ashes.°
                        Our city—
look around you, see with your own eyes—
our ship pitches wildly, cannot lift her head
from the depths, the red waves of death        30
Thebes is dying. A blight on the fresh crops
and the rich pastures, cattle sicken and die,
and the women die in labor, children stillborn,
and the plague, the fiery god of fever hurls down
on the city, his lightning slashing through us—        35
raging plague in all its vengeance, devastating
the house of Cadmus!° And black Death luxuriates
in the raw, wailing miseries of Thebes.
Now we pray to you. You cannot equal the gods,
your children know that, bending at your altar.        40
But we do rate you first of men,
both in the common crises of our lives
and face-to-face encounters with the gods.

---

21 **Zeus** chief deity on Mt. Olympus, and father of Apollo.   25 **Athena** goddess
of wisdom and protector of cities.   27 **the ashes** Diviners foretold the future
by examining the ashes of burnt offerings.   37 **Cadmus** mythical founder
of Thebes.

You freed us from the Sphinx,° you came to Thebes
and cut us loose from the bloody tribute° we had paid          45
that harsh, brutal singer. We taught you nothing,
no skill, no extra knowledge, still you triumphed.
A god was with you, so they say, and we believe it—
you lifted up our lives.
                So now again,
Oedipus, king, we bend to you, your power—                     50
we implore you, all of us on our knees:
find us strength, rescue! Perhaps you've heard
the voice of a god or something from other men,
Oedipus . . . what do you know?
The man of experience—you see it every day—                    55
his plans will work in a crisis, his first of all.

Act now—we beg you, best of men, raise up our city!
Act, defend yourself, your former glory!
Your country calls you savior now
for your zeal, your action years ago.                          60
Never let us remember of your reign:
you helped us stand, only to fall once more.
Oh raise up our city, set us on our feet.
The omens were good that day you brought us joy—
be the same man today!                                         65
Rule our land, you know you have the power,
but rule a land of the living, not a wasteland.
Ship and towered city are nothing, stripped of men
alive within it, living all as one.

OEDIPUS.                                 My children,
I pity you. I see—how could I fail to see                      70
what longings bring you here? Well I know
you are sick to death, all of you,
but sick as you are, not one is sick as I.
Your pain strikes each of you alone, each
in the confines of himself, no other. But my spirit           75
grieves for the city, for myself and all of you.
I wasn't asleep, dreaming. You haven't wakened me—
I've wept through the nights, you must know that,

---

44 **the Sphinx** a female monster (body of a lion, wings of a bird, face of a woman)
who asked the riddle "What goes on four legs in the morning, two at noon, and
three in the evening?" and who killed those who could not answer. When Oedipus
responded correctly that man crawls on all fours in infancy, walks upright in matu-
rity, and uses a staff in old age, the Sphinx destroyed herself.    45 **bloody tribute**
i.e., the young Thebans who had tried to solve the riddle and had failed.

groping, laboring over many paths of thought.
After a painful search I found one cure:                                    80
I acted at once. I sent Creon,
my wife's own brother, to Delphi°—
Apollo the Prophet's oracle—to learn
what I might do or say to save our city.

Today's the day. When I count the days gone by                              85
it torments me . . . what is he doing?
Strange, he's late, he's gone too long.
But once he returns, then, then I'll be a traitor
if I do not do all the god makes clear.
PRIEST.  Timely words. The men over there                                   90
are signaling—Creon's just arriving.
OEDIPUS. [*Sighting* CREON, *then turning to the altar.*]
                                              Lord Apollo,
let him come with a lucky word of rescue,
shining like his eyes!
PRIEST. Welcome news, I think—he's crowned, look,
and the laurel wreath is bright with berries.                               95
OEDIPUS.  We'll soon see. He's close enough to hear—

[*Enter* CREON *from the side; his face is shaded with a wreath.*]

Creon, prince, my kinsman, what do you bring us?
What message from the god?
CREON.                                        Good news.
I tell you even the hardest things to bear,
if they should turn out well, all would be well.                            100
OEDIPUS.  Of course, but what were the god's *words?* There's no hope
and nothing to fear in what you've said so far.
CREON.  If you want my report in the presence of these . . .

[*Pointing to the* PRIESTS *while drawing* OEDIPUS *toward the
palace.*]

I'm ready now, or we might go inside.
OEDIPUS.                                      Speak out,
speak to us all. I grieve for these, my people,                             105
far more than I fear for my own life.
CREON.                                      Very well,
I will tell you what I heard from the god.
Apollo commands us—he was quite clear—
"Drive the corruption from the land,

---

82 **Delphi** site of a shrine of Apollo.

don't harbor it any longer, past all cure,    110
don't nurse it in your soil—root it out!"

OEDIPUS.  How can we cleanse ourselves—what rites?
What's the source of the trouble?

CREON.  Banish the man, or pay back blood with blood.
Murder sets the plague-storm on the city.

OEDIPUS.                                    Whose murder?    115
Whose fate does Apollo bring to light?

CREON.                                    Our leader,
my lord, was once a man named Laius,
before you came and put us straight on course.

OEDIPUS.                              I know—
or so I've heard. I never saw the man myself.

CREON.  Well, he was killed, and Apollo commands us now—    120
he could not be more clear,
"Pay the killers back—whoever is responsible."

OEDIPUS.  Where on earth are they? Where to find it now,
the trail of the ancient guilt so hard to trace?

CREON.  "Here in Thebes," he said.    125
Whatever is sought for can be caught, you know,
whatever is neglected slips away.

OEDIPUS.                              But where,
in the palace, the fields or foreign soil,
where did Laius meet his bloody death?

CREON.  He went to consult an oracle, Apollo said,    130
and he set out and never came home again.

OEDIPUS.  No messenger, no fellow-traveler saw what happened?
Someone to cross-examine?

CREON.                              No,
they were all killed but one. He escaped,
terrified, he could tell us nothing clearly,    135
nothing of what he saw—just one thing.

OEDIPUS.                              What's that?
one thing could hold the key to it all,
a small beginning give us grounds for hope.

CREON.  He said thieves attacked them—a whole band,
not single-handed, cut King Laius down.

OEDIPUS.                              A thief, so daring,    140
so wild, he'd kill a king? Impossible, unless conspirators paid
him off in Thebes.

CREON.  We suspected as much. But with Laius dead
no leader appeared to help us in our troubles.

OEDIPUS.  Trouble? Your *king* was murdered—royal blood!    145
What stopped you from tracking down the killer
then and there?

CREON.                    The singing, riddling Sphinx.
She . . . persuaded us to let the mystery go
and concentrate on what lay at our feet.
OEDIPUS.                                              No,
I'll start again—I'll bring it all to light myself!                    150
Apollo is right, and so are you, Creon,
to turn our attention back to the murdered man.
Now you have *me* to fight for you, you'll see:
I am the land's avenger by all rights,
and Apollo's champion too.                                              155
But not to assist some distant kinsman, no,
for my own sake I'll rid us of this corruption.
Whoever killed the king may decide to kill me too,
with the same violent hand—by avenging Laius
I defend myself.

[*To the* PRIESTS.]

                          Quickly, my children.                        160
Up from the steps, take up your branches now.

[*To the* GUARDS.]

One of you summon the city here before us,
tell them I'll do everything. God help us,
we will see our triumph—or our fall.

[OEDIPUS *and* CREON *enter the palace, followed by the guards.*]

PRIEST. Rise, my sons. The kindness we came for                        165
Oedipus volunteers himself.
Apollo has sent his word, his oracle—
Come down, Apollo, save us, stop the plague.

[*The* PRIESTS *rise, remove their branches and exit to the side. Enter a* CHORUS, *the citizens of Thebes, who have not heard
the news that* CREON *brings. They march around the altar,
chanting.*]

CHROUS.                                              Zeus!
Great welcome voice of Zeus,° what do you bring?
What word from the gold vaults of Delphi                               170
comes to brilliant Thebes? Racked with terror—
          terror shakes my heart
and I cry your wild cries, Apollo, Healer of Delos°

_____

169 **welcome voice of Zeus** Apollo, son of Zeus, spoke for Zeus.    173 **Delos**
sacred island where Apollo was born.

I worship you in dread . . . what now, what is your price?
some new sacrifice? some ancient rite from the past                    175
come round again each spring?—
        what will you bring to birth?
Tell me, child of golden Hope
warm voice that never dies!
You are the first I call, daughter of Zeus                              180
deathless Athena—I call your sister Artemis,°
heart of the market place enthroned in glory,
        guardian of our earth—
I call Apollo, Archer astride the thunderheads of heaven—
O triple shield against death, shine before me now!                    185
If ever, once in the past, you stopped some ruin
launched against our walls
        you hurled the flame of pain
far, far from Thebes—you gods
        come now, come down once more!
                        No, no                                          190
the miseries numberless, grief on grief, no end—
too much to bear, we are all dying
O my people . . .
        Thebes like a great army dying
and there is no sword of thought to save us, no                        195
and the fruits of our famous earth, they will not ripen
no and the women cannot scream their pangs to birth—
screams for the Healer, children dead in the womb
        and life on life goes down
        you can watch them go                                          200
        like seabirds winging west, outracing the day's fire
down the horizon, irresistibly
        streaking on to the shores of Evening
                        Death
so many deaths, numberless deaths on deaths, no end—
Thebes is dying, look, her children                                    205
stripped of pity . . .
        generations strewn on the ground
unburied, unwept, the dead spreading death
and the young wives and gray-haired mothers with them
cling to the altars, trailing in from all over the city—               210
Thebes, city of death, one long cortege
        and the suffering rises
                wails for mercy rise
        and the wild hymn for the Healer blazes out

---

181 **Artemis** a goddess, sister of Apollo.

clashing with our sobs our cries of mourning—                215
O golden daughter of god,° send rescue
radiant as the kindness in your eyes!

Drive him back!—the fever, the god of death
    that raging god of war
not armored in bronze, not shielded now, he burns me,        220
battle cries in the onslaught burning on—
O rout him from our borders!
Sail him, blast him out to the Sea-queen's chamber
    the black Atlantic gulfs
    or the northern harbor, death to all                     225
where the Thracian surf comes crashing.
Now what the night spares he comes by day and kills—
the god of death.
                    O lord of the stormcloud,
you who twirl the lightning, Zeus, Father,
thunder Death to nothing!                                    230

Apollo, lord of the light, I beg you—
    whip your longbow's golden cord
showering arrows on our enemies—shafts of power
champions strong before us rushing on!

Artemis, Huntress,                                           235
torches flaring over the eastern ridges—
ride Death down in pain!

God of the headdress gleaming gold, I cry to you—
your name and ours are one, Dionysus°—
    come with your face aflame with wine                     240
    your raving women's cries
your army on the march! Come with the lightning
come with torches blazing, eyes ablaze with glory!
Burn that god of death that all gods hate!

[OEDIPUS *enters from the palace to address the* CHORUS, *as if
addressing the entire city of Thebes.*]

OEDIPUS.  You pray to the gods? Let me grant your prayers.   245
    Come, listen to me—do what the plague demands:
    you'll find relief and lift your head from the depths.
    I will speak out now as a stranger to the story,
    a stranger to the crime. If I'd been present then,
    there would have been no mystery, no long hunt           250

---

216 **golden daughter of god** Athena.     239 **Dionysus** god of wine and fertility.
He was attended by the Maenads (the "raving women" of line 241).

without a clue in hand. So now, counted
a native Theban years after the murder,
to all of Thebes I make this proclamation:
if any one of you knows who murdered Laius,
the son of Labdacus, I order him to reveal                          255
the whole truth to me. Nothing to fear,
even if he must denounce himself,
let him speak up
and so escape the brunt of the charge—
he will suffer no unbearable punishment,                           260
nothing worse than exile, totally unharmed.

[OEDIPUS *pauses, waiting for a reply.*]

                                                    Next,
if anyone knows the murderer is a stranger,
a man from alien soil, come, speak up.
I will give him a handsome reward, and lay up
gratitude in my heart for him besides.                             265

[*Silence again, no reply.*]

But if you keep silent, if anyone panicking,
trying to shield himself or friend or kin,
rejects my offer, then hear what I will do.
I order you, every citizen of the state
where I hold throne and power: banish this man—                    270
whoever he may be—never shelter him, never
speak a word to him, never make him partner
to your prayers, your victims burned to the gods.
Never let the holy water touch his hands
Drive him out, each of you, from every home.                       275
*He* is the plague, the heart of our corruption,
as Apollo's oracle has just revealed to me.
So I honor my obligations:
I fight for the god and for the murdered man.

Now my curse on the murderer. Whoever he is,                       280
a lone man unknown in his crime
or one among many, let that man drag out
his life in agony, step by painful step—
I curse myself as well . . . if by any chance
he proves to be an intimate of our house,                          285
here at my hearth, with my full knowledge,
may the curse I just called down on him strike me!

These are your orders: perform them to the last.
I command you, for my sake, for Apollo's, for this country
blasted root and branch by the angry heavens.                      290

Even if god had never urged you on to act,
how could you leave the crime uncleansed so long?
A man so noble—your king, brought down in blood—
you should have searched. But I am the king now,
I hold the throne that he held then, possess his bed    295
and a wife who shares our seed . . . why, our seed
might be the same, children born of the same mother
might have created blood-bonds between us
if his hope of offspring hadn't met disaster—
but fate swooped at his head and cut him short.    300
So I will fight for him as if he were my father,
stop at nothing, search the world
to lay my hands on the man who shed his blood,
the son of Labdacus descended of Polydorus,
Cadmus of old and Agenor, founder of the line:    305
their power and mine are one.
                                        Oh dear gods,
my curse on those who disobey these orders!
Let no crops grow out of the earth for them—
shrivel their women, kill their sons,
burn them to nothing in this plague    310
that hits us now, or something even worse.
But you, loyal men of Thebes who approve my actions,
may our champion, Justice, may all the gods
be with us, fight beside us to the end!
LEADER.  In the grip of your curse, my king, I swear    315
I'm not the murderer, I cannot point him out.
As for the search, Apollo pressed it on us—
he should name the killer.
OEDIPUS.                              Quite right,
but to force the gods to act against their will—
no man has the power.
LEADER.                          Then if I might mention    320
the next best thing . . .
OEDIPUS.                          The third best too—
don't hold back, say it.
LEADER.                          I still believe . . .
Lord Tiresias° sees with the eyes of Lord Apollo.
Anyone searching for the truth, my king,
might learn it from the prophet, clear as day.    325
OEDIPUS.  I've not been slow with that. On Creon's cue
I sent the escorts, twice, within the hour.
I'm surprised he isn't here.

---

323 **Tiresias** a blind prophet.

LEADER.                    We need him—
  without him we have nothing but old, useless rumors.
OEDIPUS.  Which rumors? I'll search out every word.          330
LEADER.  Laius was killed, they say, by certain travelers.
OEDIPUS.  I know—but no one can find the murderer.
LEADER.  If the man has a trace of fear in him
  he won't stay silent long,
  not with your curses ringing in his ears.                 335
OEDIPUS.  He didn't flinch at murder,
  he'll never flinch at words.

[*Enter* TIRESIAS, *the blind prophet, led by a boy with escorts in
attendance. He remains at a distance.*]

LEADER.  Here is the one who will convict him, look,
  they bring him on at last, the seer, the man of god.
  The truth lives inside him, him alone.
OEDIPUS.                       O Tiresias,                   340
  master of all the mysteries of our life,
  all you teach and all you dare not tell,
  signs in the heavens, signs that walk the earth!
  Blind as you are, you can feel all the more
  what sickness haunts our city. You, my lord,              345
  are the one shield, the one savior we can find.

  We asked Apollo—perhaps the messengers
  haven't told you—he sent his answer back:
  "Relief from the plague can only come one way.
  Uncover the murderers of Laius,                           350
  put them to death or drive them into exile."
  So I beg you, grudge us nothing now, no voice,
  no message plucked from the birds, the embers
  or the other mantic ways within your grasp.
  Rescue yourself, your city, rescue me—                    355
  rescue everything infected by the dead.
  We are in your hands. For a man to help others
  with all his gifts and native strength:
  that is the noblest work.
TIRESIAS.                      How terrible—to see the truth
  when the truth is only pain to him who sees!              360
  I knew it well, but I put it from my mind,
  else I never would have come.
OEDIPUS.  What's this? Why so grim, so dire?
TIRESIAS.  Just send me home. You bear your burdens,
  I'll bear mine. It's better that way,                     365
  please believe me.

OEDIPUS.                    Strange response . . . unlawful,
unfriendly too to the state that bred and reared you—
you withhold the word of god.
TIRESIAS.                         I fail to see
that your own words are so well-timed.
I'd rather not have the same thing said of me . . .          370
OEDIPUS. For the love of god, don't turn away,
not if you know something. We beg you,
all of us on our knees.
TIRESIAS.                    None of you knows—
and I will never reveal my dreadful secrets,
not to say your own.                                         375
OEDIPUS. What? You know and you won't tell?
You're bent on betraying us, destroying Thebes?
TIRESIAS. I'd rather not cause pain for you or me.
So why this . . . useless interrogation?
You'll get nothing from me.
OEDIPUS.                         Nothing! You,                380
you scum of the earth, you'd enrage a heart of stone!
You won't talk? Nothing moves you?
Out with it, once and for all!
TIRESIAS. You criticize my temper . . . unaware
of the one you live with, you revile me.                     385
OEDIPUS. Who could restrain his anger hearing you?
What outrage—you spurn the city!
TIRESIAS. What will come will come.
Even if I shroud it all in silence.
OEDIPUS. What will come? You're bound to *tell* me that.     390
TIRESIAS. I'll say no more. Do as you like, build your anger
to whatever pitch you please, rage your worst—
OEDIPUS. Oh I'll let loose, I have such fury in me—
now I see it all. You helped hatch the plot,
you did the work, yes, short of killing him                  395
with your own hands—and given eyes I'd say
you did the killing single-handed!
TIRESIAS.                         Is that so!
I charge you, then, submit to that decree
you just laid down: from this day onward
speak to no one, not these citizens, not myself.             400
*You* are the curse, the corruption of the land!
OEDIPUS. You, shameless—
aren't you appalled to start up such a story?
You think you can get away with this?
TIRESIAS.                         I have already.
The truth with all its power lives inside me.                405

OEDIPUS.  Who primed you for this? Not your prophet's trade.
TIRESIAS.  You did, you forced me, twisted it out of me.
OEDIPUS.  What? Say it again—I'll understand it better.
TIRESIAS.  Didn't you understand, just now?
    Or are you tempting me to talk?              410
OEDIPUS.  No, I can't say I grasped your meaning.
    Out with it, again!
TIRESIAS.  I say you are the murderer you hunt.
OEDIPUS.  That obscenity, twice—by god, you'll pay.
TIRESIAS.  Shall I say more, so you can really rage?      415
OEDIPUS.  Much as you want. Your words are nothing—futile.
TIRESIAS.  You cannot imagine . . . I tell you,
    you and your loved ones live together in infamy,
    you cannot see how far you've gone in guilt.
OEDIPUS.  You think you can keep this up and never suffer?  420
TIRESIAS.  Indeed, if the truth has any power.
OEDIPUS.                       It does
    but not for you, old man. You've lost your power,
    stone-blind, stone-deaf—senses, eyes blind as stone!
TIRESIAS.  I pity you, flinging at me the very insults
    each man here will fling at you so soon.
OEDIPUS.                Blind,      425
    lost in the night, endless night that cursed you!
    You can't hurt me or anyone else who sees the light—
    you can never touch me.
TIRESIAS.           True, it is not your fate
    to fall at my hands. Apollo is quite enough,
    and he will take some pains to work this out.      430
OEDIPUS.  Creon! Is this conspiracy his or yours?
TIRESIAS.  Creon is not your downfall, no, you are your own.
OEDIPUS.              O power—
    wealth and empire, skill outstripping skill
    in the heady rivalries of life,
    what envy lurks inside you! Just for this,      435
    the crown the city gave me—I never sought it,
    they laid it in my hands—for this alone, Creon,
    the soul of trust, my loyal friend from the start
    steals against me . . . so hungry to overthrow me
    he sets this wizard on me, this scheming quack,    440
    this fortune-teller peddling lies, eyes peeled
    for his own profit—seer blind in his craft!

    Come here, you pious fraud. Tell me,
    when did you ever prove yourself a prophet?
    When the Sphinx, that chanting Fury kept her deathwatch here,  445

why silent then, not a word to set our people free?
There was a riddle, not for some passer-by to solve—
it cried out for a prophet. Where were you?
Did you rise to the crisis? Not a word,
you and your birds, your gods—nothing.                    450
No, but I came by, Oedipus the ignorant,
*I* stopped the Sphinx! With no help from the birds,
the flight of my own intelligence hit the mark.

And this is the man you'd try to overthrow?
You think you'll stand by Creon when he's king?           455
You and the great mastermind—
you'll pay in tears, I promise you, for this,
this witch-hunt. If you didn't look so senile
the lash would teach you what your scheming means!
LEADER.  I would suggest his words were spoken in anger,   460
Oedipus . . . yours too, and it isn't what we need.
The best solution to the oracle, the riddle
posed by god—we should look for that.
TIRESIAS.  You are the king no doubt, but in one respect,
at least, I am your equal: the right to reply.            465
I claim that privilege too.
I am not your slave. I serve Apollo.
I don't need Creon to speak for me in public.
                                            So,
you mock my blindness? Let me tell you this.
You with your precious eyes,                              470
you're blind to the corruption of your life,
to the house you live in, those you live with—
who *are* your parents? Do you know? All unknowing
you are the scourge of your own flesh and blood,
the dead below the earth and the living here above,        475
and the double lash of your mother and your father's curse
will whip you from this land one day, their footfall
treading you down in terror, darkness shrouding
your eyes that now can see the light!
                                    Soon, soon
you'll scream aloud—what haven won't reverberate?          480
What rock of Cithaeron° won't scream back in echo?
That day you learn the truth about your marriage,
the wedding-march that sang you into your halls,
the lusty voyage home to the fatal harbor!

---

481 **Cithaeron** mountains near Thebes, where Oedipus was abandoned as
an infant.

And a crowd of other horrors you'd never dream        485
will level you with yourself and all your children.
There. Now smear us with insults—Creon, myself,
and every word I've said. No man will ever
be rooted from the earth as brutally as you.
OEDIPUS.  Enough! Such filth from him? Insufferable—        490
what, still alive? Get out—
faster, back where you came from—vanish!
TIRESIAS.  I would never have come if you hadn't called me here.
OEDIPUS.  If I thought you would blurt out such absurdities,
you'd have died waiting before I'd had you summoned.        495
TIRESIAS.  Absurd, am I! To you, not to your parents:
the ones who bore you found me sane enough.
OEDIPUS.  Parents—who? Wait . . . who is my father?
TIRESIAS.  This day will bring your birth and your destruction.
OEDIPUS.  Riddles—all you can say are riddles, murk and darkness.        500
TIRESIAS.  Ah, but aren't you the best man alive at solving riddles?
OEDIPUS.  Mock me for that, go on, and you'll reveal my greatness.
TIRESIAS.  Your great good fortune, true, it was your ruin.
OEDIPUS.  Not if I saved the city—what do I care?
TIRESIAS.  Well then, I'll be going.

[*To his attendant.*]

Take me home, boy.        505
OEDIPUS.  Yes, take him away. You're a nuisance here.
Out of the way, the irritation's gone.

[*Turning his back on* TIRESIAS, *moving toward the palace.*]

TIRESIAS.                         I will go,
once I have said what I came here to say.
I'll never shrink from the anger in your eyes—
you can't destroy me. Listen to me closely:        510
the man you've sought so long, proclaiming,
cursing up and down, the murderer of Laius—
he is here. A stranger.
you may think, who lives among you,
he soon will be revealed a native Theban        515
but he will take no joy in the revelation.
Blind who now has eyes, beggar who now is rich,
he will grope his way toward a foreign soil,
a stick tapping before him step by step.

[OEDIPUS *enters the palace.*]

Revealed at last, brother and father both        520
to the children he embraces; to his mother

son and husband both—he sowed the loins
his father sowed, he spilled his father's blood!

Go in and reflect on that, solve that.
And if you find I've lied                                               525
from this day onward call the prophet blind.

[TIRESIAS *and the boy exit to the side.*]

CHORUS.                                          Who—
  who is the man the voice of god denounces
  resounding out of the rocky gorge of Delphi?
     The horror too dark to tell,
  whose ruthless bloody hands have done the work?        530
  His time has come to fly
     to outrace the stallions of the storm
       his feet a streak of speed—
  Cased in armor, Apollo son of the Father
  lunges on him, lightning-bolts afire!                       535
  And the grim unerring Furies°
      closing for the kill.
            Look,
  the word of god has just come blazing
  flashing off Parnassus'° snowy heights!
     That man who left no trace—                            540
  after him, hunt him down with all our strength!
  Now under bristling timber
     up through rocks and caves he stalks
      like the wild mountain bull—
  cut off from men, each step an agony, frenzied, racing blind    545
  but he cannot outrace the dread voices of Delphi
  ringing out of the heart of Earth,
     the dark wings beating around him shrieking doom
      the doom that never dies, the terror—

  The skilled prophet scans the birds and shatters me with terror!    550
  I can't accept him, can't deny him, don't know what to say,
  I'm lost, and the wings of dark foreboding beating—
  I cannot see what's come, what's still to come . . .
  and what could breed a blood feud between
     Laius' house and the son of Polybus?°                   555
  I know of nothing, not in the past and not now,
  no charge to bring against our king, no cause

---

536 **Furies** avenging deities.     539 **Parnassus** a mountain associated with Apollo.
555 **son of Polybus** Oedipus is mistakenly thought to be the son of Polybus,
King of Corinth.

to attack his fame that rings throughout Thebes—
not without proof—not for the ghost of Laius,
not to avenge a murder gone without a trace.                      560

Zeus and Apollo know, they know, the great masters
    of all the dark and depth of human life.
But whether a mere man can know the truth,
whether a seer can fathom more than I—
    there is no test, no certain proof                            565
        though matching skill for skill
a man can outstrip a rival. No, not till I see
these charges proved will I side with his accusers.
We saw him then, when the she-hawk° swept against him,
saw with our own eyes his skill, his brilliant triumph—          570
    there was the test—he was the joy of Thebes!
Never will I convict my king, never in my heart.

[*Enter* CREON *from the side.*]

CREON.  My fellow-citizens, I hear King Oedipus
levels terrible charges at me. I had to come.
I resent it deeply. If, in the present crisis                     575
he thinks he suffers any abuse from me,
anything I've done or said that offers him
the slightest injury, why, I've no desire
to linger out this life, my reputation in ruins.
The damage I'd face from such an accusation                       580
is nothing simple. No, there's nothing worse:
branded a traitor in the city, a traitor
to all of you and my good friends.

LEADER.                                          True,
but a slur might have been forced out of him,
by anger perhaps, not any firm conviction.                        585

CREON.  The charge was made in public, wasn't it?
*I* put the prophet up to spreading lies?

LEADER.  Such things were said . . .
I don't know with what intent, if any.

CREON.  Was his glance steady, his mind right                     590
when the charge was brought against me?

LEADER.  I really couldn't say. I never look
to judge the ones in power.

[*The doors open.* OEDIPUS *enters.*]

                                        Wait,
here's Oedipus now.

_____

569 **the she-hawk** the Sphinx.

OEDIPUS.                    You—here? You have the gall
to show your face before the palace gates?                                    595
You, plotting to kill me, kill the king—
I see it all, the marauding thief himself
scheming to steal my crown and power!
                                        Tell me,
in god's name, what did you take me for,
coward or fool, when you spun out your plot?              600
Your treachery—you think I'd never detect it
creeping against me in the dark? Or sensing it,
not defend myself? Aren't you the fool,
you and your high adventure. Lacking numbers,
powerful friends, out for the big game of empire—        605
you need riches, armies to bring that quarry down!
CREON. Are you quite finished? It's your turn to listen
for just as long as you've . . . instructed me.
Hear me out, then judge me on the facts.
OEDIPUS. You've a wicked way with words, Creon,               610
but I'll be slow to learn—from you.
I find you a menace, a great burden to me.
CREON. Just one thing, hear me out in this.
OEDIPUS.                              Just one thing,
don't tell *me* you're not the enemy, the traitor.
CREON. Look, if you think crude, mindless stubbornness        615
such a gift, you've lost your sense of balance.
OEDIPUS. If you think you can abuse a kinsman,
then escape the penalty, you're insane.
CREON. Fair enough, I grant you. But this injury
you say I've done you, what is it?                            620
OEDIPUS. Did you induce me, yes or no,
to send for that sanctimonious prophet?
CREON. I did. And I'd do the same again.
OEDIPUS. All right then, tell me, how long is it now
since Laius . . .
CREON.            Laius—what did *he* do?
OEDIPUS.                                Vanished,              625
swept from sight, murdered in his tracks.
CREON. The count of the years would run you far back . . .
OEDIPUS. And that far back, was the prophet at his trade?
CREON. Skilled as he is today, and just as honored.
OEDIPUS. Did he ever refer to me then, at that time?
CREON.                                No,                      630
never, at least, when I was in his presence.
OEDIPUS. But you did investigate the murder, didn't you?
CREON. We did our best, of course, discovered nothing.

OEDIPUS.  But the great seer never accused me then—why not?
CREON.  I don't know.And when I don't, *I* keep quiet.                    635
OEDIPUS.  You do know this, you'd tell it too—
    if you had a shred of decency.
CREON.                              What?
    If I know, I won't hold back.
OEDIPUS.                          Simply this:
    if the two of you had never put heads together,
    we would never have heard about *my* killing Laius.              640
CREON.  If that's what he says . . . well, you know best.
    But now I have a right to learn from you
    as you just learned from me.
OEDIPUS.                        Learn your fill,
    you never will convict me of the murder.
CREON.  Tell me, you're married to my sister, aren't you?            645
OEDIPUS.  A genuine discovery—there's no denying that.
CREON.  And you rule the land with her, with equal power?
OEDIPUS.  She receives from me whatever she desires.
CREON.  And I am the third, all of us are equals?
OEDIPUS.  Yes, and it's there you show your stripes—               650
    you betray a kinsman.
CREON.                        Not at all.
    Not if you see things calmly, rationally,
    as I do. Look at it this way first:
    who in his right mind would rather rule
    and live in anxiety than sleep in peace?                         655
    Particularly if he enjoys the same authority.
    Not I, I'm not the man to yearn for kingship,
    not with a king's power in my hands. Who would?
    Now, as it is, you offer me all I need,                          660
    not a fear in the world. But if I wore the crown . . .
    there'd be many painful duties to perform,
    hardly to my taste.
                How could kingship
    please me more than influence, power
    without a qualm? I'm not that deluded yet,                       665
    to reach for anything but privilege outright,
    profit free and clear.
    Now all men sing my praises, all salute me,
    now all who request your favors curry mine.
    I am their best hope: success rests in me.                       670
    Why give up that, I ask you, and borrow trouble?
    A man of sense, someone who sees things clearly
    would never resort to treason.
    No, I've no lust for conspiracy in me,
    nor could I ever suffer one who does.                            675

Do you want proof? Go to Delphi yourself,
examine the oracle and see if I've reported
the message word-for-word. This too:
if you detect that I and the clairvoyant
have plotted anything in common, arrest me,    680
execute me. Not on the strength of one vote,
two in this case, mine as well as yours.
But don't convict me on sheer unverified surmise.
How wrong it is to take the good for bad,
purely at random, or take the bad for good.    685
But reject a friend, a kinsman? I would as soon
tear out the life within us, priceless life itself.
You'll learn this well, without fail, in time.
Time alone can bring the just man to light—
the criminal you can spot in one short day.
LEADER.                                    Good advice,    690
my lord, for anyone who wants to avoid disaster.
Those who jump to conclusions may go wrong.
OEDIPUS.  When my enemy moves against me quickly,
plots in secret, I move quickly too, I must,
I plot and pay him back. Relax my guard a moment,    695
waiting his next move—he wins his objective,
I lose mine.
CREON.            What do you want?
You want me banished?
OEDIPUS.                          No, I want you dead.
CREON.  Just to show how ugly a grudge can . . .
OEDIPUS.                                           So,
still stubborn? you don't think I'm serious?    700
CREON.  I think you're insane.
OEDIPUS.                          Quite sane—in my behalf.
CREON.  Not just as much in mine?
OEDIPUS.                              You—my mortal enemy?
CREON.  What if you're wholly wrong?
OEDIPUS.                              No matter—I must rule.
CREON.  Not if you rule unjustly.
OEDIPUS.                          Hear him, Thebes, my city!
CREON.  My city too, not yours alone!    705
LEADER.  Please, my lords.

[*Enter* JOCASTA *from the palace.*]

                          Look, Jocasta's coming,
and just in time too. With her help
you must put this fighting of yours to rest.
JOCASTA.  Have you no sense? Poor misguided men,
such shouting—why this public outburst?    710

Aren't you ashamed, with the land so sick,
to stir up private quarrels?

[*To* OEDIPUS.]

Into the palace now.And Creon, you go home.
Why make such a furor over nothing?

CREON.  My sister, it's dreadful . . . Oedipus, your husband,          715
he's bent on a choice of punishments for me,
banishment from the fatherland or death.

OEDIPUS.  Precisely. I caught him in the act, Jocasta,
plotting, about to stab me in the back.

CREON.  Never—curse me, let me die and be damned          720
if I've done you any wrong you charge me with.

JOCASTA.  Oh god, believe it, Oedipus,
honor the solemn oath he swears to heaven.
Do it for me, for the sake of all your people.

[*The* CHORUS *begins to chant.*]

CHORUS.  Believe it, be sensible          725
give way, my king, I beg you!

OEDIPUS.  What do you want from me, concessions?

CHORUS.  Respect him—he's been no fool in the past
and now he's strong with the oath he swears to god.

OEDIPUS.  You know what you're asking?

CHORUS.                              I do.

OEDIPUS.                                        Then out with it!          730

CHORUS.  The man's your friend, your kin, he's under oath—
don't cast him out, disgraced
branded with guilt on the strength of hearsay only.

OEDIPUS.  Know full well, if that is what you want
you want me dead or banished from the land.

CHORUS.                                        Never—          735
no, by the blazing Sun, first god of the heavens!
Stripped of the gods, stripped of loved ones,
let me die by inches if that ever crossed my mind.
But the heart inside me sickens, dies as the land dies
and now on top of the old griefs you pile this,          740
your fury—both of you!

OEDIPUS.                    Then let him go,
even if it does lead to my ruin, my death
or my disgrace, driven from Thebes for life.
It's you, not him I pity—your words move me.
He, wherever he goes, my hate goes with him.          745

CREON.  Look at you, sullen in yielding, brutal in your rage—
you'll go too far. It's perfect justice:
natures like yours are hardest on themselves.

OEDIPUS.  Then leave me alone—get out!

CREON.                                              I'm going.
You're wrong, so wrong. These men know I'm right.          750

[*Exit to the side. The* CHORUS *turns to* JOCASTA.]

CHORUS.  Why do you hesitate, my lady
    why not help him in?

JOCASTA.  Tell me what's happened first.

CHORUS.  Loose, ignorant talk started dark suspicions
    and a sense of injustice cut deeply too.                  755

JOCASTA.  On both sides?

CHORUS.                     Oh yes.

JOCASTA.                              What did they say?

CHORUS.  Enough, please, enough! The land's so racked already
    or so it seems to me . . .
    End the trouble here, just where they left it.

OEDIPUS.  You see what comes of your good intentions now?     760
    And all because you tried to blunt my anger.

CHORUS.                                        My king,
    I've said it once, I'll say it time and again—
        I'd be insane, you know it,
    senseless, ever to turn my back on you.
    You who set our beloved land—storm-tossed, shattered—      765
    straight on course. Now again, good helmsman,
    steer us through the storm!

[*The* CHORUS *draws away, leaving* OEDIPUS *and* JOCASTA *side
by side.*]

JOCASTA.                         For the love of god,
    Oedipus, tell me too, what is it?
    Why this rage? You're so unbending.

OEDIPUS.  I will tell you. I respect you, Jocasta,                770
    much more than these . . .

[*Glancing at the* CHORUS.]

    Creon's to blame, Creon schemes against me.

JOCASTA.  Tell me clearly, how did the quarrel start?

OEDIPUS.  He says I murdered Laius—I am guilty.

JOCASTA.  How does he know? Some secret knowledge               775
    or simple hearsay?

OEDIPUS.                 Oh, he sent his prophet in
    to do his dirty work. You know Creon,
    Creon keeps his own lips clean.

JOCASTA.                             A prophet?
    Well then, free yourself of every charge!

Listen to me and learn some peace of mind:                               780
no skill in the world,
nothing human can penetrate the future.
Here is proof, quick and to the point.

An oracle came to Laius one fine day
(I won't say from Apollo himself                                         785
but his underlings, his priests) and it said
that doom would strike him down at the hands of a son,
our son, to be born of our own flesh and blood. But Laius,
so the report goes at least, was killed by strangers,
thieves, at a place where three roads meet . . . my son—               790
he wasn't three days old and the boy's father
fastened his ankles, had a henchman fling him away
on a barren, trackless mountain.
                                        There, you see?
Apollo brought neither thing to pass. My baby
no more murdered his father than Laius suffered—                        795
his wildest fear—death at his own son's hands.
That's how the seers and all their revelations
mapped out the future. Brush them from your mind.
Whatever the god needs and seeks
he'll bring to light himself, with ease.

OEDIPUS.                                          Strange,                800
    hearing you just now . . . my mind wandered,
    my thoughts racing back and forth.

JOCASTA.   What do you mean? Why so anxious, startled?

OEDIPUS.   I thought I heard you say that Laius
    was cut down at a place where three roads meet.                     805

JOCASTA.   That was the story. It hasn't died out yet.

OEDIPUS.   Where did this thing happen? Be precise.

JOCASTA.   A place called Phocis, where two branching roads,
    one from Daulia, one from Delphi,
    come together—a crossroads.                                         810

OEDIPUS.   When? How long ago?

JOCASTA.   The heralds no sooner reported Laius dead
    than you appeared and they hailed you king of Thebes.

OEDIPUS.   My god, my god—what have you planned to do to me?

JOCASTA.   What, Oedipus? What haunts you so?

OEDIPUS.                                          Not yet.               815
    Laius—how did he look? Describe him.
    Had he reached his prime?

JOCASTA.                                          He was swarthy,
    and the gray had just begun to streak his temples,
    and his build . . . wasn't far from yours.

OEDIPUS.                              Oh no no,
  I think I've just called down a dreadful curse          820
  upon myself—I simply didn't know!
JOCASTA. What are you saying? I shudder to look at you.
OEDIPUS. I have a terrible fear the blind seer can see.
  I'll know in a moment. One thing more—
JOCASTA.                              Anything,
  afraid as I am—ask, I'll answer, all I can.            825
OEDIPUS. Did he go with a light or heavy escort,
  several men-at-arms, like a lord, a king?
JOCASTA. There were five in the party, a herald among them,
  and a single wagon carrying Laius.
OEDIPUS.                              Ai—
  now I can see it all, clear as day.                    830
  Who told you all this at the time, Jocasta?
JOCASTA. A servant who reached home, the lone survivor.
OEDIPUS. So, could he still be in the palace  even now?
JOCASTA. No indeed. Soon as he returned from the scene
  and saw you on the throne with Laius dead and gone,    835
  he knelt and clutched my hand, pleading with me
  to send him into the hinterlands, to pasture,
  far as possible, out of sight of Thebes.
  I sent him away. Slave though he was,
  he'd earned that favor—and much more.                  840
OEDIPUS. Can we bring him back, quickly?
JOCASTA. Easily. Why do you want him so?
OEDIPUS.                              I'm afraid,
  Jocasta, I have said too much already.
  That man—I've got to see him.
JOCASTA.                              Then he'll come.
  But even I have a right, I'd like to think,            845
  to know what's torturing you, my lord.
OEDIPUS. And so you shall—I can hold nothing back from you,
  now I've reached this pitch of dark foreboding.
  Who means more to me than you? Tell me,
  whom would I turn toward but you                        850
  as I go through all this?

  My father was Polybus, king of Corinth.
  My mother, a Dorian, Merope. And I was held
  the prince of the realm among the people there,
  till something struck me out of nowhere,               855
  something strange . . . worth remarking perhaps,
  hardly worth the anxiety I gave it.
  Some man at a banquet who had drunk too much

shouted out—he was far gone, mind you—
that I am not my father's son. Fighting words!    860
I barely restrained myself that day
but early the next I went to mother and father,
questioned them closely, and they were enraged
at the accusation and the fool who let it fly.
So as for my parents I was satisfied,    865
but still this thing kept gnawing at me,
the slander spread—I had to make my move.
                                        And so,
unknown to mother and father I set out for Delphi,
and the god Apollo spurned me, sent me away
denied the facts I came for,    870
but first he flashed before my eyes a future
great with pain, terror, disaster—I can hear him cry,
"You are fated to couple with your mother, you will bring
a breed of children into the light no man can bear to see—
you will kill your father, the one who gave you life!"    875
I heard all that and ran. I abandoned Corinth,
from that day on I gauged its landfall only
by the stars, running, always running
toward some place where I would never see
the shame of all those oracles come true.    880
And as I fled I reached that very spot
where the great king, you say, met his death.
Now, Jocasta, I will tell you all.
Making my way toward this triple crossroad
I began to see a herald, then a brace of colts    885
drawing a wagon, and mounted on the bench . . . a man,
just as you've described him, coming face-to-face,
and the one in the lead and the old man himself
were about to thrust me off the road—brute force—
and the one shouldering me aside, the driver,    890
I strike him in anger!—and the old man, watching me
coming up along his wheels—he brings down
his prod, two prongs straight at my head!
I paid him back with interest!
Short work, by god—with one blow of the staff    895
in this right hand I knock him out of his high seat,
roll him out of the wagon, sprawling headlong—
I killed them all—every mother's son!

Oh, but if there is any blood-tie
between Laius and this stranger . . .    900
what man alive more miserable than I?
More hated by the gods? *I* am the man

no alien, no citizen welcomes to his house,
law forbids it—not a word to me in public,
driven out of every hearth and home.                          905
And all these curses I—no one but I
brought down these piling curses on myself!
And you, his wife, I've touched your body with these,
the hands that killed your husband cover you with blood.

Wasn't I born for torment? Look me in the eyes!               910
I am abomination—heart and soul!
I must be exiled, and even in exile
never see my parents, never set foot
on native ground again. Else I am doomed
to couple with my mother and cut my father down . . .        915
Polybus who reared me, gave me life.
                                        But why, why?
Wouldn't a man of judgment say—and wouldn't he be right—
some savage power has brought this down upon my head?

Oh no, not that, you pure and awesome gods,
never let me see that day! Let me slip                        920
from the world of men, vanish without a trace
before I see myself stained with such corruption,
stained to the heart.
LEADER.    My lord, you fill our hearts with fear.
         But at least until you question the witness,         925
         do take hope.
OEDIPUS.                 Exactly. He is my last hope—
         I am waiting for the shepherd. He is crucial.
JOCASTA.    And once he appears, what then? Why so urgent?
OEDIPUS.    I will tell you. If it turns out that his story
         matches yours, I've escaped the worst.              930
JOCASTA.    What did I say? What struck you so?
OEDIPUS.                                    You said thieves—
         he told you a whole band of them murdered Laius.
         So, if he still holds to the same number,
         I cannot be the killer. One can't equal many.
         But if he refers to one man, one alone,              935
         clearly the scales come down on me:
         I am guilty.
JOCASTA.        Impossible. Trust me,
         I told you precisely what he said,
         and he can't retract it now;
         the whole city heard it, not just I.                 940
         And even if he should vary his first report
         by one man more or less, still, my lord,

he could never make the murder of Laius
truly fit the prophecy. Apollo was explicit:
my son was doomed to kill my husband . . . my son,                    945
poor defenseless thing, he never had a chance
to kill his father. They destroyed him first.

So much for prophecy. It's neither here nor there.
From this day on, I wouldn't look right or left.

OEDIPUS.   True, true. Still, that shepherd,                          950
someone fetch him—now!

JOCASTA.   I'll send at once. But do let's go inside.
I'd never displease you, least of all in this.

[OEDIPUS *and* JOCASTA *enter the palace.*]

CHORUS.   Destiny guide me always
Destiny find me filled with reverence                                955
     pure in word and deed.
Great laws tower above us, reared on high
born for the brilliant vault of heaven—
     Olympian Sky their only father,
nothing mortal, no man gave them birth,                              960
their memory deathless, never lost in sleep:
within them lives a mighty god, the god does not grow old.

Pride breeds the tyrant
violent pride, gorging, crammed to bursting
     with all that is overripe and rich with ruin—                   965
clawing up to the heights, headlong pride
crashes down the abyss—sheer doom!
     No footing helps, all foothold lost and gone.
But the healthy strife that makes the city strong—
I pray that god will never end that wrestling:                       970
god, my champion, I will never let you go.

But if any man comes striding, high and mighty
     in all he says and does,
no fear of justice, no reverence
for the temples of the gods—                                         975
     let a rough doom tear him down,
repay his pride, breakneck, ruinous pride!
If he cannot reap his profits fairly
     cannot restrain himself from outrage—
mad, laying hands on the holy things untouchable!                    980

          Can such a man, so desperate, still boast
          he can save his life from the flashing bolts of god?
               If all such violence goes with honor now
                    why join the sacred dance?

Never again will I go reverent to Delphi,                    985
    the inviolate heart of Earth
    or Apollo's ancient oracle at Abae
    or Olympia of the fires—
    unless these prophecies all come true
for all mankind to point toward in wonder.                   990
King of kings, if you deserve your titles
Zeus, remember, never forget!
You and your deathless, everlasting reign.

    They are dying, the old oracles sent to Laius,
    now our masters strike them off the rolls.                995
        Nowhere Apollo's golden glory now—
        the gods, the gods go down.

[*Enter* JOCASTA *from the palace, carrying a suppliant's branch
wound in wool.*]

JOCASTA   Lords of the realm, it occurred to me,
    just now, to visit the temples of the gods,
    so I have my branch in my hand and incense too.          1000

    Oedipus is beside himself. Racked with anguish,
    no longer a man of sense, he won't admit
    the latest prophecies are hollow as the old—
    he's at the mercy of every passing voice
    if the voice tells of terror.                             1005
    I urge him gently, nothing seems to help,
    so I turn to you, Apollo, you are nearest.

[*Placing her branch on the altar, while an old herdsman enters
from the side, not the one just summoned by the King but an
unexpected* MESSENGER *from Corinth.*]

    I come with prayers and offerings . . . I beg you,
    cleanse us, set us free of defilement!
    Look at us, passengers in the grip of fear,               1010
    watching the pilot of the vessel go to pieces.
MESSENGER.  [*Approaching* JOCASTA *and the* CHORUS.]
    Strangers, please, I wonder if you could lead us
    to the palace of the king . . . I think it's Oedipus.
    Better, the man himself—you know where he is?
LEADER.   This is his palace, stranger. He's inside.         1015
    But here is his queen, his wife and mother
    of his children.
MESSENGER.           Blessings on you, noble queen,
    queen of Oedipus crowned with all your family—
    blessings on you always!

JOCASTA.  And the same to you, stranger, you deserve it . . .     1020
  such a greeting. But what have you come for?
  Have you brought us news?
MESSENGER.                               Wonderful news—
  for the house, my lady, for your husband too.
JOCASTA.  Really, what? Who sent you?
MESSENGER.                               Corinth.
  I'll give you the message in a moment.                          1025
  You'll be glad of it—how could you help it?—
  though it costs a little sorrow in the bargain.
JOCASTA.  What can it be, with such a double edge?
MESSENGER.  The people there, they want to make your Oedipus
  king of Corinth, so they're saying now.                         1030
JOCASTA.  Why? Isn't old Polybus still in power?
MESSENGER.  No more. Death has got him in the tomb.
JOCASTA.  What are you saying? Polybus, dead?—dead?
MESSENGER.                                       If not,
  if I'm not telling the truth, strike me dead too.
JOCASTA.  [To a servant.]
  Quickly, go to your master, tell him this!                      1035
  You prophecies of the gods, where are you now?
  This is the man that Oedipus feared for years,
  he fled him, not to kill him—and now he's dead,
  quite by chance, a normal, natural death,
  not murdered by his son.
OEDIPUS.  [Emerging from the palace.]                             1040
                               Dearest,
  what now? Why call me from the palace?
JOCASTA.  [Bringing the MESSENGER closer.]
  Listen to him, see for yourself what all
  those awful prophecies of god have come to.
OEDIPUS.  And who is he? What can he have for me?
JOCASTA.  He's from Corinth, he's come to tell you              1045
  your father is no more—Polybus—he's dead!
OEDIPUS.  [Wheeling on the MESSENGER.]
  What? Let me have it from your lips.
MESSENGER.                               Well,
  if that's what you want first, then here it is:
  make no mistake, Polybus is dead and gone.
OEDIPUS.  How—murder? sickness?—what? what killed him?          1050
MESSENGER.  A light tip of the scales put old bones to rest.
OEDIPUS.  Sickness then—poor man, it wore him down.
MESSENGER.                                       That,
  and the long count of years he'd measured out.

OEDIPUS.                              So!
Jocasta, why, why look to the Prophet's hearth,
the fires of the future? Why scan the birds          1055
that scream above our heads? They winged me on
to the murder of my father, did they? That was my doom?
Well look, he's dead and buried, hidden under the earth,
and here I am in Thebes, I never put hand to sword—
unless some longing for me wasted him away,          1060
then in a sense you'd say I caused his death.
But now, all those prophecies I feared—Polybus
packs them off to sleep with him in hell!
They're nothing, worthless.
JOCASTA.                       There.
Didn't I tell you from the start?                    1065
OEDIPUS.  So you did. I was lost in fear.
JOCASTA.  No more, sweep it from your mind forever.
OEDIPUS.  But my mother's bed, surely I must fear—
JOCASTA.                                       Fear?
What should a man fear? It's all chance,
chance rules our lives. Not a man on earth           1070
can see a day ahead, groping through the dark.
Better to live at random, best we can.
And as for this marriage with your mother—
have no fear. Many a man before you,
in his dreams, has shared his mother's bed.          1075
Take such things for shadows, nothing at all—
Live, Oedipus,
as if there's no tomorrow!
OEDIPUS.                    Brave words,
and you'd persuade me if mother weren't alive.
But mother lives, so for all your reassurances       1080
I live in fear, I must.
JOCASTA.                  But your father's death,
that, at least, is a great blessing, joy to the eyes!
OEDIPUS.  Great, I know . . . but I fear her—she's still alive.
MESSENGER.  Wait, who is this woman, makes you so afraid?
OEDIPUS.  Merope, old man. The wife of Polybus.      1085
MESSENGER.  The queen? What's there to fear in her?
OEDIPUS.  A dreadful prophecy, stranger, sent by the gods.
MESSENGER.  Tell me, could you? Unless it's forbidden
other ears to hear.
OEDIPUS.            Not at all.
Apollo told me once—it is my fate—                   1090
I must make love with my own mother,

shed my father's blood with my own hands.
So for years I've given Corinth a wide berth,
and it's been my good fortune too. But still,
to see one's parents and look into their eyes                    1095
is the greatest joy I know.
MESSENGER.                                You're afraid of that?
That kept you out of Corinth?
OEDIPUS.                                My *father,* old man—
so I wouldn't kill my father.
MESSENGER.                                So that's it.
Well then, seeing I came with such good will, my king,
why don't I rid you of that old worry now?                       1100
OEDIPUS.  What a rich reward you'd have for that!
MESSENGER.  What do you think I came for, majesty?
So you'd come home and I'd be better off.
OEDIPUS.  Never, I will never go near my parents.
MESSENGER.  My boy, it's clear, you don't know what you're doing.     1105
OEDIPUS.  What do you mean, old man? For god's sake, explain.
MESSENGER.  If you ran from *them,* always dodging home . . .
OEDIPUS.  Always, terrified Apollo's oracle might come true—
MESSENGER.  And you'd be covered with guilt, from both your parents.
OEDIPUS.  That's right, old man, that fear is always with me.         1110
MESSENGER.  Don't you know? You've really nothing to fear.
OEDIPUS.  But why? If I'm their son—Merope, Polybus?
MESSENGER.  Polybus was nothing to you, that's why, not in blood.
OEDIPUS.  What are you saying—Polybus was not my father?
MESSENGER.  No more than I am. He and I are equals.
OEDIPUS.                                My father—                1115
how can my father equal nothing? You're nothing to me!
MESSENGER.  Neither was he, no more your father than I am.
OEDIPUS.  Then why did he call me his son?
MESSENGER.                                You were a gift,
years ago—know for a fact he took you
from my hands.
OEDIPUS.                No, from another's hands?                 1120
Then how could he love me so? He loved me, deeply . . .
MESSENGER.  True, and his early years without a child
made him love you all the more.
OEDIPUS.                                And you, did you . . .
buy me? find me by accident?
MESSENGER.                                I stumbled on you,
down the woody flanks of Mount Cithaeron.
OEDIPUS.                                So close,                 1125
what were you doing here, just passing through?
MESSENGER.  Watching over my flocks, grazing them on the slopes.

OEDIPUS.   A herdsman, were you? A vagabond, scraping for wages?
MESSENGER.   Your savior too, my son, in your worst hour.
OEDIPUS.                                        Oh—
   when you picked me up, was I in pain? What exactly?          1130
MESSENGER.   Your ankles . . . they tell the story. Look at them.
OEDIPUS.   Why remind me of that, that old affliction?
MESSENGER.   Your ankles were pinned together. I set you free.
OEDIPUS.   That dreadful mark—I've had it from the cradle.
MESSENGER.   And you got your name° from that misfortune too,    1135
   the name's still with you.
OEDIPUS.                      Dear god, who did it?—
   mother? father? Tell me.
MESSENGER.                  I don't know.
   The one who gave you to me, he'd know more.
OEDIPUS.   What? You took me from someone else?
   You didn't find me yourself?
MESSENGER.                    No sir,                            1140
   another shepherd passed you on to me.
OEDIPUS.   Who? Do you know? Describe him.
MESSENGER.   He called himself a servant of . . .
   if I remember rightly—Laius.

   [JOCASTA *turns sharply.*]

OEDIPUS.   The king of the land who ruled here long ago?          1145
MESSENGER.   That's the one. That herdsman was *his* man.
OEDIPUS.   Is he still alive? Can I see him?
MESSENGER.   They'd know best, the people of these parts.

   [OEDIPUS *and the* MESSENGER *turn to the* CHORUS.]

OEDIPUS.   Does anyone know that herdsman,
   the one he mentioned? Anyone seen him                          1150
   in the fields, in the city? Out with it!
   The time has come to reveal this once for all.
LEADER.   I think he's the very shepherd you wanted to see,
   a moment ago. But the queen, Jocasta,
   she's the one to say.
OEDIPUS.                 Jocasta,                                1155
   you remember the man we just sent for?
   Is *that* the one he means?
JOCASTA.                      That man . . .
   why ask? Old shepherd, talk, empty nonsense,
   don't give it another thought, don't even think—

_____
1135 **you got your name** "Oedipus" means "swollen foot."

OEDIPUS.  What—give up now, with a clue like this?       1160
    Fail to solve the mystery of my birth?
    Not for all the world!
JOCASTA.              Stop—in the name of god,
    if you love your own life, call off this search!
    My suffering is enough.
OEDIPUS.             Courage!
    Even if my mother turns out to be a slave,       1165
    and I a slave, three generations back,
    *you* would not seem common.
JOCASTA.              Oh no,
    listen to me, I beg you, don't do this.
OEDIPUS.  Listen to you? No more. I must know it all,
    must see the truth at last.
JOCASTA.             No, please—       1170
    for your sake—I want the best for you!
OEDIPUS.  Your best is more than I can bear.
JOCASTA.                  You're doomed—
    may you never fathom who you are!
OEDIPUS.  [*To a servant.*] Hurry, fetch me the herdsman, now!
    Leave her to glory in her royal birth.       1175
JOCASTA.  Aieeeeee—
             man of agony—
    that is the only name I have for you,
    that, no other—ever, ever, ever!

    [*Flinging through the palace doors. A long, tense silence
    follows.*]

LEADER.  Where's she gone, Oedipus?
    Rushing off, such wild grief . . .       1180
    I'm afraid that from this silence
    something monstrous may come bursting forth.
OEDIPUS.  Let it burst! Whatever will, whatever must!
    I must know my birth, no matter how common
    it may be—I must see my origins face-to-face.       1185
    She perhaps, she with her woman's pride
    may well be mortified by my birth,
    but I, I count myself the son of Chance,
    the great goddess, giver of all good things—
    I'll never see myself disgraced. She is my mother!       1190
    And the moons have marked me out, my blood-brothers,
    one moon on the wane, the next moon great with power.
    That is my blood, my nature—I will never betray it,
    never fail to search and learn my birth!

CHORUS.   Yes—if I am a true prophet                                          1195
        if I can grasp the truth,
    by the boundless skies of Olympus,
    at the full moon of tomorrow, Mount Cithaeron
    you will know how Oedipus glories in you—
    you, his birthplace, nurse, his mountain-mother!                    1200
    And we will sing you, dancing out your praise—
    you lift our monarch's heart!
        Apollo, Apollo, god of the wild cry
        may our dancing please you!
                                            Oedipus—
            son, dear child, who bore you?                              1205
    Who of the nymphs who seem to live forever
    mated with Pan,° the mountain-striding Father?
    Who was your mother? who, some bride of Apollo
    the god who loves the pastures spreading toward the sun?
        Or was it Hermes, king of the lightning ridges?               1210
    Or Dionysus, lord of frenzy, lord of the barren peaks—
    did he seize you in his hands, dearest of all his lucky finds?—
    found by the nymphs, their warm eyes dancing, gift
    to the lord who loves them dancing out his joy!

[OEDIPUS *strains to see a figure coming from the distance. Attended by palace guards, an old* SHEPHERD *enters slowly, reluctant
to approach the king.*]

OEDIPUS.   I never met the man, my friends . . . still,                      1215
    if I had to guess, I'd say that's the shepherd,
    the very one we've looked for all along.
    Brothers in old age, two of a kind,
    he and our guest here. At any rate
    the ones who bring him in are my own men,                          1220
    I recognize them.

[*Turning to the* LEADER.]

                            But you know more than I,
    you should, you've seen the man before.
LEADER.   I know him, definitely. One of Laius' men,
    a trusty shepherd, if there ever was one.
OEDIPUS.   You, I ask you first, stranger,                                  1225
    you from Corinth—is this the one you mean?
MESSENGER.   You're looking at him. He's your man.

---

1207 **Pan** god of shepherds (associated, like Hermes and Dionysus,
with wilderness).

OEDIPUS. [*To the* SHEPHERD.]
    You, old man, come over here—
    look at me. Answer all my questions.
    Did you ever serve King Laius?
SHEPHERD.                  So I did . . .     1230
    a slave, not bought on the block though,
    born and reared in the palace.
OEDIPUS.  Your duties, your kind of work?
SHEPHERD.  Herding the flocks, the better part of my life.
OEDIPUS.  Where, mostly? Where did you do your grazing?
SHEPHERD.                   Well,     1235
    Cithaeron sometimes, or the foothills round about.
OEDIPUS.  This man—you know him? ever see him there?
SHEPHERD.  [*Confused, glancing from the* MESSENGER *to the* KING.]
    Doing what?—what man do you mean?
OEDIPUS.  [*Pointing to the* MESSENGER.]
    This one here—ever have dealings with him?
SHEPHERD.  Not so I could say, but give me a chance,     1240
    my memory's bad . . .
MESSENGER.  No wonder he doesn't know me, master.
    But let me refresh his memory for him.
    I'm sure he recalls old times we had
    on the slopes of Mount Cithaeron;     1245
    he and I, grazing our flocks, he with two
    and I with one—we both struck up together,
    three whole seasons, six months at a stretch
    from spring to the rising of Arcturus° in the fall,
    then with winter coming on I'd drive my herds     1250
    to my own pens, and back he'd go with his
    to Laius' folds.

    [*To the* SHEPHERD.]

                 Now that's how it was,
    wasn't it—yes or no?
SHEPHERD.              Yes, I suppose . . .
    it's all so long ago.
MESSENGER.          Come, tell me,
    you gave me a child back then, a boy, remember?     1255
    A little fellow to rear, my very own.
SHEPHERD.  What? Why rake up that again?
MESSENGER.  Look, here he is, my fine old friend—
    the same man who was just a baby then.

---

1249 **Arcturus** a star whose rising signaled the end of summer.

SHEPHERD.  Damn you, shut your mouth—quiet!                    1260
OEDIPUS.  Don't lash out at him, old man—
   you need lashing more than he does.
SHEPHERD.                                               Why,
   master, majesty—what have I done wrong?
OEDIPUS.  You won't answer his question about the boy.
SHEPHERD.  He's talking nonsense, wasting his breath.          1265
OEDIPUS.  So, you won't talk willingly—
   then you'll talk with pain.

    *[The guards seize the* SHEPHERD.]

SHEPHERD.  No, dear god, don't torture an old man!
OEDIPUS.  Twist his arms back, quickly!
SHEPHERD.                                   God help us, why?—
   what more do you need to know?                          1270
OEDIPUS.  Did you give him that child? He's asking.
SHEPHERD.  I did . . . I wish to god I'd died that day.
OEDIPUS.  You've got your wish if you don't tell the truth.
SHEPHERD.  The more I tell, the worse the death I'll die.
OEDIPUS.  Our friend here wants to stretch things out, does he?   1275

    *[Motioning to his men for torture.]*

SHEPHERD.  No, no, I gave it to him—I just said so.
OEDIPUS.  Where did you get it? Your house? Someone else's?
SHEPHERD.  It wasn't mine, no. I got it from . . . someone.
OEDIPUS.  Which one of them?

    *[Looking at the citizens.]*

                 Whose house?
SHEPHERD.                                   No—
   god's sake, master, no more questions!                   1280
OEDIPUS.  You're a dead man if I have to ask again.
SHEPHERD.  Then—the child came from the house . . . of Laius.
OEDIPUS.  A slave? or born of his own blood?
SHEPHERD.                                   Oh no,
   I'm right at the edge, the horrible truth—I've got to say it!
OEDIPUS.  And I'm at the edge of hearing horrors, yes, but I must hear!   1285
SHEPHERD.  All right! His son, they said it was—his son!
   But the one inside, your wife,
   she'd tell it best.
OEDIPUS.  My wife—
   *she* gave it to you?                                     1290
SHEPHERD.  Yes, yes, my king.
OEDIPUS.  Why, what for?

SHEPHERD.  To kill it.

OEDIPUS.  Her own child,
　　how could she?                                         1295

SHEPHERD.  She was afraid—
　　frightening prophecies.

OEDIPUS.  What?

SHEPHERD.　　　　They said—
　　he'd kill his parents.

OEDIPUS.  But you gave him to this old man—why?        1300

SHEPHERD.  I pitied the little baby, master,
　　hoped he'd take him off to his own country,
　　far away, but he saved him for this, his fate.
　　If you are the man he says you are, believe me,
　　you were born for pain.

OEDIPUS.　　　　　　　　O god—                           1305
　　all come true, all burst to light!
　　O light—now let me look my last on you!
　　I stand revealed at last—
　　cursed in my birth, cursed in marriage,
　　cursed in the lives I cut down with these hands!     1310

[*Rushing through the doors with a great cry. The Corinthian*
MESSENGER, *the* SHEPHERD *and attendants exit slowly to the side.*]

CHORUS.  O the generations of men
　　the dying generations—adding the total
　　of all your lives I find they come to nothing . . .
　　　　　does there exist, is there a man on earth
　　who seizes more joy than just a dream, a vision?     1315
　　And the vision no sooner dawns than dies
　　blazing into oblivion.

　　You are my great example, you, your life
　　your destiny, Oedipus, man of misery—
　　I count no man blest.
　　　　　　　　　You outranged all men!                 1320
　　　　Bending your bow to the breaking-point
　　you captured priceless glory, O dear god,
　　and the Sphinx came crashing down,
　　　　　the virgin, claws hooked
　　like a bird of omen singing, shrieking death—        1325
　　like a fortress reared in the face of death
　　you rose and saved our land.

　　From that day on we called you king
　　we crowned you with honors, Oedipus, towering over all—
　　mighty king of the seven gates of Thebes.           1330

But now to hear your story—is there a man more agonized?
More wed to pain and frenzy? Not a man on earth,
the joy of your life ground down to nothing
O Oedipus, name for the ages—
    one and the same wide harbor served you        1335
        son and father both
son and father came to rest in the same bridal chamber.
How, how could the furrows your father plowed
bear you, your agony, harrowing on
in silence O so long?

                But now for all your power        1340
Time, all-seeing Time has dragged you to the light,
judged your marriage monstrous from the start—
the son and the father tangling, both one—
O child of Laius, would to god
    I'd never seen you, never never!        1345
        Now I weep like a man who wails the dead
and the dirge comes pouring forth with all my heart!
I tell you the truth, you gave me life
my breath leapt up in you
and now you bring down the night upon my eyes.    1350

[*Enter a* MESSENGER *from the palace.*]

MESSENGER.  Men of Thebes, always first in honor,
    what horrors you will hear, what you will see,
    what a heavy weight of sorrow you will shoulder . . .
    if you are true to your birth, if you still have
    some feeling for the royal house of Thebes.        1355
    I tell you neither the waters of the Danube
    nor the Nile can wash this palace clean.
    Such things it hides, it soon will bring to light—
    terrible things, and none done blindly now,
    all done with a will. The pains        1360
    we inflict upon ourselves hurt most of all.
LEADER.  God knows we have pains enough already.
    What can you add to them?
MESSENGER.  The queen is dead.
LEADER.                    Poor lady—how?
MESSENGER.  By her own hand. But you are spared the worst,    1365
    you never had to watch . . . I saw it all,
    and with all the memory that's in me
    you will learn what that poor woman suffered.

    Once she'd broken in through the gates,
    dashing past us, frantic, whipped to fury,        1370

ripping her hair out with both hands—
straight to her rooms she rushed, flinging herself
across the bridal-bed, doors slamming behind her—
once inside, she wailed for Laius, dead so long,
remembering how she bore his child long ago,          1375
the life that rose up to destroy him, leaving
its mother to mother living creatures
with the very son she'd borne.
Oh how she wept, mourning the marriage-bed
where she let loose that double brood—monsters—       1380
husband by her husband, children by her child.
                                    And then—
but how she died is more than I can say. Suddenly
Oedipus burst in, screaming, he stunned us so
we couldn't watch her agony to the end,
our eyes were fixed on him. Circling                   1385
like a maddened beast, stalking, here, there,
crying out to us—
                  Give him a sword! His wife,
no wife, his mother, where can he find the mother earth
that cropped two crops at once, himself and all his children?
He was raging—one of the dark powers pointing the way,  1390
none of us mortals crowding around him, no,
with a great shattering cry—someone, something leading him on—
he hurled at the twin doors and bending the bolts back
out of their sockets, crashed through the chamber.
And there we saw the woman hanging by the neck,        1395
cradled high in a woven noose, spinning,
swinging back and forth. And when he saw her,
giving a low, wrenching sob that broke our hearts,
slipping the halter from her throat, he eased her down,
in a slow embrace he laid her down, poor thing . . .   1400
then, what came next, what horror we beheld!

He rips off her brooches, the long gold pins
holding her robes—and lifting them high,
looking straight up into the points,
he digs them down the sockets of his eyes, crying, "You,  1405
you'll see no more the pain I suffered, all the pain I caused!
Too long you looked on the ones you never should have seen,
blind to the ones you longed to see, to know! Blind
from this hour on! Blind in the darkness—blind!"
His voice like a dirge, rising, over and over           1410
raising the pins, raking them down his eyes.
And at each stroke blood spurts from the roots,

splashing his beard, a swirl of it, nerves and clots—
black hail of blood pulsing, gushing down.

These are the griefs that burst upon them both,                    1415
coupling man and woman. The joy they had so lately,
the fortune of their old ancestral house
was deep joy indeed. Now, in this one day,
wailing, madness and doom, death, disgrace,
all the griefs in the world that you can name,                     1420
all are theirs forever.

LEADER.                        Oh poor man, the misery—
has he any rest from pain now?

[*A voice within, in torment.*]

MESSENGER.                                  He's shouting,
"Loose the bolts, someone, show me to all of Thebes!
My father's murderer, my mother's—"
No, I can't repeat it, it's unholy.                                1425
Now he'll tear himself from his native earth,
not linger, curse the house with his own curse.
But he needs strength, and a guide to lead him on.
This is sickness more than he can bear.

[*The palace doors open.*]

                                      Look,
he'll show you himself. The great doors are opening—              1430
you are about to see a sight, a horror
even his mortal enemy would pity.

[*Enter* OEDIPUS, *blinded, led by a boy. He stands at the palace
steps, as if surveying his people once again.*]

CHORUS.                                  O the terror—
the suffering, for all the world to see,
the worst terror that ever met my eyes.
What madness swept over you? What god,                            1435
what dark power leapt beyond all bounds,
beyond belief, to crush your wretched life?—
godforsaken, cursed by the gods!
I pity you but I can't bear to look.
I've much to ask, so much to learn,                               1440
so much fascinates my eyes,
but you . . . I shudder at the sight.

OEDIPUS.                                  Oh, Ohh—
the agony! I am agony—
where am I going? where on earth?

> where does all this agony hurl me?                    1445
> where's my voice?—
> winging, swept away on a dark tide—
> My destiny, my dark power, what a leap you made!

CHORUS.  To the depths of terror, too dark to hear, to see.

OEDIPUS.  Dark, horror of darkness                       1450
> *my* darkness, drowning, swirling around me
> crashing wave on wave—unspeakable, irresistible
> headwind, fatal harbor! Oh again,
> the misery, all at once, over and over
> the stabbing daggers, stab of memory              1455
> raking me insane.

CHORUS.                     No wonder you suffer
> twice over, the pain of your wounds,
> the lasting grief of pain.

OEDIPUS.                      Dear friend, still here?
> Standing by me, still with a care for me,
> the blind man? Such compassion,                    1460
> loyal to the last. Oh it's you,
> I know you're here, dark as it is
> I'd know you anywhere, your voice—
> it's yours, clearly yours.

CHORUS.                        Dreadful, what you've done . . .
> how could you bear it, gouging out your eyes?      1465
> What superhuman power drove you on?

OEDIPUS.  Apollo, friends, Apollo—
> he ordained my agonies—these, my pains on pains!
> But the hand that struck my eyes was mine,
> mine alone—no one else—                            1470
> I did it all myself!
> What good were eyes to me?
> Nothing I could see could bring me joy.

CHORUS.  No, no, exactly as you say.

OEDIPUS.                         What can I ever see?
> What love, what call of the heart                  1475
> can touch my ears with joy? Nothing, friends.
> Take me away, far, far from Thebes,
> quickly, cast me away, my friends—
> this great murderous ruin, this man cursed to heaven,
> the man the deathless gods hate most of all!       1480

CHORUS.  Pitiful, you suffer so, you understand so much . . .
> I wish you'd never known.

OEDIPUS.                       Die, die—
> whoever he was that day in the wilds
> who cut my ankles free of the ruthless pins,

he pulled me clear of death, he saved my life                                    1485
for this, this kindness—
   Curse him, kill him!
If I'd died then, I'd never have dragged myself,
my loved ones through such hell.
CHORUS.  Oh if only . . . would to god.
OEDIPUS.                                                   I'd never have come to this,    1490
   my father's murderer—never been branded
   mother's husband, all men see me now! Now,
   loathed by the gods, son of the mother I defiled
   coupling in my father's bed, spawning lives in the loins
that spawned my wretched life. What grief can crown this grief?    1495
   It's mine alone, my destiny—I am Oedipus!
CHORUS.  How can I say you've chosen for the best?
   Better to die than be alive and blind.
OEDIPUS.  What I did was best—don't lecture me,
no more advice. I, with *my* eyes,                                    1500
how could I look my father in the eyes
when I go down to death? Or mother, so abused . . .
I have done such things to the two of them,
crimes too huge for hanging.
                 Worse yet,
the sight of my children, born as they were born,                    1505
how could I long to look into their eyes?
No, not with these eyes of mine, never.
Not this city either, her high towers,
the sacred glittering images of her gods—
I am misery! I, her best son, reared                                    1510
as no other son of Thebes was ever reared,
I've stripped myself, I gave the command myself.
All men must cast away the great blasphemer,
the curse now brought to light by the gods,
the son of Laius—I, my father's son!                                    1515

Now I've exposed my guilt, horrendous guilt,
could I train a level glance on you, my countrymen?
Impossible! No, if I could just block off my ears,
the springs of hearing, I would stop at nothing—
I'd wall up my loathsome body like a prison,                          1520
blind to the sound of life, not just the sight:
Oblivion—what a blessing . . .
for the mind to dwell a world away from pain.

O Cithaeron, why did you give me shelter?
Why didn't you take me, crush my life out on the spot?              1525
I'd never have revealed my birth to all mankind.

O Polybus, Corinth, the old house of my fathers,
so I believed—what a handsome prince you raised—
under the skin, what sickness to the core.
Look at me! Born of outrage, outrage to the core.                    1530
O triple roads—it all comes back, the secret,
dark ravine, and the oaks closing in
where the three roads join . . .
You drank my father's blood, my own blood
spilled by my own hands—you still remember me?                       1535
What things you saw me do? Then I came here
and did them all once more!

                            Marriages! O marriage,
you gave me birth, and once you brought me into the world
you brought my sperm rising back, springing to light
fathers, brothers, sons—one murderous breed—                        1540
brides, wives, mothers. The blackest things
a man can do, I have done them all!

                                    No more—
it's wrong to name what's wrong to do. Quickly,
for the love of god, hide me somewhere,
kill me, hurl me into the sea                                        1545
where you can never look on me again.

[*Beckoning to the* CHORUS *as they shrink away.*]

                                   Closer,
it's all right. Touch the man of grief.
Do. Don't be afraid. My troubles are mine
and I am the only man alive who can sustain them.

[*Enter* CREON *from the palace, attended by palace guards.*]

LEADER.  Put your requests to Creon. Here he is,                     1550
    just when we need him. He'll have a plan, he'll act.
    Now that he's the sole defense of the country
    in your place.
OEDIPUS.           Oh no, what can I say to him?
    How can I ever hope to win his trust?
    I wronged him so, just now, in every way.                       1555
    You must see that—I was so wrong, so wrong.
CREON.  I haven't come to mock you, Oedipus,
    or to criticize your former failings.

[*Turning to the guards.*]

                               You there,
have you lost all respect for human feelings?
At least revere the Sun, the holy fire                               1560

that keeps us all alive. Never expose a thing
of guilt and holy dread so great it appalls
the earth, the rain from heaven, the light of day!
Get him into the halls—quickly as you can.
Piety demands no less. Kindred alone                              1565
should see a kinsman's shame. This is obscene.
OEDIPUS.  Please, in god's name . . . you wipe my fears away,
coming so generously to me, the worst of men.
Do one thing more, for your sake, not mine.
CREON.  What do you want? Why so insistent?                       1570
OEDIPUS.  Drive me out of the land at once, far from sight,
where I can never hear a human voice.
CREON.  I'd have done that already, I promise you.
First I wanted the god to clarify my duties.
OEDIPUS.  The god? His command was clear, every word:            1575
death for the father-killer, the curse—
he said destroy me!
CREON.  So he did. Still, in such a crisis
it's better to ask precisely what to do.
OEDIPUS.                                   So miserable—
you'd consult the god about a man like me?                       1580
CREON.  By all means. And this time, I assume,
even you will obey the god's decrees.
OEDIPUS.                                   I will,
I will. And you, I command you—I beg you . . .
the woman inside, bury her as you see fit.
It's the only decent thing,                                      1585
to give your own the last rites. As for me,
never condemn the city of my fathers
to house my body, not while I'm alive, no,
let me live on the mountains, on Cithaeron,
my favorite haunt, I have made it famous.                        1590
Mother and father marked out that rock
to be my everlasting tomb—buried alive.
Let me die there, where they tried to kill me.
Oh but this I know: no sickness can destroy me,
nothing can. I would never have been saved                       1595
from death—I have been saved
for something great and terrible, something strange.
Well let my destiny come and take me on its way!
About my children, Creon, the boys at least,
don't burden yourself. They're men,                              1600
wherever they go, they'll find the means to live.
But my two daughters, my poor helpless girls,
clustering at our table, never without me

hovering near them . . . whatever I touched,
they always had their share. Take care of them,                    1605
I beg you. Wait, better—permit me, would you?
Just to touch them with my hands and take
our fill of tears. Please . . . my king.
Grant it, with all your noble heart.
If I could hold them, just once, I'd think                         1610
I had them with me, like the early days
when I could see their eyes.

[ANTIGONE *and* ISMENE, *two small children, are led in from the
palace by a nurse.*]

                              What's that
O god! Do I really hear you sobbing?—
my two children. Creon, you've pitied me?
Sent me my darling girls, my own flesh and blood!                  1615
Am I right?

CREON.              Yes, it's my doing.
I know the joy they gave you all these years,
the joy you must feel now.

OEDIPUS.                         Bless you, Creon!
May god watch over you for this kindness,
better than he ever guarded me.
                              Children, where are you?            1620
Here, come quickly—

[*Groping for* ANTIGONE *and* ISMENE, *who approach their father
cautiously, then embrace him.*]

                         Come to these hands of mine,
your brother's hands, your own father's hands
that served his once bright eyes so well—
that made them blind. Seeing nothing, children,
knowing nothing, I became your father,                             1625
I fathered you in the soil that gave me life.

How I weep for you—I cannot see you now . . .
just thinking of all your days to come, the bitterness,
the life that rough mankind will thrust upon you.
Where are the public gatherings you can join,                      1630
the banquets of the clans? Home you'll come,
in tears, cut off from the sight of it all,
the brilliant rites unfinished.
And when you reach perfection, ripe for marriage,
who will he be, my dear ones? Risking all                          1635
to shoulder the curse that weighs down my parents,
yes and you too—that wounds us all together.

What more misery could you want?
Your father killed his father, sowed his mother,
one, one and the selfsame womb sprang you—                    1640
he cropped the very roots of his existence.

Such disgrace, and you must bear it all!
Who will marry you then? Not a man on earth.
Your doom is clear: you'll wither away to nothing,
single, without a child.

[*Turning to* CREON.]

                   Oh Creon,                    1645
you are the only father they have now . . .
we who brought them into the world
are gone, both gone at a stroke—
Don't let them go begging, abandoned,
women without men. Your own flesh and blood!                    1650
Never bring them down to the level of my pains.
Pity them. Look at them, so young, so vulnerable,
shorn of everything—you're their only hope.
Promise me, noble Creon, touch my hand!

[*Reaching toward* CREON, *who draws back.*]

You, little ones, if you were old enough                    1655
to understand, there is much I'd tell you.
Now, as it is, I'd have you say a prayer.
Pray for life, my children,
live where you are free to grow and season.
Pray god you find a better life than mine,                    1660
the father who begot you.
CREON.                                   Enough.
You've wept enough. Into the palace now.
OEDIPUS.  I must, but I find it very hard.
CREON.  Time is the great healer, you will see.
OEDIPUS.  I am going—you know on what condition?                    1665
CREON.  Tell me. I'm listening.
OEDIPUS.  Drive me out of Thebes, in exile.
CREON.  Not I. Only the gods can give you that.
OEDIPUS.  Surely the gods hate me so much—
CREON.  You'll get your wish at once.
OEDIPUS.                                   You consent?                    1670
CREON.  I try to say what I mean; it's my habit.
OEDIPUS.  Then take me away. It's time.
CREON.  Come along, let go of the children.
OEDIPUS.                                   No—
don't take them away from me, not now! No no no!

[*Clutching his daughters as the guards wrench them loose and take them through the palace doors.*]

CREON.  Still the king, the master of all things?                    1675
No more: here your power ends.
None of your power follows you through life.

[*Exit* OEDIPUS *and* CREON *to the palace. The* CHORUS *comes forward to address the audience directly.*]

CHORUS.  People of Thebes, my countrymen, look on Oedipus.
He solved the famous riddle with his brilliance,
he rose to power, a man beyond all power.                            1680
Who could behold his greatness without envy?
Now what a black sea of terror has overwhelmed him.
Now as we keep our watch and wait the final day,
count no man happy till he dies, free of pain at last.

[*Exit in procession.*]

## ▓ TOPICS FOR CRITICAL THINKING AND WRITING

### *The Play on the Page*

1. On the basis of lines 1–149, characterize Oedipus. Does he seem an effective leader? What additional traits are revealed in lines 205–491?
2. In your opinion, how fair is it to say that Oedipus is morally guilty? Does he argue that he is morally innocent because he did not intend to do immoral deeds? Can it be said that he is guilty of *hybris* but that *hybris* (see page 624) has nothing to do with his fall?
3. Oedipus says that he blinds himself in order not to look upon people he should not. What further reasons can be given? Why does he not (like Jocasta) commit suicide?
4. Does the play show the futility of human effots to act intelligently?
5. In *Oedipus,* do you find the gods evil?
6. Are the choral odes lyrical interludes that serve to separate the scenes, or do they advance the dramatic action?
7. Matthew Arnold said that Sophocles saw life steadily and saw it whole. But in this play is Sophocles facing the facts of life? Or, on the contrary, is he avoiding what we think of as normal life, and presenting a series of unnatural and outrageous coincidences? In either case, do you think the play is relevant today?
8. Can you describe your emotions at the end of the play? Do they include pity for Oedipus? Pity for all human beings, including yourself? Fear that you might be punished for some unintended transgres-

sion? Awe, engendered by a perception of the interrelatedness of things? Relief that the story is only a story? Exhilaration? Explain your reaction.

## The Play on the Stage

9. During your first consideration of the play, start with a reading of lines 1–149. Choose someone from the group to stand on a chair (Oedipus), two other readers to stand nearby (the Priest and Creon), and several others to kneel or lie on the floor (Theban citizens). After this rough enactment, ask the readers how they felt about their roles. Then discuss the ways a modern staging could create a powerful opening for the play. Some questions to consider: Do the Thebans ever touch Oedipus? Should the actor playing Oedipus make eye contact with anyone on the stage?

10. Originally the Greek chorus chanted and danced. What are your recommendations for a director today? How large a chorus would you use? Would you use dance movements? If not, in what sorts of movements might the chorus engage? Choose a particular passage from the play to illustrate your ideas.

11. Imagine that you are directing a production of *Oedipus*. Propose a cast for the principal roles, using well-known actors or people from your own circle. Explain the reasons for your choices.

12. Would you use masks for some (or all) of the characters? If so, would they be masks that fully cover the face, Greek-style, or sort of half-masks? (A full mask enlarges the face, and conceivably the mouthpiece can amplify the voice, but only an exceptionally large theater might require such help. Perhaps half-masks are enough if the aim is chiefly to distance the actors from the audience and from daily reality, and to force the actors to develop resources other than facial gestures. One director, arguing in favor of half-masks, has said that actors who wear even a half-mask learn to act not with the eys but with the neck.)

13. What might be gained or lost by performing the play in modern dress? Or is there some period other than ancient Greece—let's say the Victorian period—in which you think the play might be effectively set? Alan MacVey, who directed a production at the University of Iowa, used classical costumes but afterward said that he wished he had used a conference table as the set and had costumed the royalty in "power suits." What is your response to this idea? One argument sometimes used by those who hold that modern productions of Greek drama should use classical costumes is that Greek drama *ought* to be remote and ritualistic. Evaluate this view. What sort of modern dress might be effective?

# A NOTE ON THE ELIZABETHAN THEATER

Shakespeare's theater was wooden, round or polygonal (the Chorus in *Henry V* calls it a "wooden O"). About eight hundred spectators could stand in the yard in front of—and perhaps along the two sides of—the stage that jutted from the rear wall, and another fifteen hundred or so spectators could sit in the three roofed galleries that ringed the stage.

That portion of the galleries that was above the rear of the stage was sometimes used by actors. For instance, in *The Tempest*, 3.3, a stage direction following line 17 mentions "Prospero on the top, invisible," that is, he is imagined to be invisible to the characters in the play.

Entry to the stage was normally gained by doors at the rear, but apparently on rare occasions use was made of a curtained alcove—or perhaps a booth—between the doors, which allowed characters to be "discovered" (revealed) as in the modern proscenium theater, which normally employs a curtain. Such "discovery" scenes are rare.

Although the theater as a whole was unroofed, the stage was protected by a roof, supported by two pillars. These could serve (by an act of imagination) as trees behind which actors might pretend to conceal themselves.

A performance was probably uninterrupted by intermissions or by long pauses for the changing of scenery; a group of characters leaves the stage, another enters, and if the locale has changed the new characters somehow tell us. (Modern editors customarily add indications of locales to help a reader, but it should be remembered that the action on the Elizabethan stage was continuous.)

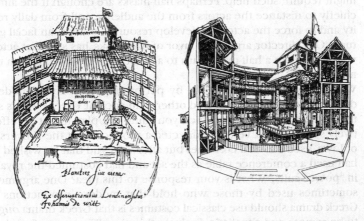

*Left:* Johannes de Witt, a Continental visitor to London, made a drawing of the Swan Theater in about the year 1596. The original drawing is lost; this is Arend van Buchel's copy of it. *Right:* C. Walter Hodges's drawing (1965) of an Elizabethan playhouse.

# A NOTE ON THE TEXTS
# OF *OTHELLO*

*Othello* was first published in 1622, in a small volume called a quarto (each sheet of paper has been folded in half, and then in half again, to make four leaves—i.e., eight pages). *Othello* was next published in 1623, in the first folio edition of Shakespeare's collected plays (a folio is a larger book—each sheet has been folded only once, producing two leaves, four pages).

The quarto (Q) contains 16 lines not in the folio (F), but the folio has about 150 lines not in the quarto. Further, there are hundreds of small but significant differences between the texts—for instance, "O God" in Q and "Oh heaven" in F—but perhaps the most important difference in a single word occurs in Othello's next-to-last speech. In Q he says his hand, "Like the base Indian, threw a pearle away, / Richer than all his Tribe." In F

Quarto, 1622    *Oth.* Soft you, a word or two,
I haue done the State some seruice, and they know't;
No more of that : I pray you in your letters,
When you shall these vnlucky deedes relate,
Speake of them as they are , nothing extenuate,
Nor set downe ought in malice; then must you speake,
Of one that lou'd not wisely, but too well :
Of one not easily iealous, but being wrought,
Perplext in the extreame ; of one whose hand,
Like the base *Indian*, threw a pearle away,
Richer then all his Tribe : of one whose subdued eyes,
Albeit vnused to the melting moode,
Drops teares as fast as the *Arabian* trees,
Their medicinall gum ; set you downe this,
And say besides; that in *Aleppo* once,
Where a *Malignant* and a *Turband Turke*,
Beate a *Venetian*, and traduc'd the State;
I tooke by th throate the circumcised dog,
And smote him thus,            *He stabs himselfe.*

Part of the page of the 1622 quarto, where Othello speaks of himself as a "base *Indian*." An Elizabethan tradition associated American Indians with ignorantly neglecting to value precious jewels and gold, so Othello here may be comparing himself to such an Indian. Most editors accept this reading.

*Note:* The technology of printing in England in Shakespeare's day was fairly low, not only by comparison with printing today but even by comparison with printing on the Continent in the early seventeenth century. With very few exceptions publishers in England produced books for a market that wanted cheap editions rather than fine editions, which means that the consumer would get pages that were unevenly inked and were sometimes printed from typefaces that were damaged.

Folio, 1623

*Oth.* Soft you; a word or two before you goe :
I haue done the State fome feruice, and they know't:
No more of that. I pray you in your Letters,
When you fhall thefe vnluckie deeds relate,
Speake of me, as I am. Nothing extenuate,
Nor fet downe ought in malice.
Then muft you fpeake,
Of one that lou'd not wifely, but too well :
Of one, not eafily Iealious, but being wrought,
Perplexed in the extreame : Of one, whofe hand
(Like the bafe Iudean) threw a Pearle away
Richer then all his Tribe: Of one, whofe fubdu'd Eyes,
Albeit vn-vfed to the melting moode,
Drops teares as faft as the Arabian Trees
Their Medicinable gumme. Set you downe this:
And fay befides, that in *Aleppo* once,
Where a malignant, and a Turbond-Turke
Beate a Venetian, and traduc'd the State,
I tooke by th'throat the circumcifed Dogge,
And fmoate him, thus.

Part of a page in the 1623 folio, where Othello speaks of himself as "the base Iudean,"
Conceivably the manuscript had *Indian* or *Indean*, but the type-setter mistakenly inverted an *n*, producing a *u*. On the other hand, Iudean (that is, Judean) makes sense,
referring either to (a) Herod the Great (king of the Jews), who murdered his wife after
she had been accused (falsely) of infidelity, or (b) Judas Iscariat, who betrayed Jesus.
(Also relevant is Matthew 13.45, in which Jesus tells a parable comparing the kingdom
of heaven to "a pearl of great price").

Othello says his hand, "(Like the base Iudean) threw a Pearle away / Richer
than all his Tribe." That is, in Q he compares himself to the ignorant savage
(perhaps a native of India, perhaps an American Indian) who did not
properly value a precious jewel. (Europeans conventionally thought that
other cultures did not value pearls.) In F he compares himself to Judas Iscariat, who betrayed Jesus, or perhaps to Herod the Great, king of the
Jews, who murdered his wife. Arguments can be made on behalf of both
readings, but perhaps the strongest is in favor of "Indian," on the grounds
that Othello is correctly saying that he acted out of ignorance (like the Indian), not out of malice (like Judas).

David Bevington, the editor of the version of *Othello* that we give,
uses F for the most part, but he sometimes draws on Q where (as in the
Indian/Judean instance) Q seems to him to be what Shakespeare probably wrote. Bevington has also added some material for the reader's convenience—for instance, indications of scene and some stage directions. His
text and notes were prepared for his book, *The Complete Works of Shakespeare*, Updated 4th ed. (New York: Longman, 1997).

# WILLIAM SHAKESPEARE

*William Shakespeare (1564–1616) was born in Stratford, England, of middle-class parents. Nothing of interest is known about his early years, but by 1590 he was acting and writing plays in London. By the end of the following decade he had worked in all three Elizabethan dramatic genres—tragedy, comedy, and history.* Romeo and Juliet, *for example, was written about 1595, the year of* Richard II, *and in the following year he wrote* A Midsummer Night's Dream. Julius Caesar *(1599) probably preceded* As You Like It *by one year, and* Hamlet *probably followed* As You Like It *by less than a year. Among the plays that followed* Othello *(1603–1604) were* King Lear *(1605–1606),* Macbeth *(1605–1606), and several "romances"—plays that have happy endings but that seem more mediatative and closer to tragedy than such comedies as* A Midsummer Night's Dream, As You Like It, *and* Twelfth Night.

A possible staging of Act 5, Scene 1, as at the Globe Theatre, by C. Walter Hodges. Successive events, shown here simultaneously, are numbered in sequence.

# Othello, the Moor of Venice     [1603–1604?]

## THE NAMES OF THE ACTORS

OTHELLO, *the Moor*
BRABANTIO, *[a senator,] father to Desdemona*
CASSIO, *an honorable lieutenant [to Othello]*
IAGO, *[Othello's ancient,] a villain*
RODERIGO, *a gulled gentleman*
DUKE *of Venice*
SENATORS *[of Venice]*
MONTANO, *governor of Cyprus*
LODOVICO *and* GRATIANO, *[kinsmen to Brabantio,] two noble Venetians*
SAILORS
CLOWN
DESDEMONA, *[daughter to Brabantio and] wife to Othello*
EMILIA, *wife to Iago*
BIANCA, *a courtesan [and mistress to Cassio]*
A MESSENGER
A HERALD
A MUSICIAN
*S*ervants, Attendants, Officers, Senators, Musicians, Gentlemen

**SCENE:** *Venice; a seaport in Cyprus]*

**1.1** *Enter* RODERIGO *and* IAGO.

RODERIGO. Tush, never tell me!° I take it much unkindly
    That thou, Iago, who hast had my purse
    As if the strings were thine, shouldst know of this.°
IAGO. 'Sblood,° but you'll not hear me.
    If ever I did dream of such a matter,                              5
    Abhor me.
RODERIGO. Thou toldst me thou didst hold him in thy hate.
IAGO. Despise me
    If I do not. Three great ones of the city,
    In personal suit to make his lieutenant,                          10
    Off-capped to him;° and by the faith of man,
    I know my price, I am worth no worse a place.
    But he, as loving his own pride and purposes,
    Evades them with a bombast circumstance°

---

**1.1 Location: Venice, a street.    1 never tell me** (An expression of incredulity,
like "tell me another one.")    **3 this** i.e., Desdemona's elopement.    **4 'Sblood**
by His (Christ's blood).    **11 him** i.e., Othello.    **14 bombast circumstance**
wordy evasion. (Bombast is cotton padding.)

Horribly stuffed with epithets of war,°                    15
And, in conclusion,
Nonsuits° my mediators. For, "Certes,"° says he,
"I have already chose my officer."
And what was he?
Forsooth, a great arithmetician,°                          20
One Michael Cassio, a Florentine,
A fellow almost damned in a fair wife,°
That never set a squadron in the field
Nor the division of a battle° knows
More than a spinster°—unless the bookish theoric,°        25
Wherein the togaed° consuls° can propose°
As masterly as he. Mere prattle without practice
In all his soldiership. Bvt he, sir, had th' election;
And I, of whom his° eyes had seen the proof
At Rhodes, at Cyprus, and on other grounds                 30
Christened° and heathen, must be beeled and calmed°
By debitor and creditor.° This countercaster,°
He, in good time,° must his lieutenant be,
And I—God bless the mark!°—his Moorship's ancient.°
RODERIGO. By heaven, I rather would have been his hangman.° 35
IAGO. Why, there's no remedy. 'Tis the curse of service;
Preferment° goes by letter and affection,°
And not by old gradation,° where each second
Stood heir to th' first. Now, sir, be judge yourself
Whether I in any just term° am affined°                    40
To love the Moor.

---

**15 epithets of war** military expressions.   **17 Nonsuits** rejects the petition of.
**Certes** certainly.   **20 arithmeti-cian** i.e., a man whose military knowledge is
merely theoretical, based on books of tactics.   **22 A . . . wife** (Cassio does not
seem to be married, but his counterpart in Shakespeare's source does have a
woman in his house. See also 4.1.127.)   **24 division of a battle** disposition of a
military unit.   **25 a spinster** i.e., a housewife, one whose regular occupation is
spinning.   **theoric** theory.   **26 togaed** wearing the toga.   **consuls** counselors,
senators.   **propose** discuss.   **29 his** i.e., Othello's.   **31 Christened** Christian.
**beeled and calm** left to leeward without wind, becalmed. (A sailing metaphor.)
**32 debitor and creditor** (A name for a system of bookkeeping, here used as a
contemptuous nickname for Cassio.)   **countercaster** i.e., bookkeeper, one who
tallies with *counters*, or "metal disks." (Said contemptuously.)   **33 in good time**
opportunely, i.e., forsooth.   **34 God bless the mark** (Perhaps originally a
formula to ward off evil; here an expression of impatience.)   **ancient** standard-
bearer, ensign.   **35 his hangman** the executioner of him.   **37 preferment**
promotion.   **letter and affection** personal influence and favoritism.   **38 old
gradation** step-by-step seniority, the traditional way.   **40 term** respect.
**affined** bound.

Laurence Fishburne as Othello.

RODERIGO.  I would not follow him then.
IAGO.  O sir, content you.°
        I follow him to serve my turn upon him.
        We cannot all be masters, nor all masters                    45
        Cannot be truly° followed. You shall mark
        Many a duteous and knee-crooking knave
        That, doting on his own obsequious bondage,
        Wears out his time, much like his master's ass,
        For naught but provender, and when he's old, cashiered.°    50
        Whip me° such honest knaves. Others there are
        Who, trimmed in forms and visages of duty,°
        Keep yet their hearts attending on themselves,
        And, throwing but shows of service on their lords,
        Do well thrive by them, and when they have lined their coats,°  55
        Do themselves homage.° These fellows have some soul,
        And such a one do I profess myself. For, sir,
        It is as sure as you are Roderigo,

---

**43 content you** don't you worry about that.    **46 truly** faithfully.    **50 cashiered**
dismissed from service.    **51 Whip me** whip as far as I'm concerned.
**52 trimmed . . . duty** dressed up in the mere form and show of dutifulness.
**55 lined their coats** i.e., stuffed their purses.    **56 Do themselves homage**
i.e., attend to self-interest solely.

Were I the Moor I would not be Iago.°
In following him, I follow but myself—                              60
Heaven is my judge, not I for love and duty,
But seeming so for my peculiar° end.
For when my outward action doth demonstrate
The native° act and figure° of my heart
In compliment extern.° 'tis not long after                          65
But I will wear my heart upon my sleeve
For daws° to peck at. I am not what I am.°

RODERIGO.  What a full° fortune does the thick-lips° owe°
   If he can carry 't thus!°

IAGO.                    Call up her father.
   Rouse him, make after him, poison his delight,                   70
   Proclaim him in the streets; incense her kinsmen,
   And, though he in a fertile climate dwell,
   Plague him with flies.° Though that his joy be joy.°
   Yet throw such changes of vexation° on 't
   As it may° lose some color.°                                     75

RODERIGO.  Here is her father's house. I'll call aloud.

IAGO.  Do, with like timorous° accent and dire yell
   As when, by night and negligence,° the fire
   Is spied in populous cities.

RODERIGO.  What ho, Brabantio! Signor Brabantio, ho!                80

IAGO.  Awake! What ho, Brabantio! Thieves, thieves, thieves!
   Look to your house, your daughter, and your bags!
   Thieves, thieves!

BRABANTIO [enters] above [at a window].°

BRABANTIO.  What is the reason of this terrible summons?
   What is the matter° there?                                      85

---

**59 Were . . . Iago** i.e., if I were able to assume command, I certainly would not
choose to remain a subordinate, or, I would keep a suspicious eye on a flattering
subordinate.   **62 peculiar** particular, personal.   **64 native** innate.   **figure**
shape, intent.   **65 compliment extern** outward show. (Conforming in this case
to the inner workings and intention of the heart.)   **67 daws** small crowlike birds,
proverbially stupid and avaricious.   **I am not what I am** i.e., I am not one who
wears his heart on his sleeve.   **68 full** swelling.   **thick-lips** (Elizabethans often
applied the term "Moor" to Negroes.)   **owe** own.   **69 carry 't thus** carry this
off.   **72–73 though . . . flies** though he seems prosperous and happy now, vex
him with misery.   **73 Though . . . be joy** although he seems fortunate and
happy. (Repeats the idea of line 72.)   **74 changes of vexation** vexing changes.
**75 As it may** that may cause it to.   **some color** some of its fresh gloss.
**77 timorous** frightening.   **78 and negligence** i.e., by negligence.   **83 s.d. at a
window** (This stage direction, from the Quarto, probably calls for an appearance
on the gallery above and rearstage.)   **85 the matter** your business.

RODERIGO.  Signor, is all your family within?
IAGO.  Are your doors locked?
BRABANTIO.                    Why, wherefore ask you this?
IAGO.  Zounds,° sir, you're robbed. For shame, put on your gown!
    Your heart is burst; you have lost half your soul.
    Even now, now, very now, an old black ram                    90
    Is tupping° your white ewe. Arise, arise!
    Awake the snorting° citizens with the bell,
    Or else the devil° will make a grandsire of you.
    Arise, I say!
BRABANTIO.          What, have you lost your wits?
RODERIGO.  Most reverend signor, do you know my voice?                    95
BRABANTIO.  Not I. What are you?
RODERIGO.  My name is Roderigo.
BRABANTIO.  The worser welcome.
    I have charged thee not to haunt about my doors.
    In honest plainness thou hast heard me say                    100
    My daughter is not for thee; and now, in madness,
    Being full of supper and distempering° drafts,
    Upon malicious bravery° dost thou come
    To start° my quiet.
RODERIGO.  Sir, sir, sir—
BRABANTIO.                    But thou must needs be sure                    105
    My spirits and my place° have in° their power
    To make this bitter to thee.
RODERIGO.                    Patience, good sir.
BRABANTIO.  What tell'st thou me of robbing? This is Venice;
    My house is not a grange.°
RODERIGO.                    Most grave Brabantio,
    In simple° and pure soul I come to you.                    110
IAGO.  Zounds, sir, you are one of those that will not serve God if the devil
    bid you. Because we come to do you service and you think we are
    ruffians, you'll have your daughter covered with a Barbary° horse;
    you'll have your nephews° neigh to you; you'll have coursers° for
    cousins° and jennets° for germans.°                    115
BRABANTIO.  What profane wretch art thou?

---

88 **Zounds** by His (Christ's) wounds.    91 **tupping** covering, copulating
with. (Said of sheep.)    92 **snorting** snoring.    93 **the devil** (The devil was
conventionally pictured as black.)    102 **distempering** intoxicating.    103 **Upon
malicious bravery** with hostile intent to defy me.    104 **start** startle, disrupt.
106 **My spirits and my place** my temperament and my authority of office.
**have in** have it in.    109 **grange** isolated country house.    110 **simple** sincere.
113 **Barbary** from northern Africa (and hence associated with Othello).
114 **nephews** i.e., grandson.    **coursers** powerful horses.    115 **cousins**
kinsmen.    **jennets** small Spanish horses.    **germans** near relatives.

IAGO.   I am one, sir, that comes to tell you your daughter and the Moor
are now making the beast with two backs.
BRABANTIO.   Thou art a villain.
IAGO.                          You are—a senator.°
BRABANTIO.   This thou shalt answer.° I know thee, Roderigo.        120
RODERIGO.   Sir, I will answer anything. But I beseech you,
    If't be your pleasure and most wise° consent—
    As partly I find it is—that your fair daughter,
    At this odd-even° and dull watch o' the night,
    Transported with° no worse nor better guard        125
    But with a knave° of common hire, a gondolier,
    To the gross clasps of a lascivious Moor—
    If this be known to you and your allowance°
    We then have done you bold and saucy° wrongs.
    But if you know not this, my manners tell me        130
    We have your wrong rebuke. Do not believe
    That, from° the sense of all civility,°
    I thus would play and trifle with your reverence.°
    Your daughter, if you have not given her leave,
    I say again, hath made a gross revolt,        135
    Tying her duty, beauty, wit,° and fortunes
    In an extravagant° and wheeling° stranger°
    Of here and everywhere. Straight° satisfy yourself.
    If she be in her chamber or your house,
    Let loose on me the justice of the state        140
    For thus deluding you.
BRABANTIO.   Strike on the tinder,° ho!
    Give me a taper! Call up all my people!
    This accident° is not unlike my dream.
    Belief of it oppresses me already.        145
    Light, I say, light!                        *Exit [above].*
IAGO.                     Farewell, for I must leave you.
    It seems not meet° nor wholesome to my place°
    To be producted°—as, if I stay, I shall—

---

119 **a senator** (Said with mock politeness, as though the word itself were an
insult.)    120 **answer** be held accountable for.    122 **wise** well-informed.
124 **odd-even** between one day and the next, i.e., without midnight.    125 **with**
by.    126 **But with a knave** than by a low fellow, a servant.    128 **allowance**
permission.    129 **saucy** insolent.    132 **from** contrary to.   **civility** good
manners, decency.    133 **your reverence** the respect due to you.    136 **wit**
intelligence    137 **extravagant** expatriate, wandering far from home.   **wheeling**
roving about, vagabond.   **stranger** foreigner.    138 **Straight** straightway.
142 **tinder** charred linen ignited by a spark from flint and steel, used to light
torches or *tapers* (lines 142, 167).    144 **accident** occurrence, event.    147 **meet**
fitting.   **place** position (as ensign).    148 **producted** produced (as a witness).

Against the Moor. For I do know the state,
However this may gall° him with some check,°                    150
Cannot with safety cast° him, for he's embarked°
With such loud reason° to the Cyprus wars,
Which even now stands in act,° for their souls,°
Another of his fathom° they have none
To lead their business; in which regard,°                        155
Though I do hate him as I do hell pains,
Yet for necessity of present life°
I must show out a flag and sign of love,
Which is indeed but sign. That you shall surely find him,
Lead to the Sagittary° the raisèd search,°                       160
And there will I be with him. So farewell.            *Exit.*

*Enter [below]* BRABANTIO *[in his nightgown°] with servants
and torches.*

BRABANTIO.  It is too true an evil. Gone she is;
And what's to come of my despisèd time°
Is naught but bitterness. Now, Roderigo,
Where didst thou see her?—O unhappy girl!—                      165
With the Moor, sayst thou?—Who would be a father!—
How didst thou know 'twas she?—O, she deceives me
Past thought!—What said she to you?—Get more tapers.
Raise all my kindred.—Are they married, think you?
RODERIGO.  Truly, I think they are.                             170
BRABANTIO.  Oh heaven! How got she out? O treason of the blood!
Fathers, from hence trust not your daughters' minds
By what you see them act. Is there not charms°
By which the property° of youth and maidhood
May be abused?° Have you not read, Roderigo,                    175
Of some such thing!
RODERIGO.                      Yes, sir, I have indeed.
BRABANTIO.  Call up my brother.—O, would you had had her!—
Some one way, some another.—Do you know
Where we may apprehend her and the Moor?

---

**150 gall** rub; oppress.   **check** rebuke.   **151 cast** dismiss.   **embarked** engaged.
**152 loud reason** unanimous shout of confirmation (in the Senate).   **153 stands
in act** are going on.   **for their souls** to save themselves.   **154 fathom** i.e.,
ability, depth of experience.   **155 in which regard** out of regard for which.
**157 life** livelihood.   **160 Sagittary** (An inn or house where Othello and
Desdemona are staying, named for its sign of Sagittarius, or Centaur.)   **raisèd
search** search party roused out of sleep.   **s.d. nightgown** dressing gown. (This
costuming is specified in the Quarto text.)   **163 time** i.e., remainder of life.
**173 charms** spells.   **174 property** special quality, nature.   **175 abused**
deceived.

RODERIGO. I think I can discover° him, if you please      180
    To get good guard and go along with me.
BRABANTIO. Pray you, lead on. At every house I'll call;
    I may command° at most.—Get weapons, ho!
    And raise some special officers of night.—
    On, good Roderigo, I will deserve° your pains.      185

*Exeunt.*

**1.2** *Enter* OTHELLO, IAGO, *attendants with torches.*

IAGO. Though in the trade of war I have slain men,
    Yet do I hold it very stuff° o' the conscience
    To do no contrived° murder. I lack iniquity
    Sometimes to do me service. Nine or ten times
    I had thought t' have yerked° him° here under the ribs.      5
OTHELLO. 'Tis better as it is.
IAGO.                 Nay, but he prated,
    And spoke such scurvy and provoking terms
    Against your honor
    That, with the little godliness I have,
    I did full hard forbear him.° But, I pray you, sir,      10
    Are you fast married? Be assured of this,
    That the magnifico° is much beloved,
    And hath in his effect° a voice potential°
    As double as the Duke's. He will divorce you,
    Or put upon you what restraint or grievance      15
    The law, with all his might to enforce it on,
    Will give him cable.°
OTHELLO.                Let him do his spite.
    My services which I have done the seigniory°
    Shall out-tongue his complaints. 'Tis yet to know°—
    Which, when I know that boasting is an honor,      20
    I shall promulgate—I fetch my life and being
    From men of royal siege,° and my demerits°

---

**180 discover** reveal, uncover.    **183 command** demand assistance.
**185 deserve** show gratitude for.    **1.2 Location: Venice, another street,
before Othello's lodgings.**    **2 very stuff** essence, basic material (continuing
the metaphor of *trade* from line 1).    **3 contrived** premeditated.    **5 yerked**
stabbed.    **him** i.e., Roderigo.    **10 I . . . him** I restrained myself with great
difficulty from assaulting him.    **12 magnifico** Venetian grandee, i.e., Brabantio.
**13 in his effect** at his command.    **potential** powerful.    **17 cable** i.e., scope.
**18 seigniory** Venetian government.    **19 yet to know** not yet widely known.
**22 siege** i.e., rank. (Literally, a seat used by a person of distinction.)    **demerits**
deserts.

May speak unbonneted° to as proud a fortune
As this that I have reached. For know, Iago,
But that I love the gentle Desdemona,                                    25
I would not my unhousèd° free condition
Put into circumscription and confine°
For the sea's worth.° But look, what lights come yond?

*Enter* CASSIO *[and certain officers°] with torches.*

IAGO.  Those are the raisèd father and his friends.
You were best go in.
OTHELLO.                    Not I. I must be found.                        30
My parts, my title, and my perfect soul°
Shall manifest me rightly. Is it they?
IAGO.  By Janus,° I think no.
OTHELLO.  The servants of the Duke? And my lieutenant?
The goodness of the night upon you, friends!                            35
What is the news?
CASSIO.                    The Duke does greet you, General,
And he requires your haste-post-haste appearance
Even on the instant.
OTHELLO.                    What is the matter,° think you?
CASSIO.  Something from Cyprus, as I may divine.°
It is a business of some heat.° The galleys                             40
Have sent a dozen sequent° messengers
This very night at one another's heels,
And many of the consuls,° raised and met,
Are at the Duke's already. You have been hotly called for;
When, being not at your lodging to be found,                           45
The Senate hath sent about° three several° quests
To search you out.
OTHELLO.                    'Tis well I am found by you.
I will but spend a word here in the house.
And go with you.                                                  [*Exit.*]

---

23 **unbonneted** without removing the hat, i.e., on equal terms. (? Or "with
hat off," "in all due modesty.")   26 **unhousèd** unconfined, undomesticated.
27 **circumscription and confine** restriction and confinement.   28 **the sea's
worth** all the riches at the bottom of the sea.   **s.d. officers** (The Quarto text
calls for "Cassio with lights, officers with torches.")   31 **My . . . soul** my natural
gifts, my position or reputation, and my unflawed conscience.   33 **Janus** Roman
two-faced god of beginnings.   38 **matter** business.   39 **divine** guess.   40 **heat**
urgency.   41 **sequent** successive.   43 **consuls** senators.   46 **about** all over the
city.   **several** separate.

CASSIO.                    Ancient, what makes° he here?
IAGO.  Faith, he tonight hath boarded° a land carrack.°                    50
    If it prove lawful prize,° he's made forever.
    CASSIO.  I do not understand.
IAGO.                         He's married.
CASSIO.                       To who?

    [*Enter* OTHELLO.]

IAGO.  Marry,° to—Come Captain, will you go?
OTHELLO.  Have with you.°
CASSIO.  Here comes another troop to seek for you.                    55

    *Enter* BRABANTIO, RODERIGO, *with officers and torches.*°

IAGO.  It is Brabantio. General, be advised.°
    He comes to bad intent.
OTHELLO.                    Holla! Stand there!
RODERIGO.  Signor, it is the Moor.
BRABANTIO.                   Down with him, thief!

    [*They draw on both sides.*]

IAGO.  You, Roderigo! Come, sir, I am for you.
OTHELLO.  Keep up° your bright swords, for the dew will rust them.        60
    Good signor, you shall more command with years
    Than with your weapons.
BRABANTIO.  O thou foul thief, where has thou stowed my daughter?
    Damned as thou art, thou hast enchanted her!
    For I'll refer me° to all things of sense,°                    65
    If she in chains of magic were not bound
    Whether a maid so tender, fair, and happy,
    So opposite to marriage that she shunned
    The wealthy curlèd darlings of our nation,
    Would ever have, t' incur a general mock,                    70
    Run from her guardage° to the sooty bosom
    Of such a thing as thou—to fear, not to delight.

---

49 **makes** does.   50 **boarded** gone aboard and seized as an act of piracy (with
sexual suggestion).   **carrack** large merchant ship.   51 **prize** booty.   53 **Marry**
(An oath, originally "by the Virgin Mary"; here used with wordplay on *married*.)
54 **Have with you** i.e., let's go.   55 **s.d. officers and torches** (The Quarto text
calls for "others with lights and weapons.")   56 **be advised** be on your guard.
60 **Keep up** keep in the sheath.   65 **refer me** submit my case.   **things of**
**sense** commonsense understandings, or, creatures possessing common sense.
71 **her guardage** my guardianship of her.

Judge me the world if 'tis not gross in sense°
That thou hast practiced on her with foul charms,
Abused her delicate youth with drugs or minerals°                          75
That weakens motion.° I'll have 't disputed on;°
'Tis probable and palpable to thinking.
I therefore apprehend and do attach° thee
For an abuser of the world, a practicer
Of arts inhibited° and out of warrant.°—                                    80
Lay hold upon him! If he do resist,
Subdue him at his peril.

OTHELLO.                         Hold your hands,
Both you of my inclining° and the rest.
Were it my cue to fight, I should have known it
Without a prompter.—Whither will you that I go                             85
To answer this your charge?

BRABANTIO.  To prison, till fit time
Of law and course of direct session°
Call thee to answer.

OTHELLO.                      What if I do obey?
How may the Duke be therewith satisfied,                                    90
Whose messengers are here about my side
Upon some present business of the state
To bring me to him?

OFFICER.                      'Tis true, most worthy signor.
The Duke's in council, and your noble self,
I am sure, is sent for.

BRABANTIO.                  How? The Duke in council?                       95
In this time of the night? Bring him away.°
Mine's not an idle° cause. The Duke himself,
Or any of my brothers of the state,
Cannot but feel this wrong as 'twere their own;
For if such actions may have passage free,°                               100
Bondslaves and pagans shall our statesmen be.

*Exeunt.*

---

73 **gross in sense** obvious.   75 **minerals** i.e., poisons.   76 **weakens motion**
impair the vital faculties.   **disputed on** argued in court by professional counsel,
debated by experts.   78 **attach** arrest.   80 **arts inhibited** prohibited arts, black
magic.   **out of warrant** illegal.   83 **inclining** following, party.   88 **course of
direct session** regular or specially convened legal proceedings.   96 **away** right
along.   97 **idle** trifling.   100 **have passage free** are allowed to go unchecked.

**1.3** *Enter* DUKE *[and]* SENATORS *[and sit at a table, with lights], and*
OFFICERS.° *[The* DUKE *and* SENATORS *are reading dispatches.]*°

DUKE.  There is not composition° in these news
    That gives them credit.
FIRST SENATOR.  Indeed, they are disproportioned.°
    My letters say a hundred and seven galleys.
DUKE.  And mine, a hundred forty.
SECOND SENATOR.                    And mine, two hundred.      5
    But though they jump° not on a just° account—
    As in these cases, where the aim° reports
    'Tis oft with difference—yet do they all confirm
    A Turkish fleet, and bearing up to Cyprus.
DUKE.  Nay, it is possible enough to judgment.              10
    I do not so secure me in the error
    But the main article I do approve°
    In fearful sense.
SAILOR  *(within)*.  What ho, what ho, what ho!

    *Enter* SAILOR.

OFFICER.  A messenger from the galleys.
DUKE.  Now, what's the business?                           15
SAILOR.  The Turkish preparation° makes for Rhodes.
    So was I bid report here to the state
    By Signor Angelo.
DUKE.  How say you by° this change?
FIRST SENATOR.                    This cannot be
    By no assay° of reason. 'Tis a pageant°                 20
    To keep us in false gaze.° When we consider
    Th' importance of Cyprus to the Turk,
    And let ourselves again but understand
    That, as it more concerns the Turk than Rhodes,
    So may he with more facile question bear it,°           25

---

**1.3 Location: Venice, a council chamber.   s.d. Enter . . . Officers** (The
Quarto text calls for the Duke and senators to "sit at a table with lights and
attendants."). **1 composition** consistency. **3 disproportioned** inconsistent.
**6 jump** agree. **just** exact. **7 the aim** conjecture. **11–12 I do not . . .
approve** I do not take such (false) comfort in the discrepancies that I fail
to perceive the main point, i.e., that the Turkish fleet is threatening.
**16 preparation** fleet prepared for battle. **19 by** about. **20 assay** test.
**pageant** mere show. **21 in false gaze** looking the wrong way. **25 So may . . .
it** so also he (the Turk) can more easily capture it (Cyprus).

For that° it stands not in such warlike brace,°
But altogether lacks th' abilities°
That Rhodes is dressed in°—if we make thought of this,
We must not think the Turk is so unskillful°
To leave that latest° which concerns him first,            30
Neglecting an attempt of ease and gain
To wake° and wage° a danger profitless.

DUKE.  Nay, in all confidence, he's not for Rhodes.

OFFICER.  Here is more news.

*Enter a* MESSENGER.

MESSENGER.  The Ottomites, reverend and gracious,            35
Steering with due course toward the isle of Rhodes,
Have there injointed them° with an after° fleet.

FIRST SENATOR.  Ay, so I thought. How many, as you guess?

MESSENGER.  Of thirty sail; and now they do restem
Their backward course,° bearing with frank appearance°       40
Their purposes toward Cyprus. Signor Montano,
Your trusty and most valiant servitor,°
With his free duty° recommends° you thus,
And prays you to believe him.

DUKE.  'Tis certain then for Cyprus.                          45
Marcus Luccicos, is not he in town?

FIRST SENATOR.  He's now in Florence.

DUKE.  Write from us to him, post-post-haste. Dispatch.

FIRST SENATOR.  Here comes Brabantio and the valiant Moor.

*Enter* BRABANTIO, OTHELLO, CASSIO, IAGO, RODERIGO, *and officers.*

DUKE.  Valiant Othello, we must straight° employ you         50
Against the general enemy° Ottoman.
[*To* BRABANTIO] I did not see you; welcome, gentle° signor.
We lacked your counsel and your help tonight.

BRABANTIO.  So did I yours. Good Your Grace, pardon me;
Neither my place° nor aught I heard of business              55
Hath raised me from my bed, nor doth the general care
Take hold on me, for my particular° grief

---

**26 For that** since.   **brace** state of defense.   **27 abilities** means of self-defense.
**28 dressed in** equipped with.   **29 unskillful** deficient in judgment.   **30 latest**
last.   **32 wake** stir up.   **wage** risk.   **37 injointed them** joined themselves.
**after** second, following.   **39–40 restem . . . course** retrace their original course.
**40 frank appearance** undisguised intent.   **42 servitor** officer under your
command.   **43 free duty** given and loyal service.   **recommends** commends
himself and reports to.   **50 straight** straightway.   **51 general enemy** universal
enemy to all Christendom.   **52 gentle** noble.   **55 place** official position.
**57 particular** personal.

Is of so floodgate° and o'erbearing nature
That it engluts° and swallows other sorrows
And it is still itself.°
DUKE.                Why, what's the matter?      60
BRABANTIO. My daughter! O, my daughter!
DUKE AND SENATORS.           Dead?
BRABANTIO.                  Ay, to me.
She is abused,° stol'n from me, and corrupted
By spells and medicines bought of mountebanks;
For nature so preposterously to err,
Being not deficient,° blind, or lame of sense,°    65
Sans° witchcraft could not.
DUKE. Whoe'er he be that in this foul proceeding
Hath thus beguiled your daughter of herself,
And you of her, the bloody book of law
You shall yourself read in the bitter letter      70
After your own sense°—yea, though our proper° son
Stood in your action.°
BRABANTIO.          Humbly I thank Your Grace.
Here is the man, this Moor, whom now it seems
Your special mandate for the state affairs
Hath hither brought.
ALL.              We are very sorry for 't.      75
DUKE. [*to* OTHELLO] What, in your part, can you say to this?
BRABANTIO. Nothing, but this is so.
OTHELLO. Most potent, grave, and reverend signors,
My very noble and approved° good masters:
That I have ta'en away this old man's daughter,      80
It is most true; true, I have married her.
The very head and front° of my offending
Hath this extent, no more. Rude° I am in my speech,
And little blessed with the soft phrase of peace;
For since these arms of mine had seven years' pith,°      85
Till now some nine moons wasted,° they have used
Their dearest° action in the tented field;

---

**58 floodgate** i.e., overwhelming (as when floodgates are opened).    **59 engluts**
engulfs.    **60 is still itself** remains undiminished.    **62 abused** deceived.
**65 deficient** defective.    **lame of sense** deficient in sensory perception.
**66 Sans** without.    **71 After . . . sense** according to your interpretation.
**our proper** my own.    **72 Stood . . . action** were under your accusation.
**79 approved** proved, esteemed.    **82 head and front** height and breadth,
entire extent.    **83 Rude** unpolished.    **85 since . . . pith,** i.e., since I was seven.
**pith** strength, vigor.    **86 Till . . . wasted** until some nine months ago (since
when Othello has evidently not been on active duty, but in Venice).    **87 dearest**
most valuable.

And little of this great world can I speak
More than pertains to feats of broils and battle,
And therefore little shall I grace my cause                     90
In speaking for myself. Yet, by your gracious patience,
I will a round° unvarnished tale deliver
Of my whole course of love—what drugs, what charms,
What conjuration, and what mighty magic,
For such proceeding I am charged withal,°                       95
I won his daughter.

BRABANTIO.                    A maiden never bold;
Of spirit so still and quiet that her motion
Blushed at herself;° and she, in spite of nature,
Of years,° of country, credit,° everything,
To fall in love with what she feared to look on!              100
It is a judgment maimed and most imperfect
That will confess° perfection so could err
Against all rules of nature, and must be driven
To find out practices° of cunning hell
Why this should be. I therefore vouch° again                  105
That with some mixtures powerful o'er the blood,°
Or with some dram conjured to this effect,°
He wrought upon her.

DUKE.                    To vouch this is no proof,
Without more wider° and more overt test°
Than these thin habits° and poor likelihoods°                 110
Of modern seeming° do prefer° against him.

FIRST SENATOR.    But Othello, speak.
Did you by indirect and forcèd courses°
Subdue and poison this young maid's affections?
Or came it by request and such fair question°                 115
As soul to soul affordeth?

OTHELLO.                    I do beseech you,
Send for the lady to the Sagittary
And let her speak of me before her father.
If you do find me foul in her report,

---

**92 round** plain.    **95 withal** with.    **97–98 her . . . herself** i.e., she blushed
easily at herself. (*Motion* can suggest the impulse of the soul or of the emotions,
or physical movement.)    **99 years** i.e., difference in age.    **credit** virtuous
reputation.    **102 confess** concede (that).    **104 practices** plots.    **105 vouch**
assert.    **106 blood** passions.    **107 dram . . . effect** dose made by magical spells
to have this effect.    **109 more wider** fuller.    **test** testimony.    **110 habits**
garments, i.e., appearances.    **poor likelihoods** weak inferences.    **111 modern
seeming** commonplace assumption.    **prefer** bring forth.    **113 forcèd courses**
means used against her will.    **115 question** conversation.

The trust, the office I do hold of you                         120
Not only take away, but let your sentence
Even fall upon my life.
DUKE.                         Fetch Desdemona hither.
OTHELLO.  Ancient, conduct them. You best know the place.

[*Exeunt* IAGO *and attendants.*]

And, till she come, as truly as to heaven
I do confess the vices of my blood,°                          125
So justly° to your grave ears I'll present
How I did thrive in this fair lady's love,
And she in mine.
DUKE.  Say it, Othello.
OTHELLO.  Her father loved me, oft invited me,                130
Still° questioned me the story of my life
From year to year—the battles, sieges, fortunes
That I have passed.
I ran it through, even from my boyish days
To th' very moment that he bade me tell it,                   135
Wherein I spoke of most disastrous chances,
Of moving accidents° by flood and field,
Of hairbreadth scapes i' th' imminent deadly breach,°
Of being taken by the insolent foe
And sold to slavery, of my redemption thence,                140
And portance° in my travels' history,
Wherein of antres° vast and deserts idle,°
Rough quarries, rocks, and hills whose heads touch heaven,
It was my hint° to speak—such was my process—
And of the Cannibals that each other eat,                     145
The Anthropophagi,° and men whose heads
Do grow beneath their shoulders. These things to hear
Would Desdemona seriously incline;
But still the house affairs would draw her thence,
Which ever as she could with haste dispatch              150
She'd come again, and with a greedy ear
Devour up my discourse. Which I, observing,
Took once a pliant° hour, and found good means
To draw from her a prayer of earnest heart

---

**125 blood** passions, human nature.    **126 justly** truthfully, accurately.    **131 Still**
continually.    **137 moving accidents** stirring happenings.    **138 imminent . . .**
**breach** death-threatening gaps made in a fortification.    **141 portance** conduct.
**142 antres** caverns.    **idle** barren, desolate.    **143 Rough quarries** rugged rock
formations.    **144 hint** occasion, opportunity.    **146 Anthropophagi** man-eaters.
(A term from Pliny's *Natural History*.)    **153 pliant** well-suiting.

That I would all my pilgrimage dilate,°                                155
Whereof by parcels° she had something heard,
But not intentively.° I did consent,
And often did beguile her of her tears,
When I did speak of some distressful stroke
That my youth suffered. My story being done,                          160
She gave me for my pains a world of sighs.
She swore, in faith, 'twas strange, 'twas passing° strange,
'Twas pitiful, 'twas wondrous pitiful.
She wished she had not heard it, yet she wished
That heaven had made her° such a man. She thanked me,                 165
And bade me, if I had a friend that loved her,
I should but teach him how to tell my story,
And that would woo her. Upon this hint° I spake.
She loved me for the dangers I had passed,
And I loved her that she did pity them.                               170
This only is the witchcraft I have used.
Here comes the lady. Let her witness it.

*Enter* DESDEMONA, IAGO, [*and*] *attendants.*

DUKE.  I think this tale would win my daughter too.
Good Brabantio,
Take up this mangled matter at the best.°                             175
Men do their broken weapons rather use
Than their bare hands.
BRABANTIO.                     I pray you, hear her speak.
If she confesses that she was half the wooer,
Destruction on my head if my bad blame
Light on the man!—Come hither, gentle mistress.                      180
Do you perceive in all this noble company
Where most you owe obedience?
DESDEMONA.                      My noble Father,
I do perceive here a divided duty.
To you I am bound for life and education;°
My life and education both do learn° me                              185
How to respect you. You are the lord of duty;°
I am hitherto your daughter. But here's my husband,
And so much duty as my mother showed
To you, preferring you before her father,

_____

155 **dilate** relate in detail.   156 **by parcels** piecemeal.   157 **intentively** with
full attention, continuously.   162 **passing** exceedingly.   165 **made her** created
her to be.   168 **hint** opportunity. (Othello does not mean that she was dropping
hints.)   175 **Take . . . best** make the best of a bad bargain.   184 **education**
upbringing.   185 **learn** teach.   186 **of duty** to whom duty is due.

So much I challenge° that I may profess　　　　　　　190
Due to the Moor my lord.
BRABANTIO.　God be with you! I have done.
　Please it Your Grace, on to the state affairs.
　I had rather to adopt a child than get° it.
　Come hither, Moor. [*He joins the hands of* OTHELLO
　　*and* DESDEMONA.]　　　　　　　　　　　　195
　I here do give thee that with all my heart°
　Which, but thou hast already, with all my heart°
　I would keep from thee.—For your sake,° jewel,
　I am glad at soul I have no other child,
　For thy escape° would teach me tyranny,　　　200
　To hang clogs° on them.—I have done, my lord.
DUKE.　Let me speak like yourself,° and lay a sentence°
　Which, as a grece° or step, may help these lovers
　Into your favor.
　When remedies° are past, the griefs are ended　　205
　By seeing the worst, which late on hopes depended.°
　To mourn a mischief° that is past and gone
　Is the next° way to draw new mischief on.
　What° cannot be preserved when fortune takes,
　Patience her injury a mockery makes.°　　　　210
　The robbed that smiles steals something from the thief;
　He robs himself that spends a bootless grief.°
BRABANTIO.　So let the Turk of Cyprus us beguile,
　We lose it not, so long as we can smile.
　He bears the sentence well that nothing bears　　215
　But the free comfort which from thence he hears,
　But he bears both the sentence and the sorrow
　That, to pay grief, must of poor patience borrow.°

---

**190 challenge** claim.　**194 get** beget.　**196 with all my heart** wherein my whole affection has been engaged.　**197 with all my heart** willingly, gladly. **198 For your sake** on your account.　**200 escape** elopement.　**201 clogs** (Literally, block of wood fastened to the legs of criminals or convicts to inhibit escape.)　**202 like yourself** i.e., as you would, in your proper temper.　**lay a sentence** apply a maxim.　**203 grece** step.　**205 remedies** hopes of remedy. **206 which . . . depended** which griefs were sustained until recently by hopeful anticipation.　**207 mischief** misfortune, injury.　**208 next** nearest.　**209 What** whatever.　**210 Patience . . . makes** patience laughs at the injury inflicted by fortune (and thus eases the pain).　**212 spends a bootless grief** indulges in unavailing grief.　**215–218 He bears . . . borrow** a person well bears out your maxim who can enjoy its platitudinous comfort, free of all genuine sorrow, but anyone whose grief bankrupts his poor parlence is left with your saying and his sorrow, too. (*Bears the sentence* also plays on the meaning, "receives judicial sentence.")

These sentences, to sugar or to gall,
Being strong on both sides, are equivocal.°                            220
But words are words. I never yet did hear
That the bruised heart was piercèd through the ear.°
I humbly beseech you, proceed to th' affairs of state.

DUKE.  The Turk with a most mighty preparation makes for Cyprus.
Othello, the fortitude° of the place is best known to you; and   225
and though we have there a substitute° of most allowed° suffi-
ciency, yet opinion, a sovereign mistress of effects, throws a more
safer voice on you.° You must therefore be content to slubber° the
gloss of your new fortunes with this more stubborn° and boister-
ous expedition.                                                       230

OTHELLO.  The tyrant custom, most grave senators,
Hath made the flinty and steel couch of war
My thrice-driven° bed of down. I do agnize°
A natural and prompt alacrity
I find in hardness,° and do undertake                                 235
These present wars against the Ottomites.
Most humbly therefore bending to your state,°
I crave fit disposition for my wife,
Due reference of place and exhibition,°
With such accommodation° and besort°                                  240
As levels° with her breeding.°

DUKE.  Why, at her father's.

BRABANTIO.                                          I will not have it so.

OTHELLO.  Nor I.

DESDEMONA.  Nor I. I would not there reside,
To put my father in impatient thoughts
By being in his eye. Most gracious Duke,                              245
To my unfolding° lend your prosperous° ear,
And let me find a charter° in your voice,
T' assist my simpleness.

---

**219–220 These . . . equivocal** these fine maxims are equivocal, either sweet or
bitter in their application.    **222 piercèd . . . ear** i.e., surgically lanced and cured
by mere words of advice.    **225 fortitude** strength.    **226 substitute** deputy.
**allowed** acknowledged.    **226–227 opinion . . . on you** general opinion,
an important determiner of affairs, chooses you as the best man.    **228 slubber**
soil, sully.    **stubborn** harsh, rough.    **233 thrice-driven** thrice sifted,
winnowed.    **agnize** know in myself, acknowledge. **235 hardness** hardship.
**237 bending . . . state** bowing or kneeling to your authority.    **239 reference .
. . exhibition** provision of appropriate place to live and allowance of money.
**240 accommodation** suitable provision.    **besort** attendance.    **241 levels**
equals, suits.    **breeding** social position, upbringing.    **246 unfolding**
explanation, proposal.    **prosperous** propitious.    **247 charter** privilege,
authorization.

DUKE. What would you, Desdemona?
DESDEMONA. That I did love the Moor to live with him,                    250
My downright violence and storm of fortunes°
May trumpet to the world. My heart's subdued
Even to the very quality of my lord.°
I saw Othello's visage in his mind,
And to his honors and his valiant parts°                                255
Did I my soul and fortunes consecrate.
So that, dear lords, if I be left behind
A moth° of peace, and he go to the war,
The rites° for why I love him are bereft me,
And I a heavy interim shall support                                     260
By his dear° absence. Let me go with him.
OTHELLO. Let her have your voice.°
Vouch with me, heaven, I therefor beg it not
To please the palate of my appetite,
Not to comply with heat°—the young affects°                             265
In me defunct—and proper° satisfaction,
But to be free° and bounteous to her mind.
And heaven defend° your good souls that you think°
I will your serious and great business scant
When she is with me. No, when light-winged toys                         270
Of feathered Cupid seel° with wanton dullness
My speculative and officed instruments,°
That° my disports° corrupt and taint° my business,
Let huswives make a skillet of my helm,
And all indign° and base adversities                                    275
Make head° against my estimation!°
DUKE. Be it as you shall privately determine,
Either for her stay or going. Th' affair cries haste,
And speed must answer it.

---

**251 My . . . fortunes** my plain and total breach of social custom, taking my
future by storm and disrupting my whole life.    **252–253 My heart's . . . lord** my
heart is brought wholly into accord with Othello's virtues; I love him for his
virtues.    **255 parts** qualities.    **258 moth** i.e., one who consumes merely.
**259 rites** rites of love (with a suggestion, too, of "rights," sharing.)    **261 dear**
(1) heartfelt (2) costly.    **262 voice** consent.    **265 heat** sexual passion.    **young
affects** passions of youth, desires.    **266 proper** personal.    **267 free** generous.
**268 defend** forbid.    **think** should think.    **271 seel** i.e., make blind (as in
falconry, by sewing up the eyes of the hawk during training).    **272 speculative** .
**. . instruments** eyes and other faculties used in the performance of duty.
**273 That** so that.    **disports** sexual pastimes.    **taint** impair.    **275 indign**
unworthy, shameful.    **276 Make head** raise an army.    **estimation** reputation.

A SENATOR.                              You must away tonight.
DESDEMONA.  Tonight, my lord?
DUKE.                              This night.
OTHELLO.                          With all my heart.                         280
DUKE.  At nine i' the morning here we'll meet again.
    Othello, leave some officer behind,
    And he shall our commission bring to you,
    With such things else of quality and respect°
    As doth import° you.
OTHELLO.                    So please Your Grace, my ancient;           285
    A man he is of honesty and trust.
    To his conveyance I assign my wife,
    With what else needful Your Good Grace shall think
    To be sent after me.
DUKE.                      Let it be so.
    Good night to everyone. [*To* BRABANTIO.] And, noble signor,    290
    If virtue no delighted° beauty lack,
    Your son-in-law is far more fair than black.
FIRST SENATOR.  Adieu, brave Moor. Use Desdemona well.
BRABANTIO.  Look to her, Moor, if thou hast eyes to see.
    She has deceived her father, and may thee.                           295

        *Exeunt* [DUKE, BRABANTIO, CASSIO, SENATORS, *and officers*].

OTHELLO.  My life upon her faith! Honest Iago,
    My Desdemona must I leave to thee.
    I prithee, let thy wife attend on her,
    And bring them after in the best advantage.°
    Come, Desdemona, I have but an hour                               300
    Of love, of worldly matters and direction,°
    To spend with thee. We must obey the time.°

                              *Exit* [*with* DESDEMONA].

RODERIGO.  Iago—
IAGO.  What sayst thou, noble heart?
RODERIGO.  What will I do, think'st thou?                               305
IAGO.  Why, go to bed and sleep.
RODERIGO.  I will incontinently° drown myself.
IAGO.  If thou dost, I shall never love thee after. Why, thou silly gentleman?

---

**284 of quality and respect** of importance and relevance     **285 import**
concern.     **291 delighted** capable of delighting.     **299 in . . . advantage** at the
most favorable opportunity.     **301 direction** instructions.     **302 the time** the
urgency of this present crisis.     **307 incontinently** immediately, without self-
restraint.

RODERIGO. It is silliness to live when to live is torment; and then have
we a prescription° to die when death is our physician. 310
IAGO. O villainous!° I have looked upon the world for four times seven
years, and, since I could distinguish betwixt a benefit and an injury,
I never found man that knew how to love himself. Ere I would say I
would drown myself for the love of a guinea hen,° I would change
my humanity with a baboon. 315
RODERIGO. What should I do? I confess it is my shame to be so fond,°
but it is not in my virtue° to amend it.
IAGO. Virtue? A *fig!*° 'Tis in ourselves that we are thus or thus. Our
bodies are our gardens to the which our wills are gardeners; so
that if we will plant nettles or sow lettuce, set hyssop° and weed 320
up thyme, supply it with one gender° of herbs or distract it with°
many, either to have it sterile with idleness° or manured with industry—why, the power and corrigible authority° of this lies in
our wills. If the beam° of our lives had not one scale of reason to
poise° another of sensuality, the blood° and baseness of our 325
natures would conduct us to most preposterous conclusions. But
we have reason to cool our raging motions,° our carnal stings, our
unbitted° lusts, whereof I take this that you call love to be a sect
or scion.°
RODERIGO. It cannot be. 330
IAGO. It is merely a lust of the blood and a permission of the will.
Come, be a man. Drown thyself? Drown cats and blind puppies. I
have professed me thy friend, and I confess me knit to thy deserving with cables of perdurable° toughness. I could never better
stead° thee than now. Put money in thy purse. Follow thou the 335
wars; defeat thy favor° with an usurped° beard. I say, put money
in thy purse. It cannot be long that Desdemona should continue
her love to the Moor—put money in thy purse—nor he his to her. It
was a violent commencement in her, and thou shalt see an

---

**309–310 prescription** (1) right based on long-established customs (2) doctor's
prescription. **311 villainous** i.e., what perfect nonsense. **314 guinea hen** (A
slang term for a prostitute). **316 fond** infatuated. **317 virtue** strength, nature.
**318 *fig*** (To give a fig is to thrust the thumb between the first and second fingers
in a vulgar and insulting gesture.) **320 hyssop** an herb of the mint family.
**321 gender** kind. **distract it with** divide it among. **322 idleness** want of
cultivation. **323 corrigible authority** power to correct. **324 beam** balance.
**325 poise** counterbalance. **blood** natural passions. **327 motions** appetites.
**328 unbitted** unbridled, uncontrolled. **329 sect or scion** cutting or offshoot.
**334 perdurable** very durable. **335 stead** assist. **336 defeat thy favor**
disguise your face. **usurped** (The suggestion is that Roderigo is not man enough
to have a beard of his own.)

swerable sequestration°—put but money in thy purse. These 340
Moors are changeable in their wills°—fill thy purse with money.
The food that to him now is as luscious as locusts° shall be to him
shortly as bitter as coloquintida.° She must change for youth;
when she is sated with his body, she will find the error of her
choice. She must have change, she must. Therefore put money in 345
thy purse. If thou wilt needs damn thyself, do it a more delicate
way than drowning. Make° all the money thou canst. If sanctimony°
and a frail vow betwixt an erring° barbarian and a supersubtle Venetian be not too hard for my wits and all the tribe of hell, thou shalt enjoy her. Therefore make money. A pox of drowning thyself! It is 350
clean out of the way.° Seek thou rather to be hanged in compass-
ing° thy joy than to be drowned and go without her.
RODERIGO.  Wilt thou be fast° to my hopes if I depend on the issue?°
IAGO.  Thou art sure of me. Go, make money. I have told thee often,
and I retell thee again and again, I hate the Moor. My cause is 355
hearted;°thine hath no less reason. Let us be conjunctive° in our
revenge against him. If thou canst cuckold him, thou dost thyself
a pleasure, me a sport. There There are many events in the womb
of time which will be delivered. Traverse,° go, provide thy
money. We wil have more of this tomorrow. Adieu.                 360
RODERIGO.  Where shall we meet i' the morning?
IAGO.  At my lodging.
RODERIGO.  I'll be with thee betimes.°                [He starts to leave.]
IAGO.  Go to, farewell.—Do you hear, Roderigo?
RODERIGO.  What say you?                                           365
IAGO.  No more of drowning, do you hear?
RODERIGO.  I am changed.
IAGO.  Go to, farewell. Put money enough in your purse.
RODERIGO.  I'll sell all my land.                          *Exit.*
IAGO.  Thus do I ever make my fool my purse;                      370
    For I mine own gained knowledge should profane
    If I would time expend with such a snipe°
    But for my sport and profit. I hate the Moor;

---

**339–340 an answerable sequestration** a corresponding separation or
estrangement.    **341 wills** carnal appetites.    **342 locusts** fruit of the carob tree
(see Matthew 3.4), or perhaps honeysuckle.    **343 coloquintida** colocynth or
bitter apple, a purgative.    **347 Make** raise, collect.    **sanctimony** sacred
ceremony.    **348 erring** wandering, vagabond, unsteady.    **351 clean . . . way**
entirely unsuitable as a course of action.    **351–352 compassing** encompassing,
embracing.    **353 fast** true.    **issue** (successful) outcome.    **356 hearted** fixed in
the heart, heartfelt.    **conjunctive** united.    **359 Traverse** (A military marching
term.)    **363 betimes** early.    **372 snipe** woodcock, i.e., fool.

And it is thought abroad° that twixt my sheets
He's done my office.° I know not if't be true;                    375
But I, for mere suspicion in that kind,
Will do as if for surety.° He holds me well;°
The better shall my purpose work on him.
Cassio's a proper° man. Let me see now:
To get his place and to plume up° my will                         380
In double knavery—How, how?—Let's see:
After some time, to abuse° Othello's ear
That he° is too familiar with his wife.
He hath a person and a smooth dispose°
To be suspected, framed to make women false.                     385
The Moor is of a free° and open° nature,
That thinks men honest that but seem to be so,
And will as tenderly° be led by the nose
As asses are.
I have 't. It is engendered. Hell and night                       390
Must bring this monstrous birth to the world's light.

[*Exit.*]


**2.1** *Enter* MONTANO *and two* GENTLEMEN.

MONTANO.  What from the cape can you discern at sea?
FIRST GENTLEMAN.  Nothing at all. It is a high-wrought flood.°
    I cannot, twixt the heaven and the main,°
    Descry a sail.
MONTANO.  Methinks the wind hath spoke aloud at land;             5
    A fuller blast ne'er shook our battlements.
    If it hath ruffianed° so upon the sea,
    What ribs of oak, when mountains° melt on them,
    Can hold the mortise?° What shall we hear of this?

---

**374 it is thought abroad** it is rumored.   **375 my office** i.e., my sexual function
as husband.   **377 do . . . surety** act as if on certain knowledge.   **holds me
well** regards me favorably.   **379 proper** handsome.   **380 plume up** put a
feather in the cap of, i.e., glorify, gratify.   **382 abuse** deceive.   **383 he** i.e.,
Cassio.   **384 dispose** disposition.   **386 free** frank, generous.   **open**
unsuspicious.   **388 tenderly** readily.   **2.1 Location: A seaport in Cyprus,
an open place near the quay.**   **2 high-wrought flood** very agitated sea.
**3 main** ocean (also at line 41).   **7 ruffianed** raged.   **8 mountains** i.e., of water.
**9 hold the mortise** hold their joints together. (A *mortise* is the socket hollowed
out in fitting timbers.)

SECOND GENTLEMAN. A segregation° of the Turkish fleet.                    10
   For do but stand upon the foaming shore,
   The chidden° billow seems to pelt the clouds;
   The wind-shaked surge, with high and monstrous mane,°
   Seems to cast water on the burning Bear°
   And quench the guards of th' ever-fixèd pole.                    15
   I never did like molestation° view
   On the enchafèd° flood.
MONTANO. If that° the Turkish fleet
   Be not ensheltered and embayed,° they are drowned;
   It is impossible to bear ir out.°                    20

*Enter a* [THIRD] GENTLEMAN.

THIRD GENTLEMAN. News, lads! Our wars are done.
   The desperate tempest hath so banged the Turks
   That their designment° halts.° A noble ship of Venice
   Hath seen a grievous wreck° and sufferance°
   On most part of their fleet.                    25
MONTANO. How? Is this true?
THIRD GENTLEMAN. The ship is here put in,
   A Veronesa;° Michael Cassio,
   Lieutenant to the warlike Moor Othello,
   Is come on shore; the Moor himself at sea,                    30
   And is in full commission here for Cyprus.
MONTANO. I am glad on 't. 'Tis a worthy governor.
THIRD GENTLEMAN. But this same Cassio, though he speak of comfort
   Touching the Turkish loss, yet he looks sadly°
   And prays the Moor be safe, for they were parted                    35
   With foul and violent tempest.
MONTANO.                                        Pray heaven he be,
   For I have served him, and the man commands
   Like a full° soldier. Let's to the seaside, ho!

---

**10 segregation** dispersal.    **12 chidden** i.e., rebuked, repelled (by the shore),
and thus shot into the air.    **13 monstrous mane** (The surf is like the mane of a
wild beast.)    **14 the burning Bear** i.e., the constellation Ursa Minor or the Little
Bear, which includes the polestar (and hence regarded as the *guards of th' ever-
fixèd pole* in the next line; sometimes the term *guards* is applied to the two
"pointers" of the Big Bear or Dipper, which may be intended here).    **16 like
molestation** comparable disturbance.    **17 enchafèd** angry.    **18 If that** if.
**19 embayed** sheltered by a bay.    **20 bear it out** survive, weather the storm.
**23 designment** design, enterprise.    **halts** is lame.    **24 wreck** shipwreck.
**sufferance** damage, disaster.    **28 Veronesa** i.e., fitted out in Verona for Venetian
service, or possibly *Verennessa* (the Folio spelling), i.e., *verrinessa*, a cutter (from
*verrinare*, "to cut through").    **34 sadly** gravely.    **38 full** perfect.

As well to see the vessel that's come in
As to throw out our eyes for brave Othello,                    40
Even till we make the main and th' aerial blue°
An indistinct regard.°
THIRD GENTLEMAN.          Come, let's do so,
For every minute is expentacy°
Of more arrivance.°

*Enter* CASSIO.

CASSIO.  Thanks, you the valiant of this warlike isle,          45
That so approve° the Moor! O, let the heavens
Give him defense against the elements,
For I have lost him on a dangerous sea.
MONTANO.  Is he well shipped?
CASSIO.  His bark is stoutly timbered, and his pilot           50
Of very expert and approved allowance;°
Therefore my hopes, not surfeited to death,°
Stand in bold cure.°
[*A cry*] *within:*          "A sail, a sail, a sail!"
CASSIO.  What noise?
A GENTLEMAN.  The town is empty. On the brow o' the sea°       55
Stand ranks of people, and they cry "A sail!"
CASSIO.  My hopes do shape him for° the governor.

[*A shot within.*]

SECOND GENTLEMAN.  They do discharge their shot of courtesy;°
Our friends at least.
CASSIO.               I pray you, sir, go forth,
And give us truth who 'tis that is arrived.                     60
SECOND GENTLEMAN.  I shall.                          *Exit.*
MONTANO.  But, good Lieutenant, is your general wived?
CASSIO.  Most fortunately. He hath achieved a maid
That paragons° description and wild fame,°
One that excels the quirks° of blazoning° pens,               65

---

**41 the main . . . blue** the sea and the sky.   **42 An indistinct regard**
indistinguishable in our view.   **43 is expectancy** gives expectations.
**44 arrivance** arrival.   **46 approve** admire, honor.   **51 approved allowance**
tested reputation.   **52 surfeited to death** i.e., overextended, worn thin through
repeated application or delayed fulfillment.   **53 in bold cure** in strong hopes
of fulfillment.   **55 brow o' the sea** cliff-edge.   **57 My . . . for** I hope it is.
**58 discharge . . . courtesy** fire a salute in token of respect and courtesy.
**64 paragons** surpasses.   **wild fame** extravagant report.   **65 quirks** witty
conceits.   **blazoning** setting forth as though in heraldic language.

And in th' essential vesture of creation
Does tire the enginer.°

*Enter* [SECOND] GENTLEMAN. °

                            How now? Who has put in?°
SECOND GENTLEMAN.  'Tis one Iago, ancient to the General.
CASSIO.  He's had most favorable and happy speed.
    Tempests themselves, high seas, and howling winds,          70
    The guttered° rocks and congregated sands—
    Traitors ensteeped° to clog the guiltless keel—
    As° having sense of beauty, do omit°
    Their mortal° natures, letting go safely by
    The divine Desdemona.
MONTANO.                 What is she?         75
CASSIO.  She that I spake of, our great captain's captain,
    Left in the conduct of the bold Iago,
    Whose footing° here anticipates our thoughts
    A sennight's° speed. Great Jove, Othello guard,
    And swell his sail with thine own powerful breath,      80
    That he may bless this bay with his tall° ship,
    Make love's quick pants in Desdemona's arms,
    Give renewed fire to our extincted spirits,
    And bring all Cyprus comfort!

*Enter* DESDEMONA, IAGO, RODERIGO, *and* EMILIA.

                        O, behold,
    The riches of the ship is come on shore!          85
    You men of Cyprus, let her have your knees.

[*The gentlemen make curtsy to* DESDEMONA.]

    Hail to thee, lady! And the grace of heaven
    Before, behind thee, and on every hand
    Enwheel thee round!
DESDEMONA.              I thank you, valiant Cassio.
    What tidings can you tell me of my lord?          90
CASSIO.  He is not yet arrived, nor know I aught
    But that he's well and will be shortly here.

---

**66–67 in . . . enginer** in her real, God-given, beauty, (she) defeats any attempt
to praise her.  **enginer** engineer, i.e., poet, one who devises.  **s.d. Second
Gentleman** (So identified in the Quarto text here and in lines 58, 61, 68, and 96;
the Folio calls him a gentleman.)  **67 put in** i.e., to harbor.  **71 guttered** jagged,
trenched.  **72 ensteeped** lying under water.  **73 As** as if.  **omit** forbear to
exercise.  **74 mortal** deadly.  **78 footing** landing.  **79 sennight's** week's.
**81 tall** splendid, gallant.

DESDEMONA.  O, but I fear—How lost you company?
CASSIO.  The great contention of the sea and skies
    Parted our fellowship.

    (*Within*) "A sail, a sail" [*A shot.*]
                                    But hark. A sail!                    95
SECOND GENTLEMAN.  They give their greeting to the citadel.
    This likewise is a friend.
CASSIO.                        See for the news.

    [*Exit* SECOND GENTLEMAN.]

    Good Ancient, you are welcome. [*Kissing* EMILIA.] Welcome, mistress.
    Let it not gall your patience, good Iago,
    That I extend° my manners; 'tis my breeding°                        100
    That gives me this bold show of courtesy.
IAGO.  Sir, would she give you so much of her lips
    As of her tongue she oft bestows on me,
    You would have enough.
DESDEMONA.  Alas, she has no speech!°                                   105
IAGO.  In faith, too much.
    I find it still,° when I have list° to sleep.
    Marry, before your ladyship, I grant,
    She puts her tongue a little in her heart
    And chides with thinking.°
EMILIA.                        You have little cause to say so.          110
IAGO.  Come on, come on. You are pictures out of doors,°
    Bells° in your parlors, wildcats in your kitchens,°
    Saints° in your injuries, devils being offended,
    Players° in your huswifery,° and huswives° in your beds.
DESDEMONA.  O, fie upon thee, slanderer!                                115
IAGO.  Nay, it is true, or else I am a Turk.°
    You rise to play, and go to bed to work.
EMILIA.  You shall not write my praise.
IAGO.                        No, let me not.
DESDEMONA.  What wouldst write of me, if thou shouldst praise me?

---

**100 extend** give scope to. **breeding** training in the niceties of etiquette.
**105 she has no speech** i.e., she's not a chatterbox, as you allege. **107 still**
always. **list** desire. **110 with thinking** i.e., in her thoughts only.
**111 pictures out of doors** i.e., silent and well behaved in public. **112 Bells**
i.e., jangling, noisy, and brazen. **in your kitchens** i.e., in domestic affairs. (Ladies
would not do the cooking.) **113 Saints** martyrs. **114 Players** idlers, triflers,
or deceivers. **huswifery** housekeeping. **huswives** hussies (i.e., women are
"busy" in bed, or unduly thrifty in dispensing sexual favors). **116 a Turk** an
infidel, not to be believed.

IAGO.  O, gentle lady, do not put me to 't,                                    120
    For I am nothing if not critical.°
DESDEMONA.  Come on, essay.°—There's one gone to the harbor?
IAGO.  Ay, madam.
DESDEMONA.  I am not merry, but I do beguile
    The thing I am° by seeming otherwise.                                  125
    Come, how wouldst thou praise me?
IAGO.  I am about it, but indeed my invention
    Comes from my pate as birdlime° does from frieze°—
    It plucks out brains and all. But my Muse labors,°
    And thus she is delivered:                                             130
    If she be fair and wise, fairness and wit,
    The one's for use, the other useth it.°
DESDEMONA.  Well praised! How if she be black° and witty?
IAGO.  If she be black, and thereto have a wit,
    She'll find a white° that shall her blackness fit.°                    135
DESDEMONA.  Worse and worse.
EMILIA.                             How if fair and foolish?
IAGO.  She never yet was foolish that was fair,
    For even her folly° helped her to an heir.°
DESDEMONA.  These are old fond° paradoxes to make fools laugh i' th'
    alehouse. What miserable praise hast thou for her that's foul and     140
    foolish?
IAGO.  There's none so foul° and foolish thereunto,°
    But does foul° pranks which fair and wise ones do.
DESDEMONA.  O heavy ignorance! Thou praisest the worst best. But what
    praise couldst thou bestow on a deserving woman indeed, one           145
    that, in the authority of her merit, did justly put on the vouch°
    of very malice itself?
IAGO.  She that was ever fair, and never proud,
    Had tongue at will, and yet was never loud,
    Never lacked gold and yet went never gay,°                            150
    Fled from her wish, and yet said, "Now I may,"°

---

121 **critical** censorious.    122 **essay** try.    125 **The thing I am** i.e., my anxious
self.    128 **birdlime** sticky substance used to catch small birds.    **frieze** coarse
woolen cloth.    129 **labors** (1) exerts herself (2) prepares to deliver a child
(with a following pun on *delivered* in line 130).    132 **The one's . . . it** i.e.,
her cleverness will make use of her beauty.    133 **black** dark-complexioned,
brunette.    135 **a white** a fair person (with word-play on "wight," a person).
**fit** (with sexual suggestion of mating).    138 **folly** (with added meaning of
"lechery, wantonness").    **to an heir** i.e., to bear a child.    139 **fond** foolish.
142 **foul** ugly.    **thereunto** in addition.    143 **foul** sluttish.    146 **put . . .
vouch** compel the approval.    150 **gay** extravagantly clothed.    151 **Fled . . .
may** avoided temptation where the choice was hers.

She that being angered, her revenge being nigh,
Bade her wrong stay° and her displeasure fly,
She that in wisdom never was so frail
To change the cod's head for the salmon's tail,°        155
She that could think and ne'er disclose her mind,
See suitors following and not look behind,
She was a wight, if ever such wight were—
DESDEMONA. To do what?
IAGO. To suckle fools° and chronicle small beer.°        160
DESDEMONA. O most lame and impotent conclusion! Do not learn of
him, Emilia, though he be thy husband. How say you, Cassio? Is
he not a most profane° and liberal° counselor?
CASSIO. He speaks home,° madam. You may relish° him more in° the
soldier than in the scholar.        165

[CASSIO *and* DESDEMONA *stand together, conversing intimately.*]

IAGO [*aside*]. He takes her by the palm. Ay, well said,° whisper. With
as little a web as this will I ensnare as great a fly as Cassio. Ay,
smile  upon her, do; I will gyve° thee in thine own courtship.° You say true;° 'tis so, indeed. If such tricks as these strip
you out of your lieutenantry, it had been better you had not kissed        170
your three fingers so oft, which now again you are most apt to play
the sir° in. Very good; well kissed! An excellent courtesy! 'Tis so,
indeed. Yet again your fingers to your lips? Would they were clyster
pipes° for your sake! [*Trumpet within.*] The Moor! I know his
trumpet.        175
CASSIO. 'Tis truly so.
DESDEMONA. Let's meet him and receive him.
CASSIO. Lo, where he comes!

*Enter* OTHELLO *and attendants.*

OTHELLO. O my fair warrior!
DESDEMONA.                            My dear Othello!
OTHELLO. It gives me wonder great as my content        180
To see you here before me. O my soul's joy,

---

**153 Bade . . . stay** i.e., resolved to put up with her injury patiently.   **155 To . . .
tail** i.e., to exchange a lackluster husband for a sexy lover (?). (*Cod's head* is slang
for "penis," and *tail* for "pudendum.")   **160 suckle fools** breastfeed babies.
**chronicle small beer** i.e., keep petty household accounts, keep track of trivial
matters.   **163 profane** irreverent, ribald.   **liberal** licentious, free-spoken.
**164 home** right to the target. (A term from fencing.)   **relish** appreciate.
**in** in the character of.   **166 well said** well done.   **168 gyve** fetter, shackle.
**courtship** courtesy, show of courtly manners.   **169 You say true** i.e., that's right,
go ahead.   **172 the sir** i.e., fine gentleman.   **174 clyster pipes** tubes used for
enemas and douches.

If after every tempest come such calms,
May the winds blow till they have wakened death,
And let the laboring bark climb hills of seas
Olympus-high, and duck again as low                                185
As hell's from heaven! If it were now to die,
'Twere now to be most happy, for I fear
My soul hath her content so absolute
That not another comfort like to this
Succeeds in unknown fate.°                                          190

DESDEMONA.                          The heavens forbid
But that our loves and comforts should increase
Even as our days do grow!

OTHELLO.  Amen to that, sweet powers!
I cannot speak enough of this content.
It stops me here; it is too much of joy.                            195
And this, and this, the greatest discords be

[*They kiss.*]°

That e'er our hearts shall make!

IAGO.  [*aside*] O, you are well tuned now!
But I'll set down° the pegs that make this music,
As honest as I am.°                                                 200

OTHELLO.  Come, let us to the castle.
News, friends! Our wars are done, the Turks are drowned.
How does my old acquaintance of this isle?—
Honey, you shall be well desired° in Cyprus;
I have found great love amongst them. O my sweet,                   205
I prattle out of fashion,° and I dote
In mine own comforts.—I prithee, good Iago,
Go to the bay and disembark my coffers.°
Bring thou the master° to the citadel;
He is a good one, and his worthiness                                210
Does challenge° much respect.—Come, Desdemona.—
Once more, well met at Cyprus!

*Exeunt* OTHELLO *and* DESDEMONA [*and all but* IAGO *and* RODERIGO].

IAGO.  [*to an attendant*] Do thou meet me presently at the harbor.
[*To* RODERIGO.]  Come hither. If thou be'st valiant—as, they say,

---

190 **Succeeds . . . fate** i.e., can follow in the unknown future.  **s.d. They kiss**
(The direction is from the Quarto.)  199 **set down** loosen (and hence untune
the instrument).  200 **As . . . I am** for all my supposed honesty.  204 **desired**
welcomed.  206 **out of fashion** irrelevantly, incoherently (?).  208 **coffers**
chests, baggage.  209 **master** ship's captain.  211 **challenge** lay claim to,
deserve.

base men° being in love have then a nobility in their natures more  215
than is native to them—list° me. The Lieutenant tonight watches
on the court of guard.° First, I must tell thee this: Desdemona is
directly in love with him.

RODERIGO.  With him? Why, 'tis not possible.

IAGO.  Lay thy finger thus,° and let thy soul be instructed. Mark me  220
with what violence she first loved the Moor, but° for bragging
and telling her fantastical lies.To love him still for prating? Let not
thy discreet heart think it. Her eye must be fed; and what delight
shall she have to look on the devil? When the blood is made dull
with the act of sport,° there should be, again to inflame it and to  225
give satiety a fresh appetite, loveliness in favor,° sympathy° in
years, manners, and beauties—all which the Moor is defective in.
Now, for want of these required conveniences,° her delicate tenderness will find itself abused,° begin to heave the gorge,° dis-
relish and abhor the Moor. Very nature° will instruct her in it  230
and compel her to some second choice. Now, sir, this granted—
as it is a most pregnant° and unforced position—who stands so
eminent in the degree of° this fortune as Cassio does? A knave
very voluble,° no further conscionable° than in putting on the
mere form of civil and humane° seeming for the better compassing  235
of his salt° and most hidden loose affection.° Why, none, why,
none. A slipper° and subtle knave, a finder out of occasions,
that has an eye can stamp° and counterfeit advantages,° though
true advantage never present itself; a devilish knave. Besides, the
knave is handsome, young, and hath all those requisites in him that  240
folly° and green° minds look after. A pestilent complete knave, and
the woman hath found him° already.

RODERIGO.  I cannot believe that in her. She's full of most blessed condition.°

IAGO.  Blessed fig's end!° The wine she drinks is made of grapes. If she
had been blessed, she would never have loved the Moor. Blessed  245

---

**215 base men** even lowly born men.    **216 list** listen to.    **217 court of guard**
guardhouse. (Cassio is in charge of the watch.)    **216 thus** i.e., on your lips.
**221 but** only.    **225 the act of sport** sex.    **226 favor** appearance.    **sympathy**
correspondence, similarity.    **228 required conveniences** things conducive
to sexual compatibility.    **229 abused** cheated, revolted.    **heave the gorge**
experience nausea.    **230–231 Very nature** her very instincts.    **232 pregnant**
evident, cogent.    **233 in . . . of** as next in line for.    **234 voluble** facile, glib.
**conscionable** conscientious, conscience-bound.    **235 humane** polite,
courteous.    **236 salt** licentious.    **affection** passion.    **237 slipper** slippery.
**238 an eye can stamp** an eye that can coin, create.    **advantages** favorable
opportunities.    **241 folly** wantonness.    **241 green** immature.    **242 found him**
sized him up, perceived his intent.    **243 condition** disposition.    **244 fig's end**
(See 1.3.316 for the vulgar gesture of the fig.)

pudding!° Didst thou not see her paddle with the palm of his
hand? Didst not mark that?

RODERIGO. Yes, that I did; but that was but courtesy.

IAGO. Lechery, by this hand. An index° and obscure° prologue to
the history of lust and foul thoughts. They met so near with their    250
lips that their breaths embraced together. Villainous thoughts,
Roderigo! When these mutualities° so marshal the way, hard at
hand° comes the master and main exercise, th' incorporate° conclusion. Pish! But, sir, be you ruled by me. I have brought you
from Venice. Watch you°  tonight; for the command, I'll lay 't     255
upon you.° Cassio knows you not. I'll not be far from you. Do you find
some occasion to anger Cassio, either by speaking too loud, or taint-
ing° his discipline, or from what other course you please, which
the time shall more favorably minister.°

RODERIGO. Well.                                                      260

IAGO. Sir, he's rash and very sudden in choler,° and haply° may strike
at you. Provoke him that he may, for even out of that will I cause
these of Cyprus to mutiny,° whose qualification° shall come into
no true taste° again but by the displanting of Cassio. So shall you
have a shorter journey to your desires by the means I shall then    265
have to prefer° them, and the impediment most profitably removed, without the the which there were no expectation of our
prosperity.

RODERIGO. I will do this, if you can bring it to any opportunity.

IAGO. I warrant° thee. Meet me by and by° at the citadel. I must fetch   270
his necessaries ashore. Farewell.

RODERIGO. Adieu.                                          *Exit.*

IAGO. That Cassio loves her, I do well believe 't;
That she loves him, 'tis apt° and of great credit.°
The Moor, howbeit that I endure him not,                             275
Is of a constant, loving, noble nature,
And I dare think he'll prove to Desdemona
A most dear husband. Now, I do love her, too,
Not out of absolute lust—though peradventure

---

246 **pudding** sausage.    249 **index** table of contents.    **obscure** (i.e., the *lust
and foul thoughts* in line 246 are secret, hidden from view.)    252 **mutualities**
exchanges, intimacies.    253 **hard at hand** closely following.    **incorporate**
carnal.    255 **Watch you** stand watch.    255–256 **for the command . . . you**
I'll arrange for you to be appointed, given orders.    257–258 **tainting**
disparaging.    259 **minister** provide.    261 **choler** wrath.    **haply** perhaps.
263 **mutiny** riot.    **qualification** appeasement.    264 **true taste** i.e., acceptable
state.    266 **prefer** advance.    270 **warrant** assure.    **by and by** immediately.
274 **apt** probable.    **credit** credibility.

I stand accountant° for as great a sin—                      280
But partly led to diet° my revenge
For that I do suspect the lusty Moor
Hath leaped into my seat, the thought whereof
Doth, like a poisonous mineral, gnaw my innards;
And nothing can or shall content my soul                     285
Till I am evened with him, wife for wife,
Or failing so, yet that I put the Moor
At least into a jealousy so strong
That judgment cannot cure. Which thing to do,
If this poor trash of Venice, whom I trace°                   290
For° his quick hunting, stand the putting on,°
I'll have our Michael Cassio on the hip,°
Abuse° him to the Moor in the rank garb—°
For I fear Cassio with my nightcap° too—
Make the Moor thank me, love me, and reward me               295
For making him egregiously an ass
And practicing upon° his peace and quiet
Even to madness. 'Tis here, but yet confused.
Knavery's plain face is never seen till used.        *Exit.*


**2.2** *Enter* OTHELLO'*s* HERALD *with a proclamation.*

HERALD. It is Othello's pleasure, our noble and valiant general, that,
upon certain tidings now arrived, importing the mere perdition°
of the Turkish fleet, every man put himself into triumph:° some
to dance, some to make bonfires, each man to what sport and revels his addiction° leads him. For, besides these beneficial news, it    5
is the celebration of his nuptial. So much was his pleasure should
be proclaimed. All offices° are open, and there is full liberty of
feasting from this present hour of five till the bell have told

---

**280 accountant** accountable.    **281 diet** feed.    **290 trace** i.e., train, or follow
(?), or perhaps *trash*, a hunting term, meaning to put weights on a hunting dog in
order to slow him down.    **291 For** to make more eager.    **stand . . . on** respond
properly when I incite him to quarrel.    **292 on the hip** at my mercy, where I
can throw him. (A wrestling term.)    **293 Abuse** slander.    **rank garb** coarse
manner, gross fashion.    **294 with my nightcap** i.e., as a rival in my bed, as
one who gives me cuckold's horns.    **297 practicing upon** plotting against.
**2.2 Location: Cyprus, a street.**    **2 mere perdition** complete destruction.
**3 triumph** public celebration.    **5 addiction** inclination.    **7 offices** rooms
where food and drink are kept.

eleven. Heaven bless the isle of Cyprus and our noble general
Othello!                                                                           10

                                                       *Exit.*

**2.3** *Enter* OTHELLO, DESDEMONA, CASSIO, *and attendants.*

OTHELLO.  Good Michael, look you to the guard tonight.
    Let's teach ourselves that honorable stop°
    Not to outsport° discretion.
CASSIO.  Iago hath direction what to do,
    But nothwithstanding, with my personal eye                        5
    Will I look to 't.
OTHELLO.             Iago is most honest.
    Michael, good night. Tomorrow with your earliest°
    Let me have speech with you. [*To Desdemona.*]
                   Come, my dear love,
    The purchase made, the fruits are to ensue;
    That profit's yet to come 'tween me and you.°—                   10
    Good night.

    *Exit* [OTHELLO, *with* DESDEMONA *and attendants*].

    *Enter* IAGO.

CASSIO.  Welcome, Iago. We must to the watch.
IAGO.  Not this hour,° Lieutenant; 'tis not yet ten o' the clock. Our gen-
    eral cast° us thus early for the love of his Desdemona; who° let
    us not therefore blame. He hath not yet made wanton the night      15
    with her, and she is sport for Jove.
CASSIO.  She's a most exquisite lady.
IAGO.  And, I'll warrant her, full of game.
CASSIO.  Indeed, she's a most fresh and delicate creature.
IAGO.  What an eye she has! Methinks it sounds a parley° to
    provovation.                                                       20
CASSIO.  An inviting eye, and yet methinks right modest.
IAGO.  And when she speaks, is it not an alarum° to love?
CASSIO.  She is indeed perfection.

---

**2.3 Location: Cyprus, the citadel.**  **2 stop** restraint.  **3 outsport** celebrate
beyond the bounds of.  **7 with your earliest** at your earliest convenience.
**9–10 The purchase . . . you** i.e., though married, we haven't yet consummated
our love.  **13 Not this hour** not for an hour yet.  **cast** dismissed.  **14 who**
i.e., Othello.  **20 sounds a parley** calls for a conference, issues an invitation.
**22 alarum** signal calling men to arms (continuing the military metaphor of
*parley,* line 19).

IAGO. Well, happiness to their sheets! Come, Lieutenant, I have a
stoup° of wine, and here without° are a brace° of Cyprus gallants
that would fain have a measure° to the health of the black
Othello.

CASSIO. Not tonight, good Iago. I have very poor and unhappy brains for
drinking. I could well wish courtesy would invent some other custom of entertainment.

IAGO. O, they are our friends. But one cup! I'll drink for you.°

CASSIO. I have drunk but one cup tonight, and that was craftily
qualified° too, and behold what innovation° it makes here.° I
am unfortunate in the infirmity and dare not task my weakness
with any more.

IAGO. What, man? 'Tis a night of revels. That gallants desire it.

CASSIO. Where are they?

IAGO. Here at the door. I pray you, call them in.

CASSIO. I'll do 't, but it dislikes me.°                          *Exit.*   35

IAGO. If I can fasten but one cup upon him,
With that which he hath drunk tonight already,
He'll be as full of quarrel and offense°
As my young mistress' dog. Now, my sick fool Roderigo,
Whom love hath turned almost the wrong side out,          40
To Desdemona hath tonight caroused°
Potations pottle-deep;° and he's to watch.°
Three lads of Cyprus—noble swelling° spirits,
That hold their honors in a wary distance,°
The very elements° of this warlike isle—                  45
Have I tonight flustered with flowing cups,
And they watch° too. Now, 'mongst this flock of drunkards
Am I to put Cassio in some action
That may offend the isle.—But here they come.

*Enter* CASSIO, MONTANO, *and* GENTLEMEN; [*servants following with
wine*].

If consequence do but approve my dream,°                  50
My boat sails freely both with wind and stream.°

---

**25 stoup** measure of liquor, two quarts.    **25 without** outside.   **brace** pair.
**26 fain have a measure** gladly drink a toast.    **31 for you** in your place.
(Iago will do the steady drinking to keep the gallants company while Cassio
has only one cup.)    **33 qualified** diluted.        **innovation** disturbance,
insurrection.    **here** i.e., in my head.    **39 it dislikes me** i.e., I'm reluctant.
**42 offense** readiness to take offense.    **45 caroused** drunk off.    **46 pottle-deep**
to the bottom of the tankard.    **watch** stand watch.    **47 swelling** proud.
**48 hold . . . distance** i.e., are extremely sensitive of their honor.    **49 very
elements** typical sort.    **51 watch** are members of the guard.    **54 If . . . dream**
if subsequent events will only substantiate my scheme.    **55 stream** current.

CASSIO.  'Fore God, they have given me a rouse° already.
MONTANO.  Good faith, a little one; not past a pint, as I am a solider.
IAGO.  Some wine, ho! [*He sings.*]
   "And let me the cannikin° clink, clink,
   And let me the cannikin clink.      60
   A soldier's a man,
   O, man's life's but a span;°
   Why, then, let a soldier drink."

  Some wine, boys!
CASSIO.  'Fore God, an excellent song.         65
IAGO.  I learned it in England, where indeed they are most potent in
  potting.° Your Dane, your German, and your swag-bellied Hollan-
  der—drink, ho!— are nothing to your English.
CASSIO.  Is your Englishman so exquisite in his drinking?
IAGO.  Why, he drinks you,° with facility, your Dane° dead drunk; he 70
  sweats not° to overthrow your Almain;° he gives your Hollander a
  vomit ere the next  pottle can be filled.
CASSIO.  To the health of our general!
MONTANO.  I am for it, Lieutenant, and I'll do you justice.°
IAGO.  O sweet England! [*He sings.*]        75

   "King Stephen was and-a worthy peer,
   His breeches cost him but a crown;
   He held them sixpence all too dear,
   With that he called the tailor lown.°

   He was a wight of high renown,      80
   And thou art but of low degree.
   'Tis pride° that pulls the country down;
   Then take thy auld° cloak about thee."

  Some wine, ho!
CASSIO.  'Fore God, this is a more exquisite song than the other.  85
IAGO.  Will you hear 't again?
CASSIO.  No, for I hold him to be unworthy of his place that does those
  things. Well, God's above all; and there be souls must be saved,
  and there be souls must not be saved.
IAGO.  It's true, good Lieutenant.         90

---

56 **rouse** full draft of liquor. 59 **cannikin** small drinking vessel. 62 **span**
brief span of time. (Compare Psalm 39.6 as rendered in the 1928 Book of
Common Prayer: "Thou hast made my days as it were a span long.") 67 **potting**
drinking. 70 **drinks you** drinks. **your Dane** your typical Dane. 71 **sweats
not** i.e., need not exert himself. **Almain** German. 74 **I'll . . . justice** i.e., I'll
drink as much as you. 79 **lown** lout, rascal. 82 **pride** i.e., extravagance in
dress. 83 **auld** old.

CASSIO. For mine own part—no offense to the General, nor any man
of quality°—I hope to be saved.

IAGO. And so do I too, Lieutenant.

CASSIO. Ay, but, by your leave, not before me; the lieutenant is to be saved
before the ancient. Let's have no more of this; let's to our af-     95
fairs.—God forgive us our sins!—Gentlemen, let's look to our
business. Do not think, gentlemen, I am drunk.This is my ancient;
this is my right hand, and this is my left. I am not drunk now. I can
stand well enough, and speak well enough.

GENTLEMEN. Excellent, well.     100

CASSIO. Why, very well then; you must not think then that I am drunk.
*Exit.*

MONTANO. To th' platform, masters. Come, let's set the watch.°

[*Exeunt* GENTLEMEN.]

IAGO. You see this fellow that is gone before.
He's a soldier fit to stand by Caesar
And give direction; and do but see his vice.     105
'Tis to his virtue a just equinox,°
The one as long as th' other. 'Tis a pity of him.
I fear the trust Othello puts him in,
On some odd time of his infirmity,
Will shake this island.

MONTANO.                    But is he often thus?     110

IAGO. 'Tis evermore the prologue to his sleep.
He'll watch the horologe a double set,°
If drink rock not his cradle.

MONTANO.                    It were well
The General were put in mind of it.
Perhaps he sees it not, or his good nature     115
Prizes the virtue that appears in Cassio
And looks not on his evils. Is not this true?

*Enter* RODERIGO.

IAGO [*aside to him*]. How now, Roderigo?
I pray you, after the Lieutenant; go.     [*Exit* RODERIGO.]

MONTANO. And 'tis great pity that the noble Moor     120
Should hazard such a place as his own second
With° one of an engaffed° infirmity.

---

92 **quality** rank.     102 **set the watch** mount the guard.     106 **just equinox**
counterpart. (Equinox is an equal length of days and nights.)     112 **watch . . . set**
stay awake twice around the clock or *horologe*.     121–122 **hazard . . . With** risk
giving such an important position as his second in command to.     122 **engaffed**
engrafted, inveterate.

It were an honest action to say so
To the Moor.
IAGO.                Not I, for this fair island.
I do love Cassio well and would do much                    125
To cure him of this evil.              [*Cry within:* "Help! Help!"]
                    But, hark! What noise?

*Enter* CASSIO, *pursuing*° RODERIGO.

CASSIO.  Zounds, you rogue! You rascal!
MONTANO.  What's the matter, Lieutenant?
CASSIO.  A knave teach me my duty? I'll beat the knave into a
      twiggen° bottle.
RODERIGO.  Beat me?                                        130
CASSIO.  Dost thou prate, rogue?           [*He strikes* RODERIGO.]
MONTANO.  Nay, good Lieutenant. [*Restraining him.*] I pray you, sir,
      hold your hand.
CASSIO.  Let me go, sir, or I'll knock you o'er the mazard.°
MONTANO.  Come, come, you're drunk.
CASSIO.  Drunk?                                   [*They fight.*]  135
IAGO [*aside to* RODERIGO].  Away, I say. Go out and cry a mutiny.°

[*Exit* RODERIGO.]

Nay, good Lieutenant—God's will, gentlemen—
Help, ho!—Lieutenant—sir—Montano—sir—
Help, masters!°—Here's a goodly watch indeed!

[*A bell rings.*]°

Who's that which rings the bell?—Diablo,° ho!          140
The town will rise.° God's will, Lieutenant, hold!
You'll be ashamed forever.

*Enter* OTHELLO *and attendants* [*with weapons*].

OTHELLO.  What is the matter here?
MONTANO.                    Zounds, I bleed still.
I am hurt to th' death. He dies! [*He thrusts at* CASSIO.]
OTHELLO.                    Hold, for your lives!

_____

**126 s.d. pursuing** (The Quarto text reads, "driving in.")  **129 twiggen** wicker-
covered. (Cassio vows to assail Roderigo until his skin resembles wickerwork or
until he has driven Roderigo through the holes in a wickerwork.)  **133 mazard**
i.e., head. (Literally, a drinking vessel.)  **136 mutiny** riot.  **139 masters** sirs.
**s.d. A bell rings** (This direction is from the Quarto, as are *Exit Roderigo* at line
114, *They fight* at line 130, and *with weapons* at line 137.)  **140 Diablo** the
devil.  **141 rise** grow riotous.

IAGO.   Hold, ho! Lieutenant—sir—Montano—gentlemen—                145
   Have you forgot all sense of place and duty?
   Hold! The General speaks to you. Hold, for shame!
OTHELLO.   Why, how now, ho! From whence ariseth this?
   Are we turned Turks, and to ourselves do that
   Which heaven hath forbid the Ottomites?°                       150
   For Christian shame, put by this barbarous brawl!
   He that stirs next to carve for° his own rage
   Holds his soul light;° he dies upon his motion.°
   Silence that dreadful bell. It frights the isle
   From her propriety.° What is the matter, masters?             155
   Honest Iago, that looks dead with grieving,
   Speak. Who began this? On thy love, I charge thee.
IAGO.   I do not know. Friends all but now, even now,
   In quarter° and in terms° like bride and groom
   Devesting them° for bed; and then, but now—                    160
   As if some planet had unwitted men—
   Swords out, and tilting one at others' breasts
   In opposition bloody. I cannot speak°
   Any beginning to this peevish odds;°
   And would in action glorious I had lost                        165
   Those legs that brought me to a part of it!
OTHELLO.   How comes it, Michael, you are thus forgot?°
CASSIO.   I pray you, pardon me. I cannot speak.
OTHELLO.   Worthy Montano, you were wont be° civil;
   The gravity and stillness° of your youth                       170
   The world hath noted, and your name is great
   In mouths of wisest censure.° What's the matter
   That you unlace° your reputation thus
   And spend your rich opinion° for the name
   Of a night-brawler? Give me answer to it.                      175
MONTANO.   Worthy Othello, I am hurt to danger.
   Your officer, Iago, can inform you—

---

**149–150 to ourselves . . . Ottomites** inflict on ourselves the harm that heaven
has prevented the Turks from doing (by destroying their fleet).   **152 carve for**
i.e., indulge, satisfy with his sword.   **153 Holds . . . light** i.e., places little value
on his life.   **upon his motion** if he moves.   **155 propriety** proper state or
condition.   **159 In quarter** in friendly conduct, within bounds.   **in terms** on
good terms.   **160 Devesting them** undressing themselves.   **163 speak** explain.
**164 peevish odds** childish quarrel.   **167 are thus forgot** have forgotten
yourself thus.   **169 wont be** accustomed to be.   **170 stillness** sobriety.
**172 censure** judgment.   **173 unlace** undo, lay open (as one might loose the
strings of a purse containing reputation).   **174 opinion** reputation.

While I spare speech, which something° now offends° me—
Of all that I do know; nor know I aught
By me that's said or done amiss this night,                    180
Unless self-charity be sometimes a vice,
And to defend ourselves it be a sin
When violence assails us.
OTHELLO.                    Now, by heaven,
My blood° begins my safer guides° to rule,
And passion, having my best judgment collied,°              185
Essays° to lead the way. Zounds, if I stir,
Or do but lift this arm, the best of you
Shall sink in my rebuke. Give me to know
How this foul rout° began, who set it on;
And he that is approved in° this offense,                      190
Though he had twinned with me, both at birth,
Shall lose me. What? In a town of° war
Yet wild, the people's hearts brim full of fear,
To manage° private and domestic quarrel?
In night, and on the court and guard of safety?°             195
'Tis monstrous. Iago, who began 't?
MONTANO [to IAGO]. If partially affined,° or leagued in office,°
Thou dost deliver more or less than truth,
Thou art no soldier.
IAGO.                    Touch me not so near.
I had rather have this tongue cut from my mouth           200
Than it should do offense to Michael Cassio;
Yet, I persuade myself, to speak the truth
Shall nothing wrong him. Thus it is, General.
Montano and myself being in speech,
There comes a fellow crying out for help,                     205
And Cassio following him with determined sword
To execute° upon him. Sir, this gentleman

[indicating MONTANO]

Steps in to Cassio and entreats his pause.°
Myself the crying fellow did pursue,
Lest by his clamor—as it so fell out—                         210

---

**178 something** somewhat.   **offends** pains.   **184 blood** passion (of anger).
**guides** i.e., reason.   **185 collied** darkened.   **186 Essays** undertakes.   **189 rout**
riot.   **190 approved in** found guilty of.   **192 town of** town garrisoned for.
**199 manage** undertake.   **195 on . . . safety** at the main guardhouse or
headquarters and on watch.   **197 partially affined** made partial by some
personal relationship.   **leagued in office** in league as fellow officers.
**207 execute** give effect to (his anger).   **208 his pause** him to stop.

The town might fall in fright. He, swift of foot,
Outran my purpose, and I returned, the rather°
For that I heard the clink of fall of swords
And Cassio high in oath, which till tonight
I ne'er might say before. When I came back—          215
For this was brief—I found them close together
At blow and thrust, even as again they were
When you yourself did part them.
More of this matter cannot I report.
But men are men; the best sometimes forget.°          220
Though Cassio did some little wrong to him,
As men in rage strike those that wish them best,°
Yet surely Cassio, I believe, received
From him that fled some strange indignity,
Which patience could not pass.°
OTHELLO.                        I know, Iago,          225
Thy honesty and love doth mince this matter,
Making it light to Cassio. Cassio, I love thee,
But nevermore be officer of mine.

*Enter* DESDEMONA, *attended.*

Look if my gentle love be not raised up.
I'll make thee an example.                            230
DESDEMONA. What is the matter, dear?
OTHELLO.                        All's well now, sweeting;
Come away to bed. [*To* MONTANO.] Sir, for your hurts,
Myself will be your surgeon.°    Lead him off.

[MONTANO *is led off.*]

Iago, look with care about the town
And silence those whom this vile brawl distracted.   235
Come, Desdemona. 'Tis the soldiers' life
To have their balmy slumbers waked with strife.

*Exit* [*with all but* IAGO *and* CASSIO].

IAGO. What, are you hurt, Lieutenant?
CASSIO. Ay, past all surgery.
IAGO. Marry, God forbid!                              240
CASSIO. Reputation, reputation, reputation! O, I have lost my reputa-
tion! I have lost the immortal part of myself, and what remains is
bestial. My reputation, Iago, my reputation!

---

**212 rather** sooner.    **220 forget** forget themselves.    **222 those . . . best** i.e.,
even those who are well disposed.    **225 pass** pass over, overlook.    **233 be your
surgeon** i.e., make sure you receive medical attention.

IAGO.  As I am an honest man, I thought you had received some bodily
wound; there is more sense in that than in reputation. Reputation  245
is an idle and most false imposition,° oft got without merit and lost
without deserving. You have lost no reputation at all, unless you
repute yourself such a loser. What, man, there are more ways to re-
cover° the General again. You are but  now cast in his mood°—a
punishment more in policy° than in malice, even  so as one would  250
beat his offense less dog to affright an imperious lion.° Sue° to him
again and he's yours.
CASSIO. I will rather sue to be despised than to deceive so good a com-
mander with so slight,° so drunken, and so indiscreet an officer.
Drunk? And speak parrot?° And squabble? Swagger? Swear? And  255
discourse fustian with one's own shadow? O thou invisible spirit
of wine, if thou hast no name to be known by, let us call thee
devil!
IAGO.  What was he that you followed with your sword? What had
he done to you?                                                                            260
CASSIO.  I know not.
IAGO.  Is 't possible?
CASSIO.  I remember a mass of things, but nothing distinctly; a quarrel,
but nothing wherefore.° O God, that men should put an enemy
in their mouths to steal away their brains! That we should, with  265
joy, pleasance, revel, and applause° transform ourselves into
beasts!
IAGO.  Why, but you are now well enough. How came you thus
recovered?
CASSIO.  It hath pleased the devil drunkenness to give place to the  270
devil wrath. One unperfectness shows me another, to make me
frankly despise myself.
IAGO.  Come, you are too severe a moraler.° As the time, the place, and
the condition of this country stands, I could heartily wish this
had not befallen; but since it is as it is, mend it for your own good.  275
CASSIO.  I will ask him for my place again; he shall tell me I am a drunkard. Had I as many mouths as Hydra,° such an answer would
stop them all. To be now a sensible man, by and by a fool, and

---

**246 false imposition** thing artificially imposed and of no real value.
**248–249 recover** regain favor with.    **249 cast in his mood** dismissed in a
moment of anger.    **250 in policy** done for expediency's sake and as a public
gesture.    **250-251 would . . . lion** i.e., would make an example of a minor offender
in order to deter more important and dangerous offenders.    **251 Sue** petition.
**254 slight** worthless.    **255 speak parrot** talk nonsense, rant.    **264 wherefore**
why.    **266 applause** desire for applause.    **273 moraler** moralizer.    **277 Hydra**
the Lernaean Hydra, a monster with many heads and the ability to grow two
heads when one was cut off, slain by Hercules as the second of his twelve labors.

presently a beast! O, strange! Every inordinate cup is unblessed,
and the ingredient is a devil.       280

IAGO. Come, come, good wine is a good familiar creature, if it be well
used. Exclaim no more against it. And, good Lieutenant, I think
you think I love you.

CASSIO. I have well approved° it, sir. I drunk!

IAGO. You or any man living may be drunk at a time,° man. I'll tell you    285
what you shall do. Our general's wife is not the general—I may say
so in this respect, for that° he hath devoted and given up himself to the contemplation, mark, and denotement° of her
parts° and graces. Confess yourself freely to her; importune her
help to put you in your place again. She is of so free,° so kind, so    290
apt, so blessed a disposition, she holds it a vice in her goodness
not to do more than she is requested. This broken joint between
you and her husband entreat her to splinter;° and, my fortunes
against any lay° worth naming, this crack of your love shall grow
stronger than it was before.       295

CASSIO. You advise me well.

IAGO. I protest,° in the sincerity of love and honest kindness.

CASSIO. I think it freely;° and betimes in the morning I will beseech the
virtuous Desdemona to undertake for me. I am desperate of my fortunes if they check° me here.       300

IAGO. You are in the right. Good night, Lieutenant. I must to the watch.

CASSIO. Good night, honest Iago.                  *Exit* CASSIO.

IAGO. And what's he then that says I play the villain,
When this advice is free° I give, and honest,
Probal° to thinking, and indeed the course       305
To win the Moor again? For 'tis most easy
Th' inclining° Desdemona to subdue°
In any honest suit; she's framed as fruitful°
As the free elements.° And then for her
To win the Moor—were 't to renounce his baptism,    310
All seals and symbols of redeemèd sin—
His soul is so enfettered to her love
That she may make, unmake, do what she list,

---

**284 approved** proved.    **285 at a time** at one time or another.    **287 in . . . that**
in view of this fact, that.    **288 mark, and denotement** (Both words mean
"observation.")    **289 parts** qualities.    **290 free** generous.    **293 splinter** bind
with splints.    **294 lay** stake, wager.    **297 protest** insist, declare.    **298 freely**
unreservedly.    **300 check** repulse.    **304 free** (1) free from guile (2) freely given.
**305 Probal** probable, reasonable.    **307 inclining** favorably disposed.    **subdue**
persuade.    **308 framed as fruitful** created as generous.    **309 free elements**
i.e., earth, air, fire, and water, unrestrained and spontaneous.

Even as her appetite° shall play the god
With his weak function.° How am I then a villain,          315
To counsel Cassio to this parallel° course
Directly to his good? Divinity of hell!°
When devils will the blackest sins put on,°
They do suggest° at first with heavenly shows,
As I do now. For whiles this honest fool                   320
Plies Desdemona to repair his fortune,
And she for him pleads stronger to the Moor,
I'll pour this pestilence into his ear,
That she repeals him° for her body's lust;
And by how much she strives to do him good,                325
She shall undo her credit with the Moor.
So will I turn her virtue into pitch,°
And out of her own goodness make the net
That shall enmesh them all.

*Enter* RODERIGO.

                         How now, Roderigo?
RODERIGO. I do follow here in the chase, not like a hound that hunts, but   330
    one that fills up the cry.° My money is almost spent; I have been
    tonight exceedingly well cudgeled; and I think the issue will be I
    shall have so much° experience for my pains, and so, with no
    money at all and a little more wit, return again to Venice.
IAGO. How poor are they that have not patience!                              335
    What wound did ever heal but by degrees?
    Thou know'st we work by wit, and not by witchcraft,
    And wit depends on dilatory time.
    Does 't not go well? Cassio hath beaten thee,
    And thou, by that small hurt, hast cashiered° Cassio.                    340
    Though other things grow fair against the sun,
    Yet fruits that blossom first will first be ripe,°
    Content thyself awhile. By the Mass, 'tis morning!
    Pleasure and action make the hours seem short.

---

**314 her appetite** her desire, or, perhaps, his desire for her.    **315 function**
exercise of faculties (weakened by his fondness for her).    **316 parallel**
corresponding to these facts and to his best interests.    **317 Divinity of hell**
inverted theology of hell (which seduces the soul to its damnation).    **318 put on**
further investigate.    **319 suggest** tempt.    **324 repeals him** attempts to get him
restored.    **327 pitch** i.e., (1) foul blackness (2) a snaring substance.    **331 fill up
the cry** merely takes part as one of the pack.    **333 so much** just so much and
no more.    **340 cashiered** dismissed from service.    **341–342 Though . . . ripe**
i.e., plans that are well prepared and set expeditiously in motion will soonest
ripen into success.

Retire thee; go where thou art billeted.
Away, I say! Thou shalt know more hereafter.
Nay, get thee gone.                          *Exit* RODERIGO.
          Two things are to be done.
My wife must move° for Cassio to her mistress;
I'll set her on;
Myself the while to draw the Moor apart                          350
And bring him jump° when he may Cassio find
Soliciting his wife. Ay, that's the way.
Dull not device° by coldness° and delay.          *Exit.*


**3.1** *Enter* CASSIO [*and*] MUSICIANS.

CASSIO.  Masters, play here—I will content your pains°—
          Something that's brief, and bid "Good morrow, General."
                                        [*They play.*]

[*Enter*] CLOWN.

CASSIO.  Why, masters, have your instruments been in Naples, that they
          speak 'i the nose° thus?
A MUSICIAN.  How, sir, how?                          5
CLOWN.  Are these, I pray you, wind instruments?
A MUSICIAN.  Ay, marry, are they, sir.
CLOWN.  O, thereby hangs a tail.
A MUSICIAN.  Whereby hangs a tale, sir?
CLOWN.  Marry, sir, by many a wind instrument° that I know. But, mas-          10
          ters, here's money for you. [*He gives money.*] And the General so
          likes your music that he desires you, for love's sake,° to make no
          more noise with it.
A MUSICIAN.  Well, sir, we will not.
CLOWN.  If you have any music that may not° be heard, to 't again; but,          15
          as they say, to hear music the General does not greatly care.
A MUSICIAN.  We have none such, sir.

---

**348 move** plead.   **351 jump** precisely.   **353 device** plot.   **coldness** lack of
seal.   **3.1 Location: Before the chamber of Othello and Desdemona.**
**1 content your pains** reward your efforts.   **3–4 speak i' the nose** (1) sound
nasal (2) sound like one whose nose has been attacked by syphilis. (Naples was
popularly supposed to have a high incidence of venereal disease.)   **10 wind
instrument** (With a joke on flatulence. The *tail*, line 8, that hangs nearby the
*wind instrument* suggests the penis.)   **12 for love's sake** (1) out of friendship
and affection (2) for the sake of lovemaking in Othello's marriage.   **15 may not**
cannot.

CLOWN.  Then put up your pipes in your bag, for I'll away.° Go, vanish
   into air, away!                              *Exeunt* MUSICIANS.
CASSIO.  Dost thou hear, mine honest friend?                          20
CASSIO.  No, I hear not your honest friend; I hear you.
CASSIO.  Prithee, keep up° thy quillets.° There's a poor piece of gold for
   thee. [*He gives money.*] If the gentle-woman that attends the
   General's wife be stirring, tell her there's one Cassio entreats her
   a little favor of speech.° Wilt thou do this?                      25
CLOWN.  She is stirring, sir. If she will stir° hither, I shall seem° to
   notify unto her.
CASSIO.  Do, good my friend.                        *Exit* CLOWN.

   *Enter* IAGO.

                              In happy time,° Iago.
IAGO.  You have not been abed, then?
CASSIO.  Why, no. The day had broke                                  30
   Before we parted. I have made bold, Iago,
   To send in to your wife. My suit to her
   Is that she will to virtuous Desdemona
   Procure me some access.
IAGO.  I'll send her to you presently;                               35
   And I'll devise a means to draw the Moor
   Out of the way, that your converse and business
   May be more free.
CASSIO.  I humbly thank you for 't.                     *Exit* IAGO.
                   I never knew
   A Florentine° more kind and honest.                               40

   *Enter* EMILIA.

EMILIA.  Good morrow, good Lieutenant. I am sorry
   For your displeasure;° but all will sure be well.
   The General and his wife are talking of it,
   And she speaks for you stoutly.° The Moor replies
   That he you hurt is of great fame° in Cyprus                      45
   And great affinity,° and that in wholesome wisdom
   He might not but refuse you; but he protests° he loves you

_____

**18 I'll away** (Possibly a misprint, or a snatch of song?)    **22 keep up** do not bring
out, do not use.    **quillets** quibbles, puns.    **25 a little . . . speech** the favor of a
brief talk.    **26 stir** bestir herself (with a play on *stirring*, "rousing herself from
rest").    **seem** deem it good, think fit.    **28 In happy time** i.e., well met.
**40 Florentine** i.e., even a fellow Florentine. (Iago is a Venetian; Cassio is a
Florentine.)    **42 displeasure** fall from favor.    **44 stoutly** spiritedly.    **45 fame**
reputation, importance.    **46 affinity** kindred, family connection.    **47 protests**
insists.

And needs no other suitor but his likings
To take the safest occasion by the front°
To bring you in again.
CASSIO.　　　　　　　　　　Yet I beseech you,　　　　　50
If you think fit, or that it may be done,
Give me advantage of some brief discourse
With Desdemona alone.
EMILIA.　Pray you, come in.
　　　　　　　　　　I will bestow you where you shall have time
To speak your bosom° freely.　　　　　　　　55
CASSIO.　I am much bound to you.　　　　　　[*Exeunt.*]


**3.2** Enter OTHELLO, IAGO, and GENTLEMEN.

OTHELLO　[*giving letters*]. These letters, give, Iago, to the pilot,
And by him do my duties° to the Senate.
That done, I will be walking on the works,°
Repair° there to me.
IAGO.　　　　　　　　Well, my good lord, I'll do 't.
OTHELLO.　This fortification, gentlemen, shall we see 't?　　5
GENTLEMEN.　We'll wait upon° your lordship.　　　　*Exeunt.*


**3.3** Enter DESDEMONA, CASSIO, and EMILIA.

DESDEMONA.　Be thou assured, good Cassio, I will do
All my abilities in thy behalf.
EMILIA.　Good madam, do. I warrant it grieves my husband
As if the cause were his.
DESDEMONA.　O, that's an honest fellow. Do not doubt, Cassio,　　5
But I will have my lord and you again
As friendly as you were.
CASSIO.　　　　　　　　Bounteous madam,
Whatever shall become of Michael Cassio,
He's never anything but your true servant.
DESDEMONA.　I know 't. I thank you. You do love my lord;　　10
You have known him long, and be you well assured

---

**49 occasion . . . front** opportunity by the forelock.　**55 bosom** inmost
thoughts.　**3.2 Location: The citadel.**　**2 do my duties** convey my respects.
**3 works** breastworks, fortifications.　**4 Repair** return, come.　**6 wait upon**
attend.　**3.3 Location: The garden of the citadel.**

He shall in strangeness° stand no farther off
Than in a politic° distance.

CASSIO.                                   Ay, but, lady,
That policy may either last so long,
Or feed upon such nice and waterish diet,°                    15
Or breed itself so out of circumstance,°
That, I being absent and my place supplied,°
My general will forget my love and service.

DESDEMONA.  Do not doubt° that. Before Emilia here
I give thee warrant° of thy place. Assure thee,             20
If I do vow a friendship I'll perform it
To the last article. My lord shall never rest.
I'll watch him tame° and talk him out of patience;°
His bed shall seem a school, his board° a shrift;°
I'll intermingle everything he does                          25
With Cassio's suit. Therefore be merry, Cassio,
For thy solicitor° shall rather die
Than give thy cause away.°

      *Enter* OTHELLO *and* IAGO [*at a distance*].

EMILIA.  Madam, here comes my lord.
CASSIO.  Madam, I'll take my leave.                          30
DESDEMONA.  Why, stay, and hear me speak.
CASSIO.  Madam, not now. I am very ill at ease,
Unfit for mine own purposes.
DESDEMONA.  Well, do your discretion.°          *Exit* CASSIO.
IAGO.  Ha! I like not that.                                  35
OTHELLO.  What dost thou say?
IAGO.  Nothing, my lord; or if—I know not what.
OTHELLO.  Was not that Cassio parted from my wife?
IAGO.  Cassio, my lord? No, sure, I cannot think it,
That he would steal away so guiltylike,                      40
Seeing you coming.
OTHELLO.  I do believe 'twas he.

_____

**12 strangeness** aloofness.   **13 politic** required by wise policy.   **15 Or . . .
diet** or sustain itself at length upon such trivial and meager technicalities.
**16 breed . . . circumstances** continually renew itself so out of chance events,
or yield so few chances for my being pardoned.   **17 supplied** filled by another
person.   **19 doubt** fear.   **20 warrant** guarantee.   **23 watch him tame** tame
him by keeping him from sleeping. (A term from falconry.)   **out of patience**
past his endurance.   **24 board** dining table.   **shrift** confessional.   **27 solic-
itor** advocate.   **28 away** up.   **34 do your discretion** act according to your
own discretion.

DESDEMONA.  How now, my lord?
　I have been talking with a suitor here,
　A man that languishes in your displeasure.                            45
OTHELLO.  Who is 't you mean?
DESDEMONA.  Why, your lieutenant, Cassio. Good my lord,
　If I have any grace or power to move you,
　His present reconciliation take;°
　For if he be not one that truly loves you,                            50
　That errs in ignorance and not in cunning,°
　I have no judgment in an honest face.
　I prithee, call him back.
OTHELLO.  Went he hence now?
DESDEMONA.  Yes, faith, so humbled                                      55
　That he hath left part of his grief with me
　To suffer with him. Good love, call him back.
OTHELLO.  Not now, sweet Desdemona. Some other time.
DESDEMONA.  But shall 't be shortly?
OTHELLO.  The sooner, sweet, for you.                                   60
DESDEMONA.  Shall 't be tonight at supper?
OTHELLO.  No, not tonight.
DESDEMONA.  Tomorrow dinner,° then?
OTHELLO.  I shall not dine at home.
　I meet the captains at the citadel.                                   65
DESDEMONA.  Why, then, tomorrow night, or Tuesday morn,
　On Tuesday noon, or night, on Wednesday morn.
　I prithee, name the time, but let it not
　Exceed three days. In faith, he's penitent;
　And yet his trespass, in our common reason°—                         70
　Save that, they say, the wars must make example
　Out of her best°—is not almost° a fault
　T' incur a private check.° When shall he come?
　Tell me, Othello. I wonder in my soul
　What you would ask me that I should deny,                             75
　Or stand so mammering on.° What? Michael Cassio,
　That came a-wooing with you, and so many a time,
　When I have spoke of you dispraisingly,

---

**49 His . . . take** let him be reconciled to you right away.   **51 in cunning**
wittingly.   **63 dinner** (The noontime meal.)   **70 common reason** everyday
judgments.   **71–72 Save . . . best** were it not that, as the saying goes, military
discipline requires making an example of the very best men. (She refers to *wars*
as a singular concept.)   **72 not almost** scarcely.   **73 private check** even a
private reprimand.   **76 mammering on** wavering about.   **80 bring him in**
restore him to favor.   **86 peculiar** particular, personal.

Hath ta'en your part—to have so much to do
To bring him in!° By 'r Lady, I could do much—                    80
OTHELLO.  Prithee, no more. Let him come when he will;
    I will deny thee nothing.
DESDEMONA.  Why, this is not a boon.
    'Tis as I should entreat you wear your gloves,
    Or feed on nourishing dishes, or keep you warm,                85
    Or sue to you to do a peculiar° profit
    To your own person. Nay, when I have a suit
    Wherein I mean to touch° your love indeed,
    It shall be full of poise° and difficult weight,
    And fearful to be granted.                                     90
OTHELLO.  I will deny thee nothing.
    Whereon,° I beseech thee, grant me this,
    To leave me but a little to myself.
DESDEMONA.  Shall I deny you? No. Farewell, my lord.
OTHELLO.  Farewell, my Desdemona. I'll come to thee straight.°    95
DESDEMONA.  Emilia, come—Be as your fancies° teach you;
    Whate'er you be, I am obedient.                 Exit [with EMILIA].
OTHELLO.  Excellent wretch!° Perdition catch my soul
    But I do love thee! And when I love thee not,
    Chaos is come again.°                                          100
IAGO.  My noble lord—
OTHELLO.  What dost thou say, Iago?
IAGO.  Did Michael Cassio, when you wooed my lady,
    Know of your love?
OTHELLO.  He did, from first to last. Why dost thou ask?          105
IAGO.  But for a satisfaction of my thought;
    No further harm.
OTHELLO.              Why of thy thought, Iago?
IAGO.  I did not think he had been acquainted with her.
OTHELLO.  O, yes, and went between us very oft.
IAGO.  Indeed?                                                     110
OTHELLO.  Indeed? Ay, indeed. Descern'st thou aught in that?
    Is he not honest?
IAGO.  Honest, my lord?
OTHELLO.  Honest. Ay, honest.

---

**80 bring him in** restore him to favor.    **86 peculiar** particular, personal.
**88 touch** test.    **89 poise** weight, heaviness; or equipoise, delicate balance
involving hard choice.    **92 Whereon** in return for which.    **95 straight** straight
way.    **96 fancies** inclinations.    **98 wretch** (A term of affectionate endearment.)
**99–100 And . . . again** i.e., my love for you will last forever, until the end of time
when chaos will return. (But with an unconscious, ironic suggestion that, if
anything should induce Othello to cease loving Desdemona, the result would
be chaos.)

IAGO.  My lord, for aught I know.                                    115
OTHELLO.  What dost thou think?
IAGO.  Think, my lord?
OTHELLO.  "Think, my lord?" By heaven, thou echo'st me,
    As if there were some monster in thy thought
    Too hideous to be shown. Thou dost mean something.     120
    I heard thee say even now, thou lik'st not that,
    When Cassio left my wife. What didst thou not like?
    And when I told thee he was of my counsel°
    In my whole course of wooing, thou criedst "Indeed?"
    And didst contract and purse° thy brow together       125
    As if thou then hadst shut up in thy brain
    Some horrible conceit.° If thou dost love me,
    Show me thy thought.
IAGO.  My lord, you know I love you.
OTHELLO.  I think thou dost;                                          130
    And, for° I know thou'rt full of love and honesty,
    And weigh'st thy words before thou giv'st them breath,
    Therefore these stops° of thine fright me the more;
    For such things in a false disloyal knave
    Are tricks of custom,° but in a man that's just        135
    They're close dilations,° working from the heart
    That passion cannot rule.°
IAGO.                         For° Michael Cassio,
    I dare be sworn I think that he is honest.
OTHELLO.  I think so too.
IAGO.                      Men should be what they seem;
    Or those that be not, would they might seem none!°    140
OTHELLO.  Certain, men should be what they seem.
IAGO.  Why, then, I think Cassio's an honest man.
OTHELLO.  Nay, yet there's more in this.
    I prithee, speak to me as to thy thinkings,
    As thou dost ruminate, and give thy worst of thoughts  145
    The worst of words.
IAGO.                    Good my lord, pardon me.
    Though I am bound to every act of duty,
    I am not bound to that° all slaves are free to.°

---

**123 of my counsel** in my confidence.   **125 purse** knit.   **127 conceit** fancy.
**131 for** because.   **133 stops** pauses.   **135 of custom** customary.   **136 close
dilations** secret or involuntary expressions or delays.   **137 That passion
cannot rule** i.e., that are too passionately strong to be restrained (referring to the
workings), or, that cannot rule its own passions (referring to the heart).   **137 For**
as for.   **140 none** i.e., not to be men, or not seem to be honest.   **148 that** that
which.   **free to** free with respect to.

Utter my thoughts? Why, say they are vile and false,
As where's the palace whereinto foul things                      150
Sometimes intrude not? Who has that breast so pure
But some uncleanly apprehensions
Keep leets and law days,° and in sessions sit
With° meditations lawful?°

OTHELLO.  Thou dost conspire against thy friend,° Iago,          155
If thou but think'st him wronged and mak'st his ear
A stranger to thy thoughts.

IAGO.                                    I do beseech you,
Though I perchance am vicious° in my guess—
As I confess it is my nature's plague
To spy into abuses, and oft my jealousy°                         160
Shapes faults that are not—that your wisdom then,°
From one° that so imperfectly conceits,°
Would take no notice, nor build yourself a trouble
Out of his scattering° and unsure observance.
It were not for your quiet nor your good,                        165
Nor for my manhood, honesty, and wisdom,
To let you know my thoughts.

OTHELLO.                            What dost thou mean?

IAGO.  Good name in man and woman, dear my lord,
Is the immediate° jewel of their souls.
Who steals my purse steals trash; 'tis something, nothing;       170
'Twas mine, 'tis his, and has been slave to thousands;
But he that filches from me my good name
Robs me of that which not enriches him
And makes me poor indeed.

OTHELLO.  By heaven, I'll know thy thoughts.                     175

IAGO.  You cannot, if° my heart were in your hand,
Nor shall not, whilst 'tis in my custody.

OTHELLO.  Ha?

IAGO.          O, beware, my lord, of jealousy.
It is the green-eyed monster which doth mock
The meat it feeds on.° That cuckold lives in bliss               180

---

153 **Keep leets and law days** i.e., hold court, set up their authority in one's heart. (*Leets* are a kind of manor court; *law days* are the days courts sit in session, or three sessions.)    154 **With** along with.    **lawful** innocent.    155 **thy friend** i.e., Othello.    158 **vicious** wrong.    160 **jealousy** suspicious nature.    161 **then** on that account.    162 **one** i.e., myself, Iago.    **conceits** judges, conjectures. 164 **scattering** random.    169 **immediate** essential, most precious.    176 **if** even if.    179–180 **doth mock . . . on** mocks and torments the heart of its victim, the man who suffers jealousy.

Who, certain of his fate, loves not his wronger;°
But O, what damnèd minutes tells° he o'er
Who dotes, yet doubts, suspects, yet fondly loves!

OTHELLO.  O misery!

IAGO.  Poor and content is rich, and rich enough,°             185
    But riches fineless° is as poor as winter
    To him that ever fears he shall be poor.
    Good God, the souls of all my tribe defend
    From jealousy!

OTHELLO.  Why, why is this?                                    190
    Think'st thou I'd make a life of jealousy,
    To follow still the changes of the moon
    With fresh suspicions?° No! To be once in doubt
    Is once° to be resolved.° Exchange me for a goat
    When I shall turn the business of my soul          195
    To such exsufflicate and blown° surmises
    Matching thy inference.° 'Tis not to make me jealous
    To say my wife is fair, feeds well, loves company,
    Is free of speech, sings, plays, and dances well;
    Where virtue is, these are more virtuous.         200
    Not from mine own weak merits will I draw
    The smallest fear of doubt of her revolt,°
    For she had eyes, and chose me. No, Iago,
    I'll see before I doubt; when I doubt, prove;
    And on the proof, there is no more but this—       205
    Away at once with love or jealousy.

IAGO.  I am glad of this, for now I shall have reason
    To show the love and duty that I bear you
    With franker spirit. Therefore, as I am bound,
    Receive it from me. I speak not yet of proof.       210
    Look to your wife; observe her well with Cassio.
    Wear your eyes thus, not° jealous nor secure.°
    I would not have your free and noble nature,

---

**181 his wronger** i.e., his faithless wife. (The unsuspecting cuckold is spared the misery of loving his wife only to discover she is cheating on him.)   **182 tells** counts.   **185 Poor . . . enough** to be content with what little one has is the greatest wealth of all. (Proverbial.)   **186 fineless** boundless.   **192–193 To follow . . . suspicions** to be constantly imagining new causes for suspicion, changing incessantly like the moon.   **194 once** once and for all.   **resolved** free of doubt, having settled the matter.   **196 exsufflicate and blown** inflated and blown up, rumored about, or, spat out and flyblown, hence, loathsome, disgusting. **197 inference** description or allegation.   **202 doubt . . . revolt** fear of her unfaithfulness.   **212 not** neither.   **secure** free from uncertainty.

Out of self-bounty,° be abused.° Look to 't.
I know our country disposition well;                              215
In Venice they do let God see the pranks
They dare not show their husbands; their best conscience
Is not to leave 't undone, but keep 't unknown.

OTHELLO.  Dost thou say so?

IAGO.  She did deceive her father, marrying you;                  220
    And when she seemed to shake and fear your looks,
    She loved them most.

OTHELLO.                          And so she did.

IAGO.                                Why, go to,° then!
    She that, so young, could give out such a seeming,°
    To seel° her father's eyes up close as oak,°
    He thought 'twas witchcraft! But I am much to blame.         225
    I humbly do beseech you of your pardon
    For too much loving you.

OTHELLO.  I am bound° to thee forever.

IAGO.  I see this hath a little dashed your spirits.

OTHELLO.  Not a jot, not a jot.

IAGO.                          I' faith, I fear it has.           230
    I hope you will consider what is spoke
    Comes from my love. But I do see you're moved.
    I am to pray you not to strain my speech
    To grosser issues° nor to larger reach°
    Than to suspicion.                                           235

OTHELLO.  I will not.

IAGO.  Should you do so, my lord,
    My speech should fall into such vile success°
    Which my thoughts aimed not. Cassio's my worthy friend.
    My lord, I see you're moved.

OTHELLO.                          No, not much moved.             240
    I do not think but Desdemona's honest.°

IAGO.  Long live she so! And long live you to think so!

OTHELLO.  And yet, how nature erring from itself—

IAGO.  Ay, there's the point! As—to be bold with you—
    Not to affect° many proposèd matches                         245
    Of her own clime, complexion, and degree,°

---

214 **self-bounty** inherent or natural goodness and generosity.    **abused**
deceived.    222 **go to** (An expression of impatience.)    223 **seeming** false
appearance.    224 **seel** blind. (A term from falconry.)    **oak** (A close-grained
wood.)    228 **bound** indebted (but perhaps with ironic sense of "tied").
234 **issues** significances.    **reach** meaning, scope.    238 **success** effect, result.
241 **honest** chaste.    245 **affect** prefer, desire.    246 **clime . . . degree** country,
color, and social position.

Whereto we see in all things nature tends—
Foh! One may smell in such a will° most rank,
Foul disproportion,° thoughts unnatural.
But pardon me. I do not in position°                              250
Distinctly speak of her, though I may fear
Her will, recoiling° to her better° judgment,
May fall to match you with her country forms°
And happily° repent.
OTHELLO.                        Farewell, farewell!
If more thou dost perceive, let me know more.                    255
Set on thy wife to observe. Leave me, Iago.
IAGO [*going*]. My lord, I take my leave.
OTHELLO. Why did I marry? This honest creature doubtless
Sees and knows more, much more, than he unfolds.
IAGO [*returning*]. My Lord, I would I might entreat your honor  260
To scan° this thing no farther. Leave it to time.
Although 'tis fit that Cassio have his place—
For, sure, he fills it up with great ability—
Yet if you please to hold him off awhile,
You shall by that perceive him and his means.°                   265
Note if your lady strain his entertainment°
With any strong or vehement importunity;
Much will be seen in that. In the meantime,
Let me be thought too busy° in my fears—
As worthy cause I have to fear I am—                             270
And hold her free,° I do beseech your honor.
OTHELLO. Fear not my government.°
IAGO. I once more take my leave.                          *Exit.*
OTHELLO. This fellow's of exceeding honesty,
And knows all qualities,° with a learnèd spirit,                 275
Of human dealings. If I do prove her haggard,°
Though that her jesses° were my dear heartstrings,
I'd whistle her off and let her down the wind°

---

**248 will** sensuality, appetite.    **249 disproportion** abnormality.    **250 position**
argument, proposition.    **252 recoiling** reverting.    **better** i.e., more natural and
reconsidered.    **253 fall . . . forms** undertake to compare you with Venetian
norms of handsomeness.    **254 happily repent** haply repent her marriage.
**261 scan** scrutinize.    **265 his means** the method he uses (to regain his post).
**266 strain his entertainment** urge his reinstatement.    **269 busy** interfering.
**271 hold her free** regard her as innocent.    **272 government** self-control,
conduct.    **275 qualities** natures, types.    **276 haggard** wild (like a wild
female hawk).    **277 jesses** straps fastened around the legs of a trained hawk.
**278 I'd . . . wind** i.e., I'd let her go forever. (To release a hawk downwind was to
invite it not to return.)

To prey at fortune.° Haply, for° I am black
And have not those soft parts of conversation°                    280
That chamberers° have, or for I am declined
Into the vale of years—yet that's not much—
She's gone. I am abused,° and my relief
Must be to loathe her. O curse of marriage,
That we can call these delicate creatures ours                    285
And not their appetites! I had rather be a toad
And live upon the vapor of a dungeon
Than keep a corner in the thing I love
For others' uses. Yet, 'tis the plague of great ones;
Prerogatived° are they less than the base.°                      290
'Tis destiny unshunnable, like death.
Even then this forkèd° plague is fated to us
When we do quicken.° Look where she comes.

*Enter* DESDEMONA *and* EMILIA.

If she be false, O, then heaven mocks itself!
I'll not believe 't.
DESDEMONA.                     How now, my dear Othello?          295
Your dinner, and the generous° islanders
By you invited, do attend° your presence.
OTHELLO.  I am to blame.
DESDEMONA.                     Why do you speak so faintly?
Are you not well?
OTHELLO.  I have a pain upon my forehead here.                    300
DESDEMONA.  Faith, that's with watching.° 'Twill away again.

[*She offers her handkerchief.*]

Let me but bind it hard, within this hour
It will be well.
OTHELLO.                     Your napkin° is too little.
Let it alone.° Come, I'll go in with you.

---

**279 prey at fortune** fend for herself in the wild.   **Haply, for** perhaps because.
**280 soft . . . conversation** pleasing graces of social behavior.   **281 cham-
berers** gallants.   **283 abused** deceived.   **290 Prerogatived** privileged (to have
honest wives).   **the base** ordinary citizens. (Socially prominent men are especially prone to the unavoidable destiny of being cuckolded and to the public
shame that goes with it.)   **292 forkèd** (An allusion to the horns of the cuckold.)
**293 quicken** receive life. (Quicken may also mean to swarm with maggots as the
body festers, as in 4.2.69, in which case lines 292–293 suggest that *even then*, in
death, we are cuckolded by *forkèd* worms.)   **296 generous** noble.   **297 attend**
await.   **301 watching** too little sleep.   **303 napkin** handkerchief.   **304 Let it
alone** i.e., never mind.

[*He puts the handkerchief from him, and it drops.*]

DESDEMONA.  I am very sorry that you are not well.                  305

*Exit* [*with* OTHELLO].

EMILIA  [*picking up the handkerchief*].  I am glad I have found this napkin.
    This was her first remembrance from the Moor.
    My wayward° husband hath a hundred times
    Wooed me to steal it but she so loves the token—
    For he conjured her she should ever keep it—            310
    That she reserves it evermore about her
    To kiss and talk to. I'll have the work ta'en out,°
    And give 't Iago. What he will do with it
    Heaven knows, not I;
    I nothing but to please his fantasy.°                   315

*Enter* IAGO.

IAGO.  How now? What do you do here alone?
EMILIA.  Do not you chide. I have a thing for you.
IAGO.  You have a thing for me? It is a common thing°—
EMILIA.  Ha!
IAGO.  To have a foolish wife.                                     320
EMILIA.  O, is that all? What will you give me now
    For that same handkerchief?
IAGO.  What handkerchief?
EMILIA.  What handkerchief?
    Why, that the Moor first gave to Desdemona;           325
    That which so often you did bid me steal.
IAGO.  Hast stolen it from her?
EMILIA.  No, faith. She let it drop by negligence,
    And to th' advantage° I, being here, took 't up.
    Look, here 'tis.
IAGO.                     A good wench! Give it me.                 330
EMILIA.  What will you do with 't, that you have been so earnest
    To have me filch it?
IAGO [*snatching it*].  Why, what is that to you?
EMILIA.  If it be not for some purpose of import,
    Give 't me again. Poor lady, she'll run mad
    When she shall lack° it.

---

**308 wayward** capricious.   **312 work ta'en out** design of the embroidery
copied.   **315 fantasy** whim.   **318 common thing** (With bawdy suggestion;
*common* suggests coarseness and availability to all comers, and *thing* is a slang
term for the pudendum.)   **329 to th' advantage** taking the opportunity.
**335 lack** miss.

IAGO.                           Be not acknown on 't.°                    335
    I have use for it. Go, leave me.                    *Exit* EMILIA.
    I will in Cassio's lodging lose° this napkin
    And let him find it. Trifles light as air.
    Are to the jealous confirmations strong
    As proofs of Holy Writ. This may do something.             340
    The Moor already changes with my poison.
    Dangerous conceits° are in their natures poisons,
    Which at the first are scarce found to distaste,°
    But with a little act° upon the blood
    Burn like the mines of sulfur.

    *Enter* OTHELLO.

                         I did say so.                    345
    Look where he comes! Not poppy nor mandragora°
    Nor all the drowsy syrups of the world
    Shall ever medicine thee to that sweet sleep
    Which thou owedst° yesterday.
OTHELLO.                       Ha, ha, false to me?
IAGO.  Why, how now, General? No more of that.                    350
OTHELLO.  Avaunt! Begone! Thou hast set me on the rack.
    I swear 'tis better to be much abused
    Than but to know 't a little.
IAGO.                          How now, my lord?
OTHELLO.  What sense had I of her stolen hours of lust?
    I saw 't not, thought it not, it harmed not me.             355
    I slept the next night well, fed well, was free° and merry;
    I found not Cassio's kisses on her lips.
    He that is robbed, not wanting° what is stolen,
    Let him not know 't and he's not robbed at all.
IAGO.  I am sorry to hear this.                    360
OTHELLO.  I had been happy if the general camp,
    Pioners° and all, had tasted her sweet body,
    So° I had nothing known. O, now, forever
    Farewell the tranquil mind! Farewell content!
    Farewell the plumèd troops and the big° wars                    365
    That makes ambition virtue! O, farewell!

---

**335 Be . . . on't** do not confess knowledge of it.    **337 lose** (The Folio spelling, *loose*, is a normal spelling for "lose," but it may also contain the idea of "let go," "release.")    **342 conceits** fancies, ideas.    **343 distaste** be distasteful.    **344 act** action, working.    **346 mandragora** an opiate made of the mandrake root. **349 thou owedst** you did own.    **356 free** carefree.    **358 wanting** missing. **362 Pioners** diggers of mines, the lowest grade of soldiers.    **363 So** provided. **365 big** stately.

Farewell the neighing steed and the shrill trump,
The spirit-stirring drum, th' ear-piercing fife,
The royal banner, and all quality,°
Pride,° pomp, and circumstance° of glorious war!　　370
And O, you mortal engines,° whose rude throats
Th' immortal Jove's dread clamors° counterfeit,
Farewell! Othello's occupation's gone.

IAGO. Is 't possible, my lord?

OTHELLO. Villain, be sure thou prove my love a whore!　　375
Be sure of it. Give me the ocular proof,
Or, by the worth of mine eternal soul,
Thou hadst been better have been born a dog
Than answer my waked wrath!

IAGO.　　　　　　　　　　Is 't come to this?

OTHELLO. Make me to see 't, or at the least so prove it　　380
That the probation° bear no hinge nor loop
To hang a doubt on, or woe upon thy life!

IAGO. My noble lord—

OTHELLO. If thou dost slander her and torture me,
Never pray more; abandon all remorse;°　　385
On horror's head horrors accumulate;°
Do deeds to make heaven weep, all earth amazed;°
For nothing canst thou to damnation add
Greater than that.

IAGO.　　　　　　O grace! O heaven forgive me!
Are you a man? Have you a soul or sense?　　390
God b' wi' you; take mine office. O wretched fool,°
That lov'st to make thine honesty a vice!°
O monstrous world! Take note, take note, O world,
To be direct and honest is not safe.
I thank you for this profit,° and from hence°　　395
I'll love no friend, sith° love breeds such offense.°

OTHELLO. Nay, stay. Thou shouldst be° honest.

---

**369 quality** character, essential nature.　**370 Pride** rich display.　**circumstance** pageantry.　**371 mortal engines** i.e., cannon (*Mortal* means "deadly.")
**372 Jove's dread clamors** i.e., thunder.　**381 probation** proof.　**385 remorse**
pity, penitent hope for salvation.　**386 horrors accumulate** add still more
horrors.　**387 amazed** confounded with horror.　**391 O wretched fool** (Iago
addresses himself as a fool for having carried honesty too far.)　**392 vice** failing,
something overdone.　**395 profit** profitable instruction.　**hence** henceforth.
**396 sith** since.　**offense** i.e., harm to the one who offers help and friendship.
**397 Thou shouldst be** it appears that you are. (But Iago replies in the sense of
"ought to be.")

IAGO.  I should be wise, for honesty's a fool
    And loses that° it works for.
OTHELLO.                              By the world,
    I think my wife be honest and think she is not;        400
    I think that thou art just and think thou art not.
    I'll have some proof. My name, that was as fresh
    As Dian's° visage, is now begrimed and black
    As mine own face. If there be cords, or knives,
    Poison, or fire, or suffocating streams,         405
    I'll not endure it. Would I were satisfied!
IAGO.  I see, sir, you are eaten up with passion.
    I do repent me that I put it to you.
    You would be satisfied?
OTHELLO.                          Would? Nay, and I will.
IAGO.  And may; but how? How satisfied, my lord?      410
    Would you, the supervisor,° grossly gape on?
    Behold her topped?
OTHELLO.                        Death and damnation! O!
IAGO.  It were a tedious difficulty, I think,
    To bring them to that prospect. Damn them then,°
    If ever mortal eyes do see them bolster°        415
    More° than their own.° What then? How then?
    What shall I say? Where's satisfaction?
    It is impossible you should see this,
    Were they as prime° as goats, as hot as monkeys,
    As salt° as wolves in pride,° and fools as gross    420
    As ignorance made drunk. But yet I say,
    If imputation and strong circumstances°
    Which lead directly to the door of truth
    Will give you satisfaction, you might have 't.
OTHELLO.  Give me a living reason she's disloyal.      425
IAGO.  I do not like the office.
    But sith° I am entered in this cause so far,
    Pricked° to 't by foolish honesty and love,
    I will go on. I lay with Cassio lately,
    And being troubled with a raging tooth        430
    I could not sleep. There are a kind of men
    So loose of soul that in their sleeps will mutter

---

**399 that** what.    **403 Dian** Diana, goddess of the moon and of chastity.
**411 supervisor** onlooker.    **414 Damn them then** i.e., they would have
to be really incorrigible.    **415 bolster** go to bed together, share a bolster.
**416 More** other.    **own** own eyes.    **419 prime** lustful.    **420 salt** wanton,
sensual.    **pride** heat.    **422 imputation . . . circumstances** strong
circumstantial evidence.    **427 sith** since.    **428 Pricked** spurred.

Their affairs. One of this kind is Cassio.
In sleep I heard him say, "Sweet Desdemona,
Let us be wary, let us hide our loves!"     435
And then, sir, would he grip and wring my hand,
Cry "O sweet creature!," then kiss me hard,
As if he plucked up kisses by the roots
That grew upon my lips; then laid his leg
Over my thigh, and sighed, and kissed, and then     440
Cried, "Cursèd fate that gave thee to the Moor!"

OTHELLO.   O monstrous! Monstrous!

IAGO.                   Nay, this was but his dream.

OTHELLO.   But this denoted a foregone conclusion.°
'Tis a shrewd doubt,° though it be but a dream.

IAGO.   And this may help to thicken other proofs     445
That do demonstrate thinly.

OTHELLO.               I'll tear her all to pieces.

IAGO.   Nay, but be wise. Yet we see nothing done;
She may be honest yet. Tell me but this:
Have you not sometimes seen a handkerchief
Spotted with strawberries° in your wife's hand?     450

OTHELLO.   I gave her such a one. 'Twas my first gift.

IAGO.   I know not that; but such a handkerchief—
I am sure it was your wife's—did I today
See Cassio wipe his beard with.

OTHELLO.            If it be that—

IAGO.   If it be that, or any that was hers,     455
It speaks against her with the other proofs.

OTHELLO.   O, that the slave° had forty thousand lives!
One is too poor, too weak for my revenge.
Now do I see 'tis true. Look here, Iago,
All my fond° love thus do I blow to heaven.     460
'Tis gone.
Arise, black vengeance, from the hollow hell!
Yield up, O love, thy crown and hearted° throne
To tyrannous hate! Swell, bosom, with thy freight,°
For 'tis of aspics'° tongues!     465

IAGO.   Yet be content.°

OTHELLO.   O, blood, blood, blood!

IAGO.   Patience, I say. Your mind perhaps may change.

---

**443 foregone conclusion** concluded experience or action.   **444 shrewd
doubt** suspicious circumstance.   **450 Spotted with strawberries** embroidered
with a strawberry pattern.   **457 the slave** i.e., Cassio.   **460 fond** foolish (but
also suggesting "affectionate").   **463 hearted** fixed in the heart.   **464 freight**
burden.   **465 aspics'** venomous serpents'.   **466 content** calm.

OTHELLO.  Never, Iago. Like to the Pontic Sea,°
    Whose icy current and compulsive course      470
    Ne'er feels retiring ebb, but keeps due on
    To the Propontic° and the Hellespont,°
    Even so my bloody thoughts with violent pace
    Shall ne'er look back, ne'er ebb to humble love,
    I that a capable° and wide revenge      475
    Swallow them up. Now, by yond marble° heaven,
    [*Kneeling*] In the due reverence of a sacred vow
    I here engage my words.
IAGO.                Do not rise yet.
    [*He kneels.*]° Witness, you ever-burning lights above,
    You elements that clip° us round about,      480
    Witness that here Iago doth give up
    The execution° of his wit,° hands, heart,
    To wronged Othello's service. Let him command,
    And to obey shall be in me remorse,°
    What bloody business ever.°      [*They rise.*]
OTHELLO.            I greet thy love,      485
    Not with vain thanks, but with acceptance bounteous,
    And will upon the instant put thee to 't.°
    Within these three days let me hear thee say
    That Cassio's not alive.
IAGO.             My friend is dead;
    'Tis done at your request. But let her live.      490
OTHELLO.  Damn her, lewd minx!° O, damn her, damn her!
    Come, go with me apart. I will withdraw
    To furnish me with some swift means of death
    For the fair devil. Now art thou my lieutenant.
IAGO.  I am your own forever.      *Exeunt.*  495

**3.4** *Enter* DESDEMONA, EMILIA *and*

DESDEMONA.  Do you know, sirrah,° where Lieutenant Cassio lies?°
CLOWN.  I dare not say he lies anywhere.

---

**469 Pontic Sea** Black Sea.    **472 Propontic** Sea of Marmara, between the Black
Sea and the Aegean.  **Hellespont** Dardanelles, straits where the Sea of Marmara
joins with the Aegean.  **475 capable** ample, comprehensive.  **476 marble**
i.e., gleaming like marble and unrelenting.  **479 s.d. He kneels** (In the Quarto
text, Iago kneels here after Othello has knelt at line 477.)  **480 clip** encompass.
**482 execution** exercise, action.  **wit** mind.  **484 remorse** pity (for Othello's
wrongs).  **485 ever** soever.  **487 to 't** to the proof.  **491 minx** wanton.
**3.4 Location: Before the citadel.**    **1 sirrah** (A form of address to an inferior.)
**lies** lodges. (But the Clown makes the obvious pun.)

DESDEMONA.  Why, man?

CLOWN.  He's a soldier, and for me to say a soldier lies, 'tis stabbing.

DESDEMONA.  Go to.Where lodges he?                                    5

CLOWN.  To tell you where he lodges is to tell you where I lie.

DESDEMONA.  Can anything be made of this?

CLOWN.  I know not where he lodges, and for me to devise a lodging and
    say he lies here, or he lies there, were to lie in mine own throat.°

DESDEMONA.  Can you inquire him out, and be edified by report?        10

CLOWN.  I will catechize the world for him; that is, make questions, and
    by them answer.

DESDEMONA.  Seek him, bid him come hither.Tell him I have moved° my
    lord on his behalf and hope all will be well.

CLOWN.  To do this is within the compass of man's wit, and therefore I   15
    will attempt the doing it.                          *Exit* CLOWN.

DESDEMONA.  Where should I lose that handkerchief, Emilia?

EMILIA.  I know not, madam.

DESDEMONA.  Believe me, I had rather have lost my purse
    Full of crusadoes,° and but my noble Moor                  20
    Is true of mind and made of no such baseness
    As jealous creatures are, it were enough
    To put him to ill thinking.

EMILIA.                              Is he not jealous?

DESDEMONA.  Who, he? I think the sun where he was born
    Drew all such humors° from him.

EMILIA.                              Look where he comes.           25

    *Enter* OTHELLO.

DESDEMONA.  I will not leave him now till Cassio
    Be called to him.—How is 't with you, my lord?

OTHELLO.  Well, my good lady. [*Aside.*] O, hardness to dissemble!—
    How do you, Desdemona?

DESDEMONA.                          Well, my good lord.

OTHELLO.  Give me your hand. [*She gives her hand.*] This hand is
    moist, my lady.                                             30

DESDEMONA.  It yet hath felt no age nor known no sorrow.

OTHELLO.  This argues° fruitfulness° and liberal° heart.
    Hot, hot, and moist.This hand of yours requires
    A sequester° from liberty, fasting and prayer,

---

**9 lie . . . throat** (1) lie egregiously and deliberately (2) use the windpipe to
speak a lie.   **13 moved** petitioned.   **20 crusadoes** Portuguese gold coins.
**25 humors** (Refers to the four bodily fluids thought to determine temperament.)
**32 argues** gives evidence of.   **fruitfulness** generosity, amorousness, and
fecundity.   **liberal** generous and sexually free.   **34 sequester** separation,
sequestration.

Much castigation,° exercise devout;°                                        35
For here's a young and sweating devil here
That commonly rebels. 'Tis a good hand,
A frank° one.

DESDEMONA.      You may indeed say so,
For 'twas that hand that gave away my heart.

OTHELLO.  A liberal hand. The hearts of old gave hands,°              40
But our new heraldry is hands, not hearts.°

DESDEMONA.  I cannot speak of this. Come now, your promise.

OTHELLO.  What promise, chuck?°

DESDEMONA.  I have sent to bid Cassio come speak with you.

OTHELLO.  I have a salt and sorry rheum° offends me;                 45
Lend me thy handkerchief.

DESDEMONA.  Here, my lord.              [*She offers a handkerchief.*]

OTHELLO.  That which I gave you.

DESDEMONA.                        I have it not about me.

OTHELLO.  Not?

DESDEMONA.  No, faith, my lord.                                        50

OTHELLO.  That's a fault. That handkerchief
Did an Egyptian to my mother give.
She was a charmer,° and could almost read
The thoughts of people. She told her, while she kept it
'Twould make her amiable° and subdue my father            55
Entirely to her love, but if she lost it
Or made a gift of it, my father's eye
Should hold her loathèd and his spirits should hunt
After new fancies.° She, dying, gave it me,
And bid me, when my fate would have me wived,              60
To give it her.° I did so; and take heed on 't;
Make it a darling like your precious eye.
To lose 't or give 't away were such perdition°
As nothing else could match.

DESDEMONA.                        Is 't possible?

OTHELLO.  'Tis true. There's magic in the web° of it.                 65
A sibyl, that had numbered in the world

---

**35 castigation** corrective discipline.   **exercise devout** i.e., prayer, religious
meditation, etc.   **38 frank** generous, open (with sexual suggestion).   **40 The
hearts . . . hands** i.e., in former times, people would give their hearts when they
gave their hands to something.   **41 But . . . hearts** i.e., in our decadent times,
the joining of hands is no longer a badge to signify the giving of hearts.
**43 chuck** (A term of endearment.)   **45 salt . . . rheum** distressful head cold
or watering of the eyes.   **53 charmer** sorceress.   **55 amiable** desirable.
**59 fancies** loves.   **61 her** i.e., to my wife.   **63 perdition** loss.   **65 web** fabric,
weaving.

The sun to course two hundred compasses,°
In her prophetic fury° sewed the work;°
The worms were hallowed that did breed the silk,
And it was dyed in mummy° which the skillful                    70
Conserved of° maidens' hearts.

DESDEMONA.                              I' faith! Is 't true?
OTHELLO.  Most veritable. Therefore look to 't well.
DESDEMONA.  Then would to God that I had never seen 't!
OTHELLO.  Ha? Wherefore?
DESDEMONA.  Why do you speak so startingly and rash?°              75
OTHELLO.  Is 't lost? Is 't gone? Speak, is 't out o' the way?°
DESDEMONA.  Heaven bless us!
OTHELLO.  Say you?
DESDEMONA.  It is not lost; but what an if° it were?
OTHELLO.  How?                                                    80
DESDEMONA.  I say it is not lost.
OTHELLO.                            Fetch 't, let me see 't.
DESDEMONA.  Why, so I can, sir, but I will not now.
    This is a trick to put me from my suit.
    Pray you, let Cassio be received again.
OTHELLO.  Fetch me the handkerchief! My mind misgives.            85
DESDEMONA.  Come, come,
    You'll never meet a more sufficient° man.
OTHELLO.  The handkerchief!
DESDEMONA.                          I pray, talk° me of Cassio.
OTHELLO.  The handkerchief?
DESDEMONA.                          A man that all his time°
    Hath founded his good fortunes on your love,                  90
    Shared dangers with you—
OTHELLO.  The handkerchief!
DESDEMONA.  I' faith, you are to blame.
OTHELLO.  Zounds!                                    Exit OTHELLO.
EMILIA.  Is not this man jealous?                                 95
DESDEMONA.  I ne'er saw this before.
    Sure, there's some wonder in this handkerchief.
    I am most unhappy in the loss of it.

---

**67 compasses** annual circlings. (The *sibyl*, or prophetess, was two hundred years
old.)    **68 prophetic fury** frenzy of prophetic inspiration.    **work** embroidered
pattern.    **70 mummy** medicinal or magical preparation drained from mummified
bodies.    **71 Conserved of** prepared or preserved out of.    **75 startingly and
rash** disjointedly and impetuously, excitedly.    **76 out o' the way** lost, misplaced.
**79 an if** if.    **87 sufficient** able, complete.    **88 talk** talk to.    **89 all his time**
throughout his career.

EMILIA.  'Tis not a year or two shows us a man.°
      They are all but stomachs, and we all but° food;       100
      They eat us hungerly,° and when they are full
      They belch us.

      *Enter* IAGO *and* CASSIO.

                    Look you, Cassio and my husband.
IAGO [*to* CASSIO].  There is no other way; 'tis she must do 't.
      And, lo, the happiness!° Go and importune her.
DESDEMONA.  How now, good Cassio? What's the news with you?       105
CASSIO.  Madam, my former suit. I do beseech you
      That by your virtuous° means I may again
      Exist and be a member of his love
      Whom I, with all the office° of my heart,
      Entirely honor. I would not be delayed.       110
      If my offense be of such mortal° kind
      That nor my service past, nor° present sorrows,
      Nor purposed merit in futurity
      Can ransom me into his love again,
      But to know so must be my benefit;°       115
      So shall I clothe me in a forced content,
      And shut myself up in° some other course,
      To fortune's alms.°
DESDEMONA.                    Alas, thrice-gentle Cassio,
      My advocation° is not now in tune.
      My lord is not my lord; nor should I know him,       120
      Were he in favor° as in humor° altered.
      So help me every spirit sanctified
      As I have spoken for you all my best
      And stood within the blank° of his displeasure
      For my free speech! You must awhile be patient.       125
      What I can do I will, and more I will
      Than for myself I dare. Let that suffice you.
IAGO.  Is my lord angry?

---

99 **'Tis . . . man** i.e., you can't really know a man even in a year or two of
experience (?), or, real men come along seldom (?).    100 **but** nothing but.
101 **hungerly** hungrily.    104 **the happiness** in happy time, fortunately met.
107 **virtuous** efficacious.    109 **office** loyal service.    111 **mortal** fatal.
112 **nor . . . nor** neither . . . nor.    115 **But . . . benefit** merely to know that my
case is hopeless will have to content me (and will be better than uncertainty).
117 **shut . . . in** confine myself to.    118 **To fortune's alms** throwing myself
on the mercy of fortune.    119 **advocation** advocacy.    121 **favor** appearance.
**humor** mood.    124 **within the blank** within point-blank range. (The *blank* is
the center of the target.)

EMILIA.                    He went hence but now,
And certainly in strange unquietness.
IAGO.   Can he be angry? I have seen the cannon                    130
When it hath blown his ranks into the air,
And like the devil from his very arm
Puffed his own brother—and is he angry?
Something of moment° then. I will go meet him.
There's matter in 't indeed, if he be angry.                    135
DESDEMONA.   I prithee, do so.                    *Exit* [IAGO].
                    Something, sure, of state,°
Either from Venice, or some unhatched practice°
Made demonstrable here in Cyprus to him,
Hath puddled° his clear spirit; and in such cases
Men's natures wrangle with inferior things,                    140
Though great ones are their object. 'Tis even so;
For let our finger ache, and it indues°
Our other, healthful members even to a sense
Of pain. Nay, we must think men are not gods,
Nor of them look for such observancy°                    145
As fits the bridal.° Beshrew me° much, Emilia,
I was, unhandsome° warrior as I am,
Arraigning his unkindness with° my soul;
But now I find I had suborned the witness,°
And he's indicted falsely.
EMILIA.                    Pray heaven it be                    150
State matters, as you think, and no conception
Nor no jealous toy° concerning you.
DESDEMONA.   Alas the day! I never gave him cause.
EMILIA.   But jealous souls will not be answered so;
They are not ever jealous for the cause,                    155
But jealous for° they're jealous. It is a monster
Begot upon itself,° born on itself.
DESDEMONA.   Heaven keep that monster from Othello's mind!
EMILIA.   Lady, amen.
DESDEMONA.   I will go seek him. Cassio, walk hereabout.                    160
If I do find him fit, I'll move your suit
And seek to effect it to my uttermost.

---

134 **of moment** of immediate importance, momentous.    136 **of state** concerning state affairs.    137 **unhatched practice** as yet unexecuted or undiscovered
plot.    139 **puddled** muddied.    142 **indues** brings to the same condition.
145 **observancy** attentiveness.    146 **bridal** wedding (when a bridegroom is
newly attentive to his bride).    **Beshrew me** (A mild oath.)    147 **unhandsome**
insufficient, unskillful.    148 **with** before the bar of.    149 **suborned the
witness** induced the witness to give false testimony.    152 **toy** fancy.    156 **for**
because.    157 **Begot upon itself** generated solely from itself.

CASSIO.  I humbly thank your ladyship.

*Exit* [DESDEMONA *with* EMILIA].

*Enter* BIANCA.

BIANCA.  Save° you, friend Cassio!

CASSIO.                           What make° you from home?

How is 't with you, my most fair Bianca?                        165

I' faith, sweet love, I was coming to your house.

BIANCA.  And I was going to your lodging, Cassio.

What, keep a week away? Seven days and nights?

Eightscore-eight° hours? And lovers' absent hours

More tedious than the dial° eightscore times?                   170

O weary reckoning!

CASSIO.                    Pardon me, Bianca.

I have this while with leaden thoughts been pressed;

But I shall, in a more continuate° time,

Strike off this score° of absence. Sweet Bianca,

[*giving her* DESDEMONA*'s handkerchief*]

Take me this work out.°

BIANCA.                       O Cassio, whence came this?         175

This is some token from a newer friend.°

To the felt absence now I feel a cause.

Is 't come to this? Well, well.

CASSIO.                         Go to, woman!

Throw your vile guesses in the devil's teeth,

From whence you have them. You are jealous now   180

That this is from some mistress, some remembrance,

No, by my faith, Bianca.

BIANCA.                      Why, whose is it?

CASSIO.  I know not, neither. I found it in my chamber.

I like the work well. Ere it be demanded°—

As like° enough it will—I would have it copied.               185

Take it and do 't, and leave me for this time.

BIANCA.  Leave you? Wherefore?

CASSIO.  I do attend here on the General,

And think it no addition,° nor my wish,

To have him see me womaned.                                     190

BIANCA.  Why, I pray you?

---

164 **Save** God save.  **make** do.  169 **Eightscore-eight** one hundred sixty-eight, the number of hours in a week.  170 **the dial** a complete revolution of the clock.  173 **continuate** uninterrupted.  174 **Strike . . . score** settle this account.  175 **Take . . . out** copy this embroidery for me.  176 **friend** mistress.  184 **demanded** inquired for.  185 **like** likely.  189 **addition** i.e., addition to my reputation.

CASSIO. Not that I love you not.

BIANCA. But that you do not love me.
    I pray you, bring° me on the way a little,
    And say if I shall see you soon at night.       195

CASSIO. 'Tis but a little way that I can bring you,
    For I attend here; but I'll see you soon.

BIANCA. 'Tis very good. I must be circumstanced.°

    *Exeunt* omnes.

## 4.1 *Enter OTHELLO and IAGO*

IAGO. Will you think so?

OTHELLO.            Think so, Iago?

IAGO.               What,
    To kiss in private?

OTHELLO.           An unauthorized kiss!

IAGO. Or to be naked with her friend in bed
    An hour or more, not meaning any harm?

OTHELLO. Naked in bed, Iago, and not mean harm?      5
    It is hypocrisy against the devil.
    They that mean virtuously and yet do so,
    The devil their virtue tempts, and they tempt heaven.

IAGO. If they do nothing, 'tis a venial° slip.
    But if I give my wife a handkerchief—        10

OTHELLO. What then?

IAGO. Why then, 'tis hers, my lord, and being hers,
    She may, I think, bestow 't on any man.

OTHELLO. She is protectress of her honor too
    May she give that?.                15

IAGO. Her honor is an essence that's not seen;
    They have it° very oft that have it not.
    But, for the handkerchief—

OTHELLO. By heaven, I would most gladly have forgot it.
    Thou saidst—O, it comes o'er my memory      20
    As doth the raven o'er the infectious house,°
    Boding to all—he had my handkerchief.

IAGO. Ay, what of that?

---

**194 bring** accompany.   **198 be circumstanced** be governed by circumstance, yield to your conditions.   **4.1 Location: Before the citadel**.   **9 venial** pardonable.   **17 They have it** i.e., they enjoy a reputation for it.   **21 raven . . . house** (Allusion to the belief that the raven hovered over a house of sickness or infection, such as one visited by the plague.)

OTHELLO.                    That's not so good now.
IAGO.                                              What
  If I had said I had seen him do you wrong?
  Or heard him say—as knaves be such abroad,°                     25
  Who having, by their own importunate suit,
  Or voluntary dotage° of some mistress,
  Convincèd or supplied° them, cannot choose
  But they must blab—
OTHELLO.                          Hath he said anything?
IAGO.  He hath, my lord; but, be you well assured,               30
  No more than he'll unswear.
OTHELLO.                          What hath he said?
IAGO.  Faith, that he did—I know not what he did.
OTHELLO.  What? What?
IAGO.  Lie—
OTHELLO.   With her?
IAGO.                  With her, on her; what you will.
OTHELLO.  Lie with her? Lie on her? We say "lie on her" when they be   35
  lie° her. Lie with her? Zounds, that's fulsome.°—Handkerchief—
  confessions—handkerchief!—To confess and be hanged for his
  labor—first to be hanged and then to confess.°—I tremble at it.
  Nature would not invest herself in such shadowing passion with-
  out some instruction.° It is not words° that shakes me thus. Pish!   40
  Noses, ears, and lips.—Is 't possible?—Confess—handkerchief!—
  O devil!

  *Falls in a trance.*

IAGO.  Work on,
  My medicine, work! Thus credulous fools are caught,
  And many worthy and chaste dames even thus,                    45
  All guiltless, meet reproach.—What, ho! My lord!
  My lord, I say! Othello!

  *Enter* CASSIO.

                          How now, Cassio?
CASSIO.  What's the matter?

---

25 **abroad** around about.    27 **voluntary dotage** willing infatuation.
28 **Convincèd or supplied** seduced or sexually gratified.    35 **belie** slander.
36 **fulsome** foul.    38 **first . . . to confess** (Othello reverses the proverbial
*confess and be hanged;* Cassio is to be given no time to confess before he dies.)
39 **Nature . . . instruction** i.e., without some foundation in fact, nature would
not have dressed herself in such an overwhelming passion that comes over me
now and fills my mind with images, or in such a lifelike fantasy as Cassio had in
his dream of lying with Desdemona.    40 **words** mere words.

IAGO.  My lord is fall'n into an epilepsy.
    This is his second fit. He had one yesterday.    50
CASSIO.  Rub him about the temples.
IAGO.                           No, forbear.
    The lethargy° must have his° quiet course.
    If not, he foams at mouth, and by and by
    Breaks out to savage madness. Look, he stirs.
    Do you withdraw yourself a little while.    55
    He will recover straight. When he is gone,
    I would on great occasion° speak with you.

    [*Exit* CASSIO.]

    How is it, General? Have you not hurt your head?
OTHELLO.  Dost thou mock me?°
IAGO.                 I mock you not, by heaven.
    Would you would bear your fortune like a man!    60
OTHELLO.  A hornèd man's a monster and a beast.
IAGO.  There's many a beast then in a populous city,
    And many a civil° monster.
OTHELLO.  Did he confess it?
IAGO.  Good sir, be a man.    65
    Think every bearded fellow that's but yoked°
    May draw with you.° There's millions now alive
    That nightly lie in those unproper° beds
    Which they dare swear peculiar.° Your case is better.°
    O, 'tis the spite of hell, the fiend's arch-mock,    70
    To lip° a wanton in a secure° couch
    And to suppose her chaste! No, let me know,
    And knowing what I am,° I know what she shall be.°
OTHELLO.  O, thou art wise. 'Tis certain.
IAGO.  Stand you awhile apart;    75
    Confine yourself but in a patient list.°
    Whilst you were here o'erwhelmèd with your grief—
    A passion most unsuiting such a man—

---

**52 lethargy** coma.  **his** its.   **57 on great occasion** on a matter of great
importance.   **59 mock me** (Othello takes Iago's question about hurting his head
to be a mocking reference to the cuckold's horns.)   **63 civil** i.e., dwelling in
a city.   **66 yoked** (1) married (2) put into the yoke of infamy and cuckoldry.
**67 draw with you** pull as you do, like oxen who are yoked, i.e., share your fate
as cuckold.   **68 unproper** not exclusively their own.   **69 peculiar** private,
their own.   **better** i.e., because you know the truth.   **71 lip** kiss.  **secure** free
from suspicion.   **73 what I am** i.e., a cuckold.  **she shall be** will happen to
her.   **76 in . . . list** within the bounds of patience.

Cassio came hither. I shifted him away,°
And laid good 'scuse upon your ecstasy,°                           80
Bade him anon return and here speak with me,
The which he promised. Do but encave° yourself
And mark the fleers,° the gibes, and notable° scorns
That dwell in every region of his face;
For I will make him tell the tale anew,                           85
Where, how, how oft, how long ago, and when
He hath and is again to cope° your wife.
I say, but mark his gesture. Marry, patience!
Or I shall say you're all-in-all in spleen,°
And nothing of a man.

OTHELLO.                    Dost thou hear, Iago?              90
I will be found most cunning in my patience;
But—dost thou hear?—most bloody.

IAGO.                              That's not amiss;
But yet keep time° in all. Will you withdraw?

[OTHELLO *stands apart*.]

Now will I question Cassio of Bianca,
A huswife° that by selling her desires                            95
Buys herself bread and clothes. It is a creature
That dotes on Cassio—as 'tis the strumpet's plague
To beguile many and be beguiled by one.
He, when he hears of her, cannot restrain°
From the excess of laughter. Here he comes.                      100

*Enter* CASSIO.

As he shall smile, Othello shall go mad;
And his unbookish° jealousy must conster°
Poor Cassio's smiles, gestures, and light behaviors
Quite in the wrong.—How do you now, Lieutenant?

CASSIO.  The worser that you give me the addition°               105
Whose want° even kills me.

IAGO.  Ply Desdemona well and you are sure on 't.
[*Speaking lower*.] Now, if this suit lay in Bianca's power,
How quickly should you speed!

CASSIO [*laughing*].  Alas, poor caitiff!°                       110

---

**79 shifted him away** used a dodge to get rid of him.    **80 ecstasy** trance.
**82 encave** conceal.    **83 fleers** sneers.    **notable** obvious.    **87 cope** encounter
with, have sex with.    **89 all-in-all in spleen** utterly governed by passionate
impulses.    **93 keep time** keep yourself steady (as in music).    **95 huswife**
hussy.    **99 restrain** refrain.    **102 unbookish** uninstructed.    **conster** construe.
**105 addition** title.    **106 Whose want** the lack of which.    **110 caitiff** wretch.

OTHELLO [*aside*]. Look how he laughs already!

IAGO. I never knew a woman love man so.

CASSIO. Alas, poor rogue! I think, i' faith, she loves me.

OTHELLO. Now he denies it faintly, and laughs it out.

IAGO. Do you hear, Cassio?

OTHELLO.               Now he importunes him     115
    To tell it o'er. Go to!° Well said,° well said.

IAGO. She gives it out that you shall marry her.
    Do you intend it?

CASSIO. Ha, ha, ha!

OTHELLO. Do you triumph, Roman?° Do you triumph?     120

CASSIO. I marry her? What? A customer?° Prithee, bear some charity to
    my wit;° do not think it so unwholesome. Ha, ha, ha!

OTHELLO. So, so, so, so! They laugh that win.°

IAGO. Faith, the cry° goes that you shall marry her.

CASSIO. Prithee, say true.     125

IAGO. I am a very villain else.°

OTHELLO. Have you scored me?° Well.

CASSIO. This is the monkey's own giving out. She is persuaded I will
    marry her out of her own love and flattery,° not out of my
    promise.     130

OTHELLO. Iago beckons me.° Now he begins the story.

CASSIO. She was here even now; she haunts me in every place. I was
    the other day talking on the seabank° with certain Venetians, and
    thither comes the bauble,° and, by this hand,° she falls me thus
    about my neck—     135

[*He embraces* IAGO.]

OTHELLO. Crying, "O dear Cassio!" as it were; his gesture imports it.

CASSIO. So hangs and lolls and weep upon me, so shakes and pulls me.
    Ha, ha, ha!

OTHELLO. Now he tells how she plucked him to my chamber. O, I see
    that nose of yours, but not that dog I shall throw it to.°     140

CASSIO. Well, I must leave her company.

---

116 **Go to** (An expression of remonstrance.)    **Well said** well done.
120 **Roman** (The Romans were noted for their *triumphs* or triumphal
processions.)    121 **customer** i.e., prostitute.    121–122 **bear . . . wit** be more
charitable to my judgment.    123 **They . . . win** i.e., they that laugh last laugh
best.    124 **cry** rumor.    126 **I . . . else** call me a complete rogue if I'm not telling
the truth.    127 **scored me** scored off me, beaten me, made up my reckoning,
branded me.    129 **flattery** self-flattery, self-deception.    131 **beckons** signals.
133 **seabank** seashore.    134 **bauble** plaything.    **by this hand** I make my vow.

IAGO.  Before me,° look where she comes.

*Enter* BIANCA [*with* OTHELLO'*s handkerchief*].

CASSIO.  'Tis such another fitchew!° Marry, a perfumed one.—What do
  you mean by this haunting of me?
BIANCA.  Let the devil and his dam° haunt you! What did you mean by   145
  that same handkerchief you gave me even now? I was a fine fool
  to take it. I must take out the work? A likely piece of work,° that
  you should find it in your chamber and know not who left it
  there! This is some minx's token, and I must take out the work?
  There; give it your hobbyhorse.° [*She gives him the hand-*   150
  *kerchief.*] Wheresoever you had it, I'll take out no work on 't.
CASSIO.  How now, my sweet Bianca? How now? How now?
OTHELLO.  By heaven, that should be° my handkerchief!
BIANCA.  If you'll come to supper tonight, you may; if you will not, come
  when you are next prepared for.°                                   155

  *Exit.*

IAGO.  After her, after her.
CASSIO.  Faith, I must. She'll rail in the streets else.
IAGO.  Will you sup there?
CASSIO.  Faith, I intend so.
IAGO.  Well, I may chance to see you, for I would very fain speak with
  you                                                               160
CASSIO.  Prithee, come. Will you?
  IAGO.  Go to.° Say no more.                               [*Exit* CASSIO.]
OTHELLO [*advancing*].  How shall I murder him, Iago?
IAGO.  Did you perceive how he laughed at his vice?
OTHELLO.  O, Iago!                                                  165
IAGO.  And did you see the handkerchief?
OTHELLO.  Was that mine?
IAGO.  Yours, by this hand. And to see how he prizes the foolish
  woman your wife! She gave it him, and he hath given it his whore.
OTHELLO.  I would have him nine years a-killing. A fine woman!   170
  A fair woman! A sweet woman!

---

**140 not . . . to** (Othello imagines himself cutting off Cassio's nose and throwing
it to a dog.)    **142 Before me** i.e., on my soul.    **143 'Tis . . . fitchew** what a
polecat she is! Just like all the others. (Polecats were often compared with
prostitutes because of their rank smell and presumed lechery.)    **145 dam**
mother.    **147 A likely . . . work** a fine story.    **150 hobbyhorse** harlot.
**153 should be** must be.    **155 when . . . for** when I'm ready for you
(i.e., never).    **162 Go to** (An expression of remonstrance.)

IAGO.  Nay, you must forget that.

OTHELLO.  Ay, let her rot and perish, and be damned tonight, for she shall
not live. No, my heart is turned to stone; I strike it, and it hurts my
hand. O, the world hath not a sweeter creature! She might lie    175
by an emperor's side and command him tasks.

IAGO.  Nay, that's not your way.°

OTHELLO.  Hang her! I do but say what she is. So delicate with her needle! An admirable musician! O, she will sing the savageness out
of a bear. Of so high and plenteous wit and invention!°    180

IAGO.  She's the worse for all this.

OTHELLO.  O, a thousand, a thousand times! And then, of so gentle a
condition!°

IAGO.  Ay, too gentle.°

OTHELLO.  Nay, that's certain. But yet the pity of it, Iago! O, Iago, the pity
of it, Iago!    185

IAGO.  If you are so fond° over her iniquity, give her patent° to offend,
for if it touch not you it comes near nobody.

OTHELLO.  I will chop her into messes.° Cuckold me?

IAGO.  O, 'tis foul in her.

OTHELLO.  With mine officer?    190

IAGO.  That's fouler.

OTHELLO.  Get me some poison, Iago, this night. I'll not expostulate with
her, lest her body and beauty unprovide° my mind again. This
night, Iago.

IAGO.  Do it not with poison. Strangle her in her bed, even the bed she    195
hath contaminated.

OTHELLO.  Good, good! The justice of it pleases. Very good.

IAGO.  And for Cassio, let me be his undertaker.° You shall hear more
by midnight.

OTHELLO.  Excellent good. [*A trumpet within.*] What trumpet is that same?    200

IAGO.  I warrant, something from Venice.

*Enter* LODOVICO, DESDEMONA, *and attendants.*

'Tis Lodovico. This comes from the Duke.    195
See, your wife's with him.

LODOVICO.  God save you, worthy General!

---

**177 your way** i.e., the way you should think of her.    **180 invention**
imagination.    **183 gentle a condition** wellborn and well-bred.    **184 gentle**
generous, yielding (to other men).    **186 fond** foolish.    **patent** license.
**188 messes** portions of meat, i. e., bits.    **193 unprovide** weaken, render unfit.
**198 be his undertaker** undertake to dispatch him.

OTHELLO.                      With all my heart,° sir.

LODOVICO [*giving him a letter*]. The Duke and the senators of Venice
 greet you.                                                                 205

OTHELLO. I kiss the instrument of their pleasures.

 [*He opens the letter, and reads.*]

DESDEMONA. And what's the news, good cousin Lodovico?

IAGO. I am very glad to see you, signor.

 Welcome to Cyprus.

LODOVICO. I thank you. How does Lieutenant Cassio?                               210

IAGO. Lives, sir.

DESDEMONA. Cousin, there's fall'n between him and my lord
 An unkind° breach; but you shall make all well.

OTHELLO. Are you sure of that?

DESDEMONA. My lord?                                                             215

OTHELLO [*reads*]. "This fail you not to do, as you will—"

LODOVICO. He did not call; he's busy in the paper.

 Is there division twixt my lord and Cassio?

DESDEMONA. A most unhappy one. I would do much
 T' atone° them, for the love I bear to Cassio.                              220

OTHELLO. Fire and brimstone!

DESDEMONA. My lord?

OTHELLO. Are you wise?

DESDEMONA. What, is he angry?

LODOVICO.                     Maybe the letter moved him;
 For, as I think, they do command him home,                                 225
 Deputing Cassio in his government.°

DESDEMONA. By my troth, I am glad on 't.°

OTHELLO. Indeed?

DESDEMONA. My lord?

OTHELLO. I am glad to see you mad.°                                             230

DESDEMONA. Why, sweet Othello—

OTHELLO [*striking her*]. Devil!

DESDEMONA. I have not deserved this.

LODOVICO. My lord, this would not be believed in Venice,
 Though I should swear I saw 't. 'Tis very much.°                            235
 Make her amends; she weeps.

---

204 **With all my heart** i.e., I thank you most heartily.  213 **unkind** unnatural,
contrary to their natures; hurtful.  220 **atone** reconcile.  226 **government**
office.  227 **on 't** of it.  230 I am . . . **mad** i.e., I am glad to see that you are
insane enough to rejoice in Cassio's promotion. (? Othello bitterly plays on
Desdemona's *I am glad.*)  235 **very much** too much, outrageous.

OTHELLO.                              O devil, devil!
   If that the earth could teem° with woman's tears,
   Each drop she falls would prove a crocodile.°
   Out of my sight!
DESDEMONA.                    I will not stay to offend you. [*Going.*]
LODOVICO.  Truly, an obedient lady.                              240
   I do beseech your lordship, call her back.
OTHELLO.  Mistress!
DESDEMONA [*returning*].  My lord?
OTHELLO.  What would you with her, sir?°
LODOVICO: Who, I, my lord?                                        245
OTHELLO.  Ay, you did wish that I would make her turn.
   Sir, she can turn, and turn, and yet go on
   And turn again; and she can weep, sir, weep;
   And she's obedient,° as you say, obedient,
   Very obedient.—Proceed you in your tears.—        250
   Concerning this, sir—O well-painted passion!°—
   I am commanded home.—Get you away;
   I'll send for you anon.—Sir, I obey the mandate
   And will return to Venice.—Hence, avaunt!

   [*Exit* DESDEMONA.]

   Cassio shall have my place. And, sir, tonight        255
   I do entreat that we may sup together.
   You are welcome, sir, to Cyprus.—Goats and monkeys!°    *Exit.*
LODOVICO.  Is this the noble Moor whom our full Senate
   Call all in all sufficient? Is this the nature
   Whom passion could not shake? Whose solid virtue        260
   The shot of accident nor dart of chance
   Could neither graze nor pierce?
IAGO.                              He is much changed.
LODOVICO.  Are his wits safe? Is he not light of brain?
IAGO.  He's that he is. I may not breathe my censure
   What he might be. If what he might he is not,        265
   I would to heaven he were!°

---

**237 teem** breed, be impregnated.    **238 falls . . . crocodile** (Crocodiles were
supposed to weep hypocritical tears for their victims.)    **244 What . . . sir**
(Othello implies that Desdemona is pliant and will do a turn, lines 239–241, for
any man.)    **249 obedient** (With much the same sexual connotation as *turn in*
lines 239–241.)    **251 passion** i. e., grief.    **257 Goats and monkeys** (See
3.3.419.)    **264-266 I may . . . were** i.e., I dare not venture an opinion as to
whether he's of unsound mind, as you suggest, but, if he isn't, then it might be
better to wish he were in fact insane, since only that could excuse his wild
behavior.

LODOVICO.                    What, strike his wife?
IAGO.  Faith, that was not so well; yet would I knew
       That stroke would prove the worst!
LODOVICO.                       Is it his use?°
       Or did the letters work upon his blood°
       And new-create his fault?
IAGO.                       Alas, alas!                                    270
       It is not honesty in me to speak
       What I have seen and known. You shall observe him,
       And his own courses will denote° him so
       That I may save my speech. Do but go after,
       And mark how he continues.                                         275
LODOVICO.  I am sorry that I am deceived in him.      *Exeunt.*


**4.2** *Enter* OTHELLO *and* EMILIA

OTHELLO.  You have seen nothing then?
EMILIA.  Nor ever heard, nor ever did suspect.
OTHELLO.  Yes, you have seen Cassio and she together.
EMILIA.  But then I saw no harm, and then I heard
       Each syllable that breath made up between them.             5
OTHELLO.  What, did they never whisper?
EMILIA.  Never, my lord.
OTHELLO.  Nor send you out o' the way?
EMILIA.  Never.
OTHELLO.  To fetch her fan, her gloves, her mask, nor nothing?    10
EMILIA.  Never, my lord.
OTHELLO.  That's strange.
EMILIA.  I durst, my lord, to wager she is honest,
       Lay down my soul at stake.° If you think other,
       Remove your thought; it doth abuse your bosom.°           15
       If any wretch have put this in your head,
       Let heaven requite it with the serpent's curse!°
       For if she be not honest, chaste, and true,
       There's no man happy; the purest of their wives
       Is foul as slander.

-----

268 **use** custom.   269 **blood** passions.   273 **courses will denote** actions will
reveal.   **4.2 Location:** The citadel.   **14 at stake** as the wager.   **15 abuse
your bosom** deceive you.   **17 the serpent's curse** the curse pronounced by
God on the serpent for deceiving Eve, just as some man has done to Othello and
Desdemona. (See Genesis 3.14.)

OTHELLO.                    Bid her come hither. Go.                    20
*Exit* EMILIA.

She says enough; yet she's a simple bawd
That cannot say as much.° This° is a subtle whore,
A closet lock and key° of villainous secrets.
And yet she'll kneel and pray; I have seen her do 't.

*Enter* DESDEMONA *and* EMILIA.

DESDEMONA.  My lord, what is your will?                    25
OTHELLO.  Pray you, chuck, come hither.
DESDEMONA.  What is your pleasure?
OTHELLO.                    Let me see your eyes.
Look in my face.
DESDEMONA.                    What horrible fancy's this?
OTHELLO [*to* EMILIA].  Some of your function,° mistress.
Leave procreants° alone and shut the door;                    30
Cough or cry "hem" if anybody come.
Your mystery, your mystery!° Nay, dispatch.

*Exit* EMILIA.

DESDEMONA [*kneeling*].  Upon my knees, what doth your speech import?
I understand a fury in your words,
But not the words.                    35
OTHELLO.  Why, what art thou?
DESDEMONA.                    Your wife, my lord, your true
And loyal wife.
OTHELLO.                    Come, swear it, damn thyself,
Lest, being like one of heaven,° the devils themselves
Should fear to seize thee. Therefore be double damned:
Swear thou art honest.
DESDEMONA.                    Heaven doth truly know it.                    40
OTHELLO.  Heaven truly knows that thou art false as hell.
DESDEMONA.  To whom, my lord? With whom? How am I false?
OTHELLO [*weeping*].  Ah, Desdemon! Away, away, away!
DESDEMONA.  Alas the heavy day! Why do you weep?
Am I the motive° of these tears, my lord?                    45
If haply you my father do suspect

---

**21–22 she's . . . much** i.e., any procuress or go-between who couldn't make up
as plausible a story as Emilia's would have to be pretty stupid.   **22 This** i.e.,
Desdemona.   **23 closet lock and key** i.e., concealer.   **29 Some . . . function**
i.e., practice your chosen profession, that of bawd (by guarding the door).
**30 procreants** mating couples.   **32 mystery** trade, occupation.   **38 being . . .
heaven** looking like an angel.   **45 motive** cause.

An instrument of this your calling back,
Lay not your blame on me. If you have lost him,
I have lost him too.
OTHELLO.                    Had it pleased heaven
To try me with affliction, had they° rained              50
All kinds of sores and shames on my bare head,
Steeped me in poverty to the very lips,
Given to captivity me and my utmost hopes,
I should have found in some place of my soul
A drop of patience. But, alas, to make me                55
A fixèd figure for the time of scorn°
To point his° slow and moving finger° at!
Yet could I bear that too, well, very well.
But there where I have garnered° up my heart,
Where either I must live or bear no life,                60
The fountain° from the which my current runs
Or else dries up—to be discarded thence!
Or keep it as a cistern° for foul toads
To knot° and gender° in! Turn thy complexion there,°
Patience, thou young and rose-lipped cherubin—           65
Ay, there look grim as hell!°
DESDEMONA.  I hope my noble lord esteems me honest.°
OTHELLO.  O, ay, as summer flies are in the shambles,°
That quicken° even with blowing.° O thou weed,
Who art so lovely fair and smell'st so sweet             70
That the sense aches at thee, would thou hadst ne'er been born!
DESDEMONA.  Alas, what ignorant° sin have I committed?
OTHELLO.  Was this fair paper, this most goodly book,
Made to write "whore" upon? What committed?
Committed? O thou public commoner!°                      75
I should make very forges of my cheeks,
That would to cinders burn up modesty,
Did I but speak thy deeds. What committed?

---

50 **they** i.e., heavenly powers.   56 **time of scorn** i.e., scornful world.   57 **his**
its.   **slow and moving finger** i.e., hour hand of the clock, moving so slowly it
seems hardly to move at all. (Othello envisages himself as being eternally pointed
at by the scornful world as the numbers on a clock are pointed at by the hour
hand.)   59 **garnered** stored.   61 **fountain** spring.   63 **cistern** cesspool.
64 **knot** couple.   **gender** engender.   **Turn . . . there** change your color,
grow pale, at such a sight.   65–66 **Patience . . . hell** (Even Patience, that rose-
lipped cherub, will look grim and pale at this spectacle.)   67 **honest** chaste.
68 **shambles** slaughterhouse.   69 **quicken** come to life.   **with blowing**
i.e., with the puffing up of something rotten in which maggots are breeding.
72 **ignorant sin** sin in ignorance.   75 **commoner** prostitute.

Heaven stops the nose at it and the moon winks;°
The bawdy° wind, that kisses all it meets,                                80
Is hushed within the hollow mine° of earth
And will not hear 't. What committed?
Impudent strumpet!
DESDEMONA.                    By heaven, you do me wrong.
OTHELLO.  Are not you a strumpet?
DESDEMONA.  No, as I am a Christian.                                      85
If to preserve this vessel° for my lord
From any other foul unlawful touch
Be not to be a strumpet, I am none.
OTHELLO.  What, not a whore?
DESDEMONA.  No, as I shall be saved.                                      90
OTHELLO.  Is't possible?
DESDEMONA.  O, heaven forgive us!
OTHELLO.                              I cry you mercy,° then.
I took you for that cunning whore of Venice
That married with Othello. [*Calling out.*] You, mistress,
That have the office opposite to Saint Peter                             95
And keep the gate of hell!

[*Enter* EMILIA]

                              You, you, ay, you!
We have done our course.° There's money for your pains.
                                          [*He gives money.*]
I pray you, turn the key and keep our counsel.            *Exit.*
EMILIA.  Alas, what does this gentleman conceive?°
How do you, madam? How do you, my good lady!               100
DESDEMONA.  Faith, half asleep.°
EMILIA.  Good madam, what's the matter with my lord?
DESDEMONA.  With who?
EMILIA.  Why, with my lord, madam.
DESDEMONA.  Who is thy lord?
EMILIA.                        He that is yours, sweet lady.     105
DESDEMONA.  I have none. Do not talk to me, Emilia.
I cannot weep, nor answers have I none
But what should go by water.° Prithee, tonight
Lay on my bed my wedding sheets, remember;
And call thy husband hither.                                    110

---

**79 winks** closes her eyes. (The moon symbolizes chastity.)    **80 bawdy**
kissing one and all.    **81 mine** cave (where the winds were thought to dwell).
**86 vessel** body.    **92 cry you mercy** beg your pardon.    **97 course** business
(with an indecent suggestion of "trick," turn at sex).    **99 conceive** suppose,
think.    **101 half asleep** i.e., dazed.    **108 go by water** be expressed by tears.

EMILIA.  Here's a change indeed!                              *Exit.*
DESDEMONA.  'Tis meet I should be used so, very meet.°
 How have I been behaved, that he might stick°
 The small'st opinion° on my least misuse?°

 *Enter* IAGO *and* EMILIA.

IAGO.  What is your pleasure, madam? How is 't with you?    115
DESDEMONA.  I cannot tell. Those that do teach young babes
 Do it with gentle means and easy tasks.
 He might have chid me so, for, in good faith,
 I am a child to chiding.
IAGO.  What is the matter, lady?                             120
EMILIA.  Alas, Iago, my lord hath so bewhored her,
 Thrown such despite and heavy terms upon her,
 That true hearts cannot bear it.
DESDEMONA.  Am I that name, Iago?
IAGO.  What name, fair lady?                                 125
DESDEMONA.  Such as she said my lord did say I was.
EMILIA.  He called her whore. A beggar in his drink
 Could not have laid such terms upon his callet.°
IAGO.  Why did he so?
DESDEMONA [*weeping*].  I do not know. I am sure I am none such.   130
IAGO.  Do not weep, do not weep. Alas the day!
EMILIA.  Hath she forsook so many noble matches,
 Her father and her country and her friends,
 To be called whore? Would it not make one weep?
DESDEMONA.  It is my wretched fortune.
IAGO.                              Beshrew° him for 't!      135
 How comes this trick° upon him?
DESDEMONA.                         Nay, heaven doth know.
EMILIA.  I will be hanged if some eternal° villain,
 Some busy and insinuating° rogue,
 Some cogging,° cozening° slave, to get some office,
 Have not devised this slander. I will be hanged else.   140
IAGO.  Fie, there is no such man. It is impossible.
DESDEMONA.  If any such there be, heaven pardon him!
EMILIA.  A halter° pardon him! And hell gnaw his bones!
 Why should he call her whore? Who keeps her company?
 What place? What time? What form?° What likelihood?     145

---

**112 meet** fitting.   **113 stick** attach.   **114 opinion** censure.   **least misuse**
slightest misconduct.   **128 callet** whore.   **135 Beshrew** curse.   **136 trick**
strange behavior, delusion.   **137 eternal** inveterate.   **138 insinuating**
ingratiating, fawning, wheedling.   **139 cogging** cheating.   **cozening** defrauding.
**143 halter** hangman's noose.   **145 form** appearance, circumstance.

The Moor's abused by some most villainous knave,
Some base notorious knave, some scurvy fellow.
O heaven, that° such companions° thou'dst unfold,°
And put in every honest hand a whip
To lash the rascals naked through the world                           150
Even from the east to th' west!

IAGO.                              Speak within door.°
EMILIA. O, fie upon them! Some such squire° he was
That turned your wit the seamy side without°
And made you to suspect me with the Moor.
IAGO. You are a fool. Go to.°
DESDEMONA.                     Alas, Iago,                             155
What shall I do to win my lord again?
Good friend, go to him; for, by this light of heaven,
I know not how I lost him. Here I kneel. [*She kneels.*]
If e'er my will did trespass 'gainst his love,
Either in discourse° of thought or actual deed,                       160
Or that° mine eyes, mine ears, or any sense
Delighted them° in any other form;
Or that I do not yet,° and ever did,
And ever will—though he do shake me off
To beggarly divorcement—love him dearly,                             165
Comfort forswear° me! Unkindness may do much,
And his unkindness may defeat° my life,
But never taint my love. I cannot say "whore."
It does abhor° me now I speak the word;
To do the act that might the addition° earn                           170
Not the world's mass of vanity° could make me.

[*She rises.*]

IAGO. I pray you, be content. 'Tis but his humor.°
The business of the state does him offense,
And he does chide with you.
DESDEMONA. If 'twere no other—                                        175
IAGO. It is but so, I warrant.              [*Trumpets within.*]
Hark, how these instruments summon you to supper!

---

148 **that** would that.  **companions** fellows.  **unfold** expose.  **151 within
door** i.e., not so loud.  **152 squire** fel-low.  **153 seamy side without** wrong
side out.  **155 Go to** i.e., that's enough.  **160 discourse of thought** process
of thinking.  **161 that** if. (Also in line 163.)  **162 Delighted them** took
delight.  **163 yet** still.  **166 Comfort forswear** may heavenly comfort forsake.
**167 defeat** destroy.  **169 abhor** (1) fill me with abhorrence (2) make me whore-
like.  **170 addition** title.  **171 vanity** showy splendor.  **172 humor** mood.

The messengers of Venice stays the meat.°
Go in, and weep not. All things shall be well.

*Exeunt* DESDEMONA *and* EMILIA.

*Enter* RODERIGO.

How now, Roderigo?                                                    180
RODERIGO. I do not find that thou deal'st justly with me.
IAGO. What in the contrary?
RODERIGO. Every day thou daff'st me° with some device,° Iago, and
    rather, as it seems to me now, keep'st from me all conveniency°
    than suppliest me with the least advantage° of hope. I will indeed   185
    no longer endure it, nor am I yet persuaded to put up° in peace
    what already I have foolishly suffered.
IAGO. Will you hear me, Roderigo?
RODERIGO. Faith, I have heard too much, for your words and perfor-
    mances are no kin together.                                          190
IAGO. You charge me most unjustly.
RODERIGO. With naught but truth. I have wasted myself out of my
    means. The  jewels you have had from me to deliver° Des-
    demona would half have corrupted a votarist.° You have told
    me she hath received them and returned me expectations and   195
    comforts of sudden respect° and acquaintance, but I find none.
IAGO. Well, go to, very well.
RODERIGO. "Very well"! "Go to"! I cannot go to,° man, nor 'tis not very
    well. By this hand, I think it is scurvy, and begin to find myself
    fopped° in it.                                                       200
IAGO. Very well.
RODERIGO. I tell you 'tis not very well.° I will make myself known
    to Desdemona. If she will return me my jewels, I will give over
    my suit and repent my unlawful solicitation; if not, assure yourself
    I will seek satisfaction° of you.                                   205
IAGO. You have said now?°
RODERIGO. Ay, and said nothing but what I protest intendment° of doing.

---

**178 stays the meat** are waiting to dine.    **183 thou daff'st me** you put me off.
**device** excuse, trick.    **184 conveniency** advantage, opportunity.    **185 advantage** increase.    **186 put up** submit to, tolerate.    **193 deliver** deliver to.
**194 votarist** nun.    **196 sudden respect** immediate consideration.    **198 I cannot go to** (Roderigo changes Iago's *go to,* an expression urging patience, to
*I cannot go to,* "I have no opportunity for success in wooing.")    **200 fopped**
fooled, duped.    **202 not very well** (Roderigo changes Iago's *very well,* "all right,
then," to *not very well,* "not at all good.") **205 satisfaction** repayment. (The term
normally means settling of accounts in a duel.)    **206 You . . . now** have you
finished?    **207 intendment** intention.

IAGO. Why, now I see there's mettle in thee, and even from this instant do build on thee a better opinion than ever before. Give me
thy hand, Roderigo. Thou hast taken against me a most just excep-   210
tion; but yet I protest I have dealt most directly in thy affair.

RODERIGO. It hath not appeared.

IAGO. I grant indeed it hath not appeared, and your suspicion is not
without wit and judgment. But, Roderigo, if thou hast that in thee
indeed which I have greater reason to believe now than ever—I    215
mean purpose, courage, and valor—this night show it. If thou the
next night following enjoy not Desdemona, take me from this
world with treachery and devise engines for° my life.

RODERIGO. Well, what is it? Is it within reason and compass?

IAGO. Sir, there is especial commission come from Venice to depute   220
Cassio in Othello's place.

RODERIGO. Is that true? Why, then Othello and Desdemona return
again to Venice.

IAGO. O, no; he goes into Mauritania and takes away with him the
fair Desdemona, unless his abode be lingered here by some acci-   225
dent; wherein none can be so determinate° as the removing of
Cassio.

RODERIGO. How do you mean, removing of him?

IAGO. Why, by making him uncapable of Othello's place—knocking out
his brains.                                                        230

RODERIGO. And that you would have me to do?

IAGO. Ay, if you dare do yourself a profit and a right. He sups tonight
with a harlotry,° and thither will I go to him. He knows not yet of
his honorable fortune. If you will watch his going thence,
which I will fashion to fall out° between twelve and one, you   235
may take him at your pleasure. I will be near to second your
attempt, and he shall fall between us. Come, stand not amazed at it,
but go along with me. I will show you such a necessity in his
death that you shall think yourself bound to put it on him. It is now
high° suppertime, and the night grows to waste.° About it.      240

RODERIGO. I will hear further reason for this.

IAGO. And you shall be satisfied.                          *Exeunt.*

**4.3** *Enter* OTHELLO, LODOVICO, DESDEMONA, EMILIA, *and attendants.*

LODOVICO. I do beseech you, sir, trouble yourself no further.

---

**218 engines for** plots against.   **226 determinate** conclusive.   **233 harlotry**
slut.   **235 fall out** occur.   **240 high** fully.   **grows to waste** wastes away.
**4.3 Location: The citadel.**

OTHELLO.  O, pardon me; 'twill do me good to walk.
LODOVICO.  Madam, good night. I humbly thank your ladyship.
DESDEMONA.  Your honor is most welcome.
OTHELLO.                                    Will you walk, sir?
    O, Desdemona!                                                        5
DESDEMONA.  My lord?
OTHELLO.  Get you to bed on th' instant.
    I will be returned forthwith. Dismiss your attendant there. Look
    't be done.
DESDEMONA.  I will, my lord.                                            10

    *Exit* [OTHELLO, *with* LODOVICO *and attendants*].

EMILIA.  How goes it now? He looks gentler than he did.
DESDEMONA.  He says he will return incontinent,°
    And hath commanded me to go to bed,
    And bid me to dismiss you.
EMILIA.  Dismiss me?                                                   15
DESDEMONA.  It was his bidding. Therefore, good Emilia,
    Give me my nightly wearing, and adieu.
    We must not now displease him.
EMILIA.  I would you had never seen him!
DESDEMONA.  So would not I. My love doth so approve him             20
    That even his stubbornness,° his checks,° his frowns—
    Prithee, unpin me—have grace and favor in them.

    [EMILIA *prepares* DESDEMONA *for bed*.]

EMILIA.  I have laid those sheets you bade me on the bed.
DESDEMONA.  All's one.° Good faith, how foolish are our minds!
    If I do die before thee, prithee shroud me                        25
    In one of these same sheets.
EMILIA.                             Come, come, you talk.°
DESDEMONA.  My mother had a maid called Barbary.
    She was in love, and he she loved proved mad°
    And did forsake her. She had a song of "Willow."
    An old thing 'twas, but it expressed her fortune,                 30
    And she died singing it. That song tonight
    Will not go from my mind; I have much to do
    But to go hang° my head all at one side
    And sing it like poor Barbary. Prithee, dispatch.
EMILIA.  Shall I go fetch your nightgown?°                            35

---

**12 incontinent** immediately.    **21 stubbornness** roughness.    **checks** rebukes.
**24 All's one** all right. It doesn't really matter.    **26 talk** i.e., prattle.    **28 mad**
wild, i.e., faithless.    **32–33 I . . . hang** I can scarcely keep myself from hanging.
**35 nightgown** dressing gown.

DESDEMONA.　No, unpin me here.
　　This Lodovico is a proper° man.
EMILIA.　A very handsome man.
DESDEMONA.　He speaks well.
EMILIA.　I know a lady in Venice would have walked barefoot to Pales-　40
　　tine for a touch of his nether lip.
DESDEMONA.　[*singing*]:
　　　　　　　　"The poor soul sat sighing by a sycamore tree,
　　　　　　　　Sing all a green willow;°
　　　　　　　　Her hand on her bosom, her head on her knee,
　　　　　　　　Sing willow, willow, willow.　　　　　　　　　　45
　　　　　　　　The fresh streams ran by her and murmured her moans;
　　　　　　　　Sing willow, willow, willow;
　　　　　　　　Her salt tears fell from her, and softened the stones—"

　　Lay by these.
　　　　　　　　[*Singing*.] "Sing willow, willow, willow—"　　　50
　　Prithee, hie thee.° He'll come anon.°
　　　　　　　　[*Singing*.] "Sing all a green willow must be my garland.
　　　　　　　　Let nobody blame him; his scorn I approve—"

　　Nay, that's not next.—Hark! Who is 't that knocks?
EMILIA.　It's the wind.　　　　　　　　　　　　　　　　55
DESDEMONA [*singing*].
　　　　　　　　"I called my love false love; but what said he then?
　　　　　　　　Sing willow, willow, willow;
　　　　　　　　If I court more women, you'll couch with more men."

　　So, get thee gone. Good night. Mine eyes do itch;
　　Doth that bode weeping?
EMILIA.　　　　　　　　　　　'Tis neither here nor there.　　60
DESDEMONA.　I have heard it said so. O, these men, these men!
　　Dost thou in conscience think—tell me, Emilia—
　　That there be women do abuse° their husbands
　　In such gross kind?
EMILIA.　　　　　　　　　There be some such, no question.
DESDEMONA.　Wouldst thou do such a deed for all the world?　　65
EMILIA.　Why, would not you?
DESDEMONA.　　　　　　　　No, by this heavenly light!
EMILIA.　Nor I neither by this heavenly light;
　　I might do 't as well i' the dark.
DESDEMONA.　Wouldst thou do such a deed for all the world?

---

**37 proper** handsome.　　**43 willow** (A conventional emblem of disappointed
love.)　　**51 hie thee** hurry.　　**anon** right away.　　**63 abuse** deceive.

EMILIA.  The world's a huge thing. It is a great price                    70
    For a small vice.
DESDEMONA.  Good troth, I think thou wouldst not.
EMILIA.  By my troth, I think I should, and undo 't when I had done.
    Marry, I would not do such a thing for a joint ring,° nor for mea-
    sures of lawn,° nor for gowns, petticoats, nor caps, nor any petty        75
    exhibition.° But for all the whole world! Uds° pity, who would not
    make her husband a cuckold to make him a monarch? I should
    venture purgatory for 't.
DESDEMONA.  Beshrew me if I would do such a wrong
    For the whole world.                                                     80
EMILIA.  Why, the wrong is but a wrong i' the world, and having the world
    for your labor, 'tis a wrong in your own world, and you might
    quickly make it right.
DESDEMONA.  I do not think there is any such woman.
EMILIA.  Yes, a dozen, and as many                                        85
    To th' vantage° as would store° the world they played° for.
    But I do think it is their husbands' faults
    If wives do fall. Say that they slack their duties°
    And pour our treasures into foreign laps,°
    Or else break out in peevish jealousies,                                 90
    Throwing restraint upon us? Or say they strike us,°
    Or scant our former having in despite?°
    Why, we have galls,° and though we have some grace,
    Yet have we some revenge. Let husbands know
    Their wives have sense° like them. They see, and smell,                  95
    And have their palates both for sweet and sour,
    As husbands have. What is it that they do
    When they change us for others? Is it sport?°
    I think it is. And doth affection° breed it?
    I think it doth. Is 't frailty that thus errs?                           100
    It is so, too. And have not we affections,
    Desires for sport, and frailty, as men have?
    Then let them use us well; else let them know,
    The ills we do, their ills instruct us so.

---

**74 joint ring** a ring made in separate halves.    **75 lawn** fine linen.
**76 exhibition** gift.    **Uds** God's.    **86 To th' vantage** in addition, to boot.
**store** populate.    **played** (1) gambled (2) sported sexually.    **88 duties** marital
duties.    **89 pour . . . laps** i.e., are unfaithful, give what is rightfully ours (semen)
to other women.    **91 Throwing . . . us** i.e., jealously restricting our freedom
to see other men.    **92 scant . . . despite** reduce our allowance to spite us.
**93 have galls** i.e., are capable of resenting injury and insult.    **95 sense** physical
sense.    **98 sport** sexual pastime.    **99 affection** passion.

DESDEMONA.  Good night, good night. God me such uses° send        105
Not to pick bad from bad, but by bad mend!°

*Exeunt.*


**5.1** *Enter* IAGO *and* RODERIGO.

IAGO.  Here stand behind this bulk.° Straight will he come.
Wear thy good rapier bare,° and put it home.
Quick, quick! Fear nothing. I'll be at thy elbow.
It makes us or it mars us. Think on that,
And fix most firm thy resolution.                                5
RODERIGO.  Be near at hand. I may miscarry in 't.
IAGO.  Here, at thy hand. Be bold, and take thy stand.

[IAGO *stands aside.* RODERIGO *conceals himself.*]

RODERIGO.  I have no great devotion to the deed;
And yet he hath given me satisfying reasons.
'Tis but a man gone. Forth, my sword! He dies.                   10

[*He draws.*]

IAGO.  I have rubbed this young quat° almost to the sense,°
And he grows angry. Now, whether he kill Cassio
Or Cassio him, or each do kill the other,
Every way makes my gain. Live Roderigo,°
He calls me to a restitution large                               15
Of gold and jewels that I bobbed° from him
As gifts to Desdemona.
It must not be. If Cassio do remain,
He hath a daily beauty in his life
That makes me ugly; and besides, the Moor                        20
May unfold° me to him; there stand I in much peril.
No, he must die. Be 't so. I hear him coming.

*Enter* CASSIO.

RODERIGO [*coming forth*].  I know his gait, 'tis he.—Villain, thou diest!

---

**105 uses** habit, practice.   **106 Not . . . mend** i.e., not to learn bad conduct from
others' badness (as Emilia has suggested women learn from men), but to mend
my ways by perceiving what badness is, making spiritual benefit out of evil and
adversity.   **5.1 Location: A street in Cyprus.   1 bulk** framework projecting
from the front of a shop.   **2 bare** un-sheathed.   **11 quat** pimple, pustule.   **to
the sense** to the quick.   **14 Live Roderigo** if Roderigo lives.   **16 bobbed**
swindled.   **21 unfold** expose.

*[He attacks* CASSIO]

CASSIO.  That thrust had been mine enemy indeed,
But that my coat° is better than thou know'st.               25
I will make proof° of thine.

*[He draws, and wounds* RODERIGO.]

RODERIGO.                    O, I am slain!          *[He falls.]*

[IAGO *from behind, wounds* CASSIO *in the leg, and exits.*]

CASSIO.  I am maimed forever. Help, ho! Murder! Murder!

*Enter* OTHELLO.

OTHELLO.  The voice of Cassio! Iago keeps his word.
RODERIGO.  O, villain that I am!
OTHELLO.  It is even so.                                     30
CASSIO.  O, help, ho! Light! A surgeon!
OTHELLO.  'Tis he. O brave Iago, honest and just,
That hast such noble sense of thy friend's wrong!
Thou teachest me. Minion,° your dear lies dead,
And your unblest fate hies.° Strumpet, I come.              35
Forth of° my heart those charms, thine eyes are blotted;
Thy bed, lust-stained, shall with lust's blood be spotted.

                                        *Exit* OTHELLO.

*Enter* LODOVICO *and* GRATIANO.

CASSIO.  What ho! No watch? No passage?° Murder! Murder!
GRATIANO.  'Tis some mischance. The voice is very direful.
CASSIO.  O, help!                                           40
LODOVICO.  Hark!
RODERIGO.  O wretched villain!
LODOVICO.  Two or three groan. 'Tis heavy° night;
These may be counterfeits. Let's think 't unsafe
To come in to° the cry without more help.                   45

*[They remain near the entrance.]*

RODERIGO.  Nobody come? Then shall I bleed to death.

*Enter* IAGO [*in his shirtsleeves, with a light*].

LODOVICO.  Hark!
GRATIANO.  Here's one comes in his shirt, with light and weapons.

---

**25 coat** (Possibly a garment of mail under the outer clothing, or simply a tougher
coat than Roderigo expected.)    **26 proof** a test.    **34 Minion** hussy (i.e., Desdemona).    **35 hies** hastens on.    **36 Forth of** from out.    **38 passage** people
passing by.    **43 heavy** thick, dark.    **45 come in to** approach.

IAGO.  Who's there? Whose noise is this that cries on° murder?
LODOVICO.  We do not know.
IAGO.                                          Did not you hear a cry?                     50
CASSIO.  Here, here! For heaven's sake, help me!
IAGO.                                          What's the matter?

   [*He moves toward* CASSIO.]

GRATIANO [*to* LODOVICO].  This is Othello's ancient, as I take it.
LODOVICO [*to* GRATIANO].  The same indeed, a very valiant fellow.
IAGO [*to* CASSIO].  What° are you here that cry so grievously?
CASSIO.  Iago? O, I am spoiled,° undone by villains!                            55
   Give me some help.
IAGO.  O me, Lieutenant! What villains have done this?
CASSIO.  I think that one of them is hereabout,
   And cannot make° away.
IAGO.                                          O treacherous villains!

   [*To* LODOVICO *and* GRATIANO.]

   What are you there? Come in, and give some help.            60
                                          [*They advance.*]
RODERIGO.  O, help me there!
CASSIO.  That's one of them.
IAGO.                                          O murderous slave! O villain!

   [*He stabs* RODERIGO.]

RODERIGO.  O damned Iago! O inhuman dog!
IAGO.  Kill men i' the dark?— Where be these bloody thieves?—
   How silent is this town!—Ho! Murder, murder!—              65
   [*To* LODOVICO *and* GRATIANO.] What may you be? Are you of good
   or evil?
LODOVICO.  As you shall prove us, praise° us.
IAGO.  Signor Lodovico?
LODOVICO.  He, sir.
IAGO.  I cry you mercy.° Here's Cassio hurt by villains.           70
GRATIANO.  Cassio?
IAGO.  How is 't, brother?
CASSIO.  My leg is cut in two.
IAGO.  Marry, heaven forbid!
   Light, gentlemen! I'll bind it with my shirt.                       75

   [*He hands them the light, and tends to* CASSIO's *wound.*]

---

**49 cries on** cries out.   **54 What** who (also at lines 60 and 66).   **55 spoiled**
ruined, done for.   **59 make** get.   **67 praise** appraise.   **70 I cry you mercy**
I beg your pardon.

*Enter* BIANCA.

BIANCA.  What is the matter, ho? Who is 't that cried?

IAGO.  Who is 't that cried?

BIANCA.                          O my dear Cassio!
My sweet Cassio! O Cassio, Cassio, Cassio!

IAGO.  O notable strumpet! Cassio, may you suspect
Who they should be that have thus mangled you?                          80

CASSIO.  No.

GRATIANO.  I am sorry to find you thus. I have been to seek you.

IAGO.  Lend me a garter. [*He applies a tourniquet.*] So.—O, for a chair,°
To bear him easily hence!

BIANCA.  Alas, he faints! O Cassio, Cassio, Cassio!                          85

IAGO.  Gentlemen all, I do suspect this trash
To be a party in this injury.—
Patience awhile, good Cassio.—Come, come;
Lend me a light. [*He shines the light on* RODERIGO.]
                          Know we this face or no?
Alas, my friend and my dear countryman                          90
Roderigo! No.—Yes, sure.—O heaven! Roderigo!

GRATIANO.  What, of Venice?

IAGO.  Even he, sir. Did you know him?

GRATIANO.  Know him? Ay.

IAGO.  Signor Gratiano? I cry your gentle° pardon.                          95
These bloody accidents° must excuse my manners
That so neglected you.

GRATIANO.                          I am glad to see you.

IAGO.  How do you, Cassio? O, a chair, a chair!

GRATIANO.  Roderigo!

IAGO.  He, he, 'tis he. [*A litter is brought in.*] O, that's well said;° the chair.  100
Some good man bear him carefully from hence;
I'll fetch the General's surgeon. [*To* BIANCA.] For you, mistress,
Save you your labor.°—He that lies slain here, Cassio,
Was my dear friend. What malice° was between you?

CASSIO.  None in the world, nor do I know the man.                          105

IAGO [*to* BIANCA].  What, look you pale?—O, bear him out o' th' air.°

[CASSIO *and* RODERIGO *are borne off.*]

Stay you,° good gentlemen.—Look you pale, mistress?—

---

**83 chair** litter.    **95 gentle** noble.    **96 accidents** sudden events.    **100 well
said** well done.    **103 Save . . . labor** i.e., never you mind tending Cassio.
**104 malice** enmity.    **106 bear . . . air** (Fresh air was thought to be dangerous
for a wound.)    **107 Stay you** (Lodovico and Gratiano are evidently about to
leave.)

Do you perceive the gastness° of her eye?—
Nay, if you stare,° we shall hear more anon.—
Behold her well; I pray you, look upon her.                    110
Do you see, gentlemen? Nay, guiltiness
Will speak, though tongues were out of use.

[*Enter* EMILIA.]

EMILIA.  'Las, what's the matter? What's the matter, husband?
IAGO.  Cassio hath here been set on in the dark
By Roderigo and fellows that are scaped.                    115
He's almost slain, and Roderigo dead.
EMILIA.  Alas, good gentleman! Alas, good Cassio!
IAGO.  This is the fruits of whoring. Prithee, Emilia,
Go know° of Cassio where he supped tonight.
[*To* BIANCA.] What, do you shake at that?                    120
BIANCA.  He supped at my house, but I therefore shake not.
IAGO.  O, did he so? I charge you go with me.
EMILIA.  O, fie upon thee, strumpet!
BIANCA.  I am no strumpet, but of life as honest°
As you that thus abuse me.                    125
EMILIA.  As I? Faugh! Fie upon thee!
IAGO.  Kind gentlemen, let's go see poor Cassio dressed.°—
Come, mistress, you must tell's another tale.
Emilia, run you to the citadel
And tell my lord and lady what hath happed.—                    130
Will you go on afore? [*Aside.*] This is the night
That either makes me or fordoes° me quite.          *Exeunt.*

**5.2** *Enter* OTHELLO [*with a light*], *and* DESDEMONA *in her bed.*

OTHELLO.  It is the cause,° it is the cause, my soul.
Let me not name it to you, you chaste stars!
It is the cause. Yet I'll not shed her blood,
Nor scar that whiter skin of hers than snow,
And smooth as monumental° alabaster.                    5

---

**108 gastness** terror.     **109 stare** (Iago pretends to interpret Bianca's wild looks as
an involuntary confession of guilt.)     **119 know** learn.     **124 honest** chaste.
**127 Cassio dressed** Cassio's wounds dressed.     **132 fordoes** undoes, ruins.
**5.2 Location:** A bedchamber in the citadel. **s.d. in her bed** (Either the
curtains are drawn back to reveal the bed in a recessed area backstage, or the bed is
"thrust out" onstage as the scene begins.)     **1 cause** i.e., cause of justice, the
offense itself, which Othello must correct as an agent of justice.     **5 monumental**
i.e., used in making tombs and funeral monuments.

Yet she must die, else she'll betray more men.
Put out the light, and then put out the light.°
If I quench thee, thou flaming minister,°
I can again thy former light restore,
Should I repent me;° but once put out thy light,                    10
Thou cunning'st pattern° of excelling nature,
I know not where is that Promethean heat°
That can thy light relume.° When I have plucked thy rose,
I cannot give it vital growth again;
It needs must wither. I'll smell thee on the tree.                    15

[*He kisses her.*]

O balmy breath, that dost almost persuade
Justice to break her sword! One more, one more.
Be thus when thou art dead, and I will kill thee,
And love thee after. One more, and that's the last.

[*He kisses her.*]

So sweet was ne'er so fatal. I must weep,                    20
But they are cruel° tears. This sorrow's heavenly;
It strikes where it doth love.° She wakes.
DESDEMONA.  Who's there? Othello?
OTHELLO.  Ay, Desdemona.
DESDEMONA.  Will you come to bed, my lord?                    25
OTHELLO.  Have you prayed tonight, Desdemon?
DESDEMONA.  Ay, my lord.
OTHELLO.  If you bethink yourself of any crime°
    Unreconciled as yet to heaven and grace,
    Solicit° for it straight.°                    30
DESDEMONA.  Alack, my lord, what may you mean by that?
OTHELLO.  Well, do it, and be brief. I will walk by.
    I would not kill thy unprepar`ed spirit.
    No, heaven forfend!° I would not kill thy soul.
DESDEMONA.  Talk you of killing?
OTHELLO.                         Ay, I do.
DESDEMONA.                                Then heaven                    35
    Have mercy on me!

---

**7 the light . . . light** the torch or lamp . . . Desdemona's life.    **8 flaming minister**
torch or lamp that serves me.    **10 repent me** change my mind.    **11 Thou . . .**
**pattern** you skillfully wrought perfect example.    **12 Promethean heat** divine
fire. (Alluding to the theft of fire from heaven by Prometheus.)    **13 relume**
rekindle.    **21 cruel** unrelenting.    **22 It . . . love** (Compare Hebrews 12.6: "For
whom the Lord loveth he chasteneth.")    **28 crime** sin.    **30 Solicit** petition,
pray.    **straight** immediately.    **34 forfend** forbid.

OTHELLO.                    Amen, with all my heart!
DESDEMONA. If you say so, I hope you will not kill me.
OTHELLO. Humh!
DESDEMONA. And yet I fear you; for you're fatal then
When your eyes roll so. Why I should fear I know not,                    40
Since guiltiness I know not; but yet I feel I fear.
OTHELLO. Think on thy sins.
DESDEMONA.                    They are loves I bear to you.°
OTHELLO. Ay, and for that thou diest.
DESDEMONA. That death's unnatural that kills for loving.
Alas, why gnaw you so your nether lip?                    45
Some bloody passion shakes your very frame.
These are portents; but yet I hope, I hope,
They do not point on° me.
OTHELLO. Peace, and be still!
DESDEMONA. I will so. What's the matter?                    50
OTHELLO. That handkerchief which I so loved and gave thee
Thou gav'st to Cassio.
DESDEMONA.                    No, by my life and soul!
Send for the man and ask him.
OTHELLO. Sweet soul, take heed, take heed of perjury.
Thou art on thy deathbed.                    55
DESDEMONA. Ay, but not yet to die.
OTHELLO.                    Yes, presently.°
Therefore confess thee freely of thy sin;
For to deny each article with oath
Cannot remove nor choke the strong conception°
That I do groan withal.° Thou art to die.                    60
DESDEMONA. Then Lord have mercy on me!
OTHELLO.                    I say, amen.
DESDEMONA. And have you mercy too! I never did
Offend° you in my life; never loved Cassio
But with such general warranty° of heaven
As I might love. I never gave him token.                    65
OTHELLO. By heaven, I saw my handkerchief in 's hand.
O perjured woman! Thou dost stone° my heart,
And makes me call what I intend to do
A murder, which I thought a sacrifice.
I saw the handkerchief.

---

**42 They are . . . you** i.e., if I sinned, it was in loving you more than my father
or more than God.    **48 point on** point at, predict what is to happen to.
**56 presently** immediately.    **59 conception** (1) belief in your guilt (2) plan
in my mind.    **60 groan withal** (1) groan at in sorrow (2) as in giving birth.
**63 Offend** wrong.    **64 warranty** sanction.    **67 stone** turn to stone, harden.

DESDEMONA.                He found it, then.                              70
  I never gave it him. Send for him hither;
  Let him confess a truth.
OTHELLO.                He hath confessed.
DESDEMONA. What, my lord?
OTHELLO. That he hath used thee.
DESDEMONA.                How? Unlawfully?
OTHELLO.                                          Ay.
DESDEMONA. He will not say so.
OTHELLO.                No, his mouth is stopped;          75
  Honest Iago hath ta'en order° for 't.
DESDEMONA. O, my fear interprets. What, is he dead?
OTHELLO. Had all his hairs been lives, my great revenge
  Had stomach for them all.
DESDEMONA. Alas, he is betrayed and I undone!          [*She weeps.*]     80
OTHELLO. Out, strumpet! Weep'st thou for him to my face?
DESDEMONA. O, banish me, my lord, but kill me not!
OTHELLO. Down, strumpet!
DESDEMONA. Kill me tomorrow; let me live tonight!
OTHELLO. Nay, if you strive—                              85
DESDEMONA. But half an hour!
OTHELLO.                Being done,° there is no pause.
DESDEMONA. But while I say one prayer!
OTHELLO.                It is too late.
    *Smothers* her,
EMILIA [*at the door*]. My lord, my lord! What, ho! My lord, my lord!
OTHELLO. What noise is this? Not dead? Not yet quite dead?
  I that am cruel am yet merciful;                     90
  I would not have thee linger in thy pain.

    [*He dispatches her.*]
                  So, so.
EMILIA [*within*]. What, ho! My lord, my lord!
OTHELLO.                Who's there?
EMILIA [*within*]. O, good my lord, I would speak a word with you!
OTHELLO. Yes, 'tis Emilia.—By and by.—She's dead.
  'Tis like° she comes to speak of Cassio's death.—     95
  The noise was here.° Ha! No more moving?
  Still as the grave. Shall she come in? Were 't good?—
  I think she stirs again. No. What's best to do?

---

**76 ta' en order** taken measures.    **86 Being done** i.e., since justice has begun its relentless course.    **95 like** likely that.    **96 here** (The Folio's *high* is possible, suggesting that the commotion of the attack on Cassio was loud.)

If she come in, she'll sure speak to my wife,
My wife! My wife! What wife? I have no wife.          100
O, insupportable! O heavy hour!
Methinks it should be now a huge eclipse
Of sun and moon, and that th' affrighted globe
Should yawn° at alteration.°
EMILIA [*within*].          I do beseech you
That I may speak with you, O, good my lord!          105
OTHELLO.  I had forgot thee. O, come in, Emilia.—
Soft,° by and by. Let me the curtains draw.—

[*He closes the bed-curtains and opens the door.*]

Where art thou?

*Enter* EMILIA.

What's the matter with thee now?
EMILIA.  O, my good lord, yonder's foul murders done!
OTHELLO.  What, now?          110
EMILIA.  But now, my lord.
OTHELLO.  It is the very error° of the moon;
She comes more nearer earth than she was wont,
And makes men mad.
EMILIA.  Cassio, my lord, hath killed a young Venetian          115
Called Roderigo.
OTHELLO.          Roderigo killed?
And Cassio killed?
EMILIA.          No, Cassio is not killed.
OTHELLO.  Not Cassio killed? Then murder's out of tune,
And sweet revenge grows harsh.
DESDEMONA.  O, falsely, falsely murdered!          120
EMILIA.  O Lord, what cry is that?
OTHELLO.  That? What?
EMILIA.  Out° and alas, that was my lady's voice.

[*She opens the bed-curtains.*]

Help, help, ho, help! O lady, speak again!
Sweet Desdemona! O sweet mistress, speak!          125
DESDEMONA.  A guiltless death I die.

---

**104 yawn** gape in amazement, i.e., move in an earthquake. (According to Pliny,
earthquakes often happen during eclipses.)   **at alteration** at these cataclysmic
events in nature, well suited to express the horror of Desdemona's death.
**107 Soft** wait a minute.   **112 error** aberration, irregularity.   **123 Out** (A cry
of dismay, intensifying *alas.*)

EMILIA.  O, who hath done this deed?
DESDEMONA.  Nobody; I myself. Farewell.
    Commend me to my kind lord. O, farewell!                    [*She dies.*]
OTHELLO.  Why, how should she be murdered?
EMILIA.                                        Alas, who knows?          130
OTHELLO.  You heard her say herself it was not I.
EMILIA.  She said so. I must needs report the truth.
OTHELLO.  She's like a liar gone to burning hell!
    'Twas I that killed her.
EMILIA.                            O, the more angel she,
    And you the blacker devil!                                    135
OTHELLO.  She turned to folly,° and she was a whore.
EMILIA.  Thou dost belie° her, and thou art a devil.
OTHELLO.  She was false as water.
EMILIA.  Thou art rash as fire to say
    That she was false. O, she was heavenly true!                 140
OTHELLO.  Cassio did top her. Ask thy husband else.°
    O, I were damned beneath all depth in hell
    But that I did proceed upon just grounds
    To this extremity. Thy husband knew it all.
EMILIA.  My husband?                                                    145
OTHELLO.  Thy husband.
EMILIA.  That she was false to wedlock?
OTHELLO.  Ay, with Cassio. Nay, had she been true,
    If heaven would make me such another world
    Of one entire and perfect chrysolite,°                        150
    I'd not have sold her for it.
EMILIA.  My husband?
OTHELLO.  Ay, 'twas he that told me on her first.
    An honest man he is, and hates the slime
    That sticks on filthy deeds.                                  155
EMILIA.  My husband?
OTHELLO.  What needs this iterance,° woman? I say thy husband.
EMILIA.  O mistress, villainy hath made mocks with° love!
    My husband say she was false?
OTHELLO.                                        He, woman;
    I say thy husband. Dost understand the word?                  160
    My friend, thy husband, honest, honest Iago.
EMILIA.  If he say so, may his pernicious soul
    Rot half a grain a day! He lies to th' heart.
    She was too fond of her most filthy bargain.

---

**136 folly** i.e., wantonness, fleshly sin.    **137 belie** slander.    **141 else** i.e., if you
don't believe me.    **150 chrysolite** precious topaz.    **157 iterance** iteration,
repetition.    **158 made mocks with** derided, made sport of.

OTHELLO. Ha?                                     [*He draws.*] 165
EMILIA. Do thy worst!
  This deed of thine is no more worthy heaven
  Than thou wast worthy her.
OTHELLO.                          Peace, you were best.°
EMILIA. Thou hast not half that power to do me harm
  As I have to be hurt.° O gull!° O dolt!                    170
  As ignorant as dirt! Thou hast done a deed—
  I care not for thy sword; I'll make thee known,
  Though I lost twenty lives.—Help! Help, ho, help!
  The Moor hath killed my mistress! Murder, murder!

*Enter* MONTANO, GRATIANO, *and* IAGO

MONTANO. What is the matter? How now, General?          175
EMILIA. O, are you come, Iago? You have done well,
  That men must lay their murders on your neck.
GRATIANO. What is the matter?
EMILIA [*to* IAGO]. Disprove this villain, if thou be'st a man.
  He says thou toldst him that his wife was false.       180
  I know thou didst not; thou'rt not such a villain.
  Speak, for my heart is full.
IAGO. I told him what I thought, and told no more
  Than what he found himself was apt° and true.
EMILIA. But did you ever tell him she was false?          185
IAGO. I did.
EMILIA. You told a lie, an odious, damnèd lie!
  Upon my soul, a lie, a wicked lie.
  She false with Cassio? Did you say with Cassio?
IAGO. With Cassio, mistress. Go to, charm° your tongue.   190
EMILIA. I will not charm my tongue; I am bound to speak.
  My mistress here lies murdered in her bed—
ALL. O heavens forfend!
EMILIA. And your reports have set the murder on.
OTHELLO. Nay, stare not, masters. It is true indeed.       195
GRATIANO. 'Tis a strange truth.
MONTANO. O monstrous act!
EMILIA.                         Villainy, villainy, villainy!
  I think upon 't—I think I smell 't! O villainy!
  I thought so then°—I'll kill myself for grief—
  O villainy, villainy!                                    200

---

**168 you were best** it would be best for you.  **170 to be hurt** i.e., to endure
hurt.  **gull** dupe.  **184 apt** plausible.  **190 charm** keep silent (as though by
a magic spell).  **199 then** (Perhaps at 3.3.331–332 and 4.2.137–154.)

IAGO.  What, are you mad? I charge you, get you home.
EMILIA.  Good gentlemen, let me have leave to speak.
    'Tis proper I obey him, but not now.
    Perchance, Iago, I will ne'er go home.
OTHELLO.  O! O! O!            [OTHELLO *falls on the bed.*°]
EMILIA.        Nay, lay thee down and roar,       205
    For thou hast killed the sweetest innocent
    That e'er did lift up eye.°
OTHELLO [*rising*].        O, she was foul!
    I scarce did know you, uncle. There lies your niece,
    Whose breath indeed these hands have newly stopped.
    I know this act shows° horrible and grim.      210
GRATIANO.  Poor Desdemon! I am glad thy father's dead.
    Thy match was mortal to him, and pure grief
    Shore his old thread° in twain. Did he live now,
    This sight would make him do a desperate turn,°
    Yea, curse his better angel from his side,      215
    And fall to reprobance.°
OTHELLO.  'Tis pitiful. But yet Iago knows
    That she with Cassio hath the act of shame
    A thousand times committed. Cassio confessed it;
    And she did gratify° his amorous works      220
    With that recognizance° and pledge of love
    Which I first gave her. I saw it in his hand;
    It was a handkerchief, an antique token
    My father gave my mother.
EMILIA.  O God! O heavenly God!      225
IAGO.  Zounds, hold your peace.
EMILIA.        'Twill out, 'twill out! I peace?
    No, I will speak as liberal as the north.°
    Let heaven and men and devils, let them all,
    All, all, cry shame against me, yet I'll speak.
IAGO.  Be wise, and get you home.
EMILIA.        I will not.

    [IAGO *threatens* EMILIA.]

GRATIANO.              Fie      230
    Your sword upon a woman?

---

**205 s.d. Othello bed** (This direction is from the Quarto, as also *He kisses her* at
line 19 and *She dies* at line 129.)    **207 lift up eye** i.e., lift her eyes to heaven.
**210 shows** looks.    **213 Shore . . . thread** sheared the thread of his old age
(as Atropos, one of the three Fates, was thought to do).    **214 turn** deed.
**216 reprobance** damnation, i.e., suicide.    **220 gratify** reward.    **221 recog-
nizance** token.    **227 liberal as the north** freely as the north wind (blows).

EMILIA.  O thou dull Moor! That handkerchief thou speak'st of
I found by fortune and did give my husband;
For often, with a solemn earnestness,
More than indeed belonged° to such a trifle,                       235
He begged of me to steal 't.
IAGO.                                   Villainous whore!
EMILIA.  She give it Cassio? No, alas! I found it,
And I did give 't my husband.
IAGO.                                   Filth, thou liest!
EMILIA.  By heaven, I do not, I do not, gentlemen.
O murderous coxcomb!° What should such a fool          240
Do with so good a wife?
OTHELLO.  Are there no stones° in heaven
But what serves for the thunder?—Precious° villain!

[*He runs at* IAGO; MONTANO *disarms* OTHELLO. IAGO, *from
behind, stabs* EMILIA.°]

GRATIANO.  The woman falls! Sure he hath killed his wife.
EMILIA.  Ay, ay. O, lay me by my mistress' side.          245

*Exit* [IAGO.]

GRATIANO.  He's gone, but his wife's killed.
MONTANO.  'Tis a notorious villain. Take you this weapon,
Which I have here recovered from the Moor.
Come, guard the door without. Let him not pass,
But kill him rather. I'll after that same villain,          250
For 'tis a damned slave.

*Exit* [*with all but* OTHELLO *and* EMILIA, *who has been laid by*
DESDEMONA's *side*].

OTHELLO.  I am not valiant neither,
But every puny whipster° gets my sword.
But why should honor° outlive honesty?°
Let it go all.
EMILIA.                  What did thy song bode, lady?          255
Hark, canst thou hear me? I will play the swan,
And die in music. [*She sings.*] "Willow, willow, willow."

---

**235 belonged** was appropriate.    **240 coxcomb** fool. (Addressed to Othello.)
**242 stones** bolts, such as those used for thunderbolts.    **243 Precious** i.e., arrant,
utter.    **s.d. He . . . Emilia** (The Quarto text reads, "The Moor runs at Iago. Iago
kills his wife." The Quarto also specifies the exit of Iago at line 245 and the death
of Emilia at line 260.)    **253 whipster** contemptible fellow (one who is always
ready to whip out his sword).    **254 honor** i.e., the bravery for which one enjoys
a soldier's reputation.    **honesty** true integrity.

Moor, she was chaste. She loved thee, cruel Moor.
So come my soul to bliss as I speak true.
So speaking as I think, alas, I die.                                    [*She dies.*]  260
OTHELLO.  I have another weapon in this chamber;
It was a sword of Spain, the ice-brook's temper° —
O, here it is. [*He finds a sword.*] Uncle, I must come forth.
GRATIANO [*within*].  If thou attempt it, it will cost thee dear.
Thou hast no weapon, and perforce must suffer.                          265
OTHELLO.  Look in upon me then and speak with me,
Or, naked° as I am, I will assault thee.

[*Enter* GRATIANO.]

GRATIANO.  What is the matter?
OTHELLO.                          Behold, I have a weapon;
A better never did itself sustain
Upon a soldier's thigh. I have seen the day                             270
That, with this little arm and this good sword,
I have made my way through more impediments
Than twenty times your stop.° But O, vain boast!
Who can control his fate? 'Tis not so now.
Be not afraid, though you do see me weaponed;                           275
Here is my journey's end, here is my butt°
And very seamark° of my utmost sail.

[GRATIANO *steps back.*]

Do you go back dismayed? 'Tis a lost° fear;
Man but a rush° against Othello's breast
And he retires. Where should Othello go?                                280

[*He turns to* DESDEMONA.]

Now, how dost thou look now? O ill-starred wench!
Pale as thy smock! When we shall meet at compt,°
This look of thine will hurl my soul from heaven,
And fiends will snatch at it. Cold, cold, my girl?
Even like thy chastity. O cursèd, cursèd slave!°                        285
Whip me, ye devils,
From the possession of this heavenly sight!
Blow me about in winds! Roast me in sulfur!

---

262 **the ice-brook's temper** tempered in ice-cold water.    267 **naked** unarmed.
273 **stop** power (to stop).    276 **butt** goal, limit. (An archery term.)    277 **sea-
mark** beacon (marking his destination or limit).    278 **lost** wasted, unneeded.
279 **Man . . . rush** wield no more than a reed.    282 **compt** account, judgment
day.    285 **slave** i.e., Othello himself.

Wash me in steep-down gulfs of liquid fire!
O Desdemon! Dead, Desdemon! Dead! O! O!                        290

*Enter* LODOVICO, CASSIO *[carried in a litter°]*, MONTANO, *and* IAGO
*[prisoner]*, *with officers.*

LODOVICO. Where is this rash and most unfortunate man?
OTHELLO. That's he that was Othello. Here I am.
LODOVICO. Where is that viper? Bring the villain forth.

[IAGO *is led forward.*]

OTHELLO. I look down towards his feet;° but that's a fable.
If that thou be'st a devil, I cannot kill thee.              295

[*He wounds* IAGO.]

LODOVICO. Wrench his sword from him. [OTHELLO *is disarmed.*]
IAGO.                            I bleed, sir, but not killed.
OTHELLO. I am not sorry neither. I'd have thee live,
For in my sense° 'tis happiness to die.
LODOVICO. O thou Othello, that was once so good,
Fall'n in the practice° of a cursèd slave,°                  300
What shall be said to thee?
OTHELLO.                    Why, anything.
An honorable murderer, if you will,
For naught I did in hate, but all in honor.
LODOVICO. This wretch hath part confessed his villainy.
Did you and he consent° in Cassio's death?                  305
OTHELLO. Ay.
CASSIO. Dear General, I never gave you cause.
OTHELLO. I do believe it, and I ask your pardon.
Will you, I pray, demand that demi-devil
Why he hath thus ensnared my soul and body?                 310
IAGO. Demand me nothing. What you know, you know.
From this time forth I never will speak word.
LODOVICO. What, not to pray?
GRATIANO. Torments° will ope your lips.
OTHELLO. Well, thou dost best.                               315
LODOVICO. Sir, you shall understand what hath befall'n,
Which, as I think, you know not. Here is a letter
Found in the pocket of the slain Roderigo;

---

**290 s.d. in a litter** (The Quarto specifies that Cassio is "in a chair.")
**294 towards his feet** i.e., to see if they are cloven, as the devil's are fabled to be.
**298 in my sense** to one who feels as I do.    **300 in the practice** through the
plotting, into the snare.    **slave** villain.    **305 consent** agree.    **314 Torments**
torture.

And here another. [*He produces letters.*] The one of them imports
The death of Cassio, to be undertook                                    320
By Roderigo.
OTHELLO.   O villain!
CASSIO.                   Most heathenish and most gross!°
LODOVICO  [*showing another paper*]. Now here's another discontented°
paper
Found in his pocket too. And this, it seems,
Roderigo meant t' have sent this damnèd villain;                        325
But that belike° Iago in the interim
Came in and satisfied him.°
OTHELLO.   O thou pernicious caitiff!—
How came you, Cassio, by that handkerchief
That was my wife's?
CASSIO.                   I found it in my chamber;                      330
And he himself confessed but even now
That there he dropped it for a special purpose
Which wrought to his desire.°
OTHELLO.                        O fool, fool, fool!
CASSIO.   There is besides in Roderigo's letter
How he upbraids Iago, that he made him                                  335
Brave° me upon the watch, whereon it came°
That I was cast;° and even but now he spake,
After long seeming dead, Iago hurt him,
Iago set him on.
LODOVICO  [*to* OTHELLO]. You must forsake this room and go with us.    340
Your power and your command is taken off,°
And Cassio rules in Cyprus. For this slave,
If there be any cunning cruelty
That can torment him much and hold him long,°
It shall be his. You shall close prisoner rest°                         345
Till that the nature of your fault be known
To the Venetian state.—Come, bring away.
OTHELLO.   Soft you;° a word or two before you go.
I have done the state some service, and they know 't.

---

322 **gross** monstrous.    323 **discontented** full of discontent.    326 **belike** most
likely.    327 **Came . . . him** interposed and gave him satisfactory explanation.
333 **wrought . . . desire** worked out as he wished, fitted in with his plan.
336 **Brave** defy.    **whereon it came** whereof it came about.    337 **cast**
dismissed.    341 **taken off** taken away.    344 **hold him long** keep him alive a
long time (during his torture).    345 **rest** remain.    348 **Soft you** one moment.

No more of that. I pray you, in your letters,                                    350
When you shall these unlucky° deeds relate,
Speak of me as I am; nothing extenuate,
Nor set down aught in malice. Then must you speak
Of one that loved not wisely but too well;
Of one not easily jealous but, being wrought,°                                   355
Perplexed° in the extreme; of one whose hand,
Like the base Indian,° threw a pearl away
Richer than all his tribe; of one whose subdued° eyes,
Albeit unusèd to the melting mood,
Drops tears as fast as the Arabian trees                                         360
Their medicinable gum.° Set you down this;
And say besides that in Aleppo once,
Where a malignant and a turbaned Turk
Beat a Venetian and traduced the state,
I took by th' throat the circumcisèd dog                                         365
And smote him, thus.                              [*He stabs himself.*°]
LODOVICO.  O bloody period!°
GRATIANO.  All that is spoke is marred.
OTHELLO.  I kissed thee ere I killed thee. No way but this,
Killing myself, to die upon a kiss.                                              370

[*He kisses* DESDEMONA *and dies.*]

CASSIO.  This did I fear, but thought he had no weapon;
For he was great of heart.
LODOVICO [*to* IAGO].                  O Spartan dog,°
More fell° than anguish, hunger, or the sea!
Look on the tragic loading of this bed.
This is thy work. The object poisons sight;                                      375
Let it be hid.° Gratiano, keep° the house,

---

**351 unlucky** unfortunate.   **355 wrought** worked upon, worked into a frenzy.
**356 Perplexed** distraught.   **357 Indian** (This reading from the Quarto pictures
an ignorant savage who cannot recognize the value of a precious jewel. The Folio
reading, Iudean or Judean, i.e., infidel or disbeliever, may refer to Herod, who
slew Miriamne in a fit of jealousy, or to Judas Iscariot, the betrayer of Christ.)
**358 subdued** i.e., overcome by grief.   **361 gum** i.e., myrrh.   **366 s.d. He
stabs himself** (This direction is in the Quarto text.)   **367 period** termination,
conclusion.   **372 Spartan dog** (Spartan dogs were noted for their savagery and
silence.)   **373 fell** cruel.   **376 Let it be hid** i.e., draw the bed curtains. (No stage
direction specifies that the dead are to be carried offstage at the end of the play.)
**keep** remain in.

*[The bed curtains are drawn]*
And seize upon° the fortunes of the Moor,
For they succeed on° you. [*To* CASSIO.] To you, Lord Governor,
Remains the censure° of this hellish villain,
The time, the place, the torture. O, enforce it!                    380
Myself will straight aboard, and to the state
This heavy act with heavy heart relate.                    *Exeunt.*

_____

**377 seize upon** take legal possession of.    **378 succeed on** pass as though by
inheritance to.    **379 censure** sentencing.


# ✺ TOPICS FOR
# CRITICAL THINKING AND WRITING

## *Act 1*

1. Iago, contemptuous of dutiful servants, compares them in 1.1.49 to
   asses. What other animal images does he use in the first scene? In
   your view, what does the use of such images tell us about Iago?
2. Is there any need to do more than knock loudly at Brabantio's door?
   What does 1.1.81–83 tell us about Iago?
3. In 1.1.111ff., and in his next speech, Iago uses prose instead of blank
   verse. What effect do you think is gained?
4. What is Iago trying to do to Othello in the first speech of 1.2? In
   1.2.29 why does Iago urge Othello to "go in"? When Othello first
   speaks (1.2.6), does he speak as we might have expected him to, given
   Iago's earlier comments about Othello? In Othello's second speech is
   there anything that resembles Iago's earlier description of him?
5. Do you think it incredible that a young woman who has rejected
   "the wealthy, curlèd darlings" (1.2.69) of Venice should choose a
   Moor? Explain your view.
6. Iago had said (1.1.14) that Othello uses "bombast circumstance." Is
   1.3.130ff. an example? Why, or why not?
7. Brabantio in 1.3.213–222 speaks in couplets (pairs of rhyming
   lines), as the Duke has just done. What is the effect of the verse?
   Does it suggest grief? Mockery?
8. Do you think the love of Othello and Desdemona is impetuous and irrational? What is their love based on?
9. The last speech in 1.3 is in verse, though previous speeches are in
   prose. How would you describe the effect of the change?
10. Is it a fault that Othello "thinks men honest that but seem to be so"
    (1.3.387)?

## Act 2

1. In 2.1.1–17, Shakespeare introduces a description of a storm. What symbolic overtones, if any, do you think it may it have?
2. What does Iago's description (2.1.148–158) of a good woman tell us about his attitude toward goodness and women?
3. In Iago's last speech in this act he gives several reasons why he hates Othello. List them, and add to the list any reasons he gave earlier. Evaluate them carefully. How convincing are they?
4. Again (2.1.273ff.) Shakespeare gives Iago verse, when alone, after prose dialogue. Why do you suppose he did this—i.e., what effect (if any) does the change have?
5. In 2.3.13–22, what sort of thing is Iago trying to get Cassio to say?
6. How does (2.3.183–196) prepare us for Othello's later tragic deed of killing Desdemona?

## Act 3

1. What is the point of the repetition (3.3.106–142) of "thought," "think," "know," and "honest"?
2. Is it surprising that Othello speaks (3.3.194) of a goat? In later scenes keep an eye out for his use of animal imagery.
3. Does one indeed smell "a will most rank" (3.3.248) in Desdemona's choice? Or had her choice been based on other qualities? If you think the latter, explain.
4. Emilia gets possession of the handkerchief by accident (3.3.306). Is it fair, then, to say that the tragic outcome is based on mere accident? And if so, is the play seriously weakened as a tragedy?
5. In 3.4.65–71 Othello is, of course, talking about a handkerchief, but he is also asking for the restoration of love. What words apply especially to love?

## Act 4

1. In 4.1.35ff. Othello uses prose. What does this shift suggest about Othello's state of mind?
2. Othello says (4.1.188) "I will chop her into messes. Cuckold me?" Do you think that in this scene Othello's ferocity toward Desdemona is chiefly motivated by a sense of personal injury? What if anything does Shakespeare do here to prevent the audience from merely loathing Othello?
3. What is Othello's emotional state in the first nineteen lines of 4.2?
4. In 4.2 Othello's baseness, very evident in the previous scene, continues here. But what lines in this scene tend to work against the view that he is merely base, and give him the stature of a tragic hero?

5. Why is it that Othello "looks gentler than he did" (4.3.11)?
6. What qualities in Desdemona's singing prevent us from regarding her as a merely pathetic figure here?

## Act 5

1. What do 5.1.19–20 tell us about Iago? How much "daily beauty" have we seen in Cassio's life? Do we assume Iago judges him incorrectly?
2. What does 5.2.16–17 tell us about the spirit with which Othello is about to kill Desdemona? Is he acting from a sense of wounded pride?
3. In 5.2.128–129 Desdemona dies with a lie on her lips. Do you think the worse of her? Why?
4. Emilia calls Othello "gull," "dolt," "ignorant as dirt" (5.2.170–171). Has she a point? If so, do these words prevent Othello from being a tragic hero?
5. T. S. Eliot, in "Shakespeare and the Stoicism of Seneca," *Selected Essays,* says of 5.2.348–366: "Othello ... is cheering himself up. He is endeavoring to escape reality, he has ceased to think about Desdemona, and is thinking about himself." Evaluate this view. To what does Othello in effect compare himself in the last line of this speech?
6. In Christian thought suicide is a sin. Do you judge it sinful here?

## General Questions

1. W. H. Auden, in *The Dyer's Hand,* says that "in most tragedies the fall of the hero from glory to misery and death is the work, either of the gods, or of his own freely chosen acts, or, more commonly, a mixture of both. But the fall of Othello is the work of another human being; nothing he says or does originates with himself. In consequence we feel pity for him but no respect; our esthetic respect is reserved for Iago." Evaluate Auden's view.
2. Harley Granville-Barker, in *Prefaces to Shakespeare,* says: "The mere sight of such beauty and nobility and happiness, all wickedly destroyed must be a harrowing one. Yet the pity and terror of it come short of serving for the purgation of our souls, since Othello's own soul stays unpurged. ... It is a tragedy without meaning, and that is the ultimate horror of it." Evaluate this view.
3. A black British actor has said,

> When a black actor plays a role written for a white actor in black make-up and for a predominantly white audience, does he not encourage the white way, or rather the wrong way, of looking at black men, namely that black men, or "Moors," are over-emotional, excitable and unstable, thereby vindicating Iago's state-

ment, "These Moors are changeable in their wills" (1.3)? Of all the parts in the canon, perhaps Othello is the one which should most definitely not be played by a black actor.

> Quoted in Lois Potter, *Shakespeare in Performance: Othello* (2002), 169

Does this view make sense to you? Why or why not?

4. How important to the play is the theme of race? Central to everything to happens? Significant but not really central? Please explain.

5. It has been said that a reader's or a spectator's interest in Iago consists of equal parts admiration and horror. Your view?

6. What does it mean to say that a tragic hero achieves self-knowledge? Is this knowledge essential to the dramatic power of a tragedy, or could a play still be tragic without it? Does Othello achieve self-knowledge in the final scene?

7. Could you imagine a different version of *Othello*, in which the play is a comedy rather than a tragedy? How would you revise the play to make everything turn out well in the end?

8. Do you think that Shakespeare is trying to teach us something special in this play? What is this "something," and where in the text do you perceive the evidence for it? What is the relationship between the action on the stage and the lives that we lead?

9. Have you read other Shakespearean tragedies beside this one? Which is your favorite? What are the reasons for your choice?

10. Shakespeare's plays have been performed and studied for centuries. Often it's said that they are inexhaustible. What does it mean to say that a literary work, by Shakespeare or some other great writer, is inexhaustible? Would you say that this is true—true for you—about *Othello*? Where in the text might you locate evidence for your view?

# A

# Remarks about Manuscript Form

## BASIC MANUSCRIPT FORM

Much of what follows is nothing more than common sense.

- Use good-quality 8½″ × 11″ paper. Make a photocopy, or if you have written on a word processor, print out a second copy, in case the instructor's copy goes astray.
- If you write on a word processor, **double-space,** and print on one side of the page only; set the printer for professional or best quality. If you submit handwritten copy, use lined paper and write on one side of the page only in black or dark blue ink, on every other line.
- Use **one-inch margins** on all sides.
- Within the top margin, put your last name and then (after hitting the space bar twice) the **page number** (in arabic numerals), so that the number is flush with the right-hand margin.
- On the first page, below the top margin and flush with the left-hand margin, put your **full name,** your **instructor's name,** the **course number** (including the section), and the **date,** one item per line, double-spaced.
- **Center the title** of your essay. Remember that the title is important—it gives the readers their first glimpse of your essay. **Create your own title**—one that reflects your topic or thesis. For example, a paper on Charlotte Perkins Gilman's "The Yellow Wallpaper" should not be called "The Yellow Wallpaper" but might be called

1112

```
            Disguised Tyranny in Gilman's
                "The Yellow Wallpaper"
    or

              How to Drive a Woman Mad
```

These titles do at least a little in the way of rousing a reader's interest.

- **Capitalize the title thus:** Begin the first word of the title with a capital letter, and capitalize each subsequent word except articles (*a, an, the*), conjunctions (*and, but, if, when,* etc.), and prepositions (*in, on, with,* etc.):

```
              A Word on Behalf of Love
```

Notice that you do *not* enclose your title within quotation marks, and you do *not* underline it—though if it includes the title of a poem or a story, *that* is enclosed within quotation marks, or if it includes the title of a novel or play, *that* is underlined (to indicate italics), thus:

```
           Gilman's "The Yellow Wallpaper"
                and Medical Practice
```

and

```
            Gender Stereotypes in Hamlet
```

- **After writing your title, double-space,** indent five spaces, and begin your first sentence.
- Unless your instructor tells you otherwise, **use a staple** to hold the pages together. (Do not use a stiff binder; it will only add to the bulk of the instructor's stack of papers.)
- Extensive revisions should have been made in your drafts, but minor **last-minute revisions** may be made—neatly—on the finished copy. Proofreading may catch some typographical errors, and you may notice some small weaknesses. You can make corrections using the following proofreader's symbols.

# CORRECTIONS IN THE FINAL COPY

**Changes** in wording may be made by crossing through words and rewriting them:

```
                                      has
    The influence of Poe and Hawthorne have greatly
                                      ∧
    diminished.
```

**Additions** should be made above the line, with a caret below the line at the appropriate place:

The influence of Poe and Hawthorne has <sub>greatly</sub> diminished.

**Transpositions** of letters may be made thus:

The influence of Poe and Hawthorne has diminished.

**Deletions** are indicated by a horizontal line through the word or words to be deleted. Delete a single letter by drawing a vertical or diagonal line through it; then indicate whether the letters on either side are to be closed up by drawing a connecting arc:

The influence of Poe and Hawthorne has great/ly
diminished.

**Separation** of words accidentally run together is indicated by a vertical line, closure by a curved line connecting the letters to be closed up:

The influence of Poe and Hawthorne has g reatly
diminished.

**Paragraphing** may be indicated by the symbol ¶ before the word that is to begin the new paragraph:

The influence of Poe and Hawthorne has greatly
diminished. ¶ The influence of Borges has very
largely replaced that of earlier writers of
fantasy.

# QUOTATIONS AND
# QUOTATION MARKS

First, a word about the *point* of using quotations. Don't use quotations to pad the length of a paper. Rather, give quotations from the work you are discussing so that your readers will see the material being considered and (especially in a research paper) so that your readers will know what some of the chief interpretations are and what your responses to them are.

*Note:* The next few paragraphs do *not* discuss how to include citations of pages, a topic taken up in the next appendix under the heading "How to Document: Footnotes, Internal Parenthetical Citations, and a List of Works Cited."

**The Golden Rule:** If you quote, *comment on* the quotation. Let the reader know what you make of it and why you quote it.

Additional principles:

1. **Identify the speaker or writer of the quotation** so that the reader is not left with a sense of uncertainty. Usually, in accordance with the principle of letting readers know where they are going, this identification precedes the quoted material, but occasionally it may follow the quotation, especially if it will provide something of a pleasant surprise. For instance, in a discussion of Flannery O'Connor's stories, you might quote a disparaging comment on one of the stories and then reveal that O'Connor herself was the speaker.

2. If the quotation is part of your own sentence, **be sure to fit the quotation grammatically and logically into your sentence.**

*Incorrect:* Holden Caulfield tells us very little about "what my lousy childhood was like."
*Correct:* Holden Caulfield tells us very little about what his "lousy childhood was like."

3. **Indicate any omissions or additions.** The quotation must be exact. Any material that you add—even one or two words—must be enclosed within square brackets, thus:

```
Hawthorne tells us that "owing doubtless to the
depth of the gloom at that particular spot [in
the forest], neither the travellers nor their
steeds were visible."
```

If you wish to omit material from within a quotation, indicate the ellipsis by three spaced periods. That is, at the point where you are omitting material, type a space, a period, a space, a period, a space, a third period. If you are omitting material from the end of a sentence, type a space after the last word that you quote, then a period, a space, a period, a space, a third period, and a period at the end of the sentence. The following example is based on a quotation from the sentences immediately above this one:

```
The instructions say, "If you . . . omit material
from within a quotation, [you must] indicate the
ellipsis . . . . If you are omitting material from
the end of a sentence, type . . . and a period to
indicate the end . . . ."
```

Notice that although material preceded "If you," periods are not needed to indicate the omission because "If you" began a sentence in the original.

Customarily, initial and terminal omissions are indicated only when they are part of the sentence you are quoting. Even such omissions need not be indicated when the quoted material is obviously incomplete—when, for instance, it is a word or phrase.

4. **Distinguish between short and long quotations,** and treat each appropriately. **Short quotations** (usually defined as fewer than five lines of typed prose or three lines of poetry) are enclosed within quotation marks and run into the text (rather than being set off, without quotation marks), as in the following example:

```
Hawthorne begins the story by telling us that
"Young Goodman Brown came forth at sunset into
the street at Salem village," thus at the outset
connecting the village with daylight. A few
paragraphs later, when Hawthorne tells us that
the road Brown takes was "darkened by all of
the gloomiest trees of the forest," he begins to
associate the forest with darkness--and a very
little later with evil.
```

If your short quotation is from a poem, be sure to follow the capitalization of the original, and use a slash mark (with a space before and after it) to indicate separate lines. Give the line numbers, if your source gives them, in parentheses, immediately after the closing quotation marks and before the closing punctuation, thus:

```
In "Diving into the Wreck," Adrienne Rich's
speaker says that she puts on "body-armor" (5).
Obviously the journey is dangerous.
```

To set off a **long quotation** (more than four typed lines of prose or more than two lines of poetry), indent the entire quotation ten spaces from the left margin. Usually, a long quotation is introduced by a clause ending with a colon—for instance, "The following passage will make this point clear:" or "The closest we come to hearing an editorial voice is a long passage in the middle of the story:" or some such lead-in. After typing your lead-in, double-space, and then type the quotation, indented and double-spaced.

5. **Commas and periods go inside the quotation marks.**

```
Chopin tells us in the first sentence that "Mrs.
Mallard was afflicted with heart trouble," and
in the last sentence the doctors say that Mrs.
Mallard "died of heart disease."
```

**Exception:** If the quotation is immediately followed by material in parentheses, close the quotation, then give the parenthetic material, and then—after closing the parenthesis—insert the comma or period.

> Chopin tells us in the first sentence that "Mrs.
> Mallard was afflicted with heart trouble" (28),
> and in the last sentence the doctors say that
> Mrs. Mallard "died of heart disease" (29).

**Semicolons, colons, and dashes** go outside the closing quotation marks.

**Question marks and exclamation points** go inside if they are part of the quotation, outside if they are your own.

In the following passage from a student's essay, notice the difference in the position of the question marks. The first question mark is part of the quotation, so it is enclosed within the quotation marks. The second question mark, however, is the student's, so it comes after the closing quotation marks.

> The older man says to Goodman Brown, "Sayest
> thou so?" Doesn't a reader become uneasy when
> the man immediately adds, "We are but a little
> way in the forest yet"?

# Quotation Marks or Underlining?

Use quotation marks around titles of short stories and other short works—that is, titles of chapters in books, essays, and poems that might not be published by themselves. Underline (to indicate italics) titles of books, periodicals, collections of essays, plays, and long poems such as *The Rime of the Ancient Mariner.* Word processing software will let you use italic type (instead of underlining) if you wish.

# A Note on the Possessive

It is awkward to use the possessive case for titles of literary works and secondary sources. Rather than "*The Great Gatsby*'s final chapter," write instead "the final chapter of *The Great Gatsby.*" Not "*The Oxford Companion to American Literature*'s entry on Emerson," but, instead, "the entry on Emerson in *The Oxford Companion to American Literature.*"

# B

# Writing a Research Paper

## WHAT RESEARCH IS NOT, AND WHAT RESEARCH IS

Because a research paper requires its writer to collect and interpret evidence—usually including the opinions of earlier investigators—it is sometimes said that a research paper, unlike a critical essay, is not the expression of personal opinion. But such a view is unjust both to criticism and to research. A critical essay is not a mere expression of personal opinions; if it is any good, it is an argument, offering evidence that supports the opinions and thus persuades the reader of their objective rightness. And a research paper is in the final analysis largely personal, because the author continuously uses his or her own judgment to evaluate the evidence, deciding what is relevant and convincing. A research paper is not the mere presentation of what a dozen scholars have already said about a topic; it is a thoughtful evaluation of the available evidence, and so it is, finally, an expression of what the author thinks the evidence adds up to.

## PRIMARY AND SECONDARY MATERIALS

The materials of literary research can be conveniently divided into two sorts, primary and secondary. The *primary materials,* or sources, are the real subject of study; the *secondary materials* are critical and historical accounts already written about these primary materials. For example, Langston Hughes wrote poems, stories, plays, and essays. For a student of Hughes, these works are the primary materials. (We include several of his works in this book.) If you want to study his ways of representing African-

American speech, or his representations of whites, or his collaboration with Zora Neale Hurston, you will read the primary material— his own writings (and Hurston's, in the case of the collaborative work). But in an effort to reach a thoughtful understanding of some aspect of his work, you will also want to look at later biographical and critical studies of his works and perhaps also at scholarly writing on such topics as Black English. You may even find yourself looking at essays on Black English that do not specifically mention Hughes but that nevertheless may prove helpful.

Similarly, if you are writing about Charlotte Perkins Gilman (we include one of her stories), the primary material includes not only other stories but also her social and political writing. If you are writing about her views of medical treatment of women, you will want to look not only at the story we reprint ("The Yellow Wallpaper") but also at her autobiography. Further, you will also want to look at some secondary material, such as recent scholarly books and articles on medical treatment of women in the late nineteenth and early twentieth centuries.

## Locating Material: First Steps

This appendix is devoted to traditional resources. Consult the next two appendices for a detailed introduction to electronic resources.

The easiest way to locate articles and books on literature written in a modern language—that is, on a topic other than literature of the ancient world—is to consult the

> *MLA International Bibliography of Books and Articles in the Modern Languages and Literatures* (1922– ),

which until 1969 was published as part of *PMLA* (*Publications of the Modern Language Association*) and since 1969 has been published separately. It is also available on CD-ROM through WilsonDisc, and in fact the disc is preferable since it is updated quarterly, whereas the print version is more than a year behind the times. Many college and university libraries also now offer the *MLA International Bibliography* as part of their package of online resources for research, and it is even more up-to-date.

*MLA International Bibliography* lists scholarly studies—books as well as articles in academic journals—published in a given year. Because of the great number of items listed, the print version of the bibliography runs to more than one volume, but material on writing in English (including, for instance, South African authors who write in English) is in one volume. To see what has been published on Langston Hughes in a given year, then, in this volume you turn to the section on American literature (as opposed to British, Canadian, Irish, and so forth), and then to the subsection labeled 1900–99, to see if anything that sounds relevant is listed.

Because your time is limited, you probably cannot read everything published on your topic. At least for the moment, therefore, you will use only the last five or ten years of this bibliography. Presumably, any important earlier material will have been incorporated into some of the recent studies listed. When you come to read these recent studies, if you find references to an article from, say, 1975 that sounds essential, of course you will read that article too.

Although *MLA International Bibliography* includes works on American literature, if you are doing research on an aspect of American literature you may want to begin with

> *American Literary Scholarship* (1965- ).

This annual publication is noted for its broad coverage of articles and books on major and minor American writers, and is especially valuable for its frank comments on the material that it lists.

On some recent topics—for instance, the arguments for and against dropping *Huckleberry Finn* from high school curricula—there may be few or no books, and there may not even be material in the scholarly journals indexed in *MLA International Bibliography.* Popular magazines, however, such as the *Atlantic Monthly, Ebony,* and *Newsweek*—unlisted in *MLA*—may include some useful material. These magazines, and about 200 others, are indexed in

> *Readers' Guide to Periodical Literature* (1900- ).

If you want to write a research paper on the controversy over *Huckleberry Finn,* or on the popular reception given to Kenneth Branagh's films of Shakespeare's *Henry V, Much Ado about Nothing,* and *Hamlet,* you can locate mate-rial (for instance, reviews of Branagh's films) through *Readers' Guide.* For that matter, you can also locate reviews of older films, let's say Olivier's films of Shakespeare's plays, by consulting the volumes for the years in which the films were released.

On many campuses *Readers' Guide* has been supplanted by

> *InfoTrac*®(1985- ),

on CD-ROM. The disc is preinstalled in a microcomputer that can be accessed from a computer terminal. This index to authors and subjects in popular and scholarly magazines and in newspapers provides access to several database indexes, including

- The *General Periodicals Index,* available in the Academic Library Edition (about 1,100 general and scholarly periodicals) and in the Public Library Edition (about 1,100 popular magazines)

- The *Academic Index* (400 general-interest publications, all of which are also available in the Academic Library Edition of the *General Periodicals Index*)
- The *Magazine Index Plus* (the four most recent years of the *New York Times,* the two most recent months of the *Wall Street Journal,* and 400 popular magazines, all of which are included in the Public Library Edition of the *General Periodicals Index*)
- The *National Newspaper Index* (the four most recent years of the *New York Times,* the *Christian Science Monitor,* the *Washington Post,* and the *Los Angeles Times*)

Once again, many college and university libraries are now making available online versions of these and similar resources for research. Some students (and faculty) prefer to use the books on the shelf, but the electronic editions have significant advantages. Often, it is easier to perform "searches" using them; and in many cases they are updated well before the next print editions are published.

## Other Bibliographic Aids

There are hundreds of guides to authors, publications, and reference works. *The Oxford Companion to African American Literature* (1997), edited by William L. Andrews, Frances Smith Foster, and Trudier Harris, provides detailed entries on authors, literary works, and many literary, historical, and cultural topics and terms, as well as suggestions for further reading. *Reader's Guide to Literature in English* (1996), edited by Mark Hawkins-Dady, is a massive work (nearly 1,000 pages) that gives thorough summaries of recent critical and scholarly writing on English and American authors.

How do you find such books? Two invaluable guides to reference works (that is, to bibliographies and to such helpful compilations as handbooks of mythology, place names, and critical terms) are

James L. Harner, *Literary Research Guide: A Guide to Reference Sources for the Study of Literatures in English and Related Topics,* 4th ed. (2002)

and

Michael J. Marcuse, *A Reference Guide for English Studies* (1990).

And there are guides to these guides: reference librarians. If you don't know where to turn to find something, turn to the librarian.

# WHAT DOES YOUR OWN INSTITUTION OFFER?

We'll mention again that many colleges and universities now offer as part of their resources for research a wide range of electronic materials and databases. At Wellesley College, for example, the library offers a detailed list of research resources, and there is another listing arranged according to department and interdisciplinary program. Some of these are open or free sites, available to anyone with a connection to the WWW. But others are by "subscription only," which means that only members of this academic community can access them.

Sign up for a library tutorial at your own school, and browse in and examine both the library's home page and the online catalog's options and directories.

One of the best research sites, to which many libraries subscribe, is the *FirstSearch* commercial database service.

*FirstSearch* enables you to find books, articles, theses, films, computer software, and other types of material for just about any field, subject, or topic. Its categories include:

Arts & Humanities
Business & Economics
Conferences & Proceedings
Consumer Affairs & People
Education
Engineering & Technology
General & Reference
General Science
Life Sciences
Medicine & Health
News & Current Events
Public Affairs & Law
Social Sciences

Within these categories, you will find a number of useful databases and resources. Make your "search" as focused as possible: Look for materials that bear on the topic that you are writing about, and, even more, that show a connection to the thesis that you are working to develop and demonstrate. Learn from what you find, but approach it critically: Is this source a good one? What are its strengths, and what are (or might be) its limitations? Keep in mind too that you engage in the process of selecting good sources in order to strengthen *your* topic and thesis. The quotations you give from the sources are there to support your ideas and insights. Above all your reader is interested in what *you* have to say.

> ## A RULE FOR WRITERS
>
> A good choice of secondary sources can help you to develop your analysis of a literary work, but remember that it is your point of view that counts. Use sources to help present your own interpretation more effectively.

---

## ✔ CHECKLIST: Evaluating Sources on the World Wide Web

❏ Focus the topic of your research as precisely as you can before you embark on a WWW search. Lots of surfing and browsing can sometimes turn up good material, but using the WWW without a focus can prove distracting and unproductive. It takes you away from library research (where the results might be better) and from the actual planning and writing of the paper.

❏ Ask the following questions:
  ❏ Does this site or page look like it can help me in my assigment?
  ❏ Whose site or page is this?
  ❏ What is the intended audience?
  ❏ Can you determine the point of view? Are there signs of a specific slant or bias?
  ❏ What is the detail, depth, and quality of the material presented?
  ❏ Is the site well constructed and well organized?
  ❏ Is the text well written?
  ❏ Can this WWW information be corroborated or supported by print sources?
  ❏ When was the site or page made available? Has it been recently revised or updated? *Reminder:* Your browser will enable you to get this information; if you are using Netscape 4.7, for example, go to View, and choose Page Info.
  ❏ Can the person or institution, company, or agency responsible for this site or page receive e-mail comments, questions, criticisms?

# TAKING NOTES

Let's assume now that you have checked some bibliographies and that you have a fair number of references you must read to have a substantial knowledge of the evidence and the common interpretations of the evidence. Most researchers find it convenient, when examining bibliographies and the library catalog, to write down each reference on a 3″ × 5″ index card—one title per card. On the card, put the author's full name (last name first), the exact title of the book or article, and the name of the journal (with dates and pages). Titles of books and periodicals (publications issued periodically—for example, monthly or four times a year) are underlined; titles of articles and of essays in books are enclosed in quotation marks. It's also a good idea to put the library catalog number on the card to save time if you need to get the item for a second look.

Next, start reading or scanning the materials whose titles you have collected. Some of these items will prove irrelevant or silly; others will prove valuable in themselves and also in the leads they give you to further references, which you should duly record on index cards. Notes—aside from these bibliographic notes—are best taken on larger index cards. The 3″ × 5″ cards are too small for summaries of useful materials; we use 4″ × 6″ cards, which allow you to record a moderate amount of information. Using these medium-sized cards rather than larger ones serves as a reminder that you need not take notes on everything. Be selective in taking notes.

# Two Mechanical Aids: The Photocopier and the Word Processor

Use the **photocopier** to make copies of material from the library (including material that does not circulate) that you know you need, or that you might want to refer to later. But remember that sometimes it is even more efficient to

- Read the material in the library,
- Select carefully what pertains to the purpose of your research, and
- Take your notes on it.

The **word processor** or **computer** is useful not only in the final stage, to produce a neat copy, but also in the early stages of research, when you are getting ideas and taking notes. With the help of the computer, you can brainstorm ideas, make connections, organize and reorganize material, and develop (and change) outlines. This file can be a kind of creative "work space" for your research paper.

# A Guide to Note Taking

Some students use note cards—we have already mentioned that we use 4″ × 6″ cards—for taking notes during the process of research. Others write on separate sheets of a notebook, or on the sheets of a yellow legal pad. Still others take their notes using a computer or word processor, and then organize and rearrange this body of material by copying and pasting, moving the notes into a coherent order. (We advise you not to delete material that, when you reread your notes, strikes you as irrelevant. It *probably* is irrelevant; but on the other hand, it may turn out to be valuable after all. Just put unwanted material into a file called "rejects," or some such thing, until you have completed the paper.)

Whichever method you prefer, keep in mind the following:

- **For everything you consult or read in detail, always specify the source,** so that you know exactly from where you have taken a key point or a quotation.
- **Write summaries (abridgments), not paraphrases (restatements).**
- **Quote sparingly.** Remember that this is *your* paper—it will present your thesis, not the thesis and arguments and analyses of someone else. Quote directly only those passages that are particularly effective, or crucial, or memorable. In your finished paper these quotations will provide authority and emphasis.
- **Quote accurately.** After copying a quotation, check your note against the original, correct any misquotation, and then put a checkmark after your quotation to indicate that it is accurate. Verify the page number also, and then put a checkmark on your note after the page number. If a quotation runs from the bottom of, say, page 306 to the top of 307, on your note put a distinguishing mark (for instance, two parallel vertical lines after the last word of the first page) so that if you later use only part of the quotation, you will know the page on which it appeared.

**Use ellipses** (three spaced periods) to indicate the omission of any words within a sentence. If the omitted words are at the end of the quoted sentence, put a period where you end the sentence, and then add three spaced periods to indicate the omission:

```
If the . . . words are at the end of the quoted
sentence, put a period where you end. . . .
```

**Use square brackets to indicate your additions to the quotation.** Here is an example:

```
Here is an [uninteresting] example.
```

- **Never copy a passage by changing an occasional word,** under the impression that you are thereby putting it into your own words. Notes of this sort may find their way into your paper, your reader will sense a style other than yours, and suspicions of plagiarism may follow. (For a detailed discussion of plagiarism, see pages 1200–1202.)

- **Comment on your notes** as you do your work, and later as you reflect on what you have jotted down from the sources. Make a special mark—we recommend using double parentheses ((. . .)) or a different-colored pen to write, for example, "Jones seriously misreads the passage," or "Smith makes a good point but fails to see its implications." As you work, consider it your obligation to *think* about the material, evaluating it and using it as a stimulus to further thought.
- **In the upper corner of each note card, write a brief key**—for example, "Swordplay in *Hamlet*"—so that later you can tell at a glance what is on the note.

# DRAFTING THE PAPER

The job of writing up your argument remains, but if you have taken good notes and have put useful headings on each note, you are well on your way.

- Read through the notes and sort them into packets of related material. Remove all notes that you now see are irrelevant to your paper. (Do not destroy them, however; you may want them later.) Go through the notes again and again, sorting and resorting, putting together what belongs together.
- Probably you will find that you have to do a little additional research—somehow you aren't quite clear about this or that—but after you have done this additional research, you should be able to arrange the packets into a reasonable and consistent sequence. You now have a kind of first draft, or at least a tentative organization for your paper.
- Beware of the compulsion to include every note in your essay; that is, beware of telling the reader, "A says . . . ; B says . . . ; C says . . ."
- You must have a point, a thesis. Make sure that you state it early, and that you keep it evident to your readers.
- Make sure that the organization is evident to the reader. When you were doing your research, and even perhaps when you were arranging your notes, you were not entirely sure where you were going; but by now, with your notes arranged into what seems to you to be the right sequence, you think you know what everything adds up to. Doubtless in the process of drafting you will make important changes in your focus, but do not abandon a draft until you think it not only says what you want to say, but says it in what seems to you to be a reasonable order. The final version of the paper should be a finished piece of work, without the inconsistencies, detours, and occasional dead ends of an early draft. Your readers should feel that

they are moving toward a conclusion (by means of your thoughtful evaluation of the evidence) rather than merely reading an anthology of commentary on the topic. And so we should get some such structure as "There are three common views on. . . . The first two are represented by A and B; the third, and by far the most reasonable, is C's view that. . . . A argues . . . but. . . . The second view, B's, is based on . . . but. . . . Although the third view, C's, is not conclusive, still. . . . Moreover, C's point can be strengthened when we consider a piece of evidence that she does not make use of. . . ."

- Preface all or almost all quotations with a lead-in, such as "X concisely states the common view" or "Z, without offering any proof, asserts that . . ." Let the reader know where you are going, or, to put it a little differently, let the reader know how the quotation fits into your argument.

Quotations and summaries, in short, are accompanied by judicious analyses of your own. By the end of the paper, your readers have not only read a neatly typed paper (see pages 1112–1114) and gained an idea of what previous writers have said but also are persuaded that under your guidance they have seen the evidence, heard the arguments justly summarized, and reached a sound conclusion.

A bibliography or list of works consulted (see pages 1134–1144) is usually appended to a research paper so that readers may easily look further into the primary and secondary material if they wish; but if you have done your job well, readers will be content to leave the subject where you left it, grateful that you have set matters straight.

# KEEPING A SENSE OF PROPORTION

Keep in mind the boundaries of the assignment.

- What is the *length* of the essay? How much *time* did the instructor give you in which to do it?
- *How many sources* did the instructor suggest that you should use? Did the instructor refer to specific kinds of sources that the paper should include—scholarly books and/or articles, other primary texts (published statements by artists, interviews with museum personnel)?
- What are the *proportions* of the essay? How much should consist of formal analysis, and how much of historical research and context?

For a **short paper**—say, two to five pages—in which you treat one or two works in a historical context, it may be sufficient if you look at two or three standard reference works. In them you will find some basic ideas—overviews of the period—and you can think about your selected works within these contexts.

For a paper of **medium length,** say five to ten or twelve pages, you almost surely will want to go beyond basic references. You probably will want to look into some of the works that these references cite, and your instructor presumably has given you enough time to look at them.

- Pay attention to *when* the books or articles were published; the most recent publications may not be the best, but they probably will give you a good sense of current thinking, and they will guide you to other recent writings.

For a **long paper**—say, fifteen to twenty-five pages—you will have to go beyond basic references and also beyond a few additional specialized sources. Your instructor almost surely will expect you to have read widely, so at the outset you may want to do a "subject" search in the online catalogs of your own library. But your library, unless it is a major research library, may not contain some work that, according to reference books, is especially important. Or even if your library does contain this title, it may appear as merely one more title in a long list, and you may not be aware of its importance. Before doing a search, then, consider the possibility of first checking reference books and compiling a short bibliography of titles that they cite. Then begin by looking at the titles especially recommended in reference books. If your library does not have some of these titles, request them by interlibrary loan.

How do you know when to stop? There is no simple answer. And almost everyone who has written a research paper has thought, "There still is one more source that I need to consult before I start drafting my paper." (In this respect the writer of a research paper is like a painter; it has been said painters never finish paintings, they just abandon them.) In the midst of a busy semester you need to make choices and to budget your time.

- Stop when you have acquired the historical knowledge that strengthens your analyses of works of literature—the knowledge that deepens your understanding of the works, and the knowledge that is sufficient for you to meet the specifications of the assignment.
- The paper should be *your* paper, a paper in which you present a thesis that you have developed, focusing on certain works. By using secondary resources you can enrich your analysis, as you place yourself in the midst of the scholarly community interested in this work or group of works. But keep a proper proportion between your thinking—again, the paper is *your* paper—and the thinking set forth in your sources.

# FOCUS ON PRIMARY SOURCES

Remember that your paper should highlight *primary* sources, the materials that are your real subject (as opposed to the secondary sources, the critical and historical discussion of these primary materials). It should be, above all, *your* paper, a paper in which you present a thesis that you have developed about the literary work or works that you have chosen to examine. In short, you are arguing a case. By using secondary sources, you can enrich your analysis, as you place yourself in the midst of the scholarly community interested in this author or authors. But keep a judicious proportion between primary sources, which should receive the greater emphasis, and secondary sources, which should be used selectively.

To help you succeed in this balancing act, when you review your draft, mark with a red pen the quotations from and references to primary sources, and then with a blue pen do the same marking for secondary sources. If, when you scan the pages of your paper-in-progress, you see a lot more blue than red, you should change the emphasis, the proportion, to what it should be. Guard against the tendency to rely heavily on the secondary sources you have compiled. The point of view that really counts is your own.

---

## ✔ CHECKLIST: Reviewing a Revised Draft

After you have written a draft and revised it at least once (better, twice or more), reread it with the following questions in mind. If possible, ask a friend to read the draft, along with the questions. If your answers or your friend's are unsatisfactory, revise.

❑ Does the draft fulfill the specifications (e.g., length, scope) of the assignment?

❑ Does the draft have a point, a focus?

❑ Is the title interesting and informative? Does it create a favorable first impression?

❑ Are the early paragraphs engaging, and do they give the reader a fairly good idea of what the thesis is and how the paper will be organized?

❑ Are arguable assertions supported with adequate evidence?

❑ Do you keep your readers in mind, for instance, by defining terms that they may be unfamiliar with?

❑ Are quotations adequately introduced with signal phrases (for instance, "An opposing view holds"), rather than just dumped into the essay? Are quotations as brief as possible? Might summaries (properly credited to the sources) be more effective than long quotations?

❑ Are quotations adequately commented on, not simply left to speak for themselves?

❑ Are *all* sources cited—not only words, but also ideas—including Internet material?

❑ Is the organization clear, reasonable, and effective? (Check by making a brief outline. Remember that the paper not only must be organized, but also that the organization must be clear to the reader. Check to see that transitions are adequate.)

❑ Does the final paragraph nicely round off the paper, or does it merely restate—unnecessarily—what is by now obvious?

❑ Does the paper include all the visual materials that the reader needs to see?

❑ Is the documentation in correct form?

# DOCUMENTATION

## What to Document: Avoiding Plagiarism

Honesty requires that you acknowledge your indebtedness for material, not only when you quote directly from a work but also when you appropriate an idea that is not common knowledge. Not to acknowledge such borrowing is plagiarism. If in doubt whether to give credit, give credit.

You ought, however, to develop a sense of what is considered **common knowledge.** Definitions in a dictionary can be considered common knowledge, so there is no need to say, "According to Webster, a novel is . . ." (This is weak in three ways: It's unnecessary, it's uninteresting, and it's unclear, since "Webster" appears in the titles of several dictionaries, some good and some bad.) Similarly, the date of first publication of *The Scarlet Letter* (1850) can be considered common knowledge. Few can give it when asked, but it can be found out from innumerable sources, and no one need get the credit for providing you with the date. The idea that Hamlet delays is also a matter of common knowledge. But if you are impressed by so-and-so's argument that Claudius has been much maligned, you should give credit to so-and-so.

Suppose that in the course of your research for a paper on Langston Hughes you happen to come across Arnold Rampersad's statement, in an essay in *Voices and Visions* (ed. Helen Vendler):

> Books alone could not save Hughes from loneliness, let alone give him the strength to be a writer. At least one other factor was essential in priming him for creative obsession. In the place in his heart, or psychology, vacated by his parents entered the black masses. (355)

This is an interesting idea, and in the last sentence the shift from heart to psychology is perhaps especially interesting. You certainly *cannot* say—

with the implication that the idea and the words are your own—something like

> Hughes let enter into his heart, or his
> psychology--a place vacated by his parents--the
> black masses.

The writer is simply lifting Rampersad's ideas and making only tiny changes in the wording. But even a larger change in the wording is unacceptable unless Rampersad is given credit. Here is a restatement that is an example of plagiarism even though the words differ from Rampersad's:

> Hughes took into himself ordinary black people,
> thus filling the gap created by his mother and
> father.

In this version, the writer presents Rampersad's idea as if it were the writer's own—and presents it less effectively than Rampersad.
  What to do? Give Rampersad credit, perhaps along these lines:

> As Arnold Rampersad has said, "in the place in
> his heart, or his psychology" where his parents
> had once been, Hughes now substituted ordinary
> black people (355).

You can use another writer's ideas, and even some of the very words, but you must give credit, and you must use quotation marks when you quote. You can

- Give credit and quote directly, or
- Give credit and summarize the writer's point, or
- Give credit and summarize the point but include—within quotation marks—some phrase you think is especially interesting.

---

## ✔ CHECKLIST: Avoiding Plagiarism

❑ In taking notes, did you make certain to indicate when you were quoting directly, when you were paraphrasing, and when you were summarizing, and did you clearly give the source of any online material that you cut and pasted into your notes? (If not, you will have to retrieve your sources and check your notes against them.)
❑ Are all quotations enclosed within quotation marks and acknowledged?
❑ Are all changes within quotations indicated by square brackets for additions and ellipses marks (. . .) for omissions?

❏ If a passage in a source is paraphrased rather than quoted directly or summarized in the paper, is the paraphrase explicitly identified as a paraphrase, and is a reason given for offering a paraphrase rather than quoting
directly (for instance, the original uses highly technical language, or the
original is confusingly written)?

❏ Are the sources for all borrowed ideas—not just borrowed words—acknowledged, and are these ideas set forth in your own words and with
your own sentence structure?

❏ Does the list of sources include all the sources (online as well as print)
that you have made use of?

*Reminder:* Material that is regarded as common knowledge, such as the
date of Shakespeare's death, is not cited because all sources give the same information—but if you are in doubt about whether something is or is not regarded as common knowledge, cite your source.

# How to Document: Footnotes, Internal Parenthetical Citations, and a List of Works Cited (MLA Format)

Documentation tells your reader exactly what your sources are. Until
fairly recently, the standard form was the footnote, which, for example,
told the reader that the source of such and such a quotation was a book
by so-and-so. But in 1984 the Modern Language Association, which had
established the footnote form used in hundreds of journals, university
presses, and classrooms, substituted a new form. It is this newer form—
parenthetical citation *within* the text (rather than at the foot of the page
or the end of the essay)—that we will discuss at length. Keep in mind,
though, that footnotes still have their uses.

## Footnotes

If you are using only one source, your instructor may advise you to give
the source in a footnote. (Check with your instructors to find out their
preferred forms of documentation.)

Let's say that your only source is this textbook. Let's say, too, that all
of your quotations will be from a single story—Kate Chopin's "The Story
of an Hour"—printed in this book on pages 00–00. If you use a word
processor, the software program can probably format the note for you. If,
however, you are using a typewriter, type the digit 1 (elevated, and
*without* a period after it) after your first reference to (or quotation from)
the story, and then put a footnote at the bottom of the page, explaining
where the story can be found. After your last line of text on the page,
triple-space, indent five spaces from the left-hand margin, and type the

arabic number 1, elevated. Do *not* put a period after it. Then type a statement (double-spaced) to the effect that all references are to this book.

Notice that although the footnote begins by being indented five spaces, if the note runs to more than one line the subsequent lines are given flush left.

> ¹Chopin's story appears in Sylvan Barnet,
> William Burto, and William E. Cain, eds.
> A Little Literature. (New York: Longman, 2007),
> 36-38.

(If a book has more than three authors or editors, give the name of only the first author or editor, and follow it with *et al.*, the Latin abbreviation for "and others.")

Even if you are writing a comparison of, say, two stories in this book, you can use a note of this sort. It might run thus:

> ¹All page references given parenthetically
> within the essay refer to stories in Sylvan
> Barnet, William Burto, and William E. Cain, eds.
> A Little Literature. (New York: Longman, 2007).

If you use such a note, you do not need to use a footnote after each quotation that follows. You can give the citations right in the body of the paper, by putting the page references in parentheses after the quotations.

### Internal Parenthetical Citations

Here we distinguish between embedded quotations (which are short, are run right into your own sentence, and are enclosed in quotation marks) and quotations that are set off on the page and are not enclosed in quotation marks (for example, three or more lines of poetry, five or more lines of typed prose).

**For an embedded quotation,** put the page reference in parentheses immediately after the closing quotation mark *without* any intervening punctuation. Then, after the parenthesis that follows the number, insert the necessary punctuation (for instance, a comma or a period):

> O'Connor begins "A Good Man Is Hard to Find" with
> a simple declarative sentence, "The grandmother
> didn't want to go to Florida" (182). O'Connor
> then goes on to give the grandmother's reason.

The period comes *after* the parenthetical citation. In the next example *no* punctuation comes after the first citation—because none is needed—and a comma comes *after* (not before or within) the second citation, because a comma is needed in the sentence:

```
This is ironic because almost at the start of
the story, in the second paragraph, Richards
with the best of motives "hastened" (36) to
bring his sad message; if he had at the start
been "too late" (38), Mallard would have arrived
at home first.
```

**For a quotation that is not embedded** within the text but is set off (by being indented ten spaces), put the parenthetical citation on the last line of the quotation, one space *after* the period that ends the quoted sentence.

Four additional points:

- The abbreviations *p., pg.,* and *pp.* are *not* used in citing pages.
- If a story is very short, perhaps running for only a page or two, your instructor may tell you there is no need to keep citing the page reference for each quotation. Simply mention in the footnote that the story appears on, say, pages 205-206.
- If you are referring to a poem, your instructor may tell you to use parenthetical citations of line numbers rather than of page numbers. But, again, your footnote will tell the reader that the poem can be found in this book, and on what page.
- If you are referring to a play with numbered lines, your instructor may prefer that in your parenthetical citations you give act, scene, and line, rather than page numbers. Use arabic (not roman) numerals, separating the act from the scene, and the scene from the line, by periods. Here, then, is how a reference to Act 3, Scene 2, line 118 would be given:

```
(3.2.118)
```

## Parenthetical Citations and List of Works Cited

Footnotes have fallen into disfavor. Parenthetical citations are now usually clarified not by means of a footnote but by means of a list, headed "Works Cited," given at the end of the essay. In this list you give alphabetically (last name first) the authors and titles that you have quoted or referred to in the essay.

Briefly, the idea is that the reader of your paper encounters an author's name and a parenthetical citation of pages. By checking the author's name in Works Cited, the reader can find the passage in the book. Suppose you are writing about Kate Chopin's "The Story of an Hour." Let's assume that you have already mentioned the author and the title of the story—that is, you have let the reader know the subject of the essay—and now you introduce a quotation from the story in a sentence such as this. (Notice the parenthetical citation of page numbers immediately after the quotation.)

```
True, Mrs. Mallard at first expresses grief when
she hears the news, but soon (unknown to her
friends) she finds joy in it. So, Richards's
"sad message" (36), though sad in Richards's
eyes, is in fact a happy message.
```

Turning to Works Cited, the reader, knowing the quoted words are by Chopin, looks for Chopin and finds the following:

```
Chopin, Kate. "The Story of an Hour." A Little
    Literature, Eds. Sylvan Barnet, William Burto,
    and William E. Cain. New York: Longman, 2007.
```

Thus the essayist is informing the reader that the quoted words ("sad message") are to be found on page 36 of this anthology.

If you have not mentioned Chopin's name in some sort of lead-in, you will have to give her name within the parentheses so that the reader will know the author of the quoted words:

```
What are we to make out of a story that ends by
telling us that the leading character has died
"of joy that kills" (Chopin 38)?
```

The closing quotation marks come immediately after the last word of the quotation; the citation and the final punctuation—in this case, the essayist's question mark—come *after* the closing quotation marks.

If you are comparing Chopin's story with Gilman's "The Yellow Wallpaper," in Works Cited you will give a similar entry for Gilman—her name, the title of the story, the book in which it is reprinted, and the page numbers that the story occupies.

If you are referring to several works reprinted within one volume, instead of listing each item fully, it is acceptable in Works Cited to list each item simply by giving the author's name, the title of the work, then a period, a space, and the name of the anthologist, followed by the page numbers that the selection spans. Thus a reference to Chopin's "The Story of an Hour" would be followed only by: Barnet 28–29. This form requires that the anthology itself be cited under the name of the first-listed editor, thus:

```
Barnet, Sylvan, William Burto, and William E.
    Cain, eds. A Little Literature, New York:
    Longman, 2007.
```

If you are writing a research paper, you will use many sources. In the essay itself you will mention an author's name, quote or summarize from this author, and follow the quotation or summary with a parenthetical citation of the pages. In Works Cited you will give the full title, place of publication, and other bibliographic material.

Here are a few examples, all referring to an article by Joan Templeton. "The *Doll House* Backlash: Criticism, Feminism, and Ibsen." The article appeared in *PMLA* 104 (1989): 28–40, but this information is given only in Works Cited, not within the text of the student's essay.

If in the text of your essay you mention the author's name, the citation following a quotation (or a summary of a passage) is merely a page number in parentheses, followed by a period, thus:

> In 1989 Joan Templeton argued that many critics,
> unhappy with recognizing Ibsen as a feminist,
> sought "to render Nora inconsequential" (29).

Or:

> In 1989 Joan Templeton noted that many critics,
> unhappy with recognizing Ibsen as a feminist,
> have sought to make Nora trivial (29).

If you don't mention the name of the author in a lead-in, you will have to give the name within the parenthetical citation:

> Many critics, attempting to argue that Ibsen was
> not a feminist, have tried to make Nora trivial
> (Templeton 29).

Notice in all of these examples that the final period comes after the parenthetical citation. *Exception:* If the quotation is longer than four lines and is therefore set off by being indented ten spaces from the left margin, end the quotation with the appropriate punctuation (period, question mark, or exclamation mark), hit the space bar twice, and type (in parentheses) the page number. In this case, do not put a period after the citation.

*Another point:* If your list of Works Cited includes more than one work by an author, in your essay when you quote or refer to one or the other you'll have to identify *which* work you are drawing on. You can provide the title in a lead-in, thus:

> In "The <u>Doll House</u> Backlash: Criticism,
> Feminism, and Ibsen," Templeton says, "Nora's
> detractors have often been, from the first, her
> husband's defenders" (30).

Or you can provide the information in the parenthetic citation, giving a shortened version of the title. This usually consists of the first word, unless it is *A, An,* or *The,* in which case including the second word is usually enough. Certain titles may require still another word or two, as in this example:

> According to Templeton, "Nora's detractors
> have often been, from the first, her husband's
> defenders" ("<u>Doll House</u> Backlash" 30).

## Forms of Citation in Works Cited

In looking over the following samples of entries in Works Cited, remember:

- The list of Works Cited appears at the end of the paper. It begins on a new page, and the page continues the numbering of the text.
- The list of Works Cited is arranged alphabetically by author (last name first).
- If a work is anonymous, list it under the first word of the title unless the first word is *A, An,* or *The,* in which case list it under the second word.
- If a work is by two authors, although the book is listed alphabetically under the first author's last name, the second author's name is given in the normal order, first name first.
- If you list two or more works by the same author, the author's name is not repeated but is represented by three hyphens followed by a period and a space.
- Each item begins flush left, but if an entry is longer than one line, subsequent lines in the entry are indented five spaces.

For details about almost every imaginable kind of citation, consult Joseph Gibaldi, *MLA Handbook for Writers of Research Papers,* 6th ed. (New York: Modern Language Association, 2003). We give here, however, information concerning the most common kinds of citations.

Here are samples of the kinds of citations you are most likely to include in your list of Works Cited.

### *A book by one author:*

> Douglas, Ann. <u>The Feminization of American</u>
> <u>Culture</u>. New York: Knopf, 1977.

Notice that the author's last name is given first, but otherwise the name is given as on the title page. Do not substitute initials for names written out on the title page, but you may shorten the publisher's name—for example, from Little, Brown and Company to Little.

Take the title from the title page, not from the cover or the spine, but disregard unusual typography—for instance, the use of only capital letters or the use of & for *and*. Underline the title and subtitle with one continuous underline, but do not underline the period. The place of publication is indicated by the name of the city. If the city is not well known or if several cities have the same name (for instance, Cambridge, Massachusetts, and Cambridge, England) the name of the state or country is added. If the title page lists several cities, give only the first.

### A book by more than one author:

> Gilbert, Sandra, and Susan Gubar. <u>The Madwoman</u>
>
> <u>in the Attic: The Woman Writer and the</u>
>
> <u>Nineteenth-Century Literary Imagination</u>.
>
> New Haven: Yale UP, 1979.

Notice that the book is listed under the last name of the first author (Gilbert) and that the second author's name is then given with first name (Susan) first. *If the book has more than three authors,* give the name of the first author only (last name first) and follow it with *et al.* (Latin for "and others.")

### A book in several volumes:

> McQuade, Donald, et al., eds. <u>The Harper</u>
>
> <u>American Literature</u>. 2nd ed. 2 vols. New
>
> York: Longman, 1994.
>
> Pope, Alexander. <u>The Correspondence of Alexander</u>
>
> <u>Pope</u>. 5 vols. Ed. George Sherburn. Oxford:
>
> Clarendon, 1955.

The total number of volumes is given after the title, regardless of the number that you have used.

If you have used more than one volume, within your essay you will parenthetically indicate a reference to, for instance, page 30 of volume 3 thus: (3: 30). If you have used only one volume of a multivolume work— let's say you used only volume 2 of McQuade's anthology—in your entry in Works Cited write, after the period following the date, Vol. 2. In your parenthetical citation within the essay you will therefore cite only the page reference (without the volume number), since the reader will (on consulting Works Cited) understand that in this example the reference is in volume 2.

If, instead of using the volumes as a whole, you used only an independent work within one volume—say, an essay in volume 2—in Works Cited omit the abbreviation *Vol.* Instead, give an arabic 2 (indicating volume 2) followed by a colon, a space, and the page numbers that encompass the selection you used:

```
McPherson, James Alan. "Why I Like Country
   Music." The Harper American Literature.
   2nd ed. 2 vols. New York: Longman, 1994.
   2: 2304-15.
```

Notice that this entry for McPherson specifies not only that the book consists of two volumes, but also that only one selection ("Why I Like Country Music," occupying pages 2304-2315 in volume 2) was used. If you use this sort of citation in Works Cited, in the body of your essay a documentary reference to this work will be only to the page; the volume number will *not* be added.

### *A book with a separate title in a set of volumes:*

```
Churchill, Winston. The Age of Revolution.
   Vol. 3 of A History of the English-Speaking
   Peoples. New York: Dodd, 1957.
Jonson, Ben. The Complete Masques. Ed. Stephen
   Orgel. Vol. 4 of The Yale Ben Jonson. New
   Haven: Yale UP, 1969.
```

### *A revised edition of a book:*

```
Chaucer, Geoffrey. The Riverside Chaucer.
   Ed. Larry Benson. 3rd ed. Boston: Houghton,
   1987.
Ellmann, Richard. James Joyce. Rev. ed. New
   York: Oxford UP, 1982.
```

### *A reprint, such as a paperback version of an older hardcover book:*

```
Rourke, Constance. American Humor. 1931. Garden
   City, New York: New York Review of Books,
   2004.
```

Notice that the entry cites the original date (1931) but indicates that the writer is using the New York Review of Books reprint of 2004.

*An edited book other than an anthology:*

> Keats, John. The Letters of John Keats. Ed.
> Hyder Edward Rollins. 2 vols. Cambridge,
> Mass.: Harvard UP, 1958.

*An anthology:*    You can list an anthology either under the editor's name or under the title.

*A work in a volume of works by one author:*

> Sontag, Susan. "The Aesthetics of Silence." In
> Styles of Radical Will. New York: Farrar,
> 1969, 3-34.

This entry indicates that Sontag's essay, called "The Aesthetics of Silence," appears in a book of hers entitled *Styles of Radical Will.* Notice that the page numbers of the short work are cited (not page numbers that you may happen to refer to, but the page numbers of the entire piece).

*A work in an anthology, that is, in a collection of works by several authors:*    Begin with the author and the title of the work you are citing, not with the name of the anthologist or the title of the anthology. The entry ends with the pages occupied by the selection you are citing:

> Ng, Fae Myenne. "A Red Sweater." Charlie Chan
> Is Dead: An Anthology of Contemporary Asian
> American Fiction. Ed. Jessica Hagedorn. New
> York: Penguin, 1993. 358-68.

Normally, you will give the title of the work you are citing (probably an essay, short story, or poem) in quotation marks. If you are referring to a book-length work (for instance, a novel or a full-length play), underline it to indicate italics. If the work is translated, after the period that follows the title, write *Trans.* and give the name of the translator, followed by a period and the name of the anthology.

If the collection is a multivolume work and you are using only one volume, in Works Cited you will specify the volume, as in the example (page 1139) of McPherson's essay. Because the list of Works Cited specifies the volume, your parenthetical documentary reference within your essay will specify (as mentioned earlier) only the page numbers, not the volume. Thus, although McPherson's essay appears on pages 2304–2315 in the second volume of a two-volume work, a parenthetical citation will refer only to the page numbers because the citation in Works Cited specifies the volume.

Remember that the pages specified in the entry in your list of Works Cited are to the *entire selection*, not simply to pages you may happen to refer to within your paper.

If you are referring to a *reprint of a scholarly article*, give details of the original publication, as in the following example:

```
Mack, Maynard. "The World of Hamlet." Yale
    Review 41 (1952): 502-23. Rpt. in Hamlet.
    By William Shakespeare. Ed. Sylvan Barnet.
    New York: Penguin Putnam, 1998. 265-87.
```

***Two or more works in an anthology:***  If you are referring to more than one work in an anthology, in order to avoid repeating all the information about the anthology in each entry in Works Cited, under each author's name (in the appropriate alphabetical place) give the author and title of the work, then a period, a space, and the name of the anthologist, followed by the page numbers that the selection spans. Thus, a reference to Shakespeare's *Othello* would be followed only by

```
Barnet, Burto, Cain 1002-1111
```

rather than by a full citation of Barnet's anthology. This form requires that the anthology itself also be listed, under Barnet.

***Two or more works by the same author:***  Notice that the works are given in alphabetical order (*Fables* precedes *Fools*) and that the author's name is not repeated but is represented by three hyphens followed by a period and a space. If the author is the translator or editor of a volume, the three hyphens are followed not by a period but by a comma, then a space, then the appropriate abbreviation (*Trans.* or *Ed.*), then the title:

```
Frye, Northrop. Fables of Identity: Studies in
    Poetic Mythology. New York: Harcourt, 1963.
---. Fools of Time: Studies in Shakespearean
    Tragedy. Toronto: U of Toronto P, 1967.
```

***A translated book:***

```
Gogol, Nikolai. Dead Souls. Trans. Andrew
    McAndrew. New York: New American Library,
    1961.
```

If you are discussing the translation itself, as opposed to the book, list the work under the translator's name. Then put a comma, a space, and "trans." After the period following "trans." skip a space, then give the title of the book, a period, a space, and then "By" and the author's name, first name first. Continue with information about the place of publication, publisher, and date, as in any entry to a book.

***An introduction, foreword, or afterword, or other editorial apparatus:***

> Fromm, Erich. Afterword. <u>1984</u>. By George Orwell.
> New American Library, 1961.

Usually a book with an introduction or some such comparable material is listed under the name of the author of the book rather than the name of the author of the editorial material (see the citation to Pope on page 1138). But if you are referring to the editor's apparatus rather than to the work itself, use the form just given.

Words such as *preface, introduction, afterword,* and *conclusion* are capitalized in the entry but are neither enclosed within quotation marks nor underlined.

***A book review:***    First, here is an example of a review that does not have a title.

> Vendler, Helen. Rev. of <u>Essays on Style</u>. Ed.
> Roger Fowler. <u>Essays in Criticism</u> 16 (1966):
> 457-63.

If the review has a title, give the title after the period following the reviewer's name, before "Rev." If the review is unsigned, list it under the first word of the title, or the second word if the first word is *A, An,* or *The.* If an unsigned review has no title, begin the entry with "Rev. of" and alphabetize it under the title of the work being reviewed.

***An encyclopedia:***    The first example is for a signed article, the second for an unsigned article.

> Lang, Andrew. "Ballads." <u>Encyclopaedia</u>
> <u>Britannica</u>. 1910 ed.
> "Metaphor." <u>The New Encyclopaedia Britannica:</u>
> <u>Micropaedia</u>. 1974 ed.

***An article in a scholarly journal:***    Some journals are paginated consecutively; that is, the pagination of the second issue picks up where the first issue left off. Other journals begin each issue with a new page 1. The forms of the citations in Works Cited differ slightly.

First, the citation of a *journal that uses continuous pagination:*

Burbick, Joan. "Emily Dickinson and the
Economics of Desire." American Literature
58 (1986): 361-78.

This article appeared in volume 58, which was published in 1986. (Notice that the volume number is followed by a space, then by the year in parentheses, and then by a colon, a space, and the page numbers of the entire article.) Although each volume consists of four issues, you do *not* specify the issue number when the journal is paginated continuously.

For a *journal that paginates each issue separately* (a quarterly journal will have four page 1's each year), give the issue number directly after the volume number and a period, with no spaces before or after the period:

Spillers, Hortense J. "Martin Luther King and
the Style of the Black Sermon." The Black
Scholar 3.1 (1971): 14-27.

**An article in a weekly, biweekly, or monthly publication:**

McCabe, Bernard. "Taking Dickens Seriously."
Commonweal 14 May 1965: 24.

Notice that the volume number and the issue number are omitted for popular weeklies or monthlies such as *Time* and *Atlantic.*

**An article in a newspaper:** Because newspapers usually consist of several sections, a section number may precede the page number. The example indicates that an article begins on page 3 of section 2 and is continued on a later page:

Wu, Jim. "Authors Praise New Forms." New York
Times 8 Mar. 1996, sec. 2: 3+.

You may also have occasion to cite something other than a printed source, for instance, a lecture. Here are the forms for the chief nonprint sources.

**An interview:**

Saretta, Howard. Personal interview. 3 Nov.
1998.

*A lecture:*

> Heaney, Seamus. Lecture. Tufts University. 15
> Oct. 1998.

*A television or radio program:*

> 60 Minutes. CBS. 25 Jan. 2004.

*A film or videotape:*

> Modern Times. Dir. Charles Chaplin. United
> Artists, 1936.

*A recording:*

> Frost, Robert. "The Road Not Taken." Robert
> Frost Reads His Poetry. Caedmon, TC 1060,
> 1956.

*A performance:*

> The Cherry Orchard. By Anton Chekhov. Dir.
> Ron Daniels. American Repertory Theatre,
> Cambridge, Mass. 3 Feb. 1994.

# Citing Sources on the World Wide Web

Scholars and reference librarians have not reached a consensus about the correct form—what should be included, and in what order—for the citation of WWW sources. But all agree on two principles: (1) Give as much information as you can; (2) Make certain that your readers can retrieve the source themselves—which means that you should check the URL carefully. For accuracy's sake, it is a good idea to copy the URL from the Location line of your browser and paste it into your list of Works Cited.

# ✔ CHECKLIST: Citing Sources on the World Wide Web

Provide the following information:

- ❏ Author
- ❏ Title
- ❏ Publication information
- ❏ Title of archive or database
- ❏ Date (if given) when the site was posted; sometimes termed the "revision" or "modification" date
- ❏ Name of institution or organization that supports or is associated with this site
- ❏ Date that you accessed this source
- ❏ URL

## A RULE FOR WRITERS

Remember that when you use a source from the World Wide Web, you need to acknowledge and cite it, just as you do when you use a print source.

# C

# Writing Essay Examinations

## WHY DO INSTRUCTORS GIVE EXAMINATIONS?

Perhaps an understanding of the nature of essay examinations will help you to write better essays.

Examinations not only measure learning and thinking, but also stimulate them. Even so humble an examination as a short-answer quiz—chiefly a device to oblige students to do the assigned reading—is a sort of push designed to move students forward. Of course, internal motivation is far superior to external, but even such crude external motivation as a quiz can have a beneficial effect. Students know this; indeed, they often will say that they have chosen to take a particular course "because I want to know something about . . . and I know that I won't do the reading on my own." (Teachers often teach a new course for the same reason; we want to become knowledgeable about, say, Asian-American literature, and we know that despite our lofty intentions we may not seriously confront the subject unless we are under the pressure of facing a class.)

In short, examinations help students to acquire learning and then to convert learning into thinking. Sometimes it is not until preparing for the final examination that students—rereading the chief texts and classroom notes—perceive what the course was really about; until this late stage, the trees obscure the forest, but now, in the process of the reviewing and sorting things out, a pattern emerges. The experience of reviewing and then of writing an examination, though fretful, can be highly exciting as connections are made and ideas take on life.

# GETTING READY

The night before the examination you will almost certainly feel that you don't know this, that, and the other thing, and you may feel that nothing short of reading all of the assignments—an impossibility, of course—can get you through the test. If indeed you have not done the reading, this feeling is warranted. The best preparation for an examination is not a panicky turning of hundreds of pages the night before the test; rather, the best preparation is to

- keep up with the reading throughout the term, and to annotate the text while reading,
- make connections among the works you study from one week to the next,
- participate in class discussion, and
- annotate the text during the class discussions.

If you engage in these practices, you will not only be preparing for the examination, but you will also be getting more out of the course—more knowledge and more *pleasure*—than if you come to class unprepared.

Nevertheless, however well prepared you are, you will want to do some intensive preparation shortly before the final examination. We suggest that you may want to reread Chapters 2, 3, 7 (all on fiction), 11, 12, 13 (all on poetry), 24 and 25 (both on drama), because these chapters discuss not only the genres but also the job of writing essays about them.

# WRITING ESSAY ANSWERS

Let's assume that before the examination you have read the assigned material, marked the margins of your books, made summaries of the longer readings and of the classroom comments, reviewed everything carefully, and had a decent night's sleep. Now you are facing the examination sheet. Here are some suggestions:

1. Before you write anything on the examination booklet beyond your name, read the entire examination. Something in the last question—maybe even a passage that is quoted—may give you an idea that will help you when you write your answer to the first question.
2. Budget your time. If the first question is worth 25%, give it about one-fourth of your time, not half the allotted time. On the other hand, do not provide perfunctory answers: If the question is worth 25%, your instructor expects a fairly detailed response.

3. Rank for yourself the degree of difficulty of the questions, from easiest to hardest. Start with the questions that you immediately know you can handle effectively, and save harder questions for later. Often those harder questions will become easier once you have gotten into the activity of writing the examination.

4. After you have thought a little about the question, before writing furiously, take a moment to jot down few ideas that strike you, as a sort of outline or source of further inspiration. You may at the outset realize that, say, you want to make three points, and unless you jot these down—three key words will do—you may spend all the allotted time on one point.

5. Answer the question. If you are asked to compare two characters, compare them; don't just write two character sketches. Take seriously such words as *compare, define, summarize,* and, especially, *evaluate.*

6. You often can get a good start merely by turning the question into an affirmation—for example, by turning "In what ways does the poetry of Louise Erdrich resemble her fiction" into "Louise Erdrich's poetry resembles her fiction in at least . . . ways."

7. Don't waste time summarizing at length what you have read unless asked to do so—but, of course, you may have to give a brief summary in order to support a point. The instructor wants to see that you can *use* your reading, not merely that you have *done* the reading.

8. Be concrete. Illustrate your arguments with facts—the names of authors, titles, dates, characters, details of plot, and quotations if possible.

9. Leave space for last-minute additions. If you are writing in an examination booklet, either skip a page between essays or write only on the right-hand pages so that on rereading you can add material at the appropriate place on the left-hand pages.

10. Reread what you have written, and make last-minute revisions. By the time you have finished writing the last essay you have probably thought of some things—for instance, some quotations may have come to mind—that might well add strength to some of the earlier essays.

Beyond these general suggestions we can best talk about essay examinations by looking at five common types of questions:

1. A passage to explicate

2. A historical question (for example, "Trace the influence of Guy de Maupassant on Kate Chopin")

3. A critical quotation to be evaluated

4. A wild question (such as "What would Flannery O'Connor think of Leslie Marmon Silko's 'The Man to Send Rain Clouds'?"; "What would Othello do if he were in Hamlet's place?")

5. A comparison (for example, "Compare Eliot's 'The Love Song of
   J.Alfred Prufrock' with Browning's 'My Last Duchess' as dramatic monologues")

A few remarks on each of these types may be helpful.

1. On explication, see pages 55–60 and pages 511–512. As a short rule,
   look carefully at the tone (speaker's attitude toward self, subject, and
   audience) and at the implications of the words (their connotations
   and associations), and see whether a pattern of imagery is evident.
   For example, religious language (*adore, saint*) in a secular love poem
   may precisely define the nature of the lover and of the beloved. Remember, *an explication is not a paraphrase* (a putting into other
   words) but an attempt to show the relations of the parts by calling attention to implications. Organization of such an essay is rarely a problem, since most explications begin with the first line and go on to the
   last. Indeed, if you glance at the poem or passage and feel worried
   that it is too difficult or obscure, don't panic. Take a breath, and begin
   with the first line or the first sentence. Explicate *that*, and then focus
   on how the next line or sentence is related to what has come just before. Proceed step by step, piece by piece, and as you do so you will
   develop a sense of the whole—which is where your explication can
   conclude.
2. A good essay on a historical question will offer a nice combination of
   argument and evidence; that is, the thesis will be supported by concrete details (names, dates, perhaps, even brief quotations). A discussion of Chopin's debt to Maupassant cannot be convincing if it does
   not specify certain works and certain characteristics. If you are asked
   to relate a writer or a body of work to an earlier writer or period, list
   the chief characteristics of the earlier writer or period, and then
   show specifically how the material you are discussing is related to
   these characteristics. If you remember and can quote some relevant
   terms, phrases, or lines from the works, your reader will feel that you
   really know the works themselves.
3. If you are asked to evaluate a critical quotation, read it carefully, and
   in your answer take account of *all* the quotation. If, for example, the
   quoted critic has said, "Louise Erdrich in her fiction always . . . but in
   her poetry rarely . . ." you will have to write about poetry and fiction;
   it will not be enough to talk only about one form or the other, unless,
   of course, the instructions on the examination ask you to take only as
   much of the quotation as you wish. Watch especially for words like
   *always, for the most part, never*; that is, although the passage may on
   the whole approach the truth, you may feel that some important qualifications are needed. This is not being picky; true thinking involves
   making subtle distinctions, yielding assent only so far and no further.

And (again) be sure to give concrete details, supporting your argument with evidence.

4. Curiously, a wild question, such as "What would Shakespeare think of *Death of a Salesman?*" or "What would J. Alfred Prufrock think if he were stopping by woods on a snowy evening?" usually produces rather tame answers: A couple of standard ideas about Shakespeare (for instance, Shakespeare chiefly wrote poetry, and he usually included some comedy in his tragedies) are mechanically applied to Arthur Miller, or a simple characterization of Prufrock is set forth, and some gross incompatibilities are revealed. But as the previous paragraph suggests, it may be necessary to do more than set up bold oppositions. The interest in such a question and in the answer to it may be largely in the degree to which superficially different figures resemble each other in some important ways. Remember that the wildness of the question does not mean that all answers are equally acceptable; as usual, any good answer will be supported by concrete detail. If time permits, you can often enrich your answer by reflecting a bit on the *other* way of looking at the issue. First, to be sure, explain what Shakespeare might have said—this is what the question asks for. But consider too how you could strengthen this answer by taking note as well of what Miller might have said about Shakespearean tragedy.

5. On comparisons, see pages 60–62. Because comparisons are especially difficult to write, be sure to take a few moments to jot down a sort of outline so that you know where you will be going. In a comparison of Browning's and Eliot's monologues, you might treat one poem by each, devoting alternate paragraphs to one author, or you might first treat one author's poem and then turn to the other's. But if you adopt this second strategy, your essay may break into two parts. You can guard against this weakness in three ways: Announcing at the outset that you will treat one author first, then the other; reminding your reader during your treatment of the first author that you will pick up certain points when you get to the second author; and briefly reminding your reader during the treatment of the second author of certain points you already made in your treatment of the first. Remember to make your points as clear and specific as you can. If you say that two authors are both "pessimistic about whether love can endure," you'll want to explain the nature of this pessimism, the reasons in each case for this view, and the precise similarities and the differences. A frequent weakness in "comparisons" is that they are too general, lacking the details that indicate subtle differences. When you review your answer, ask yourself if you have been sufficiently precise.

APPENDIX

# D

# The Pleasures of Rereading

We are always looking for new books to read, but most of us also find ourselves drawn to reread certain novels, stories, plays, and poems that affect us in special ways. A particular pleasure comes in remembering them, in recalling the thoughts and feelings they stimulated in us. These works are like old friends, and our response to them is like the state of mind that Robert Burns captures in "Auld Lang Syne" (which means "long ago times" or "times long gone"). Here is the first stanza:

> Should auld acquaintance be forgot,
>     And never brought to mind?
> Should auld acquaintance be forgot,
>     And auld lang syne?

We find that when we return to our favorite literary works, they are both the same and different. We have changed, and so have they. We see again what is familiar in them, even as we notice a phrase, an image, or a passage of dialogue whose impact we missed or that did not quite register the first time around.

In a sense, then, we live with the authors and books that we have most enjoyed; they remain with us. This group is not the same for everybody—one of the pleasures of reading literature is having the freedom to compile our own list of favorites. At the same time, it is also true that many works of literature have managed to strike a response in nearly everyone. There are many literary works that all of us remember, that possess a wonderfully captivating power. The title of "The Road Not Taken" by Robert Frost, for example, is almost unforgettable, and many readers have found that the final stanza has stayed with them permanently:

> I shall be telling this with a sigh
> Somewhere ages and ages hence:
> Two roads diverged in a wood, and I—
> I took the one less traveled by,
> And that has made all the difference.

Frost's poem is only one of many possible examples. It leads us to say that perhaps the only pastime more enjoyable than reading is rereading. We hope that this book has introduced you to poems, stories, and plays that you will look forward to reading again and living with once more. Should auld acquaintance be forgot . . . .